STRATEGIC MANAGEMENT
Concepts and Cases

A COMPETITIVE ADVANTAGE APPROACH

STRATEGIC MANAGEMENT

EIGHTEENTH EDITION

Concepts and Cases

A COMPETITIVE ADVANTAGE APPROACH

Fred R. David, PhD

University of Debrecen
Debrecen, Hungary

Forest R. David, PhD

Lenoir-Rhyne University
Hickory, North Carolina

Meredith E. David, PhD

Baylor University
Waco, Texas

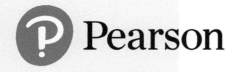 Pearson

Library of Congress Cataloging-in-Publication Data
The CIP data for this title is on file with the Library of Congress.

3 2023

ISBN-10: 0-13-789766-9
ISBN-13: 978-0-13-789766-7

Pearson's Commitment to Diversity, Equity, and Inclusion

Pearson is dedicated to creating bias-free content that reflects the diversity, depth, and breadth of all learners' lived experiences.

We embrace the many dimensions of diversity, including but not limited to race, ethnicity, gender, sex, sexual orientation, socioeconomic status, ability, age, and religious or political beliefs.

Education is a powerful force for equity and change in our world. It has the potential to deliver opportunities that improve lives and enable economic mobility. As we work with authors to create content for every product and service, we acknowledge our responsibility to demonstrate inclusivity and incorporate diverse scholarship so that everyone can achieve their potential through learning. As the world's leading learning company, we have a duty to help drive change and live up to our purpose to help more people create a better life for themselves and to create a better world.

Our ambition is to purposefully contribute to a world where:

- Everyone has an equitable and lifelong opportunity to succeed through learning.
- Our educational content accurately reflects the histories and lived experiences of the learners we serve.

- Our educational products and services are inclusive and represent the rich diversity of learners.
- Our educational content prompts deeper discussions with students and motivates them to expand their own learning (and worldview).

Accessibility

We are also committed to providing products that are fully accessible to all learners. As per Pearson's guidelines for accessible educational Web media, we test and retest the capabilities of our products against the highest standards for every release, following the WCAG guidelines in developing new products for copyright year 2022 and beyond.

 You can learn more about Pearson's commitment to accessibility at
https://www.pearson.com/us/accessibility.html

Contact Us

While we work hard to present unbiased, fully accessible content, we want to hear from you about any concerns or needs with this Pearson product so that we can investigate and address them.

 Please contact us with concerns about any potential bias at
https://www.pearson.com/report-bias.html

 For accessibility-related issues, such as using assistive technology with Pearson products, alternative text requests, or accessibility documentation, email the Pearson Disability Support team at **disability.support@pearson.com**

Brief Contents

Contents

PART 6   Strategic-Management Case Analysis   350

Cases

Preface

New to This Edition

With this edition we have updated 35 percent of the chapter material, added 11 new end-of-chapter mini-cases, and provided virtually all new examples in the chapters. We have integrated new diversity, ethics, and inclusion (DEI) content appropriately as needed in all chapters and cases for this 18th edition. For example, minorities and female "exemplary strategists" are showcased at the beginning of most chapters and the cohesion case. Specifically, new material in this edition includes the following items outlined in this section.

Chapter 1 Cohesion Case on McDonald's Corporation (2022)

Students apply strategy concepts to McDonald's through 25 new, innovative Assurance-of-Learning Exercises provided at the end of chapters. McDonald's is one of the most successful, well-known, and best-managed global companies in the world.

THE COHESION CASE

McDonald's Corporation, 2022
BY FRED R. DAVID

https://corporate.mcdonalds.com/

Headquartered in Chicago, Illinois, McDonald's is the world's largest restaurant company and the world's second-largest employer (behind Walmart). McDonald's trains its managers and franchisees at Hamburger University located at its Chicago headquarters. McDonald's is the largest private operator of playgrounds in the United States and is the largest purchaser of beef, pork, potatoes, and apples.

McDonald's operates about 40,000 restaurants in 120 countries; roughly 36,000 restaurants are franchised and only 4,000 are owned by the company. McDonald's franchised restaurants are owned and operated by independent local business owners, whereas the company-owned restaurants are used to test new products, services, and innovations. McDonald's company-owned restaurants are also used for training potential managers and testing various marketing, pricing, and operational ideas before rollout across the system.

Mini-Cases

There are 11 new mini-cases, one at the end of each chapter.

Complete with questions designed to apply chapter concepts, the new mini-cases focus on the following companies:

- Chapter 1: Ford Motor Company
- Chapter 2: JetBlue Airways
- Chapter 3: *Washington Post*
- Chapter 4: A School of Business
- Chapter 5: Macy's, Inc.
- Chapter 6: Stellantis N.V.
- Chapter 7: AstraZeneca
- Chapter 8: Microsoft Corporation
- Chapter 9: TJX Companies, Inc.
- Chapter 10: Cargill, Archer-Daniels-Midland, & Tyson Foods
- Chapter 11: Toshiba Corporation

MINI-CASE ON JETBLUE AIRWAYS

DOES JETBLUE HAVE THE BEST MISSION STATEMENT?[15]

As indicated at the website given in the Source Line, some analysts rate JetBlue Airways (JetBlue) number one as having the best mission statement among all companies, but is that true? As you know, there are recommended components and characteristics that should be included in an effective mission statement.

Headquartered in New York City, JetBlue is a *Fortune* 500 major low-cost airline operating more than 1,000 flights daily serving more than 100 domestic and international cities. JetBlue flies all over Mexico, South America, Europe, and Canada. JetBlue stock trades on the Nasdaq under the ticker symbol JBLU.

At the JetBlue corporate website, www.jetblue.com, the company does not provide a published vision or mission statement. JetBlue uses or once used the following statement, however, that was used by analysts to rate the firm as having the best mission statement:

Chapter Capsules—ALL NEW

Within each chapter, a new **EXEMPLARY STRATEGIST, GLOBAL CAPSULE,** and **ETHICS CAPSULE** are provided.

Exemplary Strategist Capsules—one at the beginning of each chapter to showcase an individual that is employing strategic management exceptionally well.

Global Capsules—provided to showcase the strategic relevance of material to global operations, issues, and conditions.

Ethics Capsules—developed to accent the fact that "good ethics is good business" across all aspects of the strategic-management process.

EXEMPLARY **STRATEGIST** SHOWCASED

Patti Poppe, CEO of Pacific Gas & Electric[1]

The CEO and chief strategist of Pacific Gas & Electric (PG&E), Patti Poppe plans to spend about $20 billion to put 10,000 miles of PG&E power lines underground, primarily to better manage and be less vulnerable to wildfires but also to reduce long-term expenditures on "vegetation management." No utility company has ever attempted to do what Poppe plans, saying such an undertaking is prohibitively expensive. Poppe... probation for vio... guilty in 2018 fo... Paradise, Californ... manslaughter for... PG&E has strugg... common cause o...

GLOBAL CAPSULE 10

Usage of DEI Metrics Across Countries[7]

Companies globally are scrambling to develop, use, monitor, and make decisions based on numerous diversity, equality, and inclusion (DEI) metrics or variables that collectively characterize an institution's overall standing on DEI, including fairness regarding race, gender, and religious variables. DEI is often viewed as an assessment of an organization's integration of minorities, including women and people of color, into the workforce, so the same metrics are applicable globally. Every country is populated by roughly 50 percent females, and inclusion of females is an almost universal key component of DEI to be measured and improved.

In the United States, research says about 14 percent of the population self-identify as Black or African American. Racial diversity is growing in most n... ed by Pew Resear... they favor a more... a diverse populat... diverse, including... Belize is also raci... Indians, and othe... East Indians, Black... countries through...

1. Diversity among applicant pool

ETHICS CAPSULE 9

Rubrik's CEO Bipul Sinha: "Achieve Exemplary Business Ethics Through Exemplary Transparency"[12]

Based in Palo Alto, California, Rubrik is a data management company whose CEO, Bipul Sinha, has established a culture of complete openness as a means of achieving superior business ethics. Sinha believes extreme honesty helps create a strong corporate culture that spurs entrepreneurialism, innovativeness, motivation, commitment, and integrity. Even the company's board of director meetings are completely open to all 600 of the company's employees, and most employ-

the *Forbes* Cloud 100 that annually ranks the world's best private cloud companies. Other firms that made the 2021 list were Stripe, Databricks, and Canva.

In contrast to Rubrik's transparency, GE's board of directors did not know until the *Wall Street Journal* reported it in 2017 that their former CEO Jeff Immelt had an extra jet follow his corporate jet on many of his overseas trips during his 16-year tenure as CEO. Immelt resigned days after the disclosure. However, an increasing number of companies and organizations are in fact providing employees with regular updates on how the firm is doing financially and what, where, when, and why. This is evident even among private (not public) companies. Approximately 43 percent of all private firms today share financial information with all employees, up from 24 percent in 2012. That is nearly a 100 percent increase. Greater communication yields greater understanding that leads to greater commitment which results in higher performance.

Chapter	Exemplary Strategist Capsules focus on the following people:	Global Capsules focus on the following topics:	Ethics Capsules address the following issues:
1	Andrew Cathy, CEO of Chick-fil-A	Companies Exiting China amid Tighter Security	Don't Just Talk the Talk, Walk the Walk
2	Patti Poppe, CEO of Pacific Gas & Electric	LinkedIn: Clear Core Values, Vision, and Mission Lead to Global Prominence	What Ethics Variable Is Most Important?
3	Chipotle's Chief Diversity, Inclusion and People Officer, Ms. Andrada, and Chief Development Officer, Ms. Zalotrawala	What Is the Fastest Growing City and Country? Perhaps Dubai and the UAE	CO_2 Emissions Across Countries
4	CEO of Nasdaq, Adena Friedman	Samsung Electronics	Unethical Hacking for Profit Increasing Fast
5	CEO of Apple, Inc.—Tim Cook and CEO of Macy's, Inc.—Jeff Gennette	Numerous Countries Downsizing Foreign Workforce, Relying on Native Residents	Ask Hobby Lobby Is Good Ethics Good Business?
6	Phebe Novakovic, Chairperson and CEO of General Dynamics Corp.	Are Foreign Takeovers Becoming Less Available?	As We Strategize, We Must Not Jeopardize Animal Welfare
7	CEO of Edward D. Jones & Co.—Penny Pennington	COVID-19 Pandemic Caused Some Hoteliers to Rethink Their Target Marketing	Do Firms Need a Cell Phone Policy to outline Acceptable Use in the Workplace?
8	CEO of TIAA—Thasunda Brown Duckett	The 10 Most (and Least) Corrupt Countries in the World in 2021	Projected Financial Statement Manipulation
9	CEO of Walgreens Boots Alliance—Rosalind Brewer	India's Big Shift Away from China on Solar Panels	Achieving Exemplary Business Ethics Through Exemplary Transparency
10	CEO of CVS Health—Karen Lynch	Usage of Diversity, Equity, and Inclusion (DEI) Metrics Across Countries	As We Strategize, We Must Not Exploit or Harm Wildlife
11	CEO of GlaxoSmithKline—Emma Walmsley	China Aims for Superiority on Rare Earth Metals Mining and Processing	Is Animal Testing a Global Ethical Issue?

Assurance-of-Learning Exercises—nearly all new and organized into four sets as follows that apply chapter concepts, tools, and techniques:

Set 1: Strategic Planning for McDonald's—26 exercises apply chapter material to the McDonald's Cohesion Case to prepare students for doing case analysis on for-profit companies.

Set 2: Strategic Planning for My University—12 exercises apply chapter material to your college or university to prepare students for doing case analysis on nonprofit organizations.

Set 3: Strategic Planning to Enhance My Employability—14 exercises apply chapter material to individuals instead of companies to prepare students for making career choices.

Set 4: Individual Versus Group Strategic Planning—12 exercises apply chapter material by comparing the effectiveness of individual versus group decisions; these are fun, in-class group exercises that yield a winning individual and winning group for each activity.

Detailed Chapter-by-Chapter Changes

Chapter 1: THE NATURE OF STRATEGIC MANAGEMENT—scores of new examples are provided to exemplify all concepts. New diversity, equity, and inclusion (DEI) material is given.

Chapter 2: BUSINESS VISION AND MISSION—new material and examples are provided for how to write effective vision, mission, and core value statements.

Chapter 3: THE EXTERNAL ASSESSMENT—new material is provided on political, economic, social, technology, environment, legal (PESTEL) framework; more guidance is provided regarding how to assign weights and ratings in matrices; new examples abound throughout.

The AQCD concept is explained and exemplified better. The discussion of Five-Forces Analysis is strengthened. Guidelines are provided for using the strategic planning template at www.strategyclub.com to develop a Competitive Profile Matrix and External Factor Evaluation Matrix.

Chapter 4: THE INTERNAL ASSESSMENT—this chapter has been revamped; the AQCD material is improved; the marketing material is enhanced; new examples abound throughout. Supply chain and robotics issues are discussed. Guidelines are provided for using the strategic planning template to develop financial ratios, financial statements, and an Internal Factor Evaluation Matrix.

Chapter 5: STRATEGIES IN ACTION—scores of new examples are provided to exemplify all concepts; the growing trend of firms divesting a segment(s) to become more homogeneous is discussed.

Chapter 6: STRATEGY ANALYSIS AND CHOICE—the presentation of this chapter that includes SWOT, Boston Consulting Group (BCG), Internal-External (IE), Strategic Position and Action Evaluation (SPACE), Grand, and Quantitative Strategic Planning Matrix (QSPM) analyses is enhanced and shortened. A new Figure 6-14 is provided to accompany enhanced SWOT analysis. The presentation of portfolio analysis is improved. Guidelines are provided for using the strategic planning template to develop all matrices.

Chapter 7: IMPLEMENTING STRATEGIES: MANAGEMENT AND MARKETING ISSUES—this chapter is fully updated and enhanced, especially with new target marketing, segmentation, and positioning analyses. New policies regarding remote work are discussed. The new Chief Diversity Officer position is discussed. Enhanced discussion of strategic business unit structures and perceptual maps is provided. A new organizational structure decision-making model is presented. Guidelines are provided for using the strategic planning template to develop perceptual maps.

Chapter 8: IMPLEMENTING STRATEGIES: FINANCE AND ACCOUNTING ISSUES—there is enhanced presentation of financial and accounting tools, such as EPS/EBIT analysis, corporate valuation, and projected financial statements; a new running example for ABC Company is provided. The increasing usage of special purpose acquisition companies (SPACs) as a form of initial public offerings is discussed. Guidelines are provided for using the strategic planning template to perform all financial analyses.

Chapter 9: STRATEGY EVALUATION AND GOVERNANCE—excellent new examples are presented to highlight new trends and concepts such as balanced scorecard usage and diversity, equity, and inclusion (DEI) considerations in governance.

Chapter 10: BUSINESS ETHICS, ENVIRONMENTAL SUSTAINABILITY, AND CORPORATE SOCIAL RESPONSIBILITY—this chapter provides updated coverage of ethics, whistleblowing, bribery, sustainability, and corporate social responsibility. This text reveals why "good ethics is good business." The diversity, ethics, and inclusion (DEI) discussion is improved to promote and encourage firms to conduct operations with respect for all individuals, an important concern for consumers, companies, society, and Association to Advance Collegiate Schools of Business (AACSB). Substantial new material is provided on livestock and wildlife welfare.

Chapter 11: GLOBAL AND INTERNATIONAL ISSUES—this chapter is enhanced and shortened but provides new coverage of cultural and conceptual strategic management differences across countries. Doing business globally has become a necessity in most industries. Full updates are provided for an ever-changing global business environment, ranging from tax rates to cultural shifts.

Part 6: STRATEGIC MANAGEMENT CASE ANALYSIS—this section that follows all chapters has been rewritten to be more concise and in providing guidelines for students performing case analysis and making oral presentations.

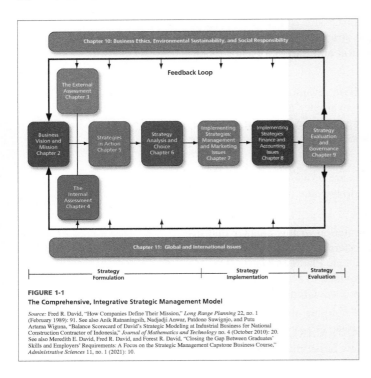

FIGURE 1-1
The Comprehensive, Integrative Strategic Management Model

Source: Fred R. David, "How Companies Define Their Mission," *Long Range Planning* 22, no. 1 (February 1989): 91. See also Anik Ratnaningsih, Nadjadji Anwar, Patdono Suwignjo, and Putu Artama Wiguna, "Balance Scorecard of David's Strategic Modeling at Industrial Business for National Construction Contractor of Indonesia," *Journal of Mathematics and Technology* no. 4 (October 2010): 20. See also Meredith E. David, Fred R. David, and Forest R. David, "Closing the Gap Between Graduates' Skills and Employers' Requirements: A Focus on the Strategic Management Capstone Business Course," *Administrative Sciences* 11, no. 1 (2021): 10.

Author-Created Videos

We have added author-created videos introducing the content of each chapter and 11 videos discussing a variety of important topics such as mission statement delivery, BCG Matrix, and corporate evaluation.

Solving Teaching and Learning Challenges

The primary challenge facing strategy professors is to keep students engaged while making sure business skills are learned. This text leads all others in being practical, skills-oriented, and unfolds in the same manner as the process of actually doing strategic planning unfolds. Students and professors alike appreciate this practical approach presented in a concise, conversational, and exciting manner—beginning with the integrative model of the strategic management process that unifies all chapters. All of the 11 end-of-chapter mini-cases, 471 review questions, and 64 Assurance-of-Learning Exercises are designed specifically to apply chapter concepts. Importantly, too, all 30 new cases in this 18th edition are written and designed to facilitate application of chapter concepts, as illustrated in the new Concepts-by-Cases matrix presented in a moment.

The Case Rationale

Case analysis remains the primary learning vehicle used in most strategic management classes, for five important reasons:

1. Analyzing cases gives students the opportunity to work in teams to evaluate the internal operations and external issues facing various organizations and to craft strategies that can lead these firms to success. Working in teams gives students practical experience in solving problems as part of a group. In the business world, important decisions are generally made within groups; strategic management students learn to deal with overly aggressive group members as well as timid, noncontributing group members. This experience is valuable because strategic management students are near graduation and will soon enter the working world full-time.

2. Analyzing cases enables students to improve their oral and written communication skills as well as their analytical and interpersonal skills by proposing and defending particular courses of action for the case companies.

3. Analyzing cases allows students to view a company, its competitors, and its industry concurrently, thus simulating the complex business world.

4. Analyzing cases allows students to apply concepts learned in many business courses. Students gain experience dealing with a wide range of organizational problems that impact all the business functions.

5. Analyzing cases gives students practice in applying concepts, evaluating situations, formulating a game plan, and resolving implementation problems in a variety of business and industry settings.

Exemplary Strategist

Strategic management students often learn best when provided with real-world examples that illustrate the application of key concepts to real-world situations. Thus, each 18th edition chapter begins by featuring an exemplary strategist to showcase and reveal the key characteristics and management approach of leading strategists in the world. We all can learn from the best strategists. These vignettes showcase the accomplishments and leadership of exemplary minorities and women who blaze a trail and set a great example for all of us to follow each day.

Ethics Capsules

Students sometimes struggle with understanding the importance of business ethics in strategic management. Ethical issues can play a key role in a firm's success (or failure). An ethics capsule appears in each chapter to showcase the overriding importance of doing business in a socially and environmentally responsible manner. These capsules exemplify across all stages of strategic management that indeed "good ethics is good business."

Global Capsules

When conducting case analyses on multinational corporations, students sometimes struggle with recognizing how essential factors of the global business environment may impact a local firm as it seeks to attract and serve customers across several countries or even continents. However, important global factors must be considered across all stages of strategic management. Thus, each 18th edition chapter contains a global capsule to showcase the relevance of the material in a global business environment and to highlight the importance of carefully considering unique factors of the global business environment when formulating, implementing, and evaluating strategies for a multinational corporation.

Implications for Strategists

Almost every company in existence could benefit from learning and applying the concepts, skills, and techniques discussed in the textbook to regularly perform strategic planning. Thousands, perhaps, millions of businesses and strategists globally use the strategic planning template and techniques discussed in this textbook to ensure that they develop an effective game plan that can be implemented to achieve sustained competitive advantage. To further assist strategists in applying the David method for strategic management, each 18th edition chapter ends by highlighting particularly important concepts and tools being used by strategists on the frontline actually doing strategic planning.

Implications for Students

A crucial challenge in teaching strategy is making sure that students actually learn the business skills needed to engage in strategic management. Students in the capstone business course increasingly must be capable of demonstrating their employability to potential employers. When considering the employability of business graduates, many employers actively seek out candidates who can demonstrate their knowledge of important business skills. The mission of this 18th edition text is to provide students with a platform whereby they can learn pivotal strategic planning skills and competencies needed to obtain a meaningful job and advance in their career. As such, each chapter ends with special strategy guidelines that can facilitate students' efforts to become meaningful contributors at their workplace and to society.

The New Concepts-by-Cases Matrix

All 30 cases in the 18th edition facilitate coverage of all strategy concepts presented in the 11 chapters, but as revealed by shaded cells (or an x) in the matrix, some cases especially exemplify particularly important strategy concepts. The Concepts-by-Cases matrix facilitates professors effectively using different cases to assure student learning of various chapter concepts. Note from the purple shaded boxes that each case is used to test at least six strategic management concepts. This new, innovative ancillary promises to elevate the case learning method to new heights in teaching strategic management. Designed and used in this manner, case analysis a better pedagogical tool even than simulations in teaching and applying key strategy concepts, tools, and techniques, so students finish the capstone course having learned and gained proficiency and competence in specific skills valued in the business world.

		Key Strategic Management Concepts	Strategy Model/Process	Vision/Mission Statements	Competitive Profile Matrix	Porter's Five Forces	EFE Matrix	PESTEL	Value Chain Analysis	IFE Matrix	Strategy Types	Porter's Two Generic Strategies
		0	0	0	0	0	0	0	0	0	0	0
US-Based Disruptive Service Companies												
Case 1	Airbnb			■			■	■				
Case 2	Uber Technologies				■	■				■	■	■
US-Based Service Companies												
Case 3	Tesla Motors		■								■	■
Case 4	First Solar											
Case 5	Cracker Barrel Old Country Store					■		■				
Case 6	Chipotle Mexican Grill	■							■		■	
Case 7	Wynn Resorts			■	■							■
Case 8	Cinemark Holdings					■						
Case 9	Meta Platforms									■		
Case 10	Electronic Arts							■				
Case 11	TJX Companies								■			■
Case 12	Citigroup								■		■	
Case 13	JetBlue Airways		■		■			■				
Case 14	FedEx Corp.				■							
Manufacturing Companies												
Case 15	Caterpillar Inc.			■		■			■			
Case 16	Chevron Corp.								■	■		
Case 17	Tyson Foods		■									
Case 18	Constellation Brands						■			■		
Case 19	Johnson Outdoors					■	■					■
Case 20	Thor Industries			■		■						
Case 21	Apple Inc.											
Case 22	IBM (International Business Machines)	■			■							
Case 23	Colgate-Palmolive							■			■	
Case 24	Helen of Troy			■		■						
Nonprofit Organizations												
Case 25	American Red Cross	■	■									
Case 26	United States Postal Service (USPS)		■				■			■	■	
Not-US-Based Companies												
Case 27	Singapore Airlines				■	■		■				■
Case 28	Danone S.A.											
Case 29	Grupo Bimbo, S.A.B. de C.V.											
Case 30	GlaxoSmithKline Plc								■		■	

First Mover Advantages	SWOT Matrix	SPACE Matrix	BCG & IE Matrices	Grand Strategy & QSPM	Organizational Structure	Organizational Culture	DEI	Market Segmentation & Product Position	EPS-EBIT Analysis	Projected Financial Statements	Company Valuation	Balanced Scorecard & Benchmarking	Governance	Business Ethics	Environmental Sustainability	Outsourcing & Reshoring	Foreign Business Culture	
6	6	6	7	6	6	6	6	8	6	6	6	6	6	8	6	6	10	

The David Approach Is Unique

This textbook is globally considered to be the most practical, skills-oriented strategic management textbook on the market. All chapters unfold from a widely used integrative model of strategic planning, so students learn the "process of doing strategic planning," rather than focusing on seminal theories in strategy. The David approach is "learning by doing"—students develop skills that can enhance their own employability through numerous features, such as 64 new Assurance-of-Learning end-of-chapter exercises in this edition. The 30 new, student friendly cases in this edition elevate this text to new highs as the go-to pedagogical platform for teaching strategic management at both the bachelor's and master's levels in colleges and universities across the globe.

In addition to offering outstanding coverage of vital strategy tools, matrices, and techniques being used by companies and organizations to do strategic planning, this 18th edition offers more coverage on topics such as social responsibility, sustainability, and diversity, ethics, and inclusion (DEI) than any other strategic management textbook, including topics such as bribery, workplace romance, devising codes of ethics, taking a position (or not) on social issues, and preserving wildlife—topics that other textbooks do not mention, even though companies continually face strategic decisions in these areas.

The Association to Advance Collegiate Schools of Business (AACSB) International increasingly advocates a more skills-oriented, practical approach in business books, which this text provides, rather than a theory-based approach. This textbook also offers more coverage of global and international issues than any other strategic management textbook, including topics such as how business culture, taxes, tariffs, political stability, and economic conditions vary across countries—all framed from a strategic planning perspective.

Lastly, this textbook is trusted across five continents to provide students (and managers) the latest skills and concepts needed to effectively formulate and efficiently implement a strategic plan—a game plan, if you will—that can lead to sustainable competitive advantages for any type of business. This text meets all AACSB International guidelines for the strategic management course at both the graduate and undergraduate levels, and previous editions have been used at more than 500 colleges and universities globally.

Developing Employability Skills

Using this text, students learn how to actually do strategic planning. This is an immense benefit for students, a critical employability skill, because employers recognize the benefits of employees having an understanding of what a firm is trying to achieve and why. Nearly all students using this text also use the free, Excel-based, strategic planning template at the www.strategyclub.com author website; many students include this skill too on their resumes, to showcase their proficiency using a template commonly used by businesses for doing strategic planning. Businesses value Excel. As professors of strategic management ourselves, we three authors know that imparting concrete skills and competencies to students enhances their chances for securing an excellent job upon graduation and advancing in their career, which is a primary part of our mission as authors and professors.

Instructor Teaching Resources

For more information and resources, visit www.pearson.com.

Acknowledgments

The strength of this text is largely attributed to the collective wisdom, work, and experiences of strategic management professors, researchers, students, and practitioners. Names of individuals whose published research is referenced in this edition are listed alphabetically in the Name Index. To all individuals involved in making this text so popular and successful, we are indebted and thankful.

Many special persons and reviewers contributed valuable material and suggestions for this edition. We would like to thank our colleagues and friends at Baylor University, Auburn University, Mississippi State University, East Carolina University, the University of South Carolina, Campbell University, the University of North Carolina at Pembroke, Francis Marion University, Lenoir-Rhyne University, and the University of Debrecen. We have taught strategic management or marketing courses at all these universities. Scores of students and professors at these schools helped shape the development of this text. We especially want to thank Dr. Andras Nabradi at the University of Debrecen for your valuable insight, encouragement, knowledge, suggestions, and friendship.

We thank you, the reader, for investing the time and effort to read and study this text. It will help you formulate, implement, and evaluate strategies for any organization with which you become associated. We hope you come to share our enthusiasm for the rich subject area of strategic management and for the systematic learning approach taken in this text. We also want to welcome and invite your suggestions, ideas, thoughts, comments, and questions regarding any part of this text or the ancillary materials.

Please contact Dr. Fred R. David at **freddavid9@gmail.com**, or write him at P.O. Box 8139, Ocean Isle Beach, NC 28469. We sincerely appreciate and need your input to continually improve this text in future editions. Your willingness to draw our attention to specific errors or deficiencies in coverage or exposition will especially be appreciated.

Thank you for using this text.

—Fred R. David

—Forest R. David

—Meredith E. David

Fred, Forest, and Meredith would like to dedicate the 18th edition of this textbook to the matriarch of the family, Fred's wife of 45 years and Forest and Meredith's mom—Joy H. David. Thank you Joy for supporting our book-writing activities for many years and for providing unending encouragement to us.

Joy H. David

About the Authors

Fred has been lead author of this textbook for nearly four decades. This text is a global leader in the field of strategic management providing an application, practitioner-oriented approach to the discipline. About 500 colleges and universities have used this textbook that is translated into numerous languages and widely used globally. Holding BS and MBA Degrees from Wake Forest University and a PhD in management from the University of South Carolina, Dr. Fred David is currently Professor Emeritus of Strategic Planning at Francis Marion University in Florence, South Carolina. He has published more than 100 academic journal articles and cases. Fred enjoys spending time with his grandsons, Everett David (age 8) and Cooper David (age 7), parents of Byron and Brooke David in South Carolina.

Fred R. David

Dr. Forest David has been a coauthor on this textbook for the 15th, 16th, 17th, and 18th editions, sole author of the *Case Instructor's Manual* for the last eight editions, and sole developer of the free Excel Strategic Planning Template found on the author website (www.strategyclub.com). Holding a PhD from the University of Debrecen in Hungary, Forest has taught management classes at Mississippi State University, Campbell University, Francis Marion University, the University of Debrecen, and Partium Christian University in Romania. Currently employed as a full-time Visiting Professor of Management at Lenoir-Rhyne University in Hickory, North Carolina, Forest has nearly a hundred business journal articles, presentations, and case publications. Forest is a licensed United States Coast Guard Master's Captain and takes people on boating charters part-time during Summers.

Forest R. David

Meredith holds a PhD in business administration from the University of South Carolina and an MBA Degree from Wake Forest University. Dr. Meredith David is currently a tenured Associate Professor of Marketing at Baylor University in Waco, Texas, where she recently received the prestigious Young Researcher Award. She has published more than 50 articles, cases, and papers on marketing and strategic management in journals such as the *Journal of Business Research, Journal of Advertising, Journal of Strategic Marketing, European Journal of Marketing*, and *Business Horizons*. Meredith has traveled the world over as a professor and student, including teaching strategic management at Jiao Tong University in Shanghai, China. In her career, Meredith has traveled to Australia, Canada, China, Costa Rica, Curacao, England, France, Germany, Hungary, Iceland, Indonesia, Ireland, Japan, Lebanon, Macau, Malaysia, Mexico, Peru, Portugal, Romania, Taiwan, and Thailand.

Meredith E. David

Fred R. David, Forest R. David, and Meredith E. David are a father–son–daughter team that has published scores of articles in top journals such as *Academy of Management Review, Academy of Management Executive, Journal of Applied Psychology, Long Range Planning, International Journal of Management, Journal of Business Strategy*, and *Advanced Management Journal*. Six recent journal articles by the authors, listed here, are changing the way strategic management courses are taught.

David, Meredith E., Fred R. David, and Forest R. David, "Testing and Enhancing a Pivotal Organizational Structure Decision-Making Model," *International Journal of Strategic Decision Sciences* 12, no. 2 (2021): 1–19.

David, Meredith E., Fred R. David, and Forest R. David, "Closing the Gap Between Graduates' Skills and Employers' Requirements: A Focus on the Strategic Management Capstone Business Course," *Administrative Sciences* 11, no. 1 (2021): 10–26.

David, Forest R., Meredith E. David, and Fred R. David, "A New and Improved Organizational Structure Decision-Making Model," *SAM Advanced Management Journal* 85, no. 4 (2020): 1–9.

David, Forest R., Meredith E. David, and Fred R. David, "Business Curricula: Coverage of Employability Skills in a Strategic Management Course," *SAM Advanced Management Journal* 85, no. 1 (2020): 1–12.

David, Fred R., Steven Creek, and Forest R. David, "What Is the Key to Effective SWOT Analysis? Including AQCD Factors," *SAM Advanced Management Journal* 84, no. 1 (2019): 25–36.

David, Meredith E., Fred R. David, and Forest R. David, "The Quantitative Strategic Planning Matrix: A New Marketing Tool," *Journal of Strategic Marketing* 25, no. 4 (2017): 342–52.

## PART 1

OVERVIEW OF STRATEGIC MANAGEMENT

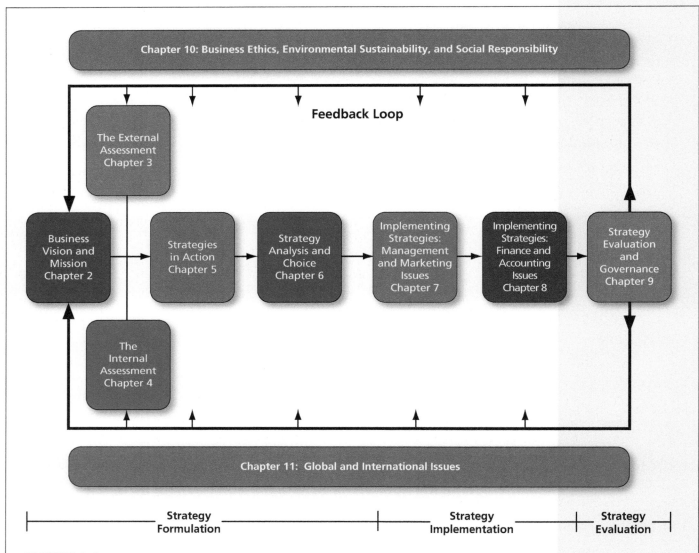

FIGURE 1-1

The Comprehensive, Integrative Strategic Management Model

Source: Fred R. David, "How Companies Define Their Mission," *Long Range Planning* 22, no. 1 (February 1989): 91. See also Anik Ratnaningsih, Nadjadji Anwar, Patdono Suwignjo, and Putu Artama Wiguna, "Balance Scorecard of David's Strategic Modeling at Industrial Business for National Construction Contractor of Indonesia," *Journal of Mathematics and Technology* no. 4 (October 2010): 20. See also Meredith E. David, Fred R. David, and Forest R. David, "Closing the Gap Between Graduates' Skills and Employers' Requirements: A Focus on the Strategic Management Capstone Business Course," *Administrative Sciences* 11, no. 1 (2021): 10.

The Nature of Strategic Management

LEARNING OBJECTIVES

After studying this chapter, you should be able to do the following:

1.1. Describe the strategic management process.

1.2. Discuss the three stages of activities for strategy formulation, implementation, and evaluation.

1.3. Explain the need for integrating analysis and intuition in strategic management.

1.4. Define and give examples of key terms in strategic management.

1.5. Describe the benefits of engaging in strategic management.

1.6. Explain why some firms do not engage in strategic planning.

1.7. Describe the pitfalls in doing strategic planning.

1.8. Discuss the connection between business and military strategies.

1.9. Explain how this course can enhance a student's employability.

ASSURANCE-OF-LEARNING EXERCISES

The following exercises are found at the end of this chapter:

SET 1:	Strategic Planning for McDonald's
EXERCISE 1A:	Gather Strategy Information for McDonald's Company
EXERCISE 1B:	Enter McDonald's Vitals into the Strategic Planning Template
SET 2:	Strategic Planning for My University
EXERCISE 1C:	Perform SWOT Analysis for My University
SET 3:	Strategic Planning to Enhance My Employability
EXERCISE 1D:	Perform SWOT Analysis on Myself
SET 4:	Individual Versus Group Strategic Planning
EXERCISE 1E:	How Detrimental Are Various Pitfalls in Strategic Planning?

Chapter 1 provides an overview of strategic management; introduces a practical, integrative model of the strategic management process (illustrated in Figure 1-1); and defines basic activities and terms in strategic management. The primary focus of this textbook is on learning by doing. From this text, students learn how to do strategic planning. The integrative model reveals the layout of this text and the process of strategic planning so students can follow the journey in a meaningful way.

An exciting new feature of this edition at the beginning of each chapter is an exemplary strategist capsule to showcase a famous strategist for doing an exemplary job applying strategic planning concepts, tools, and techniques. The first person featured for excellent strategic management practices is Andrew Cathy, CEO of Chick-fil-A, who as you see in the insert is leading one of the most successful companies anywhere. At the end of each chapter, a new, one-page, mini-case on a company is provided with respective questions that apply various concepts, tools, and techniques presented.

What Is Strategic Management?

1.1. Describe the strategic management process.

Strategic management is the art and science of formulating, implementing, and evaluating cross-functional decisions that enable an organization to achieve its objectives. As this definition implies, strategic management focuses on integrating management, marketing, finance, accounting, production, and information systems to achieve organizational success. Strategic management can also be defined as the executive-level activity of distributing resources across products and regions to gain a sustainable competitive advantage over rivals.

Firms have liberty to compete in many different ways within a variety of geographic areas, so decisions must be made regarding what markets to enter, what markets to avoid, which competitor's space to invade, and which to avoid. A firm's survival can hinge on these decisions being right; this text unveils the process needed for making effective strategic decisions. For example, Walgreens is rebranding itself as a health-care provider by attaching doctors' offices to hundreds of its drugstores; Walgreens recently paid $5.2 billion for VillageMD to help accomplish this strategy.

EXEMPLARY **STRATEGIST** SHOWCASED[1]

Andrew Cathy, CEO of Chick-fil-A

Andrew Cathy, CEO and chief strategist of Chick-fil-A, is leading one of the most well-managed companies in the world that also has a great strategic plan. Headquartered in Atlanta and founded in 1967 by Andrew Cathy's grandfather, Truett Cathy, Chick-fil-A is one of the largest and perhaps the fastest growing restaurant chains in the United States and perhaps the fastest growing. Andrew Cathy is a 43-year-old father of four who grew up in the family business and is now leading the company into bold new areas with advanced online-only items on the menu and updated drive-through lanes. Cathy says (paraphrased), "Success can be a danger for any company because you tend to hold on to yesterday while losing sight of what is needed for tomorrow."

Cathy says Chick-fil-A will never go public because the company does not need the external cash. He also says the company will always be closed on Sundays as a tribute to his grandfather who wanted people to go to church if they wanted to or just spend time with family. When asked about the company's stance on various social issues, Cathy says, "We respect everybody and are open to everybody and treat everybody with honor and dignity; we follow what my grandfather always said, 'I'm not right wing or left wing; I'm the whole chicken.'"

When asked about getting into burgers or other menu items as almost all rival chains have done, Cathy says (paraphrased), "We are trying to help the cows so we will continue encouraging customers to eat more chicken." He did say, however, that Chick-fil-A is considering some plant-based options to chicken; he revealed also that the company uses young, tender chickens rather than old, tougher hens. With

Kent D. Johnson/AP Photo

more than 2,500 restaurants in 47 states and Canada, Chick-fil-A is adding hundreds of stores, including its first six restaurants in Hawaii in 2022. Glassdoor recently named Chick-fil-A one of the top 100 best places to work in the United States.

[1]Based on Heather Haddon, "New Generation Leads at Chick-fil-A," *Wall Street Journal*, November 1, 2021, p. B5.

Formulating strategies such as deciding what to produce and where, when, and how to compete is what leads to a sustainable competitive advantage. Even the best strategies must be implemented well through operational- or tactical-level activities like hiring and motivating employees, cutting costs, benchmarking, outsourcing, securing financing, and keeping facilities warm (or cool). Implementation activities are vitally important and must be monitored by strategists, but effectively formulated strategies, more so than operational tactics, are generally what leads to sustained competitive advantages.

To gain a sustainable competitive advantage, firms need to provide unique products and services. Uniqueness matters. For example, Apple's computers, iPads, and iPhones all run on Apple's unique operating system; the only way to have an iPhone is to also be a user of Apple's operating system. To assure "effective uniqueness," firms must accept concessions in the strategy process to gain a sustainable competitive advantage as exemplified in the Apple example. Another example is Rolex, and the company not offering cheaper lines of watches. Rolex has resisted increasing market share by offering new cheaper product lines to attract new customers. Instead, Rolex has maintained its unique reputation and market share as the top luxury watch brand in the world. Rolex, and all successful firms, thus make trade-offs and tough decisions throughout the process of developing, producing, and selling products.

Chapter 2 discusses core values, vision, and mission—items that represent the starting point for developing and nurturing a firm's uniqueness. Everything in strategy flows from a particular firm's core values, vision, and mission, and all successful firms are different (unique) from rival firms in some key ways.

The term *strategic management* is used at many colleges and universities as the title for the capstone course in business administration. This course integrates material from all business courses and, additionally, introduces new strategic management concepts and techniques that are widely used by firms. Two special features of this text are a Cohesion Case (on McDonald's) and end-of-chapter assurance-of-learning exercises, as described in Table 1-1.

Strategic Planning

The term *strategic management* in this text is used synonymously with the term **strategic planning**. The latter term is more often used in the business world, whereas the former is often used in academia. Sometimes the term *strategic management* is used to refer to strategy formulation,

TABLE 1-1 A Cohesion Case and Assurance-of-Learning Exercises

A distinguishing, popular feature of this text is the Cohesion Case, named so because a written case on a company (McDonald's) appears at the end of this chapter, and then all other subsequent chapters feature end-of-chapter assurance-of-learning exercises to apply strategic planning concepts, tools, and techniques to the Cohesion Case company. McDonald's is a well-known, well-managed global firm undergoing strategic change. By working through the exercises related to McDonald's, students become prepared to develop an effective strategic plan for any company (case) assigned to them. Case analysis is a core part of almost every strategic management course globally.

   We are thrilled to provide new sets of end-of chapter assurance-of-learning exercises. All exercises have been carefully designed to "assure learning" by applying chapter concepts, tools, and techniques in a fun and meaningful way to best assure that competence is gained. Employability skills are discussed near the end of this and every other chapter. The four sets of assurance-of-learning exercises that appear at the end of each chapter are as follows:

Set 1: Strategic Planning for McDonald's—Exercises that apply chapter material to the McDonald's Cohesion Case; these exercises ready students for doing case analysis as "knowledge application and analysis" and "information technology" skills are honed.

Set 2: Strategic Planning for My University—Exercises that apply chapter material to your college or university; these exercises ready students for doing case analysis in nonprofit organizations while honing business ethics, social responsibility, and data literacy skills.

Set 3: Strategic Planning to Enhance My Employability—Exercises that apply chapter material to individuals instead of companies; these exercises prepare students for making career choices and enable students to apply strategy tools, techniques, and concepts to enhance their own career.

Set 4: Individual Versus Group Strategic Planning—Exercises that apply chapter material by comparing the effectiveness of individual versus group decisions; these are fun in-class group activities that yield a winning individual and a winning group for each exercise, while honing critical-thinking and collaboration skills.

implementation, and evaluation, with *strategic planning* referring only to strategy formulation. The purpose of strategic planning is to exploit and create new and different opportunities for tomorrow; **long-range planning**, in contrast, tries to optimize the trends of today for tomorrow.

The term *strategic planning* originated in the 1950s and was popular between the mid-1960s and the mid-1970s. During these years, strategic planning was widely believed to be the answer for all corporate problems. At the time, much of corporate America and other industrial nations were obsessed with strategic planning. Following that boom, however, strategic planning was cast aside during the 1980s because various planning models did not yield higher returns. The 1990s, however, brought the revival of strategic planning, and the process is widely practiced today in the business world.

A strategic plan is, in essence, a company's game plan. Just as an athletic team needs a good game plan to have a chance for success, a company must have a good strategic plan to compete successfully. Profit margins among firms in most industries are so slim that there is little room for error in the overall strategic plan. A strategic plan results from tough managerial choices among numerous good alternatives, and it signals commitment to specific markets, policies, procedures, and operations in lieu of other, less desirable courses of action.

The Strategic Management Model

The **strategic management model** shown in Figure 1-1 is a widely accepted, comprehensive depiction of the strategic management process.[2] The process conveyed does not guarantee success, but it does represent a clear and practical approach for formulating, implementing, and evaluating strategies. Relationships among major components of the strategic management process are shown in the model, which appears on the opening page of all subsequent chapters with the speific part of the model shaded to show the particular focus of the respective chapter. This text is organized around the model because it reveals how organizations do strategic planning. There are three important questions to answer in preparing a strategic plan:

Where are we now?

Where do we want to go?

How are we going to get there?

Identifying an organization's existing vision, mission, objectives, and strategies is the logical starting point for strategic management because a firm's present situation and condition may preclude certain strategies and may even dictate a particular course of action. Every organization has a vision, mission, objectives, and strategy, even if these elements are not consciously designed, written, or communicated. The answer to where an organization is going can be determined largely by where the organization has been!

The strategic management process is dynamic and continuous. A change in any one of the major components in the model can necessitate a change in any or all of the other components. For instance, various developing nations coming online could represent a major opportunity and require a change in long-term objectives and strategies; a failure to accomplish annual objectives might require a change in policy; or a major competitor's change in strategy might require a change in the firm's mission. The activities represented in Figure 1-1 are not independent silos; they represent an interrelated process. Thus, activities for strategy formulation, implementation, and evaluation should be performed on a continual basis and not just at the end of the year or semiannually. *The strategic management process never really ends.*

In Figure 1-1, perhaps the most important activity is the feedback loop because strategy must be thought of as a verb rather than a noun. The stages of strategic management (i.e., formulation, implementation, and evaluation) are so fluid as to be virtually indistinguishable because when one starts, the other ends. Continuous feedback enables firms to readily adapt to changing conditions; when anyone is preparing an external or internal assessment or even implementing strategies, they should be mindful of the firm's vision and mission. The feedback loop reveals that a change in any strategic planning activity can impact any or all other activities. For example, changes in a firm's mission can impact all other activities; *everything a firm does should be mission driven.*

Note in Figure 1-1 that business ethics, social responsibility, environmental sustainability, and international issues impact all activities in the model, as discussed in Chapters 10 and 11, respectively. Regarding business ethics, recent research discussed in the Ethics Capsule 1 concludes that exemplary business ethics in a company is increasingly being associated with exemplary reduction in the firm's carbon dioxide (CO_2) emissions.

ETHICS CAPSULE 1

Don't Just Talk the Talk, Walk the Walk, on Emissions[3]

akiyoko/123RF

According to Refinitiv, 67 percent of *Fortune* 500 companies at the end of 2020 had published CO_2 emissions goals, up from less than 50 percent in 2017. However, Boston Consulting Group (BCG) reports that only 11 percent of big companies met their emission-reduction goals over the past 5 years. Goals and actions are easy to state but also easy to disregard because they are difficult to track and harder to enforce. Too many companies talk the talk but for varied reasons do not walk the walk.

Just talking is changing, however, because regulators, investors, customers, and activists are increasingly scrutinizing corporate disclosures, and the Securities and Exchange Commission (SEC) is drafting specific reporting protocols that firms must follow to monitor and report their progress toward reducing emissions. Firms soon cannot simply, for example, pay for trees to be planted to offset their carbon emissions.

A major source of planet-warming CO_2 emissions is airlines, and many of those firms were at the recent United Nations conference on climate change in Glasgow. United Airlines was there and said it will replace 5 percent of its jet fuel with biofuel alternatives by 2030 and will be "100% green," having zero carbon emissions by 2050. United's carbon footprint, however, increased by 10 percent to 42 million tons from 2015 to 2019; so talk is admirable, but action is wonderful. As of October 31, 2021, among the *Fortune* 500 companies, 65 firms had net-zero targets in place.

The International Maritime Organization plans to start charging oceangoing vessels $100 for each metric ton of CO_2 emitted per trip; the World Bank says this action would raise $330 billion annually. There are about 60,000 cargo and passenger ships traveling the world's oceans. *Annual Sustainability Reports* are becoming commonplace as customers increasingly associate exemplary business ethics with exemplary reductions in CO_2 emissions.

Even as companies and countries talk the talk, the global coal-fired power generation rose 9 percent in 2021 as electricity demand surpasses the shift to cleaner energy. This increase is mainly due to China and India that together account for about 67 percent of the world's coal use. Coal use in China and India were up 9 and 12 percent, respectively, in 2021, and through 2024, will increase 4.1 and 11.0 percent, respectively, in the two countries.

[3]Based on Jean Eaglesham, "Companies' Pledges to Reduce Emissions Get a Closer Look," *Wall Street Journal*, November 6–7, 2021, p. B3. Also, Sha Hua, "Fueled by Demand, Global Coal Power Expected to Hit Record," *Wall Street Journal*, December 18–19, 2021, p. A10.

The strategic management process is not as cleanly divided and neatly performed in practice as the strategic-management model suggests. Strategists do not go through the process in lock-step fashion. Generally, there is give-and-take among hierarchical levels of an organization. To develop a strategic plan, many organizations conduct formal meetings semiannually to discuss and update the firm's vision, mission, opportunities, threats, strengths, weaknesses, strategies, objectives, policies, and performance. These meetings are commonly held off premises and are called **retreats**. The rationale for periodically conducting strategic management meetings away from the work site is to encourage more creativity and candor from participants. Good communication and feedback are needed throughout the strategic management process.

Application of the strategic management process is typically more formal in larger and well-established organizations. Formality refers to the extent that participants, responsibilities, authority, duties, and basic approach are objective and clear rather than subjective and vague. Smaller businesses tend to be less formal. Firms that compete in complex, rapidly changing environments, such as technology companies, tend to be more formal in strategic planning. Firms that have many divisions, products, markets, and technologies also tend to be more formal in applying strategic management concepts. Greater formality in applying the strategic management process is usually positively associated with organizational success.[4]

Stages of Strategic Management

1.2. Discuss the three stages of activities for strategy formulation, implementation, and evaluation.

The **strategic management process** consists of three stages: strategy formulation, strategy implementation, and strategy evaluation. **Strategy formulation** includes developing a vision and mission, identifying an organization's external opportunities and threats, determining internal strengths and weaknesses, establishing long-term objectives, generating alternative strategies, and choosing particular strategies to pursue. Strategy-formulation issues include deciding what new businesses to enter, what businesses to abandon, whether to expand operations or diversify, whether to enter international markets, whether to merge or form a joint venture, and how to avoid a hostile takeover.

Because no organization has unlimited resources, strategists must decide which alternative strategies will benefit the firm most. Strategy-formulation decisions commit an organization to specific products, markets, resources, and technologies over an extended period of time. Strategies determine long-term competitive advantages. For better or worse, strategic decisions have major multifunctional consequences and enduring effects on an organization. Top managers have the best perspective to understand fully the ramifications of strategy-formulation decisions; they have the authority to commit the resources necessary for implementation.

Strategy implementation requires a firm to establish annual objectives, devise policies, motivate employees, and allocate resources so that formulated strategies can be executed efficiently. Strategy implementation includes developing a culture supportive of the strategy, creating an organizational structure, redirecting marketing efforts, preparing budgets, developing and using information systems, devising tactics, and linking employee compensation to organizational performance. **Tactics** are actions that bring to life or execute the formulated strategies. Similar tactics can be used to implement various strategies that are different.

Strategy implementation often is called the action stage of strategic management. Implementing strategy means mobilizing employees and managers to put formulated strategies into action. Often considered to be the most difficult stage in strategic management, strategy implementation requires personal discipline, commitment, and sacrifice. Successful strategy implementation hinges on managers' abilities to motivate employees, which is more an art than a science. Strategies formulated but not implemented serve no useful purpose.

Interpersonal skills are especially critical for successful strategy implementation. Strategy-implementation activities affect all employees and managers in an organization. Every division and department must decide on answers to questions such as "What must we do to implement our part of the organization's strategy?" and "How best can we get the job done?" The challenge of implementation is to stimulate managers and employees throughout an organization to work with pride and enthusiasm toward achieving stated objectives.

Strategy evaluation is the final stage in strategic management. Managers desperately need to know when particular strategies are not working well; strategy evaluation is the primary means for obtaining this information. All strategies are subject to future modification because external and internal factors constantly change. Three fundamental strategy-evaluation activities are (1) reviewing external and internal factors that are the bases for current strategies, (2) measuring performance, and (3) taking corrective actions. Strategy evaluation is needed because success today is no guarantee of success tomorrow! Success always creates new and different problems; complacent organizations experience demise.

Formulation, implementation, and evaluation of strategy activities occur at three hierarchical levels in a large organization: corporate, divisional or strategic business unit, and functional. By fostering communication and interaction among managers and employees across hierarchical levels, strategic management helps a firm function as a competitive team. Most small businesses and some large businesses do not have divisions or strategic business units; they have only the corporate and functional levels. Nevertheless, managers and employees at these two levels should be actively involved in strategic management activities.

Peter Drucker says the prime task of strategic management is thinking through the overall mission of a business—

> that is, of asking the question, "What is our business?" This leads to the setting of objectives, the development of strategies, and the making of today's decisions for tomorrow's results. This clearly must be done by a part of the organization that can see the entire business; that can balance objectives and the needs of today against the needs of tomorrow; and that can allocate resources of men and money to key results.[5]

Integrating Analysis and Intuition

1.3. Explain the need for integrating analysis and intuition in strategic management.

W. Edwards Deming once said, "In God we trust. All others bring data." The strategic management process can be described as an objective, logical, systematic approach for making major decisions in an organization. It attempts to organize qualitative and quantitative information in a way that allows effective decisions to be made under conditions of uncertainty. Yet strategic management is not a pure science that lends itself to a nice, neat, one-two-three approach.

Based on past experiences, judgment, and feelings, many people recognize that **intuition** is essential to making good strategic decisions. Some managers and owners of businesses profess to have extraordinary abilities for using intuition alone in devising brilliant strategies. For example, Will Durant, who organized General Motors (GM), was described by Alfred Sloan as "a man who would proceed on a course of action guided solely, as far as I could tell, by some intuitive flash of brilliance. He never felt obliged to make an engineering hunt for the facts. Yet at times, he was astoundingly correct in his judgment."[6] Albert Einstein acknowledged the importance of intuition when he said, "I believe in intuition and inspiration. At times I feel certain that I am right while not knowing the reason. Imagination is more important than knowledge because knowledge is limited, whereas imagination embraces the entire world."[7]

Although some organizations today may survive and prosper because they have intuitive geniuses managing them, most are not so fortunate. Most organizations can benefit from integrating intuition and analysis in decision-making. Choosing an intuitive or analytic approach to decision-making is not an either-or proposition. Managers at all levels in an organization inject their intuition and judgment into strategic management analyses. Analytical thinking and intuitive thinking complement each other.

Operating from the I've-already-made-up-my-mind-don't-bother-me-with-the-facts mode is not management by intuition; it is management by ignorance.[8] Drucker says, "I believe in intuition only if you discipline it. 'Hunch' artists, who make a diagnosis but don't check it out with the facts, are the ones in medicine who kill people, and in management kill businesses."[9] In a sense, the strategic management process is an attempt to duplicate what goes on in the mind of a brilliant, intuitive person who knows the business and assimilates and integrates that knowledge through analysis in formulating strategies.

Adapting to Change

The strategic management process is based on the belief that organizations should continually monitor internal and external events and trends so that timely changes can be made as needed. The rate and magnitude of changes that affect organizations are increasing dramatically, as evidenced by how the coronavirus (COVID-19) pandemic caught so many firms by surprise. Firms, like organisms, must be "adept at adapting," or they will not survive.

To survive, all organizations must astutely identify and adapt to change. As indicated in Global Capsule 1, for some companies, adapting to change means downsizing or removing their operations in China. The strategic management process is aimed at allowing organizations to adapt effectively to change over the long run. Waterman noted:

> In today's business environment, more than in any preceding era, the only constant is change. Successful organizations effectively manage change, continuously adapting their bureaucracies, strategies, systems, products, and cultures to survive the shocks and prosper from the forces that decimate the competition.[10]

The need to adapt to change leads organizations to fundamental strategic management questions, such as What kind of business should we become? Are we in the right field(s)? Should we reshape our business? What new competitors are entering our industry? What strategies should we pursue? How are our customers changing? Are new technologies being developed that could put us out of business?

One way many firms are adapting to change is by acquiring their suppliers or moving production facilities closer to home to help alleviate bottlenecks resulting from supply chains. The historical practice of using inexpensive manufacturing in distant locales, outsourcing many low-skill jobs, and relying on ocean transportation to obtain needed supplies is waning rapidly. Almost all businesses are being impacted by unreliable supply chains,

GLOBAL CAPSULE 1

Companies Exiting China amid Tightening Security Measures[11]

michal812/Shutterstock

Yahoo just ceased doing business in China, on the heels of Microsoft's LinkedIn removing itself from China. China's tighter data security and privacy regulations, along with rising geopolitical tensions, have foreign firms rethinking mainland China as a profitable place to do business. China's closed border policies and crackdown on big technology firms also have many foreign multinational companies downsizing or removing operations in the country.

The world's largest videogame publisher, Tencent, is rethinking its operations in China because the country imposed restrictions that limit children's playtime on videogames to 3 hours per week; China has also put all new videogame approvals on hold. Players younger than age 18 now account for only 1.1 percent of Tencent's revenues in China; it is difficult to do business with those numbers. Tencent just withdrew the game *Fortnite* completely from China.

[11]Based on Liza Lin, "Yahoo to End Operations in China," *Wall Street Journal,* November 11, 2021, pp. B1, B2.

everything from sneakers to airlines to McDonald's. Initially, many CEOs thought supply chain bottlenecks were related to the COVID-19 pandemic, but now they realize it is also related to politics and weather. But whatever the reason, unavailable supplies can quickly put any business out of business.

Key Terms in Strategic Management

1.4. Define and give examples of key terms in strategic management.

Before we further discuss strategic management, we should define 10 key terms: *competitive advantage, strategists, vision and mission statements, external opportunities and threats, internal strengths and weaknesses, long-term objectives, strategies, SWOT analysis, annual objectives,* and *policies.*

Competitive Advantage

Strategic management is all about gaining and maintaining **competitive advantage**. This term can be defined as any activity a firm does especially well compared with activities done by rival firms or any resource a firm possesses that rival firms desire. For example, having fewer fixed assets than rival firms can provide major competitive advantages. Apple Inc. has virtually no manufacturing facilities of its own, whereas rival Sony owns 57 electronics factories. Apple relies almost entirely on contract manufacturers for production of its products.

Normally, a firm can sustain a competitive advantage for only a certain period because of rival firms imitating and undermining that advantage. Thus, it is not adequate simply to obtain competitive advantage. A firm must strive to achieve **sustained competitive advantage** by continually adapting to changes in external trends and events, internal capabilities, competencies, and resources. For example, Meta Platforms is engaged in fierce competition with TikTok. Meta recently launched its short-video product called Reels as it tries to strengthen its video business. TikTok was the most-downloaded app globally in 2021 when it overtook Meta's Instagram in popularity among coveted young users.

Strategists

Strategists are the individuals most responsible for the success or failure of an organization. They have various job titles, such as *CEO, chief strategy officer, president, owner, chair of the board, executive director, chancellor, dean,* and *entrepreneur.* Jay Conger, professor of organizational behavior at the London Business School and author of *Building Leaders*, says, "All strategists have to be chief learning officers. We are in an extended period of change. If our leaders aren't highly adaptive and great models during this period, then our companies won't adapt either, because ultimately leadership is about being a role model."

The chief strategy officer (CSO) position has become common in many organizations. Hundreds of companies have appointed a new CSO in the last couple of years, including Cheryl Policastro who was just appointed CSO of the creative commerce agency TPN headquartered in Dallas, Texas. Scott Soussa, a former senior executive of the real estate investment firm Blackstone was hired by a large rival firm, Angelo Gordon, and was appointed CSO beginning in April 2022. Adam Lurie was hired by and appointed as CSO of a leading artificial intelligence firm, Torch.AI. Also in April 2022, Starbucks hired a new CSO, Frank Britt, who now reports directly to CEO Johnson. Starbucks had not had a CSO since 2018. Mr. Britt is aiming to help curtail unionization efforts occurring throughout the Starbucks system.

Athletic coaches are also strategists. Football, basketball, baseball, soccer and, in fact, many athletic contests are often won or lost based on a team's game plan. For example, a basketball coach may plan to fast break and play up-tempo, rather than play more half-court, if the players are smaller and faster or if the team has more depth than the opposing team. Some inspirational, quotes related to strategy planning from legendary National Football League (NFL) coaches are provided in Table 1-2.

TABLE 1-2 Eight Famous Quotes Related to Strategic Planning from NFL Coaches

1. "Perfection is not attainable. But if we chase perfection, we can catch excellence."—*Vince Lombardi, Head Coach Green Bay Packers (1959–1967)*
2. "Leadership is a matter of having people look at you and gain confidence. . . . If you're in control, they're in control."—*Tom Landry, Head Coach Dallas Cowboys (1960–1988)*
3. "If you want to win, do the ordinary things better than anyone else does them, day in and day out."—*Chuck Noll, Head Coach Pittsburgh Steelers (1969–1991)*
4. "Leaders are made, they are not born. They are made by hard effort, which is the price which all of us must pay to achieve any goal that is worthwhile."—*Vince Lombardi, Head Coach Green Bay Packers (1959–1967)*
5. "You fail all the time, but you aren't a failure until you start blaming someone else."—*Bum Phillips, Head Coach Houston Oilers (1975–1980) and New Orleans Saints (1981–1985)*
6. "Success demands singleness of purpose."—*Vince Lombardi, Head Coach Green Bay Packers (1959–1967)*
7. "Stay focused. Your start does not determine how you're going to finish."—*Herm Edwards, Head Football Coach of the New York Jets (2001–2005), Kansas City Chiefs (2006–2008), and Arizona State University (2018 to present)*
8. "Nobody who ever gave his best regretted it."—*George S. Halas, Head Coach Chicago Bears (1933–1942, 1946–1955, 1958–1967)*

Source: A variety of sources.

Vision and Mission Statements

Many organizations develop a **vision statement** that answers the question "What do we want to become?" Developing a vision statement is often considered the first step in strategic planning, preceding even development of a mission statement. Many vision statements are a single sentence as revealed through numerous examples in Chapter 2.

A **mission statement** is an "enduring statement of purpose that distinguishes one business from other similar firms. A mission statement identifies the scope of a firm's operations in product and market terms."[12] It addresses the basic question that faces all strategists: What is our business? A clear mission statement describes the values and priorities of an organization. Developing a mission statement compels strategists to think about the nature and scope of present operations and to assess the potential attractiveness of future markets and activities. A mission statement broadly charts the future direction of an organization and serves as a constant reminder to its employees of why the organization exists and what the founders envisioned when they put their fame and fortune (and names) at risk to breathe life into their dreams.

External Opportunities and Threats

External opportunities and **external threats** refer to **political, economic, sociocultural, technological, environmental, legal (PESTEL)**, and competitive trends and events that could significantly benefit or harm an organization in the future. Opportunities and threats are largely beyond the control of a single organization, thus, the word *external*. Some example opportunities and threats are listed in Table 1-3. Dollars, numbers, percentages, ratios, and quantification are essential so strategists can assess the magnitude of opportunities and threats and take appropriate actions. For example, in Table 1-3, rather than saying "Marketing is moving rapidly to the internet," strategists need to conduct research and find, for example, that "spending on online advertisements globally is rising 18 percent annually and represents about 44 percent of total advertising expenditures in the United States." Strategies must be formulated and implemented based on specific factual information to the extent possible because so much is at stake in having a good game plan.

External trends and events are creating a different type of consumer and, consequently, a need for different types of products, services, and strategies. A competitor's strength could be a threat, or a rival firm's weakness could be an opportunity. A basic tenet of strategic management is that firms need to formulate strategies to take advantage of external opportunities and avoid or reduce the impact of external threats. For this reason, identifying, monitoring, and evaluating external opportunities and threats is essential for success. This process of conducting research and gathering and assimilating external information is sometimes called **environmental scanning** or *industry analysis*.

TABLE 1-3 Some Example Opportunities and Threats

- Consumer expectation for green operations and products is rising 8 percent annually in Western Europe.
- Internet marketing is growing 11 percent annually in the United States.
- Commodity food prices rose 6 percent the prior year.
- Oil and gas prices increased 8 percent in the last 12 months.
- Computer hacker problems are increasing 14 percent annually.
- Interest rates are 2 percent but are rising in the United States.
- State and local governments' finances worsened 12 percent last year.
- The number of births declined 5 percent annually in many countries over the last 3 years.
- The gross domestic product (GDP) of Brazil fell from 6 percent to 5 percent in the last year.
- Competitor XYZ just introduced product ABC at a 10 percent lower price than our product.
- Social media networking is growing 9 percent annually in China.

Internal Strengths and Weaknesses

Internal strengths and **internal weaknesses** are an organization's controllable activities that are performed especially well or poorly. They arise in the activities of management, marketing, finance/accounting, production, and information systems of a business. Identifying and evaluating organizational strengths and weaknesses in the functional areas of a business is an essential activity in strategic management. Organizations strive to pursue strategies that capitalize on internal strengths and improve internal weaknesses.

Strengths and weaknesses are determined relative to competitors. *Relative deficiency or superiority is important information.* Also, strengths and weaknesses can be determined by elements of *being* rather than *performance*. For example, a strength may involve ownership of natural resources or a historic reputation for quality. Strengths and weaknesses may be determined relative to a firm's own objectives. For instance, high levels of inventory turnover may not be a strength for a firm that seeks never to stockout.

Internal factors can be determined in a number of ways, including computing ratios, measuring performance, and making comparisons to past periods and industry averages. Various types of surveys also can be developed and administered to examine internal factors, such as employee morale, production efficiency, advertising effectiveness, and customer loyalty.

Long-Term Objectives

Objectives can be defined as specific results that an organization seeks to achieve in pursuing its mission. Long term means more than one year. Objectives are essential for organizational success because they provide direction; aid in evaluation; foster synergy; reveal priorities; focus coordination; and provide a basis for effective planning, organizing, motivating, and controlling activities. Objectives should be challenging, measurable, consistent, reasonable, and clear. In a multidivisional firm, objectives are needed both for the overall company and each division. Some companies list as objectives "to grow sales profitably" and "to maximize total shareholder return." Avoid vagueness like this throughout a strategic-planning project!

As indicated in this chapters' Ethics Capsule, most large companies and many small firms now have specific CO_2 emissions and sustainability objectives, as well as specific diversity, equity, and inclusion (DEI) objectives. For example, by 2030, McDonald's objective is to achieve a 31 percent reduction in emissions from its 2015 baseline. Be mindful that regarding annual revenue and net income objectives, shareholders expect at least a 5 percent top-line and bottom-line increase, so any strategic plan developed in this course or within a firm should strive for 5+ percent growth annually.

Strategies

Strategies are the means by which **long-term objectives** will be achieved. Business strategies may include geographic expansion, diversification, acquisition, product development, market penetration, retrenchment, divestiture, liquidation, and joint ventures. Strategies are potential actions that require top management decisions and significant amounts of the firm's resources. They affect an organization's long-term prosperity, typically for at least 5 years and, thus, are future oriented. Strategies also have multifunctional and multidivisional consequences and require consideration of both the external and internal factors facing the firm.

Strategies currently being pursued by DuPont and Coca-Cola are described in Table 1-4.

TABLE 1-4 Two Companies' Strategies in Action: DuPont and Coca-Cola

DuPont de Nemours, Inc. is actively acquiring and divesting companies as it strives to reinvent and pivot itself from being a chemicals and plastics firm to a company that capitalizes on the booming hybrid and electric vehicle industry and the high-speed 5G telecommunication networks business. Consistent with this strategy, DuPont just acquired the electronics materials maker Rogers Corporation for $5.2 billion and sold (divested) its materials, thermoplastics, nylon, and mobility segments.

Coca-Cola Company paid $5.6 billion for the remaining 70 percent of BodyArmor, based in New York, that it did not already own. The sports-drink brand BodyArmor is the major rival drink to industry-leading Gatorade that is owned by PepsiCo. Coke obtained about $1.4 billion in sales of BodyArmor in 2021, up from $250 million in 2018, but Gatorade sales annually are about $8.4 billion. Coke's Powerade has about 13 percent market share in the industry compared with BodyArmor at about 18 percent and Gatorade at about 64 percent. Part of the $5.6 billion went to three big sports investors of BodyArmor, James Harden (NBA star), the Koby Bryant estate (former NBA star), and Mike Trout (MLB star).

Source: Based on a variety of sources.

SWOT Analysis

Strengths-Weaknesses-Opportunities-Threats (SWOT) Analysis is an important matching tool that helps managers develop four types of strategies: SO (strengths-opportunities) strategies, WO (weaknesses-opportunities) strategies, ST (strengths-threats) strategies, and WT (weaknesses-threats) strategies.[13] Matching key external and internal factors is a critically important activity in strategic planning. Note in Table 1-5 that the resultant strategies 1, 2, 3, and 4 are SO, WO, ST, and WT strategies, respectively. SWOT analysis is explained further in Chapter 6, but the matching of external with internal factors to generate strategies results in a SWOT Matrix as illustrated in Figure 1-2.

Annual Objectives

Annual objectives are short-term milestones that organizations must achieve to reach long-term objectives. Like long-term objectives, annual objectives should be measurable, quantitative, challenging, realistic, consistent, and prioritized. They must also be established at the corporate,

TABLE 1-5 Matching Key External and Internal Factors to Formulate Strategies

Key Internal Factor	Key External Factor	Resultant Strategy
S1: Demand for Dunkin' up 6 percent annually (internal strength)	+ O1: Desire for healthy products up 8 percent annually (external opportunity)	= SO1: Dunkin' eliminated all artificial dyes and colors in its donuts in 2018
W1: Insufficient production capacity by 1 million units annually (internal weakness)	+ O2: Exit of two major foreign competitors from the area (external opportunity)	= WO1: Purchase competitors' production facilities
S2: R&D has developed four new products in 12 months (internal strength)	+ T1: Sugary drink consumption is declining 5 percent annually (external threat)	= ST1: Spend $1 million to promote healthiness of four new products
W2: Poor employee morale (internal weakness)	+ T2: Health-care costs rose 7 percent last year (external threat)	= WT1: Implement a new corporate wellness program

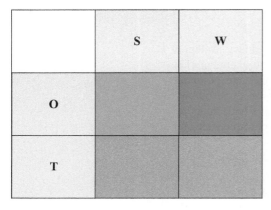

	STRENGTHS (S)	WEAKNESSES (W)
	1. 2. 3. 4. 5. 6. 7. 8. 9. 10.	1. 2. 3. 4. 5. 6. 7. 8. 9. 10.
OPPORTUNITIES (O)	**SO STRATEGIES**	**WO STRATEGIES**
1. 2. 3. 4. 5. 6. 7. 8. 9. 10.	1. 2. ETC.	1. 2. ETC.
THREATS (T)	**ST STRATEGIES**	**WT STRATEGIES**
1. 2. 3. 4. 5. 6. 7. 8. 9. 10.	1. 2. ETC.	1. 2. ETC.

FIGURE 1-2
The Basic SWOT Matrix Format

divisional, and functional levels in a large organization. Annual objectives should be stated in terms of management, marketing, finance/accounting, production, and information systems accomplishments. A set of annual objectives is needed for each long-term objective. These objectives are especially important in strategy implementation, whereas long-term objectives are particularly important in strategy formulation. Annual objectives provide the basis for allocating resources.

Policies

Policies are the means by which annual objectives will be achieved. Policies include guidelines, rules, and procedures established to support efforts to achieve stated objectives. Policies are guides to decision-making and address repetitive or recurring situations. Usually, policies are stated in terms of management, marketing, finance/accounting, production/operations, R&D, and management information systems (MIS) activities. They may be established at the corporate level and apply to an entire organization, at the divisional level and apply to a single division, or they may be established at the functional level and apply to particular operational activities or departments.

Like annual objectives, policies are especially important in strategy implementation because they outline an organization's expectations of its employees and managers. Policies allow consistency and coordination within and between organizational departments. For example, hundreds of companies are revising their policies related to employees working from home and employees' smartphone use during working hours. New policies abound related to monitoring diversity, inclusion, affirmative action, pollution abatement, and employee benefits. For example, banks are required to record employees' work-related phone calls, emails, and texts. Effective monitoring of such communications is challenging given that many bank employees today are working from home. In 2022, JP Morgan Chase paid a $200 million fine for not properly monitoring employees' messages.

Benefits of Engaging in Strategic Management

1.5. Describe the benefits of engaging in strategic management.

Strategic management allows an organization to be more proactive than reactive in shaping its own future; it allows an organization to initiate and influence (rather than just respond to) activities and, thus, exert control over its own destiny. Small business owners, CEOs, presidents, and managers of many for-profit and nonprofit organizations have recognized and realized the benefits of strategic management.

Historically, the principal benefit of strategic management has been to help organizations formulate better strategies through the use of a more systematic, logical, and rational approach for decision-making. In addition, the process, rather than the decision or document, is also a major benefit of engaging in strategic management. Through involvement in the process (i.e., dialogue and participation), managers and employees become committed to supporting the organization. *A key to successful strategic management is communication, and it may be the most important word in all of management.* Figure 1-3 illustrates this intrinsic benefit of a firm engaging in strategic planning; note that all firms need all employees "on a mission" to help the firm succeed.

Dale McConkey said, "Plans are less important than planning." The manner in which strategic management is carried out is therefore exceptionally important. A major aim of the process is to achieve understanding and commitment from all managers and employees. Understanding may be the most important benefit of strategic management, followed by commitment. When managers and employees understand what the organization is doing and why, they often feel a part of the firm and become committed to assisting it. This is especially true when employees also understand links between their own compensation and organizational performance. Managers and employees become surprisingly creative and innovative when they understand and support the firm's mission, objectives, and strategies. A great benefit of strategic management, then, is the opportunity that the process provides to empower individuals. **Empowerment** is the act of strengthening employees' sense of effectiveness by encouraging them to participate in decision-making and exercise initiative and imagination, while rewarding them for doing so. *You want your people to run the business as it if were their own.*

Strategic planning is a learning, helping, educating, and supporting process and not merely a paper-shuffling activity among top executives. Dialogue about strategic management is more important than a nicely bound document about it. A strategist must avoid developing a strategic plan alone and then presenting the plan to operating managers to execute. Through involvement in the process, line managers must become "owners" of the strategy. *Ownership of a strategic plan by the people who have to execute the plan is a key to success in any organization.*

Although making good strategic decisions is the major responsibility of an organization's owner or CEO, both managers and employees must also be involved in strategy formulation, implementation, and evaluation activities. Participation is fundamental to gaining commitment for needed changes. An increasing number of corporations and institutions are using strategic management to make effective decisions. But strategic management is not a guarantee for success; it can be dysfunctional if conducted haphazardly.

Financial Benefits

Organizations that use strategic management concepts are generally more successful, showing significant improvement in sales, profitability, and productivity, compared to firms without systematic planning activities. High-performing firms tend to do systematic planning to prepare for future fluctuations in their external and internal environments. Firms with management systems that use strategic planning concepts, tools, and techniques generally exhibit superior long-term financial performance relative to their industry.

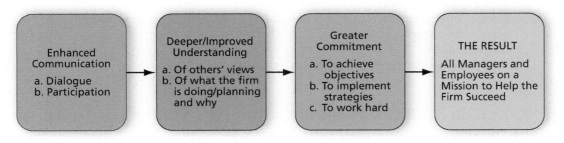

FIGURE 1-3

Benefits to a Firm that Does Strategic Planning

High-performing firms seem to make more informed decisions with good anticipation of both short- and long-term consequences. In contrast, firms that perform poorly often engage in activities that are shortsighted and do not reflect good forecasting of future conditions. Strategists of low-performing organizations are often preoccupied with solving internal problems and meeting paperwork deadlines. They typically underestimate their competitors' strengths and overestimate their own firm's strengths. They often attribute weak performance to uncontrollable factors such as a poor economy, technological change, or foreign competition.

More than 100,000 businesses in the United States fail annually. Business failures include bankruptcies, foreclosures, liquidations, and court-mandated receiverships. Although many factors besides a lack of effective strategic management can lead to business failure, the planning concepts and tools described in this text can yield substantial financial benefits for any organization.

Nonfinancial Benefits

Besides helping firms avoid financial demise, strategic management offers other tangible benefits, such as enhanced awareness of external threats, improved understanding of competitors' strategies, increased employee productivity, reduced resistance to change, and a clearer understanding of performance–reward relationships. Strategic management enhances the problem-prevention capabilities of organizations because it promotes interaction among managers at all divisional and functional levels. Firms that have nurtured their managers and employees, shared organizational objectives with them, empowered them to help improve the product or service, and recognized their contributions can turn to them for help in a pinch because of this interaction.

In addition to empowering managers and employees, strategic management often brings order and discipline to an otherwise floundering firm. It can be the beginning of an efficient and effective managerial system. Strategic management may renew confidence in the current business strategy or point to the need for corrective actions. The strategic management process provides a basis for identifying and rationalizing the need for change to all managers and employees of a firm; it helps them view change as an opportunity rather than as a threat. Some nonfinancial benefits of a firm using strategic management are increased discipline, improved coordination, enhanced communication, increased forward thinking, improved decision-making, increased synergy, and more effective allocation of time and resources.

Why Some Firms Do No Strategic Planning

1.6. Explain why some firms do not engage in strategic planning.

Some firms do not engage in formal strategic planning, and some firms do engage in strategic planning but receive little support from managers and employees. What follows are 10 reasons (excuses) often given for minimal or no strategic planning in a firm.

1. No formal training in strategic management.
2. No understanding of or appreciation for the benefits of planning.
3. No monetary rewards for planning.
4. No punishment for not planning.
5. Too busy "firefighting" (resolving internal crises) to plan ahead.
6. View planning as a waste of time because no product or service is made.
7. Laziness; effective planning takes time and effort; time is money.
8. Content with current success; failure to realize that success today is no guarantee for success tomorrow.
9. Overconfidence.
10. Prior bad experience with strategic planning done sometime, somewhere.

Pitfalls in Strategic Planning

1.7. Describe the pitfalls in doing strategic planning.

Strategic planning is an involved, intricate, and complex process that takes an organization into uncharted territory. It does not provide a ready-to-use prescription for success; instead, it takes the organization through a journey and offers a framework for addressing questions and solving problems. Being aware of potential pitfalls and being prepared to address them is essential to success. There are some pitfalls in doing strategic planning; avoid the following:

- Using strategic planning to gain control over decisions and resources.
- Doing strategic planning only to satisfy accreditation or regulatory requirements.
- Too hastily moving from mission development to strategy formulation.
- Not communicating the plan to employees, who continue working in the dark.
- Top managers making many intuitive decisions that conflict with the formal plan.
- Top managers not actively supporting the strategic planning process.
- Not using plans as a standard for measuring performance.
- Delegating planning to a "planner" rather than involving all managers.
- Not involving essential employees in all phases of planning.
- Not creating a collaborative climate supportive of change.
- Viewing planning as unnecessary or unimportant.
- Viewing planning activities as silos comprised of independent parts.
- Becoming so engrossed in current problems that insufficient or no planning is done.
- Being so formal in planning that flexibility and creativity are stifled.[14]

Comparing Business and Military Strategies

1.8. Discuss the connection between business and military strategies.

A strong military heritage underlies the study of strategic management. Terms such as *objectives, mission, strengths,* and *weaknesses* were first formulated to address problems on the battlefield. According to *Webster's New World Dictionary, strategy* is "the science of planning and directing large-scale military operations, of maneuvering forces into the most advantageous position prior to actual engagement with the enemy."[15] The word *strategy* comes from the Greek *strategos,* which refers to a military general and combines *stratos* (the army) and *agos* (to lead). The history of strategic planning began in the military. A vital aim of both business and military strategy is "to gain competitive advantage." In many respects, business strategy is like military strategy, and military strategists have learned much over the centuries that can benefit business strategists today.

Both business and military organizations try to use their own strengths to exploit competitors' weaknesses. If an organization's overall strategy is wrong (ineffective), then all the efficiency in the world may not be enough to allow success. Business or military success is generally not the happy result of accidental strategies. Rather, success is the product of both continuous attention to changing external and internal conditions and the formulation and implementation of insightful adaptations to those conditions.

Born in Pella in 356 BCE, Alexander the Great was king of Macedon, a state in northern ancient Greece. Tutored by Aristotle until the age of 16, Alexander had created one of the largest empires of the ancient world by the age of 30, stretching from the Ionian Sea to the Himalayas. Alexander was undefeated in battle and is considered one of history's most successful commanders. He became the measure against which military leaders even today compare themselves, and military academies throughout the world still teach his strategies and tactics. Alexander the Great once said, "Greater is an army of sheep led by a lion, than an army of lions led by a sheep." This quote reveals the overwhelming importance of an excellent strategic plan for any organization to succeed.

Both business and military organizations must adapt to change and constantly improve to be successful. Too often, firms do not change their strategies when their environment and competitive conditions dictate the need to change. Frederick Gluck offered a classic military example of this:

When Napoleon won, it was because his opponents were committed to the strategy, tactics, and organization of earlier wars. When he lost—against Wellington, the Russians, and the Spaniards—it was because he, in turn, used tried-and-true strategies against enemies who thought afresh, who were developing the strategies not of the last war but of the next.[16]

Sun Tzu's *The Art of War* has been applied to many fields well outside of the military. Much of the text is about how to fight wars without actually having to do battle: It gives tips on how to outsmart one's opponent so that physical battle is not necessary. As such, the book has found application as a training guide for many competitive endeavors that do not involve actual combat, such as in devising courtroom trial strategy or acquiring a rival company. Similarities can be construed from Sun Tzu's writings to the practice of formulating and implementing strategies among businesses today. Table 1-6 provides narrative excerpts from *The Art of War*. Of the principles listed, which do you believe are most applicable or analogous to companies as compared to armies?

In ancient times, a bad military strategy or game plan could result in nearly 100,000 men being killed in a single battle. For example, in the Battle of Cannae on August 2, 216 BCE, near the ancient village of Cannae in Apulia in southeast Italy, the famous leader Hannibal and his Carthaginians, surrounded and annihilated a Roman army of about 86,000 men, almost all of whom were killed on that day. The Battle of Cannae is regarded as one of the worst defeats in Roman history, but there are countless examples like this over the last 2,000 years where a weaker force, with a superior strategic plan, destroys a much larger force with an inferior plan. Survival of any entity is oftentimes at stake based on the strategic plan, both in business and military settings.

TABLE 1-6 Excerpts from Sun Tzu's *The Art of War* Writings

- Strategic planning is a matter of vital importance to the state: a matter of life or death, the road either to survival or ruin. Hence, it is imperative that it be studied thoroughly.

- Strategic planning is based on deception. When near the enemy, make it seem that you are far away; when far away, make it seem that you are near. Hold out baits to lure the enemy. Strike the enemy when he is in disorder. Avoid the enemy when he is stronger. Attack the enemy where he is unprepared. Appear where you are not expected.

- A speedy victory is the main object in strategic planning. If this is long in coming, weapons are blunted and morale depressed. When the army engages in protracted campaigns, the resources of the state will fall short. Thus, while we have heard of stupid haste in war, we have not yet seen a clever operation that was prolonged.

- Generally, in strategic planning the best policy is to take a state intact; to ruin it is inferior to this. To capture the enemy's entire army is better than to destroy it; to take intact a regiment, a company, or a squad is better than to destroy it. For to win 100 victories in 100 battles is not the epitome of skill. To subdue the enemy without fighting is the supreme excellence. Those skilled in war subdue the enemy's army without battle.

- The art of using troops is this: When 10 to the enemy's 1, surround him. When five times his strength, attack him. If double his strength, divide him. If equally matched, you may engage him with some good plan. If weaker, be capable of withdrawing. And if in all respects unequal, be capable of eluding him.

- Know your enemy and know yourself, and in a hundred battles you will never be defeated. When you are ignorant of the enemy but know yourself, your chances of winning or losing are equal. If ignorant both of your enemy and of yourself, you are sure to be defeated in every battle.

- He who occupies the field of battle first and awaits his enemy is at ease, and he who comes later to the scene and rushes into the fight is weary; those skilled in war bring the enemy to the field of battle rather than being brought there by him.

- Analyze the enemy's plans so that you will know his deficiencies as well as his strengths. Agitate him to ascertain the pattern of his movement. Lure him out to reveal his dispositions and position. Launch probing attacks to decipher strengths and weaknesses.

- Avoid strength. Strike weakness. Anyone able to win the victory by modifying his tactics in accordance with the enemy situation may be said to be divine.

- If you decide to go into battle, do not announce your intentions or plans. Project "business as usual."

- Unskilled leaders work out their conflicts on battlefields. Brilliant strategists rarely go to battle; they achieve their objectives through tactical positioning well in advance of confrontation.

- When you do decide to challenge another company (or army), much calculating, estimating, analyzing, and positioning bring triumph. Little computation brings defeat.

- Skillful leaders do not let a strategy inhibit creative counter-movement. Thus, commands from a distance should not interfere with spontaneous maneuvering at the point of attack.

- When a decisive advantage is gained over a rival, skillful leaders do not press on. They hold their position and give their rivals the opportunity to surrender or merge. Never allow your forces to be damaged by those who have nothing to lose.

Note: The word *strategic planning* is substituted for *war* or *warfare*.
Source: Based on *Sun Tzu's The Art of War* Writings, 1910, Lionel Giles.

Developing Employability Skills

1.9. Explain how this course can enhance a student's employability.

The how-to, skills-oriented, practical approach of this text's content and layout enables students to gain numerous career-enhancing (employability) skills that experts say are vital for success in the workplace of the 21st century. **Employability** skills include tools, techniques, and concepts being used by businesses and learned by students using this text; the skills can be grouped into 6 broad categories and 14 specific categories, as shown in Table 1-7.

TABLE 1-7 Employability Skills to Be Gained by Students Using This Text

Broad Skills to Be Developed
1. Critical thinking: to define and solve problems and make decisions or form judgments about a particular situation or set of circumstances.
2. Collaboration: to work with colleagues on reports, presentations, and projects.
3. Knowledge application and analysis: to learn a concept and then apply that knowledge to other challenges.
4. Business ethics and social responsibility: to know in your heart that good ethics is good business.
5. Information technology: to enhance one's word-processing, spreadsheet, database, presentation, and software skills.
6. Data literacy: to access, assess, interpret, manipulate, summarize, and communicate data.

Specific Skills to Be Gained; Learn How to:
1. Develop a 3-year strategic plan for any for-profit or nonprofit company or organization.
2. Write and evaluate vision and mission statements.
3. Conduct an external and internal strategic planning assessment.
4. Formulate strategies using SWOT analysis.
5. Develop and use a BCG and Internal-External (IE) Portfolio Matrix analysis.
6. Develop and use a Quantitative Stragegic Planning Matrix (QSPM) analysis.
7. Determine an appropriate set of recommendations with associated costs for any firm.
8. Develop and use perceptual maps to better position firms versus rival companies.
9. Determine the value of any firm using various corporate valuation methods.
10. Perform earnings per share-earnings before interest and taxes (EPS-EBIT) analysis to determine the extent that debt versus stock should be used to raise needed capital for the firm.
11. Develop and use value chain analysis, balanced scorecards, and financial ratio analysis.
12. Evaluate corporate structures and develop effective organizational charts.
13. Develop and use projected financial statements to support any proposed strategic plan.
14. Use a popular corporate strategic planning Excel template.

Means Used to Develop Skills, this text has:
11 concise chapters organized around a practical, integrative strategic planning model.

61 end-of-chapter assurance-of-learning exercises organized in four effective, fun categories.

355 end-of-chapter review questions.

30 brand-new, student-friendly cases on companies in the news undergoing change.

11 mini-cases with chapter relevant questions.

A Cohesion Case on McDonald's at the end of this chapter and many associated end-of-chapter exercises.

A popular Excel-based, Strategic Planning Template widely used by both companies and students doing strategic planning (see the author website at www.strategyclub.com)

IMPLICATIONS FOR STRATEGISTS

Figure 1-4 shows that to gain and sustain competitive advantages, a firm must create and nurture a clear vision and mission and then systematically formulate, implement, and evaluate strategies. Consistent business success rarely happens by chance; it most often results from careful planning followed by diligent, intelligent, hard work. If the process were easy, every business would be successful. Consistent success requires that strategists gather and assimilate relevant data, make tough trade-offs among various options that would benefit the firm, energize and reward employees, and continually adapt to change. To survive and prosper, a business must gain and sustain at least one major competitive advantage over rival firms. In the process, many attractive options will be discarded in favor of a few; strategic planning in a sense can be defined as "choosing what not to do."

The strategic management process represents a systematic means for creating, maintaining, and strengthening a firm's competitive advantage(s). This text provides step-by-step guidance throughout the process to help strategists gain and sustain a firm's competitive advantages. As the 11 chapters unfold, more than 100 key elements of the process, ranging from developing portfolio matrices to managing workplace romance, are examined to help strategists lead their firm in delivering prosperity to shareholders, customers, and employees. The 11 chapters provide a clear, planned, journey through the strategic management process, with numerous highlights accented along the way, so strategists can perform essential analyses and anticipate and resolve potential problems in leading their firm to success. Use the free Excel template at www.strategyclub.com to keep your firm's strategic planning process on track.

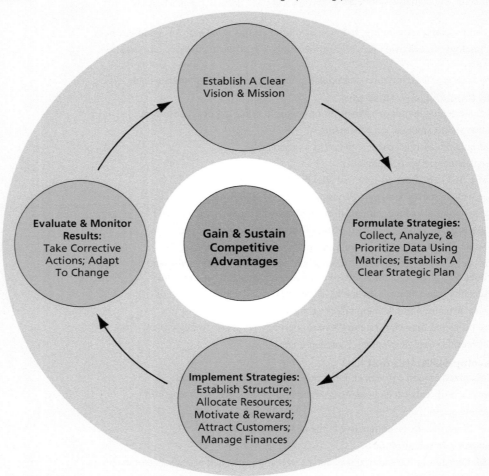

FIGURE 1-4

How to Gain and Sustain Competitive Advantages

IMPLICATIONS FOR STUDENTS

In performing strategic management case analysis, emphasize throughout your project, beginning with the first page or slide, where your firm has competitive advantages and disadvantages. More importantly, emphasize throughout how you recommend the firm sustain and grow its competitive advantages and how you recommend the firm overcome its competitive disadvantages. Pave the way early and often in your presentation for what you ultimately recommend that your firm should do over the next 3 years. The notion of competitive advantage should be integral to the discussion on every page or PowerPoint slide. Therefore, avoid being merely *descriptive* in your written or oral analysis, but, rather, be *prescriptive*, insightful, and forward-looking throughout your project.

For all the reasons given in Table 1-8, use the free Excel strategic planning template at www.strategyclub.com to develop your 3-year strategic plan for any assigned case company.

TABLE 1-8 12 Reasons Students (and Companies) Use the Strategic Planning Template at www.strategyclub.com

1. To save time in preparing a strategic management case analysis; enables user to focus on the "thinking rather than the mechanics" of developing matrices and performing analyses.
2. To follow the correct process in formulating and implementing strategies.
3. To avoid mistakes in math calculations, plotting points, and drawing graphs.
4. To develop professional-looking charts, graphs, and matrices.
5. To develop existing and projected financial ratios.
6. To correctly place firms in BCG and IE portfolio matrices.
7. To examine many different scenarios for using debt versus stock to raise needed capital, using EPS-EBIT analysis.
8. To vary weights and ratings in matrices and to see the resultant impact on total weighted scores.
9. To more easily share information with team members and colleagues.
10. To more easily develop projected financial statements to reveal the expected impact of various strategies.
11. To develop skills with perceptual mapping or product positioning.
12. To gain experience using actual corporate strategic planning software; many business jobs require proficiency in Excel, which students gain in using the template.

Chapter Summary

All firms have a strategy, even if it is informal, unstructured, and sporadic. All organizations are heading somewhere, but unfortunately some organizations do not know where they are going. The old saying "If you do not know where you are going, then any road will lead you there!" accents the need for organizations to use strategic management concepts and techniques. The strategic management process is becoming more widely used by small firms, large companies, nonprofit institutions, governmental organizations, and multinational conglomerates alike. The process of empowering managers and employees has almost limitless benefits.

Organizations should take a proactive rather than a reactive approach in their industry, and they should strive to influence, anticipate, and initiate rather than just respond to events. The strategic management process embodies this approach to decision-making. It represents a logical, systematic, and objective approach for determining an enterprise's future direction. The stakes are generally too high for strategists to use intuition alone in choosing among alternative courses of action. Successful strategists take the time to think about their businesses and then implement programs and policies to get from where they are to where they want to be in a reasonable period of time.

It is a known and accepted fact that people and organizations that plan ahead are much more likely to become what they want to become than those that do not plan at all. Good strategists plan and control their plans, whereas bad strategists rarely plan and often try to control people! This text is devoted to providing you with the tools necessary to be a good strategist.

Key Terms and Concepts

annual objectives (p. 13)
competitive advantage (p. 10)
employability (p. 19)
empowerment (p. 15)
environmental scanning (p. 12)
external opportunities (p. 12)

external threats (p. 12)
internal strengths (p. 12)
internal weaknesses (p. 12)
intuition (p. 9)
long-range planning (p. 6)
long-term objectives (p. 13)

mission statement (p. 11)
political, economic, sociocultural, technological,
  environmental, legal (PESTEL) (p. 12)
policies (p. 14)
retreats (p. 7)
strategic management (p. 4)
strategic management model (p. 6)
strategic management process (p. 7)
strategic planning (p. 5)
strategies (p. 13)

strategists (p. 10)
strategy evaluation (p. 8)
strategy formulation (p. 7)
strategy implementation (p. 8)
sustained competitive advantage (p. 10)
Strengths-Weaknesses-Opportunities-Threats (SWOT)
  analysis (p. 13)
tactics (p. 8)
vision statement (p. 11)

Issues for Review and Discussion

1-1. Why do you believe SWOT analysis is so commonly used by businesses in doing strategic planning?

1-2. What percentage of companies does the chapter say have published CO_2 emissions goals, and what percentage of those companies meet those goals? Why such a large difference? What are the implications of such a large difference?

1-3. For your college or university, identify a strategy that would exemplify the matching concept evidenced in SWOT analysis.

1-4. Diagram the comprehensive strategic management model.

1-5. Develop a diagram to reveal the benefits to a firm for doing strategic planning. Include "improved understanding," "enhanced communication," "all managers and employees on a mission," and "greater commitment"—in the correct order.

1-6. How important do you believe "having an excellent game plan" is to winning a basketball or football game against your university's major rival? Discuss.

1-7. Are *strategic management* and *strategic planning* synonymous terms? Explain.

1-8. Why do many firms move too hastily from vision and mission development to devising alternative strategies?

1-9. Why are strategic planning retreats often conducted away from the work site? How often should firms have a retreat, and who should participate in them?

1-10. Distinguish between long-range planning and strategic planning.

1-11. How important do you think "being adept at adapting" is for businesses? Explain.

1-12. As cited in the chapter, famous businessman W. Edwards Deming once said, "In God we trust. All others bring data." What did Deming mean in terms of developing a strategic plan?

1-13. What strategies do you believe can save even more newspaper companies from extinction?

1-14. Distinguish between the concepts of *vision* and *mission*.

1-15. Your university has fierce competitors. List three external opportunities and three external threats that face your university.

1-16. List three internal strengths and three internal weaknesses that characterize your university.

1-17. List reasons why objectives are essential for organizational success.

1-18. Why are policies especially important in strategy implementation?

1-19. What is a "retreat," and why do firms take the time and spend the money to have these?

1-20. Discuss the notion of strategic planning being more formal versus informal in an organization. On a 1 to 10 scale from formal to informal, what number best represents your view of the most effective approach? Why?

1-21. List what you believe are the five most important lessons for business that can be garnered from *The Art of War*.

1-22. Compare and contrast strategies with tactics. Give an example of each for (1) McDonald's Corporation and (2) your university.

1-23. Explain why the strategic management class is often called a *capstone course*.

1-24. What aspect of strategy formulation do you think requires the most time? Why?

1-25. Why is strategy implementation often considered the most difficult stage in the strategic management process?

1-26. Why is it so important to integrate intuition and analysis in strategic management?

1-27. Explain the importance of a vision and a mission statement.

1-28. Discuss relationships among objectives, strategies, and policies.

1-29. Why do you think some CEOs fail to use a strategic management approach to decision-making?

1-30. Discuss the importance of feedback in the strategic management model.

1-31. How can strategists best ensure that strategies will be effectively implemented?

1-32. Give an example of a recent political development that changed the overall strategy of an organization.

1-33. Who are the major competitors of your college or university? What are their strengths and weaknesses? What are their strategies? How successful are these institutions compared to your college?

1-34. In your opinion, what is the single major benefit of using a strategic management approach to decision-making? Justify your answer.

1-35. Most students will never become a CEO or even a top manager in a large company. So why is it important for all business majors to study strategic management?

1-36. Describe the content available at the Strategy Club website at www.strategyclub.com.

1-37. List four financial and four nonfinancial benefits of a firm engaging in strategic planning.

1-38. Why is it that a firm can normally sustain a competitive advantage for only a limited period of time?

1-39. Why it is not adequate simply to obtain a competitive advantage?

1-40. How can a firm best achieve a sustained competitive advantage?

1-41. In sequential order in the strategic planning process, arrange the following appropriately: policies, objectives, vision, strategies, mission, strengths.

1-42. Label the following as an opportunity, a strategy, or a strength.

    a. XYZ Inc. is hiring 50 more salespersons.
    b. XYZ Inc. has 50 salespersons.
    c. XYZ Inc.'s rival firm has only 150 salespersons.

1-43. Explain why internal strengths and weaknesses should be stated in divisional terms to the extent possible.

1-44. Explain why both internal and external factors should be stated in specific terms (i.e., using numbers, percentages, money ratios, and comparisons over time) to the extent possible.

1-45. Identify the three activities that comprise strategy evaluation.

1-46. List six characteristics of annual objectives.

1-47. Would strategic management concepts and techniques benefit foreign businesses as much as domestic firms? Justify your answer.

1-48. What do you believe are some potential pitfalls or risks in using a strategic management approach to decision-making?

1-49. What happened at the Battle of Cannae? What are the lessons for us today in developing strategic plans?

Writing Assignments

1-50. Strengths and weaknesses should be determined relative to competitors or by elements of being or relative to a firm's own objectives. Explain.

1-51. What are the three stages in strategic management? Which stage is more analytical? Which relies most on empowerment to be successful? Which relies most on statistics? Justify your answers.

MINI-CASE: FORD VERSUS GENERAL MOTORS

THE RACE TO BECOME ALL-ELECTRIC

Ford's world headquarters in Detroit, Michigan, is only 9 miles from the headquarters of General Motors (GM). Rivalry between the two companies has become especially bitter since Tesla's advances in electric vehicles. Both Ford and GM are shifting their overall strategic plan to become all-electric, perhaps as soon as 2030. The two companies are building their own battery factories and are partnering with technology companies to access digital innovations. Between 2021 and 2025, Ford has pledged to spend $30 billion on electric vehicles. Globally, electric vehicles comprised 9 percent of automobile sales, but only 3.6 percent in the United States, with both numbers increasing rapidly.

marekuliasz/Shutterstock

Ford recently out-negotiated GM to garner 12 percent ownership of Rivian Automotive based in Irvine, California. Rivian went public in November 2021 and produces the world's first all-electric pickup truck called the R1T, and a midsize all-electric SUV called the R1S, at its Illinois factory. Ford today has a collaboration partnership with Rivian, but GM is soon to release its own all-electric pickup truck, the GMC Hummer EV Pickup. Whichever firm, Ford or GM, best manages their shift to becoming all-electric will garner huge competitive advantages at a time when gas and diesel vehicles are both companies' bread-and-butter revenue and profit generators.

President Joe Biden's infrastructure package aims to build a national network of electric-vehicle charging stations. The level of government support for electrifying transportation in the United States is higher than ever; even school buses likely soon must be all-electric.

Questions

1. Identify two external opportunities and threats that you think face Ford and GM.
2. Pick Ford or GM. Identify two internal strengths and two weakness that you think face the firm.
3. Pick Ford or GM. Identify two strategies that may be good for the firm to pursue given your answers to questions 1 and 2. Use the SWOT framework to develop your two strategies.[17]

[17]Based on information in Mike Collas and Ben Foldy, "Ford, GM and the Race for Rivian," *Wall Street Journal*, November 6–7, 2021, pp. B1, B4.

Web Resources

1. **The Author Website** The website for this textbook is widely used by both companies and students for doing strategic planning. The downloadable template at the website receives more than 30,000 hits per year. www.strategyclub.com

2. **SWOT Analysis Narrative and Worksheet** This website explains SWOT analysis and provides a downloadable worksheet. https://www.mindtools.com/pages/article/newTMC_05.htm

3. **SWOT Analysis Images** This search result url provides more than 100 JPEG images of SWOT matrices that can be used in a case project or strategic planning report. https://www.google.com/search?q=swot+analysis&tbm=isch&tbo=u&source=univ&sa=X&ved=0ahUKEwjokNTanonWAhUIPiYKHdfeAOQQsAQIeQ&biw=1295&bih=743

4. **Strategic Planning Models** This website provides a video and narrative coverage of 16 popular strategic planning models. https://www.clearpointstrategy.com/strategic-planning-models/

5. **Strategic Management Organizations** Some popular strategy websites are as follows:

   Strategic Management Society (SMS)—https://strategicmanagement.net/—publishes the *Strategic Management Journal* and holds annual strategic management conferences
   Association for Strategic Planning—www.strategyassociation.org/—provides a Strategic Management Professional (SMP) certification program
   McKinsey & Company—www.mckinsey.com—perhaps the largest management consulting firm in the world; the company does extensive strategic planning consulting

6. **Dr. Fred David gives a video overview of Chapter 1 in the 17th edition but much info is still applicable to the current edition.** https://www.youtube.com/watch?v=-xVl5-oJcrE

7. **Dr. Fred David gives key guidelines for writing a perfect resume** https://www.youtube.com/watch?v=TLXNyD1EbT4

Current Readings

David, Forest R., Meredith David, and Fred David, "Business Curricula: Coverage of Employability Skills in a Strategic Management Course," *SAM Advanced Management Journal* 85 no. 1 (2020): 35–42.

David, Fred R., and Forest R. David, "Comparing Management Curricula with Management Practice," *SAM Advanced Management Journal* 76, no. 3 (Summer 2011): 48–55.

David, Fred R., Meredith E. David, and Forest R. David, "What Are Business Schools Doing for Business Today?" *Business Horizons* (February 2011): 51–62.

David, Meredith E., and Fred R. David, "Strategic Planning for Individuals: A Proposed Framework and Method," *SAM Advanced Management Journal* 82, no. 4 (Winter 2018): 40–51.

David, Meredith E., Fred R. David, and Forest R. David, "Closing the Gap Between Graduates' Skills and Employers' Requirements: A Focus on the Strategic Management Capstone Business Course," *Administrative Sciences* 11, no. 1 (2021): 10–26.

Gligor, David M., Millorad Novicevic, Javad Feizabadi, and Andrew Stapleton, "Examining Investor Reactions to Appointments of Black Top Management Executives and CEOs," *Strategic Management Journal* 42, no. 10 (October 2021): 1939–59.

Hannah, Douglas P., Ron Tidhar, and Kathleen M. Eisenhardt, "Analytic Models in Strategy, Organizations, and Management Research: A Guide for Consumers," *Strategic Management Journal* 42, no. 2 (February 2021): 329–60.

Hernandez, Exequiel, and Anoop Menon, "Corporate Strategy and Network Change," *Academy of Management Review* 46, 1 (January 2021): 80–107.

MacLennan, Andrew F., and Constantinos C. Markides, "Causal Mapping for Strategy Execution: Pitfalls and Applications," *California Management Review* 63, no. 4 (August 2021): 89–122.

Rindova, Violina P., and Luis L. Martins, "Shaping Possibilities: A Design Science Approach to Developing Novel Strategies," *Academy of Management Review* 46, no. 4 (October 2021): 800–22.

Vincent, Vinod W., "Integrating Intuition and Artificial Intelligence in Organizational Decision-Making," *Business Horizons* 64, no. 4 (July 2021): 425–38.

Endnotes

1. On page 4.

2. Fred R. David, "How Companies Define Their Mission," *Long Range Planning* 22, no. 1 (February 1989): 91. See also Anik Ratnaningsih, Nadjadji Anwar, Patdono Suwignjo, and Putu Artama Wiguna, "Balance Scorecard of David's Strategic Modeling at Industrial Business for National Construction Contractor of Indonesia," *Journal of Mathematics and Technology* no. 4 (October 2010): 20. See also Meredith E. David, Fred R. David, and Forest R. David, "Closing the Gap Between Graduates' Skills and Employers' Requirements: A Focus on the Strategic Management Capstone Business Course," *Administrative Sciences* 11, no. 1 (2021): 10–26.

3. On page 7.

4. G. L. Schwenk and K. Schrader, "Effects of Formal Strategic Planning in Financial Performance in Small Firms: A Meta-Analysis," *Entrepreneurship and Practice* 3, no. 17 (1993): 53–64.

5. Peter Drucker, *Management: Tasks, Responsibilities, and Practices* (New York: Harper & Row, 1974), 611.

6. Alfred Sloan, Jr., *Adventures of the White Collar Man* (New York: Doubleday, 1941), 104.

7. Quoted in Eugene Raudsepp, "Can You Trust Your Hunches?" *Management Review* 49, no. 4 (April 1960): 7.

8. Stephen Harper, "Intuition: What Separates Executives from Managers," *Business Horizons* 31, no. 5 (September–October 1988): 16.

9. Ron Nelson, "How to Be a Manager," *Success* (July–August 1985): 69.

10. Robert Waterman, Jr., *The Renewal Factor: How the Best Get and Keep the Competitive Edge* (New York: Bantam, 1987). See also *Business Week*, September 14, 1987, 100; and *Academy of Management Executive* 3, no. 2 (May 1989): 115.

11. On page 10.

12. John Pearce, II, and Fred David, "The Bottom Line on Corporate Mission Statements," *Academy of Management Executive* 1, no. 2 (May 1987): 109.

13. Heinz Weihrich, "The TOWS Matrix: A Tool for Situational Analysis," *Long Range Planning* 15, no. 2 (April 1982): 61. *Note:* Although Dr. Weihrich first modified SWOT analysis to form the TOWS matrix, the acronym SWOT is much more widely used than TOWS in practice. See also Marilyn Helms and Judy Nixon, "Exploring SWOT Analysis—Where Are We Now?" *Journal of Strategy and Management* 3, no. 3 (2010): 215–51.

14. Based on www.des.calstate.edu/limitations.html and www.entarga.com/stratplan/purposes.html

15. Victoria Neufeldt, ed. *Webster's New World Dictionary*, 4th ed. (Hoboken, NJ: Pearson, 1998). Pearson purchased this dictionary from Simon & Schuster in 1998 but sold it to IDG Books in 1999.

16. Frederick Gluck, "Taking the Mystique Out of Planning," *Across the Board* (July–August 1985), 59.

17. On page 24.

18. On page 29.

THE COHESION CASE

Ken Wolter/Alamy Photo

McDonald's Corporation, 2022

BY FRED R. DAVID

https://corporate.mcdonalds.com/

Headquartered in Chicago, Illinois, McDonald's is the world's largest restaurant company and the world's second-largest employer (behind Walmart). McDonald's trains its managers and franchisees at Hamburger University located at its Chicago headquarters. McDonald's is the largest private operator of playgrounds in the United States and is the largest purchaser of beef, pork, potatoes, and apples.

McDonald's operates about 40,000 restaurants in 120 countries; roughly 36,000 restaurants are franchised and only 4,000 are owned by the company. McDonald's franchised restaurants are owned and operated by independent local business owners, whereas the company-owned restaurants are used to test new products, services, and innovations. McDonald's company-owned restaurants are also used for training potential managers and testing various marketing, pricing, and operational ideas before rollout across the system.

Revenues and net income from franchised restaurants are not reported on McDonald's financial statements; those numbers are reported on the independent owners' financial statements. McDonald's does, however, report on their financial statements rents, royalties, and fees received from franchisees for purchases of food, drinks, and equipment. McDonald's embraces franchising that enables individuals to be their own boss/employer and to maintain control over many employment-related matters, marketing, and pricing decisions, while benefiting from the parent's reputation, operating system, and financial resources. McDonald's, however, requires all franchisees to adhere to strict operating standards, policies, and procedures to protect the company's brand, reputation, and basic uniformity globally.

McDonald's corporate website says that the company focuses on four areas that matter most: (1) Food Quality and Sourcing, (2) the Planet, (3) Community Connection, and (4) Jobs, Inclusion, and Empowerment. McDonald's strives to be exemplary in terms of sustainability, ethics, diversity, inclusion, and social responsibility. Due to rising costs, however, for paper, food, and supplies, as well as wages increasing 10 percent in 2021, McDonald's recently increased its menu prices 6 percent to help keep pace. For decades, McDonald's has been a symbol of globalization and the American way of life, but sometimes the company is criticized for contributing to obesity worldwide.

Copyright by Fred David Books LLC.

History

Founded in 1940 in San Bernardino, California, by two brothers, Richard and Maurice McDonald, the company's world renown double-arched "M" Golden Arches symbol first appeared in 1953 at a McDonald's in Phoenix, Arizona. An early franchisee and eventual CEO of McDonald's, Ray Kroc purchased the company from the two brothers in 1955. The mascot clown of the company, Ronald McDonald, was introduced in 1965 as a marketing strategy to entice children to want to eat at McDonald's. Being credited with building McDonald's into the most successful fast-food corporation in the world, Ray Kroc died in 1984 at the age of 82.

During the 1990s, McDonald's acquired a variety of restaurant chains but began divesting those chains in the 2000s. For example, McDonald's divested Chipotle Mexican Grill, Donatos Pizza, and Boston Market in the 2000s. In 2017, McDonald's began its on-demand delivery concept by forming a partnership with Uber Eats, followed by DoorDash in 2019, and then Grubhub in 2021. Sales from on-demand delivery today accounts for less than 5 percent of McDonald's revenues.

Some notable milestones in the history of McDonald's are as follows:

1961 – Hamburger University opens in Chicago; graduates receive Bachelor of Hamburgerology degrees.
1965 – The Filet-O-Fish sandwich is added to the menu.
1968 – The Big Mac is added to the menu.
1973 – The Quarter Pounder and Quarter Pounder with cheese are added to the menu.
1983 – Chicken McNuggets are added to the menu.
2002 – McDonald's publishes its first ever *Social Responsibility Report*.
2015 – McDonald's USA launched All-Day Breakfast.
2017 – McDonald's launched McDelivery with Uber Eats.
2020 – McDonald's opens its first net-zero emissions restaurant (at Walt Disney World Resort).

In Q1 of 2022, McDonald's closed its operations in Russia after that country invaded Ukraine. McDonald's "temporarily" closed 850 locations in Russia, but continued paying its 62,000 employees there and operating its Ronald McDonald House Charities, meaning that it will continue to incur costs. McDonald's restaurants in Ukraine and Russia accounted for about 9 percent of the company's 2021 revenue, since most are directly owned and operated by McDonald's, rather than being franchised. McDonald's CEO Chris Kempczinski said: "Our values mean we cannot ignore the needless human suffering unfolding in Ukraine." Similarly Starbucks, Papa John's International and Yum! Brands, the parent company of Kentucky Fried Chicken, suspended their operations while condemning Russia's invasion of Ukraine. Yum! Brands' suspension of investments and developments had a notable impact on that company's profits given they had 1,136 Russia stores, largely contained within its KFC nameplate, but of which 50 are Pizza Hut locales.

For Q1 of 2022, McDonald's perfomed exceptionally well, having reported that its global comparable sales increased 11.8 percent for Q1, as follows:

- U.S. increased 3.5%
- International Operated Markets (IOM) segment increased 20.4%
- International Developmental Licensed (IDL) Markets segment increased 14.7%

The company's Q1 2022 consolidated revenues increased 11 percent, systemwide sales increased 10 percent, consolidated operating income increased 1 percent – even though the Company temporarily suspended operations during the quarter in Russia and Ukraine as a result of the military conflict in the region.

Core Values, Vision, and Mission

McDonald's has a published set of five core values that (paraphrased) read as follows:

1. *Serve* – We put our customers and employees first;
2. *Inclusion* – We are open for everyone to partake;
3. *Integrity* – We strive to always do what is right;
4. *Community* – We work hard to be a good neighbor; and
5. *Family* – We work together to continually improve.

McDonald's appears not to have a published vision statement, but on their corporate website, a mission statement (paraphrased) is given as follows:

Our mission is to provide delicious feel-good moments easy for everyone to enjoy. This is how we uniquely feed and benefit communities. We serve delicious food at convenient locations and hours and affordable prices. We strive to offer the speed, choice, and personalization our customers expect. We serve food, but most of all our employees serve moments of feel-good using a lighthearted, unpretentious, welcoming, and dependable personality.

Internal Issues

Products

McDonald's menu varies slightly globally to suit local consumer preferences and tastes, but generally the menu includes hamburgers and cheeseburgers, Big Mac, Quarter Pounder with Cheese, Filet-O-Fish, several chicken sandwiches, Chicken McNuggets, wraps, McDonald's Fries, salads, oatmeal, shakes, McFlurry desserts, sundaes, soft serve cones, bakery items, soft drinks, coffee, McCafé beverages, and other beverages. Additionally, breakfast offerings generally include Egg McMuffin, Sausage McMuffin with Egg, McGriddles, biscuit and bagel sandwiches, oatmeal, breakfast burritos, and hotcakes.

According to the website https://www.eatthis.com/mcdonalds-least-most-popular-items/, the five most popular McDonald's products are (in rank order from the best): (1) Fries, (2) Big Mac, (3) Double Cheeseburger, (4) Chicken McNuggets, and (5) Sausage McMuffin with Egg. The same website reports that the five least popular McDonald's products are (in rank order from the worst): (1) Filet-O-Fish, (2) Sweet Tea, (3) Bacon Ranch Salad with Buttermilk Crispy Chicken, (4) Hotcakes, and (5) Egg White Delight McMuffin.

Zero Emissions and Sustainability

McDonald's is committed to achieving net-zero emissions across its global operations by 2050. Toward this end, between 2018 and 2021, McDonald's reported an 8.5 percent reduction in emissions among all its restaurants and offices and a 5.9 percent decrease in supply chain emissions, compared with a 2015 baseline. By 2030, the company's goal is to achieve a 31 percent reduction in emissions from the 2015 baseline.

McDonald's believes that lower greenhouse gas emissions and a steady rather than a rising global temperature will ultimately mean less severe weather and more favorable conditions for farmers, positively impacting restaurant operators and their communities. Thus, the company has a published and continually updated timeline for reaching its 2050 net-zero emissions progress, available at the website: https://corporate.mcdonalds.com/corpmcd/en-us/our-stories/article/ourstories.net-zero-climate.html

In a similar vein, McDonald's has pledged that globally by the end of 2025, every Happy Meal toy will be sustainable (i.e., made from renewable, recycled, or certified materials). The company recently invested in six large renewable energy projects that together will generate about 3.4 million megawatt hours of renewable energy annually, enough renewable energy to power over 8,000 McDonald's restaurants.

Strategy

McDonald's strategy revolves around what it calls the 3D's: (1) Digital, (2) Delivery, and (3) Drive-Through. The company recently entered into an agreement with IBM to enhance the development and deployment of Automated Order Taking (AOT) technology whereby IBM-acquired McD tech Labs and is advancing McDonald's Digital, Delivery and Drive-Through operations. McDonald's McD Tech Labs team are now a part of IBM's Cloud & Cognitive Software division.

The 3D strategy is described (paraphrased):

Digital: "MyMcDonald's" aims to digitalize the firm's drive-through, takeaway, delivery, curbside pick-up, and dine-in offerings. This tool enables customers to (1) receive tailored offers, (2) participate in a new loyalty program, and (3) order and receive menu items through the channel of their choice. At year-end 2021, "MyMcDonald's" was available in the company's top six markets; the company's digital sales exceeded $10 billion or nearly 20 percent of systemwide sales in 2020.

Delivery: The company is working to expand delivery beyond the 30,000 McDonald's restaurants that currently offer delivery and to introduce the McDonald's app for placing orders into markets around the world beyond where it is currently available.

Drive-Through: The company aims to increase its number of drive-through locations from about 30,000 locations presently, including nearly 95 percent of the more than 13,000 locations in the United States. McDonald's is testing new technology to enhance the drive-through customer experience, including AOT and a new drive-through express pick-up lane for customers with a digital order.

Diversity, Equity, and Inclusion (DEI)

To promote diversity, equity, and inclusion, McDonald's has a DEI strategy whereby everywhere in the world that anyone interacts with McDonald's, the company wants DEI to be evident. This includes having a diverse workforce, evidenced by inclusion of women and minorities on the company's board of directors, including the chairman of the Board. The firm wants to break down barriers to economic opportunity, improve the representation of women at all levels of the company, encourage franchisees and suppliers to embrace DEI, uphold human rights, cultivate a respectful, ethical workplace, and provide equitable pay to all employees.

The company expects its DEI strategy to accelerate inclusion of historically underrepresented groups throughout the firm. In 2021, to facilitate this goal, McDonald's incorporated quantitative human capital management-related metrics to annual incentive compensation for its executives. McDonald's executives' compensation is now based somewhat on their ability to show progress toward implementing the company's core values and DEI strategy. Note in the Exemplary Strategist capsule the leadership role of Desiree Ralls-Morrison at McDonald's.

Advertising

McDonald's expenditures for radio and television advertising, primarily in the United States, and other marketing-related expenses were in millions: $377 for 2021, $326 for 2020, $365 for 2019, and $88.0 for 2018. The big increase in 2019 was primarily due to $175 million of extra marketing being provided by McDonald's across all segments to help franchisee and company-owned restaurants recover from the COVID-19 pandemic. Additionally, in the firm's International Operated Market segment, the company spent substantial advertising monies specifically aimed at assisting

Desiree Ralls-Morrison, General Counsel and Corporate Secretary of McDonald's[18].

McDonald's is a successful company with an excellent strategic plan, due in part to the work and leadership of Desiree Ralls-Morrison, McDonald's female, minority General Counsel and Corporate Secretary. In 2019, Ralls-Morrison was named one of the most powerful women in corporate America by *Black Enterprise Magazine* and, in 2020, was named as one of the top innovative General Counsels around the world by *The Financial Times*. Ralls-Morrison oversees McDonald's global legal operations and contributes to the company's development and execution of clear strategies. Ralls-Morrison is responsible for anticipating and managing risk and advancing the company's brand and values and is a key advisor to McDonald's Board of Directors and CEO.

Before joining McDonald's, Ralls-Morrison was General Counsel and Corporate Secretary at Boston Scientific Corporation,and, before that, served as General Counsel and Corporate Secretary at Boehringer Ingelheim USA, Inc., and General Counsel of the Consumer Group at Johnson & Johnson. Ralls-Morrison currently serves on the board of directors for DICK'S Sporting Goods, Inc. and as a director for The Partnership, Inc. located in the Boston area. Ralls-Morrison earned a Juris Doctor from Harvard Law School and a Bachelor of Arts in economics and political science from Wesleyan University.

[18]Based on a variety of sources including the McDonald's corporate website and 2021 *Form 10K*.

company-owned restaurants. Understand also that franchisees independently spend considerable local monies of their own advertising; McDonald's does not pay for this activity because the company is not the primary beneficiary.

Segments

McDonald's financial statements feature three reportable segments as follows:

1. **United States** – includes both franchised and company-owned restaurants in the United States. This segment is the largest and is 95 percent franchised.
2. **International Operated Markets (IOM)** – includes both franchised and company-owned restaurants located in nine countries: Australia, Canada, France, Germany, Italy, the Netherlands, Russia, Spain, and the UK. This segment is 84 percent franchised.
3. **International Developmental Licensed Markets & Corporate (IDL)** – includes restaurants in about 80 countries other than the United States and the nine IOM countries. This segment is 98 percent franchised.

Exhibit 1 reveals that 41 percent of McDonald's revenues during the COVID-19 pandemic came from their US restaurants, up from 37 percent the prior year. However, company revenues decreased from the IOM restaurants, partly because many IOM restaurants that did not have drive-throughs so were totally closed for part of the year.

EXHIBIT 1 McDonald's Percent Revenue by Segment

	2019	2020	2021
United States	37%	41%	38%
IOM (9 countries)	54%	50%	53%
IDL (about 80 countries)	9%	9%	9%

Source: Based on information in McDonald's 2021 *Annual Report*, p. 18.

Exhibit 2 reveals that McDonald's company-owned restaurants in the United States performed comparatively better in 2021 than the company-owned restaurants located outside the United States. Be reminded that 93 percent of all McDonald's restaurants globally are franchised, not company-owned; from franchised restaurants the company derives fees (not revenues).

EXHIBIT 2 McDonald's Segments' Comparable Sales Increases and Decreases of Company-Owned Restaurants (%)

	2019	2020	2021
United States	5.0%	(4%)	9%
IOM (9 countries)	6.1%	(19.0%)	26%
IDL (about 80 countries)	7.2%	6%	13%
Total	5.9%	14%	20%

Source: Based on information in McDonald's 2021 *Annual Report*, p. 13.

Although franchised sales are not recorded as revenues by McDonald's, the total franchised sales do give excellent indication of the financial health of the franchisee base. Note from the numbers in Exhibit 3 reveals that McDonald's franchised revenues increased dramatically in 2021 as the world began to recover from the pandemic.

EXHIBIT 3 McDonald's Franchisees' Sales (in Millions)

	2019	2020	2021
United States	$5,353	$5,261	$6,094
IOM (9 countries)	$5,064	$4,348	$5,638
IDL (about 80 countries)	$1,239	$1,117	$1,353
Total	$11,656	$10,726	$13,085

Source: Based on information in McDonald's 2021 *Annual Report*, p. 19.

Note in Exhibit 4 that even though McDonald's IDL segment includes restaurants from about 80 countries, total revenues are substantially lower than from the United States or the 9 IOM countries.

EXHIBIT 4 McDonald's Revenues Derived from Company-Owned Restaurants and Fees Derived from Franchised Restaurants (in Millions)

	2019	2020	2021
United States	$7,843	$7,656	$8,711
IOM (9 countries)	$11,398	$9,462	$12,094
IDL (about 80 countries)	$1,836	$1,747	$2,068
Total	$21,077	$18,865	$22,873

Source: Based on information in McDonald's 2021 *Annual Report*, p. 15.

During 2020, McDonald's opened 977 restaurants systemwide but closed 643, with about 200 of those closures being in the United States and about half of those being inside Walmart stores. As indicated in Exhibit 5, McDonald's had 15,808 IDL restaurants at year-end 2021, but these were contributing little operating profits for the company. Note increases in all segments in Exhibit 5 except the USA segment.

EXHIBIT 5 McDonald's Number of Restaurants at Year-End

	2019	2020	2021
United States	13,846	13,682	13,438
IOM (9 countries)	10,465	19,560	10,465
IDL (about 80 countries)	14,384	14,956	15,808
Total	38,695	39,198	40,031

Source: Based on information in McDonald's 2021 *Annual Report*, p. 33.

Exhibit 6 provides a breakdown of McDonald's total revenues by segment. Note dramatic increases across the board in 2021 when the pandemic subsided.

EXHIBIT 6 A Breakdown of McDonald's Total Revenues by Segment Obtained From Both Company-Owned and Franchised Restaurants (in Millions)

	2019	2020	2021
United States	$37,923	$38,123	$43,344
IOM (9 countries)	$28,853	$25,446	$33,097
IDL (about 80 countries)	$23,981	$21,609	$26,234
Total	$90,757	$85,178	$102,675

Source: Based on information in McDonald's 2021 *Annual Report*, p. 50.

Exhibit 7 provides a breakdown of McDonald's operating income by segment.

EXHIBIT 7 A Breakdown of McDonald's Total Operating Income by Segment Obtained From Both Company-Owned and Franchised Restaurants (in Millions)

	2019	2020	2021
United States	$4,069	$3,789	$4,755
IOM (9 countries)	$4,789	$3,315	$5,130
IDL (about 80 countries)	$212	$220	$471
Total	$9,070	$7,324	$10,356

Source: Based on information in McDonald's 2021 *Annual Report*, p. 24.

Exhibit 8 provides a breakdown of McDonald's total sales (food and drink) from company-owned restaurants versus total revenues (rents, royalties, and fees) derived from franchisees. Notice that the two numbers are pretty close even though McDonald's has 30,000 franchised and 4,000 company-owned restaurants.

EXHIBIT 8 A Breakdown of McDonald's Total Revenues (in Millions)

	2019	2020	2021
Sales derived from company-operated restaurants (food and drink)	$9,420.8.	$8,139.2	$9,787
Revenues derived from franchised restaurants (rents, royalties, and fees)	$11,655.7	$10,726.1	$13,085
Other Revenues	$287.9	$342.5	$351
Total Revenues	$21,364.4	$19,207.8.	$23,223

Source: Based on information in McDonald's 2021 *Annual Report*, p. 12.

Organizational Structure

McDonald's does not provide an organizational chart on its website or in its *Annual Report*, but based on the titles of individuals, the company appears to operate from a strategic business unit (SBU) design, with the two units being United States and International.

A depiction of McDonald's probable organizational chart is given in Exhibit 9. Analysts suggest that 10 or more presidents of large geographic regions should appear below the two base levels shown, but apparently this is not currently the case within the company. Analysts also suggest that McDonald's should have a chief operating officer for the two SBU persons to report to, rather than every top executive reporting apparently to CEO Kempczinski. In fact, some analysts suggest that seven SBU's would be better than two: (1) United States, (2) Europe, (3) Asia, (4) Australia and Pacific, (5) South and Central America and Mexico, (6) Canada, and (7) Middle East and Africa.

EXHIBIT 9 McDonald's Top Executives and Probable Organizational Structure

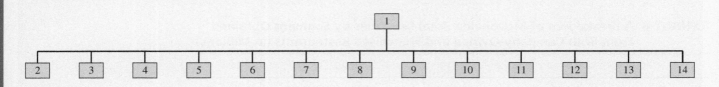

1. Chris Kempczinski, President and CEO
2. Lucy Brady, Senior Vice President, Chief Digital Customer Engagement Officer (female)
3. Heidi Capozzi, Executive Vice President, Global Chief People Officer (female)
4. Francesca DeBiase, Executive Vice President, Chief Supply Chain Officer (female)
5. Katie Beirne Fallon, Executive Vice President and Chief Global Impact Officer (female)
6. Piotr Jucha, Senior Vice President, Global Restaurant Development and Restaurant Solutions Group

7. Alistaair Macrow, Executive Vice President and Global Chief Marketing Officer
8. Mark Ostermann, Vice President, Strategic Alignment and Chief of Staff, Office of the CEO
9. Kevin Ozan, Executive Vice President and Chief Financial Officer
10. Desiree Ralls-Morrison, General Counsel and Corporate Secretary (female)
11. Daniel Henry, Executive Vice President, Global Chief Information Officer
12. Manu Steijaert, Executive Vice President and Chief Customer Officer
13. Joe Erlinger, President, McDonald's USA
14. Ian Borden, President, International

Source: Based on McDonald's corporate website, and most recent *Annual Report.*

Financial Data

The Year 2020

The years 2019 and 2020 were tough for McDonald's given the worldwide COVID-19 pandemic because restaurants in some places were forced to close completely, some just closed inside seating, and those without drive-through capabilities suffered most. Revenue declines in 2020 for McDonald's were worst in the UK, France, Germany, Italy, and Spain. As expected, comparable guest counts for McDonald's were negative across most regions and segments for the year. In fact, for the year 2020, global comparable sales decreased 7.7 percent. Comparable guest counts were negative across both the IOM and IDL outside the United States segments for the year, but comparable sales in the US increased 0.4 percent, benefiting from higher average order size check growth and growth in delivery.

Third Quarter 2021

By the third quarter (Q3) of 2021, McDonald's was performing really well again. The company's global comparable sales increased 12.7 percent in Q3 2021 versus the prior year's Q3. In the company's US segment, revenues increased 9.6 percent, led by the Crispy Chicken Sandwich that performed especially well. Company revenues derived from the IOM segment (comprised of nine countries) increased 13.9 percent, led by the UK, Canada, France, and Germany. The company's IDL segment reported that revenues increased 16.7 percent, led by Japan and Latin America, despite weak sales in China.

A summary of the company's Q3 2021 results is provided in Exhibit 10. Note the dramatic positive turnaround as the pandemic had waned in many locations globally.

EXHIBIT 10 McDonald's Comparable Q3 2021 Sales Increases and (Decreases)

	Q3 2020	Q3 2021
United States	4.6%	9.6%
IOM (9 countries)	(4.4)%	13.9%
IDL (about 80 countries)	(10.1%)	16.7%
Total	(2.2%)	12.7%

Source: Based on information in the McDonald's Q3 2021 *Quarterly Report.*

The Year 2021

The year 2021 steadily improved for McDonald's.

For 2021, as indicated in Exhibit 11 in the company's consolidated income statements, revenues increased 21 percent, operating income increased 63 percent, and net income increased 101 percent.

EXHIBIT 11 McDonald's Consolidated Income Statements (in Millions)

Income Statement	12/31/20	12/31/21		Percent Change
Revenue (Sales)	$19,208	$23,223	⬆	21%
Cost of Goods Sold	$9,189	$10,383	⬆	13%
Gross Profit	$10,019	$12,840	⬆	28%
Operating Expenses	$3,678	$2,484	⬇	−32%
EBIT (Operating Income)	$6,341)	$10,356	⬆	63%
Interest Expense	$1,183	$1,228	⬆	4%
EBT	$5,158	$9,128	⬆	77%
Tax	$1,410	$1,583	⬆	12%
Non-Recurring Events	0	0	NA	NA
Net Income	$3,748	$7,545	⬆	101%

Source: Based on information in the 2021 McDonald's *Annual Report,* p. 38. Note that the statements in Exhibit 11 are condensed from the actual statements in the *Annual Report* and, more specifically, are condensed into the template format as provided on the www.strategyclub.com author website.

Exhibit 12 provides McDonald's consolidated balance sheets for 2020 and 2021. Notice that the company carries quite a bit of Goodwill and quite a bit of long-term debt on its balance sheets.

EXHIBIT 12 McDonald's Consolidated Balance Sheets (in Millions)

Balance Sheet	12/31/20	12/31/21		Percent Change
Assets				
Cash and Short Term Investments	$3,449	$4,709	⬆	37%
Accounts Receivable	$2,110	$1,872	⬇	−11%
Inventory	$51	$56	⬆	10%
Other Current Assets	$632	$511	⬇	−19%
Total Current Assets	$6,242	$7,148	⬆	15%
Property Plant & Equipment	$24,958	$24,721	⬇	−1%
Goodwill	$2,773	$2,783	⬆	0%
Intangibles	0	0	NA	NA
Other Long-Term Assets	$18,654	$19,202	⬆	3%
Total Assets	$52,627	$53,854	⬆	2%
Liabilities				
Accounts Payable	$741	$1,007	⬆	36%
Other Current Liabilities	$5,440	$3,013	⬇	−45%
Total Current Liabilities	$6,181	$4,020	⬇	−35%
Long-Term Debt	$35,197	$35,623	⬆	1%
Other Long-Term Liabilities	$19,074	$18,812	⬇	−1%
Total Liabilities	$60,452	$58,455	⬇	−3%
Equity				
Common Stock	$17	$17	⬇	0%
Retained Earnings	$53,908	$57,535	⬆	7%
Treasury Stock	($67,066)	($67,810)	⬆	1%
Paid in Capital & Other	$5,316	$5,657	⬆	6%
Total Equity	($7,825)	($4,601)	NA	NA
Total Liabilities and Equity	**$52,627**	**$53,854**	⬆	2%

Source: Based on information in the 2021 McDonald's *Annual Report*, p. 40. Note that the statements in Exhibit 12 are condensed from the actual statements in the *Annual Report* and, more specifically, are condensed into the template format as provided on the www.strategyclub.com author website.

Exhibit 13 provides a summary of McDonald's year-end $EPS, $ Dividends Paid, and # of Shares Outstanding. Note the resounding improvement in 2021.

EXHIBIT 13 A Summary of McDonald's Year-End $ EPS, $ Dividends Paid, and # of Shares Outstanding

	2019	2020	2021
$ EPS	$7.95	$6.35	$10.04
$ Dividends Paid	$4.73	$5.04	$5.52
# of Shares Outstanding (in millions)	$758.1	$744.6	$740.0

Source: Based on information in McDonald's 2021 *Annual Report*, p. 40, and https://finance.yahoo.com/quote/MCD/key-statistics?p=MCD

External Issues

About 70 percent of consumers in mid-2021 reported purchasing takeout food more than ever. The fast-food restaurant industry recovered nicely in 2021 amid an increase in vaccine rollout and the lifting of dine-in restrictions. This rebound is evidenced in the Consumer Confidence Index (CCI) increasing to 129.1 in July 2021 after a drastic drop to 85.7 in April 2020. The CCI averaged 128.3 in 2019.

Thanks to a resumption of inside seating amid the vaccine rollout, customer traffic entering restaurants is accelerating globally. This trend accelerated in 2021–2022 as dining rooms resumed normal scheduling and capacity limits. Analysts project real gross domestic product (GDP) in the United States to increase 6.4 percent in 2021 after declining 3.4 percent in 2020, and up from 2.3 percent in 2019. These numbers reflect higher consumer spending and higher business fixed investment.

Digitalization

Restaurants performing the best today are those that have embraced new technologies to accommodate an avalanche of customers craving to dine-in or dine-out at their establishment. Many restaurants now have a dedicated line both inside and outside to accommodate digital order customers. More than ever, customers hate frustrating long queues and slow service; customers love quick-service and convenience and are willing to pay the price. A good example of this is the system experienced at Chick-fil-A.

A crowdsourced local business review and social networking firm named Yelp reported in May 2021 that more than 3.7 million diners used their app to book for dine-in, the highest totals ever. The number of customers seated via Yelp was up by 48 percent year-over-year in May 2021. In the fast-food restaurant industry, analysts expect further acceleration in the deployment of digital ordering via customized websites and dedicated mobile apps (mobile order and pay), plus the rollout of digital self-order kiosks to ease ordering, payment, and pickup.

The National Restaurant Association (NRA) reports that the most popular off-premise options are curbside takeout, followed by delivery (third party and in-house), and drive-through. Some restaurants are now customizing their takeout menus, whereas others are offering promotions such as free or discounted delivery and more efficient curbside pickup. Initiated by the pandemic months, use of off-premises foodservice is here to stay and is booming as the strict lockdowns of the pandemic fade out.

The skyrocketing popularity of digital and mobile orders is spurring consumers to download restaurant apps and to sign up for restaurant loyalty programs. NPD Group reports that for the year ending March 2021 (a period covering a full year since the pandemic's start), restaurant digital orders grew 124 percent compared with the previous period. Surging by 130 percent, digital orders for carry-out comprised 62 percent of all digital orders. Similarly, digital order for delivery, which held 38 percent share of total restaurant digital orders, increased by 140 percent compared to the prior year.

The increased popularity of takeout and delivery offerings has resulted in more digital reliance on third-party delivery services such as DoorDash, Uber Eats, and Grubhub, which generally take a commission of 20 to 30 percent per sale. Such companies are innovating, providing free delivery for all mobile orders, offering daily (versus weekly) payouts for restaurants, and suspending collection fees partially or wholly.

A worrisome risk associated with increased digitalization, however, is the potential for security and data breaches. Breaches can crush brand perception and customer loyalty and undermine the overall customer experience as well. McDonald's and other such companies are also wary of new (and potentially onerous) privacy regulations that could significantly restrict the collection and use of consumers' personal information by digital platforms and vendors.

Worker Shortages

One Fair Wage (OFW) is an organization that advocates ending "subminimum wages for workers." OFW reports that 53 percent of all restaurant workers are considering leaving their job, with 76 percent mentioning low wages and tips as the reason. Thousands of restaurants globally have "Help Wanted" signs or notifications posted due to a "shortage" of people willing to work for the wages paid.

The worker shortage issue is really a double-whammy because restaurants face price-sensitive customers. Any businessperson knows that it is difficult if not impossible at times to pay high wages and simultaneously offer low prices. It takes well-trained and highly motivated employees to prepare and deliver food and drinks, in a uniform manner globally, especially using varied off-premise means such as takeout, drive-through, delivery, catering, kiosks, and/or food trucks.

Competitors

There are millions of international, national, regional and local, private mom-and-pop, and public large-chain retailers of quick-service and fast-casual eating establishments that compete with McDonald's based on price, convenience, service, experience, menu variety, and product quality. McDonald's routinely compares itself to rivals using Euromonitor International's informal-eating-out (IEO) segment information, which includes all quick-service restaurants. According to Euromonitor International, the global IEO segment was composed of about 9 million restaurants and generated $1.2 trillion in annual sales in 2019, with McDonald's accounting for only 0.4 percent of those outlets and 8.4 percent of the sales.

Major quick-service chains that compete with McDonald's include Wendy's, Burger King, Subway, and Yum! Brands (parent of Kentucky Fried Chicken, Taco Bell, and Pizza Hut). Home of the Whopper that challenges the Big Mac, Burger King is probably the single-most direct competitor for McDonald's. Burger King is owned by Restaurant Brands International that also owns Tim Hortons and Popeyes.

Fast-casual restaurants are also close competitors of McDonald's and include firms like Chipotle Mexican Grill, Panera Bread Company, and Five Guys Burgers and Fries. Fast-casuals promise higher quality food than traditional fast-food restaurants but at a lower price point than full-service restaurants. Meals generally range in price from $8 to $12. Fast-casual restaurants are currently doing so well in fact that companies in other segments are renovating and upgrading to attract fast-casual customers.

Starbucks is a specialty quick-service brand that has some products, especially coffee, that overlap with McDonald's. Headquartered in Atlanta, Georgia, privately owned Chick-fil-A is a large, rapidly growing rival to McDonald's, especially in the United States.

Exhibit 14 provides a revenue synopsis of the leading fast-food industry companies. Notice that Chick-fil-A is doing outstanding as is Domino's, but note that Subway is struggling.

EXHIBIT 14 A Total Revenue Analysis of the Fast-Food Industry Top 10 (in Millions)

Company	2019	2020	Change (%)
McDonald's	$40,412	$40,517	0.3
Starbucks	$21,380	$18,485	(13.5)
Chick-fil-A	$11,320	$13,745	21.4
Taco Bell	$11,293	$11,294	0.0
Wendy's	$9,762	$10,231	4.8
Burger King	$10,204	$9,657	(5.3)
Dunkin'	$9,228	$8,762	(5.0)
Subway	$10,200	$8,318	(18.5)
Domino's Pizza	$7,044	$8,287	17.6
Chipotle Mexican	$5,509	$5,921	7.5

Source: Based on a variety of sources, including information at S&P NetAdvantage's *Industry Survey*, August 2021, p. 18.

Burger King

Headquartered in Miami, Florida, Burger King reported more than $20 billion in worldwide revenues for 2020 when it operated more than 18,000 locations in more than 100 countries and served roughly 11 million daily visitors. Independent franchisees own nearly all Burger King restaurants.

Wendy's

Headquartered in Dublin, Ohio, Wendy's is a fast-food restaurant chain with more than 6,800 locations worldwide. Like Burger King and McDonald's, Wendy's focuses on burgers, fries, and other classic American food.

Yum! Brands

Headquartered in Louisville, Kentucky, Yum! Brands owns and operates Taco Bell, KFC (Kentucky Fried Chicken), and Pizza Hut. Yum! Brands has more than 50,000 restaurants in more than 150 countries; more than 98 percent of the firm's restaurants are franchised.

Subway

Headquartered in Milford, Connecticut, and featuring a menu primarily of sandwiches and salads, Subway is one of the largest restaurant chains in the world with more than 37,000 locations in nearly 100 countries. Privately held, Subway does not publish exact revenues, but *Restaurant Business* says the company's 2019 sales were about $10.2 billion in the United States.

Starbucks

Headquartered in Seattle, Washington, Starbucks is the world's largest coffeehouse chain. At year-end 2020, the company operated more than 32,000 stores in 76 countries, including more than 18,000 in the United States. Starbucks serves coffee, espresso, cappuccino, tea, pastries, sandwiches, and other foods and, for 2020, reported total revenue of $23.5 billion.

Conclusion

As the world returns to the "new normal" of millions of customers daily desiring to eat at quick-service and fast-casual restaurants, McDonald's needs a clear strategic plan to hold off rival firms determined to take their market share. Note in the case that there are about 80 countries that comprise the company's IDL segment, and yet this segment delivers vastly lower revenues and operating profits than the company's IOM segment, which is composed of just 9 countries. Tough regional decisions need to be made by McDonald's going forward regarding where to locate new restaurants globally given varying opportunities to operate profitably.

Digitalization is a key to success going forward, but as the case mentions, firms such as DoorDash, Uber Eats, and Grubhub expect commissions of 20 to 30 percent per sale. Thus, McDonald's must invest further in expanding its mobile and digital technologies and should teach these concepts and tools at Hamburger University. Safeguards must be strengthened to address security and privacy concerns in using customer-derived information. The company must continue making progress on its 3D strategy: Digital, Delivery, and Drive-Through.

Acquisitions may be an attractive strategy moving forward to both reduce competition in various regions and to grow more quickly, especially in the face of shortages of workers in the restaurant business (and in the construction industry). Because fast-casual restaurants such as Five Guys are outperforming quick-service companies such as McDonald's, perhaps a firm such as Five Guys could be acquired at a reasonable price.

McDonald's prides itself on its core values that include ethics, diversity, inclusion, accessibility, and sustainability. Recall from the case that the company has established quantitative measures to assess each of these values. Amid its future growth of at least an annual 5 percent top-line and bottom-line increase as expected by shareholders, the core values mentioned must be strengthened.

As indicated, McDonald's needs an improved organizational structure. The division-head persons likely should be based on regions, and the company needs a chief operating officer. The bottom line is that McDonald's needs a clear strategic plan moving forward. This is a price-sensitive, low profit margin, highly competitive industry. Be reminded that McDonald's derives more revenue and net income from its IOM segment composed of nine countries, than from its US or IDL segments, as indicated in Exhibit 15.

EXHIBIT 15 McDonald's Percent Revenues by Segment

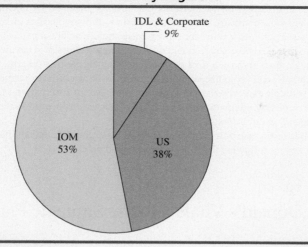

Source: McDonald's 2021 *Form 10K*, p. 12.

Prepare a comprehensive strategic plan for McDonald's CEO Chris Kempczinski.

References

1. McDonald's 2020 and 2021 *Annual Reports.*
2. McDonald's Q3 2021 *Quarterly Report.*
3. S&P NetAdvantage's *Industry Surveys* for the Restaurant Industry, August 2021.
4. https://www.eatthis.com/mcdonalds-least-most-popular-items/

ASSURANCE-OF-LEARNING EXERCISES

SET 1: STRATEGIC PLANNING FOR MCDONALD'S CORPORATION

EXERCISE 1A

Gather Strategy Information for McDonald's Corporation

Purpose

The primary purpose of this exercise is to show students how to obtain vital information for doing case analysis or preparing a strategic plan for any publicly held firm. The secondary purpose is to familiarize you with (1) strategy terms introduced in this chapter and (2) key sources of information for doing strategic planning. Generally in a strategic management course, teams of students prepare a strategic plan (case analysis) for some assigned company, so this exercise can assist in learning how to get started in such a project.

Instructions

Step 1   Read the McDonald's Cohesion Case, and list what you consider to be the firm's strengths, weaknesses, opportunities, and threats. Then, go to the corporate website at https://corporate.mcdonalds.com/, scroll down to the bottom of the website, and click on *Investors*. Click on *View All Financial Information*. Scroll down to Annual Reports. Click *Annual Reports* and then click *2021 Annual Report or Form 10K*. Download this pdf file to your desktop; peruse the information and add to your list of McDonald's strengths, weaknesses, opportunities, and threats.

Step 2   Go online or to your college library website and download to your desktop Standard & Poor's *Industry Surveys* PDF file for the restaurant industry. Use this information to add to your list of McDonald's strengths, weaknesses, opportunities, and threats.

Step 3   Go to the www.finance.yahoo.com website. Enter the stock symbol MCD. Note the wealth of information on McDonald's that may be obtained by clicking any item along the row below the company name. Use this data to refine your lists of key external and internal factors. Each factor listed for this exercise should include a percentage, number, dollar, or ratio to reveal some quantified fact or trend. These factors provide the underlying basis for a strategic plan because a firm strives to take advantage of strengths, improve weaknesses, avoid threats, and capitalize on opportunities. Avoid vagueness in strategic planning.

Step 4   Through class discussion, compare your lists of external and internal factors to those developed by other students and modify your lists as needed. Save this information for use in exercises in the text.

Step 5   Whatever case company you work on this semester, update the information on your company by following the steps listed outlined here.

EXERCISE 1B

Enter McDonald's Vitals into the Strategic Planning Template

Purpose

The purpose of this exercise is to give you practice using resources at the author website (www.strategyclub.com), especially the Excel strategic planning template. Thousands of students annually find the author website resources to be immensely useful in preparing and delivering a strategic management case analysis.

Instructions

Step 1   Go to the www.strategyclub.com website. Review the following resources:
- Excel student template
- Sample case analysis in Word (.docx)
- Live author videos
- Guidelines for presenting a strategic plan or case analysis

Step 2   Download the free Excel strategic planning template. Read carefully instructions given with the template.

Step 3   Using your Exercise 1A results, enter McDonald's strengths, weaknesses, opportunities, and threats into the Excel template.

Step 4   Save this file for use in later exercises.

SET 2: STRATEGIC PLANNING FOR MY UNIVERSITY

EXERCISE 1C

Perform SWOT Analysis for My University

Purpose

The purpose of this exercise is to apply SWOT analysis to a nonprofit organization, namely your college or university. SWOT analysis is the most widely used of all strategic planning tools and techniques because it is conceptually simple and lends itself readily to discussion among managers. SWOT analysis formulates strategies by matching an organization's internal strengths and weaknesses with external opportunities and threats to generate feasible strategies to be considered.

For a university, external factors could include declining numbers of high school graduates; population shifts; community relations; increased competitiveness among colleges and universities; rising numbers of adults returning to college; decreased support from local, state, and federal agencies; increasing numbers of foreign students attending US colleges; and a rising number of internet courses.

Internal factors of a college or university could be related to faculty, students, staff, alumni, athletic programs, physical plant, grounds and maintenance, student housing, administration, fundraising, academic programs, food services, parking, placement, clubs, fraternities, sororities, and public relations.

Instructions

Step 1   For your university, identify four external opportunities, four external threats, four internal strengths, and four internal weaknesses.

Step 2   Match your external with internal factors to develop or generate two SO strategies, two WO strategies, two ST strategies, and two WT strategies. For example, a SO strategy to "Double the number of online course offerings in 3 years" could be developed or generated based on a strength "world renown faculty" coupled with an opportunity "rising interest in online courses."

Step 3   Discuss your key factors and strategies as a class.

Step 4   What new things did you learn about your university from the class discussion? How could this type of discussion benefit an organization? Save your answers and work for use in late exercises.

SET 3: STRATEGIC PLANNING TO ENHANCE MY EMPLOYABILITY

EXERCISE 1D
Perform SWOT Analysis on Myself

Purpose

This exercise can help you decide on the best career path for yourself. Individuals and organizations are alike in many ways. Each has competitors and each should plan for the future. Every individual (and organization) faces some external opportunities and threats, some internal strengths and weaknesses, and reaches pivotal forks in the road. These and other similarities make it possible for individuals to use many corporate strategic management concepts and tools such as SWOT analysis.

Instructions

Introduced in this chapter, SWOT analysis a popular strategic planning tool that can help individuals in career planning. Individuals can perform SWOT analysis by completing the following six steps:

1. Identify four external opportunities you face.
2. Identify four external threats you face.
3. Identify four of your personal strengths.
4. Identify four personal weaknesses.
5. Develop SO (strength-opportunity), WO (weakness-opportunity), ST (strength-threat), WT (weakness-threat) strategies—two strategies of each type—and, thus, eight strategies total.
6. Select three strategies to implement.

An external opportunity could be, for example, that your university offers a graduate program that interests you, whereas an external threat could be that interest rates are rising precluding getting a loan. A weakness could be a low grade-point average, whereas a personal strength may be three years of work experience. Strategy is sometimes defined as "the match" a person (or firm) makes between its internal resources and skills and the opportunities and risks created by its external factors. When a person has major weaknesses, they should strive to overcome them and perhaps convert them into strengths. When a person faces major threats, they should seek to avoid or mitigate the effects of them to focus on opportunities. Even though SWOT analysis is explained considerably more in Chapter 6, give it a try here to help in planning your next career move.

Source: Based on Meredith E. David, Fred R. David, and Forest R. David, "Closing the Gap Between Graduates' Skills and Employers' Requirements: A Focus on the Capstone Business Course," *Administrative Sciences* 11, no. 1 (2021): 10–26. Also, Forest R. David, Meredith David, and Fred David, "Business Curricula: Coverage of Employability Skills in a Strategic Management Course," *SAM Advanced Management Journal* 85, no. 1 (2020): 35–42. Also, Meredith E. David, and Fred R. David, "Strategic Planning for Individuals: A Proposed Framework and Method," *SAM Advanced Management Journal* 82, no. 4 (Winter 2018): 40–51.

SET 4: INDIVIDUAL VERSUS GROUP STRATEGIC PLANNING

EXERCISE 1E

How Detrimental Are Various Pitfalls in Strategic Planning?

Purpose

Whenever a firm engages in strategic planning, there are certain potholes or pitfalls that need to be avoided. Being aware of potential pitfalls and being prepared to address them is essential to success. A list of 13 pitfalls that commonly plague firms and undermine strategic planning efforts follows. These can be ranked in terms of how potentially detrimental or severe they are in doing strategic planning. This exercise reveals the authors' ranking of the 13 pitfalls in terms of how potentially detrimental or severe they are in doing strategic planning.

Pitfalls

1. Using strategic planning to gain control over decisions and resources.
2. Doing strategic planning only to satisfy accreditation or regulatory requirements.
3. Too hastily moving from mission development to strategy formulation.
4. Failing to communicate the plan to employees, who continue working in the dark.
5. Top managers making many intuitive decisions that conflict with the formal plan.
6. Top managers not actively supporting the strategic planning process.
7. Failing to use plans as a standard for measuring performance.
8. Delegating planning to a "planner" rather than involving all managers.
9. Failing to involve key employees in all phases of planning.
10. Failing to create a collaborative climate supportive of change.
11. Viewing planning as unnecessary or unimportant.
12. Becoming so engrossed in current problems that insufficient or no planning is done.
13. Being so formal in planning that flexibility and creativity are stifled.

The purpose of this exercise is to examine and discuss how potentially detrimental or severe the various pitfalls are in doing strategic planning. In addition, the purpose of this exercise is to examine whether individual decision-making is better than group decision-making. Academic research suggests that groups make better decisions than individuals about 80 percent of the time.

Steps

1. Fill in Column 1 in Table 1-9 to reveal your individual ranking of how potentially detrimental to strategic planning the pitfalls are, where 1 = most detrimental to 13 = least detrimental. For example, if you feel Pitfall 1 is the fifth-most detrimental, then enter a 5 in the table in Column 1 beside Pitfall 1.
2. Fill in Column 2 in Table 1-9 to reveal your group's ranking of the 13 pitfalls.
3. Fill in Column 3 in Table 1-9 to reveal the expert's ranking of the 13 pitfalls. (To be provided by your professor, the expert rankings are based on the authors' experience and the end of the chapter).
4. Fill in Column 4 in Table 1-9 to reveal the absolute difference between Column 1 and Column 3 to reveal how well you performed as an individual in this exercise. (Note: For absolute difference, disregard negative numbers).
5. Fill in Column 5 in Table 1-9 to reveal the absolute difference between Column 2 and Column 3 to reveal how well your group performed in this exercise.
6. Sum Column 4. Sum Column 5.
7. Compare the Column 4 sum with the Column 5 sum. If your Column 4 sum is less than your Column 5 sum, then you performed better as an individual than as a group. Normally, group decision-making is superior to individual decision-making, so if you did better than your group, you did excellent.
8. The Individual Winner(s): The individual(s) with the lowest Column 4 sum is the WINNER.
9. The Group Winners(s): The group(s) with the lowest Column 5 score is the WINNER.

TABLE 1-9 Pitfalls in Doing Strategic Planning: Comparing Individual Versus Group Decision-Making

Pitfalls to Avoid in Doing Strategic Planning	Column 1	Column 2	Column 3	Column 4	Column 5
1.					
2.					
3.					
4.					
5.					
6.					
7.					
8.					
9.					
10.					
11.					
12.					
13.					
SUM					

## PART 2

STRATEGY FORMULATION

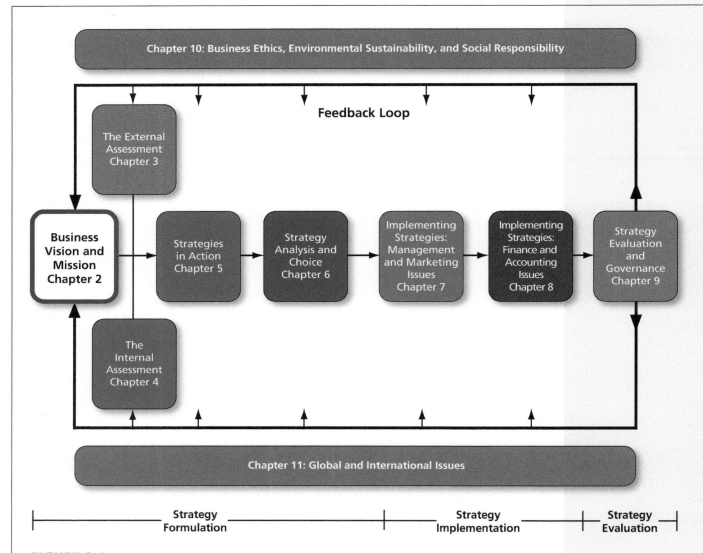

FIGURE 2-1

The Comprehensive, Integrative Strategic Management Model

Source: Fred R. David, "How Companies Define Their Mission," *Long Range Planning* 22, no. 1 (February 1989): 91. See also Anik Ratnaningsih, Nadjadji Anwar, Patdono Suwignjo, and Putu Artama Wiguna, "Balance Scorecard of David's Strategic Modeling at Industrial Business for National Construction Contractor of Indonesia," *Journal of Mathematics and Technology* no. 4 (October 2010): 20. See also Meredith E. David, Fred R. David, and Forest R. David, "Closing the Gap Between Graduates' Skills and Employers' Requirements: A Focus on the Strategic Management Capstone Business Course," *Administrative Sciences* 11, no. 1 (2021): 10–26.

Business Vision
and Mission

LEARNING OBJECTIVES

After studying this chapter, you should be able to do the following:

2.1. Explain the need for core values statements in strategic management.

2.2. Describe the nature and role of vision statements in strategic management.

2.3. Identify the characteristics of a vision statement.

2.4. Describe the nature and role of mission statements in strategic management.

2.5. Identify and discuss the characteristics of an effective mission statement.

2.6. Identify and discuss the components of mission statements.

2.7. Discuss the benefits of a firm having clear vision and mission statements.

2.8. Evaluate and write vision and mission statements for different organizations.

ASSURANCE-OF-LEARNING EXERCISES

The following exercises are found at the end of this chapter:

SET 1:	Strategic Planning for McDonald's
EXERCISE 2A:	Develop an Improved McDonald's Vision Statement
EXERCISE 2B:	Develop an Improved McDonald's Mission Statement
EXERCISE 2C:	Compare McDonald's Mission Statement to a Rival Firm's
SET 2:	Strategic Planning for My University
EXERCISE 2D:	Compare Your University's Vision and Mission Statements to Those of a Rival Institution
SET 3:	Strategic Planning for Myself
EXERCISE 2E:	Develop a Vision and Mission Statement for Yourself
SET 4:	Individual Versus Group Strategic Planning
EXERCISE 2F:	What Is the Relative Importance of Each of the Nine Components of a Mission Statement?

Chapter 2 focuses on the concepts and tools needed to evaluate and write core values, vision, and mission statements. As illustrated with white shading in Figure 2-1, carefully prepared statements of vision and mission are widely recognized by both practitioners and academicians as the first step in strategic management. Actual vision and mission statements from large and small organizations and for-profit and nonprofit enterprises are presented and critiqued.

The exemplary strategist showcased in this chapter is the CEO of Pacific Gas & Electric, Patti Poppe, who has a bold new vision for one of the largest electric utility companies in the United States. Poppe is on a mission to bury all the company's power lines.

We can perhaps best understand core values, vision, and mission by focusing on a business when it is first started. In the beginning, a new business is simply a collection of ideas. Starting a new business rests on a set of beliefs that the organization can offer some product or service to some customers in some geographic area using some type of technology at a profitable price. A new business owner typically believes their philosophy of the new enterprise will result in a favorable public image, and the business concept can be effectively communicated to and adopted by important constituencies. When the ideas and beliefs about a business at its inception are put into writing, the resulting documents mirror the same basic ideas that underlie core values, vision, and mission statements. As a business grows, owners or managers may revise the founding set of beliefs, but those original ideas usually are still reflected in core values, vision, and mission statements. These beliefs can aid in holding a company together during tough times.

Core values, vision, and mission statements often can be found in the front of annual reports and commonly displayed throughout a firm's premises and distributed with company information sent to constituencies. These statements are part of numerous internal reports, such as loan requests, supplier agreements, labor relations contracts, business plans, and customer service agreements. However, too many companies and organizations today have no core values, vision, or mission statement, thus missing out on an incredible opportunity to motivate and energize customers, employees, and shareholders, while also jeopardizing their strategic planning efforts.

Core Values Statements: What Is Our Foundation?

2.1. Explain the need for core values statements in strategic management.

Core values provide the needed ethical foundation for creating an excellent vision and mission. A **core values statement** specifies a firm's commitment to integrity, fairness, discipline, equal employment opportunity, teamwork, accountability, continuous improvement, or other such exemplary attributes.

EXEMPLARY **STRATEGIST** SHOWCASED

Patti Poppe, CEO of Pacific Gas & Electric[1]

The CEO and chief strategist of Pacific Gas & Electric (PG&E), Patti Poppe plans to spend about $20 billion to put 10,000 miles of PG&E power lines underground, primarily to better manage and be less vulnerable to wildfires but also to reduce long-term expenditures on "vegetation management." No utility company has ever attempted to do what Poppe plans, saying such an undertaking is prohibitively expensive. Poppe joined PG&E in January 2021 as the firm was on probation for violating federal pipeline safety laws. PG&E was found guilty in 2018 for igniting the Camp Fire that destroyed the town of Paradise, California, and more recently was charged for involuntary manslaughter for its role in sparking a wildfire near the Oregon border. PG&E has struggled for years to clear power lines of nearby trees, a common cause of wildfires.

Robert Clay/Alamy Photo

PG&E is submitting a plan to the California Public Utilities Commission for permission to substantially raise rates, even though it has among the highest rates in the United States already. Poppe is fighting an uphill battle to achieve her objective, partly because nationwide only about 20 percent of utilities' power lines are underground. Poppe says power lines can be buried for about $2 million per mile, and buried lines offset the need for continual cutting, trimming, and removal of trees. PG&E spends about $1.4 billion annually on vegetation management. Live power lines can spark when any vegetation touches them, producing arcs of electricity that can ignite anything dry. California of late is amid a major drought.

Poppe "leads with love" as she daily interacts extensively with company employees. She is a huge advocate for utilities shifting from coal to renewable energy sources—and for burying power lines. Patti Poppe is setting an excellent example for perhaps all CEOs of utility companies in the United States.

[1]Based on Katherine Blunt, "Can She Bury PG&E's Biggest Problem?" *Wall Street Journal*, November 6–7, 2021, pp. B1, B6.

GLOBAL CAPSULE 2

LinkedIn: Clear Core Values, Vision, and Mission Lead to Global Prominence[2]

jejim120/Alamy Photo

Should You Join Our Network?

The social networking site, LinkedIn, has a network of more than 500 million registered users in 200 countries. LinkedIn has grown globally as fast as almost any other firm, partly by having a clear vision. LinkedIn's former CEO Jeff Weiner has been voted the best CEO in the United States. Weiner's outstanding leadership style has earned him the trust and admiration of all LinkedIn employees. Weiner says, "a manager is someone who tells others what to do, whereas a leader inspires others to do great things." When Weiner spoke at the Wisdom 2.0 conference in San Francisco, he identified and explained the three most important ingredients for being a great leader. **Weiner says the most important ingredient for a great leader is for that person to be clear about the organization's vision.** Fred Kofman is LinkedIn's vice president of leadership and organizational development; Kofman says:

Most CEOs sit at the front of a boat and tell their employees where they need to row; Weiner grabs a surfboard and catches a huge wave, inspiring everyone behind him to do the same. The surfers are all riding the same wave, sharing the same vision, but are putting much more of their heart and personality into their work than the grunts in the rowboat.

According to Weiner, the second-most important ingredient for a leader is to be brave. Weiner says (paraphrased):

If you have true vision and you want to try something that has not been done before, there will be a lot of doubters, skeptics, people who feel threatened, and people who get in your way. Thus, you have to exude confidence to be able to overcome those challenges and for people to want to follow you. You have to be authentic and have true conviction or no one will get behind you.

According to Weiner, the third-most important ingredient necessary to be a great leader is to be an effective communicator.

He explains that whenever a leader has these three ingredients, led by core values, vision, and mission, the job at hand becomes "a matter of what objective you're trying to achieve and then surrounding yourself with the best talent you can."

[2]Based on http://jobs.aol.com/articles/2015/07/06/linkedin-ceo-jeff-weiner-leadership-qualities/?SiteID=cbaolcompromotion_july_14.Also, https://www.cnbc.com/2017/06/28/linkedin-ceo-jeff-weiner-heres-what-separates-leaders-from-managers.html and https://www.consciousculturegroup.com/linkedin-vision-values-insights/

For example, LinkedIn's core values (paraphrased) are (1) customers first, (2) relationships matter, (3) be open and honest, (4) require excellence, (5) take intelligent risks, and (6) act like an owner. Great firms possess core values that remain fixed and almost never change. The core values of any firm should transcend technological changes, fads, product life cycles, and globalization.

Because vision and mission statements change over time, it is vital to know who you are before you can discuss what you want to become, what business you are in, or how will you get there. Generally, if core values are open for change in the future, they are not core values. Disney, for example, has a core value "to make people happy;" a technology firm may have a core value "to connect the world." Tyson Foods' core values statement that guides the firm's operations follows (paraphrased):

We are engaged in the production of food, seeking to pursue truth and integrity, while creating value for our shareholders, customers, employees, and communities. We strive to be an honorable, faith-friendly company composed of diverse people. We feed the world with trusted food products while being excellent stewards of the animals, land, and environment entrusted to us.

The Global Capsule 2 reveals how LinkedIn's core values led to a vision and mission that catapulted the company to global prominence.

Vision Statements: What Do We Want to Become?

2.2. **Describe the nature and role of vision statements in strategic management.**

It is especially important for managers and executives in any firm to agree on the basic vision the organization strives to achieve in the long term. A **vision statement** should answer the basic question, "What do we want to become?" A clear vision provides the foundation for developing a comprehensive mission statement. Many organizations have both a vision and mission statement, but the vision statement should be established first. Examples of vision statements are provided in Table 2-1. The vision statement should be short, preferably one sentence, and as many managers as possible should have input into developing the statement. In the book of Proverbs in the Bible, Chapter 29, Verse 18 says, "Where there is no vision, the people perish."

TABLE 2-1 Six Exemplary Vision Statements (Paraphrased)

- Dr Pepper Snapple: to be the best beverage business globally; our brands are synonymous with refreshment, fun, and flavor today and tomorrow.
- IBM: to be the world's most successful information technology company focused on helping customers apply technology to solve their problems now and in the future.
- Hilton Worldwide: to fill the Earth with the light and warmth of hospitality by delivering exceptional experiences—every hotel and guest for all time.
- Starbucks: to be the premier purveyor of the finest coffee in the world while maintaining uncompromising principles as we steadily grow.
- Kellogg: to enrich and delight the world through foods and brands that matter today and tomorrow.
- Harley-Davidson: to fulfill dreams through the experiences of motorcycling for all time.

For many corporations, profit rather than vision or mission is the primary motivator, but profit alone is not enough to motivate people. It is not uncommon that profit is perceived negatively by many stakeholders of a firm. For example, employees could see profit as something that they earn and management then uses and even gives away to shareholders. Although this perception is undesired and disturbing to management, it clearly indicates that both profit and vision are needed to motivate a workforce effectively. Reuben Mark, former CEO of Colgate, maintains that a clear vision increasingly must make sense internationally. Mark's thoughts on vision follow:

> When it comes to rallying everyone to the corporate banner, it's essential to push one vision globally rather than trying to drive home different messages in different cultures. The trick is to keep the vision simple but elevated: "We make the world's fastest computers" or "Telephone service for everyone." You're never going to get anyone to charge the machine guns only for financial objectives. It's got to be something that makes people feel better, feel a part of something.[3]

When employees and managers together shape or fashion a vision statement of a firm, the resultant document can reflect the personal visions that managers and employees have in their hearts and minds about their own futures. Shared vision creates a commonality of interests that can lift workers out of the monotony of daily work and put them into a new world of opportunity, challenge, and belongingness. The motivation, dedication, and commitment associated with shared vision is an immense potential benefit for any firm or organization.

Characteristics of a Vision Statement

2.3. Identify the characteristics of a vision statement.

A vision statement should reveal the type of business the firm conducts. For example, a vision that says, "to become the best retail firm in the United States," is too broad because that firm could be selling anything from apples (A) to zebras (Z). Although typically a single sentence, vision statements need to do more than identify the product or service a firm offers; vision statements should be written from a customer perspective. Ideally every organization wants its employees and customers to align their actions with the firm's vision. To fulfill this need, an excellent vision statement describes a desired future state. Being futuristic enables vision statements to be used to facilitate organizational change. The statement needs to be doable but challenging.

In summary, effective vision statements exhibit the following five characteristics; these five attributes can be used as guidelines for writing or evaluating vision statements. Any vision statement that scores a 5 out of 5 on these characteristics is exemplary. Let's call this vision assessment technique "the 5-out-of-5 test."

1. **Clear:** reveals the type of industry and what the firm strives to become.
2. **Futuristic:** reveals what the firm strives to become or accomplish within 5 years.
3. **Concise:** one sentence in length.
4. **Unique:** reveals the firm's competitive advantage.
5. **Inspiring:** motivates the readers to support the firm.

Vision Statement Analysis

There is no one best vision statement for a particular company in a given industry, but the 5-out-of-5 test can be used to both develop and evaluate vision statements. Six exemplary vision statements that meet the 5-out-of-5 test are provided in Table 2-1. Notice the Harley-Davidson statement meets the five criteria in just 11 words.

Four vision statements that do *not* meet the 5-out-of-5 test are provided in Table 2-2.

TABLE 2-2 Four Nonexemplary Vision Statements (paraphrased)

1. Avon Products, Inc.: to be the firm that best understands and satisfies the product and service needs of women globally. *Author Comment:* Lacks Characteristics 1, 2, and 4.
2. Charles Schwab Corporation: to help investors help themselves. *Author Comment:* Lacks Characteristics 2, 4, and 5.
3. Instagram: to capture and share the world's moments. *Author Comment:* Lacks Characteristics 1, 2, 4, and 5.
4. Zappos.com: to deliver happiness to customers, employees, and vendors. *Author Comment:* Lacks Characteristics 1, 2, 4, and 5.

Mission Statements: What Is Our Business?

2.4. Describe the nature and role of mission statements in strategic management.

Current thought on mission statements is based largely on guidelines set forth in the mid-1970s by Peter Drucker, who is often called "the father of modern management" for his pioneering studies at General Motors and for his 22 books and hundreds of articles. Drucker believes that asking the question "What is our business?" is synonymous with asking "What is our mission?" An enduring statement of purpose that distinguishes one organization from other similar enterprises, the **mission statement**, is a declaration of an organization's "reason for being." It answers the pivotal question "What is our business?" A clear mission statement is essential for effectively establishing objectives and formulating strategies.

Sometimes called a **creed statement**, a statement of purpose, a statement of philosophy, a statement of beliefs, a statement of business principles, or a statement "defining our business," a mission statement reveals what an organization wants to be and who it wants to serve. All organizations have a reason for being, even if strategists have not consciously transformed this reason into writing. Drucker has the following to say about mission statements (paraphrased):

> A mission statement is the foundation for priorities, strategies, plans, and work assignments. It is the starting point for the design of jobs and organizational structures. Nothing may seem simpler or more obvious than to know what a company's business is. A lumber mill makes lumber, an airline carries passengers and freight, and a bank lends money. But "What is our business?" is almost always a difficult question and the right answer is usually anything but obvious. The answer to this question is the first responsibility of strategists.[4]

Some strategists spend almost every moment of every day on administrative and tactical concerns; those who rush quickly to establish objectives and implement strategies often overlook the development of a vision and mission statement. This problem is so widespread that many corporations, organizations, and small businesses in the United States have not yet developed a formal vision or mission statement.

Some companies develop mission statements simply because owners or top management believe it is fashionable, rather than out of any real commitment. However, firms that develop and systematically revisit their vision and mission statements, treat them as living documents, and consider them to be an integral part of the firm's culture realize great benefits. For example, managers at Johnson & Johnson (J&J) meet regularly with employees to review, reword, and reaffirm the firm's mission. The entire J&J workforce recognizes the value that top management places on this exercise, and these employees respond accordingly.

Characteristics of a Mission Statement

2.5. Identify and discuss the characteristics of an effective mission statement.

A mission statement is a declaration of attitude and outlook. It usually is broad in scope for at least two major reasons. First, a quality mission statement allows for the generation and consideration of a range of feasible alternative objectives and strategies without unduly stifling management creativity. Excess specificity would limit the potential of creative growth for the organization. However, an overly general statement that does not exclude any strategy alternatives could be dysfunctional. Apple's mission statement, for example, should not open the possibility for diversification into pesticides—or Ford Motor Company's into food processing.

Second, a mission statement needs to be broad to reconcile differences among and appeal to an organization's diverse **stakeholders**, the individuals and groups of individuals who have a special stake or claim on the company. Thus, a mission statement should be **reconciliatory**. Stakeholders include employees, managers, stockholders, boards of directors, customers, suppliers, distributors, creditors, governments (local, state, federal, and foreign), unions, competitors, environmental groups, and the general public. Stakeholders affect and are affected by an organization's strategies, yet the claims and concerns of diverse constituencies vary and often conflict. For example, the general public is especially interested in social responsibility, whereas stockholders are more interested in profitability. Stakeholder expectations leveled on any business literally may number in the thousands, and they often include clean air, jobs, taxes, investment opportunities, career opportunities, equal employment opportunities, employee benefits, salaries, wages, clean water, and community services. All stakeholders' expectations of an organization cannot be pursued with equal emphasis. A quality mission statement reveals that the organization will strive to meet the varied expectations of stakeholders.

The statement of mission should be sufficiently broad to allow judgments about the most promising growth directions and those considered less promising. Numbers should not be included in a mission statement. George Steiner offers the following insight on the need for a mission statement to be broad in scope:

> Mission statements are not designed to express concrete ends, but rather to provide motivation, general direction, an image, a tone, and a philosophy to guide the enterprise. An excess of detail could prove counterproductive since concrete specification could be the base for rallying opposition; all in the firm need to be onboard with the firm's mission.[5]

An effective mission statement should not be too lengthy; the recommended length is fewer than 100 words. An effective mission statement should arouse positive feelings and emotions about an organization; it should be inspiring in the sense that it motivates readers to action. A mission statement should be enduring but never cast in stone, meaning that a statement may need to be changed at any time depending on changes anywhere in the integrative model of strategic management. This dynamic nature of both vision and mission statements is conveyed in Figure 2-1 through the feedback loop. An effective mission statement generates the impression that a firm is successful, has direction, and is worthy of time, support, and investment from all stakeholders.

A business mission reflects judgments about future growth directions and strategies that are based on forward-looking external and internal analyses. The statement should provide useful criteria for selecting among alternative strategies. A clear mission statement provides a basis for generating and screening strategic options. A mission statement should (1) define what the organization is, (2) be limited enough to exclude some ventures and broad enough to allow for creative growth, (3) distinguish a given organization from all others, (4) serve as a framework for evaluating both current and prospective activities, and (5) be stated in terms sufficiently clear to be widely understood throughout the organization.[6] The mission statement should reflect the anticipations of customers. Rather than developing a product and then trying to find a market, the operating philosophy of organizations should be to identify customers' needs and then provide a product or service to fulfill those needs.

Table 2-3 summarizes 10 desired characteristics of an effective mission statement.

TABLE 2-3 Characteristics of a Mission Statement

1. Broad in scope; does not include monetary amounts, numbers, percentages, ratios, or objectives.
2. Concise; fewer than 100 words in length.
3. Inspiring.
4. Identifies the utility of a firm's products.
5. Reveals that the firm is socially responsible.
6. Reveals that the firm is environmentally responsible.
7. Includes nine components: customers, products or services, markets, technology, concern for survival, growth, and profits, philosophy, distinctive competence, concern for public image, and concern for employees.
8. Reconciliatory; resolves divergent views among stakeholders.
9. Enduring but never cast in stone.
10. Attracts customers; is written from a customer perspective.

Quality mission statements identify the utility (value) of a firm's products to its customers. This is why Verizon's mission statement focuses on communication rather than on telephones; it is why ExxonMobil's mission statement focuses on energy rather than on oil and gas; it is why Union Pacific's mission statement focuses on transportation rather than on railroads; it is why Universal Studios' mission statement focuses on entertainment rather than on movies. A major reason for developing a mission statement is to attract customers; all companies and organizations must continually attract customers.

The following utility statements are relevant in developing a mission statement:

Do not offer me things. Offer me benefits.

Do not offer me clothes. Offer me attractive looks.

Do not offer me shoes. Offer me comfort for my feet and the pleasure of walking.

Do not offer me a house. Offer me security, comfort, and a place that is clean and happy.

Do not offer me books. Offer me hours of pleasure and the benefit of knowledge.

Do not offer me food. Offer me health and nutrition.

Do not offer me tools. Offer me the benefits and the pleasure that come from making beautiful things.

Do not offer me furniture. Offer me comfort and the quietness of a cozy place.

Do not offer me things. Offer me ideas, emotions, ambience, feelings, and benefits.

Please, do not offer me *things*.

Managers often perceive customer satisfaction as a valuable intangible asset to a firm; research suggests that customer satisfaction has a strong positive relationship with organizational performance.[7] When written from a customer perspective, mission statements can spur employees, salespersons, and managers to provide exemplary customer service, which arguably would enhance customer loyalty and translate into customers being "on a mission" to seek out, use, and promote the firm's products and services.

Components of a Mission Statement

2.6. Identify and discuss the components of mission statements.

Most practitioners and academicians of strategic management agree there are nine **mission statement components** to be included in an exemplary statement. Because a mission statement is often the most visible and public part of the strategic management process, it is important that it includes both the 10 characteristics summarized previously and the following nine components:

1. *Customers*—Who are the firm's present and potential customers?
2. *Products or services*—What are the firm's major products or services?
3. *Markets*—Geographically, where does the firm compete?

4. *Technology*—Is the firm technologically current?
5. *Concern for survival, growth, and profitability*—Is the firm committed to growth and financial soundness?
6. *Philosophy*—What are the basic beliefs, values, aspirations, and ethical priorities of the firm?
7. *Distinctive competence*—What is the firm's major competitive advantage?
8. *Concern for public image*—Is the firm responsive to social, community, and environmental concerns?
9. *Concern for employees*—Are employees a valuable asset of the firm?[8]

To exemplify how mission statements should be written to include all nine components, a component-by-component example for a charter boat fishing company is provided in Table 2-4. Note the charter company's customers are "outdoor enthusiasts." "Customers" is an important component to include in a mission statement, so merely including the word *customer* is not sufficient or adequate because that word alone will not attract customers. The statement needs to identify more precisely the target groups of customers. In fact, all nine components should be written from a customer perspective, as given in the Table 2-4 example. For example, regarding the product/service component, the charter fishing company provides "memories for a lifetime"—thus revealing the utility of the service offered and appealing to people who may not like to "just go fishing." Regarding the distinctive competence component, whereby the firm reveals the major competitive advantage its products or services provide, the statement says: "for customer enjoyment and safety, we provide the most experienced staff in the industry." A concise, inspiring, exemplary mission statement that could be derived from the component-by-component example shown in Table 2-4 follows.

Our fleet of fast, clean deep sea fishing boats (products) offers outdoor enthusiasts (customers) an exciting fishing adventure off the coast of North Carolina (markets). Using the latest safety and fishing finding equipment (technology), as well as emission-friendly engines (public image), our friendly captain and first mate are the most experienced in the industry (distinctive competence). Ensuring that customers "catch rather than just fish," our staff of experienced captains and first mates (employees) follows the Golden Rule (philosophy) and creates lifelong memories for customers, all while charging the lowest possible prices and fostering repeat customers (survival, growth, profitability). (85 words)

Regarding the survival, growth, and profitability component, for publicly held firms, shareholders often expect at least a 5 percent annual growth in revenues because otherwise individuals could redirect their money to achieve this rate of growth (usually) in the stock market. Regarding the

TABLE 2-4 Mission Statement Components Written from a Customer Perspective

1. *Customers:* Our customers are outdoor enthusiasts seeking fishing excitement and adventure.
2. *Products or services:* We provide fast, clean boats, all the bait and tackle needed, and friendly first mates to create memories for a lifetime.
3. *Markets:* Our fleet of fast, clean vessels operate all along the North Carolina coast.
4. *Technology:* Our vessels are equipped with the very latest safety and fish finding equipment to ensure that customers comfortably are "catching rather than just fishing."
5. *Survival, growth, and profitability:* Our prices are as low as possible to garner repeat customers and a reasonable return for our owners.
6. *Philosophy:* We assure customers the utmost courtesy and care as our motto on every vessel is to follow the Golden Rule.
7. *Distinctive competence:* For customer enjoyment and safety, we provide the most experienced staff in the industry.
8. *Public image:* Our vessels use emission-friendly engines; we strive to bring repeat tourists to all communities where we operate.
9. *Employees:* Our captains and first mates are "on a mission" to help customers have a great time.

Source: Based on Meredith E. David, Forest R. David, & Fred R. David, "Mission Statement Theory and Practice: A Content Analysis and New Direction," *International Journal of Business, Marketing, and Decision Sciences* 7, no. 1 (Summer 2014): 95–109.

philosophy component, recent research discussed in the Ethics Capsule 2 concludes that trustworthiness is the most important variable in doing business. Note: The authors feel that component 7 (distinctive competence) is the most important among the nine, followed by customers and then philosophy, but all nine components are important and need including.

ETHICS CAPSULE 2

What Ethics Variable Is Most Important in Doing Business?[9]

Lucky Business/Shutterstock

Who Is This Approaching?

Three professors from Harvard Business School, Amy Cuddy, Susan Fiske, and Peter Glick, recently revealed in a new book, *Presence*, that the most important variable in doing business with someone you do not know is trustworthiness. The authors say that within seconds of meeting someone, people determine first and foremost the extent that the person is trustworthy. They say that variable is far more important than competence, intelligence, looks, strength, height, and numerous other variables.

Professor Cuddy explains, "From an evolutionary perspective, it was more crucial to our survival that we know quickly whether a person(s) deserves our trust." In other words, for nearly a million years of man's evolution, when people first met other people, they assessed within seconds whether the new person(s) was trustworthy, meaning is this person going to steal from us or try to kill us. Trustworthiness, these authors report, was always assessed before competence (i.e., can this person start a fire or catch a fish). Cuddy says competence is evaluated today only after trust is established because physically and psychologically, man today is the result of various traits being promoted and others extinguished over the millennia, and trustworthiness is number one according to these researchers.

Cuddy, Fiske, and Glick go on to say that focusing too much today on displaying your strengths or that you are smart, whether in a job interview or in seeking to do business with someone, can backfire. Cuddy says, "A warm, trustworthy person who is also strong elicits admiration, but only after you've established trust does your strength become a gift, rather than a threat."

[9]Based on Jenna Goudreau, A Harvard Psychologist Says People Judge You Based on 2 Criteria When They First Meet You," http://www.aol.com/article/2016/01/16/a-harvard-psychologist-says-people-judge-you-based-on-2-criteria/21298315/?cps=gravity_4816_5749740174701162847

The Importance (Benefits) of Vision and Mission Statements

2.7. Discuss the benefits of a firm having clear vision and mission statements.

A meta-analysis of 20 years of empirical research on mission statements concluded there is a positive relationship between mission statements and measures of financial performance.[10] In actual practice, wide variations exist in the nature, composition, and use of both vision and mission statements. King and Cleland recommend that organizations carefully develop a written mission statement to reap the following benefits:

1. To make sure all employees and managers understand the firm's purpose or reason for being.
2. To provide a basis for prioritization of key internal and external factors used to formulate feasible strategies.
3. To provide a basis for the allocation of resources.
4. To provide a basis for organizing work, departments, activities, and segments around a common purpose.[11]

Another benefit of developing a comprehensive mission statement is that divergent views among managers can be uncovered and resolved through the process. The question "What is our business?" can create controversy. Raising the question often reveals differences among strategists in the organization. Individuals who have worked together for a long time and who think they know each other suddenly may realize that they are in fundamental disagreement.

For example, in a college or university, divergent views among faculty regarding the relative importance of teaching, research, and service often are expressed during the development of the mission statement. Negotiation, compromise, and eventual agreement on important issues are needed before people in any organization or company can focus on more specific activities related to formulating strategy.

Considerable disagreement among an organization's strategists over vision and mission statements can cause trouble if not resolved. For example, unresolved disagreement over the business mission was one of the reasons for W.T. Grant's 1975 bankruptcy and eventual liquidation. Top executives of the firm, including Ed Staley and Lou Lustenberger, were firmly entrenched in opposing positions that W.T. Grant should be like Kmart or JCPenney, respectively. W.T. Grant decided to adopt attributes of both Kmart and JCPenney; this compromise was a huge strategic mistake. In other words, top executives of W.T. Grant never resolved their vision or mission issue, which ultimately led to the firm's disappearance.[12]

Too often, strategists develop vision and mission statements only when the organization is in trouble. Of course, the documents are needed then. Developing and communicating these statements during troubled times indeed may have spectacular results and may even reverse decline. However, to wait until an organization is in trouble to develop a vision and mission statement is a gamble that characterizes irresponsible management. According to Drucker, as indicated, the most important time to ask seriously, "What do we want to become?" and "What is our business?" is when a company is successful:

> Success always obsoletes the very behavior that achieved it, always creates new realities, and always creates new and different problems. Only the fairy tale story ends, "They lived happily ever after." It is never popular to argue with success or to rock the boat. It will not be long before success will turn into failure. Sooner or later, even the most successful answer to the question "What is our business?" becomes obsolete.[13]

In multidivisional organizations, strategists should ensure that divisional units perform strategic management tasks (sometimes referred to as *business-level strategy*), including the development of a statement of vision and mission for their unique division. Each division should involve its own managers and employees in developing vision and mission statements that are consistent with and supportive of the corporate mission. The benefits of having a clear vision and mission are summarized in Table 2-5.

An organization that fails to develop an effective vision and mission statement loses the opportunity to present itself favorably to existing and potential stakeholders. All organizations need customers, employees, and managers, and most firms need creditors, suppliers, and distributors. Vision and mission statements are effective vehicles for communicating with important internal and external stakeholders. The principal benefit of these statements as tools of strategic management is derived from their specification of the ultimate aims of a firm. Vision and mission statements reveal the firm's shared expectations internally among all employees and managers and, for external constituencies, reveal the firm's long-term commitment to responsible, ethical action in providing a needed product or service to customers.

TABLE 2-5 10 Benefits of Having a Clear Vision and Mission

1. Achieve clarity of purpose among all managers and employees.
2. Provide a basis for all other strategic planning activities, including internal and external assessment, establishing objectives, developing strategies, choosing among alternative strategies, devising policies, establishing organizational structure, allocating resources, and evaluating performance.
3. Provide direction.
4. Provide a focal point for all stakeholders of the firm.
5. Resolve divergent views among managers.
6. Promote a sense of shared expectations among all managers and employees.
7. Project a sense of worth and intent to all stakeholders.
8. Project an organized, motivated organization worthy of support.
9. Achieve higher organizational performance.
10. Achieve synergy among all managers and employees.

The Process of Developing Vision and Mission Statements

As many managers as possible should be involved in the process of developing these statements because, through involvement, people become committed to an organization. An effective approach to developing vision and mission statements is first to ask all managers to read this chapter as background information. Then, managers are asked to individually prepare vision and mission statements for the organization. A facilitator or committee of top managers should then merge these statements into a single document and distribute the draft statements to all managers. A request for modifications, additions, and deletions is needed next, along with a meeting to revise the document. To the extent that all managers have input into and support the final documents, organizations can more easily obtain managers' support for other strategy formulation, implementation, and evaluation activities. Thus, the process of developing vision and mission statements represents a great opportunity for strategists to obtain needed support from all managers in the firm.

Some organizations use discussion groups of managers to develop and modify existing statements. Other organizations hire an outside consultant or facilitator to manage the process and help draft the language. At times an outside person with expertise in developing such statements, who has unbiased views, can manage the process more effectively than an internal group or committee of managers.

When an effective process is followed, developing a mission statement can create an emotional bond and sense of mission among employees and customers. Commitment to a company's strategy and intellectual agreement on the strategies to be pursued do not necessarily translate into an emotional bond; hence, strategies that have been formulated may not be implemented. An emotional bond comes when an individual personally identifies with the underlying values and behavior of a firm, thus turning intellectual agreement and commitment to strategy into a sense of mission. Involving marketers and sales representatives in the development of the mission statement and writing statements from a customer perspective could enable firms to create an emotional bond with customers and enhance the likelihood that salespersons would be "on a mission" to provide excellent customer service.

Evaluating and Writing Vision and Mission Statements

2.8. Evaluate and write vision and mission statements for different organizations.

There is a right way for both vision and mission statements to be developed and communicated as described in this chapter. Recall in Global Capsule 2 that the former CEO of LinkedIn says the most important ingredient for a great leader is for that person to be clear about the organization's vision.

A mission statement should provide more than mere inclusion of a single word such as products or employees regarding a respective component. Why? Because the statement should motivate stakeholders to action, as well as be customer-oriented, informative, inspiring, and enduring.

Perhaps the best way to develop a skill for evaluating and writing vision and mission statements is to study actual (or proposed) statements and critique them. What follows in this section therefore is a quick focus on the vision and mission statement situation at three companies: Nestlé S.A, Adidas AG, and Emirates Group.

Nestlé S.A.

Headquartered in Vevey, Switzerland, and serving 186 countries, Nestlé S.A. is the largest food-producing company in the world, selling ready-for-consumption food products. But Nestlé does not have a vision statement published on either their corporate website or in the firm's *Annual Report*. A viable vision statement for Nestlé could be as follows:

> We strive to produce the most healthy and tasty food with the aim to improve life for everyone on Earth now and for future generations.

The proposed statement meets the 5-out-of-5 test presented because it includes the five desired characteristics: Clear, Futuristic, Concise, Unique, and Inspiring.

Nestlé also does not have a published mission statement, but a viable statement could be as follows:

> Our philosophy at Nestlé is to hire the most talented scientists (4) and most devoted employees (9) as we strive to provide the most nutritious foods, drinks, and pet foods (2) to our customers. Quality, healthy, affordable foods (7) should be available to everyone around the world (1, 3). We are committed to controlling costs (5) and conducting business in an ethical way (6) that has a neutral impact on the environment (8). (64 words)

Although there is always room for improvement, the proposed Nestlé mission statement arguably incudes the nine components indicated with numbers in parentheses: 1. *Customers*, 2. *Products or services*, 3. *Markets*, 4. *Technology*, 5. *Concern for survival, growth, and profitability*, 6. *Philosophy*, 7. *Distinctive competence*, 8. *Concern for public image*, and 9. *Concern for employees*.

The proposed Nestlé mission statement is only 64 words, so it is concise and arguably also includes the 10 mission statement characteristics presented as desirable in this chapter.

Adidas AG

Headquartered in Herzogenaurach, Germany, Adidas AG is a sports apparel and footwear manufacturer that also produces accessory products such as bags, shirts, watches, eyewear, and other sports- and clothing-related goods. The company is the largest sportswear manufacturer in Europe and the second-biggest sportswear manufacturer in the world, with Nike being the largest. Adidas states on their corporate website that their mission is (paraphrased):

To be the best sports brand in the world.

However, this statement likely fits better as a vision statement.

The Adidas vision statement arguably meets no criteria among the 5-out-of-5 test. Their vision statement is too broad. Vision statements need to do more than identify the product or service a firm offers; vision statements should be written from a customer perspective. Ideally every organization wants its employees and customers to align their actions with the firm's vision. To fulfill this need, an excellent vision statement describes a desired future state. Being futuristic enables vision statements to be used to facilitate organizational change. The Adidas statement needs to be doable but challenging.

A new and improved Adidas vision statement could read something like this:

We strive to continually improve upon our world reputation as one of the largest and best suppliers and retailers of sports footwear, apparel, equipment, and accessories.

Because Adidas does not have a published mission statement, a proposed statement could read something like the following:

At Adidas we are committed to hiring a globally (3) diverse workforce (9) to design, promote and sell top-of-the-line athletic footwear, apparel, and accessories (2, 7). We strive to use the latest e-commerce technology (4) to provide better shopping experiences for our customers of all ages (1) globally. We are an inclusive company (6) that is active in philanthropy (8) as we strive to provide excellent rewards for our shareholders (5). (62 words)

The proposed Adidas statement arguably includes all nine components and all 10 characteristics identified as needed to be exemplary.

Emirates Group

The name "Emirates Group" (Emirates) includes two entities: the well-known Emirates Airline and the aviation services company Dubai National Air Transport Association (dnata). Headquartered in Garhoud, Dubai, UAE, near the Dubai International Airport, Emirates Airline (or simply Emirates) is the state-owned global airline of Dubai. The largest airline in the Middle East, Emirates provides passenger and freight services to about 100 countries, while dnata provides ground handling, cargo, catering, and travel services in 35 countries.

Emirates does not have a written vision statement, at least not made available on either the corporate website or the *Annual Report*. A possible vision statement could read something like this perhaps:

To provide efficient, innovative passenger and cargo air flight services wherever people live and work today and tomorrow.

This proposed vision statement for Emirates arguably meets all criteria among the 5-out-of-5 test presented in this chapter.

Emirates does not really have a published mission statement, so the following statement could be proposed. Note that the proposed statement arguably includes the nine desired components and the 10 desired characteristics:

We strive to offer the best award-winning passenger and cargo jet services (7) as well as on-the-ground airport services (2) around the world (3) and to set an excellent example for integrity (6) and humility for all. We strive to hire the best employees (9) and use the latest technology (4) to assure that passengers (1) and communities are safe and happy, as we endeavor to meet and exceed the expectations of our shareholders (5) and the silent needs of the natural environment (8). (75 words)

IMPLICATIONS FOR STRATEGISTS

Figure 2-2 reveals that establishing and nurturing an effective vision and mission is a vital first step in gaining and maintaining competitive advantages. Businesses succeed by attracting and keeping customers, and they do this by providing value for customers through unique experiences, products, or services. Firms nurture their uniqueness as evidenced in the distinctive competence component in mission statements. Marketers continually assess customers' changing needs and wants and make appropriate adjustments in the design and delivery of products and services to sustain competitive advantage. Developing and communicating a clear business vision and mission is essential because without effective vision and mission statements, a firm's short-term actions may be counterproductive to long-term interests. A clear vision and mission provides direction for all subsequent activities that endeavor to see customers, employees, and shareholders concurrently on a mission to see the firm succeed.

Vision and mission statements are not just words that look nice when framed or engraved; they provide a basis for strategy

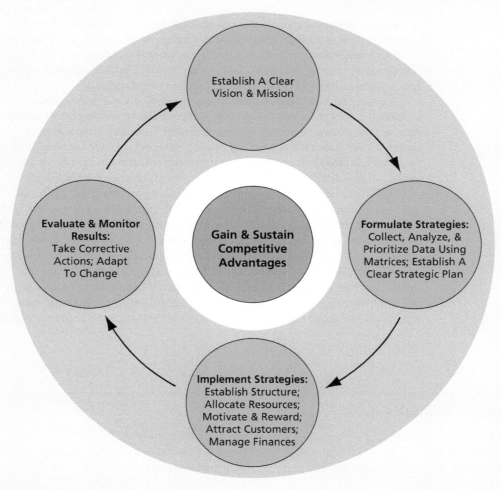

FIGURE 2-2

How to Gain and Sustain Competitive Advantages

and action; they reveal the reason a business opens its doors every day, the reason salespersons sell, the reason customers buy, and the reason employees work. The statements ideally are the passion behind the company, the foundation for employee morale, and the basis for customer loyalty. Written from a customer perspective and included in both oral and written communication with customers, the statements could be used to attract and keep customers. Vision and mission statements do matter. Marketers pursue projects and managers make daily decisions mindful of the firm's basic vision, mission, and resources. Managers work hard every day to motivate employees. Executives are on a mission to present the firm favorably to many stakeholders. A clear vision and mission enables strategists to lead the way as a firm strives to gain, sustain, and grow its customer base and competitive advantages.

IMPLICATIONS FOR STUDENTS

Because gaining and sustaining competitive advantage is the essence of strategic management, when presenting your vision and mission statements as part of a case analysis, be sure to address the distinctive competence component. Compare your recommended vision and mission statements with the firm's existing statements and with rival firms' statements to clearly reveal how your recommendations or strategic plan enables the firm to gain and sustain competitive advantage. Your proposed mission statement should certainly include the 10 characteristics and nine components, but in your discussion about the vision or mission, focus on competitive advantage. In other words, be prescriptive, forward-looking, and insightful—couching your vision or mission overview in terms of how you believe the firm can best gain and sustain competitive advantage versus major rivals. Do not be content with merely showing a nine-component comparison of your proposed statement with rival firms' statements, although that would be nice to include in your analysis.

Chapter Summary

Every organization has a unique purpose and reason for being. This uniqueness should be reflected in vision and mission statements. The nature of a business' core values, vision, and mission can represent either a competitive advantage or disadvantage for the firm. An organization achieves a heightened sense of purpose when strategists, managers, and employees develop and communicate clear core values, vision, and mission. Drucker says that developing a clear business vision and mission is the "first responsibility of strategists."

A quality mission statement reveals an organization's customers; products or services; markets; technology; concern for survival, growth, and profitability; philosophy; distinctive competence; concern for public image; and concern for employees. These nine basic components serve as a practical framework for evaluating and writing mission statements. As the first step in strategic management, the vision and mission statements provide direction for all planning activities. As indicated next in the mini-case, even JetBlue Airways' vision and mission statements can be improved.

Well-designed vision and mission statements are essential for formulating, implementing, and evaluating strategy. Developing and communicating a clear business vision and mission are the most commonly overlooked tasks in strategic management. Without clear statements of vision and mission, a firm's short-term actions can be counterproductive to long-term interests. Vision and mission statements always should be subject to revision, but if carefully prepared, they will require infrequent major changes. Vision and mission statements should serve as guidance and be reviewed often when divergent views arise among managers on various strategies to implement. Organizations usually reexamine their vision and mission statements annually. Effective vision and mission statements stand the test of time.

Key Terms and Concepts

concern for employees (p. 50)
concern for public image (p. 50)
concern for survival, growth, and profitability (p. 50)
core values statement (p. 44)
creed statement (p. 47)
customers (p. 49)
distinctive competence (p. 50)
markets (p. 49)

mission statement (p. 47)
mission statement components (p. 49)
philosophy (p. 50)
products or services (p. 49)
reconciliatory (p. 48)
stakeholders (p. 48)
technology (p. 50)
vision statement (p. 45)

Issues for Review and Discussion

2-1. This chapter's exemplary strategist is CEO of PG&E, Patti Poppe, who has a bold new vision to put all PG&E power lines underground. How closely aligned do you think Poppe's personal vision would be or should be with her corporate vision statement?

2-2. In Ethics Capsule 2, what variable among all variables is most important in doing business and important in developing a mission statement?

2-3. Regarding the "survival, growth, and profitability component" for publicly held firms, shareholders oftentimes expect at least a 5 percent annual growth in revenues (top line) and net income (bottom line). Explain why this statement is true.

2-4. Explain the 5-out-of-5 test associated with vision statements.

2-5. At the website http://www.themarketingblender.com/vision-mission-statements/, it defines vision as "the dreaming piece" and defines mission as "the doing piece." How effective is this distinction?

2-6. Discuss the relative importance of vision and mission documents for managers compared with employees, customers, and shareholders.

2-7. Define *reconciliatory*, and give an example of how this characteristic can be met in a mission statement.

2-8. Which mission statement component most closely reveals the firm's competitive advantage? Give an example.

2-9. Critique the following vision statement by Stokes Eye Clinic: "Our vision is to take care of your vision."

2-10. For a university, students are the customer. Write a single sentence that could be included in your university's mission statement to reveal the institution's market components written from a customer perspective.

2-11. Some excellent nine-component mission statements consist of just two sentences. Write a two-sentence mission statement for a company of your choice.

2-12. How do you think an organization can best align company mission with employee mission?

2-13. What are some different names for mission statement, and where will you likely find a firm's mission statement?

2-14. If your company does not have a vision or mission statement, describe a good process for developing these documents.

2-15. Explain how developing a mission statement can help resolve divergent views among managers in a firm.

2-16. Drucker says the most important time to seriously reexamine the firm's vision or mission is when the firm is successful. Why is this?

2-17. Explain why a mission statement should not include monetary amounts, numbers, percentages, ratios, goals, or objectives.

2-18. Discuss the meaning of the following statement: "Good mission statements identify the utility of a firm's products to its customers."

2-19. Distinguish between the distinctive competence and the philosophy components in a mission statement. Give an example of each for your university.

2-20. When someone or some company is "on a mission" to achieve something, many times the person or company cannot be stopped. List three things in prioritized order that you are on a mission to achieve in life.

2-21. Compare and contrast vision statements with mission statements in terms of composition and importance.

2-22. Do local service stations need to have written vision and mission statements? Why or why not?

2-23. Why do you think organizations that have a comprehensive mission tend to be high performers? Does having a comprehensive mission cause high performance?

2-24. What is your college or university's distinctive competence? How would you state that in a mission statement?

2-25. Explain the principal value of a vision and a mission statement.

2-26. Why is it important for a mission statement to be reconciliatory?

2-27. In your opinion, what are the three most important components that should be included when writing a mission statement? Why?

2-28. How would the mission statements of a for-profit and a nonprofit organization differ?

2-29. Write a vision and mission statement for an organization of your choice.

2-30. Who are the major stakeholders of the bank that you do business with locally? What are the major claims of those stakeholders?

2-31. List eight benefits of having a clear mission statement.

2-32. How often do you think a firm's vision and mission statement should be changed?

2-33. What four characteristics can be used to evaluate the quality of a vision statement?

2-34. Explain the importance of core values in establishing vision and mission statements.

2-35. According to the textbook authors, what are the three most important mission statement components in rank order?

Writing Assignments

2-36. Explain why a mission statement should not include strategies and objectives.

2-37. List seven characteristics of a mission statement.

Ken Wolter/Alamy Photo

ASSURANCE-OF-LEARNING EXERCISES

SET 1: STRATEGIC PLANNING FOR MCDONALD'S

EXERCISE 2A

Develop an Improved McDonald's Vision Statement

Purpose

As indicated in the Cohesion Case in Chapter 1, McDonald's appears not to have a published vision statement. The purpose of this exercise is to develop an excellent proposed vision statement for McDonald's, one that meets the 5-out-of-5 test discussed in this chapter.

Instructions

Step 1   Review the Cohesion Case and the McDonald's corporate website at https://corporate.mcdonalds.com/corpmcd/our-purpose-and-impact.html

Step 2   Develop a proposed vision statement for the company.

Step 3   Write a paragraph explaining how and why your proposed vision statement is excellent.

Step 4   Email your work to your professor for evaluation.

Step 5   Recall from the Battle of Cannae discussed in Chapter 1, clear vision and mission are the basis for an excellent strategic plan and, thus, can be vital to company survival.

EXERCISE 2B

Develop an Improved McDonald's Mission Statement

Purpose

As indicated in the Cohesion Case in Chapter 1, McDonald's has a published mission (Purpose) statement. The purpose of this exercise is to evaluate McDonald's Purpose Statement and to prepare a revised, improved statement.

Instructions

Step 1   Review the Cohesion Case and the McDonald's corporate website at https://corporate.mcdonalds.com/corpmcd/our-purpose-and-impact.html

Step 2   Critique the existing McDonald's Purpose statement by determining which of the nine desired components and which of the 10 recommended characteristics are not included.

Step 3   Develop a proposed Purpose Statement for the company, one that includes the necessary components and characteristics discussed in this chapter.

Step 4   Email your work to your professor for evaluation.

Step 5   Recall from the Battle of Cannae discussed in Chapter 1, clear vision and mission are the basis for an excellent strategic plan and, thus, can be vital to company survival.

EXERCISE 2C

Compare McDonald's Mission Statement to a Rival Firm's

Purpose

Burger King is considered globally to be McDonald's major competitor. It is appropriate therefore to compare and contrast the two companies' vision and mission statements because those documents represent the foundation or basis for developing an excellent strategic plan.

Instructions

Step 1   In a word document, prepare a 14 × 4 matrix. Place the nine desired mission statement components down the left column followed by the five variables recommended to be included in an effective vision statement. Across the top, let Column 1 be your proposed vision statement for McDonald's and Column 2 be the Burger King vision statement provided. Let Column 3 represent your proposed mission statement for McDonald's and Column 4 be the Burger King mission statement.

Step 2	Critique your proposed statements with the Burger King statements provided.
Step 3	Write *Included* or *Not Included* in each cell of your 14 × 4 matrix.
Step 4	Write a half-page summary of your analysis.
Step 5	Email your work to your professor for evaluation.

The following statements (paraphrased) for Burger King can be used for this exercise:

Vision statement: To be the most profitable fast-food-restaurant in the world, with great people serving the best burgers in the world.

Mission statement: To offer the best-value, quality food, served quickly, in an attractive, clean environment.[14]

SET 2: STRATEGIC PLANNING FOR MY UNIVERSITY

EXERCISE 2D

Compare Your University's Vision and Mission Statements to Those of a Rival Institution

Purpose

Most colleges and universities have vision and mission statements. The purpose of this exercise is to give you practice comparing the effectiveness of vision and mission statements. Compare your university (or school of business) with a rival institution.

Instructions

Step 1	Determine whether your institution has a vision or mission statement. Look online or in the front of your college handbook. Analyze your college's vision and mission statements in light of the concepts presented in this chapter.
Step 2	Compare the vision statement and the mission statement of your college or university to those of a leading rival institution.
Step 3	Write a one-page summary of your analysis of the statements as per the needed 5-out-of-5 vision elements, the 10 mission characteristics, and nine mission components.

SET 3: STRATEGIC PLANNING FOR MYSELF

EXERCISE 2E

Develop a Vision and Mission Statement for Yourself

Purpose

A personal vision and mission statement can be helpful to an individual in job-related decisions and career paths. This exercise will give you practice developing and writing vision and mission statements from a personal perspective. For most college students nearing graduation, it is nearly inevitable to be faced with employability decisions. Developing vision and mission statements compels an individual to think about the nature and scope of their skills and abilities and to assess the potential attractiveness of future job opportunities and activities. These statements broadly chart the future direction of a person's life and serve as a motivating force and constant reminder of why the individual continuously gets up in the morning and works hard.

Instructions

| Step 1 | Develop a professional vision statement for yourself. Your statement should answer the question "What and where do I want to be professionally and personally in 3 to 5 years?" |
| Step 2 | Develop a professional mission statement for yourself. Your statement should answer the question "What do I want to accomplish professionally and personally in the next 1 to 3 years?" |

SET 4: INDIVIDUAL VERSUS GROUP STRATEGIC PLANNING

EXERCISE 2F

What Is the Relative Importance of Each of the Nine Components of a Mission Statement?

Purpose

Research reveals that a mission statement should include all nine components to be most effective. For some companies or organizations, some components may be more important to include than others. Based on their experience, this exercise reveals the authors' ranking of the relative importance of the nine mission components recommended for inclusion in an exemplary statement.

The purpose of this exercise is to examine how well students understand the components of a mission statement. In addition, the purpose of this exercise is to examine whether individual decision-making is better than group decision-making. Academic research suggests that groups make better decisions than individuals about 80 percent of the time.

Instructions

Rank the nine mission statement components as to their relative importance (1 = most important, 9 = least important). First, rank the components as an individual. Then, rank the components as part of a group of three. Thus, determine what person(s) and what group(s) can come closest to the expert ranking. This exercise enables examination of the relative effectiveness of individual versus group decision-making in strategic planning.

Steps

1. Fill in Column 1 in Table 2-6 to reveal your individual ranking of the relative importance of the nine components (1 = most important, to 9 = least important). For example, if you feel the Customer component is the fifth-most important, then enter a 5 in Column 1 beside Customers.

2. Fill in Column 2 in Table 2-6 to reveal your group's ranking of the relative importance of the nine components (1 = most important, to 9 = least important).

3. Fill in Column 3 in Table 2-6 to reveal the expert's ranking (provided by your professor) of the nine components.

TABLE 2-6 Mission Statement Analysis: Comparing Individual Versus Group Decision-Making

Components	Column 1	Column 2	Column 3	Column 4	Column 5
1. Customers					
2. Products					
3. Markets					
4. Technology					
5. Survival/Growth					
6. Philosophy					
7. Distinctive Competence					
8. Public Image					
9. Employee					
Sums					

4. Fill in Column 4 in Table 2-6 to reveal the absolute difference between Column 1 and Column 3 to reveal how well you performed as an individual in this exercise. (Note: Absolute difference disregards negative numbers.)

5. Fill in Column 5 in Table 2-6 to reveal the absolute difference between Column 2 and Column 3 to reveal how well your group performed in this exercise.

6. Sum Column 4. Sum Column 5.

7. Compare the Column 4 sum with the Column 5 sum. If your Column 4 sum is less than your Column 5 sum, then you performed better as an individual than as a group. Normally, group decision-making is superior to individual decision-making, so if you did better than your group, you did excellent.

8. The Individual Winner(s): The individual(s) with the lowest Column 4 sum is the WINNER.

9. The Group Winners(s): The group(s) with the lowest Column 5 score is the WINNER.

MINI-CASE ON JETBLUE AIRWAYS

DOES JETBLUE HAVE THE BEST MISSION STATEMENT?[15]

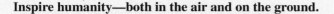

As indicated at the website given in the Source Line, some analysts rate JetBlue Airways (JetBlue) number one as having the best mission statement among all companies, but is that true? As you know, there are recommended components and characteristics that should be included in an effective mission statement.

Markus Mainka/Shutterstock

Headquartered in New York City, JetBlue is a *Fortune* 500 major low-cost airline operating more than 1,000 flights daily serving more than 100 domestic and international cities. JetBlue flies all over Mexico, South America, Europe, and Canada. JetBlue stock trades on the Nasdaq under the ticker symbol JBLU.

At the JetBlue corporate website, www.jetblue.com, the company does not provide a published vision or mission statement. JetBlue uses or once used the following statement, however, that was used by analysts to rate the firm as having the best mission statement:

Inspire humanity—both in the air and on the ground.

JetBlue has historically sought to distinguish itself from rival airlines by offering outstanding amenities such as nice seats, television, Sirius XM radio, and movies at every seat. Sometimes JetBlue ties Southwest Airlines as being ranked the "Highest in Customer Satisfaction Among Low-Cost Carriers" by J.D. Power. Southwest's mission (purpose) statement is given at https://www.southwest.com/html/about-southwest/index.html?clk=GFOOTER-ABOUT-ABOUT as follows (paraphrased):

Connect people to what's important in their lives through friendly, reliable, and low-cost air travel.

Questions

1. In light of the concepts in this chapter, how would you compare the mission statement of JetBlue to that of Southwest Airlines? Which statement is exemplary, if either? Which statement is better with regard to components needed compared with characteristics needed?
2. Develop an exemplary mission statement for JetBlue Airways.

[15]Based on https://www.fond.co/blog/best-mission-statements/

Web Resources

1. **Example vision statements** This website provides excellent videos, guidelines, and examples for developing a vision and mission statement.
   https://www.themarketingblender.com/vision-mission-statements/
2. **Example vision statements** This website provides about 100 example vision statements.
   https://www.cascade.app/blog/examples-good-vision-statements
3. **Example mission statements** This website provides more than 100 example mission statements from *Fortune* 500 companies.
   https://www.missionstatements.com/fortune_500_mission_statements.html
4. **Example mission statements** This website provides 51 example mission statements from some of the world's leading companies.
   https://alessiobresciani.com/foresight-strategy/51-mission-statement-examples-from-the-worlds-best-companies/
5. **Author-supplied video** Fred David gives a video overview of Chapter 2 in the prior edition, but much info is still applicable to the 18th edition.
   https://www.youtube.com/watch?v=yX4NDAUM8vk

Current Readings

Abdurakhmonov, Mirzokhidjon, Jason W. Ridge, and Aaron D. Hill, "Unpacking Firm External Dependence: How Government Contract Dependence Affects Firm Investments and Market Performance," *Academy of Management Journal* 64, no. 1 (February 2021): 327–50.

Apaydin, Marina, Guoliang Frank Jiang, Mehmet Demirbag, and Dima Jamali, "The Importance of Corporate Social Responsibility Strategic Fit and Times of Economic Hardship," *British Journal of Management* 32, no. 2 (April 2021): 399–415.

Daspit, Joshua J., James J. Chrisman, Pramodita Sharma, Allison W. Pearson, and Rebecca G. Long, "A Strategic Management Perspective of the Family Firm: Past Trends, New Insights, and Future Directions," *Journal of Managerial Issues* 29, no. 1 (Spring 2017): 6–29.

David, Fred R., Forest R. David, and Meredith E. David, "Benefits, Characteristics, Components, and Examples of Customer-Oriented Mission Statements," *International Journal of Business, Marketing, and Decision Sciences* 9, no. 1 (Fall 2016): 1–14.

David, Meredith E., Forest R. David, and Fred R. David, "Mission Statement Theory and Practice: A Content Analysis and New Direction," *International Journal of Business, Marketing, and Decision Sciences* 7, no. 1 (Summer 2014): 95–109.

Eshima, Yoshihiro, and Brian S. Anderson, "Firm Growth, Adaptive Capability, and Entrepreneurial Orientation," *Strategic Management Journal* 38, no. 3 (March 2017): 770–79.

Levine, Sheen, Mark Bernard, and Rosemarie Nagel, "Strategic Intelligence: The Cognitive Capability to Anticipate Competitor Behavior," *Strategic Management Journal* 38, no. 12 (December 2017): 2390–423.

Miller, Danny, and Isabelle Le Breton-Miller, "Paradoxical Resource Trajectories: When Strength Leads to Weakness and Weakness Leads to Strength," *Journal of Management* 47, no. 7 (September 2021): 1899–914.

Rodríguez, Omar, and Sundar Bharadwaj, "Competing on Social Purpose: Brands That Win By Tying Mission to Growth," *Harvard Business Review* 95, no. 5 (September–October 2017): 94–101.

Saarikko, Ted, Ulrika H. Westergren, and Tomas Blomquist, "The Internet of Things: Are You Ready for What's Coming?" *Business Horizons* 60, no. 5 (September 2017): 667–76.

Yan, Shipeng, Juan Almandoz, and Fabrizio Ferraro, "The Impact of Logic (In) Compatibility: Green Investing, State Policy, and Corporate Environmental Performance," *Administrative Science Quarterly* 66, no. 4 (December 2021): 903–44.

Endnotes

1. On page 44.
2. On page 45.
3. Brian Dumaine, "What the Leaders of Tomorrow See," *Fortune* (July 3, 1989): 50.
4. Peter Drucker, *Management: Tasks, Responsibilities, and Practices* (New York: Harper & Row, 1974), 61.
5. George Steiner, *Strategic Planning: What Every Manager Must Know* (New York: The Free Press, 1979): 160.
6. John Pearce II, "The Company Mission as a Strategic Tool," *Sloan Management Review* 23, no. 3 (Spring 1982): 74.
7. Raj Devasagayam, Nicholas R. Stark, and Laura Spitz Valestin, "Examining the Linearity of Customer Satisfaction: Return on Satisfaction as an Alternative," *Business Perspectives and Research* 1, no. 2 (January 2013): 1. Xueming Luo, Jan Wieseke, and Christian Homburg, "Incentivizing CEOs to Build Customer- and Employee-Firm Relations for Higher Customer Satisfaction and Firm Value," *Journal of the Academy of Marketing Science* 40, no. 6 (2012): 745.
8. Meredith E. David, Forest R. David, and Fred R. David, "Mission Statement Theory and Practice: A Content Analysis and New Direction," *International Journal of Business, Marketing, and Decision Sciences* 7, no. 1 (Summer 2014): 95–109.
9. On page 51.
10. Sebastian Desmidt, Anita Prinzie, and Adelien A. Decramer, "Looking for the Value of Mission Statements: A Meta-Analysis of 20 Years of Research," *Management Decision* 49, no. 3 (2011): 468.
11. W. R. King and D. I. Cleland, *Strategic Planning and Policy* (New York: Van Nostrand Reinhold, 1979): 124.
12. "How W. T. Grant Lost $175 Million Last Year," *Business Week* (February 25, 1975): 75. Drucker, *Management: Tasks, Responsibilities, and Practices*, 88.
13. Drucker, *Management: Tasks, Responsibilities, and Practices*, 88.
14. Based on http://panmore.com/burger-king-vision-statement-mission-statement
15. On page 61.

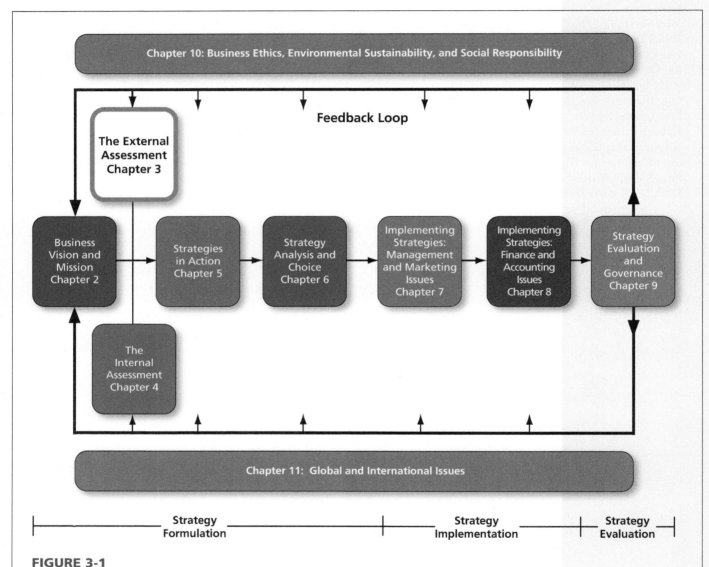

FIGURE 3-1

The Comprehensive, Integrative Strategic Management Model

Source: Fred R. David, "How Companies Define Their Mission," *Long Range Planning* 22, no. 1 (February 1989): 91. See also Anik Ratnaningsih, Nadjadji Anwar, Patdono Suwignjo, and Putu Artama Wiguna, "Balance Scorecard of David's Strategic Modeling at Industrial Business for National Construction Contractor of Indonesia," *Journal of Mathematics and Technology* no. 4 (October 2010): 20. See also, Meredith E. David, Fred R. David, and Forest R. David, "Closing the Gap Between Graduates' Skills and Employers' Requirements: A Focus on the Strategic Management Capstone Business Course," *Administrative Sciences* 11, no. 1 (2021): 10–26.

The External Assessment

LEARNING OBJECTIVES

After studying this chapter, you should be able to do the following:

3.1. Describe the nature and purpose of an external assessment in formulating strategies.

3.2. Identify and discuss the PESTEL external forces that impact organizations.

3.3. Explain Porter's Five-Forces Model and competitive forces that impact organizations.

3.4. Describe key sources of information for identifying opportunities and threats.

3.5. Discuss forecasting tools and techniques.

3.6. Explain how to develop and use an External Factor Evaluation (EFE) Matrix.

3.7. Explain how to develop and use a Competitive Profile Matrix (CPM).

ASSURANCE-OF-LEARNING EXERCISES

The following exercises are found at the end of this chapter:

SET 1:	Strategic Planning for McDonald's
EXERCISE 3A:	Develop an EFE Matrix for McDonald's
EXERCISE 3B:	Develop a Competitive Profile Matrix for McDonald's
SET 2:	Strategic Planning for My University
EXERCISE 3C:	Develop an EFE Matrix for Your College or University
EXERCISE 3D:	Develop a Competitive Profile Matrix for Your College or University
SET 3:	Strategic Planning to Enhance My Employability
EXERCISE 3E:	How Competitive Is Your State Among All States for Finding a Job?
EXERCISE 3F:	Compare and Contrast CareerBuilder, Glassdoor, Monster Jobs, and ZipRecruiter
EXERCISE 3G:	A Template Competency Test
SET 4:	Individual Versus Group Strategic Planning
EXERCISE 3H:	What External Forces Are Most Important in Strategic Planning?

Companies and organizations continually deal with external uncertainties and must quickly adapt to change to survive, as indicated in the following story:

Once there were two company presidents who competed in the same industry. These two presidents decided to go on a camping trip to discuss a possible merger. They hiked deep into the woods. Suddenly, they came upon a grizzly bear that rose up on its hind legs and snarled. Instantly, the first president took off his knapsack and got out a pair of jogging shoes. The second president said, "Hey, you can't outrun that bear." The first president responded, "Maybe I can't outrun that bear, but I surely can outrun you!"

As illustrated in Figure 3-1, this chapter focuses on the concepts and tools needed to manage external uncertainties by conducting an **external audit** (sometimes called **industry analysis**). An external audit focuses on identifying and evaluating trends and events beyond the control of a single firm, such as increased foreign competition, population shifts to coastal areas, an aging society, and technological advancements in metaverse, augmented reality, robotics, and quantum mechanics. An external audit reveals key opportunities and threats confronting an organization; an external audit guides managers in formulating strategies that take advantage of the opportunities and avoid or reduce the impact of threats.

This chapter presents a practical framework for gathering, assimilating, analyzing, and prioritizing external information that provides a foundation for formulating strategies effectively. Specifically, the first two-thirds of this chapter address external opportunity and threat areas in terms of what, where, how, and why to obtain this information; the latter one-third of this chapter explains how to develop and use an External Factor Evaluation (EFE) Matrix and Competitive Profile Matrix (CPM) to assimilate all the opportunity and threat factors and information.

The exemplary strategists showcased in this chapter, Marissa Andrada and Tabassum Zalotrawala, lead Chipotle Mexican Grill's Diversity, Equity, and Inclusion efforts and are vital individuals designing a winning strategy for that popular, fast-casual restaurant company.

EXEMPLARY **STRATEGIST** SHOWCASED

Andrada and Zalotrawala Lead the Way at Chipotle[1]

Headquartered in Newport Beach, California, Chipotle Mexican Grill has two exemplary female strategists: Marissa Andrada, Chief Diversity, Inclusion and People Officer, and Tabassum Zalotrawala, Chief Development Officer.

Andrada manages diversity, equity, and inclusion (DEI) strategy across all levels of the Chipotle company. She develops and nurtures a culture of well-being to inspire mutual learning, development, and personal and career growth. She has revamped Chipotle's benefits, launching a new tuition assistance program, access to mental healthcare, and a quarterly bonus option open to Chipotle's more than 85,000 employees. Prior to joining Chipotle, Andrada held similar positions at Kate Spade & Company, Starbucks Coffee Company, GameStop Corporation, and Red Bull North America. She has an MBA from Pepperdine University and was a 2020 American Business Award Gold Stevie winner in the HR Executive of the Year category. She is an exemplary strategist today at Chipotle.

Zalotrawala joined Chipotle as Chief Development Officer in December 2018 and oversees the restaurant's real estate, design, construction, facilities, and strategic sourcing activities. She has established innovative formats including the Chipotlane, which was named one of 'The Most Innovative Architecture Projects of 2020' by *Fast Company*. Prior to joining Chipotle, Zalotrawala performed similar leadership roles at Panda Restaurant Group, and before that at Arby's and Wendy's. She started her career in luxury hospitality,

Helen Sessions/Alamy Photo

designing high-profile palaces and mosques in Muscat, Sultanate of Oman. She holds a BFA degree in interior design from the American Intercontinental University and completed the Harvard Business School Advanced Management Program. She received the Exceptional Women Award in 2020. She is an exemplary strategist today at Chipotle.

[1]Based on information at https://ir.chipotle.com/management

The External Assessment Phase of Strategy Formulation

3.1. Describe the nature and purpose of an external assessment in formulating strategies.

The purpose of an external audit is to develop a finite list of both opportunities that could benefit a firm and threats that should be avoided or mitigated. As the term *finite* suggests, the external audit is not aimed at developing an exhaustive list of every possible factor that could influence the business; rather, it is aimed at identifying strategic variables that offer **actionable responses**. Firms should be able to respond either offensively or defensively to the factors by formulating strategies that capitalize on external opportunities or that minimize the impact of potential threats. Figure 3-1 illustrates with white shading how the external audit fits into the strategic management process.

Key External Forces

The major **external forces** that impact organizations can be divided into six groups: political, economic, sociocultural, technological, environmental, and legal. PESTEL is the acronym for these six forces. Key external factors are commonly derived by identifying and analyzing these forces that impact many differing industries, followed by conducting a Five-Forces analysis, which is significantly more refined and focuses on competitors, suppliers, and distributors in a particular industry. **PESTEL analysis** and Five-Forces analysis together yield key opportunities and threats facing the firm.

Research reveals that the broad PESTEL factors can account for up to 25 percent of firm performance, whereas competitor, supplier, distributor, and consumer factors related to the industry-specific Five-Forces Model explain 20 percent of firm performance.[2] PESTEL analysis may include highly unpredictable yet profound events, called ***Black Swan* events**, such as the COVID-19 pandemic. The remaining 55 percent of variance that explains firm performance is comprised of internal factors discussed in Chapter 4.

Relationships among these forces and an organization are depicted in Figure 3-2. External trends and events, such as increasing cybersecurity concerns, changing consumer behavior and demand, and political transitions, significantly affect products, services, markets and, thus, the strategies of organizations worldwide.

FIGURE 3-2

How Are Key External Factors Identified in Performing Strategic Planning in a Firm?

The Actionable-Quantitative-Comparative-Divisional (AQCD) Test

When identifying and prioritizing essential PESTEL and Five-Forces external factors in strategic planning, make sure the factors selected meet the following four criteria to the extent possible:

1. Actionable (i.e., meaningful and helpful in ultimately deciding what actions or strategies a firm should consider pursuing);
2. Quantitative (i.e., include percentages, ratios, dollars, and numbers to the extent possible);
3. Comparative (i.e., reveals changes over time); and
4. Divisional (relates to the firm's products or regions (rather than consolidated) so inferences can be drawn regarding what products and regions are doing well or not).[3]

Factors that meet these four criteria pass what can be called the Actionable-Quantitative-Comparative-Divisional (AQCD) test, which is a measure of the quality of an external factor. In addition to passing the AQCD test, make sure that external factors are indeed external (not internal), and make sure that external factors, particularly opportunities, are stated as external trends, events, or facts, rather than being stated as strategies the firm could pursue. Also, make sure the external factors relate closely to the firm achieving its mission (opportunities) or hindering its mission (threats). Factors selected for inclusion in an external assessment should be driven by the company's mission.

Regarding the AQCD criteria, strive to include all high-quality factors in an external assessment for a firm. External factors are deemed high quality if they meet three or four of the AQCD criteria; a low-quality factor will meet two or fewer of the AQCD criteria. When performing an external assessment, engage in an engineering hunt for facts to make sure as many factors as possible pass the AQCD test. It is important to state external factors to the extent possible in actionable, quantitative, comparative, and divisional terms.

High-quality and low-quality external factors for Walmart are given to further exemplify this important AQCD concept. For example, the online grocery shopping example is actionable because of the fact that Walmart perhaps should take actions to enhance its online retail business.

	ASK YOURSELF, "IS THE FACTOR..."			
	Actionable	Quantitative	Comparative	Divisional
A High-Quality External Factor				
Online retail grocery shopping grew from 12% to 16% in 2022.	yes	yes	yes	yes
A Low-Quality External Factor				
Consumers' average disposable incomes increased greatly in 2022.	no	no	no	no

Changes in external forces translate into changes in demand for both industrial and consumer goods and services. External forces affect the types of products developed, the nature of market segmentation and positioning strategies, the range of services offered, and the choice of businesses to acquire or sell. External forces have a direct impact on both suppliers and distributors. Identifying and evaluating external opportunities and threats enables organizations to revise their vision and mission statements if needed and to design strategies to achieve long-term objectives and develop policies to achieve annual objectives.

PESTEL External Forces that Impact Organizations

3.2. Identify and discuss the PESTEL external forces that impact organizations.

Political Forces

Governments and legislators can and often do impact strategic decisions. Federal, state, local, and foreign governments are major regulators, deregulators, subsidizers, employers, and customers

GLOBAL CAPSULE 3

What Is the Fastest Growing City and Country? Perhaps Dubai and the UAE[4]

IR Stone/Shutterstock

Dubai and the UAE just revamped their political and governmental systems to accelerate their economy, boost business, and open their arms to the whole world. On the Persian Gulf, Dubai and the UAE offer beautiful skyscrapers and beaches, open borders, zero taxes, a 10-year visa, decriminalization of cohabitation for unmarried couples, consumption of alcohol without a license, vaccine rates above 90 percent, and a new workweek effective as of December 2021 from Monday through Friday, rather than the Middle East standard of Sunday through Thursday. From 2021 to 2023, Dubai and the UAE have become arguably the fastest-growing economy in the world. Dubai's bars, restaurants, and hotels are packed with locals, travelers, tourists, visitors, and businesspeople from all over the world.

The UAE, including both Dubai and Abu Dhabi, recently hosted the successful Expo 2020, the Cricket T20 World Cup rugby tournament, and one of the largest professional gold events on the European Tour. Business license applications increased 70 percent in the UAE in 2021. The new restaurant, Aura, located on the 50th floor of a skyscraper in Dubai, has a one-month waiting list for a table. Aura has the world's highest 360-degree infinity pool. Hundreds of restaurants in the UAE have a long waiting list for dining.

Globally, companies are relocating their headquarters to the UAE for many reasons, including to take advantage of zero taxes, but also to enjoy openness as they provide millions of customers with all kinds of products and services.

[4] Rory Jones and Stephen Kalin, "High Vaccine Rates and Zero Taxes Make Dubai a Boomtown," *Wall Street Journal*, December 11, 2021, p. A11.

of organizations. Political and governmental factors, therefore, can represent major opportunities or threats for both small and large organizations. For industries and firms that depend heavily on government contracts or subsidies, such as Boeing or Lockheed, political forecasts can be the most important part of an external audit.

State and local income taxes and property taxes, for example, impact where companies locate facilities and where people desire to live. Seven US states, for example, have zero state income tax: Alaska, Florida, Nevada, South Dakota, Texas, Washington, and Wyoming. Example political variables that often yield AQCD opportunities and threats to organizations are provided in Table 3-1. Political/governmental factors must be stated in AQCD terms to the extent possible to be useful in strategic planning. Many companies have altered or abandoned strategies in the past because of political or governmental actions.

As indicated in Global Capsule 3, political factors are benefiting firms in Dubai immensely. Specifically, zero taxes, high vaccine rates, a 10-year visa, decriminalization of cohabitation for unmarried couples, consumption of alcohol without a license, a new workweek from Monday through Friday rather than the Middle East standard of Sunday through Thursday, and more have led Dubai and the UAE to become arguably the most booming economy in the world.

Between 2016 and 2020, FedEx invested $71 million on campaign contributions and lobbying, and the company received tax credits of $877 million between 2018 and 2020. Over the same time, Charter Communications invested $64 million on lobbying. Companies' dedication to lobbying reveal their concern that significant opportunities or potentially detrimental threats can arise from the P in PESTEL.

TABLE 3-1 Examples of Political Variables to Be Monitored

Natural environmental regulations	United States versus other country relationships
Protectionist actions by countries	Political conditions in countries
Changes in patent laws	Global price of oil changes
Equal employment opportunity laws	Local, state, and federal laws
Level of defense expenditures	Import–export regulations
Unionization trends	Tariffs, particularly on steel and aluminum
Antitrust legislation	Local, state, and national elections

Economic Forces

Economic factors have a direct impact on the potential attractiveness of various strategies. An example of an economic variable is "value of the dollar," which can have a significant effect on financial results of companies with global operations. Domestic firms with significant overseas sales, such as McDonald's, are hurt by a strong dollar. If the dollar appreciates 10 percent relative to the local currency of a particular country in which a US company has $100 million in revenues, that company's revenues would decrease by $10 million as they are translated into US dollars. For foreign firms with relatively large US sales, however, a strong dollar provides a boost. A strong dollar enables US firms to purchase raw materials more cheaply from other countries.

In April 2022, the U.S. dollar reached a two-year high as interest rates continued to rise towards 6 percent. Just in the first four months of 2022, the U.S. dollar rose 10 percent against the Japanese yen and more than 5 percent against the euro. A high value of the U.S. dollar boosts profits at U.S. companies that import goods from abroad and boosts the purchasing power of consumers buying goods from overseas. However, a high value of the U.S. dollar threatens U.S. multinationals by making their products less competitive abroad and a high value also hurts the U.S. because associated rising interest rates make interest payments on the U.S.'s $29 trillion national debt increase dramatically.

Favorable economic conditions bode well for many firms because economic growth typically reduces unemployment, boosts consumer confidence, and increases disposable income. A few categories of economic variables that often yield AQCD opportunities and threats for organizations are provided in Table 3-2. Economic factors must be stated in AQCD terms to the extent possible to be useful in strategic planning.

TABLE 3-2 Example Economic Categories to Be Monitored

Shift to a service economy	Demand shifts for different goods and services
Availability of credit	Income differences by region and consumer groups
Level of disposable income	Price fluctuations
Propensity of people to spend	Foreign countries' economic conditions
Interest rates	Monetary and fiscal policies
Inflation rates	Stock market trends
Gross domestic product (GDP) trends	Tax rate variation by country and state
Import/export factors	European Economic Community (EEC) policies
Unemployment trends	Organization of Petroleum Exporting Countries (OPEC) policies
Value of the dollar in world markets	

Sociocultural Forces

Sociocultural forces impact strategic decisions on virtually all products, services, markets, and customers. Small, large, for-profit, and nonprofit organizations in all industries are being staggered and challenged by the opportunities and threats arising from changes in sociocultural variables. These forces are shaping the way people live, work, produce, and consume. New trends are creating a shift in consumer demands and, consequently, a need for different products, new services, and updated strategies.

An example sociocultural factor relates to demand for packaged foods. In the US food industry, demand for processed packaged foods is declining because consumers are showing increased preferences for freshly prepared food options. Packaged food companies such as Kellogg are trying to quickly adapt to mitigate this external threat; Kellogg recently hired a new CEO, Steven Cahillane, who comes with extensive experience leading the health and wellness company, Nature's Bounty.

Consumer tastes and trends constantly change; people wander through stores less, opting increasingly to use their mobile phones and computers to research prices and cherry-pick promotions. Brick-and-mortar retail department stores consequently are struggling as consumers increasingly turn to online retailers and smaller specialty stores. These external trends have prompted many retail chains to slow or cease store openings.[5]

The United States (and the world) is also becoming older. Individuals ages 65 and older in the United States, as a percentage of the population, will rise to 19 percent by 2030. The trend toward an older society is good news for restaurants, hotels, airlines, cruise lines, tours, travel services, pharmaceutical firms, and funeral homes. Older people are especially interested in health care, financial services, travel, crime prevention, and leisure. The aging population affects the strategic orientation of nearly all organizations.

Example categories of sociocultural variables that often yield AQCD opportunities and threats for organizations are given in Table 3-3.

TABLE 3-3 Key Sociocultural Variables

Population changes by race, age, and geographic area	Life expectancy rates
Regional changes in tastes and preferences	Per-capita income
Number of marriages	Social media pervasiveness
Number of divorces	Attitudes toward retirement
Number of births	Attitudes toward product quality
Number of deaths	Attitudes toward customer service
Immigration and emigration rates	Social programs
Social Security programs	Social responsibility issues

Technological Forces

A variety of new technologies such as the Internet of Things (IoT), three-dimensional (3D) printing, predictive analytics, quantum computing, robotics, and artificial intelligence (AI) are fueling innovation in many industries and impacting strategic planning decisions. Businesses are using mobile technologies and applications to better determine customer trends and are employing advanced analytics to make enhanced strategy decisions. The vast increase in the amount of data coming from mobile devices and social media sites is astonishing. A primary reason that Cisco Systems recently entered the data analytics business is that sales of hardware, software, and services connected to the IoT is expected to increase dramatically.

Advances in technology impact the manufacturing labor market. Ben Pring, Director of Cogniant's Center for the Future of Work estimates that nearly 19 million jobs in the United States will become obsolete or be replaced by automation in the next 15 years.[6] In a dramatic shift from employing people with low wages in countries outside of the United States, Adidas is shifting to produce footwear in developed countries using fully robotic plants called "speed-factories." Adidas' speed factories are now located across the world, including in Germany, the United States, France, China, and Japan. This shift from low-wage employees to complete automation is a technological revolution occurring in the footwear industry. Before new speed factories, Adidas owned no factories, instead using more than 1,000 suppliers that employ millions of people to assemble shoes at low-wage facilities globally. Adidas' new strategy aims to eventually surpass its major rival Nike.

No company or industry today is insulated against emerging technological developments. In high-tech industries, identification and evaluation of key technological opportunities and threats can be the most important part of the external strategic management audit. In performing an external assessment, technology-related factors must be stated in AQCD terms to the extent possible to be useful in strategic planning. Technological advancements impact firms in countless ways, such as the following:

1. They can dramatically affect organizations' products, services, markets, suppliers, distributors, competitors, customers, manufacturing processes, marketing practices, and competitive position.
2. They can create new markets, result in a proliferation of new and improved products, change the relative competitive cost positions in an industry, and render existing products and services obsolete.

3. They can reduce or eliminate cost barriers between businesses, create shorter production runs, create shortages in technical skills, and result in changing values and expectations of employees, managers, and customers.

4. They can create new competitive advantages that are more powerful than existing advantages.

The **metaverse** is creating new products and services across all industries. What is the metaverse? It is an online 3D, virtual or augmented reality (AR) world where individuals, companies, and organizations can interact and share quality time with others and spend money as avatars on products and services. The defining aspect of the metaverse is that you are not just looking in from the outside, but you are privately inside (seemingly) the other entity's dominion. In some cases, virtual and AR headsets are used. **Avatars** are digital objects that can become "you" or "anyone" or "anything" and interact with you as if you and the entity are actually together. Consumers can now access the metaverse on a range of devices from smartphones to PCs. As avatars, people can work, learn, play, shop, purchase, talk, trade services and properties, and experience entertainment just as if they are right beside the other entity. The metaverse enables people to seemingly teleport themselves to practically anywhere in the world in a moment.

IBM and Honeywell are leading the way on rapid advances in quantum computing. IBM just introduced Eagle, a powerful quantum computing processor that within this decade is expected to transform drug manufacturing, lead to creation of new materials, products, and services, boost cybersecurity, improve defense capabilities, and much more. The largest quantum computing company today is the new Quantinuum, formed by the merger of Honeywell's Quantum Solutions and the UK quantum software company Cambridge Quantum. Quantinuum just released the world's first commercial quantum-computing product, an encryption key generator called Quantum Origin, now being purchased by financial services companies, cybersecurity firms, telecommunications, and defense firms.

A **chief information officer (CIO)** and **chief technology officer (CTO)** are common positions in firms today, reflecting the growing importance of **information technology (IT)** in strategic management. A CIO and CTO work together to ensure that information needed to formulate, implement, and evaluate strategies is available on demand. The CIO is primarily a manager, managing the firm's relationship with stakeholders; the CTO is primarily a technician, focusing on technical issues such as data acquisition, data processing, decision support systems, and software and hardware acquisition.

Environmental Forces

The second E in the PESTEL category of external variables that represent key opportunities and threats for companies stands for environmental forces and includes climate change, carbon dioxide (CO_2) emissions, pollution abatement, water quality, air quality, ecological factors, and even the weather. Thousands of companies on their websites now provide their goals, objectives, plans, metrics, and progress being made across numerous environmental variables. For example, in March 2021, Chipotle introduced a new environmental, social, and governance (ESG) metric that ties executive compensation to ESG goals. There are three categories of the ESG: (1) Food and Animals, (2) People, and (3) the Environment. Under the ESG system, 10 percent of Chipotle's executive leadership team's annual incentive bonus is tied to the company's progress toward achieving specific goals in the three areas. ESG mandates that Chipotle's top executives be evaluated on the company's progress toward meeting overarching company goals in the three sustainability areas.

A environmental and ecological trend impacting thousands of companies is the rapid electrification of automobiles, homes, manufacturing plants, office buildings, appliances, and much more. Solar and hydrogen panels and cells, and associated high-tech batteries, are going to replace gasoline and diesel sooner rather than later and eventually will replace even traditional electricity. The world is not there yet, but it is moving rapidly to a scenario where all automobiles, homes, and offices will have solar or hydrogen panels and high-tech batteries alongside to store energy. Be mindful that alternating current (AC) electricity cannot be stored, and many traditional methods of producing electricity are not environmentally friendly. Solar and hydrogen power are becoming cost effective to use and are more readily accepted as being environmentally friendly. With the increase in energy-efficient lighting, appliances, and even automobiles, buses, and trains, local direct current (DC) battery power is now an option for many. Powering homes

ETHICS CAPSULE 3

CO_2 Emissions Vary Substantially Across Countries[7]

Eye35.pix/Alamy Photo

Carbon tariffs, also called *border adjustments*, may soon become common. This is where a country imposes a tax on imports of certain products, such as aluminum, steel, cement, and fertilizer, that entail bad CO_2 emission processes. Steel made from high-polluting blast furnaces in the Ukraine and China, for example, soon face substantial border adjustments. European officials are implementing carbon tariffs to reduce continental emissions by 55 percent by 2030, led by the UK that plans to require all automobiles sold in the country to be all-electric vehicle sales by 2030.

The Climate Leadership Council reports that products made in the United States on average produce 40 percent less CO_2 than the global average. Note in the following chart that the United States and the EU

are comparatively low polluters, whereas Russia, India, and China are comparatively higher polluters. Carbon tariffs are an essential external variable in many firms' strategic plans in terms of where to locate or withdraw operations and where to obtain needed products.

CO_2 Emissions by Country per Million Dollars of GDP (listed best to worst):

EU	264
United States	286
Brazil	298
Canada	382
Mexico	411
China	983
India	1,068
Russia	1,213

[7]Based on Yuka Hayashi and Jacob Schlesinger, "Carbon Tariffs Gain Momentum," *Wall Street Journal*, November 3, 2021, pp. A1, A12.

and businesses and eventually manufacturing plants and cities with DC energy is also a national security issue because using these sources can aid in mitigating a country's risk of a foreign nation infiltrating the country's electrical grid and turning off the power. All homes, businesses, and countries need independence from, or at a minimum backup from, reliance on the grid.

Pollution is a growing concern among companies and countries. Ethics Capsule 3 reveals how CO_2 emissions vary across countries. Note that Russia, India, and China are the worst polluters; this could be an essential external factor in any company's strategic plan regarding where to locate or withdraw operations. In performing strategic planning and case analysis, relevant environmental and ecological factors must be stated in AQCD terms to the extent possible to be useful in strategic planning.

Legal Forces

The *L* in the PESTEL category of external variables that impact companies' strategic planning includes all the regulations and laws imposed on various businesses globally. These forces vary considerably across countries and are a primary reason why companies sometimes avoid operations outside the United States. Even within the United States, mandatory minimum wage increases, labor laws, consumer laws, antitrust laws, and even changing tax and accounting regulations and laws can represent major factors to consider in strategic planning. Keeping up with the various minimum wage rate changes can be a daunting task. For example, some states are on a schedule for an annual increase in the minimum wage to eventually reach $15 an hour, but more than 20 states follow the federal minimum, which is $7.25 and has not changed since 2009. By 2022 for large businesses and 2023 for small businesses, California is the first state to require a $15.00 minimum wage rate.

Competitive Analysis and Porter's Five-Forces Model

3.3. **Explain Porter's Five-Forces Model and competitive forces that impact organizations.**

Competitive Analysis

Arguably the most important part of an external audit is identifying rival firms and determining their strengths, weaknesses, capabilities, objectives, and strategies. George Salk stated, "If you're not faster than your competitor, you're in a tenuous position, and if you're only half as fast, you're terminal."

Competition in virtually all industries is intense—and sometimes cut-throat. Addressing questions about competitors, such as those presented in Table 3-4, is essential in performing an external audit. **Competitive intelligence (CI)**, as formally defined by the Society of Competitive Intelligence Professionals (SCIP), is a systematic and ethical process for gathering and analyzing information about the competition's activities and general business trends to further a business' own goals (SCIP website). Quality competitive intelligence in business, as in the military, is one of the keys to success. Major competitors' weaknesses can represent external opportunities; major competitors' strengths may represent key threats.

TABLE 3-4 Key Questions About Competitors

1. What are the strengths and weaknesses of our major competitors?
2. What products and services do we offer that are unique in the industry?
3. What are the objectives and strategies of our major competitors?
4. How will our major competitors most likely respond to current political, economic, sociocultural, technological, environmental, and legal trends affecting our industry?
5. How vulnerable are our major competitors to our new strategies, products, and services?
6. How vulnerable is our firm to successful counterattack by our major competitors?
7. How does our firm compare to rivals in mastering the social media conversation in this industry?
8. To what extent are new firms entering and old firms leaving this industry?
9. What key factors have resulted in our present competitive position in this industry?
10. How are supplier and distributor relationships changing in this industry?

Various legal and ethical ways to obtain competitive intelligence include the following:

- Reverse-engineer rival firms' products.
- Use surveys and interviews of customers, suppliers, and distributors of rival firms.
- Analyze the rival firm's *Form 10-K*.
- Conduct fly-over and drive-by visits to rival firm operations.
- Search online databases and websites such as www.owler.com.
- Contact government agencies for public information about rival firms.
- Monitor relevant trade publications, magazines, and newspapers.
- Purchase social media data about customers of all firms in the industry.
- Hire top executives from rival firms.

Information gathered from employees, managers, suppliers, distributors, customers, creditors, and consultants can make the difference between having superior or just average intelligence and overall competitiveness. All members of an organization—from the CEO to custodians—are valuable intelligence agents for a firm. Special characteristics of a successful CI program include flexibility, usefulness, timeliness, and cross-functional cooperation. CI is not corporate espionage. Unethical tactics such as bribery, wiretapping, and computer hacking should never be used to obtain information. Due to cybersecurity threats, CI must assure that persons in a firm cannot access data and information unrelated to their job description because hackers exploit this avenue in firms. In performing an external assessment, competitor-related factors must be stated in AQCD terms to the extent possible to be useful in strategic planning.

Five-Forces Model

Harvard Business School Professor, Michael Porter, suggests that firms should strive to compete in attractive industries, avoid weak or faltering industries, and gain a full understanding of key external factors within the attractive industry. Given that competitive positioning within an industry is a key determinant of competitive advantage, Porter established the Five-Forces Model.

One of the major contributions of Porter's work is a shift in focus away from viewing competition directed toward a few rival firms and to a broader analysis that includes forces from current competitors, new competitors, substitute products, suppliers, and buyers. Competitive advantage can be created in each area of the five forces by offering value to the consumer that exceeds cost. Rather than focusing solely on a top competitor, it is important that firms examine

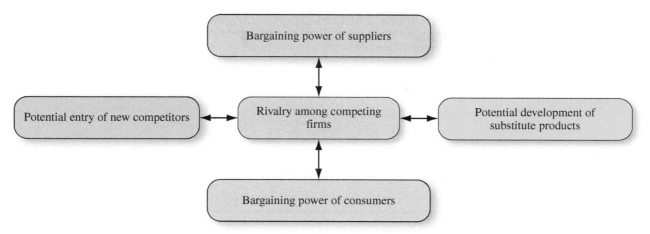

FIGURE 3-3

The Five-Forces Model of Competition

how suppliers and others listed in the five forces are trying to siphon off as much value as possible in all business transactions.

Porter's model is also used to determine which industries to enter because generally the stronger the five forces are, the less profitable the industry. Porter is an advocate of external variables rather than internal ones being a larger driver of competitive advantage, similar to a rising or falling tide; it is difficult to overcome a rising tide no matter your internal capabilities. Porter's model also prompts managers to focus on the medium- and longer-term factors that determine competitiveness, rather than short-term factors such as stock market movements, who won the election, or even something as trivial as inclement weather, which is often an excuse proposed by pundits on TV to explain slow Christmas sales. It is not that short-term factors are not important or have no impact, but they simply do not affect competition to the degree that long-term factors do, as revealed in the Five-Forces Model.

As illustrated in Figure 3-3, **Porter's Five-Forces Model** offers guidance to strategists in formulating strategies to keep rival firms at bay. According to Porter, the nature of competitiveness in a given industry can be viewed as a composite of five forces:

1. Rivalry among competing firms
2. Bargaining power of suppliers
3. Bargaining power of consumers
4. Potential entry of new competitors
5. Potential development of substitute products

RIVALRY AMONG COMPETING FIRMS   Rivalry among competing firms is usually the most powerful of the five competitive forces and the most traditional factor analyzed by managers. It is also the only factor highly affected by changes in the other four factors. Strategies pursued by one firm can be successful only to the extent that they provide competitive advantage over the strategies pursued by rival firms. Intense rivalry among competitors in an industry can decrease overall industry profits because firms often lower prices or spend extra on advertising to maintain market share, often transferring profits directly to consumers and other players in the Five-Forces Model. Rivalry among competing firms increases for numerous reasons as shown in Table 3-5, including an increase in the number of competitors and a shift towards competitors becoming more equal in size and capability.

As rivalry among competing firms intensifies, industry profits decline, in some cases to the point where an industry becomes inherently unattractive. Changes in strategy by one firm may be met with retaliatory countermoves, such as lowering prices, enhancing quality, adding features, providing services, extending warranties, and increasing advertising—especially when a firm senses weakness from another. Although avoiding high-rivalry industries would be ideal, that is often easier said than done. At times it may be best to look for an industry with more favorable five forces and reduced rivalry, but firms can also compete within a similar or subindustry

TABLE 3-5 Conditions that Cause High Rivalry Among Competing Firms

1. When the number of competing firms is high
2. When competing firms are of similar size
3. When competing firms have similar capabilities
4. When demand for the industry's products is changing rapidly
5. When price cuts are common in the industry
6. When consumers can switch brands easily
7. When barriers to leaving the market are high
8. When barriers to entering the market are low
9. When fixed costs are high among competing firms
10. When products are perishable or have short product life cycles

by offering products targeting different customer groups with differentiated products. Offering differentiation helps all firms in the industry by moving away from competing on cost, where unique customers can be better served while maintaining profits for firms.

BARGAINING POWER OF SUPPLIERS The bargaining power of suppliers refers to the ability of suppliers to raise the price of any inputs into the industry. This force affects the intensity of competitiveness in an industry, especially when there are few substitutes available for the product offered by suppliers, when the cost of switching to an alternative product offered by a different supplier is high, when the industry is not a key source of the supplier's revenues, or when there are few suppliers.

In some cases, firms pursue a backward-integration strategy to compete with suppliers. This strategy is especially effective when suppliers are unreliable, too costly, not capable of meeting a firm's needs on a consistent basis, or simply have too much bargaining power and are able to charge absorbent prices. Boeing and Airbus, the two largest jetliner manufacturers, are beginning to make a portion of the parts that go into planes because both firms determined too high of a proportion of industry profitability was going to suppliers. A key lesson for suppliers is that if your customer has the means to backward-integrate, it may be best to renegotiate prices.

Overall, firms are in a better position when numerous suppliers exist. It is often in the best interest of both suppliers and producers to assist each other with reasonable prices, improved quality, development of new services, just-in-time deliveries, and reduced inventory costs, thus enhancing long-term profitability for all concerned. In more and more industries, sellers are forging strategic partnerships with select suppliers in an effort to (1) reduce inventory and logistics costs, (2) accelerate the availability of next-generation components, (3) reduce defect rates, and (4) squeeze out important cost savings for both themselves and their suppliers.[8]

BARGAINING POWER OF CONSUMERS Bargaining power of buyers refers to the ability of buyers to drive down prices for products offered by companies in a given industry. This force is strong when firms operate in industries that contain a limited number of buyers or that are made up of buyers that have multiple choices of where to buy from; this force is also strong when buyers purchase in volume or have low switching costs. Consumers (buyers) gain bargaining power under the following circumstances:

1. If they can inexpensively switch to competing brands or substitutes
2. If they are particularly important to the seller
3. If sellers are struggling in the face of falling consumer demand
4. If they are informed about sellers' products, prices, and costs
5. If they have discretion in whether and when they purchase the product[9]

The impact of this force on industry competitiveness is higher when the products being purchased are standard or undifferentiated, enabling consumers to negotiate selling price, warranty coverage, and accessory packages to a greater extent. Rival firms may offer extended warranties or special services to gain customer loyalty whenever the bargaining power of consumers is substantial. New car buyers, for example, often compare prices of their desired car across several dealerships, often negotiating lower prices and additional services from dealerships in exchange for their business.

POTENTIAL ENTRY OF NEW COMPETITORS   Whenever new firms can easily enter a particular industry, existing firms are likely to face threats of reduced market share. In such industries, a firm's strategies should deter new firms from entering the market to avoid further saturation of the market. Example barriers to entry can include economies of scale, specialized know-how, strong brand reputation, established customer loyalty, high capital requirements, absolute cost advantages, highly efficient supply chains, specialized distribution channels, access to key raw materials, and possession of patents. The automotive oil-change industry, for example, has relatively low barriers to entry; whereas the smartphone industry has much higher barriers to entry.

Despite numerous barriers to entry, new firms sometimes enter industries with higher-quality products, lower prices, and substantial marketing resources. When the threat of new firms entering the market is strong, incumbent firms generally fortify their positions and take swift actions to deter new entrants, such as lowering prices, extending warranties, adding features, or offering financing specials. Even the threat of new entrants can increase rivalry and thus reduce profitability.

Eliminating competition is a possibility and common strategy employed by firms in an industry with high rivalry. Firms use mergers and acquisitions and purchase suppliers or buyers (distributors) all as a means to eliminate rivalry, but there are problems associated with this level of thinking. Acquiring the competition often is associated with paying a premium and dealing with different organizational cultures; although there may be no competitors currently, new competitors may enter with different products and ultimately better serve many current customers. Purchasing suppliers or distributors takes a firm away from the business they do best, possibly allowing competitors to further develop and improve their products without being bogged down with supply chain issues they know little about.

POTENTIAL DEVELOPMENT OF SUBSTITUTE PRODUCTS   In many industries, firms are in close competition with producers of substitute products in other industries. Examples are beer, wine, and liquor; public transportation and car, bike, and taxi/Uber; natural gas, electricity, and solar power; glass bottles, paperboard containers, and aluminum cans. A high threat of substitutes exists when consumer needs can easily be filled by one or more substitute products outside of the firm's industry. Competitive pressures arising from substitute products increase as the relative price of substitute products decline and as consumers' costs of switching decrease.

The presence of substitute products puts a ceiling on the price that can be charged before consumers will switch to the substitute product. Price ceilings equate to profit ceilings and more intense competition among rivals. Producers of eyeglasses and contact lenses, for example, face increasing competitive pressures from laser eye surgery. Producers of sugar face similar pressures from artificial sweeteners. Newspapers and magazines face substitute-product competitive pressures from the internet and 24-hour cable television. Substitute products can also come from places not normally expected. For example, a diamond producer may not consider a honeymoon package as a substitute for a less expensive ring. The bottom line with this force is that strategists must manage the potential threat of substitute products.

As a result of Porter's Five Forces, the intensity of competition among firms varies widely across industries. Table 3-6 reveals the average net profit margin for firms in different industries. Note substantial variation among industries, with the lowest being for construction and retail. The collective impact of competitive forces is so brutal in some industries that the market is clearly unattractive from a profit-making standpoint. Strategists must continually monitor the five forces to identify new opportunities and threats facing the firm and alter strategies accordingly.

In conclusion, when studying competition from an industry perspective, do not focus totally on the closest rival firm because the Five-Forces Model teaches that suppliers, distributors, and consumers are attempting to siphon off industry profits just as a firm's direct competitor is attempting. Several pitfalls firms should avoid when using the Five-Forces analysis, include (1) placing equal weight on all five forces instead of identifying the most pressing forces for their industry, (2) defining the industry too broad or too narrow, and (3) using the five forces to pin labels such as attractive or unattractive on an industry rather than using the model to more efficiently formulate strategies. When using Porter's Five-Forces Model as an external assessment tool in doing strategic planning, strive to identify AQCD opportunities and threats most important for success in a given industry and most relevant to the firm's vision and mission.

TABLE 3-6 Competitiveness Across a Few Industries (2021 data)

Industry	Net Profit Margin (%)
Auto Repair and Maintenance	12
Construction	05
Hotels and Hospitality	08
Maintenance Services	10
Restaurants/Food	15
Retail	05
Tax Services	20
Transportation	19

Source: Based on https://www.caminofinancial.com/profit-margin-by-industry/

Key Sources of Information for an External Audit

3.4. **Describe key sources of information for identifying opportunities and threats.**

A wealth of strategic information is available to organizations from both published and unpublished sources. Unpublished sources include customer surveys, market research, speeches at professional and shareholders' meetings, television programs, interviews, and conversations with stakeholders. Published sources of strategic information include periodicals, journals, reports, government documents, abstracts, books, directories, newspapers, and manuals. A company website is usually an excellent place to start to find information about a firm, particularly on the Investor Relations web pages.

There are many excellent websites for gathering strategic information, but seven outstanding ones that the authors use routinely in performing an external audit are:

1. http://finance.yahoo.com
2. www.hoovers.com
3. www.morningstar.com
4. www.mergentonline.com
5. http://globaledge.msu.edu/industries/
6. Corporate website of companies
7. www.comparably.com

The fifth website listed is operated by Michigan State University and provides industry profiles that are an excellent source for information, news, events, and statistical data for any industry. Most college libraries subscribe to excellent online business databases that can then be used for free by students to gather information to perform a strategic management case analysis. Simply ask your reference librarian. Some outstanding library database sources of external audit information are described in Table 3-7; the authors use all of these sources, especially S&P Net Advantage's *Industry Surveys* and IBISWorld, to obtain AQCD external factors for inclusion in an external assessment. Note also in Table 3-7, the PrivCo source is helpful for obtaining information about privately held firms; use www.owler.com for information about rival firms.

The website www.comparably.com listed as *#7* gives great studies, articles, and comparative information for any publicly held company as "compared" to the firm's major rivals. This website is outstanding for gathering external strategy assessment information because it compares any firm to rival firms on diversity, culture, leadership, marketing, pricing, and numerous other variables.

Forecasting and Making Assumptions

3.5. **Discuss forecasting tools and techniques.**

Forecasts are educated assumptions about future trends and events. Forecasting is a complex activity because of factors such as technological innovation, cultural changes, new products, improved services, stronger competitors, shifts in government priorities, changing social values,

TABLE 3-7 Excellent Online Sources to Obtain EFE Matrix Factor Information

- **IBISWorld**—Provides online USA Industry Reports (NAICS), US Industry iExpert Summaries, and US Business Environment Profiles. A global version of IBIS is also available.
- **Lexis-Nexis Academic**—Provides online access to newspaper articles (including *New York Times* and *Washington Post*) and business information (including SEC filings).
- **Lexis-Nexis Company Dossier**—Provides online access to extensive, current data on 13 million companies. It collects and compiles information into excellent documents.
- **Mergent Online**—Provides online access to *Mergent's Manuals*, which include trend, descriptive, and statistical information on hundreds of public companies and industries. Unconsolidated company income statements and balance sheets are provided.
- **PrivCo**—Provides information on privately held companies, including private financials and revenues; private merger and acquisition deals and deal multiples, private firm valuations, venture capitalist funding, private equity deal history. (Go to www.owler.com for information about competitors.)
- **Regional Business News**—Provides comprehensive full-text coverage for regional business publications; incorporates coverage of more than 80 regional business publications covering all metropolitan and rural areas within the United States.
- **Standard & Poor's NetAdvantage**—Provides online access to Standard & Poor's (S&P) *Industry Surveys*, stock reports, corporation records, *The Outlook*, mutual fund reports, and more. Locate the "Company" tab at the top of the page or the "Simple Search" option located on the right side of the page. Use the "Company Profile" option.
- **Value Line Investment Survey**—Provides excellent online information and advice on approximately 1,700 stocks, more than 90 industries, the stock market, and the economy. Company income statements and balance sheets are provided.
- **US Securities and Exchange Commission (SEC)**—Provides the *Form 10K* for publicly held companies in the United States. Use the search box at the top of the page or look under the "Filings" tab along the top of the page.
- **Company *Annual Reports* On-Line (CAROL)**—Provides direct links to publicly held companies' financial statements in both Europe and the United States.

Source: Based on information at www.fmarion.edu/library

unstable economic conditions, and unforeseen events. Managers often must rely on published forecasts to effectively identify key external opportunities and threats.

A sense of the future permeates all action and underlies every decision a person makes. People eat expecting to be satisfied and nourished in the future. People sleep assuming that in the future they will feel rested. They invest energy, money, and time because they believe their efforts will be rewarded in the future. They build highways assuming that automobiles and trucks will need them in the future. Parents educate children on the basis of forecasts that they will need certain skills, attitudes, and knowledge when they grow up. The truth is we all make implicit forecasts throughout our daily lives. The question, therefore, is not whether we should forecast but rather how we can best forecast to enable us to move beyond our ordinarily unarticulated assumptions about the future. Can we obtain information and use it to make educated assumptions (forecasts) that better guide our current decisions and foster a more desirable future state of affairs? Assumptions must be made based on facts, figures, trends, and research. Strive for the firm's assumptions to be more accurate than rival firms' assumptions.

No forecast is perfect; some are even wildly inaccurate. This fact accents the need for strategists to devote sufficient time and effort to study the underlying bases for published forecasts and to develop internal forecasts of their own. Key external opportunities and threats can be effectively identified only through good forecasts.

Making Assumptions

Planning would be impossible without assumptions. McConkey defines assumptions as the "best present estimates of the impact of major external factors, over which managers have little if any control, but which may exert a significant impact on performance or the ability to achieve desired results."[10] Strategists are faced with countless variables and imponderables that can be neither controlled nor predicted with 100 percent accuracy. *Wild guesses should never be made in formulating strategies, but reasonable assumptions based on available information must always be made.*

By identifying future occurrences that could have a major effect on the firm and by making reasonable assumptions about those factors, strategists can carry the strategic management process forward. Assumptions are needed only for future trends and events that are most likely to have a significant effect on the company's business. Based on the best information at the time, assumptions serve as checkpoints on the validity of strategies. If future occurrences deviate significantly from assumptions, strategists know that corrective actions may be needed. Firms that compile the best information generally make the most accurate assumptions, which can lead to major competitive advantages.

The External Factor Evaluation Matrix

3.6. Explain how to develop and use an External Factor Evaluation (EFE) Matrix.

An **External Factor Evaluation (EFE) Matrix** allows strategists to summarize and evaluate PESTEL external forces and competitive information. The EFE Matrix provides an empirical assessment of how well a firm is handling external factors overall, including the firm's effectiveness at capitalizing on opportunities and minimizing threats.

Steps to Develop an EFE Matrix

An EFE Matrix can be developed in five steps.

STEP 1: DEVELOP A FULL AND NARROW LIST OF KEY EXTERNAL FACTORS   Conduct research about the focal company using the resources listed in Table 3-7. Compile and organize information into two data sets, opportunities and threats, developing a full list of perhaps 50 opportunities and 50 threats that are AQCD to the extent possible. Brainstorming sessions are commonly used to accomplish this task because substantial, genuine input is needed in this initial gathering of information. Include factors most important to your firm's industry, vision, mission, and strategies, considering PESTEL and the Five Forces. Then, narrow your data sets down to 20 key external factors that include specifically 10 opportunities and 10 threats. (Note: We use 10 and 10 because organizations commonly use this breakdown and the template at www.strategyclub.com uses 10 and 10). List opportunities first and then threats. Also, do not include strategies as opportunities, so for example, "to build two new manufacturing plants in Europe" is a strategy and not an opportunity; there may be an underlying opportunity that could make that strategy reasonable, such as "eight European countries have repealed restrictions on the sale of generic drugs."

Firms reduce the full list of 50 factors down to 20 factors usually by asking respondents to rank each factor according to importance (1 = most important to 50 = least important), then summing the rankings from respondents, and finally using the 20 factors with the lowest cumulative scores.

Take care that your selected 20 factors are somewhat distinct from each other. When determining particular factors to include in an EFE Matrix, and when assigning weights and ratings (Step 2 and 3), focus on a narrow industry perspective. For example, for Spirit Airlines, the industry is discount airlines, rather than all airlines, and for Lamborghini, the industry is high-end sports cars and not simply automobiles. Focusing external analyses on the parent industry and supporting industries is important to facilitate external factors being stated in terms that meet the AQCD test. The industry perspective described above centers more on the Five Forces Model than the PESTEL analysis. However, if PESTEL factors play a major role, then be sure to include them as some of your 10 opportunities or 10 threats as well, but try to avoid including broad PESTEL factors at the expense of a detailed industry analysis. Quality external audits take time.

Be ever mindful of the AQCD test because excessive vagueness gives analysts no guidance in assigning weights or ratings in developing an EFE Matrix. Recall that W. Edwards Deming said, "In God we trust. Everyone else bring data." An important point here is that companies (and students) never should include just the first 20 factors that come to mind. For example, someone recently included as a threat in an EFE Matrix that "a hurricane can come." Ninety-nine percent of the time that factor should not be included in the matrix; instead, conduct research to identify external factors that relate to the firm's vision, mission, strategies, and competitive advantages.

STEP 2: ASSIGN WEIGHTS TO KEY EXTERNAL FACTORS   In developing an EFE Matrix, assign a weight that ranges from 1.00 (all-important) to 0.01 (not important) for each factor. The weight assigned to a given factor indicates the relative importance of the factor for being successful in the firm's industry relative to other factors included in the EFE Matrix. For example, a factor receiving a weight of 0.06 is mathematically 200 percent more important than a factor receiving a weight of 0.02 for success in the industry. Regardless of whether a key factor for a particular firm is an opportunity or threat, factors considered to have the greatest effect on organizational performance of all firms in a specific industry should be assigned the highest weights. The sum of all weights must equal 1.0. Do not try to even weights out to total 0.50 for opportunities and 0.50 for threats. In fact, if rivalry is high in a given industry, as discussed in the Porter's Five Forces section, then the sum of weights assigned to threats could be higher than the sum for opportunities.

Weights are industry-based and not company-based. In an EFE Matrix, list opportunities from highest weight to lowest weight; do the same for threats. Also, do not be alarmed to significantly weigh the top 2 or 3 opportunities and top 2 or 3 threats more than the remaining opportunities and threats. In fact, it would not be incorrect to weigh the top 5 external factors with 50 percent of the total weight and the remaining 15 factors with the remaining 50 percent of the weight. Firms cannot address every opportunity or threat equally (or even close to equally) and unfortunately must make difficult choices on where to commit time, money, and resources.

Don't overweigh factors. For example, if you determine after a detailed analysis of the industry that e-commerce should account for 10 percent of the total weight of an EFE Matrix, and you include three detailed e-commerce factors meeting an AQCD design, ensure the three sum to around 10 percent. A mistake students and strategists commonly make is they will weigh each of the AQCD e-commerce factors 10 percent, bringing the total e-commerce element to 30 percent total weight.

STEP 3: ASSIGN RATINGS TO KEY EXTERNAL FACTORS   In developing an EFE Matrix, assign a rating between 4 to 1 to each key external factor to indicate how effectively (or ineffectively) the firm's current strategies are responding to the most current opportunity or threat, where 4 = the response is superior, 3 = the response is above average, 2 = the response is average, and 1 = the response is poor. Both opportunities and threats can receive a rating of 4, 3, 2, or 1 at any time. Ratings are based on the effectiveness of a firm's strategies in capitalizing on opportunities or avoiding and mitigating threats. Ratings are company-based and not industry-based.

Assignment of numerical values down the rating column in an EFE Matrix should be with consideration that companies carve out niches in industries that enable them to gain and sustain competitive advantages through effective strategies. These niches are most often based on capitalizing on some opportunities more effectively than rivals. This is not to say that threats are not important, they are; some threats can wipe a firm out. However, if a firm faces many opportunities, this is likely the result of effective strategies positioning the firm well, so higher ratings are often warranted for opportunities; higher ratings increase the total weighted score in an EFE Matrix.

STEP 4: OBTAIN WEIGHTED SCORES   Along each row in an EFE Matrix, multiply the factor's weight by its rating to determine a weighted score for each factor.

STEP 5: OBTAIN TOTAL WEIGHTED SCORE   Sum the weighted scores to determine the total weighted score for the organization. Regardless of how many factors are included in an EFE Matrix, the total weighted score can range from a high of 4.0 to a low of 1.0, with the average score being 2.5. Total weighted scores well below 2.5 characterize the current strategies an organization is pursuing are weak at responding to most recent external factors identified in the EFE Matrix, implying that new strategies are likely needed and perhaps so is a new direction, new vision, or new mission. Total weighted scores well above 2.5 indicate a strong external position, whereby a continuation of current strategies may be prudent, being ever mindful that there is always room for improvement. A total weighted score of 3.5 for example indicates that an organization is responding in an outstanding way to existing opportunities and threats in its industry. In other words, the firm's strategies effectively take advantage of existing opportunities and minimize the potential adverse effects of external threats. A total weighted score of 1.5 indicates that the firm's strategies are not capitalizing on opportunities or avoiding external threats.

Pay particular attention to factors with a high weight and low rating in addition to the total weighted score. It is possible for a weighted score to be above average but a factor receiving a high relative weight to be rated a 2 or 1, indicating a new strategy revolving around this single factor may be needed. Making "small" decisions regarding weights and ratings in matrices is essential for making effective big strategy decisions later in the strategic planning process; for example, a billion dollars may be at stake in choosing a particular strategy over another to implement, and the EFE Matrix with its factors, weights, and ratings is helpful in making that type of choice.

An Example EFE Matrix

An example EFE Matrix is provided in Table 3-8 for a local 10-theater cinema complex. Observe in the table that the most important factor to being successful in this industry is the "Trend toward healthy eating eroding concession sales," as indicated by the 0.12 weight. Also note that the local cinema is doing excellent (received a rating of 4) in regard to its handling of two external factors, "TDB University is expanding 6 percent annually" and "Trend toward healthy eating eroding concession sales." Perhaps the cinema is placing flyers on campus and also adding yogurt and healthy drinks to its concession menu.

Overall, the total weighted score of 2.58 is above the average (midpoint) of 2.5, so this cinema business is doing slightly above average taking advantage of the external opportunities and minimizing external threats facing the firm. There is definitely room for improvement, though, because the highest total weighted score would be 4.0. As indicated by ratings of 1, the business needs to capitalize more on the "Two new neighborhoods developing within 3 miles" opportunity and work to avoid the "movies rented from . . . Time Warner" threat. But take care to note, although both these factors receive a 1 rating, the weight for the opportunity in question is 0.09, which is 50 percent more important for industry success than the 0.06 weight for the threat in question.

Recall that mathematically, 0.04 is 33 percent more important than 0.03, and a rating of 3 is 50 percent higher than a rating of 2. Small judgments regarding assignment of weights and ratings in matrices are vital for making effective larger decisions related to deployment of resources and money across regions and products.

TABLE 3-8 EFE Matrix for a Local 10-Theater Cinema Complex

Key External Factors	Weight	Rating	Weighted Score
Opportunities			
1. Two new neighborhoods developing within 3 miles	0.09	1	0.09
2. TDB University is expanding 6 percent annually	0.08	4	0.32
3. Major competitor across town recently closed	0.08	3	0.24
4. Demand for going to cinemas growing 10 percent	0.07	2	0.14
5. Disposable income among citizens up 5 percent in prior year	0.06	3	0.18
6. Rowan County is growing 8 percent annually in population	0.05	3	0.15
7. Unemployment rate in county declined to 3.1 percent	0.03	2	0.06
Threats			
1. Trend toward healthy eating eroding concession sales	0.12	4	0.48
2. County and city property taxes increasing 25 percent	0.08	2	0.16
3. Movies rented at local Redboxes up 12 percent	0.08	2	0.16
4. Demand for online movies growing 10 percent	0.06	2	0.12
5. Commercial property adjacent to cinemas for sale	0.06	3	0.18
6. Movies rented last quarter from Time Warner up 15 percent	0.06	1	0.06
7. Local religious groups object to R-rated movies	0.04	3	0.12
8. TDB University installing an on-campus movie theater	0.04	3	0.12
Total	**1.00**		**2.58**

Note: The point of this example is to illustrate the mechanics of developing an EFE Matrix rather than having actual industry-specific factors.

The Competitive Profile Matrix

3.7. Explain how to develop and use a Competitive Profile Matrix (CPM).

The **Competitive Profile Matrix (CPM)** reveals how a focal firm compares to major competitors across a range of key factors. This comparative analysis provides important strategic information regarding a firm's competitive advantages or disadvantages in a given industry. In determining what factors to include in a CPM, tailor the factors to the particular industry. For example, in the airline industry, such factors as on-time arrival, leg room in planes, and routes served are far better factors to include than merely including "quality of service" or "financial condition" as factors.

An excellent website for comparing rival firms across nine management and marketing variables is www.comparably.com. For example, in Table 3-9, FedEx Corporation is compared with its major competitors that include DHL, C. H. Robinson, UPS, and TNT. The table provides information regarding how FedEx ranks on nine quality variables compared with its rival firms. Note that FedEx ranks number one on four variables: product quality, customer service, happy employees, and minority employees. Overall, note that FedEx is second-best behind DHL as indicated by the total score of 16 versus 15 (lower sum is better as you see in Column 10). This website provides useful information in preparing a CPM.

TABLE 3-9 Comparing FedEx Versus Rival Firms (Ranking 1 = Best; 5 = Worst)

	Variables									
	1	2	3	4	5	6	7	8	9	10
FedEx	3	1	2	2	1	2	3	1	1	16
UPS	5	3	3	3	3	4	4	3	3	31
DHL	1	2	1	1	2	1	1	4	2	15
TNT	4	5	5	5	5	5	5	-	-	34+
C. H. Robinson	2	4	4	4	4	3	2	2	4	29

Variables

1. Effectiveness of CEO
2. Product quality
3. Do customers recommend company products to friends?
4. Pricing
5. Customer service
6. Overall culture
7. Do employees recommend company products to friends?
8. How happy are the women employees at the firm?
9. How happy are minority employees at the firm?
10. Summed score (lower sum the better)

Source: Based on https://www.comparably.com/companies/fedex/competitors

Similar to an EFE Matrix, a CPM uses weights that quantify the importance of a given factor to the industry, as well as ratings that quantify how well a given firm's strategies are doing relative to the other firms evaluated in the CPM. Weights in a CPM are industry-based and sum to 1.0. Ratings in a CPM are assigned to quantify how well a firm and its key competitors' strategies are performing on each critical success factor; ratings reveal the degree of effectiveness of the firm's strategies. Assign a rating between 4 and 1 to each key factor to indicate how effectively the firm's current strategies respond to the factor, where 4 = the response is superior, 3 = the response is above average, 2 = the response is average, and 1 = the response is poor. Ratings are company-based; weights are industry-based.

The weights and ratings are then multiplied together to achieve a weighted score and then summed for each firm in the CPM. The key difference between a CPM and EFE Matrix is that a CPM compares the strategies of several firms, whereas an EFE Matrix analyzes how effectively the strategies of one firm are aligned with the most recent opportunities and threats facing the firm. Critical success factors within a CPM include points of competitive advantage within an industry, as well as other factors that are crucial for a firm to succeed within a given industry; *critical success factors* in a CPM can include both internal and external issues. List critical success factors from highest weight to lowest weight in a CPM.

A sample CPM is provided in Table 3-10. In this example, the two most important factors to being successful in the industry are "advertising" and "global expansion," as indicated by weights of 0.20. If there were no weight column in this analysis, note that each factor then would be equally important. Thus, including a weight column yields a more robust analysis because it enables the analyst to capture perceived or actual levels of importance. Note in Table 3-10 that Company 1's strategies are responding in a superior fashion to "product quality," as indicated by a rating of 4, whereas Company 2's strategies are superior regarding "advertising." Overall, Company 1's strategies are responding best, as indicated by the total weighted score of 3.15 and Company 3 is responding worst. Never duplicate ratings in a row in a CPM; go ahead and make judgments or decisions as to appropriate ratings based on your research and knowledge of the focal firm and rival companies. Always list factors from high weight to low weight, rather than in random order to make interpretation easier for the reader.

Other than the critical success factors listed in the sample CPM, factors often included in this analysis include breadth of product line, effectiveness of sales distribution, proprietary or patent advantages, location of facilities, production capacity and efficiency, experience, union relations, technological advantages, and e-commerce expertise. In generating the list of critical success factors, strive to include factors that differentiate firms within the industry (i.e., factors that determine competitive advantages).

Just because one firm receives a 3.15 overall total weighted score and another receives a 2.50 in a CPM, it does not necessarily follow that the first firm is precisely 26 percent better than the second, but it does suggest that the first firm is performing better on the variables included in the CPM. Regarding weights in a CPM or EFE Matrix, be mindful that 0.08 is mathematically 33 percent higher than 0.06, so even small differences can reveal important perceptions regarding the relative importance of various factors. The aim with numbers is to assimilate and evaluate information in a meaningful way that aids in decision-making.

TABLE 3-10 An Example CPM

Critical Success Factors	Weight	Company 1		Company 2		Company 3	
		Rating	Score	Rating	Score	Rating	Score
Advertising	0.20	1	0.20	4	0.80	3	0.60
Global expansion	0.20	4	0.80	1	0.20	2	0.40
Financial position	0.15	4	0.60	2	0.30	3	0.45
Management	0.10	4	0.40	2	0.20	1	0.10
Product quality	0.10	4	0.40	3	0.30	2	0.20
Customer loyalty	0.10	4	0.40	3	0.30	2	0.20
Price competitiveness	0.10	3	0.30	2	0.20	1	0.10
Market Share	0.05	1	0.05	4	0.20	3	0.15
Total	**1.00**		**3.15**		**2.50**		**2.20**

Note: The ratings values are as follows: 4 = response is superior, 3 = response is above average, 2 = response is average, 1 = response is poor. As indicated by the total weighted score of 2.20, Company 3 strategies are aligned relatively worse on the eight critical success factors when compared to Company 1 and Company 2. Only eight critical success factors are included for simplicity; in actuality, however, this is too few. The template asks that 12 factors be included and to tailor factors to a given industry.

IMPLICATIONS FOR STRATEGISTS

Figure 3-4 reveals that to gain and sustain competitive advantages, strategists must collect, analyze, and prioritize information regarding the firm's competitors, as well as identify and consider relevant social, demographic, economic, and technology trends and events impacting the firm and its industry. It is not uncommon for there to be substantial discussing, perhaps even some cussing, in deliberating what external factors should be included in an EFE Matrix because factors included ultimately impact the firm's strategies and direction. An engineering hunt for AQCD external factors is essential because resultant strategies can be expensive and sometimes irreversible. Survival of the firm can hinge on an effective and thorough external assessment being performed. Recall the Battle of Cannae story in Chapter 1.

The Process of Performing an External Audit

In performing an external audit, involve as many managers and employees as possible because involvement leads to understanding and commitment; individuals appreciate having the opportunity to contribute ideas and to gain a better understanding of their firm's industry, competitors, markets, and strategies. An effective way to gather competitive intelligence and information across the PESTEL and Five-Forces analyses discussed in this chapter is to ask various managers to monitor particular sources of information, such as key magazines, trade journals, newspapers, and online sources. These persons can submit periodic scanning reports to the person(s) who coordinates the external audit. This approach provides a continuous stream of timely strategic information and involves many individuals in the process of external auditing. Suppliers, distributors, salespersons, customers, and competitors represent other sources of vital information.

After AQCD external audit information is gathered and a full list of 50 factors is reduced to a narrow list of 20 as described in this chapter, the resultant 20 factors should be assimilated into an EFE Matrix and CPM as described. Prioritization is absolutely essential in strategic planning because no organization can do everything that would benefit the firm; tough choices between good options have to be made; in both an EFE Matrix and CPM, factors are listed from most important (highest weight) to least important. Even a full list of more than 50 factors can be reduced to the 20 most important in the manner described in this chapter.

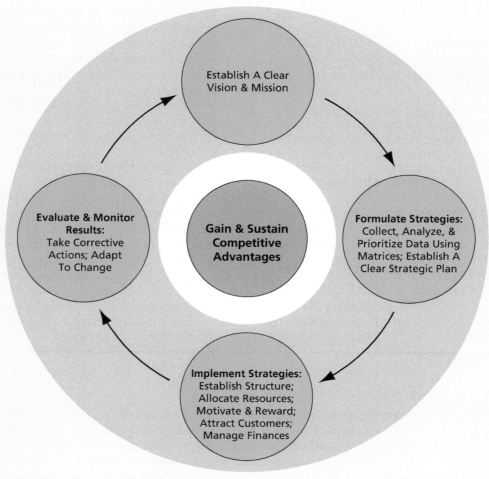

FIGURE 3-4

How to Gain and Sustain Competitive Advantages

IMPLICATIONS FOR STUDENTS

In developing and presenting the external assessment for your firm, be mindful that gaining and sustaining competitive advantage is the overriding purpose of developing the EFE Matrix and CPM. During this external section of your written or oral project, emphasize how and why particular factors can yield competitive advantage for the firm. In other words, instead of robotically going through the weights and ratings (which, by the way, are critically important), highlight various factors in light of where you are leading the firm. Make it abundantly clear in your discussion how your firm, with your recommendations, can subdue rival firms or at least profitably compete with them. Showcase during this part of your project the key underlying reasons how and why your firm can prosper among rivals. Remember to be *prescriptive*, rather than *descriptive*, in the manner that you present your entire project. If presenting your project orally, be self-confident and passionate rather than timid and uninterested. Definitely "bring the data" throughout your project because "vagueness" is the most common downfall of students in doing case analysis. To obtain the most recent information about your case company, read the firm's most recent quarterly report; the narrative that accompanies quarterly reports is excellent. It is necessary for students in developing an EFE Matrix to include specific (AQCD) factors related to the six PESTEL forces and competitive factors associated with Porter's Five-Forces Model.

Template Considerations

When using the template to perform an EFE Matrix and CPM analysis, enter all your data into the respective sections of Excel Tab Part I using the following techniques.

1. Enter in 10 opportunities and 10 threats (you do not have to list them by the most important at this step) into Part I under the respective opportunities and threats sections. Highlight the opportunities and threats, and right-click the mouse, choose format/alignment, and then click wrap text. If wrap text is already clicked, simply unclick the box and reclick. This procedure will alleviate any cut off text.
2. Provide the weights for each opportunity and threat. The weights with their corresponding factors do not have to be in largest to smallest order at this point. Feel free to adjust the weights for the respective factors as you deem appropriate. Once satisfied with the weights and factors and after ensuring the total is 1.0 (Excel calculates this for you), continue to step 3.
3. Highlight the opportunities section (Column B on the template) over to the weights section (Column D on the template) under Part I Tab in Excel and then click the sort button in Excel; be sure

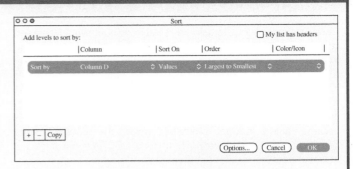

not to jointly perform this task for threats at this point. The sort button is found at the top of the page and to the far right of the Home page. Click custom sort and adjust the Column box to Column D (your weights), Sort On Box should be checked to values, and the Order Box should be "largest to smallest." The following figure is how your Excel should look after following these steps. Repeat this process for Threats.

4. For the CPM, after entering in 12 critical success factors in any order you desire, then supply the weights as you deem appropriate in any order you desire. Be sure your total weight adds to 1.0. Once satisfied with the weights with respect to the critical success factors, highlight Column B to Column D for the CPM in Part I and sort in the same manner you did for the EFE Matrix; this will arrange everything from largest weight to smallest weight while maintaining the correct weights of respective critical success factors.
5. After the respective critical success factors and weights are in order from highest to lowest, enter in the name of your firm and two rivals and supply the respective ratings as outlined in the textbook.
6. After completing the EFE Matrix and CPM, proceed to the EFE Matrix and CPM Tabs at the bottom of Excel. Take care to notice if the respective text for your opportunities and threats is cut off on the EFE Matrix. If so, move your mouse between the numbers on the left side of Excel on the EFE Tab and expand the cells to include all of your text. Cut and paste the matrices into your PowerPoint or Word file. It is best to either use the Paste Special feature (with no links) or simply take a screen shot of the matrix by using Shift, Command, 4 on a Mac or press Windows Key, Shift, S on a Windows machine to open the Snip tool.
7. Only Enter this data into Part I, the EFE Matrix and CPM Tabs are protected and cannot be adjusted.

Chapter Summary

Increasing turbulence in markets and industries around the world reveals the external audit has become an explicit and vital part of the strategic management process. This chapter provided a framework for collecting and evaluating political, economic, sociocultural, technological, environmental, legal, and competitive information. The AQCD test was explained to assure that opportunities and threats as stated in an EFE Matrix are actionable, qualitative, comparative, and divisional to the extent possible.

Firms that do not mobilize and empower their managers and employees to identify, monitor, forecast, and evaluate key external forces may fail to anticipate emerging opportunities and threats and, consequently, may pursue ineffective strategies, miss opportunities, and invite organizational demise. Firms not taking advantage of e-commerce and social media networks are technologically falling behind.

A major responsibility of strategists is to ensure development of an effective external audit system. This includes using information technology to devise a competitive intelligence system that works. The EFE Matrix, CPM, and Porter's Five-Forces Model can help strategists evaluate their market and industry, but these tools must be accompanied by good intuitive judgment. Multinational firms especially need a systematic and effective external audit system because external forces among foreign countries vary so greatly.

Key Terms and Concepts

actionable responses (p. 67)
avatars (p. 72)
Black Swan events (p. 67)
chief information officer (CIO) (p. 72)
chief technology officer (CTO) (p. 72)
competitive intelligence (CI) (p. 74)
Competitive Profile Matrix (CPM) (p. 83)
external audit (p. 66)

External Factor Evaluation (EFE) Matrix (p. 80)
external forces (p. 67)
industry analysis (p. 66)
information technology (IT) (p. 72)
metaverse (p. 72)
PESTEL analysis (p. 67)
Porter's Five-Forces Model (p. 75)

Issues for Review and Discussion

3-1. Explain why it is important to develop both a full and narrow list of key external factors in developing an EFE Matrix.

3-2. Explain the significance of an EFE Matrix total weighted score of 3.67 versus 1.59.

3-3. What does a CPM total weighted score of 1.88 imply for a company?

3-4. In an EFE Matrix, should the weights for opportunities be designed to roughly equal the weights for threats? Why?

3-5. List the six PESTEL external forces discussed in this chapter. When and why would some forces be more important than others?

3-6. How have external factors resulted in a major overhaul to the traditional retail industry as we once knew it?

3-7. Provide a synopsis of IBISWorld, Mergent Online, and PrivCo.

3-8. Compare and contrast the EFE Matrix with a CPM in terms of value provided for a strategist in performing an external assessment.

3-9. Mathematically, how much more important is a rating of 4 compared to a rating of 3? Why is this concept important in developing strategic planning matrices?

3-10. Describe how political elections can be an important external factor for companies to consider. Select an industry and reveal some key political factors impacting firms.

3-11. List some legal or ethical ways to gather competitive intelligence. List some illegal or unethical ways.

3-12. As the value of the dollar rises, US firms doing business abroad see their profits fall, so some firms raise prices of their products to offset the decrease in profits. What are some risks of raising prices?

3-13. Does McDonald's Corp. benefit from a low or high value of the dollar? Explain why.

3-14. Explain how Facebook, Twitter, and Instagram can represent a major threat or opportunity for a company.

3-15. If your CPM has three firms and they all end up with the same total weighted score, would the analysis still be useful? Why?

3-16. What industries are initially being most affected by the metaverse? Why? Which PESTEL force would metaverse best be categorized as?

3-17. Governments sometimes use protectionism to cope with economic problems, imposing tariffs and subsidies on foreign goods as well as placing restrictions and incentives on their own firms to keep jobs at home. What are the strategic implications of protectionism for international commerce?

3-18. Rank order the relative importance of Porter's Five Forces in the business of operating a college or university.

3-19. Let's say you work for McDonald's and you applied Porter's Five-Forces Model to study the fast-food industry. Rank the five forces as to relative importance for strategic planning at McDonald's.

3-20. Explain why it is appropriate for ratings in an EFE Matrix to be 4, 3, 2, or 1 for any opportunity or threat.

3-21. Why is inclusion of about 20 factors recommended in the EFE Matrix rather than about 10 factors or about 40 factors?

3-22. In developing an EFE Matrix, explain why is it advantageous to arrange your opportunities according to the highest weight, and your threats likewise?

3-23. In developing an EFE Matrix, would it be best to have 10 opportunities and 10 threats or would 17 opportunities (or threats) be fine with 3 of the other to achieve a total of 20 factors as desired?

3-24. Could or should critical success factors in a CPM include external factors? Explain.

3-25. Explain how to conduct an external strategic management audit in a business versus as a student performing case analysis.

3-26. Identify a recent economic, social, political, or technological trend that significantly affects the local Pizza Hut.

3-27. Discuss the following statement: Major opportunities and threats usually result from an interaction among key environmental trends rather than from a single external event or factor.

3-28. Use Porter's Five-Forces Model to evaluate competitiveness within the US banking industry.

3-29. How does the external audit affect other components of the strategic management process?

3-30. Construct an EFE Matrix for an organization of your choice.

3-31. Let's say your boss develops an EFE Matrix that includes 62 factors. How would you suggest reducing the number of factors to 20?

3-32. Discuss the ethics of gathering competitive intelligence.

3-33. Discuss the ethics of cooperating with rival firms.

3-34. Do you agree with Porter's view that competitive positioning within an industry is a strategic determinant of competitive advantage(s)?

3-35. Define, compare, and contrast the weights versus ratings in an EFE Matrix.

3-36. What is the difference between factors listed in an EFE Matrix and critical success factors listed in a CPM? In which matrix is it particularly important to include specific, actionable factors? Why?

3-37. List a hypothetical AQCD PESTEL factor for each of the six fundamental external forces that give rise to opportunities and threats.

3-38. Why do annual reports often state external risk information in really vague terms; why should strategists avoid including such vagueness in developing an EFE Matrix?

3-39. Explain the AQCD test for determining the quality of an external factor. Why should the AQCD test be met to the extent possible in performing an external assessment?

Writing Assignments

3-40. Describe the process of performing an external audit in an organization doing strategic planning for the first time.

3-41. Compare and contrast the duties and responsibilities of a CIO with a CTO in a large firm.

ASSURANCE-OF-LEARNING EXERCISES

SET 1: STRATEGIC PLANNING FOR MCDONALD'S

EXERCISE 3A

Develop an EFE Matrix for McDonald's

Ken Wolter/Alamy Photo

Purpose

This exercise will give you practice in developing an EFE Matrix. An EFE Matrix summarizes the results of an external audit. This is an important strategic planning tool widely used by strategists.

Instructions

Step 1 Get familiar with the template at the www.strategyclub.com website; click on EFE Matrix. Use the template to save immense time in completing this exercise. Be mindful, however, that the template does not itself access the internet to find key opportunities and threats. You need to do that and then enter that information into the template. The template is widely used by companies in preparing an EFE Matrix.

Step 2 Join with two other students in class and prepare an EFE Matrix for McDonald's. Refer to the Cohesion Case and to Exercise 1A and 1B in Chapter 1, if necessary, to identify external opportunities and threats. Make sure the factors you include are actionable, quantitative, comparative, and specific. Use the online sources listed in Table 3-7. Be sure not to include strategies as opportunities; but do include as many monetary amounts, percentages, numbers, and ratios as possible.

Step 3   All three-person teams participating in this exercise should record their EFE total weighted scores on the board. Put your initials after your score to identify it as your team's score.

Step 4   Compare the total weighted scores. Which team's score came closest to the instructor's answer? Discuss reasons for variation in the scores reported on the board.

EXERCISE 3B

Develop a Competitive Profile Matrix for McDonald's

Purpose

Monitoring competitors' performance and strategies is a key aspect of an external audit. This exercise is designed to give you practice in evaluating the competitive position of organizations in a given industry and assimilating that information in a CPM.

Instructions

Step 1   Get familiar with the template at the www.strategyclub.com website; you can click on CPM. Use the template to save you time in completing this exercise. Be mindful that the template does not itself access the internet to find key factors to include in a CPM. You need to do that and then enter that information into the template. The template is widely used by organizations in preparing a CPM.

Step 2   Turn back to the Cohesion Case in Chapter 1 and review the section on competitors. Also view online resources that compare McDonald's with Burger King. Use the sources listed in Table 3-7.

Step 3   Prepare a CPM that includes McDonald's and Burger King.

Step 4   Turn in your CPM for a classwork grade.

SET 2: STRATEGIC PLANNING FOR MY UNIVERSITY

EXERCISE 3C

Develop an EFE Matrix for Your College or University

Purpose

Most colleges and universities do strategic planning. Institutions are consciously and systematically identifying and evaluating external opportunities and threats facing higher education in your state, the nation, and the world.

Instructions

Step 1   Join with two other individuals in class and jointly prepare an EFE Matrix for your institution.

Step 2   Go to the board and record your total weighted score in a column that includes the scores of all three-person teams participating. Put your initials after your score to identify it as your team's score.

Step 3   Which team viewed your college's strategies most positively? Which team viewed your college's strategies most negatively? Discuss the nature of the differences.

EXERCISE 3D

Develop a Competitive Profile Matrix for Your College or University

Purpose

Your college or university competes with all other educational institutions in the world, especially those in your own state. State funds, students, faculty, staff, endowments, gifts, and federal funds are areas of competitiveness. Other areas include athletic programs, dorm life, academic reputation, location, and career services. The purpose of this exercise is to give you practice in thinking competitively about the business of education in your state.

Instructions

Step 1   Identify two colleges or universities in your state that compete directly with your institution for students. Interview several persons, perhaps classmates, who are aware of particular strengths and weaknesses of those universities. Record information about the two competing universities.

Step 2	Prepare a CPM that includes your institution and the two competing institutions. Include the following 12 factors in your analysis:

1. Tuition costs
2. Quality of faculty
3. Academic reputation
4. Average class size
5. Campus landscaping
6. Athletic programs
7. Quality of students
8. Graduate programs
9. Location of campus
10. Campus culture
11. Variety of undergraduate degree programs offered
12. Number of undergraduate degree programs offered

Step 3	Submit your CPM to your instructor for evaluation.

SET 3: STRATEGIC PLANNING TO ENHANCE MY EMPLOYABILITY

EXERCISE 3E

How Competitive Is Your State Among All States for Finding a Job?

Purpose

Just like companies, states compete against each other across numerous variables. Various research firms rank states annually with regard to their unemployment rate, job growth and labor force participation rate. Labor force participation rate measures the percentage of persons that are either employed or actively looking for a job. Unemployment rate measures the percentage of the labor force that is out of work. Colorado ranks first in the nation for employment at the website mentioned below, but Utah, Massachusetts, Idaho, and Virginia are also excellent.

The purpose of this exercise is to determine how your state ranks in terms of its job outlook and prospects. This information can enhance your job search as you near completion of a business administration degree.

Instructions

Step 1	Review information provided at the following website: https://www.usnews.com/news/best-states/rankings/economy/employment
Step 2	Determine where your state ranks among all states for finding a job.
Step 3	What actions could your state take to improve its competitiveness overall? How do nearby states to yours compare in attractiveness for finding a job?

EXERCISE 3F

Compare and Contrast CareerBuilder, Glassdoor, Monster Jobs, and ZipRecruiter

Purpose

Job hunting websites compete against each other for your business. Both job seekers and companies with job openings use job hunting websites, especially CareerBuider, Glassdoor, Monster Jobs, and ZipRecruiter. The purpose of this exercise is to familiarize you with the operation, strengths, and weaknesses of these four websites.

Instructions

Step 1	Review the four named websites taking note of what you especially like and dislike.
Step 2	Prepare a CPM for CareerBuilder. Include the three rival websites in your analysis.

EXERCISE 3G

A Template Competency Test

Purpose

The free Excel strategic planning template at www.strategyclub.com is widely used for strategic planning by students and small businesses; this exercise aims to enhance your familiarity with the template. Developing competence with the template will enable you to place this skill appropriately on your resume, in addition to facilitating your development of a comprehensive strategic plan for an assigned case company.

Instructions

Answer the following questions about the template. Discuss your answers with classmates to determine any issues or concerns.

Questions

1. How many factors does the template include in an EFE Matrix? In a CPM?
2. What happens using the template if you enter an inappropriate rating or weight such as a weakness rating of 5 or a weight of 1.2?
3. In using the template, why are changes to a matrix done on Part I or Part II rather than on a matrix itself?
4. What are key differences between Part I and Part II in the template?
5. Does the template address vision and/or mission statements?

SET 4: INDIVIDUAL VERSUS GROUP STRATEGIC PLANNING

EXERCISE 3H

What External Forces Are Most Important in Strategic Planning?

Purpose

A prioritized list of external factors is needed for effective strategic planning. Often, the process entails all managers individually ranking the factors identified, from 1 (most important) to 20 (least important). Prioritization is absolutely essential in strategic planning because no organization can do everything that would benefit the firm; tough choices between good options have to be made.

External forces can be divided into several categories: (1) political forces; (2) economic forces; (3) sociocultural forces; (4) technological forces; (5) environmental forces; (6) legal forces (PESTEL); and (7) competitive forces associated with Porter's Five-Forces Model. For some companies or organizations at various times, some forces may be more important to include than others. This exercise reveals the authors' ranking of the relative importance of external forces for inclusion in an external assessment.

The purpose of this exercise is to examine more closely the external areas of a business. In addition, the purpose of this exercise is to examine whether individual decision-making is better than group decision-making. Academic research suggests that groups make better decisions than individuals about 80 percent of the time.

Instructions

Rank the seven external forces as to their relative importance (1 = most important, 7 = least important). First, rank the forces as an individual. Then, rank the forces as part a group of three. Thus, determine what person(s) and what group(s) can come closest to the expert ranking. This exercise enables examination of the relative effectiveness of individual versus group decision-making in strategic planning.

Steps

1. Fill in Column 1 in Table 3-11 to reveal your individual ranking of the relative importance of the seven forces (1 = most important, 2 = next most important, etc.). For example, if you feel Economic factors are the fourth-most important external force, then enter a 4 in Table 3-11 in Column 1 beside Economic.
2. Fill in Column 2 in Table 3-11 to reveal your group's ranking of the relative importance of the seven forces (1 = most important, 2 = next most important, etc.).
3. Fill in Column 3 in Table 3-11 to reveal the expert's ranking of the seven forces.
4. Fill in Column 4 in Table 3-11 to reveal the absolute difference between Column 1 and Column 3 to reveal how well you performed as an individual in this exercise. (Note: Absolute difference disregards negative numbers.)
5. Fill in Column 5 in Table 3-11 to reveal the absolute difference between Column 2 and Column 3 to reveal how well your group performed in this exercise.

6. Sum Column 4. Sum Column 5.
7. Compare the Column 4 sum with the Column 5 sum. If your Column 4 sum is less than your Column 5 sum, then you performed better as an individual than as a group. Normally, group decision-making is superior to individual decision-making, so if you did better than your group, you did excellent.
8. The Individual Winner(s): The individual(s) with the lowest Column 4 sum is the WINNER.
9. The Group Winners(s): The group(s) with the lowest Column 5 score is the WINNER.

TABLE 3-11 External Force Analysis: Comparing Individual Versus Group Decision-Making

External Forces	Column 1	Column 2	Column 3	Column 4	Column 5
1. Political					
2. Economic					
3. Sociocultural					
4. Technological					
5. Environment					
6. Legal					
7. Competitive					
Sums					

MINI-CASE ON *WASHINGTON POST*

WASHINGTON POST NEEDS A STRATEGY TO DEAL WITH ITS SHARP DECLINE IN ONLINE READERSHIP

PJiiiJane/Shutterstock

Founded in 1877, the iconic, daily *Washington Post* newspaper published in Washington DC has a large national audience, especially in Maryland and Virginia. But the *Post* is facing a dramatic drop in its online readership. It experienced boom increases in readership during the Trump presidency years with inclusion of many politically related articles when consumers wanted that product, but the company says political articles are now not widely desired or read, so the *Post* likely has to start including much more nonpolitical articles.

In October 2021, the *Post* had 66 million monthly unique visitors, down 28 percent from the prior October. The *Post* had 2.7 million digital subscribers in October 2021, down from 3.0 million just 9 months earlier. The *Post*'s traffic from nonsubscribers was off 35 percent in 2020–2021. Only 14 percent of the *Post*'s subscribers are younger than age 55, compared with 61 percent of the US adult population.

Rival newspapers such as the *New York Times* and the *Wall Street Journal* have reported growing readership by offering articles such as features and culture rather than focusing on politics that is cyclical in consumer interest. New strategies at the *Post* will largely be based on the company successfully identifying, rating, and weighting key external opportunities and threats.

The newspaper publishing industry in general faces numerous external threats as consumers increasingly use their smartphones, social media, and other outlets for what news they want to read. There are some important opportunities too that must be capitalized on for any newspaper, including the *Washington Post,* to prosper in the coming years.[11]

Questions

1. Consider the following two-dimensional matrix with weights on the *y*-axis and ratings on the *x*-axis, as shown in Figure 3-5. What are example opportunities and threats that could possibly characterize *Washington Post* in the four corners of the matrix? Develop a hypothetical opportunity and threat for the *Post* that could be positioned in each of the four corners of the matrix. Give a supporting rationale for each factor. What box in Figure 3-5 is most pressing for a firm to address if many factors line up in that box? What box is least important?

2. Consider the following Answer given. Study the Answer given and see if you agree. Justify your thinking.

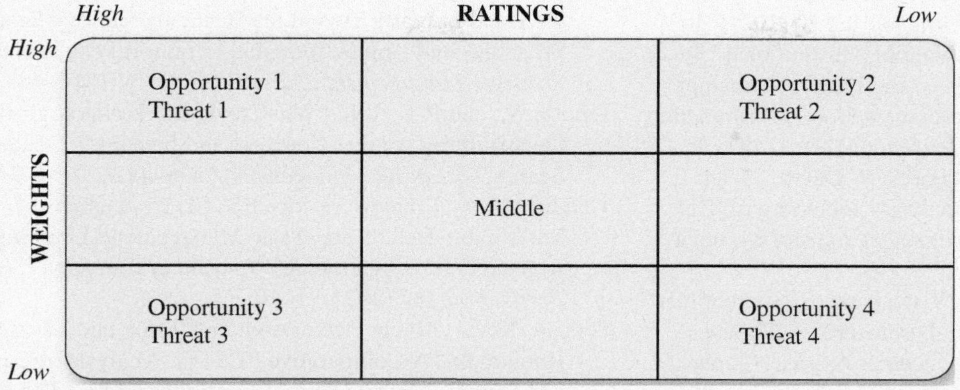

FIGURE 3-5

A Weights-by-Ratings Matrix to Exemplify EFE Matrix Logic

Note: A purpose of this mini-case is to give students practice thinking about when, in developing an EFE Matrix, could a particular factor receive the following weights and ratings:
1. a high weight and high rating
2. a high weight and low rating
3. a low weight and high rating
4. a low weight and low rating

Answer
1. The most important box for maintaining a competitive advantage is Box 1 (continue current strategies).
2. The most important box to have significant changes in strategy is Box 2 (high weight and current strategies either do not exist or are poorly addressing the factor).
3. The box in which our resources are possibly being misplaced the most is Box 3. The opportunities and threats that matter the least (of the included ones in the EFE) are the ones that support our current strategies the most. This represents a waste of resources!
4. The least important box is Box 4 because it is not as important for industry success (lower weights), and the firm is really not focused there anyway.

Web Resources

1. http://finance.yahoo.com
2. www.hoovers.com
3. www.morningstar.com
4. www.mergentonline.com
5. http://globaledge.msu.edu/industries/
6. See Table 3-7 for Excellent Library Databases

7. Fred David gives a video overview of Chapter 3 in the prior edition, but much info is still applicable to the 18th edition. First Half of Chapter 3: https://www.youtube.com/watch?v=r8eqv4P7qX4
Second Half of Chapter 3: https://www.youtube.com/watch?v=izd1Y4vUOOg

Current Readings

Allen, W. D., D. J. Schepker, and C. Chadwick, "Firms' Responses to Changes in Frictions in Related Human Capital Factor Markets," *Strategic Management Journal* (2021): 1–27.

Brunzel, Johannes, "Making Use of Quantitative Content Analysis: Insights from Academia and Business Practice," *Business Horizons* 64, no. 4 (July 2021): 453–64.

Capps, Charles J. I., Christopher M. Cassidy, Renee Gravois, and Janis A. Warner, "Expanding the Competitive Profile Matrix: Introducing the Production/Operations Management, Marketing, Human Resources Management, Finance/Accounting, Research and Development, and Information Systems Competitive Profile Matrices," *Journal of Business Strategies* 36, no. 1 (Spring 2019): 59–69.

Choi, Wonseok, Sukjae Jeong, and Jang Yeop Kim, "The Evaluation of the Export Competitiveness of Weapon Systems in Emerging Market Using Five Forces Model," *Academy of Strategic Management Journal* 20 (2021): 1–20.

Conti, R., O. Kacperczyk, and G. Valentini, "Institutional Protection of Minority Employees and Entrepreneurship: Evidence from the LGBT Employment Non-Discrimination Acts," *Strategic Management Journal* (2021): 1–34.

David, Fred R., Steven Creek, and Forest R. David, "What Is the Key to Effective SWOT Analysis? Including AQCD Factors," *SAM Advanced Management Journal* 84, no. 1 (2020): 25–36.

Flammer, C., M. W. Toffel, and K. Viswanathan, "Shareholder Activism and Firms' Voluntary Disclosure of Climate Change Risks," *Strategic Management Journal* 42, no. 10 (2021): 1850–79.

Hou, Y., and D. Yao, "Pushed into a Crowd: Repositioning Costs, Resources, and Competition in the RTE Cereal Industry," *Strategic Management Journal* 43, no. 1 (2021): 3–29.

Morandi Stagni, R, A. Fosfuri, and J. Santaló, "A Bird in the Hand Is Worth Two in the Bush: Technology Search Strategies and Competition due to Import Penetration," *Strategic Management Journal* 42 (2021): 1516–44.

Tandon, V., and P. K. Toh, "Who Deviates? Technological Opportunities, Career Concern, and Inventor's Distant Search," *Strategic Management Journal* (2021): 1–34.

Thakur, Vikas, "Framework for PESTEL Dimensions of Sustainable Healthcare Waste Management: Learnings from COVID-19 Outbreak," *Journal of Cleaner Production* 287 (2021): 1–14.

Zentner, Kevin, Alycia Fritze, Andrea Kloster, and Larysa Romaniuk, "A Comparative PESTEL Analysis of Canada and China's Management of Energy Markets," *The Journal of Applied Business and Economics* 22, no. 12 (2020): 253–73.

Endnotes

1. On page 66.

2. R. P. Rumelt, 'How Much Does Industry Matter?' *Strategic Management Journal* 12, no. 3 (1991): 167–85.

3. Fred R. David, Steven Creek, and Forest R. David, "What Is the Key to Effective SWOT Analysis? Including AQCD Factors," *SAM Advanced Management Journal* 84, no. 1 (2020): 25–36.

4. On page 69.

5. Shelly Banjo and Paul Ziobro, "Shoppers Flee Physical Stores," *Wall Street Journal*, August 6, 2014, p. B1.

6. Based on Vanessa Fuhrmans, "A Future Without Jobs? Think Again," *Wall Street Journal*, November 16, 2017, p. B5.

7. On page 73.

8. Arthur Thompson, Jr., A. J. Strickland III, and John Gamble, *Crafting and Executing Strategy: Text and Readings* (New York: McGraw-Hill/Irwin, 2005): 63.

9. Michael E. Porter, *Competitive Strategy: Techniques for Analyzing Industries and Competitors* (New York: Free Press, 1980): 24–27.

10. Dale McConkey, "Planning in a Changing Environment," *Business Horizons* 31, no. 5 (September–October 1988): 67.

11. Based on Benjamin Mullin and Alexandra Bruell, "*Washington Post* Seeks to Stem Drop in Readership," *Wall Street Journal*, December 17, 2021, p. B6.

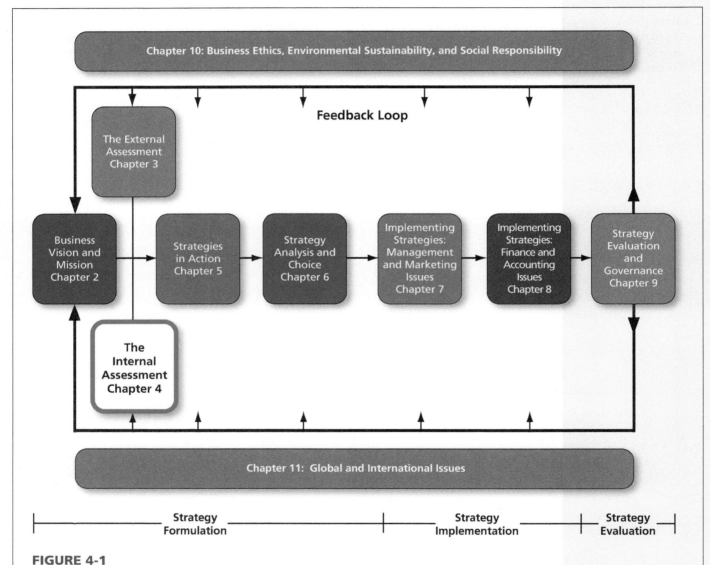

FIGURE 4-1

The Comprehensive, Integrative Strategic Management Model

Source: Fred R. David, "How Companies Define Their Mission," *Long Range Planning* 22, no. 1 (February 1989): 91. See also Anik Ratnaningsih, Nadjadji Anwar, Patdono Suwignjo, and Putu Artama Wiguna, "Balance Scorecard of David's Strategic Modeling at Industrial Business for National Construction Contractor of Indonesia," *Journal of Mathematics and Technology* no. 4 (October 2010): 20. See also Meredith E. David, Fred R. David, and Forest R. David, "Closing the Gap Between Graduates' Skills and Employers' Requirements: A Focus on the Strategic Management Capstone Business Course," *Administrative Sciences* 11, no. 1 (2021): 10–26.

The Internal Assessment

LEARNING OBJECTIVES

After studying this chapter, you should be able to do the following:

4.1. Describe the nature and role of an internal assessment in formulating strategies.

4.2. Discuss the nature and role of management in formulating strategies.

4.3. Discuss the nature and role of marketing in formulating strategies.

4.4. Discuss the nature and role of finance and accounting in formulating strategies.

4.5. Discuss management information systems (MIS) in terms of formulating strategies.

4.6. Explain how to develop and use an Internal Factor Evaluation (IFE) Matrix.

ASSURANCE-OF-LEARNING EXERCISES

The following exercises are found at the end of this chapter:

SET 1:	Strategic Planning for McDonald's
EXERCISE 4A:	Perform a Financial Ratio Analysis for McDonald's
EXERCISE 4B:	Develop an IFE Matrix for McDonald's
SET 2:	Strategic Planning for My University
EXERCISE 4C:	Construct an IFE Matrix for Your College or University
SET 3:	Strategic Planning for Myself
EXERCISE 4D:	Construct an IFE Matrix for Yourself
SET 4:	Individual Versus Group Strategic Planning
EXERCISE 4E:	What Internal Functional Areas Are Most Important to Examine in Strategic Planning?

This chapter focuses on identifying and evaluating a firm's strengths and weaknesses in the functional areas of business, including management, marketing, finance, accounting, and management information systems (MIS). Careful evaluation of a business' functional areas is necessary to determine the firm's core competencies and understand whether the firm's current strategy is effectively working to provide a sustainable competitive advantage. One excellent way to evaluate the effectiveness of a firm's strategy is to study the firm's financial performance relative to competitors and industry averages. Financial information alone, however, cannot provide a complete assessment of the effectiveness of a firm's strategy, and strategists as well as students of strategy must dig deep into management, marketing, finance, accounting, and MIS issues simultaneously to fully understand why a firm's strategy is effective or not.

The first two-thirds of this chapter addresses potential strengths and weaknesses in the functional areas cited in terms of what, where, how, and why to obtain this information; the latter one-third of this chapter explains how to assimilate and use this information through development and evaluation of an Internal Factor Evaluation (IFE) Matrix.

Showcased as the exemplary strategist for this chapter is Adena Friedman, CEO of Nasdaq, Inc. Headquartered in New York City, Nasdaq owns and operates the Philadelphia Stock Exchange and the Boston Stock Exchange, as well as Nasdaq Copenhagen, Nasdaq Helsinki, Nasdaq Iceland, Nasdaq Riga, Nasdaq Stockholm, Nasdaq Tallinn, and Nasdaq Vilnius.

The Internal Assessment Phase of Strategy Formulation

4.1. Describe the nature and role of an internal assessment in formulating strategies.

All organizations have strengths and weaknesses in the functional areas of business. No enterprise is equally strong or weak in all areas. Objectives and strategies are established with the intention of capitalizing on internal strengths and overcoming weaknesses. The internal-audit part of the strategic management process is illustrated in Figure 4-1 with white shading.

EXEMPLARY **STRATEGIST** SHOWCASED

Adena Friedman, CEO of Nasdaq, Inc.[1]

Adena Friedman has been CEO of Nasdaq since 2017. Friedman has led Nasdaq to post record revenues and net income and a 200+ percent increase in Nasdaq's share price during her tenure. Nasdaq's revenues are nearly $4 billion annually, up nearly 60 percent since 2017, while earnings-per-share are approaching 8.0. CEO Friedman is on a mission to grow Nasdaq quickly and responsibly as she invests in "all technology all the time while continuously fighting financial crime and fraud." Nasdaq acquired the data-and-transaction-security firm Verafin for $2.8 billion in 2021 and uses their software to discover and prevent crime and fraud. Friedman is also on a mission at Nasdaq to open "many doors of opportunity for minorities and disadvantaged persons." She says: "In order to successfully motivate, you need a plan." This is why she oversees a continuous strategic review of everything Nasdaq does. She says she leads a team of 50 executives at Nasdaq to develop and coalesce around a vision for the future. Because of Friedman, more than 130 stock exchanges around the world use Nasdaq technology to manage their operations. She has led Nasdaq to evolve from being a U.S.-focused stock exchange to a global technology company.

Admirably, Friedman has two grown sons and a husband and is proud of having always managed her personal and business lives with success. Regarding her leadership style, Friedman says it is important to do a lot more listening than speaking and never assume you are the smartest person in the room; be open-minded. She says being a CEO is analogous to being a parent in that you are

E.J. Baumeister Jr/Alamy Photo

successful only when your children are successful and able to take on the challenges that life brings them. A company executive at Nasdaq says: "What is remarkable about Adena is her combination of visionary leadership with a machinelike understanding of the operations details; it's extraordinarily rare." Nasdaq's CEO is an exemplary strategist—the United States and the whole world are better off having Adena Friedman at the helm.

[1]Based on Bruce Horovitz, "Plucking Four-Leaf Clovers Isn't Nasdaq ECO's Secret," *Investor's Business Daily*, November 8, 2021, p. A4.

Some researchers emphasize the importance of the internal audit part of the strategic management process by comparing it to the external audit in importance. Robert Grant, for example, concluded that the internal audit is more important, saying:

> In a world where customer preferences are volatile, the identity of customers is changing, and the technologies for serving customer requirements are continually evolving, an externally focused orientation does not provide a secure foundation for formulating long-term strategy. When the external environment is in a state of flux, the firm's own resources and capabilities may be a much more stable basis on which to define its identity. Hence, a definition of a business in terms of what it is capable of doing may offer a more durable basis for strategy.[2]

Resource-Based View

The **resource-based view (RBV)** approach to competitive advantage contends that internal resources are more important for a firm than external factors in achieving and sustaining competitive advantage. Proponents of RBV theory contend that a firm's performance is primarily determined by internal resources that enable the firm to exploit opportunities and neutralize threats. A firm's resources can be tangible, such as labor, capital, land, plant, and equipment, or intangible, such as culture, knowledge, brand equity, reputation, and intellectual property. Because tangible resources can more easily be bought and sold, intangible resources are often more important for gaining and sustaining competitive advantages.

A resource can be considered valuable to the extent that it is (1) rare, (2) hard to imitate, or (3) not easily substitutable. Often called **empirical indicators**, these three characteristics of resources enable a firm to implement strategies that improve its efficiency and effectiveness and lead to a sustainable competitive advantage. The more a resource(s) is rare (not held by many firms in the industry), hard to imitate (hard to copy or achieve), and not easily substitutable (invulnerable to threat of substitution from different products), the stronger a firm's competitive advantage will be and the longer the advantage will last. Valuable resources comprise strengths that a firm can capitalize on to prosper within a given industry.

The basic premise of RBV theory is that the mix, type, amount, and nature of a firm's internal resources should be considered first and foremost in devising strategies that can lead to sustainable competitive advantages. Managing strategically according to the RBV involves developing and exploiting a firm's unique resources and capabilities and continually maintaining and strengthening those resources.

Key Internal Forces

An internal strategic management assessment includes analysis of how strong or weak a firm is in each functional area of business, including management, marketing, finance, accounting, and MIS. Uniqueness or distinctive competencies a firm has or lacks in each area provides the foundation for identifying strength and weakness factors. Strengths that cannot be easily matched or imitated by competitors are called **distinctive competencies**. It is of paramount importance in strategic planning to capitalize on and nurture strengths because competitive advantages generally arise more from strengths, uniqueness, and distinctive competencies than from weaknesses. Improving on weaknesses, however, is a vital task for all organizations and generally helps to improve efficiencies. Weaknesses are unlikely to develop into sustainable competitive advantages, thus stressing the importance of nurturing strengths.

It is impossible in a strategic management text to review in-depth all the material presented in prior business courses; there are many subareas within these functions, such as customer service, warranties, advertising, packaging, and pricing under marketing. However, strategic planning must include a detailed assessment of how the firm is doing in all internal areas. Thus, an overview of each of the functional business areas from a strategy perspective is provided here. Regardless of the type or size of firm, effective strategic planning hinges on identification and prioritization of internal strengths and weaknesses because a firm must continually capitalize on its strengths and improve on its weaknesses to gain and sustain a competitive advantage.

Management

4.2. Discuss the nature and role of management in formulating strategies.

There are four basic activities that comprise **management**: planning, organizing, motivating, and controlling. An overview of these activities is provided in Table 4-1; an organization should continually capitalize on its strengths and improve on its weaknesses in these four areas.

TABLE 4-1 The Basic Functions of Management

Function	Description	Stage of Strategic Management Process When Most Important
Planning	Planning consists of all managerial activities related to preparing for the future, such as establishing objectives, devising strategies, and developing policies.	Strategy Formulation
Organizing	Organizing includes all managerial activities that result in a structure of task and authority relationships, such as organizational design, job specialization, job descriptions, span of control, job design, and job analysis.	Strategy Implementation
Motivating	Motivating involves efforts directed toward shaping human behavior, such as leadership, communication, teamwork, job enrichment, and human resource management (HRM).	Strategy Implementation
Controlling	Controlling refers to all managerial activities that compare actual results with planned results, such as quality control, financial control, inventory control, expense control, analysis of variances, rewards, and sanctions.	Strategy Evaluation

Planning

Planning is the essential bridge between the present and the future; planning increases the likelihood of achieving desired results. Even though planning is considered the foundation of management, it is the task that managers most commonly neglect. Planning enables a firm to:

1. Take into account relevant factors and focus on the critical ones.
2. Ensure that the firm is prepared for all reasonable eventualities and can make timely changes and adapt as needed.
3. Gather the resources needed and carry out tasks in the most efficient way possible.
4. Conserve its own resources and avoid wasting natural resources.
5. Assess whether the effort, costs, and implications associated with achieving desired objectives are warranted.
6. Be proactive, anticipate, and influence the future.

Planning is more than simply projecting past and present trends into the future (long-range planning). Planning also includes revising a firm's vision and mission, forecasting future events and trends, establishing objectives, and choosing strategies to pursue. Successful organizations strive to guide their own futures rather than merely react to external forces and events as they occur. Historically, organisms and organizations that adapt well to changing conditions survive and prosper; others become extinct.

An organization can develop synergy through planning. **Synergy** exists when everyone pulls together as a team that knows what it wants to achieve; synergy is the $2 + 2 = 5$ effect. By establishing and communicating clear objectives, employees and managers can work together toward desired results. Synergy can result in powerful competitive advantages. The strategic management process itself is aimed at creating synergy in an organization.

Strengths and weaknesses with respect to planning could relate to: (1) quality of a firm's vision or mission and how well the firm's strategies support the vision or mission, (2) divisions' relative contribution to the firm's performance, and (3) resource allocation across regions and products.

Organizing

The purpose of **organizing** is to achieve coordinated effort by defining task and authority relationships. Organizing means determining who does what and who reports to whom. There are countless examples in history of well-organized enterprises successfully competing against—and in

GLOBAL CAPSULE 4

Samsung Is Reorganizing to Develop an "Apple" Ecosystem[3]

Based in Seoul, South Korea, Samsung Electronics is the world's largest maker of smartphones, semiconductors, and televisions. Led by 53-year-old Lee Jae-Yong, grandson of the founder of the company, Samsung recently replaced all three of its co-CEOs with a new generation of executives. Samsung's mobile and consumer electronics units were merged into a single division. Lee wants Samsung's smartphones to become a fulcrum that links all the company's products and appliances. Samsung just merged its smartphone operations with its home appliance operations. Samsung Galaxy phones have fallen behind Apple's iPhones.

Samsung is investing $17 billion in Taylor, Texas, to produce semiconductors because its two rival semiconductor firms, Taiwan Semiconductor Manufacturing and Intel, are outperforming Samsung. A total reorganization is going on at Samsung because the company feels substantial heat from rival firms on all fronts. Despite numerous conglomerate firms in the last 2 years divesting or spinning off homogeneous parts, there is no word of Samsung considering that strategy. Time will tell if a big diversified company like Samsung going forward can outperform rivals across products ranging from televisions to semiconductors.

[3]Based on Jiyoung Sohn, "Samsung Acts to Spark Growth," *Wall Street Journal*, December 8, 2021, pp. B1, B2.

some cases defeating—much stronger but less-organized firms. A well-organized firm generally has motivated managers and employees who are committed to seeing the organization succeed. Resources are allocated more effectively and used more efficiently in a well-organized firm.

The organizing function of management can be viewed as consisting of three sequential activities: breaking down tasks into jobs, combining jobs to form departments, and delegating authority. In *The Wealth of Nations*, published in 1776, Adam Smith cited the advantages of work specialization in the manufacture of pins:

> One man draws the wire, another straightens it, a third cuts it, a fourth points it, a fifth grinds it at the top for receiving the head. Ten men working in this manner can produce 48,000 pins in a single day, but if they had all wrought separately and independently, each might at best produce twenty pins in a day.[4]

Organizing includes developing an appropriate structure, span of control, and chain of command. Structure dictates how resources are allocated and how objectives are established in a firm. Changes in strategy often require changes in structure because positions may be created, deleted, or merged. The most common types of structure are discussed in Chapter 7. Strengths and weaknesses with respect to organizing could relate to (1) how well the firm's current structure matches the various divisions and strategy of the firm, (2) the degree to which a clear chain of command is displayed through executive titles, and (3) the extent of overlap among related jobs and job descriptions.

As indicated in the Global Capsule 4, Samsung Electronics is reorganizing its management structure substantially to develop an ecosystem similar to Apple Inc. where many of its products are linked and "talk" to each other.

Motivating

Motivating is the process of influencing people to accomplish specific objectives. Motivation helps explain why some people work hard and others do not. Strategies have little chance of succeeding if employees are not motivated to implement them once they are formulated. The motivating function of management includes such activities as developing leaders, managing groups, communicating effectively, and managing organizational change.

When managers and employees of a firm strive to achieve high levels of productivity, this indicates that the firm's strategists are excellent leaders—persons that establish rapport with subordinates, empathize with their needs and concerns, set a good example, and are trustworthy and fair. An excellent leader communicates a vision of the firm's future and inspires people to work hard to achieve that vision. Stressing the importance of leadership, Sun Tzu stated, "Weak leadership can wreck the soundest strategy." According to Peter Drucker:

> Leadership is not a magnetic personality. That can just as well be demagoguery. It is not "making friends and influencing people." That is flattery. Leadership is the lifting of a person's vision to higher sights, the raising of a person's performance to a higher standard, the building of a person's personality beyond its normal limitations.[5]

An organization's system of communication determines whether strategies can be implemented successfully. Good two-way communication is vital for gaining support for departmental and divisional objectives and policies. Top-down communication can encourage bottom-up communication. The strategic management process becomes a lot easier when subordinates are encouraged to discuss their concerns, reveal their problems, provide recommendations, and give suggestions. A primary reason for instituting strategic management is to build and support effective communication networks throughout the firm.

Human resource management (HRM) includes activities such as recruiting, interviewing, testing, selecting, orienting, training, developing, caring for, evaluating, rewarding, disciplining, promoting, transferring, demoting, and dismissing employees, as well as managing union relations. The complexity and importance of HRM has increased to such a degree that all but the smallest organizations generally have a full-time human resource manager. As employees and managers come and go, HRM must manage this process effectively to maintain employee morale and minimize workplace stress. Table 4-2 reveals several of many ways that effective HRM can help create and maintain a competitive advantage for organizations. The type of HRM information listed in Table 4-2 could be the source of a firm's strengths or weaknesses with respect to the overall motivation of managers and employees.

TABLE 4-2 Six Ways Human Resource Management Can Provide a Competitive Advantage

1. Analyze turnover rates to determine where problems are.
2. Measure and monitor employee engagement and morale scores.
3. Track employee data to identify high and low performers.
4. Determine going market rates for talent and align compensation with company goals.
5. Design employee development and training pathways that take into account the strategic and long-term needs of the organization.
6. Provide guidance on legal issues related to all personnel matters.

Source: Based on information from http://hrdailyadvisor.blr.com/2017/08/21/using-hr-competitive-advantage/

Controlling

All managers in an organization have controlling responsibilities, such as conducting performance evaluations and taking necessary action to minimize inefficiencies. The controlling function of management is particularly important for effective strategy evaluation (the focal topic of Chapter 9). **Controlling** consists of four basic steps:

1. Establishing performance standards.
2. Measuring individual and organizational performance.
3. Comparing actual performance to planned performance standards.
4. Taking corrective actions.

The **production/operations** portion of a business consists of all those activities that transform inputs (i.e., raw materials, labor, capital, machines, and facilities) into finished goods and services. The extent to which a manufacturing plant's output reaches its full potential output is called **capacity utilization**, a key strategic variable. The higher the capacity utilization, the better; otherwise, equipment may sit idle. For example, if a manufacturing firm's plants are averaging 60 percent capacity utilization, that would represent a severe weakness of the firm. The website https://www.tysonfoods.com/who-we-are/our-story/what-we-do gives Tyson Foods' capacity utilization information across all its facilities. Note that for Fiscal 2021 across 14 beef facilities, Tyson's capacity utilization was 78 percent compared to across 7 pork facilities where the firm's capacity utilization was 88 percent.

TABLE 4-3 The Basic Decision Areas Within Production/Operations

Decision Areas	Example Decisions
1. Process	Robotics, facility layout, process flow analysis, line balancing, process control, and transportation analysis
2. Capacity	Forecasting, facilities planning, aggregate planning, scheduling, capacity planning, queuing analysis, and capacity utilization
3. Inventory	Level of raw materials, work-in-process, finished goods, what to order, when to order, how much to order, and materials handling
4. Workforce	Managing the skilled, unskilled, clerical, and managerial employees by caring for job design, work measurement, job enrichment, work standards, and motivation techniques
5. Quality	Quality control, sampling, testing, quality assurance, and cost control

Source: Based on a variety of sources.

As indicated in Table 4-3, Roger Schroeder suggests that production/operations comprises five decision areas: process, capacity, inventory, workforce, and quality. Production/operations activities often represent the largest part of an organization's human and capital assets. In many industries, the major costs of producing a product are incurred within operations, so production/operations can have great value as a competitive weapon in a company's overall strategy. Strengths and weaknesses in the five areas of production can mean the success or failure of an enterprise.

Increasingly in production settings, a new breed of robots called **collaborative machines** are working alongside people. Priced as low as $20,000 and becoming widely used even in small businesses, robots do not take lunch breaks or sick days or require health insurance, and they can work nonstop all night tirelessly if needed. Collaborative machines are more flexible, often doing one task one day and a different task the next day. During the first nine months of 2021 alone, companies in the United States ordered 29,000 robots, partly due to labor shortages throughout manufacturing and in many industries.

About two-thirds of robotics orders are in non-automobile-related industries; robots are becoming especially common in the metals, consumer goods, food, and semiconductors industries. Tyson Foods recently announced that it is spending an additional $1.3 billion over the next 3 years to further automate the most labor-intensive parts of its production processes. This expenditure comes on the heels of Tyson spending nearly $1 billion over the last few years to develop robotic meat-processing systems. Tyson's traditional labor force just cannot keep up with increasing demand, especially as childcare and pandemic issues hamper attendance. Artificial intelligence (AI) systems are rapidly advancing, enabling robots to be more productive and "smarter."[6] Strengths and weaknesses with respect to controlling could relate to (1) inventory turnover levels versus competitors, (2) how well or poorly the firm's operations are performing across various geographical regions, and (3) how cost efficient the firm is in acquiring needed supplies.

Integrating Strategy and Culture

The functions of management can be performed best when a firm's strategy and culture are integrated. Every business entity has a unique organizational culture that impacts strategic planning activities. **Organizational culture** is "a pattern of behavior that has been developed by an organization as it learns to cope with its problem of external adaptation and internal integration, and that has worked well enough to be considered valid and to be taught to new members as the correct way to perceive, think, and feel."[7] This definition emphasizes the importance of matching external with internal factors in making strategic decisions. Organizational culture captures the subtle, elusive, and largely unconscious forces that shape a workplace. Remarkably resistant to change, culture can represent a major strength or weakness for any firm.

The strategic management process takes place largely within a particular organization's culture. A culture ideally supports the collective commitment of its people to a common purpose. It must foster competence and enthusiasm among managers and employees. If strategies can capitalize on cultural strengths, such as a strong work ethic or highly ethical beliefs, then management often can swiftly and easily implement changes. However, if the firm's culture is not supportive, strategic changes may be ineffective or even counterproductive. A firm's culture can become antagonistic to new strategies, with the result being confusion and disorientation.

To achieve and maintain competitive advantage, firms must continually learn, adapt, and evolve. Adapting to change can be difficult, particularly when change includes forging new alliances, partnerships, or mergers between different companies, each of which likely has its own unique culture and identity. Table 4-4 provides some example (possible) aspects of an organization's culture and possible considerations for identifying strengths and weaknesses within the firm.

When one firm acquires another firm, integrating the two cultures effectively can be vital for success. For example, in Table 4-4, one firm may score mostly 1s (low) and the other firm may score mostly 5s (high), which would present a challenging strategic problem. Regardless of a firm's industry, geography, or company history, it is imperative that firms effectively integrate corporate strategy and culture, even as they continuously adapt and evolve overtime.

An organization's culture should infuse individuals with enthusiasm for implementing strategies. Internal strengths and weaknesses associated with a firm's culture sometimes are overlooked because of the interfunctional nature of this phenomenon. This is a fundamental reason why strategists need to view and understand their firm as a sociocultural system. Success is often determined by links between a firm's culture and strategies. The challenge of strategic management today is to bring about the changes in organizational culture and individual mindsets that are needed to support the formulation, implementation, and evaluation of strategies.

TABLE 4-4 15 Aspects of an Organization's Culture

Dimension	Low		Degree		High
1. Strong work ethic; arrive early and leave late	1	2	3	4	5
2. High ethical beliefs; clear code of business ethics followed	1	2	3	4	5
3. Formal dress; shirt and tie expected	1	2	3	4	5
4. Informal dress; many casual dress days	1	2	3	4	5
5. Socialize together outside of work	1	2	3	4	5
6. Do not question supervisor's decision	1	2	3	4	5
7. Encourage whistleblowing	1	2	3	4	5
8. Be health conscious; have a wellness program	1	2	3	4	5
9. Allow substantial "working from home"	1	2	3	4	5
10. Encourage creativity, innovation, and open-mindedness	1	2	3	4	5
11. Support women and minorities; no glass ceiling	1	2	3	4	5
12. Be highly socially responsible; be philanthropic	1	2	3	4	5
13. Have numerous meetings	1	2	3	4	5
14. Have a participative management style	1	2	3	4	5
15. Preserve the natural environment; have a sustainability program	1	2	3	4	5

Management Audit Checklist of Questions

The following checklist of questions can help determine specific strengths and weaknesses in the management functional area of business. An answer of *no* to any question could indicate a potential weakness, although the strategic significance and implications of negative answers, of course, will vary by organization, industry, and severity of the weakness. Positive or *yes* answers to the checklist questions suggest potential areas of strength.

1. Does the firm use strategic management concepts?
2. Are company objectives and goals measurable and well communicated?
3. Do managers at all hierarchical levels plan effectively?
4. Do managers delegate authority well?
5. Is the organization's structure appropriate?
6. Are job descriptions and job specifications clear?
7. Is employee morale high?
8. Are employee turnover and absenteeism low?
9. Are organizational reward and control mechanisms effective?

Marketing

4.3. Discuss the nature and role of marketing in formulating strategies.

Marketing can be described as the process of defining, anticipating, and fulfilling consumers' needs and wants. Marketing is about satisfying current and potential customers' needs. Excellent marketing can provide firms with a competitive advantage. Table 4-5 lists the top 10 best companies in customer satisfaction according to the *Wall Street Journal*.

Marketing consists of five basic activities: (1) marketing research and target market analysis, (2) product planning, (3) pricing products, (4) promoting products, and (5) placing or distributing products. Understanding these activities helps strategists identify and evaluate marketing strengths and weaknesses—a vital activity in strategy formulation.

TABLE 4-5 The 10 Best (Among 250) Companies in Customer Satisfaction According to the *Wall Street Journal*

Company	Customer Satisfaction Score
IBM	84.2
Caterpillar Inc.	76.6
Agilent Technologies Inc.	76.1
Procter & Gamble Company	75.1
Cisco Systems Inc.	74.2
Accenture PLC	73.3
Clorox Company	72.5
Molson Coors Beverage Company	72.3
Ford Motor Company	71.7
TE Connectivity Ltd.	71.6

Source: Based on information from https://www.wsj.com/articles/top-companies-for-customer-satisfaction-11613492860

Marketing Research and Target Market Analysis

Marketing research is the systematic gathering, recording, and analyzing of data to identify and define opportunities and problems related to the marketing of goods and services. Marketing research is often used to help firms evaluate and formulate strategies. Marketing researchers employ numerous scales, instruments, procedures, concepts, and techniques to gather information; their research can uncover critical strengths and weaknesses. Organizations that possess excellent marketing research skills have a competitive advantage. According to the former president of PepsiCo:

> Looking at the competition is the company's best form of market research. The majority of our strategic successes are ideas that we borrow from the marketplace, usually from a small regional or local competitor. In each case, we spot a promising new idea, improve on it, and then out-execute our competitor.[8]

An important use of marketing research involves **target market analysis**—the examination and evaluation of consumer needs and wants. Marketing research involves methods such as administering customer surveys, analyzing consumer information, evaluating market positioning strategies, developing customer profiles, and determining optimal market segmentation strategies, all of which contribute to effective customer analysis.

Successful organizations continually monitor present and potential customers' buying patterns and engage in extensive marketing research to understand the needs and wants of different segments of customers. Firms tailor their product offerings to fit the needs of their target market(s). Many companies have recently shifted their target markets to focus on younger consumers, and particularly millennials because these individuals now make up the largest group of U.S. consumers. For example, Home Depot, Procter & Gamble, Williams-Sonoma Inc., Sherwin-Williams Co., and Scotts Miracle-Gro Company are now targeting millennials by offering online lessons aimed at teaching basic skills such as how to mow a lawn, use a tape measure, hammer a nail, and care for plants.

With a clearly defined target market, marketers can best use their strategic toolbox to ensure that their firm's offering delivers value to target customers. A clear understanding of a firm's target market(s) serves as the foundation on which the marketing mix is designed. Commonly referred to as the "four Ps of marketing," the marketing mix includes product, price, promotion, and place, as indicated in Table 4-6. Marketers design a marketing mix to fit the unique needs of each target market. Table 4-6 reveals key areas to consider when searching for and identifying possible strengths and weaknesses related to the marketing functional area of a firm.

TABLE 4-6 The Marketing Mix Component Variables

Product	Place	Promotion	Price
Quality	Distribution channels	Advertising	Level
Features and options	Distribution coverage	Personal selling	Discounts
Style and brands	Outlet location	Sales promotion	Allowances
Packaging	Sales territories	Publicity	Payment terms
Product line	Inventory levels		
Warranty and services	Transportation carriers		

Source: Based on a variety of sources.

Product Planning

Products can be physical goods, services, ideas, or anything a company offers to satisfy individual or business customer needs through the exchange process. Product planning includes devising warranties; packaging; determining product options, features, brand style, and quality; deleting old products; and providing customer service. Product planning is particularly important when a company is pursuing product development or diversification. In such cases, companies often must decide whether to extend an existing product line or create an entirely new product line. In implementing a product development strategy, the Campbell Soup Company, for example, may consider extending its line of soups by developing a new soup or entering a new category of products by perhaps offering a marinade.

One important part of product planning involves **test marketing**, which allows an organization to examine alternative marketing plans, learn about potential problems with the product, uncover ways to better market the product, or forecast future sales of new products. In conducting a test-market project, an organization must decide how many cities to include, which cities to include, how long to run the test, what information to collect during the test, and what action to take after the test has been completed. Test marketing is used more frequently by consumer goods companies than industrial goods companies. The technique can enable an organization to avoid substantial losses by revealing weak products and ineffective marketing approaches before large-scale production begins.

Another important part of product planning is research and development (R&D). Many firms today conduct no R&D, and yet many other companies depend on successful R&D activities for survival. Firms pursuing a product-development strategy especially need to have a strong R&D orientation. High-tech firms, such as Microsoft, spend a much larger proportion of their revenues on R&D. A crucial decision for many firms is whether to be a "first mover" or a "fast follower" (i.e., spend heavily on R&D to be the first to develop radically new products or spend less on R&D by imitating, duplicating, or improving on products after rival firms develop them).

Most firms have no choice but to continually develop new and improved products because of changing consumer needs and tastes, new technologies, shortened product life cycles, and increased domestic and foreign competition. A shortage of ideas for new products, increased global competition, increased market segmentation, strong special interest groups, and increased government regulations are several factors making the successful development of new products more and more difficult, costly, and risky. In the pharmaceutical industry, for example, only one of every few thousand drugs created in the laboratory ends up on pharmacists' shelves.

Strengths and weaknesses with respect to products could relate to (1) the value of a firm's brands relative to competitors' brands, (2) the firm's product assortment or cannibalism among the firm's existing products, or (3) features of the firm's products relative to those of similar products found in the marketplace.

Pricing

Pricing refers to deciding the amount an individual must exchange to receive a firm's product offering. Pricing objectives often include setting prices at levels that maximize profit, sales, or market share, or setting prices to foster customer satisfaction or to enhance the image and prestige of a product. Pricing strategies are often based on costs, demand, the competition, or on customers' needs. Chipotle is just the latest company to raise its menu prices, following McDonald's and Starbucks, with these firms saying the increases are needed to offset rising wage rates and the overall cost of raw materials. Chipotle is opening about 250 new stores per year in the U.S. and most of these include drive-throughs dedicated to online orders.

Widespread internet use and advances in technology have enabled firms to quickly adjust prices to meet changes in the marketplace. In dynamic pricing strategies, the same product may be sold to different customers for different prices or even to the same customer for different prices. Intense price competition, coupled with internet price-comparative shopping, has reduced profit margins to bare minimum levels for many companies. Target and Best Buy are among the many companies that now offer to match online prices of rival retailers. Both companies are seeking to combat "showrooming" by shoppers who check out products in their stores but buy them on rivals' websites. Issues related to pricing can represent key strengths or weaknesses for firms.

Firms must be aware of government constraints on pricing, including regulations regarding price fixing, price discrimination, predatory pricing, unit pricing, price advertising, and price controls. For example, the Robinson-Patman Act prohibits manufacturers and wholesalers from discriminating in price among channel member purchasers (retailers and wholesalers) if competition is lessened. Strengths and weaknesses with respect to pricing could relate to whether or not the focal firm price matches and how the firm's prices (including currencies in which the products can be paid) compare to similar products sold by competitors.

Promotion

Successful strategy implementation generally rests on the ability of an organization to sell some good or service. **Promotion** includes many marketing activities, such as advertising, sales promotion, public relations, personal selling, and direct marketing. Common promotional tools designed to inform consumers about products include TV advertising, magazine ads, billboards, websites, and public relations, among others. Discounts, coupons, and samples are often used to encourage purchase. Promotional tools such as personal selling, buzz building, and social media are often used to build relationships with customers. The effectiveness of various promotional tools for consumer and industrial products varies. Personal selling is especially important for industrial goods companies, whereas advertising and social media marketing are more important for consumer goods companies. Determining organizational strengths and weaknesses in the promotional function of marketing is an important part of performing an internal strategic management audit.

Promotion in general and advertising in particular can be expensive, a primary reason marketing is a major business function to be studied carefully. Without marketing, even the best products have little chance of being successful. Many successful brands are now using digital platforms and social media to build relationships and establish emotional bonds with consumers. As social networks, virtual worlds, product review sites, and location-based social apps become increasingly popular among consumers, marketers spend heavily on social media marketing. In performing a strategic planning analysis, in addition to comparing rival firms' websites, it is important to compare rival firms' handling of social media issues.

Strengths and weaknesses with respect to promotion could relate to a firm's (1) website and social media engagement (or lack thereof), (2) association with key celebrities or spokespersons, or (3) advertising and brand slogans or images.

Channels of Distribution

Channels of distribution is a term that refers to the various intermediaries that take a product from a producer to an end customer. These intermediaries bear a variety of names such as wholesalers, retailers, brokers, facilitators, agents, vendors—or simply distributors. In this regard, marketers often make decisions related to warehousing, distribution channels, distribution coverage, retail site locations, sales territories, inventory location, transportation carriers, wholesaling, and retailing.

Marketers must determine how widely available their product should be for consumers to find and purchase. Some firms offer their products through as many wholesalers and retailers that will sell them, whereas other firms offer products only through several select outlets or authorized dealers. For example, the Dasani brand of bottled water, which has a relatively broad target market, is much more readily available than some other brands, such as Fiji Artesian Water and Voss bottled water, which target smaller, higher-end markets.

Some of the most complex and challenging decisions facing firms concern product distribution. Successful organizations identify and evaluate alternative ways to reach their ultimate market. Many companies today are increasingly making their products available for purchase online, directly through their website, but this practice can upset retailers. Efficient supply chain and distribution systems are essential for any firm to gain and sustain a competitive advantage. Strengths and weaknesses with respect to place could relate to the effectiveness of brick-and-mortar versus online sales or the average return on investment (ROI) of various purchase locations.

Marketing Audit Checklist of Questions

The following types of questions about marketing must be examined in performing an internal assessment:

1. Are markets segmented effectively?
2. Is the organization positioned well among competitors?
3. Are present channels of distribution reliable and cost-effective?
4. Is the firm conducting and using market research effectively?
5. Are product quality and customer service good?
6. Are the firm's goods and services priced appropriately?
7. Does the firm have an effective promotional strategy?
8. Is the firm's internet presence excellent as compared to rivals?

Finance and Accounting

4.4. Discuss the nature and role of finance and accounting in formulating strategies.

Financial condition is often considered the single-best measure of a firm's competitive position and overall attractiveness to investors. Table 4-7 lists top companies for financial strength according to the *Wall Street Journal*. Note that Microsoft Corporation heads the list. Determining an

TABLE 4-7 The 10 Best (Among 250) Companies for Financial Strength According to the *Wall Street Journal*.

Company	Financial Strength Score
Microsoft Corporation	90.9
Apple Inc.	90.3
Amazon.com Inc.	90.1
Alphabet Inc.	84.2
Meta Platforms	83.8
Philip Morris International Inc.	80.9
Mastercard Inc.	80.2
Cisco Systems Inc.	80.1
Etsy Inc.	78.3
Intel Corporation	78.2

Source: Based on https://www.wsj.com/articles/top-companies-for-financial-strength-11618350537

organization's financial strengths and weaknesses is essential in formulating strategies. A firm's liquidity, leverage, working capital, profitability, asset utilization, cash flow, and equity can eliminate some strategies as being feasible alternatives. Financial factors often impact existing strategies and influence strategy implementation plans.

Finance and Accounting

According to James Van Horne, finance and accounting activities can be categorized into three decision areas: the investment decision, the financing decision, and the dividend decision.[9] The **investment decision**, also called **capital budgeting**, is the allocation and reallocation of capital and resources to projects, products, assets, and divisions of an organization. After strategies are formulated, capital budgeting decisions are required to successfully implement strategies. The **financing decision** determines the best capital structure for the firm and includes examining various methods by which the firm can raise capital (for example, by issuing stock, increasing debt, selling assets, or using a combination of these approaches). The financing decision must consider both short-term and long-term needs for working capital. Two crucial financial ratios that indicate whether a firm's financing decisions have been effective are the debt-to-equity ratio and the debt-to-total-assets ratio.

Dividend decisions concern issues such as the dollar amount per share to pay quarterly to stockholders, the stability of dividends paid over time, and the repurchase or issuance of stock. Dividend decisions determine the amount of funds that are retained in a firm compared with the amount paid out to stockholders. Three financial ratios that are helpful in evaluating a firm's dividend decisions are the earnings-per-share ratio, the dividends-per-share ratio, and the price-earnings ratio. The benefits of paying dividends to investors must be balanced against the benefits of internally retaining funds, and there is no set formula on how to balance this trade-off. Sometimes to appease shareholders, dividends are paid out (1) even when the firm has incurred a negative annual net income, (2) even when the firm has to obtain outside sources of capital to pay for the dividends, and (3) even when the funds were needed for reinvestment in the business. Reasons for this practice are as follows:

1. Paying cash dividends is customary for some firms. Failure to do so could be thought of as a stigma. A dividend change is a signal about the future.
2. Dividends represent a sales point for investment bankers. Some institutional investors can buy only dividend-paying stocks.
3. Shareholders often demand dividends, even in companies with great opportunities for reinvesting all available funds.
4. A myth exists that paying dividends will result in a higher stock price.

Financial Ratios

Financial ratio analysis is the most widely used method for determining an organization's strengths and weaknesses in the investment, financing, and dividend areas. Because the functional areas of business are so closely related, financial ratios can actually signal strengths or weaknesses anywhere up and down a firm's value chain from suppliers through production to distribution.

Financial ratios are computed from an organization's income statement and balance sheet. Computing financial ratios is like taking a photograph: The results reflect a situation at just one point in time. Comparing ratios over time and to industry averages is more likely to result in meaningful statistics that can be used to identify and evaluate strengths and weaknesses. Financial ratio trend analysis, illustrated in Figure 4-2, is a useful technique that incorporates both the time and industry average dimensions of financial ratios. Note that the dotted lines reveal projected ratios.

Financial ratios are equally applicable in for-profit and nonprofit organizations, but the ratios vary considerably across types of industries. Even though nonprofit organizations would not have return-on-investment or earnings-per-share ratios, they would routinely monitor many other special ratios. For example, a religious organization or place of worship would monitor the ratio of dollar contributions to the number of members, whereas a zoo would monitor dollar food sales to number of visitors. A university would monitor number of students divided by number

Current ratio

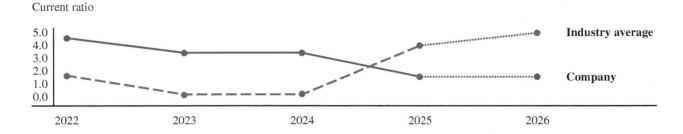

Profit margin

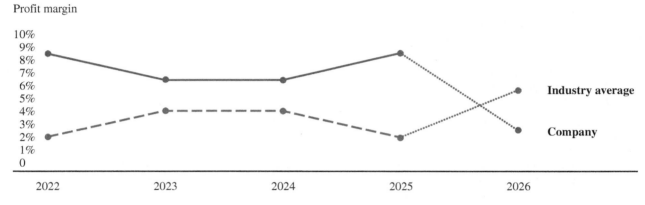

FIGURE 4-2

Financial Ratio Trend Analysis

of professors. Nonprofit organizations strive to be financially sound just as for-profit firms do and they need strategic planning just as much as for-profit firms.

Financial ratio analysis should be conducted on three separate fronts:

1. *How has each ratio changed over time?* This information provides a means of evaluating historical trends. Examine whether each ratio has been historically increasing, decreasing, or nearly constant. Analysts often calculate the percentage change in a ratio from 1 year to the next to assess historical financial performance on that dimension. Large percentage changes can be especially relevant, but be mindful that if base numbers are small, then large percentage changes can ensue more easily.

2. *How does each ratio compare with industry norms?* A firm's inventory turnover ratio may appear impressive at first glance but may pale when compared to industry standards or norms. Industries can differ dramatically on certain ratios. For example, grocery companies have a high inventory turnover, whereas automobile dealerships have a lower turnover. Therefore, comparison of a firm's ratios within its particular industry can be essential in determining strengths and weaknesses.

3. *How does each ratio compare with key competitors?* Often competition is more intense between several competitors in a given industry or location than across all rival firms in the industry. When this is true, financial ratio analysis should include comparison to those key competitors. For example, if a firm's profitability ratio is trending up over time and compares favorably to the industry average but is trending down relative to its leading competitor, there may be reason for concern.

Excellent free online and subscription (fee-based) resources for obtaining financial information about firms and industries are provided in Table 4-8. Some sources listed provide financial ratios. The free Excel template at www.strategyclub.com calculates both existing and projected financial ratios once students enter in relevant data.

Financial ratio analysis is not without some limitations. For example, financial ratios are based on accounting data, and firms differ in their treatment of items such as depreciation, inventory valuation, R&D expenditures, pension plan costs, mergers, and taxes. Also, seasonal factors

TABLE 4-8 Excellent Websites to Obtain Strategic Information (Including Financial Ratios) on Companies and Industries

1. Online Free Resources.
   a. *Form 10K* or *Annual Report*
   b. https://finance.yahoo.com
   c. www.hoovers.com
   d. https://globaledge.msu.edu/industries/
   e. www.morningstar.com

2. Online Subscription Resources (Likely Subscribed to by Your University Library)
   a. Mergent Online: www.mergentonline.com
      At this website, financial statements seem to be more complete than at other sites. You can also search for companies with the same SIC or NAICS code and then create a comparison financial ratio report. A number of different ratios can be used as comparison criteria to create a tailored report that can then be exported into a Microsoft Excel format. Alternatively, use the Competitors Tab in Mergent to build a list of companies and compare their ratios. Your college library likely subscribes to this service.
   b. Factiva: https://new.dowjones.com/products/factiva/
      At this website, first use the Companies & Markets tab to search for a company. Next, click "Reports" and choose the "Ratio Comparison Report" to get a company's ratios compared to industry averages. Your college library likely subscribes to this service.
   c. S&P NetAdvantage: https://www.standardandpoors.com/products-services/industry_surveys/en/us
      This website provides company and industry ratios and information in two sections of the database: (1) the Compustat Excel Analytics section of a particular company's information page and (2) the S&P Industry Surveys.
   d. Onesource: www.avention.com/OneSource
      This is a widely used source for financial ratio information. Search for a particular company and then click on the link for "Ratio Comparisons" on the left side of the company information page. The data in Onesource will compare your company against the industry, against the sector, and against the stock market as a whole.
   e. Yahoo Industry Center: https://biz.yahoo.com/ic/
      This is an excellent free resource that allows a user to browse industries by performance rankings, including return on equity, price-earnings ratio, market cap, price change, profit margin, price-to-book value, long-term debt, and more.

3. Hardcopy Reference Books for Financial Ratios in Most Libraries
   a. Robert Morris Associate's *Annual Statement Studies:* An excellent source of financial ratio information.
   b. Dun & Bradstreet's *Industry Norms & Key Business Ratios:* An excellent source of financial ratio information.

Source: Based on a variety of sources.

can influence comparative ratios. Therefore, conformity to industry composite ratios does not establish with certainty that a firm is performing normally or that it is well managed. Likewise, departures from industry averages do not always indicate that a firm is doing especially well or poorly. For example, a high inventory turnover ratio could indicate efficient inventory management and a strong working capital position, but it also could indicate a serious inventory shortage and a weak working capital position.

Another limitation of financial ratios in terms of including them as key internal factors in the upcoming IFE Matrix is that financial ratios are not actionable in terms of revealing potential strategies needed (i.e., because they generally are based on performance of the overall firm). For example, to include as a key internal factor that the firm's current ratio increased from 1.8 to 2.1 is not very actionable because the factor does not specify which current assets or current liabilities were most significant in contributing to the change. In contrast, a factor such as the firm's fragrance division's revenues increased 18 percent in Africa in 2022 would be considerably more actionable because more insight is provided as to actions needed to address the issue. Recall from the prior chapter the importance of factors being stated in actionable terms. The Actionable-Quantitative-Comparative-Divisional (AQCD) test discussed in the prior chapter for performing an external assessment is equally important in performing an internal assessment.

Table 4-9 provides a summary of essential financial ratios showing how each ratio is calculated and what each ratio measures. However, all the ratios are *not* significant for all industries and companies. For example, accounts receivable turnover and average collection period are not meaningful to a company that takes only cash receipts. As indicated in Table 4-9, main financial ratios can be classified into the following five types: liquidity (how is the firm's cash position), leverage (how is the firm's debt position), activity (how efficient are the firm's operations), profitability (how is the firm performing), and growth (is the firm meeting shareholders' expectations).

The website www.comparably.com gives great studies, articles, and comparative information for any publicly-held company as "compared" to the firm's major rivals. This website is

TABLE 4-9 A Summary of Essential Financial Ratios

Ratio	How Calculated	What It Measures
I. Liquidity Ratios		
Current Ratio	$\dfrac{\text{Current assets}}{\text{Current liabilities}}$	The extent to which a firm can meet its short-term obligations
Quick Ratio	$\dfrac{\text{Current assets minus inventory}}{\text{Current liabilities}}$	The extent to which a firm can meet its short-term obligations without relying on the sale of its inventories
II. Leverage Ratios		
Debt-to-Total-Assets Ratio	$\dfrac{\text{Total debt}}{\text{Total assets}}$	The percentage of total funds provided by creditors
Debt-to-Equity Ratio	$\dfrac{\text{Total debt}}{\text{Total stockholders' equity}}$	The percentage of total funds provided by creditors versus by owners
Long-Term Debt-to-Equity Ratio	$\dfrac{\text{Long-term debt}}{\text{Total stockholders' equity}}$	The balance between debt and equity in a firm's long-term capital structure
Times-Interest-Earned Ratio	$\dfrac{\text{Profits before interest and taxes}}{\text{Total interest charges}}$	The extent to which earnings can decline without the firm becoming unable to meet its annual interest costs
III. Activity Ratios		
Inventory Turnover	COGS/Inventory	Whether a firm holds excessive stocks of inventories and whether a firm is slowly selling its inventories compared to the industry average
Fixed Assets Turnover	$\dfrac{\text{Sales}}{\text{Fixed assets}}$	Sales productivity and plant and equipment utilization
Total Assets Turnover	$\dfrac{\text{Sales}}{\text{Total assets}}$	Whether a firm is generating a sufficient volume of business for the size of its asset investment
Accounts Receivable Turnover	Sales/Accounts receivable	The average length of time it takes a firm to collect credit sales (in percentage terms)
Average Collection Period	$\dfrac{\text{Accounts receivable}}{\text{Total credit sales/365 days}}$	The average length of time it takes a firm to collect on credit sales (in days)
IV. Profitability Ratios		
Gross Profit Margin	Gross profit/Sales	The total margin available to cover operating expenses and yield a profit
Operating Profit Margin	$\dfrac{\text{EBIT}}{\text{Sales}}$	Profitability without concern for taxes and interest
Net Profit Margin	$\dfrac{\text{Net income}}{\text{Sales}}$	After-tax profits per dollar of sales
Return on Total Assets (ROA)	$\dfrac{\text{Net income}}{\text{Total assets}}$	After-tax profits per dollar of assets; this ratio is also called *return on investment* (ROI)
Return on Stockholders' Equity (ROE)	$\dfrac{\text{Net Income}}{\text{Total stockholders' equity}}$	After-tax profits per dollar of stockholders' investment in the firm
Earnings per Share (EPS)	$\dfrac{\text{Net income}}{\text{Number of shares of common stock outstanding}}$	Earnings available to the owners of common stock
Price-Earnings Ratio	$\dfrac{\text{Market price per share}}{\text{Earnings per share}}$	Attractiveness of firm on equity markets
V. Growth Ratios		
Sales	$\dfrac{(\text{Sales 2023 - Sales 2022})}{\text{Sales 2022}}$	Firm's annual growth rate in sales
Net Income	$\dfrac{(\text{Net Income 2023 - Net Income 2022})}{\text{Net Income 2022}}$	Firm's annual growth rate in profits
Earnings per Share	$\dfrac{(\text{EPS 2023 - EPS 2022})}{\text{EPS 2022}}$	Firm's annual growth rate in EPS
Dividends per Share	$\dfrac{(\text{Div. per Share 2023-Div. per Share 2022})}{\text{Dividends Per Share 2022}}$	Firm's annual growth rate in dividends per share

COGS = cost of goods sold; EBIT = earnings before interest and taxes; Div. = dividends

outstanding for gathering internal strategy assessment information because it compares any firm to rival firms on diversity, culture, leadership, marketing, pricing, and numerous other variables.

Finance and Accounting Audit Checklist

Strengths and weaknesses in finance and accounting are often identified by answering the following types of questions:

1. Where is the firm financially strong and weak as indicated by financial ratio analysis?
2. Can the firm raise needed short-term capital?
3. Should the firm raise needed long-term capital through debt or equity?
4. Does the firm have sufficient working capital?
5. Are capital budgeting procedures effective?
6. Are dividend payout policies reasonable?
7. Does the firm have excellent relations with its investors and stockholders?
8. Are the firm's financial managers experienced and well trained?
9. Is the firm's debt situation excellent?

Financial analysis provides an excellent tool for identifying many strengths and weaknesses of the firm, but the numbers themselves generally do not reveal the source of issues, which could stem for example from marketing and promotional effectiveness, HRM and employee productivity, accounting errors, and so on. Therefore, carefully study your firm's *Form 10K* or *Annual Report* and other company documents, including quarterly reports, to uncover strengths and weaknesses within the functional areas. Finance and accounting strengths and weaknesses could relate to issues such as the firm's use of debt versus equity to raise capital, the firm's dividend policy, or the firm's acquisition versus organic growth practices.

Management Information Systems

4.5. Discuss management information systems (MIS) in terms of formulating strategies.

Information ties all business functions together and provides the basis for all managerial decisions. Information can represent a major source of competitive advantage or disadvantage and a major source of a firm's internal strength and weakness factors. A **management information system (MIS)** collects, codes, stores, synthesizes, and presents information in such a manner that it aids in operational and strategic decision-making. The heart of an information system is a database containing the kinds of records and data important to managers. If a business fails to manage information well, this is an internal weakness that needs fixing.

Business Analytics

Business analytics is a business technique that involves using software to mine huge volumes of data to help executives make decisions. Sometimes called *predictive analytics, machine learning,* or *data mining*, this procedure enables a researcher to assess and use the aggregate experience of an organization, which is a priceless strategic asset for a firm. The history of a firm's interaction with its customers, suppliers, distributors, employees, rival firms, and more can all be tapped with **data mining** to generate predictive models. Business analytics is similar to the actuarial methods used by insurance companies to rate customers by the chance of positive or negative outcomes. Every business is basically a risk management endeavor! Therefore, like insurance companies, all businesses can benefit from measuring, tracking, and computing the risk associated with hundreds of strategic and tactical decisions made every day.

Strategists use business analytics to provide a firm with proprietary business intelligence regarding, for example, which segment(s) of customers choose your firm versus those who defer, delay, or defect to a competitor and why. In addition to understanding consumer behavior better, which yields more effective and efficient marketing, business analytics also is being used to slash expenses by, for example, withholding retention offers from customers who are going to stay with the firm anyway or managing fraudulent transactions involving invoices, credit card purchases, tax returns, insurance claims, mobile phone calls, online ad clicks, and more. Business analytics can also reveal where competitors are weak so that marketing activities can be directly targeted to take advantage of resultant opportunities.

ETHICS CAPSULE 4

Unethical Hacking for Profit Increasing Fast[10]

Andrey_Popov/Shutterstock

Ransomware a decade ago was mainly where an individual's personal computer was hacked, their photos and files were encrypted, and they got them back for $100, but now, organized criminal groups are hacking big corporations and organizations demanding upwards of $10 million per incident. In Q3 2021 alone, the average ransomware payment was $139,739, which was up from $41,198 just 2 years before. The way cyber extortionists typically work is

they seize a firm's computer system online by installing malware and lock up the victim's computers with data-encrypting software. Therefore, whether at work or home, be careful never to download something suspicious to your desktop, anytime, anywhere.

The cyberattack in May 2021 on Colonial Pipeline took down the largest fuel pipeline in the United States. Other recent publicized incidents include Solarwinds, JBS, and Kaseya. Due to this external threat becoming so severe, companies can now purchase cyber insurance. About one-third of large U.S. firms now have this insurance. Unfortunately, hackers try to identify insured victims to get paid quicker. Cyber insurance premiums are rising about 20 percent annually, and insurers such as Vantage Group and Travelers are demanding greater and greater security measures be in place before they will insure a firm. Companies such as Dell Technologies, Hewlett-Packard, and Nutanix have increased the power (and price) of their antivirus software products and services.

[10]Reinhardt Krause, "The Extortion Economy," *Investor's Business Daily*, December 13, 2021, pp. A1, A10.

Business analytics enables a firm to learn from experience and to make current and future decisions based on prior information. Deriving robust predictive models from data mining to support hundreds of commonly occurring business decisions is the essence of learning from experience. The mathematical models and analysis of thousands, millions, or even billions of prior data points can reveal patterns of behavior for optimizing the deployment of resources and can dramatically enhance decision-making at all organizational levels and all stages of strategic management. Business analytics can identify and analyze patterns, but perhaps more importantly, they can reveal the likelihood of an event, and that information can be worth millions of dollars to companies, organizations, and governments.

In terms of cyberthreats, a recent *Wall Street Journal* article revealed what companies should be most concerned about and what they can do to mitigate the threat.[11] The biggest threat currently facing firms is that too many people in too many organizations have too much access to too much information not needed to do their particular job, whether it is access to sales data, patent information, or even material about the next new product being developed. Technical controls must be put in place in organizations to prevent employees from having broad access to company information and data because hackers from various countries and companies and lone wolves are increasingly gaining access to corporate files through employees and managers who unknowingly allow the access to seemingly honest "constituencies."

In November 2021, the computer systems of Robinhood Markets Inc. were hacked; about 5 million email addresses and another 2 million full names with information were stolen by the intruder, who demanded a ransom. Cybercriminals are targeting employees and customers of companies worldwide. The FBI reported that victims of phishing, vishing, and cybercrime in the United States lost about $54 million in 2020. As indicated in Ethics Capsule 4, ransomware attacks besiege Corporate America as unethical hackers engage in extortion and bribery for profit. Cybersecurity spending worldwide increased 13 percent in 2021 to nearly $175 billion and is expected to increase another 11 percent annually in both 2022 and 2023.[12]

The Internal Factor Evaluation (IFE) Matrix

4.6.   **Explain how to develop and use an Internal Factor Evaluation (IFE) Matrix.**

The internal topics discussed so far in this chapter provide a foundation for identifying strengths and weaknesses of a firm as they relate to a firm's current strategies, paying careful attention to strengths and weaknesses that are unique and lead to or hinder sustaining a competitive advantage. An internal assessment reveals key strengths and weaknesses confronting an organization;

this is vital information for managers in formulating strategies that capitalize on strengths and mitigate, overcome, and improve on weaknesses.

The Actionable-Quantitative-Comparative-Divisional (AQCD) Test

As discussed analogously in the prior chapter for external factors, when identifying and prioritizing key internal factors in strategic planning, make sure the factors selected meet the following four criteria to the extent possible:

1. Actionable (i.e., meaningful and helpful in ultimately deciding what actions or strategies a firm should consider pursuing);
2. Quantitative (i.e., include percentages, ratios, dollars, and numbers to the extent possible);
3. Comparative (i.e., reveals changes over time), and
4. Divisional (relates to the firm's products or regions (rather than consolidated) so inferences can be drawn regarding what products and regions are doing well or not).[13]

As mentioned in the prior chapter, factors that meet the four criteria pass what can be called the Actionable-Quantitative-Comparative-Divisional (AQCD) test, that is a measure of the quality of an internal factor. In addition to passing the AQCD test, make sure that internal factors are indeed internal (not external). Also, make sure the internal factors relate closely to the firm achieving its mission (strengths) or hindering its mission (weaknesses). Factors selected for inclusion in an internal assessment should be driven by the company's mission.

Regarding the AQCD criteria, strive to include all high-quality factors in an internal assessment for a firm. A high-quality factor will meet three or four of the AQCD criteria; a low-quality factor will meet two or fewer of the AQCD criteria. Engage in an engineering hunt for facts to make sure as many factors as possible pass the AQCD test. It is important to state internal factors to the extent possible in actionable, quantitative, comparative, and divisional terms. Vagueness in stating factors must be avoided because vagueness gives little guidance for assigning weights or ratings in developing an IFE Matrix.

High quality and low-quality internal factors (hypothetical) for Exxon Mobil Corporation are given to further exemplify this important concept:

	Ask Yourself Is the Factor...			
	Actionable	Quantitative	Comparative	Divisional
A High-Quality Internal Factor				
Exxon's natural gas segment sales grew 14% in 2022 in Europe compared with 8% in 2021.	yes	yes	yes	yes
A Low-Quality Internal Factor				
Exxon's price earnings ratio in 2022 was 14.4.	no	yes	no	no

Steps in Developing an IFE Matrix

An internal strategic management audit includes development of an **Internal Factor Evaluation (IFE) Matrix**. This tool for strategy formulation weighs and rates major strengths and weaknesses in the functional areas of a business, providing a total weighted score indicating the overall strength of a firm's internal position. The IFE Matrix is an evaluation of the effectiveness of the firm's current strategies, not taking into account opportunities and threats. The purpose of the IFE Matrix and the internal assessment as a whole is to determine how effective the firm's current strategies are based on the firm's strengths and weaknesses.

Strategists analyze the firm's response to key strengths and weaknesses (the ratings in step 3) with respect to how well the firm's strategies capitalize on the particular strengths or improve on the weaknesses. The weights in step 2 are based on how important the respective factor is to being successful in the industry. The resulting total weighted score (step 5) indicates the internal effectiveness of the current strategies. The IFE Matrix total weighted score is suggestive of whether a continuation of strategy is warranted (scores above 2.5) or a change in strategy is needed (scores below 2.5). Used in conjunction with the EFE Matrix and CPM discussed in Chapter 3, the IFE Matrix provides the input needed to perform strategy-matching analyses described in Chapter 6.

An IFE Matrix can be developed in five steps:

Step 1: Develop a Full and Narrow List of Key Internal Factors

Conduct research about the focal company using the resources listed in Table 4-8. Perhaps use a brainstorming session to compile and organize information into two data sets, strengths and weaknesses, developing a full list of perhaps 50 strengths and weaknesses. Be sure to include factors from management, marketing, finance, accounting, and MIS that are of strategic importance. Then, narrow your data sets down to 20 critical internal factors that include specifically 10 strengths and 10 weaknesses. (Note: We use 10 and 10 because organizations commonly use this breakdown, and the template at www.strategyclub.com uses 10 and 10). List strengths first and then weaknesses.

Firms reduce the full list of 50 factors down to 20 factors usually by asking respondents to rank each factor according to importance (1 = most important to 50 = least important), then summing the rankings from respondents, and finally using the 20 factors with the lowest cumulative score. An important point here is that companies (and students) never should include just the first 20 factors that come to mind. For example, a student recently included as a weakness in their IFE Matrix for a college that "there are feral cats on campus;" but most of the time that factor will not rise to the level of importance to be included in the matrix. Instead, conduct research to identify internal factors that relate to the university's vision, mission, strategies, and competitive advantage(s).

When determining respective factors to include in an IFE Matrix and when assigning weights and ratings, focus on a narrow industry perspective. Within the narrow industry, consider the vision and mission of the firm and the firm's current strategies (i.e., when selecting factors and assigning weights and ratings). For example, for McDonald's, the industry is fast-food restaurants, rather than restaurants in general, and for Porsche, the industry is luxury sports cars, and not simply automobiles. This narrow industry perspective is important, as indicated in Table 4-10.

TABLE 4-10 Guidelines for Developing an IFE Matrix

1. Use the Narrow (Not Broad) Industry in Which the Firm Competes

Example: Burger King (owned by Restaurant Brands International) competes in the fast-food industry (as opposed to the more general restaurant industry). Therefore, for Burger King, if including a weakness regarding the lack of healthy options on their menu, this factor should likely receive a low weight because healthy menu options are not as vital to the fast-food industry, whose customer base mostly desire quick service, good taste, cheap prices, and filling food. Similarly, Burger King's weakness related to low-quality meats should not receive a high weight either because quality meats are not that important in the fast-food industry; customers simply are not willing to pay for them. Similarly, Burger King's strength of providing low-priced coffee would receive a high weight if the analyst views coffee as being especially important for success in the fast-food industry. If, however, the analyst views coffee not to be especially important for success in the fast-food industry, then this strength of Burger King should receive a relatively low weight.

2. State Factors so They Pass the AQCD Test

Example: A firm's revenues may have decreased 15 percent from 1 year to the next, but stated in this manner, this "weakness" is not actionable because it does not reveal the reason, or reasons, why revenues declined; the reason(s) could range from competition driving down prices to raw materials being unavailable for one product or division of the firm. Nonactionable factors could lead managers astray if they make false assumptions regarding what to do about the factor. Therefore, state the "revenue decline factor" perhaps as follows: Revenues in the chocolate segment of the firm declined 21 percent in the most recent quarter because of factory recall problems. Now the factor passes the AQCD test in providing insightful, relevant, useful, information for formulating strategies.

Step 2: Assign Weights to Key Internal Factors

In developing an IFE Matrix, assign a weight that ranges from 0.01 (not important) to 1.0 (all-important) for each factor. The weight assigned to a given factor indicates the relative importance of the factor for being successful in the firm's industry relative to other factors included in the IFE Matrix. For example, a factor receiving a weight of 0.04 is 100 percent more important for success in the industry than a factor receiving a weight of 0.02. Regardless of whether a key factor for a particular firm is a strength or weakness, factors considered to have the greatest effect on organizational performance of all firms in a specific industry should be assigned the highest weights. The sum of all weights must equal 1.0. Do not attempt to even weights out to total 0.50 for strengths and 0.50 for weaknesses. Weights are industry-based and not company-based. List strengths from highest weight to lowest weight; do the same for weaknesses.

Step 3: Assign Ratings to Key Internal Factors

In developing an IFE Matrix, assign a rating between 4 and 1 to each key internal factor to indicate how effectively (or ineffectively) the firm's strategies are responding to the strength or weakness, where 4 = the response is superior, 3 = the response is above average, 2 = the response is average, and 1 = the response is poor. Even though both strengths and weaknesses can receive a rating of 4, 3, 2, or 1 at any time, generally there should be a compelling reason to assign a rating of 4 or 3 to a weakness; but, if the firm has excellent strategies in place to resolve or mitigate the weakness, then the firm's response can be considered superior and a 4 is possible. It is more common for a firm to be responding in a superior fashion to strengths; competitive advantages are built on strengths, and strategies that result in strengths are generally excellent.

Responding well to a weakness may not lead to a competitive advantage, whereas turning a strength into a distinctive competency could yield a competitive advantage. Ratings are based on the effectiveness of a firm's strategies in capitalizing on strengths or improving weaknesses. Ratings are company-based and not industry-based.

Assignment of numerical values down the rating column in an IFE Matrix should be with consideration that companies carve out niches in industries that enable them to gain and sustain competitive advantages through effective strategies. These niches are most often based on some unique strength that yields prosperity amid rivals.

Step 4: Obtain Weighted Scores

Along each row in an IFE Matrix, multiply the factor's weight by its rating to determine a weighted score for each factor.

Step 5: Obtain Total Weighted Score

Sum the weighted scores to determine the total weighted score for the organization. Regardless of how many factors are included in an IFE Matrix, the total weighted score can range from a high of 4.0 to a low of 1.0, with the average score being 2.5. Total weighted scores well below 2.5 characterize organizations that are weak internally, implying that new strategies are likely needed, including perhaps a new direction, new vision, or mission. Total weighted scores well above 2.5 indicate a strong internal position, whereby a continuation of current strategies may be prudent. In addition to the total weighted score, also pay careful attention to the weights and ratings of the top two or three strengths and top two or three weaknesses for possible continuations or changes in strategy. (Note: The IE Matrix presented in Chapter 6 focuses on matching EFE and IFE total weighted scores in formulating strategies.)

An Example IFE Matrix

An example IFE Matrix is provided in Table 4-11 for a retail computer store. The table reveals that the two most important factors to be successful in the retail computer store business (as indicated by the highest weighted factors) are Strength 1: Revenues from repair/service in the store, and Weakness 1: Location of store negatively impacted by new Highway 34. Note that among the strengths, the store's strategies are not responding well (rating is 2) to two factors: Average customer purchase increased from $97 to $128 and Debt-to-total-assets ratio declined to 34%, as indicated by the assigned 2 ratings. Regarding the store's weaknesses, note that the owner's strategies are responding superiorly to two factors: (1) Location of store negatively

TABLE 4-11 Sample IFE Matrix for a Retail Computer Store

Key Internal Factors	Weight	Rating	Weighted Score
Strengths			
1. Revenues from repair/service in the store up 16%.	0.15	3	0.45
2. Employee morale is excellent.	0.10	3	0.30
3. Average customer purchase increased from $97 to $128.	0.07	2	0.14
4. In-store promotions resulted in 20% increase in sales.	0.05	3	0.15
5. In-store technical support personnel have MIS college degrees.	0.05	4	0.20
6. Inventory turnover increased from 5.8 to 6.7.	0.05	3	0.15
7. Debt-to-total-assets ratio declined to 34%.	0.03	2	0.06
8. Newspaper advertising expenditures increased 10%.	0.02	3	0.06
9. Revenues per employee up 19%.	0.02	3	0.06
Weaknesses			
1. Location of store negatively impacted by new Highway 34.	0.15	4	0.60
2. Revenues from software segment of store down 12%.	0.10	2	0.20
3. Often customers wait 15 minutes to check out.	0.05	1	0.05
4. Store has no website.	0.05	2	0.10
5. Revenues from service segment down 8%.	0.04	1	0.04
6. Supplier on-time delivery increased to 2.4 days.	0.03	1	0.03
7. Carpet and paint in store somewhat in disrepair.	0.02	3	0.06
8. Bathroom in store needs refurbishing.	0.02	4	0.08
Total	**1.00**		**2.73**

impacted by new Highway 34, as indicated by the rating of 4 (because plans are underway to perhaps relocate the store), and (2) Bathroom needs refurbishing, as indicated by the rating of 4 (because the bathroom is in the process of being remodeled). Note that the store's IFE Matrix overall contains numerous dollars, numbers, percentages, and ratios, rather than vague statements; this is excellent. This store receives a 2.73 total weighted score, which on a 1- to 4-scale, indicates some success, but there is room for improvement in store operations, strategies, policies, and procedures.

Coupled with the EFE Matrix, the IFE Matrix provides important information for strategy formulation. For example, this retail computer store might want to hire another checkout person and repair its carpet and paint. Also, the store may want to increase advertising for its repair services because that is a relatively significant (weight 0.15) factor to being successful in this business.

In multidivisional firms, each autonomous division or strategic business unit should construct their own IFE Matrix (and their own EFE Matrix). Divisional matrices then can be integrated to develop an overall corporate IFE Matrix. Be as divisional as possible when developing a corporate IFE Matrix. Also, in developing an IFE Matrix, do not allow more than 30 percent of the key factors to be financial ratios. Financial ratios are generally the result of many factors, so it is difficult to know what particular strategies should be considered based on financial ratios. For example, a firm would have no insight on whether to sell in Brazil or South Africa to take advantage of a high corporate ROI ratio.

An actual IFE Matrix is provided in Table 4-12 for Shell Corporation. Note in Table 4-12 the most important internal factor for success in the oil and gas industry relates in fact to oil and gas becoming a frowned-on commodity on which Shell and similar companies highly depend. Note that Shell's key internal factors are listed from high weight (most important) to low weight (least important) in the matrix. As indicated by the total weighted score of 2.50, Shell's performance at capitalizing on strengths and improving on weaknesses is only average, although there is room for improvement, especially on the solar, wind, and hydrogen factor that received a Rating of 1.

TABLE 4-12 An Actual IFE Matrix for Shell Corporation

Strengths	Weight	Rating	Weighted Score
1. Shell's Oil Products Segment generates more revenue than all other segments combined but there was a huge drop in relative revenues in this segment in 2020 compared to the other segments.	0.12	3	0.36
2. Shell is investing around $900 million annually in renewables. A few notable accomplishments, in the UK, 900 thousand homes are supplied with natural gas and smart home technology mostly in European homes.	0.07	2	0.14
3. Shell's Integrated Gas, Renewables, & Energy Solutions segment generates the second most revenue than all other segments with the best profit margin of all divisions at over 20%.	0.06	3	0.18
4. Shell is in the process of transforming its business more toward biofuels, hydrogen charging for electric automobiles, and focusing increasingly on solar and wind technology. This is a slow process for Shell though as the firm has a stated goal of increasing biofuels and hydrogen in transportation from 3% to 10% by 2030.	0.06	1	0.06
5. LNG Canada is a huge Shell natural gas project under construction off the west coast of British Columbia, Canada, but 10 years away from completion. Shell owns 40% of this project.	0.05	4	0.20
6. Shell is attempting to shift its resources to becoming a net zero emissions firm with a target by 2050 of reaching that goal. In fact, in 2021, Shell introduced its Powering Progress initiative to accelerate the transition to a net zero emission business.	0.05	3	0.15
7. Shell operates chemical plants worldwide and supplied 1,000 industrial customers with over 15 million tons of petrochemicals in 2020.	0.04	4	0.16
8. Shell focuses on safety with Goal Zero, meaning zero harm to its people or the environment.	0.03	3	0.09
9. By 2030, Shell aims to provide renewable electricity to 50 million households and offer 2.5 million electric charging ports for automobiles	0.03	2	0.06
10. There are more women than men on Shell's Board of Directors.	0.01	4	0.04

IMPLICATIONS FOR STRATEGISTS

Figure 4-3 illustrates that to gain and sustain competitive advantages, a firm must formulate strategies that capitalize on internal strengths and continually improve on internal weaknesses. Firms must nurture and build on competitive advantages embedded largely within the list of strengths included in an IFE Matrix. Coupled with the vision or mission and external audit, the internal audit must be performed methodically and carefully because survival of the firm could hinge on the strategic plan that ensues from these assessments. Do not let assignment of weights and ratings become based on mere guessing, emotion, and opinion; use the sources of information mentioned in this chapter and others to extract actionable, quantitative, comparative, and divisional factors for inclusion in matrices. Use the AQCD test as a guide for developing effective, useful strength and weakness factors.

The Process of Performing an Internal Audit

The process of performing an **internal audit** closely parallels the process of performing an external audit. Representative managers and employees throughout the firm need to be involved in determining a firm's strengths and weaknesses. The internal audit requires gathering, assimilating, and prioritizing information about the firm's management, marketing, finance, accounting, and MIS operations to reveal the firm's most important strengths and most severe weaknesses.

Compared to the external audit, the process of performing an internal audit provides more opportunity for participants to understand how their jobs, departments, and divisions fit into the whole organization. This is a great benefit because managers and employees perform better when they understand how their work affects other areas and activities of the firm. For example, when marketing and manufacturing managers jointly discuss issues related to internal strengths and weaknesses, they gain a better appreciation of the issues, problems, concerns, and needs of all the functional areas. Thus, performing an internal audit is an excellent vehicle or forum for improving the process of communication in an organization.

William King believes a task force of managers from different units of the organization, supported by staff, should be charged with determining the 20 most important strengths and weaknesses that should influence the future of the firm. According to King,

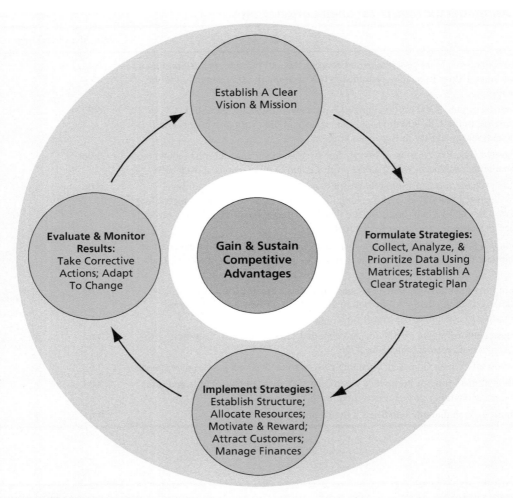

FIGURE 4-3

How to Gain and Sustain Competitive Advantages

The development of conclusions on the 20 most important organizational strengths and weaknesses can be, as any experienced manager knows, a difficult task, when it involves managers representing various organizational interests and points of view. Developing a 20-page list of strengths and weaknesses could be accomplished relatively easily, but a list of the 20 most important ones involves significant analysis and negotiation. This is true because of the judgments that are required and the impact that such a list will inevitably have as it is used in the formulation, implementation, and evaluation of strategies.[14]

Strategic planning is most successful when managers and employees from all functional areas work together to provide ideas and information. Financial managers, for example, may need to restrict the number of feasible options available to operations managers, or R&D managers may develop products for which marketing managers need to set higher objectives.

A key to organizational success is effective coordination and understanding among managers from all functional business areas. Through involvement in performing an internal strategic management audit, managers from different departments and divisions of the firm come to understand the nature and effect of decisions in other functional business areas in their firm. Knowledge of these relationships is critical for effectively establishing objectives and strategies. Financial ratio analysis, for example, exemplifies the complexity of relationships among the functional areas of business. A declining ROI or profit margin ratio could, for example, be the result of ineffective marketing, poor management policies, R&D errors, or a weak MIS.

Strategists should follow the guidelines presented in this chapter and throughout this text to help assure that their firm is heading in the right direction for the right reasons and rewarding the right people for doing the right things, in the right places.

IMPLICATIONS FOR STUDENTS

To obtain the most recent management, marketing, and financial information about your case company, read the firm's most recent quarterly report; the narrative that accompanies quarterly reports is excellent for revealing what a company is doing and the most recent financial results. Use these reports to obtain comparative information for developing an IFE Matrix.

Gaining and sustaining competitive advantage is the essence or purpose of strategic planning. In the internal portion of your case analysis, emphasize how and why your internal strengths and weaknesses can both be leveraged to gain competitive advantage and overcome competitive disadvantage, in light of the direction you are taking the firm. Maintain your project's upbeat, insightful, and forward-thinking demeanor during the internal assessment, rather than being mundane, descriptive, and vague. Focus on how your firm's resources, capabilities, structure, and strategies, with your recommended improvements, can lead the firm to prosperity.

Although the numbers must provide the basis for your analysis and must be accurate and reasonable, do not bore a live audience or class with overreliance on numbers. In contrast, throughout your presentation or written analysis, refer to your recommendations, explaining how your plan of action will improve the firm's weaknesses and capitalize on strengths in light of anticipated competitor countermoves. Keep your audience's attention, interest, and suspense, rather than reading to them or defining ratios for them.

The strategic planning template at www.strategyclub.com is widely used in businesses and among students to develop a company or organization's IFE Matrix. Conduct research regarding your company, its industry, and competitors as discussed in this chapter and compile and assimilate your major strengths and weaknesses in an IFE Matrix using the template. Note the first two end-of-Chapter 4 exercises ask you to get familiar with the process of using the template both for developing financial ratios and preparing an IFE Matrix for the McDonald's Cohesion Case.

Template Considerations Regarding Financial Statements and Financial Ratios

The process for entering data into the IFE Matrix is the same as described in detail in Chapter 3 under Template Considerations, so here let's move onto discussing the template as a tool for developing financial statements and ratios.

Note along the bottom row of the strategic planning template at www.strategyclub.com there is an icon "Financial Ratios" and also an icon "Projected Financial Ratios." The template will calculate these ratios and give you the percentage change from 1 year to the next. However, as you know, ratios are calculated based on financial statements, so it is important in preparing a comprehensive strategic plan using the template to convert your company's existing financial statements into the template format. This is easy to do and is explained here. Converting existing statements into the template formatted statements will enable the template to calculate all your projected financial ratios based on your projected financial statements, which will be developed after you decide what the firm needs to do going forward and how much capital will be needed.

Plan to use the strategic planning template provided at the www.strategyclub.com website because it allows you to efficiently calculate both existing and projected financial ratios. Follow the guidelines given because this will save you immense time in preparing a comprehensive strategic planning project.

1. Enter your company's financial statements into the template's standard format for an income statement and balance sheet using the Part II tab. Note the template statements go left to right, so enter the oldest year on the far left, and then in the column to the far right, enter the most current year. The template will let you enter the dates in reverse order, but don't because all percentage change and ratios are generated assuming the data was entered in oldest (left) to most recent (right). It can be tricky because some companies' actual statements may be entered going in the reverse order. The template is designed for financial data to be entered left to right because this leads well into the projected statements, all flowing left to right from oldest to most current year.

2. Data entry should be entered only on the Part II tab; the other tabs are protected so you will not accidently delete formulas. So, pull up your company's latest financial statements from www.finance.yahoo.com or from your company's Form 10K and, even though the template standard rows do not match perfectly with your actual statements, convert your actual financial statements to the template format, keeping major rows on Part II such as revenues, tax, plant, and property & equipment identical in the template to the actual row in your company's statements. After entering in the data on Part II, click on the financial statements tab at the bottom of Excel to ensure your major lines such as net income, total assets, total liabilities, and total equity are the same as on the company's reported statements. The ideal place to make any adjustments (return to Part II) on the income statement is with the nonrecurring events line item and the ideal place on the balance sheet is with the "other" line items such as "other current assets" and "other long-term-assets;" this will help ensure that after you make any adjustments, the total assets on your balance sheet will equal the total assets on the firm's balance sheet.

3. Regarding converting your company's balance sheets into template format, be mindful that a balance sheet needs to balance, so make it balance. Use the "other" line items described in point 2 to ensure your current assets, total assets, current liabilities, total liabilities, and total equity match the firm's respective totals. For example, the template only has two line items for current liabilities, accounts payable, and other current liabilities. If the firm you are studying reports $10,000 for total current liabilities and has four entries under current liabilities, all you need to do is simply enter in the entry your firm used for accounts payable (assume this was $2,000) and then simply enter in the remainder or $8,000 into "other current liabilities," making your total current liabilities match the firm's total current liabilities of $10,000. It is that easy!

4. Once you have finished entering in your data into Part II, click on the financial statements tab and check the major line items to ensure they match your firm's statements. Also check to ensure the statements balance. If you have a mistake, return to Part II and

make the necessary adjustments. Once the statements are correct, return to the financial statements tab in Excel and select the entire statement with your mouse, copy and paste your financial statements from the template now into Word or PowerPoint as you gradually during the semester build a .docx comprehensive strategic plan for your case company. It is best to use the paste special feature and decline the option to paste a link. You could also create a small screen shot of the financial statements and paste this picture into Word or PowerPoint. It may seem like a waste of time to enter the financial data into the template format when you could simply cut and paste the statements from the company's Annual

Report, but the extra time spent to enter the data into the template format will produce financial ratios automatically and guide you to quickly producing projected income statements, balance sheets, and projected ratios, thus saving you tremendous time.

5. Once you have your existing financial statements entered into the template format, and your balance sheet balances as needed, click on the lower right financial ratios tab on the template screen. There you will see all the ratios that were automatically calculated year-over-year. Some of this financial ratio info might represent strengths or weaknesses in your IFE Matrix. Transfer the financial ratios into Word or PowerPoint in same manner described for the financial statements.

Chapter Summary

Management, marketing, finance and accounting, and MIS represent the core operations of most businesses and the sources of competitive advantages. A strategic management audit of a firm's internal operations is vital to organizational health. Many companies still prefer to be judged solely on their bottom-line performance. However, it is essential that strategists identify and evaluate internal strengths and weaknesses to effectively formulate and choose among alternative strategies. The IFE Matrix, coupled with the CPM and the EFE Matrix in Chapter 3, as well as clear statements of vision and mission in Chapter 2, provides the basic information needed to successfully formulate competitive strategies. The process of performing an internal audit represents an opportunity for managers and employees throughout the organization to participate in determining the future of the firm. Involvement in the process can energize and mobilize managers and employees.

Understanding both external and internal factors and relationships between them (see SWOT analysis in Chapter 6) is the key to effective strategy formulation. Because both external and internal factors continually change, strategists seek to identify and take advantage of positive changes and buffer against negative changes in a continuing effort to gain and sustain a firm's competitive advantage. This is the essence and challenge of strategic management, and often survival of the firm hinges on this work. Adherence to the AQCD test regarding internal (and external) factors will enable excellent matching matrices to be constructed (in Chapter 6).

Key Terms and Concepts

activity ratios (p. 112)
business analytics (p. 113)
capacity utilization (p. 102)
capital budgeting (p. 109)
channel of distribution (p. 107)
collaborative machines (p. 103)
controlling (p. 102)
data mining (p. 113)
distinctive competencies (p. 99)
dividend decisions (p. 109)
empirical indicators (p. 99)
financial ratio analysis (p. 109)
financing decision (p. 109)
growth ratios (p. 112)
human resource management (HRM) (p. 102)
internal audit (p. 119)
Internal Factor Evaluation (IFE) Matrix (p. 115)
investment decision (p. 109)

leverage ratios (p. 112)
liquidity ratios (p. 112)
management (p. 100)
management information system (MIS) (p. 113)
marketing (p. 105)
marketing research (p. 105)
motivating (p. 101)
organizational culture (p. 103)
organizing (p. 100)
planning (p. 100)
production/operations (p. 102)
profitability ratios (p. 112)
promotion (p. 107)
resource-based view (RBV) (p. 99)
synergy (p. 100)
target market analysis (p. 105)
test marketing (p. 106)

Issues for Review and Discussion

4-1. Explain why strengths are more important than weaknesses in strategic planning.

4-2. What is test marketing? Explain when and why a firm may want to engage in test marketing.

4-3. Do strengths always receive higher weights than weaknesses? Explain why.

4-4. Do strengths always receive higher ratings than weaknesses? Explain why.

4-5. Should assignment of weights down an IFE Matrix weight column be contingent on intensity of industry rivalry? Discuss.

4-6. Explain why it is so important to focus on a firm's narrow industry rather than its broader industry in developing an IFE Matrix.

4-7. Explain the concept of factors being actionable.

4-8. Explain why companies develop a list of 50 (to 100) internal factors before reducing the list to 20 to include in an IFE Matrix?

4-9. Describe two ways how a firm can determine from a list of 50 (to 100) internal factors the 20 most important factors to include in an IFE Matrix.

4-10. Discuss strategic implications of a firm receiving a total weighted IFE Matrix score of 1.5 versus 3.5.

4-11. If IFE Matrix strength factor 4 receives a rating of 4, what does that signify for the analyst? If weakness factor 4 receives a rating of 4, what does that signify?

4-12. The primary means for gaining and sustaining competitive advantages for most companies are shifting downstream. Explain and discuss this statement.

4-13. In analyzing big data, there is a shift from focusing largely on aggregates or averages to also focusing on outliers because outliers often reveal (predict) critical innovations, trends, disruptions, and revolutions on the horizon. Explain and discuss this statement.

4-14. What are some limitations of financial ratio analysis?

4-15. Does RBV theory determine diversification targets? Explain and discuss.

4-16. True or False: Personal selling is typically more useful for industrial goods companies, whereas advertising is typically more effective for consumer goods companies. Explain.

4-17. What are collaborative machines?

4-18. Identify some excellent online resources for finding financial ratio information.

4-19. How might elements of the marketing mix, particularly price and place, vary for common household goods compared with luxury products?

4-20. Is a capacity utilization rate of 50 percent good? Why?

4-21. Explain why *communication* may be the most important word in management. What do you think is the most important word in marketing? In finance? In accounting?

4-22. Discuss how the nature of marketing has changed in the last few years.

4-23. Explain why it is best not to have more than 30 percent of the factors in an IFE Matrix be financial ratios.

4-24. List three firms you are familiar with and give a distinctive competency for each firm.

4-25. Give some key reasons why it is essential to prioritize strengths and weaknesses.

4-26. Why may it be easier in performing an internal assessment to develop a list of 80 strengths and weaknesses than to decide on the top 20 to use in formulating strategies?

4-27. Think of an organization with which you are familiar. List three resources of that entity that are empirical indicators.

4-28. Think of an organization with which you are familiar. Rate that entity's organizational culture on the 15 example dimensions listed in Table 4-4.

4-29. If you and a partner were going to visit a foreign country where you have never been before, how much planning would you do ahead of time? What benefit would you expect that planning to provide?

4-30. Even though planning is considered the foundation of management, why do you think it is commonly the task that managers neglect most?

4-31. Are you more organized than the person sitting beside you in class? If not, what problems could that present in terms of your performance and rank in the class? How analogous is this situation to rival companies?

4-32. List the three ways that financial ratios should be compared or used. Which of the three comparisons do you feel is most important? Why?

4-33. In an IFE Matrix, would it be advantageous to list your strengths, and then your weaknesses, in order of decreasing weight? Why?

4-34. In an IFE Matrix, a critic may say there is no significant difference between a weight of 0.08 and 0.06. How would you respond? What is the mathematical difference?

4-35. Why do many firms consistently pay out dividends?

4-36. What is marketing promotion? Name several example forms of promotion commonly used by marketers.

4-37. Explain why prioritizing the relative importance of strengths and weaknesses in an IFE Matrix is an important strategic management activity.

4-38. How can delegation of authority contribute to effective strategic management?

4-39. Explain how you would motivate managers and employees to implement a major new strategy.

4-40. Why do you think production and operations managers often are not directly involved in activities for strategy formulation? Why can this be a major organizational weakness?

4-41. Give two examples of HRM strengths and two examples of HRM weaknesses of an organization with which you are familiar.

4-42. Define, compare, and contrast weights versus ratings in an EFE Matrix versus an IFE Matrix.

4-43. If a firm has zero debt in its capital structure, is that always an organizational strength? Why or why not?

4-44. After conducting an internal audit, a firm discovers a total of 100 strengths and 100 weaknesses. What procedures then could be used to determine the most important of these? Why is it important to reduce the total number of essential factors?

4-45. Why is it important for companies to conduct marketing research? What type of information might they discover from marketing research?

4-46. What are 10 activities that comprise HRM?

4-47. Explain the difference between *data* and *information* in terms of each being useful to strategists.

4-48. What are the most important characteristics of an effective management information system?

4-49. Do you agree or disagree with RBV theorists that internal resources are more important for a firm than external factors in achieving and sustaining competitive advantage? Explain your position.

4-50. What makes a resource valuable to a company?

4-51. List five financial ratios that may be used by your university to monitor operations.

4-52. What is the most severe cyberthreat facing companies today, and how can firms best mitigate against this threat?

Writing Assignments

4-53. List three ways that financial ratios should be compared or used. Which of the three comparisons do you feel is most important? Why?

4-54. Would you ever pay out dividends when your firm's annual net profit is negative? Why or why not? What effect could this have on a firm's strategies?

ASSURANCE-OF-LEARNING EXERCISES

SET 1: STRATEGIC PLANNING FOR MCDONALD'S

EXERCISE 4A

Perform a Financial Ratio Analysis for McDonald's

Ken Wolter/Alamy Stock Photo

Purpose

Financial ratio analysis is one of the best techniques for identifying and evaluating internal strengths and weaknesses. Potential investors and current shareholders look closely at firms' financial ratios, making detailed comparisons to industry averages and to previous periods of time. Financial ratio analyses provide vital input information for developing an IFE Matrix.

Note along the bottom row of the strategic planning template at www.strategyclub.com there is an icon Financial Ratios and also an icon Projected Financial Ratios. The template will thus calculate these ratios and give you the percentage change from 1 year to the next. However, as you know, ratios are calculated based on financial statements, so it is important in preparing a comprehensive strategic plan using the template to convert your company's existing financial statements into the template format. This is well worth the effort and is explained near the end of this chapter.

Instructions

Step 1   Using the resources listed in Table 4-8, find as many of McDonald's financial ratios as possible. Record your sources. Report your research to your classmates and your professor.

Step 2   Given the Template Considerations for Financial Ratios provided near the end of this chapter, try to convert McDonald's actual (most recent) financial statements into the template format, and get the template to then calculate associated financial ratios and changes year-over-year.

EXERCISE 4B

Develop an IFE Matrix for McDonald's

Purpose

This exercise will give you experience in developing an IFE Matrix. Identifying and prioritizing factors to include in an IFE Matrix fosters communication among functional and divisional managers. Preparing an IFE Matrix allows managers to articulate their concerns and thoughts regarding the business condition of the firm. This results in an improved collective understanding of the business.

Instructions

Step 1   Get familiar with the template at the www.strategyclub.com website. You can click on IFE Matrix and use the template to save immense time in completing this exercise. Be mindful, however, that the template does not itself access the internet to find key strengths and weaknesses. You need to do that and then enter that information into the template. The template is widely used by companies (and students) in preparing an IFE Matrix.

Step 2   Join with two other individuals to form a three-person team. Develop a team IFE Matrix for McDonald's. Use information from Exercise 1B from Chapter 1.

Step 3   Compare your team's IFE Matrix to other teams' IFE matrices. Discuss any major differences.

Step 4   What strategies do you think would allow McDonald's to capitalize on its major strengths? What strategies would allow McDonald's to improve on its major weaknesses?

SET 2: STRATEGIC PLANNING FOR MY UNIVERSITY

EXERCISE 4C
Construct an IFE Matrix for Your College or University

Purpose
This exercise gives you the opportunity to evaluate your university's major strengths and weaknesses. As will become clearer in the next chapter, an organization's strategies are largely based on striving to take advantage of strengths and improve on weaknesses.

Instructions
Step 1   Join with two other individuals to form a three-person team. Develop a team IFE Matrix for your university.

Step 2   What was your team's total weighted score?

Step 3   Compare your team's IFE Matrix to other teams' IFE matrices. Discuss any major differences.

Step 4   What strategies do you think would allow your university to capitalize on its major strengths? What strategies would allow your university to improve on its major weaknesses?

SET 3: STRATEGIC PLANNING FOR MYSELF

EXERCISE 4D
Construct an IFE Matrix for Yourself

Purpose
This exercise gives you the opportunity to evaluate your own personal strengths and weaknesses. As will become clearer in the next chapter, an organization's strategies are largely based on striving to take advantage of strengths and improve on weaknesses. Similarly, in planning for your career, you should formulate and implement personal strategies based on capitalizing on your strengths and improving on your weaknesses.

Instructions
Step 1   Develop an IFE Matrix for yourself. As you assign weights, consider the relative importance of each factor for success in your desired career.

Step 2   Compare your total weighted score to the average score of 2.5.

Step 3   What strategies might enable you to capitalize on your major strengths? What strategies might help you improve on your major weaknesses?

SET 4: INDIVIDUAL VERSUS GROUP STRATEGIC PLANNING

EXERCISE 4E
What Internal Functional Areas Are Most Important to Examine in Strategic Planning?

Purpose
A prioritized list of internal factors is needed for effective strategic planning. Often, the process entails all managers individually ranking the factors identified, from 1 (most important) to 20 (least important). Prioritization is absolutely essential in strategic planning because no organization can do everything that would benefit the firm; tough choices between good alternatives have to be made.

Internal functional areas that yield strengths and weaknesses can be divided into five broad categories or areas: (1) management, (2) marketing, (3) finance, (4) accounting, and (5) MIS. For some companies or organizations at various times, some areas are more important than others. This exercise reveals the authors' ranking of the relative importance of five functional areas for inclusion in a strategic planning internal assessment.

The purpose of this exercise is to examine more closely the functional areas of business. In addition, the purpose of this exercise is to examine whether individual decision-making is better than group decision-making. Academic research suggests that groups make better decisions than individuals about 80 percent of the time.

Instructions

Rank the five internal areas as to their relative importance (1 = most important, 5 = least important) in doing strategic planning. First, rank the areas as an individual. Then, rank the areas as a group of three. Thus, determine what person(s) and what group(s) can come closest to the expert ranking. This exercise enables examination of the relative effectiveness of individual versus group decision-making in strategic planning.

Steps

1. Fill in Column 1 in Table 4-13 to reveal your individual ranking of the relative importance of the five areas (1 = most important, 2 = next most important, etc.). For example, if you feel management is the third-most important functional area in doing strategic planning, then enter a 3 in Table 4-13 in Column 1 beside Management.
2. Fill in Column 2 in Table 4-13 to reveal your group's ranking of the relative importance of the five areas (1 = most important, 2 = next most important, etc.).
3. Fill in Column 3 in Table 4-13 to reveal the expert's ranking of the relative importance of the five functional areas.
4. Fill in Column 4 in Table 4-13 with the absolute difference between Column 1 and Column 3 to reveal how well you performed as an individual in this exercise. (Note: Absolute difference disregards negative numbers.)
5. Fill in Column 5 in Table 4-13 with the absolute difference between Column 2 and Column 3 to reveal how well your group performed in this exercise.
6. Sum Column 4. Sum Column 5.
7. Compare the Column 4 sum with the Column 5 sum. If your Column 4 sum is less than your Column 5 sum, then you performed better as an individual than as a group. Normally, group decision-making is superior to individual decision-making, so if you did better than your group, you did excellent.
8. The Individual Winner(s): The individual(s) with the lowest Column 4 sum is the WINNER.
9. The Group Winners(s): The group(s) with the lowest Column 5 score is the WINNER.

TABLE 4-13 Internal Functional Area Analysis: Comparing Individual Versus Group Decision-Making

Internal Functional Areas	Column 1	Column 2	Column 3	Column 4	Column 5
1. Management					
2. Marketing					
3. Finance					
4. Accounting					
5. MIS					
Sums					

MINI-CASE ON A SCHOOL OF BUSINESS

HOW IMPORTANT ARE UNCOMMON RATIOS FOR A SCHOOL OF BUSINESS' SUCCESS?

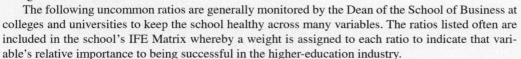
Goodluz/Shutterstock

In performing an internal strategic management assessment, there are two broad categories of important ratios: (1) Common ratios calculated across industries, such as all the ratios mentioned in this chapter, and (2) Uncommon ratios that relate to a particular industry. For example, in the airline industry, there are dozens of important ratios not mentioned in this chapter, just as there are many important uncommon ratios regularly monitored by hotel and motel firms, banks, hospitals, and even colleges and universities.

The following uncommon ratios are generally monitored by the Dean of the School of Business at colleges and universities to keep the school healthy across many variables. The ratios listed often are included in the school's IFE Matrix whereby a weight is assigned to each ratio to indicate that variable's relative importance to being successful in the higher-education industry.

Business schools in nearly all colleges and universities have a strategic plan that includes an internal assessment, including a ratio analysis. Business schools compete for resources with other schools such as Nursing and Education at the institution. Rank the ratios listed from 1 (most important) to 15 (least important) in terms of their relative importance to being successful in managing a School of Business. Justify your rankings.

1. Number of online classes versus on-campus classes
2. Number of students per number of faculty
3. Number of male students per total number of students
4. Number of female students per total number of students
5. Number of minority students per total number of students
6. Number of international students per total number of students
7. Number of out-of-state students per total number of students
8. Number of students majoring in business per total number of students
9. Number of MBA students this year versus last year
10. Number of BBA students this year versus last year
11. Number of accounting majors per number of BBA students
12. Number of management majors per number of BBA students
13. Number of finance majors per number of BBA students
14. Number of marketing majors per number of BBA students
15. Number of economics majors per number of BBA students

Web Resources

1. See Table 4-8 for excellent websites for obtaining strategic information about companies and industries.
2. Fred David gives a video overview of Chapter 4 in the prior edition, but much info is still applicable to the 18th edition.

a. First half of Chapter 4: https://www.youtube.com/watch?v=sPNyN1ZkT4U
b. Second half of Chapter 4: https://www.youtube.com/watch?v=fzMFvGGhSds

Current Readings

Baer, Michael D., Emma Frank, Fadel Matta, Margaret Luciano, and Ned Wellman, "Undertrusted, Overtrusted, or Just Right? The Fairness of (In)Congruence Between Trust Wanted and Trust Received," *Academy of Management Journal* 64, no. 1 (February 2021): 180–206.

Cardador, M. Teresa, Patrick L. Hill, and Arghavan Salles, "Unpacking the Status-Leveling Burden for Women in Male-Dominated Occupations," *Administrative Science Quarterly*, August 20, 2021, p. 1.

David, Fred R., Steven Creek, and Forest R. David, "What Is the Key to Effective SWOT Analysis? Including AQCD Factors," *SAM Advanced Management Journal* 84, no. 1 (2020): 25–36.

Davis, Gerald F., and Theodore DeWitt, "Organization Theory and the Resource-Based View of the Firm: The Great Divide," *Journal of Management* 47, no. 7 (September 2021): 1684–97.

Dlugos, Kathryn, and J. R. Keller. "Turned Down and Taking Off? Rejection and Turnover in Internal Talent Markets," *Academy of Management Journal* 64, no. 1 (February 2021): 63–85.

Felten, Edward, Manav Raj, and Robert Seamans, "Occupational, Industry, and Geographic Exposure to Artificial Intelligence: A Novel Dataset and its Potential Uses," *Strategic Management Journal* 42, no. 12 (December 2021): 2195–217.

Freeman, R. Edward, Sergiy D. Dmytriyev, and Robert A. Phillips, "Stakeholder Theory and the Resource-Based View of the Firm," *Journal of Management* 47, no. 7 (September 2021): 1757–70.

Kalnins, Arturs, and Michele Williams, "The Geography of Female Small Business Survivorship: Examining the Roles of Proportional Representation and Stakeholders," *Strategic Management Journal* 42, no. 7 (July 2021): 1247–74.

Li, Jiangyan, Wei Shi, Brian L. Connelly, Xiwei Yi, and Xin Qin. "CEO Awards and Financial Misconduct," *Journal of Management* 48, no. 2 (February 2022): 380–409.

Miller, Danny, and Isabelle Le Breton-Miller, "Paradoxical Resource Trajectories: When Strength Leads to Weakness and Weakness Leads to Strength," *Journal of Management* 47, no. 7 (September 2021): 1899–914.

Naumovska, Ivana, Edward Zajac, and Peggy Lee, "Strength and Weakness in Numbers? Unpacking the Role of Prevalence in the Diffusion of Reverse Mergers," *Academy of Management Journal* 64, no. 2 (April 2021): 409–34.

Rahman, Mahabubur, M. Ángeles Rodríguez-Serrano, and Mathew Hughes, "Does Advertising Productivity Affect Organizational Performance? Impact of Market Conditions," *British Journal of Management* 32, no. 4 (October 2021): 1359–83.

Richard, Orlando C., Maria Del Carmen Triana, and Mingxiang Li, "The Effects of Racial Diversity Congruence Between Upper Management and Lower Management on Firm Productivity," *Academy of Management Journal* 64, no. 5 (October 2021): 1355–82.

Wang, Yaopeng, Hisham Farag, and Wasim Ahmad, "Corporate Culture and Innovation: A Tale from an Emerging Market," *British Journal of Management* 32, no. 4 (October 2021): 1121–40.

Yan, Shipeng, Juan Almandoz, and Fabrizio Ferraro, "The Impact of Logic (In)Compatibility: Green Investing, State Policy, and Corporate Environmental Performance," *Administrative Science Quarterly* 66, no. 4 (December 2021): 903–44.

Zhu, David H., and James D. Westphal, "Structural Power, Corporate Strategy, and Performance," *Strategic Management Journal* 42, no. 3 (March 2021): 624–51.

Endnotes

1. On page 98.
2. Robert Grant, "The Resource-Based Theory of Competitive Advantage: Implications for Strategy Formulation," *California Management Review* (Spring 1991): 116.
3. On page 101.
4. Adam Smith, *The Wealth of Nations* (New York: Modern Library, 1937), 3–4.
5. Peter Drucker, *Management Tasks, Responsibilities, and Practice* (New York: Harper & Row, 1973), 463.
6. Allison Prang, "Sales of Robotics Increase with U.S. Labor Shortage," *Wall Street Journal*, November 12, 2021, p. B4.
7. Edgar Schein, *Organizational Culture and Leadership* (San Francisco: Jossey-Bass, 1985), 9.
8. Quoted in Robert Waterman, Jr., "The Renewal Factor," *BusinessWeek*, September 14, 1987, p. 108.
9. J. Van Horne, *Financial Management and Policy* (Upper Saddle River, NJ: Prentice-Hall, 1974): 10.
10. On page 114.
11. Stephen Schmidt and Scott Smith, "Where the Cyberthreats Are," *Wall Street Journal*, December 19, 2017, p. R1.
12. Reinhardt Krause, "The Extortion Economy," *Investor's Business Daily*, December 13, 2021, pp. A1, A10.
13. Fred R. David, Steven A. Creek, and Forest R. David, "What Is the Key to Effective SWOT Analysis? Including AQCD Factors," *SAM Advanced Management Journal* 84, no. 1 (2020): 25–36.
14. William King, "Integrating Strength–Weakness Analysis into Strategic Planning," *Journal of Business Research* 11: 475–87.

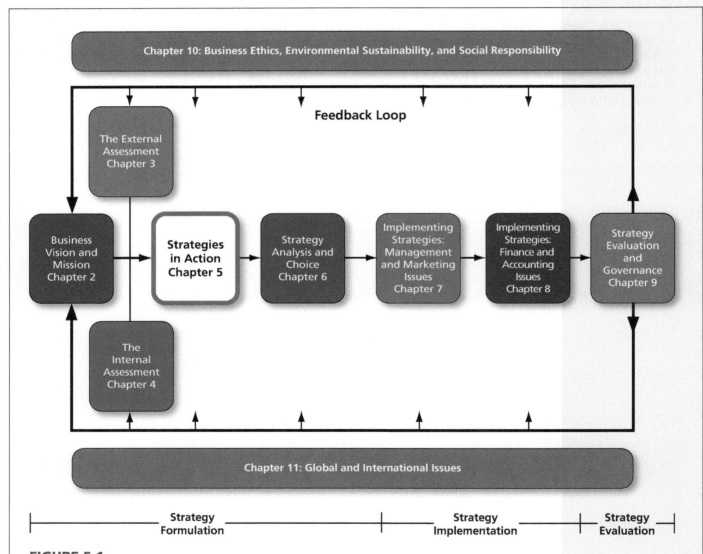

FIGURE 5-1

The Comprehensive, Integrative Strategic Management Model

Source: Fred R. David, "How Companies Define Their Mission," *Long Range Planning* 22, no. 1 (February 1989): 91. See also Anik Ratnaningsih, Nadjadji Anwar, Patdono Suwignjo, and Putu Artama Wiguna, "Balance Scorecard of David's Strategic Modeling at Industrial Business for National Construction Contractor of Indonesia," *Journal of Mathematics and Technology* no. 4 (October 2010): 20. See also, Meredith E. David, Fred R. David, and Forest R. David, "Closing the Gap Between Graduates' Skills and Employers' Requirements: A Focus on the Strategic Management Capstone Business Course," *Administrative Sciences* 11, no. 1 (2021): 10–26.

Strategies in Action

LEARNING OBJECTIVES

After studying this chapter, you should be able to do the following:

5.1. Identify and discuss 5 characteristics and 10 benefits of clear objectives.

5.2. Define and give an example of 11 types of strategies.

5.3. Identify and discuss the three types of integration strategies.

5.4. Give specific guidelines for when market penetration, market development, and product development are especially effective strategies.

5.5. Explain when diversification is an effective business strategy.

5.6. List guidelines for when retrenchment, divestiture, and liquidation are especially effective strategies.

5.7. Explain value chain analysis and benchmarking in strategic management.

5.8. Identify and discuss Porter's two generic strategies: cost leadership and differentiation.

5.9. Compare and contrast when companies should build, borrow, or buy as key means for achieving strategies.

5.10. Discuss first-mover advantages and disadvantages.

5.11. Explain how strategic planning differs in for-profit, not-for-profit, and small firms.

ASSURANCE-OF-LEARNING EXERCISES

The following exercises are found at the end of this chapter:

SET 1:	Strategic Planning for McDonald's
EXERCISE 5A:	Develop Hypothetical McDonald's Corporation Strategies
EXERCISE 5B:	Should McDonald's Build, Borrow, or Buy in 2023–2026?
SET 2:	Strategic Planning for My University
EXERCISE 5C:	Develop Alternative Strategies for Your University
SET 3:	Strategic Planning for Myself
EXERCISE 5D:	The Key to Personal Strategic Planning: Simultaneously Build and Borrow
SET 4:	Individual Versus Group Strategic Planning
EXERCISE 5E:	What Is the Best Mix of Strategies for McDonald's Corporation?

Hundreds of companies have embraced strategic planning in their quest for higher revenues and profits. Kent Nelson, former chair and CEO of UPS, explains why his company created a new strategic planning department: "Because we're making bigger bets on investments in technology, we can't afford to spend a whole lot of money in one direction and then find out five years later it was the wrong direction."[1] As illustrated in Figure 5-1, long-term objectives are needed before strategies can be generated, evaluated, and selected.

This chapter brings strategic management to life with many contemporary examples. Different types of strategies are defined and exemplified, including Michael Porter's generic strategies: cost leadership and differentiation. Guidelines are presented for determining when each strategy is most appropriate to pursue. The integral importance of value chain analysis and benchmarking in strategic planning is revealed. An overview of strategic management in nonprofit organizations, governmental agencies, and small firms is provided. As showcased, CEOs Tim Cook and Jeff Gennette are two of the best strategists on the planet; Cook has led Apple to be the most admired company in the world. Read to see why Cook and Gennette are outstanding.

Long-Term Objectives

5.1. Identify and discuss 5 characteristics and 10 benefits of clear objectives.

Long-term objectives represent the results expected from pursuing certain strategies. Strategies represent the actions to be taken to accomplish long-term objectives. The time frame for objectives and strategies should be consistent, usually from 2 to 5 years. Without long-term objectives, an organization would drift aimlessly toward some unknown end or become too focused on short-term fads and stray away from the firm's mission.

It is hard to imagine an organization or an individual being successful without clear objectives. You probably have worked hard the last few years striving to achieve an objective to graduate with a business degree. Success rarely occurs by accident; rather, it is the result of hard work directed toward achieving certain objectives.

EXEMPLARY **STRATEGISTS** SHOWCASED

Tim Cook and Jeff Gennette, CEO of Apple Inc. and Macy's, Inc. Respectively[2]

There are only a few LGBTQ CEOs in the *Fortune* 500, but two that are exemplary strategists are Tim Cook of Apple and Jeff Gennette of Macy's. Under Gennette's leadership, Macy's sales increased from $17 billion in 2020 to $24 billion in 2021 as the 164-year-old retailer is performing great even amid the COVID-19 pandemic.

The editor of *Businessweek*, Megan Murphy, recently asked the CEO of Apple, Tim Cook, what he thought his legacy at Apple would be. Cook responded: "To be honest I don't think about it; I think about doing stuff." He went on to explain how and why Apple's founder, Steve Jobs, rather than himself, should be the person revered forever as Apple's supreme strategist extraordinaire. Cook told Megan that Apple in the past, present, and future is all about its founder Jobs. Cook explained that Jobs' "DNA" or "ethos" is and always will be Apple's "Constitution" or guiding set of principles. According to Cook, Jobs' ethos ingrained into Apple forever include the following items (paraphrased):

1. Pay acute attention to detail.
2. Keep it simple and genuinely care.
3. Focus on the user and user experience.
4. Focus on building the best.
5. Follow the motto "good isn't good enough;" every product and process must be, as Jobs often said, "insanely great."
6. Apple should own the proprietary technology it uses to control its own quality of product and user experience.

dpa picture alliance/Alamy Photo

7. Walk away and be honest with yourself when you do something wrong.
8. Never get married to your position or pride.
9. Invest for the long-term rather than striving to be the first to market with a product.

[2]Based on Megan Murphy, "Tim Cook," *Bloomberg Businessweek*, June 19, 2017, pp. 52–56. Also based on Phil Wahba, "The Conversation with Jeff Gennette," *Fortune*, December/January 2022, pp. 18–22.

Characteristics and Benefits of Objectives

Objectives should be quantitative, understandable, challenging, compatible (consistent vertically and horizontally in a chain of command), and obtainable. Each objective should also be associated with a timeline. Objectives are commonly stated in terms such as *growth in assets, growth in sales, profitability, market share, degree and nature of diversification, degree and nature of vertical integration, earnings per share*, and *social responsibility*. (Note: Do not emulate many *Annual Reports* that print really vague objectives for the firm, such as "to grow sales profitably" and "to improve return on invested capital." Such statements are useless in strategic planning.)

Clearly established objectives offer many benefits. They provide direction, allow synergy, assist in evaluation, establish priorities, reduce uncertainty, minimize conflicts, stimulate exertion, and aid in both the allocation of resources and the design of jobs. Objectives provide a basis for consistent decision-making by managers whose values and attitudes differ. Objectives serve as standards by which individuals, groups, departments, divisions, and entire organizations can be evaluated.

Table 5-1 and Table 5-2 summarize the desired characteristics and benefits, respectively, of clear objectives.

TABLE 5-1 Five Characteristics of Objectives

1. Quantitative: measurable
2. Understandable: clear
3. Challenging: achievable
4. Compatible: consistent vertically and horizontally in a chain of command
5. Obtainable: realistic

TABLE 5-2 10 Benefits of Having Clear Objectives

1. Provide direction by revealing expectations.
2. Allow synergy.
3. Assist in evaluation by serving as standards.
4. Establish priorities.
5. Reduce uncertainty.
6. Minimize conflicts.
7. Stimulate exertion.
8. Aid in allocation of resources.
9. Aid in design of jobs.
10. Provide basis for consistent decision making.

Financial Versus Strategic Objectives

Two types of objectives are especially common in organizations: financial and strategic objectives. **Financial objectives** include those associated with growth in revenues, growth in earnings, higher dividends, larger profit margins, greater return on investment, higher earnings per share, a rising stock price, improved cash flow, and all other objectives relating to the financial position of the firm, whereas **strategic objectives** focus on goals for obtaining a competitive advantage, including factors such as a larger market share, quicker on-time delivery than rivals, lower costs than rivals, higher product quality than rivals, wider geographic coverage than rivals, achieving technological leadership, and consistently getting new or improved products to market ahead of rivals.

Often there is a trade-off between financial and strategic objectives such that crucial decisions need to be made. For example, a firm can do certain activities to maximize short-term financial objectives that would harm long-term strategic objectives. To improve financial position in the short run through higher prices may, for example, jeopardize long-term market share. The dangers associated with trading off long-term strategic objectives with near-term bottom-line performance are especially severe if competitors relentlessly pursue increased market share at the expense of short-term profitability. Amazon, for example, operated for decades without concern for profits and instead concentrated on gaining market share. There are other trade-offs between financial and strategic objectives, related to riskiness of actions, concern for business ethics, the need to preserve the natural environment, and social responsibility issues. Both financial and strategic objectives should include annual and long-term performance targets. Ultimately, the best way to sustain competitive advantage is to relentlessly pursue strategic objectives that strengthen a firm's business position over rivals.

Avoid Managing by Crisis, Hope, Extrapolation, and Mystery (CHEM)

Derek Bok, former President of Harvard University, once said, "If you think education is expensive, try ignorance." The idea behind this saying also applies to establishing objectives because strategists should avoid managing by crisis, hope, extrapolation, and mystery (CHEM).

- *Managing by Crisis*—Based on the belief that the true measure of a really good strategist is the ability to solve problems. Because there are plenty of crises and problems to go around for every person and organization, strategists ought to bring their time and creative energy to bear on solving the most pressing problems of the day. Managing by crisis is actually a form of reacting, letting events dictate the *what* and *when* of management decisions.
- *Managing by Hope*—Based on the fact that the future is laden with great uncertainty and that if we try and do not succeed, then we hope our second (or third) attempt will succeed. Decisions are predicated on the hope that they will work and that good times are just around the corner, especially if luck and good fortune are on our side.
- *Managing by Extrapolation*—Adheres to the principle "If it ain't broke, don't fix it." The idea is to keep on doing the same things in the same ways because things are going well.
- *Managing by Mystery*—Built on the idea that there is no general plan for which way to go and what to do; just do the best you can to accomplish what you think should be done. In short, "Do your own thing, the best way you know how" (sometimes referred to as *the mystery approach to decision-making* because subordinates are left to figure out what is happening and why).[3]

Types of Strategies

5.2. Define and give an example of 11 types of strategies.

Defined and exemplified in Table 5-3, alternative strategies that an enterprise could pursue can be categorized into 11 actions: forward integration, backward integration, horizontal integration, market penetration, market development, product development, related diversification, unrelated diversification, retrenchment, divestiture, and liquidation. Each alternative strategy has countless variations. For example, market penetration can include adding salespersons, increasing advertising expenditures, couponing, and using similar actions to increase market share in a given geographic area. Note for a particular company the example strategy is specific; be specific to the extent possible in all aspects of strategic planning.

Most organizations simultaneously pursue a combination of two or more strategies, but a **combination strategy** can be exceptionally risky if carried too far. No organization can afford to pursue all the strategies that might benefit the firm; priorities must be established. Difficult decisions must be made. Organizations, like individuals, have limited resources. Both organizations and individuals must choose among alternative strategies and avoid excessive indebtedness.

Strategic planning thus involves choices that risk resources, and trade-offs that sacrifice opportunity. In other words, if you have a strategy to go north in the United States, then you must buy snowshoes and warm jackets (spend resources) and forgo the opportunity of faster population growth in southern states. You cannot have a strategy to go north and then take a step east, south, or west "just to be on the safe side." Strategy is all about what to do and what *not* to do.

Firms spend resources and focus on a finite number of opportunities in pursuing strategies to achieve an uncertain outcome in the future. Strategic planning is much more than a roll of the dice; it is an educated wager based on predictions and hypotheses that are continually tested and refined by knowledge, research, experience, and learning. Survival of the firm often hinges on an excellent strategic plan.[4]

Organizations cannot excel in multiple different strategic pursuits because resources and talents get spread thin and competitors gain advantage. In large, diversified companies, a combination strategy is commonly employed when different divisions pursue different strategies. Organizations struggling to survive may simultaneously employ a combination of several defensive strategies, such as divestiture and retrenchment.

TABLE 5-3 Alternative Strategies Defined and Recent Examples Given

Strategy	Definition	Example
Forward Integration	Gaining ownership or increased control over distributors or retailers	Amazon is adding 500 new distribution centers globally to speed up its deliveries
Backward Integration	Seeking ownership or increased control over suppliers	Ford is joining with GlobalFoundries, Inc. to produce needed semiconductors
Horizontal Integration	Seeking ownership or increased control over competitors	Skillsoft Corp. acquired rival U.S.-based education technology firm Codecademy
Market Penetration	Seeking increased market share for present products in present markets through greater marketing	Cryptocurrency firm Crypto.com ran its first Super Bowl commercial in 2022
Market Development	Introducing present products into a new geographic area	Costco is adding 20 new stores annually; low-cost grocer Lidl is building 50 new stores
Product Development	Seeking increased sales by improving present products or developing new ones	Dollar Tree, owner of Family Dollar, is expanding its offerings of fresh produce
Related Diversification	Adding new but related products	Fenway Sports Group that owns the Boston Red Sox just acquired the Pittsburgh Penguins hockey team
Unrelated Diversification	Adding new, unrelated products	The security firm ADT just acquired Sunpro Solar for $825 million
Retrenchment	Regrouping through cost and asset reduction to reverse declining sales and profit	General Mills laid off 1,400 employees in 2021
Divestiture	Selling a division or part of an organization	AT&T divested its online advertising segment, Xandra, to Microsoft
Liquidation	Selling all of a company's assets, in parts, for their tangible worth	Mom-and-pop restaurant DEF Inc. sold all its assets and ceased doing business

Levels of Strategies

Developing strategy is not just a task for top executives. Middle- and lower-level managers also must be involved in the strategic planning process to the extent possible. In large firms, there are actually four levels of strategies: corporate, divisional, functional, and operational—as illustrated in Figure 5-2. However, in small firms, there are three levels of strategies: company, functional, and operational.

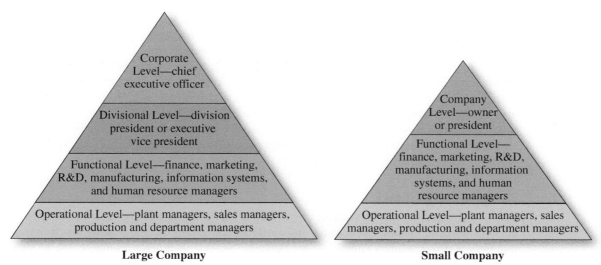

Large Company

Small Company

FIGURE 5-2

Levels of Strategies with Persons Most Responsible

The persons primarily responsible for having effective strategies at the various levels include the CEO at the corporate level; the president of segments at the divisional level; the chief finance officer (CFO), chief information officer (CIO), human resource manager (HRM), chief marketing officer (CMO), and other executives at the functional level, and the plant manager, regional sales manager, and so on at the operational level. It is important that all managers at all levels participate and understand the firm's strategic plan to help ensure coordination, facilitation, and commitment, while avoiding inconsistency, inefficiency, and miscommunication.

Long-term objectives are needed at the corporate, divisional, functional, and operational levels of an organization. They are an important measure of managerial performance. Bonuses or merit pay for managers today should be based to a greater extent on long-term objectives and strategies. An example framework for relating objectives to performance evaluations is provided in Table 5-4. A particular organization could tailor these guidelines to meet their own needs, but incentives should be attached to both long-term and annual objectives.

TABLE 5-4 Varying Performance Measures by Organizational Level

Organizational Level	Basis for Annual Bonus or Merit Pay
Corporate: overall firm	75% based on long-term objectives
	25% based on annual objectives
Divisional (such as by product or region)	50% based on long-term objectives
	50% based on annual objectives
Functional (such as marketing or finance)	25% based on long-term objectives
	75% based on annual objectives
Operational (such as manufacturing plants)	25% based on long-term objectives
	75% based on annual objectives

Integration Strategies

5.3. Identify and discuss the three types of integration strategies.

Forward integration and backward integration are sometimes collectively referred to as **vertical integration**. Vertical integration strategies allow a firm to gain control over distributors or suppliers, whereas **horizontal integration** refers to gaining ownership or control over competitors. Vertical and horizontal actions by firms are broadly referred to as **integration strategies**.

Historically, vertical integration strategies have been difficult to implement because of the firm operating in businesses out of its core competency and because large fixed costs are generally associated with such strategies. For example, if Coke wished to vertically integrate, it could acquire sugar farms to gain control over its suppliers and open its own brick-and-mortar stores to gain control of distributors. Both would be excessively costly and divert Coke from what it does best: producing beverage products. Although the risk of depending on suppliers and distributors may be high, owning these businesses is often associated with even greater risks. Viable options to vertical integration are joint ventures and strategic alliances discussed later in the chapter. Opportunity costs associated with the resources used for vertical integration usually could be more effectively deployed to other endeavors.

Forward Integration

Forward integration involves gaining ownership or increased control over distributors or retailers as a means of moving closer to the end customer and cutting out the middleman. Increasing numbers of manufacturers (suppliers) are pursuing forward integration to market the products they produce. For example, Nike sells millions of shoes and shirts in a variety of retail stores ranging from Foot Locker to JCPenney, but the company is rapidly boosting its direct-to-consumer business, bypassing, and in some cases infuriating, retail stores. Nike's forward-integration strategy has hundreds of retail stores upset.

Target is engaging in forward integration by building four large distribution centers in the US in order to move its inventory management and distribution in-house rather than being outsourced. This new strategy will increase Target's distribution warehouses to over 50 total located in about 25 states. Target is also building ten new sortation centers nationwide to help fulfill online orders more quickly. In another forward integration move, the U.K.-based food delivery company called Deliveroo PLC has begun building and operating pizza parlors. The new restaurants are called Pizza Paradiso, and the first one was located in London.

In another forward integration move, Roku, Inc. the nation's largest television streaming service, is now developing more than 50 original shows of its own. Roku wants to better monetize its 155 million customers who watch the Roku Channel for on average 3.5 hours per day. Roku's strategy has evolved over recent years from just selling streaming devices, to also selling advertisements, to additionally developing and marketing its own television shows and movies.

Forward integration is an increasingly popular strategy among U.S.-based retail pharmacy companies. CVS Health recently announced that for the first time the company is actively working with "speed and urgency" to establish physician-staffed primary-care practices inside their stores. Walgreens is also seeking to rebrand itself as a health-care provider by attaching doctors' offices to hundreds of its drugstores; Walgreens paid $5.2 billion for VillageMD to accomplish this strategy.

An effective means of implementing forward integration is **franchising**. Approximately 2,000 companies in about 50 different industries in the United States use franchising to distribute their products or services. Businesses can expand rapidly by franchising because costs and opportunities are spread among many individuals. Total sales by franchises in the United States exceed $1 trillion annually. The following six guidelines indicate when forward integration may be an especially effective strategy.[5]

1. An organization's present distributors are especially expensive, unreliable, or incapable of meeting the firm's distribution needs.
2. The availability of quality distributors is so limited a rival could potentially sign an exclusive contract, thus locking down a competitive advantage.
3. An organization competes in an industry that is growing and is expected to continue to grow markedly.
4. An organization has both the capital and human resources needed to manage the new business of distributing its own products.
5. The advantages of stable production are particularly high; this is a consideration because an organization can increase the predictability of the demand for its output through forward integration.
6. Present distributors or retailers have high-profit margins; this situation suggests that a company could profitably distribute its own products and price them more competitively by integrating forward.

Backward Integration

Backward integration is a strategy of seeking ownership or increased control of a firm's suppliers. This strategy can be especially appropriate when a firm's current suppliers are unreliable, too costly, or cannot meet the firm's needs. An excellent example of backward integration is occurring in the U.S. steel-production business where companies such as Nucor, Cleveland-Cliffs, and Steel Dynamics are aggressively acquiring scrap businesses. Record high prices for steel and unreliability of supply chains has spurred this acquisition spree. For example, Cleveland-Cliffs just acquired Ferrous Processing that operates 22 scrap sites in the U.S. and Canada.

Similarly, Aluminum companies such as Norsk Hydro ASSA, Novelis Inc, and Canada's Matalo are aggressively trying to secure scrap metal and are building factories to process the metal as securing sufficient supplies of raw material has become a major problem. This backward integration strategy in the aluminum industry is evidenced for example by the new Norsk Hydro plant in Cassopollis, Michigan, that annually now produces 120,000 metric tons of new aluminum from scrap metal.

Some industries are reducing their historical pursuit of backward integration; this practice is called **de-integration**. Instead of owning their suppliers, companies negotiate with outside suppliers. Ford and Chrysler buy more than half of their component parts from outside suppliers such as TRW, Eaton, General Electric (GE), and Johnson Controls. This makes sense in industries that have global sources of supply. Today, companies shop around, play one seller against another, and go with the best deal. Global competition is also spurring firms to reduce their number of suppliers and to demand higher levels of service and quality from those they keep. Although traditionally relying on many suppliers to ensure uninterrupted supplies and low prices, many U.S. firms now are following the lead of Japanese firms, which have far fewer suppliers and closer, long-term relationships with those few. "Keeping track of so many suppliers is onerous," said Mark Shimelonis, formerly of Xerox.

American Eagle Outfitters (AEO), the large apparel retailer, just acquired one of its suppliers, the digital fulfillment company Quiet Logistics, to take better control over its supply chain. Retailers such as AEO are struggling to get goods into their stores. Quiet Logistics has eight fulfillment centers in six cities where workers and robots fulfill digital orders for shipping apparel. AEO's digital sales account for 35 percent of all their sales and that percentage is increasing rapidly.

Home Depot and other mass retailers have recently begun chartering their own oceangoing container ships to move goods from overseas. This strategy could be considered backward integration aimed at reducing reliance on suppliers' transportation logistics. Home Depot is also working with suppliers by introducing alternative products to keep their shelves full for customers to have broad selections.

In another backward integration move, Ford and General Motors (GM) are entering the semiconductor business because of unreliable suppliers. Ford is establishing ties with GlobalFoundries, while GM is forging ties with Qualcomm and NXP Semiconductors NV. Ford plans to eventually bring chip development in-house, designing its own chips. Relying on suppliers in distant lands that are subject to local lockdowns, closing, and restrictions has companies in numerous industries considering backward integration as a necessary strategy to pursue.

Seven guidelines for when backward integration may be an especially effective strategy are:[6]

1. An organization's present suppliers are especially expensive, unreliable, or incapable of meeting the firm's needs for parts, components, assemblies, or raw materials.
2. The number of suppliers is small and the number of competitors is large.
3. An organization competes in an industry that is growing rapidly.
4. An organization has both capital and human resources to manage the new business of supplying its own raw materials.
5. The advantages of stable prices of raw materials are of utmost importance.
6. Present suppliers have high-profit margins, which suggests that the business of supplying products or services in a given industry may be a worthwhile venture.
7. Whenever various resources may be needed quickly.

Horizontal Integration

Horizontal integration is a strategy aimed at gaining control over a firm's competitors; this is arguably the most common growth strategy. Thousands of mergers, acquisitions, and takeovers among competitors are consummated annually and most aim for increased economies of scale, enhanced transfer of resources and competencies, reduced competition, and fewer price wars. Kenneth Davidson makes the following observation about horizontal integration:

> The trend towards horizontal integration seems to reflect strategists' misgivings about their ability to operate many unrelated businesses. Mergers between direct competitors are more likely to create efficiencies than mergers between unrelated businesses, both because there is a greater potential for eliminating duplicate facilities and because the management of the acquiring firm is more likely to understand the business of the target.[7]

One of the most pronounced horizontal integration deals in the U.S. recently occurred when Denver-based Frontier Group agreed to acquire Ft. Lauderdale-based Spirit Airlines for

$2.9 billion to create arguably the largest discount-airline corporation. Ultra-low-cost airlines such as Frontier and Spirit are adding capacity more rapidly than traditional-fare carriers. The combined companies plan to hire an additional 10,000 employees by 2026.

The videogame company Unity Software recently purchased the Weta Digital studio that owns visual effects tools that create high-quality realistic-looking characters and objects such as you see in *Lord of the Rings* and *Game of Thrones* videogames and movies. Unity says the acquisition of Weta will enable it to develop metaverse products whereby users can interact as digital avatars. Weta owns tools that Unity wants, such as Lumberjack that allows users to digitally grow plants and Barbershop that enables users to draft real-looking mustaches on characters. Unity paid $1.63 billion for Weta.

The huge beauty products company, Waldencast just acquired (1) the skin-care company Obagi whose products are mainly available through dermatologists and (2) the makeup company Milk Makeup, a vegan makeup brand that is sold at Sephora and other retailers. Based in White Plains, New York, Waldencast's ticker symbol on the Nasdaq is WALDU. In another horizontal integration move, Toronto, Canada-based TD Bank recently acquired Tennessee-based First Horizon for $13.4 billion. That deal will close during Q1 2023 as TD Bank has long desired to enter the Southeast US banking business.

Verizon Communications recently acquired TracFoneWireless for $6.25 billion in a horizontal integration move. The acquisition extended Verizon's lead as the nation's largest wireless-network operator in terms of subscribers, followed by T-Mobile and AT&T. Two of the world's largest ocean tanker companies, Norway-based Frontline Ltd. and Belgium's Euronav NV recently merged, creating one of the world's biggest tanker companies owning 69 vessels. The new company is named Frontline and has a market capitalization of around $4.5 billion.

The following six guidelines indicate when horizontal integration may be an especially effective strategy:[8]

1. An organization can gain monopolistic characteristics in a particular area or region without being challenged by the federal government for "tending substantially" to reduce competition.
2. An organization competes in a growing industry.
3. Increased economies of scale provide major competitive advantages.
4. An organization has both the capital and human talent needed to successfully manage an expanded organization.
5. When competitors are faltering and can be acquired at a discount.
6. When a firm desires to enter a new geographic market quickly.

Intensive Strategies

5.4. Give specific guidelines for when market penetration, market development, and product development are especially effective strategies.

Market penetration, market development, and product development are sometimes referred to as **intensive strategies** because they require intensive efforts if a firm's competitive position with existing products is to improve. Intensive strategies are normally good options because they involve a firm sticking to what it does best with the only variation being (1) redoubling its effort (market penetration), (2) taking what it does best on the "road" (market development), or (3) improving on what it does best (product development). In contrast, forward and backward integration and diversification strategies take firms away from their core products, services, or competencies.

Market Penetration

A **market penetration** strategy seeks to increase market share for present products or services in present markets through greater marketing efforts. This strategy is widely used alone and in combination with other strategies. Market penetration includes increasing the number of salespersons, increasing advertising expenditures, offering extensive sales promotions, or increasing publicity efforts.

Bank of America (BoA) is engaged in a market penetration strategy; the company just launched an expanded customer loyalty program with additional, new levels of Preferred Rewards tiers and more opportunities to earn rewards and advance up the Preferred Rewards Tier system. By offering a newly expanded and more exciting loyalty program, BoA is hoping to make customers feel valued and increase customer loyalty. Additionally, BoA is likely hoping that the new rewards program will encourage current customers to expand the range of services they currently have with BoA. The newly upgraded loyalty and rewards program offered by BoA is designed to foster customer commitment and attachment to the company by providing current clients newly expanded options and opportunities for earning and redeeming rewards. Loyalty programs are among one of the most common marketing tactics used to successfully implement a market penetration strategy.

The following five guidelines indicate when market penetration may be an especially effective strategy.[9]

1. Current markets are not saturated with a particular product or service.
2. The usage rate of present customers could be increased significantly.
3. The market shares of major competitors have been declining, whereas total industry sales have been increasing.
4. The correlation between dollar sales and dollar marketing expenditures historically has been high.
5. Increased economies of scale provide major competitive advantages.

Market Development

Market development involves introducing present products or services into new geographic areas. For example, Heineken NV is quickly expanding its operations across Africa. Heineken recently acquired two African alcohol companies: (1) Distell Group Holdings, which makes cider, wine, and spirits, and (2) Namibia Breweries Ltd. The world's second-largest brewer behind Anheuser-Busch InBev, Heineken says Africa has exceptionally high long-term potential for beer consumption because outside of South Africa and Angola, people in Africa drink about 12 liters of beer per capita, compared with 73 liters per capita in North America. Heineken does not want rivals Diageo PLC or Anheuser to gain further footholds across Africa.

Market development is not always a successful strategy. For example, the huge German digital bank N26 recently discontinued its operations in the United States after launching there 2 years before. N26 says there is simply higher demand for its products in Eastern Europe and other parts of the world, and its shareholders demand 5+ percent top-line (revenues) and bottom-line (net income) growth annually, which is the common expectation of shareholders across all industries and continents.

Owner of the most successful food-delivery app in the United States, San Francisco-based Door Dash is now rapidly expanding globally, primarily through acquisitions. Door Dash just paid $8 billion to acquire the European food-delivery company, Helsinki-based Wolt Enterprises, enabling Door Dash to now compete with Uber Eats in Europe. Door Dash is now active in 29 countries globally. Food delivery is a booming business evidenced by Grubhub recently acquiring Europe's Just Eat Takeaway and Uber Technologies acquiring Postmates.

As companies such as Door Dash increase the number of countries in which they do business, firms are finding that foreign countries are relying increasingly on their native workforce rather than using migrant labor. As indicated in Global Capsule 5, Malaysia is a good example country that recently closed its borders to migrant labor during the pandemic and kept the borders closed after the pandemic.

Millions of small businesses annually add a second, third, or fourth store, office, or restaurant in new locations; that is market development. Dollar General is adding 1,000 new stores every 12 months across the United States, and there are presently more than 17,000 one-story plain yellow-and-black Dollar Generals in the United States, more than Starbucks' two-tailed green mermaid stores. Starting in 2022, Dollar General is extending its footprint internationally for the first time by opening new stores in Mexico.

GLOBAL CAPSULE 5

Numerous Countries Downsizing Their Foreign Workforce, Relying on Native Residents.[10]

pat13824l/123RF

Many countries closed their borders to foreign or migrant workers during the pandemic of 2020–2022. Many of these same countries are keeping their borders closed, such as Malaysia, or have introduced levies on companies that employ foreigners, such as Saudi Arabia, or are reducing immigration to raise local wages and productivity, such as the UK.

Along with curtailing the influx of migrant workers, many countries, such as Indonesia and Bangladesh, are providing incentives for companies to automate. To lure locals to jobs, in the absence of foreigners, companies are raising wages and increasing benefits offered to workers. The reduction in foreign labor in numerous countries has contributed substantially to global supply chain shortages and outages of everything from food to semiconductors, but countries say in the long-run tight or closed borders will benefit their economy and raise the standard of living in their country for citizens.

Under the Biden administration, the United States seems to be an outlier in this regard because migrant workers and immigrants often enter illegally at the border. This soft position stands in sharp contrast even to the EU, which is explicitly paying for fences at their borders. Poland and other Eastern European countries are forcing immigrants back at the border. Poland, Latvia, and Lithuania, three EU countries, have requested financing from the European Council, which has approved funds to build walls and fences along EU countries' borders.

[10]Based on Jon Emont, "Malaysia Tries Smaller Foreign Workforce," *Wall Street Journal*, November 15, 2021, p. A10. Also, Drew Hinshaw and Bojan Pancevski, "Europe Shifts Stance, Weighs Border Barriers," *Wall Street Journal*, November 12, 2021, p. A9.

These following seven guidelines indicate when market development may be an especially effective strategy.[11]

1. New channels of distribution are available that are reliable, inexpensive, and of good quality.
2. An organization is successful at what it does.
3. New untapped or unsaturated markets exist.
4. An organization has the needed capital and human resources to manage expanded operations.
5. An organization has excess production capacity.
6. An organization's basic industry is rapidly becoming global in scope.
7. Consumption habits of the firm's products are similar in other geographic areas.

Product Development

Product development is a strategy that seeks increased sales by improving or modifying present products or services. Product development usually entails large R&D expenditures. The candymaker Hershey is pushing much further into the salty snack business by its two recent acquisitions of Dot's Homestyle Pretzels (based in North Dakota) and Pretzels Inc. (based in Bluffton, Indiana), respectively, for $1.2 billion total. Hershey already owns SkinnyPop popcorn and Pirate's Booty cheese puffs, but plain pretzels are a new product for the company, whose stated vision is to become a snacking behemoth.

Hertz Global Holdings exited bankruptcy in June 2021 and, within weeks, negotiated with Tesla to take delivery of 100,000 Tesla electric cars during 2022–2023. Hertz is changing the look of its product offerings for customers renting vehicles, gradually shifting to all-electric and hybrid vehicles. Based on the price of a Tesla Model 3, the cost to Hertz is expected to be about $4 billion.

Global semiconductor and computer chip shortages have led to hundreds of companies redesigning their products to use fewer chips and computers. Some vehicles now for example use single integrated processor boards rather than several smaller boards. Many products now are produced and sold with fewer electronic features and less technology, ranging from automatic door locks to GPS screens.

The largest videogame company by market capitalization, Roblox Corporation, based in San Mateo, California, is developing three new metaverse games for middle-school, high-school, and college students. Previously providing mostly videogames for children, Roblox' three new products will teach students about (1) robotics, (2) space exploration, and (3) careers and concepts in computer science, engineering, and biomedical science, respectively.

Coca-Cola is deepening its entry into the liquor business by sealing a deal with Constellation Brands to introduce a line of cocktails under its existing Fresca brand. The new product is called Fresca Mixed. This Coca-Cola strategy makes sense because roughly 50 percent of its customers of Fresca already mix the drink with spirits. This entry follows the recent Topo Chico hard seltzer product produced by Coca-Cola in partnership with Molson Coors. Similarly, rival PepsiCo recently introduced an alcoholic version of Mountain Dew in a partnership with Boston Beer Company.

Product development overall is an excellent option because a firm does not stray far from what it does best. The following five guidelines indicate when product development may be an especially effective strategy to pursue.[12]

1. An organization has successful products that are in the maturity stage of the product life cycle; the idea here is to attract satisfied customers to try new (improved) products as a result of their positive experience with the organization's present products or services.
2. An organization competes in an industry that is characterized by rapid technological developments.
3. Major competitors offer better-quality products at comparable prices.
4. An organization competes in a high-growth industry.
5. An organization has especially strong research and development capabilities.

Diversification Strategies

5.5. Explain when diversification is an effective business strategy.

The two general types of **diversification strategies** are **related diversification** and **unrelated diversification**. Businesses are said to be *related* when their value chains possess competitively valuable cross-business strategic fits; businesses are said to be *unrelated* when their value chains are so dissimilar that few competitively valuable cross-business relationships exist.[13] Most companies favor related diversification strategies to capitalize on synergies such as:

- Transferring competitively valuable expertise, technological know-how, or other capabilities from one business to another.
- Combining related activities of separate businesses into a single operation to achieve lower costs.
- Exploiting common use of a well-known brand name.
- Cross-business collaboration to create competitively valuable resource strengths and capabilities.[14]

Diversification strategies are becoming less popular because organizations are finding it more difficult to manage diverse business activities. In the 1960s and 1970s, the trend was to diversify to avoid being dependent on any single industry, but the 1980s saw a general reversal of that thinking. Diversification is still on the retreat. Michael Porter, of the Harvard Business School, commented, "Management found it couldn't manage the beast." Businesses are still selling, closing, or spinning off less profitable or "different" divisions to focus on their core businesses. For example, the CEO of JPMorgan Chase, Jamie Dimon agrees with Porter. Dimon is a big advocate for economies of scale, arguing that growth for the sake of growth is a misguided strategy. He suggests firms should be careful not to venture into areas outside their corporate strategy and instead deploy resources into areas that will build economies of scale because this is often more advantageous to customers, shareholders, and ultimately for the entire economy. Dimon even has joked before that without economies of scale, we might still be living in tents and hunting for our own food—revealing just how important he considers economies of scale to be for all businesses across various industries. Basically Dimon is talking about the advantages of being homogeneous rather than heterogeneous in terms of products and industries within which the firm competes.

Rapidly appearing new technologies, new products, and fast-shifting buyer preferences make diversification difficult. The 2022–2023 breakup of General Electric (GE) into three separate public companies is indicative of how difficult life has become for highly diversified companies. There is a profound business trend toward large conglomerates dismantling. A spokesperson at T. Rowe Price speaking about the GE breakup recently said (paraphrased): "In the last five years, there is strong evidence in the business world that highly diversified firms do substantially better as separate entities because they can be more focused." The breakup of GE comes on the heels of other major, voluntary breakups of conglomerate firms, including Emerson Electric, Siemens AG, United Technologies, Honeywell International, and DowDuPont.

Although the retreat to being more focused is especially appropriate for manufacturing firms, being diversified may still be a viable strategy for high-tech firms because the internet and cloud underpin diverse industries; Microsoft, Amazon, Meta Platform, and Alphabet are good examples. Many high-tech, highly diversified firms are flourishing as modern neo-conglomerates that intimately link all their diverse products and services within a given firm via online sharing networks and operating systems, so a new customer in any segment becomes linked to all other segments. Diversification, therefore, in the high-tech industry likely has a bright future, in contrast to old traditional conglomerates such as GE and others that are breaking apart.

Diversification must do more than simply spread business risks across different industries; after all, shareholders could accomplish this by simply purchasing equity in different firms across different industries or by investing in mutual funds. Diversification makes sense only to the extent that the strategy adds more to shareholder value than what shareholders could accomplish acting individually. Any industry chosen for diversification must be attractive enough to yield consistently high returns on investment and offer potential synergies across the operating divisions that are greater than those entities could achieve alone. Many strategists contend that firms should "stick to the knitting" and not stray too far from the firms' basic areas of competence. However, in an unattractive industry, diversification makes sense, such as for Philip Morris, because cigarette consumption is declining, product liability suits are a risk, and some investors reject tobacco stocks on principle.

Related Diversification

In a related diversification move, Google recently invested $1 billion in a partnership with the futures-exchange company, CME Group, enabling Google's Cloud segment to eventually power financial markets that handle trillions of dollars in trades each day. Although Google already competes with Amazon and Microsoft in the cloud provider service industry, the CME partnership gives Google a new competitive advantage in the financial services part of the cloud. CME is the world's largest exchange company, recently overtaking Hong Kong Exchanges & Clearing Ltd.

Fenway Sports Group that owns both the Boston Red Sox and the Liverpool Football Club recently purchased the Pittsburgh Penguins hockey team. The Penguins have won five Stanley Cups and are an iconic and successful franchise, but this is Fenway Sports' first foray into professional hockey. Among the four major U.S. sports leagues, the National Hockey League (NHL) relies most heavily on ticket revenue, so they were most negatively impacted by the pandemic and low attendance. The Penguins too have not been doing well of late.

In a related diversification move, Chevron recently acquired Renewable Energy Group for $3.15 billion that makes diesel and other fuels from corn and cooking oil. Chevron and other energy companies are facing intense pressure to move away for such heavy reliance on fossil fuels.

Five guidelines for when related diversification may be an effective strategy are as follows.[15]

1. An organization competes in a no-growth or a slow-growth industry.
2. Adding new, but related, products would significantly enhance the sale of current products.
3. New, but related, products could be offered at highly competitive prices.
4. New, but related, products have seasonal sales levels that counterbalance an organization's existing peaks and valleys.
5. An organization has a strong management team.

Unrelated Diversification

An unrelated diversification strategy favors capitalizing on a portfolio of businesses that are capable of delivering excellent financial performance in their respective industries, rather than striving to capitalize on strategic fit among the businesses. Firms that employ unrelated diversification continually search across different industries for companies that can be acquired for a deal and yet have the potential to provide a high return on investment. Pursuing unrelated diversification entails being on the hunt to acquire companies whose assets are undervalued, companies that are financially distressed, or companies that have high-growth prospects but are short on investment capital.

In an unrelated diversification move, the home security company, ADT Inc. just acquired the leading solar-panel-installation company, Sunpro Solar, for $825 million. Owner of the blue sign in your yard, ADT is confident that it can cross-sell to customers both home security systems and solar panels. ADT security systems are already in 6 million homes; the company has a large, reputable sales team marketing security and now solar.

The cinema chain, AMC Entertainment, is diversifying big time by acquiring a 22 percent stake in a Nevada-based gold and silver mining company, Hycroft Mining Holding that owns a 70,000-acre mine in Nevada. Hycroft had previously gone public in 2020 in a SPAC (special purpose acquisition company) deal by merging with Mudrick Capital Acquistion. However, an analyst for Wedbuh Securities, Michael Pachter, says this acquisition by AMC "makes no sense whatsoever."

Amazon is diversifying further by recently acquiring a fleet of about 3,000 Internet satellites that may compete with Elon Musk's SpaceX company. Amazon's Project Kuiper has nearly one hundred planned launches of satellites as the company races ahead to send broadband satellites into low-Earth orbit.

Five guidelines for when unrelated diversification may be an especially effective strategy follow.[16]

1. Existing markets for an organization's present products are saturated.
2. An organization competes in a highly competitive or a no-growth industry, as indicated by low industry profit margins and returns.
3. An organization's present channels of distribution can be used to market new products to current customers.
4. New products have countercyclical sales patterns compared to an organization's present products.
5. An organization has the capital and managerial talent needed to compete successfully in a new industry.

Defensive Strategies

5.6. List guidelines for when retrenchment, divestiture, and liquidation are especially effective strategies.

In addition to integrative, intensive, and diversification strategies, organizations also could pursue defensive strategies such as retrenchment, divestiture, or liquidation. Retrenchment is a broad term that can include divestiture and liquidation.

Retrenchment

Retrenchment occurs when an organization regroups through cost and asset reduction to reverse declining sales and profits. Sometimes called a **turnaround strategy**, retrenchment is designed to fortify an organization's basic distinctive competence. During retrenchment, strategists work with limited resources and face pressure from shareholders, employees, and the media. Retrenchment can involve selling off land and buildings to raise needed cash, pruning product lines, closing marginal businesses, closing obsolete factories, automating processes, reducing the number of employees, and instituting expense control systems. Bed Bath & Beyond recently closed 37 of its 900+stores in a retrenchment strategy aimed at improving the company's profitability. Peloton Interactive just cut 2,800 jobs and its CEO resigned as the exercise equipment and virtual classes became less popular given changing consumer behavior. The company's retrenchment strategy and personnel changes are expected to spur a rebound for the firm.

In some cases, declaring **bankruptcy** can be an effective retrenchment strategy. Bankruptcy can allow a firm to avoid major debt obligations and to void union contracts. **Chapter 11 bankruptcy** allows organizations to retrench, reorganize, and come back after filing a petition for protection. The number of U.S. retail companies declaring bankruptcy exploded in 2020, but began in 2021 to wane back to levels similar to before the COVID-19 pandemic. Firms declaring bankruptcy in 2020–2021 included Belk, Century 21, Chuck E. Cheese, Francesca's, GNC, Hertz, JCPenney, Paper Source, Solstice Marketing Concepts, Stein Mart, Lord & Taylor, Lucky Brand, New York & Company, Tuesday Morning, and the U.S. arm of L'Occitane. A major problem for retail firms is shoppers' discount addiction spurred by Amazon's prowess and also smartphone-shopping tools and apps prompting never-ending price-cutting, price matching, and price wars. The dramatic shift to online purchasing has generally curtailed the need for brick-and-mortar stores of all kinds.

Sears Holding Company is currently engaged in drawn-out bankruptcy proceedings. There are lawsuits ongoing against Sears alleging that the company stripped away its Lands' End and its Sears Hometown stores out of the firm illegally before or during the bankruptcy. However, the total number of bankruptcies reported in 2021 in the U.S. were the lowest reported in more than 15 years, despite the Covid-19 pandemic. The sharp decline was due to stimulus money from the government coupled with relaxed covenants on debt and even more debt available and approved during the Covid crisis.

Three guidelines reveal when retrenchment may be an especially effective strategy to pursue.[17]

1. An organization is plagued by inefficiency, low profitability, poor employee morale, and pressure from stockholders to improve performance.
2. An organization has failed to capitalize on external opportunities, minimize external threats, take advantage of internal strengths, and overcome internal weaknesses over time; that is, the organization's strategic managers have failed (and possibly will be replaced by more competent individuals).
3. An organization has grown so large so quickly that major internal reorganization is needed.

Divestiture

Selling a division or part of an organization is called **divestiture**. It is often used to raise capital for further strategic acquisitions or investments. Divestiture can be part of an overall retrenchment strategy to rid an organization of businesses that are unprofitable, that require too much capital, or that do not fit well with the firm's other activities. Divestiture has also become a popular strategy for firms to refocus on their core businesses and become less diversified.

A form of divestiture occurs when a corporation splits into two or more parts. Most often, divested segments become separate, publicly traded companies. Many large conglomerate firms are employing this strategy. Sometimes this strategy is a prelude to the firm selling the separated part(s) to a rival firm. Corporations annually split off about $2 trillion worth of subsidiaries. Part of the reason for splitting diversified firms is that the homogenous parts are generally much more attractive to potential buyers. Many times, the acquiring firms desire to promote homogeneity to complement their own operations, rather than heterogeneity, and are willing to pay for homogeneity. For example, Johnson & Johnson is splitting into two companies: (1) Consumer Products such as Band-Aid bandages, baby powder, Neutrogena, Aveeno, Zarbee's, vitamins, minerals, etc., and (2) Prescription and over-the-counter-drugs and medical-devices such as Motrin and Nicorette. GE recently split into three companies, and Japan's Toshiba Corporation also is splitting into three companies. Conglomerates often have trouble selling themselves; the value of firms in homogenous parts almost always today exceeds the heterogeneous big unit.

Unilever is the world's largest tea maker, with brands that include Lipton, Brooke Bond, and PG Tips. However, the London-based company makes more money on other products such as Dove soap, Hellmann's mayonnaise, and Ben & Jerry's ice cream, and its shareholders are not happy with underperforming products. Therefore, Unilever just divested its tea business that includes 34 tea brands, 11 factories, and Unilever's tea estates in three countries, all for €4.5 billion to CVC Capital Partners. Prior to selling its tea business, Unilever sold its struggling margarine-and-spreads business to KKR & Co. for $8 billion.

IBM in mid-2022 divested its Watson Health business to Francisco Partners, as IBM refocuses on its core business around the cloud. Watson uses artificial intelligence (AI) to analyze diagnostic tests and manage care. Just months earlier, IBM divested its Kyndryl Holdings IT-services business, again trying to become more homogeneous around the cloud. Here are some guidelines for when divestiture may be an especially effective strategy to pursue.[18]

1. An organization has pursued a retrenchment strategy and failed to accomplish needed improvements.
2. A division is responsible for an organization's overall poor performance.
3. A division is a misfit with the rest of an organization; this can result from radically different markets, customers, managers, employees, values, or needs.
4. A large amount of cash is needed quickly and cannot be obtained reasonably from other sources.
5. Government antitrust action threatens an organization.

Liquidation

Selling all of a company's assets, in parts, for their tangible worth is called **liquidation**. Liquidation is a recognition of defeat and consequently can be an emotionally difficult strategy. However, it may be better to cease operating than to continue losing large sums of money. **Chapter 7 bankruptcy** is a liquidation procedure used only when a corporation sees no hope of being able to operate successfully or to obtain the necessary creditor agreement. All the organization's assets are sold in parts for their tangible worth. Several hundred thousand companies declare Chapter 7 bankruptcy annually with most of the firms being small. In fact, during the 2020–2022 COVID-19 pandemic, thousands of bankrupt companies liquidated, just went out of business totally, such as mom-and-pop restaurants globally, due to mandatory closures and too few (or no) customers.

Two guidelines reveal when liquidation may be an especially effective strategy to pursue.[19]

1. An organization has pursued both a retrenchment strategy and a divestiture strategy, and neither has been successful.
2. The shareholders of a firm can minimize their losses by selling the organization's assets.

Value Chain Analysis and Benchmarking

5.7. Explain value chain analysis and benchmarking in strategic management.

Whenever a customer buys a product it is because that consumer feels the value to be derived from that product in terms of price paid versus benefits received is worthwhile. However, the ultimate price paid by a consumer for a product is determined from scores of activities that went into producing that product, from raw materials to suppliers, to production processes, to distributors, etc. This collection of activities that leads to the ultimate price of a product is commonly referred to as a firm's **value chain**.[20] Firms seek competitive advantages anywhere they can up and down their value chain to ultimately provide some product at some price and some level of quality that consumers will perceive to be of sufficient value to warrant the purchase. The value chain concept, as illustrated in Figure 5-3, is important in strategic management.

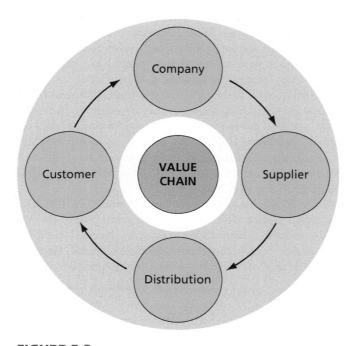

FIGURE 5-3

A Value Chain Illustrated

Value chain analysis (VCA) can be defined as the process whereby a firm determines the value (price minus cost) of each and all activities that went into producing and marketing a product, from purchasing raw materials to manufacturing, distributing, and marketing those products. VCA is an excellent way to identify both external opportunities and threats and internal strengths and weaknesses of a firm. Companies strive to gain competitive advantages wherever possible up and down their value chain because such value activities are not easily duplicated or imitable by rival firms. In contrast, just lowering the price of an end product or hiring a celebrity to promote an end product is easily imitable; such actions do not represent a sustainable competitive advantage. In other words, at every step along a firm's value chain, the firm strives to create value (price minus cost) that can ultimately be transferred to the end user (customers), so customers will buy the product at some price to obtain the perceived value.

Substantial judgment may be required in performing a VCA because different items along the value chain may impact other items positively or negatively, at times creating complex interrelationships. For example, exceptional customer service may be especially expensive yet may reduce the costs of returns and increase revenues. Cost and price differences among rival firms can have their origins in activities performed by suppliers, distributors, creditors, or even shareholders.

The initial step in implementing VCA is to divide a firm's operations into specific activities or business processes. Then the analyst attempts to attach a cost of each discrete activity versus the price to be paid; the costs could be in terms of both time and money. Finally, the analyst converts the value data into information by looking for competitive opportunities and threats or strengths and weaknesses that may yield competitive advantage or disadvantage. Conducting a VCA is supportive of the resource-based view's examination of a firm's assets and capabilities as sources of distinctive competence.

When a major competitor or new market entrant offers products or services at low prices, this may be because that firm has substantially lower value chain costs or perhaps the rival firm is just waging a desperate attempt to gain sales or market share. VCA enables a firm to examine and monitor the extent that its prices and costs are competitive throughout the value chain; those value segments lead cumulatively to the customers' perceived value received by paying some price for some end product.

A value chain is illustrated in Figure 5-4. There can be more than a hundred particular value-creating activities associated with the business of producing and marketing a product or service, and each one of the activities can represent a sustainable competitive advantage or disadvantage for the firm. The combined costs of all the various activities in a company's value chain define the firm's cost of doing business. Firms should determine where cost advantages and disadvantages in their value chain occur *relative* to the value chain of rival firms.

Value chains differ immensely across industries and firms. Whereas a paper products company, such as Stone Container, would include on its value chain timber farming, logging, pulp mills, and papermaking, a company such as Hewlett-Packard would include programming, peripherals, mining of metals, licensing, software, hardware, and laptops. A motel would include food, housekeeping, check-in and check-out operations, website, reservations system, where they order supplies, and so on.

All firms should use VCA to develop and nurture a core competence and convert this competence into a distinctive competence. A **core competence** is any element of a firm's value chain that performs especially well (yields high value). When a core competence evolves into a major competitive advantage, then it is called a *distinctive competence.* Figure 5-5 illustrates this process.

More and more companies are using VCA to gain and sustain competitive advantage by becoming especially efficient and effective along various parts of the value chain. For example, Walmart has built powerful value advantages by focusing on exceptionally tight inventory control and volume purchasing of products. In contrast, computer companies compete aggressively along the distribution end of the value chain.

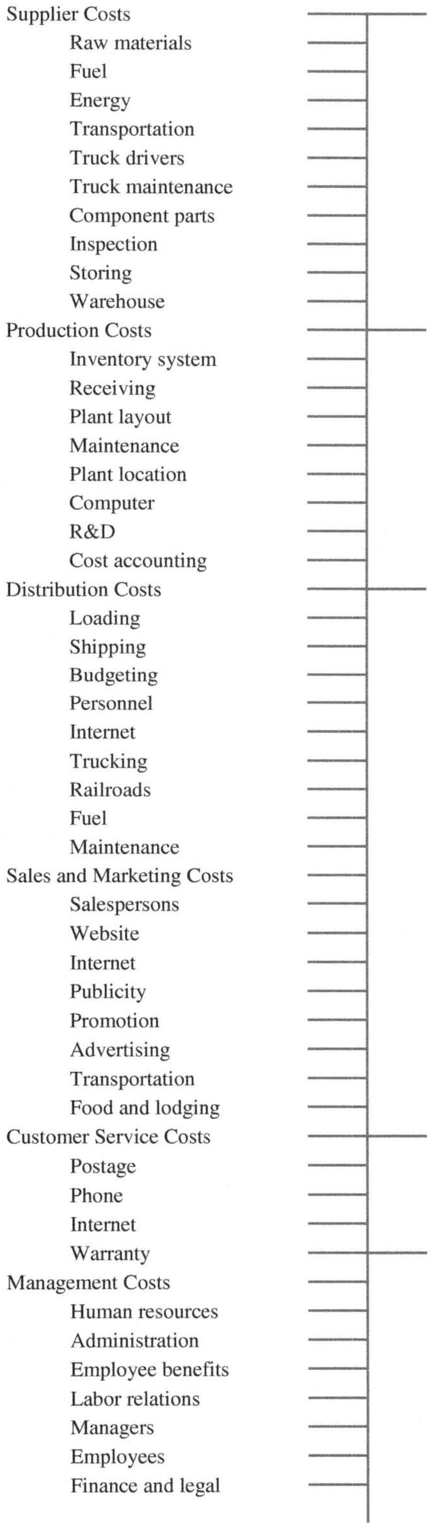

Supplier Costs
    Raw materials
    Fuel
    Energy
    Transportation
    Truck drivers
    Truck maintenance
    Component parts
    Inspection
    Storing
    Warehouse
Production Costs
    Inventory system
    Receiving
    Plant layout
    Maintenance
    Plant location
    Computer
    R&D
    Cost accounting
Distribution Costs
    Loading
    Shipping
    Budgeting
    Personnel
    Internet
    Trucking
    Railroads
    Fuel
    Maintenance
Sales and Marketing Costs
    Salespersons
    Website
    Internet
    Publicity
    Promotion
    Advertising
    Transportation
    Food and lodging
Customer Service Costs
    Postage
    Phone
    Internet
    Warranty
Management Costs
    Human resources
    Administration
    Employee benefits
    Labor relations
    Managers
    Employees
    Finance and legal

FIGURE 5-4

An Example Value Chain for a Typical Manufacturing Company

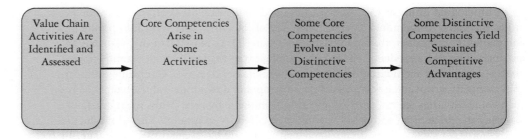

FIGURE 5-5

Transforming Value Chain Activities into Sustained Competitive Advantages

Price competitiveness is a strategic component of competitiveness for both mass retailers and computer firms.

To gain and sustain competitive advantage, a firm must create value for a product or service that exceeds the value offered by rivals.[21] This is commonly done in one of two ways: (1) operating at the lowest cost or (2) commanding a premium price. A few firms try to do both simultaneously. The bottom line, however, is that a business needs to be better than rivals on many points along its value chain because these points likely cannot be easily copied; thus, they are sustainable. Rival firms ask, "How do they do it?" The answer for many successful firms is through effective value chain analysis.

VCA focuses on the quality differences in activities among rival firms. Not all firms in a given industry will place equal weights on various value chain items. For example, Rolex and Timex both produce watches, yet each value chain will differ substantially on key areas. Rolex creates value for the customer through prestige and elegance, whereas Timex creates value through price and utility. Each firm creates value so long as consumers feel they are getting value for the price paid for the product or service and each firm can have its own competitive advantage in the watch industry. Even though the weights on various value chain items can differ within the same industry, firms should strive to understand not only their own value chain operations but also those of the industry, competitors, suppliers, and distributors.

VCA is a tool used to examine each step along the path of creating value from upstream operations such as suppliers all the way to downstream operations of delivering the product to customers. One of the main benefits of VCA is that each activity from start to finish has a value element that can be improved. Pay careful attention to areas along the value chain that are likely to lead to higher quality or lower costs. Also, be mindful it is generally more advantageous to choose a path of being different than a rival on select value chain activities than simply trying to compete with them on every item. The jewelry firms Tiffany (owned by Louis Vuitton SE) and Blue Nile are great examples of firms that have chosen to be different in the way they create value for customers.

Benchmarking

Benchmarking is another analytical tool used to determine whether a firm's value chain is competitive compared to those of rivals and, thus, conducive to winning in the marketplace. Benchmarking entails examination of value chain activities across an industry to determine best practices among competing firms; firms engage in benchmarking for the purpose of duplicating or improving on those best practices. Similar to VCA, benchmarking is an analytical tool used to identify key external opportunities and threats and internal strengths and weaknesses. Benchmarking enables a firm to take action to improve its competitiveness by identifying (and improving on) value chain activities where rival firms have comparative advantages in cost, service, reputation, or operation.

A challenging part of benchmarking can be gaining access to other firms' VCAs with associated costs. Typical sources of benchmarking information, however, include published reports, trade publications, suppliers, distributors, customers, partners, creditors, shareholders, lobbyists, and willing rival firms. Some rival firms share benchmarking data. However, the International Benchmarking Clearinghouse provides guidelines to help ensure that restraint of trade, price fixing, bid rigging, bribery, and other improper business conduct does not arise between participating firms.

Although benchmarking is useful, strategists should be mindful of their firm's unique position and how their firm differs from rivals when selecting which factors along a value chain to benchmark. Never hastily benchmark variable after variable without discretion. For example, Five Guys who specializes in burgers made to order with quality ingredients should not benchmark McDonald's service time component, just as McDonald's should not benchmark Five Guys' quality component. Five Guys benchmarking and attempting to compete with McDonald's on service time would be dysfunctional to Five Guys' unique strategy and position of offering higher quality burgers; erroneous benchmarking could lead a firm away from what made the firm successful. This is not to say improving on service time is not important; it is just that Five Guys should not sacrifice made to order burgers for premade burgers simply to benchmark McDonald's service time component. Recall that uniqueness is important in strategic management, so use benchmarking wisely.

Michael Porter's Two Generic Strategies

5.8. Identify and discuss Porter's two generic strategies: cost leadership and differentiation.

According to Michael Porter, strategies allow organizations to gain competitive advantage from two different bases: cost leadership and differentiation. Porter calls these bases **generic strategies** because generally firms should be mindful that it is often best to develop product lines that compete on cost or compete on unique value; it is difficult to compete on both simultaneously. **Cost leadership** emphasizes producing standardized products or services at a low per-unit cost for consumers who are price sensitive. **Differentiation** is a strategy aimed at producing products and services considered unique to the industry and directed at consumers who are relatively price insensitive. Unlike with cost leadership where a firm examines how to reduce costs all along its value chain, with differentiation the firm looks to maximize value all along its value chain.

Cost Leadership

As indicated in Table 5-5, there are two types of cost leadership strategies. Type 1 is a *broad* low-cost strategy that offers products or services to a wide range of customers at one of the lowest prices available on the market. Type 2 is a *narrow* or *focused* low-cost strategy that offers products or services to a smaller range of customers at one of the lowest prices on the market. A cost leadership strategy aims to offer customers a range of products or services at the lowest price available compared to a rival's products with similar attributes.

Walmart could serve as an example firm pursuing a Type 1 cost leadership strategy because the company serves a broad range of market segments with varied socioeconomic backgrounds. Dollar General would serve as an example of Type 2 focusing mostly on rural areas, limited product lines, less décor devoted to the stores, and less service. Both Type 1 and Type 2 strategies target a large market. This is an important distinction of any cost leadership market; to achieve economies of scale, there must be large market potential. Both Walmart and Dollar General meet the large market potential criteria, even though Dollar General has a significantly more focused target customer base. Amazon is potentially another example of Type 1 cost leadership; Jiffy Lube, Little Caesars Pizza, and Spirit Airlines are all examples of successful Type 2 cost-leadership strategies, as well as examples of firms "saying no and accepting trade-offs" as a part of their cost leadership strategy.

Striving to be the low-cost producer in an industry can be especially effective when the market is composed of many price-sensitive buyers, when there are few ways to achieve product

TABLE 5-5 The Four Types of Generic Strategies

	Generic Strategies	
	Cost Leadership	Differentiation
Market Segments		
Broad	Type 1	Type 3
Narrow	Type 2	Type 4

differentiation, when buyers do not care much about differences from brand to brand, or when there are a large number of buyers with significant bargaining power. The basic idea is to under-price competitors and thereby gain market share and sales, likely driving some competitors out of the market. Companies employing a cost-leadership strategy must achieve their competitive advantage in ways that are difficult for competitors to copy or match. If rivals find it relatively easy or inexpensive to imitate the leader's cost-leadership methods, the leader's advantage will not last long enough to yield a valuable edge in the marketplace. In other words, firms try to gain competitive advantages all along their value chain, so the firm can ultimately provide some product at a price low enough to yield compelling value to customers.

For a resource to be valuable, it must be either rare, hard to imitate, or not easily substitutable. To employ a cost-leadership strategy successfully, a firm must ensure that its total costs across its overall value chain are lower than competitors' total costs. A key way to first ensure the firm is maintaining its cost-leadership competitive advantage is to routinely examine every level of its value chain relative to rival firms for areas of possible cost savings. A successful cost-leadership strategy usually permeates the entire firm, as evidenced by high efficiency, low overhead, limited perks, intolerance of waste, intensive screening of budget requests, wide spans of control, rewards linked to cost containment, and broad employee participation in cost control efforts.

Some risks of pursuing cost leadership are that competitors may imitate the strategy, thus driving overall industry profits down; technological breakthroughs in the industry may make the strategy ineffective; or buyer interest may swing to other differentiating features besides price; simply cutting retail prices will not yield a cost leadership position because such actions are easily copied and will erode margins.

Differentiation

There are two levels of a successful differentiation strategy, Type 3 having a wide target market and Type 4 having a narrow target market, as revealed in Table 5-5. Under differentiation strategies, firms are not as reliant on economies of scale, so targeting a small group of customers can be advantageous if they are willing to pay a premium for the products or services offered. A differentiation strategy should be pursued only after a careful study of buyers' needs and preferences has determined the feasibility of incorporating one or more differentiating features into a unique product that showcases the desired attributes. A successful differentiation strategy allows a firm to charge a higher price for its product and to gain customer loyalty because consumers may become strongly attached to the differentiating features, such as superior service, spare parts availability, engineering design, product performance, useful life, gas mileage, or ease of use.

Examples of firms employing Type 3-wide differentiation strategies would include Monster Beverage, Apple, and BMW; these firms employ a strategy that adds perceived value at significantly higher prices than their counterparts. All three also target a wider audience than brands like Louis Vuitton, Rolex, or Maserati, which operate under a Type 4 strategy. A firm does not have to offer extremely expensive products to use a Type 4 strategy, but generally this is the case because creating value at every step of the value chain is expensive and with limited buyers reducing economies of scale prices tend to be expensive.

Generally, environments favorable to differentiation are those where buyers have many different tastes or application needs. For example, the quality and type of food desired by consumers varies greatly, leading to many different types of restaurants. When technology is changing rapidly, firms can release new products and often have customers "trained" to purchase the latest and greatest. Apple enjoys being differentiated through its own iOS software. All the other leading phone manufacturers use Android, Windows, or some other operating system created by different firms. Whenever customers view products as commodities, there is a need for differentiation; even "commodities" such as milk or eggs can often be differentiated through marketing, attractive packaging, and other tactics, leading to prices often twice as high as competitors.

Differentiation does not guarantee competitive advantage, especially if standard products sufficiently meet customer needs or if rapid imitation by competitors is possible. Products protected by barriers that prevent quick copying by competitors are best. Successful differentiation can mean greater product flexibility, greater compatibility, lower costs, improved service, less maintenance, greater convenience, or more features. Product development is an example of a strategy that offers the advantages of differentiation.

A risk of pursuing a differentiation strategy is that the unique product may not be valued highly enough by customers to justify the higher price. When this happens, a cost-leadership strategy will easily defeat a differentiation strategy. Another risk of pursuing a differentiation strategy is that competitors may quickly develop ways to copy the differentiating features. Thus, firms must find durable sources of uniqueness that cannot be imitated quickly or inexpensively by rival firms.

Common organizational requirements for a successful differentiation strategy include strong coordination among the R&D and marketing functions and substantial amenities to attract scientists and creative people. Firms can pursue a differentiation strategy based on many different competitive aspects. Differentiation opportunities exist or can potentially be developed anywhere along the firm's value chain, including supply chain activities, product R&D activities, production and technological activities, manufacturing activities, human resource management activities, distribution activities, or marketing activities.

The most effective differentiation bases are those that are difficult or expensive for rivals to duplicate. Competitors are continually trying to imitate, duplicate, and outperform rivals along any differentiation variable that yields competitive advantage. Firms must be careful when employing a differentiation strategy because buyers will not pay a higher price unless the perceived benefits of the differentiated offering exceed its price and thus provide overall value.[22]

Means for Achieving Strategies

5.9. **Compare and contrast when companies should build, borrow, or buy as key means for achieving strategies.**

Companies are under continual pressure from stockholders to maintain top-line (revenues) and bottom-line (net income) growth (usually 5+ percent) and pay higher dividends. To accomplish this end, firms are often faced with a build, borrow, or buy decision. Building is growing internally (organically); borrowing is growing externally using means such as partnerships, joint ventures, and alliances; and buying includes mergers and acquisitions. Let's look at build, borrow, or buy options a bit closer.

Build from Within to Grow

When firms build from within, sometimes called **organic growth**, as a means for achieving strategies, strategists must consider how well current internal resources match the capabilities needed to grow (5+ percent). Building from within can include new training programs, hiring new employees, building (instead of buying rival's) stores, or developing a "blue ocean strategy." A **blue ocean strategy** aims to target a new market where competition is not yet present, thus creating a "blue ocean" as opposed to a red ocean where many firms are competing often on price, and the gains of one firm are often at the expense of another. Blue ocean strategy is similar to being a first mover seeking market space not yet occupied by rivals.

Kim and Mauborgne's research on blue oceans revealed that existing line extensions account for 86 percent of new products created; only 14 percent of new ventures are targeted at new markets or industries.[23] Blue ocean thinking in developing news markets and products can provide benefits far greater than competing in traditional markets. Apple's development of the PC and smartphone were blue ocean examples where customers did not even know they desired the products before they were brought to market by Apple. However, the blue ocean environment did not last long for Apple on either product because competitors entered quickly, forcing Apple to operate under what Porter would classify as a differentiation strategy.

Netflix, Southwest, eBay, and Amazon, like Apple, were all derived partly from blue ocean thinking. These examples are of blue oceans where there was no defined industry or market for the products previously, but according to Kim and Mauborgne, blue oceans can arise from already established industries as well. It is likely blue oceans within current industries will not be as sustainable and may even erode a firm's mission, moving it away from its core competencies. Extra care should be taken when considering blue ocean thinking while operating within an already established industry. However, a firm does not have to have a blue ocean to build.

ETHICS CAPSULE 5

Ask Hobby Lobby Is Good Ethics Good Business?[24]

Betty LaRue/Alamy Photo

Based in Oklahoma City and having more than 900 stores in the United States, Hobby Lobby increased its minimum full-time hourly wage to $18.50 at the beginning of 2022. Hobby Lobby is growing fast, opening 25 new stores in 2021. The company has raised its minimum hourly wage 12 times over the last 13 years and was one of the first retailers to establish a nationwide minimum hourly

wage well above the federal minimum wage. The largest arts-and-crafts home décor company in the world, Hobby Lobby is a privately held, U.S. firm with more than $5 billion in annual sales.

CEO David Green at Hobby Lobby says, "the secret to being a great manager is to manage by the book." The book Green refers to is the Bible, as evidenced by his company being closed on Sundays to allow employees to be with their families and attend a house of worship. All Hobby Lobby employees earn more than twice the federal minimum wage; the company offers generous employee benefits; and all stores close at 8 p.m. Green says, "The Bible has everything one needs to know about good leadership." Hobby Lobby employees are trained to always be positive; there is little employee turnover, even though turnover among other retail companies' hourly employees is about 65 percent. Hobby Lobby has zero long-term debt and about one-half of the firm's pretax earnings are donated to charities as CEO Green reveals in his book *Giving It All Away… And Getting It Back Again*. Green's leadership guides include to: "always put integrity at the core of your business; never compromise principles to make more money; and make sure you never stop thinking about the customer's perspective."

[24]Based on https://newsroom.hobbylobby.com. Also, Scott Smith, "Why Retail's David Green Manages by 'The Book,'" *Investor's Business Daily*, May 22, 2017, p. A4.

Flawed thinking a few years ago in the retail business was that e-commerce would replace brick-and-mortar. Instead, the online and in-store experience have become more strongly linked. Brick-and-mortar stores are needed as hubs for customer pickup, to try on merchandise, and as distribution centers. Brick-and-mortar stores have evolved into interactive platforms with digital touches everywhere for mobile checkout and artificial intelligence to stock merchandise tailored to local tastes and needs. For example, the retailer Dick's Sporting Goods is adding to its more than 800 stores. New and remodeled Dick's stores feature concepts that include House of Sport, Public Lands, and Golf Galaxy, as well as batting cages, rock-climbing walls, and putting greens. Other retailers are also adding brick-and-mortar stores for the same reasons, including Levi Strauss and UNTUCKit. Although e-commerce is booming, for the first time since 2017, U.S. retailers opened more stores in 2021 than they closed for the reasons mentioned here. Thousands of retailers are "building from within to grow."

Headquartered in Oklahoma City, Hobby Lobby is rapidly adding to its nearly 1,000 stores across the United States. Hobby Lobby is the largest privately owned arts-and-crafts retailer in the world with about 45,000 employees. CEO David Green and wife Barbara Green attribute everything their company has achieved to exemplary business ethics, as evidenced in Ethics Capsule 5.

Borrow from Others to Grow

Firms tend to "borrow" capabilities through joint ventures or strategic alliances when the (1) firm does not believe it can develop the necessary resources internally or (2) the costs and risks of merging are too high. **Joint venture** occurs when two or more companies form a temporary partnership or consortium for the purpose of capitalizing on some opportunity and having shared equity ownership in the new entity. Joint ventures are being used increasingly because they allow companies to improve communications and networking, to globalize operations, and to minimize risk. They are formed when a given opportunity is too complex, uneconomical, or risky for a single firm to pursue alone or when an endeavor requires a broader range of competencies and know-how than any one firm possesses. Joint ventures are less common than alliances but more common than mergers or acquisitions.

Kathryn Rudie Harrigan summarizes the trend toward increased joint venturing: "In today's global business environment of scarce resources, rapid rates of technological change, and rising capital requirements, the important question is no longer 'Shall we form a joint venture?' Now the question is 'Which joint ventures and cooperative arrangements are most appropriate for our needs and expectations?' followed by 'How do we manage these ventures most effectively?'"[25] Four common reasons joint ventures struggle include:

1. Managers who must collaborate daily in operating the venture are not involved in forming or shaping the venture.
2. The venture may benefit the partnering companies but may not benefit customers, who then complain about poorer service or criticize the companies in other ways.
3. The venture may not be supported equally by both partners. If supported unequally, problems arise.
4. The venture may begin to compete more with one of the partners than the other.[26]

Six guidelines for when a joint venture may be an especially effective means for pursuing strategies are:[27]

1. A privately-owned firm forms a joint venture with a publicly-owned organization. The advantages to being privately held, such as closed ownership, and the advantages of being publicly held, such as access to stock issuances as a source of capital, can sometimes be synergistically combined in a joint venture.
2. A domestic firm forms a joint venture with a foreign company. A joint venture can provide a domestic firm with the opportunity for obtaining local management in a foreign country, thereby reducing risks such as expropriation and harassment by host country officials.
3. The distinct competencies of two or more firms complement each other especially well.
4. A particular project is potentially profitable but requires overwhelming resources and risks.
5. Two or more smaller firms have trouble competing with a large firm.
6. There is a need to quickly introduce a new technology.

Cooperation among competitors is becoming more common. For collaboration to succeed, both firms must contribute something distinctive, such as technology, distribution, basic research, or manufacturing capacity. But a major risk is that unintended transfers of important skills or technology may occur at organizational levels below where the deal was signed.[28] Information not covered in the formal agreement often gets traded in the day-to-day interactions and dealings of engineers, marketers, and product developers. Firms often give away too much information to rival firms when operating under cooperative agreements! Tighter formal agreements are needed.

Perhaps the best example of rival firms in an industry forming alliances to compete against each other is the airline industry. Today, there are three major alliances: Star, SkyTeam, and Oneworld. Joint ventures and cooperative arrangements among competitors demand a certain amount of trust if companies are to combat paranoia about whether one firm will injure the other. Increasing numbers of domestic firms are joining forces with competitive foreign firms to reap mutual benefits. Kathryn Harrigan at Columbia University contends, "Within a decade, most companies will be members of teams that compete against each other."

General Motors and Honda Mote recently formed a partnership to jointly develop a line of affordable electric vehicles, including Sport-utility vehicles, priced below $30,000. In fact, automobile manufacturers are increasingly joining forces to defray the high costs of developing electric cars. As of mid-2022, the average cost of an EV is about $60,000 compared to about $40,000 for non-EV's.

Often, U.S. companies enter alliances primarily to reduce costs and risks of entering new businesses or markets. In contrast, *learning from the partner* is a major reason why Asian and European firms enter into cooperative agreements. U.S. firms, too, should place learning high on the list of reasons to be cooperative with competitors. Companies in the United States often form alliances with firms in Asia to gain an understanding of their manufacturing excellence, but manufacturing competence of firms in Asia is not easily transferable. Manufacturing excellence is a complex system that includes employee training and involvement, integration with suppliers, statistical process controls, value engineering, and design. In contrast, U.S. firms' know-how in technology and related areas can be imitated more easily. Therefore, firms in the United States need to be careful not to give away more intelligence than they receive in cooperative agreements with rival Asian firms.

Buy Others to Grow

Merger and acquisition refers to firms buying others to grow. A **merger** occurs when two organizations of about equal size unite to form one enterprise. An **acquisition** occurs when a large organization purchases (acquires) a smaller firm or vice versa. If a merger or acquisition is not desired by both parties, it is called a **hostile takeover**, as opposed to a **friendly merger**. Most mergers are friendly, but the number of hostile takeovers is on the rise. A hostile takeover is not unethical as long as it is conducted in a civil and legal manner.

Not all mergers are effective and successful. For example, soon after Halliburton acquired Baker Hughes, Halliburton's stock price declined 11 percent. So, a merger between two firms can yield great benefits, but the price and reasoning must be right. More than 10,000 mergers transpire annually in the United States, with same-industry combinations predominating. A general market consolidation is occurring in most industries.

Six reasons why many mergers and acquisitions fail are provided in Table 5-6. Table 5-7 presents the potential benefits of merging with or acquiring another firm.

A **leveraged buyout (LBO)** occurs when a firm's shareholders are bought (hence, *buyout*) by the company's management and other private investors using borrowed funds (hence, *leverage*). Besides trying to avoid a hostile takeover, other reasons for initiating a LBO include instances when a particular division(s) lacks fit with an overall corporate strategy, as well as when selling a division could raise needed cash. A LBO converts a public firm into a private company.

Another popular way for firms to grow occurs whenever a **private equity firm** acquires and takes private some target firm. For example, private equity firms in the United States announced a record $1 trillion of buyouts in 2021, nearly three times the amount of the prior year and more than double the amount ever in a single year (2007). Among the largest private equity firms leading the way are KKR & Co., Carlyle Group, Thomas Bravo, Permira Advisers, Bain Capital, and Hellman & Friedman LLC. For example, Advent International and Permira purchased McAfee for $11.8 billion, and Bain Capital and Hellman & Friedman purchased Athenahealth for $17 billion.

The intent of virtually all private equity acquisitions is to buy firms at a low price and sell them later at a high price, which is arguably just good business.

TABLE 5-6 Six Reasons Why Many Mergers and Acquisitions Fail

1. Integration difficulties up and down the two value chains
2. Taking on too much new debt the target firm owes or to buy the target
3. Inability to achieve synergy
4. Too much diversification
5. Difficult to integrate different organizational cultures
6. Reduced employee morale due to layoffs and relocations

TABLE 5-7 12 Potential Benefits of Merging with or Acquiring Another Firm

1. To provide improved capacity utilization
2. To make better use of the existing sales force
3. To reduce managerial staff
4. To gain economies of scale
5. To smooth out seasonal trends in sales
6. To gain access to new suppliers, distributors, customers, products, and creditors
7. To gain new technology
8. To gain market share
9. To enter global markets
10. To gain pricing power
11. To reduce tax obligations
12. To eliminate competitors

First-Mover Advantages

5.10.   Discuss first-mover advantages and disadvantages.

First-mover advantages refer to the benefits a firm may achieve by entering a new market or developing a new product or service prior to rival firms. As indicated in Table 5-8, some advantages of being a first mover include securing access to rare resources, gaining new knowledge of key factors and issues, and carving out market share and a position that is easy to defend and costly for rival firms to overtake. First-mover advantages are analogous to taking the high ground first, which puts one in an excellent strategic position to launch aggressive campaigns and to defend territory. Being the first mover can be an excellent strategy when such actions (1) build a firm's image and reputation with buyers; (2) produce cost advantages over rivals in terms of new technologies, new components, or new distribution channels; (3) create highly loyal customers; and (4) make imitation or duplication by a rival difficult or unlikely.

TABLE 5-8 Six Benefits of a Firm Being the First Mover

1. Secure access and commitments to rare resources
2. Gain new knowledge of critical success factors and issues
3. Gain market share and position in the best locations
4. Establish and secure long-term relationships with customers, suppliers, distributors, and investors
5. Gain customer loyalty and commitment
6. Gain patent protection early

One of the keys in deciding to be a first mover is how quickly will a new technology, product, or service catch on with a target market. Quicker adoption by the bulk of the customer base enhances the incentive to be a first mover. Quick adoption may especially be likely in industries such as pharmaceuticals where patent protection can virtually lock out anyone other than the first mover.

To sustain the competitive advantage gained by being the first mover, a firm needs to be a fast learner. There are, however, risks associated with being the first mover, such as unanticipated problems and costs that occur from being the first firm doing business in the new market. Therefore, being a slow mover (also called *fast follower* or *late mover*) can be effective when a firm can easily copy or imitate the lead firm's products or services, especially when initial costs are high. If technology is advancing rapidly, slow movers can often leapfrog a first mover's products with improved second-generation products, so being a late mover has potential advantages.

In some industries, being a fast follower (or the first to get it right) may be the better strategy, such as in the electric car business where most customers have not quickly adopted the new technology, due to high switching costs, lack of infrastructure of charging stations, and uneasiness. In iPods and iPhones, Apple was a first mover and continues to enjoy many benefits of entering the market first and profiting from high-switching costs that customers would incur by switching from Apple's unique operating system and ecosystem whereby its products can interact.

Strategic Management in Nonprofit and Small Firms

5.11.   Explain how strategic planning differs in for-profit, not-for-profit, and small firms.

Nonprofit organizations are similar to for-profit companies in virtually evey respect except for two major differences: (1) Nonprofits do not pay taxes, and (2) nonprofits do not have shareholders to provide capital. Nonprofits have employees, customers, creditors, suppliers, and distributors as well as financial budgets, income statements, balance sheets, cash flow statements, and so on. Nonprofit organizations embrace strategic planning as much as for-profit firms and, perhaps, even more. Both nonprofit and for-profit organizations have competitors that want to put them out of business.

The strategic management process is being used effectively by countless nonprofit and governmental organizations, such as the Girl Scouts, Boy Scouts, the Red Cross, chambers of commerce, educational institutions, medical institutions, public utilities, libraries, government agencies, zoos, cities, and places of worship. Many nonprofit and governmental organizations outperform private firms and corporations on innovativeness, motivation, productivity, and strategic management.

Compared to for-profit firms, nonprofit and governmental organizations may be totally dependent on outside financing. Especially for these organizations, strategic management provides an excellent vehicle for developing and justifying requests for needed financial support. Nonprofits and governmental organizations owe it to their constituencies to garner and use monies wisely; that requires excellent strategy formulation, implementation, and evaluation.

Educational Institutions

Accrediting bodies that audit colleges and universities (such as SACS and AACSB) require continuous strategic planning. College enrollments in general are declining. State and federal support and monies given to institutions of higher learning in the United States is dropping more than 5 percent annually. All these factors make strategic planning essential for institutions of higher learning.

Population shifts nationally from the Northeast and Midwest to the Southeast and West are another threat. To cope with severe external threats, educational institutions are more frequently using strategic management concepts, tools, and techniques.

Both BBA and MBA programs nationally are shifting to become more skills oriented. Recent research reveals that salaries for new MBAs are reaching new highs as a tight labor market has consulting firms, banks, technology firms, and other companies hiring top graduates from business schools. The University of Pennsylvania's Wharton School and the University of Chicago's Booth School of Business report that entry-level MBAs received an average salary of $155,000 in 2021, a new high and up $5,000 from the prior year.[29] New MBAs from the Duke University Fuqua School of Business average salaries rose 4 percent to a new high of $141,000. The median MBA salary across the United States for 2021 was flat at $115,000. Among all MBAs graduating in the United States in 2021, female enrollment hit a high of 41 percent, up from 39 percent the prior year; starting salaries of new MBA women average about 20 percent less than male counterparts.

Governmental Agencies and Departments

Federal, state, county, and municipal agencies and departments, such as police departments, chambers of commerce, forestry associations, and health departments, are responsible for formulating, implementing, and evaluating strategies that use taxpayers' dollars in the most cost-effective way to provide services and programs. Strategic management concepts are generally required and, thus, widely used to enable governmental organizations to be more effective and efficient.

Strategists in governmental organizations operate with less strategic autonomy than their counterparts in private firms. Public enterprises generally cannot diversify into unrelated businesses or merge with other firms. Governmental strategists usually enjoy little freedom in altering the organization's mission or redirecting objectives. Legislators and politicians often have direct or indirect control over major decisions and resources. Strategic issues get discussed and debated in the media and legislatures. Issues become politicized, resulting in fewer strategic choice alternatives. However, government agencies and departments are finding that their employees get excited about the opportunity to participate in the strategic management process and thereby have an effect on the organization's core value, vision, mission, objectives, strategies, and policies. In addition, government agencies are using a strategic management approach to develop and substantiate formal requests for additional funding.

Small Firms

"Becoming your own boss" is a dream for millions of people and a reality for millions more. Almost everyone wants to own a business—from teens and college students, who are signing up for entrepreneurial courses in record numbers, to those older than age 65, who are forming more companies every year. However, the percentage of people younger than age 30 who own private businesses has reached a 24-year low in the United States, to about 3.6 percent, down from 10.6 percent in 1989. The stereotype that 20-somethings are entrepreneurial risk-takers is simply false, as millions of young adults struggle in underpaid jobs to maintain their own households, rather than living with their parents. Reasons for the decline vary, but reduced bank lending for small business start-ups, more indebtedness among young people, and increasing numbers of competitors because of the internet, all contribute to a more risk-averse, younger-than-30 age group.

The strategic management process is just as vital for small companies as it is for large firms. From their inception, all organizations have a strategy, even if the strategy just evolves from day-to-day operations. Even if conducted informally or by a single owner or entrepreneur, the strategic management process can significantly enhance small firms' growth and prosperity. However, a lack of strategic management knowledge is a serious obstacle for many small business owners, as is a lack of sufficient capital to exploit external opportunities and a day-to-day cognitive frame of reference. Research indicates that strategic management in small firms is more informal than in large firms, but small firms that engage in strategic management generally outperform those that do not.

IMPLICATIONS FOR STRATEGISTS

Figure 5-6 reveals that to gain and sustain competitive advantages, firms must collect, analyze, and prioritize large amounts of information to make excellent decisions. A strategic plan is much akin to an athletic team's game plan in the sense that both a strategic plan and a game plan are developed after carefully studying rival firms (teams); success of the firm (or team) depends greatly on that plan being a better plan than the rival's plan. Any strategist, much like any coach, puts their firm in great jeopardy of failure if the opposing strategist (coach) has a better strategic plan.

VCA and benchmarking are required to create, identify, nurture, and exploit sustained competitive advantages that can lead to success. Parity (and commoditization) is becoming commonplace in both business and athletics; as parity increases, the intrinsic value of the overarching strategic plan, or game plan, increases exponentially. For example, in college football, great

parity exists among teams such as Auburn, Alabama, Ohio State, Florida State, Kansas State, Oregon, Arizona State, Michigan State, and Michigan, so the game plan can make the difference between winning and losing.

Most of the strategies described in this chapter would separately yield substantial benefits for firms, but no firm has sufficient resources to pursue more than a few basic strategies. Thus, strategists must select from a number of excellent alternatives, eliminate other excellent options, and consider risks, trade-offs, costs, and other key factors. Any strategist, or coach, that gets "outstrategized" by their opposing strategist (or coach) puts their firm (or team) at a major disadvantage. Being outcoached can doom even a superior team (or firm). Therefore, in Chapter 6 we examine six additional analytical tools being widely used by strategists to help develop a winning strategic plan.

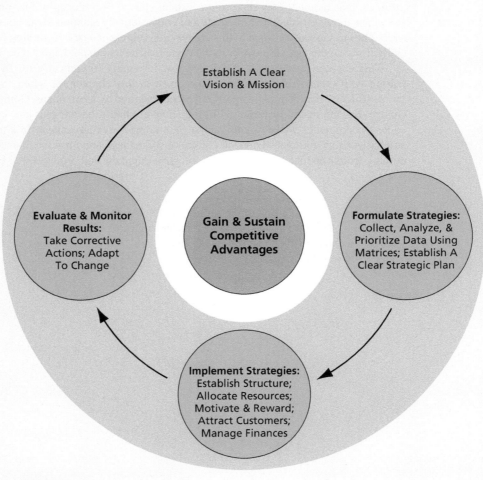

FIGURE 5-6

How to Gain and Sustain Competitive Advantages

IMPLICATIONS FOR STUDENTS

Numerous alternative strategies and means to achieve those strategies, as described in this chapter, could benefit any firm, but your strategic management case analysis should result in specific recommendations whereby you decide what actions will best provide the firm with competitive advantages. Ultimately you will be transforming some of the general strategies and actions defined in this chapter into specific recommendations with projected costs. Because your recommendations with costs comprise the most important pages or slides in your case project, Chapter 6 will go into further detail on this topic. In giving an oral written presentation or paper, introduce bits of your recommendations early to "pave the way" for costs shown later on your recommendations page. Your recommendations page(s) itself should, therefore, be a summary of suggestions mentioned throughout your paper or presentation, rather than being a surprise shock to your reader or audience. You may even want to include with your recommendations insight as to why certain other strategies and means to achieve those actions were not chosen for implementation. That information, too, should be anchored in the notion of competitive advantage and disadvantage with respect to perceived costs and benefits. You may ask: "What is the difference between recommendations and strategies?" The answer is: "Recommendations are strategies *generated and selected for implementation.*"

Chapter Summary

The main appeal of any managerial approach is the expectation that it will enhance organizational performance. This is especially true of strategic management. Through involvement in strategic management activities, managers and employees achieve a better understanding of an organization's priorities and operations. Strategic management allows organizations to be efficient, but more importantly, it allows them to be effective. Although strategic management does not guarantee organizational success, the process allows proactive rather than reactive decision-making. Strategic management may represent a radical change in philosophy for some organizations, so strategists must be trained to anticipate and constructively respond to questions and issues as they arise. The strategies discussed in this chapter can represent a new beginning for many firms, especially if managers and employees in the organization understand and support the plan for action.

This chapter reveals that firms can grow internally (organically) or by acquiring or cooperating with other firms. Guidelines are given in this chapter for when firms have been most successful historically pursuing particular strategies and by what means. Companies and industries change, but the material presented in this chapter should be relevant and useful for decades to come as companies strive to gain and sustain competitive advantage. In a nutshell, this chapter emphasizes that companies need to continuously manage and improve their value chain activities ranging from raw material securement to marketing their end product(s) to be successful.

Key Terms and Concepts

acquisition (p. 154)
backward integration (p. 137)
bankruptcy (p. 144)
benchmarking (p. 148)
blue ocean strategy (p. 151)
Chapter 7 bankruptcy (p. 146)
Chapter 11 bankruptcy (p. 144)
combination strategy (p. 134)
core competence (p. 147)
cost leadership (p. 149)
de-integration (p. 138)
differentiation (p. 149)
diversification strategies (p. 142)
divestiture (p. 145)
financial objectives (p. 133)
first-mover advantages (p. 155)
forward integration (p. 136)
franchising (p. 137)
friendly merger (p. 154)
generic strategies (p. 149)
horizontal integration (p. 136)

hostile takeover (p. 154)
integration strategies (p. 136)
intensive strategies (p. 139)
joint venture (p. 152)
leveraged buyout (LBO) (p. 154)
liquidation (p. 146)
long-term objectives (p. 132)
market development (p. 140)
market penetration (p. 139)
merger (p. 154)
organic growth (p. 151)
private-equity firms (p. 154)
product development (p. 141)
related diversification (p. 142)
retrenchment (p. 144)
strategic objectives (p. 133)
turnaround strategy (p. 144)
unrelated diversification (p. 142)
value chain (p. 146)
value chain analysis (VCA) (p. 147)
vertical integration (p. 136)

Issues for Review and Discussion

5-1. Define and discuss vertical integration.

5-2. Identify the advantages and disadvantages of vertical integration.

5-3. Define and give an example of a blue ocean strategy.

5-4. Identify and discuss three common ways to build capabilities internally.

5-5. What are the advantages of being a first mover in a particular industry?

5-6. What are the two key differences between for-profit and not-for-profit organizations, besides one type seeks to make a profit and the other does not.

5-7. Define and discuss whether it is best for a small firm to build, borrow, or buy to grow.

5-8. Provide reasons why so many companies are divesting (spinning off) key segments or divisions of the firm.

5-9. When is a leveraged buyout an appropriate strategy to pursue?

5-10. Provide actual examples of how Amazon is forward integrating and diversifying at the same time.

5-11. Explain the following statement: Unlike with cost leadership where a firm examines how to reduce costs along its value chain, with differentiation one looks to maximize value along each level of the value chain.

5-12. Define and explain benchmarking.

5-13. The number and dollar value of hostile takeovers are on the rise. Give two reasons for this trend.

5-14. How are for-profit firms different from nonprofit firms in terms of business? What are the implications for strategic planning?

5-15. If the CEO of a beverage company such as Dr Pepper Snapple asked you whether backward or forward integration would be better for the firm, how would you respond?

5-16. In order of importance, list the characteristics of objectives.

5-17. In order of importance, list the benefits of objectives.

5-18. Also called de-integration, there appears to be a growing trend for firms to become more backward integrated. Discuss why.

5-19. What conditions, externally and internally, would be desired or necessary for a firm to diversify?

5-20. There is a growing trend of increased collaboration among competitors. List the benefits and drawbacks of this practice.

5-21. List major benefits of forming a joint venture to achieve desired objectives.

5-22. List major benefits of acquiring another firm to achieve desired objectives.

5-23. List reasons why many mergers or acquisitions historically have failed.

5-24. Can you think of any reasons why not-for-profit firms would benefit less from doing strategic planning than for-profit companies?

5-25. Discuss how important it is for a college football or basketball team to have a good game plan for the big rival game this coming weekend. How much time and effort do you feel the coaching staff puts into developing that game plan? Why is such time and effort essential?

5-27. How does strategy formulation differ for a small versus a large organization? How does it differ for a for-profit versus a nonprofit organization?

5-28. Give hypothetical examples of market penetration, market development, and product development.

5-29. Give hypothetical examples of forward integration, backward integration, and horizontal integration.

5-30. Give hypothetical examples of related and unrelated diversification.

5-31. Give hypothetical examples of joint venture, retrenchment, divestiture, and liquidation.

5-32. Are hostile takeovers unethical? Why or why not?

5-33. What are the major advantages and disadvantages of diversification?

5-34. What are the major advantages and disadvantages of an integrative strategy?

5-35. How does strategic management differ in for-profit and nonprofit organizations?

5-36. Why is it not advisable to pursue too many strategies at once?

5-37. Compare and contrast financial objectives with strategic objectives. Which type is more important in your opinion? Why?

5-38. How do the levels of strategy differ in a large firm versus a small firm?

5-39. List 11 types of strategies. Give a hypothetical example of each strategy listed.

5-40. Define and explain first-mover advantages.

5-41. Give some advantages and disadvantages of cooperative versus competitive strategies.

5-42. What are the two major differences between for-profit and not-for-profit organizations?

5-43. Give some guidelines for when forward integration is an excellent strategy to pursue.

5-44. Give some guidelines for when backward integration is an excellent strategy to pursue.

5-45. Give some guidelines for when horizontal integration is an excellent strategy to pursue.

5-46. Give some guidelines for when market penetration is an excellent strategy to pursue.

5-47. Give some guidelines for when market development is an excellent strategy to pursue.

5-48. Give some guidelines for when product development is an excellent strategy to pursue.

5-49. Give some guidelines for when divestiture is an excellent strategy to pursue.

5-50. Give some guidelines for when retrenchment is an excellent strategy to pursue.

5-51. Give some guidelines for when liquidation is an excellent strategy to pursue.

5-52. Give some guidelines for when unrelated diversification is an excellent strategy to pursue.

5-53. Give some guidelines for when related diversification is an excellent strategy to pursue.

5-54. What is the difference between recommendations and strategies?

5-55. Why do *annual reports* often state objectives in really vague terms, such as to "hire good people" or to "stay ahead of trends"; why should strategists avoid including such vagueness in preparing a strategic plan?

Writing Assignment

5-56. If a company has $1 million to spend on a new strategy and is considering market development versus product development, what determining factors would be most important to consider?

Ken Wolter/Alamy Photo

ASSURANCE-OF-LEARNING EXERCISES

SET 1: STRATEGIC PLANNING FOR MCDONALD'S

EXERCISE 5A

Develop Hypothetical McDonald's Corporation Strategies

Purpose

This chapter identifies, defines, and exemplifies 11 key types of strategies available to firms. This exercise will give you practice formulating possible strategies within each broad category.

Instructions

Step 1   Review the Cohesion Case and your answers to the prior end-of-chapter assurance-of-learning exercises.

Step 2   For the 11 strategies given in Table 5-3, identify a feasible alternative strategy that could reasonably benefit the McDonald's Corporation.

EXERCISE 5B

Should McDonald's Build, Borrow, or Buy in 2023–2024?

Purpose

Comparing *what is planned* versus *what you recommend* is an important part of case analysis. Do not recommend what the firm actually plans, unless in-depth analysis of the situation reveals those strategies to be best among all feasible alternatives. This exercise gives you experience conducting research to determine what a firm is doing in 2022–2023 and should do in 2023–2026.

Instructions

Step 1   Go to the McDonald's corporate website and click on "Press Center." Read through the most recent 10 press releases.

Step 2   Determine two strategies that McDonald's *is* actually pursuing. Give some pros and cons of those two strategies in light of the guidelines presented in this chapter.

Step 3   Determine two strategies that McDonald's is *not* pursuing. Give some pros and cons of those two strategies in light of the guidelines presented in this chapter.

SET 2: STRATEGIC PLANNING FOR MY UNIVERSITY

EXERCISE 5C

Develop Alternative Strategies for Your University

Purpose

It is important for representatives from all areas of a college or university to identify and discuss alternative strategies that could benefit faculty, students, alumni, staff, and other constituencies. As you complete this exercise, notice the learning and understanding that occurs as people express differences of opinion. Recall that *the process of planning is more important than the document.*

Instructions

Step 1   Recall or locate the external opportunity and threat and internal strength and weakness factors that you identified previously as part of Exercise 1C. If you did not do that exercise, discuss now as a class, important external and internal factors facing your college or university.

Step 2   Identify and put on the screen 10 alternative strategies that you feel could benefit your college or university. Your proposed actions should allow the institution to capitalize on particular strengths, improve on certain weaknesses, avoid external threats, or take advantage of particular external opportunities. Number the strategies as they are written on the screen from 1 to 10. State each strategy in specific terms, such as Build two new dormitories, rather than in vague terms, such as Do market penetration.

Step 3   On a separate sheet of paper, number from 1 to 10. Everyone in class individually should rate the strategies identified, using a 1 to 3 scale, where 1 = I do not support implementation, 2 = I am neutral about implementation, and 3 = I strongly support implementation. In rating the strategies, recognize that no institution has sufficient funds to do everything desired or potentially beneficial.

Step 4   Your professor will now pick up the rating sheets and have a student add up the scores for each strategy. That is, sum the ratings for each strategy, so that a prioritized list of recommended strategies is obtained. The higher the sum, the more attractive the strategy. This prioritized list reflects the collective wisdom of your class. Strategies with the highest score are deemed best.

Step 5   Discuss how this process could enable organizations to achieve understanding and commitment from individuals.

SET 3: STRATEGIC PLANNING FOR MYSELF

EXERCISE 5D

The Key to Personal Strategic Planning: Simultaneously Build and Borrow

Purpose

As a means to achieve various strategies, companies usually choose among build, borrow, and buy to grow. However, individuals must build and borrow. This exercise gives you insight on how to build and borrow to launch a successful career.

Instructions

Step 1   List four ways you can build (i.e., grow internally) to advance your career opportunities.

Step 2   List four ways you can borrow (i.e., grow using others) to advance your career opportunities.

Step 3   Compare and contrast your lists with those of other students. Collectively decide on the four best build and four best borrow means to achieve your objectives.

SET 4: INDIVIDUAL VERSUS GROUP STRATEGIC PLANNING

EXERCISE 5E

What Is the Best Mix of Strategies for McDonald's Corporation?

Purpose

Strategic management classes are usually composed of teams of students who perform case analyses. The purpose of this exercise is to examine whether individual decision-making is better than group decision-making. Academic research suggests that groups make better decisions than individuals about 80 percent of the time. No company has sufficient resources to implement all strategies that would benefit the firm. Thus, tough choices have to be made. Ranking strategies as to their relative attractiveness (1 = most attractive, 2 = next most attractive, etc.) is a commonly used procedure to help determine which actions to actually fund. Often, a group of managers will jointly rank strategies and compare their ranking to other groups. This ranking process may be used to determine the relative attractiveness of feasible alternative strategies.

The purpose of this exercise is to examine how well students understand the advantages and disadvantages of a firm pursuing the strategic options described in this chapter. This is a fun exercise that also gives you experience selecting among feasible alternative strategies for a company.

Situation

McDonald's is doing really well but strives to do better. It is trying to decide what strategies would be best for the company going forward. Seven strategies discussed in this chapter are being seriously considered, as listed.

Strategies

Production operations

1. Forward integration: Form partnerships with both Uber Eats and Door Dash to deliver meals
2. Backward integration: Acquire a 10,000-acre cattle ranch in Texas
3. Horizontal integration: Acquire Chick-fil-A
4. Market development: Double the number of restaurants in Africa within 3 years
5. Market penetration: Triple the level of advertising for Chicken McNuggets and Crispy Chicken Sandwich
6. Product development: Begin offering veggie burgers and veggie smoothies
7. Unrelated diversification: Acquire the ABC Construction company to build new and remodel old restaurants to offer dual lines for pickup and a new line for online orders

Task

Rank the seven strategies listed in terms of their relative attractiveness for McDonald's, where 1 = the most attractive strategy to pursue, 2 = the next most attractive strategy, etc., to 7 = the least attractive strategy to pursue. Rank the strategies first as an individual and then as part of a group. Then, listen to the expert ranking and rationale. In this manner, this exercise enables you to determine what individual(s) and what group(s) in class make the best strategic decisions (i.e., that come closest to the expert ranking).

Steps

1. Fill in Column 1 in Table 5-9 to reveal your individual ranking of the relative attractiveness of the proposed strategies. For example, if you feel backward integration is the seventh-best option, then in Table 5-9, enter a 7 in Column 1 beside Backward Integration.
2. Fill in Column 2 in Table 5-9 to reveal your group's ranking of the relative attractiveness of the proposed strategies. For example, if your group feels backward integration is the third-best option, then enter 3 into Column 2 beside Backward Integration.
3. Fill in Column 3 in Table 5-9 to reveal the expert's ranking of the relative attractiveness of the proposed strategies.

4. Fill in Column 4 in Table 5-9 with the absolute difference between Column 1 and Column 3 to reveal how well you performed as an individual in this exercise. (Note: Absolute difference disregards negative numbers.)

5. Fill in Column 5 in Table 5-9 with the absolute difference between Column 2 and Column 3 to reveal how well your group performed in this exercise.

6. Sum Column 4. Sum Column 5.

7. Compare the Column 4 sum with the Column 5 sum. If your Column 4 sum is less than your Column 5 sum, then you performed better as an individual than as a group. If you did better than your group, you did excellent.

8. The Individual Winner(s): The individual(s) with the lowest Column 4 sum is the WINNER.

9. The Group Winners(s): The group(s) with the lowest Column 5 score is the WINNER.

TABLE 5-9 Strategic Planning for McDonald's: Individual Versus Group Decision-Making

The Strategies	Column Number				
	(1) My Rank	(2) Group Rank	(3) Expert Rank	(4) Absolute Value 1–3	(5) Absolute Value 2–3
1. Backward integration Acquire a 10,000-acre cattle ranch in Texas					
2. Forward integration Form partnerships with both Uber Eats and Door Dash to deliver meals					
3. Horizontal integration Acquire Chick-fil-A					
4. Market development Double the number of restaurants in Africa within 3 years					
5. Market penetration Triple the level of advertising for Chicken McNuggets and Crispy Chicken Sandwich					
6. Product development Begin offering veggie burgers and veggie smoothies					
7. Unrelated diversification Acquire the ABC Construction company to build new and remodel old restaurants to offer dual lines for pickup including a new line for online orders					

MINI-CASE ON MACY'S INC.

IS DIVESTITURE THE MOST COMMON CORPORATE STRATEGY TODAY?[30]

Helen89/Shutterstock

Hundreds of companies nationwide and globally are divesting parts of their business, trying to become more homogeneous and take advantage of the realization that their separate parts are worth more than the firm's combined parts. Hudson's Bay Company and Saks Fifth Avenue recently spun-off (divested) their e-commerce operations from their brick-and-mortar retail business. Macy's Inc. was considering a similar spin-off in 2022 that would divest its digital operations from the traditional in-store operations. Usually, however, such divestitures are based on products that are completely different, such as pharmaceuticals versus personal care products. Separating digital from traditional is quite a new divestiture strategy.

Despite receiving pressure from an activist investor to divest the e-commerce operations, Macy's has managed to enhance its online presence at www.bloomingdales.com and www.macys.com and total digital sales in 2021 increased 13% over 2020 and 39% over 2019. Going into 2022, Macy's is reportedly in a stronger and better position than before the pandemic and the firm is no longer considering a spin-off. The company's CEO, Jeff Gennette recently stated (paraphrased): "In every scenario we considered, it was clear that Macy's has a stronger future as a fully integrated business that combines our digital and physical assets to build our national footprint through offering customers a broad range of brands both in-store and through our profitable digital platform." In Macy's fiscal year 2021, digital sales comprised about 35% of total sales and by 2023, the company expects to generate $10 billion in annual sales from its digital offerings.

Macy's is doing great financially and it appears that an omnichannel strategy may be optimal; the firm's digital sales are three times higher in locales with brick-and-mortar Macy's stores than in markets without physical storefronts. Net sales for fiscal year 2021 were $24.5 billion, compared to $17.4 billion in 2020 and $24.6 billion in 2019. For other firms in the industry, however, including Hudson's Bay, Saks Fifth Avenue, and soon maybe even Kohl's and other department stores, divestiture and spin-offs have been the preferred strategy.

Questions

1. What are potential drawbacks of a firm separating into separate companies its digital operations from its traditional stores or businesses? For example, could a rival firm acquire just one of the segments and compromise effectiveness of the other segment(s)?
2. Is the most common corporate strategy now divestiture? Name a type of strategy more commonly being pursued today than divestiture.

[30]Based on Charity Scott and Suzanne Kapner, "Macy's Mulls Spinning Off Digital Unit," *Wall Street Journal*, November 19, 2021, pp. B1, B2. Also based on information from "Macy's rejects e-commerce spinoff as it looks to build on digital growth," and "Macy's Opts Against Separation of E-Commerce Business," accessed on May 6, 2022 from https://www.retaildive.com/news/macys-rejects-e-commerce-spinoff-as-it-looks-to-build-on-digital-growth/619197/ and https://www.wsj.com/articles/macys-posts-quarterly-gains-helped-by-digital-sales-11645536430, respectively.

Web Resources

1. This website defines and gives an example of benchmarking: https://asq.org/quality-resources/benchmarking
2. This website defines and gives an example of value chain analysis: https://online.hbs.edu/blog/post/what-is-value-chain-analysis
3. Fred David gives a video overview of Chapter 5 in the prior edition, but much info is still applicable to the 18th edition: https://www.youtube.com/watch?v=jhOqAXCDQOY

Current Readings

Amirhossein, Sadoghi, and Jan Vecer, "Optimal Liquidation Problem in Illiquid Markets," *European Journal of Operational Research* 296, no. 3 (2022): 1050–66.

Bettinazzi, Emanuele, and Emilie Feldman, "Stakeholder Orientation and Divestiture Activity," *Academy of Management Journal* 64, no. 4 (August 2021): 1078–96.

Choi, Jaeho, Anoop Menon, and Haris Tabakovic, "Using Machine Learning to Revisit the Diversification-Performance Relationship," *Strategic Management Journal* 42, no. 9 (September 2021): 1632–61.

Feldman, Emilie R., and Arkadiy V. Sakhartov, "Resource Redeployment and Divestiture as Strategic Alternatives," *Organization Science* (epub ahead of print). https://doi.org/10.1287/orsc.2021.1474

Girardi, Giulio, Kathleen W. Hanley, Stanislava Nikolova, Loriana Pelizzon, and Mila Getmansky Sherman, "Portfolio Similarity and Asset Liquidation in the Insurance Industry," *Journal of Financial Economics* 142 no. 1, (2021): 69–96.

Hu Yihong, Shengnan Qu, Guo Li, and Suresh P. Sethi. "Power Structure and Channel Integration Strategy for Online Retailers," *European Journal of Operational Research* 294, no. 3 (2021): 951–64.

Lee, Chi-Hyon, Manuela N. Hoehn-Weiss, and Samina Karim, "Competing Both Ways: How Combining Porter's Low-Cost and Focus Strategies Hurts Firm Performance," *Strategic Management Journal* 42, no. 12 (December 2021): 2218–44.

Li Pei, Dan Tan, Guangyong Wang, Hang Wei, and Jilan Wu, "Retailer's Vertical Integration Strategies Under Different Business Modes," *European Journal of Operational Research* 294, no. 3, (2021): 965–75.

Pearce, John A., and Pankaj C. Patel, "Reaping the Financial and Strategic Benefits of a Divestiture by Spin-off," *Business Horizons* 65, no. 3 (2022): 291–301. https://doi.org/10.1016/j.bushor.2021.03.001

Prashantham, Shameen, "Partnering with Startups Globally: Distinct Strategies for Different Locations," *California Management Review* 63, no. 4 (August 2021): 123–45.

Endnotes

1. John Byrne, "Strategic Planning—It's Back," *BusinessWeek*, August 26, 1996, p. 46.

2. On page 132.

3. Steven C. Brandt, *Strategic Planning in Emerging Companies* (Reading, MA: Addison-Wesley, 1981). Reprinted with permission of the publisher.

4. F. Hansen and M. Smith, "Crisis in Corporate America: The Role of Strategy," *Business Horizons*, January–February 2003, p. 9.

5. Based on F. R. David, "How Do We Choose Among Alternative Growth Strategies?" *Managerial Planning* 33, no. 4 (January–February 1985): 14–17, 22.

6. Ibid.

7. Kenneth Davidson, "Do Megamergers Make Sense?" *Journal of Business Strategy* 7, no. 3 (Winter 1987): 45.

8. David, "How Do We Choose."

9. Ibid.

10. On page 141.

11. Ibid.

12. Ibid.

13. Arthur Thompson Jr., A. J. Strickland III, and John Gamble, *Crafting and Executing Strategy: Text and Readings* (New York: McGraw-Hill/Irwin, 2005), 241.

14. Michael E. Porter, *Competitive Strategy: Techniques for Analyzing Industries and Competitors* (New York: Free Press, 1980), 53–57, 318–19.

15. David, "How Do We Choose."

16. Ibid.

17. Ibid.

18. Ibid.

19. Ibid.

20. Porter, *Competitive Strategy*, 34–44.

21. Porter, *Competitive Strategy*, 160–62.

22. Porter, *Competitive Strategy*, 160–62.

23. https://www.audible.com/pd/Business/Summary-of-Blue-Ocean-Strategy-by-W-Chan-Kim-and-Renee-A-Mauborgne-Audiobook/B01L06M29Y?gclid=Cj0KCQiA_5_QBRC9ARIsADVww15mWwiWvtZ5ci2wnBjmZlXczGUkKktkDjWHt9wQ7pzwDYIi_R3UxSkaAt7QEALw_wcB&pcrid=158258695641&cvo_pid=5075902449&mkwid=DSATitle_dc&pmt=b&cvosrc=ppc+dynamic+search.google.97175169&cvo_crid=158258695641&pkw=&source_code=GO1GB907OSH060513

24. On page 152.

25. Kathryn Rudie Harrigan, "Joint Ventures: Linking for a Leap Forward," *Planning Review* 14, no. 4 (July–August 1986): 10.

26. Matthew Schifrin, "Partner or Perish," *Forbes*, May 21, 2001, p. 32.

27. David, "How Do We Choose."

28. Gary Hamel, Yves Doz, and C. K. Prahalad, "Collaborate with Your Competitors—and Win," *Harvard Business Review* 67, no. 1 (January–February 1989): 133.

29. Patrick Thomas, "M.B.A. Graduates' Salaries Are Soaring," *Wall Street Journal*, November 12, 2021, p. A13. Also, Meredith E. David, Fred R. David, and Forest R. David, "Closing the Gap Between Graduates' Skills and Employers' Requirements: A Focus on the Strategic Management Capstone Business Course." *Administrative Sciences* 11, no. 1 (2021): 10–26.

30. On page 164.

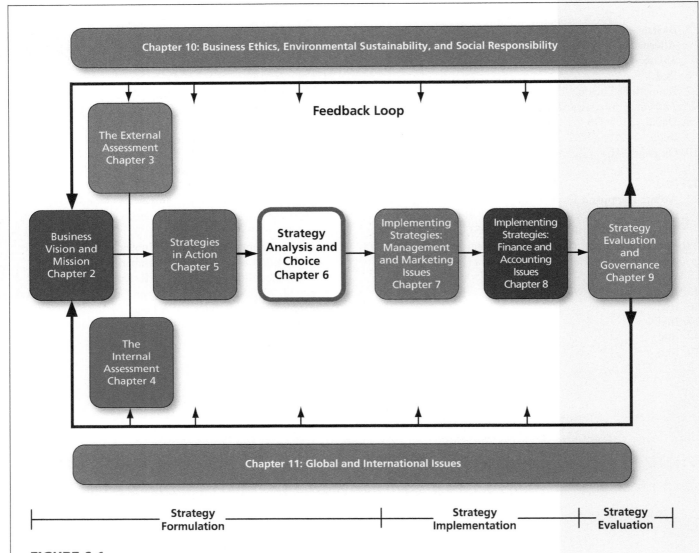

FIGURE 6-1

The Comprehensive, Integrative Strategic Management Model

Source: Fred R. David, "How Companies Define Their Mission," *Long Range Planning* 22, no. 1 (February 1989): 91. Also Anik Ratnaningsih, Nadjadji Anwar, Patdono Suwignjo, and Putu Artama Wiguna, "Balance Scorecard of David's Strategic Modeling at Industrial Business for National Construction Contractor of Indonesia," *Journal of Mathematics and Technology* no. 4 (October 2010): 20. Also, Meredith E. David, Fred R. David, and Forest R. David, "Closing the Gap Between Graduates' Skills and Employers' Requirements: A Focus on the Strategic Management Capstone Business Course," *Administrative Sciences* 11, no. 1 (2021): 10.

Strategy Analysis and Choice

LEARNING OBJECTIVES

After studying this chapter, you should be able to do the following:

6.1. Describe the strategy analysis and choice process.

6.2. Diagram and explain the three-stage strategy formulation analytical framework.

6.3. Construct and apply the Strengths-Weaknesses-Opportunities-Threats (SWOT) Matrix.

6.4. Construct and apply the Strategic Position and Action Evaluation (SPACE) Matrix.

6.5. Construct and apply the Boston Consulting Group (BCG) Matrix.

6.6. Construct and apply the Internal-External (IE) Matrix.

6.7. Construct and apply the Grand Strategy Matrix.

6.8. Construct and apply the Quantitative Strategic Planning Matrix (QSPM).

6.9. Explain how to estimate costs associated with recommendations.

6.10. Discuss the role of organizational culture in strategic analysis and choice.

6.11. Identify and discuss important political considerations in strategy analysis and choice.

ASSURANCE-OF-LEARNING EXERCISES

The following exercises are found at the end of this chapter:

SET 1:	Strategic Planning for McDonald's
EXERCISE 6A:	Perform a SWOT Analysis for McDonald's
EXERCISE 6B:	Develop a SPACE Matrix for McDonald's
EXERCISE 6C:	Develop a BCG Matrix for McDonald's
EXERCISE 6D:	Develop a QSPM for McDonald's
SET 2:	Strategic Planning for My University
EXERCISE 6E:	Develop a BCG Matrix for My University
SET 3:	Strategic Planning to Enhance My Employability
EXERCISE 6F:	Perform QSPM Analysis on Yourself
EXERCISE 6G:	A Template Competency Test
SET 4:	Individual Versus Group Strategic Planning
EXERCISE 6H:	How Severe Are Various Subjective Threats in Strategic Planning?

Strategy analysis and choice largely involve making subjective decisions based on objective information. Prior chapters in this text focused on obtaining the objective information needed in this chapter to formulate strategies and decide which particular strategies to implement. This chapter introduces important concepts that enable strategists to generate feasible alternatives, evaluate those alternatives, and choose a specific course of action. Behavioral aspects of strategy formulation are also covered in this chapter, including considerations of politics, culture, ethics, and social responsibility. Modern tools for formulating strategies are described. Material in this chapter, as well as in prior chapters, largely follows the flow of the Excel strategic planning template at www.strategyclub.com that is available for students to use freely, if desired.

Strategy Analysis and Choice

6.1. Describe the strategy analysis and choice process.

As indicated by Figure 6-1 with white shading, this chapter focuses on generating and evaluating alternative strategies, as well as selecting strategies to pursue. Strategy analysis and choice seek to determine alternative courses of action that could best enable the firm to achieve its mission and objectives. The firm's present strategies, objectives, vision, and mission, coupled with the external and internal audit information, provide a basis for generating and evaluating feasible alternative strategies. This systematic approach is an effective way to avoid an organizational crisis. Rudin's Law states, "When a crisis forces choosing among alternatives, most people choose the worst possible one."

Unless underlying external factor evaluation, internal factor evaluation, and competitive profile matrices produced really low total weighted scores, alternative strategies will likely represent incremental steps that move the firm from its present position to a desired future position. Alternative strategies should not come out of the wild blue yonder; they are derived from the firm's vision, mission, objectives, external audit, and internal audit; they are consistent with, or build on, past strategies that have worked well.

As indicated in the Exemplary Strategist capsule, the CEO of General Dynamics is Phebe Novakovic, who is an experienced, exemplary strategist that has been overseeing outstanding strategic planning at General Dynamics for more than a decade.

EXEMPLARY **STRATEGIST** SHOWCASED

Phebe Novakovic, Chairperson and CEO of General Dynamics Corporation[1]

Originally of Serbian descent, Phebe Novakovic has for a decade, and continues today, to perform exemplary strategic work as the CEO and Chairperson of General Dynamics, one of the largest aerospace and defense companies in the world. Headquartered in Reston, Virginia, General Dynamics just introduced two new business Gulfstream jets and is producing the first Columbia-class guided-missile, nuclear-powered submarines, along with numerous other cutting-edge military, aerospace, and high-tech advanced products. General Dynamics employs more than 100,000 people in 50 countries and generates more than $40 billion in annual revenues with exemplary profits. The third-largest defense contractor in the world, General Dynamics provides extensive maintenance and repair services for many of the U.S. Navy's warships.

Novakovic received an MBA in 1988 from the Wharton School of Business at the University of Pennsylvania in Philadelphia. In 2021, Novakovic was listed as the world's 30th most powerful woman in business by *Forbes* magazine. She is a member of the board of directors of both Abbott Laboratories and JPMorgan Chase. For more than a decade before working with General Dynamics, Novakovic was an officer in the Central Intelligence Agency (CIA). She has extensive global connections with suppliers, distributors, customers, and gov-

ernments, and uses these relationships to enable General Dynamics to formulate and implement outstanding strategies, amid numerous rival firms and the pandemic.

[1]Based on https://www.forbes.com/power-women/#30bface75e25

The Process of Generating and Selecting Strategies

Strategists never consider all feasible strategies that could benefit the firm because there is an infinite number of possible actions and an infinite number of ways to implement those actions. Therefore, a manageable set of the most attractive alternative strategies must be developed, examined, prioritized, and selected. The advantages, disadvantages, trade-offs, costs, and benefits of these strategies should be determined.

Identifying and evaluating strategies should involve many of the managers and employees who previously assembled the organizational vision and mission statements, performed the external audit, and conducted the internal audit. Representatives from each department and division of the firm should be included in this process, as was described in previous chapters. Involvement provides the best opportunity for managers and employees to gain an understanding of what the firm is doing and why and to become committed to helping the firm accomplish its objectives.

All participants in the strategy analysis and choice activity should have the firm's external and internal audit information available. This information, coupled with the firm's vision and mission statements, will help participants crystallize in their own minds particular strategies that they believe could benefit the firm most. Creativity should be encouraged in this thought process. At a bare minimum, a SWOT analysis should be performed by participants as described in this chapter. Additionally, BCG, IE, SPACE, GRAND, and QSPM analyses are always immensely helpful in strategic planning as will be outlined in this chapter.

The Strategy Formulation Analytical Framework

6.2. Diagram and explain the three-stage strategy formulation analytical framework.

Important strategy formulation techniques can be integrated into a three-stage decision-making framework, as shown in Figure 6-2. The tools presented in this framework are applicable to all sizes and types of organizations and can help strategists identify, evaluate, and select strategies. The tools enable firms to break down complex data and ultimately establish an effective strategic plan. The tools shown anchor the analytical strategic planning process advocated by the authors and this text.

All nine techniques included in the **strategy formulation analytical framework** require the integration of intuition and analysis. Autonomous divisions in an organization commonly use strategy formulation techniques to develop strategies and objectives. Divisional analyses provide a basis for identifying, evaluating, and selecting among alternative corporate-level strategies.

Strategists themselves, not analytical tools, are always responsible and accountable for strategic decisions. Lenz emphasized that the shift from a words-oriented to a numbers-oriented planning process can give rise to a false sense of certainty; it can reduce dialogue, discussion, and argument as a means for exploring understandings, testing assumptions, and fostering organizational learning.[2] Strategists, therefore, must be wary of this possibility and use analytical

STAGE 1: THE INPUT STAGE		
External Factor Evaluation (EFE) Matrix	Competitive Profile Matrix (CPM)	Internal Factor Evaluation (IFE) Matrix

STAGE 2: THE MATCHING STAGE				
Strengths-Weaknesses-Opportunities-Threats (SWOT) Matrix	Strategic Position and Action Evaluation (SPACE) Matrix	Boston Consulting Group (BCG) Matrix	Internal-External (IE) Matrix	Grand Strategy Matrix

STAGE 3: THE DECISION STAGE
Quantitative Strategic Planning Matrix (QSPM)

FIGURE 6-2

The Strategy Formulation Analytical Framework

tools wisely to facilitate, rather than to diminish, communication. Without objective information and analysis, however, personal biases, politics, prejudices, emotions, personalities, and halo error (the tendency to put too much weight on a single factor) often play too dominant of a role in the strategy formulation process, undermining effectiveness. Thus, an analytical approach is essential for achieving maximum effectiveness in strategic planning.

Stage 1: The Input Stage

Stage 1 of the strategy formulation analytical framework consists of the External Factor Evaluation (EFE) Matrix, the Internal Factor Evaluation (IFE) Matrix, and the Competitive Profile Matrix (CPM). Called the **input stage**, Stage 1 summarizes the basic input information needed to formulate strategies. Procedures for developing EFE, CPM, and IFE matrices were presented in Chapter 3 and Chapter 4, respectively. Information derived from those analytical tools provides basic input information for the matching and decision stage matrices described in this chapter. The input tools require strategists to quantify subjectivity during early stages of the strategy formulation process. Making small decisions in the input matrices regarding the relative importance of external and internal factors allows strategists to more effectively generate, prioritize, evaluate, and select among alternative strategies. Good intuitive judgment is always needed in determining appropriate weights and ratings; but keep in mind that a rating of 3, for example, is mathematically 50 percent larger than a rating of 2, so small differences matter.

Stage 2: The Matching Stage

Stage 2, called the **matching stage**, focuses on generating feasible alternative strategies by aligning key external and internal factors. Stage 2 techniques include the **Strengths-Weaknesses-Opportunities-Threats (SWOT) Matrix**, the Strategic Position and Action Evaluation (SPACE) Matrix, the Boston Consulting Group (BCG) Matrix, the Internal-External (IE) Matrix, and the Grand Strategy Matrix.

Strategy is sometimes defined as the match an organization makes between its internal resources and skills and the external opportunities and risks facing the firm.[3] The matching stage of the strategy formulation framework consists of five techniques: the SWOT Matrix, the SPACE Matrix, the BCG Matrix, the IE Matrix, and the Grand Strategy Matrix. These tools rely on information derived from the input stage to match external opportunities and threats with internal strengths and weaknesses. SWOT analysis is commonly performed first and is generally considered the most important tool.

Matching external and internal key factors is essential for effectively generating feasible alternative strategies. In most situations, external and internal relationships are complex, and matching requires multiple alignments for each strategy generated. Successful matching of key external and internal factors depends on those underlying key factors being *actionable, quantitative, comparative*, and *divisional* (AQCD) to the extent possible, as described in Chapter 3 and Chapter 4, respectively. Recall that the basic concept of matching was introduced in Chapter 1.

Stage 3: The Decision Stage

Stage 3, called the **decision stage**, involves a single technique, the Quantitative Strategic Planning Matrix (QSPM). A QSPM uses input information from Stage 1 to objectively evaluate feasible alternative strategies identified in Stage 2. QSPM analysis reveals the relative attractiveness of alternative strategies and, thus, provides an objective basis for selecting specific strategies. The QSPM is a more robust way to determine the relative attractiveness of strategies than the summed ranking method described below.

Alternative strategies proposed by SWOT, BCG, IE, SPACE, and GRAND analyses should be considered and discussed in a meeting or series of meetings. Proposed strategies should be listed in writing. When all feasible strategies identified by participants are stated in specific terms and understood, the strategies should be individually ranked from 1 to however many feasible alternative strategies have been identified, in order of attractiveness, perhaps where 1 is the best and 30 (if there are 30 strategies) is the worst. Then, collect the participants' ranking sheets and sum the ratings given for each strategy to end up with a useful ranking of the strategies. Strategies with the lowest sums may be deemed the most attractive, so this process results in a prioritized list of best strategies that reflects the collective wisdom of the group. In terms of how to rank a given strategy, respondents should consider the firm's vision, mission, objectives, and associated costs, as well as any highly weighted external and internal factors.

Rather than, or in conjunction with this ranking method, the QSPM, detailed later in this chapter, offers a more robust procedure to determine the relative attractiveness of alternative strategies. We say "in conjunction with" because the resultant top strategies, perhaps the top 10 to 15, could be evaluated further in a QSPM analysis described later in this chapter.

The SWOT Matrix

6.3. Construct and apply the Strengths-Weaknesses-Opportunities-Threats (SWOT) Matrix.

SWOT analysis was introduced in Chapter 1 because it is arguably the most important and most widely used matching tool. There are four sets of strategies developed in SWOT analysis: SO, WO, ST, and WT.

SO strategies use a firm's internal strengths to take advantage of external opportunities. All managers would like their organization to be in a position in which internal strengths can be used to take advantage of external trends and events. Organizations generally will pursue WO, ST, or WT strategies to more effectively position themselves into situations in which they can apply SO strategies. Using the template, generally four strategies should be formulated and included within each of the four SWOT sets of strategies, but any number of strategies could be included within each set. Be mindful, however, that no firm can pursue everything that could benefit the firm; tough choices have to be made. Prioritization is important throughout the strategic planning process.

WO strategies aim at improving internal weaknesses by taking advantage of external opportunities. Sometimes key external opportunities exist, but a firm has internal weaknesses that prevent it from exploiting those opportunities. For example, for an auto parts manufacturer, the rising demand for electric cars (external opportunity), coupled with the firm having limited batteries to offer (internal weakness), suggests that the firm should consider developing and producing a new line of batteries.

ST strategies use a firm's strengths to avoid or reduce the impact of external threats. An example ST strategy could be when a firm uses its excellent legal department (a strength) to collect millions of dollars in damages from rival firms that infringe on its patents. Rival firms that copy ideas, innovations, and patented products are a threat to many industries. When an organization faces major threats, it will seek to avoid them while concentrating on opportunities. For example, when an organization has both the capital and human resources needed to distribute its own products (internal strengths) and distributors are unreliable, costly, or incapable of meeting the firm's needs (external threats), forward integration (gaining control of distributors) can be an attractive ST strategy.

WT strategies are defensive tactics directed at reducing internal weaknesses and avoiding external threats. An organization faced with numerous external threats and internal weaknesses may indeed be in a precarious position. In fact, such a firm may have to fight for its survival, merge, retrench, declare bankruptcy, or choose to liquidate. For example, some restaurant chains do business with suppliers that treat livestock inhumanely (internal weakness) and face growing customer awareness of the need to preserve wildlife and treat animals with respect (external threat)—resulting in a WT strategy to cease using certain suppliers. As another example, when a firm has excess production capacity (internal weakness) and its basic industry is experiencing declining annual sales and profits (external threat), related diversification can be an effective WT strategy. Whatever strategies are ultimately chosen for implementation, ethics issues are a consideration. For example, as indicated in Ethics Capsule 6, consumers are more sensitive to how animals are treated than ever before.

An example SWOT Matrix is illustrated in Figure 6-3. As shown, there are nine cells: four key factor cells, four strategy cells, and one cell that is always left blank (the upper-left cell). The four strategy cells, labeled *SO, WO, ST,* and *WT*, are developed after completing the four key factor cells, labeled *S, W, O,* and *T*. (*Author comment:* The strategic planning template at www.strategyclub.com simply leaves a space to type in SO, WO, ST, and WT strategies.) The process of constructing a SWOT Matrix can be summarized in eight steps, as follows:

1. List the firm's key AQCD internal strengths.
2. List the firm's key AQCD internal weaknesses.
3. List the firm's key AQCD external opportunities.
4. List the firm's key AQCD external threats.
5. Match internal strengths with external opportunities to develop specific SO strategies.
6. Match internal weaknesses with external opportunities to develop specific WO strategies.
7. Match internal strengths with external threats to develop specific ST strategies.
8. Match internal weaknesses with external threats to develop specific WT strategies.

ETHICS CAPSULE 6

As We Strategize We Must Not Jeopardize Animal Welfare[4]

Travel Stock/Shutterstock

Consumers are increasingly resentful of companies that harm wildlife or treat animals inhumanely. According to the *World Wildlife Fund's Living Planet Report*, the world's animal species are dying, and humans are a big reason why. The report reveals that global populations of wild mammals, fish, birds, amphibians, and reptiles declined 58 percent on average in the last 45 years. Specifically, land animals declined by 38 percent, marine species incurred a 36 percent drop, and the number of freshwater species decreased by 81 percent.

According to a United Nations report released in May 2021, up to 1 million species are at risk of extinction because of human activities. Species like eastern and western gorillas are nearly extinct and poaching has decimated both elephant and northern white rhino populations. Even vulture populations are headed toward extinction as are certain species of bees. Other causes of the mass extinction of wildlife include urban development, overhunting, pollution, disease, and climate change—all of which are tied to humans. In many respects, the Earth is becoming inhospitable to animals and humans. SWOT factors and strategies often address this business ethics issue.

Dr. John J. Wiens of the University of Arizona has studied this extinction phenomena and says: "If humans cause larger temperature increases, we could lose more than a third or even half of all animal and plant species." Wiens also says: "If we stick to the Paris Agreement to combat climate change, we may lose fewer than 2 out of every 10 plant and animal species on Earth by 2070."

[4]Based on https://www.usatoday.com/story/news/nation/2020/02/14/climate-change-study-plant-animal-extinction/4760646002

	Strengths	Weaknesses
	1. Inventory turnover up 5.8 to 6.7 2. Average customer purchase up $97 to $128 3. Employee morale is excellent 4. In-store promotions = 20 percent increase in sales 5. Newspaper advertising expenditures down 10 percent 6. Revenues from repair and service in store up 16 percent 7. In-store technical support persons have MIS degrees 8. Store's debt-to-total-assets ratio down 34 percent 9. Revenues per employee up 19 percent	1. Software revenues in store down 12 percent 2. Location of store hurt by new Hwy 34 3. Carpet and paint in store in disrepair 4. Bathroom in store needs refurbishing 5. Total store revenues down 8 percent 6. Store has no website 7. Supplier on-time-delivery up to 2.4 days 8. Customer checkout process too slow
Opportunities	**SO Strategies**	**WO Strategies**
1. Population of city growing 10 percent 2. Land is available 1 mile away 3. Vehicle traffic passing store up 12 percent 4. Vendors average six new products a year 5. Older adults' use of computers up 8 percent 6. Small business growth in area up 10 percent 7. Desire for websites up 18 percent by realtors 8. Desire for websites up 12 percent by small firms	1. Add 4 new in-store promotions monthly (S4, O3) 2. Add two new repair and service persons (S6, O5) 3. Send flyer to all adults older than age 55 (S5, O5)	1. Purchase land to build new store (W2, O2) 2. Install new carpet, paint, and bath (W3, W4, O1) 3. Up website services by 50 percent (W6, O7, O8) 4. Launch mailout to all realtors in city (W5, O7)
Threats	**ST Strategies**	**WT Strategies**
1. Best Buy opening new store in 1 year nearby 2. Local university offers computer repair 3. New bypass Hwy 34 in 1 year will divert traffic 4. New mall being built nearby 5. Gas prices up 14 percent 6. Vendors raising prices 8 percent	1. Hire two more repair persons and market these new services (S6, S7, T1) 2. Purchase land to build new store (S8, T3) 3. Raise out-of-store service calls from $60 to $80 (S6, T5)	1. Hire two new cashiers (W8, T1, T4) 2. Install new carpet, paint, and bath (W3, W4, T1)

FIGURE 6-3

A SWOT Matrix for a Retail Computer Store

Some important aspects of a SWOT Matrix are evidenced in Figure 6-3. For example, note that both the internal and external factors and the SO, ST, WO, and WT strategies are stated in specific terms. This is important! For example, regarding the second SO strategy (SO2), if the analyst simply said, "Add new repair and service persons," the reader may conclude that 20 new repair and service persons are needed, when only 2 are needed. So, in stating strategies, be as quantitative and divisional as possible. Furthermore, remember to consult the vision and mission statements of the firm, and keep in mind what the firm considers to be its competitive advantages or core competencies based on its value chain analysis. Take care to develop SO, WO, ST, and WT strategies based on these considerations as well as the factors receiving the highest weights from your EFE and IFE matrices.

Regarding specificity, for each SWOT strategy included in the matrix, ask yourself this question: "Is the strategy stated specifically enough to estimate the cost (or savings) if it is selected for implementation?" If the answer is NO, then the strategy is too vaguely stated. Thus, whenever words such as "expand, increase, decrease, more, or reduce" are used in a SWOT Matrix, clarify with a percentage or number exactly what you are proposing. There is no need to give estimated costs in a SWOT Matrix, but the information must be specific enough to generate these numbers if the particular strategy is selected for implementation. Vagueness is disastrous in strategic planning, especially in a SWOT Matrix.

As shown in Figure 6-3, it is important to include the "S1, O2" notation after each strategy in a SWOT Matrix. This notation reveals the rationale for each alternative strategy in terms of the internal and external factors that were "matched" to formulate desirable strategies. For example, note that this retail computer store business may need to "purchase land to build a new store" because a new Highway 34 will make the current location less desirable. The "S8, T3" type of notation, given after each strategy in a SWOT Matrix, accents that *strategies do not come out of the blue yonder.*

The purpose of SWOT analysis and each Stage 2 matching tool is to generate a list of feasible, specific alternative strategies, not to select or determine which strategies are best. Not all of the strategies developed in the SWOT Matrix will be selected for implementation. No firm has sufficient capital or resources to implement every strategy formulated. As a rule of thumb, include at least four strategies in each SO, ST, WO and WT quadrant to encompass all aspects of the business; usually a SWOT matrix, thus, will include at least 16 strategies total.

In a SWOT matrix, avoid ever putting dollar amounts needed among the strategies. SWOT strategies need to be stated in specific terms with numbers. For example, an SO2 strategy might be to "Add 250 new stores in the Southeast United States annually for the next 3 years." However, estimated dollar total amounts for respective strategies do not need to be provided because this information will be provided later in the analysis with the recommendations (strategies selected for implementation). It is just premature among alternative strategies in a SWOT matrix to provide total dollar amounts needed; unfortunately doing so is often misconstrued by students or managers to satisfy the "specific" requirement for SWOT strategies. The numbers among SWOT strategies should relate to specifically what is being suggested, how many stores for example, rather than some random dollar amount with no clue given regarding what the dollars are being spent for specifically.

Although the SWOT Matrix is widely used in strategic planning, the analysis does have limitations.[5] First, SWOT analysis does not reveal how to achieve a competitive advantage, so it must not be an end in itself. The analysis should be the starting point for a discussion on how proposed strategies could be implemented as well as cost-to-benefit, uniqueness, and trade-off considerations that ultimately could lead to competitive advantage. Second, SWOT is a static assessment (or snapshot) in time. As circumstances, capabilities, threats, and strategies change, the dynamics of a competitive environment may not be revealed in a single matrix. Third, there are interrelationships among the key internal and external factors that SWOT does not reveal but which may be important in devising strategies. Finally, the relative attractiveness of alternative strategies is not provided.

The Strategic Position and Action Evaluation (SPACE) Matrix

6.4. Construct and apply the Strategic Position and Action Evaluation (SPACE) Matrix.

The **Strategic Position and Action Evaluation (SPACE) Matrix** is another Stage 2 matching tool that uses two axes and four quadrants to reveal whether aggressive, conservative, defensive, or competitive strategies are most appropriate for a given organization. Axes of the SPACE Matrix represent two internal dimensions (**financial position [FP]** and **competitive position [CP]**) and two external dimensions (**stability position [SP]** and **industry position [IP]**). To perform SPACE analysis, simply rate a company on each of the four dimensions (axes) named above and revealed in Figure 6-4.[6]

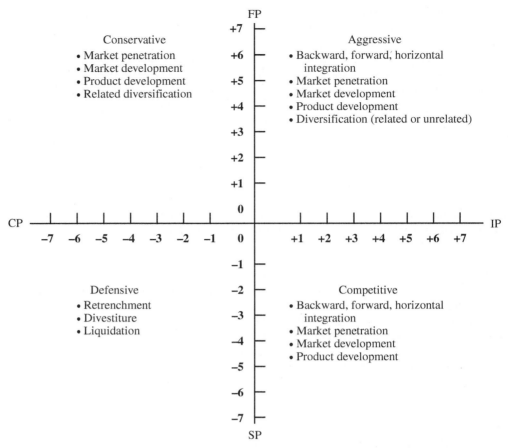

FIGURE 6-4

The SPACE Matrix

Source: Based on H. Rowe, R. Mason, and K. Dickel, *Strategic Management and Business Policy: A Methodological Approach* (Reading, MA: Addison-Wesley Publishing Co. Inc., © 1982), 155.

Depending on the type of organization, numerous variables could make up each of the dimensions represented on the axes of the SPACE Matrix. Factors that were included in the firm's EFE and IFE matrices should be considered in developing a SPACE Matrix. Other variables commonly included in a SPACE analysis are given in Table 6-1. For example, return on investment, leverage, liquidity, working capital, and cash flow are commonly considered to be determining factors of an organization's financial position (FP). Like the SWOT Matrix, the SPACE Matrix should be tailored to the particular organization being studied and based on factual information to the extent possible. Include specific factors; for example, Delta Airlines may include "volatility of oil prices" as a factor under SP with a rating of −6. To the degree factors are unique to a particular firm and industry, the more effective the SPACE results will be in suggesting possible generic strategies to implement. *Note*: If using the template to help perform your SPACE analysis, you may use the general factors provided, but try to determine key factors related to your company and industry in the same manner you did previously in Chapter 3 with the CPM. When using the template, the calculations are done automatically and the rating scale is provided.

Steps in Performing SPACE Analysis

The process of developing a SPACE Matrix can be summarized in six steps.

Step 1   Select a set of variables to define financial position (FP), competitive position (CP), stability position (SP), and industry position (IP).
   1. Let's first elaborate on the difference between the SP and IP axes. The term SP refers to the volatility of profits and revenues for firms in a given industry based

TABLE 6-1 Example Factors That Make Up the SPACE Matrix Axes

Internal Strategic Position	External Strategic Position
Financial Position (FP)	*Stability Position (SP)*
Return on investment	Technological changes
Leverage	Rate of inflation
Liquidity	Demand variability
Working capital	Price range of competing products
Cash flow	Barriers to entry into market
Inventory turnover	Competitive pressure
Earnings per share	Ease of exit from market
Price earnings ratio	Risk involved in business
Competitive Position (CP)	*Industry Position (IP)*
Market share	Growth potential
Product quality	Profit potential
Product life cycle	Financial stability
Customer loyalty	Extent leveraged
Capacity utilization	Resource utilization
Technological know-how	Ease of entry into market
Control over suppliers and distributors	Productivity, capacity utilization

Source: Based on H. Rowe, R. Mason, & K. Dickel, *Strategic Management and Business Policy: A Methodological Approach* (Reading, MA: Addison-Wesley Publishing Co. Inc., 1982); 155–156.

on the factors considered in the SPACE. Thus, SP volatility (stability) is based on the expected impact of changes in profits by volatility in core external factors such as technology, the economy, demographics, seasonality, and so on. The higher the frequency and magnitude of profitability changes in a given industry, the more unstable the SP becomes. An industry can be stable or unstable on SP, yet high or low on IP. The robotics industry, for instance, would be unstable (−7) on the SP axis due to constant developments and upgrades, yet high growth on the IP axis (+7), whereas the canned food industry would be stable (−1) on the SP axis, yet low growth on the IP axis (+1). IP simply refers to how attractive a particular industry is going forward with regard to growth, revenues, and profits.

Regarding the FP axis, simply rate the firm on numerous financial variables where +7 is really strong and +1 is really weak. Similarly, on the CP axis, simply rate the firm as per its relative position on numerous variables versus rival firms, where −7 is really weak and −1 is really strong.

Step 2   Assign a numerical value ranging from +1 (worst) to +7 (best) to each of the variables that make up the FP and IP dimensions. Assign a numerical value ranging from −1 (best) to −7 (worst) to each of the variables that make up the SP and CP dimensions. On the FP and CP axes, make comparisons to competitors. For example, a +7 on any FP or IP factor is outstanding, whereas a +1 is terrible. On the IP and SP axes, make comparisons to other industries. On the SP axis, know that a −7 on any factor denotes a highly unstable industry condition (unattractive), whereas −1 denotes a highly stable industry condition (attractive).

Step 3   Compute an average score for FP, CP, IP, and SP by summing the values given to the variables of each dimension and then by dividing by the number of variables included in the respective dimension.

Step 4   Plot the average scores for FP, IP, SP, and CP on the appropriate axes in the SPACE Matrix.

Step 5   Add the two scores on the *x*-axis (CP and IP) and plot the resultant point on X. Add the two scores on the *y*-axis (FP and SP) and plot the resultant point on Y. Plot the intersection of the new (*x, y*) coordinate.

Step 6   Draw a **directional vector** from the origin of the SPACE Matrix (0,0) through the new (*x, y*) coordinate. That vector, being located in a particular quadrant, reveals particular strategies the firm should consider. *Author comment: The template plots the new (x, y) coordinate, rather than drawing a vector; the template also lets you estimate (x, y) coordinates for rival firms without averaging the SP, CP, IP, and FP values. You may also elect to estimate a new (x, y) point for your firm after your new strategies are implemented to show improvements in the firm's position within the SPACE Matrix.*

SPACE Matrix Quadrants

Some example strategy profiles that can emerge from SPACE analysis are shown in Figure 6-5. The directional vector associated with each profile suggests the type of strategies to pursue: aggressive, conservative, competitive, or defensive. Specifically, when a firm's directional vector is located in the **Aggressive Quadrant** (upper right) of the SPACE Matrix, an organization is in an excellent position to use its internal strengths to (1) take advantage of external opportunities, (2) overcome internal weaknesses, and (3) avoid external threats. Therefore, as indicated in Figure 6-4, market penetration, market development, product development, backward integration, forward integration, horizontal integration, or diversification, can be feasible, depending on the specific circumstances that face the firm.

When performing SPACE analysis for a particular firm, be specific in terms of recommended strategies. For example, instead of saying market penetration is a recommended strategy when a vector is located in the Aggressive Quadrant, say "adding 34 new stores in India is the proposed strategy." This is an important point for students doing case analyses because whenever a particular company is known, then the terms learned in Chapter 5, such as market development, must be quantified to enable specific recommendations to be proposed. The term "market development" could refer to adding a manufacturing plant in Thailand, Mexico, or Kenya. Thus, be *specific* to the extent possible regarding implications of all the matrices presented in this chapter. Vagueness is disastrous in strategic management. Avoid terms such as *expand, increase, decrease*, and *grow*, unless accompanying numbers are provided.

The SPACE directional vector may appear in the **Conservative Quadrant** (upper left), which implies staying close to the firm's basic competencies and not taking excessive risks. As indicated in Figure 6-4, conservative strategies most often include market penetration, market development, product development, and related diversification. The SPACE directional vector may be located in the **Defensive Quadrant** (lower left), which suggests the firm should focus on improving internal weaknesses and avoiding external threats. Defensive strategies include retrenchment, divestiture, and liquidation. Finally, the SPACE directional vector may be located in the **Competitive Quadrant** (lower right), indicating competitive strategies. Competitive strategies include backward, forward, and horizontal integration; market penetration; market development; and product development—as indicated in Figure 6-4.

SPACE analysis is an excellent tool for transferring complex information into a manageable list of strategies to consider for implementation. SPACE analysis can be helpful in deciding how aggressive or defensive a firm should be, so it's important to always include SPACE analysis in doing strategic planning.

A SPACE Matrix analysis has some limitations as follows:

1. It is a snapshot in time.
2. There are more than four dimensions that firms could or should be rated on.
3. The directional vector could fall directly on an axis or could even go nowhere if the coordinate is (0,0). Whenever this happens, analysts usually add a few more evaluative criteria that comprise the FP (and any other) axis to make the vector shift into a particular quadrant.
4. Implications of the exact angle of the vector within a quadrant are unclear.
5. The relative attractiveness of alternative strategies generated is unclear.

Aggressive Profiles

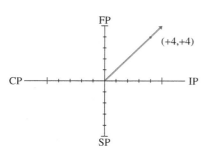

A financially strong firm that has achieved major competitive advantages in a growing and stable industry

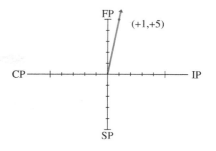

A firm whose financial strength is a dominating factor in the industry

Conservative Profiles

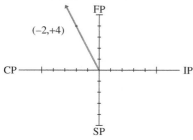

A firm that has achieved financial strength in a stable industry that is not growing; the firm has few competitive advantages

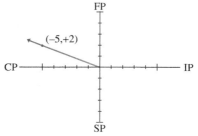

A firm that suffers from major competitive disadvantages in an industry that is technologically stable but declining in sales

Competitive Profiles

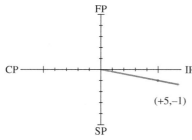

A firm with major competitive advantages in a high-growth industry

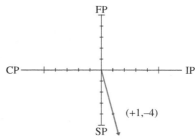

An organization that is competing fairly well in an unstable industry

Defensive Profiles

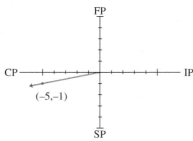

A firm that has a very weak competitive position in a negative growth, stable industry

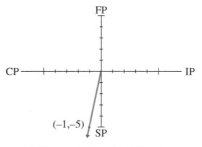

A financially troubled firm in a very unstable industry

FIGURE 6-5
Example Strategy Profiles

Source: Based on H. Rowe, R. Mason, and K. Dickel, *Strategic Management and Business Policy: A Methodological Approach* (Reading, MA: Addison-Wesley Publishing Co. Inc., © 1982), 155.

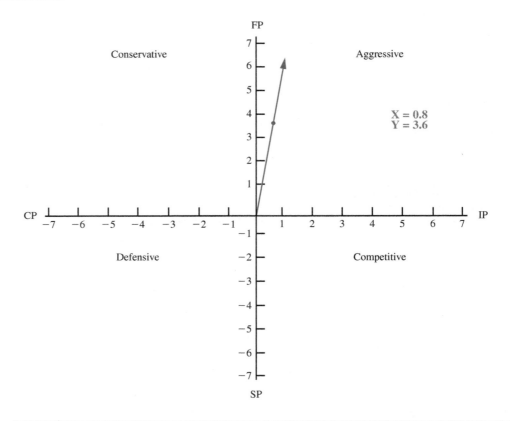

FIGURE 6-6

A SPACE Matrix for ABC Company

Internal Analysis:		External Analysis:	
Financial Position (FP)		**Stability Position (SP)**	
Debt Ratio	7	Competitive Pressure	−4
Liquidity	7	Price Comparison	−2
Current Ratio	7	Product Demand	−2
EPS	7	Diversity of Social Media Interest Served	−3
ROA	4	Number of Inactive Accounts	−3
Financial Position (FP) Average	**6.4**	**Stability Position (SP) Average**	**−2.8**

Internal Analysis:		External Analysis:	
Competitive Position (CP)		**Industry Position (IP)**	
Cash Flow	−2	Growth Potential	6
Social Networking Market Share	−1	Cyber Security Concerns	2
Professional Networking Market Share	−6	Ease of Entry into Market	2
Product Variety	−5	Profit Potential	5
Use of Technology	−2	Alternative Products	5
Competitive Position (CP) Average	**−3.2**	**Industry Position (IP) Average**	**4.0**

The SPACE Matrix has been used to help determine ABC Company's overall strategic position as provided in Figure 6-6. As noted in Figure 6-6, ABC Company falls in the Aggressive Quadrant.

The Boston Consulting Group (BCG) Matrix

6.5. Construct and apply the Boston Consulting Group (BCG) Matrix.

BCG is a private management consulting firm that specializes in strategic planning. Based in Boston, Massachusetts, and employing 6,200 consultants worldwide, BCG has approximately

90 offices in 50 countries, and annually ranks in the top five on *Fortune*'s list of the "100 Best Companies to Work For."

Autonomous divisions (also called *segments* or *profit centers*) of an organization make up what is called a **business portfolio**. When a firm's divisions compete in different industries, a separate strategy must often be developed for each business. The **Boston Consulting Group (BCG) Matrix** is designed specifically to enhance a multidivisional firm's efforts to formulate strategies. Allocating resources across divisions is arguably the most important strategic decision facing multidivisional firms. Multidivisional firms range in size from small, three-restaurant, mom-and-pop firms, to huge conglomerates such as Walt Disney Company, to universities that have various schools or colleges—and they all need to use **portfolio analysis**—a tool that compares divisions of a firm to determine how best to allocate resources among those divisions.

In a *Form 10K* or *Annual Report*, and sometimes in quarterly reports, most companies disclose revenues and sometimes operating profits by segment. Reasons to disclose by-segment financial information in a *Form 10K* more than offset the reasons not to disclose, as indicated in Table 6-2. BCG portfolio analysis can be performed based on whatever information is provided, such as the location of all the firm's stores or branches, product lines offered, the business process, or any other manner to provide segment data. In the BCG matrices in this chapter, the size of circles corresponds to segment revenues (or number of stores), and pie slices within circles correspond to segment operating profits.

TABLE 6-2 Reasons to (or Not to) Disclose Financial Information by Segment (by Division)

Reasons to Disclose	Reasons Not to Disclose
1. Stakeholders will better understand the firm, which leads to greater support.	1. To avoid rival firms obtaining free competitive information.
2. Managers and employees will better understand the firm, which leads to greater commitment.	2. To avoid performance failures being exposed.
	3. To avoid rivalry among segments becoming too intense.
3. Disclosure enhances communication process both within the firm and with outsiders.	4. To avoid lucrative markets being revealed to rival firms.

The BCG Matrix graphically portrays differences among divisions based on two dimensions: (1) relative market share position on the *x*-axis, and (2) industry growth rate on the *y*-axis. The BCG Matrix allows a multidivisional organization to manage its portfolio of businesses by examining these two dimensions for each division relative to other divisions in the organization. **Relative market share position (RMSP)** is defined as the ratio of a division's own market share (or revenues or number of stores) in a particular industry to the market share (or revenues or number of stores) held by the largest rival firm (leader) in that industry. In the U.S. candy industry, for example, Nestle's relative market share position is Nestle's market share divided by Mars' market share, or $1.3/20.8 = 0.063$; similarly, Hershey's relative market share position is $13.8/20.8 = 0.664$, as indicated in Table 6-3.

TABLE 6-3 Market Share Data for the U.S. Candy Industry

Company	Market Share (percent)	BCG: Relative Market Share Position
Mars	20.8	$20.8/20.8 = 1.000$
Hershey	13.8	$13.8/20.8 = 0.664$
Jelly Belly	3.4	$3.4/20.8 = 0.164$
Mondelez	3.3	$3.3/20.8 = 0.159$
Tootsie Roll	3.0	$3.0/20.8 = 0.144$
Nestle	1.3	$1.3/20.8 = 0.063$

Source: Based on Dmitry Diment's 2021 Industry Report on Candy Production in the US, *IBIS World*, August 2021, p. 1.

The midpoint for relative market share position usually is set at 0.50, corresponding to a division that has half the market share of the leading firm in the industry. The *y*-axis represents the **industry growth rate** (IGR) in sales, measured in percentage terms—that is, the average annual increase or decrease in revenue for all firms in an industry. The growth rate percentages on the *y*-axis could range from −20 to +20 (or −10 to +10) percent, with 0.0 being the midpoint. The average annual increase in revenues for several leading firms in the industry would be a good estimate for the IGR value. Also, various sources, such as the *S&P Industry Surveys* and www.finance.yahoo.com would provide this value. Be mindful that a negative IGR does not indicate revenues were negative, rather that industry revenues were less than they were the previous period.

Based on each division's respective (*x, y*) coordinate, each segment can be properly positioned in a BCG Matrix. Divisions located in Quadrant I (upper right) of the BCG Matrix are called "Question Marks," those located in Quadrant II (upper left) are called "Stars," those located in Quadrant III (lower left) are called "Cash Cows," and those divisions located in Quadrant IV (lower right) are called "Dogs." The four BCG quadrants are described as follows:

- *Question Marks*—Divisions in Quadrant I (upper right) have a low relative market share position, yet they compete in a high-growth industry. Generally, these firms' cash needs are high and their cash generation is low. These businesses are called **question marks** because the organization must decide whether to strengthen them by pursuing an intensive strategy (i.e., market penetration, market development, or product development) or to sell them. An example question mark could be Snap's portfolio of virtual reality technology devices; virtual reality is a high-growth industry, but Snap has a low relative market share. Another way to view *Question Marks* is that rivals have beaten you to the market. If the industry is still new, there is more incentive to pursue intensive strategies because the top firms are likely not generating significant revenues either, but as the industry in question becomes more mature, then selling this business off becomes more attractive.
- *Stars*—Divisions in Quadrant II (upper left) represent the organizations' best long-run opportunities for growth and profitability and are therefore called **stars**. Divisions with a high relative market share and a high IGR should receive substantial investment to maintain or strengthen their dominant positions. Forward, backward, and horizontal integration; market penetration; market development; and product development are appropriate strategies for these divisions to consider, as indicated in Figure 6-7. A star example could be Meta's (Facebook's parent) portfolio of virtual reality devices; Meta is one of the leaders in the industry in revenues in these devices.
- *Cash Cows*—Divisions in Quadrant III (lower left) have a high relative market share position but compete in a low-growth industry; they are called **cash cows**. Because they generate cash in excess of their needs, they are often milked. Many of today's cash cows were yesterday's stars. Cash cow divisions should be managed to maintain their strong position for as long as possible. Product development, or diversification, may be an attractive strategy for strong cash cows. However, as a cash cow division becomes weak, retrenchment or divestiture can become more appropriate. A cash cow example is Hewlett-Packard (HP) with its desktop computers; HP is a market leader in terms of revenues, but desktop computers are a low-growth industry. Another way to think of cash cows is the industry is slowly giving way to newer technology or consumer tastes and experiencing declining sales, but these sales remain robust enough to finance other aspects of the business.
- *Dogs*—Divisions in Quadrant IV (lower right) have a low relative market share position and compete in a slow- or no-market-growth industry; they are **dogs** in the firm's portfolio. Because of their weak internal and external position, these businesses are often liquidated, divested, or trimmed down through retrenchment. When a division first becomes a dog, retrenchment can be the best strategy to pursue because many dogs have bounced back after strenuous asset and cost reduction to become viable, profitable divisions.

The basic BCG Matrix appears in Figure 6-7. Each circle represents a separate division. The size of the circle corresponds to the proportion of corporate revenue generated by that business unit, and the pie slice indicates the proportion of corporate profits generated by that division.

The major benefit of the BCG Matrix is that it draws attention to the cash flow, investment characteristics, and needs of an organization's various divisions. The divisions of many firms evolve over time: Dogs become question marks, question marks become stars, stars become cash cows, and cash cows become dogs in an ongoing counterclockwise motion. Less frequently, stars

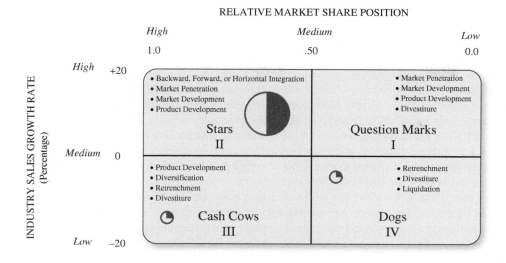

RELATIVE MARKET SHARE POSITION

FIGURE 6-7

The BCG Matrix

Source: Based on the BCG Portfolio Matrix from the Product Portfolio Matrix, © 1970, The Boston Consulting Group.

become question marks, question marks become dogs, dogs become cash cows, and cash cows become stars (in a clockwise motion). In some organizations, no cyclical motion is apparent. Over time, organizations should strive to achieve a portfolio of divisions that are stars.

An example of a BCG Matrix is provided in Figure 6-8, which illustrates an organization composed of five divisions with annual sales ranging from $5,000 to $60,000. Division 1 has the greatest sales volume, so the circle representing that division is the largest one in the matrix. The circle corresponding to Division 5 is the smallest because its sales volume ($5,000) is least among all the divisions. The pie slices within the circles reveal the percent of corporate profits contributed by each division. As shown, Division 1 contributes the highest profit percentage, 40 percent, as indicated by 40 percent of the area within circle 1 being shaded. Notice in the diagram that Division 1 is considered a star, Division 2 is a question mark, Division 3 is also a question mark, Division 4 is a cash cow, and Division 5 is a dog.

RELATIVE MARKET SHARE POSITION IN THE INDUSTRY

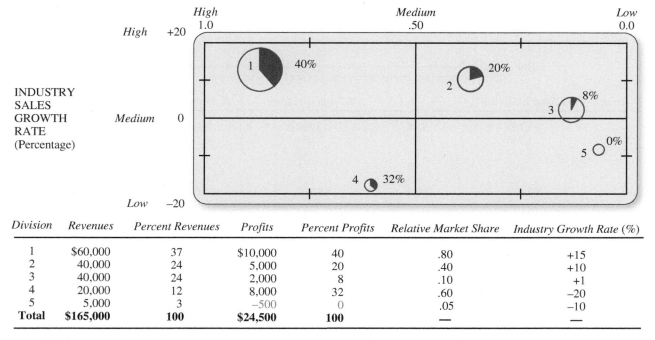

Division	Revenues	Percent Revenues	Profits	Percent Profits	Relative Market Share	Industry Growth Rate (%)
1	$60,000	37	$10,000	40	.80	+15
2	40,000	24	5,000	20	.40	+10
3	40,000	24	2,000	8	.10	+1
4	20,000	12	8,000	32	.60	−20
5	5,000	3	−500	0	.05	−10
Total	**$165,000**	**100**	**$24,500**	**100**	—	—

FIGURE 6-8

An Example BCG Matrix

The BCG Matrix, like all analytical techniques, has some limitations. For example, viewing every business as a star, cash cow, dog, or question mark is an oversimplification; many businesses fall right in the middle of the BCG Matrix and, thus, are not easily classified. Furthermore, the BCG Matrix does not reflect if various divisions or their industries are growing over time; that is, the matrix has no temporal qualities. For this reason, students (and companies) often develop and compare a Before Recommendations versus After Recommendations BCG Matrix, an excellent way to reveal expected results of your recommendations versus prior positioning of segments.

Another limitation of BCG analysis is that other variables besides relative market share position and IGR in sales, such as the size of the market and competitive advantages, are important in making strategic decisions about various divisions. A final limitation is the BCG is not comparing the firm's own divisions to each other; it only compares each division to its respective industry. For this reason, the firm's smallest segment can be a star. The Internal-External Matrix (upcoming) would likely not allow this as the divisions are compared to one another (at least in some indirect capacity) because of the methodology of identifying the SWOTs, then weighting them, and finally revealing how well our current strategies are responding to each. The IE Matrix process is thus more robust, resulting likely in lower scores for a fledging division because firms cannot be responding equally to all strategies across all divisions.

Another example BCG Matrix is provided in Figure 6-9. As you can see, Division 5 had an operating loss of $188 million as indicated by its red shading. The remaining pie slices add up to more than 100 percent profits to account for negative net income associated with Division 5 (this is a different way to portray divisional losses in a BCG matrix analysis).

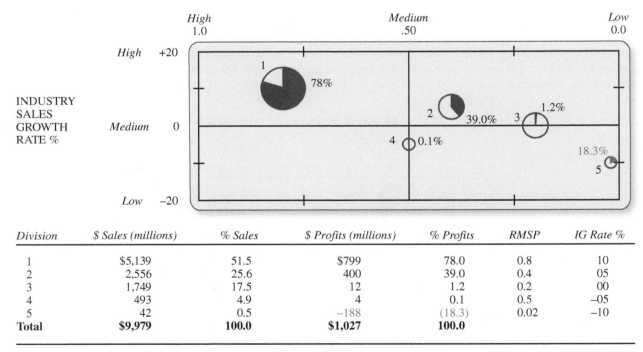

RELATIVE MARKET SHARE POSITION (RMSP)

Division	$ Sales (millions)	% Sales	$ Profits (millions)	% Profits	RMSP	IG Rate %
1	$5,139	51.5	$799	78.0	0.8	10
2	2,556	25.6	400	39.0	0.4	05
3	1,749	17.5	12	1.2	0.2	00
4	493	4.9	4	0.1	0.5	−05
5	42	0.5	−188	(18.3)	0.02	−10
Total	**$9,979**	**100.0**	**$1,027**	**100.0**		

FIGURE 6-9

An Example BCG Matrix

The Internal-External (IE) Matrix

6.6. Construct and apply the Internal-External (IE) Matrix.

The **Internal-External (IE) Matrix** positions an organization's various divisions (segments) in a nine-cell display, as illustrated in Figure 6-10. The IE Matrix is similar to the BCG Matrix in that both tools involve plotting a firm's divisions in a schematic diagram; this is why both tools are

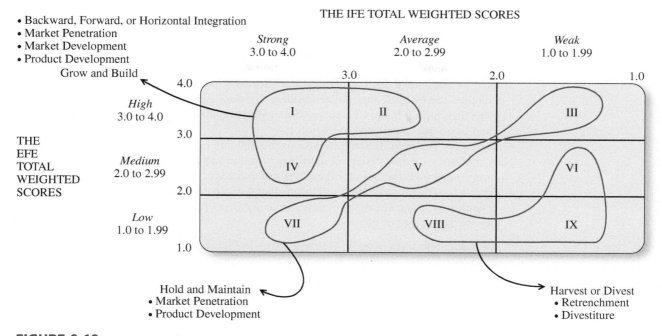

FIGURE 6-10

The Internal-External (IE) Matrix

Source: Based on: The IE Matrix was developed from the General Electric (GE) Business Screen Matrix. For a description of the GE Matrix, see Michael Allen, "Diagramming GE's Planning for What's WATT," in R. Allio and M. Pennington, eds., *Corporate Planning: Techniques and Applications* l par; New York: AMACOM, 1979.

forms of portfolio analysis. In both the BCG and IE matrices, the size of each circle represents the percentage of revenues or number of stores each division contributes, and pie slices reveal the percentage of operating profits contributed by each division. But there are four important differences between the BCG Matrix and the IE Matrix, as follows:

1. The *x*- and *y*-axes are different.
2. The IE Matrix requires more information about the divisions than does the BCG Matrix. Thus, the placing of divisions in the IE Matrix is much more accurate than in a BCG Matrix.
3. The strategic implications of each matrix are different.
4. The IE Matrix has nine quadrants versus four in a BCG Matrix.

For these reasons, strategists in multidivisional firms often develop both the BCG Matrix and the IE Matrix in formulating alternative strategies. A common practice is to develop a BCG Matrix and an IE Matrix for the present and then develop projected matrices to reflect expectations of the future. This before-and-after analysis can be quite effective in an oral presentation, enabling students (or strategists) to pave the way for (justify or give some rationale for) their recommendations across divisions of the firm. Also, commonly a BCG Matrix will be developed by region and an IE Matrix by product, or vice versa.

The IE Matrix is based on two crucial dimensions: (1) the IFE total weighted scores on the *x*-axis and (2) the EFE total weighted scores on the *y*-axis. Recall that each division of an organization should construct an IFE Matrix and an EFE Matrix for its part of the organization, but usually in performing case analysis, strategic management students simply estimate divisional IFE and EFE scores rather than prepare those underlying matrices for every division. Regardless, it is the total weighted scores derived from the divisions that allow construction of the corporate-level IE Matrix. On the *x*-axis of the IE Matrix, an IFE total weighted score of 1.0 to 1.99 represents a weak internal position; a score of 2.0 to 2.99 is considered average; and a score of 3.0 to 4.0 is strong. Similarly, on the *y*-axis, an EFE total weighted score of 1.0 to 1.99 is considered weak; a score of 2.0 to 2.99 is average; and a score of 3.0 to 4.0 is strong. Circles, representing divisions, are positioned in an IE Matrix based on their respective IFE and EFE total weighed scores.

Despite having nine cells, the IE Matrix has three major regions that have different strategy implications, as follows:

- *Region 1*—The prescription for divisions that fall into cells I, II, or IV can be described as *grow and build*. Intensive (market penetration, market development, and product development) or integrative (backward integration, forward integration, and horizontal integration) strategies can be most appropriate for these divisions. This is the best region for divisions, given their high IFE and EFE scores. Successful organizations are able to achieve a portfolio of businesses positioned in Region 1.
- *Region 2*—The prescription for divisions that fall into cells III, V, or VII can be described as *hold and maintain* strategies; market penetration and product development are two commonly employed strategies for these types of divisions.
- *Region 3*—The prescription for divisions that fall into cells VI, VIII, or IX can be described as *harvest or divest* strategies; retrenchment and divestiture are two commonly used strategies for these types of divisions.

An example four-division IE Matrix is given in Figure 6-11. As indicated by the positioning of the four circles, grow and build strategies are appropriate for Divisions 1, 2, and 3. But Division 4 is a candidate for harvest or divest. Division 2 contributes the greatest percentage of company sales and, thus, is represented by the largest circle. Division 1 contributes the greatest proportion of total profits; it has the largest-percentage pie slice.

An example five-division IE Matrix is given in Figure 6-12. Note that Division 1 has the largest revenues (as indicated by the largest circle) and the largest profits (as indicated by the largest pie slice) in the matrix. It is common for organizations to develop both geographic and product-based IE matrices to more effectively formulate strategies and allocate resources among divisions.

Important Note: Whenever a particular company is known, such as in doing case analysis or in the real world, be more specific with proposed strategies rather than using generic terms in regard to resultant IE Matrix strategies. Couch your strategies in quantitative and divisional terms to the extent possible. (This is true also with strategies derived from the BCG, SPACE, GRAND, and even SWOT analyses; specificity is golden—avoid vagueness.)

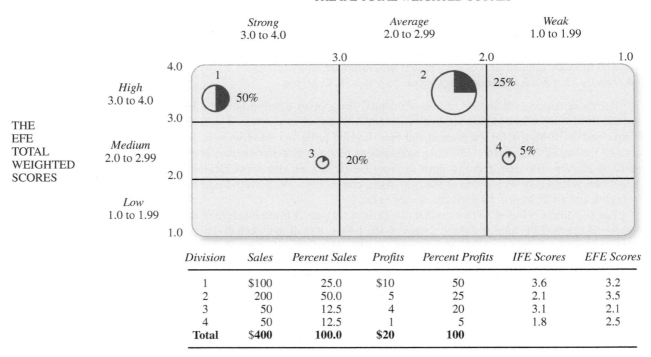

THE IFE TOTAL WEIGHTED SCORES

Division	Sales	Percent Sales	Profits	Percent Profits	IFE Scores	EFE Scores
1	$100	25.0	$10	50	3.6	3.2
2	200	50.0	5	25	2.1	3.5
3	50	12.5	4	20	3.1	2.1
4	50	12.5	1	5	1.8	2.5
Total	**$400**	**100.0**	**$20**	**100**		

FIGURE 6-11

An Example IE Matrix

THE IFE TOTAL WEIGHTED SCORES

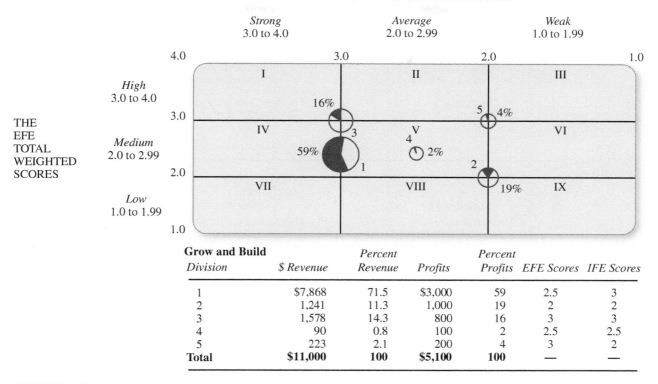

| Grow and Build | | Percent | | Percent | | |
Division	$ Revenue	Revenue	Profits	Profits	EFE Scores	IFE Scores
1	$7,868	71.5	$3,000	59	2.5	3
2	1,241	11.3	1,000	19	2	2
3	1,578	14.3	800	16	3	3
4	90	0.8	100	2	2.5	2.5
5	223	2.1	200	4	3	2
Total	**$11,000**	**100**	**$5,100**	**100**	—	—

FIGURE 6-12
The IE Matrix

The Grand Strategy Matrix

6.7. Construct and apply the Grand Strategy Matrix.

In addition to the SWOT Matrix, SPACE Matrix, BCG Matrix, and IE Matrix, the **Grand Strategy Matrix** is a popular tool for formulating alternative strategies. All organizations can be positioned in one of the Grand Strategy Matrix's four strategy quadrants. A firm's divisions likewise could be positioned. As illustrated in Figure 6-13, the Grand Strategy Matrix is based on two evaluative dimensions: (1) competitive position on the *x*-axis and (2) market (industry) growth on the *y*-axis. Any industry whose annual growth in sales exceeds 5 percent could be considered to have rapid growth. Appropriate strategies for an organization to consider are listed in sequential order of attractiveness in each quadrant of the Grand Strategy Matrix.

Firms located in Quadrant I of the Grand Strategy Matrix are in an excellent strategic position. For these companies, continued concentration on current markets (market penetration) and products (product development and/or market development) are appropriate strategies. It is unwise for a Quadrant I firm to shift notably from its established competitive advantages, yet all firms seek continual improvement. Thus, when a Quadrant I organization has excessive resources, then backward, forward, or horizontal integration may be considered. When a Quadrant I firm is too heavily committed to a single product, then related diversification may reduce the risks associated with a narrow product line. Quadrant I firms can afford to take advantage of external opportunities and take increased risks when necessary.

Firms positioned in Quadrant II need to evaluate their present approach to the marketplace seriously. Although their industry is growing, they are unable to compete effectively; they need to determine why the firm's current approach is ineffective and how the company can best change to improve its competitiveness. Because Quadrant II organizations are in a rapid market growth industry, an intensive strategy (as opposed to integrative or diversification) is usually the first option that should be considered. However, if the firm is lacking a distinctive competence or competitive advantage, then horizontal integration is often a desirable alternative. As a last

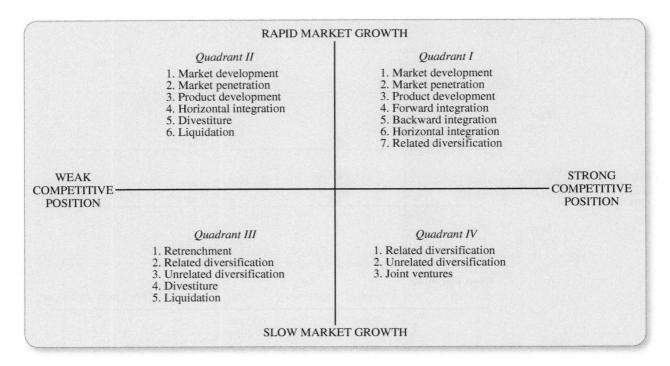

FIGURE 6-13

The Grand Strategy Matrix

Source: Based on Roland Christensen, Norman Berg, and Malcolm Salter, *Policy Formulation and Administration* (Homewood, IL: Richard D. Irwin, 1976), 16–18.

resort, divestiture or liquidation should be considered. Divestiture can provide funds needed to acquire other businesses or buy back shares of stock.

Quadrant III organizations compete in slow-growth industries and have weak competitive positions. These firms must make drastic changes quickly to avoid further decline and possible liquidation. Extensive cost and asset reduction (retrenchment) should be pursued first. An alternative strategy is to shift resources away from the current business into different areas (diversify). If all else fails, the final options for Quadrant III businesses are divestiture or liquidation.

Finally, Quadrant IV businesses have a strong competitive position but are in a slow-growth industry. These firms have the strength to launch diversified programs into more promising growth areas: Quadrant IV businesses have characteristically high cash-flow levels and limited internal growth needs and often can pursue related or unrelated diversification successfully. Quadrant IV firms also may pursue joint ventures.

Even with the Grand Strategy Matrix, be certain that you always, whenever possible, state your alternative strategies in specific terms to the extent possible. For example, avoid using terms such as "divestiture." Rather, specify the exact division to be sold. Also, be sure to use the free Excel student template at www.strategyclub.com that facilitates construction of all strategic planning matrices.

If using the strategic planning template at www.strategyclub.com to perform GRAND analysis, you may use the 1 to 9 scale offered on the template, where 1 = the weakest competitive position and also the slowest industry growth rate, and 9 = the strongest competitive position and the fastest industry growth rate. Also, the template enables up to six points (coordinates) to be plotted in a Grand Strategy Matrix, analogous to various divisions of a firm, or rival firms, or even years to depict expected results of proposed recommendations. You may be creative in this regard, simply label everything accordingly within the template.

Feedback Among the Matching Tools

As strategies are identified using BCG, IE, GRAND, and SPACE analyses, Figure 6-14 reveals that those strategies ideally should be framed in SWOT terms. In other words, broad generic

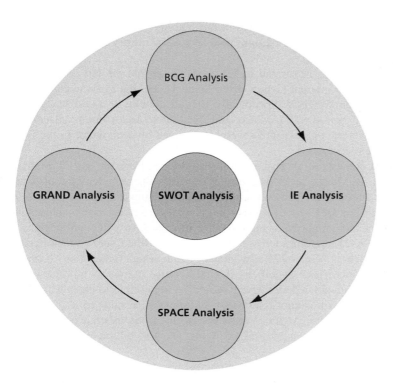

FIGURE 6-14

Relationships Among the Five Matching Tools

terms such as market development recommended perhaps from a BCG analysis should be (1) made more specific in terms of what countries or regions and how many stores or distribution centers or whatever are being suggested, and (2) the more specific, narrowed strategy should be associated with a set of S, W, O, T factors analogously as discussed in the SWOT Matrix section. If a particular narrowed strategy, perhaps coming from a BCG analysis, cannot be anchored in underlying external or internal factors outlined from the SWOT strategies, this should be a concern to be considered. Figure 6-14 uses arrows to signify that the outer four tools are commonly used to generate additional SWOT feasible alternative strategies. The firm will ultimately prioritize all the SWOT strategies and determine the ideal set of strategies to move onto Recommendations to be implemented.

The Decision Stage: The QSPM

6.8. Construct and apply the Quantitative Strategic Planning Matrix (QSPM).

Other than ranking strategies to achieve the prioritized list, as mentioned previously in this chapter, there is only one analytical technique in the literature designed to determine the relative attractiveness of feasible alternative plans or actions. The **Quantitative Strategic Planning Matrix (QSPM)**, which comprises Stage 3 of the strategy formulation analytical framework, objectively indicates which alternative strategies are the most attractive.[7] The QSPM uses input from Stage 1 analyses and matching results from Stage 2 analyses to decide more objectively among alternative strategies. That is, the EFE Matrix, IFE Matrix, and CPM that comprise Stage 1, coupled with the SWOT Matrix, SPACE Matrix, BCG Matrix, IE Matrix, and Grand Strategy Matrix that comprise Stage 2, provide the needed information for setting up the QSPM (Stage 3). The QSPM is a tool that allows strategists to evaluate alternative strategies objectively, based on previously identified external and internal key success factors. Like other strategy formulation analytical tools, the QSPM requires the assignment of ratings (called "attractiveness scores"), but making "small" rating decisions enable strategists to make effective "big" decisions, such as which country to spend a billion dollars in to sell a product.

The basic format of the QSPM is illustrated in Table 6-4. Note that the left column of a QSPM consists of key external and internal factors (from Stage 1), and the top row consists of feasible alternative strategies (from Stage 2). Specifically, the left column of a QSPM consists of information obtained directly from the EFE Matrix and IFE Matrix. In a column adjacent to the key internal and external factors, the respective weights received by each factor in the EFE Matrix and the IFE Matrix are recorded.

The top row of a QSPM consists of alternative strategies derived from the SWOT Matrix, SPACE Matrix, BCG Matrix, IE Matrix, and Grand Strategy Matrix. These matching tools usually generate similar feasible alternatives. However, not every strategy suggested by the matching techniques has to be evaluated in a QSPM. Strategists should compare several viable alternative strategies in a QSPM, perhaps including two or more SWOT strategies, so you could designate your QSPM strategies using SWOT notation such as SO4 versus WT3. Make sure your strategies are stated in specific terms, such as "Open 275 new stores in Indonesia" rather than "Expand globally" or "Open new stores in Africa." Specificity is vital because ultimately a dollar value must be established for each recommended strategy; it would be impossible to establish a dollar value for "expand globally." If you cannot reasonably assign a dollar value to a QSPM (or SWOT) strategy, then the strategy is too vague. Vagueness is disastrous in strategic planning because no one knows what you really are suggesting or saying, and a $1 billion investment may be on the line.

Conceptually, the QSPM determines the relative attractiveness of various strategies based on the extent that key external and internal factors are capitalized on or improved. The relative attractiveness of each strategy is computed by determining the cumulative impact of each external and internal factor. Any number of strategies can be included in the QSPM.

A QSPM for a retail computer store is provided in Table 6-5. This example illustrates all the components of the QSPM: strategic alternatives, key factors, weights, attractiveness scores (AS), total attractiveness scores (TAS), and the sum total attractiveness score (STAS). The three new terms just introduced—(1) attractiveness score, (2) total attractiveness score, and (3) the sum

TABLE 6-4 The Quantitative Strategic Planning Matrix (QSPM)

Key Factors	Weight	Strategic Alternatives		
		Strategy 1	Strategy 2	Strategy 3
Key External Factors				
Political				
Economic				
Sociocultural				
Technological				
Environmental				
Legal				
Competitive				
Key Internal Factors				
Management				
Marketing				
Finance/Accounting				
Production/Operations				
Research and Development				
Management Information Systems				

TABLE 6-5 A QSPM for a Retail Computer Store

		STRATEGIC ALTERNATIVES			
		1 Buy New Land and Build New, Larger Store		2 Fully Renovate Existing Store	
Key Factors	*Weight*	*AS*	*TAS*	*AS*	*TAS*
Opportunities					
1. Population of city growing 10%	0.10	4	0.40	2	0.20
2. Land is available 1 mile away	0.10	2	0.20	4	0.40
3. Vehicle traffic passing store up 12 percent	0.08	1	0.08	4	0.32
4. Vendors average six new products a year	0.05	—		—	
5. Older adults' use of computers up 8 percent	0.05	—		—	
6. Small business growth in an area up 10 percent	0.05	—		—	
7. Desire for websites up 18 percent by realtors	0.04	—		—	
8. Desire for websites up 12 percent by small firms	0.03	—		—	
Threats					
1. Best Buy opening new store nearby in 1 year	0.15	4	0.60	3	0.45
2. New bypass for Highway 34 in 1 year will divert traffic	0.12	4	0.48	1	0.12
3. Local university offers computer repair	0.08	—		—	
4. New mall being built nearby	0.08	2	0.16	4	0.32
5. Gas prices up 14 percent	0.04	—		—	
6. Vendors raising prices 8 percent	0.03	—		—	
Total	**1.00**				
Strengths					
1. Revenues from repair/service in the store up 16 percent	0.15	4	0.60	3	0.45
2. Employee morale is excellent	0.10	—		—	
3. Average customer purchase increased from $97 to $128	0.07	2	0.14	4	0.28
4. Inventory turnover increased from 5.8 to 6.7	0.05	—		—	
5. In-store promotions resulted in 20 percent increase in sales	0.05	—		—	
6. In-store technical support personnel have MIS college degrees	0.05	—		—	
7. Store's debt-to-total-assets ratio declined to 34 percent	0.03	4	0.12	2	0.06
8. Newspaper advertising expenditures increased 10 percent	0.02	—		—	
9. Revenues per employee up 19 percent	0.02	—		—	
Weaknesses					
1. Location of store negatively impacted by new Highway 34	0.15	4	0.60	1	0.15
2. Revenues from software segment of store down 12 percent	0.10	—		—	
3. Often customers have to wait to check out	0.05	2	0.10	4	0.20
4. Store has no website	0.05	—		—	
5. Revenues from businesses down 8 percent	0.04	3	0.12	4	0.16
6. Supplier on-time delivery increased to 2.4 days	0.03	—		—	
7. Carpet and paint in store somewhat in disrepair	0.02	1	0.02	4	0.08
8. Bathroom in store needs refurbishing	0.02	1	0.02	4	0.08
Total	**1.00**		**3.64**		**3.27**

total attractiveness score—are defined and explained as the six steps required to develop a QSPM are discussed:

Step 1   *Make a list of the firm's key external opportunities and threats and internal strengths and weaknesses in the left column of the QSPM.* This information should be taken directly from the EFE Matrix and IFE Matrix. (The Excel Template at www .strategyclub.com will facilitate this process.)

Step 2   *Assign weights to each key external and internal factor.* These weights are identical to those in the EFE Matrix and IFE Matrix. The weights are presented in a straight column just to the right of the external and internal factors.

Step 3   *Examine the Stage 2 (matching) matrices, and identify alternative strategies that the organization should consider implementing.* Record these strategies in the top row of the QSPM, perhaps selecting two or more of your SO, WO, ST, or WT strategies.

Step 4   *Determine the Attractiveness Scores (AS),* defined as numerical values that indicate the relative attractiveness of each strategy considering a single external or internal factor. **Attractiveness Score (AS)** is determined by examining each key external or internal factor, one at a time, and asking the question, "Does this factor affect the choice of strategies being made?" If the answer to this question is *yes,* then the strategies should be compared relative to that key factor. Specifically, ASs should be assigned to each strategy to indicate the relative attractiveness of one strategy over others, considering the factor. The range for ASs is 1 = *not attractive*, 2 = *somewhat attractive*, 3 = *reasonably attractive*, and 4 = *highly attractive.* By "attractive," we mean the extent that one strategy, compared with others, enables the firm to either capitalize on the strength, improve on the weakness, exploit the opportunity, or avoid the threat. Work row by row in developing a QSPM. If the answer to the previous question is *no*, indicating the respective key factor has no effect on the specific choice being made, then do not assign ASs to the strategies in that set. Use a dash (or 0 if using the template) to indicate that the key factor does not affect the choice being made. *Note:* If you assign an AS to one strategy, then assign an AS to the other; in other words, if one strategy receives a dash (or 0)—then all others must receive a dash (or 0) in a given row.

Step 5   *Compute the Total Attractiveness Scores.* **Total Attractiveness Score (TAS)** is defined as the product of multiplying the weights (Step 2) by the AS (Step 4) in each row. The TASs indicate the relative attractiveness of each alternative strategy, considering only the impact of the adjacent external or internal critical success factor. The higher the TASs, the more attractive the strategic alternative (considering only the adjacent critical success factor).

Step 6   *Compute the Sum Total Attractiveness Score.* Add TASs in each strategy column of the QSPM. The **Sum Total Attractiveness Score (STAS)** reveals which strategy is most attractive in each set of alternatives. Higher scores indicate more attractive strategies, considering all the relevant external and internal factors that could affect the strategic decisions. The magnitude of the difference between the STASs in a given set of strategic alternatives indicates the relative desirability of one strategy over another.

In Table 6-5, two alternative strategies—(1) buy new land and build new larger store and (2) fully renovate existing store—are being considered by a computer retail store. Note by the STASs of 3.64 versus 3.27 that the analysis indicates the business should buy new land and build a new larger store. Note the use of dashes to indicate which factors do not affect the strategy choice being considered. If a particular factor affects one strategy, but not the other, it affects the choice being made, so ASs should be recorded for both strategies. Never rate one strategy and not the other. Note also in Table 6-5 that there are no consecutive 1s, 2s, 3s, or 4s across any row in a QSPM; never assign the same AS across a row. Always prepare a QSPM working row by row. Also, if you have more than four strategies in the QSPM, then let the ASs range from 1 to "the number of strategies being evaluated." This will enable you to have a different AS for each strategy. These are all important guidelines to follow in developing a QSPM. In practice, the store did purchase the new land and build a new store; the business also did some minor refurbishing until the new store was operational.

There should be a rationale for each AS assigned. Note in the first row of Table 6-5 that the "Population of city growing 10 percent" opportunity could be capitalized on best by Strategy 1, "Buy New Land and Build New, Larger Store," so an AS score of 4 was assigned to Strategy 1. ASs, therefore, are not mere guesses; they should be rational, defensible, and reasonable.

Mathematically, the AS of 4 in row 1 suggests Strategy 1 is 100 percent more attractive than Strategy 2, whose AS was 2 (since $4 - 2 = 2$ and 2 divided by $2 = 100$ percent).

Positive Features and Limitations of the QSPM

A positive feature of the QSPM is that sets of strategies can be examined sequentially or simultaneously. For example, corporate-level strategies could be evaluated first, followed by division-level strategies, and then function-level strategies. There is no limit to the number of strategies that can be evaluated or the number of sets of strategies that can be examined at once using the QSPM.

Another positive feature of the QSPM is that it requires strategists to integrate pertinent external and internal factors into the decision process. Developing a QSPM makes it less likely that key factors will be overlooked or weighted inappropriately. It draws attention to important relationships that affect strategic decisions. Although developing a QSPM requires decisions about ASs, those small decisions enhance the probability that the final strategic decisions will be best for the organization. A QSPM can be used by small and large, for-profit and nonprofit organizations, and even can be used by individuals in making career choices.[8]

The QSPM has two limitations. First, it always requires informed judgments regarding ASs, but quantification is helpful throughout the strategic planning process to minimize halo error and various biases. ASs are not mere guesses. Be reminded that a 4 is 33 percent more important than a 3; making informed small decisions is important for making effective big decisions, such as deciding among various strategies to implement. Second, a limitation of the QSPM is that its factors and strategy choices are based on underlying input and matching matrices and analysis.

How to Estimate Costs Associated with Recommendations

6.9. **Explain how to estimate costs associated with recommendations.**

The SWOT, SPACE, BCG, IE, and GRAND matrices are used in strategic planning to generate feasible alternative strategies that could benefit the firm. The term **recommendation** is used to refer to "any alternative strategy that is selected for implementation." Due to monetary or nonmonetary constraints, no firm can implement all alternative strategies proposed in the matching matrices, so firms use the QSPM and expert judgment to select particular strategies. Perhaps the most important page in a student's strategic planning case project is their **Recommendations Page**—a page where recommendations are listed along with an estimated dollar (respective currency) amount for the expected cost (or savings) of each recommendation over the next 3 years. The dollar amounts should all be added to reveal a total amount of new capital needed over the 3 years.

As indicated in Global Capsule 6, acquiring foreign companies is becoming less and less an option among recommendations as countries become increasingly wary of foreign entities acquiring and extracting national security information from host countries. Sometimes the acquiring company is just a shell company headquartered somewhere "friendly" but owned by a potential adversary country that could have harmful ulterior motives for the acquisition.

So, how much does it cost to build a manufacturing plant? Guidance is given in Table 6-6 for determining the estimated cost (or savings) of various recommendations. Table 6-6 gives six example actions that could be recommendations for a firm, along with a rationale and author comment for how dollar values can be estimated on a recommendations page. As indicated, an approach using cost per square foot may be used to estimate the total cost of building manufacturing plants, retail stores, distribution centers, or warehouses. Another way to estimate various costs is to find costs incurred for similar expenditures by other firms. Also, look in the firm's Form 10K because costs are often given for previous expenditures, and these dollar values can give guidance for estimating costs associated with new recommendations. Avoid wild cost guesses; ask "experts" in the field if needed.

Cultural Aspects of Strategy Analysis and Choice

6.10. **Discuss the role of organizational culture in strategic analysis and choice.**

As defined in Chapter 4, Organizational culture includes the set of shared values, beliefs, attitudes, customs, norms, rites, rituals, personalities, heroes, and heroines that describe a firm. Culture is the unique way an organization does business. It is the human dimension that creates solidarity and meaning, and it inspires commitment and productivity in an organization when strategy changes are made. All humans have a basic need to make sense of the world, to feel in control, and to have meaning.

GLOBAL CAPSULE 6

Are Foreign Takeovers Becoming Less Available? The Answer Is Yes.[9]

JHVEPhoto/Shutterstock

In the UK, 16 percent of residents already work for a foreign-owned company, compared with only 5 percent in the United States. As this number increases, the UK, and also Germany, Spain, and Italy, have recently tightened takeover defenses of their domestic companies. Nvidia Corp. based in Santa Clara, California, announced in 2020 that it would pay $40 billion for the UK chip designer Arm Holdings; however, this attempted acquisition never went through and was terminated in 2022 due to significant regulatory challenges. Currently Parker-Hannifin Corp. wants to acquire Meggitt PLC, one of the UK's last independent defense companies. This and other potential acquisitions across Europe may not go through because of national security concerns.

In January 2022, the UK began requiring companies in 17 sensitive sectors to notify the government about any foreign takeover or investments in their company. Prior to that date, notification of the government was voluntary. Potentially hostile countries, such as China, have been acquiring high-technology companies in other countries for years, especially in sensitive industries such as artificial intelligence, semi-conductors, robotics, and even energy. In the UK, most of the country's utilities and automakers, and even soccer teams, are owned by foreign companies. But this is rapidly changing, especially in the 17 technology-related, including pharmaceutical-related, industries.

[9]Based on Alistair MacDonald and Ben Dummett,"U.K. Looks Closely at Foreign Takeovers," *Wall Street Journal*, December 13, 2021, p. B6. Also based on Ian King, Giles Turner, and Peter Elstrom, "Nvidia Quietly Prepares to Abandon $40 Billion Arm Bid," *Bloomberg*, January 25, 2022, https://www.bloomberg.com/news/articles/2022-01-25/nvidia-is-said-to-quietly-prepare-toabandon-takeover-of-arm

When events threaten meaning, individuals react defensively. Managers and employees may even sabotage new strategies in an effort to recapture the status quo. For these reasons, it is beneficial to view strategy analysis and choice from a cultural perspective because success often rests on the degree of support that strategies receive from a firm's culture. If a firm's strategies are supported by an organization's culture, then managers often can implement changes swiftly and easily. However, if a supportive culture does not exist and is not cultivated, then strategy changes may be difficult to implement.

Strategies that require fewer cultural changes may be more attractive because extensive changes can take considerable time and effort. Whenever two firms merge, it becomes especially important to evaluate and consider culture-strategy linkages. Organizational culture can be the primary reason for difficulties a firm encounters when it attempts to shift its strategic direction, as the following statement explains:

> Not only has the "right" corporate culture become the essence and foundation of corporate excellence, but success or failure of needed corporate reforms hinges on management's sagacity and ability to change the firm's driving culture in time and in tune with required changes in strategies.[10]

The Politics of Strategy Analysis and Choice

6.11. **Identify and discuss important political considerations in strategy analysis and choice.**

All organizations are political. Unless managed, political maneuvering consumes valuable time, subverts organizational objectives, diverts human energy, and results in the loss of valuable employees. Sometimes political biases and personal preferences get unduly embedded in strategy choice decisions. Internal politics affect the choice of strategies in all organizations. The hierarchy of command in an organization, combined with the career aspirations of different people and the need to allocate scarce resources, guarantees the formation of coalitions of individuals who strive to take care of themselves first and the organization second, third, or fourth. Coalitions of individuals often form around strategic issues that face an enterprise. A major responsibility of strategists is to guide the development of coalitions, to nurture an overall team concept, and to gain the support of key individuals and groups of individuals.

In the absence of objective analyses, strategy decisions often are based on the politics of the moment. With the development of improved strategy formation analytical tools, political factors

TABLE 6-6 Recommendations and Associated Costs with Rationale

Recommendation with Total Cost Rationale

1. Build one new manufacturing plant. $40M = ($400 per sq. ft. × 100K sq. ft. = $40M)
Author Comment—Depending on the size of the plant, cost of the land, and complexity of the plant, the dollar amount could be higher or lower. Often a *Form 10K* will reveal the actual cost of a similar plant recently built. Another way to estimate this cost is to divide the firm's total property, plant, and equipment on their balance sheet by the number of manufacturing plants to get an average for one and use this as a basis for the cost of building a new plant. A good rule of thumb is to spread the cost of building a new manufacturing plant over 2 years.

2. Open 200 new retail stores. $300M = (200 stores × 10K sq. ft. per store × $150 per sq. ft = $300M)
Author Comment—Depending on the average store size and cost of land, the dollar amount could be higher or lower. Another way to estimate this cost is to divide the firm's total property, plant, and equipment on their balance sheet by the number of existing stores to get an average for one store and use this as a basis for opening 200 new stores. Be mindful that many firms use a franchise instead of a company-owned business model, whereby most costs are borne by the franchisee; also, many firms lease instead of own retail space. If the 200 new stores are to come online over 3 years, spread the total cost over 3 years.

3. Hire 100 new salespersons. $7.5M = (100 × $75K annual pay = $7.5M)
Author Comment—The cost could be higher or lower depending on the average salary plus commission and amenities to be paid to salespersons in each industry.

4. Divest our fragrance division. The fragrance segment comprises 27 percent of firm's revenues; total revenue of firm is $640M. So, 27% × $640M = $172.8M (revenue).
Author Comment—Besides going into debt, issuing stock, or using net income, a way to raise needed funds is to divest a segment. Divestiture may be needed if the segment is performing poorly, if the firm desires to become less diversified, or if the firm needs to realign its portfolio of businesses with its new or existing mission statement.

5. Increase R&D expenditures 10% annually for 3 years. If $50M is the current R&D annual expenditure, then: $55M + $60.5M + $66.55M = $182.05M.
Author Comment—As a percentage of revenue, R&D expenditures can range from zero for low-tech firms to upward of 20 percent of revenue for high-tech firms.

6. Acquire the jewelry segment of a rival firm. If the jewelry segment comprises 15 percent of the total value, assets, and revenues of the rival firm and that total value is $1.5B, then 15 percent of $1.5B = $225M.
Author Comment—Firms need to show 5+ percent annual growth in revenues to keep shareholders pleased. An acquisition is widely used to achieve this need, especially if internal (organic) growth is not sufficient. Companies, like individuals, negotiate to try to buy low and sell high.

become less important in making strategic decisions. In the absence of objectivity, political factors sometimes dictate strategies, and this is unfortunate. Managing political relationships is an integral part of building enthusiasm and esprit de corps in an organization.

A classic study of strategic management in nine large corporations examined the political tactics of successful strategists and found that these persons let weakly supported ideas and proposals die through inaction and established additional hurdles or tests for strongly supported ideas considered unacceptable, but not openly opposed.[11] Successful strategists keep a low political profile on unacceptable proposals and strive to let most negative decisions come from subordinates or a group consensus, thereby reserving their personal vetoes for big issues and crucial moments. Successful strategists do a lot of chatting and informal questioning to stay abreast of how things are progressing and to know when to intervene. Successful strategists lead strategy but do not dictate it. They give few orders, announce few decisions, depend heavily on informal questioning, and seek to probe and clarify until a consensus emerges.

Successful strategists generously and visibly reward key thrusts that succeed. They assign responsibility for major new thrusts to **champions**, the individuals most strongly identified with the idea or product and whose futures were linked to its success. They stay alert to the symbolic impact of their own actions and statements so as not to send false signals that could stimulate movements in unwanted directions.

Because strategies must be effective in the marketplace and capable of gaining internal commitment, the following tactics used by politicians for centuries can aid strategists:

1. Achieving desired results is more important than imposing a particular method; therefore, consider various methods and choose, whenever possible, the one(s) that will afford the greatest commitment from employees and managers.
2. Achieving satisfactory results with a popular strategy is generally better than trying to achieve optimal results with an unpopular strategy.
3. Often, an effective way to gain commitment and achieve desired results is to shift from short-term to long-term issues and concerns.
4. Middle-level managers must be genuinely involved in and supportive of strategic decisions because successful implementation will hinge on their support.[12]

IMPLICATIONS FOR STRATEGISTS

This chapter has revealed six new matrices widely used by strategists to gain and sustain a firm's competitive advantages, the core purpose of strategic planning, as illustrated in Figure 6-15. Five of the six are matching tools, SWOT, SPACE, BCG, IE, and GRAND, coupled with the single decision-making tool, QSPM. Whereas some consulting firms and some textbooks advocate using only one or two matrices in strategic planning, our experience is that all six tools introduced in this chapter are uniquely valuable. Coupled with the EFE Matrix, the CPM, and the IFE Matrix from previous chapters, the nine tools together supply strategists the appropriate means for leading a firm down the narrow path to success. Rarely is the path to success wide or easy, due to parity, commoditization, imitation, duplication, substitute products, global competitors, and the willingness and ability of consumers to switch allegiances and loyalties. Employees expect strategists to formulate a superior "game plan," so their hard work implementing the strategic plan will yield job security, good compensation, and ultimately happiness for employees.

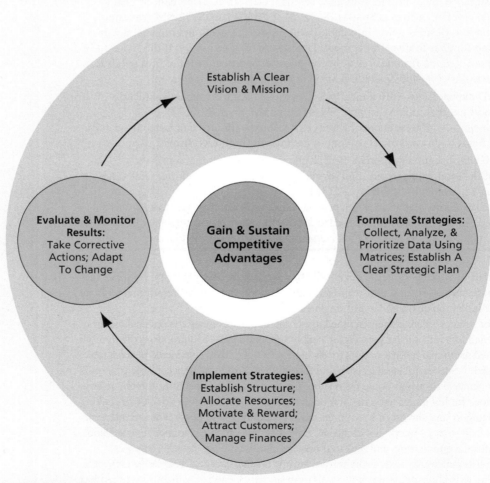

FIGURE 6-15

How to Gain and Sustain Competitive Advantages

IMPLICATIONS FOR STUDENTS

In preparing the strategy formulation matrices, avoid wild guesses, but become comfortable with "excellent estimates," as needed, based on research, to move forward with appropriate matrices. Sometimes students are so accustomed (due to their accounting and finance classes especially) to being counted wrong if their answer is off at the third decimal place, it takes a while in a strategic management class to realize that businesses make excellent estimates based on research *all the time* because no business is sure what tomorrow will bring. So, if you can make reasonable estimates, move forward with particular matrices. For example, with the IE Matrix, if segment information is not provided, enter only a single circle in the matrix to represent the overall firm, rather than two or more circles for the divisions. But be mindful that multiple circles could be included based on the number of stores, or the number of customers, rather than traditional dollar revenue information; so do not rush to the conclusion that portfolio information is not available. Also, prepare all matrices based on the point in time of your analysis rather than a desired future point in time—but seriously consider performing a before and after analysis whereby you show for example the existing IE Matrix placement of segments versus your expected future placement.

To generate and decide on alternative strategies that will best gain and sustain competitive advantages, your SWOT, SPACE, BCG, IE, and GRAND matrices and QSPM need to be developed accurately. However, in covering those matrices in an oral presentation, focus more on the implications of those analyses than the nuts-and-bolts calculations. In other words, as you go through those matrices in a presentation, your goal is not to prove to the class that you did the calculations correctly. They expect accuracy and clarity, and certainly you should have that covered. It is the implications of each matrix that your audience will be most interested in, so use these matrices to pave the way for your recommendations with costs, which generally come just a page or two deeper into the project. A good rule of thumb is to spend at least an equal amount of time on the implications as the actual calculations of each matrix when presented. This approach will improve the delivery aspect of your presentation or paper by maintaining the high-interest level of your audience. Focusing on implications rather than calculations will also encourage questions from the audience when you finish. Silence from an audience is not good because silence means your audience either fell asleep or was disinterested, unconvinced, or unimpressed. Use the free Excel student template at www.strategyclub.com as needed.

Template Considerations

When using the template to create your SWOT, IE, BCG, SPACE, and GRAND matrices, it is best to avoid overlapping words plotting on top of each other. To avoid this problem, create a legend for each matrix or graph; in the template just number your divisions or segments 1, 2, 3, 4, so that only numbers print inside the matrix or graph. Then in your Word (.docx) strategic planning document, provide a legend (1, 2, 3, 4) that reveals the names of the segments. In fact, prepare your whole strategic planning document as a .docx file, and simply cut and paste all Excel matrices and graphs from the Excel template into your Word document. That way you never need to unlock the template and you also can easily avoid overlapping words plotting on top of each other in various matrices and graphs. In rare situations, Excel will place the labels in a difficult to read area of our matrix. If you encounter this problem, you may click on the Review tab at the top of Excel then click "unprotect sheet" and adjust as needed. Be sure to re-click "protect sheet" before leaving the page. To copy and paste your matrices into PowerPoint, Keynote, or Word, follow the instructions provided under Template Considerations in Chapter 3.

Chapter Summary

The essence of strategy formulation is an assessment of whether an organization is doing the right things and how it can be more effective in what it does. Every organization should be wary of becoming a prisoner of its own strategy, for even the best strategies become obsolete sooner or later. Regular reappraisal of strategy helps management avoid complacency. Objectives and strategies should be consciously developed and coordinated and should not merely evolve out of day-to-day operating decisions.

An organization with no sense of direction and no coherent strategy precipitates its own demise. When an organization does not know where it wants to go, it usually ends up someplace it does not want to be. Every organization needs to consciously establish and communicate clear objectives and strategies. Any organization, whether military, product-oriented, service-oriented, governmental, or even athletic, must develop and execute effective strategies to win. An excellent offense without an excellent defense, or vice versa, usually leads to defeat. Developing strategies that use strengths to capitalize on opportunities could be considered offensive, whereas strategies designed to improve on weaknesses while avoiding threats could be considered defensive. Every organization has numerous external opportunities and threats and internal strengths and weaknesses that can be aligned to formulate feasible alternative strategies.

Modern strategy formulation tools and concepts described in this chapter are integrated into a practical three-stage framework. Tools such as the SWOT Matrix, SPACE Matrix, BCG Matrix, IE Matrix, and Grand Strategy Matrix can significantly enhance the quality of strategic decisions, but they should never be used to dictate the choice of strategies. Behavioral, cultural, and political aspects of strategy generation and selection are always important to consider and manage. Because of increased legal pressure from outside groups, boards of directors are assuming a more active role in strategy analysis and choice. This is a positive trend for organizations.

Key Terms and Concepts

Aggressive Quadrant (p. 176)
Attractiveness Score (AS) (p. 190)
Boston Consulting Group (BCG) Matrix (p. 179)
business portfolio (p. 179)
cash cows (p. 180)
champions (p. 193)
competitive position (CP) (p. 173)
Competitive Quadrant (p. 176)
Conservative Quadrant (p. 176)
decision stage (p. 170)
Defensive Quadrant (p. 176)
directional vector (p. 176)
dogs (p. 180)
financial position (FP) (p. 173)
Grand Strategy Matrix (p. 185)
industry growth rate (IGR) (p. 180)
industry position (IP) (p. 173)
input stage (p. 170)
Internal-External (IE) Matrix (p. 182)
matching (p. 170)

matching stage (p. 170)
portfolio analysis (p. 179)
Quantitative Strategic Planning Matrix (QSPM) (p. 187)
question marks (p. 180)
recommendation (p. 191)
Recommendations Page (p. 191)
relative market share position (RMSP) (p. 179)
SO strategies (p. 171)
stability position (SP) (p. 173)
stars (p. 180)
Strategic Position and Action Evaluation (SPACE) Matrix (p. 173)
strategy formulation analytical framework (p. 169)
Strengths-Weaknesses-Opportunities-Threats (SWOT) Matrix (p. 170)
ST strategies (p. 171)
Sum Total Attractiveness Score (STAS) (p. 190)
Total Attractiveness Score (TAS) (p. 190)
WO strategies (p. 171)
WT strategies (p. 171)

Issues for Review and Discussion

6-1. Explain the difference between strategies and recommendations.

6-2. Explain how to estimate costs associated with recommendations.

6-3. Why is it essential for a SWOT strategy to be stated specifically enough to estimate the cost (or savings)?

6-4. Why is it important to treat all animals, even cattle, pigs, and chickens, with care and respect?

6-5. A 2021 *IBIS World Industry Report* for "Chocolate Production in the US" states that Mars leads the market with 35.4 percent market share, followed by Ferrero and then Hershey, which have 18.6 percent and 17.2 percent market share, respectively. With regard to a BCG Matrix, what is the relative market share position for each of these three firms?

6-6. List five limitations of a SPACE Matrix.

6-7. List the pros and cons of a firm disclosing by-segment corporate information in a *Form 10K*.

6-8. What are some key differences between the BCG and the IE portfolio matrices?

6-9. In developing a QSPM, if 10 strategies are being compared simultaneously, what would be a good scale for the ASs? Why?

6-10. In developing a BCG Matrix or an IE Matrix, what would be a good surrogate for revenues for Target Corp., Burger King, Bank of America, and Spirit Airlines?

6-11. In developing a SPACE Matrix, what would you expect the SP average to be for Apple, Heinz, Verizon, Amazon, and Kroger? Diagram and explain.

6-12. Rather than developing a QSPM, what is an alternative procedure for prioritizing the relative attractiveness of alternative strategies?

6-13. Overlay a BCG Matrix with a Grand Strategy Matrix and discuss similarities in terms of format and implications. Diagram and explain.

6-14. Define halo error. How can halo error inhibit selecting the best strategies to pursue?

6-15. List six drawbacks of using only subjective information in formulating strategies.

6-16. For a firm that you know well, give an example of SO strategy showing how an internal strength can be matched with an external opportunity to formulate a strategy.

6-17. For a firm that you know well, give an example WT strategy, showing how an internal weakness can be matched with an external threat to formulate a strategy.

6-18. List three limitations of the SWOT Matrix and analysis.

6-19. For the following three firms using the given factors, calculate a reasonable stability position (SP) coordinate to go on their SPACE Matrix axis, given what you know about the nature of those industries.

Factors	Winnebago	Apple	U.S. Postal Service	SP Score
Barriers to entry into market				
Seasonal nature of business				
Technological changes				

6-20. Would the angle or degrees of the vector in a SPACE Matrix be important in generating alternative strategies? Diagram and explain.

6-21. On the competitive position (CP) axis of a SPACE Matrix, what level of capacity utilization would be necessary for you to give the firm a negative 1? Negative 7? Why? Diagram and explain.

6-22. If a firm has a weak financial position (FP) and competes in an unstable industry, in which quadrant will the SPACE vector lie? Diagram and explain.

6-23. Describe a situation where the SPACE analysis would have no vector. In other words, describe a situation where the SPACE analysis coordinate would be (0,0). What should an analyst do in this situation?

6-24. Develop a BCG Matrix for your university. Because your college does not generate profits, what would be a good surrogate for the pie slice values? How many circles do you have and how large are they? Explain.

6-25. In a BCG Matrix, would the question mark quadrant or the cash cow quadrant be more desirable? Diagram and explain.

6-26. Would a BCG Matrix and analysis be worth performing if you do not know the profits of each segment? Why?

6-27. What major limitations of the BCG Matrix does the IE Matrix overcome? Diagram and explain.

6-28. In an IE Matrix, do you believe it is more advantageous for a division to be located in Quadrant II or IV? Why? Diagram and explain.

6-29. Develop a 2 × 2 × 2 × 2 × 2 QSPM for an organization of your choice (i.e., two strengths, two weaknesses, two opportunities, two threats, and two strategies). Follow all the QSPM guidelines presented in the chapter.

6-30. How would application of the strategy formulation analytical framework differ from a small to a large organization?

6-31. What types of strategies would you recommend for an organization that achieves total weighted scores of 3.6 on the IFE Matrix and 1.2 on the EFE Matrix? Diagram and explain.

6-32. Given the following information, develop a SPACE Matrix for the XYZ Corporation: FP = +2; SP = − 6; CP = −2; IP = +4. Diagram and explain.

6-33. Given the information in the following table, develop a BCG Matrix and an IE Matrix.

Divisions	1	2	3
Profits	$10	$15	$25
Sales	$100	$50	$100
Relative Market Share	0.2	0.5	0.8
Industry Growth Rate	+.20	+.10	−.10
IFE Total Weighted Scores	1.6	3.1	2.2
EFE Total Weighted Scores	2.5	1.8	3.3

6-34. How would you develop a portfolio matrix for your school of business?

6-35. Explain how to estimate the cost of building one new manufacturing plant for a company.

6-36. Discuss the limitations of various strategy formulation analytical techniques.

6-37. Explain why cultural factors should be an important consideration when analyzing and choosing among alternative strategies.

6-38. How would for-profit and nonprofit organizations differ in their applications of the strategy formulation analytical framework?

6-39. Develop a SPACE Matrix for a company that is financially weak and is a weak competitor. The industry for this company is pretty stable, but the industry's projected growth in revenues and profits is not good. Label all axes and quadrants.

6-40. List four limitations of a BCG Matrix. Diagram and explain.

6-41. Provide an example to show clearly and completely that you can develop an IE Matrix for a three-division company, where each division has $10, $20, and $40 in revenues and $2, $4, and $1 in profits, respectively. State other assumptions needed. Label the axes and quadrants.

6-42. What procedures could be necessary if the SPACE vector falls right on the axis between the competitive and defensive quadrants? Diagram and explain.

6-43. In a BCG Matrix or the Grand Strategy Matrix, what would you consider to be a rapid market (or industry) growth rate?

6-44. Why is it important to work row-by-row instead of column-by-column in preparing a QSPM?

6-45. Why should one avoid putting double 4s in a row in preparing a QSPM?

6-46. Envision a QSPM with no weight column. Would that still be a useful analysis? Why or why not? What do you lose by deleting the weight column?

6-47. Prepare a BCG Matrix for a two-division firm with sales of $5 and $8 versus profits of $3 and $1, respectively. State assumptions for the RMSP and IGR axes to enable you to construct the diagram.

6-48. Consider developing a before and after BCG or IE Matrix to reveal the expected results of your proposed strategies. What limitation of the analysis would this procedure overcome somewhat?

6-49. If a firm has the leading market share in its industry, where on the BCG Matrix would the circle lie? Diagram and explain.

6-50. If a firm competes in an unstable industry, such as telecommunications, where on the SP axis of the SPACE Matrix would you plot the appropriate point? Diagram and explain, stating assumptions as necessary.

6-51. Why do you think the SWOT Matrix is the most widely used of all strategy matrices?

6-52. What are two limitations of the QSPM discussed in the chapter?

Writing Assignments

6-55. Explain the steps involved in developing a QSPM.

6-56. How are the SWOT Matrix, SPACE Matrix, BCG Matrix, IE Matrix, and Grand Strategy Matrix similar? How are they different?

Ken Wolter/Alamy Photo

ASSURANCE-OF-LEARNING EXERCISES

SET 1: STRATEGIC PLANNING FOR MCDONALD'S

EXERCISE 6A

Perform a SWOT Analysis for McDonald's

Purpose

The SWOT Matrix is the most widely used of all strategic planning tools and techniques because it is conceptually simple and lends itself readily to discussion among executives and managers. The SWOT Matrix is effective in formulating strategies because it clearly matches a firm's internal strengths and weaknesses with the firm's external opportunities and threats to generate feasible strategies that should be considered. This exercise gives you practice in performing SWOT analysis for a large corporation.

Instructions

Step 1   Join with two other students in class. Together, develop a SWOT Matrix for McDonald's. Follow guidelines provided in the chapter, including notation (e.g., S4, T3) at the end of each strategy. Include two strategies in each of the four (SO, ST, WT, WO) quadrants. Be specific regarding your strategies, avoiding generic terms such as "forward integration." Use the Cohesion Case, your answers to Assurance-of-Learning Exercise 1B, and the company's most recent quarterly report as given at the corporate website.

Step 2   Turn in the SWOT Matrix your team developed to your professor for a classwork grade. Note: Feel free to list factors and strategies vertically on a page rather than necessarily fitting everything into a nine-cell array.

EXERCISE 6B

Develop a SPACE Matrix for McDonald's

Purpose

The SPACE Matrix is one of five matching strategic management tools widely used to formulate feasible strategies. Used in conjunction with the SWOT, BCG, IE, and GRAND matrices, the SPACE Matrix can be helpful in devising a strategic plan because hard choices normally must be made between attractive strategic options. This exercise gives you practice in developing a SPACE Matrix.

Instructions

Step 1   Review McDonald's business as described in the Cohesion Case as well as the company's most recent *Form 10K* and quarterly report.

Step 2   Review industry and competitive information pertaining to McDonald's.

Step 3   Develop a SPACE Matrix for McDonald's. What strategies do you recommend for McDonald's given your SPACE analysis? Avoid generic, vague terms such as "market development."

EXERCISE 6C

Develop a BCG Matrix for McDonald's

Purpose

Portfolio matrices are widely used by multidivisional organizations to help identify and select strategies to pursue. A BCG analysis identifies particular divisions that should receive fewer resources than others. It may identify some divisions that need to be divested. This exercise gives you practice in developing a BCG Matrix.

Instructions

Step 1   Place the following five column headings at the top of a separate sheet of paper: Divisions, Revenues, Profits, Relative Market Share Position, and Industry Growth Rate. Down the far left of your page, list McDonald's divisions and segments. Now turn back to the Cohesion Case and find information to fill in all the cells in your data table.

Step 2   Based on McDonald's segment data given in the Cohesion Case, complete a BCG Matrix for the company.

Step 3   Compare your BCG Matrix to other students' matrices. Discuss any major differences.

EXERCISE 6D

Develop a QSPM for McDonald's

Purpose

This exercise gives you practice in developing a QSPM to determine the relative attractiveness of various strategic alternatives.

Instructions

Step 1   Join with two other students in class to develop a joint QSPM for McDonald's.

Step 2   Compare your team's QSPM to those of other teams.

Step 3   Discuss any major differences.

SET 2: STRATEGIC PLANNING FOR MY UNIVERSITY

EXERCISE 6E

Develop a BCG Matrix for My University

Purpose

Developing a BCG Matrix for many nonprofit organizations, including colleges and universities, is a useful exercise. Of course, there are no profits for each division or department and, in some cases, no revenues. However, be creative in performing a BCG Matrix. For example, the pie slice in the circles can represent the number of majors receiving jobs on graduation, the number of faculty teaching in that area, or some other variable that you believe is important to consider. The size of the circles can represent the number of students majoring in particular departments or areas.

Instructions

Step 1   Develop a BCG Matrix for your university. Include all academic schools, departments, or colleges.

Step 2   Diagram your BCG Matrix on paper.

Step 3   Discuss differences among the BCG Matrices developed in class.

SET 3: STRATEGIC PLANNING TO ENHANCE MY EMPLOYABILITY

EXERCISE 6F

Perform QSPM Analysis on Yourself

Purpose

QSPM analysis is designed to determine the relative attractiveness of feasible alternative actions. Although primarily used in a business setting, QSPM analysis can enable individuals to objectively determine which alternative strategies are best to pursue. The purpose of this exercise is to showcase how individuals can use QSPM analysis to make career choices.

Instructions

Step 1   Follow the steps provided in Chapter 6 for developing a QSPM analysis, but do so for yourself rather than a company. Use the external and internal factor information about yourself that you developed in Exercise 1D to get started.

Step 2   Across the top row of your QSPM, consider two strategies as follows:
             (1) Go to graduate school or (2) Go to work full-time.

Step 3	To keep this example simple, do not include a weight column, as some firms also prefer; simply add the ASs to obtain your recommended best strategy, rather than multiplying across rows and then summing TASs.
Step 4	Share with the class what strategy, More School or More Work, yields the highest TAS in your personal analysis.

EXERCISE 6G
A Template Competency Test

Purpose

The free Excel strategic planning template at www.strategyclub.com is widely used for strategic planning by students and small businesses; this exercise aims to enhance your familiarity with the template. Developing competence with the template will enable you to place this skill appropriately on your resume, in addition to facilitating your development of a comprehensive strategic plan for an assigned case company.

Instructions

Answer the following questions about the template. Discuss your answers with classmates to determine any issues or concerns.

1. In performing SPACE analysis, does the template allow you to show your firm and rival firms? If yes, would a legend be nice to create to organize information? Why?
2. In performing BCG analysis, how does the template address firms competing in markets with over or under 20 percent IGR?
3. Using the template, what is a good way to show a before and after (your recommendations) BCG?
4. In performing IE portfolio analysis using the template, are your EFE and IFE Matrix total weighted scores automatically plotted after you finish those matrices? For divisions, does the template call for all "divisional" EFE and IFE matrices?
5. Why is it best to label divisions 1, 2, 3, etc. on BCG and IE matrices and thereby create a legend, rather than let division names plot in the matrix?
6. In performing GRAND analysis, how many firms, divisions, or scenarios does the template allow to be considered or placed in the matrix? Why is this a nice feature? What are some scenarios you could examine?
7. Why is there no need to reenter weights when performing QSPM analysis using the template?

SET 4: INDIVIDUAL VERSUS GROUP STRATEGIC PLANNING

EXERCISE 6H
How Severe Are Various Subjective Threats in Strategic Planning?

Purpose

As discussed in this chapter, without objective information and analysis, six subjective threats (i.e., personal biases, politics, prejudices, emotions, personalities, and halo error) often play a dominant role in the strategy formulation process, undermining effectiveness. Halo error is the tendency to put too much weight on a single factor.

The purpose of this exercise is to examine more closely various threats of relying too heavily on subjectivity in formulating strategies. A secondary purpose of this exercise is to examine whether individual decision-making is better than group decision-making. Academic research suggests that groups make better decisions than individuals about 80 percent of the time.

Instructions

Rank the six subjective threats as to their relative severity (1 = most severe, 6 = least severe). First, rank the threats as an individual. Next, rank the threats as part of a group of three. Thus, determine what person(s) and what group(s) here today can come closest to the expert ranking.

This exercise enables examination of the relative effectiveness of individual versus group decision-making in strategic planning.

The Steps

1. Fill in Column 1 in Table 6-7 to reveal your individual ranking of the relative severity of the six subjective threats (1 = most severe to 6 = least severe). For example, if you think Personal Biases is the third-most severe threat, then enter a 3 in Table 6-7 in Column 1 beside Personal Biases.
2. Fill in Column 2 in Table 6-7 to reveal your group's ranking of the relative severity of the six threats (1 = most severe to 6 = least severe).
3. Fill in Column 3 in Table 6-7 to reveal the expert's ranking of the six threats. To be provided by your professor, the expert rankings are based on the authors' experience, rather than on findings from empirical research.
4. Fill in Column 4 in Table 6-7 with the absolute difference between Column 1 and Column 3 to reveal how well you performed as an individual in this exercise. (Note: Absolute difference disregards negative numbers.)
5. Fill in Column 5 in Table 6-7 with the absolute difference between Column 2 and Column 3 to reveal how well your group performed in this exercise.
6. Sum Column 4. Sum Column 5.
7. Compare the Column 4 sum with the Column 5 sum. If your Column 4 sum is less than your Column 5 sum, then you performed better as an individual than as a group. Normally, group decision-making is superior to individual decision-making, so if you did better than your group, you did excellent.
8. The Individual Winner(s): The individual(s) with the lowest Column 4 sum is the WINNER.
9. The Group Winners(s): The group(s) with the lowest Column 5 score is the WINNER.

TABLE 6-7 Assessing Severity of Being Too Subjective in Making Strategic Decisions: Comparing Individual Versus Group Decision-Making

Threats of Being Too Subjective	Column 1	Column 2	Column 3	Column 4	Column 5
1. Personal Biases					
2. Politics					
3. Prejudices					
4. Emotions					
5. Personalities					
6. Halo error					
Sums					

MINI-CASE ON STELLANTIS NV

WHAT AUTO COMPANY WILL HAVE THE BEST SMART COCKPIT BY 2025?[13]

Fiat Chrysler Automobiles NV and France's PSA Group merged in early 2021 to form Stellantis NV. Since then, Stellantis has embarked on a mission to have the best smart cockpit among all vehicles by 2025. To accomplish this objective, Stellantis is hiring 3,500 new software engineers between 2022 and 2024. Stellantis is the parent company for Jeep, Chrysler, and Peugot. By developing, producing, and marketing smart cockpits, Stellantis expects its annual revenues to exceed $20 billion euros (about US$21.5 billion) by 2030. Stellantis envisions its new cockpits to feature extensive downloadable software available both for a fee and free and to interact easily with smartphones and numerous other devices in a new metaverse or augmented world.

MikeDotta/Shutterstock

Ford, General Motors, Tesla, and other firms are planning similar smart cockpits but primarily plan to subcontract this work out to other companies and are seemingly not as determined as Stellantis. By 2030,

Stellantis says it will have about 34 million vehicles that generate revenue for the company by periodically downloading updated software of all kinds to continually enhance their vehicle cockpits. Stellantis is redesigning all of its vehicles' dashboards that are command centers for ultra-connected vehicles.

To accomplish its objectives, Stellantis is collaborating with Foxconn Technology Group to develop exclusive semiconductors for its vehicles. CEO Carlos Tavares of Stellantis says his company's technology-packed vehicles, all 14 brands, will soon feature amazing cockpits that enable downloadable software to keep the vehicles up-to-date and modern throughout the life of the vehicle. Stellantis plans to soon generate extensive revenue not just on the one-time-sell of a vehicle but continuously from owners downloading amazing software updates for each brand the company sells.

Questions

1. Would Stellantis' strategy to hire 3,500 new software engineers be considered a SO, WO, ST, or WT strategy? What would be the key underlying internal and external factors that form the basis of this strategy?
2. Stellantis' Chief Software Officer says his company plans to control much more of the software value chain in the coming years. What are the benefits and risks of this strategy? Do you think controlling more of the value chain is a wise strategy or not and why?
3. In a BCG Matrix, would Stellantis be classified as a Star, Question Mark, Cash Cow, or Dog? Why?

[13]Based on Nick Kostov and Nora Naughton, "Jeep Make Stellantis Bets on Software," *Wall Street Journal*, December 8, 2021, p. B3.

Web Resources

1. **BCG Matrix Images** This website provides more than 100 JPEG images of BCG matrices that can be used in a case project or strategic planning report.
https://www.google.com/search?q=bcg+matrix&tbm=isch&ved=2ahUKEwjrpZKGson1AhUB2qwKHSA0B LUQ2-cCegQIABAA&oq=BCG+&gs_lcp=CgNp bWcQARgAMgcIABCxAxBDMggIABCABBC xAzIICAAQgAQQsQMyBAgAEEMyBAgAEEMyBA gAEEMyBQgAEIAEMgUIABCABDIECAAQQz IECAAQQzoHCCMQ7wMQJzoICAAQsQMQgwFQ_ hNY1BpgqCBoAHAAeACAAVGIAfYCkgEBNZgBA KABAaoBC2d3cy13aXotaW1nwAEB&sclient=img&ei= pIfMYevDOYG0swWg6JCoCw&bih=657&biw=1366 &rlz=1C1GCEU_enUS819US819

2. **The QSPM Matrix** This website provides numerous PDF files that discuss and exemplify the QSPM Matrix in further detail.
https://scholar.google.com/scholar?hl=en&as_sdt=0%2C6 &q=quantitative+strategic+planning+matrix%2C+QSPM &btnG=

3. **Strategic Planning Template** This website offers the best strategic planning template available for developing a three-year strategic plan, and it is free. All six new matrices introduced in Chapter 6 (SWOT, SPACE, BCG, IE, GRAND, QSPM) are included in the template.
http://www.strategyclub.com

4. **Author-Developed Videos** Fred David gives a video overview of Chapter 6 in the prior edition, but much info is still applicable in the 18th edition.
Part 1 of Chapter 6: https://www.youtube.com/ watch?v=-03weLqsgDM
Part 2 of Chapter 6: https://www.youtube.com/ watch?v=Jz7kY9drjuI

Current Readings

Abdurakhmonov, Mirzokhidjon, Jason W. Ridge, and Aaron D. Hill, "Unpacking Firm External Dependence: How Government Contract Dependence Affects Firm Investments and Market Performance," *Academy of Management Journal* 64, no. 1 (February 2021): 327–50.

Apaydin, Marina, Guoliang Frank Jiang, Mehmet Demirbag, and Dima Jamali, "The Importance of Corporate Social Responsibility Strategic Fit and Times of Economic Hardship," *British Journal of Management* 32, no. 2 (April 2021): 399–415.

Boghossian, Johnny, and Robert J. David, "Under the Umbrella: Goal-Derived Category Construction and Product Category Nesting," *Administrative Science Quarterly* 66, no. 4 (December 2021): 1084–129.

Cascio, Wayne F., Arjun Chatrath, and Rohan A. Christie-David, "Antecedents and Consequences of Employee and Asset Restructuring," *Academy of Management Journal* 64, no. 2 (April 2021): 587–613.

David, Meredith E., Fred R. David, and Forest R. David, "The Quantitative Strategic Planning Matrix: A New Marketing Tool," *Journal of Strategic Marketing* 3 (April 2016): 1–11.

Li, Xu, and Freek Vermeulen, "High Risk, Low Return (and Vice Versa): The Effect of Product Innovation on Firm Performance in a Transition Economy," *Academy of Management Journal* 64, no. 5 (October 2021): 1383–418.

Luciano, Margaret M., Virgil Fenters, Semin Park, Amy L. Bartels, and Scott I. Tannebaum, "The Double-Edged Sword of Leadership Task Transitions in Emergency Response Multiteam Systems," *Academy of Management Journal* 64, no. 4 (August 2021): 1236–64.

Martignoni, Dirk, and Thomas Keil, "It Did Not Work: Unlearn and Try Again – Unlearning Success and Failure Beliefs in Changing Environments," *Strategic Management Journal* 42, no. 6 (June 2021): 1057–82.

Miller, Danny, and Isabelle Le Breton-Miller, "Paradoxical Resource Trajectories: When Strength Leads to Weakness and Weakness Leads to Strength," *Journal of Management* 47, no. 7 (September 2021): 1899–914.

Rahman, Mahabubur, Serrano, M. Ángeles Rodríguez, and Mathew Hughes, "Does Advertising Productivity Affect Organizational Performance? Impact of Market Conditions," *British Journal of Management* 32, no. 4 (October 2021): 1359–83.

Sajko, Miha, Christophe Boone, and Tine Buyl, "CEO Greed, Corporate Social Responsibility, and Organizational Resilience to Systemic Shocks," *Journal of Management* 47, no. 4 (April 2021): 957–92.

Wang, Yaopeng, Hisham Farag, and Wasim Ahmad, "Corporate Culture and Innovation: A Tale from an Emerging Market," *British Journal of Management* 32, no. 4 (October 2021): 1121–40.

Endnotes

1. On page 168.
2. R. T. Lenz, "Managing the Evolution of the Strategic Planning Process," *Business Horizons* 30, no. 1 (January–February 1987): 37.
3. Robert Grant, "The Resource-Based Theory of Competitive Advantage: Implications for Strategy Formulation," *California Management Review*, Spring 1991, p. 114.
4. On page 172.
5. Greg Dess, G. T. Lumpkin, and Alan Eisner, *Strategic Management: Text and Cases* (New York: McGraw-Hill/Irwin, 2006), 72.
6. Adapted from H. Rowe, R. Mason, and K. Dickel, *Strategic Management and Business Policy: A Methodological Approach* (Reading, MA: Addison-Wesley, 1982), 155–156.
7. Fred David, "The Strategic Planning Matrix—A Quantitative Approach," *Long Range Planning* 19, no. 5 (October 1986): 102; Andre Gib and Robert Margulies, "Making Competitive Intelligence Relevant to the User," *Planning Review* 19, no. 3 (May–June1991): 21.
8. Meredith E. David, Forest R. David, and Fred R. David, "The QSPM: A New Marketing Tool," Presented at

the International Academy of Business and Public Administration Disciplines (IABPAD) Meeting in Dallas, Texas, April 2015. Also, Meredith E. David and Fred R. David. "Strategic Planning for Individuals: A Proposed Framework and Method?" 2017 Academy of Business Research (ABR) Conference in Atlantic City, New Jersey, September 20, 2017.

9. On page 192.
10. Y. Allarie and M. Firsirotu, "How to Implement Radical Strategies in Large Organizations," *Sloan Management Review* 26, no. 3 (Spring 1985): 19. Another excellent article is P. Shrivastava, "Integrating Strategy Formulation with Organizational Culture," *Journal of Business Strategy* 5, no. 3 (Winter 1985): 103–11.
11. James Brian Quinn, *Strategies for Changes: Logical Incrementalism* (Homewood, IL: Irwin, 1980), 128–45. These political tactics are listed in A. Thompson and A. Strickland, *Strategic Management: Concepts and Cases* (Plano, TX: Business Publications, 1984), 261.
12. William Guth and Ian Macmillan, "Strategy Implementation versus Middle Management Self-Interest," *Strategic Management Journal* 7, no. 4 (July–August 1986): 321.
13. On page 202.

## PART 3

STRATEGY IMPLEMENTATION

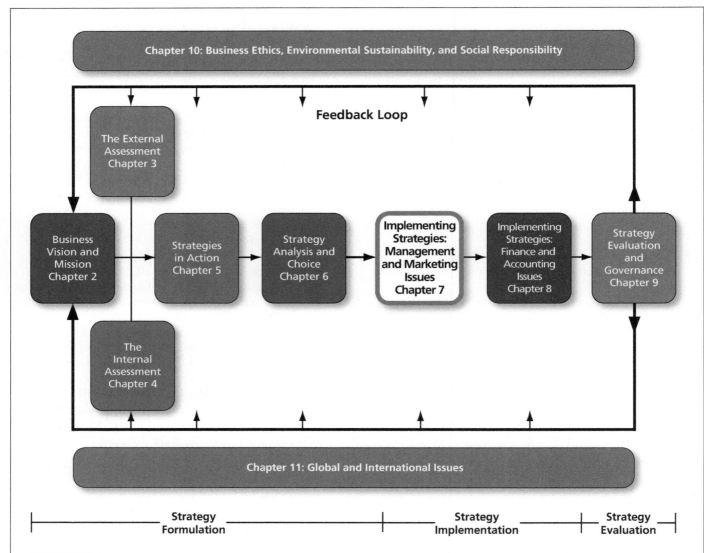

FIGURE 7-1

The Comprehensive, Integrative Strategic Management Model

Source: Fred R. David, "How Companies Define Their Mission," *Long Range Planning* 22, no. 1 (February 1989): 91. See also Anik Ratnaningsih, Nadjadji Anwar, Patdono Suwignjo, and Putu Artama Wiguna, "Balance Scorecard of David's Strategic Modeling at Industrial Business for National Construction Contractor of Indonesia," *Journal of Mathematics and Technology* no. 4 (October 2010): 20. Also, Meredith E. David, Fred R. David, and Forest R. David, "Closing the Gap Between Graduates' Skills and Employers' Requirements: A Focus on the Strategic Management Capstone Business Course," *Administrative Sciences* 11, no. 1 (2021): 10–26.

Implementing Strategies: Management and Marketing Issues

LEARNING OBJECTIVES

After studying this chapter, you should be able to do the following:

7.1. Describe the transition from formulating to implementing strategies.

7.2. Discuss reasons why annual objectives are essential for effective strategy implementation.

7.3. Identify and discuss the nature and role of policies in strategy implementation.

7.4. Explain the roles of resource allocation and managing conflict in strategy implementation.

7.5. Discuss the need to match a firm's structure with its strategy.

7.6. Identify, diagram, and discuss different types of organizational structure.

7.7. Identify and discuss 15 do's and don'ts in constructing organizational charts.

7.8. Discuss three strategic production/operations issues vital for strategy implementation.

7.9. Discuss seven strategic human resource issues vital for strategy implementation.

7.10. Describe key strategic marketing issues vital for implementing strategies.

ASSURANCE-OF-LEARNING EXERCISES

The following exercises are found at the end of this chapter:

SET 1:	Strategic Planning for McDonald's
EXERCISE 7A:	Compare and Contrast McDonald's Marketing Expenses Versus Rival Firms
EXERCISE 7B:	Diagram an Existing and Proposed Organizational Chart for McDonald's
SET 2:	Strategic Planning for My University
EXERCISE 7C:	Develop a Perceptual Map for My University
SET 3:	Strategic Planning to Enhance My Employability
EXERCISE 7D:	Marketing Yourself to Best Achieve Your Career Objectives
SET 4:	Individual Versus Group Strategic Planning
EXERCISE 7E:	What Are the Most Important Benefits of Having a Diverse Workforce?

The strategic management process does not end with deciding what strategy or strategies to pursue. There must be a translation of strategic thought into action. This translation is significantly easier when managers and employees of the firm understand the business, feel a part of the company, and have become committed to helping the organization succeed through involvement in strategy formulation activities. Without understanding and commitment, strategy implementation efforts face major problems. Vince Lombardi commented, "The best game plan in the world never blocked or tackled anybody."

Even the most technically perfect strategic plan will serve little purpose if it is not implemented. Many organizations tend to spend an inordinate amount of time, money, and effort on developing the strategic plan, all the while treating the means and circumstances under which it will be implemented as afterthoughts! Change comes through implementation and evaluation, not through the plan. A technically imperfect plan that is implemented well will achieve more than a perfect plan that never gets off the paper on which it is written.[1]

Implementing strategy affects an organization from top to bottom, including all the functional and divisional areas of a business. This chapter focuses on management and marketing issues most critical for successful strategy implementation, whereas Chapter 8 focuses on analogous finance and accounting issues. Showcased as the exemplary strategist for this chapter is Penny Pennington, CEO of Edward D. Jones & Co. Headquartered in St. Louis, Missouri, Edward Jones has about 25,000 locations in the United States and Canada serving about 7 million clients.

Transitioning from Formulating to Implementing Strategies

7.1. Describe the transition from formulating to implementing strategies.

The strategy implementation stage of the strategic management process is illustrated with white shading in Figure 7-1 on the first page of this chapter. Successful strategy formulation does not guarantee successful strategy implementation. It is always more difficult to do something (strategy implementation) than to say you are going to do it (strategy formulation)! Although inextricably linked, strategy implementation is fundamentally different from strategy formulation.

EXEMPLARY **STRATEGIST** SHOWCASED

Penny Pennington, CEO of Edward D. Jones & Co.[2]

Penny Pennington worked her way up from being an Edward Jones financial advisor in Livonia, Michigan, in 2000 to becoming CEO of the company. Pennington, age 58, was recently named to *Fortune Magazine*'s Most Powerful Women in Business list; she is the only woman running a major U.S. brokerage. Today Pennington is responsible for the Edward Jones' strategic direction, working with the more than 49,000 associates (financial advisors) across the United States and Canada to make a meaningful difference in customers' lives, who have entrusted roughly $1.6 trillion in client assets under their care.

Pennington suggests the following ways to climb the corporate ladder and become a successful leader:

1. Go out of your way to learn all the blocking and tackling basics of your industry.
2. View setbacks positively as an excellent way to improve.
3. Find ways to learn more and more about your industry.

4. Learn to be uncomfortable. Ask questions. Play Devil's Advocate. Ask why even when surrounded by status quo persons.
5. Value (cherish and capitalize) lifelong learning.

[2]Based on Beth Kowitt, "Value Lifelong Learning," *Investor's Business Daily*, November 8, 2021, p. A4.

In all but the smallest organizations, the transition from strategy formulation to strategy implementation requires a shift in responsibility from strategists to divisional and functional managers. Implementation problems can arise because of this shift in responsibility, especially if strategy formulation decisions come as a surprise to middle- and lower-level managers. Managers and employees are motivated more by perceived self-interests than by organizational interests, unless the two coincide. This is a primary reason why divisional and functional managers should be involved as much as possible in activities for both strategy formulation and strategy implementation. Strategy formulation and implementation can be contrasted in the ways illustrated in Figure 7-2.

Concepts and tools for strategy formulation do not differ greatly for small, large, for-profit, or nonprofit organizations. However, in contrast, strategy implementation varies substantially among different types and sizes of organizations. Implementing strategies requires actions such as altering sales territories, adding new departments, closing facilities, hiring new employees, changing an organization's pricing strategy, developing financial budgets, developing new employee benefits, establishing cost-control procedures, changing advertising strategies, building new facilities, training new employees, transferring managers among divisions, and building a better management information system. These types of activities obviously differ greatly across manufacturing, service, and governmental organizations.

The Need for Clear Annual Objectives

7.2. **Discuss reasons why annual objectives are essential for effective strategy implementation.**

Annual objectives are desired milestones an organization should achieve to ensure successful strategy implementation. Annual objectives are essential for strategy implementation for five primary reasons:

1. They represent the basis for allocating resources.
2. They are a primary mechanism for evaluating managers.
3. They enable effective monitoring of progress toward achieving long-term objectives.
4. They establish organizational, divisional, and departmental priorities.
5. They are essential for keeping a strategic plan on track.

Considerable time and effort should be devoted to ensuring that annual objectives are well conceived, consistent with long-term objectives, and supportive of strategies to be implemented. Active participation in establishing annual objectives is needed for the reasons already listed. Approving, revising, or rejecting annual objectives is much more than a rubber-stamp activity. The purpose of annual objectives can be summarized as follows:

Annual objectives serve as guidelines for action, directing, and channeling efforts and activities of organization members. They provide a source of legitimacy in an enterprise by justifying activities to stakeholders. They serve as standards of performance. They serve as an important source of employee motivation and identification. They give incentives for managers and employees to perform. They provide a basis for organizational design.[3]

Clearly stated and communicated objectives are critical to success in all types and sizes of firms. Annual objectives are often stated in terms of profitability, growth, and market share by business segment, geographic area, customer group, and product. Figure 7-3 illustrates how the Stamus Company could establish annual objectives based on long-term objectives. Table 7-1 reveals associated revenue figures that correspond to the objectives outlined in Figure 7-3. Note that, according to plan, the Stamus Company will slightly exceed its long-term objective of doubling company revenues between 2023 and 2025. Figure 7-3 also reflects how a hierarchy of annual objectives can be established based on an organization's structure.

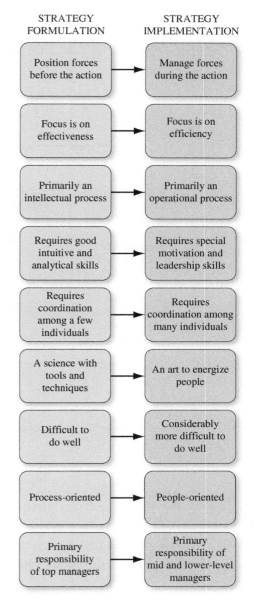

FIGURE 7-2

Contrasting Strategy Formulation with Strategy Implementation

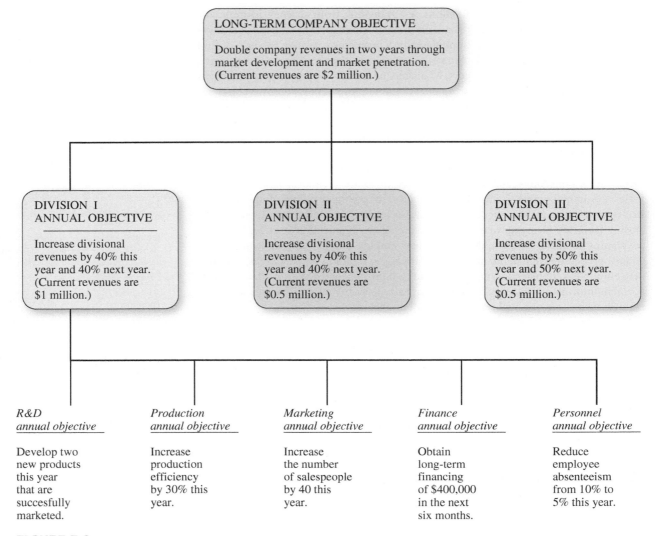

FIGURE 7-3

The Stamus Company's Hierarchy of Aims

Objectives should be consistent across both horizontal (i.e., functional, departmental, staff) and vertical (top to lower managers) levels in a chain of command. **Horizontal consistency of objectives**, such as pertaining to a chief financial officer (CFO), chief marketing officer (CMO), chief information officer (CIO), chief strategy officer (CSO), or human resources manager (HRM) laterally across a chart, is as important as **vertical consistency of objectives**, such as pertaining to a chairperson, CEO, division president, or plant manager downward in a chart. For example, vertically if the firm has a 10 percent annual growth in revenues objective, then horizontally production/manufacturing needs an annual objective to produce 10 percent more product.

Annual objectives should be measurable, consistent, reasonable, challenging, clear, communicated throughout the organization, characterized by an appropriate time dimension, and

TABLE 7-1 The Stamus Company's Revenue Expectations (in millions, $)

	2023	2024	2025
Division I Revenues	1.00	1.40	1.96
Division II Revenues	0.50	0.70	0.98
Division III Revenues	0.50	0.75	1.12
Total Company Revenues	**2.00**	**2.85**	**4.06**

accompanied by commensurate rewards and sanctions. These elements are often called the *characteristics of objectives*. Too often, objectives are stated in generalities, with little operational usefulness. Annual objectives, such as "to improve communication" or "to improve performance," are not clear, specific, or measurable. Objectives should state quantity, quality, cost, and time—and also be verifiable. Terms and phrases such as "maximize," "minimize," "as soon as possible," and "adequate" should be avoided. For example, an annual objective could be "increase sales of brand ABC to 1,000 units yielding $20,000 in revenue annually."

Annual objectives should be supported by clearly stated policies. It is important to tie rewards and sanctions to annual objectives so that employees and managers understand that achieving objectives is critical to successful strategy implementation. Clear annual objectives do not guarantee successful strategy implementation, but they do increase the likelihood that personal and organizational aims can be accomplished. Overemphasis on achieving objectives can result in undesirable conduct, such as faking the numbers, distorting the records, and letting objectives become ends in themselves. Wells Fargo had a problem with this a few years ago in regard to employees opening new customer accounts to meet quotas.

Based on management activities such as establishing clear annual objectives, *Fortune* recently asked 4,170 executives, directors, and securities analysts to select 10 companies they admired the most, and the top 12 firms are shown in Table 7-2. Note that Apple is number one, partly because of its unique ecosystem of superior products that "talk to each other," a feature unrivaled in the industry.

TABLE 7-2 The Most Admired Companies in the World

Rank	Company	Author Comment
1	Apple	Has a unique ecosystem that links its products
2	Amazon.com	Building hundreds of new distribution centers to speed delivery to your door
3	Microsoft	The most popular computing software firm
4	Walt Disney	Produces great movies; owns ESPN and ABC Sports
5	Starbucks	Offers tea, beer, wine, lunch, and dinner
6	Berkshire Hathaway	Highly diversified; owns many companies
7	Alphabet	Owns Google, the best search engine anywhere
8	JPMorgan Chase	World's largest bank by market capitalization
9	Netflix	Offers streaming services to more than 214 million subscribers worldwide
10	Costco Wholesale	Ranked 10th on *Fortune*'s 2021 list of largest U.S. firms by total revenue
11	Walmart	Ranked first on the *Fortune* 500 list of the largest U.S.-based firms
12	Salesforce	Owns Tableau Software, Pardot, and MuleSoft

Source: Based on information at https://fortune.com/worlds-most-admired-companies/

Establish Policies

7.3. **Identify and discuss the nature and role of policies in strategy implementation.**

Policies refer to specific guidelines, methods, procedures, rules, forms, and administrative practices established to support and encourage work toward stated goals. Changes in a firm's strategic direction do not occur automatically. On a day-to-day basis, policies are needed to make a strategy work. Policies facilitate solving recurring problems and guide the implementation of strategy. Policies are essential instruments for strategy implementation, for at least six reasons:

1. Policies set boundaries, constraints, and limits on the kinds of administrative actions that can be taken to reward and sanction behavior.
2. Policies let both employees and managers know what is expected of them, thereby increasing the likelihood that strategies will be implemented successfully.
3. Policies provide a basis for management control and allow coordination across organizational units.
4. Policies reduce the amount of time managers spend making decisions. Policies also clarify what work is to be done and by whom.
5. Policies promote delegation of decision making to appropriate managerial levels where various problems usually arise.
6. Policies clarify what can and cannot be done in pursuit of an organization's objectives.

New policies and practices are being devised to get employees back to the office, at least for 3 days a week, because substantial research suggests employees are more productive at the office than working at home. But how can firms get employees to work from the office rather than working from home without losing their best talent or having disgruntled employees? One answer is that firms should make employees want to come back to the office; this can be done in the following ways:

1. Provide excellent conditions at the office where employees can avoid distractions or problems at home, such as a lousy printer, uncomfortable desk setup, suboptimal lighting, unstable Wi-Fi, and distractions from children, family members, or social media.
2. Provide a safe, clean, and healthy environment at the office.
3. Allow more social time at work and more brainstorming, engagement, camaraderie, collegiality, interaction, and conversation at lunch and other appropriate times at the office. Do not sequester people in solitary cubicles.
4. Provide abundant low-cost conveniences at the office, such as a well-stocked kitchen area, three-ply toilet paper, luxury hand cream and soap in the bathroom, etc.
5. Make sure the office is a happy and well-organized place where employees can truly be productive; provide incentives and bonuses for employees when they are more productive.

In essence, the office must be a place where employees can be happy, more productive, and potentially earn more money, compared with working from home.[4] As discussed in Ethics Capsule 7, there is an increasing need for firms to establish policies regarding employees' use of personal smartphones at work; distractions caused by such behavior can undermine employee morale, not to mention productivity.

Many organizations have a policy manual that serves to guide and direct behavior. Policies can apply to all divisions and departments, such as: "We are an equal opportunity employer," or to a single department, such as: "Employees in this department must take at least one training and development course each year." Whatever their scope and form, policies serve as a mechanism for implementing strategies and obtaining objectives. Policies should be stated in writing whenever possible. They represent the means for carrying out strategic decisions. Examples of policies that support a company strategy, a divisional objective, and a departmental objective are provided in Table 7-3. Some example issues that may require a management policy are provided in Table 7-4.

ETHICS CAPSULE 7

Do Firms Need a Cell Phone Policy to Outline Acceptable Use in the Workplace?[5]

Edhar Yuralaits/123RF

Recent research on worker productivity suggests that the majority of employers view employees' smartphones as the biggest source of workplace distraction. One in 5 employers report that, in a typical workday, their employees are productive for less than 5 hours. Smartphone use in the workplace does not affect just a focal employee's productivity, but it can also negatively affect surrounding others. For example, research on boss **phubbing** (short for phone snubbing), which occurs when a manager uses or is distracted by his/her cell phone during time spent with an employee, albeit during a meeting, at lunch, or in other workplace settings, has shown that boss phubbing negatively impacts employee job performance. Specifically, employees that feel phubbed by their boss report having less trust for their boss and lower job satisfaction, which in turn results in lower job performance.

Companies should consider setting formal cell phone policies, which outline clear rules for personal phone use and access, as well as consequences for violating those rules. Setting specific boundaries and guidelines for cell phone use at work will ensure that managers and employees have a consistent understanding of when and where cell phones are permitted in the workplace. Without such a cell phone policy, employees across all levels of the organization will likely increase their use of cell phones during work for purposes unrelated to work.

[5]James A. Roberts, and Meredith E. David, "Boss Phubbing, Trust, Job Satisfaction and Employee Performance," *Personality and Individual Differences* 155, no. 1 (2020): 1–8.

TABLE 7-3 A Hierarchy of Policies

Company Strategy

Acquire a chain of retail stores to meet our sales growth and profitability objectives.

Supporting Policies

1. "All stores will be open from 8 a.m. to 8 p.m. Monday through Saturday."
2. "All stores must support company advertising by contributing 5 percent of their total monthly revenues for this purpose."

Divisional Objective

Increase the division's revenues from $10 million in 2022 to $15 million in 2023.

Supporting Policies

1. "Beginning in January 2023, each one of this division's salespersons must file a weekly activity report that includes the number of calls made, the number of miles traveled, the number of units sold, the dollar volume sold, and the number of new accounts opened."
2. "Beginning in January 2023, this division will return to its employees 5 percent of its gross revenues in the form of a Christmas bonus."

Production Department Objective

Increase production from 20,000 units in 2022 to 30,000 units in 2023.

Supporting Policies

1. "Beginning in January 2023, employees will have the option of working up to 20 hours of overtime per week."
2. "Beginning in January 2023, perfect attendance awards in the amount of $100 will be given to all employees who do not miss a workday in a given year."

TABLE 7-4 Example Issues that May Require a Management Policy

- To offer extensive or limited management development workshops and seminars
- To recruit through employment agencies, college campuses, or newspapers
- To promote from within or to hire from the outside
- To promote on the basis of merit or on the basis of seniority
- To tie executive compensation to long-term or annual objectives
- To allow heavy, light, or no overtime work
- To establish a high- or low-safety stock of inventory

Allocate Resources and Manage Conflict

7.4.   Explain the roles of resource allocation and managing conflict in strategy implementation.

Allocate Resources

All organizations have at least four types of resources (or assets) that can be used to achieve desired objectives: (1) financial resources, (2) physical resources, (3) human resources, and (4) technological resources. **Resource allocation** can be defined as distributing an organization's assets across products, regions, and segments according to priorities established by annual objectives. Allocating resources is a vital strategy implementation activity. Strategic management itself is sometimes referred to as a *resource-allocation process*. In fact, allocating resources across business segments (divisions) is arguably the *most important strategic* decision facing large companies annually.

In organizations that do no strategic planning, resource allocation is often based on political or personal factors and bias, rather than on clear analysis and thought. Strategists should be wary of a number of factors that commonly prohibit effective resource allocation, including overprotection of resources, too great an emphasis on short-run financial criteria, organizational politics, vague strategy targets, a reluctance to take risks, and a lack of sufficient knowledge. Below the corporate level, there often exists an absence of systematic thinking about resources allocated and strategies of the firm. Effective resource allocation does not guarantee successful strategy implementation because programs, personnel, controls, and commitment must breathe life into the resources provided.

Manage Conflict

Honest differences of opinion, turf protection, and competition for limited resources can inevitably lead to conflict. **Conflict** can be defined as a disagreement between two or more parties on one or more issues. Establishing annual objectives can lead to conflict because individuals have different expectations, perceptions, schedules, pressures, obligations, and personalities. Misunderstandings between line managers (such as production supervisors) and staff managers (such as human resource specialists) can occur. For example, a collection manager's objective of reducing bad debts by 50 percent in a given year may conflict with a divisional objective to increase sales by 20 percent. Conflict must be managed for strategy implementation to be successful. Managing conflict is a strategic issue in most, if not all, organizations.

Establishing objectives can lead to conflict because managers and strategists must make trade-offs, such as whether to emphasize short-term profits or long-term growth, profit margin or market share, market penetration or market development, growth or stability, high risk or low risk, and social responsiveness or profit maximization. Trade-offs are necessary because no firm has sufficient resources to pursue all strategies that could benefit the firm. Table 7-5 reveals some important management trade-off decisions required in strategy implementation. Strategic planning necessitates making effective trade-off decisions.

TABLE 7-5 Some Management Trade-Off Decisions Required in Strategy Implementation

1. To emphasize short-term profits or long-term growth
2. To emphasize profit margin or market share
3. To emphasize market development or market penetration
4. To lay off or furlough
5. To seek growth or stability
6. To be more socially responsible or more profitable
7. To outsource jobs or pay more to keep jobs at home
8. To acquire externally or to build internally
9. To use leverage or equity to raise funds
10. To use part-time or full-time employees

Conflict is not always bad. An absence of conflict can signal indifference and apathy. Conflict can serve to energize opposing groups into action and may help managers identify problems. General George Patton once said, "If everyone is thinking alike, then somebody isn't thinking."

Various approaches for managing and resolving conflict range from ignoring the problem in hopes that the conflict will resolve itself or physically separating the conflicting individuals, to compromising, to exchanging members of conflicting parties so that each can gain an appreciation of the other's point of view, or even holding a meeting at which conflicting parties present their views and work through their differences.

Match Structure with Strategy

7.5. Discuss the need to match a firm's structure with its strategy.

Alfred Chandler promoted the notion that "changes in strategy lead to changes in organizational structure." Structure should be designed to facilitate the strategic pursuit of a firm and, therefore, follow strategy. Without a strategy or reason for being (mission), companies find it difficult to design an effective structure.

Changes in strategy often require changes in structure for two major reasons. First, structure largely dictates how objectives and policies will be established. For example, objectives and policies established under a geographic organizational structure are couched in geographic terms. Objectives and policies are stated largely in terms of products in an organization whose structure is based on product groups. The structural format for developing objectives and policies can significantly impact all other strategy-implementation activities.

The second major reason why changes in strategy often require changes in structure is that structure dictates how resources will be allocated. If an organization's structure is based on customer groups, then resources are allocated in that manner. Similarly, if an organization's structure is designed along functional business lines, then resources are allocated by functional areas. Unless new or revised strategies place emphasis in the same areas as old strategies, structural reorientation commonly becomes a part of strategy implementation.

When a firm changes its strategy, the existing organizational structure may become ineffective. As indicated in Table 7-6, symptoms of an ineffective organizational structure include too many levels of management, too many meetings attended by too many people, too much attention being directed toward solving interdepartmental conflicts, too large a span of control, and too many unachieved objectives. Changes in structure can facilitate strategy implementation efforts, but changes in structure should not be expected to make a bad strategy good, to make bad managers good, or to make bad products sell.

TABLE 7-6 Symptoms of an Ineffective Organizational Structure

1. Too many levels of management
2. Too many meetings attended by too many people
3. Too much attention being directed toward solving interdepartmental conflicts
4. Too large a span of control
5. Too many unachieved objectives
6. Declining corporate or business performance
7. Losing ground to rival firms
8. Revenue or earnings divided by number of employees or number of managers is low compared to rival firms

Structure undeniably can and does influence strategy. Strategies formulated must be workable, so if a certain new strategy requires massive structural changes, it may not be an attractive choice. In this way, structure can shape the choice of strategies. But a more important concern is determining what types of structural changes are needed to implement new strategies and how these changes can best be accomplished. There is no one optimal organizational design or structure for a given strategy or type of organization. What is appropriate for one organization may not be appropriate for a similar firm, although successful firms in a given industry do tend to organize themselves in a similar way. For example, consumer goods companies tend to emulate the divisional structure-by-product form of organization. Small firms tend to be functionally structured (centralized). Medium-sized firms tend to be divisionally structured (decentralized). Large firms tend to use a strategic business unit (SBU) structure or matrix structure. These types of structure are discussed in the next section.

Types of Organizational Structure

7.6. Identify, diagram, and discuss different types of organizational structure.

There are seven basic types of organizational structure: (1) functional, (2) divisional-by-region, (3) divisional-by-product, (4) divisional-by-customer, (5) divisional-by-process, (6) strategic business unit (SBU), and (7) matrix.[6] Companies, like people and armies, strive to be better organized or structured than rivals because better organization can yield tremendous competitive advantages. There are countless examples throughout history of incidents, battles, and companies where superior organization overcame massive odds against the entity, such as the Battle of Cannae mentioned in Chapter 1.

The Functional Structure

The most widely used organizational structure is the functional or centralized type because this structure is the simplest and least expensive of the seven alternatives. A **functional structure** groups tasks and activities by business function, such as marketing or finance. For example, a university may structure its activities by major functions that include academic affairs, student services, alumni relations, athletics, maintenance, and accounting.

Under a functional structure, divisions or segments of the firm are not delegated authority, responsibility, and accountability for revenues or profits; rather, key decisions are made centrally. For example, a small business composed of three restaurants in three adjacent towns is functionally structured if all hiring, firing, promotion, and advertising decisions are made centrally, but this same small business is divisionally structured if those decisions are delegated to each restaurant manager. Besides being simple and inexpensive, a functional structure also promotes specialization of labor, encourages efficient use of managerial and technical talent, minimizes the need for an elaborate control system, allows rapid decision-making, and enables uniformity across stores and product offerings.

Some disadvantages of a functional structure are that it forces accountability to the top, minimizes career development opportunities, and is sometimes characterized by low employee morale, line or staff conflicts, poor delegation of authority, and inadequate planning for products and markets. For these reasons, most large companies have abandoned the functional structure in favor of decentralization and improved accountability. Table 7-7 summarizes the advantages and disadvantages of a functional organizational structure.

TABLE 7-7 Advantages and Disadvantages of a Functional Organizational Structure

Advantages	Disadvantages
1. Simple and inexpensive	1. Accountability forced to the top
2. Capitalizes on specialization of business activities such as marketing and finance	2. Delegation of authority and responsibility not encouraged
3. Minimizes need for elaborate control system	3. Minimizes career development
4. Allows for rapid decision-making	4. Low employee and manager morale
5. Enables uniformity across stores and product offerings	5. Inadequate planning for products and markets
	6. Leads to short-term, narrow thinking
	7. Leads to communication problems

A functional structure often leads to short-term and narrow thinking that may undermine what is best for the firm as a whole. For example, the R&D department may strive to overdesign products and components to achieve technical elegance, whereas manufacturing may argue for low-frills products that can be mass-produced more easily. Thus, communication is often not as good in a functional structure. Schein gives an example of a communication problem in a functional structure:

> The word "marketing" will mean product development to the engineer, studying customers through market research to the product manager, merchandising to the salesperson, and constant change in design to the manufacturing manager. Then when these managers try to work together, they often attribute disagreements to personalities and fail to notice the deeper, shared assumptions that vary and dictate how each function thinks.[7]

The Divisional Structure

The **divisional (decentralized) structure** is the second-most common type. Divisions are sometimes referred to as *segments, profit centers,* or *business units.* As a small organization grows, it has more difficulty managing different products in different markets. Some form of divisional structure generally becomes necessary to motivate employees, control operations, and compete successfully in diverse locations. The divisional structure can be organized in one of four ways: (1) by region, (2) by product, (3) by customer, or (4) by process. With a divisional structure, functional activities are performed both centrally and in each separate division. For example, Ford recently established a new division named Ford Model E to house it electronic vehicle (EV) production and marketing of the new Mustang Mach E and F-150 Lightning. Analysts say this change in structure might be a forerunner to Ford divesting off its EV business to Tesla, Rivian, or Lucid.

A divisional structure has some clear advantages. First and perhaps foremost, accountability is clear. That is, divisional managers can be held responsible for sales and profit levels. Because a divisional structure is based on extensive delegation of authority, managers and employees can easily see the results of their good or bad performances. As a result, employee morale is generally higher in a divisional structure than in a centralized structure. Other advantages of the divisional design are that it creates career development opportunities for managers, allows local control of situations, leads to a competitive climate within an organization, and allows new businesses and products to be added easily.

The divisional design is not without some limitations, however. Perhaps the most important limitation is that a divisional structure is costly, for a number of reasons. First, each division requires functional specialists who must be paid. Second, there exists some duplication of staff services, facilities, and personnel; for instance, functional specialists are also needed centrally (at headquarters) to coordinate divisional activities. Third, managers must be well qualified because the divisional design forces delegation of authority; better-qualified individuals require higher salaries. A divisional structure can also be costly because it requires an elaborate, headquarters-driven control system. Fourth, competition between divisions may become so intense that it is dysfunctional and leads to limited sharing of ideas and resources for the common good of the firm. Table 7-8 gives the advantages and disadvantages of a divisional organizational structure.

TABLE 7-8 Advantages and Disadvantages of a Divisional Organizational Structure

Advantages	Disadvantages
1. Clear accountability	1. Can be costly due to duplication of functional activities
2. Allows local control of local situations	
3. Creates career development chances	2. Can hamper efforts for uniformity across stores and product offerings
4. Promotes delegation of authority	
5. Leads to competitive climate internally	3. Requires a skilled management force
6. Allows easy adding of new products or regions	4. Requires an elaborate control system
	5. Competition among divisions can become so intense as to be dysfunctional
7. Allows strict control and attention to products, customers, or regions	6. Can lead to limited sharing of ideas and resources
	7. Some regions, products, or customers may receive special treatment

A *divisional-by-region* type of structure is appropriate for organizations whose strategies need to be tailored to fit the particular needs and characteristics of customers in different geographic areas. This type of structure can be most appropriate for organizations that have similar branch facilities located in widely dispersed areas. A divisional-by-region structure allows local participation in decision-making and improved coordination within a region. Divisional-by-region is good when regions are different across a myriad of variables but actual consumption of product lines are similar. This design thus may be effective for a computer company.

The *divisional-by-product (or service)* type of structure is most effective for implementing strategies when specific products need special emphasis. Also, this type of structure is widely used when an organization offers only a few products or when an organization's products or services differ substantially. The divisional-by-product structure allows strict control over and attention to product lines, but it may also require a more skilled management force and reduced top management control. For example, the maker of Hellmann's mayonnaise, Axe deodorant, Dove soap, and Suave shampoo, Unilever is pursuing retrenchment in 2022 along with laying off several thousand of its 149,000 total number of employees. Additionally, Unilever is restructuring its operations into five stand-alone product-based divisions, as follows: 1) Beauty and Wellbeing, 2) Personal Care, 3) Home Care, 4) Nutrition, and 5) Ice Cream. Previously, there were three Unilever divisions: 1) Food and Refreshments, 2) Beauty and Personal Care, and 3) Home Care. The new structure will enable accountability and responsibility to be much clearer within the firm.

A *divisional-by-customer* type of structure can be the most effective way to implement strategies when a few major customers are of paramount importance and many different services are provided to these customers. This structure allows an organization to cater effectively to the requirements of clearly defined customer groups. For example, book publishing companies often organize their activities around customer groups, such as colleges, secondary schools, and private commercial schools. Some airline companies have two major customer divisions: (1) passengers and (2) freight or cargo services. Utility companies often use (1) commercial, (2) residential, and (3) industrial as their divisions by customer.

A *divisional-by-process* type of structure is similar to a functional structure because activities are organized according to the way work is actually performed. However, a key difference between these two designs is that functional departments are not accountable for profits or revenues, whereas divisional process departments are evaluated on these criteria. An example of a divisional-by-process structure is a manufacturing business organized into six divisions: electrical work, glass cutting, welding, grinding, painting, and foundry work. In this case, all operations related to these specific processes would be grouped under the separate divisions. Each process (division) would be responsible for generating revenues and profits. The divisional-by-process structure can be particularly effective in achieving objectives when distinct production processes represent the thrust of competitiveness in an industry. Even the common breakdown of company-owned versus franchise-owned restaurants or stores could be considered divisional-by-process.

The Strategic Business Unit Structure

As the number, size, and diversity of divisions in an organization increase, controlling and evaluating divisional operations becomes increasingly difficult for strategists. Increases in sales often are not accompanied by similar increases in profitability. The span of control becomes too large at top levels of the firm. For example, in a large conglomerate organization composed of more than 80 divisions or brands, such as Conagra Brands, the CEO could have difficulty even remembering the first names of divisional presidents. In multidivisional organizations, a **strategic business unit (SBU) structure** can greatly facilitate strategy-implementation efforts.

An SBU structure simply groups similar divisions together into "units" and delegates authority and responsibility for each unit to a senior executive who reports directly to the CEO. This change in structure can facilitate strategy implementation by improving coordination between similar divisions and channeling accountability to distinct business units. In a 100-division conglomerate, the divisions could perhaps be regrouped into 10 SBUs according to certain common characteristics, such as competing in the same industry, being located in the same area, or having the same customers.

A disadvantage of an SBU structure is that it requires an additional layer of management, which increases salary expenses. However, this limitation does not outweigh the advantages of improved coordination and accountability. Another advantage of the SBU structure is that it makes the tasks of planning and control by the corporate office more manageable. The popularity of an SBU type structure is growing. For example, Alibaba's CEO Daniel Zhang recently transferred much of his power to the separate SBU headpersons to become more agile in management and to pave the way for anticipated spinoffs (divestitures). This 2021–2023 shift in structure at Alibaba reverses the push toward more centralization over the preceeding 3 years. Alibaba is another one of those high-tech conglomerates doing well in contrast to traditional manufacturing firms. Zhang recently said in a speech (paraphrased) "if your company can support 10 million profitable businesses on a single platform, this is called an economy; our Alibaba Economy is functioning well."

The Matrix Structure

A **matrix structure** is an organizational design in which vertical and horizontal flows of authority and communication (hence the term *matrix*) are created whereby functions are horizontally arrayed and divisions, products, or projects are vertically arrayed. In contrast, functional and divisional structures depend primarily on a vertical chain of command and authority. A matrix structure can result in higher overhead because it creates more management positions. Other disadvantages of a matrix structure that contribute to overall complexity include dual lines of budget authority (a violation of the unity of command principle), dual sources of reward and punishment, shared authority, dual reporting channels, and a need for an extensive and effective communication system.

The matrix structure is often used in the construction and health-care industries. For example, in the construction industry, a matrix structure would work well for Bechtel Corporation and Fluor Corporation because every construction project has a head project person, and if the project is large, each project also has a head human resources person, who reports both to the head project person and the corporate head HR person.

As indicated in Table 7-9, some advantages of a matrix structure are that project objectives are clear, there are many channels of communication, workers can see the visible results of their work, shutting down a project can be accomplished relatively easily, and it facilitates the use of specialized personnel, equipment, and facilities. Functional resources are shared in a matrix structure, rather than duplicated as in a divisional structure. Individuals with a high degree of expertise can divide their time as needed among projects, and they in turn develop their own skills and competencies more than in other structures.

A typical matrix structure, inclusive of typical executive titles, is illustrated in Figure 7-4. Note that the letters (A through Z4) refer to managers. For example, if you were manager A,

TABLE 7-9 Advantages and Disadvantages of a Matrix Structure

Advantages	Disadvantages
1. Clear project objectives	1. Requires excellent vertical and horizontal flows of communication
2. Employees clearly see results of their work	2. Costly because creates more manager positions
3. Easy to shut down a project	3. Violates unity of command principle
4. Facilitates uses of special equipment, personnel, and facilities	4. Creates dual lines of budget authority
5. Shared functional resources instead of duplicated resources, as in a divisional structure	5. Creates dual sources of reward and punishment
	6. Creates shared authority and reporting
	7. Requires mutual trust and understanding

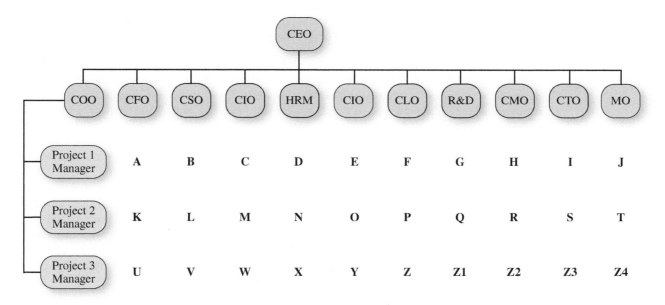

Note: Titles spelled out as follows.

Chief Executive Officer (CEO)
Chief Operating Officer (COO)
Chief Finance Officer (CFO)
Chief Strategy Officer (CSO)
Chief Information Officer (CIO)
Human Resources Manager (HRM)
Competitive Intelligence Officer (CIO)
Chief Legal Officer (CLO)
Research & Development Officer (R&D)
Chief Marketing Officer (CMO)
Chief Technology Officer (CTO)
Maintenance Officer (MO)

FIGURE 7-4

A Typical Matrix Structure with Typical Executive Titles in a Large Firm

you would be responsible for financial aspects of Project 1, and you would have two bosses: the Project 1 Manager on site and the chief financial officer (CFO) off site.

Do's and Don'ts in Developing Organizational Charts

7.7. **Identify and discuss 15 do's and don'ts in constructing organizational charts.**

Students analyzing strategic management cases (and actual corporate executives) often revise and improve a firm's organizational structure. This section provides basic guidelines and several do's and don'ts in regard to developing organizational charts, especially for midsize to large firms. First of all, reserve the title of CEO for the top executive of the firm. Do not use the title "president" for the top person; use it for the division's top managers if there are divisions within the firm. Also, do not use the title president for functional business executives. They should have the title "chief," "vice president," "manager," or "officer," such as "chief information officer," or "VP of human resources." Furthermore, do not recommend a dual title (such as CEO and president) for just one executive.

Do not let a single individual be both chairman of the board and CEO of a company. Of note, chairperson or chair is much better than chairman for the top board person's title. Corporate America is splitting the chair of the board and the CEO positions in publicly held companies. This movement includes asking the New York Stock Exchange and Nasdaq to adopt listing rules that would require separate positions. About 59 percent of companies in the S&P 500 stock index have separate positions, up from 37 percent in 2011. Many more European and Asian companies split the two positions. For example, 80 percent of British companies split the positions, and virtually all German and Dutch companies split the positions.

Directly below the CEO, it is best to have a chief operating officer (COO) with any division presidents reporting directly to the COO. On the same level as the COO and also reporting to the CEO are functional business executives, such as a chief financial officer (CFO), VP of human resources, chief strategy officer (CSO), chief information officer (CIO), chief marketing officer (CMO), VP of R&D, VP of legal affairs, an investment relations officer, maintenance officer, and so on. Note in Figure 7-4 that these positions are labeled and placed appropriately in a matrix structure, which, as shown, generally include project managers rather than division presidents reporting to a COO.

The COO position is increasingly being deleted in U.S. companies. In fact, the percentage of large companies in the United States with COOs has declined almost every year for a decade, to about 35 percent today. Health-care and industrial companies are least likely to have a COO. An accounting firm, PricewaterhouseCoopers, suggests there are four reasons why companies are phasing out the COO position: (1) to flatten their structure, (2) eliminate a layer of management, (3) reduce costs, and (4) expand the CEO's authority and responsibility. Digital communications and even social media today enable a CEO often to perform COO duties. Many companies now delegate the traditional duties of a COO to the CEO or to other positions, such as the CFO or chief brand officer. Deleting the COO position does increase the CEO's span of control, spreading the CEO thinly, which is not a good idea for many companies.

In developing an organizational chart, avoid having a particular individual reporting to more than one person in the chain of command (except in a matrix structure). This would violate the unity of command principle of management that "every employee should have just one boss." Also, do not have any functional positions such as CFO, CIO, CSO, and human resource officer report to the COO. All these positions report directly to the CEO.

In contrast to the COO position, the number of chief accounting officers (CAO) among U.S. companies is increasing. CAOs now do much more than just manage the company's books and prepare financial statements. They stand up and debate strategic issues related to how best to balance the balance sheet, when and how to recognize revenue, and know how to report results using both U.S. and foreign standards (generally accepted accounting procedures [GAAP] vs. international financial reporting standards [IFRS]). CAOs are more commonly signing the company's financial filings, making them personally liable for any mistakes or improprieties—along with the CFO and CEO.

Gary Kabureck, former CAO at Xerox Corp. says: "I think what happened over the last 15 years in the USA is that the accounting function started to separate from the controller function." In a firm, a controller is typically more focused on budgeting and planning, whereas the CAO is responsible for the ins and outs of global bookkeeping. The CAO also interacts closely with the board's audit committee, as well as with outside firms auditing the company.

A relatively new top management position that is quickly becoming mainstream is the Chief Diversity Officer (CDO). The Chief Diversity Officer's role is to assure that a firm's goals, objectives, and policies related to diversity, equity, and inclusion (DE&I) are met, all the while facilitating a corporate culture that values diversity, equity, and inclusion. The CDO should report directly to the CEO. Mita Mallick, a DE&I expert says that, "If you want to be a competitive company in ten years, you have to have this role."[8] Data from Axios and LinkedIn shows a 68 percent increase in the number of CDO positions in corporations from 2015 to 2020. This is still an evolving position, however, and several large companies including Morgan Stanley have had diversity officers resign out of frustration from not being able to make change within their firm. As stated by Eli Lilly's CDO, Joy Fitzgerald, in an interview with the *Wall Street Journal*, "You're dealing with polarizing topics, and these topics and issues are very nuanced. There are not a lot of best practices you can point to that are easy or quick."

One never knows for sure if a proposed or actual structure is indeed most effective for a particular firm. Declining financial performance signals a need for altering the structure. Important guidelines to follow in devising organizational charts for companies are provided in Table 7-10.

TABLE 7-10 Guidelines for Developing an Organizational Chart

1. Instead of *chairman* of the board, make it *chairperson* (or just *chair*) of the board.
2. Make sure the board of directors includes diversity in race, ethnicity, gender, and age.
3. Make sure the chair of the board is not also the CEO or president of the company.
4. Make sure the CEO of the firm does not also carry the title *president*.
5. Reserve the title *president* for the division heads of the firm.
6. Include a COO if divisions are large or geographically dispersed.
7. Make sure only presidents of divisions report to the COO.
8. Make sure functional executives such as CFO, CIO, CMO, CSO, R&D, chief learning officer (CLO), chief technology officer (CTO), and HRM report to the CEO, not the COO.
9. Make sure every executive has one boss, so lines in the chart should be drawn accordingly, assuring unity of command.
10. Make sure span of control is reasonable, probably no more than 10 persons reporting to any other person.
11. Make sure diversity in race, ethnicity, gender, and age is well represented among corporate executives.
12. Avoid a functional type structure for all but the smallest firms.
13. Decentralize, using some form of divisional structure, whenever possible.
14. Use a SBU type structure for large firms with more than 10 divisions.
15. Make sure executive titles match product names as best possible in divisional-by-product and SBU-designated firms.

How to Depict an Organizational Chart

For whatever reason, companies rarely provide a diagram of their organizational chart, neither in their *Form 10K* or on their corporate website. Therefore, students often wrestle with actually drawing an existing chart and devising a new and improved organizational chart. Nearly all companies provide, however, a list of their top executives and associated titles. This "title" information can be used to develop existing and proposed charts. Follow three simple steps to develop organizational charts:

Step 1. List executive positions by title and number. Numbering positions enables numbers, rather than boxes or circles, to be used in a structure diagram to reveal reporting relationships; it is just easier to use numbers.

Step 2.   Using numbers to denote positions, devise your chart to show reporting relationships, consistent with guidelines presented in this chapter.

Step 3.   Draw lines connecting numbers to reveal reporting relationships. Be mindful that a line connecting one number to another means that person reports to the other; so do not connect, for example, a CFO to a CMO.

Figure 7-5 and Figure 7-6 give an existing and improved organizational chart for ABC Company, respectively. ABC Company's example charts demonstrate how to apply the three steps given. In devising any organizational chart, do not be concerned with the names of executives because people come and go in a firm; positions stay relatively constant. Also, do not be overly concerned with the existing chart reporting relationships because those are usually unknown to all but corporate insiders; your new and improved chart is of paramount importance. Also, do not include the 20 or so lower and mid-level managers in a chart; similarly, do not include the board of director members in a chart. It's not that lower-level and mid-level managers and board members are not important because they are. It is just that reporting relationships among the top executives in a firm reveals the type of structure and chain of command. The firm must get those two aspects correct to effectively implement any strategy.

Figure 7-7 give Winnebago Industries, Inc.'s actual and improved organizational chart respectively, further illustrating how to apply the three steps. Headquartered in Forest City, Iowa, Winnebago manufactures and sells recreation vehicles (RVs), including motor homes, travel trailers, and fifth wheel trailers under the Winnebago brand name; component parts for other manufacturers; motorhome shells for law enforcement command centers, mobile medical clinics, and mobile office space; and commercial vehicles as bare shells to third parties. Winnebago sells products primarily through independent dealers in the United States and Canada.

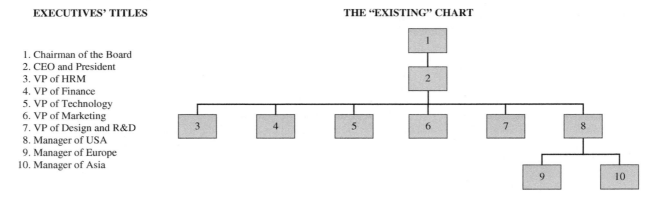

EXECUTIVES' TITLES

1. Chairman of the Board
2. CEO and President
3. VP of HRM
4. VP of Finance
5. VP of Technology
6. VP of Marketing
7. VP of Design and R&D
8. Manager of USA
9. Manager of Europe
10. Manager of Asia

FIGURE 7-5

ABC Company's Existing (Not Good) Organizational Chart

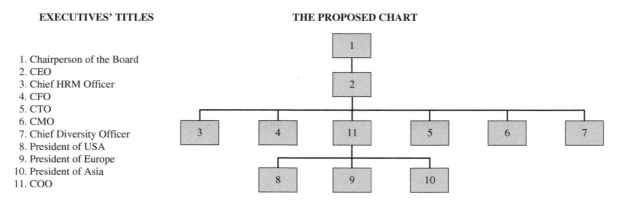

EXECUTIVES' TITLES

1. Chairperson of the Board
2. CEO
3. Chief HRM Officer
4. CFO
5. CTO
6. CMO
7. Chief Diversity Officer
8. President of USA
9. President of Europe
10. President of Asia
11. COO

FIGURE 7-6

ABC Company's Improved (Excellent) Organizational Chart

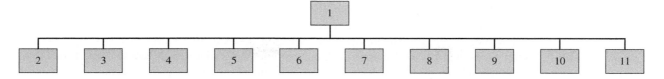

1. Michale Happe, President and CEO
2. Ashis Bhattacharya, SVP – Business Development, Advanced Technology, and Enterprise Marketing
3. Stacy Bogart, SVP, General Counsel, Secretary and Corporate Responsibility and President, Winnebago Industries Foundation
4. Bryan Hughes, CFO, SVP – Finance, IT, and Strategic Planning
5. Sri Koneru, VP, Information Technology

6. Chris West, SVP, Enterprise Operations
7. Bret Woodson, SVP, Human Resources and Corporate Relations
8. Huw Bower, President, Winnebago Outdoors
9. Donald Clark, President, Grand Design RV
10. Stephen Heese, President, Chris-Craft
11. Bill Fenech, President Barletta Boats

FIGURE 7-7

Winnebago's Actual (Not Good) Organizational Chart

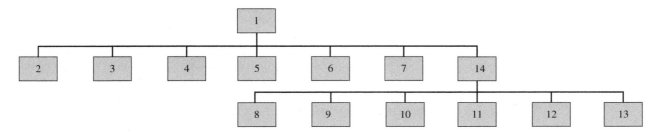

1. Michale Happe, CEO
2. Ashis Bhattacharya, SVP – Business Development, Advanced Technology, and Enterprise Marketing
3. Stacy Bogart, SVP, General Counsel, Secretary and Corporate Responsibility and President, Winnebago Industries Foundation
4. Bryan Hughes, CFO, SVP – Finance, IT, and Strategic Planning
5. Sri Koneru, VP, Information Technology
6. Chris West, SVP, Enterprise Operations

7. Bret Woodson, SVP, Human Resources and Corporate Relations
8. Huw Bower, President, Winnebago Outdoors
9. Donald Clark, President, Grand Design RV
10. Stephen Heese, President, Chris-Craft
11. Bill Fenech, President, Barletta Boats
12. Lady Two, President, Motor Homes
13. Lady Three, President, Towables
14. Lady One, COO

FIGURE 7-8

Winnebago's Improved (Excellent) Organizational Chart

Only recently has Winnebago added boats to its product mix. Note in the improved Winnebago chart, the title president is dropped from the CEO position, and a COO is added because this is a large firm with diverse products, and the company is more clearly arrayed using a divisional-by-product design.

Strategic Production/Operations Issues

7.8. Discuss three strategic production/operations issues vital for strategy implementation.

Production/operations capabilities, limitations, and policies can significantly enhance or inhibit the attainment of objectives. Production processes may constitute more than 70 percent of a firm's total assets. Thus, a major part of the strategy implementation process takes place at the production site. Decisions related to strategic production on plant size, plant location, product design, choice of equipment, kind of tooling, size of inventory, inventory control, quality control, cost control, use of standards, job specialization, employee training, equipment and resource utilization, shipping and packaging, and technological innovation can determine the success or failure of strategy implementation efforts.

Three production/operations issues, restructuring/reengineering, managing resistance to change, and deciding where and how to produce goods, are especially important for successful strategy implementation and are, therefore, discussed next.

Restructuring and Reengineering

Restructuring and reengineering are forms of retrenchment discussed in Chapter 5. **Restructuring**, sometimes called *downsizing*, involves reducing the size of the firm in terms of number of employees, number of divisions or units, and number of hierarchical levels in the firm's organizational structure. This reduction in size is intended to improve both efficiency and effectiveness. Restructuring is concerned primarily with shareholder well-being rather than employee well-being. The primary benefit sought from restructuring is cost reduction. But the downside of restructuring can be reduced employee commitment, creativity, and innovation associated with pending and actual employee layoffs.

Job security in European companies is slowly moving toward a U.S. business model, in which firms lay off almost at will. From banks in Milan to factories in Mannheim, European employers are starting to show people the door in an effort to streamline operations, increase efficiency, and compete against already slim-and-trim U.S. firms. European firms still prefer to downsize by attrition and retirement, rather than by blanket layoffs because of culture, laws, and unions.

In contrast to restructuring, reengineering is concerned more with employee and customer well-being than shareholder well-being. **Reengineering** involves reconfiguring or redesigning work, jobs, and processes for the purpose of improving cost, quality, service, and speed. Reengineering does not usually affect the organizational structure or chart, nor does it imply job loss or employee layoffs. Whereas restructuring is concerned with eliminating or establishing, shrinking or enlarging, and moving organizational departments and divisions, the focus of reengineering is changing the way work is actually carried out. Reengineering is characterized by many tactical (short-term, business-function-specific) decisions, whereas restructuring is characterized by strategic (long-term, affecting all business functions) decisions.

Manage Resistance to Change

No organization or individual can escape change. But the thought of change raises anxieties because people fear economic loss, inconvenience, uncertainty, and a break in normal social patterns. Almost any change in structure, technology, people, or strategies has the potential to disrupt comfortable interaction patterns. For this reason, people resist change. The strategic management process can impose major changes on individuals and processes. Reorienting an organization to get people to think and act strategically is not an easy task. Strategy implementation can pose a threat to many managers and employees. New power and status relationships are anticipated and realized. New formal and informal groups' values, beliefs, and priorities may be largely unknown. Managers and employees may become engaged in resistance behavior as their roles, prerogatives, and power in the firm change. Disruption of social and political structures that accompany strategy execution must be anticipated and considered during strategy formulation and managed during strategy implementation.

Resistance to change may be the single greatest threat to successful strategy implementation. Resistance regularly occurs in organizations in the form of sabotaging production machines, absenteeism, filing unfounded grievances, and an unwillingness to cooperate. People often resist strategy implementation because they do not understand what is happening or why changes are taking place. In that case, employees may simply need accurate information. Successful strategy implementation hinges on managers' abilities to develop an organizational climate conducive to change. Change must be viewed by managers and employees as an opportunity for the firm to compete more effectively, rather than being seen as a threat to everyone's livelihood.

Strategists can take a number of positive actions to minimize managers' and employees' resistance to change. For example, individuals who will be affected by a change should be involved in the decision to make the change and in decisions about how to implement the change. Strategists should anticipate changes and develop and offer training and development workshops so that managers and employees can adapt to those changes. They also need to effectively communicate the need for changes.

Decide Where and How to Produce Goods

In China, about 700,000 assembly workers at manufacturing contractors such as Foxconn put together Apple products. It would be difficult to bring those jobs to the United States for at least three reasons. First, Foxconn—China's largest private employer and the manufacturer of an estimated 40 percent of the world's consumer electronic devices—pays its assembly workers far less than U.S. labor laws would allow. A typical salary is about $18 a day. Second, Foxconn and other Chinese manufacturing operations house employees in dormitories and can send hundreds of thousands of workers to the assembly lines at a moment's notice. On the lines, workers are subjected to what most Americans would consider unbearably long hours and tough working conditions. That system gives tech companies the efficiency needed to race products out the door, so speed is a bigger factor than pay. Finally, most of the component suppliers for Apple and other technology giants are also in China or other Asian countries. That geographic clustering gives companies the flexibility to change a product design at the last minute and still ship on time.

Examples of adjustments in production systems that could be required to implement various strategies are provided in Table 7-11 for both for-profit and nonprofit organizations. The largest bicycle company in the United States, Huffy, recently ended its own production of bikes and now contracts out those services to Asian and Mexican manufacturers. Huffy focuses instead on the design, marketing, and distribution of bikes, but it no longer produces bikes themselves. The Dayton, Ohio, company closed its plants in Ohio, Missouri, and Mississippi.

TABLE 7-11 Production Management and Strategy Implementation

Type of Organization	Strategy Being Implemented	Production System Adjustments
Hospital	Adding a cancer center (Product Development)	Purchase specialized equipment and add specialized people
Bank	Adding 10 new branches (Market Development)	Perform site location analysis
Beer brewery	Purchasing a barley farm operation (Backward Integration)	Revise the inventory control system
Steel manufacturer	Acquiring a fast-food chain (Unrelated Diversification)	Improve the quality control system
Computer company	Purchasing a retail distribution chain (Forward Integration)	Alter the shipping, packaging, and transportation systems

Factors that should be studied before locating production facilities include the availability of major resources, the prevailing wage rates in the area, transportation costs related to shipping and receiving, the location of major markets, political risks in the area or country, currency and tax considerations, language and legal issues, and the availability of trainable employees. Some of these factors explain why many manufacturing operations in China are moving back to Mexico, to Vietnam, or even back to the United States. Former President Donald Trump pledged to create such a pro-business environment that companies would reshore (relocate) their manufacturing facilities to the United States.

Strategic Human Resource Issues

7.9. Discuss seven strategic human resource issues vital for strategy implementation.

Any organization is only as good as its people! Thus, human resource issues can make or break successful strategy implementation. The CEO of JPMorgan Chase, Jamie Dimon, is widely considered to be one of the world's preeminent human resource strategists. Dimon says strategic planning has more to do with heart than mind. He says this means recognize people, admit you do not have all the answers, value others' expertise and experiences, provide people a platform to contribute, applaud people for their contributions, and basically let people know you care. Dimon says to avoid finger-pointing and scapegoating and focus on improved relations and collaboration. He contends that most business decisions lead to better outcomes after detailed analyses are performed and multiple people from various departments (finance, management information system [MIS], accounting, marketing, and others) are involved in the decision-making process.

Thus, seven human resource issues are discussed further in this section, as follows: (1) linking performance and pay to strategy, (2) balancing work life with home life, (3) developing a diverse workforce, (4) using caution in hiring a rival's employees, (5) creating a culture that supports strategy, (6) using caution in monitoring employees' social media, and (7) developing a corporate well-being program.

Link Performance and Pay to Strategy

An organization's compensation system needs to be aligned with strategic outcomes. Decisions on salary increases, promotions, merit pay, and bonuses need to support the long-term and annual objectives of the firm. A dual bonus system based on both annual and long-term objectives can be helpful in linking performance and pay to strategies. The percentage of a manager's annual bonus attributable to short-term versus long-term results should vary by hierarchical level in the organization. It is important that bonuses not be based solely on short-term results because such a system ignores long-term company strategies and objectives and could reward unnecessary risk-taking and cost-cutting.

Criteria such as sales, profit, production efficiency, quality, and safety could also serve as bases for an effective bonus system. If an organization meets certain understood, agreed-on profit objectives, every member of the enterprise should share in the harvest. A bonus system can be an effective tool for motivating individuals to support efforts toward strategy implementation.

A combination of reward strategy incentives, such as salary raises, stock options, employee benefits, promotions, praise, recognition, increased job autonomy, and awards, can be used to encourage managers and employees to push hard for successful strategic implementation. The range of options for getting people, departments, and divisions to actively support activities for strategy implementation in a particular organization is almost limitless. A firm, for example, could give its employees a 10-year option to buy up to 1,000 shares of company stock at a set price lower than the current market price.

Balance Work Life and Home Life

Work and family strategies now represent a competitive advantage for those firms that offer such benefits as elder-care assistance, flexible scheduling, job sharing, adoption benefits, on-site summer camp, employee help lines, pet care, and even lawn service referrals. New corporate titles such as Work and Life Coordinator are becoming common. Globally, it is widely acknowledged that the best countries for gender equality in the workforce are Iceland, Finland, Norway, and Sweden, all of which rate above the United States. According to the 2021 *World Economic Forum's Global Gender Gap Index Report*, the United States is, in fact, ranked 30th overall.

In a recent 12-month study on Work-Life Balance conducted by Comparably.com, thousands of employees from more than 10,000 North American companies anonymously rated their employers and responded to a series of questions related to work-life balance; the top 10 best large and small/midsize companies for work-life balance in 2021 are provided in Table 7-12.

A good home life contributes immensely to a good work life. Some specific measures that firms are taking to address this issue are providing spouse relocation assistance as an employee benefit; supplying company resources for family recreational and educational use; establishing employee country clubs, such as those at IBM and Bethlehem Steel; and creating family and work interaction opportunities. Similarly, some organizations have developed family days, when family members are invited into the workplace, taken on plant or office tours, invited to dinner with management, and given a chance to see exactly what other family members do each day. Family days are inexpensive and increase the employee's pride in working for the organization.

TABLE 7-12 Top 10 Large and Small/Midsize Companies for Work-Life Balance

Large Companies	Small/Midsize Companies
1. HubSpot (Cambridge, MA)	1. Course Hero (Redwood City, CA)
2. Chegg (Santa Clara, CA)	2. Namely (New York, NY)
3. ZipRecruiter (Santa Monica, CA)	3. Strava (San Francisco, CA)
4. Farmers Insurance (Woodland Hills, CA)	4. Kyruus (Boston, MA)
5. nCino (Wilmington, NC)	5. Verisys Corporation (Louisville, KY)
6. Momentive (formerly Survey Monkey) (San Mateo, CA)	6. Fetch Rewards (Chicago, IL)
7. Elsevier (New York, NY)	7. Mixpanel (San Francisco, CA)
8. 23andMe (Sunnyvale, CA)	8. GoSite (San Diego, CA)
9. Trimble (Sunnyvale, CA)	9. Rev.com (Austin, TX)
10. Smartsheet (Bellevue, WA)	10. Motivosity (Lehi, UT)

Source: Based on information at https://www.businessinsider.com/large-companies-best-work-life-balance-comparably-ranking-2021-10#22-gympass-4, https://www.comparably.com/news/best-work-life-balance-2021/, and a variety of other sources.

Flexible working hours during the week are another human resource response to the need for individuals to balance work life and home life. Employee engagement and productivity is likely to be the greatest in firms where employees feel that their company's policies, benefits, and culture advocate work-life balance and in firms where employees feel appreciated and are empowered to take time off when needed.

Promote Diversity

The term **glass ceiling** refers to the invisible barrier in many firms that bars women and minorities from top-level management positions. In 2021, the number of women as CEOs leading *Fortune* 500 companies increased to an all-time record of 41, or 8.2 percent. Two of these women are black, making 2021 the first year in history that two black women served as CEOs of *Fortune* 500 companies in the same year. Thus, progress in this regard is slow, even in the United States.

Having a diverse and inclusive organization can seem like an overly optimistic goal, particularly for small, highly localized firms, but it can be a worthwhile goal. Six benefits among many of having a diverse workforce are as follows:

1. Women and minorities have different insights, opinions, and perspectives that should be considered.
2. A diverse workforce portrays a firm committed to nondiscrimination.
3. A workforce that mirrors a diverse customer base can help attract customers, build customer loyalty, and design or offer products and services that meet customer needs and wants.
4. A diverse workforce helps protect the firm against discrimination lawsuits.
5. Individuals in minority groups, including those based on ethnicity, race, sexual orientation, gender identity, and religious beliefs, represent a huge additional pool of qualified applicants.
6. A diverse workforce strengthens a firm's social responsibility and ethical position.

A recent study by *Forbes* and Statista surveyed 50,000 employees to determine "America's Top Employers for Diversity in 2021." Results of the study indicate that JLL (Jones Lang LaSalle), the commercial real estate firm headquartered in Chicago, holds the top spot, with 75 percent of its board of directors representing gender or racial diversity. Of the thousands of firms included in the study, 60 percent (up from 28 percent in 2020) of them explicitly report on their websites their actions taken to promote diversity, and 28 percent (up from 18 percent in 2020) of the firms have a senior leader whose role is dedicated solely to DE&I initiatives. Bloomberg reporter Jeff Green says that, "While 85 of the nation's top 100 corporations tracked by Bloomberg for corporate diversity have a chief diversity officer, representation of minorities within their workforce continues to lag behind. Recruiting a new leader sends a strong signal, but it takes more than one executive to make an impact in the face of institutional pushback."

Use Caution in Hiring a Rival's Employees

An article titled "Do's and Don'ts of Poaching Workers" in *Investor's Business Daily* gives guidelines to consider before hiring a rival firm's employees.[9] The practice of hiring employees from rival firms has a long tradition, but increasingly in our lawsuit-happy environment, firms must consider whether that person(s) had access to the "secret sauce formula, customer list, programming algorithm, or any proprietary or confidential information" of the rival firm. If the person has that information and joins your firm, lawsuits could follow that hiring, especially if the person was under contract at the rival firm or had signed a "noncompete agreement." The article says that to help safeguard the firm from this potential problem, a "well-written employee handbook" addressing the issue is necessary.

According to Wayne Perrett, human resource manager for ComAp in Roscoe, Illinois, "A company does not want to become known as one that 'steals' employees from competitors; that is bad for ethics and bad for business." It is not illegal to interview and hire employees from rival firms, and it has been done for centuries, but increasingly this is becoming a strategic issue to be managed, to avoid litigation. For example, in a huge employee-poaching move, Microsoft recently had about 100 HoloLens augmented-reality employees quit and go to other technology firms, especially Meta Platforms. As craze for metaverse expertise intensifies, rival firms are paying double existing salaries to attract competent, experienced, "metaverse" employees. Apple and other similar firms have also been losing employees to Meta Platforms, as elaborated upon in the *Wall Street Journal* article (1-11-22, p. A1).

GlaxoSmithKline PLC hired rival Pfizer Inc.'s top vaccine scientist, Dr. Philip Dormitzer, just as pharmaceutical firms were scrambling to assess how their vaccines would combat the new Omicron variant of COVID-19. Dormitzer replaces vaccine specialist Emanuel Hanon who had departed Glaxo for rival company Viome. Such hirings across rival firms do occur, but firms must be careful and cautious to avoid lawsuits related to patent and trademark infringements.

Create a Culture Supportive of Strategy

All organizations have a unique **culture**. For example, at Meta Platforms, Inc. (the parent company of Facebook), employees are given unusual freedom to choose and change assignments. Even low-level employees are encouraged to question and criticize managers. Meta employees are rated on a normal distribution curve (Bell curve), which creates a hectic, intense work environment where past accomplishments mean little compared to what you have done lately for the firm. Managers are not revered at Meta as bosses; rather, they are regarded as helpers.

Strategists should strive to preserve, emphasize, and build on aspects of an existing culture that support proposed new strategies. Aspects of an existing culture that are antagonistic to a proposed strategy should be identified and changed. Changing a firm's culture to fit a new strategy is usually more effective than changing a strategy to fit an existing culture. As indicated in Table 7-13, numerous techniques are available to alter an organization's culture, including recruitment, training, transfer, promotion, restructure of an organization's design, role modeling, positive reinforcement, and mentoring.

TABLE 7-13 Ways and Means for Altering an Organization's Culture

1. Recruitment
2. Training
3. Transfer
4. Promotion
5. Restructuring
6. Reengineering
7. Role modeling
8. Positive reinforcement
9. Mentoring
10. Revising vision or mission
11. Redesigning physical spaces or facades
12. Altering reward systems
13. Altering organizational policies, procedures, and practices

Use Caution in Monitoring Employees' Social Media

Many companies monitor employees' and prospective employees' social media activities and have the legal right to do so; there are many pros and cons of this activity. Proponents of companies monitoring employees' social media activities emphasize that (1) a company's reputation in the marketplace can easily be damaged by disgruntled employees venting on social media sites and (2) social media records can be subpoenaed, like email, and used as evidence against the company. Proponents say companies have a responsibility to know the nature of employees' communications through social media as related to clients, patients, suppliers, distributors, coworkers, managers, technology, patents, procedures, policies, and much more. To ignore social media communication by employees, proponents say, is irresponsible and too risky for the firm. Some companies use social media to research and screen job candidates, sometimes finding provocative or inappropriate photos and information related to potential employees' biases, stereotypes, prejudices, drinking, and drug use. Companies however should never use social media to discriminate based on age, race, ethnic background, religion, sexuality, or disability.

Arguments against the practice of companies monitoring employees' social media activities say it is an invasion of privacy and too often becomes "a fishing expedition" sifting through tons of personal information irrelevant to a company or its business. Positions on political issues, gun rights, voting accessibility, or immigration are example topics where company researchers may "not like" individuals with belief systems different from their own. Given new global, societal, and corporate awareness and concern for DE&I, companies must be careful not to discriminate based on social media findings.

On balance, companies should monitor employee and potential employee's social media activities whenever they have a reason to believe the person is engaged in illegal or unethical conduct, but to systematically investigate every employee and job candidate's social media activities is arguably counterproductive. The bottom line is that companies have the *legal right* to monitor employees' conduct but have the *legal duty* to do so only if there is sufficient reason for concern.

Develop a Corporate Well-Being Program

Corporate wellness has become a major strategic issue in companies. If you owned a company and paid the health insurance of employees, would you desire to have a healthy workforce? Healthy employees are more productive and less absent from work.

The notion of corporate wellness is rapidly shifting from health assessment, weight loss, and biometric screenings to also include financial well-being, social networks, work-life balance, and overall well-being. The focus now is thus on lifestyle management rather than just cholesterol management; this shift includes such things as sit-stand desks in the workspace and access to the outdoors while at work. The term *corporate wellness* has largely been replaced with *corporate well-being*, and these newly designed programs are being used in recruitment and retention; the programs are being intertwined with company goals and objectives.

Corporate wellness is especially important today because (1) the U.S. Labor Department and Census Bureau report that in 2021–2025 older workers are 'unretiring' and re-entering the labor force, and (2) the pandemic raised everyone's awareness of the importance of corporate wellness. About 3 percent of retired U.S. workers are returning to the workforce, spurred by wage increases, higher benefit offerings, availability of remote work, vaccines controlling the pandemic, and literally thousands of job openings; the U.S. Bureau of Labor Statistics reports that "the U.S. labor force participation rate is the lowest since 1977."[10]

Strategic Marketing Issues

7.10. **Describe key strategic marketing issues vital for implementing strategies.**

Countless marketing considerations affect the success or failure of strategy implementation efforts, such as the following:

1. How to make advertisements more interactive to be more effective
2. How to take advantage of social media conversations about the company and industry
3. To use exclusive dealerships or multiple channels of distribution
4. To use heavy, light, or no TV advertising versus online advertising
5. To limit (or not) the share of business done with a single supplier or business customer
6. To be a price leader or a price follower
7. To offer a complete or limited warranty
8. To extend an existing product line or create a new line of products

Market segmentation, target marketing, and product positioning are among marketing's most important contributions to strategic management. Strategies such as market development, product development, market penetration, and diversification require increased sales through new markets or products. To implement strategies successfully, effective segmentation, targeting, and positioning are required as discussed next.

Segment and Target Markets Effectively

As illustrated in Figure 7-9, companies engage in market segmentation first, then target marketing, and then position products among industry offerings. Because consumers vary in their needs and wants, undifferentiated marketing is rarely an effective strategy. Thus, firms engage in **market segmentation**, dividing a market into distinct subsets of customers that differ from one another in product needs or buying habits. The segments are created based on unique demographic, geographic, psychographic, or behavioral characteristics of consumers. Successful strategy implementation requires effective (and efficient) marketing.

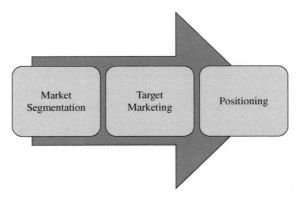

FIGURE 7-9

Segment, Target, and Position: The Key to Marketing Strategy

Source: Based on a variety of sources.

Market segmentation requires strategists to determine the characteristics and needs of consumers, to analyze consumer similarities and differences, and to develop consumer group profiles. After segmenting markets, companies select particular segment(s) to target. Individual market segments differ in consumer needs and buying habits so firms carefully select segment(s) to target. Firms such as Marriott, InterContinental, and Wyndham have multiple brands of hotels so they can market varied offerings tailored to particular target segments.

The COVID-19 pandemic negatively affected business of all types, and firms within the tourism and hospitality industries were hit particularly hard. As discussed in Global Capsule 7, the pandemic created a new threat with continued travel restrictions and bans being put in place, but to some hoteliers, the pandemic also created a new opportunity to market "staycations." Strategies aimed at mitigating the threat of continued travel restrictions and exploiting the "staycation" opportunity required hoteliers to alter their market segmentation and shift their target markets. This segmentation, targeting, and positioning was essential to the implementation of a new strategy formulated in response to the global pandemic. Market segmentation and targeting decisions directly affect the **marketing mix variables**: product, place, promotion, and price (discussed in Chapter 4).

Product Positioning

After markets have been segmented and one or more segments have been selected as the target market(s), firms engage in positioning. **Positioning** entails designing a marketing mix that offers unique value to target customers. The product offering, its price, the way it is promoted or advertised, and the channels through which it is sold all complement one another and are designed to attract a particular target market. As illustrated in Figure 7-10, product, price, promotion, and place aspects of any offering collectively yield value to a target market, resulting in consumer demand being high (or low) versus rival offerings.

GLOBAL CAPSULE 7

How the COVID-19 Pandemic Caused Some Hoteliers to Rethink Their Target Marketing[11]

Salvador Maniquiz/Shutterstock

The tourism and hospitality industries were severely hurt by COVID. Strict travel restrictions halted international travel and drastically reduced domestic travel, leaving most hotels with extremely low occupancy numbers. The pandemic created a new threat with continued travel restrictions and bans being put in place, but to some hoteliers, the pandemic also created a new opportunity to market "staycations." Strategies aimed at mitigating the threat of continued travel restrictions and exploiting the "staycation" opportunity required hoteliers to alter their market segmentation and shift their target markets. Many hoteliers shifted their market to locals rather than tourists and then segmented the local market as needed, perhaps by the type of consumption experience desired.

In 2020, HVS, a global consulting firm specializing in hospitality conducted a survey of consumers and hoteliers and found that 75 percent of consumers had considered booking a staycation, while 75 percent of hoteliers reported that they were targeting staycation demand. Data from the HVS survey was further analyzed to understand variations in demand patterns and segment the local market. Three subsegments were identified: "Staycation Dreamers" (i.e., locals who want to disconnect and recharge through impeccable service and amenities), "Staycation Explorers" (i.e., locals who want to deepen a connection to local culture through curated experiences), and "Businesss Staycationers" (i.e., local professionals who seek flexible and smart work spaces). Hoteliers then repositioned their offerings to fit the distinct needs of one or more segments of potential staycationers. The Canadian hotel group, Germain Hotels, repositioned itself to target Staycation Explorers by partnering with local restaurants to deliver private and gourmet but localized "In-Room Gastronomy" experiences that would not be available otherwise. This segmentation, targeting, and positioning was essential to the implementation of a new strategy aimed at attracting the market segment of "Staycation Explorers."

[11]Based on https://www.hvs.com/article/9080-Targeting-Hotel-Staycation-Demand-in-Canada-and-Beyond and a variety of sources.

Through marketing, Procter & Gamble (P&G) has effectively implemented strategies for product development and market penetration. Consider the following P&G laundry detergent brands, for example: Gain provides "a scent you can wear all day long;" Cheer provides "exceptional color-protection;" and Dreft "gently and safely cleans baby clothing." These detergents target unique segments and are positioned as such.

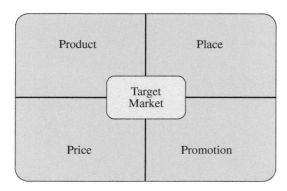

FIGURE 7-10

Positioning Products to Meet Target Market Needs

Source: Based on a variety of sources.

Perceptual Mapping

Firms continuously monitor the image of their brands as perceived by consumers. A product-positioning tool widely used in marketing is perceptual mapping, or developing schematic representations to reflect how a firm's goods or services compare to competitors' in the mind of consumers. Perceptual mapping is widely used for deciding how to better meet the needs and wants of particular consumer groups. The technique can be summarized in five steps:

1. Select key criteria that effectively differentiate products in the industry. Specifically, consider the key characteristics of your brand offerings that provide unique value to your target customers.
2. Diagram a two-dimensional product-positioning map with specified criteria on each axis.
3. Plot major competitors' brands in the resultant four-quadrant matrix.
4. Assess whether your brand's location in the matrix is ideal, especially relative to competitors. That is, consider whether your brand's position, as perceived by consumers, offers unique value.
5. Reposition your brand's offering as needed to shift consumers' perceptions of the brand to a location that provides a competitive advantage over rival brands.

An effective strategy for product positioning uniquely distinguishes a company from the competition. Companies commonly develop **perceptual maps** to better understand current and potential competitive advantages and disadvantages versus rival companies, rival products, or in-house products. Figure 7-11 shows a perceptual map of domestic commercial airlines. Consider for example that Delta is implementing a strategy for market penetration with objectives aimed at increasing revenue; the perceptual map in Figure 7-11 may help guide Delta managers by suggesting that the firm needs to either focus on improving the availability of flight offerings or lowering prices.

Perceptual maps can also be helpful in fostering the implementation of strategies for incumbent firms that may be planning to enter a new market as part of a diversification strategy. Perceptual maps also reveal unclaimed space that may contain a market segment not yet targeted by any major firms in the industry. Figure 7-11 indicates that several firms already offer average range prices and availability of flight offerings, but a firm could perhaps differentiate itself by offering an enhanced availability of flight offerings for moderate prices (while remaining below American Airlines). Perceptual maps can also help firms identify any areas where they may be over- or underserving customers and costing the firm money. Delta is possibly overpricing its flights; sure many business customers will accept this, but Delta could likely get more business, including perhaps taking business from American or United, by lowering its prices a little.

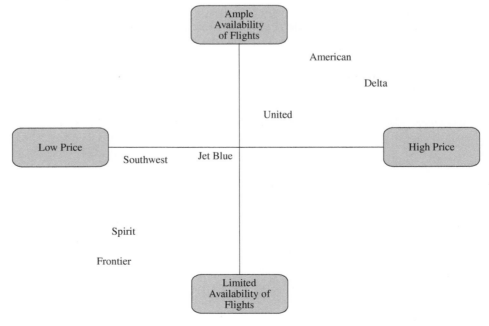

FIGURE 7-11

A Perceptual Map for Domestic Airline Brands

Source: Based on a variety of sources.

Perceptual maps are also often used by firms with multiple different brands. For example, when implementing strategies, Marriott could use a perceptual map to illustrate how its many different brands compare to or are differentiated from one another, to identify potential problems with underperforming brands or to visualize potential markets that could best serve as a focus for a new brand of Marriott hotels. For example, the addition of another midrange hotel brand may cannibalize sales of existing Marriott brands, but the addition of an economy brand of hotels may be fruitful for Marriott to consider as a means of implementing a growth strategy.

Engage Customers in Social Media

Social media marketing has become an important strategic issue and an effective way to understand consumers' perceptions of brands. Marketing has evolved to be more about building a two-way relationship with consumers than just informing consumers about a product or service. Marketers increasingly strive to get customers involved in the company website and social media pages and solicit suggestions in terms of product development, customer service, and ideas. Companies want customers to interact with the firm on such social media networks as Twitter, LinkedIn, Instagram, Facebook, Pinterest, and Foursquare. To manage this process, many larger companies have hired social media managers to be the face or voice of the company on social and digital media sites. These managers respond to comments and problems, track negative or misleading statements, manage the online discussion about a firm, and gather valuable information about opinions and desires—all of which can be vital for monitoring the strategy implementation progress and making appropriate changes.

The online community of customers increasingly mirrors the offline community; online engagement can be a much quicker, cheaper, and effective source for gathering market research data than traditional focus groups and surveys. Successful strategy implementation requires a firm to know what people are saying about it and its products. Social media posts, blog discussions, tweets, emails, and conversations with family and friends represent valuable content for brand management. Excellent firms today embrace consumers' opinions, desires, and feelings, and learn from, and leverage consumer-generated content to improve the effectiveness of their marketing mix.

Firms benefit immensely by providing incentives to customers to share their thoughts, opinions, and experiences on the company website. Firms should encourage customers to network among themselves on topics of their choosing on the company website. The company website must not be just about the company; it must be all about the customer, too. Offering points, discounts, or coupons on the website for customers who provide ideas, suggestions, or feedback can be helpful. Driving traffic to the company website and then keeping customers at the website for as long as possible with daily new material, updates, excitement, and offers is effective marketing.

Customers trust other customers' opinions more than a company's marketing pitch, and the more they talk freely, the more the firm can learn how to improve its overall marketing mix. Marketers should monitor blogs daily to determine, evaluate, and influence opinions being formed by customers. Customers must not feel like they are a captive audience for advertising at a firm's website. Table 7-14 provides some key principles of marketing communications.

TABLE 7-14 Key Principles of Marketing Communications

1. Reach – Do not just focus on current heavy users; reach beyond existing heavy users.
2. Attention – Loyal users will be inclined to pay attention, but you must earn the attention of new and light users.
3. Creativity – Be novel and not obvious in the communications; when multiple similar things are shown, the one that differs the most is likely to be the one remembered most.
4. Distinctiveness – Distinctive brand assets help create a frame of reference in one's memory, fostering brand recall and purchase likelihood.
5. Consistency – Arguably one of the most neglected aspects of communication, consistency is key; be consistently distinctive with your communications.
6. Emotion – As stated by Phil Barden, "Communications evoking emotional responses have better attention, deeper processing of the content, better memory-encoding and retrieval."
7. Motivation – Communicate what the brand helps one achieve (i.e., your prospective buyer's implicit goal).

Source: Based on https://www.marketingweek.com/principles-effective-marketing-communication/

Millennials spend more time weekly on the internet than watching television, listening to the radio, and watching movies combined. Thus, social media ads are often a better means of reaching younger customers than traditional yellow pages, television, magazine, radio, or newspaper ads. However, substantial traffic on the internet is reportedly fake, being the result of bogus computers programmed to visit websites to take advantage of marketers who typically pay for ads whenever a user visits a webpage, regardless if the user is an actual person. Criminals can erect websites and deliver phony traffic and collect payments from advertisers through middlemen. Although the exponential increase in social media engagement has created huge opportunities for marketers, it also has produced severe threats; any kind of negative publicity travels fast online. Seemingly minor ethical and questionable actions can catapult into huge public relations problems for companies as a result of the monumental online social and business communications.

IMPLICATIONS FOR STRATEGISTS

New Organizational Structure Decision-Making Model

For thousands of years strategists have realized that being effectively organized is commonly the main difference between success and failure. Examples abound historically where armies or institutions with far less resources and manpower, but better organized, overcame, outperformed, and defeated stronger rivals. Until the year 2020 however, strategists lacked an objective, decision-making model regarding how to best organize or structure their firm. Specifically, until publication of the two articles listed, no mathematical model was available for companies to help determine the best structure to use. Based on an extension of this chapter, the landmark articles cited here reveal that there are (1) 10 key characteristics of a firm that significantly impact structural design and (2) seven basic types of structure. The full articles are provided for download under Resources at the author website at www.strategyclub.com.

Meredith E. David, Forest R. David, and Fred R. David, "Testing and Enhancing a Pivotal Organizational Structure Decision-Making Model," *International Journal of Strategic Decision Sciences* 12, no. 2 (2021): 1–19.

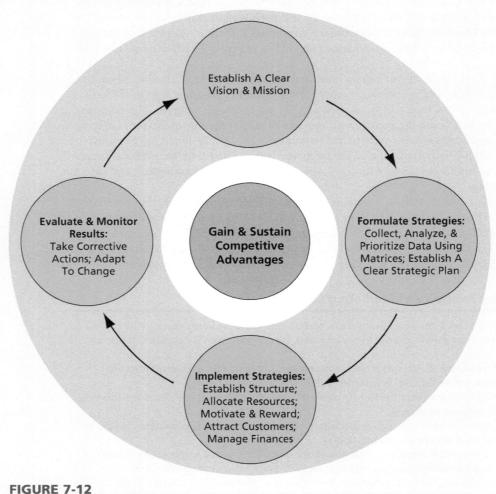

FIGURE 7-12

How to Gain and Sustain Competitive Advantages

Forest R. David, Meredith E. David, and Fred R. David, "A New and Improved Organizational Structure Decision-Making Model," *SAM Advanced Management Journal* 85, no. 4 (2020): 25–39.

The two articles reveal that as a firm's underlying characteristics change, structural changes may be needed. Firms can potentially manage structural change more effectively by continually monitoring changes in the 10 identified organizational characteristics. The articles reveal that various types of structure are more desirable than others across continuums associated with various organizational characteristics. The two articles can aid firms in reorganizing across various regions, products, customers, and the like. The first article develops and presents the model, and the second article empirically tests and refines the model.

There is no one optimal organizational structure for a given strategy or for a given size of firm, but the two articles suggest that the best structure depends on a particular firm's position along 10 literature-derived organizational characteristics. Pending future research aimed at continual improvement, strategists hopefully will use the guidelines provided in this chapter, coupled with the decision-making model presented in the two articles, to make organizational-design decisions that can lead to success.

Conclusion

Figure 7-12 reveals that to gain and sustain competitive advantages, firms must be exceptionally well organized and must allocate resources appropriately across products, services, and regions. Employees must know clearly what rewards and benefits they will receive if the firm does well; this knowledge will help motivate the workforce to work hard. As indicated in this chapter, other management policies and procedures also are needed to facilitate superior strategic implementation, including creating an inclusive organization, linking compensation to firm performance, encouraging corporate well-being, and nurturing an organizational culture that treats all people with respect. If strategists do an exceptional job with the management and marketing issues related to strategy implementation, the firm is well on its way to success.

Perceptual mapping and market segmentation especially are vitally important tools for strategists to make sure that monies devoted to advertising, promotion, publicity, and selling are wisely used. Marketing expenditures can be unnecessarily exorbitant if not based on clear product positioning analyses and target marketing.

IMPLICATIONS FOR STUDENTS

An integral part of managing a firm is continually and systematically seeking to gain and sustain competitive advantage through effective planning, organizing, motivating, and controlling. Rival firms engage in these same activities, so emphasize in your strategic management case analysis how your firm can best implement your recommendations. Remember to be prescriptive rather than descriptive on every page or slide in your project, meaning to be insightful, forward-looking, and analytical, rather than just describing operations. It is easy to *describe* a company, but it is difficult to *analyze* a company. Strategic-management case analysis is about *analyzing* a company and its industry, uncovering ways and means for the firm to best gain and sustain competitive advantage. So, communicate throughout your project how your firm, and especially your recommendations, will lead to improved growth and profitability versus rival firms. Avoid vagueness and generalities throughout your project because your audience or reader seeks great ideas backed up by great analyses. Be analytical and prescriptive rather than vague and descriptive in highlighting every slide you show an audience.

A crucial consideration in devising an organizational structure concerns the divisions. Note whether the divisions (if any) of a firm presently are established based on geography, customer, product, or process. If the firm's organizational chart is not available, you often can devise a chart based on the titles of executives. An important case analysis activity is for you to decide how the divisions of a firm should be organized for maximum effectiveness. Even if the company presently has no divisions, determine whether it would operate better with divisions. In other words, which type of divisional breakdown do you (or your group or team) feel would be best for the firm in allocating resources, establishing objectives, and devising compensation incentives? This important strategic decision faces many midsize and large firms (and teams of students analyzing a strategic-management case).

Be mindful that all firms have functional staff below their top executive and often readily provide this information, so be wary of concluding prematurely that a particular firm uses a functional structure. If you see the word "president" in the titles of executives, coupled with financial reporting segments, such as by product or geographic region, then the firm is currently divisionally structured.

Capitalize on your expertise in marketing in regard to proposing how best to segment, target, and position your firm's products to facilitate effective strategy implementation. Use the template at the author website to develop several perceptual maps to lay the foundation for spending resources to best position a firm's products to gain and sustain competitive advantages. To develop your perceptual maps, find data tables using a Google search that compare your firm and its products to rival firms, and give the reference(s) as a source for each map.

Template Considerations

The strategic planning template at www.strategyclub.com is not useful for developing organizational charts, but the template is excellent for developing perceptual maps. Perceptual map data is entered into Part I of the template. The template will allow for up to 10 products to be considered at one time. Enter as many products as you deem necessary based on your x- and y-axis labels using the 1 to 9 scale described in the template. Take care in the naming of your axes. For example, for the fast-food industry naming the x-axis "low quality" to "high quality" and the y-axis "low price" to "high price" would not be nearly as effective as naming the x-axis "short-wait time" to "long-wait time" and the y-axis "low price" to "high price." With the second set of axes, plausible business opportunities could better be determined in each quadrant because various sets of consumers may be willing to pay for (1) short wait time high price, (2) short wait time low price, (3) long wait time low price, and (4) long wait time high price. Possibly choice 4 here could be Five Guys. However, it is unlikely anyone will be willing to pay a high price for low quality. Everyone is willing to pay a low price for high quality, but this business model would not be financially feasible to operate. Therefore, with poor axis naming choices, the product positioning map could be reduced to only one quadrant, significantly defeating the benefits of a true four quadrant map.

Chapter Summary

Successful strategy formulation does not guarantee successful strategy implementation at all. Although inextricably interdependent, strategy formulation and strategy implementation are characteristically different. It is widely agreed that *the real work begins after strategies are formulated*. Successful strategy implementation requires the support of, as well as discipline and hard work from, motivated managers and employees. It is sometimes frightening to think that a single individual can irreparably sabotage efforts for strategy implementation.

Formulating the effective strategies is not enough because managers and employees must be motivated to implement those strategies. Management issues considered central to strategy implementation include matching organizational structure with strategy, linking performance and pay to strategies, creating an organizational climate conducive to change, managing political relationships, creating a culture supportive of strategy, adapting production and operations processes, and managing human resources. Establishing annual objectives, devising policies, and allocating resources are common central activities for strategy implementation in all organizations. Depending on the size and type of the organization, other management issues could be equally important to successful strategy implementation. Similarly, depending on the size and type of firm, marketing issues, practices, and policies may vary, but effective segmentation, target marketing, and positioning is required for organizational success.

Key Terms and Concepts

annual objectives (p. 207)	perceptual map (p. 230)
conflict (p. 212)	phubbing (p. 210)
culture (p. 226)	policies (p. 209)
divisional (decentralized) structure (p. 214)	positioning (p. 228)
functional structure (p. 213)	reengineering (p. 222)
glass ceiling (p. 225)	resistance to change (p. 222)
horizontal consistency of objectives (p. 208)	resource allocation (p. 211)
market segmentation (p. 228)	restructuring (p. 222)
marketing mix variables (p. 228)	strategic business unit (SBU) structure (p. 216)
matrix structure (p. 216)	vertical consistency of objectives (p. 208)

Issues for Review and Discussion

7-1. What are the benefits and drawbacks of employees working from home? On balance, do you believe the benefits offset the drawbacks?

7-2. Where is the best location, place, or position on a perceptual map for introducing a new product line?

7-3. From a human resource management perspective, explain the difference between corporate wellness and corporate well-being.

7-4. As indicated in the chapter, workplace well-being is gaining steam. Explain the term and give three examples.

7-5. Array correctly in sequential order market positioning, segmenting, and targeting.

7-6. Identify and discuss three reasons why market segmentation is so important in strategy implementation.

7-7. What is the "marketing mix," and why is it so important in strategy implementation?

7-8. Advertisements are getting more and more lengthy, annoying, and intrusive on both television and social media platforms. On television, for example, sometimes eight ads will play on a commercial break. How lengthy of a commercial break will you tolerate before switching the channel to some other program, 1 minute, 3 minutes, 5 minutes, or 10 minutes? Despite the rising cost of placing an ad, could the annoyance factor offset the potential benefits of an ad? How can firms best counter this growing problem in strategy implementation?

7-9. What policy do you recommend for companies regarding employees spending time on their personal Facebook and other social media accounts during the workday? Could your policy be enforced? How? Why?

7-10. List five important benefits of a company or organization having a diverse workforce.

7-11. Explain how a large firm such as Proctor & Gamble could use a perceptual map as a tool for assessing the positioning of its brands from several product categories.

7-12. Discuss the "Do's and Don'ts of Poaching Workers" from rival firms.

7-13. Discuss recent trends and facts regarding corporate well-being programs in the United States.

7-14. Should companies monitor employees' social media? Why or why not? If yes, how?

7-15. List four reasons why companies are phasing out the COO position.

7-16. Discuss three ways for linking performance and pay to strategies.

7-17. List the different types of organizational structure. Diagram what you think is the most complex of these structures and label your chart clearly.

7-18. List the advantages and disadvantages of a functional versus a divisional organizational structure.

7-19. Why is perceptual mapping an important marketing tool in strategy implementation?

7-20. In the beverage soda industry, what two variables would be helpful to include in a perceptual map? Why?

7-21. List seven guidelines to follow in developing an organizational chart.

7-22. Women comprise less than 20 percent of boards of directors. Why is this a problem globally for many companies and countries?

7-23. Some head football coaches get paid millions, presumably because there is so much money involved in college football, the need to win is paramount. However, head coaches are often fired when a season goes badly, with huge payouts to the coach by contract. How could a head coach's compensation package be better structured to encourage winning and, at the same time, not be so potentially costly to a university?

7-24. *Businessweek* says firms should "base executive compensation on actual company performance, rather than on the company's stock price." For example, Target Corp. bases executive pay on same-store sales growth rather than stock price. Discuss.

7-25. Explain why firms need a policy against workplace phubbing.

7-26. Strategy formulation focuses mainly on effectiveness, whereas strategy implementation often focuses on efficiency. Which is more important, effectiveness or efficiency? Give an example of each concept.

7-27. In stating objectives, why should terms such as "increase," "minimize," "maximize," "as soon as possible," "adequate," and "decrease "be avoided?

7-28. Among the three marketing activities (product positioning, target marketing, market segmentation), which activity comes first, second, and third?

7-29. Explain why Alfred Chandler's strategy–structure relationship commonly exists among firms.

7-30. If you owned and opened three restaurants after you graduated, would you operate from a functional or divisional structure? Why?

7-31. Explain how to choose between a divisional-by-product and a divisional-by-region organizational structure.

7-32. Think of a company that would operate best, in your opinion, using a division-by-process organizational structure. Explain your reasoning.

7-33. Identify and discuss pros and cons of keeping the COO position in a corporate design.

7-34. In order of importance, in your opinion, list six advantages of a matrix organizational structure.

7-35. Why should division head persons have the title president rather than vice president?

7-36. In order of importance, in your opinion, list six techniques or activities widely used to alter an organization's culture.

7-37. Allocating resources can be a political and an ad hoc activity in firms that do not use strategic management. Why is this true? Does adopting strategic management ensure easy resource allocation? Why?

7-38. Describe the relationship between annual objectives and policies.

7-39. Identify and discuss three policies that apply to your present strategic management class.

7-40. Explain the following statement: Horizontal consistency of goals is as important as vertical consistency.

7-41. To conflict problems, how would you resolve a disagreement between a human resource manager and a sales manager over the firing of a particular salesperson? Why?

7-42. Describe the organizational culture of your college or university.

7-43. Explain why organizational structure is so important in strategy implementation.

7-44. In your opinion, how many separate divisions could an organization reasonably have without using an SBU organizational structure? Why?

7-45. Do you believe expenditures for childcare or fitness facilities are warranted from a cost-to-benefit perspective? Why or why not?

7-46. Explain why successful strategy implementation often hinges on whether the strategy formulation process empowers managers and employees.

7-47. Identify and discuss four primary reasons why annual objectives are so essential for effective strategy implementation.

7-48. Identify and discuss eight characteristics of objectives.

7-49. Why is it essential for organizations to segment markets and target particular groups of consumers?

7-50. Why did Facebook change its corporate name to Meta Platforms in 2021?

7-51. Develop a perceptual map for five colleges and universities in your state. Explain the potential value of your map for the president of your institution.

7-52. Under the marketing mix factor of price, what are three considerations or decisions many firms face?

7-53. Under the marketing mix factor of promotion, list three subsets or decision areas.

Writing Assignments

7-54. What are the two major disadvantages of an SBU organizational structure? What are the two major advantages? At what point in a firm's growth do you feel the advantages offset the disadvantages? Explain.

7-55. Would you recommend a divisional structure by geographic area, product, customer, or process for a medium-sized bank in your local area? Why?

Ken Wolter/Alamy Photo

ASSURANCE-OF-LEARNING EXERCISES

SET 1: STRATEGIC PLANNING FOR MCDONALD'S

EXERCISE 7A

Compare and Contrast McDonald's Marketing Expenses Versus Rival Firms

Purpose

Marketing is expensive. For example, a 30-second ad spot during the annual NFL Super Bowl costs about $6 million. Yet, firms must do marketing otherwise even the best products in the world can go unnoticed. But firms can go broke doing marketing. These are reasons why marketing is a key business function and an important issue in strategy implementation. This exercise can give you experience comparing and contrasting McDonald's marketing expenditures versus two major rivals: Restaurant Brands (owns Burger King) and Yum Brands (owns Taco Bell and Pizza Hut). Analysis in this regard can provide guidance on whether to increase or decrease McDonald's marketing expenditures.

Instructions

Step 1	Go online to the McDonald's (https://www.mcdonalds.com), Restaurant Brands International (https://www.rbi.com), and Yum Brands (https://www.yum.com) websites at the respective Investor Relations page and download the three *Form 10Ks* for the respective firms.
Step 2	Look in the Table of Contents of each Form 10K to find the pages that reveal the three firms' marketing or advertising expenditures.
Step 3	Prepare a comparative data table to consolidate this information.
Step 4	Prepare a report to suggest implications for McDonald's in terms of marketing or advertising expenditures going forward as needed to implement strategies.

EXERCISE 7B

Diagram an Existing and Proposed Organizational Chart for McDonald's

Purpose

Organizational structure matters because being well organized is vital for success in all aspects of business (and personal) endeavors. This exercise gives you experience developing an existing organizational chart for a company and, based on the chapter guidelines, proposing a new and improved design for a firm. Rarely do companies publicly provide an organizational chart, but nearly all publicly held firms provide a list of their top executives in the annual Form 10K, as does McDonald's. Based on that document, McDonald's top management team is as follows:

1. Chris Kempczinski, President and CEO
2. Lucy Brady, SVP, Chief Digital Customer Engagement Officer (female)
3. Heidi Capozzi, EVP, Global Chief People Officer (female)
4. Francesca DeBiase, EVP, Chief Supply Chain Officer (female)
5. Katie Beirne Fallon, EVP and Chief Global Impact Officer (female)
6. Piotr Jucha, SVP, Global Restaurant Development & Restaurant Solutions Group
7. Alistaair Macrow, SVP and Global Chief Marketing Officer
8. Mark Ostermann, VP, Strategic Alignment and Chief of Staff, Office of the CEO

9.   Kevin Ozan, EVP and Chief Financial Officer
10. Desiree Ralls-Morrison, General Counsel and Corporate Secretary (female)
11. Daniel Henry, EVP, Global CIO
12. Manu Steijaert, EVP and Chief Customer Officer
13. Joe Erlinger, President, McDonald's USA
14. Ian Borden, President, International

Instructions

As indicated in the Cohesion Case, some analysts suggest that seven SBUs would be better than two for McDonald's, as follows: (1) United States, (2) Europe, (3) Asia, (4) Australia and Pacific, (5) South America, Central America, and Mexico, (6) Canada, and (7) Middle East and Africa. Based on this suggestion, coupled with the guidelines and do's and don'ts provided in this chpater, develop a new and improved organizational chart for McDonald's.

SET 2: STRATEGIC PLANNING FOR MY UNIVERSITY

EXERCISE 7C
Develop a Perceptual Map for My University

Purpose

The purpose of this exercise is to give you practice developing product-positioning maps. Nonprofit organizations, such as universities, increasingly use perceptual maps to determine effective ways to implement strategies.

Instructions

Step 1   Join with two other people in class to form a group of three.
Step 2   Jointly prepare a product positioning (perceptual) map that includes your institution and four other colleges or universities in your state.
Step 3   Compare your map to other teams' maps. Discuss differences.
Step 4   How can your college or university best take advantage of the information revealed in the diagrams developed?

SET 3: STRATEGIC PLANNING TO ENHANCE MY EMPLOYABILITY

EXERCISE 7D
Marketing Yourself to Best Achieve Your Career Objectives

Purpose

As indicated in this chapter, establishing annual objectives and marketing products or services is vital for successful strategy implementation in companies, but these two activities are equally important for an individual in career planning. This exercise offers guidelines for you to better market yourself to meet your career objectives. In particular, 10 guidelines are provided for enhancing your resume.

1.   Meticulously make certain there are no typos, not even a comma missing.
2.   Include no personal pronouns, such as my or I, and no abbreviations, such as Rd. or St. anywhere in your resume.
3.   Looks matter, so use 12-point font throughout; manage white space margins well; double space after headings; use bullets to showcase points; never repeat wording in bullets.
4.   Include your highest GPA four ways: (1) in your major, (2) in the business school, (3) overall at the university, or (4) your last 60 hours, if that highest score is 2.75 or higher.
5.   Begin with a Job Objective saying something like "To gain an entry level position in accounting with a large manufacturing firm." Tailor this wording to the prospective firm of interest.
6.   List Education before Work Experience unless you have substantial work experience.
7.   Make sure you list your degree, your major, and when you expect your degree.
8.   Do not list courses completed but do list skills gained in courses, such as when using this textbook say: "Learned how to use a popular, Excel-based strategic planning template" or "Gained experience developing strategic plans for a wide variety of firms."

9. Make sure you use business terms in describing your work experience, saying something like "Learned the value of hard work, dependability, and reliability," or "Gained experience with customer service, pricing, and inventory control," focusing on skills learned rather than duties performed.

10. Unless constrained otherwise, include three reference persons with their titles and contact information; reveal their professional association with you; place horizontal or vertical depending on spacing; do not have only references on second page.

Instructions

Step 1	Use the guidelines listed to polish up your resume.
Step 2	Email your resume to your professor or your academic advisor or career counselor and ask for their feedback.

SET 4: INDIVIDUAL VERSUS GROUP STRATEGIC PLANNING

EXERCISE 7E

What Are the Most Important Benefits of Having a Diverse Workforce?

Purpose

Sometimes students, and even managers and executives, do not realize or appreciate why it is important to have a diverse workforce and management team. As discussed in this chapter, there are six (of many) major benefits of having a diverse workforce, as follows:

1. Women and people of color have different insights, opinions, and perspectives that should be considered.
2. A diverse workforce portrays a firm committed to nondiscrimination.
3. A workforce that mirrors a diverse customer base can help attract customers, build customer loyalty, and design or offer products and services that meet customer needs and wants.
4. A diverse workforce helps protect the firm against discrimination lawsuits.
5. Individuals in minority groups, including those based on ethnicity, race, sexual orientation, gender identity, and religious beliefs, represent a huge additional pool of qualified applicants.
6. A diverse workforce strengthens a firm's social responsibility and ethical position.

The purpose of this exercise is to examine more closely the benefits of having a diverse workforce and management team. In addition, the purpose of this exercise is to examine whether individual decision-making is better than group decision-making. Academic research suggests that groups make better decisions than individuals about 80 percent of the time.

Instructions

1. Individually think of four more benefits for having a diverse workforce.
2. Meet with two other persons in your class.
3. Compare your list of four benefits with other persons in your group.
4. What additional benefits did you become aware of in your discussion with the group?

MINI-CASE 7 ON ASTRAZENECA PLC

Grand Warszawski/Shutterstock

CAN YOU IMPROVE ASTRAZENECA'S ORGANIZATIONAL STRUCTURE?[12]

Headquartered in Cambridge, UK, AstraZeneca (AZ) is a huge pharmaceutical firm that focuses on four product areas: (1) Oncology, (2) Cardiovascular, (3) Renal and Metabolism, and (4) Respiratory, Immunology, and Other. AZ employs nearly 80,000 persons globally.

AZ's current executives with their respective titles are given below. Note the mix of by-product and by-region titles among executives. Note there is no COO but there are four females among the 12 top persons.

1. Pascal Soriot – CEO
2. Marc Dunoyer – CFO
3. Katarina Ageborg – Executive VP, Sustainability and Chief Compliance Officer
4. Jose Baselga – Executive VP, Oncology R&D
5. Pam Cheng – Executive VP Operations & Information Technology
6. Ruud Dobber – Executive VP, BioPharmaceuticals Business Unit
7. David Fredrickson – Executive VP, Oncology Business Unit
8. Menelas Pangalos – Executive VP, Biopharmaceuticals R&D
9. Jeff Pott – General Counsel and Chief Human Resources Officer
10. Iskra Reic – Executive VP, Europe and Canada
11. Leon Wang – Executive VP, International and China President
12. Fiona Cicconi – Executive VP Human Resources

Based on the titles of executives and your understanding of this chapter, can you diagram a probable organizational chart for AZ and a new and improved design? Consider that the authors suggest that AZ develop and use a product-based SBU type structure with four new group presidents. The authors suggest there should be four by-region presidents that report to each group president, as follows: (1) President of the United States, (2) President of Europe, (3) President of emerging markets, and (4) President of rest of world.

Questions

1. Diagram a probable existing organizational chart for AZ. Simply draw lines in your chart to connect numbers that stand for the respective executives in the list given.
2. Develop a new set of top executives for AZ. (Hint: About half of the titles in the provided list should be changed, and potentially 16 new executives added to your new list. Do not worry about persons' names; but do give the titles of all persons in your new list.)
3. Diagram your new and improved design for AZ given the authors input and the guidelines in this chapter. Simply draw lines in your chart to connect numbers that stand for the executives in your new list.
4. Can you identify five advantages of your new design versus your probable existing design?

[12]Based on Meredith E. David, Forest R. David, and Fred R. David, "Testing and Enhancing a Pivotal Organizational Structure Decision-Making Model," *International Journal of Strategic Decision Sciences* 12, no. 2 (2021): 1–19.

Web Resources

1. **Organizational Chart Images** This website provides more than 100 free organizational chart images used by various organizations.
   https://www.google.com/search?rls=en&sxsrf=AOaemvKg
   QkeuJO-S78_O572Q8XkhETjJ6w:1639684962817&sourc
   e=univ&tbm=isch&q=organizational+chart+template&
   client=safari&fir=cHktzn0Cr_GORM%252CGNHm_ci3Oi
   QNvM%252C_%253BQW38y8b6Rbk_5M%252Cv3maY
   APW5yzA4M%252C_%253BgFmQYFgCVEQdfM%252
   Cv3maYAPW5yzA4M%252C_%253BYe_GQYylz73ltM
   %252CYZeFfEbOLJyPuM%252C_%253BKF21gNQdzQe
   FxM%252CGNHm_ci3OiQNvM%252C_%253BT0pL_qF
   OfmLamM%252CXrgUVE7kzxLKGM%252C_
   %253B4zM1aPNpX0Z7dM%252CPxF5hIxFX22
   UvM%252C_%253BWsdpqroin2oXJM%252CG
   NHm_ci3OiQNvM%252C_%253BaoB4G3YNq_fO
   YM%252Cv3maYAPW5yzA4M%252C_%2

   53BW8Jmf0_H2Q6qdM%252CuM5MvELh-
   5VMBM%252C_&usg=AI4_-kSIyXoeB0oCPPf1AoY
   KsryNsR4N6Q&sa=X&ved=2ahUKEwjC3oG-jun0A
   hXukOAKHUFhBdUQjJkEegQIBRAC&biw=1308&
   bih=927&dpr=2

2. **Positioning Map Images** This website provides more than 100 free perceptual maps used by various organizations.
   https://www.shutterstock.com/search/
   product+positioning+map

3. Dr. Fred David gives a video overview of Chapter 7 in the prior edition, but much info is still applicable to the 18th edition.
   Part 1 of Chapter 7: https://www.youtube.com/
   watch?v=gf-1m3ifvdU
   Part 2 of Chapter 7: https://www.youtube.com/
   watch?v=_OlwLdjIPBo

Current Readings

Amis, John, Shelly Brickson, Patrick Haack, and Morela Hernandex, "Taking Inequality Seriously," *Academy of Management Review* 46, 3 (July 2021): 431–39.

Cascio, Wayne F., Arjun Chatrath, and Rohan A. Christie-David, "Antecedents and Consequences of Employee and Asset Restructuring," *Academy of Management Journal* 64, no. 2 (April 2021): 587–613.

Chen, Yan, Igor Pereira, and Pankaj C. Patel, "Decentralized Governance of Digital Platforms," *Journal of Management* 47, no. 5 (May 2021): 1305–37.

Choudhury, Raj, Cirrus Foroughi, and Barbara Larson, "Work-from-Anywhere: The Productivity Effects of Geographic Flexibility," *Strategic Management Journal* 42, no. 4 (April 2021): 655–83.

David, Forest R., Meredith David, and Fred David, "A New and Improved Organizational Structure Decision-Making Model," *SAM Advanced Management Journal* 85, no. 4 (2020): 1–9.

David, Meredith E., and Fred R. David, "Are Key Marketing Topics Adequately Covered in Strategic Management?" *Journal of Strategic Marketing* 24 (2016): 1–13.

David, Meredith E., Fred R. David, and Forest R. David, "Testing and Enhancing a Pivotal Organizational Structure Decision-Making Model," *International Journal of Strategic Decision Sciences* 12, no. 2 (2021): 1–19.

David, Fred R., Meredith E. David, and Forest R. David, "The Integration of Marketing Concepts in Strategic Management Courses: An Empirical Analysis," *SAM Advanced Management Journal* 82, no. 1 (2017): 26–35.

DesJardine, Mark R., and Wei Shi, "How Temporal Focus Shapes the Influence of Executive Compensation on Risk Taking," *Academy of Management Journal* 64, no. 1 (February 2021): 265–92.

Dlugos, Kathryn, and JR Keller, "Turned Down and Taking Off? Rejection and Turnover in Internal Talent Markets," *Academy of Management Journal* 64, no. 1 (February 2021): 63–85.

He, Wei, Shao-Long Li, Jie Feng, Guanglei Zhang, and Michael C. Sturman. "When Does Pay for Performance Motivate Employee Helping Behavior? The Contextual Influence of Performance Subjectivity," *Academy of Management Journal* 64, no. 1 (February 2021): 293–326.

Honglei Zhang, Zhenbo Zang, Hongjun Zhu, M. Irfan Uddin, and M. Asim Amin, "Big Data-Assisted Social Media Analytics for Business Model for Business Decision Making System Competitive Analysis," *Information Processing & Management* 59, no. 1 (2022): 1–14.

Kahn, William A., and Elizabeth D. Rouse, "Navigating Space for Personal Agency: Auxiliary Routines as Adaptations in Toxic Organizations," *Academy of Management Journal* 64, no. 5 (October 2021): 1419–44.

Li, Xu, and Freek Vermeulen, "High Risk, Low Return (and Vice Versa): The Effect of Product Innovation on Firm Performance in a Transition Economy," *Academy of Management Journal* 64, no. 5 (October 2021): 1383–418.

Methot, Jessica R., Emily H. Rosado-Solomon, Patrick E. Downes, and Allison S. Gabriel, "Office Chitchat as a Social Ritual: The Uplifting Yet Distracting Effects of Daily Small Talk at Work," *Academy of Management Journal* 64, no. 5 (October 2021): 1445–71.

Richard, Orlando C., Maria Del Carmen Triana, and Mingxiang Li, "The Effects of Racial Diversity Congruence between Upper Management and Lower Management on Firm Productivity," *Academy of Management Journal* 64, no. 5 (October 2021): 1355–82.

Yan, Shipeng, Juan Almandoz, and Fabrizio Ferraro, "The Impact of Logic (In) Compatibility: Green Investing, State Policy, and Corporate Environmental Performance," *Administrative Science Quarterly* 66, no. 4 (December 2021): 903–44.

Endnotes

1. Dale McConkey, "Planning in a Changing Environment," *Business Horizons* (September–October 1988): 66.

2. On page 206.

3. A. G. Bedeian and W. F. Glueck, *Management*, 3rd ed. (Chicago: Dryden, 1983), 212. Boris Yavitz and William Newman, *Strategy in Action: The Execution, Politics, and Payoff of Business Planning* (New York: The Free Press, 1982), 195.

4. Alexandra Samuel, "Come Back to the Office, Pretty Please," *Wall Street Journal*, November 1, 2021, p. R1 and R8.

5. On page 210.

6. Meredith E. David, Fred R. David, and Forest R. David, "Testing and Enhancing a Pivotal Organizational Structure Decision-Making Model," *International Journal of Strategic Decision Sciences* 12, no. 2 (2021): 1–19. Also, Forest R. David, Meredith David, and Fred David, "A New and Improved Organizational Structure Decision-Making Model," *SAM Advanced Management Journal* 85, no. 4 (2020): 1–9.

7. E. H. Schein, "Three Cultures of Management: The Key to Organizational Learning," *Sloan Management Review* 38, no. 1 (1996): 9–20. Joann Lublin, "Chairman-CEO Split Gains Allies," *Wall Street Journal*, March 30, 2009, p. B4.

8. Based on information at https://www.axios.com/chief-diversity-officer-hiring-frenzy-289877ce-ce65-4169-b414-79982e856281.html; https://www.forbes.com/sites/mariaminor/2021/05/03/heres-the-bottom-line-reason-why-companies-need-a-chief-diversity-officer/; https://www.diversityinc.com/hiring-of-chief-diversity-officers-triples-over-past-16-months-but-representation-in-the-workforce-is-still-lagging/; and https://www.govexec.com/management/2022/01/opm-issues-guidance-agency-hiring-chief-diversity-officers/360565/

9. Sheila Riley, "The Dos and Don'ts of Poaching Workers," *Investor's Business Daily*, March 31, 2014, p. A10.

10. https://www.aol.com/finance/older-workers-unretiring-leaving-workforce-210235261.html. Also, https://www.aol.com/finance/worker-shortage-employers-rolling-red-214448917.html

11. On page 229.

12. On page 239.

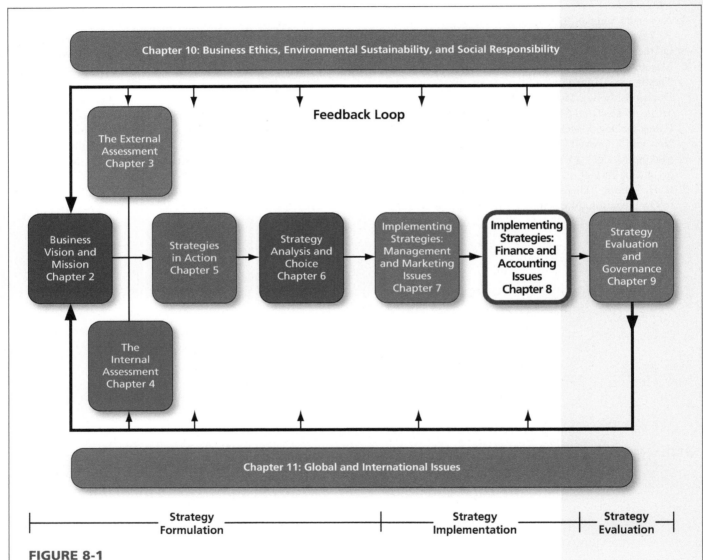

FIGURE 8-1

The Comprehensive, Integrative Strategic Management Model

Source: Fred R. David, "How Companies Define Their Mission," *Long Range Planning* 22, no. 1 (February 1989): 91. See also Anik Ratnaningsih, Nadjadji Anwar, Patdono Suwignjo, and Putu Artama Wiguna, "Balance Scorecard of David's Strategic Modeling at Industrial Business for National Construction Contractor of Indonesia," *Journal of Mathematics and Technology* no. 4 (October 2010): 20. Also, Meredith E. David, Fred R. David, and Forest R. David, "Closing the Gap Between Graduates' Skills and Employers' Requirements: A Focus on the Strategic Management Capstone Business Course," *Administrative Sciences* 11, no. 1 (2021): 10–26.

Implementing Strategies: Finance and Accounting Issues

LEARNING OBJECTIVES

After studying this chapter, you should be able to do the following:

8.1. Determine an appropriate capital structure for a firm by performing EPS/EBIT analysis to compare the relative attractiveness of debt versus stock as a source of capital to implement strategies.

8.2. Develop projected financial statements to reveal the impact of recommendations with associated costs.

8.3. Determine the cash value of the firm, or a division of the firm, using four corporate valuation methods.

8.4. Discuss financial ratios, initial public offerings (IPOs), special purpose acquisition companies (SPACs), and issuing bonds as strategic decisions.

ASSURANCE-OF-LEARNING EXERCISES

The following exercises are found at the end of this chapter:

SET 1:	Strategic Planning for McDonald's
EXERCISE 8A:	Perform an EPS/EBIT Analysis for McDonald's
EXERCISE 8B:	Prepare Projected Financial Statements for McDonald's
EXERCISE 8C:	Determine the Cash Value of McDonald's
EXERCISE 8D:	Prepare Projected Financial Ratios for McDonald's
SET 2:	Strategic Planning for My University
EXERCISE 8E:	Determine the Cash Value of My University
SET 3:	Strategic Planning to Enhance My Employability
EXERCISE 8F:	Developing Personal Financial Statements
EXERCISE 8G:	A Template Competency Test
SET 4:	Individual Versus Group Strategic Planning
EXERCISE 8H:	How Severe Are the Seven Limitations of EPS/EBIT Analysis?

S trategies can be implemented successfully only when an organization manages its finances effectively, as illustrated in Figure 8-1. This chapter examines important finance and accounting topics associated with implementing strategies. An actual working example for ABC Company is provided to illustrate and explain key finance and accounting topics. A proposed set of ABC Company recommendations with associated costs is presented, followed by an EPS/EBIT analysis to determine the most appropriate means for raising capital, projected financial statements to show the expected impact of those recommendations, and projected financial ratios. Corporate valuation is also discussed, because firms sometimes acquire other firms or may be the target of an acquisition.

Strategy implementation generally impacts the lives of everyone in an organization; thus, all employees need to buy in and support the firm's efforts to succeed in the face of numerous rival firms counterattacking. When employees understand the thinking that goes into strategy formulation and understand their roles, they will be more inclined to accept the work required for strategy implementation.

A football quarterback can call the best play possible in the huddle, but that does not translate into the play going for a touchdown. The team may even lose yardage, illustrating the importance of everyone working together to ensure the play is properly executed (implemented). Headquartered in New York City, the Teachers Insurance and Annuity Association of America (TIAA) is implementing strategies especially well, led by its finance/accounting Exemplary Strategist, CEO Thasunda Duckett.

A sampling of issues that may require finance and accounting policies, decisions, analyses, and actions in implementing strategies include the following:

EXEMPLARY **STRATEGIST** SHOWCASED

Thasunda Brown Duckett, CEO of TIAA[1]

In the 67-year history of the *Fortune* 500 list of companies, there was only one black female CEO of a *Fortune* 500 company, Ursula Burns of Xerox. That changed in 2021 when Rosalind Brewer became CEO of Walgreens Boots Alliance, and Thasunda Brown Duckett became CEO of Teachers Insurance and Annuity Association of America (TIAA), the No. 81 company on the *Fortune* 500 list.

This exemplary strategist capsule focuses on Thasunda Brown Duckett, who previously was the chief consumer banking top executive at JPMorgan Chase after being CEO of Chase Auto Finance. In 2021, Duckett ranked No. 10 on *Fortune's Most Powerful Women* list. This chapter is all about finance and accounting, and Duckett built her career climbing up the ladder among finance companies. After starting her career at Fannie Mae, Duckett enrolled in Baylor University's Executive MBA program where she received her MBA degree in 2001. Interestingly at TIAA, Duckett followed retiring TIAA CEO Roger Ferguson Jr., one of only five black CEOs in the *Fortune* 500.

In an interview, Duckett said (paraphrased): "I am extraordinarily grateful for the opportunity to lead a company that has helped millions of people retire with 'enough' to live in dignity. I recall many years ago when my father asked me to help him plan his retirement, and I had to tell him 'dad, your pension is not enough for you to pay your bills.'"

Duckett says she is excited about the opportunity to help TIAA chart its next 100 years. Duckett is a great role model for millions of women of all races, nationalities, and ethnicities.

Kathy Hutchins/Shutterstock

[1]Based on https://fortune.com/2021/02/25/thasunda-brown-duckett-tiaa-ceo-black-women-ceos-fortune-500/

1. To raise capital with short- or long-term debt, a bond issuance, divestiture, or a preferred or common stock issuance
2. To lease or buy fixed assets
3. To determine an appropriate dividend payout ratio
4. To use last-in-first-out (LIFO), first-in-first-out (FIFO), or a market-value accounting approach
5. To extend the time of accounts receivable or not
6. To establish a certain percentage discount on accounts within a specified period of time
7. To determine the amount of cash to be kept on hand
8. To purchase additional treasury stock or not
9. To determine whether to accept a merger offer
10. To determine how much to ask (or pay) for a division of the firm to be divested

Five especially important finance and accounting activities central to strategy implementation are listed and discussed sequentially in this chapter:

1. Determine capital structure: acquire needed capital to implement strategies; perform EPS/EBIT analysis.
2. Develop projected financial statements: show expected impact of recommendations.
3. Perform corporate valuation: in the event an offer is received or a rival firm is to be acquired.
4. Analyze financial ratios.
5. Manage initial public offerings (IPOs), cash levels, special purpose acquisiton companies (SPACs), and corporate bonds.[2]

Capital Structure

8.1. **Determine an appropriate capital structure for a firm by performing EPS/EBIT analysis to compare the relative attractiveness of debt versus stock as a source of capital to implement strategies.**

After developing a set of recommendations with associated costs (as explained in Chapter 6), a firm must determine the most profitable means for raising needed capital. Occasionally, cash on hand can finance small projects, but much of the cash on a firm's balance sheet may not be readily accessible without incurring taxes depending on what country the cash resides. Another way to raise the capital for new projects is to divest existing businesses. Annual net income is also available for implementing strategies, but usually all debt, all stock, or some combination of debt and stock is necessary to implement a set of recommendations. The proportion of debt-to-equity on a balance sheet is often referred to as a firm's **capital structure**; performing an EPS/EBIT analysis is a common way to determine the appropriate capital structure needed.

Before explaining EPS/EBIT analysis, let's be clear on some accounting terms as follows:

1. EPS is *earnings per share*, which is net income divided by number of shares outstanding.
2. EBIT is *earnings before interest and taxes*, or as it is sometimes called, *operating income*.
3. *Shares outstanding* is similar to *shares issued* except shares issued also includes shares of stock that a firm has repurchased (**treasury stock**). The denominator of EPS is shares outstanding; this number is reduced when a firm repurchases a portion of its own stock, thus increasing the overall EPS value. Most large firms have treasury stock, but some do not, such as Starbucks Corporation.
4. *Shares authorized* are the number of shares a firm has approval to issue in total, normally considerably more than the number of shares outstanding.
5. EBT is *earnings before tax*; EAT is *earnings after tax*. Another term for earnings is *profits* or *net income*.

Successful strategy implementation often requires additional capital beyond net income from operations or the sale of assets. Two primary sources of capital are debt and equity. Determining an appropriate mix of debt and equity in a firm's capital structure is an important strategy implementation decision. **EPS/EBIT analysis** is a widely used technique for determining whether debt, stock, or a combination of the two is the best alternative for raising capital to implement strategies. This technique involves an examination of the impact that debt versus stock financing has on EPS under various expectations for EBIT, given specific recommendations (strategies to be implemented).

Theoretically, an enterprise should carry enough debt in its capital structure to boost its return on investment in projects earning more than the cost of the debt. In low-earning periods, excessive debt in the capital structure of an organization can endanger stockholders' returns and jeopardize company survival. Fixed debt obligations must be met, regardless of circumstances, to avoid default. Avoiding debt obligations, however, does not automatically make financing through equity a more attractive means for raising capital. When the cost of capital (interest rate) is low, debt may be more attractive than stock to obtain capital, but the analysis still must be performed because high stock prices usually accompany low interest rates, making stock issuances attractive for obtaining capital. Some special concerns with stock issuances include dilution of ownership, increased takeover risk, effect on stock price, the need to pay dividends on the additional shares if the firm pays dividends, and lower EPS.

EPS is perhaps the most common measure of success of a company, so it is widely used in making the capital acquisition decision. EPS reflects the common "maximizing shareholders' wealth" overarching corporate objective, in contrast to maximizing profits in the short run. If profit maximization is the primary objective of the firm, then in performing an EPS/EBIT analysis, you may focus more on the EAT rather than EPS.

EPS/EBIT Analysis: Steps to Complete

There are four steps to complete in performing EPS/EBIT analysis:

Step 1: Gather the Input Data Needed; Determine the Following Numbers:

  a. The dollar amount of capital the firm needs to raise; i.e., the total associated costs of recommendations.
  b. Number of shares outstanding; usually found on a firm's balance sheet or by dividing market capitalization by the current stock price.
  c. Interest rate (%) at which funds can be borrowed (use 3 to 5 percent).
  d. Tax rate (%) the firm is paying (calculated from a firm's income statement; i.e., taxes or provision for taxes divided by EBT).
  e. The estimated dollar amount of EBIT range; use the most recent year EBIT number plus or minus the impact of recommendations to determine a range; select a low, medium, and high dollar amount of EBIT to simulate pessimistic, realistic, and optimistic values for the year ahead.

Step 2: Set Up a Computation Table as Follows

	All-Stock Financing			All-Debt Financing			50-50 Stock-Debt Financing		
	Pessimistic	Realistic	Optimistic	Pessimistic	Realistic	Optimistic	Pessimistic	Realistic	Optimistic
$ EBIT									
$ Interest									
$ EBT									
$ Taxes									
$ EAT									
# Shares Issued									
$ EPS									

Step 3: Insert Numbers in the Table Following These Row-by-Row Steps/Guidelines

  a. For the $ EBIT row, select a pessimistic (low), realistic (medium), and optimistic (high) $ amount for EBIT based on the previous year EBIT plus what you expect your recommendations to yield; use large ranges to get variation; place these three $ EBIT numbers across the EBIT row under each capital structure scenario; thus, place the three sets of three estimated EBIT values across the first row into each estimated economic scenario (pessimistic, realistic, and optimistic).

b. For the $ Interest row, in the three All-Stock columns, place zeros because no new interest will be paid if the firm elects to use the All-Stock approach. In the interest row for the All-Debt columns, multiply the $ capital needed times the interest rate and place the resultant amount in the three All-Debt columns. Similarly, in the 50-50 Combo columns, multiply the $ capital needed (50% of total) times the interest rate and place the resultant amount in the 50-50 Combo columns. (Note: Change the percentage if using a different combination such as 70-30 stock-debt.)

c. For the $ EBT row, subtract row 2 from row 1, in each respective column.

d. For the $ Taxes row, multiply row 3 by the tax percentage, in each respective column.

e. For the $ EAT row, subtract row 4 from row 3, in each respective column.

f. For the # Shares Issued row, in the three All-Stock columns, divide the $ capital needed by the stock price and add that number to the existing number of shares outstanding and place the resultant number in the All-Stock columns. In the three All-Debt columns, simply enter the existing number of shares outstanding because no new shares are being added. In the three 50-50 Combo columns, multiply the $ capital needed by 50 percent; then divide this number by the stock price and add the resultant number to the existing number of shares outstanding to determine the numbers for the 50-50 Combo columns. (Note: Change the percentage if using a different mix of stock versus debt.)

g. For the $ EPS row, divide row 5 by row 6, in each respective column. Take notice of which EPS values are highest along the row for each capital structure scenario. The highest EPS values reveal the "best" financing decision. If the EPS values are the same or nearly the same across the bottom row for the same level of EBIT, then the amount of funds raised may be too low to reveal significant differences based on the current interest rates or stock price, or the EBIT range may be too narrow. If you are recommending strategies that require high capital requirements, there should be differences in EPS values between All-Debt and All-Stock for the same level of EBIT.

Step 4:   Graph Your EPS/EBIT Analysis
Simply place the top row ($ EBIT) on the *x*-axis and place the bottom row ($ EPS) on the *y*-axis. Then plot three resultant lines for All-Stock, All-Debt, and 50-50 Stock-Debt Combo, respectively. The highest line in the graph reveals the highest EPS that maximizes shareholder value; select this highest EPS financing option unless you have a compelling reason(s) to overturn this decision as per limitations of this analysis discussed in Table 8-3.

EPS/EBIT Analysis: An Example

Perhaps the best way to explain EPS/EBIT analysis is by working through an example for the ABC Company, examining the All-Stock, All-Debt, and 60-40 Stock-Debt Combo financing alternatives. Following Steps 1 to 3, the needed input data and computations are given in Table 8-1 and Table 8-2, respectively.

TABLE 8-1 ABC Company Input Data Needed for EPS/EBIT Analysis

ABC Company Input Data	The Number
$ Amount of Capital Needed	$5,000 million
EBIT Range	$10,000 to $18,000 million
Interest Rate	5%
Tax Rate	23%
Stock Price	$94.17
# Shares Outstanding	2,550 million

TABLE 8-2 ABC Company Computations in Performing EPS/EBIT Analysis (in Millions, Except the EPS Row)

	Common Stock Financing			Debt Financing			Stock 60%	Debt	40%
	Pessimistic	Realistic	Optimistic	Pessimistic	Realistic	Optimistic	Pessimistic	Realistic	Optimistic
EBIT	$10,000	$15,000	$18,000	$10,000	$15,000	$18,000	$10,000	$15,000	$18,000
Interest	0	0	0	250	250	250	100	100	100
EBT	10,000	15,000	18,000	9,750	14,750	17,750	9,900	14,900	17,900
Taxes	2,300	3,450	4,140	2,243	3,393	4,083	2,277	3,427	4,117
EAT	7,700	11,550	13,860	7,508	11,358	13,668	7,623	11,473	13,783
#Shares	2,603	2,603	2,603	2,550	2,550	2,550	2,582	2,582	2,582
EPS	$2.96	$4.44	$5.32	$2.94	$4.45	$5.36	$2.95	$4.44	$5.34

Note when EBIT is forecasted as pessimistic, then equity financing is more attractive than debt financing, as indicated by the EPS value of $2.96 compared to the debt financing EPS value of $2.94. However, as the economy or projected EBIT improves, All-Debt financing will maximize ABC Company's EPS, as revealed by a $5.36 EPS for All-Debt versus a $5.32 EPS for All-Stock financing. Our conclusion is that ABC Company should use stock to raise capital under the pessimistic forecast, but if the economy is forecasted to be realistic or optimistic, then debt is the most attractive financing alternative. An important note to consider is some financial experts would suggest there may be increased financial risk with selecting the highest EPS value for the same forecasted economic condition.

Following Step 4, a graph of the ABC Company EPS/EBIT analysis is provided in Figure 8-2. The intersection points near the $15,000 level of EBIT are break-even points where one method of financing becomes more attractive than another. Note at the $10,000 level of EBIT, All-Stock yields the highest EPS, and at the $18,000 level, All-Debt financing yields the highest EPS. So, the analyst is faced with a decision regarding what to recommend based on their confidence levels for the EBIT ranges and the limitations discussed in Table 8-3. Note in Table 3 that the limitations of EPS/EBIT analysis can be grouped into seven categories beginning with Flexibility.

Be mindful that large companies may have millions of shares outstanding, so even small differences in EPS across different financing options, such as in this example, can equate to large sums of money gained by using that highest EPS value alternative. For example, ABC Company has 2,550 million shares outstanding, so the $0.04 difference you see in EPS at

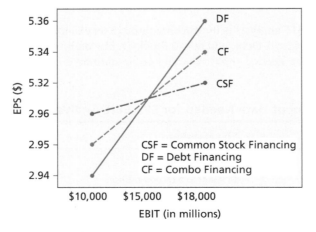

FIGURE 8-2

ABC Company's EPS/EBIT Chart

TABLE 8-3 Limitations/Considerations Associated with EPS/EBIT Analysis

1. *Flexibility.* As a firm's capital structure changes, so does its flexibility for considering future capital needs. Using all debt or all stock to raise capital today may impose fixed obligations, restrictive covenants, or other constraints tomorrow that could reduce or enhance a firm's ability to raise additional capital.

2. *Dilution of Ownership.* When additional stock is issued to finance strategy implementation, ownership and control of the enterprise are diluted. This can be a serious concern in today's business environment of hostile takeovers, mergers, and acquisitions. If dilution of ownership is a concern, then debt could be more attractive than stock, even if EPS values are higher with stock.

3. *Timing.* If interest rates are expected to rise, then debt may be more attractive than stock (assuming a fixed rate is locked in), even if EPS values are higher with stock. In times of high stock prices, stock may be more attractive than debt.

4. *Leveraged Situation.* If the firm is currently too highly leveraged versus industry average ratios, then financing through stock may be more attractive than debt, even if EPS values are higher for debt.

5. *Continuity.* The analysis assumes stock price, tax rate, and interest rates stay constant across pessimistic, realistic, and optimistic conditions.

6. *EBIT Ranges.* The EBIT values are estimated based on the prior year, plus the impact of strategies to be implemented.

7. *Dividends.* If EPS values are highest for all-stock, and if the firm pays dividends, then more funds will leave the firm as per dividends if all-stock financing is selected.

---

the \$18,000 level translates into $2,550 \times 0.04 = \$102$ million in potential monies that ABC Company would have if the firm uses debt financing over common stock financing at the \$18,000 level of EBIT.

Any number of combination stock/debt (S/D) scenarios, such as 70/30 S/D or 30/70 S/D, may be examined in an EPS/EBIT analysis to determine expected EPS values. The free Excel template at www.strategyclub.com enables easy calculation of various financing options.

EPS/EBIT Analysis: Limitations

All analytical tools have limitations, including EPS/EBIT analysis. But unless you have a compelling reason to overturn the highest last row EPS values dictating the best financing option, then indeed those highest values along the bottom row should dictate the financing decision. EPS is an excellent measure of organizational performance and, thus, is an excellent variable to examine in deciding which financing option to use. EPS/EBIT analysis itself does not alert the analyst of potential limitations discussed in Table 8-3.

Projected Financial Statements

8.2. Develop projected financial statements to reveal the impact of recommendations with associated costs.

Projected financial statements are income statements and balance sheets developed for future years to forecast the potential impacts of various recommendations proposed for implementation. Recall from Chapter 6 that all recommendations carry with them an estimated cost value. Most financial institutions require 3 years of projected financial statements whenever a business seeks capital. On financial statements, different companies use different terms for various items. For example, *revenues* or *sales* can refer to the same item; *net income, earnings*, or *profits* can refer to the same item; *capital surplus* or *paid-in-capital* can refer to the same item. A term sometimes used for *retained earnings* is *accumulated equity* or (if losses) *accumulated deficit.*

The Free Excel Strategic Planning Template at www.strategyclub.com

Many practitioners and students of strategic planning use the template to develop existing and projected financial statements to reveal the expected impact of proposed recommendations for the firm. Do not expect the template to do the thinking for you in terms of projecting each row on both the income statements and balance sheets. The template does the calculating for you, but you must supply the thinking regarding the amount to alter each row given the expected impact of your recommendations. The template can be used for any accounting system (GAAP or IFRS). For anyone using the template to develop actual and projected financial statements, Table 8-4 provides author comments.

TABLE 8-4 Template Considerations in Developing Financial Statements

Almost every row of the template's projected financial statements is to be forecasted by the user to reveal the expected impact of their recommendations for the firm. However, a few rows in the template's projected statements are automatically calculated (rather than forecasted) as discussed here.

1. Make Conversions. Convert (enter) your firm's most recent *Form 10K* actual income statements and balance sheets into the template-formatted statements on Part II of the Template. Doing this will greatly facilitate development of projected financial statements and ratios. In making this conversion, use the *nonrecurring events* row to house extraneous items on the income statements; on the balance sheets, use the *other current or other long-term assets*, the *other current or other long-term liabilities*, or the *paid in capital & other* rows under the equity section. Work to ensure on the existing income statements that revenues, EBIT, interest expense, EBT, tax, and income match your existing statements. The other line items you can adjust slightly to ensure the above items match perfectly. If having an issue with EBIT perfectly matching the *Form 10K*, simply subtract EBIT from Gross Profit on the *Form 10K* and enter this number for Operating Expenses. This procedure will ensure your template EBIT matches the EBIT from your firm's *Form 10K* because sometimes the Operating Expenses line is difficult to transfer over perfectly; it is okay if your template Operating Expenses do not perfectly match the *Form 10K* as long as EBIT does. Net income is automatically calculated from your other income statement forecasts, so the net income row is not forecasted.

2. Projected Income Statements. The template on Part II offers excellent suggestions for entering in your data. Be sure to enter in revenue numbers (and all line items for that fact) that reflect the new changes you are recommending. The template to the left provides the percentage increase or decrease for all line items from the 2 most recent years; however, do not use this number blindly. For example, if this number reveals that revenues increased 10 percent last year, but you are recommending divesting half of the company, then you likely need to reduce revenues by a significant margin rather than increase them by 10 percent simply because that is what happened last year! Use the nonrecurring events row to adjust for divesting a division or any other extraneous events in order for your firm's *Form 10K* revenues.

3. Projected Retained Earnings (RE) Row. The RE row on the template's projected balance sheets is automatically calculated because the RE row is determined by carrying over the net income less dividends annually from the income statement to the RE row near the bottom of the balance sheet.

4. Projected Balance Sheets. Work row-by-row from the bottom to the top making changes as needed to reflect the impact of your recommendations on each row. Leave forecasted items and rows the same as the prior year if you expect no change in that row given your recommendations. The template has a note to the right of each row to aid in how to enter the numbers. Work from the bottom of the projected balance sheet to the top on Part II.

5. Projected Cash. The template uses the balance sheet cash row as a plug figure to make the projected balance sheet balance, so this row is automatically calculated. Often the cash figure will be abnormally high after forecasting all other rows; in this situation make appropriate adjustments in the assets, liability or equity sections, usually using the long-term-debt or paid-in-capital rows to offset the amount you increase or decrease the cash row to keep liquidity in line with industry averages. Making adjustments, even to other items on the balance sheet, is good practice and routinely done by all accountants, so do not feel you are cheating the system until you get the numbers reasonable. Projected statements are a good-faith estimate, and a high cash figure only indicates other estimates need to be reconsidered. Also, check for typos or miscalculations on both the projected income statement and balance sheet. For example, it is possible you are over- or underestimating the (1) revenue impacts of your recommendations or (2) the amount of capital needed to implement your recommendations. Also, experiment with adjusting the historical percentages on both asset and liability items such as accounts payable or accounts receivable; it is possible the historical number needs to be increased on asset line items or decreased on liability items if the firm is operating more efficiently, and the result will bring cash down. Also, double-check plant, property, and equipment because a high cash figure may indicate you are underestimating how much these assets will cost. Once you make one change, revaluate the cash figure on the new projected balance sheet and continue until you find the cash number reasonable. Accountants do this all the time, striving for excellent, reasonable, and truthful projected statements. Ethics Capsule 8 and Global Capsule 8 address the truthfulness or reasonableness aspect of projected financial statements. Note that New Zealand and the Nordic countries lead the world in being best for having the lowest overall corruption.

    Another great place to check if your estimates are feasible or not is by studying the projected financial ratios that are automatically calculated compared to historical averages considering your recommendations. This technique is especially useful because the ratios consisting of numerator and denominator can give you a general idea what line items to examine first for adjustments. But remember the projected income statement and projected balance sheet are linked through retained earnings, so any change in the income statement is likely to filter its way all the way through the income statement into the balance sheet's retained earnings, all the way up to the cash row in the balance sheet. This could mean your high cash or any other issues are traced back to over estimating projected revenues!

6. Financial Ratios. The template will automatically calculate actual and forecasted financial ratios once both the actual and forecasted income statement and balance sheet data are entered. When compared to prior years and industry averages, financial ratios provide valuable insights for implementing strategies. (Financial ratios were discussed in Chapter 4.)

ETHICS CAPSULE 8

Projected Financial Statement Manipulation[3]

NicoElNino/Shutterstock

Investors, shareholders, and others need to know that top executives can legally manipulate financial statements to inflate or deflate expected results, and they often do. Firms may inflate or present an overly rosy picture of projected financial statements to garner support from a wide range of constituencies for a variety of reasons. But you may wonder why would executives present a deflated or unfavorable picture of the future? Reasons to deflate include (1) to discourage potential acquirers or (2) to load bad financial information into a particular accounting period so that periods beyond will look better. In the famous book *Financial Shenanigans* (2002) by

Dr. Howard Schilit, five ways are discussed in which top executives manipulate financial statements, as follows:

1. Record revenue prematurely.
2. Record fictitious revenue.
3. Increase net income with one-time gains.
4. Shift current expenses to an earlier or later period.
5. Failure to record certain liabilities.

The Securities and Exchange Commission (SEC) has taken steps to curtail projected financial statement manipulation, but this remains an ethical issue in Corporate America (and globally).

[3]Based on information at https://www.investopedia.com/articles/fundamental-analysis/financial-statement-manipulation.asp, http://www.understand-accounting.net/TheReliabilityandAccuracyoffinancialstatements.html, and https://us.aicpa.org/content/dam/aicpa/research/standards/auditattest/downloadabledocuments/at-00301.pdf

GLOBAL CAPSULE 8

What Are the Top 10 Most (and Least) Corrupt Countries in the World in 2021?[4]

Corruptness can lead to misleading projected financial statements both in the corporate and governmental world. The organization Transparency.org has created the Corruption Perceptions Index that ranks countries based upon their perceived level of corruption, a term used to describe dishonest or fraudulent behavior by someone in power who abuses their power, takes bribes, and/or commits fraud to increase their own wealth and/or power oftentimes at the expense of people they are meant to serve. The Corruption Perceptions Index (CPI), published annually by Transparency International, rates 180 countries on a scale of 0 (highly corrupt) to 100 (very clean) based upon their perceived levels of public sector corruption. The average score in 2021 was 43. The top ten least (and most) corrupt countries appear in this capsule.

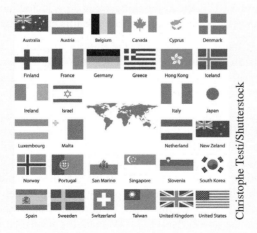

Christophe Testi/Shutterstock

Most Corrupt

Ranking	Country	2021 CPI	2022 Population
1	South Sudan	11	11,618,511
2	Syria	13	19,364,809
3	Somalia	13	16,841,795
4	Venezuela	14	29,266,991
5	Afghanistan	16	40,754,388
6	Yemen	16	31,154,867
7	North Korea	16	25,990,679
8	Libya	17	7,040,745
9	Equatorial Guinea	17	1,496,662
10	Democratic Republic of Congo	19	95,240,792

Least Corrupt

Ranking	Country	2021 CPI	2022 Population
1	New Zealand	88	4,898,203
2	Finland	88	5,554,960
3	Denmark	88	5,834,950
4	Norway	85	5,511,370
5	Singapore	85	5,943,546
6	Sweden	85	10,218,971
7	Switzerland	84	8,773,637
8	Netherlands	82	17,211,447
9	Luxembourg	81	642,371
10	Germany	80	83,883,596

[4]Based on https://worldpopulationreview.com/country-rankings/most-corrupt-countries

Steps to Develop Projected Financial Statements

Whether or not you use the free Excel strategic-planning template, projected financial statement analysis can be explained in seven steps. The template may do some of the calculating steps for you automatically.

Step 1. Prepare the projected income statement before the balance sheet. Start by forecasting sales (revenues) as accurately as possible to reveal the expected impact of recommendations being implemented. In forecasting revenues, do not blindly push historical revenue growth percentages into the future without considering ventures the firm undertook in prior years to achieve those results. What a firm did previously to achieve those past sales increases may or may not be appropriate for the future, depending on whether your recommendations take similar or analogous actions (e.g., such as opening a similar number of stores). If dealing with a manufacturing firm, also be mindful that if the firm is operating at 100 percent capacity running three 8-hour shifts per day, then probably new manufacturing facilities (land, plant, and equipment) will be needed to increase sales further.

Step 2. Use the percentage-of-sales method to project cost of goods sold (COGS) and the Operating Expenses in the income statement. For example, if COGS is 50 percent of sales in the prior year, then use a similar percentage to calculate COGS in the future year—unless there is a reason to use a different percentage. Items such as interest, dividends, and taxes must be treated independently and cannot be forecasted using the percentage-of-sales method.

Step 3. Calculate the projected net income (NI).

Step 4. Subtract from the NI any dividends to be paid. The remaining NI is retained earnings (RE). Bring the RE amount over to the balance sheet by adding it to the prior year's RE amount on the balance sheet. In other words, every year, a firm adds its RE (which is NI – Dividends for that particular year) to its historical RE total on the balance sheet. Therefore, the RE amount on the balance sheet is a cumulative number rather than money available for strategy implementation. Note that RE is the first projected balance sheet item to be entered. As a result of this accounting procedure in developing projected financial statements, the RE amount on the balance sheet is usually a large number; it is a cumulative number of dollars reinvested into the company over many years; it is *not* cash in the bank; it can be a low or even negative number if the firm has been incurring losses or paying dividends that exceed NI. In fact, the most common ways for RE to decrease from one year to the next on the balance sheet is (1) if the firm incurred an earnings loss that year or (2) the firm had positive NI for the year but paid out dividends in excess of the net income. Be mindful that RE is the key link between a projected income statement and projected balance sheet, so be careful to make this calculation correctly.

Step 5. Project the balance sheet items working from the bottom to the top. Begin with the RE row; then forecast the remaining equity items, followed by forecasting the long-term liabilities, current liabilities, long-term assets, and current assets (in that order), working from the bottom to the top.

Step 6. Use cash as the plug figure—that is, project every line item on the projected balance sheet except cash (and RE); use the cash account to make the assets equal to the sum of the liabilities and shareholders' equity. Then make appropriate adjustments. For example, if the cash needed to balance the statements is too small (or too large), consider making appropriate changes to borrow more (or less) money than planned and revaluate line items such as inventory, accounts receivable, plant property and equipment or other asset lines. For example, if cash is too high, (1) consider paying off some long-term debt; (2) reevaluate the projected percentage increase of various liabilities because it is possible the firm may be operating more efficiently or have greater economies of scale, or (3) increase your treasury stock. Rarely is the cash account number perfect on the first pass-through, so adjustments are needed and made.

Step 7. List commentary or notes below the projected statements to clarify for the reader why significant changes were made on particular items or rows in one year versus the next. Notes are essential for a reader to understand the changes made on certain rows. The template does not prepare notes because notes reflect your thinking regarding the impact of your recommendations and your associated costs.

Nonprofit Organizations

The steps outlined for preparing projected financial statements apply equally to nonprofit organizations; prepare the projected income statements first then the projected balance sheets. Because nonprofits never pay dividends, simply add the nonprofit's net income (usually called Net Assets) to their balance sheet retained earnings row (usually called Net Assets as shown in the American Red Cross' financial statements given at https://www.redcross.org/content/dam/redcross/about-us/publications/2022-publications/FY21-RedCross-Audited-Financial-Statement.pdf). If the cash account is too high or too low, just make adjustments as needed to the nonprofit's assets or liabilities sections of the balance sheets because there is no equity section (except for Net Assets). So, the projected financial statement steps/process (and template steps/process) is equally applicable to both for-profit firms and nonprofit organizations. Of course, taxes paid by nonprofits is zero, and there is zero paid-in-capital, treasury stock, and common stock.

ABC Company's Actual Financial Statements

To further explain projected financial statement analysis, let's work through an actual example for ABC Company. ABC's actual income statements and balance sheets for Year 1 and Year 2 are given in Table 8-5 and Table 8-6, respectively. Notice that ABC's actual *Form 10K* statements are converted or condensed into the "template format." (Note: About 95 percent of all strategic-management students using this textbook, as well as thousands of corporate practitioners, use this template for doing strategic planning and developing projected financial statements; if you use the template put on your resume that you "gained experience using strategic-planning software.")

Notice in Table 8-5 and Table 8-6 that ABC's actual *Form 10K* revenues declined in Year 2 and their current ratio (current assets divided by current liabilities) was less than 1.0.

Note on ABC's actual income statements in Table 8-5 the large increase in nonrecurring events in Year 2; this change was because of the company divesting various businesses to streamline the firm and better align its activities with its mission. Divestitures explain much of the large increase in ABC's net income for Year 2 and the large increase in retained earnings on the balance sheet. Without further similar divestitures moving forward, net income will likely decline the following year, whereas revenues may actually increase. This example illustrates the importance of studying the Annual Report to determine what likely caused the changes in the current financial statements; then carefully consider how your recommendations will impact the projected statements. Simply pushing forward historical numbers on every line item is a common mistake in projected financial statement development.

TABLE 8-5 ABC's Actual Income Statements for Year 1 and Year 2 (in Millions)

Income Statement	Year 1	Year 2		Percentage Change
Revenues	$65,299	$65,058	⇩	−0.37%
Cost of Goods Sold	32,909	32,535	⇩	−1.14%
Gross Profit	32,390	32,523	⇧	0.41%
Operating Expenses	18,442	18,801	⇧	1.95%
EBIT	13,948	13,722	⇩	−1.62%
Interest Expense	579	465	⇩	−19.69%
EBT	13,369	13,257	⇩	−0.84%
Tax	3,342	3,063	⇩	−8.35%
Non-Recurring Events	481	5,132	⇧	966.94%
Net Income	10,508	15,326	⇧	45.85%

TABLE 8-6 ABC's Actual Balance Sheets for Year 1 and Year 2 (in Millions)

Balance Sheet	Year 1	Year 2		Percentage Change
Assets				
Cash and Equivalents	$7,102	$5,569	⇩	−22%
Accounts Receivable	5,880	4,594	⇩	−22%
Inventory	4,716	4,624	⇩	−2%
Other Current Assets	16,084	11,707	⇩	−27%
Total Current Assets	33,782	26,494	⇩	−22%
Property Plant & Equipment	19,385	19,893	⇧	3%
Goodwill	44,350	44,699	⇧	1%
Intangibles	24,527	24,187	⇩	−1%
Other Long-Term Assets	5,092	5,133	⇧	1%
Total Assets	**127,136**	**120,406**	⇩	**−5%**
Liabilities				
Accounts Payable	16,774	16,656	⇩	−1%
Other Current Liabilities	13,996	13,554	⇩	−3%
Total Current Liabilities	30,770	30,210	⇩	−2%
Long-Term Debt	18,945	18,038	⇩	−5%
Other Long-Term Liabilities	19,438	16,380	⇩	−16%
Total Liabilities	69,153	64,628	⇩	−7%
Equity				
Common Stock	4,009	4,009	⇨	0%
Retained Earnings	87,953	96,124	⇧	9%
Treasury Stock	(82,176)	(93,715)	⇧	14%
Paid in Capital & Other	48,197	49,360	⇧	2%
Total Equity	57,983	55,778	⇩	−4%
Total Liabilities and Equity	**$127,136**	**$120,406**	⇩	**−5%**

Note on ABC's actual balance sheets in Table 8-6 the $11.5 billion increase in treasury stock from Year 1 to Year 2, indicating substantial stock buybacks by ABC. Lately, many companies have been aggressively buying their own stock, reflecting optimism about their future. However, some analysts argue that stock buybacks eat cash that a firm could better use to grow the firm. Stock buybacks do however reduce a firm's number of shares outstanding, thus increasing EPS; so firms reap this "intangible benefit" with stock buybacks. Sometimes firms will even increase their Treasury Stock near the end of the quarter, or near the end of the year, to "artificially" inflate their EPS to meet/beat EPS projections to perhaps avoid a stock price decline.

Note on ABC's actual balance sheets in Table 8-6 that about 50 percent of total assets are in the form of **goodwill** and intangibles; some financial experts suggest these items to be simply "smoke" because they are not physical assets that can easily be transferred into cash. ABC's history of acquiring firms for over book value (market capitalization value) is the reason for the firm's large goodwill values.

ABC's Projected Financial Statements

Let's propose that the ABC Company goes forward with the following four recommendations with associated costs and comments; then we follow the impact of the costs on the firm's projected financial statements:

1. Five new plants will be built in each of the 3 forecasted years (Year 3, Year 4, and Year 5) at $250 million each ($1,250 million per year attributed to plant, property, and

equipment) with adjustments to long-term debt and paid in capital, as described in number 4 below.

2. Raise an additional $1,250 million to finance R&D and new advertising. The total amount of capital being raised is $5 billion.
3. Increase dividends by 1 percent in each of the 3 forecasted years (these funds are derived from net income so no need to raise additional capital for them).
4. Forty percent of the capital needed will be financed through debt ($2,000 million) in projected Year 3 and 60 percent ($3,000 million) through equity in projected Year 4. Note $2,000 + $3,000 = $5,000$, which is the total cost of recommendations not considering dividends.

Table 8-7 and Table 8-8 reveal ABC's projected income statements and balance sheets, respectively, given the four recommendations with associated costs listed previously and the annual retained earnings carried forward to the projected balance sheet. Note, on the projected income statement in Table 8-7 both projected revenues and net income are increasing, but projected net income is down significantly from the prior year, largely because (as mentioned) there are no major divestitures (recorded as nonrecurring events on the income statement) in any projected years.

TABLE 8-7 ABC's Projected Income Statements for Year 3, Year 4, and Year 5 (in Millions)

Projected Income Statement	Year 3	Year 4	Year 5
Revenues	$66,359	$68,350	$72,451
Cost of Goods Sold	33,180	34,175	36,225
Gross Profit	33,180	34,175	36,225
Operating Expenses	20,571	21,188	22,460
EBIT	12,608	12,986	13,766
Interest Expense	565	562	559
EBT	12,043	12,424	13,207
Tax	2,770	2,858	3,302
Non-Recurring Events	0	0	0
Net Income	$9,273	$9,567	$9,905

TABLE 8-8 ABC's Projected Balanced Sheets for Year 3, Year 4, and Year 5 (in Millions)

Projected Balance Sheet	Year 3	Year 4	Year 5
Assets			
Cash and Equivalents	$3,015	$7,409	$9,552
Accounts Receivable	4,645	4,784	5,072
Inventory	4,645	4,784	5,072
Other Current Assets	11,945	12,303	13,041
Total Current Assets	24,250	29,281	32,736
Property Plant & Equipment	21,143	22,393	23,643
Goodwill	44,699	44,699	44,699
Intangibles	24,187	24,187	24,187
Other Long-Term Assets	5,309	5,468	5,796
Total Assets	**119,588**	**126,028**	**131,061**
Liabilities			
Accounts Payable	15,926	16,404	17,388

(*Continued*)

TABLE 8-8 (*Continued*)

Projected Balance Sheet	Year 3	Year 4	Year 5
Other Current Liabilities	11,281	11,619	12,317
Total Current Liabilities	27,207	28,023	29,705
Long-Term Debt	20,038	20,038	20,038
Other Long-Term Liabilities	14,599	15,037	15,939
Total Liabilities	61,844	63,098	65,682
Equity			
Common Stock	4,009	4,009	4,009
Retained Earnings	98,089	100,275	102,725
Treasury Stock	(93,715)	(93,715)	(93,715)
Paid in Capital & Other	49,360	52,360	52,360
Total Equity	57,743	62,929	65,379
Total Liabilities and Equity	**119,588**	**126,028**	**131,061**

Note on the projected balance sheets in Table 8-8, the increase in long-term debt from Year 2 to projected Year 3, indicating the proportion (40 percent) of debt financing based on the recommendations, along with the increase in paid-in-capital from projected Year 3 to projected Year 4 representing the proportion (60 percent) of common stock financing per our recommendations. Table 8-9 provides author comments regarding the projected income statement and balance sheet changes to reveal rationales for various changes in the statements.

TABLE 8-9 Author Comments Regarding ABC's Financial Statements (in Millions of USD)

Projected Income Statement	Comments	Year 3	Year 4	Year 5
Revenues	Revenues were flat from Year 1 to Year 2 partly due to significant divestitures and other nonrecurring events totaling more than $5 billion offsetting gains in revenues.	2% increase based on current operations and new revenues generated from increased advertising.	3% increase based on current operations and new revenues generated from increased advertising.	6% increase based on current operations and new revenues generated from increased advertising and from new plants providing new products to sell.
Cost of Goods Sold	Historically 50% of revenues.	50%	50%	50%
Operating Expenses	Historically 29% of revenues adjusted to 31% to account for increased R&D expenditures and increased advertising.	31%	31%	31%
Interest Expense	Financing $2,000 million by debt in Year 3 at 5%. Slight interest deduction in Year 4 and Year 5 as debts are paid, but interest expense is much higher than in Year 2 when ABC did not service this new debt.	$2,000 \times 0.05 = \$100$	−$3	−$3
Tax	Tax rate remains constant at 23% until Year 5 when increased revenues eventually move ABC into higher tax brackets in some markets; some countries have higher tax rates than the 28% U.S. corporate rate.	23%	23%	25%
Nonrecurring Events	No selling of properties or any other major one year changes such as divestitures	0	0	0

Projected Balance Sheet	Comments	Year 3	Year 4	Year 5
Cash	Cash is the plug figure used to balance the projected balance sheets; it is calculated automatically with the template. No entry or estimations for cash are required whether using the template or performing by hand. Simply enter the number for Cash that creates balance where Total Assets = Total Liabilities + Owners Equity.	3,015	7,409	9,552
Accounts Receivable	Historically 7% of revenue	7%	7%	7%
Inventory	Historically 7% of revenue	7%	7%	7%
Other Current Assets	Historically 18% of revenue	18%	18%	18%
Property Plant & Equipment	Adding five new plants per year at $250 million each. Note ABC will not see substantial revenue from the new plants until the plants are completed in Year 5.	$1,250	$1,250	$1,250
Goodwill	No new acquisitions	0	0	0
Intangibles	No new patents	0	0	0
Other Long-Term Assets	Historically 8% of revenue	8%	8%	8%
Liabilities				
Accounts Payable	Historically 26% of revenue; forecasting firm operates more efficiently after restructuring over Year 1 and Year 2.	24%	24%	24%
Other Current Liabilities	Historically 21% of revenue; expecting firm to operate more efficiently after restructuring over Year 1 and Year 2.	17%	17%	17%
Long-Term Debt	Adjust Year 3 to account for debt financing. No debt financing in either Year 4 or Year 5.	$2,000	0	0
Other Long-Term Liabilities	Historically 25% of revenue; expecting firm to operate more efficiently after restructuring over Year 1 and Year 2.	22%	22%	22%
Equity				
Common Stock	Function of par value when the stock was issued × shares outstanding. Keep at 0.	0	0	0
Treasury Stock	No stock buybacks recommended by firm.	0	0	0
Paid in Capital and Other	Financed $3,000 million through equity in Year 4.	0	$3,000	0
Additional Retained Earnings	Net Income Current Year (or latest projected year) — current dividends to be paid = new *additional* retained earnings.	$1,965	$2,186	$2,450
Total Dividends to Pay	Increase dividends by 1% each year.	$7,308	$7,381	$7,455

ABC's Retained Earnings Data Table

As indicated in the prior pages, the key link between a projected income statement and balance sheet is the annual transfer of a firm's net income less dividends (i.e., the retained earnings) to the firm's balance sheet. In light of the importance of this transaction, an ABC retained earnings (RE) data table is given in Table 8-10 to show specifically how this annual transfer of money is made.

TABLE 8-10 ABC's Retained Earnings Data Table (in Millions)

	Dividend Information		Balance Sheet Information		
	1	2	3	4	5
	Net Income	− Dividends Paid	= RE	+ Prior Year BSheet RE	= Current Year BSheet RE
Year 3	$ 9,273	$ 7,308	$ 1,965	$ 96,124	$ 98,089
Year 4	$ 9,567	$ 7,381	$ 2,186	$ 98,089	$ 100,275
Year 5	$ 9,905	$ 7,455	$ 2,450	$ 100,275	$ 102,725

Corporate Valuation

8.3. **Determine the cash value of the firm, or a division of the firm, using four corporate valuation methods.**

Evaluating the worth of a business is central to strategy implementation because firms acquire other firms, divisions of other firms, or even divest part of their own firm. Thus, thousands of transactions occur each year in which businesses are bought or sold for some dollar amount in the United States and around the world. In fact, Statista says there were 1.5 billion transactions globally in 2021, down from 4.7 billion in 2015. (Here is the link: https://www.statista.com/statistics/267369/volume-of-mergers-and-acquisitions-worldwide/).

Corporate valuation is not an exact science; value is sometimes in the eye of the beholder. Companies desire to sell high and buy low, and negotiation normally takes place in both situations. The valuation of a firm's worth is based on financial facts, but common sense and good judgment enter into the process because it is difficult to assign a monetary value to some factors—such as a loyal customer base, a history of growth, legal suits pending, dedicated employees, a favorable lease, a bad credit rating, or valuable patents—that may not be fully reflected in a firm's financial statements. Also, different valuation methods will yield different totals for a firm's worth. Evaluating the worth of a business truly requires both qualitative and quantitative skills.

Sometimes it is OK to pay more for a company than its book value (market capitalization = number of shares outstanding × stock price) if the firm has technology or patents you need or economies of scale you desire, possibly to gain a better hold on distribution or even to reduce competitive pricing pressure. However, buying a company is like buying a house in that paying a "premium" (defined as the amount of money paid for an acquisition over the market capitalization amount) is usually not financially prudent.

Stockholm-based Ericsson AB recently acquired Holmdel, New Jersey-based Vonage for $6.2 billion in a deal whereby the Swedish telecommunications maker paid a 28 percent premium for the cloud-communications software company. This industry is called "communications platform-as-a-service" and includes companies that provide tools that other companies use to interact with employees and customers by text, WhatsApp, chat, video, and voice.

In addition to preparing to buy or sell a business, corporate valuation analysis is often performed when dealing with the following finance and accounting issues: bank loans, tax calculations, retirement packages, death of a principal, partnership agreements, and IRS audits. Practically, it is just good business to know what your firm is worth. This knowledge protects the interests of all parties involved. To estimate the value of a division or segment of a firm, some analysts calculate the total corporate value and multiply that number by the percentage of revenues the division contributes to the firm.

Corporate Valuation Methods

There are numerous methods to determine the worth of a company, but four methods are most often used, as described:

METHOD 1 **The Net Worth Method** = Shareholders' Equity (SE) − (Goodwill + Intangibles) Other terms for SE are Owners' Equity, Total Equity, or Net Worth, but this line item near the bottom of a balance sheet represents the sum of common stock, additional paid-in capital, retained earnings, treasury stock, and other equity items. After calculating total SE,

TABLE 8-11 Company Worth Analysis for ABC (in Millions)

The Input Data	
Shareholders' Equity	$ 55,778
Net Income	$ 15,326
Stock Price	$ 94.17
EPS	$ 6.01019
Number of Shares Outstanding	2,550
Goodwill	$ 44,699
Intangibles	$ 24,187
The Four Valuation Methods	
Stockholders' Equity − (Goodwill + Intangibles)	($ 13,108)
Net Income × 5	$ 76,630
(Share Price/EPS) × Net Income	$ 240,134
Number of Shares Outstanding × Share Price	$ 240,134
Method Average	**$ 135,947**

subtract goodwill and intangibles if these items appear as assets on the firm's balance sheet. Whereas intangibles include copyrights, patents, and trademarks, goodwill arises when a firm acquires another firm and pays more than the book value for that firm. Note in Table 8-11 that ABC's goodwill + intangibles exceeds the firm's SE, resulting in a negative valuation. As a result, Method 1 is not likely a good indicator of ABC's market value; however, it should raise concern for shareholders, managers, and potential firms looking to acquire ABC that most of the firm's assets are intangible in nature.

METHOD 2   The Net Income Method = Net Income × Five

The second approach for measuring the monetary value of a company grows out of the belief that the worth of any business should be based largely on the future benefits its owners may derive through net profits. A conservative rule of thumb is to establish a business's worth as five times the firm's current annual profit. A 5-year average profit level could also be used. When using this approach, remember that firms may suppress earnings in their financial statements to minimize taxes. Note in Table 8-11 that Method 2 results in a low corporate valuation. If you were acquiring a business, this might be a good first offer, but likely Method 2 does not produce a value you would want to begin with if you are selling your business. If a firm's net income is negative, theoretically Method 2 would imply that the firm would pay you to acquire them. Of course, when you acquire another firm, you obtain all of the firm's debt and liabilities, so theoretically this would be possible. In general, this method is more feasible for small business evaluation.

METHOD 3   Price-Earnings Ratio Method = (Stock Price ÷ EPS) × NI

To use the **price-earnings ratio method**, divide the market price of the firm's common stock by the annual EPS and multiply this number by the firm's average net income for the past 5 years. Notice in Table 8-11 this method yields the same value as Method 4. Algebraically, this method is identical to Method 4 if earnings and number of shares figures are taken at the same point in time. In Table 8-11, ABC's Year 2 net income was used as opposed to a 5-year average.

METHOD 4   Outstanding Shares Method = Number of Shares Outstanding × Stock Price

To use the **outstanding shares method**, simply multiply the number of shares outstanding by the market price per share. If the purchase price is higher than this amount, the additional dollars are called a **premium**. The outstanding shares method may also be called the **market value** or **market capitalization** or **book value** of the firm. The premium is a per-share dollar amount that a person or organization is willing to pay beyond the book value of the firm to control (acquire) the company. If you pay less for a firm than the market cap number, the difference is called a **discount**.

In January 2022, Apple became the first publicly-traded company ever whose market capitalization surpassed $3 trillion. The $3 trillion mark came less than two years after Apple's market cap hit $2 trillion. Microsoft is also potentially on its way to the $3 trillion mark after topping $2 trillion in June 2021. Apple's rise to $3 trillion resulted from the incredible success of its

TABLE 8-12 The Top 20 Most Profitable College Football Programs (in Millions of $)

Rank	University	Profits (in Millions of $)
1.	Texas	92
2.	Tennessee (SEC)	70
3.	LSU (SEC)	58
4.	Michigan	56
5.	Notre Dame	54
6.	Georgia (SEC)	50
7.	Ohio State	50
8.	Oklahoma	48
9.	Auburn (SEC)	47
10.	Alabama (SEC)	46
11.	Oregon	40
12.	Florida State	39
13.	Arkansas (SEC)	38
14.	Washington	38
15.	Florida (SEC)	37
16.	Texas A&M (SEC)	37
17.	Penn State	36
18.	Michigan State	32
19.	USC	29
20.	South Carolina (SEC)	28

Source: Based on https://247wallst.com/media/2021/10/28/texas-longhorns-is-americas-most-profitable-college-football-team/

iPhone line, which has spawned accessories like the Apple Watch and AirPods, not to mention services like AppleCare, the App Store, Apple Music+, and Apple TV+.

Table 8-12 reveals the most profitable college football teams in the United States. Using Method 2, you can extrapolate the value of these teams. Note there are 9 Southeastern Conference (SEC) teams listed among the top 20 most profitable.

Manage Financial Ratios, IPOs, and Bonds

8.4. Discuss financial ratios, initial public offerings (IPOs), special purpose acquisition companies (SPACs), and issuing bonds as strategic decisions.

Financial Ratio Analysis

Introduced in Chapter 4, financial ratios are an important tool used to assess a firm's financial situation at one point in time. Financial ratios are examined based on (1) how they change over time, (2) how they compare to industry norms, and (3) how they compare with key competitors. Financial ratios based on actual financial statements reveal strengths and weaknesses of the firm; ratios based on projected financial statements reveal potential problems and successes likely to occur if a particular set of recommendations is implemented. For example, if a current ratio skyrockets or plummets versus industry averages, then cash (and other short-term assets) must be managed.

Continuing with our ABC Company example, Table 8-13 and Table 8-14, respectively, reveal the company's actual (historical) and projected financial ratios, both calculated using the template. Comparing the actual to the projected leverage and activity ratios does not indicate any serious abnormalities or changes, suggesting the four recommendations to be implemented indeed are feasible and doable. Note a significant drop in ABC's return on equity (ROE) and return on assets (ROA) ratios from Year 2 in the projected years because ABC's divestitures ceased in Year 2-Year 5. It is important to note, the projected ratios for ABC in Table 8-14 were not derived from the first

TABLE 8-13 ABC's Actual Financial Ratios

	Historical Ratios	
	Year 1	Year 2
Current Ratio	1.10	0.88
Quick Ratio	0.94	0.72
Total Debt-to-Total-Assets Ratio	0.54	0.54
Total Debt-to-Equity Ratio	1.19	1.16
Times-Interest-Earned Ratio	24	30
Inventor/Turnover	6.98	7.04
Fixed Assets Turnover	3.37	3.27
Total Assets Turnover	0.51	0.54
Accounts Receivable Turnover	11	14
Average Collection Period	32.87	25.77
Gross Profit Margin %	50%	50%
Operating Profit Margin %	21%	21%
ROA %	8%	13%
ROE %	18%	27%

Note: These are ABC's financial ratios computed by the template based on ABC's actual financial statements.

TABLE 8-14 ABC's Projected Financial Ratios

	Projected Ratios		
	Year 3	Year 4	Year 5
Current Ratio	0.89	1.04	1.10
Quick Ratio	0.71	0.86	0.91
Debt-to-Total-Assets Ratio	0.52	0.50	0.50
Debt-to-Equity Ratio	1.07	1.00	1.00
Times-Interest-Earned Ratio	22	23	25
Inventory Turnover	6.71	6.46	6.40
Fixed Assets Turnover	3.14	3.05	3.06
Total Assets Turnover	0.55	0.54	0.55
Accounts Receivable Turnover	14	14	14
Average Collection Period	25.55	25.55	25.55
Gross Profit Margin %	50%	50%	50%
Operating Profit Margin %	19%	19%	19%
ROA %	8%	8%	8%
ROE %	16%	15%	15%

Note: These are ABC's projected financial ratios computed by the template based on ABC's projected financial statements.

attempt at creating projected income statements and projected balance sheets. They are the result of several different interactions and adjustments to the projected statements before the projected ratios were reasonable. Take care to make adjustments as needed to your respective projected statements as well to produce both feasible projected statements and resulting projected ratios.

Go Public with an IPO?

Hundreds of companies annually hold **initial public offerings (IPOs)** to move from being private to being public. "Going public" means selling off a percentage of a company to others to raise capital; this action dilutes the owners' control of the firm. Going public is not recommended for companies with less than $10 million in sales because the initial costs can be too high for the firm to generate sufficient cash flow to make going public worthwhile. One dollar in four is the average total cost paid to lawyers, accountants, and underwriters when an initial stock issuance is less than $1 million; $1 in $20 will go to cover these costs for issuances more than $20 million. In addition to initial costs involved with a stock offering, there are costs and obligations associated with reporting and management in a publicly held firm. The new equity capital derived from going public can enable firms to develop new products, build plants, remodel stores, enter foreign countries, and market products and services more aggressively.

One of the largest IPOs in the United States in nearly a decade occurred in late 2021 when Rivian Automotive debuted on the public markets and closed at $100.73 a share, well above its $78 initial offering price. The electric-vehicle maker's debut actually defied typical market fundamentals because that price valued the startup firm to be worth more than Ford Motor and on par with General Motors. That IPO accented the dramatic shift in the automobile industry to all-electric vehicles. Rivian will "soon" produce the first all-electric pickup truck named RIT and an all-electric SUV named RIS.

In 2021, there were by far more IPOs than ever in the United States, about 1,000 total if you count startup companies going public (special purpose acquisition companies). Reasons for the big spike in IPOs include a long-running bull market, historically low interest rates, high stock liquidity, and hundreds of companies that need external funds to implement bold new strategic plans. Some high-profile IPO's in the United States in 2021 other than Rivian included Roblox, Coupang, DiDi Global, Bumble, and Robinhood Markets that popularized no-fee stock trading, and Coinbase, the largest US cryptocurrency exchange. Technology companies have historically led the IPO market because they need large investments and grow fast, but in recent years biotech and health-care companies have taken the lead.

Not all IPOs are successful. For example, Casper Sleep Inc.'s IPO for $12 per share in 2020 resulted in failure; the mattress-in-a-box maker went back private in late 2021 when Durational Capital Management, a private-equity firm, bought Casper for $6.90 per share. Soon after the Casper IPO, other companies developed and began selling their own bed-in-a-box mattresses, including Serta Simmons Bedding, Tempur Sealy International, and even Amazon began making their own mattresses. Such is the nature of business. It is simply tough to generate a profit competing in most if not all industries; that is a key reason why it is so important to carefully and correctly formulate, implement, and evaluate strategies. Rivian's stock price in May 2022 was about $20 per share, down from its $100 debut the prior year.

A relatively new but hot new way for a company to go public without going through the IPO process is to merge with a **special purpose acquisition company (SPAC)** that is already publicly traded. A SPAC merger circumvents the need for an IPO and entails the SPAC company raising money on public markets for the new firm, then merging with the new firm so that the new firm has its own publicly traded stock. For example, in 2022, Harley-Davidson sold (divested) its electric-motorcycle division (named LiveWire) to AEA-Bridges Impact Corporation (the SPAC) and then became a public company that today trades under the ticker symbol LVW on the New York Stock Exchange. Many companies have recently used the SPAC approach, including Lucid Group Inc., Nikola Corporation, and the personal-finance startup company named Dave Inc. that merged with VPC Impact Acquisition Holdings III Inc. (the SPAC).

A SPAC basically is a blank-check, shell company that raises money from investors and then lists publicly the target company on a stock exchange for the sole purpose of merging with the private firm to take it public. The "blank-check go public" business model often referred to as SPAC has taken off even in Singapore where companies are raising money to go public. SPACs are shell companies that raise money from public investors and get listed on the stock exchange and then strive to merge with private companies, sometimes called a de-SPAC deal. These business deals are a more streamlined approach to going public as compared to IPO. Hong Kong also has become a popular place for launching SPACs. However, about one half of all SPAC startups with less than $10 billion in annual revenue that went public in 2021 either failed or are falling far short of revenue and profitability expectations. For example, the bus and van maker Arrival SA's merger with a SPAC resulted in their CEO Denis Sverdlov substantially downgrading his company's lofty financial goals and expectations that were the foundation of the firm going public. In mid-2022, Westrock Coffee Holdings LLC based in Little Rock, Arkansas linked up with a SPAC (Riverview Acquisition Corporation) to go public with a valuation of about $1.2 billion.

Issue Bonds to Raise Capital?

Another popular way for a company to raise capital is to issue corporate bonds, which is analogous to going to the bank and borrowing money, except that with bonds, the company obtains the funds from investors rather than banks. On a balance sheet, bonds are included in the long-term debt row. Especially when a company's balance sheet is strong and its credit rating is excellent, issuing bonds can be an effective way to raise needed capital. Corporate bond prices are less sensitive to daily or quarterly firm operations compared to stock prices. For example, an expected equity price forecasted to finance potential recommended strategies may be significantly higher or lower than forecasted, but bond prices and rates will be more in line with the forecast based on unforeseen events such as CEO succession, new competitors emerging, a bad earnings surprise, and other factors. Smaller firms or firms with negative earnings will also likely have higher rates associated with their bonds, possibly resulting in bond issuance (debt) being a more expensive alternative than equity. Bonds are also used because sometimes banks do not want to lend money for long periods of time to fund business operations.

The practice of firms issuing bonds to buy back their own stock and to pay cash dividends to shareholders has become a concern in terms of being financially prudent. A strategic decision facing corporations therefore, is whether to issue bonds to raise capital to pacify shareholders with cash dividends and purchase company stock, or to issue bonds to finance strategies carefully formulated to yield greater revenues and profits.

A 3-16-22 *Wall Street Journal* article (p. B1) reported that companies are repurchasing their own shares of stock at a record pace. For example, Union Pacific has plans for buying back $25 billion of its stock, while PepsiCo, Amazon, and Linde PLC have all announced plans to increase their Treasury Stock by $10+ billion. Goldman analysts forecast a total of $1 trillion in Treasury Stock increases in 2022 in the U.S., up 12 percent from the prior year. In contrast, Starbucks recently suspended its stock buyback program saying the company has decided to invest those monies into its employees and also into building more restaurants. This decision is an example of what strategic planning is all about, deciding where best to invest available monies.

IMPLICATIONS FOR STRATEGISTS

Figure 8-3 reveals that to gain and sustain competitive advantages, firms must manage their finances more efficiently than rival firms, by using tools like EPS/EBIT analysis, projected financial statement analysis, and corporate valuation analysis, as described herein. As you know, it is difficult to make a dollar of profit; every dollar saved is like a dollar earned. Dollars matter and successful strategy implementation is dependent on superior "dollar management." The concepts, tools, and techniques presented in this chapter can make the difference between success and failure in implementing strategies in many companies and organizations.

IMPLICATIONS FOR STUDENTS

A personal note from the authors to students; we are exceptionally proud of you for mastering this chapter. At student international case competitions, we have witnessed numerous teams of students win case competitions largely because they are able to demonstrate that their recommendations are financially feasible and reasonable and will lead to excellent financial returns for the firm. We know this chapter is a bit tough but hopefully you find it to be concise, accurate, and easy to follow. Mastering the skills conveyed in this chapter will provide you a competitive advantage over other students and provide you a financial knowledge base to use in your business career and personal lives.

Whenever the opportunity arises in your oral or written project, reveal how your firm can gain and sustain competitive advantage using the finance and accounting concepts and analyses present-ed in this chapter. Continuously compare your firm to rivals and draw insights and conclusions so that your recommendations come across as well conceived. Never shy away from the EPS/EBIT analysis, projected financial statement analysis, or corporate valuation analyses because your audience must be convinced that what you recommend is financially feasible and worth the dollars to be spent. Spend sufficient time on the nuts-and-bolts of those analyses as needed, so fellow students (and your professor) will be assured the analyses are correct and reasonable. Too often, when students rush at the end of an oral presentation, it means their financial statements are nonexistent or incorrectly developed—so avoid that issue. Use the free Excel strategic planning template at www.strategyclub.com and consider putting on your resume that you have "Gained experience using strategic-planning software."

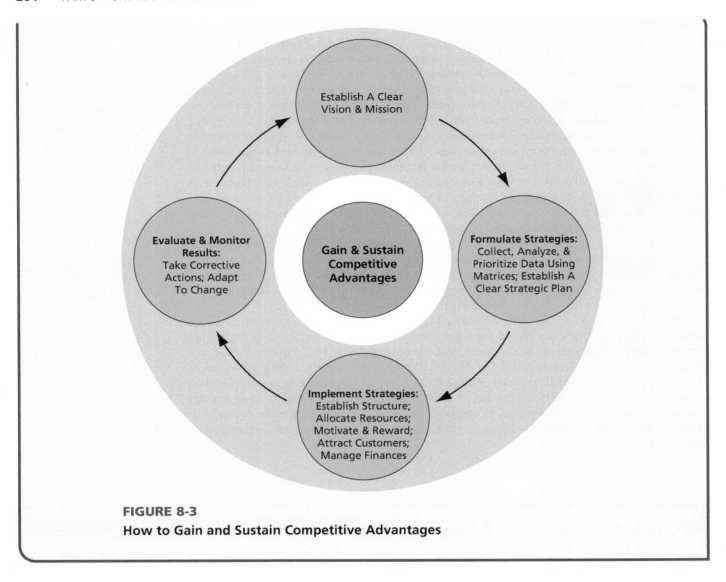

FIGURE 8-3
How to Gain and Sustain Competitive Advantages

Chapter Summary

Finance and accounting managers must devise effective strategy implementation approaches at low cost and minimum risk to the firm. The nature and role of finance and accounting activities, coupled with the management and marketing activities described in the prior chapter, largely determine organizational success. An excellent capital structure can be a competitive advantage; EPS/EBIT analysis is needed to make capital structure decisions. Projected financial statements are vital for anticipating the impact of various recommendations. Corporate valuation methods are used all the time to acquire, merge, divest, and manage a firm's finances. Together these finance concepts, tools, and techniques can help assure effective and efficient strategy implementation.

Key Terms and Concepts

book value (p. 259)

capital structure (p. 245)

discount (p. 259)

EPS/EBIT analysis (p. 245)

goodwill (p. 254)

initial public offering (IPO) (p. 261)

market capitalization (p. 259)

market value (p. 259)

outstanding shares method (p. 259)

premium (p. 259)

price-earnings ratio method (p. 259)

projected financial statement (p. 249)

special purpose acquisition company (SPAC) (p. 262)

treasury stock (p. 245)

Issues for Review and Discussion

8-1. True or False? Acquisition premiums the last few years have averaged 25 to 40 percent, but sometimes exceed 100 percent; prior research suggests that high premiums generally have negative impacts on acquisition performance. Explain.

8-2. Explain why increasing treasury stock will increase EPS in any corporation.

8-3. Some analysts say that huge New York Stock Exchange IPOs from companies such as Alibaba, headquartered in China, should be illegal in the United States because under communist governments there are not sufficient safeguards in place for financial transactions. Do you agree or disagree? Why?

8-4. True or False? In the United States, no federal laws prevent businesses from using GPS devices to monitor employees, nor does federal law require businesses to disclose to employees whether they are using such techniques. What are the implications for employees and companies?

8-5. To raise capital, what are the pros and cons of selling bonds compared to issuing stock or borrowing money from a bank?

8-6. Many companies are aggressively buying their own stock. What are situations when this practice is recommended or especially beneficial? What are the pros and cons of increasing treasury stock on the balance sheet?

8-7. Hewlett-Packard has more goodwill ($) than the book value ($) of the firm. Explain what this means, how it could occur, and what can be done about this situation.

8-8. Give a hypothetical example where Company A buys Company B for a 15 percent premium.

8-9. Give a hypothetical example where Company A buys Company B for a 15 percent discount.

8-10. What is treasury stock? When should a company purchase treasury stock?

8-11. What is an IPO? When is an IPO good for a company?

8-12. Generally speaking, how large should a firm be to justify having an IPO? Explain the IPO process.

8-13. How could or would dividends affect an EPS/EBIT analysis? Would it be correct to refer to "earnings after taxes, interest, and dividends" as retained earnings for a given year?

8-14. In performing an EPS/EBIT analysis, where do the first-row (EBIT) numbers come from?

8-15. In performing an EPS/EBIT analysis, where does the tax rate percentage come from?

8-16. Show algebraically that the price-earnings ratio formula is identical to the number of shares outstanding multiplied by the stock price formula. Why are the values obtained from these two methods sometimes different?

8-17. In accounting terms, distinguish between intangibles and goodwill on a balance sheet. Why do these two items generally stay the same on projected financial statements?

8-18. Explain four methods often used to calculate the total worth of a business.

8-19. Explain how and why top executives can and do, on occasion, legally manipulate financial statements to inflate or deflate expected results.

8-20. Explain why EPS/EBIT analysis is a central strategy implementation technique.

8-21. Identify and discuss the limitations of EPS/EBIT analysis.

8-22. True or False? Retained earnings on the balance sheet are not monies available to finance strategy implementation. Explain.

8-23. Explain why projected financial statement analysis is considered both a strategy formulation and a strategy implementation tool.

8-24. Complete the following EPS/EBIT analysis for a company whose stock price is $20, interest rate on funds is 5 percent, tax rate is 20 percent, number of shares outstanding is 500 million, and EBIT range is $100 million to $300 million. The firm needs to raise $200 million in capital. Use the following table to complete the work.

	100% Common Stock	100% Debt Financing	20% Debt–80% Stock Financing
EBIT			
Interest			
EBT			
Taxes			
EAT			
#Shares			
EPS			

8-25. Under what conditions would retained earnings on the balance sheet decrease from 1 year to the next?

8-26. In your own words, list all the steps in developing projected financial statements.

8-27. Based on the financial statements provided for McDonald's in the Cohesion Case, what dollar amount of dividends did McDonald's pay in 2021?

8-28. Why should you be careful not to use historical percentages blindly in developing projected financial statements?

Writing Assignments

8-29. In developing projected financial statements, what should you do if the dollar amount you must put in the cash account (to make the statement balance) is far more (or less) than desired?

8-30. Explain how you would estimate the total worth of a business.

Ken Wolter/Alamy Photo

ASSURANCE-OF-LEARNING EXERCISES

SET 1: STRATEGIC PLANNING FOR MCDONALD'S

EXERCISE 8A

Perform an EPS/EBIT Analysis for McDonald's

Purpose

An EPS/EBIT analysis is one of the most widely used techniques for determining the extent that debt or stock should be used to finance strategies to be implemented. This exercise can give you practice performing EPS/EBIT analysis. For this exercise, it is best to use the strategic planning template. Just open the template and click on the EPS/EBIT icon, enter the appropriate information given below, and analyze the results. You may do this exercise manually, but the template is fast and effective and widely used globally by both businesses and students. (We authors want you to be able to say on your resume that you are "proficient using excel-based strategic planning software," so potential employers will be impressed).

Instructions

Amount McDonald's needs: $5,000 million to build 500 new restaurants outside the United States.

> Interest rate: 3%
> Tax rate: 28%
> Stock price: $250
> Number of shares outstanding: 750 million
> EBIT: Pessimistic: $7,000 million; Realistic: $9,000 million; Optimistic: $10,000 million

Steps

1. Prepare an EPS/EBIT analysis for McDonald's. Determine whether the company should use all debt, all stock, or a 50-50 combination of debt and stock to finance this strategy for market development.
2. Develop an EPS/EBIT chart after completing the EPS/EBIT table.
3. Next, give a three-sentence recommendation for McDonald's CFO.

EXERCISE 8B

Prepare Projected Financial Statements for McDonald's

Purpose

This exercise is designed to give you experience preparing projected financial statements. This analysis is a strategic finance and accounting issue because it allows managers to anticipate and evaluate the expected results of various strategy implementation approaches. For this exercise, it is best to use the strategic planning template. Just open the template and click on the Projected Financial Statements icon and work from there. You may want to refer back to Exercise 4A at the end of Chapter 4 where you perhaps (hopefully) entered McDonald's existing financial statements into the template format. If you did not do that then, do this now following guidelines given both in the template and in Table 8-4 in this chapter. You may do this exercise by hand, but the template is fast and effective and widely used globally by both businesses and students. (Plus on your resume you may then say you are "experienced using excel-based strategic planning software," so potential employers will be impressed with your skills and abilities).

Instructions

Step 1   Work with a classmate. Develop a projected income statement and balance sheet for McDonald's. Assume that McDonald's needs to raise $1 billion to increase its market share and plans to obtain 50 percent financing from a bank and 50 percent financing from a stock issuance. Make other assumptions as needed, and state them clearly in written form.

Step 2   Bring your projected statements to class and discuss any problems or questions you encountered.

Step 3   Compare your projected statements to the statements of other students. What major differences exist between your analysis and the work of other students?

EXERCISE 8C

Determine the Cash Value of McDonald's

Purpose

It is simply good business to continually know the cash value (corporate valuation) of your company. This exercise gives you practice in determining the total worth of a company using several methods. To perform this analysis, use McDonald's financial statements as given in the Cohesion Case.

Instructions

Step 1   Calculate the financial worth of McDonald's based on four approaches: (1) the net worth method, (2) the net income method, (3) the price-earnings ratio method, and (4) the outstanding shares method.

Step 2   Get an average of the four methods. In a dollar amount, how much is McDonald's worth?

Step 3   Compare your analyses and conclusions with those of other students.

EXERCISE 8D

Prepare Projected Financial Ratios for McDonald's

Purpose

Financial ratios are vastly more than just an exercise for students to perform. If any firm's financial ratios get out of line with industry averages or decline over time, investors can withdraw support literally overnight. Projected financial ratios are an excellent means for anticipating financial results so as to avoid overnight calamities. The template will generate projected financial ratios after you convert your firm's financial statements to the template format and then develop projected financial statements based on recommended strategies.

Step 1   Use your Exercise 8B work. Scroll to the bottom of the template and move to the far right along the bar and click on the icon Projected Financial Ratios.

Step 2   See the ratios calculated automatically and the percentage changes provided.

Step 3   Based on the projected ratios you see, what are McDonald's two major strengths and two major weaknesses going forward? Justify your reasoning.

SET 2: STRATEGIC PLANNING FOR MY UNIVERSITY

EXERCISE 8E

Determine the Cash Value of My University

Purpose

It is simply good business to continually know the cash value (corporate valuation) of any organization, including colleges and universities. The four largest private universities in the United States by total student enrollment (in parentheses) are as follows: Southern New Hampshire University (134,345), Liberty University (93,349), New York University (52,775), and University of Southern California (46,287). https://www.collegesimply.com/colleges/rank/private-colleges/largest-enrollment/. The four largest public universities in the United States are the University of Central Florida (71,948), Texas A&M University (71,109), Ohio State University (61,369), and Florida International University (58,928). https://www.worldatlas.com/articles/10-largest-universities-in-the-united-states.html. This exercise gives you practice in determining the total worth of an organization using two methods.

Instructions

Step 1   Locate your university's most recent income statement and balance sheet.

Step 2   Calculate the financial worth of your university based on two approaches: (1) the net worth method and (2) the net income method.

Step 3   Get an average of the two methods. In a dollar amount, how much is your university worth?

Step 4   Compare your analyses and conclusions with those of other students.

SET 3: STRATEGIC PLANNING TO ENHANCE MY EMPLOYABILITY

EXERCISE 8F

Developing Personal Financial Statements

Purpose

Banks require individuals to develop personal financial statements whenever a mortgage or loan is requested. Managing your personal finances is important before and after you begin working full-time. This exercise gives you a heads up on the process of developing an income statement and balance sheet for yourself.

Instructions

Step 1   Develop an income statement and balance sheet for yourself using the free Excel template at www.strategyclub.com. Follow the steps outlined in this chapter.

Step 2   Determine your net worth which equals your total assets minus your total liabilities.

Step 3   Explain why managing personal finances is important to enhance your employability.

EXERCISE 8G

A Template Competency Test

Purpose

The free Excel strategic planning template at www.strategyclub.com is widely used for strategic planning by students and small businesses; this exercise aims to enhance your familiarity with the template. Developing competence with the template will enable you to place this skill appropriately on your resume, in addition to facilitating your development of a comprehensive strategic plan for an assigned case company.

Instructions

Answer the following questions about the template. Discuss your answers with classmates to identify and resolve any issues or concerns.

1. Why is it helpful to take the time to enter your financial statements into the template format rather than simply copying and pasting financial statements off line?

2. Does this chapter focus on Part I or Part II of the template?

3. If the EPS ranges for equity and debt for a given level of EBIT are identical, what change in the analysis would likely provide the most variance: (1) Adjusting the amount of capital needed by 25%, (2) increasing the interest rate by 1% (100 basis points), or (3) increasing the tax rate by 5% (500 basis points)? Why?

4. Which of the following methods will never maximize EPS: (1) 100% equity financing, (2) 100% debt financing, or (3) combination financing? Why?

5. Explain how analyzing projected financial ratios generated by the template can be helpful in making adjustments to your projected financial statement estimates?

6. Do you physically have to calculate any number on the projected statements when using the template?

7. The template assures your projected balance sheets are in balance every time by using what line item to achieve the balancing?

8. If you notice your current ratio went from a historical 1.0 to a projected 5.0, what are some steps you should consider taking?

9. When entering treasury stock on the template, why do you enter a negative number?

10. If you desire to quit paying dividends in projected years, what entry is needed for the template to make this calculation?

11. If current plant property and equipment were $500 million and you wish to increase plant property and equipment by $50 million in the first fiscal year, what number would you enter into Part II of the template by plant property equipment under the first projected fiscal year?

12. If you sold $100 million of common stock, what line item on the projected balance sheet on Part II of the template would you make this entry?

13. Just to the right of each line item on Part II of the projected income statement and projected balance sheet, the template provides what type of hint?

14. Why should a student enter into the template their existing and projected financial data, from oldest year to most recent year, even though the template will allow students to enter in dates in any sequence desired and even though many published statements may enter the data in reverse order?

SET 4: INDIVIDUAL VERSUS GROUP STRATEGIC PLANNING

EXERCISE 8H

How Severe Are the Seven Limitations to EPS/EBIT Analysis?

Purpose

As discussed in this chapter, EPS/EBIT analysis is the most widely used financial tool to determine whether debt or equity is better to raise needed capital. However, all analytical tools have some limitations. This chapter identifies and discusses seven limitations of EPS/EBIT analysis, as follows:

1. Flexibility
2. Control
3. Timing
4. Extent leveraged
5. Continuity
6. EBIT ranges
7. Dividends

The purpose of this exercise is to examine more closely the limitations of EPS/EBIT analysis in terms of their relative severity. In addition, the purpose is to examine whether individual decision making is better than group decision-making. Academic research suggests that groups make better decisions than individuals about 80 percent of the time.

Instructions

Rank the seven limitations of EPS/EBIT analysis as to their severity, where 1 = most severe to 7 = least severe. Use Table 8-15. First, rank the limitations as an individual. Then, rank the limitations as part of a group of three. Thus, determine what person(s) and what group(s) can come closest to the expert ranking. This exercise enables examination of the relative effectiveness of individual versus group decision making in strategic planning.

Steps

1. Fill in Column 1 in Table 8-15 to reveal your individual ranking of the severity of the seven limitations (1 = most severe to 7 = least severe). For example, if you think Limitation 1 (Flexibility) is the fourth-most severe limitation, then enter a 4 in Table 8-15 in Column 1 beside Flexibility.
2. Fill in Column 2 in Table 8-15 to reveal your group's ranking of the severity of the seven limitations (1 = most severe to 7 = least severe).
3. Fill in Column 3 in Table 8-15 to reveal the expert's ranking of the seven limitations.
4. Fill in Column 4 in Table 8-15 with the absolute difference between Column 1 and Column 3 to reveal how well you performed as an individual in this exercise. (Note: Absolute difference disregards negative numbers.)
5. Fill in Column 5 in Table 8-15 with the absolute difference between Column 2 and Column 3 to reveal how well your group performed in this exercise.
6. Sum Column 4. Sum Column 5.
7. Compare the Column 4 sum with the Column 5 sum. If your Column 4 sum is less than your Column 5 sum, then you performed better as an individual than as a group. Normally, group decision-making is superior to individual decision-making, so if you did better than your group, you did excellent.
8. The Individual Winner(s): The individual(s) with the lowest Column 4 sum is the WINNER.
9. The Group Winners(s): The group(s) with the lowest Column 5 score is the WINNER.

TABLE 8-15 Assessing EPS/EBIT Limitations: Comparing Individual Versus Group Decision-Making

Limitations	Column 1	Column 2	Column 3	Column 4	Column 5
1. Flexibility					
2. Control					
3. Timing					
4. Extent leveraged					
5. Continuity					
6. EBIT ranges					
7. Dividends					
Sums					

MINI-CASE ON THE MICROSOFT CORPORATION

JeanLucIchard/Shutterstock

MICROSOFT RATED THE BEST MANAGED COMPANY IN 2021 (AND 2020) BY THE DRUCKER INSTITUTE AT THE CLAREMONT GRADUATE UNIVERSITY[5]

Among the 846 largest U.S. companies, for the second year in a row, Microsoft is the best managed company, according to the prestigious Drucker Institute. The Institute annually rates companies on five criteria—(1) employee engagement and development, (2) innovation, (3) social responsibility, (4) financial strength, and (5) customer satisfaction—and identifies the best 250 firms. Microsoft scored among the top six firms in four of the five criteria, lacking only in customer satisfaction. Second, third, fourth, and fifth in the overall rankings of the best managed firms were Amazon, Apple, IBM, and Intel, ironically all five being high-tech companies.

The tallest person ever recorded was 8-foot-11 Robert Wadlow. He was to height as Microsoft has been to management. Microsoft has been the best managed company in recent years by pursuing some of the following strategies:

1. Let go of the old and continually move onto new products and services.
2. Create systems for continuous improvement of products.
3. Capitalize on successes and stop doing things that provide low value or return.
4. Create a different tomorrow that replaces even the most successful products of today.
5. Show continual improvement on the 17 United Nations' Sustainable Development Goals (SDG). Use the SDG's as a roadmap for company operations and compensation systems.

Questions

1. The institute does not reveal its weighting as to importance of the five criteria used in its annual ranking. What weights would you deem best? Would you place a 20 percent weight on all five criteria? Why or why not?
2. Microsoft was rated number 261 on customer satisfaction. Why do you think Microsoft was rated so low on that factor? Does such a low rating on that factor imply a low weight for that factor given that Microsoft is number 1 overall in management effectiveness?

[5]Based on Patrick Thomas, "Journal Report: C-Suite Strategies, The Best-managed Companies of 2021," *Wall Street Journal*, pp. R1-R10.

Web Resources

1. Fred David gives a video overview of Chapter 8 in the prior edition, but much info is still applicable to the 18th edition.
   Part 1 of Chapter 8: https://www.youtube.com/watch?v=RcCsn6_wguk
   Part 2 of Chapter 8: https://www.youtube.com/watch?v=LhCqORjgOIQ
   Part 3 of Chapter 8: https://www.youtube.com/watch?v=TWgPN77O58Y

2. This website gives excellent discussion about the importance of and procedures for developing projected financial statements.
   https://www.fool.com/the-blueprint/financial-projections/

3. This website gives excellent narrative regarding how to determine the cash value of any business.
   https://www.thehartford.com/business-insurance/strategy/selling-a-business/determining-market-value

4. This website gives excellent guidelines for determining the best mix of debt versus equity in a firm's capital structure.
   https://corporatefinanceinstitute.com/resources/knowledge/finance/debt-vs-equity/

Current Readings

Black, Dirk E., Ervin L. Black, Theodore E. Christensen, Kurt H. Gee, "Comparing Non-GAAP EPS in Earnings Announcements and Proxy Statements," *Management Science* (2021), https://doi.org/10.1287/mnsc.2020.3928

Cerpentier, Maarten, Tom Vanacker, Ine Paeleman, and Katja Bringmann, "Equity Crowdfunding, Market Timing, and Firm Capital Structure," *The Journal of Technology Transfer* (2021): 1–28.

Chadha, Saurabh, and Himanshu Seth, "Ownership Structure and Capital Structure: A Panel Data Study," *International Journal of Business Innovation and Research* 24, no. 3 (2021): 385–96.

Chahine, Salim, Igor Filatotchev, Garry D. Bruton, and Mike Wright, "'Success by Association': The Impact of Venture capital Firm Reputation Trend on Initial Public Offering Valuations," *Journal of Management* 47, no. 2 (2021): 368–98.

David, Fred R., Meredith E. David, and Forest R. David, "How Important is Finance Coverage in Strategic Management? A Content Analysis of Textbooks," *International Journal of Management and Human Resources* 4, no. 1 (2016): 64–78.

Feldman Emilie, R., and Arkadiy V. Sakhartov, "Resource Redeployment and Divestiture as Strategic Alternatives," *Organization Science* forthcoming.

García, C. José, and Begoña Herrero, "Female Directors, Capital Structure, and Financial Distress," *Journal of Business Research* 136 (2021): 592–601.

Giulio Girardi, Kathleen W. Hanley, Stanislava Nikolova, Loriana Pelizzon, and Mila Getmansky Sherman, "Portfolio Similarity and Asset Liquidation in the Insurance Industry," *Journal of Financial Economics* 142 no. 1, (2021): 69–96.

Krause, Ryan, Juanyi Chen, Garry D. Bruton, and Igor Filatotchev, "Chief Executive Officer Power and Initial Public Offering Underpricing: Examining the Influence of Demand–Side Cultural Power Distance," *Global Strategy Journal* 11, no. 4 (2021): 686–708.

Kuvshinov, Dmitry, and Kaspar Zimmermann, "The Big Bang: Stock Market Capitalization in the Long Run," *Journal of Financial Economics* (2021), https://doi.org/10.1016/j.jfineco.2021.09.008

Laeven, Luc, "Pandemics, Intermediate Goods, and Corporate Valuation," *Journal of International Money and Finance* 120 (2022): 102505.

Nugroho, M., D. Arif, and A. Halik, "The Effect of Loan-Loss Provision, Non-Performing Loans and Third-Party Fund on Capital Adequacy Ratio," *Accounting* 7, no. 4 (2021): 943–50.

Pearce, John, A., and Pankaj C. Patel, "Reaping the Financial and Strategic Benefits of a Divestiture by Spin-off," *Business Horizons*, forthcoming (2021), https://doi.org/10.1016/j.bushor.2021.03.001

Endnotes

1. On page 244.
2. Fred R. David, Meredith E. David, and Forest R. David, "How Important is Finance Coverage in Strategic Management? A Content Analysis of Textbooks," *International Journal of Management and Human Resources* 4, no. 1 (2016): 64–78.
3. On page 251.
4. On page 251.
5. On page 270.

## PART 4

STRATEGY EVALUATION AND GOVERNANCE

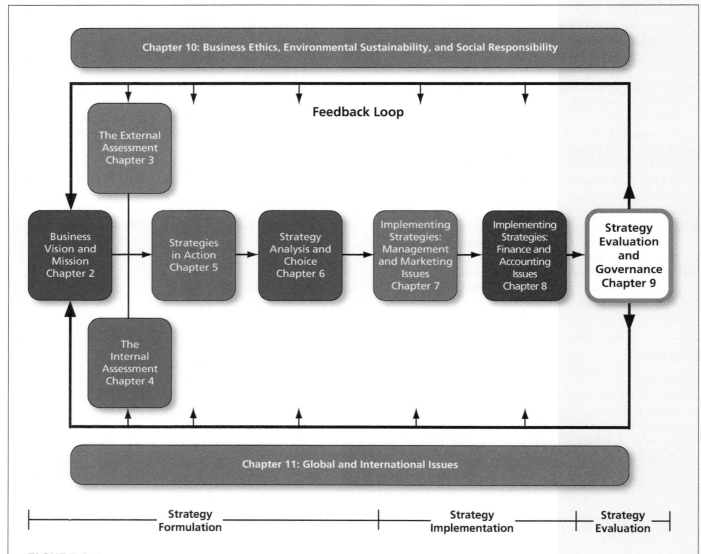

FIGURE 9-1

The Comprehensive, Integrative Strategic Management Model

Source: Fred R. David, "How Companies Define Their Mission," *Long Range Planning* 22, no. 1 (February 1989): 91. See also Anik Ratnaningsih, Nadjadji Anwar, Patdono Suwignjo, and Putu Artama Wiguna, "Balance Scorecard of David's Strategic Modeling at Industrial Business for National Construction Contractor of Indonesia," *Journal of Mathematics and Technology*, no. 4 (October 2010): 20. Also, Meredith E. David, Fred R. David, and Forest R. David, "Closing the Gap Between Graduates' Skills and Employers' Requirements: A Focus on the Strategic Management Capstone Business Course," *Administrative Sciences* 11, no. 1 (2021): 10–26.

Strategy Evaluation and Governance

LEARNING OBJECTIVES

After studying this chapter, you should be able to do the following:

9.1. Discuss the strategy evaluation process.

9.2. Discuss three activities that comprise strategy evaluation.

9.3. Describe and develop a Balanced Scorecard.

9.4. Discuss the role of a board of directors (governance) in strategic planning.

9.5. Identify and discuss four challenges in strategic management.

9.6. Identify and describe 17 guidelines for effective strategic management.

ASSURANCE-OF-LEARNING EXERCISES

The following exercises are found at the end of this chapter:

SET 1:	Strategic Planning for McDonald's
EXERCISE 9A:	Develop a Balanced Scorecard for McDonald's
SET 2:	Strategic Planning for My University
EXERCISE 9B:	Prepare a Strategy Evaluation Report for My University
SET 3:	Strategic Planning to Enhance My Employability
EXERCISE 9C:	A Balanced Scorecard to Evaluate My Professional Versus Personal Objectives
SET 4:	Individual Versus Group Strategic Planning
EXERCISE 9D:	How Important Are Various Guidelines for Effective Strategic Management?

The best formulated and implemented strategies become obsolete as a firm's external and internal environments change. It is essential, therefore, that strategists systematically evaluate the execution of strategies, as illustrated and highlighted in Figure 9-1. This chapter presents a framework that can guide managers' efforts to evaluate strategies, to make sure they are working, and to make timely changes.

Boards of directors evaluate strategies as part of their job description, so governance issues are discussed in this chapter. Guidelines are presented in this chapter for actually doing strategic planning because board members are increasingly involved in the process with top management. Special challenges impacting strategic planning activities also are discussed.

The exemplary strategist showcased in this chapter is the CEO of Walgreens Boots Alliance, Rosalind Brewer, who previously was COO of Starbucks. This chapter is all about evaluating strategies, and CEO Brewer has focused extensively on evaluating strategies at Walgreens as the company was instrumental in leading cities, towns, and communities out of the pandemic and into a healthier society.

The Strategy Evaluation Process

9.1. Discuss the strategy evaluation process.

The strategic management process results in decisions that can have significant, long-lasting consequences. Erroneous strategic decisions can inflict severe penalties and can be exceedingly difficult, if not impossible, to reverse. Therefore, most strategists agree that strategy evaluation is vital to an organization's well-being; timely evaluations can alert management to problems or potential problems before a situation becomes critical. The strategy evaluation process includes three basic activities:

1. Examine the underlying bases of a firm's strategy.
2. Compare expected results with actual results.
3. Take corrective actions to ensure that performance conforms to plans.

EXEMPLARY **STRATEGIST** SHOWCASED

Ms. Rosalind Brewer, CEO of Walgreens Boots Alliance[1]

Nearing the end of 2021, there were a record 41 female CEOs among the *Fortune* 500, including two Black women for the first time ever: Rosalind Brewer of Walgreens Boots Alliance and Thasunda Brown Duckett of Teachers Insurance and Annuity Association of America (TIAA). The only other Black woman to ever be CEO of a *Fortune* 500 company was Ursula Burns, the former CEO of Xerox who today is a member of the board of directors of Uber Technologies and of VEON. (Mary Winston, also a Black woman, was at one time interim CEO of Bed, Bath & Beyond). Walgreens is 19th on the *Fortune* 500 list of the largest companies in the United States.

A chemist by trade, Brewer says science has proven that we all should take the vaccine, a reason why she has mandated vaccines in her office and is trying to roll that mandate out company-wide to all stores. A scientist, Brewer says she is frustrated at people not paying attention to the facts because vaccines are saving millions of lives. She is a huge advocate of corporate wellness and is moving Walgreens to lead society to become healthier every day.

In the United States alone, Walgreens has 9,100 stores and serves about 8 million customers online daily. When asked about fringe rivals such as Amazon, Microsoft, and Apple having health and fitness apps, Brewer says she wants to partner with those companies to deliver great

Jonathan Weiss/Shutterstock

health care globally. Brewer's overall objective at Walgreens is to help create a healthier society, so she is moving the firm much more into prevention, convenience, and digital health care. Walgreens is now adding physicians' offices within or attached to all Walgreens' stores.

[1]Based on Beth Kowitt, "The Conversation with Rosalind Brewer," *Fortune*, October/November 2021, pp. 12–16.

Adequate and timely feedback is the cornerstone of effective strategy evaluation. Strategy evaluation can be no better than the information on which it is based. Too much pressure from top managers may result in lower-level managers contriving numbers they think will be satisfactory. Strategy evaluation can be a complex and sensitive undertaking. Too much emphasis on evaluating strategies may be expensive and counterproductive. No one likes to be evaluated too closely! Yet too little or no evaluation can create even worse problems. Strategy evaluation is essential to ensure that stated objectives are being achieved. Strategists need to create an organizational culture where strategy evaluation is viewed as an opportunity to make the firm better, so the firm can compete better, and so everyone in the firm can share in the firm's increased profitability. This chapter reveals how to evaluate strategies.

In many organizations, strategy evaluation is simply an appraisal of how well an organization has performed. Have the firm's assets increased? Has there been an increase in profitability? Have sales increased? Have productivity levels increased? Have profit margin, return on investment, and earnings-per-share ratios increased? Some firms argue that their strategy must have been correct if the answers to these types of questions are affirmative. Well, the strategy or strategies may have been correct, but this type of reasoning can be misleading because strategy evaluation must have both a long-run and short-run focus. Bad strategies may not affect short-term operating results until it is too late to make needed changes, and excellent strategies may take several years instead of months to produce great results. Short-term results can be from factors other than your strategy (good or bad); an effective strategy evaluation process deciphers such issues.

Strategy evaluation is important because firms face dynamic environments in which key external and internal factors often change quickly and dramatically. Success today is no guarantee of success tomorrow! Joseph Stalin was a ruthless leader beginning in 1928 and became Premier of the Soviet Union in 1941 until his death in 1953. A famous quote from Stalin was: "History shows that there are no invincible armies." This quote reveals that even the mightiest, most successful firms must continually evaluate their strategies and be wary of rival organizations. A firm should never be lulled into complacency with success. Countless firms have thrived 1 year only to struggle for survival the following year. According to Peter Drucker, "Unless strategy evaluation is performed seriously and systematically, and unless strategists are willing to act on the results, energy will be used up defending yesterday."

It is impossible to demonstrate conclusively that a particular strategy is optimal or even to guarantee that it will work. But any strategy must provide for the creation or maintenance of a competitive advantage in a selected area of activity. Competitive advantages normally are the result of superiority in one of three areas: (1) resources, (2) skills, or (3) position. The idea that the positioning of one's resources can enhance their combined effectiveness is familiar to military theorists, chess players, and diplomats. Position can also play a crucial role in an organization's strategy. Once gained, a strong position is defensible—meaning that it is so costly to capture that rivals are deterred from full-scale attacks. Positional advantage tends to be self-sustaining so long as the underlying external and internal factors remain stable. This is why entrenched firms can be difficult to unseat, even if their raw skill levels are only average.[2]

Strategy evaluation is becoming increasingly difficult because today's domestic and world economies are more interrelated, product life cycles are shorter, technological advancements are faster, change occurs rapidly, competitors abound globally, planning cycles are shorter, and social media and smartphones have changed everything. A fundamental problem facing managers today is how to effectively manage a workforce that increasingly demands fairness, openness, transparency, flexibility, and involvement. Managers need empowered employees acting responsibly. Otherwise the costs to companies in terms of damaged reputations, fines, missed opportunities, and diversion of management's attention can be enormous; bad news can spread like wildfire over social media. Too much pressure to achieve specific goals can lead to dysfunctional behavior.

Evaluating strategies on a continuous rather than on a periodic basis allows benchmarks of progress to be established and more effectively monitored. Some strategies take years to implement; consequently, associated results may not become apparent for years. Successful strategies combine patience with a willingness to promptly take corrective actions when necessary. There always comes a time when corrective actions are needed in an organization! Monitoring

GLOBAL CAPSULE 9

India's Big Shift Away from China on Solar Panels[3]

Instead of building massive solar farms using cheap panels imported from China, India has switched abruptly to building its own solar panels. India says being dependent on importing fossil fuels from other countries as they do now is not much different than being dependent on importing solar panels from China; both strategies make India dependent, and India needs to be independent on energy. So, India has instructed its energy companies, such as Re-New Energy Global PLC and Acme Solar Holdings Ltd., to begin to produce solar panels and components on a large scale as the country draws down on its imports from China.

Prime Minister Narendra Modi of India has pledged to the world that by 2070 his country will eliminate net carbon emissions and that India will meet half of its own energy requirements with renewable energy by 2030. These plans regarding renewable energy are considered to be perhaps the most aggressive and far-reaching of all countries. To facilitate the strategic transition, the Indian government is employing

Paulose NK/Shutterstock

new tactics that include (1) placing high tariffs on solar panel imports, (2) providing huge subsidies for in-house companies to build solar panel and components factories inside India, and (3) banning imports of solar panels from China. First Solar Inc., based in the United States, is among a dozen companies now building or planning to build solar panel factories in India to avoid high duties and tariffs and to help India help the world with its new agenda.

[3]Based on Phred Dvorak, "India Seeks Its Own Solar Industry," *Wall Street Journal*, December 16, 2021, p. B4.

and managing change is vital. Centuries ago, a writer (perhaps Solomon) made the following observations about change:

> There is a time for everything,
> A time to be born and a time to die,
> A time to plant and a time to uproot,
> A time to kill and a time to heal,
> A time to tear down and a time to build,
> A time to weep and a time to laugh,
> A time to mourn and a time to dance,
> A time to scatter stones and a time to gather them,
> A time to embrace and a time to refrain,
> A time to search and a time to give up,
> A time to keep and a time to throw away,
> A time to tear and a time to mend,
> A time to be silent and a time to speak,
> A time to love and a time to hate,
> A time for war and a time for peace.[4]

Managers and employees of a firm should be kept up-to-date regarding progress being made toward achieving a firm's objectives. If assumptions, expectations, or results deviate significantly from forecasts, then strategy evaluation is needed. Evaluating strategies is like formulating and implementing strategies in the sense that people make the difference. Through involvement in the process of evaluating strategies, managers and employees become committed to keeping the firm moving steadily toward achieving objectives.

As indicated in the Global Capsule 9, even countries engage in the three strategy evaluation activities revealed and discussed in this chapter. India has reevaluated its strategy for becoming much less reliant on fossil fuels and much more reliant on renewable energy, especially solar; India has made a dramatic shift in its tactics.

Three Strategy Evaluation Activities

9.2. Discuss three activities that comprise strategy evaluation.

Table 9-1 summarizes three strategy evaluation activities in terms of key questions that should be addressed, alternative answers to those questions, and appropriate actions for an organization to take. Notice that corrective actions are almost always needed except when (1) external and internal factors have not significantly changed and (2) the firm is progressing satisfactorily toward achieving stated objectives.

TABLE 9-1 A Strategy Evaluation Assessment Matrix

Have Major Changes Occurred in the Firm's Internal Strategic Position?	Have Major Changes Occurred in the Firm's External Strategic Position?	Has the Firm Progressed Satisfactorily Toward Achieving Its Stated Objectives?	Result
No	No	No	Take corrective actions
Yes	Yes	Yes	Take corrective actions
Yes	Yes	No	Take corrective actions
Yes	No	Yes	Take corrective actions
Yes	No	No	Take corrective actions
No	Yes	Yes	Take corrective actions
No	Yes	No	Take corrective actions
No	No	Yes	Continue present strategic course

Reviewing Bases of Strategy

Relationships among strategy evaluation activities are illustrated in Figure 9-2. As shown, **reviewing the underlying bases of an organization's strategy** could be approached by developing a revised External Factor Evaluation (EFE) Matrix and Internal Factor Evaluation (IFE) Matrix. A **revised IFE Matrix** should focus on changes in the organization's management, marketing, finance, accounting, production, and management information systems (MIS) strengths and weaknesses. A **revised EFE Matrix** should indicate how effective a firm's strategies have been in response to new opportunities and threats. This analysis could also address such questions as the following:

1. How have competitors reacted to our strategies?
2. How have competitors' strategies changed?
3. Have major competitors' strengths and weaknesses changed?
4. Why are competitors making certain strategic changes?
5. Why are some competitors' strategies more successful than others?
6. How satisfied are our competitors with their present market positions and profitability?
7. How far can our major competitors be pushed before retaliating?
8. How could we more effectively cooperate with our competitors?

Numerous external and internal factors can prevent firms from achieving long-term and annual objectives. Externally, actions by competitors, changes in demand, changes in technology, economic changes, demographic shifts, and governmental actions may prevent objectives from being accomplished. Internally, ineffective strategies may have been chosen or implementation activities may have been poor. Objectives may have been too optimistic. Thus, failure to achieve objectives may not be the result of unsatisfactory work by managers and employees. All organizational members need to know this to encourage their support for strategy evaluation activities. Organizations desperately need to know as soon as possible when their strategies are not effective. Sometimes managers and employees on the front lines discover this well before strategists. It is not a question of *whether* underlying key external and internal factors will change, but rather *when* they will change and in what ways. Here are some key questions to be answered in performing a revised EFE Matrix and IFE Matrix in evaluating strategies:

1. Are our internal strengths still strengths?
2. Have we added other internal strengths? If so, what are they?
3. Are our internal weaknesses still weaknesses?
4. Do we now have other internal weaknesses? If so, what are they?
5. Are our external opportunities still opportunities?
6. Are there now other external opportunities? If so, what are they?
7. Are our external threats still threats?
8. Are there now other external threats? If so, what are they?
9. Are we vulnerable to a hostile takeover?

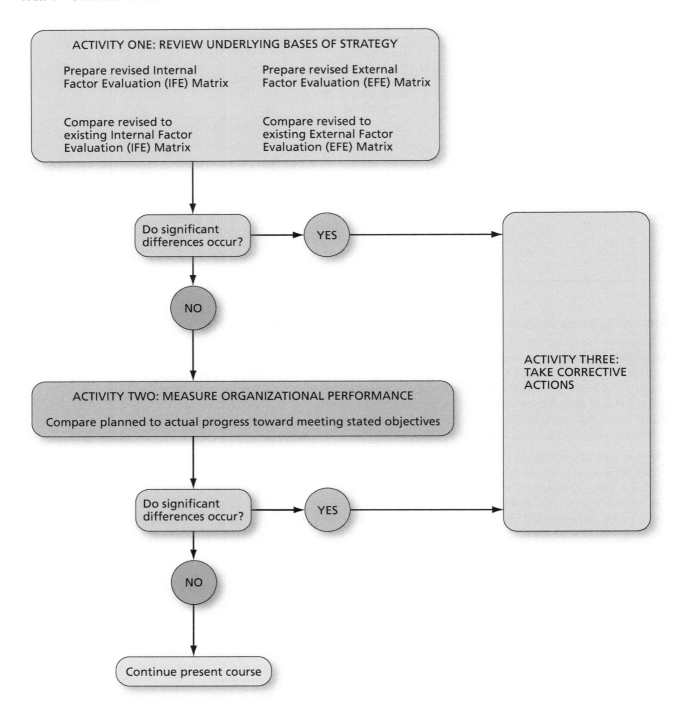

FIGURE 9-2

A Strategy Evaluation Framework

Measuring Organizational Performance

Another important strategy evaluation activity is **measuring organizational performance**. This activity includes comparing expected results to actual results, investigating deviations from plans, evaluating individual performance, and examining progress being made toward meeting stated objectives. Both long-term and annual objectives are commonly used in this process. Criteria for evaluating strategies should be measurable and easily verifiable. Criteria that predict results may be more important than those that reveal what already has happened. For example, rather than simply being informed that sales in the last quarter were 20 percent under what was expected, strategists need to know that sales in the next quarter may be 20 percent below standard unless some action is taken to counter the trend. Really effective control requires accurate forecasting.

Failure to make satisfactory progress toward accomplishing long-term or annual objectives signals a need for corrective actions. Many factors, such as unreasonable policies, unexpected turns in the economy, unreliable suppliers or distributors, or ineffective strategies, can result in unsatisfactory progress toward meeting objectives. Problems can result from ineffectiveness (not doing the right things) or inefficiency (poorly doing the right things).

Determining which objectives are most important in the evaluation of strategies can be difficult. Strategy evaluation is based on both quantitative and qualitative criteria. Selecting the exact set of criteria for evaluating strategies depends on a particular organization's size, industry, strategies, and management philosophy. An organization pursuing a retrenchment strategy, for example, could have a different set of evaluative criteria than an organization pursuing a strategy for market development. Quantitative criteria commonly used to evaluate strategies are financial ratios, often monitored for each segment of the firm. Strategists use financial ratios to make three critical comparisons:

1. Compare the firm's performance over different time periods.
2. Compare the firm's performance to competitors.
3. Compare the firm's performance to industry averages.

Many variables can and should be included in measuring organizational performance. Monitoring various key ratios can help identify problems because you know the numerator and denominator and thus the relationship, so an unexpected ratio can quickly point to a possible issue or area to investigate. As indicated in Table 9-2, typically a favorable or unfavorable variance is recorded monthly, quarterly, and annually, and resultant actions needed are then determined.

TABLE 9-2 A Sample Framework for Assessing Organizational Performance

Factor	Actual Result	Expected Result	Variance	Action Needed
Corporate Revenues				
Corporate Profits				
Corporate ROI				
Region 1 Revenues				
Region 1 Profits				
Region 1 ROI				
Region 2 Revenues				
Region 2 Profits				
Region 2 ROI				
Product 1 Revenues				
Product 1 Profits				
Product 1 ROI				
Product 2 Revenues				
Product 2 Profits				
Product 2 ROI				

Potential problems are associated with using only quantitative criteria for evaluating strategies. First, most quantitative criteria are geared toward annual objectives rather than long-term objectives. Also, different accounting methods can provide different results on many quantitative criteria. Third, intuitive judgments are almost always involved in deriving quantitative criteria. Thus, qualitative criteria are also important in evaluating strategies. Human factors such as high absenteeism and turnover rates, poor production quality and quantity rates, or low employee satisfaction can be underlying causes of declining performance. Marketing, finance, accounting, or MIS factors can also cause financial problems. The need for a "balanced" quantitative/qualitative approach in evaluating strategies gives rise in a moment to discussion of the balanced scorecard.

Several additional key questions that reveal the need for qualitative judgments in strategy evaluation are as follows:

1. How effective is the firm's balance of investments between high-risk and low-risk projects?
2. How effective is the firm's balance of investments between long-term and short-term projects?
3. How effective is the firm's balance of investments between slow-growing markets and fast-growing markets?
4. How effective is the firm's balance of investments among different divisions?
5. To what extent are the firm's alternative strategies socially responsible?
6. What are the relationships among the firm's key internal and external strategic factors?
7. How are major competitors likely to respond to particular strategies?

Taking Corrective Actions

The final strategy evaluation activity, **taking corrective actions**, requires making changes to competitively reposition a firm for the future. As indicated in Table 9-3, examples of changes that may be needed are altering an organization's structure, replacing one or more key individuals, selling a division, or revising a business mission. Other changes could include establishing or revising objectives, devising new policies, issuing stock to raise capital, adding additional salespersons, allocating resources differently, or developing new performance incentives. Taking corrective actions does not necessarily mean that existing strategies will be abandoned or even that new strategies must be formulated.

TABLE 9-3 Corrective Actions Possibly Needed to Correct Unfavorable Variances

1. Alter the firm's structure.
2. Replace one or more key individuals.
3. Divest a division.
4. Alter the firm's vision or mission.
5. Revise objectives.
6. Alter strategies.
7. Devise new policies.
8. Install new performance incentives.
9. Raise capital with stock or debt.
10. Add or terminate salespersons, employees, or managers.
11. Allocate resources differently.
12. Outsource (or reshore) business functions.

If either the actions or results of employees, departments, or divisions do not comply with preconceived or planned achievements, then corrective actions are needed. No organization can survive as an island; no organization can escape change. Taking corrective actions is necessary to keep an organization on track toward achieving stated objectives. In his thought-provoking books *Future Shock* and *The Third Wave*, Alvin Toffler argued that business environments are becoming so dynamic and complex that they threaten people and organizations with **future shock**, which occurs when the nature, types, and speed of changes overpower an individual's or organization's ability and capacity to adapt. Strategy evaluation enhances an organization's ability to adapt successfully to changing circumstances.

Taking corrective actions raises employees' and managers' anxieties. Research suggests that participation in strategy evaluation activities is one of the best ways to overcome individuals' resistance to change. According to Erez and Kanfer, individuals accept change best when they have a cognitive understanding of the changes, a sense of control over the situation, and an awareness that necessary actions are going to be taken to implement the changes.[5] The most successful organizations today continuously adapt to changes in the competitive environment. It is not sufficient today to simply react to change. Managers must anticipate change and be the creator of change.

Strategy evaluation can lead to strategy formulation or strategy implementation changes, or no changes at all. Strategists cannot escape having to revise strategies and implementation approaches sooner or later. Hussey and Langham offered the following insight on taking corrective actions:

> Resistance to change is often emotionally based and not easily overcome by rational argument. Resistance may be based on such feelings as loss of status, implied criticism of present competence, fear of failure in the new situation, annoyance at not being consulted, lack of understanding of the need for change, or insecurity in changing from well-known and fixed methods. It is necessary, therefore, to overcome such resistance by creating situations of participation and full explanation when changes are envisaged.[6]

Corrective actions should place an organization in an improved position to capitalize on internal strengths; to take advantage of key external opportunities; to avoid, reduce, or mitigate external threats; and to improve internal weaknesses. Corrective actions should have a proper time horizon and an appropriate amount of risk. They should be internally consistent and socially responsible. Perhaps most important, corrective actions strengthen an organization's competitive position in its basic industry. Continuous strategy evaluation keeps strategists close to the pulse of an organization and provides information needed for an effective strategic management system. Carter Bayles described the benefits of strategy evaluation as follows:

> Evaluation activities may renew confidence in the current business strategy or point to the need for actions to correct some weaknesses, such as erosion of product superiority or technological edge. In many cases, the benefits of strategy evaluation are much more far-reaching, for the outcome of the process may be a fundamentally new strategy that will lead, even in a business that is already turning a respectable profit, to substantially increased earnings. It is this possibility that justifies strategy evaluation, for the payoff can be very large.[7]

The Balanced Scorecard

9.3. Describe and develop a Balanced Scorecard.

Do a Google search using the keywords *balanced scorecard images*, and you will see more than a hundred currently used balanced scorecards. Note the wide variation in format evidenced through the images. Developed in the early 1990s by Harvard Business School professors Robert Kaplan and David Norton, and refined continually through today, the **balanced scorecard** is a strategy evaluation and control technique. The technique is based on the need of firms to "balance" financial measures that are often used exclusively in strategy evaluation with nonfinancial measures such as product quality, business ethics, environmental sustainability, employee morale, pollution abatement, community involvement, and customer service. The rationale behind the balanced scorecard is that financial measures report what has already happened, whereas nonfinancial metrics have a tendency to better predict what will happen in the future. An effective balanced scorecard contains a carefully chosen combination of strategic and financial objectives tailored to the company's business.

As a tool to manage and evaluate strategy, the balanced scorecard is currently in use at United Parcel Service (UPS), 3M Corporation, Heinz, and hundreds of other firms. For example, 3M Corporation has a financial objective to achieve annual growth in earnings per share of 10 percent or better, as well as a strategic objective to have at least 30 percent of sales come from products introduced in the past 4 years. The overall aim of a balanced scorecard is to "balance" shareholder objectives with customer and operational objectives. These sets of objectives interrelate and many even conflict. For example, customers want low price and high service, which may conflict with shareholders' desire for a high return on their investment.

A sample balanced scorecard is provided in Table 9-4. Notice that the firm examines six key issues in evaluating its strategies: (1) Customers, (2) Managers/Employees, (3) Operations/Processes, (4) Community/Social Responsibility, (5) Business Ethics/Natural Environment, and (6) Financial. The balanced scorecard approach to strategy evaluation aims to balance long-term with short-term concerns, to balance financial with nonfinancial concerns, and to balance internal with external concerns. The balanced scorecard could be constructed differently—that is, adapted to particular firms in various industries with the underlying theme or thrust being the same, which is to evaluate the firm's strategies based on both key quantitative and qualitative measures. Companies strive to achieve both quantitative and qualitative objectives all along their value chain, from end-users to raw materials, as discussed in Chapter 5.

TABLE 9-4 An Example Balanced Scorecard

Area of Objectives	Measure or Target	Time Expectation	Primary Responsibility
Customers			
1.			
2.			
3.			
4.			
Managers/Employees			
1.			
2.			
3.			
4.			
Operations/Processes			
1.			
2.			
3.			
4.			
Community/Social Responsibility			
1.			
2.			
3.			
4.			
Business Ethics/Natural Environment			
1.			
2.			
3.			
4.			
Financial			
1.			
2.			
3.			
4.			

Boards of Directors: Governance Issues

9.4. Discuss the role of a board of directors (governance) in strategic planning.

A **board of directors** is a group of individuals at the top of an organization with oversight and guidance over management and who look out for shareholders' interests. The act of oversight and direction is referred to as **governance**. The National Association of Corporate Directors defines *governance* as "the characteristic of ensuring that long-term strategic objectives and plans are established and that the proper management structure is in place to achieve those objectives, while at the same time making sure that the structure functions to maintain the corporation's integrity, reputation, and responsibility to its various constituencies." Boards are held accountable for the entire performance of an organization. Boards of directors are increasingly sued by shareholders for mismanaging their interests. New accounting rules in the United States and Europe now enhance corporate governance codes and require much more extensive financial disclosure among publicly held firms. The roles and duties of a board of directors can be divided into four broad categories, as indicated in Table 9-5.

TABLE 9-5 Board of Director Duties and Responsibilities

1. Control and Oversight over Management

   a. Select the CEO.
   b. Sanction the CEO's team.
   c. Provide the CEO with a forum.
   d. Ensure managerial competency.
   e. Evaluate management's performance.
   f. Set management's salary levels, including fringe benefits.
   g. Guarantee managerial integrity through continuous auditing.
   h. Evaluate corporate strategies.
   i. Devise and revise policies to be implemented by management.

2. Adherence to Legal Prescriptions

   a. Keep abreast of new laws.
   b. Ensure the entire organization fulfills legal prescriptions.
   c. Pass bylaws and related resolutions.
   d. Select new directors.
   e. Approve capital budgets.
   f. Authorize borrowing, new stock issues, bonds, and so on.

3. Consideration of Stakeholders' Interests

   a. Monitor product quality.
   b. Facilitate upward progression in employee quality of work life.
   c. Review labor policies and practices.
   d. Improve the customer climate.
   e. Keep community relations at the highest level.
   f. Use influence to better governmental, professional association, and educational contacts.
   g. Maintain good public image.

4. Advancement of Stockholders' Rights

   a. Preserve stockholders' equity.
   b. Stimulate corporate growth so that the firm will survive and flourish.
   c. Guard against equity dilution.
   d. Ensure equitable stockholder representation.
   e. Inform stockholders through letters, reports, and meetings.
   f. Declare proper dividends.
   g. Guarantee corporate survival.
   h. Guarantee the firm's financial statements are feasible and accurate.

Shareholders are increasingly wary of boards of directors. Most directors globally have ended their image as rubber-stamping friends of CEOs. Boards are more autonomous than ever and continually mindful of and responsive to legal and institutional-investor scrutiny. Boards are more cognizant of auditing and compliance issues and more reluctant to approve excessive compensation and perks. Boards stay much more abreast today of public scandals that attract shareholder and media attention. Increasingly, boards of directors monitor and review executive performance carefully without favoritism to executives, representing shareholders rather than the CEO. Boards are more proactive today, whereas in years past they were often merely reactive. These are all reasons why the chair of the board of directors should not also serve as the firm's CEO. In North America, the number of new incoming CEOs that also serve as chair of the board has declined to about 10 percent today from about 50 percent 15 years ago.

Until recently, individuals serving on boards of directors did most of their work sitting around polished mahogany tables. However, Hewlett-Packard's directors, among many others, now log on to their own special board website twice a week and conduct business based on extensive confidential briefing information posted there by the firm's top management team. Then the board members meet face-to-face every 2 months to discuss consequential, prominent issues facing the firm. New board involvement policies are aimed at curtailing lawsuits against board members.

Research reveals that companies with fewer board members outperform those with larger boards, largely because having fewer directors facilitates deeper debates, more nimble decision-making, and greater accountability.[8] Also, among companies with a market capitalization of at least $10 billion, smaller boards produce substantially higher shareholder returns. Specifically, 9-person boards perform much better, for example, than 14- to 15-member boards. Thus, many companies are reducing their number of board members. As part of a major restructuring, GE recently reduced the size of its board from 18 to 13. This change brings GE closer to the national average of 10 board members per US firm with a market capitalization of at least $10 billion.

Another benefit of fewer board members is that CEOs are more often reprimanded (or dismissed) if needed. Dr. David Yermack, a finance professor at New York University's business school, reports that smaller boards are generally more decisive, more cohesive, more hands-on, and have more informal meetings and fewer committees. Bank of America has 14 directors (as of May 2022)—too many to be efficient. In addition, the chair of the board should rarely, if ever, be the same person as the CEO, as discussed. In summary, companies should seek to reduce their board of directors to fewer than 10 persons, whenever possible—and strategy students should examine this issue in their assigned case companies.

Today, boards of directors are composed mostly of outsiders who are becoming more involved in organizations' strategic management. The trend in the United States is toward much greater board member accountability with smaller boards, now averaging 10 members rather than 18 as they did a few years ago.

BusinessWeek provides the following "principles of good governance":

1. Never have more than two of the firm's executives (current or past) on the board.
2. Never allow a firm's executives to serve on the board's audit, compensation, or nominating committee.
3. Require all board members to own a large amount of the firm's equity.
4. Require all board members to attend at least 75 percent of all meetings.
5. Require the board to meet annually to evaluate its own performance, without the CEO, COO, or top management in attendance.
6. Never allow the CEO to be chairperson of the board.
7. Never allow interlocking directorships (where a director or CEO sits on another director's board).[9]

Jeff Sonnenfeld, Senior Associate Dean of the Yale School of Management, comments, "Boards of directors are now rolling up their sleeves and becoming much more closely involved with management decision making." Company CEOs and boards are required to personally certify financial statements; company loans to company executives and directors are illegal; and there is faster reporting of insider stock transactions. Just as directors place more emphasis on staying informed about an organization's health and operations, they are also taking a more active role in ensuring that publicly issued documents are accurate representations of a firm's status. Failure to accept responsibility for auditing or evaluating a firm's strategy is considered a serious breach of a director's duties. Legal suits are becoming more common against directors for fraud, omissions, inaccurate disclosures, lack of due diligence, and culpable ignorance about a firm's operations.

Challenges in Strategic Management

9.5. Identify and discuss four challenges in strategic management.

Four particular challenges that face all strategists today are (1) deciding whether the process should be more an art or a science, (2) deciding whether strategies should be visible or hidden from stakeholders, (3) contingency planning, and (4) auditing.

The Art or Science Issue

This book is consistent with most of the strategy literature in advocating that strategic management be viewed more as a science than an art. This perspective contends that firms need to systematically assess their external and internal environments, conduct research, carefully evaluate the pros and cons of various alternatives, perform analyses, and then decide on a particular course of action. In contrast, Mintzberg's notion of "crafting" strategies embodies the artistic model, which suggests that strategic decision-making be based primarily on holistic thinking, intuition, creativity, and imagination.[10] Mintzberg and his followers reject strategies that result from objective analysis, preferring instead subjective imagination. In contrast, "strategy scientists" reject strategies that emerge from emotion, hunch, creativity, and politics. Proponents of the artistic view often consider strategic planning exercises to be time poorly spent. The Mintzberg philosophy insists on informality, whereas strategy scientists (including this text's authors) insist on more formality. Mintzberg refers to strategic planning as an "emergent" process, whereas strategy scientists use the term *deliberate* process.[11]

The answer to the art-versus-science question is one that strategists must decide for themselves, and certainly the two approaches are not mutually exclusive. The CEO of Williams-Sonoma, Laura Alber, recently stated, "I've found that the very best solutions arise from a willingness to blend art with science, ideas with data, and instinct with analysis." In deciding which approach is more effective, however, consider that the business world today has become increasingly complex and more intensely competitive. There is less room for error in strategic planning. Recall that Chapter 1 discussed the importance of intuition, experience, and subjectivity in strategic planning, and even the weights and ratings discussed in Chapter 3, Chapter 4, and Chapter 6 certainly require good judgment. But the idea of deciding on strategies for any firm without thorough research and analysis, at least in the mind of these authors, is unwise. Certainly, in smaller firms there can be more informality in the process compared to larger firms, but even for smaller firms, a wealth of competitive information is available on the internet and elsewhere and should be collected, assimilated, and evaluated before deciding on a course of action on which survival of the firm may hinge. The livelihood of countless employees and shareholders may hinge on the effectiveness of strategies selected. Too much is at stake to be less than thorough in formulating strategies. It is not wise for a strategist to rely too heavily on gut feeling and opinion instead of research data, competitive intelligence, and analysis in formulating strategies.

The Visible or Hidden Issue

An interesting aspect of any competitive analysis discussion is whether strategies themselves should be secret or open within firms. The mini-case at the end of this chapter examines this issue for TJX Companies, a secretive company. The Chinese warrior Sun Tzu and military leaders today strive to keep strategies secret because war is based on deception. But for business organizations, secrecy may not be best. Keeping strategies secret from employees and stakeholders at large could severely inhibit employee and stakeholder communication, understanding, and commitment, as well as forgo valuable input that these persons could have regarding formulation or implementation of those strategies. As indicated in the Ethics Capsule 9, CEO Bipul Sinha considers transparency to be the key to his company's success.

Strategists must decide for themselves whether the risk of rival firms easily knowing and exploiting a firm's strategies is worth the benefit of improved employee and stakeholder motivation and input. Most executives agree that some strategic information should remain confidential to top managers and that steps should be taken to ensure that such information is not disseminated beyond the inner circle. For a firm that you may own or manage, would you advocate more openness or secrecy in regard to strategies being formulated and implemented?

There are excellent reasons to keep the strategy process and strategies themselves visible and open rather than hidden and secret. There are also excellent reasons to keep strategies hidden from all but top-level executives. Strategists must decide for themselves what is most effective for their firms. This text comes down largely on the side of being visible and open, but certainly this approach may not be most effective for all strategists and all firms. As pointed out in Chapter 1, Sun Tzu argued that all war is based on deception and that the best maneuvers are those not easily predicted by rivals. Business and war are analogous in many respects.

Four reasons to be primarily open with the strategy process and resultant decisions are as follows:

1. Managers, employees, and other stakeholders can readily contribute to the process. They often have excellent ideas. Secrecy would forgo many excellent ideas.
2. Investors, creditors, and other stakeholders have greater basis for supporting a firm when they know what the firm is doing and where the firm is going.

ETHICS CAPSULE 9

Rubrik's CEO Bipul Sinha: "Achieve Exemplary Business Ethics Through Exemplary Transparency"[12]

Based in Palo Alto, California, Rubrik is a data management company whose CEO, Bipul Sinha, has established a culture of complete openness as a means of achieving superior business ethics. Sinha believes extreme honesty helps create a strong corporate culture that spurs entrepreneurialism, innovativeness, motivation, commitment, and integrity. Even the company's board of director meetings are completely open to all 600 of the company's employees, and most employees either attend in person or via teleconference to listen, view, and ask questions. The only aspect of company operations off limits or secret within the firm is confidential client information. Led by CEO Sinha, Rubrik was ranked for the fifth time in 2021 as being among the *Forbes* Cloud 100 that annually ranks the world's best private cloud companies. Other firms that made the 2021 list were Stripe, Databricks, and Canva.

In contrast to Rubrik's transparency, GE's board of directors did not know until the *Wall Street Journal* reported it in 2017 that their former CEO Jeff Immelt had an extra jet follow his corporate jet on many of his overseas trips during his 16-year tenure as CEO. Immelt resigned days after the disclosure. However, an increasing number of companies and organizations are in fact providing employees with regular updates on how the firm is doing financially and what, where, when, and why. This is evident even among private (not public) companies. Approximately 43 percent of all private firms today share financial information with all employees, up from 24 percent in 2012. That is nearly a 100 percent increase. Greater communication yields greater understanding that leads to greater commitment which results in higher performance.

[12]Based on: John Simons, "A Startup Where Board Meetings Are Open to All," *Wall Street Journal*, October 30, 2017, p. R11. Also, Thomas Gryta, Joann Lublin, and Mark Maremont, "GE Board in Dark on CEO's Use of Extra Jet," *Wall Street Journal*, October 30, 2017, p. B1.

3. Visibility promotes democracy, whereas secrecy promotes autocracy. Domestic firms and most foreign firms prefer democracy over autocracy as a management style.
4. Participation and openness enhance understanding, commitment, and communication within the firm.

Four reasons why some firms prefer to conduct strategic planning in secret and keep strategies hidden from all but the highest-level executives are as follows:

1. Free dissemination of a firm's strategies may easily translate into competitive intelligence for rival firms who could exploit the firm given that information.
2. Secrecy limits criticism, second-guessing, and hindsight.
3. Participants in a visible strategy process become more attractive to rival firms who may lure them away.
4. Secrecy limits rival firms from imitating or duplicating the firm's strategies and undermining the firm.

The obvious benefits of the visible versus hidden extremes suggest that a working balance must be sought between the apparent contradictions. Parnell says that in a perfect world all key individuals both inside and outside the firm should be involved in strategic planning, but in practice, particularly sensitive and confidential information should always remain strictly confidential to top managers.[13] This balancing act is difficult but essential for survival of the firm.

Promote Workplace Democracy

Employees at more and more companies are voting on more and more issues. For example, employees at InContext Solutions recently voted on whether to play music in office common areas. Employees at Whole Foods Market vote quite often on issues. Research suggests that giving employees a voice or vote on even small issues such as holiday parties helps to spark loyalty to the company. InContext employees recently voted on whether to have cubicles or open tables and even on which brews to keep in the company keg. Expensify employees vote on the pay of other Expensify employees, including the CEO's pay.

Whole Foods employees vote on whether to keep new employees beyond a trial period of up to 90 days. Menlo Innovations employees vote on job applicants after observing how candidates work during a trial period. 1Sale.com employees recently voted to do away with free lunches in favor of lower health insurance premiums. Social Tables Inc. employees recently voted on the company's core values, as well as the company's conference room themes and the company theme song played at corporate events. The strategic decision at hand for many companies increasingly is the extent to allow or encourage employee voting on numerous large and small issues that affect workplace productivity and morale.

A recent *Wall Street Journal* article titled "Pay Is Less Secretive in Millennial Workforce" reveals that in this day and age of sharing social contacts, pictures, and videos, millennials are issuing in a new corporate culture of democracy and openness (rather than secrecy), even with compensation systems. Research reveals that roughly one-third of US workers ages 18 to 36 say they are comfortable discussing pay with their coworkers, unlike baby boomers, ages 53 to 71, who are four times more likely to want to keep pay secret. More than half of all millennials talk about pay with their friends whether pay is secret or not.

Contingency Planning

A basic premise of excellent strategic management is that firms strive to be proactive, planning ways to deal with unfavorable and favorable events before they occur. Too many organizations prepare contingency plans just for unfavorable events; this is a mistake because both minimizing threats and capitalizing on opportunities can improve a firm's competitive position.

Regardless of how carefully strategies are formulated, implemented, and evaluated, unforeseen events, such as strikes, boycotts, natural disasters, arrival of foreign competitors, and government actions, can make a strategy obsolete. To minimize the impact of potential threats and capitalize on opportunities, organizations should develop contingency plans as part of their strategy evaluation process. **Contingency plans** can be defined as alternative plans that can be put into effect if certain key events do not occur as expected. Only high-priority areas require the insurance of contingency plans. Strategists cannot and should not try to cover all bases by planning for all possible contingencies. But in any case, contingency plans should be as simple as possible.

Some contingency plans commonly established by firms include the following:

1. If a major competitor withdraws from particular markets as intelligence reports indicate, what actions should our firm take?
2. If our sales objectives are not reached, what actions should our firm take to avoid profit losses?
3. If demand for our new product exceeds plans, what actions should our firm take to meet the higher demand?
4. If certain disasters occur—such as loss of computer capabilities; a hostile takeover attempt; loss of patent protection; or destruction of manufacturing facilities because of earthquakes, tornadoes, or hurricanes—what actions should our firm take?
5. If a new technological advancement makes our new product obsolete sooner than expected, what actions should our firm take?

Too many organizations discard alternative strategies not selected for implementation although the work devoted to analyzing these options would render valuable information. Alternative strategies not selected for implementation can serve as contingency plans in case the strategy or strategies selected do not work. When strategy evaluation activities reveal the need for a major change quickly, an appropriate contingency plan can be executed in a timely way. Contingency plans can promote a strategist's ability to respond quickly to key changes in the internal and external bases of an organization's current strategy. For example, if underlying assumptions about the economy turn out to be wrong and contingency plans are ready, then managers can make appropriate changes promptly. Sometimes, external or internal conditions present unexpected opportunities. When such opportunities occur, contingency plans could allow an organization to quickly capitalize on them. Linneman and Chandran report that contingency planning gives users, such as DuPont, Dow Chemical, Consolidated Foods, and Emerson Electric, three major benefits, as follows:

1. It enables quick responses to change.
2. It prevents panic in crisis situations.
3. It makes managers more adaptable by encouraging them to appreciate just how variable the future can be.

In addition, Linneman and Chandran suggest that effective contingency planning involves a five-step process, as follows:

1. Identify both good and bad events that could jeopardize strategies.
2. Determine when the good and bad events are likely to occur.
3. Determine the expected pros and cons of each contingency event.
4. Develop contingency plans for key contingency events.
5. Determine early warning trigger points for key contingency events.[14]

Auditing

A frequently used tool in strategy evaluation is the audit. **Auditing** is defined by the American Accounting Association (AAA) as "a systematic process of objectively obtaining and evaluating evidence regarding assertions about economic actions and events to ascertain the degree of correspondence between these assertions and established criteria, and communicating the results to interested users."[15]

Auditors examine the financial statements of firms to determine whether they have been prepared according to **generally accepted accounting principles (GAAP)** and whether they fairly represent the activities of the firm. Independent auditors use a set of standards called **generally accepted auditing standards (GAAS)**. Public accounting firms often have a consulting arm that provides strategy evaluation services.

The new era of **international financial reporting standards (IFRS)** is approaching in the United States, and businesses need to go ahead and get ready to use IFRS. Many US companies now report their finances using both the old GAAP and the new IFRS. "If companies don't prepare, if they don't start three years in advance," warns business professor Donna Street at the University of Dayton, "they're going to be in big trouble." The GAAP standards are comprised of 7,592 pages, whereas the IFRS comprises 4,640 pages, so in that sense IFRS is less cumbersome.

Most large accounting firms and multinational firms favor the switch to IFRS, saying it will simplify accounting, make it easier for investors to compare firms across countries, and make it easier to raise capital globally. But many smaller firms oppose the upcoming change, believing it will be too costly; some firms are uneasy about the idea of giving an international body the authority to write accounting rules for the United States. Some firms also would pay higher taxes because last in, first out (LIFO) inventory methods are not allowed under IFRS. The International Accounting Standards Board (IASB) has publicly expressed "regret" over the slowness in the United States of adopting IFRS.

The US Chamber of Commerce supports a change, saying it will lead to much more cross-border commerce and will help the United States compete in the world economy. Already the European Union and 120 nations have adopted or soon plan to use international rules, including Australia, China, India, Mexico, and Canada. So, the United States is likely to adopt IFRS rules, but this switch could unleash a legal and regulatory nightmare. A few US multinational firms already use IFRS for their foreign subsidiaries, such as United Technologies (UT), which derives more than 60 percent of its revenues from abroad and is already training its entire staff to use IFRS.

Guidelines for Effective Strategic Management

9.6. Identify and describe 17 guidelines for effective strategic management.

Failing to follow certain guidelines in conducting strategic management can foster criticisms of the process and create problems for the organization. Issues such as "Is strategic management in our firm a people process or a paper process?" should be addressed. Some organizations spend an inordinate amount of time developing a strategic plan, but then fail to follow through with effective implementation. Change and results in a firm come through implementation, not through formulation, although effective formulation is critically important for successful implementation. Continual evaluation of strategies is also essential because the world changes so rapidly that existing strategies can need modifying often.

Strategic management must not become a self-perpetuating bureaucratic mechanism. Rather, it must be a self-reflective learning process that familiarizes managers and employees in the organization with key strategic issues and feasible alternatives for resolving those issues. Strategic management must not become ritualistic, stilted, orchestrated, or too formal, predictable, and rigid. Words supported by numbers, rather than numbers supported by words, should represent the medium for explaining strategic issues and organizational responses. A key role of strategists is to facilitate continuous organizational learning and change.

R. T. Lenz offers six guidelines for effective strategic management:

1. Keep the process simple and easily understandable.
2. Eliminate vague planning jargon.
3. Keep the process nonroutine; vary assignments, team membership, meeting formats, settings, and even the planning calendar.
4. Welcome bad news and encourage devil's advocate thinking.
5. Do not allow technicians to monopolize the planning process.
6. To the extent possible, involve managers from all areas of the firm.[16]

An important guideline for effective strategic management is open-mindedness. A willingness and eagerness to consider new information, new viewpoints, new ideas, and new possibilities is essential; all organizational members must share a spirit of inquiry and learning. Strategists such as CEOs, presidents, owners of small businesses, and heads of government agencies must commit themselves to listen to and understand managers' positions well enough to be able to restate those positions to the managers' satisfaction. In addition, managers and employees throughout the firm should be able to describe the firm's strategies to the satisfaction of the strategists. This degree of discipline will promote understanding and learning.

Strategy evaluation activities must be economical; too much information can be as detrimental as too little information, and too many controls can do more harm than good. Strategy evaluation activities also should be meaningful; they should specifically relate to a firm's objectives. They should provide managers with useful information about tasks over which they have control and influence. Strategy evaluation activities should provide timely information; on occasion and in some areas, managers may need information on a daily or even continuous basis. For example, when a firm has diversified by acquiring another firm, evaluative information may be needed frequently. In contrast, in an R&D department, daily or even weekly evaluative information could be unnecessary. Approximate information that is timely is generally more desirable as a basis for strategy evaluation than accurate information that does not depict the present. Frequent measurement and rapid reporting may frustrate control rather than give better control. The time dimension of control must coincide with the time span of the event being measured.

Strategy evaluation processes should be designed to provide a true picture of what is happening. For example, in a severe economic downturn, productivity and profitability ratios may drop alarmingly, although employees and managers may actually be working harder. Strategy evaluations should fairly portray this type of situation. Information derived from the strategy evaluation process should facilitate action and should be directed to those individuals in the organization who need to take action based on it. Managers commonly ignore evaluative reports that are provided only for informational purposes; not all managers need to receive all reports. Controls need to be action-oriented rather than information-oriented. The strategy evaluation process should not dominate decisions; it should foster mutual understanding, trust, and common sense. No department should fail to cooperate with another in evaluating strategies. Strategy evaluations should be simple, not too cumbersome, and not too restrictive. Complex strategy evaluation systems often confuse people and accomplish little. The test of an effective evaluation system is its usefulness, not its complexity.

Large organizations require a more elaborate and detailed strategy evaluation system because it is more difficult to coordinate efforts among different divisions and functional areas. Managers in small companies often communicate daily with each other and their employees and do not need extensive evaluative reporting systems. Familiarity with local environments usually makes gathering and evaluating information much easier for small organizations than for large businesses. But the key to an effective strategy evaluation system may be the ability to convince participants that failure to accomplish certain objectives within a prescribed time is not necessarily a reflection of their performance.

There is no one ideal strategy evaluation system. The unique aspects of an organization, including its size, management style, purpose, problems, and strengths, can determine a strategy evaluation and control system's final design. Robert Waterman offered the following observation about successful organizations' strategy evaluation and control systems:

> Successful companies treat facts as friends and controls as liberating. Successful companies have a voracious hunger for facts. They see information where others see only data. Successful companies maintain tight, accurate financial controls. Their people don't regard controls as an imposition of autocracy but as the benign checks and balances that allow them to be creative and free.[17]

No organization has unlimited resources. No firm can take on an unlimited amount of debt or issue an unlimited amount of stock to raise capital. Therefore, no organization can pursue all the strategies that potentially could benefit the firm. Strategic decisions, then, always have to be made to eliminate some courses of action and to allocate organizational resources among others. Most organizations can afford to pursue only a few corporate-level strategies at any given time. It is a critical mistake for managers to pursue too many strategies at the same time, thereby spreading the firm's resources so thin that all strategies are jeopardized.

Strategic decisions require tradeoffs such as long-range versus short-range considerations or maximizing profits versus increasing shareholders' wealth. There are ethics issues, too. Strategy trade-offs require subjective judgments and preferences. In many cases, a lack of objectivity in formulating strategy results in a loss of competitive posture and profitability. Most organizations today recognize that strategic management concepts and techniques can enhance the effectiveness of decisions. Subjective factors such as attitudes toward risk, concern for social responsibility, and organizational culture will always affect strategy formulation decisions, but organizations need to be as objective as possible in considering qualitative factors. Table 9-6 summarizes important guidelines for the strategic-planning process to be effective.

TABLE 9-6 17 Guidelines for the Strategic-Planning Process to Be Effective

1. It should be a people process more than a paper process.
2. It should be a learning process for all managers and employees.
3. It should be words supported by numbers rather than numbers supported by words.
4. It should be simple, nonroutine, economical, and provide timely information.
5. It should vary assignments, team memberships, meeting formats, and even the planning calendar.
6. It should challenge the assumptions underlying the current corporate strategy.
7. It should welcome bad news and provide a true picture of what is happening.
8. It should welcome open-mindedness and a spirit of inquiry and learning.
9. It should not be a bureaucratic mechanism.
10. It should not become ritualistic, stilted, or orchestrated.
11. It should not be too formal, predictable, or rigid.
12. It should not contain jargon or arcane planning language.
13. It should not be a formal system for control and should not dominate decisions.
14. It should not disregard qualitative information.
15. It should not be controlled by "technicians."
16. Do not pursue too many strategies at once.
17. Continually strengthen the "good ethics is good business" policy.

IMPLICATIONS FOR STRATEGISTS

Figure 9-3 reveals on the far left that strategists must systematically, continuously, and carefully evaluate and monitor results by product, region, territory, segment, store, department, and even by individual, so that timely corrective actions can be taken to keep the firm on track. Quarterly, weekly, and even daily, companies have to adapt to changes that occur externally and internally because even the best strategic plan needs periodic adjusting as rival firms adjust and launch new initiatives and products in new areas. As described in this chapter, the balanced scorecard is widely used by strategists to help manage the strategy evaluation process.

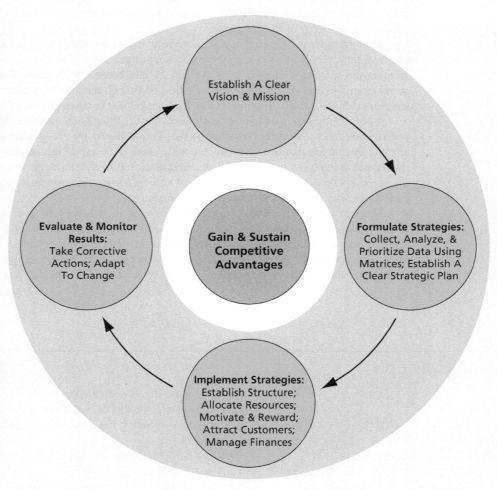

FIGURE 9-3

How to Gain and Sustain Competitive Advantages

IMPLICATIONS FOR STUDENTS

In performing your case analysis, develop and present a balanced scorecard that you recommend to help your firm monitor and evaluate progress toward stated objectives. Effective, timely evaluation of strategies can enable a firm to adapt quickly to changing conditions, and a balanced scorecard can assist in this endeavor. Couch your discussion of the balanced scorecard in terms of competitive advantages versus rival firms.

Chapter Summary

Effective strategy evaluation allows an organization to capitalize on internal strengths as they develop, to exploit external opportunities as they emerge, to recognize and defend against threats, and to mitigate or improve weaknesses before they become detrimental.

Strategists in successful organizations take the time to formulate, implement, and then evaluate strategies deliberately and systematically. Exemplary strategists move their organization forward with purpose and direction, continually evaluating and improving the firm's external and internal strategic positions. Strategy evaluation allows an organization to shape its own future rather than allowing it to be constantly shaped by remote forces that have little or no vested interest in the well-being of the enterprise.

Although not a guarantee for success, strategic management allows organizations to make effective long-term decisions, to execute those decisions efficiently, and to take corrective actions as needed to ensure success. Computer networks and the internet help to coordinate strategic management activities and to ensure that decisions are based on timely, accurate information. A key to effective strategy evaluation and to successful strategic management is an integration of intuition and analysis.

A potentially fatal problem is the tendency for analytical and intuitive issues to polarize. This polarization leads to strategy evaluation that is dominated by either analysis or intuition or to strategy evaluation that is discontinuous, with a lack of coordination among analytical and intuitive issues. Strategists in successful organizations realize that strategic management is first and foremost a people process. It is an excellent vehicle for fostering organizational communication. People are what make the difference in organizations.

The real key to effective strategic management is to accept the premise that the planning process is more important than the written plan, that the manager is continuously planning and does not stop planning when the written plan is finished. The written plan is only a snapshot as of the moment it is approved. If the manager is not planning on a continuous basis—planning, measuring, and revising—the written plan can become obsolete the day it is finished.

Key Terms and Concepts

auditing (p. 288)
balanced scorecard (p. 281)
board of directors (p. 282)
contingency plans (p. 287)
future shock (p. 280)
generally accepted accounting principles (GAAP) (p. 288)
generally accepted auditing standards (GAAS) (p. 288)
governance (p. 282)

international financial reporting standards (IFRS) (p. 288)
measuring organizational performance (p. 278)
reviewing the underlying bases of an organization's strategy (p. 277)
revised EFE Matrix (p. 277)
revised IFE Matrix (p. 277)
taking corrective actions (p. 280)

Issues for Review and Discussion

9-1. Do a Google search using the terms *balanced score-card images*. Review the many different formats of the balanced scorecard currently being used by organizations. Decide on three formats that you believe are particularly effective.

9-2. Do a Google search using the terms *balanced score-card adopters*. Review the many different organizations currently using the balanced scorecard as part of their strategic planning. Select three different companies or organizations. Compare and contrast their use of the balanced scorecard technique.

9-3. Give several hypothetical situations whereby a company should establish contingency plans.

9-4. Explain why companies continually evaluate their strategies, rather than waiting until the end of the quarter or fiscal year to engage in the three core strategy evaluation activities discussed in this chapter.

9-5. Which of the three core strategy evaluation activities do you think is most critical to be performed well? Why?

9-6. If a firm has two regions and two products, develop a sample framework for measuring organizational performance.

9-7. Compare strategy formulation with strategy implementation in terms of each being an art or a science.

9-8. Discuss the pros and cons of a transparent management style similar to that used by CEO Bipul Sinha of Rubrik.

9-9. How does an organization know if it is pursuing "optimal" strategies?

9-10. Discuss the nature and implications of the anticipated accounting switch from GAAP to IFRS in the United States.

9-11. Ask an accounting professor at your college or university the following question and report back to the class: "To what extent would learning the IFRS standards on my own give me competitive advantage in the job market?"

9-12. Evaluating strategies on a continuous rather than a periodic basis is desired. Discuss the pros and cons of this statement.

9-13. Why has strategy evaluation become so important in businesses today?

9-14. What types of quantitative and qualitative criteria should be used to evaluate a company's strategy?

9-15. As owner of a local, independent barbecue restaurant, explain how you would evaluate the firm's strategy.

9-16. Under what conditions are corrective actions (contingency plans) not required in the strategy evaluation process?

9-17. Identify types of organizations that may need to evaluate strategy more frequently than others. Justify your choices.

9-18. As executive director of the local Chamber of Commerce, in what way and how frequently would you evaluate the organization's strategies?

9-19. Identify some key financial ratios that would be important in evaluating a bank's strategy.

9-20. Strategy evaluation allows an organization to take a proactive stance toward shaping its own future. Discuss the meaning of this statement.

9-21. Diagram and discuss the balanced scorecard.

9-22. Develop a balanced scorecard for a local movie cinema complex.

9-23. Do you believe strategic management is more an art or a science? Explain.

9-24. Regarding the strategic planning process, give four "should be" guidelines and four "should not be" guidelines.

9-25. Researchers say contingency planning is a five-step process. Identify and discuss the five steps.

9-26. Identify and discuss five characteristics of effective strategy evaluation.

9-27. Identify and discuss four reasons to be open (visible) in regard to the strategic planning process and outcomes.

9-28. Identify and discuss four reasons to be closed (secret) in regard to the strategic planning process and outcomes.

Writing Assignments

9-29. Why is the balanced scorecard an important topic both in devising objectives and in evaluating strategies?

9-30. Do you believe strategic management should be more visible or hidden as a process in a firm? Explain.

ASSURANCE-OF-LEARNING EXERCISES

SET 1: STRATEGIC PLANNING FOR MCDONALD'S

EXERCISE 9A

Develop a Balanced Scorecard for McDonald's

Ken Wolter/Alamy Photo

Purpose

Balanced scorecards are widely used by companies to "balance" their financial with nonfinancial objectives. Do a Google search using the phrase "McDonald's balanced scorecard" or "balanced scorecard images" or "balanced scorecard examples" to see examples.

Instructions

Step 1   Prepare a new and improved balanced scorecard for McDonald's.

Step 2   Explain why your recommended balanced scorecard is best for McDonald's.

SET 2: STRATEGIC PLANNING FOR MY UNIVERSITY

EXERCISE 9B

Prepare a Strategy Evaluation Report for My University

Purpose

Virtually all institutions of higher learning monitor financial and other operating ratios such as those listed here, and take appropriate corrective actions as needed to address unfavorable variances. Be mindful that all companies and organizations, even colleges, develop unique sets of ratios to measure performance.

Ratios Monitored by Colleges and Universities	Actual Value	Expected Value	Variance
1. Tuition monies ($) received per student (#)			
2. Number of students (#) per faculty (#)			
3. Number of faculty (#) per grant monies ($) received			
4. Contributions ($) per contributor (#)			
5. Number of male students (#) per total of students (#)			
6. Number of female students (#) per total of students (#)			
7. Number of minority students (#) per total of students (#)			
8. Number of international students (#) per total of students (#)			
9. Increase/decrease (%) in number of students (#)			
10. Increase/decrease (%) in number of out-of-state students (#)			
11. Increase/decrease (%) in number of international students (#)			
12. Increase/decrease (%) in number of minority students (%)			
13. Long-term debt ($) to total assets ($)			
14. Current assets ($) to current liabilities ($)			
15. Number of business students (#) per total students (#)			
16. Number of out-of-state students (#) per total students (#)			
17. Growth/decline (%) in number of MBA students (#)			
18. Growth/decline (%) in number of BBA students (#)			
19. Number of accounting majors (#) per number of BBA students (#)			
20. Number of management majors (#) per number of BBA students (#)			
21. Number of finance majors (#) per number of BBA students (#)			
22. Number of marketing majors (#) per number of BBA students (#)			

Instructions

Step 1	Review your college's website and annual report to obtain as much comparative information as possible to fill in the table. Review your college's most recent accreditation report, such as the Southern Association of Colleges and Schools (SACS) Accreditation Report.
Step 2	Speak with the School of Business Dean's Office personnel to gather additional information to complete the above table.
Step 3	Based on the information gathered, prepare a strategy evaluation report for your college or university.

SET 3: STRATEGIC PLANNING TO ENHANCE MY EMPLOYABILITY

EXERCISE 9C

A Balanced Scorecard to Evaluate My Professional versus Personal Objectives

Purpose

A balanced scorecard can be used by individuals to help balance their professional and personal objectives and lives. Some variables commonly included are given in Table 9-7:

TABLE 9-7 A Balanced Scorecard for Individual Assessment

Area of Objectives	Expected Target	Actual Target	Variance	Action Needed
Professional				
A. Current Employer				
1. Pay				
2. Benefits				
3. Potential for Growth				
B. Potential Future Employer				
1. Pay				
2. Benefits				
3. Potential for Growth				
Personal				
A. Social				
1. Marital status				
2. Friend status				
3. Online activity				
4. Offline activity				
B. Health				
1. Body weight				
2. Nutrition intake				
3. Exercise quotient				
4. Stress level				

Instructions

Step 1	In Table 9-7, reveal your professional and personal objectives, and your progress to date on achieving those objectives.
Step 2	In Table 9-7, in the variance column, indicate Very Favorable (VF), Favorable (F), Unfavorable (U), or Very Unfavorable (VU) to reveal your status on each item measured.
Step 3	In Table 9-7, reveal corrective actions that you plan going forward. A corrective action should be stated for each item that has a less than Favorable variance.

SET 4: INDIVIDUAL VERSUS GROUP STRATEGIC PLANNING

EXERCISE 9D

How Important Are Various Guidelines for Effective Strategic Management?

Purpose

This chapter discusses numerous guidelines that should be followed in formulating, implementing, and evaluating strategies. Ten guidelines associated with the strategic planning process are as follows:

1. It should be a people process more than a paper process.
2. It should be a learning process for all managers and employees.
3. It should be words supported by numbers rather than numbers supported by words.

4. It should vary assignments, team memberships, meeting formats, and even the planning calendar.
5. It should challenge the assumptions underlying the current corporate strategy and welcome bad news.
6. It should welcome open-mindedness and a spirit of inquiry and learning.
7. It should not become ritualistic, stilted, orchestrated, or rigid.
8. It should not be a formal system for control.
9. It should not be controlled by "technicians."
10. Do not pursue too many strategies at once.

The purpose of this exercise is to examine more closely guidelines for the strategic planning process to be most effective. In addition, the purpose of this exercise is to examine whether individual decision-making is better than group decision-making. Academic research suggests that groups make better decisions than individuals about 80 percent of the time.

Instructions

Rank the 10 guidelines as to their relative importance for the strategic planning process to be effective, where 1 = most important to 10 = least important. First, rank the guidelines as an individual. Then, rank the guidelines as part of a group of three. Thus, determine what person(s) and what group(s) come closest to the expert ranking. This exercise enables examination of the relative effectiveness of individual versus group decision-making in strategic planning.

Steps

1. Fill in Column 1 in Table 9-8 to reveal your individual ranking of the relative importance of the 10 guidelines (1 = most important, 2 = next most important, to 10 = least important). For example, if you think Guideline 1 (People Process) is the eighth-most important guideline, then enter an 8 in Table 9-8 in Column 1 beside Guideline 1.
2. Fill in Column 2 in Table 9-8 to reveal your group's ranking of the relative importance of the 10 guidelines (1 = most important, 2 = next most important, to 10 = least important).
3. Fill in Column 3 in Table 9-8 to reveal the expert's ranking of the 10 guidelines.
4. Fill in Column 4 in Table 9-8 with the absolute difference between Column 1 and Column 3 to reveal how well you performed as an individual in this exercise. (Note: Absolute difference disregards negative numbers.)
5. Fill in Column 5 in Table 9-8 with the absolute difference between Column 2 and Column 3 to reveal how well your group performed in this exercise.
6. Sum Column 4. Sum Column 5.
7. Compare the Column 4 sum to the Column 5 sum. If your Column 4 sum is less than your Column 5 sum, then you performed better as an individual than as a group. Normally, group decision-making is superior to individual decision making, so if you did better than your group, you did excellent.
8. The Individual Winner(s): The individual(s) with the lowest Column 4 sum is the WINNER.
9. The Group Winners(s): The group(s) with the lowest Column 5 score is the WINNER.

TABLE 9-8 Strategic-Planning Guidelines Analysis: Comparing Individual Versus Group Decision-Making

Strategic-Planning Guidelines	Column 1	Column 2	Column 3	Column 4	Column 5
1.					
2.					
3.					
4.					
5.					
6.					
7.					
8.					
9.					
10.					
Sums					

MINI-CASE ON TJX COMPANIES, INC. (TJX)

SECRET STRATEGIC PLANNING WORKS GREAT FOR TJX[18]

2p2play/Shutterstock

Headquartered in Framingham, Massachusetts, TJX Companies is a discount apparel and home fashions retailer in the United States and abroad. The company owns T.J. Maxx, Marshalls, HomeGoods, TJX Canada, TJX Europe, HomeSense, and Sierra—operating 4,665 stores in nine countries: United States, Canada, UK, Ireland, Germany, Poland, Austria, the Netherlands, and Australia. TJX's annual sales and profits are increasing nicely. The number of stores at year-end 2021 include 1,285 T.J. Maxx, 1,145 Marshalls, 846 HomeGoods, 52 Sierra, and 39 HomeSense stores, as well as tjmaxx.com and sierratradingpost.com in the United States; 292 Winners, 147 HomeSense, and 105 Marshalls stores in Canada; 616 T.J. Maxx and 78 HomeSense stores, as well as tjmaxx.com, in Europe; and 66 T.J. Maxx stores in Australia.

Regarding its corporate strategic planning and evaluation process, TJX is one of the most secretive of all publicly held retailers. As discussed in this chapter, there are numerous advantages and disadvantages of being secretive rather than open in revealing corporate strategy. TJX's former CEO, Carol Meyrowitz, as well as her top executives, rarely gave interviews and never discussed corporate strategy. TJX does not talk about its corporate strategy in part because rival firms are eager to learn this information to duplicate, imitate, undermine, and replicate. However, *Fortune* reports that "excellent inventory control" is a secret to the strategic success of TJX, including the following practices:

1. Turn inventory over quickly. According to Morningstar, TJX turns over inventory every 55 days, versus 85 days for its peer group. TJX is structured to quickly buy and sell merchandise. Often, merchandise is sold before TJX has paid its vendors. Quick inventory turnover keeps new merchandise on the floor so customers rarely see the same items on repeat visits. TJX trains employees to "buy when you see it; otherwise it will be gone."
2. Provide "value, trendy merchandise," not "cheap, leftover merchandise."
3. Promote the "treasure hunt" experience rather than catering to lower-income customers. Even high-income customers love the treasure hunt experience in TJX stores.
4. Train buyers extensively and then give buyers autonomy to negotiate millions of dollars of purchases from suppliers. Purchase inventory year-round, continuously rather than seasonally, and purchase as close to the time of need as possible to negotiate a better price and be assured of the latest fashion trend. Negotiate low prices for purchases even if it means often purchasing "all available items in a category."

Questions

1. What are the advantages and disadvantages of keeping the strategic planning process secret versus placing the firm's strategic plan on the corporate website and discussing strategies and planning publicly?
2. What are three types of industries where secrecy is warranted and three industries where secrecy is not warranted, or does type of industry even matter?
3. Many colleges and universities have their strategic plan posted on their website. What are the advantages and disadvantages of this practice?
4. Rank order the four "secret" practices listed in terms of how important you think the items are to TJX's overall success. Rank the four items from 1 = most important to 4 = least important.

[18]Based on a variety of sources and on information at http://fortune.com/2014/07/24/t-j-maxx-the-best-retail-store/?icid=maing-grid7%7Chtmlws-main-bb%7Cdl30%7Csec1_lnk3%26pLid%3D508272 and at https://investor.tjx.com/news-releases/news-release-details/tjx-companies-inc-reports-very-strong-q3-fy22-sales-and-eps

---

Web Resources

1. Fred David gives a video overview of Chapter 9 in the prior edition, but much info is still applicable to the 18th edition: https://www.youtube.com/watch?v=hj2tC_UKqEE

2. This search result url gives many balanced scorecard examples and images: https://www.google.com/search?q=balanced+scorecard+images&client=safari&channel=mac_bm&sxsrf=AOaemvLloLNw5Cn8G7ZIQMXfEzZugviFzQ%

3A1639687337635&source=hp&ei=qaS7YbbpIpHKytMP
wtiF8AM&iflsig=ALs-wAMAAAAAYbuyuf6X2YKZq
UoCj9AMVGem_wg34fZT&ved=0ahUKEwj24bGql-
n0AhURpXIEHUJsAT4Q4dUDCAw&uact=5&oq=
balanced+scorecard+images&gs_lcp=Cgdnd3Mtd2l6
EAMyBQgAEIAEOgQIIxAnOgoILhDHARDRAxAnOg
UIABCRAjoOCC4QgAQQsQMQxwEQowI6CAgu
ELEDEIMBOgsILhCABBDHARCjAjoICAAQg
AQQsQM6EAgAEIAEEIcCELEDEIMBEBQ6
EQguEIAEELEDEIMBEMcBEKMCOgUILhCABDo

LCC4QgAQQxwEQrwE6CAguEIAEELEDOg4
ILhCABBCxAxDHARDRAzoLCAAQgAQQsQMQgw
E6CggAEIAEEIcCEBQ6DQgAEIAEEIc
CELEDEBQ6BggAEBYQHjoICAAQFhAKEB5QAFj2
KWDfLmgAcAB4AIABd4gBzBGSAQQyMi4zm
AEAoAEB&sclient=gws-wiz

3. The following website gives excellent narrative and guidelines for corporate governance: https://corpgov.law.harvard.edu/2021/03/03/2021-global-and-regional-trends-in-corporate-governance/

Current Readings

Amer, Faten, Sahar Hammoud, Haitham Khatatbeh, Szimonetta Lohner, Imre Boncz, and Dóra Endrei, "The Deployment of Balanced Scorecard in Health Care Organizations: Is it Beneficial? A Systematic Review," *BMC Health Services Research* 22, no. 1 (2022): 1-14.

Balaji, M., S. N. Dinesh, P. Manoj Kumar, and K. Hari Ram, "Balanced Scorecard Approach in Deducing Supply Chain Performance," *Materials Today: Proceedings* 47 (2021): 5217-22.

Boivie, Steven, Michael C. Withers, Scott D. Graffin, and Kevin G. Corley, "Corporate Directors' Implicit Theories of the Roles and Duties of Boards," *Strategic Management Journal* 42, no. 9 (September 2021) 1662–95.

Camilleri, Mark Anthony, "Using the Balanced Scorecard as a Performance Management Tool in Higher Education," *Management in Education* 35, no. 1 (2021): 10-21.

Gai, Shelby L., J. Yo-Jud Cheng, and Andy Wu, "Board Design and Governance Failures at Peer Firms," *Strategic Management Journal* 42, no. 10 (October 2021): 1909–38.

García, C. José, and Begoña Herrero, "Female Directors, Capital Structure, and Financial Distress," *Journal of Business Research* 136 (2021): 592–601.

Hawn, Olga, "How Media Coverage of Corporate Social Responsibility and Irresponsibility Influences Cross-Border Acquisitions," *Strategic Management Journal* 42, no. 1 (2021): 58–83.

Jaber, Ahmad A. Abu, and Abdulqadir J. Nashwan, "Balanced Scorecard-Based Hospital Performance Measurement Framework: A Performance Construct Development Approach," *Cureus* 14, no. 5 (2022).

Mio, Chiara, Antonio Costantini, and Silvia Panfilo, "Performance Measurement Tools for Sustainable Business: A Systematic Literature Review on the Sustainability Balanced Scorecard Use," *Corporate Social Responsibility and Environmental Management* 29, no. 2 (2022): 367-84.

Ongsakul, Viput, Sirimon Treepongkaruna, Pornsit Jiraporn, and Ali Uyar, "Do Firms Adjust Corporate Governance in Response to Economic Policy Uncertainty? Evidence from Board Size," *Finance Research Letters* 39 (2021): 101613.

Pierce, Elizabeth, "A Balanced Scorecard for Maximizing Data Performance," *Frontiers in Big Data* 5 (2022).

Post, Corinne, David J. Ketchen Jr., and Kaitlin D. Wowak, "Should Governments Mandate More Female Board Representation? Possible Intended and Unintended Consequences," *Business Horizons* 64, no. 3 (2021): 379–84.

Quesado, Patrícia, Salomé Marques, Rui Silva, and Alexandrino Ribeiro, "The Balanced Scorecard as a Strategic Management Tool in the Textile Sector," *Administrative Sciences* 12, no. 1 (2022): 38.

Schnatterly, Karen, Felipe Calvano, John P. Berns, and Chaoqun Deng, "The Effects of Board Expertise-Risk Misalignment and Subsequent Strategic Board Reconfiguration on Firm Performance," *Strategic Management Journal* 42, no. 11 (2021): 2162–91.

Tibiletti, Veronica, Pier Luigi Marchini, Katia Furlotti, and Alice Medioli, "Does Corporate Governance Matter in Corporate Social Responsibility Disclosure? Evidence from Italy in the 'Era of Sustainability'." *Corporate Social Responsibility and Environmental Management* 28, no. 2 (2021): 896–907.

Veltrop, Dennis B., Pieteer-Jan Bezemer, Gavin Nicholson, and Amedeo Pugliese, "Too Unsafe to Monitor? How Board-CEO Cognitive Conflict and Chair Leadership Shape Outside Director Monitoring," *Academy of Management Journal* 64, no. 1 (2021): 207–34.

Endnotes

1. On page 274.
2. Richard Rumelt, "The Evaluation of Business Strategy," in W. F. Glueck (ed.), *Business Policy and Strategic Management* (New York: McGraw-Hill, 1980), 359–67.
3. On page 276.
4. Ecclesiastes. 3:1–8.
5. M. Erez and F. Kanfer, "The Role of Goal Acceptance in Goal Setting and Task Performance," *Academy of Management Review* 8, no. 3 (1983): 457.
6. D. Hussey and M. Langham, *Corporate Planning: The Human Factor* (Oxford, England: Pergamon, 1979), 138.

7. Carter Bayles, "Strategic Control: The President's Paradox," *Business Horizons* 20, no. 4 (1977): 18.

8. Joann Lublin, "Are Smaller Boards Better for Investors?" *Wall Street Journal*, August 27, 2014. Also based on Den Favaro, Per-Ola Karlsson, and Gary Neilson, "The $112 Billion CEO Succession Problem," *Strategy + Business*, PwC Strategy (May 4, 2015).

9. Louis Lavelle, "The Best and Worst Boards," *BusinessWeek*, October 7, 2002, pp. 104–10.

10. Henry Mintzberg, "Crafting Strategy," *Harvard Business Review* (July–August 1987): 66–75.

11. Henry Mintzberg and J. Waters, "Of Strategies, Deliberate and Emergent," *Strategic Management Journal* 6, no. 2 (1985): 257–72.

12. On page 286.

13. John Parnell, "Five Critical Challenges in Strategy Making," *SAM Advanced Management Journal* 68, no. 2 (2003): 15–22.

14. Robert Linneman and Rajan Chandran, "Contingency Planning: A Key to Swift Managerial Action in the Uncertain Tomorrow," *Managerial Planning* 29, no. 4 (1981): 23–27.

15. American Accounting Association, *Report of Committee on Basic Auditing Concepts*, 1971, 15–74.

16. R. T. Lenz, "Managing the Evolution of the Strategic Planning Process," *Business Horizons* 30, no. 1 (1987): 39.

17. Robert Waterman, Jr., "How the Best Get Better," *BusinessWeek*, September 14, 1987, p. 105.

18. On page 297.

## PART 5

KEY STRATEGIC MANAGEMENT TOPICS

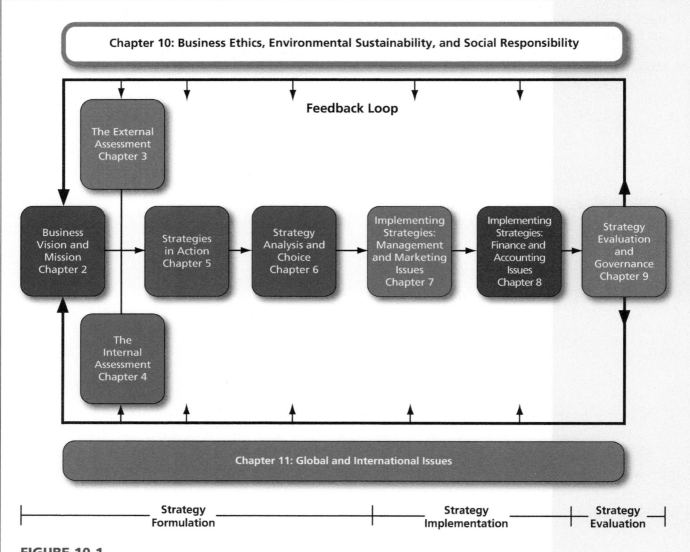

FIGURE 10-1

The Comprehensive, Integrative Strategic Management Model

Source: Fred R. David, "How Companies Define Their Mission," *Long Range Planning* 22, no. 1 (February 1989): 91. See also Anik Ratnaningsih, Nadjadji Anwar, Patdono Suwignjo, and Putu Artama Wiguna, "Balance Scorecard of David's Strategic Modeling at Industrial Business for National Construction Contractor of Indonesia," *Journal of Mathematics and Technology* no. 4, (October 2010): 20. Also, Meredith E. David, Fred R. David, and Forest R. David, "Closing the Gap Between Graduates' Skills and Employers' Requirements: A Focus on the Strategic Management Capstone Business Course," *Administrative Sciences* 11, no. 1 (2021): 10–26.

Business Ethics, Environmental Sustainability, and Corporate Social Responsibility

LEARNING OBJECTIVES

After studying this chapter, you should be able to do the following:

10.1. Explain why good ethics is good business in strategic management.

10.2. Explain why whistleblowing, bribery, and workplace romance are strategic issues.

10.3. Discuss why environmental sustainability is a key issue in strategic planning.

10.4. Discuss why corporate social responsibility (CSR) is a key issue in strategic planning.

ASSURANCE-OF-LEARNING EXERCISES

The following exercises are found at the end of this chapter:

SET 1:	Strategic Planning for McDonald's
EXERCISE 10A:	Does McDonald's (MCD) or Restaurant Brands International (RBI) Win on Diversity, Equity, and Inclusion (DEI)?
SET 2:	Strategic Planning for My University
EXERCISE 10B:	How Does My University Compare to Others on the Use of Green Power?
SET 3:	Strategic Planning for Myself
EXERCISE 10C:	What Is My Business Ethics Quotient?
SET 4:	Individual Versus Group Strategic Planning
EXERCISE 10D:	How Potentially Severe Are the Various Reasons Why Workplace Romance Should Be Discouraged?

Organizational performance entails more than simply profits. "People" and "Planet," collectively with "Profits," are commonly referred to as the three "Ps" that largely explain organizational performance. Increasingly, companies are following a **triple-bottom-line** approach, in which success depends on (1) the financial bottom line (profits), (2) the social bottom line (people), and (3) the natural environment bottom line (planet). Following a triple-bottom-line philosophy, organizations make conscious and strategic efforts to provide both financial profits to shareholders and contributions to communities in which the firm operates, all while minimizing damage to the environment.

Business ethics are "principles of conduct within organizations that guide decision-making and behavior." Good business ethics is a prerequisite for good strategic management; good ethics is good business! Ethics is about integrity, honesty, and fairness. **Social responsibility** refers to actions an organization takes beyond what is legally required to protect or enhance the well-being of all living things, including employees. Socially responsible actions would include providing daycare for employees' children or paying for college tuition for employees. **Sustainability** refers to the extent that an organization's operations and actions protect, mend, and preserve rather than harm or destroy the environment. Switching your firm's primary energy source to solar power is an example.

Business ethics, social responsibility, and environmental sustainability issues are interrelated and impact all areas of the strategic management process, as illustrated in Figure 10-1. The new CEO of CVS Health is Karen Lynch, a remarkable Exemplary Strategist who equates business ethics and corporate social responsibility with providing convenient, affordable health care to millions of people. In mid-2022, CVS Health is the fourth-largest US company (behind Walmart, Amazon, and Apple) and the highest-ranking *Fortune* 500 company to be run by a female.

All strategy formulation, implementation, and evaluation decisions have ethical ramifications. Strategists such as CEOs and business owners are the persons primarily responsible for

EXEMPLARY **STRATEGIST** SHOWCASED

Karen Lynch, CEO of CVS Health[1]

CEO Lynch's bold new strategy at CVS is to transform the company from being your local drugstore to being your local primary care all-in-one location for exemplary health care. Under CEO Lynch's leadership, CVS has transformed more than 1,000 of its 9,600 stores into HealthHUBs rather than just drugstores, and hundreds more CVS pharmacies are being transformed daily. Lynch believes that exemplary business ethics and social responsibility begins with exemplary health care, and she is steering CVS to lead the way in the United States to achieve the goal.

Lynch foresees thousands of CVS stores nationwide providing urgent care, primary care, and total care for all Americans that use the company's online services and walk-in medical doctor offices attached to or contained within CVS stores. She is transforming CVS into a provider of wellness, testing, counseling, and doctoring, rather than half of the retail space in many CVS stores that currently house retail products, snacks, gift cards, food, and beauty products.

Lynch is on a mission to prevent peoples' chronic conditions from getting worse and more costly. She is all about prevention, early detection, personal health, and wellness, with thousands of remodeled CVS locations now offering affordable, convenient urgent care, primary care, counseling, and treatment. Lynch is laser focused on the five long-lasting illnesses that account for 80 percent of the annual $3.8 trillion medical costs in the United States: (1) diabetes, (2) hypertension, (3) cardiac disease, (4) asthma, and (5) depression; half of all adult Americans suffer from one or more of those five ailments.

CVS is quickly evolving into providing three types of stores: (1) Super-Clinics that provide everything discussed in this capsule, (2) HealthHUBs that provide about three-fourths of what is discussed, and (3) MinuteClinics that will provide about half of the products and services discussed. But

JHVEPhoto/Shutterstock

among the three types of stores, the number of Super-Clinics is growing rapidly, while the number of HealthHUBs and MinuteClinics is staying constant. The company is actually closing 900 stores in 2022–2023 that cannot be easily transformed into the new CVS.

CVS' brightest future rests on being the US leader in business ethics and corporate social responsibility, which Lynch equates to exemplary, convenient, comprehensive, and affordable health care available for everyone at their neighborhood CVS.

[1]Based on Shawn Tully, "Karen Lynch, CEO, 58, CVS Health," *Fortune*, October/November 2021, pp. 60–61. Also, Sharon Terlep and Michael Dabaie, "CVS to Close 900 Stores in Shift Toward Offering Medical Services," *Wall Street Journal*, November 19, 2021, pp. B1 and B2.

ensuring that high ethical principles are espoused and practiced within an organization. Literally hundreds of business actions are unethical, including:

1. Misleading advertising or labeling
2. Causing environmental harm
3. Producing unsafe products or services
4. Padding expense accounts
5. Insider trading
6. Dumping banned or flawed products in foreign markets
7. Discriminating against women and people of color
8. Overpricing or price gouging
9. Sexual harassment, bullying, and favoritism
10. Using company resources for personal gain
11. Laundering money or engaging in bribery
12. Treating animals inhumanely
13. Overusing personal smartphone while at work
14. Polluting with inappropriate waste disposal
15. Engaging in a conflict of interest
16. Failing to protect employee and customer privacy
17. Giving inappropriate gifts
18. Failing to properly secure company records
19. Engaging in internet fraud or theft
20. Hacking into company computers
21. Phubbing (phone snubbing, such as being on your phone when meeting with others)

Why "Good Ethics Is Good Business"

10.1. Explain why good ethics is good business in strategic management.

A rising tide of consciousness regarding the importance of business ethics is sweeping the United States and the rest of the world. Moral breaches of ethical conduct by both public and private organizations are reported hourly on internet websites, newspapers, magazines, social media, news media, emails, and texts—quickly spreading fact and rumor pertaining to the inside dealings of firms.

Increasingly, executives' and managers' personal and professional decisions are placing them in the crosshairs of angry shareholders, disgruntled employees, and even their own board of directors—making the once imperious CEO far more vulnerable to personal, public, and corporate missteps. One reason CEO salaries are high is that they must take the moral risks of the firm. Strategists are responsible for developing, communicating, and enforcing a code of business ethics for their organizations. An integral part of the responsibility of all managers is to provide ethical leadership by constant example and demonstration. Managers hold positions that enable them to influence and educate many people; managers are responsible for developing and implementing ethical decision-making. Gellerman offers some good advice for managers:

> All managers risk giving too much because of what their companies demand from them. But the same superiors who keep pressing you to do more, or to do it better, or faster, or less expensively, will turn on you should you cross that fuzzy line between right and wrong. They will blame you for exceeding instructions or for ignoring their warnings. The smartest managers already know that the best answer to the question "How far is too far?" is "Don't try to find out."[2]

Does It Pay to Be Ethical?

The Institute of Business Ethics (IBE) recently conducted a study titled "Does Business Ethics Pay?" and concluded that companies displaying a "clear commitment to ethical conduct" consistently outperform companies that do not display ethical conduct. Table 10-1 provides some results of the IBE study. Similar research at DePaul University by Frigo and Litman suggests that it pays to be ethical. These researchers studied the financial performance of more than 15,000 public companies using 30 years of financial data and found that high-performing companies

TABLE 10-1 Seven Principles of Admirable Business Ethics

1. Be trustworthy; no individual or business wants to engage in business with an organization it does not trust.
2. Be open-minded, continually asking for "ethics-related feedback" from all internal and external stakeholders.
3. Honor all commitments and obligations.
4. Avoid misrepresenting, exaggerating, or misleading with print materials, actions, or words.
5. Visibly be a responsible community citizen.
6. Use your accounting practices to identify and eliminate questionable activities.
7. Follow the Golden Rule: "Do unto others as you would have them do unto you."

Source: Based on http://sbinformation.about.com/od/bestpractices/a/businessethics.htm

generally exhibit high business ethics.[3] Similarly, results of a 7-year study by Fred Kiel, author of *Return on Character*, which followed 8,000 employees and 84 top executives of *Fortune* 500 companies, indicated that character-driven leaders deliver five times greater profitability results and 26 percent higher workforce engagement than self-focused leaders. Being unethical is a recipe for headaches, inefficiency, and waste.

Bad ethics can derail even the best strategic plans. Drucker explained the following in terms of ethical leadership:

A man (or woman) might know too little, perform poorly, lack judgment and ability, and yet not do too much damage as a manager. But if that person lacks character and integrity—no matter how knowledgeable, how brilliant, or how successful—he destroys. He destroys people, the most valuable resource of the enterprise. He destroys spirit. And he destroys performance. This is particularly true of the people at the head of an enterprise because the spirit of an organization is created from the top. If an organization is great in spirit, it is because the spirit of its top people is great. If it decays, it does so because the top rots. As the proverb states, "Trees die from the top." No one should ever become a strategist unless he or she is willing to have his or her character serve as the model for subordinates.[4]

Reverend Billy Graham once said, "When wealth is lost, nothing is lost; when health is lost, something is lost; when character is lost, all is lost." An ethics "culture" needs to permeate organizations. No society anywhere in the world can compete long term or successfully with people stealing from one another or not trusting one another, with every bit of information requiring notarized confirmation, with every disagreement ending up in litigation, or with government having to regulate businesses to keep them honest. Recent examples of bad corporate cultures are Uber Technologies and Wells Fargo & Company where lawsuits specifically zeroed in on the firms' culture.

How to Establish an Ethics Culture

A key ingredient for establishing an ethics culture is to develop a clear **code of business ethics**; however, simply having a code of ethics is not sufficient to ensure ethical business behavior. Managers must take care in considering the specific details of the content of the code, how it will be implemented, and how adherence to it will be monitored. Otherwise, a code of ethics may not even be read, understood, or believed by employees, and the code itself may well be viewed as a public relations gimmick, a set of platitudes, or window dressing. Once implemented, the code of ethics should be reinforced by showing employees examples of punishment for violating the code. The website www.ethicsweb.ca/codes provides guidelines on how to write an effective code of ethics.

Companies should take active steps to ensure that the code is read, understood, believed, and remembered. Firms should consider implementing the following four practices recommended by the CEO of Better.com to adapt a firm's culture for better business ethics.[5]

1. Identify and correct any inconsistencies between what's preached and what's practiced.
2. Identify environmental changes that warrant new behaviors and adjust strategies accordingly.
3. Create a supportive culture and internal whistleblower process.
4. Encourage, reinforce, and reward desired behaviors.

Companies are increasingly formalizing cultural oversight within the organization. For example, board members at Whirlpool closely monitor the firm's culture through annual employee surveys, executive performance evaluations, and analysis of whistleblower activities. Citigroup and CACI International as well as many other firms have established formal committees designed to monitor corporate culture. To help create an ethics culture, Citicorp developed an interactive business ethics board game that is played by thousands of employees worldwide called "The Word Ethic." This game asks players business ethics questions, such as "How do you deal with a customer who offers you football tickets in exchange for a new, backdated IRA?"

History has proven that the greater the trust and confidence of people in the ethics of an institution or society, the greater its economic strength. Business relationships are built mostly on mutual trust and reputation. Short-term decisions based on greed and questionable ethics will preclude the necessary self-respect to gain the trust of others. More and more firms believe that ethics training and an ethical culture can create strategic advantage. According to Max Killan, "If business is not based on ethical grounds, it is of no benefit to society, and will, like all other unethical combinations, pass into oblivion." Several key ethical issues are discussed in greater detail in this chapter.

Being unethical is not abnormal or rare. Donald Palmer reports that misconduct is a normal phenomenon, that wrongdoing is as prevalent as "rightdoing," and that misconduct is most often done by people who are primarily good, ethical, and socially responsible.[6] Palmer reports that individuals engage in unethical activities because of a plethora of structure, processes, and mechanisms inherent in the functioning of organizations—and, importantly, all of us are candidates to be unethical in the right circumstances in any organization. Implications of this research abound for managers.

Increasingly across the globe, being an exemplary company regarding diversity, equity, and inclusion (DEI) issues is viewed admirably. Note in Global Capsule 10 that diversity varies substantially across countries.

GLOBAL CAPSULE 10

Usage of DEI Metrics Across Countries[7]

Companies globally are scrambling to develop, use, monitor, and make decisions based on numerous diversity, equality, and inclusion (DEI) metrics or variables that collectively characterize an institution's overall standing on DEI, including fairness regarding race, gender, and religious variables. DEI is often viewed as an assessment of an organization's integration of minorities, including women and people of color, into the workforce, so the same metrics are applicable globally. Every country is populated by roughly 50 percent females, and inclusion of females is an almost universal key component of DEI to be measured and improved.

In the United States, research says about 14 percent of the population self-identify as Black or African American. Racial diversity is growing in most nations, and according to a recent survey conducted by Pew Research Center, nearly 50 percent of individuals say that they favor a more racially diverse nation. Many nations already have a diverse population. For example, Trinidad and Tobago are quite diverse, including East Indians, Afro-Trinidadians, and mixed races. Belize is also racially diverse, including Mestizos, Kriols, Mayans, East Indians, and other races. Guyana is also racially diverse, including East Indians, Blacks, mixed races, and Chinese. Other racially diverse countries throughout the world include:

- Brazil
- Canada
- Colombia
- Panama
- Suriname
- United States

Some common metrics being used by companies to evaluate themselves, as well as their key suppliers and distributors, are:

Shutterstock

1. Diversity among applicant pool
2. Diversity among hiring panel
3. Diversity among new hires
4. Diversity among existing employees
5. Diversity among managers
6. Diversity among executives
7. Diversity among board of directors
8. Diversity among persons leaving the firm
9. Diversity among persons being promoted
10. Diversity among a firm's customer base
11. Variance on job satisfaction surveys by race, gender, and religion
12. Diversity among a firm's advertisements
13. To what extent are managers and executives' compensation or bonuses linked to progress being made on DEI variables?

[7]Based on https://www.cultureamp.com/blog/dei-metrics and https://www.pewresearch.org/social-trends/fact-sheet/facts-about-the-us-black-population/. Also, https://worldpopulationreview.com/country-rankings/most-racially-diverse-countries and https://www.govexec.com/management/2022/01/opm-issues-guidance-agency-hiring-chief-diversity-officers/360565/

Whistleblowing, Bribery, and Workplace Romance

10.2. **Explain why whistleblowing, bribery, and workplace romance are strategic issues.**

As social media and technology have become commonplace globally, three business ethics topics—whistleblowing, bribery, and workplace romance—have become important strategic issues facing companies. Missteps in any of these three areas can severely harm an organization.

Whistleblowing

Whistleblowing refers to employees reporting any unethical violations they discover or see in the firm. Employees should practice whistleblowing, and organizations should have policies that encourage whistleblowing. Thousands of firms warn managers and employees that failing to report an ethical violation by others could bring discharge.

The Securities and Exchange Commission's (SEC) whistleblowing policies virtually mandate that anyone seeing unethical activity must report such behavior. The website www.whistleblower.org describes dozens of recent whistleblower cases and rewards to individuals. Whistleblowers in the United States are protected under both the Sarbanes–Oxley and Dodd–Frank legislation.

Whistleblowers in the corporate world receive up to 25 percent of the proceeds of legal proceedings against firms for wrongdoing. Such payouts are becoming more and more common. Sean McKessy, a former SEC whistleblower top executive explains, "Whistleblowers from all over the world should feel similarly incentivized to come forward with credible information about potential violations of the U.S. securities laws." The SEC has paid more than $1 billion in whistleblower rewards over the past decade.

Ethics training programs should include messages from the CEO or owner of the business emphasizing ethical business practices, discussing the codes of ethics, and detailing procedures for reporting unethical behavior. Firms can align ethical and strategic decision-making by incorporating ethical considerations into strategic planning, integrating ethical decision-making into the performance-appraisal process, encouraging whistleblowing, and monitoring departmental and corporate performance regarding ethical issues.

The International Standards Organization (ISO), which is discussed later in this chapter, recently developed a new standard related specifically to whistleblowing. Specifically, ISO 37002 is the "Whistle-blowing Management Systems Standard" that provides guidance to organizations of all types and sizes regarding how to develop and maintain an effective whistle-blowing management system. The ISO 37002 includes guidance and standards for receiving, assessing, addressing, and concluding reports of whistleblowing wrongdoing.

Avoid Bribery

Bribery is defined by *Black's Law Dictionary* as the offering, giving, receiving, or soliciting of any item of value to influence the actions of an official or other person in performing a public or legal duty. A **bribe** is a gift bestowed to influence a recipient's conduct. The gift may be money, goods, actions, property, preferment, privilege, objects of value, advantage, or merely a promise or undertaking to induce the action, vote, or influence of a person in an official or public capacity.

Bribery is a crime in most countries, including the United States. Even in sports, bribery is unlawful. Antibribery and extortion initiatives are advocated by many global organizations, including the World Bank, the International Monetary Fund, the EU, the Council of Europe, the Organization of American States, the Pacific Basin Economic Council, the Global Coalition for Africa, and the United Nations. Tipping is even now considered bribery in some countries. Taking business associates to lavish dinners and giving them expensive holiday gifts and even outright cash may have been expected in some countries, such as South Korea and China, but there is now increased enforcement of bribery laws virtually everywhere. Countries with the lowest corruption rates include Denmark, New Zealand, Finland, Sweden, Switzerland, Norway, Singapore, Germany, and the UK. Information such as this impacts company strategic decisions regarding where in the world to do business.

Discussed later in this chapter, the ISO has a specific standard, ISO 37001, that addresses bribery by or of an organization, its personnel, or business associates. First established in 2016, the ISO 37001 is the "Anti-bribery Management Systems Standard" that helps organizations establish, implement, and maintain an effective antibribery compliance program. Microsoft recently fired some employees and terminated several partnerships due to allegations of bribery in some of its operations in the Middle East. The bribery allegations assert that throughout the Middle East, certain sales of Microsoft products were consummated with local third-party companies with kickbacks going to government officials and Microsoft employees.

Workplace Romance

Workplace romance is an intimate relationship between two consenting employees, as opposed to **sexual harassment**, which the Equal Employment Opportunity Commission (EEOC) defines broadly as unwelcome sexual advances, requests for sexual favors, and other verbal or physical conduct of a sexual nature. Sexual harassment (and discrimination) is illegal, unethical, and detrimental to any organization and can result in expensive lawsuits, lower morale, and reduced productivity. In 2022, Activision Blizzard fired or pushed out more than three dozen employees and disciplined another 40 related to allegations of sexual harassment and other misconduct at the videogame company.

Workplace romance between two consenting employees simply happens, so the question is generally not whether to allow the practice, or even how to prevent it, but rather how best to manage it. A recent survey by CareerBuilder found that nearly 40 percent of workers have dated a coworker, and approximately 30 percent of those relationships resulted in marriage.[8] An organization should not strictly forbid workplace romance because such a policy could be construed as an invasion of privacy, overbearing, or unnecessary. Some romances actually improve work performance, adding a dynamism and energy that translates into enhanced morale, communication, creativity, and productivity.[9] However, workplace romance could be detrimental to workplace morale and productivity for a number of reasons that include:

1. Favoritism complaints can arise.
2. Confidentiality of records can be breached.
3. Reduced quality and quantity of work can become a problem.
4. Personal arguments can lead to work arguments.
5. Whispering secrets can lead to tensions and hostilities among coworkers.
6. Sexual harassment (or discrimination) charges may ensue.
7. Conflicts of interest can arise, especially when the well-being of the partner trumps the well-being of the company.

In some states, such as California, managers can be held personally liable for damages that arise from workplace romance. Organizations should establish guidelines and policies that address workplace romance, for at least six reasons:

1. Guidelines can enable the firm to better defend against and avoid sexual harassment or discrimination charges.
2. Guidelines can specify reasons (such as the seven listed previously) why workplace romance may not be a good idea.
3. Guidelines can specify resultant penalties for romancing partners if problems arise.
4. Guidelines can promote a professional and fair work atmosphere.
5. Guidelines can help assure compliance with federal, state, and local laws, as well as recent court cases.
6. Lack of any guidelines sends a lackadaisical message throughout the firm.

A *Wall Street Journal* article recaps US standards regarding supervisor and subordinate romantic relationships at work.[10] The report reveals that only 5 percent of all firms sampled have no restrictions on such relationships; 80 percent of firms have policies that prohibit relationships between a supervisor and a subordinate; 4 percent of firms strictly prohibit all such relationships; 39 percent have policies that require individuals to inform their supervisors whenever a romantic relationship begins with a coworker; and 24 percent of firms require the two persons to be in different departments. *Wall Street Journal* (3-3-22, p. A15) reports that since transformation to remote work and Zoom meetings, workplace romance has increased dramatically. The article says remote work is boring and has spurred the need for remote relationships. In response to the rapid revival in workplace romance, many companies now require disclosure of any sexual relationships, just so the firm can better manage the drawbacks of such interactions at work or home, such as favoritism and breakup problems spilling over to become company problems.

In Europe, romantic relationships at work are largely viewed as private matters, and most firms have no policies on the practice. However, European firms are increasingly adopting explicit, US-style sexual harassment and workplace romance laws. The US military strictly bans officers from dating or having sexual relationships with enlistees. At the World Bank, sexual relations between a supervisor and an employee are considered "a de facto conflict of interest which must be resolved to avoid favoritism."

In general, company guidelines or policies should discourage workplace romance because "the downside risks generally exceed the upside benefits" for the firm. Workplace romance guidelines should specify certain situations in which affairs are especially discouraged, such as between a supervisor and subordinate, and should also detail the types of relationships allowed, such as between peer-level employees in different departments who also have different career paths. Importantly, the workplace romance policy guidelines should apply to all employees at all levels of the firm and should clearly state the actions management will take if employees violate any terms of the policy.

As a result of increasing sexual misconduct allegations across companies and organizations, more and more firms are requiring their employees to complete sexual harassment training. Most universities require all faculty to complete training regarding how to handle situations where a student mentions experiencing some form of sexual harassment by another student, faculty, or staff member. US laws require that faculty report any instance, claim, or even suggestion of sexual harassment from a student to university administrators.

Environmental Sustainability

10.3. Discuss why environmental sustainability is a key issue in strategic planning.

The ecological challenge facing all organizations requires managers to formulate strategies that preserve and conserve natural resources and control pollution. Special natural environment issues include global warming, depletion of rain forests, destruction of animal habitats, protecting endangered species, and waste management. Firms are increasingly developing green product lines that are biodegradable or made from recycled products. Managing the health of the planet requires an understanding of how international trade, competitiveness, and global resources are connected. Managing environmental affairs, for example, can no longer be simply a technical function performed by specialists in a firm; more emphasis must be placed on developing an environmental perspective among all employees and managers of the firm.

Businesses must not exploit and decimate the natural environment. Mark Starik at George Washington University believes, "Halting and reversing worldwide ecological destruction and deterioration is a strategic issue that needs immediate and substantive attention by all businesses and managers." According to the ISO, the word **environment** is defined as surroundings in which an organization operates, including air, water, land, natural resources, flora, fauna, humans, and their interrelation. Many firms are gaining competitive advantage by being good stewards of the natural environment. Green products sell well.

Employees, consumers, governments, and societies are often resentful of firms that harm rather than protect the natural environment. Conversely, people today are especially appreciative of firms that conduct operations in a way that mends, conserves, and preserves the natural environment. Consumer interest in businesses preserving nature's ecological balance and fostering a clean, healthy environment is at an all-time high.

Sustainability Reports and the Environmental Protection Agency (EPA)

A **sustainability report** reveals how a firm's operations impact the natural environment. This document discloses to shareholders information about the firm's labor practices, product sourcing, energy efficiency, environmental impact, and business ethics practices. For example, Coca-Cola's annual sustainability reports are provided online at http://www.coca-colacompany.com/stories/sustainability-reports.

No business wants the reputation of being a polluter. For the first time ever in the United States, cars, trucks, planes, and trains have displaced power plants as the biggest polluters. This trend is accelerating, as the nation's electrical grid gets cleaner faster than the transportation industry.

A poor sustainability record will hurt any firm in any market, jeopardize its standing in the community, and invite scrutiny by regulators, investors, and environmentalists. Governments increasingly demand businesses to behave responsibly and require, for example, that businesses publicly report the pollutants and wastes their facilities produce. It is simply good business for any organization to provide a sustainability report annually to the public. The Global Reporting Initiative provides a set of detailed reporting guidelines specifying what information should go into sustainability reports (https://www.globalreporting.org/information/sustainability-reporting/Pages/default.aspx).

Around the world, political and corporate leaders now realize that the "green business" topic is not going away and, in fact, is gaining ground rapidly. A few years ago, firms could get away with placing "green" terminology on their products and labels, using such terms as *organic, green, safe, earth-friendly, nontoxic,* or *natural* because there were no legal or formally accepted definitions. Today, however, these terms carry much more specific connotations and expectations. Uniform standards defining environmentally responsible company actions are rapidly being incorporated into the legal landscape. Strategically, companies more than ever must demonstrate to their customers and stakeholders that their green efforts are substantive and set the firm apart from competitors. A firm's social and environmental performance (facts and figures) must back up its rhetoric and be consistent with sustainability standards.

Many companies are moving the corporate environmental group to report directly to the CEO. Firms that manage environmental affairs will enhance relations with consumers, regulators, vendors, and other industry players, substantially improving their prospects of success. Environmental strategies could include the following:

1. Developing or acquiring green businesses
2. Divesting or altering environment-damaging businesses
3. Becoming a low-cost producer through waste minimization and energy conservation
4. Pursuing a differentiation strategy through green product features
5. Including an environmental or sustainability representative on their board of directors
6. Conducting regular environmental audits
7. Implementing bonuses for favorable environmental or conservation-related results
8. Becoming involved in environmental issues and programs
9. Incorporating environmental values in mission statements
10. Establishing environmentally oriented objectives
11. Acquiring "green" skills
12. Providing environmental training programs for company employees and managers

Through its Green Power Partnership, the EPA works with organizations to increase the use of green power. The Tractor Supply Company is one of the latest to join the EPA's Green Power Partnership. Noni Ellison, senior vice president of Tractor Supply says, "Using green power helps us reduce air pollution and lower our emissions footprint, which is an important step as we work towards our vision of a more sustainable future. Being named a Green Power Partner is validation for our commitment in creating energy and carbon efficiencies in our stores and distribution centers."[11]

Table 10-2 and Table 10-3 reveal the top 15 "green" companies and universities, respectively, based on green power percentage of total electricity use. (Note: Green power is renewable, such as wind, solar, and water, as opposed to fossil fuels, such as oil, gas, and coal that are not renewable). Note that Estée Lauder and Georgetown University are the green power usage leaders for companies and higher education institutions, respectively. Many commercial and residential builders now offer solar panels as standard equipment on homes and offices. Solar panels have become quite cost effective and they "exhume good ethics rather than bad fumes."

TABLE 10-2 The Top 15 Companies That Use the Highest Percentage of Green Energy

Company Name	Annual Green-Power Usage (kWh)	Green Power of Total Electricity Use (%)	Green Power Resources
1. The Estée Lauder Companies Inc.	91,843,084	139	Solar, Wind
2. Voya Financial	40,000,000	120	Wind
3. BNY Mellon	268,000,000	113	Wind
4. Sephora	112,323,000	112	Wind
5. Bank of America	1,855,505,589	109	Various
6. Church & Dwight Co.	159,445,000	107	Wind
7. Google LLC	7,492,567,647	106	Solar, Wind
8. The Hartford Financial Services Group	68,835,000	106	Solar, Wind
9. Wells Fargo	1,843,545,975	105	Solar, Wind
10. Equinix	2,360,296,352	104	Solar, Wind
11. State Street Corporation	158,991,503	104	Solar, Wind
12. Aldi	984,430,521	103	Various
13. Apple Inc.	20,000,000	101	Biogas, Biomass, Small Hydro, Solar, Wind
14. Starbucks	15,212,943	101	Solar, Wind
15. TD Bank	15,064,852	101	Solar, Wind

Note: More than 100% means the company produces more green energy than it needs, so it can share (or sell).

Source: Based on https://www.visualcapitalist.com/ranked-the-50-companies-that-use-the-highest-percentage-of-green-energy/

International Standardization Organization (ISO) Certification

Based in Geneva, Switzerland, the ISO is a network of national standards institutes of 165 countries, with one member per country. The ISO is the world's largest developer of sustainability standards. ISO has published nearly 22,000 international standards covering almost every industry, from health care to agriculture to food safety to technology. ISO standards reveal "required" specifications for products, services, and systems to ensure quality, safety, and efficiency; ISO standards facilitate international trade and commerce.

Widely accepted all over the world, ISO standards are voluntary because the organization itself does not regulate or legislate. Governmental agencies in various countries, such as the US Environmental Protection Agency (EPA), have adopted ISO standards as part of their regulatory framework, and the standards are the basis of much legislation. Adoptions are sovereign decisions by the regulatory authorities, governments, or companies concerned. Businesses and municipalities should consider becoming ISO certified to help attract business.

ISO 14000 refers to a series of voluntary standards in the environmental field. The ISO 14000 family of standards concerns the extent to which a firm minimizes harmful effects on the environment caused by its activities and continually monitors and improves its own environmental performance. These standards have been adopted by thousands of firms and municipalities worldwide to certify to their constituencies that they are conducting business in an environmentally friendly manner; these standards offer a universal technical benchmark for environmental compliance that more and more firms are requiring not only of themselves but also of their suppliers and distributors. Included in the ISO 14000 series are the **ISO 14001** standards in fields such as environmental auditing, environmental performance evaluation, pollution prevention, environmental labeling, and life-cycle assessment. According to the ISO 14001 standard, a community or organization is required to put in place and implement a series of practices and

TABLE 10-3 The Top 15 Universities That Use the Highest Percentage of Green Energy

University Name	Green Power of Total Electricity Use (%)	Green Power Resources	Athletic Conference
1. Georgetown University	127	Wind	Big East Conference
2. Carnegie Mellon University	111	Solar, Wind	University Athletic Association
3. Saint Louis University	105	Wind	Atlantic 10 Conference
4. University at Buffalo, the State University of New York	102	Solar, Wind	Mid-American Conference
5. Columbia University	100	Various	Ivy League
6. Boston University	100	Wind	Patriot League
7. Northeastern University	100	Wind	Colonial Athletic Association
8. Tarrant County College District	100	Solar, Wind	n/a
9. City Colleges of Chicago	100	Wind	n/a
10. Southern Illinois University Edwardsville	100	Wind	Ohio Valley Conference
11. Rochester Institute of Technology	97	Various	Liberty League
12. Arizona State University	78	Various	Pac-12 Conference
13. University of North Texas	74	Solar, Wind	American Athletic Conference
14. Ohio University	74	Solar, Wind	Mid-American Conference
15. University of Oklahoma	72	Wind	Big 12 Conference

Source: Based on information at https://www.epa.gov/greenpower/green-power-partnership-top-30-college-university, https://environmentamerica.org/sites/environment/files/reports/AME%20Campus%20Renewables%20Report%20Sum20cc-web_0.pdf, and various university's websites.

procedures that, when taken together, result in an **environmental management system (EMS)**. Not being certified with ISO 14001 can be a strategic disadvantage for towns, counties, and companies because people today expect organizations to minimize or, even better, to eliminate environmental harm they cause.

Preserving the environment should be a permanent part of doing business, for the following reasons:

1. Consumer demand for environmentally safe products and packages is increasingly high.
2. Public opinion demanding that firms conduct business in ways that preserve the natural environment is strong.
3. Environmental advocacy groups now have more than 20 million Americans as members.
4. Federal and state environmental regulations are changing rapidly and becoming more complex.
5. More lenders are examining the environmental liabilities of businesses seeking loans.
6. Many consumers, suppliers, distributors, and investors shun doing business with environmentally weak firms.
7. Liability suits and fines against firms having environmental problems are on the rise.

Consumers are increasingly realizing the impact of their consumption on the environment, including the types of behaviors and products that contribute most to their own carbon footprint. Companies should increasingly provide concrete guidance as to how they and their consumers can make the most climate-friendly consumption decisions. Mintel recently published a 2022 *Global Consumer Trend Report on Climate Complexities*; the report indicates that consumers over the next several years will increasingly begin to demand information about the overall carbon footprint of products, including details on the individual components of that footprint (e.g., agriculture, transportation, processing). Details of the key findings from the report for various industries are provided in Table 10-4.

TABLE 10-4 Implications of Climate Complexities for Consumers and Brands Across Various Industries

Automotive

As electric vehicles become more accessible, more and more consumers will reject fossil fuel-dependent automobiles as they turn to more accessible electric vehicles. Consumers will increasingly demand transparency and details about how brands are reducing the lifetime carbon footprints of automobiles.

Beauty and Personal Care

Consumers will learn new consumption habits, including using waterless, concentrated products, upcycled ingredients, and refillable packaging when possible. For example, eco-friendly brands will reposition products such as bar soap as more sustainable, plastic-free, and waterless options for laundry and dish detergents.

Financial Services

Consumers will increasingly prefer financial institutions that adhere to climate-friendly, sustainable practices, and actively encourage more eco-friendly behavior, perhaps through lower interest rates or other incentives for carbon neutrality.

Food and Drink

Consumers will increasingly look for more plant-based (and climate-friendly) alternatives as consumption of animal products, and red meat in particular, is associated with increased carbon emissions. Beef and cow's milk are among the top contributors to global emissions.

Pet Supplies

Pet parents will increasingly look for information related to the carbon "pawprint" of their pets. Brands will begin to offer alternatives to the typical heavily processed, meat-based foods offered by most cat and dog food manufacturers.

Retail

Consumers will start to learn about the carbon footprint of retailers and the products they stock. Retailers should source locally to the extent possible, while also communicating to consumers how buying local is often more environmentally friendly. Eco-friendly retailers will become the norm as more and more retailers get creative with their buildings, for example, by turning roof space into solar panels and shifting to more renewable energy sources.

Source: Based on Mintel's Global Consumer Trend 2022 Report, *Climate Complexity*, published by the Mintel Group Ltd. on November 19, 2021.

Corporate Social Responsibility (CSR)

10.4. Discuss why corporate social responsibility (CSR) is a key issue in strategic planning.

Social responsibility refers to a firm's obligation to care for its employees, customers, communities, and society in which it operates. For example, the food seasoning firm McCormick & Company states that its corporate social responsibility (CSR) goals for 2025 include working "to improve the health and well-being of all people, build vibrant communities around the world, and positively impact the planet." Some strategists agree with Ralph Nader, who proclaims that organizations have tremendous social obligations. Nader points out, for example, that ExxonMobil has more assets than most countries, and because of this, such firms have an obligation to help society cure its many ills. Other people, however, agree with the economist Milton Friedman, who asserts that organizations have no obligation to do any more for society than is legally required. Friedman may contend that it is irresponsible for a firm to give monies to charity.

Do you agree more with Nader or Friedman? Surely, we can all agree that the first social responsibility of any business must be to make enough profit to cover the firm's costs of the future, because if this is not achieved, no other social responsibility can be met. Indeed, no social need can be met if the firm fails. Many economists suggest that firms should not engage much, if any, in philanthropy because simply making a profit is difficult, and shareholders expect a high return on their investment. However, substantial research reveals an inverted u-shaped relationship between CSR and corporate financial performance, whereby firms with moderate CSR are generally also the firms with the highest financial performance; firms often see diminishing returns from overly high investments in CSR.

Strategists should examine social problems in terms of potential costs and benefits to the firm and focus on social issues that could benefit the firm most. For example, if a firm avoids cutting jobs to protect employees' livelihood, and that decision forces the firm to liquidate, then all the employees lose their jobs. Walmart selectively engages in social responsibility efforts that directly complement its business initiatives.

The ISO's ISO 26000 provides guidance to businesses and organizations committed to operating in a socially responsible way. The underlying framework for socially responsible decision-making outlined in the ISO 26000 is based on seven key principles: accountability, transparency, ethical behavior, respect for stakeholder interests, respect for the rule of law, respect for international norms of behavior, and respect for human rights. The ISO says that applying the ISO 26000 guidelines is a great way to demonstrate an organization's commitment to sustainability, and it is "the right thing to do."

Animal Welfare, Including Wildlife and Livestock Welfare

CSR also extends to animal welfare. Consumers globally are becoming increasingly intolerant of any business or nation that directly or indirectly destroys wildlife, especially endangered wildlife, such as tigers, elephants, whales, songbirds, and coral reefs. Affected businesses range from retailers that sell ivory chess pieces to restaurants that sell whale meat. As indicated in Ethics Capsule 10, many animals are in trouble. Consumers are increasingly resentful of companies that harm wildlife or treat animals inhumanely, and countries, municipalities, and companies run the risk of being boycotted and exposed for direct or indirect wildlife endangering practices.

CSR extends to the 9-plus billion land animals raised in the United States annually for food; many of these animals live their short lives in inhumane factory-like structures. Animal welfare concerns are on the rise among consumers; retailers are beginning to respond to such concerns by increasingly demanding that food suppliers provide humane treatment of animals. A large-scale survey by the American Society for the Prevention of Cruelty to Animals (ASPCA) found that US consumers (89 percent to be exact) are concerned about industrial animal agriculture, including animal welfare which is a key concern. ASPCA believes that "animals are entitled to kind and respectful treatment at the hands of humans and must be protected under the law."

Policies aimed at improving livestock welfare are increasingly being developed and approved by lawmakers around the world. In addition to newly emerging, more stringent regulations surrounding livestock welfare, substantive scientific research studies are beginning to reveal significant financial benefits of enhanced animal welfare guidelines. For example, heat stress and rough handling often lower the quality, safety, and value of livestock by bruising the meat, reducing growth, and even inhibiting reproduction. Animal welfare and the humane treatment of animals raised for food will soon become a new standard shaped by next-generation consumer expectations. As a result, large food companies such as Whole Foods, Bon Appétit, Sodexo, and Aramark have implemented more animal-friendly policies and have also begun exploring new plant-based food innovations. For example, Aramark reduced the amount of red meat in its recipes by 12 percent from 2015 to 2020, while also creating over 400 new plant-based recipes, all as a part of its "plant-forward marketing program."

Independent organizations have also implemented marketing campaigns aimed at encouraging consumers to make more ethical consumption-related decisions. For example, the ASPCA launched the "Factory Farm Detox" campaign that seeks to get consumers to "join the detox" by committing to eliminate all factory-farmed foods from their diet for 1 week.[12] A similar campaign more widely marketed to consumers globally is the "Meatless Monday" initiative, which has been implemented by many businesses, cities, public institutions, and communities around the world (https://www.mondaycampaigns.org/meatless-monday).

ETHICS CAPSULE 10

As We Strategize We Must Not Exploit or Harm Wildlife[13]

Françoise EMILY/Alamy Photo

The world's animal species are dying, and humans are a big reason why. A World Wildlife Fund Report reveals that global populations of wild mammals, fish, birds, amphibians, and reptiles have declined about 40 percent. Poaching has decimated both elephants and rhinos. Causes of extinction of wildlife include poaching, urban development, overhunting, overfishing, pollution, disease, and climate change—all of which are tied to humans.

The International Union for the Conservation of Nature (IUCN) annually publishes a "Red List of Threatened Species." There are currently 41,415 species of plants and animals on the IUCN Red List; 16,306 animals are endangered, up from 16,118 the prior year. The following 10 animals are nearly extinct, listed in order of being closest to extinction worldwide according to IUCN.

1. Javan Rhinoceros – Less than 70 adults remain in the world; they are confined to the island of Java in Indonesia.
2. Vaquita – A small harbor porpoise that lives in the northern part of the Gulf of California, Mexico, is almost extinct.
3. Mountain Gorilla – This large primate is almost extinct, living only in Rwanda, Uganda, and the Congo.
4. Tiger – Largest of all cats and almost extinct are the Bengal, Indochinese, Sumatran, Siberian, and Malayan tigers.
5. Asian Elephant – The last few of these gentle giants live in Southeast Asia, mainly Thailand and Sri Lanka.

6. Orangutans – Both Bornean and Sumatran orangutans are nearly extinct; their habitat in Sumatra and Borneo is being cleared for conversion to palm oil plantations.
7. Leatherback Sea Turtles – The largest and most migratory of all sea turtles, this species is nearly extinct due to extensive egg collection and bycatch in fishing gear.
8. Snow Leopards – Living mainly above the tree line up to 18,000 feet in elevation in the Himalayas in central and southern Asia, these big cats are nearly extinct.
9. Irrawaddy Dolphins – Swimming often from freshwater and saltwater and confined largely to the Mekong River area of Southeast Asia, only about 92 of these dolphins are alive today according to the World Wildlife Fund.
10. Atlantic Bluefin Tuna – Overfishing and illegal fishing are decimating the giant tuna population globally, due to demand for tuna in high-end sushi markets.

Consumers globally are becoming increasingly intolerant of any business or nation that directly or indirectly harms wildlife, especially endangered wildlife, such as tigers, elephants, whales, songbirds, and coral reefs. Affected businesses range from retailers that sell ivory chess pieces to restaurants that sell whale meat. In terms of whaling for example, only three countries—Japan, Iceland, and Norway—favor and engage in commercial whaling. Japan and Norway have been criticized globally in recent years for continuously launching whale-hunting expeditions and killing more than 1,000 whales each year, many of them pregnant females. Countries, municipalities, and companies run the risk of being boycotted and exposed for direct or indirect wildlife endangering practices.

[13]Based on https://www.animalsaroundtheglobe.com/the-10-most-endangered-animals/ and https://us.whales.org/our-4-goals/stop-whaling/

What Firms Are the Best CSR Stewards?

Newsweek recently partnered with Statista to determine the top-rated companies for giving back to the communities where they operate. Table 10-5 reveals that Hewlett-Packard was rated as the best company in the United States for giving back to communities.

TABLE 10-5 Top-Rated Companies for Giving Back to Communities

1. Hewlett-Packard
2. Nvidia Corporation
3. Microsoft Corporation
4. Cisco Systems
5. Qualcomm
6. General Mills
7. Whirlpool Corporation
8. Illumina
9. Citigroup Inc.
10. Dell Technologies Inc.
11. Lam Research
12. General Motors Corporation

Source: Based on https://www.rankingthebrands.com/The-Brand-Rankings.aspx?rankingID=448&year=1351

Firms should strive to engage in social activities that have economic benefits. Merck & Co. once developed the drug ivermectin for treating river blindness, a disease caused by a fly-borne parasitic worm endemic in poor tropical areas of Africa, the Middle East, and Latin America. In an unprecedented gesture that reflected its corporate commitment to social responsibility, Merck then made ivermectin available at no cost to medical personnel throughout the world. Merck's action highlights the dilemma of orphan drugs, which offer pharmaceutical companies no economic incentive for profitable development and distribution. Merck did, however, garner substantial favor among its stakeholders for its actions. Firms are becoming more proactive by doing more than the bare minimum to develop and implement strategies that preserve the environment and help local communities.

IMPLICATIONS FOR STRATEGISTS

Figure 10-2 reveals that the entire strategic management process is designed to gain and sustain competitive advantages, but all can be lost with ethical violations, ranging from bribery to sexual harassment to selling whale meat. Consider this: Trees die from the top; strategists are at the top of the firm, meaning that ethical problems at the top of a firm spell dire consequences for lower levels. Strategists must set an exemplary example personally and professionally to establish and continually reinforce an organizational culture for "doing the right thing." Social responsibility and environmental sustainability policies, practices, and procedures must reinforce a "triple-bottom-line" approach that emphasizes "good ethics is good business" and "good ethics is the foundation for everything we do and say."

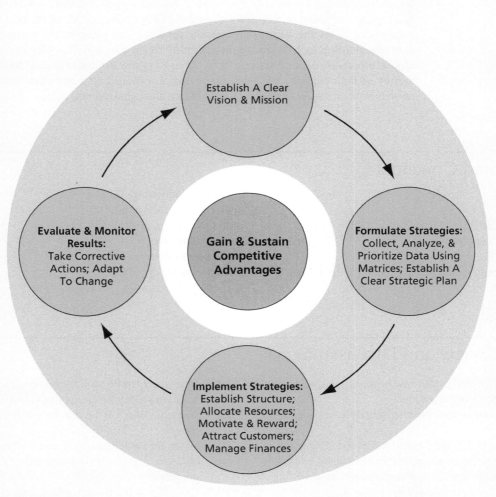

FIGURE 10-2

How to Gain and Sustain Competitive Advantages

IMPLICATIONS FOR STUDENTS

No company or individual wants to do business with someone who is unethical or insensitive to natural environment concerns. To survive, companies must be environmentally proactive; it is expected, and in many respects, is the law. On a daily basis, firms are being compared to rival firms on sustainability and ethics behavior. Issues presented in this chapter, therefore, comprise a competitive advantage or disadvantage for all organizations. Thus, you should include in your case analysis recommendations for your firm to exceed stakeholder expectations on ethics, sustainability, and social responsibility. Make comparisons to rival firms to show how your firm can gain or sustain competitive advantage on these issues. Reveal financially sound suggestions for the firm to be a good corporate citizen and promote that for competitive advantage. Although the first responsibility of any business is to stay in business, the triple-bottom-line approach can be an effective means for framing your entire project.

Chapter Summary

In a final analysis, ethical standards come out of history and heritage. Our predecessors left us with an ethical foundation on which to build. Even the legendary football coach Vince Lombardi knew that some things were worth more than winning, and he required his players to have three kinds of loyalty: to God, to their families, and to the Green Bay Packers, "in that order." Employees, customers, and shareholders have become less and less tolerant of ethical violations in firms, and more and more appreciative of model ethical firms. Information sharing across the Internet increasingly reveals such model firms versus irresponsible firms.

Consumers across the country and around the world appreciate firms that do more than is legally required to be socially responsible. But staying in business, while adhering to all laws and regulations, must be a primary objective of any business. One of the best ways to be socially responsible is for the firm to proactively conserve and preserve the natural environment. For example, developing a corporate sustainability report annually is not legally required, but such a report, based on concrete actions, goes a long way toward assuring stakeholders that the firm is worthy of their support. Business ethics, social responsibility, and environmental sustainability are interrelated and key strategic issues facing all organizations.

Key Terms and Concepts

bribe (p. 306)
bribery (p. 306)
business ethics (p. 302)
code of business ethics (p. 304)
environment (p. 308)
environmental management system (EMS) (p. 311)
ISO 14000 (p. 310)
ISO 14001 (p. 310)

sexual harassment (p. 307)
social responsibility (p. 302)
sustainability (p. 302)
sustainability report (p. 308)
triple-bottom-line (p. 302)
whistleblowing (p. 306)
workplace romance (p. 307)

Issues for Review and Discussion

10-1. Explain the triple-bottom-line approach to managing any business or organization.

10-2. What are some of the most racially diverse countries in the world?

10-3. As a part of its Global Coalition Against Corruption, Transparency International publishes annual corruption perception indices that rank countries according to their relative corruption levels. Name three countries in the top 20 (least corrupt).

10-4. What do whales, sharks, songbirds, and coral reefs have in common? What are the implications for companies?

10-5. Does it pay to be socially responsible? In general, economists say *no* and philanthropists say *yes*. What do you say? Why? What are the implications for companies?

10-6. What are some important metrics being used by companies globally to assess their DEI situation and progress?

10-7. Chick-fil-A is closed on Sundays. Is that wise management or irresponsible activism? Discuss.

10-8. List five reasons why workplace romance can be detrimental to workplace morale and productivity.

10-9. List five benefits of having workplace romance guidelines in a workplace.

10-10. Discuss the ethics of workplace romance.

10-11. Explain why concern for wildlife is a strategic issue for firms.

10-12. Explain why whistleblower payouts by the federal government to informants are becoming more and more common.

10-13. AOL has 100 lobbyists on its payroll and spends about $20 million on lobbying in Washington, DC, annually. Is this ethical?

10-14. If you owned a small business, would you develop a code of business conduct? If yes, what variables would you include? If no, how would you ensure that ethical business standards were being followed by your employees?

10-15. What do you feel is the relationship between personal ethics and business ethics? Are they or should they be the same?

10-16. How can firms best ensure that their code of business ethics is read, understood, believed, remembered, and acted on, rather than ignored?

10-17. Why is it important *not* to view the concept of whistleblowing as "tattle-telling" or "ratting" on another employee?

10-18. List several desired results of "ethics training programs" in terms of recommended business ethics policies and procedures in the firm.

10-19. Discuss bribery. Would actions such as politicians adding earmarks in legislation or pharmaceutical salespersons giving away drugs to physicians constitute bribery? Identify three business activities that would constitute bribery and three actions that would not.

10-20. How could a strategist's attitude toward social responsibility affect a firm's strategy? On a 1 to 10 scale ranging from Nader's view (1) to Friedman's view (10), what is your attitude toward social responsibility?

10-21. What is the International Standardization Organization (ISO)? What is the purpose of the ISO 14001 standards, and what types of entities can receive these certifications?

10-22. How are policies and procedures changing regarding growing animals for slaughter for supermarkets?

10-23. Is it a conflict of interest for companies to encourage employee whistleblowing because the firm could be fined heavily or incur worse penalties? Explain.

Writing Assignments

10-24. Firms should formulate and implement strategies from an environmental perspective. List eight ways firms can do this.

10-25. Discuss the major requirements of an EMS under ISO 14001.

ASSURANCE-OF-LEARNING EXERCISES

SET 1: STRATEGIC PLANNING FOR MCDONALD'S

EXERCISE 10A

Does McDonald's (MCD) or Restaurant Brands International (RBI) Win on Diversity, Equity, and Inclusion (DEI)?

Ken Wolter/Alamy Photo

Purpose

DEI initiatives, objectives, and metrics are easy to establish but more difficult to achieve and easy to disregard, partly because they are difficult to track and harder to enforce. Too many companies talk the talk but do not walk the walk with regard to DEI. Just talking is changing however because regulators, investors, customers, employees, and activists are increasingly scrutinizing corporate disclosures.

In this exercise, compare MCD's DEI initiatives, objectives, and metrics with those of major rival RBI that owns Burger King and other fast-food restaurants that compete with MCD.

Instructions

Step 1   Compare MCD's DEI progress to RBI's progress as evidenced and showcased at the MCD website and the RBI website.

MCD Website: https://corporate.mcdonalds.com/corpmcd/our-purpose-and-impact/jobs-inclusion-and-empowerment/diversity-and-inclusion.html

RBI Website: https://www.rbi.com/English/sustainability/diversity-and-inclusion/default.aspx

Step 2	Review the Corporate Equality Index (CEI) 2021 and 2022 Reports. Review information at both https://hbr.org/2021/05/how-to-measure-inclusion-in-the-workplace and https://www.hrc.org/resources/corporate-equality-index regarding how to best walk the walk on DEI.
Step 3	Identify five areas where MCD can be compared to RBI in the most recent 2 years. Decide which firm is better on each of your five criteria or areas. Overall, what grade (A, B, C, D, or F) would you give MCD and RBI on DEI? Write up your findings in a one-page summary document for your professor.

SET 2: STRATEGIC PLANNING FOR MY UNIVERSITY

EXERCISE 10B

How Does My University Compare to Others on the Use of Green Power?

Purpose

Green energy sources include wind, geothermal, hydro, and solar energy. Wind and hydro sources generate energy through the movement of air and water, whereas geothermal and solar sources generate energy through heat. All, however, provide renewable, reliable energy and protect the environment. In contrast, fossil-fuel energy sources, such as oil, gas, and coal, are not renewable and pollute the environment. The purpose of this exercise is to determine where your university would rank among all universities on its reliance of green energy.

Instructions

Step 1	The following website reveals colleges and universities rated according to the extent that they use green energy sources to operate. https://www.epa.gov/greenpower/green-power-partnership-top-30-college-university Even if your university is not listed in the current report by the EPA, conduct research to determine where your institution would rank.
Step 2	Develop an action plan to move your university toward greater reliance on green energy.

SET 3: STRATEGIC PLANNING FOR MYSELF

EXERCISE 10C

What Is My Business Ethics Quotient?

Purpose

This chapter reveals that being unethical is not abnormal or rare. Misconduct is a normal phenomenon and wrongdoing is as prevalent as "rightdoing." Misconduct is most often done by people who are primarily good, ethical, and socially responsible. Palmer reports that individuals engage in unethical activities because of a plethora of structure, processes, and mechanisms inherent in the functioning of organizations, and, importantly, all of us are candidates to be unethical under the right circumstances in any organization. Implications of this new research abound for managers.

The purpose of this exercise is to determine your business ethics quotient. We can use the word *quotient* to refer to the extent that your attitudes and behavior are good or bad compared to your fellow business students. In this exercise, your business ethics quotient can range from very bad (total score of 16) to very good (total score of 80). (Donald Palmer, "The New Perspective on Organizational Wrongdoing," *California Management Review* 56, no. 1 [2013]: 5–23).

Instructions

Step 1	Rate your personal attitudes and behavior on the following dimensions using a 1 to 5 scale where 1 is really bad, 2 is bad, 3 is OK, 4 is good, and 5 is really good. Beside each word given, rate yourself compared to your fellow business students.

1. Trustworthy
2. Reliable
3. Dependable

4. Caring
5. Humble
6. Considerate
7. Compassionate
8. Forgiving
9. Loving
10. Courteous
11. Respectful
12. Reverent
13. Supportive
14. Encouraging
15. Helpful
16. Giving

Step 2   Sum your ratings to determine your total business ethics quotient score. Are you pleased with your score? Do you need to improve your score? How can you improve your score? Would a business thinking of hiring you be pleased with your score?

SET 4: INDIVIDUAL VERSUS GROUP STRATEGIC PLANNING

EXERCISE 10D

How Potentially Severe Are the Various Reasons Why Workplace Romance Should Be Discouraged?

Purpose

This chapter discusses workplace romance as being potentially detrimental to workplace morale and productivity, for a number of reasons that include:

1. Favoritism complaints can arise.
2. Confidentiality of records can be breached.
3. Reduced quality and quantity of work can become a problem.
4. Personal arguments can lead to work arguments.
5. Whispering secrets can lead to tensions and hostilities among coworkers.
6. Sexual harassment (or discrimination) charges may ensue, either by the involved person or a third party.
7. Conflicts of interest can arise, especially when wellbeing of the partner trumps wellbeing of the firm.

The purpose of this exercise is to examine more closely the reasons why workplace romance can cause problems. In addition, the purpose of this exercise is to examine whether individual decision-making is better than group decision-making. Academic research suggests that groups make better decisions than individuals about 80 percent of the time.

Instructions

Rank the seven reasons why workplace romance can cause problems as to their relative importance (potential severity), where 1 = most important, to 7 = least important). Use Table 10-6. First, rank the reasons as an individual. Then, rank the seven reasons as part of a group of three. Thus, determine what person(s) and what group(s) can come closest to the expert ranking. This exercise enables examination of the relative effectiveness of individual versus group decision-making in strategic planning.

Steps

1. Fill in Column 1 in Table 10-6 to reveal your individual ranking of the relative importance of the seven reasons (1 = most important, 2 = next most important, etc.) in terms of how potentially damaging each reason can be. For example, if you think Reason 1 (Favoritism) is the seventh-most important (potentially severe) reason, then enter a 7 in Table 1 in Column 1 beside Favoritism.
2. Fill in Column 2 in Table 10-6 to reveal your group's ranking of the relative importance of the seven reasons (1 = most important, 2 = next most important, etc.) in terms of how potentially damaging each reason can be.
3. Fill in Column 3 in Table 10-6 to reveal the expert's ranking of the seven reasons in terms of how potentially damaging each reason can be.

4. Fill in Column 4 in Table 10-6 with the absolute difference between Column 1 and Column 3 to reveal how well you performed as an individual in this exercise. (Note: Absolute difference disregards negative numbers.)

5. Fill in Column 5 in Table 10-6 with the absolute difference between Column 2 and Column 3 to reveal how well your group performed in this exercise.

6. Sum Column 4. Sum Column 5.

7. Compare the Column 4 sum with the Column 5 sum. If your Column 4 sum is less than your Column 5 sum, then you performed better as an individual than as a group. Normally, group decision-making is superior to individual decision-making, so if you did better than your group, you did excellent.

8. The Individual Winner(s): The individual(s) with the lowest Column 4 sum is the WINNER.

9. The Group Winners(s): The group(s) with the lowest Column 5 score is the WINNER.

TABLE 10-6 Workplace Romance Analysis: Comparing Individual Versus Group Decision-Making

Reasons Why Workplace Romance Is Not Recommended	Column 1	Column 2	Column 3	Column 4	Column 5
1. Favoritism complaints can arise.					
2. Confidentiality of records can be breached.					
3. Reduced quality and quantity of work can become a problem.					
4. Personal arguments can lead to work arguments.					
5. Whispering secrets can lead to tensions and hostilities among coworkers.					
6. Sexual harassment (or discrimination) charges may ensue, either by the involved person or a third party.					
7. Conflicts of interest can arise, especially when well-being of the partner trumps well-being of the firm.					
Sums					

MINI-CASE ON CARGILL, ARCHER-DANIELS-MIDLAND, AND TYSON FOODS

Scott Sinklier/Alamy Photo

WHAT COMPANY CARES MOST ABOUT ANIMAL WELFARE?[14]

Headquartered in New York City and founded in 1866 to prevent cruelty to animals throughout the United States, the American Society for the Prevention of Cruelty to Animals (ASPCA) is one of the largest humane societies in the world. ASPCA promotes the belief that animals are entitled to kind and respectful treatment at the hands of humans and must be protected under the law. ASPCA provides an extensive list of companies that take care of the animals they process for food. We are referring here to ways in which animals are grown, slaughtered, and processed, including, for example, obtaining eggs from free-range chickens rather than caged-chickens and growing cows without them being given antibiotics and growth hormones, and using "factory farms."

Headquartered in Austin, Texas, the Global Animal Partnership (GAP) certifies chicken, turkey, beef, hog, lamb, goat, and bison farms for humane treatment of animals. The GAP works with ASPCA. GAP has a third-party audit team that visits farms on request every 15 months and certifies the farm at the particular level they are operating. GAP rates companies and farms on a 1 to 6 scale from weak to strong regarding how animals are treated and raised, where:

1 = Base Certification
2 = Enriched Environment
3 = Outdoor Access
4 = Pasture Raised
5 = Animal Centered
6 = Entire Life on a Farm

Consumers are increasingly examining companies regarding their treatment of animals, and companies are increasingly examining their suppliers and distributors on the same issue. Much of the meat consumed by people in the United States comes from three of the largest food companies in the world, listed below:

Company	Headquarters	Website
Cargill, Inc.	Minnetonka, Minnesota	http://www.cargill.com
Archer-Daniels-Midland Company (ADM)	Chicago, Illinois	http://www.adm.com
Tyson Foods	Springdale, Arizona	http://www.tysonfoods.com

Questions

1. Visit and study the websites of the three large food companies noted.
2. Determine three variables to evaluate the three companies to assess their animal welfare effectiveness.
3. Rank the three companies on the three variables overall from best to worst on their animal welfare effectiveness.
4. Determine the best and worst firm. Justify your rankings.
5. Discuss implications for the companies, their employees, and ultimately consumers.

[14] Based on https://globalanimalpartnership.org/faq/. Also, https://www.aspca.org/protecting-farm-animals

Web Resources

1. Fred David gives a video overview of Chapter 10 in the prior edition, but much info is still applicable to the 18th edition.
   https://www.youtube.com/watch?v=7zcw61ho274
2. The following websites provide information to consumers regarding how they can make more humane, sustainable, and ethical decisions for themselves and those they love, including their pets:
   https://globalanimalpartnership.org/pet-parents/

   https://globalanimalpartnership.org/shoppers/
   https://awionline.org/content/making-better-food-choices
   https://awionline.org/content/5-ways-you-can-help-farm-animals
   https://certifiedhumane.org/our-standards/
3. Individuals can join the "Factory Farm Detox" by visiting the following website:
   https://secure.aspca.org/take-action/detox?ms=wb_top_swyh-ffd-20200102&initialms=wb_top_swyh-ffd-20200102#signup

Current Readings

Altmann, Brianne A., Sven Anders, Antje Risius, and Daniel Mörlein "Information Effects on Consumer Preferences for Alternative Animal Feedstuffs," *Food Policy* 106 (2022): 102192.

Andrew, Lynn, "Why 'Doing Well by Doing Good' Went Wrong: Getting Beyond 'Good Ethics Pays,' Claims in Managerial Thinking," *Academy of Management Review* 46, 3 (July 2021): 512–33.

Apaydin, Marina, Guoliang Frank Jiang, Mehmet Demirbag, and Dima Jamali, "The Importance of Corporate Social Responsibility Strategic Fit and Times of Economic Hardship," *British Journal of Management* 32, no. 2 (April 2021): 399–415.

Derchi, G. B., L. Zoni, and A. Dossi, "Corporate Social Responsibility Performance, Incentives, and Learning Effects," *Journal of Business Ethics* 173 (2021): 617–41.

DesJardine, Mark R., Emilio Marti, and Rodolphe Durand, "Why Activist Hedge Funds Target Socially Responsible Firms: The Reaction Costs of Signaling Corporate Social Responsibility," *Academy of Management Journal* 64, no. 3 (June 2021): 851–72.

Felix, Reto, Eva M. Gonzalez, Raquel Castaño, Lorena Carrete, and Richard T. Gretz, "When the Green in Green Packaging Backfires: Gender Effects and Perceived Masculinity of Environmentally Friendly Products," *International Journal of Consumer Studies* 46, no. 3 (2022): 925–43.

Kim, Peter H., Scott S. Wiltermuth, and David T. Newman, "A Theory of Ethical Accounting and Its Implications for Hypocrisy in Organizations," *Academy of Management Review* 46, no. 1 (January 2021): 172–91.

Kim, Sol, Geul Lee, and Hyoung-Goo Kang, "Risk Management and Corporate Social Responsibility,"

Strategic Management Journal 42, no. 1 (January 2021): 202–30.

Koo, Jayoung, and Barbara Loken, "Don't Put All Your Green Eggs in One Basket: Examining Environmentally Friendly Sub-branding Strategies," *Business Ethics, the Environment & Responsibility* 31, no. 1 (2022): 164–76.

Kovács, Tünde Z., Forest David, Adrián Nagy, István Szűcs, and András Nábrádi, "An Analysis of the Demand-Side, Platform-Based Collaborative Economy: Creation of a Clear Classification Taxonomy," *Sustainability* 13, no. 5 (2021): 2817. https://doi.org/10.3390/su13052817

Lahouel, Béchir Ben, Younes Ben Zaied, Shunsuke Managi, and Lotfi Taleb, "Re-thinking about U: The Relevance of Regime-switching Model in the Relationship Between Environmental Corporate Social Responsibility and Financial Performance," *Journal of Business Research* 140 (2022): 498–519.

Li, Qiang, Wenjuan Ruan, Huimin Shi, Erwei Xiang, and Feida Zhang, "Corporate Environmental Information Disclosure and Bank Financing: Moderating Effect of Formal and Informal Institutions," *Business Strategy and the Environment* (2022), forthcoming.

Lynn, Andrew, "Why 'Doing Well by Doing Good' Went Wrong: Getting Beyond 'Good Ethics Pays' Claims in Managerial Thinking," *Academy of Management Review* 46, no. 3 (July 2021): 512–33.

Martinez, Cecilia, Ann Skeet, and Pedro M. Sasia, "Managing Organizational Ethics: How Ethics Becomes Pervasive Within Organizations," *Business Horizons* 64, no. 1 (January 2021): 83–92.

Meier, Olivier, Philippe Naccache, and Guillaume Schier, "Exploring the Curvature of the Relationship Between HRM–CSR and Corporate Financial Performance," *Journal of Business Ethics* 170, no. 4 (2021): 857–73.

Nickerson, Dionne, Michael Lowe, Adithya Pattabhiramaiah, and Alina Sorescu, "The Impact of Corporate Social Responsibility on Brand Sales: An Accountability Perspective," *Journal of Marketing* 86, no. 2 (2021): 5–28.

Sajko, Miha, Christophe Boone, and Tine Buyl, "CEO Greed, Corporate Social Responsibility, and Organizational

Resilience to Systemic Shocks," *Journal of Management* 47, no. 4 (April 2021): 957–92.

Seo, Haram, Jiao Luo, and Aseem Kaul, 'Giving a Little to Many or a lot to a Few,' The Returns to Variety in Corporate Philanthropy," *Strategic Management Journal* 42, no. 9 (September 2021): 1734–64.

Shi, W., and K. Veenstra, "The Moderating Effect of Cultural Values on the Relationship Between Corporate Social Performance and Firm Performance," *Journal of Business Ethics* 174 (2021): 89–107.

Silvestre, Winston Jerónimo, Ana Fonseca, and Sandra Naomi Morioka, "Strategic Sustainability Integration: Merging Management Tools to Support Business Model Decisions," *Business Strategy and the Environment* (2022), forthcoming.

Sun, Wenbin, Shanji Yao, and Rahul Govind, "Reexamining Corporate Social Responsibility and Shareholder Value: The Inverted-U-shaped Relationship and the Moderation of Marketing Capability," *Journal of Business Ethics* 160, no. 4 (2019): 1001–17.

Tibiletti, Veronica, Pier Luigi Marchini, Katia Furlotti, and Alice Medioli, "Does Corporate Governance Matter in Corporate Social Responsibility Disclosure? Evidence from Italy in the 'Era of Sustainability,'" *Corporate Social Responsibility and Environmental Management* 28, no. 2 (2021): 896–907.

Tsai, H. J., and Y. Wu, "Changes in Corporate Social Responsibility and Stock Performance," *Journal of Business Ethics*, https://doi.org/10.1007/s10551-021-04772-w

Yan, Shipeng, Juan Almandoz, and Fabrizio Ferraro, "The Impact of Logic (In)Compatibility: Green Investing, State Policy, and Corporate Environmental Performance," *Administrative Science Quarterly* 66, no. 4 (December 2021): 903–44.

Zipay, Kate P., Marie Mitchell, Michael Baer, Hudson Sessions, and Robert Bies, "Lenient Reactions to Misconduct: Examining the Self-conscious Process of Being Lenient to Others at Work," *Academy of Management Journal* 64, no. 2 (April 2021): 351–77.

Endnotes

1. On page 302.
2. Saul Gellerman, "Why 'Good' Managers Make Bad Ethical Choices," *Harvard Business Review* 64, no. 4 (July–August 1986): 88.
3. Based on Mark L. Frigo and Joel Litman, *DRIVEN: Business Strategy, Human Actions and the Creation of Wealth, Strategy and Execution* (Chicago: Strategy & Execution LLC, 2008).
4. Peter Drucker, *Management: Tasks, Responsibilities, and Practices* (New York: Harper & Row, 1974): 462, 463.
5. Gaurav Gupta, "Adapting Corporate Culture—Before It's Too Late: Lessons from Better.com," *Forbes*. https://www.forbes.com/sites/johnkotter/2022/01/04/adapting-corporate-culture-before-its-too-late-lessons-from-bettercom/?sh=2a52e4ba735d.
6. Donald A. Palmer, "The New Perspective on Organizational Wrongdoing," *California Management Review* 56, no. 1 (November 2013): 5–23.
7. On page 305.

8. http://www.usatoday.com/money/companies/management/story/2012-05-14/ceo-firings/54964476/1

9. http://www.businessknowhow.com/manage/romance.htm

10. Phred Dvorak, Bob Davis, and Louise Radnofsky, "Firms Confront Boss-Subordinate Love Affairs," *Wall Street Journal*, October 27, 2008, p. B5.

11. https://lbmjournal.com/tractor-supply-joins-epas-green-power-partnership/

12. https://secure.aspca.org/take-action/detox?ms=wb_top_swyh-ffd-20200102&initialms=wb_top_swyh-ffd-20200102#signup

13. On page 314.

14. On page 321.

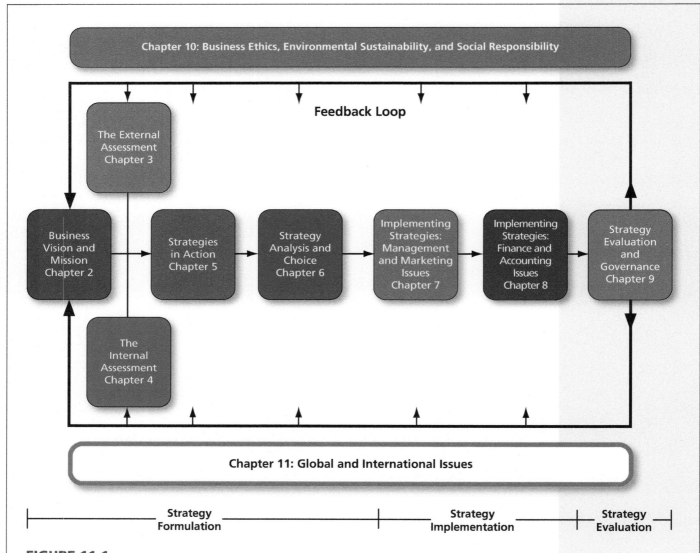

FIGURE 11-1

The Comprehensive, Integrative Strategic Management Model

Source: Fred R. David, "How Companies Define Their Mission," *Long Range Planning* 22, no. 1 (February 1989): 91. See also Anik Ratnaningsih, Nadjadji Anwar, Patdono Suwignjo, and Putu Artama Wiguna, "Balance Scorecard of David's Strategic Modeling at Industrial Business for National Construction Contractor of Indonesia," *Journal of Mathematics and Technology* no. 4, (October 2010): 20. Also, Meredith E. David, Fred R. David, and Forest R. David, "Closing the Gap Between Graduates' Skills and Employers' Requirements: A Focus on the Strategic Management Capstone Business Course," *Administrative Sciences* 11, no. 1 (2021): 10–26.

Global and International Issues

LEARNING OBJECTIVES

After studying this chapter, you should be able to do the following:

11.1. Discuss the nature of doing business globally, including labor union issues and tax rates.

11.2. Explain the advantages and disadvantages of doing business globally.

11.3. Discuss the global challenge facing firms, including outsourcing and reshoring.

11.4. Compare and contrast US business culture versus foreign business cultures; explain why this is a strategic issue.

11.5. Discuss business culture, with emphasis on Mexico, Japan, China, and India.

11.6. Discuss business climate in nations across the globe.

ASSURANCE-OF-LEARNING EXERCISES

The following exercises are found at the end of this chapter:

SET 1:	Strategic Planning for McDonald's
EXERCISE 11A:	Business Culture Variation Across Countries: A Report for McDonald's
EXERCISE 11B:	McDonald's Wants to Further Penetrate Africa. Can You Help Them?
SET 2:	Strategic Planning for My University
EXERCISE 11C:	Does My University Recruit in Foreign Countries?
SET 3:	Strategic Planning to Enhance My Employability
EXERCISE 11D:	How Well-Traveled Are You Compared with Your Colleagues?
SET 4:	Individual Versus Group Strategic Planning
EXERCISE 11E:	How Important Are Various Potential Advantages to Initiating, Continuing, or Expanding a Firm's International Operations?

Global considerations impact virtually all strategic decisions, as illustrated with white shading in Figure 11-1. The boundaries of countries can no longer define the limits of our imaginations. To see and appreciate the world from the perspective of others has become a matter of survival for many businesses. To survive and grow, more and more companies are monitoring and capitalizing on changes in competitors, markets, prices, suppliers, distributors, governments, creditors, shareholders, and customers worldwide.

The price and quality of a firm's products must be competitive on a worldwide basis and not just on a local basis. Shareholders expect substantial revenue growth; doing business globally is an excellent way to achieve this end. More and more countries are developing the capacity and will to compete aggressively in world markets. Foreign businesses and countries are willing to learn, adapt, innovate, and invent to compete successfully on a global scale.

Fortune annually identifies the world's "Most Powerful Women in Business," and for 2021, a key business woman on the list was Emma Walmsley, the CEO of GlaxoSmithKline. Walmsley is an Exemplary Strategist who in fact was the top female on *Fortune*'s global list the prior year also. She has been CEO and a member of the GSK board of directors since 2017.

The Nature of Doing Business Globally

11.1. **Discuss the nature of doing business globally, including labor union issues and tax rates.**

Exports of goods and services from the United States account for only 12 percent of US gross domestic product (GDP), so the nation is still largely a domestic, continental economy. In contrast, as a percentage of GDP, exports comprise 46 percent of the German economy, 20 percent of the Chinese economy, and 172 percent of the Singapore economy. Singapore's number is so high because it imports oil and other products and then reexports them globally. A point here is that, with exports making up just 12 percent of the country's GDP, the United States has substantial room for improvement in doing business.

A world market has emerged from what previously was a multitude of distinct national markets, and the climate for international business today is more favorable than in years past. Mass communication and high technology have created similar patterns of consumption across diverse cultures worldwide. Consequently, companies may find it difficult to survive by relying solely on domestic markets.

Globalization is a process of doing business worldwide, such that strategic decisions are made based on global profitability of the firm rather than just domestic considerations. A global strategy seeks to meet the needs of customers worldwide, with the highest value at the lowest cost. This may mean locating production in countries with lower labor costs or abundant natural resources, locating research and complex engineering centers where skilled scientists and engineers can be found, and locating marketing activities close to the markets to be served.

A **global strategy** includes designing, producing, and marketing products with global needs in mind rather than considering just a home country. A global strategy integrates actions against

---

Emma Walmsley, CEO of GlaxoSmithKline (GSK) plc[1]

Headquartered in London, England, GlaxoSmithKline (GSK) is the sixth-largest pharmaceutical company in the world, but GSK in 2022 is splitting into two separate companies: 1) pharmaceutical-focused business and 2) consumer health. CEO Emma Walmsley is leading this transformation. Being an exemplary strategist however does not insulate anyone from facing dissent from activists; Walmsley faces duress and dissent.

Walmsley faces calls for her ouster from Bluebell Capital Partners who recently took a £10 million (about $13.6 million) stake in GSK. Bluebell is urging the GSK board to replace Walmsley. Another activist investor, Elliott Management has called for Walmsley to resign. The activists' reasoning centers on Walmsley having "insufficient scientific and pharmaceutical experience compared to her counterparts at other large drug companies."

GSK's split into two companies is coming in mid-2022. The standalone pharmaceutical business will be named New GSK and will

Kevin Dietsch/UPI/Shutterstock

have a projected revenue of about $46 billion by 2031. Walmsley says the New GSK will focus on four core therapeutic areas: (1) infectious diseases, (2) HIV, (3) oncology, and (4) Immunology/Respiratory. GSK has a pipeline of 20 vaccines and 42 drugs, many dubbed the best in the industry.

Although Walmsley faces challenges from activist investors, she has won backing from an unexpected source, AstraZeneca's CEO of 10 years Pascal Soriot. AstraZeneca is a rival large, UK-based pharmaceutical firm. Soriot rejects the idea that Walmsley is unfit for leading New GSK after the corporate split. Soriot says you simply surround yourself with smart scientists, which Walmsley has done. Soriot recently offered Walmsley some advice on how to handle investor activism:

"If you are challenged by another company, the key is to have a good plan and stick to it and implement."

Walmsley is openly supported by BlackRock, GSK's largest investor. BlackRock is also AstraZeneca's largest shareholder. At the present time, the GSK board also supports Walmsley, partly because she has brought in top scientific talent to the leadership team, including Hal Barron as chief scientific officer and head of research and development.

[1]Based on https://www.biospace.com/article/another-activist-investor-group-calls-for-walmsley-s-ouster-as-ceo-ahead-of-gsk-split/. Also, https://www.fiercepharma.com/pharma/astrazeneca-chief-soriot-lends-glaxosmithkline-s-walmsley-ceo-wisdom-support-amid-investor

competitors into a worldwide plan. Today, many global buyers and sellers have mastered capabilities for instant transmission of money and information across continents.

In any industry that is global, it can be a risky posture to remain a domestic competitor because more aggressive rival firms may use global growth to capture economies of scale and learning. The domestic firm could then face an attack on domestic markets using different (and possibly superior) technology, product design, manufacturing, marketing approaches, and economies of scale. As a point of global reference, the largest companies in 25 different countries are listed in Table 11-1, as determined from equally weighted measures of revenue, profits, assets, and market value.

TABLE 11-1 The Largest Company (in Revenues) in 25 Different Countries

Company	Country
Walmart	United States
Brookfield	Canada
Gazprom	Russia
Hon Hai Precision Industry	Taiwan
Samsung Electronics	South Korea
Toyota Motor	Japan
America Movil	Mexico
State Grid	China
Koc	Turkey
Petronas	Malaysia
Trafigura	Singapore
Reliance Industries	India
PTT	Thailand
Saudi Aramco	Saudi Arabia
BHP Group	Australia
Pertamina	Indonesia
Arcelormittal	Luxembourg
Volvo	Sweden
Maersk	Denmark
Volkswagen	Germany
Accenture	Ireland
Royal Dutch Shell	Netherlands
BP	Britain
Anheuser-Busch Inbev	Belgium
Banco Santander	Spain

Source: Based on https://fortune.com/longform/biggest-companies-in-every-country-global-500/

Multinational Firms

Organizations that conduct business operations across national borders are called **international firms** or **multinational firms**. The strategic management process is conceptually the same for multinational firms as for purely domestic firms; however, the process is more complex as a result of more variables and relationships. The external opportunities and threats that face multinational firms are almost limitless, and the number and complexity of these factors increase dramatically with the number of products produced and the number of geographic areas served. Millions of small businesses do business everyday outside their home country by interacting with customers though websites, smartphones, and social media.

More time and effort are required to identify and evaluate external trends and events in multinational firms. Geographic distance, cultural and national differences, and variations in business practices often make communication between domestic headquarters and overseas operations difficult. Strategy implementation can be more difficult because different cultures have different norms, values, and work ethics. Multinational firms face unique and diverse risks, such as expropriation of assets, currency losses through exchange rate fluctuations, unfavorable foreign court interpretations of contracts and agreements, social/political disturbances, import/export restrictions, tariffs, and trade barriers. Strategists in global firms are often confronted with the need to be globally competitive and nationally responsive at the same time. With the rise in world commerce, government and regulatory bodies are more closely monitoring foreign business practices. The US Foreign Corrupt Practices Act, for example, monitors business practices in many areas.

Before entering international markets, firms should scan relevant journals and patent reports, seek the advice of academic and research organizations, participate in international trade fairs, form partnerships, and conduct extensive research to broaden their contacts and diminish the risks of doing business in new foreign markets. Firms can also offset some risks of doing business internationally by obtaining insurance from the US International Development Finance Corporation (DFC), which was formerly called the Overseas Private Investment Corporation (OPIC).

The decision to expand operations into foreign markets—that is, to globalize—is one of the most important strategic decisions made by companies. Variables that influence how, when, where, and why to internationalize have attracted much attention in scholarly journals. Recent research reveals that countries are attractive not only because of their own institutions but also as a function of their serving as a platform for entry into other regions.[2] Therefore, multinational firms make globalization decisions with special consideration in mind for how a particular region or country will facilitate the firm's further globalization into other regions and countries. Also important is the need to align any strategy with a firm's vision and mission and an assessment of the potential to gain and sustain competitive advantages.

Labor Unions

The existence or prevalence of labor unions can be an important factor in many strategic decisions, such as where to locate stores or factories because companies often like to avoid unions. The presence of unions raises wage rates for companies. In the US energy industry, for example, non-union wage rates are around $17/hour for the solar segment and around $21/hour for the wind segment; this compares to typical union wage rates of about $28/hour for the solar and wind segments. Union membership varies widely across Europe, ranging from 74 percent of employees in Finland, 70 percent in Sweden, 67 percent in Denmark, and 8 percent in Lithuania and France. In general, the popularity of unions across Europe is declining and has been for a decade.

The average level of union membership across the whole of the EU, weighted by the numbers employed in the different member states is 23 percent, compared with about 11 percent in the United States. The European average is held down by relatively low levels of membership in some of the larger EU states: Germany with 18 percent, France with 8 percent, Spain with 19 percent, and Poland with 12 percent. Overall, worldwide trade union membership has been gradually declining over the past couple decades despite increases in some African and Latin American countries.

Tax Rates

Tax rates in countries can represent an important strategic consideration regarding where to build manufacturing facilities or retail stores or even where to acquire other firms. High corporate tax rates deter investment in new factories and also provide strong incentives for corporations to avoid and evade taxes. Corporate tax rates vary considerably across countries and companies.

Corporate tax rates in general are decreasing globally. In 2021, three countries—Bangladesh, Argentina, and Gibraltar increased their top corporate tax rates, whereas 17 countries—including Chile, Tunisia, and France—reduced their corporate tax rates. Three countries with really high corporate tax rates are Comoros (50 percent), Puerto Rico (37.5 percent), and Suriname (36 percent), while Barbados (5.5 percent), Uzbekistan (7.5 percent), and Turkmenistan (8 percent) levy the lowest corporate rates. However, 15 countries now have 0 percent corporate tax, although this number is set to drop in 2023 as the United Arab Emirates (UAE) just announced that it will introduce its first-ever federal corporate income tax on business profits beginning on June 1, 2023, at a rate of 9 percent.

The worldwide average statutory corporate income tax rate, measured across 180 countries, is 23.54 percent. Regarding continents, Asia has the lowest regional average rate, at 19.62 percent, and Africa has the highest regional average rate, at 27.97 percent.

The average top corporate rate among the European Union (EU) member countries is 21.30 percent compared with 23.04 percent among Organization for Economic Cooperation and Development (OECD) countries. However, the EU, composed of 27 countries, has agreed to impose a minimum tax on corporations of 15 percent, but the proposal is pending approval of legislatures. Approval by the EU could come first with other countries following suit. In the U.S. the 15 percent minimum rule is being sponsored by Democrats, but Republicans largely oppose the potential law. This proposal by the EU is designed to spur business development globally rather than businesses having to face varied tax laws everywhere which complicates business transactions.

There is a good reason why companies such as Signet Jewelers Ltd, owner of Kay Jewelers, Zale Corporation, and Jared Jewelry, are headquartered in Hamilton, Bermuda—to pay 0 corporate tax as indicated in Table 11-2.

TABLE 11-2 Corporate Tax Rates for Various Countries in 2021 (from High to Low)

Country	Continent	Corporate Tax Rate
Argentina	South America	35
Brazil	South America	34
Australia	Australia	30
India	Asia	30
Nigeria	Africa	30
Mexico	North America	30
Germany	Europe	29.94
Japan	Asia	29.74
France	Europe	28.41
Canada	North America	26.5
USA	North America	25.75
China	Asia	25
Malaysia	Asia	24
Egypt	Africa	22.5
Indonesia	Asia	22
Turkey	Asia	20
Poland	Europe	19
Singapore	Asia	17
Ireland	Europe	12.5
Chile	South America	10
Hungary	Europe	9
Bermuda	North America	0
Cayman Islands	North America	0
Turks and Caicos Islands	North America	0

Source: Based on https://taxfoundation.org/corporate-tax-rates-by-country-2021/

Advantages and Disadvantages of Doing Business Globally

11.2. **Explain the advantages and disadvantages of doing business globally.**

Firms have numerous reasons for formulating and implementing strategies that initiate, continue, or expand involvement in business operations across national borders. Perhaps the greatest advantage is that firms can gain new customers for their products and services, thus increasing revenues. Growth in revenues and profits is a common organizational objective and often an expectation of shareholders because it is a measure of organizational success. Potential advantages of initiating, continuing, or expanding international operations are as follows:

1. Firms can gain new customers for their products.
2. Foreign operations can absorb excess capacity, reduce unit costs, and spread economic risks over a wider number of markets.
3. Foreign operations can allow firms to establish low-cost production facilities in locations close to raw materials or cheap labor.
4. Competitors in foreign markets may not exist, or competition may be less intense than in domestic markets.
5. Foreign operations may result in reduced tariffs, lower taxes, and favorable political treatment.
6. Multinational joint ventures can enable firms to learn the technology, culture, and business practices of other people and to make contacts with potential customers, suppliers, creditors, and distributors in foreign countries.
7. Economies of scale can be better achieved from operation in global rather than solely domestic markets. Larger-scale production and better efficiencies allow higher sales volumes and lower-price offerings.
8. A firm's power and prestige in domestic markets may be significantly enhanced if the firm competes globally. Enhanced prestige can translate into improved negotiating power among creditors, suppliers, distributors, and other important groups.

The availability, depth, and reliability of economic and marketing information in different countries varies extensively, as do industrial structures, business practices, and the number and nature of regional organizations. There are also numerous potential disadvantages of initiating, continuing, or expanding business across national borders, such as the following:

1. Foreign operations could be seized by nationalistic factions.
2. Firms confront different and often little understood social, cultural, demographic, environmental, political, governmental, legal, technological, economic, and competitive forces when doing business internationally.
3. Weaknesses of competitors in foreign lands are often overestimated, and strengths are often underestimated. Keeping informed about the number and nature of competitors is more difficult when doing business internationally.
4. Language, culture, and value systems differ among countries, which can create barriers to communication and problems managing people.
5. Gaining an understanding of regional organizations such as the European Economic Community, the Latin American Free Trade Area, the International Bank for Reconstruction and Development, and the International Finance Corporation is difficult, but is often required in doing business internationally.
6. Dealing with two or more monetary systems can complicate international business operations.

For these reasons and more, firms must be thorough in their research related to expanding a firm's operations into a new country or region. As revealed in Ethics Capsule 11, differences in laws and regulations across countries may prevent a firm from legally being able to conduct business in a particular country. For example, China's regulations surrounding animal testing are stricter than perhaps anywhere, requiring that any and all cosmetic products made, marketed, or sold within China must be tested on animals.

ETHICS CAPSULE 11

Is Cosmetics Animal Testing a Global Ethical Issue?[3]

unoL/Shutterstock

Experts estimate that over 110 million animals across the globe suffer from cruel animal testing each year. A large portion of this animal testing occurs for the global cosmetics industry. In 2021, Mexico became the first North American country to ban animal testing for cosmetics. The legislation also bans the importation and marketing of cosmetics that have been tested on animals.

Antón Aguilar, executive director of Humane Society International (HSI) in Mexico, thanked the Mexican government "for showing leadership on this important issue," and commented on the new law saying: "This is a monumental step forward for animals, consumers and science in Mexico, and this ground-breaking legislation leads the way for the Americas to become the next cruelty-free beauty market and brings us one bunny-leap closer to a global ban." The new Mexican law prohibits "manufacturing, importing or marketing cosmetic products that have been tested on animals or contain ingredients or combinations of ingredients that have been tested on animals." Similar bans are already in place in 41 countries globally, as well as 10 states in Brazil and 7 US states.

There are 22 million research animals in US laboratories at any given time, and nearly 200 million research animals spread across the globe. Nearly one-third of all animal testing experiments invoke moderate to severe suffering on the subject animal, yet test animals rarely receive any pain relief. The United States is the leader in the highest number of animal tests conducted annually, and nearly $20 billion in US taxpayer dollars is spent on animal testing each year. This may be surprising given estimates that animal testing has a 96 percent failure rate, meaning that only 4 of every 100 products or ingredients tested on animals actually make it through the testing phases and into the real world.

An increasing number of national and international specialists and institutions now feel that cosmetic testing on animals should be discontinued, calling animal testing ineffective and unnecessary. The National Research Council (NRC) of the National Academies of Sciences, Engineers, and Medicine (NASEM) is one such organization with this view. Additionally, many other institutions and more than 150 US companies have petitioned the federal government to place a ban on unnecessary cosmetics animal testing. However, other institutions, companies, and even countries have seemingly outdated, cruel, and inhumane perspectives of animal testing. China, or the Chinese government better yet, requires animal testing on all cosmetics manufactured or sold in China. With a growing number of consumers globally preferring "cruelty-free" products that have not been subject to any form of animal testing, should China reconsider its stance on the issue?

[3]Based on information at https://plantbasednews.org/culture/ethics/mexico-ban-animal-testing/, https://crueltyfreesoul.com/animal-testing-banned-countries/, https://spots.com/animal-testing-statistics/, and https://www.globalcosmeticsnews.com/mexico-becomes-first-north-american-country-to-pass-bill-to-ban-animal-testing/

The Global Challenge

11.3. Discuss the global challenge facing firms, including outsourcing and reshoring.

Few companies can afford to ignore the presence of international competition. Firms that seem insulated and comfortable today may be vulnerable tomorrow; for example, foreign banks do not yet compete or operate in most of the United States, but this is quickly changing.

The US economy is becoming much less American and more global. A globalized world economy and monetary system are emerging. Corporations in every corner of the globe are taking advantage of the opportunity to obtain customers globally. Markets are shifting rapidly and, in many cases, converging in tastes, trends, and prices. Innovative transport systems are accelerating the transfer of technology. Shifts in the nature and location of production systems, especially to China and India, are reducing the response time associated with changing market conditions. China has more than one billion residents, including a dramatically growing middle class that is eager to buy goods and services.

Many countries are quite protectionist, and this position can impact companies' strategic plans. **Protectionism** refers to countries imposing tariffs, taxes, and regulations on firms outside the country to favor their own companies and people. The United States and China often impose various tariffs on each other's products imported, although the number and magnitude of tariffs and taxes typically vary depending on US presidential elections. Former President Donald Trump implemented strict sanctions on Chinese goods, many of which the Biden administration has kept in place. Most economists argue that protectionism harms the world economy because it inhibits trade among countries and invites retaliation.

Advancements in telecommunications are drawing countries, cultures, and organizations worldwide closer together. Foreign revenue as a percentage of total company revenues already exceeds 50 percent in hundreds of US firms, including ExxonMobil, Gillette, Dow Chemical, Citicorp, Colgate-Palmolive, and Texaco. A primary reason why most domestic firms do business globally is that growth in demand for goods outside the United States is considerably higher than inside. For example, the domestic food industry is growing just 3 percent per year, so Kraft Foods, the second-largest food company in the world behind Nestlé, is focusing on foreign acquisitions. Shareholders and investors of virtually all companies expect sustained (more than 5 percent) growth in revenues from firms; that level of growth for many firms can only be achieved by capitalizing on demand outside the United States. Joint ventures and partnerships between domestic and foreign firms are becoming the rule rather than the exception!

Fully 95 percent of the world's population lives outside the United States, and this group is growing 70 percent faster than the US population. The lineup of competitors in virtually all industries is global. General Motors and Ford compete with Toyota and Hyundai. General Electric and Westinghouse Electric battle Siemens and Mitsubishi. Caterpillar and John Deere compete with Komatsu. Goodyear battles Michelin, Bridgestone/Firestone, and Pirelli. Boeing competes with Airbus. Only a few US industries—such as furniture, printing, retailing, consumer-packaged goods, and retail banking—are not yet greatly challenged by foreign competitors. But many products and components in these industries too are now manufactured in foreign countries. International operations can be as simple as exporting a product to a single foreign country or as complex as operating manufacturing, distribution, and marketing facilities in many countries.

The US automotive industry is experiencing significant foreign competition as Toyota and Hyundai compete with GM and Ford for US market share. History was made in 2021 when for the first time ever Toyota surpassed General Motors in US auto sales. This is the first time in the industry's nearly 120-year history that a foreign manufacturer achieved the status of being the top-selling automaker in the US. One factor working in Toyota's favor during 2021 was the global chip shortage that hurt GM and Ford but had a relatively minute impact on Toyota. Erik Gordon, a business professor at the University Michigan, explained Toyota's success within the US market as follows:

> The dominance of the US automakers of the US market is just over. Toyota might not beat G.M. again this year, but the fact that they did it is symbolic of how the industry changed. No U.S. automaker can think of themselves as entitled to market share just because they're American.

Different industries become global for different reasons. The need to amortize massive R&D investments over many markets is a major reason why the aircraft manufacturing industry became global. Monitoring globalization in one's industry is an important strategic management activity. Knowing how to use that information for one's competitive advantage is even more important. For example, firms may look around the world for the best technology and select one that has the most promise for the largest number of markets. When firms design a product, they design it to be marketable in as many countries as possible. When firms manufacture a product, they select the lowest-cost source, which may be Japan for semiconductors, Sri Lanka for textiles, Malaysia for simple electronics, and Europe for precision machinery.

Outsourcing and Reshoring

Outsourcing involves companies hiring other companies to take over various parts of their functional operations, such as human resources, information systems, payroll, accounting, customer service, and even marketing. For more than a decade, US and European companies have been outsourcing their manufacturing, tech support, and back-office work, but most insisted on keeping R&D activities in-house. However, an ever-growing number of firms today are outsourcing their product design to Asian developers. China and India have become important suppliers of intellectual property. The details of what work to outsource, to whom, where, and for how much can challenge even the biggest, most sophisticated companies. India is a booming place for outsourcing. China requires many firms to share their technological knowledge as a condition of doing business in that country; this is a growing problem for US firms and the United States in general.

Table 11-3 reveals potential benefits that firms strive to achieve through outsourcing. Notice from the first benefit that outsourcing is often used to access lower wages in foreign countries.

TABLE 11-3 Potential Benefits of Outsourcing

1. *Cost savings:* Access lower wages in foreign countries.
2. *Focus on core business:* Focus resources on developing the core business rather than being distracted by other functions.
3. *Cost restructuring:* Outsourcing changes the balance of fixed costs to variable costs by moving the firm more to variable costs.
4. *Improve quality:* Improve quality by contracting out various business functions to specialists.
5. *Knowledge:* Gain access to intellectual property and wider experience and knowledge.
6. *Contract:* Gain access to services within a legally binding contract with financial penalties and legal redress. This is not the case with services performed internally.
7. *Access to talent:* Gain access to a larger talent pool and a sustainable source of skills, especially science and engineering.
8. *Catalyst for change:* Use an outsourcing agreement as a catalyst for major change that cannot be achieved alone.
9. *Reduce time to market:* Accelerate development or production of a product through additional capability brought by the supplier.
10. *Risk management:* Manage risk by partnering with an outside firm.
11. *Tax benefit:* Capitalize on tax incentives to locate manufacturing plants to avoid high taxes in various countries.

Reshoring refers to US companies moving a portion of their manufacturing back to the United States. The strength of the dollar, however, has led some US firms to look outside the United States to produce goods. A high value of the dollar makes US goods more expensive overseas and makes imports to the United States cheaper. Overall, however, benefits of reshoring are as follows:

1. Reliable energy at a relatively low cost, lower transportation and shipment costs
2. A large, skilled workforce with US laws that protect employees, including females and people of color
3. Greater security and ability to protect designs and intellectual property from theft and overseas copycats
4. Closer tabs on quality control and supply chains, enabling enhanced customer responsiveness
5. More efficient production capacity and inventory management
6. Simplified legal and tax-related issues
7. Foster participation in the US economy by providing new jobs and developing "made in America" products

USA Versus Foreign Business Culture

11.4. Compare and contrast US business culture versus foreign business cultures; explain why this is a strategic issue.

To be successful in world markets, US managers must obtain a better knowledge of historical, cultural, and religious forces that motivate and drive people in other countries. For multinational firms, knowledge of business culture variation across countries can be essential for gaining and sustaining competitive advantage. An excellent website to visit on this topic is www.worldbusinessculture .com, where you can select any country in the world and see how business culture varies in that country versus others. In Japan, for example, business relations operate within the context of **Wa**, which stresses group harmony and social cohesion. In China, business behavior revolves around **guanxi**, or personal relations. In South Korea, activities involve concern for **inhwa**, or harmony based on respect of hierarchical relationships, including obedience to authority.

A weakness of some US firms in competing with foreign firms is a lack of understanding of foreign cultures, including how business people in other countries think and behave. Table 11-4 lists other cultural differences that managers may benefit from considering when doing business in other countries. The table shows information related to the attitude, time

TABLE 11-4 Components of Business Culture Across Various Countries

Country	Business Attitude Win-Lose to Win-Win	Time Sensitivity Low to High	Style Informal to Formal	Communication Indirect to Direct
Australia	5.0	4.0	2.0	5.0
Brazil	3.0	1.0	2.0	3.0
Canada	5.0	4.5	3.0	5.0
China	2.0	2.0	5.0	1.0
France	3.0	1.0	4.0	3.0
Germany	3.5	5.0	5.0	4.0
India	3.0	2.0	3.0	2.0
Indonesia	4.0	2.5	4.5	1.0
Italy	3.5	3.5	3.0	2.5
Japan	4.0	3.0	5.0	1.0
Malaysia	4.0	2.0	3.5	2.0
Mexico	3.5	2.0	3.0	2.0
Nigeria	2.0	1.0	3.0	2.5
South Korea	2.0	3.0	5.0	2.0
Sweden	4.0	4.0	5.0	5.0
United Arab Emirates	3.0	2.0	2.0	2.0
UK	4.0	4.0	4.0	3.0
United States	3.0	5.0	3.0	5.0

Source: Based on information from the World Trade Press' Global Road Warrior database available at https://www.globalroadwarrior.com/

sensitivity, style, and communication nature when doing business in various countries. Each element in Table 11-4 is scored on a 1.0 to 5.0 scale; scores on business attitude reflect the extent to which negotiation styles are based on achieving win-lose solutions (1.0) versus win-win solutions (5.0); scores on time sensitivity indicate the importance of timeliness from low (1.0) to high (5.0); scores on style reflect the extent to which personal style among businesspeople is informal (1.0) versus formal (5.0); and scores in communication indicate the extent to which business communications are generally indirect (1.0) versus direct (5.0). Notice for example that the business attitude in China tends to be more win-lose, as opposed to other countries such as Australia which tend to have a win-win attitude in business negotiations. Also note that China and Japan tend to have a formal style in business environments and formal behavior is expected at most meetings, but businesspeople in these countries tend to communicate much more indirectly than in other countries such as Germany and Sweden.

Managers from the United States place greater emphasis on short-term results than do foreign managers. In marketing, for example, Japanese managers strive to achieve "everlasting customers," whereas many Americans strive to make a one-time sale. Marketing managers in Japan see making a sale as the beginning, not the end, of the selling process. This is an important distinction. Japanese managers often criticize US managers for worrying more about shareholders, whom they do not know, than employees, whom they do know. Americans refer to "hourly employees," whereas many Japanese companies still refer to "lifetime employees."

Rose Knotts summarized some important cultural differences between US and foreign managers.[4] Awareness and consideration of these differences can enable a manager to be more effective, regardless of their nationality.

1. Americans place an exceptionally high priority on time, viewing time as an asset and punctuality as vital. Many foreigners place more worth on family and relationships. This difference results in foreign managers often viewing US managers as "more interested in business than people."
2. Personal touching and distance norms differ around the world. Americans generally stand about 3 feet from each other when carrying on business conversations, but Arabs and Africans stand about 1 foot apart. Touching another person with the left hand in business dealings is taboo in some countries.

3. Family roles and relationships vary in different countries. For example, males are valued more than females in some cultures, and peer pressure, work situations, and business interactions reinforce this phenomenon.

4. Business and daily life in some societies is governed by religious factors. Prayer times, holidays, daily events, and dietary restrictions, for example, need to be respected by managers regardless of their own nationality and cultural norms.

5. Many cultures around the world value modesty, team spirit, collectivity, and patience much more than competitiveness and individualism, which are so important in the United States.

6. Eating habits also differ dramatically across cultures. For example, belching is acceptable in some countries as evidence of satisfaction with the food that has been prepared. Chinese culture considers it good manners to sample a portion of each food served.

7. To prevent social blunders when meeting with managers from other lands, one must learn and respect the rules of etiquette of others. Leaving food or drink after dining is considered impolite in some countries but not in China. Bowing instead of shaking hands is customary in many countries. Some cultures view Americans as unsanitary for locating toilet and bathing facilities in the same area, whereas Americans view people of some cultures as unsanitary for not taking a bath or shower every day.

8. Americans often do business with individuals they do not know, unlike businesspersons in many other cultures. In Mexico and Japan, for example, an amicable relationship is often mandatory before conducting business.

In many countries, effective managers are those who are best at negotiating with government bureaucrats, rather than those who inspire workers. The United States provides legal protection against sexual harassment and discrimination based on race, sexual orientation, religion, and so on, but not all countries offer the same legal protections. US managers in China have to be careful about how they arrange office furniture because Chinese workers believe in **feng shui**, the practice of harnessing natural forces. Also, US managers in Japan have to be careful about **nemaswashio**, whereby Japanese workers expect supervisors to alert them privately of changes rather than informing them in a meeting.

Probably the biggest obstacle to the effectiveness of US managers—or managers from any country working in another—is the fact that it is almost impossible to change the attitude of a foreign workforce. "The system drives you; you cannot fight the system or culture," says Bill Parker, former executive vice president of Phillips Petroleum Worldwide. For example, in the Middle East, be careful of alcohol and pork because many Muslims do not eat pork or drink alcohol. In India, cows are revered, so no leather gifts.

Communication Differences Across Countries

Communication may be the most important word in strategic management. Americans increasingly interact with managers in other countries, so it is important to understand communication differences across countries. Americans sometimes come across as intrusive, manipulative, and garrulous; this impression may reduce their effectiveness in communication. Asian managers view extended periods of silence as important for organizing and evaluating one's thoughts, whereas US managers have a low tolerance for silence. Sitting through a conference without talking is unproductive in the United States but may be viewed as positive in Japan as one's silence helps preserve unity. Managers from the United States are much more action-oriented than their counterparts around the world; they rush to appointments, conferences, and meetings—and then feel the day has been productive. But for many foreign managers, resting, listening, meditating, and thinking is considered productive.

Most Japanese managers are reserved, quiet, distant, introspective, and others-oriented, whereas most US managers are talkative, direct, and individual-oriented. Unlike Japanese managers, US managers often use blunt criticism, ask prying questions, and make quick decisions. These kinds of communication differences have disrupted many potentially productive Japanese–US business endeavors. Viewing the Japanese communication style as a prototype for all Asian cultures is a stereotype that must be avoided.

Like many Asian and African cultures, the Japanese are nonconfrontational. They have a difficult time saying "no," so you must be vigilant at observing their nonverbal communication.

Rarely refuse a request, no matter how difficult or nonprofitable it may appear at the time. In communicating with Japanese businesspeople, phrase questions so that they can answer *yes*—for example, "Do you disagree with this?" Group decision-making and consensus are vitally important. The Japanese often remain silent in meetings for long periods of time and may even close their eyes when they want to listen intently.

Business Culture Across Countries[5]

11.5. **Discuss business culture, with emphasis on Mexico, Japan, China, and India.**

Managers, marketers, salespersons, and virtually all businesspersons can be more effective in doing business with persons and companies in other countries if they have an understanding and appreciation of business culture variation across countries. One aspect of business culture common across countries is appreciation for excellent customer service. Airlines fly people from nation to nation all over the world. For a flavor of how cultures vary across continents, let's examine four countries: Mexico, Japan, China, and India.

Mexico

Mexico is an authoritarian society in terms of schools, churches, businesses, and families. In general, employers seek workers who are agreeable, respectful, and obedient, rather than innovative, creative, and independent. When visitors walk into a Mexican business, they are met with a cordial, friendly atmosphere. This is almost always true because Mexicans' desire for harmony is part of the social fabric in worker–manager relations. There is a much lower tolerance for adversarial relations or friction at work in Mexico than in the United States.

Mexican employers generally provide workers with more than a paycheck, but in return they expect allegiance. Weekly food baskets, free meals, free bus service, and free day care are often part of compensation. The ideal working condition for a Mexican worker is the family model, with people all working together, doing their share, according to their designated roles. Mexican workers do not expect or desire a work environment in which self-expression and initiative are encouraged. US business embodies individualism, achievement, competition, curiosity, pragmatism, informality, spontaneity, and doing more than expected on the job, whereas Mexican businesses stress collectivism, continuity, cooperation, belongingness, formality, and doing exactly what is told. Meeting times for appointments are not rigid. Tardiness is common everywhere. Effectively doing business in Mexico requires knowledge of the Mexican way of life, culture, beliefs, and customs. Do not get irritated at the lack of punctuality in Mexico.

Japan

Japan's workforce population ages 15 to 64 is declining about 500,000 each year, so the country is facing its tightest labor market in 40 years. This shift toward an older population has forced Japan to increasingly open its doors to immigrant workers, which has increased demand for housing and international goods. The world's third-largest economy, Japan is undergoing an economic turnaround where business confidence is approaching its highest point in decades.

The Japanese people place great importance on group loyalty and consensus—a concept called **Wa**. Corporate activities in Japan encourage Wa among managers and employees. Wa requires that all members of a group agree and cooperate; this results in constant discussion and compromise. Japanese managers evaluate the potential attractiveness of alternative business decisions in terms of the long-term effect on the group's Wa. This is why silence, used for pondering alternatives, can be a plus in a formal Japanese meeting. Discussions potentially disruptive to Wa are generally conducted in informal settings, such as at a bar, so as to minimize harm to the group's Wa. Entertaining is an important business activity in Japan because it strengthens Wa. Formal meetings are often conducted in informal settings. When confronted with disturbing questions or opinions, Japanese managers tend to remain silent, whereas Americans tend to respond directly, defending themselves through explanation and argument.

In Japan, a person's age and status are of paramount importance, whether in the family unit, the extended family, or a social or business situation. Schoolchildren learn early that the oldest person in the group is to be honored. Older folks are served first and their drinks are poured for them. Greetings in Japan are formal and ritualized, so wait to be introduced because it may be viewed as impolite to introduce yourself, even in a large gathering. Foreigners may shake hands, but the traditional form of greeting in Japan is to bow. The deeper you bow, the more respect you show, but at least bow the head slightly in greetings.

In Japan, build and maintain relationships by sending greeting, thank-you, birthday, and seasonal cards. You need to be a good "correspondent" to effectively do business with the Japanese. Punctuality is important, so arrive on time for meetings and be mindful that it may take several meetings to establish a good relationship. The Japanese are looking for a long-term relationship. Always give a small gift as a token of your appreciation, and present it to the most senior person at the end of any meeting.

Business cards are exchanged in Japan constantly and with excitement. Invest in quality business cards and keep them in pristine condition. Do not write on them. Have one side of your card translated in Japanese and give it to the person with the Japanese side facing the recipient. Business cards are generally given and received with two hands and a slight bow. Examine any business card you receive carefully because this shows care and appreciation.

China

In China, greetings are formal and the oldest person is always greeted first. Like in the United States, handshakes are the most common form of greeting. Many Chinese will look toward the ground when greeting someone. The Chinese have an excellent sense of humor, often laughing at themselves if they have a comfortable relationship with the other person. Never give clocks, handkerchiefs, flowers, or straw sandals because they are associated with funerals. Do not wrap gifts in white, blue, or black paper. In China, the number 4 is unlucky, so do not give four of anything. Eight is the luckiest number, so giving eight of something is a great idea.

The Chinese rarely do business with companies or people they do not know. Your position on an organizational chart is extremely important in business relationships. Gender bias is generally not an issue. Meals and social events are not the place for business discussions. There is a demarcation between business and socializing in China, so try to be careful not to intertwine the two. Like in the United States and Germany, punctuality is important in China. Arriving late to a meeting is an insult and could negatively affect your relationship. Meetings require patience because mobile phones ring frequently and conversations may be boisterous. Never ask the Chinese to turn off their mobile phones because this causes you both to "lose face."

As indicated in the Global Capsule 11, China is on a mission to gain technological superiority among all nations in the next decade, through quantum computing, artificial intelligence, robotics, cybersecurity, mining (70%), and processing (90%) of the world's 17 rare Earth metals that are vital in the operation of batteries, computers, turbines, lasers, iPhones, jet engines, missile guidance systems, satellites, and superconductors.

India

India's rate of female participation in the labor force is about 35 percent, which is quite low, especially considering that women make up about 42 percent of college graduates in India. Even Indian women with a college degree are expected to let their careers take a back seat to caring for their spouse, children, and elderly parents. Like in many Asian cultures, people in India do not like to say *no*, verbally or nonverbally. Rather than disappoint you, they often will say something is not available, will offer you the response that they think you want to hear, or will be vague with you. This behavior should not be considered dishonest. Shaking hands is common in India, especially in the large cities among the more educated who are accustomed to dealing with westerners. Men may shake hands with other men and women may shake hands with other women; however, there are seldom handshakes between men and women because of religious beliefs.

Be mindful that neither Hindus nor Sikhs eat beef, and many are vegetarians. Lamb, chicken, and fish are the most commonly served main courses. Table manners are somewhat formal, but much Indian food is eaten with the fingers. Like most places in the world, wait to be told where and when to sit at dinner. Women in India typically serve the men and eat later. You may be asked to wash your hands before and after sitting down to a meal. Always use your right hand to eat, whether using utensils or your fingers. Leave a small amount of food on your plate to indicate

GLOBAL CAPSULE 11

China Aims for Superiority on Rare Earth Metals Mining and Processing[6]

WDG Photo/Shutterstock

Rare Earth metals are a group of 17 elements: lanthanum, cerium, praseodymium, neodymium, promethium, samarium, europium, gadolinium, terbium, dysprosium, holmium, erbium, thulium, ytterbium, lutetium, scandium, and yttrium. These elements are vital in the operation of batteries, computers, turbines, lasers, iPhones, jet engines, missile guidance systems, satellites, and superconductors. A potentially severe problem is that mainland China ominously controls the world's mining (70%) and processing (90%) of rare metals. To further strengthen its stranglehold on the mining and processing of rare Earth metals, China recently merged all its rare Earth assets and companies such as China Minmetals, Aluminum Corp. of China, and Ganzhou Rare Earth Group into one new company: China Rare Earth Group, based in the resource-rich Jiangzi province in southern China.

Companies such as Raytheon, Lockheed Martin, Boeing, BAE Systems plc, and other defense companies all make sophisticated missiles that use rare Earth metals in their guidance systems and sensors. Apple and other computer companies use rare Earth elements in touchscreens, speakers, cameras, and the so-called "haptic" engines that makes phones vibrate. Rare Earth metals are not available from traditional recyclers because they are used in such small amounts they cannot be recovered. Many companies and countries worry that China could use its dominance in the rare Earth mining and processing industry as a geopolitical weapon. People worry too because a monopolistic situation of this magnitude could conceivably be used to jeopardize a nation's electric grid system and electric vehicles; a country's national defense itself could be compromised. This is also worrisome because China's National Laboratory for Quantum Information Science in Hefei, Anhui province, has arguably already achieved the related quantum computing/mechanics superiority globally, more advanced even than Google, Microsoft, Apple, IBM, and Intel.

California's Mountain Pass mine in San Bernardino County is the only operating US rare Earth facility. But even MP Materials, owner of Mountain Pass, ships about 50,000 tons of its rare Earth concentrate annually from California to China for processing. Australia's Lynas Corporation recently signed a memorandum of understanding with Texas-based Blue Line Corporation to build a rare Earth processing facility in the United States, but this could be too little too late. Rare Earth metals are also mined in India, South Africa, Canada, Australia, Estonia, Malaysia, and Brazil but collectively only small amounts compared to operations in China.

A 2022 bipartisan Senate bill aims to ban defense contractors from obtaining rare Earth mineral materials from China. In an interview with Yahoo Finance Live, the bill's co-sponsor Sen. Mark Kelly (D, AZ) called Chinese rare Earth minerals "a national security risk" and urged the Pentagon to act quickly to eliminate the metals from military weapons systems.

"We've got to stop relying on Chinese rare Earth in our defense industry. It's a national security risk to us. If China decided to cut us off on those rare Earth minerals right now, this would have a serious impact on our national defense," Kelly said. "So, this requires that DOD and the Department of Interior work together to build a stockpile of rare Earth minerals."

The bill marks the latest U.S. attempt to break China's near monopoly on the 17 metals that are crucial to the development of everything from smart electronic devices to wind turbines. The Kelly bill is named the Restoring Essential Energy and Security Holdings Onshore for Rare Earths Act of 2022. This Act requires the U.S. Department of Defense and Interior to stockpile rare Earth minerals, and it bans the use of rare Earth metals from being obtained from China when being used in sensitive military systems.

[6]Based on Keith Zhai, "China to Create National Rare-Earths Giant," *Wall Street Journal*, December 4, 2021, p. B3. Also, https://www.reuters.com/article/us-usa-china-rareearth-explainer/explainer-chinas-rare-earth-supplies-could-be-vital-bargaining-chip-in-u-s-trade-war-idUSKCN1T00EK. Also, Source: https://www.aol.com/chinese-rare-earth-minerals-national-141923376.html

that you are satisfied. Finishing all your food means that you are still hungry, which is also true in Egypt, China, Mexico, and many countries.

Indians prefer to do business with those whom they have established a relationship with that is built on mutual trust and respect. Punctuality is important. Indians generally do not trust the legal system, and someone's word is often sufficient to reach an agreement. Do not disagree publicly with anyone in India. Titles such as professor, doctor, or engineer are important in India, as is a person's age, university degree, caste, and profession. Use the right hand to give and receive business cards. Business cards need not be translated but should be presented so that the recipient can read the card as it is handed to him or her. This is a nice, expected gesture in most countries around the world.

Business Climate Across Countries

11.6. Discuss business climate in nations across the globe.

The 2022 *World Citizenship Report* (WCR) ranked 187 countries in terms of their respective value through the lens of a global citizen. The report ranks nations from best to worst using a WCR rating. For each nation, the rating is calculated as the weighted average of five key motivators including (1) safety and security (25%), (2) economic opportunity (25%), (3) quality of life (25%), (4) global mobility (15%), and (5) financial freedom (10%).

Table 11-5 reveals the *World Citizenship Report's* 2022 rankings for the top 10 nations for economic opportunity, or conceivably the "world's most sought-after business hubs." Note, for example, that the United States is rated the second-best country on the planet for doing business, and the UK is ranked tenth. This information can be helpful for strategists (and students) deciding where to locate new operations and where to focus new efforts.

TABLE 11-5 The Top 10 Nations That Are Best for Doing Business in 2022

Ranking	Country	Continent	World Citizenship Rating
1.	Singapore	Asia	84.8
2.	United States	North America	83.7
3.	Hong Kong	Asia	83.1
4.	Netherlands	Europe	82.4
5.	Japan	Asia	82.3
6.	Switzerland	Europe	82.3
7.	Germany	Europe	81.8
8.	Denmark	Europe	81.2
9.	Sweden	Europe	81.2
10.	United Kingdom	Europe	81.2

Source: Based on information at https://ceoworld.biz/2022/02/28/the-best-places-to-do-business-in-2022-according-to-the-world-citizenship-report/, retrieved on May 31, 2022.

IMPLICATIONS FOR STRATEGISTS

Figure 11-2 reveals that doing business globally is increasingly a prerequisite for success even for the smallest of firms. About 95 percent of consumers globally live outside the United States; firms can grow and gain economies of scale by serving these consumers. Whatever product a company has to offer, it would likely be well received in many nations. It may be strategically best for your firm to outsource operations, procure resources, and use a labor force away from home to gain and sustain competitive advantages at home.

More and more countries around the world are welcoming foreign investment and capital. As a result, labor markets have steadily become more international. The drive to improve the efficiency of global business operations is leading to greater functional specialization. This is not limited to a search for the familiar low-cost labor in Latin America or Asia. Other considerations include the cost of energy, availability of resources, inflation rates, tax rates, and the nature of trade regulations.

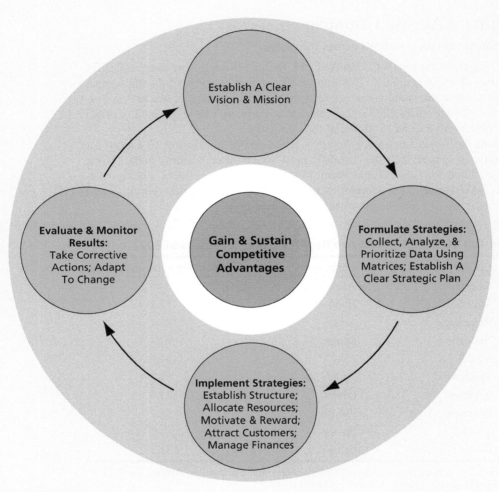

FIGURE 11-2

How to Gain and Sustain Competitive Advantages

IMPLICATIONS FOR STUDENTS

Even the smallest businesses today regularly serve customers globally and gain competitive advantages and economies of scale by doing so. Many iconic US businesses, such as Tupperware, obtain more than 80 percent of their revenue from outside the United States. Therefore, in performing a strategic management case analysis, you must evaluate the scope, magnitude, and nature of what your company is doing globally compared to rival firms. Then, determine what your company should be doing to garner global business. Continuously throughout your presentation or written report, compare your firm to rivals in terms of global business and make recommendations based on careful analysis. Be "prescriptive and insightful" rather than "descriptive and mundane" with every slide presented to pave the way for your specific recommendations with costs regarding global reach of your firm. Continually compare and contrast what you are recommending compared with what the company is actually doing or planning to do.

Chapter Summary

The population of the world has surpassed 7.5 billion. Businesses more than ever before are now searching for new opportunities beyond their national boundaries. There has never been a more internationalized and economically competitive society than today's. Some US industries, such as textiles, steel, and consumer electronics, are in disarray as a result of the international challenges of globalization.

Success in business increasingly depends on offering products and services that are competitive on a world basis and not just on a local basis. If the price and quality of a firm's products and services are not competitive with those available elsewhere in the world, the firm may soon face extinction. Global markets have become a reality in all but the most remote areas of the world. Certainly throughout the United States, even in small towns, firms feel the pressure of world competitors.

This chapter has provided some basic global information that can be essential to consider in developing a strategic plan for any organization. Business culture and climate across countries are particularly important topics in strategic planning. The advantages of engaging in international business may well offset the drawbacks for most firms. It is important in strategic planning to be effective, and the nature of global operations may be the crucial component in a plan's overall effectiveness.

Key Terms and Concepts

feng shui (p. 335)
global strategy (p. 326)
globalization (p. 326)
guanxi (p. 333)
inhwa (p. 333)
international firms (p. 328)

multinational firms (p. 328)
nemaswashio (p. 335)
outsourcing (p. 332)
protectionism (p. 331)
reshoring (p. 333)
Wa (p. 333)

Issues for Review and Discussion

11-1. *Wa, guanxi,* and *inhwa* are important management terms in Japan, China, and South Korea, respectively. What would be analogous terms to describe US management practices?

11-2. Discuss the climate for doing business in India. What are the implications for companies?

11-3. How would you describe the business climate globally in 2022–2024? What are the implications for companies?

11-4. Why are some industries more "global" than others? Discuss.

11-5. List four benefits and four drawbacks of reshoring.

11-6. Why do many Europeans find the notion of "team spirit" in a work environment difficult to grasp?

11-7. In China, *feng shui* is important in business, whereas in Japan, *nemaswashio* is important. What are analogous US terms and practices?

11-8. What areas of business does China seek superiority in within a decade?

11-9. Compare tax rates in the United States with other countries. What impact could these differences have on "keeping jobs at home"?

11-10. Give specifics regarding the nature and role of "Union Membership across Europe." What are the strategic implications of these facts and figures?

11-11. Give specifics regarding income tax rates and practices across countries and associated strategic implications.

11-12. Exports from the United States comprise about 12 percent of GDP, compared to about 45 percent of Germany's GDP. What are the implications of this for US firms doing business globally?

11-13. A company is planning to begin operations in Switzerland. That company's external factor evaluation (EFE) Matrix includes 20 factors. How much weight (1.0 to 0.01) would you place on the corporate tax rate factor? Discuss.

11-14. Explain how awareness of business culture across countries can enhance strategy implementation.

11-15. Describe the business culture in China.

11-16. Describe the business culture in India.

11-17. Describe the business culture in Mexico.

11-18. Describe the business culture in Japan.

11-19. Do some research on Singapore to determine whether you agree that the country merits its number 1 or 2 ranking globally in attractiveness for doing business.

11-20. About 53 percent of people in Belgium are members of a labor union. Compare the labor union situation across European countries and comment on the positive or negative impact this factor has on attracting business investment into those countries.

11-21. Explain why consumption patterns are becoming similar worldwide. What are the strategic implications of this trend?

11-22. What are the major differences between domestic and multinational operations that affect strategic management?

11-23. Why is globalization of industries a common factor today?

11-24. Compare the United States with foreign cultures in terms of doing business.

11-25. List six reasons that strategic management is more complex in a multinational firm.

11-26. Do you feel that protectionism is good or bad for the world economy? Why?

Writing Assignments

11-27. Make a good argument for returning the statutory corporate tax rate in the USA to the previous 21 percent.

11-28. What are the advantages and disadvantages of beginning export operations in a foreign country?

Ken Wolter/Alamy Photo

ASSURANCE-OF-LEARNING EXERCISES

SET 1: STRATEGIC PLANNING FOR MCDONALD'S

EXERCISE 11A

Business Culture Variation Across Countries: A Report for McDonald's Company

Purpose

Various websites give excellent detail that compare business culture across countries. One excellent website is http://www.kwintessential.co.uk/resources/country-profiles.html, where you can click on more than 100 countries and obtain a synopsis of a country's business culture. After clicking on a country at that website, you may scroll down to reach the section titled "Business Etiquette and Protocol."

This exercise will expand your knowledge about how business culture varies across countries. Being knowledgeable of various countries' business culture can make you a more effective manager and communicator with people and organizations globally. This knowledge is especially helpful for firms that desire to grow globally. There are about 190 different countries with different business cultures, creating many options. Business culture is an important variable in global expansion decisions.

Instructions

Step 1   Go to http://www.kwintessential.co.uk/resources/country-profiles.html. Click on three countries located on different continents. Scroll down to the "Business Etiquette and Protocol" section of each country.

Step 2   Come to class prepared to give an oral presentation that compares the business culture in the three countries you selected. Frame your presentation as if you are giving advice to top managers at McDonald's regarding expansion into those three countries.

EXERCISE 11B

McDonald's Wants to Further Penetrate Africa. Can You Help Them?

Purpose

More and more companies every day decide to launch operations in Africa. McDonald's sees millions of potential customers in Africa. Research is necessary to determine the best strategy for being the first mover in many African countries.

Instructions

Step 1	View a map of Africa.
Step 2	Compare demographic data across eight African countries.
Step 3	Gather competitive information regarding the presence of Burger King in Africa. Recall that Burger King is owned by Restaurant Brands International (RBI).
Step 4	Develop a prioritized list of eight African countries in which you would recommend McDonald's build distribution warehouses. Country 1 is your best, and country 2 is your next best. List in prioritized order two cities in each of your eight African countries where you believe McDonald's should focus distribution and retail efforts. Justify your choices.

SET 2: STRATEGIC PLANNING FOR MY UNIVERSITY

EXERCISE 11C

Does My University Recruit in Foreign Countries?

Purpose

A competitive climate exists among colleges and universities around the world. Colleges and universities in Europe and Japan are increasingly recruiting US students to offset declining enrollments. Foreign students already make up more than a third of the student body at many US universities. The purpose of this exercise is to identify particular colleges and universities in foreign countries that recruit US students.

Instructions

Step 1	Select a foreign country. Conduct research to determine the number and nature of colleges and universities in that country. What programs are institutions in those countries recognized for offering? What percentage of undergraduate and graduate students attending those institutions are US citizens? Do these institutions actively recruit US students? Are any of the schools of business at the various universities AACSB International accredited?
Step 2	Prepare a report that summarizes your research findings. Present your report to the class.

SET 3: STRATEGIC PLANNING TO ENHANCE MY EMPLOYABILITY

EXERCISE 11D

How Well-Traveled Are You Compared with Your Colleagues?

Purpose

How well-traveled are students, including yourself, at your university? To what extent do students consider their travels to be helpful in becoming an effective businessperson? Generally speaking, the more one has traveled, especially outside the United States, the more tolerant, understanding, and appreciative one is for diversity.[7] Many students even state on their résumé the extent to which they have traveled, both across the United States and perhaps around the world.

Instructions

Step 1   Administer the following survey to at least 30 business students, including your classmates in the strategic management course.

Step 2   Administer the following survey to yourself.

Step 3   Analyze the results with special emphasis comparing yourself to your colleagues. Give a 15-minute presentation to your class regarding your findings and implications.

The Survey

1. How many states in the United States have you visited?
2. How many states in the United States have you lived in for at least 3 months?
3. How many countries outside the United States have you visited?
4. List the countries outside the United States that you have visited.
5. How many countries outside the United States have you lived in for at least 3 months?
6. List the countries outside the United States that you have lived in for at least 3 months.
7. To what extent do you feel that traveling across the United States can make a person a more effective businessperson? Use a 1 to 10 scale, where 1 is "Does Not Make a Difference" and 10 is "Makes a Tremendous Difference."
8. To what extent do you feel that visiting countries outside the United States can make a person a more effective businessperson? Use a 1 to 10 scale, where 1 is "Does Not Make a Difference" and 10 is "Makes a Tremendous Difference."
9. To what extent do you feel that living in another country can make a person a more effective businessperson? Use a 1 to 10 scale, where 1 is "Does Not Make a Difference" and 10 is "Makes a Tremendous Difference."
10. What three important ways do you feel that traveling or living outside the United States would be helpful to a person in being a more effective businessperson?

SET 4: INDIVIDUAL VERSUS GROUP STRATEGIC PLANNING

EXERCISE 11E

How Important Are Various Potential Advantages to Initiating, Continuing, or Expanding a Firm's International Operations?

Purpose

This chapter discusses potential advantages (and disadvantages) to initiating, continuing, or expanding international operations. Some important advantages are as follows:

1. Firms can gain new customers for their products.
2. Foreign operations can absorb excess capacity, reduce unit costs, and spread economic risks over a wider number of markets.
3. Foreign operations can allow firms to establish low-cost production facilities in locations close to raw materials or cheap labor.

4. Competitors in foreign markets may not exist, or competition may be less intense than in domestic markets.

5. Foreign operations may result in reduced tariffs, lower taxes, and favorable political treatment.

6. Joint ventures can enable firms to learn the technology, culture, and business practices of other people and to make contacts with potential customers, suppliers, creditors, and distributors in foreign countries.

7. Economies of scale can be achieved from global operations rather than solely domestic markets. Larger-scale production and better efficiencies allow higher-sales volumes and lower-price offerings.

8. A firm's power and prestige in domestic markets may be significantly enhanced if the firm competes globally. Enhanced prestige can translate into improved negotiating power among creditors, suppliers, distributors, and other important groups.

The purpose of this exercise is to examine more closely eight potential advantages for a firm to initiate, continue, or expand international operations. In addition, the purpose of this exercise is to examine whether individual decision-making is better than group decision-making. Academic research suggests that groups make better decisions than individuals about 80 percent of the time.

Instructions

Rank the eight potential advantages for a firm to initiate, continue, or expand international operations, as to their relative importance, where 1 = most important, to 8 = least important. First, rank the advantages as an individual. Then, rank the advantages as part of a group of three. Thus, determine what person(s) and what group(s) here today can come closest to the expert ranking. This exercise enables examination of the relative effectiveness of individual versus group decision-making in strategic planning.

Steps

1. Fill in Column 1 in Table 11-6 to reveal your individual ranking of the relative importance of the eight advantages (1 = most important, 2 = next most important, etc.). For example, if you think Advantage 1 (New Customers) is the second-most important advantage, then place a 2 in Table 1 in Column 1 by the first advantage listed (new customers).

2. Fill in Column 2 in Table 11-6 to reveal your group's ranking of the relative importance of the eight advantages (1 = most important, 2 = next most important, etc.).

3. Fill in Column 3 in Table 11-6 to reveal the expert's ranking of the eight advantages for a firm to initiate, continue, or expand international operations.

4. Fill in Column 4 in Table 11-6 to reveal the absolute difference between Column 1 and Column 3 to reveal how well you performed as an individual in this exercise. (Note: Absolute difference disregards negative numbers.)

5. Fill in Column 5 in Table 11-6 to reveal the absolute difference between Column 2 and Column 3 to reveal how well your group performed in this exercise.

6. Sum Column 4. Sum Column 5.

7. Compare the Column 4 sum with the Column 5 sum. If your Column 4 sum is less than your Column 5 sum, then you performed better as an individual than as a group. Normally, group decision-making is superior to individual decision-making, so if you did better than your group, you did excellent.

8. The Individual Winner(s): The individual(s) with the lowest Column 4 sum is the WINNER.

9. The Group Winners(s): The group(s) with the lowest Column 5 score is the WINNER.

TABLE 11-6 How Important Are Various Potential Advantages to Initiating, Continuing, or Expanding a Firm's International Operations? Comparing Individual Versus Group Decision-Making

Advantages of Doing Business Globally	Col. 1	Col. 2	Col. 3	Col. 4	Col. 5
1. Firms can gain new customers for their products.					
2. Foreign operations can absorb excess capacity, reduce unit costs, and spread economic risks over a wider number of markets.					
3. Foreign operations can allow firms to establish low-cost production facilities in locations close to raw materials or cheap labor.					
4. Competitors in foreign markets may not exist, or competition may be less intense than in domestic markets.					
5. Foreign operations may result in reduced tariffs, lower taxes, and favorable political treatment.					
6. Joint ventures can enable firms to learn the technology, culture, and business practices of other people and to make contacts with potential customers, suppliers, creditors, and distributors in foreign countries.					
7. Economies of scale can be achieved from operation in global rather than solely domestic markets. Larger-scale production and better efficiencies allow higher sales volumes and lower-price offerings.					
8. A firm's power and prestige in domestic markets may be significantly enhanced if the firm competes globally. Enhanced prestige can translate into improved negotiating power among creditors, suppliers, distributors, and other important groups.					
Sums					

MINI-CASE ON TOSHIBA CORPORATION

show999/Shutterstock

IS *KEIRETSU* GONE IN JAPAN? IF YES, IS THIS GOOD FOR JAPAN?[8]

US diversified companies such as General Electric and Johnson & Johnson and numerous others commonly split up into homogeneous parts, but this activity is a rarity in Japan, historically because of *keiretsu*. The term *keiretsu* is a system in Japan where suppliers, distributors, banks, and client companies organize, own, support, and rescue each other in tough times. This good-old-boy antiquated, outdated, interlocking management system in Japan is, however, coming to a rapid end. A symbol of the end of keiretsu is the expected breakup in 2022–2023 of one of Japan's oldest diversified companies, Toshiba Corporation, headquartered in Minato, Japan. Analysts say the impending end of keiretsu is potentially the end of a major flaw in Japanese business management.

Whereas about 50 percent of a Japanese company's outstanding shares in 1989 were owned by its suppliers, distributors, and lenders, that percentage has slowly declined to about 3 percent today. At the same time, foreign ownership of those outstanding shares in Japan has risen to about 40 percent today. So now, when Japanese companies such as Toshiba face turmoil and declining finances, activists can force splits as they commonly do in US firms. Heretofore in Japan, activist, major shareholder firms were intertwined with the company's whole value chain of other firms, so their whole mindset was to help rather than to split up the firm and oust the firm's CEO.

Questions

1. What are the advantages and disadvantages of a diversified firm splitting up into homogeneous parts?
2. How can the demise of keiretsu benefit and hamper Japanese companies?
3. Is the demise of keiretsu a net plus or negative for the country of Japan? Why?

[8]Based on Joseph Sternberg, "The Toshiba Split: A Farewell to Poor Japanese Management?" *Wall Street Journal*, November 19, 2021, p. A17.

Web Resources

1. Fred David gives a video overview of Chapter 11 in the prior edition, but much info is still applicable to the 18th edition. https://www.youtube.com/watch?v=aSKfF5UUkE4
2. This website provides objective measures of business regulations and their enforcement across 183 economies and selected cities at the subnational and regional level. https://www.doingbusiness.org/en/doingbusiness
3. This website provides an online, multilingual database and provides access to more than 3 million time-series and cross-sectional data relating to food and agriculture. It also contains data for 200 countries and more than 200 primary products and inputs, just in its core.
4. https://www.fao.org/faostat/en/#home
5. The following websites provide information related to doing business internationally, including information from the Bureau of Labor Statistics:
   https://www.wri.org/
   https://www.intracen.org/
   https://www.bls.gov/fls/
   https://www.imf.org/en/Home

Current Readings

Boute, Robert N., Stephen M. Disney, Joren Gijsbrechts, and Jan A. Van Mieghem, "Dual Sourcing and Smoothing under Nonstationary Demand Time Series: Reshoring with Speed Factories," *Management Science* 68, no. 2 (2022): 1039–57.

Brouthers, Keith D., Liang Chen, Sali Li, and Noman Shaheer, "Charting New Courses to Enter Foreign Markets: Conceptualization, Theoretical Framework, and Research Directions on Non-traditional Entry Modes," *Journal of International Business Studies* (2022): 1–28.

Buckley, Peter J., Surender Munjal, and Ignacio Requejo, "How Does Offshore Outsourcing of Knowledge-Intensive Activities Affect the Exports and Financial Performance of Emerging Market Firms?," *Journal of International Business Studies* (2022): 1–26.

Butollo, Florian, "Digitalization and the Geographies of Production: Towards Reshoring or Global Fragmentation?" *Competition & Change* 25, no. 2 (2021): 259–78.

Chadha, Saurabh, and Himanshu Seth, "Ownership Structure and Capital Structure: A Panel Data Study," *International Journal of Business Innovation and Research* 24, no. 3 (2021): 385–96.

Contractor, Farok J, "The World Economy Will Need Even More Globalization in the Post-Pandemic 2021 Decade," *Journal of International Business Studies* 53, no. 1 (2022): 156–71.

Deng, Chun-Ping, Tao Wang, Thompson SH Teo, and Qi Song, "Organizational Agility Through Outsourcing: Roles of IT Alignment, Cloud Computing and Knowledge Transfer," *International Journal of Information Management* 60 (2021): 102385.

Fathollahi-Fard, Amir M., Mostafa Hajiaghaei-Keshteli, Reza Tavakkoli-Moghaddam, and Neale R. Smith, "Bi-Level Programming for Home Health Care Supply Chain Considering Outsourcing," *Journal of Industrial Information Integration* (2021): 100246.

Garcia-Bernardo, Javier, Petr Janský, and Thomas Tørsløv, "Multinational Corporations and Tax Havens: Evidence from Country-By-Country Reporting," *International Tax and Public Finance* (2021): 1–43.

Gil, Ricard, Myongjin Kim, and Giorgio Zanarone, "Relationships Under Stress: Relational Outsourcing in the US Airline Industry After the 2008 Financial Crisis," *Management Science* 68, no. 2 (2022): 1256–77.

Krause, Ryan, Juanyi Chen, Garry D. Bruton, and Igor Filatotchev, "Chief Executive Officer Power and Initial Public Offering Underpricing: Examining the Influence of Demand-Side Cultural Power Distance," *Global Strategy Journal* 11, no. 4 (2021): 686–708.

Lahiri, Somnath, Amit Karna, Sai Chittaranjan Kalubandi, and Saneesh Edacherian, "Performance Implications of Outsourcing: A Meta-Analysis." *Journal of Business Research* 139 (2022): 1303–1316.

Lartey, Theophilus A., Joseph Amankwah-Amoah, Albert Danso, Samuel Adomako, Zaheer Khan, and Shlomo Y. Tarba, "Environmental Sustainability Practices and Offshoring Activities of Multinational Corporations Across Emerging and Developed Markets," *International Business Review* 30, no. 5 (2021): 101789.

Liang, Yanze, Axèle Giroud, and Asmund Rygh, "Strategic Asset-Seeking Acquisitions, Technological Gaps, and Innovation Performance of Chinese Multinationals," *Journal of World Business* 57, no. 4 (2022): 101325.

Madan, Shilpa, Krishna Savani, and Constantine S. Katsikeas, "Privacy Please: Power Distance and People's Responses to Data Breaches Across Countries." *Journal of International Business Studies* (2022): 1–24.

McIvor, Ronan, and Lydia Bals, "A Multi-Theory Framework for Understanding the Reshoring Decision," *International Business Review* (2021): 101827.

Pedersen, Torben, and Stephen Tallman, "Global Strategy Collections: Emerging Market Multinational Enterprises," *Global Strategy Journal* 12, no. 2 (2022): 199–208.

Ponomareva, Yuliya, Timur Uman, Virginia Bodolica, and Karl Wennberg, "Cultural Diversity in Top Management Teams: Review and Agenda for Future Research," *Journal of World Business* 57, no. 4 (2022): 101328.

Röell, Christiaan, Ellis Osabutey, Peter Rodgers, Felix Arndt, Zaheer Khan, and Shlomo Tarba, "Managing Socio-Political Risk at the Subnational Level: Lessons from MNE Subsidiaries in Indonesia," *Journal of World Business* 57, no. 3 (2022): 101312.

Stallkamp, Maximilian, and Andreas P. J. Schotter, "Platforms Without Borders? The International Strategies of Digital Platform Firms," *Global Strategy Journal* 11, no. 1 (2021): 58–80.

Stendahl, Emma, Esther Tippmann, and Ali Yakhlef, "Practice Creation in Multinational Corporations: Improvisation and the Emergence of Lateral Knowledge," *Journal of World Business* 57, no. 3 (2022): 101287.

Yasuda, Naoki, and Masaaki Kotabe, "Political Risks and Foreign Direct Investments by Multinational Corporations: A Reference Point Approach," *Global Strategy Journal* 11, no. 2 (2021): 156–84.

Yildiz, H. Emre, Sergey Morgulis-Yakushev, Ulf Holm, and Mikael Eriksson, "A Relational View on the Performance Effects of International Diversification Strategies," *Journal of International Business Studies* (2022): 1–15.

Xu, Shichun, and Andy Hao, "Understanding the Impact of National Culture on Firms' Benefit-Seeking Behaviors in International B2B Relationships: A Conceptual Model and Research Propositions," *Journal of Business Research* 130 (2021): 27–37.

Zeng, Jing, "Orchestrating Ecosystem Resources in a Different Country: Understanding the Integrative Capabilities of Sharing Economy Platform Multinational Corporations," *Journal of World Business* 57, no. 6 (2022): 101347.

Endnotes

1. On page 327.
2. Based on Jean-Luc Arregle, Tuyah Miller, Michael Hitt, and Paul Beamish, "Do Regions Matter?" An Integrated Institutional and Semi-Globalization Perspective on the Internationalization of MNEs," *Strategic Management Journal* 34 (2013): 910–34.
3. On page 331.
4. Rose Knotts, "Cross-Cultural Management: Transformations and Adaptations," *Business Horizons* (January–February 1989): 29–33.
5. Some of the narrative in this section is based on information at http://kwintessential.co.uk/resources/country-profiles.html and http://www.kwintessential.co.uk/resources/global-etiquette/
6. On page 338.
7. Based on Stone, Matthew J., and James F. Petrick, "The Educational Benefits of Travel Experiences: A Literature Review," *Journal of Travel Research* 52, no. 6 (2013): 731–44; Chaochang Wang, "Attitudes Towards English Diversity of Students in the International College and the Non-IC Programmes at a University in Taiwan," *RELC Journal* 50, no. 2 (2019): 300–13; Bethany Wetzel, "South to South: Connections in the Ordinary, Fostering Empathy by Encouraging Travel Through Design," Jackson State University, Jacksonville, Alabama, MFA thesis (2021); and also information available at https://www.jrpass.com/blog/why-experiencing-a-new-culture-is-good-for-you and https://travindy.com/2020/07/does-travel-increase-cultural-understanding/
8. On page 346.

## PART 6

STRATEGIC-MANAGEMENT CASE ANALYSIS

Rido/Shutterstock

How to Prepare and Present a Case Analysis

LEARNING OBJECTIVES

After studying Part 6, you should be able to do the following:

1. Discuss guidelines for preparing to discuss a case in class.

2. Discuss guidelines for developing a written comprehensive case analysis.

3. Discuss guidelines for giving an effective oral case analysis presentation.

4. Discuss special tips for doing a case analysis.

The purpose of this section is to help you analyze strategic management cases. Numerous guidelines and suggestions are presented as are steps to follow. Be sure to use the author website (www.strategyclub.com), which provides sample case analyses, sample presentations, author videos, and especially the free Excel strategic planning template.

A strategic management case describes an organization's external and internal conditions and raises issues concerning the firm's vision, mission, strategies, objectives, and policies. Most of the information in a case is established fact, but some information may be opinions, judgments, and beliefs. Strategic management cases are more comprehensive than those you may have studied in other courses. For example, a marketing case would focus on how some company does marketing. But a strategic management case focuses on how a firm can generate a sustainable competitive advantage and, thus, requires careful consideration of all the functional areas of business as well as external contingencies.

A case puts you at the scene of the action by describing a firm's situation at some point in time and asking you to recommend an effective path or plan forward. Strategic management cases are written to give you practice applying strategic management concepts. The case method for studying strategic management is *learning by doing*, meaning you will usually be asked to prepare a 3-year strategic plan for a firm, just as if you were among top management of the firm or a consultant tasked with this work.

Guidelines for Preparing to Discuss a Case in Class

The case method of teaching can involve a classroom situation where your professor facilitates discussion by asking questions and encouraging student interaction regarding ideas, analyses, and recommendations. Be prepared for a discussion along the lines of "What would you do, why would you do it, when would you do it, and how would you do it?" Prepare answers to the following types of questions:

- What are the firm's most important external opportunities and threats?
- What are the organization's major strengths and weaknesses?
- How would you describe the organization's financial condition?
- What are the firm's existing strategies and objectives?
- Who are the firm's competitors, and what are their strategies?
- What objectives and strategies do you recommend for this organization? Explain your reasoning. How does what you recommend compare to what the company plans?
- How could the organization best implement what you recommend? What implementation problems do you envision? How could the firm avoid or solve those problems?
- How is your firm unique to the competition? What products and services are different? Where along the value chain does your firm have uniqueness and a competitive advantage—and how will your proposed recommendations enhance the firm's competitiveness?
- Are revised vision and mission statements needed given your strategic plan for the firm?

Your professor may ask the whole class to prepare a case for class discussion. Preparing a case for class discussion means that you need to read the case before class, make notes regarding the organization's external opportunities and threats as well as internal strengths and weaknesses, perform appropriate analyses, and come to class prepared to offer and defend some specific recommendations. Be excited about strategic management because in practice, the firm's survival, and, thus, many people's jobs may depend on your decisions. Guidelines for participating in a case analysis class discussion are as follows:

Be Practical

There is no such thing as a complete case, and no case ever provides all the information needed for conducting analyses and making recommendations. Likewise, in the business world, strategists never have all the information they need to make decisions. Information may be unavailable or too costly to obtain, or it may take too much time to obtain. So, in analyzing cases, do what strategists do every day, make reasonable assumptions about unknowns, perform appropriate analyses, and make decisions. *Be practical.* For example, in performing a projected financial analysis, make reasonable assumptions and proceed to show what impact your recommendations are expected to have on the organization's financial position. Avoid saying, "I don't have enough information." Always supplement the information provided in a case with internet and library research.

Be Thorough

There is no single best solution or one right answer to a strategic management case, so it is important to give ample justification for your recommendations. In the business world, strategists often do not know if their decisions are right until resources have been allocated and consumed. Then it is often too late to reverse a decision. Therefore, in your project, be thorough in justifying your thought process and recommendations from the beginning to the end of your written or oral presentation.

Be Realistic

Avoid recommending a course of action beyond an organization's means. *Be realistic.* No organization can possibly pursue all the strategies that could potentially benefit the firm. Estimate how much capital will be required to implement your recommendation. Determine whether debt, stock, or a combination of debt and stock could be used to obtain the capital. Make sure your suggestions are feasible. Do not prepare a case analysis that omits all arguments and information not supportive of your recommendations. Rather, present the major advantages and disadvantages of several feasible alternatives. Try not to exaggerate, stereotype, prejudge, or overdramatize. Strive to demonstrate that your interpretation of the evidence is reasonable and objective.

Be Specific

Do not make broad generalizations such as, "The company should pursue a market penetration strategy." Be specific by telling *what, why, when, how, where*, and *who.* Failure to use specifics is the single major shortcoming of most oral and written case analyses. Vagueness in stating factors and performing analyses is disastrous in strategic management case analysis. For example, in an internal audit, rather than saying "The firm's financial condition is bad," instead say "The firm's current ratio fell from 2.2 in 2022 to 1.3 in 2023, and this is considered to be a major weakness." Recall that external and internal factors need to be actionable, quantitative, comparative, and divisional (AQCD) to the extent possible. Rather than concluding from a SPACE Matrix that a firm should be defensive, be more specific, saying, "The firm should consider closing three plants, laying off 280 employees, and divesting itself of its chemical division, for a net savings of $20.2 million in 2024." Use ratios, percentages, numbers, and dollar estimates. Businesspeople dislike generalities and despise vagueness.

Be Original

Do not necessarily recommend the course of action that the firm plans to undertake. The aim of case analysis is for you to consider all the facts and information relevant to the organization at the time, to generate feasible alternative strategies, to choose among those alternatives, and to defend your recommendations. Support your position with charts, graphs, ratios, analyses, and the like. *Be original.* Compare and contrast what you recommend versus what the company plans to do or is doing.

Listen and Contribute

Strategy decisions are commonly made by a group of individuals rather than by a single person. Your professor will likely divide the class into three- or four-person teams and ask you to prepare written or oral case analyses. Members of a team, in class or in the business world, differ on their aversion to risk, their concern for short-run versus long-run benefits, their attitudes toward social responsibility, and their views concerning globalization. Be open-minded to others' views. Learn from each other since everyone has different skill sets.

Developing and Delivering a Written Case Analysis

Rather than have students analyze multiple cases during a semester, you may be asked to prepare a comprehensive written case analysis similar to the sample case analysis project provided on the author website at www.strategyclub.com. Or your professor could ask you or your team to focus the written case analysis on a particular aspect of the strategic management process, such as (1) to identify and evaluate the organization's existing vision, mission, objectives, and strategies; (2) to propose and defend specific recommendations for the company; or (3) to develop an industry analysis by describing the competitors, products, selling techniques, and market conditions in a given industry.

In preparing a comprehensive case analysis, you could follow the table of contents (TOC) given in Table 1; sequence your analyses according to the TOC given. The TOC sequence matches/follows the strategic management process, stages, and chapters in this text. In your written project (strategic plan) file, provide a narrative after each analysis or matrix to reveal specific implications of that particular tool or technique for the focal firm. Avoid vagueness anywhere in the project file. See the author comments in Table 1 for additional information regarding how to effectively develop and deliver a written comprehensive case analysis on a company.

TABLE 1 A Sample Table of Contents (with Author Comments)

1. Introduction: Give a one-page overview of the firm.
2. Vision Statement: Present the firm's vision statement versus your proposed statement.
3. Mission Statement: Present the firm's mission statement versus your proposed statement.
4. EFE Matrix: Include the 10 most important external opportunities and 10 most important external threats.
5. CPM: Include the firm and two rival firms compared across 10 to 20 key variables (the template allows inclusion of 12 factors).
6. Most Recent Income Statement and Balance Sheets: Provide here to enable ratio analysis to come next (Note: Convert your firm's actual *Form 10K* statements to the template-formatted statements to enable financial ratio analyses and development of projected financial statements later in project).
7. Financial Ratio Analysis: Show template-calculated or internet-derived ratios and comment on key ones; do not give definitions of the ratios and do not highlight all the ratios.
8. IFE Matrix: Include the most important 10 strengths and 10 weaknesses.
9. SWOT Analysis: Include four SO, WO, ST, WT strategies (16 total) and make sure the strategies are specific so you can reasonably estimate a cost (dollar value) for any strategy that makes it to recommendations page.
10. BCG: Prepare two BCG matrices, one by geographic area and the other by product, if possible; focus more on the implications than the numbers or mechanics of the matrix; strategies must be specific; avoid vague terms such as *market penetration*.
11. IE Matrix: Prepare two IE matrices, one by geographic area and the other by product, if possible; focus more on the implications than the numbers. For example, state how a division located in the hold and maintain quadrant will move to the grow and build quadrant after your strategies are implemented. This approach is more effective than simply stating the division is located in the grow and build quadrant. Gradually introduce your recommendations during your written project or oral presentation—to facilitate the audience following your thought process throughout and to enhance their interest in your work. If you attempt to "save" your recommendations to the end as a surprise, you risk losing the audience.
12. SPACE Matrix: Prepare a detailed analysis for the focal firm; also show plots for two rival firms; focus more on the implications than the numbers. For example, describe how your firm will move within the SPACE graph/matrix after your recommendations are implemented. Comment specifically on a few axis variables and how your actions will improve them and thus the position of the firm in the SPACE. As with any matrix, do not teach the mechanics of the matrix during your presentation.
13. Grand Strategy Matrix: Include the focal firm and two rival firms in your matrix.
14. QSPM: Select the two most attractive SWOT strategies to include along the top row of your QSPM.

15. Perceptual Maps: Include two maps, be creative as per the dimensions; frame your discussion in terms of competitive advantage of the focal firm versus rivals as per your proposed strategic plan. Discuss any market space that is not yet used by rivals and the benefits or drawbacks of serving this market space. Comment on how rival firms are repositioning versus how you plan the focal firm to reposition given your recommendations.

16. Organizational Structure: Include (1) the existing chart developed based on executive titles, and (2) your proposed chart based on the guidelines provided in Chapter 7.

17. Corporate Valuations: Include (1) focal firm, (2) rival firm, and (3) potential firm to be acquired.

18. Recommendations: Include at least 10 with costs for each given and summed; divide your strategies (1) existing strategies to be continued and (2) new strategies to be started.

19. EPS/EBIT Analysis: Include (1) all stock, (2) all debt, and (3) some combination of stock and debt.

20. Projected Financial Statements: Provide 3 years to show the expected impact of your recommendations.

21. Projected Financial Ratios: Show template-calculated ratios and comment on key ones.

22. Retained Earnings Table: Make sure the far right column of table matches the retained earnings row on your projected balance sheets (see Chapter 8).

23. Executive Summary: Give a one-page overview of your strategic plan for the firm.

Making an Oral Presentation

Your professor may ask you to present your analysis to the class. Oral presentations are usually graded on two parts: content and delivery. Content refers to the quality, quantity, correctness, and appropriateness of analyses presented, including such dimensions as logical flow through the presentation, coverage of major issues, use of specifics, avoidance of generalities, absence of mistakes, and feasibility of recommendations. Delivery includes such dimensions as audience attentiveness, clarity of visual aids, appropriate dress, persuasiveness of arguments, tone of voice, eye contact, and posture. Great ideas are of no value unless others can be convinced of their merit through clear communication. Avoid "rote reading" of anything to anyone anytime because it can be boring; instead highlight, elaborate and be insightful and prescriptive.

The guidelines presented here can help you make an effective oral presentation. Present a united front when presenting as a team. Always say "we did" and "we recommend," rather than, "I did the financial ratios" or "I recommend boosting advertising by 30 percent." A light or humorous introduction can be effective at the beginning of a presentation.

Controlling Your Voice

An effective rate of speaking ranges from 100 to 125 words per minute. Practice your presentation aloud to determine if you are talking too fast. Individuals commonly speak too fast when they are nervous. Breathe deeply before and during the presentation to help yourself slow down. Have a cup of water available; pausing to take a drink will wet your throat, take your time to collect your thoughts, control your nervousness, slow yourself down, and signal to the audience a change in topic.

Avoid a monotone voice by placing emphasis on different words or sentences. Speak loudly and clearly, but do not shout. Silence can be used effectively to break a monotone voice. Stop at the end of each sentence, rather than running sentences together with *and, uh, uhm,* or *"you know."*

Managing Body Language

Be sure not to fold your arms, lean on the podium, put your hands in your pockets, or put your hands behind you. Maintain a straight posture, with one foot slightly in front of the other. Above all, do not turn your back to the audience; doing so is not only rude but it also prevents your voice from projecting well. Avoid using too many hand gestures, too. On occasion, leave the podium or table and walk toward your audience, but do not walk around too much. Never block the audience's view of your visual aids.

Maintain good eye contact throughout the presentation. This is the best way to persuade your audience. There is nothing more reassuring to a speaker than to see members of the audience nod in agreement or smile. Try to look everyone in the eye at least once during your presentation, but focus more on individuals who look interested than on those who seem bored. To stay in touch with your audience, use humor and smiles as appropriate throughout your presentation. No presentation should ever be dull!

Speaking from Slides

Be sure *not* to read to your audience; reading puts people to sleep, and to be quite honest, reading to an audience is demeaning. Know your project well enough to present it from a dozen or so PowerPoint slides. Generally, there should be no more than four to six lines of text on each slide. Use clear headings and subheadings. Do not use many handouts or your audience may concentrate on them instead of you during the presentation. Do not read from notecards.

Answering Questions

It is best to field questions at the end of your presentation, rather than during the presentation itself. Do not abruptly exit the stage or close your last PowerPoint slide when you finish speaking; genuinely seek to answer questions. Encourage questions and take your time to respond to each one. Answering questions can be persuasive because it involves you with the audience. During the question-and-answer period, be polite, confident, and courteous. Avoid verbose responses. Do not get defensive with your answers, even if a hostile or confrontational question is asked. Staying calm during potentially disruptive situations such as a calculation mistake, reflect self-confidence, maturity, poise, and command of the particular company and its industry.

Presenting a Case Analysis Orally

Your professor may allow between 10 and 30 minutes for your case presentation. Be sure in an oral presentation to manage time, knowing that your recommendations and associated costs are the most important part. Your project file should be a .docx, but if giving a presentation also, develop a dozen or more PowerPoint slides to anchor your presentation.

On the strategyclub.com website, a breakdown is given for a 10- and a 15-minute oral case presentation. Once at the www.strategyclub.com website, simply click on "Student Resources" and then download the files needed. Whatever amount of time is allowed, you want to use the time effectively, so be sure to practice before actual delivery.

Tips for Success in Case Analysis

Strategic management students who have used this text across 18 editions offer you the following 22 tips for success in doing case analysis. The tips are provided in Table 2.

TABLE 2 Tips for Being Successful in Developing and Presenting a Strategic Management Case Analysis

---

1. Use the www.strategyclub.com website resources. The free Excel student template is especially useful as are the sample PowerPoint case analyses.
2. In preparing your external assessment, use the online databases subscribed to by your college library as identified in Chapter 3 and Chapter 4.
3. View your case analysis and presentation as a product that must have some competitive factor to favorably differentiate it from the case analyses of other students, such as wear clothes of the focal firm or show a compelling 30-second video.
4. Seek the help of professors in other specialty areas when necessary, and mention them by name in your presentation.
5. A goal of case analysis is to improve your ability to think clearly in uncertain situations; do not get frustrated that there is no single best answer.

6. Develop confidence in using quantitative tools for analysis. Being a business major, never shy away from quantitative analyses. Exude self-confidence when speaking.

7. Strive for excellence in writing. Avoid typos and sloppiness. Neatness is important.

8. Pay attention to detail. Be meticulous. Employers want careful, meticulous employees.

9. Do not merely recite ratios or present figures. Rather, develop ideas and conclusions concerning the possible trends. Use figures to support what your team is recommending.

10. Emphasize the recommendations and strategy implementation sections. A common mistake is to spend too much time on the external or internal analysis parts of your paper or presentation. The recommendations and implementation sections including projected financial statements are the most important parts.

11. Throughout your case analysis, emphasize how your proposed strategic plan will enable the firm to gain and sustain a competitive advantage.

12. When working as a team, do most of the work individually. Use team meetings mostly to assimilate work. This approach is most efficient.

13. During the presentation, keep good posture, eye contact, and voice tone, and project confidence. Do not get defensive under any conditions or with any questions. Ask the audience to point out any mistakes seen or any work that is unclear. Do not read notecards.

14. Capitalize on the strengths of each member of the group; volunteer your services in your areas of strength.

15. Think of your case analysis as if you were really doing this for a company. For example, do not invest much time describing what the firm has been doing; spend considerable time describing what needs to be done. After all, this is what the firm would have paid you to do, they likely already know what they are doing.

16. Develop a presentation style that is direct, assertive, enthusiastic, and convincing; be concise, precise, fluent, and accurate.

17. Enjoy strategic management and your project while you can; it may be several years before you are playing CEO again.

18. Let someone else read and critique your project file and your presentation several times a few days before you deliver a written project or present a project orally.

19. Include this project on your resume and include that you "gained experience using business strategic planning software." Include other employability skills as listed in Chapter 1.

20. Apply for a full-time job at the case company for which you prepared a comprehensive strategic plan.

21. For every slide you show in an oral presentation, point out how the information supports your recommendations for the firm.

22. Make certain that your key external and internal factors are actionable, quantitative, comparative, and divisional (AQCD) to the extent possible.

ASSURANCE-OF-LEARNING EXERCISE

STRATEGIC PLANNING TO ENHANCE MY EMPLOYABILITY: HOW IMPORTANT ARE VARIOUS REASONS TO USE THE FREE EXCEL STRATEGIC PLANNING TEMPLATE AT WWW.STRATEGYCLUB.COM?

Purpose

There are numerous reasons why the free Excel strategic planning template is used globally in doing strategic planning. This exercise aims to enhance your familiarity with the template, so you ultimately will be comfortable using and referring to this skill in your career progression in business.

Instructions

Rank order the following 12 reasons according to why students (and companies) like using the template at www.strategyclub.com. Let 1 = the most important reason, 2 = next most important reason, all the way to 12 = the least important reason. Compare your answers to fellow students and to your professor's expected/expert answer.

_____ 1. To save time in preparing a strategic management case analysis; to focus on the "thinking rather than the mechanics" of developing matrices and performing analyses.

_____ 2. To follow the correct process in formulating and implementing strategies.

_____ 3. To avoid mistakes in math calculations, plotting points, and drawing graphs.

_____ 4. To develop charts, graphs, and matrices that look professional.

_____ 5. To develop existing and projected financial ratios.

_____ 6. To correctly place firms in BCG and IE portfolio matrices.

_____ 7. To examine different scenarios for using debt versus stock to raise needed capital, using EPS/EBIT analysis.

_____ 8. To vary weights and ratings in matrices and to see the resultant impact on total weighted scores.

_____ 9. To more easily share information with team members, colleagues, or a professor.

_____ 10. To more easily develop projected financial statements to reveal the expected impact of various strategies.

_____ 11. To develop skills with perceptual mapping or product positioning.

_____ 12. To gain experience using corporate strategic planning software; many business jobs require proficiency in Excel, which students obtain using the template. After obtaining proficiency, you may include two competencies on your resume: (1) Excel and (2) using strategic planning software.

Airbnb, Inc., 2022

www.airbnb.com, (NASDAQ: ABNB)

Headquartered in San Francisco, California, Airbnb, Inc. is a US company that operates an on-line lodging business via its website and mobile app, primarily homestays and vacation rentals. Airbnb is a shortened version of its company's original name, AirBedandBreakfast.com. Airbnb owns none of its "million" listed properties, instead profiting by receiving a commission from each property rented through its website. Airbnb connects owners of properties with people desiring to rent a property on vacation or for relatively short periods of time being a few weeks or months or less.

Although performing exceptionally well financially, Airbnb has been criticized for possibly driving up home and vacation rentals and creating nuisances for those living near leased properties. Airbnb operates under different regulations in different jurisdictions and cities globally. Airbnb is the stalworth company in the new "sharing economy" whereby people share what they own with others for a fee, including other such companies as Uber, DoorDash, Hubble, Lyft, Lime, JustPark, Zipcar, Fon, Spotahome, Stashbee, Omni, Fiverr, Silvernest, and VRBO (vacation rental by owner) that is owned by HomeAway.com, Inc. (Airbnb's major competitor).

Airbnb is credited with starting the "sharing economy" business, that is, the peer-to-peer business model in which people can access the assets and services of other people through short-term rentals. Thanks to the relatively new sharing economy, anyone can rent a car parking space, Wi-Fi, storage space, cars, cottages, flats, rooms, offices, bicycles, and even a lawnmower or picnic basket—all on an on-demand basis. Airbnb turns property owners into hospitality entrepreneurs.

A 4-13-22, p. A10 article in *Wall Street Journal* details how people are expecting exceptional cleanliness in the aftermath of Covid, and Airbnb's high cleaning fees are irking guests, especially on weekly-or-less stays as compared to over-a-week stays. Customers really compare rival VRBO (Vacation Rental by Owner) cleaning fees to Airbnb since both companies' fees can be 50 percent or more of the nightly fee at some places.

Copyright by Fred David Books LLC; written by Fred R. David.

History

Airbnb was founded in 2008 by three college roommates, Brian Chesky, Nathan Blecharczyk, and Joe Gebbia, who came up with the idea of putting air mattresses in their living room and renting space as a bed and breakfast. They put together a website that offered short-term living quarters and breakfast for anyone who was unable to book a hotel in the saturated San Francisco market. The business was incorporated in 2008 as AirBed & Breakfast, Inc., a Delaware corporation. The guys changed the name of their business to Airbnb in 2010.

Airbnb grew rapidly in the United States and established an office in London, England, and Hamburg, Germany, in 2011, and in Sydney, Australia, in 2012, and Singapore the next year. Today Airbnb rents properties all over the Americas, Europe, Australia, and Asia, including Japan. In 2020, Airbnb raised $3.5 billion by going public with an initial public offering (IPO). Many cities globally have strict and varying regulations regarding short-term-rentals, so Airbnb conforms to varying requirements almost everywhere. Airbnb's major competitor is HomeAway but the company competes actually in the entire hotel, motel, lodging industry.

Some fast facts about Airbnb as of late 2021 are listed as follows:

1. There are 5.6 million Airbnb listings worldwide.
2. There are more than 100,000 cities and towns with active Airbnb listings.
3. There are more than 220 countries and regions with Airbnb listings.
4. There are more than 4 million hosts on Airbnb.
5. There have been over 1 billion Airbnb guest arrivals all time.
6. Airbnb hosts have earned all-time more than $110 billion in revenues.
7. The average annual earnings per host at Airbnb is $9,600.

Internal Issues

Vision/Mission/Values

The website https://www.comparably.com/companies/airbnb/mission provides vision, mission, and core value statements for Airbnb, as paraphrased below. Although the vision is a nice catchy two words, it does not meet any of the five criteria commonly noted as needed for inclusion in an exemplary vision. Similarly, the mission statement is a nice phrase, but it does not include many of the nine components or the 10 characteristics commonly denoted as needed for inclusion in an exemplary mission statement.

Vision: "Belong Anywhere."

Mission: "To help create a world where anyone can belong anywhere and live or vacation almost anywhere."

Core Values: "Embrace the Mission, Be a Host, Simplify, Every Person Matters, Be an Entrepreneur, Embrace Adventure"

Organizational Structure

In early 2021, Airbnb had 5,600 employees in 27 cities around the world, including about 1,500 engineers that maintain and continually enhance the company's technology platform and including about 2,500 employees that live and work outside the United States. Airbnb's top executives are listed and arrayed in Exhibit 1. The titles of executives imply that Airbnb is organized functionally (centralized) rather than divisionally (decentralized), especially because there are no presidents of geographic regions. To operate in 220+ countries as indicated and to have no regional presidents is inconsistent with Chapter 7 guidelines.

EXHIBIT 1 Airbnb's Top Executives Listed and Arrayed

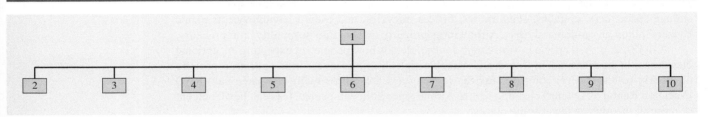

1. Brian Chesky, Cofounder and CEO
2. Nathan Blecharczyk, Cofounder, Chief Strategy Officer, Chairman of Airbnb China
3. Joe Gebbia, Cofounder, Chairman of Samara and Airbnb.org
4. Tatr Bunch, Global Head of Operations
5. Hiroki Asai, Global Head of Marketing
6. Rich Baer, Chief Legal Officer
7. Ari Balogh, Chief Technology Officer
8. Chris Lehane, Global Head of Policy and Communications
9. Catherine Powell, Global Head of Hosting
10. Dave Stephenson, CFO

Source: Based on https://investors.airbnb.com/governance/default.aspx#management

Diversity, Equity, and Inclusion (DEI)

At https://www.airbnb.com/diversity, Airbnb details their initiatives and progress toward making sure that everyone everywhere associated with Airbnb respects DEI. For example, the company describes at this website the Toolkit and the Help Center the firm has created and uses to promote DEI. In early 2021, underrepresented minority populations represented 12 percent of Airbnb's US-based employees, with women comprising 47 percent of their global employees. By the end of 2025, Airbnb aims to have 20 percent of all their employees be underrepresented minorities and 50 percent of all employees at all levels be women. By 2022, Airbnb aims to have 20 percent of their board of directors and executive team, collectively, to be people of color.

Segments

Two important metrics that Airbnb monitors are (1) Nights and Experiences Booked (NEB) and (2) Gross Booking Value (GBV). NEB represents the sum of the total number of nights booked for stays in a given period. GBV represents the net dollar value of bookings on the Airbnb platform in a period and is inclusive of host earnings, service fees, cleaning fees, and taxes. Exhibit 2 additionally provides data on these two metrics for recent years. For 2020, as indicated, Airbnb's NEB in North America were 75.5 million compared with 67.7 million in EMEA, 27.6 million in Asia Pacific, and 22.4 million in Latin America. GBV was $13.2 billion in North America compared with $6.6 billion in EMEA, $2.4 billion in Asia Pacific, and $1.7 billion in Latin America in 2020.

EXHIBIT 2 Airbnb's Business Metrics Across Regions (in Millions for NEB; in Billions for GBV)

	2020	Total, %
Nights and Experiences Booked (NEB)		
North America	75.5	39
EMEA	67.7	35
Asia Pacific	27.6	14
Latin America	22.4	12
Total	193.2	
Gross Booking Value (GBV)		
North America	13.2	55
EMEA	6.6	28
Asia Pacific	2.4	10
Latin America	1.7	07
Total	23.9	

Source: Based on Airbnb's 2020 *Form 10K*, p. 57 and 61.

Airbnb reports revenues by region as indicated in Exhibit 3. The company's total revenue in 2020 was $1.8 billion in North America compared with $1.0 billion in EMEA, $0.3 billion in Asia Pacific, and $0.3 billion in Latin America. Note in Exhibit 3 that Latin America, South America, and Australia appear to be especially fertile areas for Airbnb to seek hosts and guests in the coming years. Exhibit 4 provides a color histogram of this data to highlight the magnitude of Airbnb's reliance on North American hosts.

EXHIBIT 3 Airbnb's Revenues Across Regions (in Billions $)

	2020	Total, %
Total Revenues		
North America	1.8	53
EMEA	1.0	30
Asia Pacific	0.3	10
Latin America	0.3	07
Total	3.4	

Source: Based on Airbnb's 2020 *Form 10K*, p. 57 and 61.

Finances

Airbnb's recent income statements and balance sheets are provided in Exhibit 5 and Exhibit 6, respectively. Note the company is still unprofitable at year-end 2021.

EXHIBIT 4 A Histogram of Airbnb's Revenues Across Regions (%)

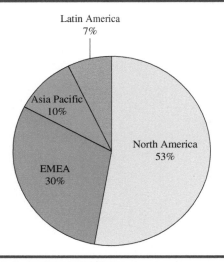

Source: Based on Airbnb's 2020 *Form 10K*, p. 57 and 61.

EXHIBIT 5 Airbnb's Recent Income Statements (in Millions)

Income Statement	12/31/20	12/31/21		Percentage Change
Revenue (Sales)	$3,378,199	$5,991,760	⬆	77%
Cost of Goods Sold	0	0	NA	NA
Gross Profit	3,378,199	5,991,760	⬆	77%
Operating Expenses	6,968,346	5,562,443	⬇	−20%
EBIT (Operating Income)	(3,590,147)	429,317	⬇	−112%
Interest Expense	144,571	424,865	⬆	194%
EBT	(3,734,718)	4,452	⬇	−100%
Tax	(97,222)	51,827	NA	NA
Nonrecurring Events	(947,220)	(304,659)	NA	NA
Net Income	($4,584,716)	($352,034)	NA	NA

Source: Based on: https://s26.q4cdn.com/656283129/files/doc_financials/2021/q4/Airbnb_Q4-2021-Shareholder-Letter_Final.pdf, p. 25. Also, Airbnb's 2020 *Form 10K*, p. 83.

EXHIBIT 6 Airbnb's Recent Balance Sheets (in Millions)

Balance Sheet	12/31/20	12/31/21		Percentage Change
Assets				
Cash and Short-Term Investments	$5,480,557	$6,067,438	⬆	11%
Accounts Receivable	2,181,329	3,715,471	⬆	70%
Inventory	0	0	NA	NA
Other Current Assets	1,254,500	2,603,471	⬆	108%
Total Current Assets	8,916,386	12,386,380	⬆	39%
Property Plant & Equipment	270,194	156,585	⬇	−42%
Goodwill	655,801	652,602	⬇	0%
Intangibles	75,886	52,308	⬇	−31%
Other Long-Term Assets	573,232	460,599	⬇	−20%
Total Assets	**10,491,499**	**13,708,474**	⬆	**31%**

Balance Sheet	12/31/20	12/31/21		Percentage Change
Liabilities				
Accounts Payable	79,898	118,361	⬆	48%
Other Current Liabilities	5,059,881	6,240,921	⬆	23%
Total Current Liabilities	5,139,779	6,359,282	⬆	24%
Long-Term Debt	1,815,562	1,982,537	⬆	9%
Other Long-Term Liabilities	634,375	590,942	⬇	−7%
Total Liabilities	**7,589,716**	**8,932,761**	⬆	**18%**
Equity				
Common Stock	60	63	⬆	5%
Retained Earnings	(6,005,707)	(6,357,741)	NA	NA
Treasury Stock	0	0	NA	NA
Paid in Capital & Other	8,907,430	11,133,391	⬆	25%
Total Equity	**2,901,783**	**4,775,713**	⬆	**65%**
Total Liabilities and Equity	**$10,491,499**	**$13,708,474**	⬆	**31%**

Source: Based on: https://s26.q4cdn.com/656283129/files/doc_financials/2021/q4/Airbnb_Q4-2021-Shareholder-Letter_Final.pdf, p. 26. Airbnb's 2020 *Form 10K*, p. 82.

EXHIBIT 7 Airbnb's Major Competitors

1. Online travel agencies: Booking Holdings (including the brands Booking.com, KAYAK, Priceline.com, and Agoda.com); Expedia Group (including the brands Expedia, Vrbo, HomeAway, Hotels.com, Orbitz, and Travelocity); Trip.com Group (including the brands Ctrip.com, Trip.com, Qunar, Tongcheng-eLong, and SkyScanner); Meituan Dianping; Fliggy (a subsidiary of Alibaba); Despegar; MakeMyTrip
2. Internet search engines: Google, including its travel search products; Baidu
3. Listing and search websites: TripAdvisor, Trivago, Mafengwo, AllTheRooms.com, Craigslist
4. Hotel chains: Marriott, Hilton, Accor, Wyndham, InterContinental, OYO, and Huazhu, as well as boutique hotel chains and independent hotels; Chinese short-term rental competitors, such as Tujia, Meituan B&B, and Xiaozhu
5. Online platforms: Viator, GetYourGuide, Klook, Traveloka, and KKDay

Source: Based on Airbnb's fiscal 2020 *Form 10K*, p. 16.

Competitors

A 3-16-22 article in *Wall Street Journal* recently described how Airbnb and other rival companies are creating a marketplace for renting offices rather than residences. The flexible-office company based in Switzerland, IWG PLC, in partnership with Instant Group for example is investing $350 million to develop and operate an online listing site for office space. As many companies embrace hybrid-work schedules, the demand for short-term office space is soaring. Another flexible-office operator, WeWork Inc. is profitably competing with Airbnb in this growing segment of the industry.

Broadly speaking, Airbnb has millions of competitors. Every hotel and motel for example could be viewed as a rival company. Airbnb lists in its *Annual Report* what it views to be their five categories of competitors, as described in Exhibit 7.

The website www.comparably.com recently ranked Airbnb on nine management and marketing variables against four competitors including Booking.com, Expedia Group, and KAYAK, as indicated in Exhibit 8. Note that Airbnb rates outstanding on most variables, and best on three variables, but worst on the eighth variable (How Happy Are the Women Employees at the Firm?). The lowest sum in column 10 is best, so overall Airbnb is ranked best, followed by Tripadvisor with the second lowest sum.

Expedia Group (NASDAQ: EXPE)

Headquartered in Seattle, Washington, Expedia Group owns Vacation Rental by Owner (VRBO) www.vrbo.com that competes directly with Airbnb. Expedia also owns Hotwire.com, Orbitz,

EXHIBIT 8 Comparing Airbnb Versus Rival Firms (Ranking 1 = Best; 6 = Worst)

	Variables									
	1	2	3	4	5	6	7	8	9	10
Airbnb	1	2	1	3	2	3	2	5	1	20
Expedia Group	2	5	5	5	5	4	4	4	5	39
Booking.com	3	4	2	4	3	1	1	3	3	24
Tripadvisor	4	1	3	1	1	2	5	2	2	21
KAYAK	5	3	4	2	4	5	3	1	4	31

Variables

1. Effectiveness of CEO
2. Product Quality
3. Do Customers Recommend Company Products to Friends?
4. Pricing
5. Customer Service
6. Overall Culture
7. Do Employees Recommend Company Products to Friends?
8. How Happy Are the Women Employees at the Firm?
9. How Happy Are Minority Employees at the Firm?
10. Summed Score (lower sum the better)

Source: Based on https://www.comparably.com/companies/airbnb/competitors

Travelocity, Trivago, and CarRentals.com. Airbnb's number-one competitor, VRBO has more than 2 million bookable vacation rentals. Just like Airbnb, VRBO connects homeowners with families and vacationers worldwide. Both Airbnb and VRBO offer condos, cabins, lake rentals, beach cottages, and more. However, there are some differences between Airbnb and VRBO:

1. Airbnb has only a Trust & Safety page, whereas VRBO has that page, plus a Book with Confidence Guarantee.
2. VRBO charges a refundable security deposit to your credit card at the time of booking, whereas Airbnb simply places these funds on hold and does not charge your credit card unless or if the property owner files a claim.
3. Airbnb displays the price per night and does not specify whether a cleaning fee is included. Guests do not know the cleaning fee until checkout, and this fee contributes to the Airbnb service fee, which drives the final price. In contrast, VRBO requires hosts to clearly display the cleaning fee on the property listing page, and the cleaning fee is a separate charge from the rental fee.
4. Airbnb users can rent shared spaces. VRBO users cannot. This is a big difference.
5. Airbnb offers one-of-a-kind stays in tiny houses, castles, treehouses, yurts, and even private islands. Such unusual properties are rarely offered by VRBO.
6. There is a high concentration of Airbnbs in cities. VRBO focuses exclusively on private residences, which is why VRBO has fewer property listings than Airbnb; VRBO is known more for their large inventories in touristy destinations.

External Issues

The term "sharing economy" refers to an economic system in which assets or services that are owned by one person can be shared with other persons, either free or for a fee, typically by means of the internet. Worldwide today, you can quite easily rent out your car, apartment, bike, cottage, home, parking space, or even your Wi-Fi network to others, when you do not need to use the asset. Examples of sharing economy companies are Airbnb, VRBO, Uber Technologies, and many others.

People have shared assets for thousands of years, but advancements in technology and the use of big data now enables asset owners and the ones seeking those assets to find each other. Other names for the sharing economy include collaborative economy, collaborative consumption, or peer economy. Sharing economies is quite honestly a booming business because it allows individuals and groups to earn money from their "idle" assets by renting them out. Millions of people are moving away from traditional capitalism into a system that allows for greater collaboration and less expensive sharing of resources, information, ideas, and services.

There are numerous trends that favorably impact the hospitality and vacation rental industries moving forward. A few trends that Airbnb should consider and capitalize on are presented and discussed in Exhibit 9. Exhibit 10 gives the forecasted vacation rental vs hotel market out through 2026.

EXHIBIT 9 Eight Trends Shaping the Hospitality Industry in 2022–2025

1. Working Remotely: Remote working has now become the norm for many employees, and this means individuals can travel more, vacation more, and rent more properties as guests from hosts. In 2021 alone, the percentage of workers around the world that are permanently working remotely roughly doubled from the prior year.

2. Digitalized Guest Experiences: Apps are increasingly important in the way companies such as Airbnb and VRBO manage the services they provide to their customers. The trend toward digital and contactless services has gained new momentum due to more widespread use of technology-assisted options, such as mobile check-in, contactless payments, voice control, and biometrics. Related technology expenditures on a firm's reservation platform are vital for future success.

3. Personalization: Guests in the short-term-rental industry have grown to expect to be recognized and treated as individuals. Tools such a Mailchimp and Zoho Establishments are going the extra mile to personally greet their guests; such tools have made personalized email marketing accessible to the masses, enabling hosts to tailor their offers and promotions, and automatically provide similar services to previous stays. Firms such as VRBO and Airbnb should invest in capitalizing on this trend. For example, AI-powered chatbots are increasingly being used to enhance the customer experience.

4. More Compassion: Travelers are less often seeking lavish displays of wealth, preferring instead to spend purposefully and positively impact society. Especially in demand are unique experiences that give back to local communities and niche properties, adventurous holidays, and relaxation retreats, which is more in line with what VRBO currently offers as compared to Airbnb.

5. Solo travel: People are increasingly embracing the meditative value of spending time alone and traveling globally unencumbered, interacting and making friends as desired. To accommodate this trend, barriers between hotel staff (or hosts) and guests are being lowered, interior design choices made to evoke a sense of homeliness and an informal atmosphere cultivated. Airbnb and VRBO could provide advice and assistance to hosts in this regard.

6. Sustainability: Short-term renters are increasingly expecting eco-friendly features throughout places they rent, ranging from miniature toiletries to bedsheets made from organic materials and LED bulbs, and even vegan options for food made available.

Source: Based on https://hospitalityinsights.ehl.edu/hospitality-industry-trends

EXHIBIT 10 Vacation Rental Forecast (in Billions $)

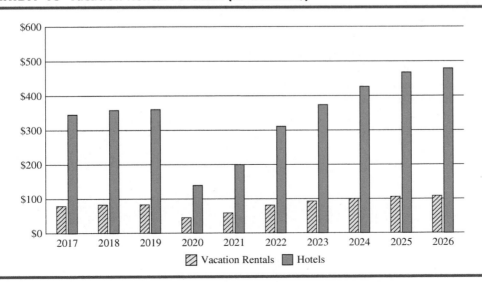

Source: Based on *Statista Travel and Tourism Report*, p. 7. Also, study_id40460_travel-tourism.pdf.

Conclusion

Given the vision and mission statements in this case, Airbnb needs to improve those documents that serve as a basis for any excellent strategic plan. Given the organizational structure discussion in this case, Airbnb needs to consider redesigning to probably use a divisional-by-region type array. This could mean adding presidents of Asia Pacific, Australia, South America, Latin America, EMEA, and North America to better obtain hosts and guests from areas not currently served and to better manage business in the current areas being served.

Given the differences between Airbnb and VRBO as listed in this case, Cofounder and CEO Brian Chesky needs to consider making some operational changes to minimize perceived advantages of a host listing their property with VRBO instead of Airbnb. Operational changes could also enable the company to obtain potentially millions more guests who may otherwise choose VRBO to select their vacation or business away-from-home places to rent.

Due to remote work, millions of people are now more flexible about where they live and work and as a result are vacationing to thousands of towns and cities, staying for weeks, months, or even entire seasons at a time. Airbnb's Q1 2022 revenue of $1.5 billion grew 70 percent year-over-year, but the company reported a Q1 net loss of $19 million so an excellent strategic plan is needed. In Q1 2022, Airbnb's Nights and Experiences Booked surpassed pre-pandemic levels and exceeded 100 million for the first time ever. The company's Q1 2022 "gross nights booked" grew 32 percent compared to Q1 2019 despite ongoing pandemic concerns and the war in Ukraine. As of the end of April 2022, Airbnb reported 30 percent more nights booked for the summer travel season than at the same time in 2019. Additionally, the company reported that its long-term stays of 28 days or more represented their fastest-growing category by trip length compared to 2019. Customers' long-term stays are at an all-time high, more than doubling in size from Q1 2019.

CEO Chesky needs a clear strategic plan for the coming years. He knows the basic external and internal factors that characterize his company, but he needs to know the relative importance of those factors as underlying bases for an effective strategic plan. In this vein, he needs you to prepare an EFE Matrix and IFE Matrix. Chesky also needs to know the relative attractiveness of various strategies that Airbnb should purse in the coming years. In this vein, prepare SWOT, BCG, and QSPM analysis for him and his top management team.

Develop a set of recommendations for Airbnb with associated costs, as well as projected financial statements to reveal the expected impact of your proposed strategic plan.

References

1. https://www.comparably.com/companies/airbnb/mission
2. https://investors.airbnb.com/governance/default.aspx#management
3. https://www.airbnb.com/diversity
4. Airbnb's fiscal 2020 *Form 10K*.
5. Airbnb's fiscal 2021 *Form 10K*.
6. https://www.comparably.com/companies/airbnb/competitors
7. https://hospitalityinsights.ehl.edu/hospitality-industry-trends
8. *Statista Travel and Tourism Report*, p. 7.
9. Study_id40460_travel-tourism.pdf.

Uber Technologies, Inc., 2022

www.uber.com, (NYSE: UBER)

Headquartered in San Francisco, California, Uber Technologies (Uber) is a global operator of mobility services, using online-secured taxi-cab-type services via individual drivers. Uber is sometimes credited, along with Airbnb, as starting the "sharing economy" industry whereby a business exists and profits by matching a person's needs with another person's assets or ability to provide those needs. Fares charged by Uber for transportation services vary based on local supply and demand at the time of the booking.

Uber focuses on ride-hailing that operates almost like taxi services except individuals use their personal vehicles to pick up persons who have used the Uber app to find someone who will give them a ride from point A to point B. Uber also owns Uber Eats that focuses on delivering food for companies, and they own Postmates that delivers packages. Uber has a partnership with Lime that owns electric bicycles and motorized scooters that persons can rent.

Uber owns no vehicles, instead receiving a 25 percent commission on each booking. Uber has slightly more than 100 million monthly active users globally. In the United States, Uber has about a 69 percent market share for ride-sharing and a 26 percent market share for food delivery. The major competitor of Uber is Lyft Inc., another ride-sharing company that ironically is also headquartered in San Francisco and roughly has about a 31 percent market share in the United States. Lyft also owns no vehicles and as of now only operates in the United States and Canada. Lyft began business in 2012 as a by-service of Zimride, a long-distance intercity carpooling company.

We authors have used Uber hundreds of times, and they are fast, safe, reliable, clean, and relatively inexpensive. In case you have never used Uber for a ride, the way Uber works is as follows:

1. Download the Uber app to your phone.
2. Whenever you need a ride, open the app and enter your destination in the Where To box.
3. A nearby driver will see and accept your request.
4. You will see on the app where the driver is and the minutes until they pick you up.
5. The driver picks you up and delivers you to your destination.
6. You rate the driver and the driver rates you.

Copyright by Fred David Books LLC; written by Fred R. David.

History

Uber was founded in 2009 by Garrett Camp, a computer programmer who named his company Ubercab, and Travis Kalanick, who sold his Red Swoosh startup business in 2007. In 2010, Ryan Graves became the first Uber employee and the company's first CEO. Uber's services and mobile app launched publicly in San Francisco in 2011.

For the first few years, Uber drivers had to have a luxury vehicle, but this changed in 2013 as the company had expanded to 35 cities. Uber became a public company officially in 2019 with an initial public offering (IPO) and by this time was a global force in ride-hailing.

Uber acquired Postmates and Careem in 2020 and acquired Drizly, an alcohol delivery service, in 2021. Uber owns 27.5 percent of Grab, a ride-hailing service in Southeast Asia and is a partial owner of Yandex, a similar service in Russia and Eastern Europe. Uber is one of the leading companies in the world competing in the shared economy industry, whereby individuals use their personal assets to help others for a fee, usually through internet contact, as for example is done with Airbnb and VRBO (Vacation Rental by Owner) matching owners/hosts with rental guests/vacationers.

Internal Issues

Vision/Mission/Core Values

Uber does not have a published vision statement on its corporate website, but it does have a lengthy mission statement provided at the website https://www.uber.com/us/en/about/

Vision, mission, and core value statements are presented for Uber at the www.comparably.com/companies/uber/mission website, as paraphrased:

Vision: *We embrace the sharing economy to enhance the way the world moves.*

Mission: *We help people travel speedily, economically, and safely anywhere, anytime, for any purpose.*

Core Values: *We welcome people from all backgrounds to help us transport people globally, adhering to the following core values: Go to the person in need; Assure safety; See the big and small picture; Do unto others as you would want them to do unto you.*

Strategy

Uber Freight in November 2021 acquired Transplace from TPG Capital for about $2.25 billion. Headquartered in Frisco, Texas, Transplace has advanced technology and operational solutions for shippers and carriers. The acquisition created one of the world's leading logistics technology platforms to meet the rapidly evolving needs of shippers and carriers. For Uber, the acquisition accelerated the company's objective to provide a seamless freight ecosystem and create the world's first true freight operating system.

According to Uber's corporate website, the joining of Transplace with Uber Freight unlocks efficiencies worth $16 billion of Freight Under Management (FUM) and reduces transportation costs, improves service, and automates processes for freight shippers of all sizes. The combined networks of Uber Freight and Transplace now comprise the world's largest network of digitally enabled carriers with a combined reach of 135,000 high-quality carriers operating across North America and Europe, including intermodal, cross border, and expedited.

At the time of this acquisition, Transplace operated one of the largest managed transportation and logistics networks in the world, and Uber Freight had more than 100,000 carriers in its network and thousands of shippers as customers, from small businesses to *Fortune* 500 companies, including AB Inbev, Nestle, LG, Land O'Lakes, and many more.

Uber uses and reports performance on two key metrics as follows:

1. Monthly Active Platform Consumers (MAPCs): a metric that Uber tracks defined as the number of unique consumers who completed a Mobility or New Mobility ride or received a delivery meal or grocery order on the Uber platform at least once in a given month. Uber's MAPC was 329 million in 2020.
2. Trips: an Uber metric defined as the number of completed consumer Mobility or New Mobility rides or deliveries of a meal or groceries. For 2020, there were 5.025 billion trips performed by Uber drivers.

Organizational Structure

Uber's top executives are listed and arrayed in Exhibit 1. Note there are no divisional presidents by region. It appears that Uber operates from a functional (centralized) structure rather than a divisional (decentralized) design. The latter likely would be more effective because it would enhance accountability and performance across regions, otherwise no top person is responsible for various vast regions.

Segments

Uber has four reportable segments:

1. Mobility: this segment connects consumers with mobility drivers. In 2020, Uber acquired Dubai-based Careem that connects consumers with drivers all over the Middle East, North Africa, and Pakistan.
2. Delivery enables consumers to order food from restaurants and have it delivered to their residence. This segment enables Mobility Drivers to make more money by delivering food from restaurants. This segment provides merchants with instant mobile presence. In 2020, Uber acquired Cornershop Cayman, an online grocery-delivery service in Chile and Mexico. Uber also in 2020 acquired Postmates in the United States.

EXHIBIT 1 Uber's Top Executives Listed and Arrayed

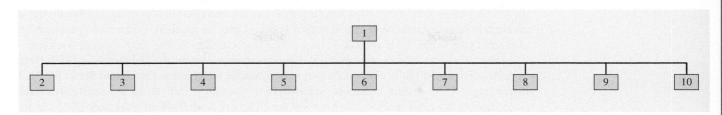

1. Dara Khosrowshahi, CEO
2. Nelson Chai, CFO
3. Jill Hazelbaker, SVP, Marketing & Public Affairs
4. Nikki Krishnamurthy, Chief People Officer
5. Tony West, Chief Legal Officer
6. Gus Fulcher, VP, Safety and Core Services
7. Pierre-Dimitri Gore-Coty, SVP, Delivery
8. Sundeep Jain, Chief Product Officer
9. Bo Young Lee, Chief Diversity and Inclusion Officer
10. Andrew Macdonald, SVP, Mobility & Business Operations

Source: Based on https://www.uber.com/newsroom/leadership/

3. Freight and Advanced Technologies Group (ATG): Uber sold this segment in January 2021 to Aurora Innovation, Inc.
4. Other Technology Programs.

Uber's revenues by segment are provided in Exhibit 2. Note that the Mobility segment generated the most revenue in 2020, but the Delivery segment grew the most year-over-year and dominated in 2021. Note that the company's revenues from its Freight division doubled in 2021. If you view the segments in terms of rides, eats, and freight as shown in Exhibit 3, notice that revenue from rides is falling but from eats is rising.

EXHIBIT 2 Uber's Revenues by Segment (in Millions)

Segment	2019	2020	2021
Mobility	$10,707	$6,089	$6,953
Delivery	1,401	3,904	8,362
Freight	731	1,011	2,132
ATG and Other	42	100	-
All Other	119	35	8
Total	$13,000	$11,139	$17,455

Source: Based on Uber's 2020 and 2021 *Form 10K*, p. 65 and 58 respectively.

EXHIBIT 3 Uber's Revenue from 2017 to 2020, by Segment (in Million US$)

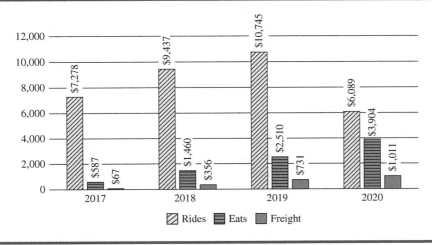

Source: Based on Uber's 2020 *Form 10K*, p. 108.

Sustainability

Uber's stated goal is to become a fully electric, zero-emission platform by 2040, with 100 percent of rides taking place in zero-emission vehicles; so if you are interested in becoming an Uber driver, an all-electric vehicle would be desirable and, in a decade, may be required. Being the largest mobility platform in the world, Uber considers it to be their responsibility to help reduce global warming.

Uber is helping drivers go electric, making transparency a priority, and partnering with Hertz to make up to 50,000 fully electric Tesla rentals available to drivers in the United States by 2023. Interestingly, Uber drivers in Europe are switching to electric vehicles (EVs) nearly five times faster than in the mass market. Uber reports the company is on track to meet their 2025 electrification commitment across seven key European capitals: Amsterdam, Berlin, Brussels, Lisbon, London, Madrid, and Paris.

Diversity, Equity, and Inclusion (DEI)

Uber provides a *People and Culture Report* at https://www.uber.com/us/en/about/diversity/ that details what the company is doing and plans to do on the DEI front. As you see in Exhibit 1, Bo Young Lee is Uber's Chief Diversity and Inclusion Officer. The company itemizes specific DEI goals and objectives at its corporate website, including items such as the following:

1. Double Black representation in leadership by 2025 through pipeline development and hiring. Leadership is defined as the five most senior levels at Uber.
2. In addition to committing $1 million to the Equal Justice Initiative and Center for Policing Equity, Uber recently committed to $10 million over the next two years to advance the success of Black-owned small businesses.

Finance

Uber's recent income statements and balance sheets are provided in Exhibit 4 and Exhibit 5, respectively. Note the dramatic improvement in both revenues and net income in 2021.

EXHIBIT 4 Uber's Recent Income Statements (in Millions)

Income Statement	12/31/20	12/31/21		Percentage Change
Revenue (Sales)	$11,139	$17,455	⇧	57%
Cost of Goods Sold	5,154	9,351	⇧	81%
Gross Profit	5,985	8,104	⇧	35%
Operating Expenses	10,848	11,938	⇧	10%
EBIT (Operating Income)	(4,863)	(3,834)	NA	NA
Interest Expense	(458)	(483)	NA	NA
EBT	(4,405)	(3,351)	⇩	−24%
Tax	(192)	(492)	⇧	156%
Nonrecurring Events	(2,555)	2,363	⇩	−192%
Net Income	($6,768)	($496)	NA	NA

Source: Based on Uber's 2021 *Form 10K,* p. 75.

Competitors

A 3-25-22 article in *Wall Street Journal* recently detailed how Uber is joining forces with former rivals - taxi companies. For example, Uber just agreed to list all 14,000 New York City taxis on the Uber app. New York City cab drivers can now take Uber customers. Although once determined to disrupt if not replace the U.S. taxi industry, Uber now is counting on traditional taxis globally to fuel its next wave of growth. Uber's new goal is to have every taxi in the world on its app and their CEO Khosrowshahi says the goal is possible to achieve. Historically, Uber indirectly modernized the taxi industry, lowered the barriers to entry, and enabled riders to secure service with the touch of a button. Taxi companies historically and globally fought Uber in court and protested against Uber sometimes in the streets such as in London, Paris, and Rome, but increasingly taxi companies and Uber are "partners." Uber expects to reap an early-mover-advantage over

EXHIBIT 5 Uber's Recent Balance Sheets (in Millions)

Balance Sheet	12/31/20	12/31/21		Percentage Change
Assets				
Cash and Short-Term Investments	$5,647	$4,295	⇩	−24%
Accounts Receivable	1,073	2,439	⇧	127%
Inventory	0	0	NA	NA
Other Current Assets	3,162	2,085	⇩	−34%
Total Current Assets	9,882	8,819	⇩	−11%
Property Plant & Equipment	1,814	1,853	⇧	2%
Goodwill	6,109	8,420	⇧	38%
Intangibles	1,564	2,412	⇧	54%
Other Long-Term Assets	13,883	17,270	⇧	24%
Total Assets	**33,252**	**38,774**	⇧	**17%**
Liabilities				
Accounts Payable	235	860	⇧	266%
Other Current Liabilities	6,630	8,164	⇧	23%
Total Current Liabilities	6,865	9,024	⇧	31%
Long-Term Debt	7,560	9,276	⇧	23%
Other Long-Term Liabilities	5,073	5,125	⇧	1%
Total Liabilities	**19,498**	**23,425**	⇧	**20%**
Equity				
Common Stock	0	0	NA	NA
Retained Earnings	(23,130)	(23,626)	NA	NA
Treasury Stock	0	0	NA	NA
Paid in Capital & Other	36,884	38,975	⇧	6%
Total Equity	**13,754**	**15,349**	⇧	**12%**
Total Liabilities and Equity	**$33,252**	**$38,774**	⇧	**17%**

Source: Based on Uber's 2021 *Form 10K*, p. 76.

rival Lift in the "taxi arena," but some Uber drivers are not happy about the "taxi partnerships" because it hurts their entrepreneurial business.

Uber's competitors across its segments include the following:

Mobility: Lyft, Didi, OLA, Bolt, and Yandex

Delivery: DoorDash, GrubHub, Deliveroo, Glovo, Rappi, IFood, Delivery Hero, Just Eat Takeaway, and Amazon

Freight: Total Quality Logistics, XPO Logistics, Convoy, Echo Global Logistics, Coyote, Transfix, DHL, and NEXT Trucking

Uber's primary competitors in its Mobility segment include Taxify, Lyft, Turo, and Easy Taxi. A recent study compared Uber on nine management and marketing variables with five of its competitors and reported the findings provided in Exhibit 6. Note that Uber ranks better than Lyft on every variable. Uber ranks number one on four variables, by far the best among the five companies ranked.

Lyft operates in the United States and Canada. Uber operates in the United States and Canada and also many cities in Europe, Central and South America, Africa, Asia, Australia, and New Zealand. Exhibit 7 compares Lyft, DoorDash, and Uber on many variables. Note that Uber is a much larger company than the other two rivals, but it also generates larger losses.

EXHIBIT 6 Comparing Uber Technologies Against Four Rival Firms (Ranking 1 = Best; 6 = Worst)

	Variables									
	1	2	3	4	5	6	7	8	9	10
Uber Technologies	3	1	1	2	1	2	3	1	2	16
Lyft, Inc.	6	4	3	4	4	5	5	3	3	37
Turo	2	3	2	3	3	4	2	-	-	19+
Taxify	4	-	-	-	-	3	4	-	-	11++
Easy Taxi	5	-	-	-	-	6	2	-	4	17++

Variables

1. Effectiveness of CEO
2. Product Quality
3. Do Customers Recommend Company Products to Friends?
4. Pricing
5. Customer Service
6. Overall Culture
7. Do Employees Recommend Company Products to Friends?
8. How Happy Are the Women Employees at the Firm?
9. How Happy Are Minority Employees at the Firm?
10. Summed Score (lower sum the better)

Source: Based on https://www.comparably.com/companies/uber/competitors

EXHIBIT 7 Rival Comparison Compared Financially: Uber, Lyft, and DoorDash

	Uber	Lyft	DoorDash
Market Capitalization	$86 billion	$18 billion	$71 billion
EPS	−1.29	−3.67	−2.23
Revenue	$15 billion	$3 billion	$4.6 billion
Net Income	−$2.4 billion	−$1.2 billion	−$625 million
Total Debt	$11.2 billion	$1.1 billion	$366 million
Total Debt/Equity	78.44	68.82	7.84
Current Ratio	1.19	1.21	3.52
# Full-time Employees	24,700	4,370	3,886
Stock Price	$45	$46	$144

Source: Based on https://finance.yahoo.com/quote/UBER?p=UBER&.tsrc=fin-srch on 1-15-22

Lyft, Inc. (NASDAQ: LYFT)

Lyft became a public company in 2019 when it raised $2.34 billion in an IPO. Early in 2020, Lyft acquired Halo Cars, which pays drivers to display digital advertisements on top of their vehicles. In late 2020, Lyft began a partnership with rental car company Sixt to let users access rental cars that are owned and operated by Sixt that has 85 locations in the United States. Lyft receives commissions from rentals. In 2021, Lyft sold its self-driving car operations to Toyota for $550 million. Lyft plans to launch a multicity robotaxi service in the United States in 2023 with Motional.

DoorDash, Inc. (NYSE: DASH)

Headquartered in San Francisco, DoorDash is the largest online food ordering and food delivery platform in the United States, having roughly a 60 percent market share. DoorDash connects people to restaurants through couriers. DoorDash uses a logistics platform that connects merchants, consumers, and dashers in the United States and Canada. The company operates DoorDash Marketplace, DoorDash Drive, and DoorDash Storefront.

External Issues

The term "sharing economy" refers to an economic system in which assets or services that are owned by one person can be shared with other persons, either free or for a fee, typically by means of the internet. Worldwide today, you can quite easily rent out your car, apartment, bike, cottage, home, parking space, or even your Wi-Fi network to others, when you do not need to use the asset. Examples of sharing economy companies are Airbnb, VRBO, Uber Technologies, and many others.

People have shared assets for thousands of years, but advancements in technology and the use of big data now enables asset owners and the ones seeking those assets to find each other. Other names for the sharing economy include collaborative economy, collaborative consumption, or peer economy. Sharing economies is quite honestly a booming business because it allows individuals and groups to earn money from their "idle" assets by renting them out. Millions of people are moving away from traditional capitalism into a system that allows for greater collaboration and less expensive sharing of resources, information, ideas, and services.

Restaurant delivery companies such as Uber Eats, GrubHub, and DoorDash now enable most restaurants in your area to be reachable via a third-party app. Exhibit 8 reveals seven statistics about the food online ordering and delivery business. Exhibit 9 provides forecasts of expected revenues from drive-sharing in various countries through 2025.

EXHIBIT 8 Some Statistics Regarding Online Ordering and Delivery of Food

1. There are 330 million people in the United States. More than 112 say they have used a food delivery service. About 60 Americans order takeout or delivery at least once a week.
2. The online food delivery industry generates almost $30 billion per year but, by 2024, will exceed $32 billion industry.
3. Rather than calling a restaurant directly, about 31 percent of Americans use third-party food delivery services at least twice a week, but 70 percent of consumers would prefer to order directly from a restaurant rather than use (and pay for) a third-party service.
4. Online ordering is growing 300 percent faster than inside-restaurant dining.
5. Almost 60 percent of millennial restaurant orders are for takeout or delivery.
6. About one-third of consumers say they would pay a higher fee for faster delivery.
7. GrubHub is the most popular food delivery service in New York City, DoorDash is top in San Francisco, Uber Eats is top in Miami with 62 percent market share, and Postmates is top in Los Angeles. Uber Eats only has 14 percent market share in its home-base city of San Francisco, compared with DoorDash's 65 percent.

Source: Based on https://www.fundera.com/resources/food-delivery-statistics

EXHIBIT 9 Expected Revenue in Car-Sharing Industry by Country, 2017 to 2025 (in Million US$)

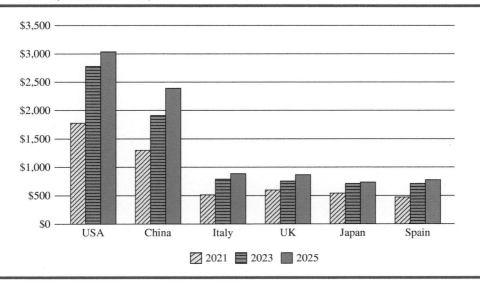

Source: Based on Statista *Mobility Market Outlook,* May 2021.

Conclusion

CEO Dara Khosrowshahi at Uber needs a clear strategic plan for the future. Through 2021 Uber was losing money annually. As indicated in the case, Uber needs a new and improved vision and mission statement. And the company would likely benefit immensely from using a divisional-by-region organizational structure rather than a functional (centralized) structure. As indicated in the competitor section of this case, Uber's rival firms are many and varied and aggressive. An excellent strategic plan moving forward will be vital for Uber to be successful.

For Q1 of 2022, Uber's Gross Bookings increased 35 percent year-over-year ("YoY") to $26.4 billion, with Mobility Gross Bookings growing to $10.7 billion (+58% YoY) and Delivery Gross Bookings rising to $13.9 billion (+12% YoY). Trips reported during Q1 2022 rose 18 percent YoY to 1.71 billion, or approximately 19 million trips per day on average. Also for Q1 of 2022, Uber's Revenue grew 136 percent YoY to $6.9 billion, or 141 percent. However, the company reported a Net Loss of $5.9 billion in Q1 2022, so Uber needs a clear strategic plan moving forward.

In developing an excellent strategic plan, Khosrowshahi knows the basic underlying external opportunities and threats and internal strengths facing Uber, but he is unsure about the relative importance of those factors. He thus needs and external and internal assessment performed, anchored by development of an EFE Matrix and IFE Matrix as described in Chapter 3 and Chapter 4 of the David textbook. Khosrowshahi also needs to know the relative attractiveness of alternative strategies facing the company, so he needs a SWOT, BCG, and QSPM analyses performed.

Let's say that Khosrowshahi has asked you to develop the comprehensive strategic plan that he needs. In addition to the analyses mentioned, include in your report a perceptual map, a set of proposed recommendations with associated costs, and an EPS-EBIT analysis to reveal whether debt or stock or some combination of debt and stock is best to obtain the needed funds. Also include projected financial statements to show the expected impact on Uber if Khosrowshahi adopts your proposed strategic plan. If further acquisitions are needed by Uber to grow its top line (revenues) and bottom line (net income) 5+ percent annually in the years to come, identify the best candidate firms for Uber to acquire. If Uber should expand organically (internally) into other regions, countries, and continents, include direction for Khosrowshahi in this regard.

All of Uber's top executives, board of directions, drivers, shareholders, and employees will benefit from and be thankful for your work developing and proposing a clear roadmap for their future. Good luck on this endeavor. We authors are confident you can do a wonderful job performing this task, following the guidelines presented in the David strategic management textbook and using the strategic planning template provided at www.strategyclub.com.

References

1. https://www.comparably.com/companies/uber/competitors
2. https://finance.yahoo.com/quote/UBER?p=UBER&.tsrc=fin-srch
3. https://www.uber.com/newsroom/leadership/
4. Uber's 2020 and 2021 *Form 10K*.
5. https://www.uber.com/us/en/about/diversity/
6. https://www.uber.com/us/en/about/
7. Statista, *Mobility Market Outlook*, May 2021.

Tesla, Inc., 2022

www.tesla.com, (NASDAQ: TSLA)

Headquartered in Austin, Texas, Tesla, Inc. is a US electric vehicle and clean energy company that designs and manufacturers electric cars, batteries, solar panels, and solar roof tile. Tesla has a market capitalization higher than any other car manufacturer in the world. Through its subsidiary Tesla Energy, the company is perhaps the largest global supplier of battery energy storage systems and photovoltaic systems. The company's name is a tribute to the famous US-Serbian inventor and electrical engineer, Nikola Tesla (1856–1943).

On June 10, 2020, Tesla's market capitalization surpassed those of BMW, Daimler, and Volkswagen combined and, within months, reached a valuation of $206 billion, surpassing Toyota's $202 billion to become the world's most valuable automaker by market capitalization. In October 2021, when the Hertz car rental company ordered 100,000 Tesla cars for its fleet, Tesla's market capitalization reached $1 trillion, the sixth company ever in the United States to reach that value.

Tesla today offers the Model S, Model 3, Model X, Model Y, Solar Roofs, and Solar Panels as well as accessories to all these products. For the year 2021, Tesla delivered more than 936,000 vehicles. Including 24,964 Model S and X (S/X) and 911,208 Model 3 and Y (3/Y). Tesla manufacturing facilities are located in Fremont, Texas; Shanghai, China; Reno, Nevada; Buffalo, New York; Bay Area, California; and soon in Berlin-Brandenburg, Germany.

In April 2022 after posting a record quarterly profit of $3.32 billion, CEO Must says that Tesla would likely produce more than 1.5 million vehicles in 2022, up more that 60 percent over the prior year. In Q1 2022, Tesla delivered about 310,000 vehicles globally, up from 184,877 a year earlier. Global supply chain problems however plague Tesla as U.S. buyers wait about eight months for a new long-range Model Y compact sport utility vehicle, rather than the normal eight weeks.

Tesla's first factory in Europe, named Gigafactory Europe, opened in March 2022 just outside Berlin, Germany, and aims to employ 12,000 people and make up to 500,000 vehicles annually, starting with the Model Y, a sporty crossover. The plant produced about 100,000 vehicles in 2022 as supply chain issues curtailed operations.

Exhibit 1 provides the range of several electric vehicles in 2021 in miles. Note the Tesla Model S has the largest range.

EXHIBIT 1 The Range of Electric Vehicles (EVs) in 2021 (in Miles)

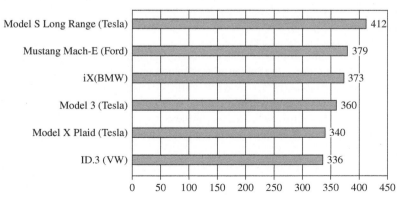

Source: Based on Worldwide; MSN; Motoring Research; Model Year 2021.

Copyright by Fred David Books LLC; written by Fred R. David.

History

Tesla was founded in 2003 by a group of engineers, including Margin Ebeerhard, Marc Tarpenning, and current CEO Elon Musk, who wanted to prove that electric vehicles can be better, quicker, as affordable, and more fun to drive than gasoline cars. The following year, Musk became the company's largest shareholder and Chairman of the Board; Musk has been CEO of Tesla since 2008.

Tesla's first car produced was the Roadster in 2009, followed up by the Model S sedan in 2012 and the Tesla Model X SUV in 2015, the Model 3 sedan in 2017, and the Model Y crossover in 2020. The Model 3 is the all-time best-selling plug-in electric car in the world with more than a million units sold. Tesla has built and operates a network of over 23,000 Superchargers 480-volt fast-charging Superchargers in more than 2,300 stations worldwide. All Tesla vehicles (except the first Roadsters) have hardware to charge at Superchargers.

In late 2016, Tesla acquired Solar City, a solar photovoltaics installation company and merged those operations into the existing battery energy storage products division to form the Tesla Energy subsidiary. Tesla manufactures three products that enable homeowners, businesses, and utilities to manage renewable energy generation, storage, and consumption: Powerwall, Powerpack, and Solar Roof.

Tesla opened its first "Gigafactory" outside the United States in Shanghai, China, in 2019. This manufacturing plant was the first automobile factory in China to be fully owned by a foreign company. Tesla today has built another Gigafactory in Berlin, Germany, and another in Texas in the United States.

At Space Exploration Technologies Corp., Tesla's CEO Elon Musk recently noticed a group of interns wandering around while waiting in a line for coffee. Musk reportedly threatened to fire them all if it happened again, and had security cameras installed to monitor compliance. Employees at Twitter (nearly acquired by Tesla in 2022), one of the most prominent companies to allow permanent remote work, may soon be in for a rude awakening because everyone at Tesla is required to spend a minimum of 40 hours in the office per week. In May 2022, CEO Musk, the world's richest man, agreed to buy Twitter for roughly $44 billion, or $54.20 a share, a 38 percent premium over the company's share price, representing the largest deal to take a company private — something Mr. Musk has said he will do with Twitter — in at least two decades. Musk says, "Free speech is the bedrock of a functioning democracy, and Twitter is the digital town square where matters vital to the future of humanity are debated; Twitter has tremendous potential — I look forward to working with the company and the community of users to unlock it." Musk has more than 83 million followers on Twitter and he wants to "transform" the platform by promoting more free speech and giving users more control over what they see on it. With more than 225 million daily users, Twitter is a small social platform compared with billions of daily users on Facebook and Instagram — but Twitter does shape narratives around the world since political leaders have used it as a megaphone, while companies, celebrities and others have employed it for image-making and brand building.

Vision and Mission

Tesla does not have a vision statement provided on its corporate website or in its *Annual Report*. However, a vision statement is provided for Tesla at https://visionarybusinessperson.com/tesla-mission-statement/ and reads (paraphrased): "To drive the world's transition to electric vehicles."

Tesla's mission statement, however, is given and reads: "to accelerate the world's transition to sustainable energy," as indicated at https://www.tesla.com/about.

Neither Tesla's vision nor mission statement meets the guidelines presented in Chapter 2 of the David textbook.

Internal Issues

Strategy

Unlike almost all other automakers, Tesla does not rely on franchised independent auto dealerships to sell vehicles. Instead, Tesla sells vehicles through its website and a network of company-owned stores sometimes called galleries that "educate and inform customers about Tesla products" rather than selling products.

Tesla does not pay for direct advertising, instead relying totally on educating customers through its showrooms and galleries situated in malls and other high-traffic areas. Tesla is known to be the first automaker in the United States to sell cars directly to consumers.

Tesla is highly vertically integrated producing vehicle components, vehicles, proprietary stations where customers can charge their vehicles, and handling all marketing and distribution internally. This extent of vertical integration is nonexistent elsewhere in the automotive industry.

Tesla surprisingly allows its competitors to license its technology, stating that it wants to help its competitors accelerate the world's use of sustainable energy. However, the licensing agreements state that the rival firm agrees not to file patent suits against Tesla or to copy its designs directly. Tesla retains strict control of its trademarks and trade secrets to prevent direct copying of its technology.

Tesla is growing organically (internally) its manufacturing capacity as quickly as possible and plans to achieve 50 percent average annual growth in vehicle deliveries, pending operational efficiency, capacity and stability of the supply chain, and regional permitting constraints. Tesla is making fast progress on the industrialization of Cybertruck, which is currently planned for production in Austin, Texas, subsequent to Model Y.

Legal Issues

Several lawsuits and controversies have arisen at Tesla from statements and acts of Musk, ranging from allegations of creative accounting, whistleblower retaliation, and worker rights violations to technical problems with their products. Complaints prompted the National Highway Traffic Safety Administration (NHTSA) in September 2021 to order Tesla to submit data pertaining to all sold US vehicles equipped with the company's self-driving autopilot feature.

Organizational Structure

Tesla has about 72,000 employees, with about 45 persons in leadership positions. The leadership team roughly is composed, according to https://www.zippia.com/tesla-careers-11363/executives/, as follows:

- 21% of management female
- 53% of management is white
- 13% of management is Hispanic or Latino
- 9% of management is Black or African American

Tesla's top executives are listed and arrayed in Exhibit 2. Because there is a COO position and at least one President position, it appears that Tesla may operate from a divisional (decentralized) design, but this is not clear from the company's website or *Annual Report*. There certainly are no clear Presidents by region or Presidents by segment, which would be recommended based on Chapter 7 of the David textbook.

EXHIBIT 2 Tesla's Top Executives Listed and Arrayed

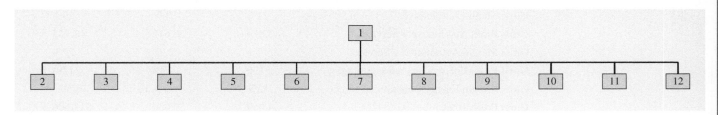

1. Elon Musk, CEO
2. Siji Varghese, COO
3. Zachary Kirkhorn, CFO
4. Vaibhav Taneja, Controller and Chief Accounting Officer
5. Andrew Baglino, SVP of Powertrain & Energy Engineering
6. JB Straubel, CTO
7. Franz von Holzhausen, Chief Designer
8. Jerome Guillen, President
9. Arnnon Geshuri, Chief HRM Officer
10. Alan Prescott, VP of Legal
11. Dave Arnold, Sr., Director of Global Communications
12. Brian Scelfo, Sr., Director of Corporate Development

Source: Based on https://www.zippia.com/tesla-careers-11363/executives/

Marketing

Tesla describes and sells vehicles primarily through their corporate website but also through an international network of company-owned stores. The company also has built galleries to educate and inform customers about Tesla products, but the galleries do not perform actual sales of vehicles. Tesla is also actively engaged in selling used Tesla vehicles. The Tesla (and non-Tesla) vehicles that the company acquires as trade-ins are subsequently remarketed, either directly by Tesla or through third parties. Tesla additionally remarkets Tesla vehicles acquired from other sources including lease returns.

Segments

Tesla operates as four reportable segments as follows:

1. Automotive Sales: includes the design, production, sales, and leasing of electric vehicles, and services and other that includes nonwarranty after-sales vehicle services, sales of used vehicles, and retail merchandise. This segment includes the Model 3 (a four-door mid-size sedan), the Model Y (a compact SUV built on the Model 3 platform, Model S (a four-door full-size sedan, and the Model X (a mid-size SUV with seating up to seven).
2. Automotive Leasing: includes all Tesla leases to Hertz and other companies and individuals.
3. Services and Other: includes various financing options and leasing, insurance, and loan options for its vehicle and solar customers.
4. Energy Generation and Storage: includes the design, production, installation, sales, and leasing of solar-energy generation and energy-storage products and related services and sales of solar energy systems incentives.

Tesla's revenues by product segment are provided in Exhibit 3. Note the dramatic increases year-over-year. Tesla's gross profit by segment is provided in Exhibit 4. Note dramatic increases year-over-year.

EXHIBIT 3 Tesla's Revenues by Segment (in Millions $)

	2019	2020	2021
Automotive sales	$19,952	$26,184	$44,125
Automotive leasing	869	1,052	1,642 + 1,465 (of auto credits)
Services and other	2,226	2,306	3,802
Energy generation/storage	1,531	1,994	2,789
Total	$24,578	$31,536	$53,823

Source: Based on Tesla's 2020 and 2021 *Form 10K*, p. 40 and p. 37 respectively.

EXHIBIT 4 Tesla's Gross Profit and Gross Margin by Segment (in Millions $)

	2019	2020	2021
Gross Profit Automotive	$4,423	$6,977	$13,839
Gross Margin Automotive	21%	26%	29%
Gross Profit Automotive + Services	3,879	6,612	13,735
Gross Margin Automotive + Services	17%	22%	27%
Gross Profit Energy Generation/Storage	190	18	(129)
Gross Margin Energy Generation/Storage	12%	1%	(4.6%)
Gross Profit Total	$4,069	$6,630	$13,606
Gross Margin Total	17%	21%	25.3%

Source: Based on Tesla's 2020 and 2021 *Form 10K,* p. 41 and p. 38 respectively.

Tesla's revenues by geographic region are provided in Exhibit 5. Note the United States, then China, and then all other countries are reported categories for the revenues. Note the dramatic increases in 2021 across all regions.

EXHIBIT 5 Tesla's Revenues by Region (in Millions $)

	2019	2020	2021
United States	$12,653	$15,207	$23,973
China	2,979	6,662	13,844
All Other Regions	8,946	9,667	16,606
Total	$24,578	$31,536	$53,823

Source: Based on Tesla's 2020 and 2021 *Form 10K*, p. 104 and p. 94 respectively.

Finances

Tesla's recent income statements and balance sheets are provided in Exhibit 6 and Exhibit 7, respectively. Note the dramatic increases.

EXHIBIT 6 Tesla's Recent Income Statements (in Millions)

Income Statement	12/31/20	12/31/21		Percentage Change
Revenue (Sales)	$31,536	$53,823	⇧	71%
Cost of Goods Sold	24,906	40,217	⇧	61%
Gross Profit	6,630	13,606	⇧	105%
Operating Expenses	4,636	7,083	⇧	53%
EBIT (Operating Income)	1,994	6,523	⇧	227%
Interest Expense	840	180	⇩	−79%
EBT	1,154	6,343	⇧	450%
Tax	292	699	⇧	139%
Nonrecurring Events	(141)	(125)	NA	NA
Net Income	$721	$5,519	⇧	665%

Source: Based on Tesla's 2021 *Form 10K*, p. 49.

EXHIBIT 7 Tesla's Recent Balance Sheets (in Millions)

Balance Sheet	12/31/20	12/31/21		Percent Change
Assets				
Cash and Short-Term Investments	$19,384	$17,576	⇩	−9%
Accounts Receivable	1,886	1,913	⇧	1%
Inventory	4,101	5,757	⇧	40%
Other Current Assets	1,346	1,854	⇧	38%
Total Current Assets	26,717	27,100	⇧	1%
Property Plant & Equipment	12,747	18,884	⇧	48%
Goodwill	207	200	⇩	−3%
Intangibles	313	257	⇩	−18%
Other Long-Term Assets	12,164	15,690	⇧	29%
Total Assets	**52,148**	**62,131**	⇧	**19%**
Liabilities			⇧	
Accounts Payable	6,051	10,025	⇧	66%

(Continued)

EXHIBIT 7 Tesla's Recent Balance Sheets (in Millions) (*Continued*)

Balance Sheet	12/31/20	12/31/21		Percent Change
Other Current Liabilities	8,197	9,680	⇧	18%
Total Current Liabilities	14,248	19,705	⇧	38%
Long-Term Debt	9,556	5,245	⇩	−45%
Other Long-Term Liabilities	4,614	5,598	⇧	21%
Total Liabilities	**28,418**	**30,548**	⇧	**7%**
Equity				
Common Stock	1	1	⇩	0%
Retained Earnings	(5,399)	331	⇩	−106%
Treasury Stock	0	0	NA	NA
Paid in Capital & Other	29,128	31,251	⇧	7%
Total Equity	**23,730**	**31,583**	⇧	**33%**
Total Liabilities and Equity	**$52,148**	**$62,131**	⇧	**19%**

Source: Based on Tesla's 2021 *Form 10K*, p. 50.

Competitors

Tesla has many competitors within its Automotive segment, and many different rival firms in its Energy Generation and Storage segment. Tesla's automotive industry competitors include Rivian, Volkswagen, Toyota, Honda, BMW Group, Ford Motor Company, Audi, General Motors, and Lexus. A recent study compared Tesla on nine management and marketing variables with five of its automotive competitors and reported the findings provided in Exhibit 8. Note that Tesla ranks first on three variables, including CEO effectiveness. As indicated by the low sum score of 24 in column 10, Tesla ranks second best overall behind BMW.

EXHIBIT 8 Comparing Tesla Against Rival Auto Firms (Ranking 1 = Best; 6 = Worst)

	Variables									
	1	2	3	4	5	6	7	8	9	10
Tesla Motors	1	2	1	1	2	4	5	5	3	24
BMW Group	2	1	4	2	1	1	3	3	4	21
Audi	3	3	3	3	3	3	2	2	2	24
Ford Motor	4	5	5	5	4	2	4	1	1	31
General Motors	5	6	6	6	6	5	6	4	5	49
Lexus	6	4	2	4	5	6	1	6	6	40

Variables

1. Effectiveness of CEO
2. Product Quality
3. Do Customers Recommend Company Products to Friends?
4. Pricing
5. Customer Service
6. Overall Culture
7. Do Employees Recommend Company Products to Friends?
8. How Happy Are the Women Employees at the Firm?
9. How Happy Are Minority Employees at the Firm?
10. Summed Score (lower sum the better)

Source: Based on https://www.comparably.com/companies/tesla-motors/competitors

In Exhibit 9, Tesla is compared to Ford Motor and General Motors. Note that Tesla has far fewer employees than Ford or GM but has a much larger market capitalization (number of shares outstanding × stock price).

EXHIBIT 9 Rivals Compared: Tesla, Ford Motor, and General Motors

	Tesla	Ford	General Motors
Market Capitalization	$1.05 trillion	$100 billion	$89 billion
EPS	3.06	0.71	7.47
Revenue	$47 billion	$135 billion	$91 billion
Net Income	$3.5 billion	$2.9 billion	$11 billion
Total Debt	$10.2 billion	$146 billion	$110 million
Total Debt/Equity	35.7	397	182
Current Ratio	1.38	1.20	1.08
# Full-time Employees	70,760	186,000	155,000
Stock Price	$1,050	$25	$62

Source: Based on https://finance.yahoo.com/quote/TSLA/key-statistics?p=TSLA

Exhibit 10 provides the all-electric car sales in Q1–Q3 2021 (vs previous year Q1–Q3). Specific numbers for Exhibit 10 are as follows:

1. Tesla: 627,371 and 21.5% share (vs 26%)
2. SAIC Motor (incl. SAIC-GM-Wuling): 411,164 and 14.1% share (vs 8%)
3. Volkswagen Group: 292,769 and 10.1% share (vs 10%)
4. BYD Auto: 185,796 and 6.4% share
5. Hyundai Motor Group: 139,889 and 4.8% share (vs 7%)

Top Five Brands Total: 1,656,989 vehicles (56.9% share)
All Other Brands Total: 1,254,436 vehicles (43.1% share)
Grand Total: 2,911,425 vehicles

EXHIBIT 10 Market Share of Electric Car Brands: 2020 vs 2021

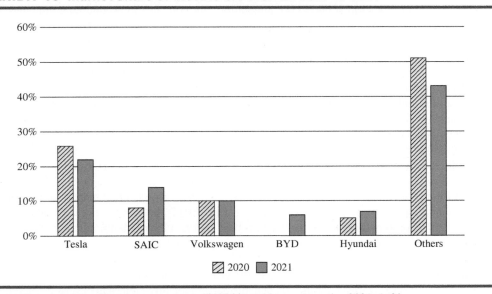

Source: Based on https://insideevs.com/news/544766/world-top-oem-sales-2021q1q3/

External Issues

The transformation globally and in the United States to electric vehicles (EVs) is accelerating, growing 88 percent in 2021 alone, but still only 3.2 percent of automobiles sold in the United States in 2021 were all-electric, according to the automobile research firm Motor Intelligence. Car companies have a long ways to go to convince consumers to abandon gasoline-powered vehicles. Big percentage increases are easy to showcase when you are working with small numbers as the basis.

A pivotal article published in the *Wall Street Journal* (January 10, 2022, pp. A1, A4) provided numerous facts that summarize the nature of the EV industry. Dozens of new EV models and vehicle types are being released by a dozen automobile manufacturers in 2022 alone. Intensity of competition is heating up in this industry. Ford's new all-electric F-150 Lightning is being released Spring 2022 and just the announcement launched Ford's stock price significantly. And the new battery-powered GM Chevy Silverado truck is to be released March 2023, along with what GM's CEO Mary Barra says will be 10 new GM EVs within two years.

Stellantis is the global automaker than owns Jeep, Ram, Chrysler, and other auto brands. Stellantis announced in January 2022 that the 100-year-old Chrysler brand will go exclusively electric by 2028. Stellantis is also set to sell electric vans to Amazon, as rival start-up Rivian Automotive is doing. In total in 2022, the aforementioned *Wall Street Journal* article says 22 new EV models will be released, followed by 27 in 2023, 24 in 2024, and 15 in 2025. EV startup company based in Irvine, California, Rivian Automotive, is building a second manufacturing plant in Georgia that will have an annual capacity of 400,000 vehicles, with production to start in 2024.

Total deliveries of Tesla EV's in 2021 were up 87 percent to 986,000 vehicles, including 352,000 vehicles sold in the United States alone, which comprised 72 percent of all EVs sold in the United States in 2021. By comparison in 2021 in the United States, Ford sold 27,000 EVs and GM sold about 25,000 EVs—but for both Ford and GM those numbers represented less than 2 percent of their total sales in the United States. The point here is although EV is the big buzzword and is no doubt a fast-growing industry, gasoline vehicle sales are what pay the bills at almost all automobile companies. Gas vehicles are generally more affordable and charging station availability is still a major problem in most geographic areas. However, some recent research provided by consulting firm AlixPartners LLP reveals that 19 percent of consumers in the United States report that their next automobile purchase will likely be EV, up from 5 percent in 2019. (Ben Foldy and Nora Eckert, "Race for Electric Vehicles Revs Up," *Wall Street Journal*, January 10, 2022, pp. A1, A4).

Conclusion

Elon Musk needs a clear 3-year strategic plan for Tesla. For years, Tesla had the market somewhat cornered on EVs and solar energy generation, but now, nearly a hundred companies have entered the EV manufacturing and energy generation business. Intensity of competition and rivalry among firms is accelerating. Tesla's profit margins are excellent within its automobile segment but weak within its energy generation segment.

The vision/mission and organizational structure sections of this case reveal that there is substantial room for improvement for Tesla in both areas. Musk knows the basic underlying external opportunities and threats and internal strengths facing Tesla, but he is unsure about the relative importance of those factors. He thus needs an external and internal assessment performed, anchored by development of an EFE Matrix and IFE Matrix as described in Chapter 3 and Chapter 4 of the David textbook. Musk also needs to know the relative attractiveness of alternative strategies facing the company, so he needs a SWOT, BCG, and QSPM analyses performed.

Let's say that Musk has asked you to develop the comprehensive strategic plan that he needs. In addition to the analyses mentioned, include in your report a perceptual map, a set of proposed recommendations with associated costs, and an EPS-EBIT analysis to reveal whether debt or stock or some combination of debt and stock is best to obtain the needed funds. Also include projected financial statements to show the expected impact on Tesla if Musk adopts your proposed strategic plan. If further acquisitions are needed by Tesla to grow its top line (revenues) and bottom line (net income) 5+ percent annually in the years to come, identify the best candidate firms for Tesla to acquire. If Tesla should expand further organically (internally) into other regions, countries, and continents, include direction for Musk in this regard.

All of Tesla's top executives, board of directions, drivers, shareholders, and employees will benefit from and be thankful for your work developing and proposing a clear roadmap for their future. Good luck on this endeavor. We authors are confident you can do a wonderful job performing this task, following the guidelines presented in the David textbook and using the strategic planning template provided at www.strategyclub.com.

References

1. https://www.zippia.com/tesla-careers-11363/executives/
2. https://finance.yahoo.com/quote/TSLA/key-statistics?p=TSLA
3. https://visionarybusinessperson.com/tesla-mission-statement/
4. https://finance.yahoo.com/quote/TSLA/key-statistics?p=TSLA
5. https://www.comparably.com/companies/tesla-motors/competitors
6. Worldwide; MSN; Motoring Research; Model Year 2021.
7. Tesla's 2020 and 2021 *Form 10K*.
8. Based on https://insideevs.com/news/544766/world-top-oem-sales-2021q1q3/
9. Ben Foldy and Nora Eckert, "Race for Electric Vehicles Revs Up," *Wall Street Journal*, January 10, 2022, pp. A1, A4.

First Solar, Inc., 2022

www.firstsolar.com, (NASDAQ: FSLR)

Headquartered in Tempe, Arizona, First Solar is one of the world's largest manufacturers, distributors, and operators of solar panels and solar power plants. The company develops, constructs, finances, and operates some of the world's largest solar grid-connected power plants. A photovoltaic (PV) system refers to the components, hardware, software, wiring, and panels that enable sunlight to be converted into electricity. First Solar is the world's largest thin film PV solar module manufacturer and the largest PV solar module manufacturer in the Western Hemisphere.

A key competitive advantage for First Solar is its thin film PV technology that has about half the carbon footprint of conventional crystalline silicon PV modules. First Solar's CdTe solar modules offer key advantages over conventional crystalline silicon solar modules by delivering more efficiency, energy yield, high wattage, and reliability. The company's Series 6 module technology delivers up to 8 percent more usable energy per nameplate watt than crystalline silicon technologies in most geographic markets.

First Solar provides PV solar energy solutions globally, including markets throughout the Americas, Asia, the Middle East, and Africa. First Solar has offices in eight cities: Houston, San Francisco, Ciudad de Mexico, Sao Paulo (Brazil), Brussels (Belgium), Frankfurt (Germany), Singapore, Tokyo (Japan), and New Delhi (India). The company has six manufacturing plants in three cities: Perrysburg, Ohio; Ho Chi Minh City, Vietnam; and Kulim, Malaysia.

First Solar's sales for Q1 2022 were $367 million, a decrease of $540 million from the prior quarter, primarily due to a decrease in the company's module sold volume, a decrease in the module average selling price, and lower project revenue in Japan. In May 2022, First Solar sold to PAG Real Assets ("PAG") of Japan its 293 megawatts $(MW)_{DC}$ utility-scale solar project development platform, and a solar operations and maintenance (O&M) platform with approximately 665 MW_{DC} under management, in Japan. PAG is a leading Asia Pacific-focused private investment manager with more than $50 billion in assets under management and is adding First Solar's project development platform to its existing portfolio of solar farms in Japan, creating one of Japan's largest renewable operators with over 600 MW_{DC} of capacity.

Back in 2021, PAG had acquired two projects under development by First Solar in Japan with a total capacity of 50 MW_{DC}. Jon-Paul Toppino, executive director and president of PAG, said, "First Solar has an unmatched reputation in this region and we are pleased to have such an experienced, professional team join the PAG family." Mark Widmar, First Solar's CEO said: "The sale of these platforms marks the completion of First Solar's strategic shift to focus on developing, scaling, and selling our advanced module technology." First Solar is the only US-headquartered company among the world's ten largest solar manufacturers. First Solar is building two new manufacturing facilities in the United States and India, which will double its nameplate manufacturing capacity to 16 gigawatts $(GW)_{DC}$ in 2024.

Copyright by Fred David Books LLC; written by Fred R. David.

History

In 1984, inventor and entrepreneur, Harold McMaster started a business named Glasstech Solar. He renamed the business Solar Cells, Inc. (SCI) in 1990. In 1999, SCI was acquired by True North Partners, LLC, who gave the company its name today: First Solar, Inc. The company went public in 2006 with an initial public offering (IPO) on the Nasdaq. The CEO of First Solar since 2016 has been Mark Widmar.

Since its founding, First Solar has been a fast-growing company that was ranked first on *Forbes*' 2011 list of America's 25 fastest-growing technology companies. The company was also listed as number one in *Solar Power World* magazine's 2012 and 2013 rankings of solar contractors.

In March 2021, First Solar completed two divestitures: the sale of its US Project Development business to Leeward Renewable Energy and the same of its North American O&M business to NovaSource Power Services. First Solar has an excellent balance sheet, and all seems well, especially given that PV installations globally are expected to double between 2022 and 2024. However, the next paragraph reveals an impending threat.

In November 2021, a US trade court reduced tariff rates on solar panels. This decision was called a "win" for the solar panel industry because it made it cheaper to install solar panels, but the ruling severely hurts First Solar because it allows foreign companies to undercut pricing on solar panel installations in the United States. With lower tariffs on competitors' products, First Solar could lose substantial business. The tariffs were first imposed by the Trump administration to counter the Chinese government's subsidies for its solar industry, which had enabled China to undercut US manufacturers on price. First Solar worries that cheap solar panels made in China could now potentially flood the US market and enable China to perhaps dominate the US utility scale market.

First Solar's fiscal year ends December 31. The company's sales for Q3 2021 were $584 million, a decrease of $46 million from Q3 2020, primarily due to lower systems segment revenue, which was partially offset by an increase in module segment revenue. The company's CEO Mark Widmar needs a clear strategic plan for the next 3 to 5 years to prosper in the fast-growing but precarious solar energy industry.

Vision/Mission

First Solar does not provide a written vision statement at its corporate website or its most recent *Annual Report*. The company's vision statement however reportedly reads (paraphrased):

> Vision Statement: *"To lead the world's sustainable energy future by driving innovation across the solar value chain."*

The company's mission statement reads as follows (paraphrased from the corporate website):

> *"To create enduring value by enabling a world powered by clean, affordable solar electricity. We are a leading global provider of comprehensive photovoltaic (PV) solar energy solutions through innovation, customer engagement, industry leadership, and operational excellence."*

Internal Issues

Organizational Structure

Early in 2021, First Solar had about 5,100 employees, including about 4,000 working in the Modules business and about 400 working in the company's Systems business. Most of these employees work in the United States, Malaysia, and Vietnam. The remaining 700 employees are in R&D, sales and marketing, and general and administrative positions. No First Solar employees are currently represented by labor unions or covered by a collective bargaining agreement.

First Solar seems to operate from a functional, centralized organizational structure because there is no COO and no top executives with the title president of any geographic regions or product types. The company seems focused more on manufacturing and operations than on marketing and sales. The top 10 executives of First Solar are listed and arrayed in Exhibit 1.

EXHIBIT 1 First Solar's Top Executives Listed and Arrayed

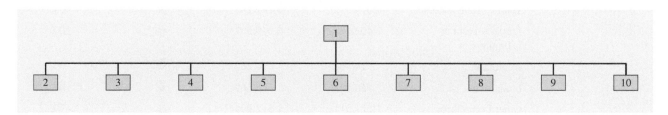

1. Mark Widmar, CEO
2. Philip deJong, COO (retired April 2021 and has not been replaced)
3. Alex Bradley, CFO
4. Georges Antoun, Chief Commercial Officer
5. Michael Koralewski, Chief Manufacturing Operations Officer
6. Kuntal Kumar Verma, Chief Manufacturing Engineering Officer
7. Pat Buehler, Chief Quality and Reliability Officer
8. Markus Gloeckler, Chief Technology Officer
9. Caroline Stockdale, Chief People and Communications Officer
10. Jason Dymbort, General Counsel and Secretary

Source: Based on https://www.firstsolar.com/About-Us/Leadership

Strategy

First Solar continues to invest substantial financial resources in R&D, striving to lead where possible technological advances in the solar industry can be found. The company continuously improves their products and processes, including advancements to the Series 6 module technology and manufacturing capabilities, such as the implementation of a copper replacement (CuRe) program and implementation of module form factor, referred to as Series 6 Plus.

Financials

First Solar's recent income statements are provided in Exhibit 2. The company's recent balance sheets are provided in Exhibit 3.

EXHIBIT 2 First Solar's Recent Income Statements (in Thousands)

Income Statement	12/31/20	12/31/21		Percentage Change
Revenue (Sales)	$2,711,332	$2,923,377	⇧	8%
Cost of Goods Sold	2,030,659	2,193,423	⇧	8%
Gross Profit	680,673	729,954	⇧	7%
Operating Expenses	363,184	143,203	⇩	−61%
EBIT (Operating Income)	317,489	586,751	⇧	85%
Interest Expense	24,299	14,589	⇩	−40%
EBT	293,190	572,162	⇧	95%
Tax	(105,165)	103,469	NA	NA
Nonrecurring Events	0	0	NA	NA
Net Income	$398,355	$468,693	⇧	18%

Source: Based on First Solar's 2021 *Form 10K*, p. 72.

EXHIBIT 3 First Solar's Recent Balance Sheets (in Thousands)

Balance Sheet	12/31/20	12/31/21		Percentage Change
Assets				
Cash and Short-Term Investments	$1,227,002	$1,450,654	⇧	18%
Accounts Receivable	520,066	375,389	⇩	−28%
Inventory	567,587	666,299	⇧	17%
Other Current Assets	699,880	698,901	⇩	0%
Total Current Assets	3,014,535	3,191,243	⇧	6%
Property Plant & Equipment	2,402,285	2,649,587	⇧	10%
Goodwill	14,462	14,462	⇩	0%
Intangibles	56,138	45,509	⇩	−19%
Other Long-Term Assets	1,621,511	1,512,945	⇩	−7%
Total Assets	**7,108,931**	**7,413,746**	⇧	**4%**
Liabilities				
Accounts Payable	183,349	193,374	⇧	5%

Other Current Liabilities	664,049	533,504	⬇	−20
Total Current Liabilities	847,398	726,878	⬇	−14%
Long-Term Debt	237,691	236,005	⬇	−1%
Other Long-Term Liabilities	502,914	491,312	⬇	−2%
Total Liabilities	**1,588,003**	**1,454,195**	⬇	**−8%**
Equity				
Common Stock	106	106	⬇	0%
Retained Earnings	2,715,762	3,184,455	⬆	17%
Treasury Stock	0	0	NA	NA
Paid in Capital & Other	2,805,060	2,774,990	⬇	−1%
Total Equity	**5,520,928**	**5,959,551**	⬆	**8%**
Total Liabilities and Equity	**$7,108,931**	**$7,413,746**	⬆	**4%**

Source: Based on First Solar's 2021 *Form 10K*, p. 71.

Segments

First Solar operates their business in two segments:

1. Modules: Basically these are solar panels. This segment includes the design, manufacture, and sale of CdTe modules (panels) that convert sunlight into electricity.
2. Systems: Basically these are solar energy power generation stations or plants. This segment includes project development, engineering, procurement, construction, and operation services.

Modules Segment

Within the modules segment, First Solar is vertically integrated, from advanced research to product development, manufacturing, and applications. The company's R&D efforts generally focus on continually improving the wattage and energy yield of solar modules. First Solar currently holds two world records for CdTe PV cell efficiency, achieving an independently certified research cell efficiency of 22.1 percent, an aperture area module efficiency of 19.0 percent, and potential long-term module efficiency of more than 25 percent.

First Solar sells most of its solar modules to third-party integrators and operators of solar energy generation systems in the United States and France. Third-party module sales comprise almost 65 percent of the company's total net sales. During 2020, Longroad Energy, NextEra Energy, and Softbank each accounted for more than 10 percent of the company's modules sales. First Solar also sells modules to wholesale commercial and industrial market companies. As more and more companies, towns, and cities commit to zero emissions by 2030 or 2040 and other sustainability goals, demand is increasing for solar module sales.

Within the Modules segment, First Solar provides a limited PV solar module warranty covering defects in materials and workmanship under normal use and service conditions for up to 12 years. The company also warrants that modules installed will produce at least 98 percent of their labeled power output rating during the first year, but then slowly degrade during their 30-year life.

Systems Segment

First Solar's Systems customers include utility companies, independent power producers, commercial and industrial companies, and others. However, on January 24, 2021, First Solar agreed to sell most of its systems business, including about 10 GW_{AC} utility-scale solar project pipeline, including the advanced-stage Horizon, Madison, Ridgely, Rabbitbrush, and Oak Trail projects that are expected to commence construction before 2025; the 30 MW$_{AC}$ Barilla Solar project, which is operational; and certain other equipment.

Segment Financials

Exhibit 4 reveals First Solar's revenues by segment. Note the substantial increase in Modules revenue and gross profit but decreases in the company's Systems revenue.

EXHIBIT 4   First Solar's Revenues and Gross Profit by Segment (in Thousands)

	2019	2020	2021
Modules Revenues	$1,460,116	$1,736,060	$2,331,380
Modules Cost of Sales	1,170,037	1,306,929	1,858,454
Modules Gross Profit	290,079	429,131	472,926
Systems Revenues	1,603,001	975,272	591,997
Systems Cost of Sales	1,343,868	723,730	334,969
Systems Gross Profit	259,133	201,542	257,028
Total Revenues	3,063,117	2,711,332	2,923,377
Total Cost of Sales	2,513,905	2,030,659	2,193,423
Total Gross Profit	$549,212	$680,673	$729,954

Source: Based on First Solar's 2020 and 2021 *Form 10K*, pp. 61, 62 and 50-51 respectively.

Exhibit 5 reveals First Solar's revenues derived from various regions. Note declines everywhere in 2021 except in the United States. Exhibit 6 provides a color schematic of First Solar's percentage revenues across regions.

EXHIBIT 5   First Solar's Revenues by Region (in Thousands)

	2019	2020	2021
United States	$2,659,940	$1,843,433	$2,456,597
Japan	34,234	469,657	207,609
France	88,816	127,097	121,537
Canada	5,944	118,865	5,288
India	7,451	33,848	37,650
Chile	138,327	20,788	11,814
All Other Countries	128,405	97,644	82,882
Total	$3,063,117	$2,711,332	$2,923,377

Source: Based on First Solar's 2020 and 2021 *Form 10K*, p. 139 and 122 respectively.

Competitors

First Solar has many small and large competitors, but some key rivals include SolarCity, Canadian Solar, Direct Energy, Trina Solar, SunPower, IXYS, Canadian Solar, Trina Solar, Meyer Burger, Victron Energy, Zenernet, Hanwha Q CELLS, Jakson, Sungrow, Fronius, and Alpha Technologies. The website https://craft.co/first-solar/competitors compares some of these rival firms on about 20 variables.

A recent study compared First Solar to three rival firms on seven management and marketing variables. The results are provided in Exhibit 7. Note that First Solar is not ranked first (best) on any variable. Owned by Tesla, SolarCity overall is best as indicated by the lowest summed score in column 8. Exhibit 8 provides a nine-variable comparison of First Solar with its major rivals. Note in Exhibit 8 that Canadian Solar has more than twice the number of employees as First Solar.

EXHIBIT 6 **First Solar's Percentage Revenues Across Regions in 2020**

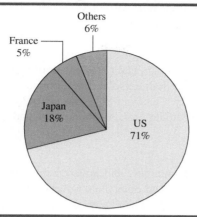

Source: Based on First Solar's 2020 *Form 10K*, p. 139.

EXHIBIT 7 **Comparing First Solar with Rival Firms (Ranking 1 = Best; 6 = Worst)**

	Variables							
	1	2	3	4	5	6	7	8 (Sum)
First Solar	2	3	2	2	3	1	2	15
SolarCity	1	2	1	2	2	2	1	11
Direct Energy	3	4	3	4	4	4	3	25
Canadian Solar	4	1	-	1	1	3	4	14+

Variables

1. Effectiveness of CEO
2. Product Quality
3. Do Customers Recommend Company Products to Friends?
4. Pricing
5. Customer Service
6. Overall Culture
7. Do Employees Recommend Company Products to Friends?
8. Summed Score (lower sum the better)

Source: Based on https://www.comparably.com/companies/first-solar/competitors

EXHIBIT 8 **Rival Solar Energy Firms Compared Financially**

	First Solar	SunPower	SolarEdge	Canadian Solar
	FSLR	SPWR	SEDG	CSIQ
Market	$9 billion	$4.0 billion	$13.5 billion	$1.7 billion (Cap)
EPS	$4.24	$2.03	$2.67	$1.19
Revenue	$2.6 billion	$1.3 billion	$1.8 billion	$4.79 billion
Net Income	$453 million	$355million	$145 million	$76 million
Total Debt	$466 million	$580 billion	$677 million	$2.2 billion
Total Debt/Equity	8.00	158	54.57	109
Current Ratio	4.26	2.89	3.83	1.10
#Full-time Employees	5,100	2,200	3,175	12,774
Stock Price	$85	$20	$250	$29

Source: Based on https://finance.yahoo.com/quote/FSLR?p=FSLR&.tsrc=fin-srch

Canadian Solar (NASDAQ: CSIQ)

Headquartered in Guelph, Canada, Canadian Solar designs, develops, manufactures, and sells solar ingots, wafers, cells, modules, standard solar modules, specialty solar products, and solar system kits that are a ready-to-install packages comprising inverters, racking systems, and other accessories. Canadian Solar also provides engineering, procurement, construction, and maintenance services, including inspections, repair, and replacement of plant equipment and site management and administrative support services for solar power projects. The company also operates solar power plants and sells electricity. Canadian Solar has operations in North America, South America, Europe, South Africa, the Middle East, Australia, Asia, and internationally.

External Issues

Most organizations, companies, communities, and governments globally have embraced sustainability and established related goals and objectives. Solar energy is consequently one of the fastest-growing forms of renewable energy. There may come a day when most houses and buildings will be solar powered because the price of PV solar power systems is declining and the cost of producing electricity from such systems has dropped to levels that are competitive with or below the wholesale price of electricity. As mentioned previously in the case however, reducing tariffs on solar panel imports from China is hurting First Solar. It is one thing for any company or business to generate revenue but quite another issue to generate sufficient profit to prosper.

This rapid price decline in solar panel and energy systems in many locations is associated with limited or no financial incentives. Energy storage capabilities are improving dramatically, spurring a continued shift to solar. An advantage of PV solar power is that the system can function for over 35 years with relatively less maintenance or oversight compared to many other forms of generation.

Solar energy has substantial environmental benefits because PV solar power systems generate no greenhouse gas or other emissions and use minimal amounts of water compared with traditional energy generation assets. For this and financial reasons, most states in the United States have enacted legislation adopting Renewable Portfolio Standard (RPS) mechanisms whereby utility companies are required to obtain a specified percentage of their total retail electricity sales to end-user customers from eligible renewable resources, such as solar.

California's RPS program is one of the most robust in the United States and has historically been a key region for First Solar and has led the western United States in renewable energy demand for the past several years. Since the passage of SB100 by the California legislature in 2018, the California RPS program requires utilities and other obligated load-serving entities to procure 60 percent of their total retail electricity demand from eligible renewable resources by 2030 and 100 percent of such electricity demand from carbon-free resources by 2045.

Energy Issues by Country

United States The United States accounts for almost 70 percent of First Solar's sales. It offers strong demand for renewable energy generation and abundant sunshine and technology and transportation systems. Solar energy tax incentive programs in the United States at the federal, state, and local levels are substantial in the form of investment and production tax credits, accelerated depreciation, and sales and property tax exemptions and abatements. For example, in 2015, the US Congress extended the 30 percent federal energy investment tax credit (ITC) for both residential and commercial solar installations through 2019. Projects that started in 2019 and 2020–2022 were eligible for a 30 percent and 26 percent ITC credit, respectively. The ITC reduces to 22 percent for projects that commence construction in 2023 and 10 percent for projects that commence construction thereafter. Generally, however, the ITC has been an important economic driver of solar installations in the United States.

Japan The PV solar energy industry in Japan is growing rapidly for several reasons. First, Japan has limited fossil fuel resources and relies heavily on fossil fuel imports. Second, following the Fukushima earthquake in 2011, the country reduced its reliance on nuclear power. Third, the Japanese government has a long-term goal of dramatically increasing installed solar power capacity and, thus, provides various incentives for solar power installations. In 2020, First Solar completed the sale of multiple projects in Japan totaling 116 MW_{AC} and expect to annually increase their business throughout Japan.

Europe   Across Europe, there is strong demand for PV solar energy rather than having to import so much oil and gas from Russia or the Middle East due to its ability to compete economically with more traditional forms of energy generation. France, Germany, Greece, Italy, the Netherlands, Portugal, and Spain are all operating large utility-scale PV solar projects. EU directives on renewable energy have set targets for all EU member states in support of the goal of a 55 percent share of energy from renewable sources in the EU by 2030.

India   With such a huge population, growing economy, and historical reliance on CO_2-emitting coal-powered plants, India is one of the largest and fastest-growing markets for PV solar energy with an installed generation capacity of over 40 GW_{DC} and over 30 GW_{DC} of new procurement projects underway. The Indian government has established aggressive renewable energy targets, which include increasing the country's solar capacity to 100 GW_{AC} by 2022 and the overall renewable energy target of 450 GW_{DC} of installed capacity by 2030. First Solar does substantial business in India and expects to accelerate that business, with about 4 GW_{DC} of installed modules already in operation.

Exhibit 9 provides the annual solar PV Installations globally in 2020 by region. Note there is huge potential for solar energy construction across Africa, Australia, and other regions.

EXHIBIT 9   Solar PV Installations Across Regions in 2020 in Megawatts

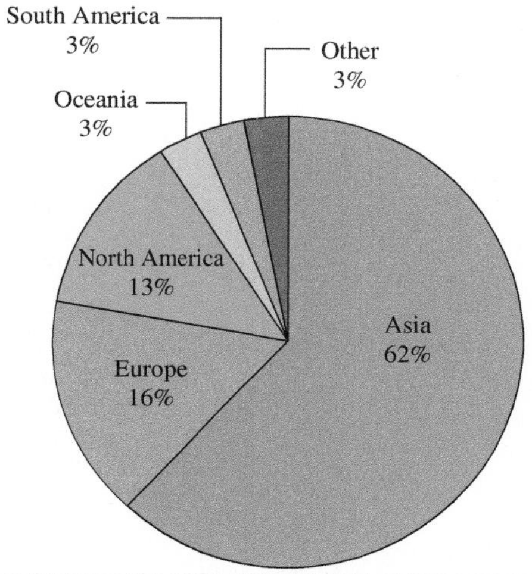

Source: Based on https://www.irena.org/publications/2021/March/Renewable-Capacity-Statistics-2021

Conclusion

CEO Mark Widmar needs a clear 3-year strategic plan for First Solar. Intensity of competition and rivalry among firms such as Canadian Solar, SolarEdge, and SolarPower are accelerating. The vision/mission and organizational structure sections of this case reveal that there is substantial room for improvement for First Solar in both areas. Widmar knows the basic underlying external opportunities and threats and internal strengths facing First Solar, but he is unsure about the relative importance of those factors. He thus needs an external and internal assessment performed, anchored by development of an EFE Matrix and IFE Matrix as described in Chapter 3 and Chapter 4 of the David textbook. Widmar also needs to know the relative attractiveness of alternative strategies facing the company, so he needs SWOT, BCG, and QSPM analyses performed.

Let's say Widmar asks you to develop the comprehensive strategic plan that he needs. In addition to the analyses mentioned, include in your report a perceptual map, a set of proposed recommendations with associated costs, and an EPS-EBIT analysis to reveal whether debt or stock or some combination of debt and stock is best to obtain the needed funds. Also include projected financial statements to show the expected impact on First Solar if Widmar adopts your proposed strategic plan. If further acquisitions are needed by First Solar to grow its top line (revenues) and bottom line (net income) 5+ percent annually in the years to come, identify the best candidate firms for First Solar to acquire. If First Solar should expand further organically (internally) into other regions, countries, and continents, include direction for Widmar in this regard.

All of First Solar's top executives, board of directors, shareholders, and employees will benefit from and be thankful for your work developing and proposing a clear roadmap for their future. Good luck on this endeavor. We authors are confident you can do a wonderful job performing this task, following the guidelines presented in the David textbook and using the strategic planning template provided at www.strategyclub.com.

References

1. https://www.firstsolar.com/About-Us/Leadership
2. https://www.comparably.com/companies/first-solar/competitors
3. https://finance.yahoo.com/quote/FSLR?p=FSLR&.tsrc=fin-srch
4. First Solar's 2020 *Form 10K*.
5. First Solar's 2021 *Form 10K*.
6. https://www.irena.org/publications/2021/March/Renewable-Capacity-Statistics-2021

Cracker Barrel Old Country Store, Inc., 2022

www.crackerbarrel.com, (NASDAQ: CBRL)

Headquartered in Lebanon, Tennessee, Cracker Barrel is an iconic US chain of restaurant combined with gift stores that provide Southern-style country meals and products with appearance and decor designed to resemble an old-fashioned general store from the early 1900s. Each location features a front porch with about a dozen wooden rocking chairs and several large barrels. Inside, a spacious, open dining area features a large stone fireplace often with logs burning, and decorative artifacts from the local area are displaced on the walls.

As you enter the front door at Cracker Barrel, you are in a unique, local-oriented gift shop that sells toys representative of the 1950s and 1960s, puzzles, woodcrafts, country music CDs, DVDs of early classic television, cookbooks, kitchen novelty decor, and early classic brands of candy and snack foods such as pecan rolls. Breakfast is served all day. There are two menus at Cracker Barrel, one for breakfast, and one for lunch and dinner.

The company strives to offer a friendly, family atmosphere, and affordable prices on country cooked meals all day long. As of September 15, 2021, there are 664 Cracker Barrel stores in 45 states. No stores are franchised. All stores are designed to appeal to both the traveler and the local customer. All stores are freestanding buildings and consist of about 20 percent floor space being devoted to the gift shop and the remainder dedicated to restaurant, training, and storage areas. All stores have stone fireplaces and antique furnishings.

Cracker Barrel's fiscal year ends on July 30. For Q1 2022 that ended October 29, 2021, the company reported total revenue of $784.9 million, up 21.4 percent from the prior year period; and net income of $33.4 million, down 80.4 percent from the prior year. The company's retail gift shops sales are performing substantially better than the firm's restaurants.

Copyright by Fred David Books LLC; written by Fred R. David.

History

Founded in 1969 by Dan Evins, Cracker Barrel restaurants/shops were at first positioned near interstate highway exits and located in the southeastern and midwestern United States. Evins intended to attract the interest of highway travelers. The name Cracker Barrel comes from "cracker barrels" in old-time country stores that were used to transport soda crackers and then repurposed into tables. People would stand around the barrels chatting and catching up on local events while having a drink or eating, or just socializing.

The first Cracker Barrel was built just off I-40 in Lebanon, Tennessee, and opened in September 1969. Like today, that restaurant served Southern cuisine that included biscuits, grits, country ham, corn bread, dumplings, and turnip greens. Cracker Barrel was incorporated in 1970 and for a decade featured gas pumps on-site because Dan bought out gas stations near interstate highways and converted them into restaurants. Gas pumps were phased out in the 1980s but initially were available at every Cracker Barrel.

Cracker Barrel launched an initial public offering (IPO) in 1981 when it became public. By 1987, the company was a chain of more than 50 restaurants in eight states, with annual net sales of almost $81 million. Growth flourished for Cracker Barrel. In 2019, Cracker Barrel acquired the 35-restaurant chain Maple Street Biscuit Company. In Fall 2020, there were 665 Cracker Barrel stores in 45 states and in Fall 2021 there were 664 restaurants. In 2021, the company opened its first West Coast Ghost Kitchen in the Hollywood area. Named Cracker Barrel Kitchen, this is a delivery-only restaurant that uses DoorDash, Uber Eats, and Grubhub to deliver Southern cuisine to customers.

Beginning in 2020, a few Cracker Barrel restaurants began serving beer and wine. This program expanded such that beer and wine service is today offered in 480, or about 72 percent of all Cracker Barrels. Restaurants generate about 79 percent of all revenues for the company; gift shop revenues comprise 21 percent. The average check per guest at Cracker Barrel during 2021 was $11.40, which represents a 2.4 percent increase over the prior year. A typical Cracker Barrel serves about 5,500 restaurant guests per week. As a percentage of overall sales in 2021, breakfast generated 25 percent, lunch 38 percent, and dinner 37 percent.

Internal Issues

Vision/Mission

Cracker Barrel does not have a published vision statement on its corporate website or most recent *Annual Report*. The company's mission statement however is two words: *Pleasing People*. Cracker Barrel has what it calls a People Promise whereby the company strives to have every employee and guest feel at home with a family atmosphere offered for everyone.

Cracker Barrel's two-word mission statement has been in place since 1969. The company strives to live up to the mission of Pleasing People each day, trying hard to assure that every employee and guest feels at home, feels cared for like family, and feels like they belong. Cracker Barrels do exemplify a culture of hospitality that's welcoming, respectful, and inclusive to everyone who walks through the front door.

Organizational Structure

Cracker Barrel seems to operate using a divisional-by-product (decentralized) organizational design because there is a top executive responsible for the restaurant operations and revenues and a separate top executive responsible for the retail operations. However, as indicated in the list of top executives given here, the structure and exact delegation of authority is unclear. Note from the list provided in Exhibit 1, there is no COO and no division-by-region top executives at Cracker Barrel. Note the CEO is female as are 3 of 10 top executives, and 3 of the 11 members of the company's board of directors.

EXHIBIT 1 Cracker Barrel's Top Executives and Probable Organizational Chart

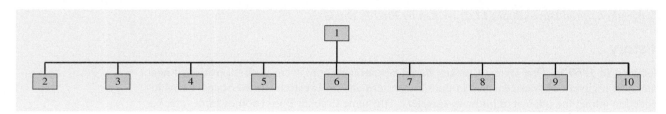

1. Sandra B. Cochran – President and CEO
2. Doug Couvillion – SVP and Interim CFO
3. Laura Daily – SVP, Retail
4. Jill Golder – SVP and Chief Financial Officer
5. Michael Hackney – SVP, Restaurant and Retail Operations
6. Rich Wolfson – SVP, General Counsel and Corporate Secretary
7. Bruce Hoffmeister, SVP and CIO
8. Jennifer Tate, SVP and Chief Marketing Officer
9. Donna Roberts, VP and Chief Human Resources Officer
10. Kara Jacobs, VP and Corporate Controller

Source: Based on information at https://investor.crackerbarrel.com/corporate-governance/management

Diversity, Equity, and Inclusion (DEI)

Cracker Barrel's dining room and gift shop are places where people of all ages, races, genders, ethnicities, walks of life, political preferences, and sexual orientations are welcome and feel at home. Openness and hospitality for all is part of the company's People Promise and mission of Pleasing People. The company strives to hire, develop, retain, and promote diverse talent that reflects the communities it serves. There is no union at Cracker Barrel. No metrics are given on the corporate website or most recent *Annual Report* regarding company performance and progress on DEI companywide.

As of July 30, 2021, more than 33 percent of Cracker Barrel's employees were racial and ethnic minorities and about 68 percent were female. The company has established Employee Resource Groups (ERGs) to allow employees to feel valued, respected, included, and connected through a wide range of programs, events, and community outreach projects. Currently, there are six ERGs functioning in the Cracker Barrel organization:

1. **LGBT Alliance:** Promote LGBT awareness and inclusion in the workplace
2. **United Cultural Awareness Network (UCAN):** Embrace culture to enhance the work experience
3. **Women's Connect:** Inspire women leaders
4. **Veteran and Military Volunteers (VERG):** Supporting veterans and military-affiliated employees
5. **B-WELL:** Sponsor health and wellness activities that nurture employees' physical, emotional, financial, and intellectual well-being
6. **Millennial ERG (MERGE):** Grow millennial talent.

Marketing

Outdoor advertising (i.e., billboards and state department of transportation signs) is Cracker Barrel's largest advertising vehicle used to reach travelers and local patrons. In fiscal 2021, the company had more than 1,500 billboards, and this expense comprised about 33 percent of the company's total advertising spent for the year. For the other 67 percent, Cracker Barrel uses television and social media and a customer relationship management (CRM) program that uses email, text messages, push, notifications, and an exclusive music program to energize desire for the brand and affinity with our guests. Cracker Barrel's advertising expenses in 2019, 2020, and 2021 were $81.8 million, $79.1 million, and $83.6 million, respectively.

Finance

Cracker Barrel's fiscal year ended on July 30, 2021; the company reported 2021 revenues of $2.81 billion, up 11.8 percent from the prior year. Comparable store restaurant sales for fiscal 2021 increased 8.4 percent versus fiscal 2020, led by a 5.3 percent increase in store traffic and a 3.1 percent increase in average check. Comparable store retail (gift shop) sales for fiscal 2021 increased 20.9 percent compared with fiscal 2020, substantially better than restaurant sales. The company reported fiscal 2021 net income of $254.5 million. Thus, Cracker Barrel overall is doing excellent, with the gift shop performing outstanding.

Cracker Barrel's fiscal 2021 income statement and balance sheet are provided in Exhibit 2 and Exhibit 3, respectively. Note the dramatic improvements in 2021 due in part to customers returning to dine-in seating as the pandemic subsides.

EXHIBIT 2 Cracker Barrel's Recent Income Statements (in Thousands)

Income Statement	7/31/20	7/30/21		Percentage Change
Revenues (Sales)	$2,522,792	$2,821,444	⇧	12%
Cost of Goods Sold	779,937	865,261	⇧	11%
Gross Profit	1,742,855	1,956,183	⇧	12%
Operating Expenses	1,639,244	1,589,524	⇩	–3%
EBIT (Operating Income)	103,611	366,659	⇧	254%
Interest Expense	22,327	56,108	⇧	151%
EBT	81,284	310,551	⇧	282%
Tax	(28,683)	56,038	NA	NA
Nonrecurring Events	(142,442)	0	NA	NA
Net Income (Loss)	($32,475)	$254,513	NA	NA

Source: Based on Cracker Barrel's Fiscal 2021 *Annual Report*, p. 49–55.

EXHIBIT 3 Cracker Barrel's Recent Balance Sheets (in Thousands)

Balance Sheet	7/31/20	7/30/21		Percentage Change
Assets				
Cash and Short-Term Investments	$436,996	$144,593	⇩	−67%
Accounts Receivable	20,157	27,372	⇧	36%
Inventory	139,091	138,320	⇩	−1%
Other Current Assets	46,768	43,311	⇩	−7%
Total Current Assets	643,012	353,596	⇩	−45%
Property Plant & Equipment	1,130,061	979,850	⇩	−13%
Goodwill	4,690	4,690	⇩	0%
Intangibles	20,960	21,285	⇧	2%
Other Long-Term Assets	745,535	1,032,273	⇧	38%
Total Assets	**2,544,258**	**2,391,694**	⇩	**−6%**
Liabilities				
Accounts Payable	103,504	135,176	⇧	31%
Other Current Liabilities	347,552	330,086	⇩	−5%
Total Current Liabilities	451,056	465,262	⇧	3%
Long-Term Debt	910,000	327,253	⇩	−64%
Other Long-Term Liabilities	764,813	935,546	⇧	22%
Total Liabilities	**2,125,869**	**1,728,061**	⇩	**−19%**
Equity				
Common Stock	237	235	⇩	−1%
Retained Earnings	438,498	663,398	⇧	51%
Treasury Stock	0	0	NA	NA
Paid in Capital & Other	(20,346)	0	NA	NA
Total Equity	**418,389**	**663,633**	⇧	**59%**
Total Liabilities and Equity	**$2,544,258**	**$2,391,694**	⇩	**−6%**

Source: Based on Cracker Barrel's Fiscal 2021 *Annual Report*, p. 49–55.

Q1 and Q2 of 2022

Many restaurant companies compare 2021 results to 2019 rather than 2020 because pandemic closures were bad for all dine-in restaurants. For Cracker Barrel's Q1 2022 that ended October 31, 2021, compared with Q1 2019, Cracker Barrel's comparable store restaurant sales increased 1.4 percent and comparable store retail (gift shop) sales increased 17.6 percent. For Q1 2022, the company's net income was $33.4 million and declared a quarterly dividend of $1.30 per share, payable on February 1, 2022 to shareholders of record on January 14, 2022.

Recall that shareholders of all firms expect a 5+ percent growth annually on both revenues and net income, so Cracker Barrel is doing excellent. Cracker Barrel's total revenue of $784.9 million for Q1 2022 represented an increase of 21.4 percent compared with Q1 2021 and an increase of 7.0 percent compared with the first quarter of 2019.

Compared to Q2 of fiscal 2019, Cracker Barrel's total revenue in Q2 2022 increased 6.2 percent, including a comparable store restaurant sales increase of 1.9 percent and a comparable store retail sales increase of 13.7 percent, as well as 7 new Cracker Barrel and 31 new

Maple Street net additions. For Q2 2022, the company's comparable store off-premise restaurant sales grew 123 percent versus Q2 2019 and comprised 24 percent of restaurant sales.
Specifically in Q2 2022, the company reported total revenue of $862.3 million, up 27.3 per-
cent compared to Q2 2021, and a net income of $37.6 million that represented a 169 percent
increase compared to the prior year quarter. Cracker Barrel is bullish on itself, repurchasing
$34.2 million in shares during its Q2 2022, and concurrently paid out $30.7 million in dividends that quarter.

By-Segment Information

About 83 percent of all Cracker Barrels are located along interstate highways. The remaining
17 percent are located off interstate or near tourist destinations. Each location offers the combo
of gift shop and restaurant, unique, effective, friendly, Southern, inclusive atmosphere. Exhibit 4
and Exhibit 5 give Cracker Barrel's revenues by segment. Note that the restaurant generates four
times the revenue of the gift shop.

EXHIBIT 4 Cracker Barrel's Revenues by Segment (in Thousands $)

	2019	2020	2021
Restaurant	$2,482,377	$2,032,030	$2,227,246
Retail (Gift Shop)	589,574	490,762	594,198
Total	$3,071,951	$2,522,792	$2,821,444

Source: Based on Cracker Barrel's 2021 *Form 10K*, p. 35.

EXHIBIT 5 A Histogram of Cracker Barrel's Revenues by Segment (in Millions $)

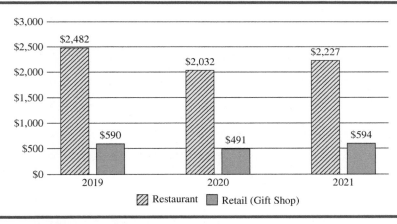

Source: Based on Cracker Barrel's 2021 *Form 10K*, p. 35.

Retail Sales (Gift Shop)

Cracker Barrel gift shops (retail sales) derive revenue from five basic product groupings: Apparel
and Accessories, Food, Décor, Toys, and Media. The percentage that each product group contributed to 2021 total retail (gift shop) sales were 29, 18, 13, 13, and 8 percent, respectively. About
33 percent of all items sold in the gift shops are purchased from vendors in China.

Restaurant

Cracker Barrel opened two new stores in fiscal 2021 and plans to open three new stores during
2022. That really is not much given there are 664 Cracker Barrels open as of September 15, 2021.
The company owns the land and buildings for 360 stores, while the other 304 properties are either
ground leases or ground and building leases. The typical store has about 8,900 square feet, including about 1,900 square feet of retail selling space and dining room seating for about 170 guests.

Maple Street Biscuit Company (MSBC) and Holler & Dash Concepts

In 2019, Cracker Barrel acquired MSBC, a breakfast and lunch fast-casual restaurant that offers biscuit-inspired meals with coffee and a limited selection of beer and wine in some locations. MSBC is open only for breakfast and lunch. In 2016, the company started its own breakfast and lunch fast-casual restaurant named Holler & Dash Biscuit House.

During 2020, Cracker Barrel converted six Holler & Dash locations into MSBC locations. As of September 15, 2021, there are 37 company-owned MSBC locations open in leased properties in Alabama, Florida, Georgia, Kentucky, North Carolina, South Carolina, Tennessee, and Texas and seven franchised MSBC restaurants were open.

Competitors

There are thousands of competitors in the full-service restaurant business that compete with Cracker Barrel, including thousands of mom-and-pop restaurants. Some analysts suggest however that there are five major rival companies: Darden Restaurants, Golden Corral, IHOP, Denny's, and Bob Evans.

Exhibit 6 reveals how Cracker Barrel recently was rated on a variety of issues as compared with its five major rival companies. Note the total score of 19 is excellent, with only Darden Restaurants being a better place to dine. Note also that Cracker Barrel was the best on gender equity and customer satisfaction. Note also that Darden is a formidable competitor.

EXHIBIT 6 How Does Cracker Barrel Compare to Rival Companies (1 = Best; 6 = Worst)?

	Cracker B.	Darden R.	Golden C.	IHOP	Denny's	Bob Evans
Criterion						
CEO Effectiveness	2	1	3	5	4	6
Product Quality	2	1	4	3	6	5
Prices vs Value	2	1	3	4	5	6
Customer Service	4	1	3	2	5	6
Employee Culture	2	1	3	4	5	6
Employee Satisfaction	2	1	4	5	3	6
Gender Equity	1	2	4	5	6	3
Diversity Excellence	3	1	5	6	4	2
Customer Satisfaction	1	2	3	4	5	6
Total	19	11	32	38	43	46

Source: Based on information https://www.comparably.com/companies/cracker-barrel/competitors

Darden Restaurants

Headquartered in Orlando, Florida, Darden Restaurants (stock symbol DRI) is the parent company for many popular restaurant chains, including Olive Garden, LongHorn Steakhouse, Bahama Breeze, Seasons 52, Yard House, Cheddar's Scratch Kitchen, Eddie V's Prime Seafood, and The Capital Grille. With more than1,800 restaurants and 160,000 employees, Darden is one of the 50 largest private employers in the United States. Golden Gate Capital purchased Red Lobster from Darden Restaurants in August 2020.

Business at Darden Restaurants is booming. For example, Q1 2022 sales increased 51 percent to $2.31 billion when the company added 34 new restaurants on top of its existing restaurants performing really well. During that Q1, Darden's earnings were $232 million, and the company bought back $186 million of its outstanding stock in anticipation of continued success and a rising stock price. Darden expects its total sales for fiscal 2022 to be about $9.5 billion with same-restaurant sales up about 30 percent from the prior fiscal year.

Golden Corral

Headquartered in Raleigh, North Carlina, Golden Corral is a privately held US chain of restaurants operating in 43 states. Golden Corral offers the iconic, popular endless buffet for breakfast, lunch, and dinner. It is a favorite family restaurant among adults and children and competes directly with and close to Cracker Barrel in hundreds of locations.

Bloomin' Brands

Headquartered in Tampa, Florida, Bloomin' Brands (BLMN stock symbol) is a large restaurant holding company that owns Outback Steakhouse, Carrabba's Italian Grill, Bonefish Grill, Aussie Grill by Outback, Fleming's Prime Steakhouse, and Aberaccio (Brazin only). Thousands of customers daily choose to dine at one of these Bloomin' brands rather than Cracker Barrel. One of the world's largest casual dining companies with almost 80,000 employees and more than 1,450 restaurants in 47 states, Puerto Rico, Guam, and 20 countries, Bloomin' Brands was recently named to the *Forbes*' list of America's Best Employers for Diversity for the third year in a row. Bloomin' Brands was honored as one of America's Best Large Employers in 2021. Just go to www.bloominbrands.com, and you will see that this company is a formidable rival to Cracker Barrel.

External Information

Cracker Barrel operates in the full-service segment of the restaurant industry; MSBC operates in the fast-casual segment. As of the end of June 2021, 39 states had reopened to 100 percent indoor capacity, whereas 11 states were open at 50 to 80 percent capacity. Restaurant menu prices in 2021 are about 4 percent higher than the prior year period largely because wholesale food prices are increasing steadily. The following data defines Cracker Barrel:

Industry: Restaurants and Bars (ICB 40501040)
Industry: Eating places (SIC 5812)
Industry: Full-Service Restaurants (NAICS 722511)
Number of Employees: 70,000 (Approximate Full-Time as of 07/30/2021)

Partly due to labor shortages, many full-service restaurant chains have recently invested in labor-saving technology to cut costs and have redesigned their restaurants to create a more-modern ambiance. However, the full-service restaurant industry is projected to return to rapid growth over the 5 years to 2026 as pent-up demand from the pandemic spurs away-from-home dining and government regulations diminish. Full-service restaurant revenue is forecast to grow at an annualized rate of 5.2 percent to $192.6 billion during the 5-year period. Consumers are increasing going out to eat as the economy improves and consumer confidence returns to growth, and people are traveling more; Cracker Barrel caters to travelers.

Full-service restaurants are facing increased competition from a growing number of fast-casual restaurants that serve high-quality food at reasonable prices, such as Chipotle Mexican Grill and Panera Bread. These restaurant chains with low overhead costs continue to threaten full-service restaurants. In response, many full-service restaurant chains are expanding operations abroad to emerging economies to meet their shareholder expected level of annual growth, typically 5+ percent top line and bottom line on an income statement.

The Omicron and Delta variants of COVID-19 are worrisome variables for all restaurants, including Cracker Barrel. Further local and state-mandated closures and restrictions on seating capacity would negatively impact Cracker Barrel's revenues and profits. Perhaps Cracker Barrel should more extensively embrace companies such as UberEats or DoorDash or even launch their own "remote kitchen services."

Conclusion

A careful analysis of the competitors and available opportunities across regions is needed along with Cracker Barrel's strengths and weaknesses to plot a strategy for the company moving forward. How aggressively should Cracker Barrel build and open new restaurants, and where? Should the company consider franchising, something it has historically avoided in the past? For their fiscal 2022 full year, Cracker Barrel plans to open three new Cracker Barrel locations and 15 new Maple Street Biscuit Company locations.

Remember, your job as the student is not to describe what Cracker Barrel is currently doing or what Cracker Barrel plans to do based on reading press releases or the company *Annual Report*, but rather your job is to consider that you have been hired by Cracker Barrel to develop and provide a 3-year strategic plan. Cracker Barrel's upper management, and in this case your classmates and professor, are looking for you (or paying you a high fee if hired by Cracker Barrel) to recommend what you feel is the best direction for the firm moving forward based on your strategic management research, knowledge, and expertise. Recall that the case says Cracker Barrel opened two new stores in fiscal 2021 and plans to open $3 + 15 = 18$ new stores during 2022; that really is not much. Shareholders of nearly all companies expect a minimum of 5 percent annual growth on both revenues and net income, so Cracker Barrel likely needs to build new restaurants more aggressively.

Consumers are increasingly price sensitive while at the same time demanding high quality in their away-from-home dining. This is partly why fast-casual restaurants, such as Chipotle Mexican Grill, Schlotzsky's, Qdoba Mexican Eats, and Panera Bread, are performing so well and taking business away from full-service restaurants such as Cracker Barrel. Should Cracker Barrel acquire one or more of these high-performing fast-casual, sit-down-inside restaurants? Recall that both of Cracker Barrel's major competitors, Darden and Bloomin', are holding companies for several successful restaurant chains.

Prepare a clear 3-year strategic plan for Cracker Barrel indicating the direction you think will be most advantageous for management moving forward. Deciding how to allocate resources across regions is a difficult yet major challenge and job of a strategist. Prepare projected financial statements if possible to reveal your expectations regarding the financial impact of your proposed strategies.

References

1. https://www.comparably.com/companies/cracker-barrel/competitors
2. Cracker Barrel's 2021 *Form 10K*.
3. https://investor.crackerbarrel.com/corporate-governance/management
4. www.bloominbrands.com

Chipotle Mexican Grill, Inc., 2022

www.chipotle.com, (NYSE: CMG)

Headquartered in Newport Beach, California, Chipotle Mexican Grill is a US chain of fast-casual restaurants providing Mexican food to customers in the United States, Canada, UK, Germany, and France. All of Chipotle's restaurants are company-owned, rather than being franchised. The Chipotle menu basically consists of five items: burritos, bowls, tacos, quesadillas, and salads. Most of the food served in a Chipotle restaurant is prepared in each restaurant, except for the beans and carnitas, which are prepared at a central kitchen in Chicago.

No Chipotle restaurants have freezers, microwave ovens, or can openers so you know the food is fresh. Chipotle has about 3,000 company-owned restaurants with more than 85,000 employees. Most reviews at websites such as https://www.influenster.com/reviews/chipotle-mexican-grill indicate that the food is great and the prices are excellent at Chipotle, but the company is facing some labor and supply-chain problems. Intensity of competition is growing in the fast-casual restaurant business, so CEO Brian Niccol needs a clear strategic plan for Chipotle.

In May 2022, Chipotle market tested a new Garlic Guajillo Steak at 102 restaurants in Denver, Indianapolis, and Orange County, California. Chipotle also in that month offered a $0 delivery fee with promo code DELIVER at U.S. restaurants.

Copyright by Fred David Books LLC; written by Fred R. David.

History

Chipotle was founded in 1993 by culinary expert Steve Ells. The first restaurant was in Denver, Colorado, near the University of Denver campus. After 1 month in business, the restaurant was selling more than1,000 burritos per day. A second store opened in 1995. Chipotle had 16 restaurants (all in Colorado) when McDonald's became a major investor in 1998. McDonald's fully divested itself from Chipotle in 2006 when the chain had grown to more than 500 locations. The first Chipotle outside of Colorado was located in Kansas City, Missouri, in 1998. Chipotle became a public company in 2006.

Chipotle expanded to Europe with the first European restaurant opening in London in May 2010, and then opened a restaurant in Paris in May 2012, and then in Frankfurt in 2013. In 2015, Chipotle reportedly became the first restaurant to quit serving genetically modified corn and soybeans in their foods, cooking completely GMO free. With more than 2,000 locations, Chipotle had a net income of $475.6 million and a staff of more than 45,000 employees in 2015. In 2018, Chipotle relocated its corporate headquarters from Denver to Newport Beach.

Ells remained Chairman and CEO of Chipotle until 2018 when Taco Bell CEO Brian Niccol replaced Ells, who remained Chairman of the Board. In 2019, Chipotle paid $6.5 million to settle a lawsuit where the plaintiffs claimed that the company's food "may have been sourced from livestock that consumed GMO animal feed." In March 2020, Ells resigned as Chairman of the Board at Chipotle and departed from the company's board of directors.

Vision/Mission

Chipotle's vision statement is sometimes stated to be (paraphrased): "*To do more than just prepare tacos while working to cultivate a better world.*" Chipotle's purpose is to "*Cultivate a better world.*" The company's mission statement is sometimes stated to be: "*To provide food with integrity.*" Chipotle's core values are sometimes stated to be: "We are committed to best ingredients, doing it for everyone, sourcing from farms, and emphasizing on both quality and responsibility." (See https://mission-statement.com/chipotle/.)

Internal Issues

Organizational Structure

Brian Niccol is Chairman of the Board and CEO of Chipotle Mexican Grill. Niccol became Chairman in March 2020 but has been CEO since March 2018. Chipotle's top executives are listed and arrayed in Exhibit 1. Because there is no COO, and no presidents or regions, it appears that Chipotle operates using a functional (centralized) organizational structure. This would be surprising because this is a large firm that likely would be most effective using a decentralized (divisional) type design by region.

EXHIBIT 1 Chipotle's Top Executives Listed and Arrayed

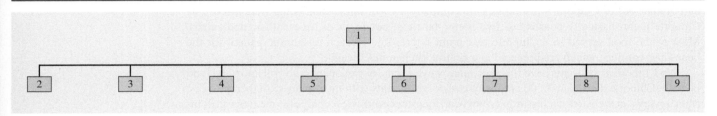

1. Brian Niccol, Chairman of the Board of Directors and CEO
2. Chris Brant, Chief Marketing Officer
3. Curt Garner, Chief Technology Officer
4. John Hartung, CFO
5. Laurie Schalow, Chief Corporate Affairs and Food Officer
6. Marissa Andrada, Chief Diversity, Inclusion, and People Officer
7. Scott Boatwright, Chief Restaurant Officer
8. Roger Theodoredis, Chief Legal Officer
9. Tabassum Zalotrawala, Chief Development Officer

Source: Based on https://ir.chipotle.com/management

Diversity, Equity, and Inclusion (DEI) and Sustainability

Chipotle has two exemplary female strategists: Marissa Andrada, Chief Diversity, Inclusion and People Officer, and Tabassum Zalotrawala, Chief Development Officer. During her 4 years at Chipotle, Andrada manages DEI strategy across all levels of the company. She develops and nurtures a culture of well-being to inspire mutual learning, development, and personal and career growth. She has revamped Chipotle's benefits, launching a new tuition assistance program, access to mental health care and a quarterly bonus option open to Chipotle's 85,000+ employees.

In March 2021, Chipotle introduced a new environmental, social, and governance (ESG) metric that ties executive compensation to ESG goals. There are three categories of the ESG: Food and Animals, People, and the Environment. Under the ESG system, 10 percent of Chipotle's executive leadership team's annual incentive bonus is tied to the company's progress toward achieving specific goals in the three areas. ESG mandates that Chipotle's top executives be evaluated on the company's progress toward meeting overarching company goals in the three sustainability areas. The People category includes numerous DEI initiatives and objectives regarding the company's hiring, promoting, and evaluating female and underrepresented groups of employees.

Chipotle prints in its annual *Form 10K* detailed data regarding its DEI performance. For example, in the company's 2020 *Form 10K* (p. 5), it says the company's employee population is 54 percent female, 45 percent male, and 1 percent not indicated. Also, the employee population is 38 percent Hispanic or Latino, 31 percent white, 18 percent Black or African American, and 13 percent Other.

Sustainability

In April 2022, Chipotle published its 2021 *Sustainability Report Update* that showcased the company's efforts across People, Food and Animals, and the Environment. For example, Chipotle enhanced its employee offerings in 2021 with leading wages, referral bonuses, and cleared pathways for advancement. Crew members can become a Restaurateur, the highest General Manager position, in as little as three and a half years, with potential total compensation of $100,000 USD while leading a multi-million-dollar growing business. The new report states that 90 percent of Chipotle restaurant management roles in 2021 came from internal promotions, and on average, six employees were promoted per restaurant for a total of nearly 19,000 promotions. Other highlights from Chipotle's 2021 *Sustainability Report Update* include:

People: 90% of restaurant management roles were internal promotions; promoted almost 19,000 team members; established an inclusive, award-winning culture.

Food & Animals: purchased over 40 million pounds of organic & transitional ingredients; purchased over 35 million pounds of local produce—an investment of more than $40 million in support of local food systems in Chipotle's communities; pledged over $1 million of the $5 million committed to young farmers by 12-31-25.

Environment: 100% of new restaurant openings participated in Chipotle's food donation "Harvest Program"; diverted 2.6 million cubic yards of waste through recycling, composting, and waste to energy.

Strategy

In January 2022, Chipotle announced availability of its plant-based chorizo for a limited time at US locations. A new, protein, plant-based chorizo is made using all real, fresh ingredients grown on a farm and can be ordered on the Chipotle app, Chipotle.com, and third-party delivery partners. The new Chipotle menu was tested in both Denver and Indianapolis and consumer response was excellent, so now it is available in all Chipotle restaurants in the United States.

In December 2021, Chipotle opened its first Chipotlane Digital Kitchen, a bit smaller facility than the traditional Chipotlane but still with no dining room access for guests or a front line, but it does offer patio seating for guests. Chipotle's new kitchen is equipped with a make line dedicated to digital orders placed through the Chipotle app and Chipotle.com, as well as marketplace partners. Guests and delivery drivers can collect their digital orders through the Chipotlane drive-thru or walk-up window. Chipotle's 300 Chipotlanes are performing really well, so the company plans to build many more of them, along with many more Chipotlane Digital Kitchens.

Chipotle is spending more and more annually on advertising and marketing. These expenses totaled $158,570, $141,567, and $111,695 for the years ended December 31, 2020, 2019, and 2018, respectively. However, nowhere in the company's *Form 10K* or on the corporate website is any indication given about segments (i.e., across regions or menu items in terms of revenues or gross profits numbers). This is a competitive business, so Chipotle maintains secrecy regarding its segments.

Finance

Chipotle's recent income statements are provided in Exhibit 2. The company's recent balance sheets are provided in Exhibit 3. Note dramatic increases in 2021 in both revenues and net income.

EXHIBIT 2 Chipotle's Recent Income Statements (in Thousands)

Income Statement	12/31/20	12/31/21		Percentage Change
Revenue (Sales)	$5,984,634	$7,547,061	⬆	26%
Cost of Goods Sold	5,420,621	5,840,052	⬆	8%
Gross Profit	564,013	1,707,009	⬆	203%
Operating Expenses	273,849	902,066	⬆	229%
EBIT (Operating Income)	290,164	804,943	⬆	177%
Interest Expense	(3,617)	(7,820)	⬆	116%
EBT	293,781	812,763	⬆	177
Tax	(61,985)	159,779	NA	NA
Nonrecurring Events	0	0	NA	NA
Net Income	$355,766	$652,984	⬆	84%

Source: Based on Chipotle's 2021 *Form 10K*, p. 33.

EXHIBIT 3 Chipotle's Recent Balance Sheets (in Thousands)

Balance Sheet	12/31/20	12/31/21		Percentage Change
Assets				
Cash and Short-Term Investments	$607,987	$815,374	⇧	34%
Accounts Receivable	104,500	99,599	⇩	−5%
Inventory	26,445	32,826	⇧	24%
Other Current Assets	681,305	433,765	⇩	−36%
Total Current Assets	1,420,237	1,381,564	⇩	−3%
Property Plant & Equipment	1,584,311	1,381,564	⇩	−13%
Goodwill	21,939	21,939	⇩	0%
Intangibles	0	0	NA	NA
Other Long-Term Assets	2,956,409	3,867,891	⇧	31%
Total Assets	**5,982,896**	**6,652,958**	⇧	**11%**
Liabilities				
Accounts Payable	121,990	163,161	⇧	34%
Other Current Liabilities	700,209	710,521	⇧	1%
Total Current Liabilities	822,199	873,682	⇧	6%
Long-Term Debt	2,952,296	3,301,601	⇧	12%
Other Long-Term Liabilities	188,266	180,301	⇩	−4%
Total Liabilities	**3,962,761**	**4,355,584**	⇧	**10%**
Equity				
Common Stock	367	371	⇧	1%
Retained Earnings	3,276,163	3,929,147	⇧	20%
Treasury Stock	(2,802,075)	(3,356,102)	NA	NA
Paid in Capital & Other	1,545,680	1,723,958	⇧	12%
Total Equity	**$2,020,135**	**$2,297,374**	⇧	**14%**
Total Liabilities and Equity	**$5,982,896**	**$6,652,958**	⇧	**11%**

Source: Based on Chipotle's 2021 *Form 10K*, p. 32.

Competitors

Capitalizing on the rising influence of Hispanic culture in the United States and the nation's growing appetite for fast-casual dining, Chipotle is one of the fastest-growing companies in the restaurant industry. Categorized as a fast-casual Mexican-food restaurant, Chipotle's primary competitors include Qdoba Mexican Eats (owned by Apollo Global Management), Moe's Southwest Grill (owned by Focus Brands), Baja Fresh Mexican Grill (owned by MTY Food Group), and Rubio's Coastal Grill. The largest Mexican-style restaurant chain in the world, Taco Bell (owned by Yum! Brands) is a fast-food (rather than fast-casual) restaurant and dwarfs Chipotle in terms of number of restaurants.

Chipotle faces hundreds of rival firms, including McDonald's (NYSE: MCD) and Sweetgreen. Headquartered in Los Angeles, Sweetgreen (NYSE: SG) is a fast-casual restaurant that mainly serves salads. Exhibit 4 compares Chipotle to four rival companies. Note Chipotle is less than half the size of McDonald's but still is a large company.

EXHIBIT 4 Rival Firms Compared Financially

	Chipotle	Yum! Brands	Sweetgreen	McDonald's
	CMG	YUM	SG	MCD
Market Capitalization	$42 billion	$37 billion	$2.5 billion	$192 billion
EPS	$25	$5.2	−5.4	9.7
Revenue	$7.2 billion	$6.5 billion	$303 million	$23 billion
Net Income	$711 million	$1.6billion	−$128 million	$7.3 billion
Total Debt	$3.5 billion	$12 billion	N/A	$48 billion
Total Debt/Equity	151	N/A	N/A	N/A
Current Ratio	1.78	1.52	3.10	1.33
# Full-time Employees	95,000	38,000	5,400	200,000
Stock Price	$1,470	$125	$24	$255

Source: Based on https://finance.yahoo.com/quote/CMG?p=CMG&.tsrc=fin-srch

A recent study compared Chipotle to MCD and SG on nine management and marketing variables and reported the findings provided in Exhibit 5. Note that Chipotle ranks best (number one) on every variable, implying this is a well-managed and marketed company.

EXHIBIT 5 Comparing Chipotle with Rival Firms (Ranking 1 = Best; 6 = Worst)

	Variables									
	1	2	3	4	5	6	7	8	9	10
Chipotle (CMG)	1	1	1	1	1	1	1	1	1	09
Sweetgreen (SG)	2	3	3	3	3	2	2	2	2	22
McDonald's (MCD)	3	2	2	2	2	3	3	3	3	23

Variables

1. Effectiveness of CEO
2. Product Quality
3. Do Customers Recommend Company Products to Friends?
4. Pricing
5. Customer Service
6. Overall Culture
7. Do Employees Recommend Company Products to Friends?
8. How Happy Are the Women Employees at the Firm?
9. How Happy Are Minority Employees at the Firm?
10. Summed Score (lower sum the better)

Source: Based on https://www.comparably.com/companies/chipotle/competitors

Exhibit 6 provides a comparison of the five most popular Mexican restaurants in the Unites States.

EXHIBIT 6 Favorite Mexican Restaurant Chains Among US Consumers

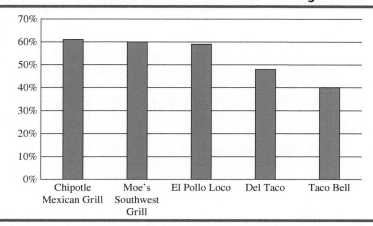

Source: Based on study_id31640_chipotle-mexican-grill-statista-dossier.pdf. Also, July 2019 restaurantmagazine.com

Qdoba Mexican Eats

A large Mexican fast-casual restaurant chain, there are today more than 700 Qdoba restaurants in the United States and Canada. Rather than all company-owned like Chipotle, about half of Qdoba's restaurants are franchises. Headquartered in San Diego, California, Qdoba is owned by Apollo Global Management that also owns Chuck E. Cheese's and Peter Piper Pizza.

Moe's Southwest Grill

Owned by Focus Brands and mostly franchised rather than company-owned, Moe's Southwest Grill has more than 700 restaurants, mostly located east of the Mississippi River. Moe's strategy is to differentiate itself with a fun and offbeat environment and with menu items named after TV and movie stars. Focus Brands owns other restaurant chains, including Auntie Anne's, Carvel, Cinnabon, Jamba, McAlister's Deli, Schlotzsky's, and Seattle's Best Coffee. When Chipotle recently added a new queso recipe to its menu, Moe's responded by offering customers free queso under the slogan "Free Queso Is Better than Some New Queso Recipe." Moe's is an aggressive, strong rival of Chipotle.

Baja Fresh Mexican Grill

MTY Food Group owns and operates both company-owned and franchised Baja Fresh Mexican Grill that is headquartered in Scottsdale, Arizona. A subsidiary of Baja Fresh is La Salsa Fresh Mexican Grill that says its major advantage over Chipotle is its use of fresh farm produce. Baja advertises on its website that its restaurants have no microwaves, no freezers, no can openers, never processed, farm-fresh, and handmade daily.

Rubio's Coastal Grill

Rubio's was founded 10 years before Chipotle and is still privately owned. It is another Mexican-style fast-casual dining chain and based mostly in the western United States but expanded into Florida in 2019. There are Rubio's restaurants in more than 200 locations. Rubio's tries to set itself apart from Chipotle and other competitors by offering fresh fish items and giving some of its California restaurants a beach-like look. In October 2020, Rubio's filed for bankruptcy after it failed to repay roughly $82.3 million in outstanding debt obligations, but the company has since exited bankruptcy and now competes fiercely for the Mexican-food industry market share.

Taco Bell

Irvine-based fast-casual chain fast-food giant Taco Bell is owned by Yum! Brands. Taco Bell has more than 7,500 locations and is the largest fast-food chain that competes directly against Chipotle. Taco Bell offers nachos, burritos, tacos, and quesadillas and has made excellent changes to keep up with shifts in consumer preferences. Taco Bell has introduced a Fresco menu featuring healthier fare and has improved the quality of their ingredients during the last decade.

External Issues

As of the end of June 2021, 39 states had reopened to 100 percent indoor capacity, whereas 11 states were open at 50 to 80 percent capacity. Restaurant menu prices in 2021 are about 4 percent higher than the prior year period largely because wholesale food prices are increasing steadily. Fast-casual is a separate category in the fast-food restaurant industry; the term refers to a growing group of restaurant operators such as Chipotle that offer higher quality, fresher food than traditional fast-food restaurants such as McDonald's but at a lower price than full-service restaurants. The typical cost per meal at a fast-casual restaurant ranges from $8 to $12. Some of the largest and most successful fast-casual restaurant chains are Panera Bread Co., Chipotle Mexican Grill, and Five Guys Burgers and Fries. Success of fast-casuals (sometimes called quick-casual or limited-service) is spurring full-service restaurants to renovate and upgrade their offerings to compete and drive more traffic.

Partly due to labor shortages, many restaurant chains have recently invested in labor-saving technology to cut costs and have redesigned their restaurants to create a more-modern ambiance. However, restaurants are projected to return to rapid growth over the 5 years to 2026 as pent-up demand from the pandemic spurs away-from-home dining and government regulations diminish. Full-service restaurant revenue is forecast to grow at an annualized rate of 5.2 percent to $192.6 billion during the 5-year period. Consumers are increasingly going out to eat as the economy improves and consumer confidence returns to growth, and people are traveling more; Chipotle caters to both residents and travelers.

Restaurants are facing increased competition from a growing number of fast-casual restaurants that serve high-quality food at reasonable prices, such as Chipotle Mexican Grill and Panera Bread. These restaurant chains that have low overhead costs continue to threaten full-service restaurants. In response, many restaurant chains are expanding operations abroad to emerging economies to meet their shareholder expected level of annual growth, typically 5+ percent top line and bottom line on an income statement.

The Omicron and Delta variants of COVID-19 are worrisome variables for all restaurants, including Chipotle. Further local and state-mandated closures and restrictions on seating capacity would negatively impact Chipotle's revenues and profits. Perhaps Chipotle should more extensively embrace companies such as UberEats or DoorDash or even launch their own "remote kitchen services." Restaurants of all size and type are shifting to digital ordering and third-party delivery at growing rates. Technology, online ordering, and third-party delivery are increasingly becoming a competitive advantage or disadvantage for restaurant companies.

The restaurant industry is facing both a hiring crunch and a supply crunch. Trouble on either front can shut a restaurant or chain down and is thus a deep concern for companies like Chipotle. Exhibit 7 provides a brand value analysis of eight restaurants, including Chipotle.

EXHIBIT 7 Brand Value of 8 Valuable Restaurant Brands Worldwide in 2021 (in Billion US$)

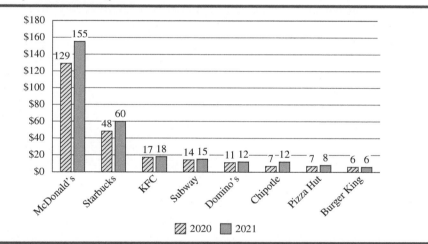

Source: Based on https://adobeindd.com/view/publications/8757d1d4-4a45-44a2-816d-601070c88b98/yup4/publication-web-resources/pdf/BZ_2021_Global_Report_FINAL.pdf

Conclusion

A careful analysis of the competitors and available opportunities across regions is needed along with Chipotle's strengths and weaknesses to plot a strategy for the company moving forward. How aggressively should Chipotle build and open new restaurants and where? Should the company consider franchising, something it has historically avoided in the past?

Remember, your job as the student is not to describe what Chipotle is currently doing or what Chipotle plans to do based on reading press releases or the company *Annual Report*, but rather your job is to consider that you have been hired by CEO Brian Niccol to develop and provide a 3-year strategic plan. Chipotle's upper management, and in this case your classmates and professor, are looking for you (or paying you a high fee if hired by Chipotle) to recommend what you feel is the best direction for the firm moving forward based on your strategic management research, knowledge, and expertise. Be mindful that shareholders of nearly all companies expect a minimum of 5 percent annual growth on both revenues and net income, so Chipotle likely needs to build new restaurants more aggressively.

Consumers are increasingly price sensitive while at the same time demanding high quality in their away-from-home dining. This is partly why fast-casual restaurants, such as Chipotle

Mexican Grill, Schlotzsky's, Qdoba Mexican Eats, and Panera Bread, are performing so well and taking business away from full-service restaurants such as Cracker Barrel. Should Chipotle acquire one or more of these high-performing fast-casual, sit-down-inside restaurants?

Prepare a clear 3-year strategic plan for CEO Niccol indicating the direction you think will be most advantageous for management moving forward. Deciding how to allocate resources across regions is a difficult yet major challenge and job of a strategist. Prepare projected financial statements if possible to reveal your expectations regarding the financial impact of your proposed strategies.

References

1. https://ir.chipotle.com/management
2. https://finance.yahoo.com/quote/CMG?p=CMG&.tsrc=fin-srch
3. https://www.comparably.com/companies/chipotle/competitors
4. Chipotle's 2020 *Form 10K*.
5. Chipotle's 2021 *Form 10K*.
6. https://mission-statement.com/chipotle/
7. https://www.influenster.com/reviews/chipotle-mexican-grill
8. study_id31640_chipotle-mexican-grill-statista-dossier.pdf.
9. July 2019 restaurantmagazine.com.
10. study_id31640_chipotle-mexican-grill-statista-dossier.pdf. Also, July 2019 restaurantmagazine.com.

Wynn Resorts, Limited, 2022

www.wynnresorts.com, (NASDAQ: WYNN)

Headquartered in Paradise, Nevada, Wynn Resorts, Ltd. (Wynn) is a well-known, large, global, high-end, casino and lodging company, with four properties: Wynn and Encore Las Vegas, Encore Boston Harbor, Wynn and Encore Macau, and Wynn Palace, Cotai (an island beside Macau). Wynn consists of Wynn Las Vegas (wynnlasvegas.com), Encore Boston Harbor (encoreboston-harbor.com), Wynn Macau (wynnmacau.com), and Wynn Palace, Cotai (wynnpalace.com). Wynn and Encore Las Vegas are two luxury hotel towers with 4,748 hotel rooms, suites and villas, about 194,000 square feet of casino space, 21 dining experiences, 513,000 rentable square feet of meeting and convention space, 155,000 square feet of retail space, two theaters, two nightclubs, a beach club, and Wynn Golf Club, an 18-hole, 128-acre championship golf course.

Located on the waterfront along the Mystic River in Everett, Massachusetts, Wynn's Encore Boston Harbor offers 211,000 square foot casino, 671 hotel rooms, specialty retail, 16 dining and lounge venues, 71,000 square feet of ballroom and meeting spaces, a six-acre public park and Harborwalk along the shoreline. Encore is the largest private, single-phase development in the history of Massachusetts.

Located in the Macau Special Administrative Region of China, Wynn Macau is a luxury hotel and casino resort with two hotel towers, 1,010 rooms and suites, 252,000 square feet of casino space, 14 food and beverage spots, 31,000 square feet of meeting and convention space, 59,000 square feet of retail space, and more. Also located in Macau, Wynn Palace is a luxury integrated resort with 1,706 rooms, suites and villas, 424,000 square feet of casino space, 14 food and beverage spots, 37,000 square feet of meeting and convention space, 107,000 square feet of designer retail, SkyCabs that traverse an eight-acre Performance.

The global pandemic and lingering effects crushed casinos and the whole hospitality industry from mid-2020 through 2021. But Wynn quickly recovered in 2022 becoming very profitable again. In April 2022, Wynn was honored on Forbes Travel Guide (FTG) Five-Star Awards list, earning an impressive 24 Five-Star recognitions across the company's global portfolio. This year, Encore Boston Harbor joins the Five-Star collection of resorts, receiving top marks for hotel and spa. Wynn is actually the global leader receiving the most Five-Star awards than any company on the planet. Also, interestingly in April 2022, Encore Boston Harbor was noted as the largest Five-Star regional resort casino in North America; and Wynn Macau was the only resort world-wide with eight individual Five-Star awards, achieving this for the sixth consecutive year; and Wynn Palace for the third straight year received the most Five-Star restaurants of any individual resort in the world, achieving this for the third consecutive year; and Wing Lei at Wynn Las Vegas for the sixth straight year was the only Five-Star Chinese restaurant in North America.

Wynn and rivals are quickly going digital. Wynn Interactive now offers digital and interactive sports betting and gaming through the betting app, WynnBET, which is currently operational in New Jersey, Colorado, Michigan, and soon will be available in Indiana, Iowa, Ohio, Tennessee, Virginia, and Massachusetts.

Copyrighted by Fred David Books LLC; written by Fred R. David.

History

Wynn Resorts was founded in 2002 by Steve Wynn who was the CEO and chairman at the time of Mirage Resorts. Wynn launched its initial public offering (IPO) in October 2002 and the company's first property was the Wynn Las Vegas that officially opened in April 2005. Wynn Macau, the company's second project, opened in 2006 and is the largest-grossing casino in that region.

Encore, an extension to Wynn Las Vegas, was completed in 2008, followed by Encore at Wynn Macau that opened in 2010. Wynn Macau is one of only five hotels in Asia to receive the

Forbes Five-Star Award and is the only resort worldwide to win that award eight times. Wynn Palace, Cotai, opened Macau in August 2016.

Wynn has a big part of the gaming and gambling operations in Macau, the island-city-resort located 1-hour boat ride offshore of Hong Kong or via landing at the Macau International Airport situated at the eastern end of Taipa Island. Macau is the largest gambling destination in the world, even larger than Las Vegas. Exhibit 1 reveals all the revenue derived from casino gaming and gambling from that island city in 2010 to 2020. Note the COVID-19-related drop in revenues to in 2020, but everything rebounded in 2021–2023.

EXHIBIT 1 **All Macau Casinos' Gaming & Gambling Revenue in Billions of Macanese Pataca (the Currency): 2010 to 2020**

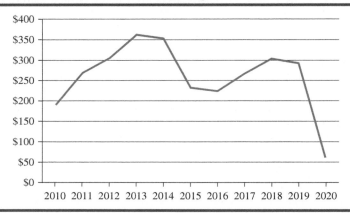

Source: Based in information at the Gaming Inspection and Coordination Bureau in Macao, April 2021, Dicj.gov.mo

In February 2022, Wynn was recognized as one of *Forbes* America's Best Employers 2022, ranking within the Top 5 companies in the Travel and Leisure category; Wynn rose an impressive 123 spots on the prior year's list. That same month, Wynn was honored on *FORTUNE* Magazine's 2022 World's Most Admired Companies list in the hotel, casino and resort category; Wynn placed first overall in the group for Quality of Products/Services.

Internal Issues

Vision/Mission/Core Values

Neither at Wynn's corporate website nor in the most recent company *Annual Report* is there a published vision or mission statement, but the company talks about its three pillars being: People, Communities, and Planet. A possible vision statement for Wynn could read something like this: "*To be the world leader in luxury resorts in the gaming sector, providing the best customer service and the best work environment in the industry*." Another possible vision statement, along with a possible mission statement and core values statement (all paraphrased) are given in Exhibit 2.

EXHIBIT 2 **Possible Vision, Mission, and Core Value Statements for Wynn Resorts**

Vision Statement: *Be the best luxury resort in the gaming industry, with unrivaled customer service. We will utilize the latest advances in gaming innovations and resort amenities to differentiate our brand from competitors and to maximize shareholder wealth. We will provide a wonderful work environment where employees are provided with endless opportunities for success and advancement.*

Mission Statement: *We have received more Forbes Travel Guide Five-Star Awards than any other gaming company in the world. Wynn offers award-winning restaurants, entertainment, nightlife, spas, salons, and luxury shopping. We strive to make every visit a once-in-a-lifetime experience for our guests.*

Core Values: *Respect everyone and everything. Embrace excellence and attention to details. Be artistic and responsible. Always strive to innovate and improve.*

Source: Based on https://www.comparably.com/companies/wynn-resorts/mission. Also, Wynn's 2020 *Form 10K*, p. 5.

Organizational Structure

The long-time CEO of Wynn Resorts, Matt Maddox, was replaced by Wynn Resort's president and CFO, Craig Billings on February 1, 2022. Wynn Resorts operates using a divisional-by-region organizational structure. The company's senior managers are listed and arrayed in Exhibit 3. Note there are five women among the top 11 executives.

EXHIBIT 3 Wynn Resorts' Top Executives Listed and Arrayed

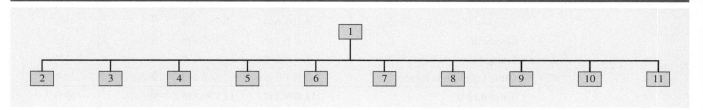

1. Craig Billings, CEO
2. Julie Cameron Doe, CFO (female)
3. Ellen Whittemore, EVP, General Counsel & Secretary (female)
4. Marilyn Spiegel, President, Wynn Las Vegas (female)
5. Linda Chen, President, Wynn International Marketing (female)
6. Ian Coughlan, President, Wynn Macau
7. DeRuyter Butler, EVP of Architecture, Design, & Development
8. Brian Gullbrants, President, Wynn MA
9. Dean Lawrence, SVP and CFO of Wynn Las Vegas
10. Craig Fullalove, SVP and CFO of Wynn Resorts Macau
11. Allison Rankin, CFO, Wynn MA (female)

Source: Based on information at https://wynnresortslimited.gcs-web.com/corporate-governance/management
Note: #9 reports to #4, #10 reports to #6, and #11 reports to #8.

CO_2 Emissions

Wynn Las Vegas procures 75 percent of their peak energy demand from renewable resources. The company has an overall goal to procure or produce 50 percent of their energy from renewable sources by 2030, with 2030 being the last year in which the company will allow a year-over-year increase in carbon emissions; after 2030, each year will be a reduction, according to plan.

Finance

Wynn's recent income statements and balance sheets are provided in Exhibit 4 and Exhibit 5, respectively. Note that Wynn was still unprofitable at year-end 2021.

EXHIBIT 4 Wynn Resorts' Recent Income Statements (in Thousands)

Income Statement	12/31/20	12/31/21		Percentage Change
Revenue (Sales)	$2,095,861	$3,763,664	⇧	80%
Cost of Goods Sold	1,743,219	2,558,581	⇧	47%
Gross Profit	352,642	1,205,083	⇧	242%
Operating Expenses	1,584,687	1,599,624	⇧	1%
EBIT (Operating Income)	(1,232,045)	(394,541)	NA	NA
Interest Expense	530,230	616,975	⇧	16%
EBT	(1,762,275)	(1,011,516)	NA	NA
Tax	564,671	474	⇩	−100%
Nonrecurring Events	259,701	256,204	⇩	−1%
Net Income	($2,067,245)	($755,786)	NA	NA

Source: Based on Wynn's 2021 *Form 10K*, p. 62.

EXHIBIT 5 Wynn Resorts' Recent Balance Sheets (in Thousands)

Balance Sheet	12/31/20	12/31/21		Percentage Change
Assets				
Cash and Short-Term Investments	$3,482,032	$2,522,530	⇩	−28%
Accounts Receivable	200,158	199,463	⇩	0%
Inventory	66,285	69,967	⇧	6%
Other Current Assets	64,672	83,957	⇧	30%
Total Current Assets	3,813,147	2,875,917	⇩	−25%
Property Plant & Equipment	9,196,644	8,765,308	⇩	−5%
Goodwill	278,195	307,578	⇧	11
Intangibles	0	0	NA	NA
Other Long-Term Assets	581,561	582,023	⇧	0%
Total Assets	**13,869,547**	**12,530,826**	⇩	**−10%**
Liabilities				
Accounts Payable	148,478	170,542	⇧	15%
Other Current Liabilities	1,732,410	1,117,338	⇩	−36%
Total Current Liabilities	1,880,888	1,287,880	⇩	−32%
Long-Term Debt	12,469,362	11,884,546	⇩	−5%
Other Long-Term Liabilities	256,614	194,615	⇩	−24%
Total Liabilities	**14,606,864**	**13,367,041**	⇩	**−8%**
Equity				
Common Stock	1,235	1,314	⇧	6%
Retained Earnings	(1,532,420)	(2,288,078)	⇧	49%
Treasury Stock	(1,422,531)	(1,436,373)	⇧	1%
Paid in Capital & Other	2,216,399	2,886,922	⇧	30%
Total Equity	**($737,317)**	**($836,215)**	⇧	**13%**
Total Liabilities and Equity	**$13,869,547**	**$12,530,826**	⇩	**−10%**

Source: Based on Wynn's 2021 *Form 10K*, p. 61.

Segments

Wynn reports operating results within four segments: Wynn Palace, Wynn Macau, Las Vegas Operations, and Encore Boston Harbor. Exhibit 6 reveals Wynn's revenues by location in recent years. Note the pandemic dramatic drop in revenues in 2020 and note that Wynn's revenues derived from Macau are larger than Las Vegas and Boston Harbor combined. Also note the huge increases in 2021 in all areas.

EXHIBIT 6 Wynn's Revenues by Location (in Thousands)

	2019	2020	2021
Macau Operations			
Wynn Palace	$2,543,694	$505,420	$883,007
Wynn Macau	2,070,029	474,657	626,015
Las Vegas Operations	1,633,457	747,947	1,503,681
Encore Boston Harbor	363,919	361,666	691,523
Corporate and Other	—	6,171	59,438
Total	$6,611,099	$2,095,861	$3,763,664

Source: Based on Wynn's 2020 and 2021 *Form 10K*, p. 41 and p. 40 respectively.

Wynn also reports their revenues by product as provided in Exhibit 7. Note that Wynn's casino revenues are more than their combined revenues obtained from rooms, food, beverage, shows, and retail.

EXHIBIT 7 Wynn's Revenues by Product (in Thousands)

	2019	2020	2021
Casino revenues	$4,573,924	$1,237,230	$2,133,420
Room revenues	804,162	307,973	592,571
Food and beverage revenues	818,822	329,584	633,911
Entertainment, retail, other revenues	414,191	221,074	403,762
Total	$6,611,099	$2,095,861	$3,763,664

Source: Based on Wynn's 2020 and 2021 *Form 10K*, p. 42 and p. 41 respectively.

Wynn also reports their net income (loss) before interest, income taxes, depreciation and amortization (EBITDA) by location, as provided in Exhibit 8. Note pandemic crushing losses incurred in 2020. Note in 2021 that the company's Las Vegas operations were much more profitable than the company's Macau operations. Even the company's Boston operations were more profitable than their casinos in Macau.

EXHIBIT 8 Wynn's EBITDA by Location (in Thousands)

	2019	2020	2021
Macau EBITDA			
Wynn Palace	$729,535	($149,647)	$91,646
Wynn Macau	648,837	(87,189)	4,209
Total Macau	1,378,372	(236,836)	95,855
Las Vegas EBITDA	413,886	(56,356)	530,878
Encore Boston Harbor EBITDA	23,150	(23,762)	210,068
Corporate and Other EBITDA	—	(7,351)	(267,360)
Total EBITDA	1,815,408	(324,305)	569,441
Other Operating Expenses	937,103	907,740	963,982
Operating income (loss)	878,305	(1,232,045)	(394,541)
Net income (loss)	$122,985	($2,067,245)	($755,786)

Source: Based on Wynn's 2020 and 2021 *Form 10K*, p. 109 and p. 47 and p. 106 respectively.

Competitors

Wynn faces more than 100 rival firms, but their biggest rivals are Las Vegas Sands (LVS), MGM Resorts International (MGM), Caesars Entertainment (CZR), Marriott International (MAR), Station Casinos, Century Casinos (CNTY), and Penn National Gaming (PENN). Exhibit 9 provides a comparison of Wynn with three big rivals. Note that Wynn is smallest among the four companies.

EXHIBIT 9 Rival Firms Compared Financially

	Wynn Resorts	Caesars	MGM Resorts	Marriott
	WYNN	CZR	MGM	MAR
Market Capitalization	$10 billion	$16.6 billion	$20 billion	$50 billion
EPS	−$7.6	−$5.4	1.25	1.43
Revenue	$3.4 billion	$8.4 billion	$7.8 billion	$2.85 billion
Net Income	−$848 million	−$1.1 billion	$615 million	$467 million
Total Debt	$11.9 billion	$27 billion	$25 billion	$10.7 billion
Total Debt/Equity	N/A	545	209	1,164
Current Ratio	2.2	1.19	1.96	0.50
# Full-time Employees	27,500	54,000	45,000	121,000
Stock Price	$90	$78	$42	$154

Source: Based on https://finance.yahoo.com/quote/WYNN?p=WYNN&.tsrc=fin-srch

A recent study compared Wynn with Las Vegas Sands (LVS), CZR, MGM Resorts, Station Casinos, and Century Casinos (CNTY) on nine management and marketing variables. The findings are reported in Exhibit 10. Note that Wynn ranks best (number one) on three variables, implying this is a well-managed and marketed company, but there is a perceived problem with Wynn's CEO, as indicated by number six ranking in column 1. Based on the analysis, MGM is a strong rival to Wynn, perhaps more so than Caesars, as indicated in column 10 with the low sum score of 20.

EXHIBIT 10 Comparing Wynn with Rival Firms (Ranking 1 = Best; 6 = Worst)

	Variables									
	1	2	3	4	5	6	7	8	9	10
Wynn Resorts	6	1	2	1	1	4	4	3	4	26
Las Vegas Sands	1	3	1	2	2	2	3	NA	NA	14+
MGM Resorts	4	2	3	3	3	1	2	1	1	20
Caesars Entertain	5	5	5	6	5	3	5	2	3	39
Century Casinos	2	6	6	5	6	6	6	NA	NA	37+
Station Casinos	3	4	4	4	4	5	1	4	2	31

Variables

1. Effectiveness of CEO
2. Product Quality
3. Do Customers Recommend Company Products to Friends?
4. Pricing
5. Customer Service
6. Overall Culture
7. Do Employees Recommend Company Products to Friends?
8. How Happy Are the Women Employees at the Firm?
9. How Happy Are Minority Employees at the Firm?
10. Summed Score (lower sum the better)

Source: Based on https://www.comparably.com/companies/wynn-resorts/competitors

Caesars Entertainment (NASDAQ: CZR)

A major rival to Wynn is Caesars, the world's largest and most diversified collection of gaming brands, including Caesars Palace, Harrah's, Horseshoe, Eldorado, Silver Legacy, Circus Circus Reno, Circus Circus Las Vegas, Tropicana and Bally's Atlantic City, Isle Capri, Rio, Flamingo, and many others. Caesars is the global leader in gaming and hospitality, providing extensive family-style services, amenities, restaurants, shows, conference rooms, sports betting, poker, roulette, slot machines, all kinds of table games like blackjack, and exhilarating (or demoralizing) experiences.

MGM Resorts International (NYSE: MGM)

Headquartered in Las Vegas, MGM owns and operates casino, hotel, gaming, sports betting, iGaming through BetMGM, convention, retail, and entertainment resorts in the United States and Macau. The company's *Form 10K* reveals three segments: Las Vegas Strip Resorts, Regional Operations, and MGM China. MGM's casino resorts offer gaming, hotel, convention, dining, entertainment, retail, and other resort amenities. MGM's portfolio consists of 29 hotel and destination gaming offerings including the Fallen Oak golf course.

Las Vegas Sands (NYSE: LVS)

Headquartered in Las Vegas, LVS competes aggressively against Wynn both in Las Vegas and Macau. LVS coined the name Macao referring to its properties on the Cotai Strip adjacent to Macau. LVS develops, owns, and operates integrated gaming and other resorts in Asia and the United States. LVS properties include The Venetian Macao Resort Hotel, the Londoner Macao, The Parisian Macao, The Plaza Macao, Four Seasons Hotel Macao, and The Sands Macao. LVS also owns the Marina Bay Sands in Singapore. LVS owns and operates The Sands Expo and Convention Center in Las Vegas and the Venetian Resort Hotel Casino in Las Vegas. LVS's integrated resorts feature accommodations, gaming, entertainment, retail malls, convention and exhibition facilities, celebrity chef restaurants, and other amenities.

Station Casinos LLC

Based in the Las Vegas suburb of Summerlin South, Nevada, Station Casinos is a US hotel and casino company that owns such brands and properties as Palms Casino Resort, Texas Station, Santa Fe Station, Fiesta Rancho, NP Durango, NP Gold Rush, NP Boulder, NP Magic Star, NP Tropicano, Lake Mead Station, and others.

Century Casinos, Inc. (NASDAQ: CNTY)

Based in Colorado Springs, Colorado, CNTY operates eight casinos in Colorado, Missouri, and West Virginia, and five casinos in Edmonton, Calgary, and Alberta, Canada. CNTY also operates casinos on four cruise ships for TUI Cruises. In Q3 2021, CNTY achieved their highest quarterly net operating revenue and net income in the company's history and an EBITDA margin of 28.3 percent. CNTY has a strong balance sheet with cash of more than $100 million and no substantial debt maturities before 2026.

External Issues

Gaming in the United States

Some of the largest hotels in the Unites States, with more than 2,000 rooms each, are located in gaming markets such as Las Vegas and Atlantic City. Smaller, regional casino markets in the United States are recovering much faster than in Las Vegas, which relies more heavily on air travel and business conventions. The legalization or development of new US gaming markets is spurring growth in the industry, with casino gambling now legal in 30 states, and gaming machines and racetracks allowed in other states.

The lifting of federal US bans on sports betting in 2018 catapulted the launch of online sports book (OSB) and online casino gaming (iGaming) businesses, which has led to a strong growth for the first half of 2021. Analysts expect this growing online betting market to reach $25 billion to $42 billion by 2030. New Jersey has seen average online bets placed rocket to more than $670 million per month. MGM Resorts recently partnered with the world's largest online betting technology company, Entain Holdings, to form Bet MGM, a US online sports betting and online gaming company to capitalize on these new external opportunities.

In 2018 the US Supreme Court delivered a landmark decision to strike down the federal ban on sports gambling and allowed individual states to decide for themselves the legality of sports gambling; many states have legalized sports betting or are in the process of doing it. Prior to the Supreme Court ruling, Nevada was the only state that was allowed to engage in betting on the outcome of sporting events. Websites such as https://www.cbssports.com/general/news/wanna-bet-explaining-where-all-50-states-stand-on-legalizing-sports-gambling/ reveal state-by-state the status of casino approvals and online gambling.

Exhibit 11 reveals the percentage of total gaming revenue of all casinos located in the United States in 2020 by state. Note that Nevada is highest at 29 percent, followed by New Jersey at

EXHIBIT 11 Total Gaming Revenue of All Casinos Located in the United States in 2020 by State (in Percentage of Millions of US$)

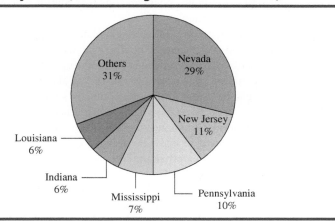

Source: Based on https://www.statista.com/statistics/187926/gross-gaming-revenue-by-state-us/, May 2021 release date.

Note: Others = 24 states.

11 percent. Note that New Jersey's gaming revenues, including Atlantic City, are down from a much higher percentage a decade ago because casinos have spread all over the United States. For example, players used to drive for 1 hour from Philadelphia to Atlantic City to gamble, but now Philly has its own casinos, as does West Virginia, so no need to drive or fly necessarily to Atlantic City.

Gaming in Macau

Macau is an island located 37 miles southwest of Hong Kong, reachable from Hong Kong in 15 minutes by helicopter, 30 minutes by road on the Hong Kong-Zhuhai-Macau Bridge that opened in 2018, and 1 hour by jetfoil ferry. Macau has been a casino destination for more than 50 years, and today is home to 41 casinos. About 95 percent of the visitors to Macau come from China, Hong Kong, and Taiwan. Annual gaming revenues in Macau grew from $2.9 billion in 2002 to $36.5 billion in 2019, before falling to $7.6 billion in 2020. Tourist arrivals in Macau decreased 85.0 percent in 2020 to 5.9 million, compared with 39.4 million visitors in 2019.

Wynn's Macau operations face competition from the other casinos in Macau, plus from casinos located throughout the world, including Singapore, South Korea, the Philippines, Vietnam, Cambodia, Malaysia, Australia, Las Vegas, cruise ships in Asia that offer gaming, and other casinos throughout Asia. Various Asian countries and regions plan to legalize gaming soon, including Japan, Taiwan, and Thailand, which would further increase competition for Wynn's Macau operations. Macau/Macao's gaming industry recovered nicely in 2021–2022. The first half of 2021 revealed that Macau/Macao casinos recorded gross game revenue (GGR) of $6.13 billion, up 45 percent from the same period in 2020, due to easing of bans on foreign entries.

As of early 2020, only six companies—SJM, Melco, Galaxy Entertainment, Wynn Macau, Sands China, and MGM China—however were licensed to run casinos in Macau due to pandemic restrictions. Each company purchased a "concession," auctioned by the government, permitting them to open gaming rooms. All six concessions are set to expire in June 2022. Macau local authorities seek to diversify the local economy away from gambling. They want casino operators to invest in alternative entertainment facilities, which provide lower rates of return to Wynn and rival firms, but casino executives are reluctant to diversify due to already strict demands, low profitability due to high fixed assets, and too few gamblers due to negative COVID tests being required for entry and 14-day quarantines being required even for persons "exposed" to COVID.

Conclusion

As indicated in the case, regionally located casinos where visitors can drive for an hour or two and play their chosen game are growing nicely, but gaming spots like Las Vegas and Macau that rely heavily on air flights are not recovering as fast due to lingering pandemic problems. Wynn is most heavily invested in Las Vegas and Macau, so this is a problem. Perhaps acquiring more regional brands or companies should be considered, such as Station Casinos or Century Casinos that are well-known and making money?

CEO Craig Billings at Wynn needs clear strategic plan because his company faces scores of competitors of all sizes, located everywhere, globally. And his company relies perhaps too heavily on Las Vegas and Macau tourists. Wynn needs also to bring own more states to use its digital online gaming products, including sports betting. Recall that shareholders expect annual growth of at least 5 percent top line and bottom line on the company's income statement.

Billings knows the basic underlying external opportunities and threats facing his company, as well as the basic internal strengths and weaknesses, but he needs to know the relative importance of those factors. He also needs to know the relative attractiveness of alternative strategies to be derived from those underlying external and internal factors. In other words, Billings needs strategy analyses performed, including IFE Matrix, EFE Matrix, SWOT, IE Matrix, perceptual mapping, EPS-EBIT analysis, and projected financial statement analysis. Let's say that Billings hires you to develop a comprehensive strategic plan for his company. Beginning with improved vision and mission statements, perform the analysis that is requested, develop some recommendations with associated costs, and present your findings and research to your professor and fellow students.

References

1. www.wynnresorts.com
2. https://wynnresortslimited.gcs-web.com/corporate-governance/management
3. Wynn Resorts 2020 *Form 10K*.
4. Wynn Resorts 2021 *Form 10K*.
5. https://www.comparably.com/companies/wynn-resorts/competitors
6. https://www.statista.com/statistics/187926/gross-gaming-revenue-by-state-us/, May 2021 release date.
7. S&P NetAdvantage, *Industry Surveys*, Hotels, Gaming, and Leisure, August 2021.
8. https://www.cbssports.com/general/news/wanna-bet-explaining-where-all-50-states-stand-on-legalizing-sports-gambling/
9. https://fortune.com/2021/08/17/macau-casino-opening-covid-tourism-recovery/
10. https://finance.yahoo.com/quote/WYNN?p=WYNN#amp;.tsrc=fin-srch
11. https://www.comparably.com/companies/wynn-resorts/mission

Cinemark Holdings, Inc., 2022

https://ir.cinemark.com, (NYSE: CNK)

Headquartered in Plano, Texas, Cinemark Holdings (Cinemark) owns and operates hundreds of movie theaters in the United States and South America. In Brazil, Cinemark has a leading 30 percent of the market. Various movie theater brands owned by Cinemark include Century Theatres, Tinseltown, CineArts, and Rave Cinemas. Cinemark derives revenues not only from the sale of movie admission tickets and concessions but also by allowing businesses to advertise on their screens before movies begin and via a Lobby Entertainment Network (LEN), which consists of hundreds of 42-inch flat screens in high-traffic areas of lobbies devoted to advertisers. There is also lobby advertising via posters, signs, and banners, and box office handouts, exit samples, and table promotions.

Concession sales are Cinemark's second-largest revenue source, historically representing about 35 percent of total revenues. Some Cinemark customers prefer to visit theatres and stay with their family or friend group, so the company recently introduced Private Watch Parties that allows guests to rent an entire auditorium to watch a film and bring up to 20 guests for a price range of $99 to $149.

A few fast facts about Cinemark are as follows:

- Is the third-largest chain of movie theaters in the United States with 324 theatres and 4,440 screens in 42 states.
- Has been ranked either number one or number two by box office revenues in 20 of their top 25 US markets at year end 2019.
- Has 200 theatres and 1,457 screens in 15 countries in Latin and South America as of Fall 2021.
- Has a presence in 15 of the top 20 metropolitan areas in South America at year-end 2020.

As of mid-2022, Cinemark operates 520 theatres with 5,849 screens in 42 states domestically and 15 countries throughout South and Central America. Cinemark's total revenues for its Q1 2022 that ended March 31, 2022, increased 303 percent to $460.5 million compared with $114.4 million for the three months that ended March 31, 2021. Also for Q1 2022, the company's admissions revenues were $235.8 million and concession revenues were $173.0 million, driven by attendance of 33.1 million patrons; average ticket price was $7.12, and concession revenues per patron were $5.23. However for Q1 2022, Cinemark's net income was negative $74.0 million compared with negative $208.3 million for the three months ended March 31, 2021. As of March 31, 2022, the company's aggregate screen count was 5,849, and the firm had commitments to open three new theatres and 42 screens during the remainder of 2022, and nine new theatres and 70 screens subsequent to 2022.

Copyright by Fred David Books LLC; written by Fred R. David.

History

Cinemark was founded in 1960 when two brothers J.C. and Lee Roy Mitchell created Mitchell Theatres, Inc. By 1972, the company was named Texas Cinema Corporation, but Lee Roy Mitchell soon formed another group of theaters under the Cinemark name in 1977. Cinemark and Texas Cinema merged in 1979 creating a mix of 25 theaters in Texas and New Mexico under the Cinemark brand. The company continued acquiring and building theaters and in 1987 acquired Plitt Theatres. Cinemark sold all its Mexican theaters to Cinemex in 2013.

Due to the COVID-19 pandemic, on March 18, 2020, Cinemark closed all its 345 theaters in the United States indefinitely, but by year end 2020, Cinemark had reopened 217 domestic theatres and 129 international theatres. By May 2021, 98 percent of Cinemark's theaters in the United States had reopened, but only 50 percent of the Cinemark theaters in South America had reopened due to government restrictions. Cinemark in Latin and South

America currently owns and operates 200 theatres and 1,457 screens in 15 countries. In late 2020, Cinemark implemented mobile concession ordering at about half of their US theatres allowing guests to prepay for select concession products and pick them up on arrival or have them delivered to their seat.

In June 2022, Cinemark Movie Club surpassed 1 million active members, and leads the industry with more than 3,000 members per theatre across its U.S. circuit. Launched in December 2017, Cinemark Movie Club was the first North American exhibitor-developed paid monthly membership program. The distinctive, transaction-based program is the first domestic theater subscription to achieve the 1-million-member milestone, underscoring its tremendous value proposition with guest satisfaction scores in excess of 90 percent. Cinemark's Movie Club offers reduced ticket prices and a 20 percent discount on concessions. Movie Club members visit Cinemark theatres three times more often than our average moviegoer with more frequent visits to the concession stand. For $9.99 per month, Cinemark's Movie Club members experience unparalleled benefits.

Internal Issues

Vision/Mission/Core Values

The case author could not find a published vision or mission statement at the Cinemark corporate website or the most recent *Annual Report*. However, possible vision or mission statements could include the following:

> *"To make the movie experience memorable, 'One Guest at a time.'"*
>
> *"To take care of customers and investors and to provide a learning and growing experience for all employees."*

A set of core values for Cinemark could not be located on the corporate website, but possibly could read something like the following:

> *"Act with honesty and integrity.*
> *Respect and care for each other and all others.*
> *Provide a safe environment for everyone.*
> *Aim to be the best at what we do."*

Organizational Structure

It appears from the position titles of executives that Cinemark operates using a functional (centralized) organizational structure, given at present there is not a president of the US segment and no COO. Cinemark's top executives are listed and arrayed in Exhibit 1.

EXHIBIT 1 Cinemark's Executives Listed and Arrayed

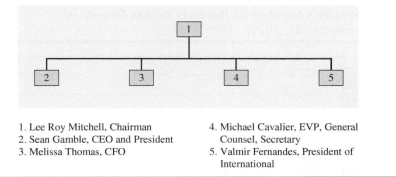

1. Lee Roy Mitchell, Chairman
2. Sean Gamble, CEO and President
3. Melissa Thomas, CFO
4. Michael Cavalier, EVP, General Counsel, Secretary
5. Valmir Fernandes, President of International

Source: Based on https://ir.cinemark.com/company-information/management-team

Segments

Concession sales are their second-largest revenue source, historically representing approximately 35 percent of total revenues. We have devoted considerable management effort to expanding concession sales by enhancing our offerings and adapting to our customers' changing preferences, as will be discussed.

Cinemark manages its operations under two divisions or segments: US Markets and International Markets. The international markets include 15 countries in Latin and South America. Exhibit 2 reveals the companies leased versus owned theaters in the United States and in International markets. Note that Cinemark leases most of its cinema land and property. Note also the decline in 2021. Shareholders like growth, not declines, top line (revenues) and bottom line (net income).

EXHIBIT 2 Cinemark's Leased Versus Owned Theaters (December 31, 2021)

	12-31-20		12-31-21	
	Leased	Owned	Leased	Owned
United States	$288	$43	$279	$42
International	200	00	201	00
Total	$488	$43	$480	$42

Source: Based on Cinemark's 2020 and 2021 *Form 10K*, p. 23 and p. 19 respectively.

Exhibit 3 provides data regarding Cinemark's revenues by product type. Note that movie ticket admission revenues are nearly double concession revenues, but this industry is in trouble with all the steep declines.

EXHIBIT 3 Cinemark's Revenues by Product (in Millions)

	2019	2020	2021
Admissions	$1,805	$356	$779
United States	1,432	291	671
International	373	65	108
Concessions	1,161	231	562
United States	936	190	483
International	225	41	79
Other	317	99	139
Total	$3,283	$686	$1,480

Source: Based on Cinemark's 2020 and 2021 *Form 10K*, p. 25 and 34, and p. 28 respectively.

Cinemark's number of theaters across countries is illustrated in Exhibit 4.

EXHIBIT 4 Cinemark's Number of Theaters Across Countries (December 31, 2021)

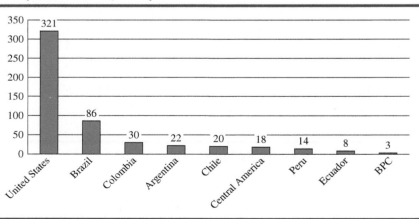

Source: Based on Cinemark's 2021 *Form 10K*, p. 6.

Note: BPC = Bolivia, Paraguay, Curaçao. Also, Central America = Honduras, El Salvador, Nicaragua, Costa Rica, Panama, and Guatemala.

Finance

Cinemark's recent income statements and balance sheets are provided in Exhibit 5 and Exhibit 6, respectively. Note the 2021 increase in revenue but continued net income loss.

EXHIBIT 5 Cinemark's Recent Income Statements (in Millions)

Income Statement	12/31/20	12/31/21		Percentage Change
Revenue (Sales)	$686	$1,511	⇧	120%
Cost of Goods Sold	236	513	⇧	117%
Gross Profit	450	998	⇧	122%
Operating Expenses	1,205	1,250	⇧	4%
EBIT (Operating Income)	(755)	(252)	NA	NA
Interest Expense	171	188	⇧	10%
EBT	(926)	(440)	NA	NA
Tax	(309)	(17)	NA	NA
Nonrecurring Events	0	0	NA	NA
Net Income	$(617)	$(423)	NA	NA

Source: Based on Cinemark's 2021 *Form 10K*, p. F-6.

EXHIBIT 6 Cinemark's Recent Balance Sheets (in Millions)

Balance Sheet	12/31/20	12/31/21		Percentage Change
Assets				
Cash and Short-Term Investments	$655	$707	⇧	8%
Accounts Receivable	25	69	⇧	176%
Inventory	13	15	⇧	15%
Other Current Assets	200	83	⇩	−59%
Total Current Assets	893	874	⇩	−2%
Property Plant & Equipment	1,615	1,383	⇩	−14%
Goodwill	1,254	1,249	⇩	0
Intangibles	314	311	⇩	−1%
Other Long-Term Assets	1,487	1,414	⇩	−5%
Total Assets	**5,563**	**5,231**	⇩	**−6%**
Liabilities				
Accounts Payable	71	76	⇧	7%
Other Current Liabilities	535	693	⇧	30%
Total Current Liabilities	606	769	⇧	27%
Long-Term Debt	2,377	2,476	⇧	4%
Other Long-Term Liabilities	1,781	1,651	⇩	−7%
Total Liabilities	**4,764**	**4,896**	⇧	**3%**
Equity				
Common Stock	0	0	NA	NA
Retained Earnings	28	(389)	⇩	−1489%
Treasury Stock	(87)	(91)	NA	NA
Paid in Capital & Other	858	815	⇩	−5%
Total Equity	**799**	**335**	⇩	**−58%**
Total Liabilities and Equity	**$5,563**	**$5,231**	⇩	**−6%**

Source: Based on Cinemark's 2021 *Form 10K*, p. F-5.

Competitors

Cinemark's primary US competitors are Regal Cinemas and AMC Entertainment. The company's primary international competitors include Cinépolis, Cine Colombia, CinePlanet, Kinoplex (GSR), Village Cines, Hoyts Chile, SuperCines, and Araujo. Other competitors include Cineplex, IMAX, Carmike Cinemas, IPIC, and Showtime. Even Netflix could be considered a competitor.

Exhibit 7 compares Cinemark with AMC, IMAX, and Cineplex. Note that AMC is by far the largest company among the three. Note also that all four companies are losing money. The pandemic crushed the moviegoing cinema industry, and firms such as Roku and Netflix are substantially hurting the going-out-to-the-movie industry, especially as pandemic concerns linger.

EXHIBIT 7 Rival Firms Compared Financially

	Cinemark	AMC Entertainment	IMAX Corp	Cineplex
	CNK	AMC	IMAX	CGX.TO
Market Capitalization	$1.9 billion	$9.2 billion	$1.1 billion	$780 million
EPS	−$5.6	−$5.4	−$0.92	−$7.22
Revenue	$942 million	$1.5 billion	$202 million	$409 million
Net Income	−$660 million	−$2.1 billion	−$54 million	−$457 million
Total Debt	$4 billion	$11 billion	$248 million	$1.9 billion
Total Debt/Equity	1,260	N/A	59.01	N/A
Current Ratio	1.04	1.10	5.8	0.25
# Full-time Employees	7,550	3,450	622	10,000
Stock Price	$16	$18	$16	$12

Source: Based on https://finance.yahoo.com/quote/CNK?p=CNK&.tsrc=fin-srch

A recent study compared Cinemark to Regal, Cinepolis, and AMC on nine management and marketing variables. The findings are reported in Exhibit 8. Note that Cinemark ranks number two on six variables, implying this is a well-managed and marketed company, but there is a perceived problem with the company culture, as indicated by the number four ranking in column 6. Based on the analysis, Regal is a strong rival to Cinemark, as indicated in five number-one rankings.

EXHIBIT 8 Comparing Cinemark Versus Rival Firms (Ranking 1 = Best; 6 = Worst)

	Variables									
	1	2	3	4	5	6	7	8	9	10
Cinemark	3	2	2	2	2	4	2	2	3	22
Cinepolis	2	3	1	3	3	2	1	1	1	17
AMC Theaters	4	4	3	4	4	3	3	3	2	30
Regal	1	1	NA	1	1	1	NA	NA	NA	5+

Variables

1. Effectiveness of CEO
2. Product Quality
3. Do Customers Recommend Company Products to Friends?
4. Pricing
5. Customer Service
6. Overall Culture
7. Do Employees Recommend Company Products to Friends?
8. How Happy Are the Women Employees at the Firm?
9. How Happy Are Minority Employees at the Firm?
10. Summed Score (lower sum the better)

Source: Based on https://www.comparably.com/companies/cinemark-usa/competitors

Exhibit 9 provides a comparison of the largest cinema chains in the Americas and Canada based on the number of screens. Note that AMC is by far the largest.

EXHIBIT 9 The Largest Cinema Chains in the Americas (as of August 18, 2021)

Company	Number of Screens	Number of Locations	Number of Screens per Location
AMC Entertainment	$11,041	$1,004	$11.0
Cinemark Holdings	5,957	533	11.2
Cinepolis	5,251	335	15.7
Cinemex	2,861	332	08.6
Cineplex	$1,676	$164	$10.2

Source: Based on S&P *Industry Surveys*, Entertainment, August 2021, p. 25.

IMAX Corporation (NASDAQ: IMAX)

Headquartered in Mississauga, Ontario, Canada, IMAX is a global entertainment firm with technology that digitally enhances the image resolution, visual clarity, and sound quality of motion picture films for projection on IMAX screens. IMAX trade names include IMAX Dome, IMAX 3D, IMAX 3D Dome, Experience It in IMAX, The IMAX Experience, An IMAX Experience, An IMAX 3D Experience, IMAX DMR, DMR, IMAX nXos, and Films To The Fullest. Early in 2021, operating in 81 countries and territories, there were 1,650 IMAX theater systems comprising 1,562 commercial multiplexes, 12 commercial destinations, and 76 institutional facilities.

Cineplex Inc. (CGX.TO)

Headquartered in Toronto, Ontario, Cineplex operates 165 theatres across Canada under numerous brands, including Cineplex Cinemas, Cineplex Odeon, SilverCity, Galaxy Cinemas, and Cinema City.

Regal Cinemas

Headquartered in Knoxville, Tennessee, Regal Cinemas is a US movie theater chain that is a division of Cineworld. Regal operates the second-largest theater circuit in the United States, with more than 7,200 screens in 549 theaters as of October 2019.

External Issues

Some interesting quick facts about the cinema movie industry in the United States and Canada in 2021 are given in Exhibit 10. Note the average price paid for a movie ticket was $9.37.

EXHIBIT 10 Going to a Cinema to See a Movie in the United States or Canada? Some 2021 Facts.

1. The average price of a ticket to go see a movie at a cinema in the United States = $9.37.
2. The number of cinema sites in the United States = 5,800.
3. Box office revenue in the United States and Canada = $4.48 billion.
4. The number of movie tickets sold in the United States and Canada = 224 million.
5. Best-paid actress worldwide = Sofia Vergara.
6. Best-paid actor worldwide = Dwayne Johnson.
7. Highest-grossing film director in history = Steven Spielberg.
8. Top three movies with the most Facebook fans: *Harry Potter, Titanic, Avatar.*

Source: Based on https://www.statista.com/topics/964/film/#dossierKeyfigures

It may be that Cinemark should expand globally in some manner. Exhibit 11 therefore reveals the percentage of movie tickets sold globally by country. Note that China and the United States comprise 60 percent of the global total, with India coming in at 14 percent.

EXHIBIT 11 Percentage of Movie Tickets Sold Globally by Country

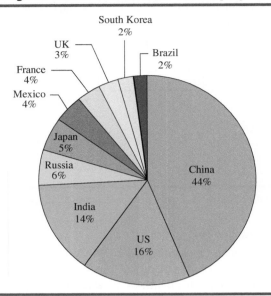

Source: Based on https://www.statista.com/statistics/252729/leading-film-markets-worldwide-by-number-of-tickets-sold/

Revenue for the movie theaters industry declined about 61 percent in 2020 due to the pandemic and social distancing measures that left theaters closed for months. Industry revenue partially recovered in 2021, but companies such as Cinemark still contend with financial scars caused by such a sharp decline in 2020. Most firms are now highly leveraged and continue to struggle despite relaxation of restrictions, but revenues on average were up about 35 percent in 2021 alone. The industry includes cinemas, drive-in and outdoor movie theaters, and film festival exhibitors.

Performance has been mixed for the cinema industry for the 5 years leading up to 2021, partly due to video streaming services such as Netflix, Hulu, and Amazon. Even premium cable networks such as Showtime, HBO, and Starz face pressure competition from streaming services. Many premium cable networks have created their own streaming platforms such as HBO Max, Showtime Streaming, and ViacomCBS to expand their reach beyond traditional video bundles. In becoming more like a streaming service provider, cable networks could benefit from having more control over customer relationships.

Conclusion

CEO Sean Gamble at Cinemark needs a clear strategic plan because his company faces scores of competitors of all sizes, facing the company from all directions. The lingering pandemic is a major concern for the movie industry. External threats from companies like Hulu, Netflix, Disney, and Roku are eroding more and more into the notion of someone paying $10 per ticket to go see a movie at a theater across town.

Gamble knows the basic underlying external opportunities and threats facing Cinemark, as well as the basic internal strengths and weaknesses, but he needs to know the relative importance of those factors. He also needs to know the relative attractiveness of alternative strategies to be derived from those underlying external and internal factors. In other words, Gamble needs strategy analyses performed, including IFE Matrix, EFE Matrix, SWOT, IE Matrix, perceptual mapping, EPS-EBIT analysis, and projected financial statement analysis.

Let's say that Gamble hires you to develop a comprehensive strategic plan for Cinemark. Begin with developing an effective vision and mission statement, which as you see early in the case, the company needs assistance on in this area and include a new, improved organizational chart, which the case also reveals the company needs assistance on improving. Perform the analysis that is requested, develop some recommendations with associated costs, and present your findings and research to your professor and fellow students.

How can the cinema industry and Cinemark adapt to an ever-changing world? Movie developers keep developing movies and people enjoy movies as much as ever, but customers are increasingly choosing to wait to see the movies online. What does Cinemark need to do in the next 3 years to effectively adapt to be a profitable company over the next 3 decades?

References

1. https://www.comparably.com/companies/cinemark-usa/competitors
2. https://www.owler.com/company/cinemark/competitors
3. https://ir.cinemark.com/company-information/management-team
4. https://finance.yahoo.com/quote/CNK?p=CNK&.tsrc=fin-srch
5. S&P *Industry Surveys*, Entertainment, August 2021, p. 25.
6. https://www.statista.com/topics/964/film/#dossierKeyfigures
7. https://www.statista.com/statistics/252729/leading-film-markets-worldwide-by-number-of-tickets-sold/
8. Cinemark's 2020 and 2021 *Form 10K*.

Meta Platforms, Inc. (formerly Facebook, Inc.), 2022

https://about.facebook.com, (NASDAQ: META)

Headquartered in Menlo Park, California, Meta Platforms (formerly Facebook), Inc. is the world's largest online social networking company. Meta Platforms (Meta) include Facebook, Instagram, WhatsApp, Oculus, and numerous other businesses. Meta is currently concentrating on shifting gears to the metaverse. Meta uses virtual and augmented reality (AR) products that enable users to connect with each other through mobile devices, personal computers, smartphones, and other platforms.

So what is the metaverse? It is an online 3D, virtual or AR world where individuals, companies, and organizations can interact and share quality time with others and spend money as avatars. The defining aspect of the metaverse is that you are not just looking in from the outside, but you are privately inside (seemingly) the other entity's dominion. In some cases, virtual and AR headsets are used. Avatars are digital objects that can become "you" or "anyone" or "anything" and interact with you as if you and the entity are together. You can now access the metaverse from a range of devices from Smartphones to PCs. As avatars, people can work, learn, play, shop, purchase, talk, trade services and properties, and experience entertainment just as if you are right beside the other entity. The metaverse is a bit like Google's Waze app where people can share detailed information like traffic accidents and police speed traps and people can teleport themselves to practically anywhere in the world in a moment.

Meta's advertising revenues were about $114 billion in 2021, up nearly 37 percent from the prior year, but it is expected to slow to a 12 percent growth rate by 2024. About 46 percent of Meta's advertising revenues come from the United States and Canada. CEO Mark Zuckerberg says he expects the metaverse to be "the next generation of the Internet and the next chapter in the life of Mata Platforms Inc." Zuckerberg at Meta has often said that the metaverse is the successor to the current mobile internet. He anticipates that people will soon jump in and out of a 3D virtual space, like those in *The Matrix* and *Ready Player One*.

Copyright by Fred David Books LLC; written by Fred R. David.

History

The original Facebook, Inc. was founded in 2004 in Cambridge, Massachusetts, by Mark Zuckerberg, along with Dustin Moskovitz, Chris R. Hughes, Andrew McCollum, and Eduardo Saverin. The company had its initial public offering (IPO) in January 2012 and raised $16 billion, the third-largest IPO ever.

Since 2020, Facebook has faced numerous lawsuits including antitrust and advertising litigation. In 2020, Facebook spent $19.7 million on lobbying, having 79 lobbyists, up from the prior year when the company spent $16.7 million on lobbying with a team of 71 lobbyists, up from $12.6 million and 51 lobbyists in 2018.

Facebook changed its name to Meta Platforms in late 2021 for a variety of reasons, including that the company's US daily active user base in 2021 was unchanged from the prior year. Also, the company's largest user base are persons aged 18 to 29, and there were declines in retention, sessions, and messaging on Instagram, whereas rival TikTok more than doubled its US user base over the last 6 months, while the same metric at Meta was up only 6 percent. Also, Facebook's Messenger was losing ground to Apple's iMessage and to Snapchat, especially among US teenagers. Another reason for the name change was that there was substantial negative publicity about the company.

Zuckerberg simply decided to rebrand the company, framing the change in terms of an evolution into metaverse rather than total reliance on social media products. The name change at Facebook was analogous to Google changing its name to Alphabet a few years previously, or Apple dropping the word Computers from its official name. Today Meta is building a social platform for the metaverse called Horizon.

There have been some early critics of Meta and particularly Facebook in 2022 for allegedly spreading misinformation about the COVID vaccine and calls for the company to be "broken up" because it is too powerful. Representative Alexandria Ocasio-Cortez (D-NY) was one politician advocating this action by the government, saying Meta "exploits its overlapping lines of business as a platform, vendor, and advertiser."

Vision/Mission

Meta's vision statement is to "help bring the metaverse to life." (See https://about.facebook.com/meta/)

Meta provides a mission statement on its corporate website, and it reads (paraphrased): "*To provide people with power to promote community and world togetherness.*"

Neither of these statements meet the guidelines provided in Chapter 2 for developing and writing a vision and mission statement, so the company needs to improve these documents.

Internal Issues

Strategy

Meta is retooling all its apps to be tailored more for young adults, even though the company acknowledges this new strategy may come at the expense of other demographics. Meta believes that virtual and AR is the new wave of interest for young people, and Zuckerberg does not want TikTok, Apple, Microsoft, and other rival firms to get the lead on this dimension of business. Meta is actively evolving from a social media company into a metaverse company.

Early in 2022, Meta's fintech (financial technology) unit, Diem Association with its intellectual property and other assets, was sold to crypto-focused bank Silvergate Capital. This divestiture ended for the moment Meta's plan to get its billions of users transacting in its own currency. This divestiture raises questions about how Meta plans to handle commerce in the metaverse, a futuristic digital environment that Zuckerberg had said would be "the successor to the mobile internet with transactions for digital goods and services being done using cryptocurrencies." Despite the sale of Diem, Meta is testing Novi in Guatemala and the United States using the stable coin Pax Dollar, but Meta still faces pushback from some US congressmen (and women) who say Meta cannot be trusted to manage cryptocurrency.

Advertising

The clothing company Patagonia recently withdrew all its paid advertising on Facebook due to thousands of internal Facebook documents prompting the *Wall Street Journal* to publish a series of stories called "The Facebook Files." The files allege that Facebook platforms are riddled with problems that can harm people, spread misinformation about climate change and politics, and even spread criminal activity. Partly in response to the Patagonia issue, in 2022 Meta moved to eliminate microtargeting options for advertisers on political and other sensitive topics. The change in strategy was rolled out across all Meta platforms, including Facebook, Instagram, and Messenger.

Means Used for Global Growth Criticized

Meta promotes that it helps millions of the poorest people globally get online through free apps and services, but analysts reveal that many if not most of these people end up being charged fees that collectively add up to millions of dollars of revenue per month for Meta. Here is how it supposedly works. To attract new users in lower-per-capita income countries such as Pakistan, Indonesia, the Philippines, and much of Africa, Meta makes deals with cellular carriers in these countries to let low-income people use a limited version of Facebook and browse some other websites without data charges. However, because many of the users have inexpensive cellphone plans that cost just a few dollars a month, often prepaid, for phone service and a small amount of internet data, and due to reported software problems at Facebook, people using the free apps get unexpectedly charged by local cellular carriers for using data. Often the user discovers this when their prepaid plans are drained of funds.

For the 12 months that ended July 2021, charges made by the cellular carriers to users of Facebook's free-data products grew to an estimated total of $7.8 million a month, from about $1.3 million a year previously, according to a Facebook document reviewed by the *Wall Street Journal* that were written in fall 2021. Facebook calls the problem "leakage" and is part of its program called Facebook Connectivity that delivers continued growth in poor but populous countries such as Indonesia, Bangladesh, the Philippines, Brazil, and much of sub-Saharan Africa because Facebook's user growth has stalled in prosperous countries.

In Asia, for example, Facebook's top markets have a population of one billion, but about 50 percent of this population is still unconnected. The company has a goal to increase the number of people in Asia who get online monthly through its initiatives to 10 times the current 1.65 million, the documents say. There are more than two dozen countries where this hidden charging is a problem, but especially in Pakistan, the Philippines, Peru, and Indonesia and especially within the Facebook free-data program named Discover. https://www.wsj.com/articles/facebook-free-india-data-charges-11643035284

Organizational Structure

Based on the titles of top executives, Meta's organizational structure appears to be decentralized, divisional-by-region, but this is not clearly the case. There is a COO, but there are no regional presidents, except for an executive over Africa and one over the central region, whatever that region comprises.

A more effective organizational structure for Meta would likely be a strategic business unit (SBU) with two units that coincide with the two segments of the firm: Family of Apps (FOA) segment that includes Facebook, Instagram, Messenger, WhatsApp and other services, and the newly formed Facebook Reality Labs (RL) segment, which includes virtual and AR-related consumer hardware, software, and content. Then, perhaps have a dozen or more regional presidents reporting to those two top SBU executives.

Meta's current organizational structure as best as can be determined at the moment is provided in Exhibit 1. The company's top executives are listed and arrayed in Exhibit 1.

EXHIBIT 1 Meta's Top Executives Listed and Arrayed

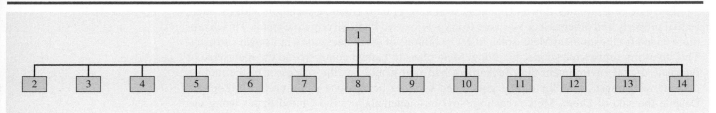

1. Mark Zuckerberg, Chairman and CEO
2. Sheryl Sandberg, COO
3. Dawn Carfora, VP, Business Planning and Operations
4. Michael Schroepfer, Chief Technology Officer
5. David Wehner, CFO
6. Atish Banerjea, CIO
7. Jennifer Newstead, Chief Legal Officer

8. Chris Cox, Chief Product Officer
9. Roy Austin, VP, Civil Rights and Compliance Officer
10. Caitlin Kalinowski, Head, VR Hardware
11. Ime Archibong, Head, New Product Experimentation
12. Henry Moniz, Chief Ethics and Compliance Officer
13. Nunu Ntshingila, Regional Director, Africa Region
14. Angelika Gifford, VP, Central Region

Source: Based on https://www.wsj.com/market-data/quotes/FB/company-people
Note: #13 and #14 report to #2

Segments

Meta operates through two segments: the FOA segment that includes Facebook, Instagram, Messenger, WhatsApp, and other services, and the newly formed Facebook RL segment, which includes virtual and AR-related consumer hardware, software, and content. Meta's revenues and income by segment are revealed in Exhibit 2.

EXHIBIT 2 Meta's Segment Revenues and Net Income (in Millions)

	2020	2021
Revenue		
Advertising	$84,169	$114,934
Other	657	721
Family of Apps	84,826	115,655
Reality Labs	1,139	2,274
Total Revenue	**85,965**	**117,929**
Income (Loss) from Operations		
Family of Apps	39,294	56,946
Reality Labs	(6,623)	(10,193)
Total Income from Operations	**$32,671**	**$46,753**

Source: Based on Meta Platforms' 2021 *Form 10K*, p. 51 and 65.

Exhibit 3 reveals Facebook's audience size by country in October 2021. Note that India has substantially more active users than the United States.

EXHIBIT 3 Facebook Audience Size by Country in October 2021 (in Millions)

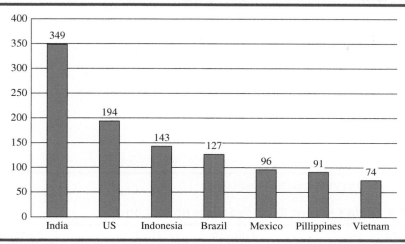

Source: Based on Study_id9711_facebook-statista-dossier.pdf, p. 7.

Meta provides a breakdown of the company's revenues by country, as indicated in Exhibit 4. Note the United States comprises almost half of the company's global revenues but also note dramatic increases globally in 2021.

EXHIBIT 4 Meta's Revenues by Country (in Millions)

	2020	2021
USA	$36.25	$48.38
Canada	2.18	3.16
Total USA & Canada	38.43	51.54
Europe, Russia, & Turkey	20.35	29.06
Asia—Pacific	19.85	26.74
Rest of the World (Africa, Latin America, Middle East)	$7.34	$10.59

Source: Based on Meta's 2021 *Form 10K*, p. 94.

Finance

For Q1 of 2022 that ended 3-31-22, Meta performed well, growing modestly, as indicated by the following metrics:

1. Q1 Family daily active people (DAP) – DAP was 2.87 billion on average, an increase of 6% year-over-year.
2. Q1 Family monthly active people (MAP) – MAP was 3.64 billion, an increase of 6% year-over-year.
3. Q1 Facebook daily active users (DAUs) – DAUs were 1.96 billion on average, an increase of 4% year-over-year.
4. Q1 Facebook monthly active users (MAUs) – MAUs were 2.94 billion, an increase of 3% year-over-year.
5. Q1 Ad impressions and price per ad – Ad impressions delivered across the Family of Apps increased by 15% year-over-year and the average price per ad decreased by 8% year-over-year.
6. Q1 Share Repurchases – Meta repurchased $9.39 billion of its Class A common stock.
7. Q1 Headcount – Meta's headcount was 77,805, an increase of 28% year-over-year.

Meta's recent income statements and balance sheets are provided in Exhibit 5 and Exhibit 6, respectively.

EXHIBIT 5 Meta's Recent Income Statements (in Millions)

Income Statement	12/31/20	12/31/21		Percentage Change
Revenues	$21,454	$25,371	⇧	18%
Cost of Goods Sold	0	0	NA	NA
Gross Profit	21,454	25,371	⇧	18%
Operating Expenses	18,165	21,109	⇧	16%
EBIT	3,289	4,262	⇧	30%
Interest Expense	0	0	NA	NA
EBT	3,289	4,262	⇧	30%
Tax	863	(70)	⇩	−108%
Nonrecurring Events	1,776	(163)	⇩	−109%
Net Income	$4,202	$4,169	⇩	−1%

Source: Based on Meta Platforms' 2021 *Form 10K*, p. 111.

EXHIBIT 6 Meta's Recent Balance Sheets (in Millions)

Balance Sheet	12/31/20	12/31/21		Percentage Change
Assets				
Cash and Short-Term Investments	$4,794	$5,197	⇧	8%
Accounts Receivable	577	800	⇧	39%
Inventory	0	0	NA	NA
Other Current Assets	45,624	46,577	⇧	2%
Total Current Assets	50,995	52,574	⇧	3%
Property Plant & Equipment	1,807	1,909	⇧	6%
Goodwill	9,135	11,454	⇧	25%
Intangibles	1,048	1,332	⇧	27%
Other Long-Term Assets	7,394	8,534	⇧	15%
Total Assets	**70,379**	**75,803**	⇧	**8%**
Liabilities				
Accounts Payable	252	197	⇩	−22%
Other Current Liabilities	38,195	42,832	⇧	12%
Total Current Liabilities	38,447	43,029	⇧	12%
Long-Term Debt	8,939	8,049	⇩	−10%
Other Long-Term Liabilities	2,930	2,998	⇧	2%
Total Liabilities	**50,316**	**54,076**	⇧	**7%**
Equity				
Common Stock	0	0	NA	NA
Retained Earnings	12,366	16,535	⇧	34%
Treasury Stock	(8,507)	(11,880)	⇩	−40%
Paid in Capital & Other	16,204	17,072	⇧	5%
Total Equity	**20,063**	**21,727**	⇧	**8%**
Total Liabilities and Equity	**$70,379**	**$75,803**	⇧	**8%**

Source: Based on Meta Platforms' 2021 *Form 10K*, p. 111.

Research and Development

Meta's research and development expenses in 2021 increased $6.21 billion, or 34 percent, to $24.655 billion, compared to 2020's $18.447 billion. The increase was primarily due to an increase in payroll related to a 30 percent growth in the number of employees in engineering and other technical functions. Realty Labs technology development costs also increased.

Marketing and Sales

Meta's marketing and sales expenses in 2021 increased $2.45 billion, or 21 percent, to $14.043 billion, compared to 2020's $11.591 billion. The increase was primarily due to an increase in the company's sales force payroll and promotion expenses. Realty Labs technology development costs also increased.

Competitors

Different companies see the metaverse differently especially with regard to how best to monetize the new phenomena. Whereas Meta and Roblox see metaverse as mostly for social interactions, Microsoft sees it as a business collaboration tool. Companies such as Nvidia and Unity Software see the metaverse as a huge opportunity for them to sell tools to further advance the functionality and authenticity of metaverse interactions, efficiency, and effectiveness.

Niantic is a Google spinoff company known for its popular AR game *Pokémon Go*. Niantic is expected to soon release new smart-glasses capable of making the user believe they are in a 3D world, says CEO John Hanke. Qualcomm is working on the metaverse and smart-glasses that their Vice President Hugo Swart says will one day be light and sleek enough to be worn all day.

Early versions of metaverse products have been developed and offered by Roblox Corp. and Epic Games Inc. and a few other companies such as Vuzix, an AR headset company that already has sleek smart-glasses called the Vuzix Shielf. Virtual and AR smart-glasses and headsets as of today are still cumbersome and inefficient compared to what companies envision with new products available by 2024. There are other companies that currently are or soon could be major rivals to Meta Platforms as Meta evolves more from social media into the metaverse.

Microsoft just became a big rival to Meta Platforms because Microsoft acquired Activision Blizzard for $68.7 billion, the most expensive video game acquisition of all time. Activision owns many video games, such as *Call of Duty, World of Warcraft, Diablo*, and *Candy Crush*, and Microsoft wants to put all the games on its Xbox Game Pass subscription service. Microsoft is doubling down on the future of the metaverse, which is Meta Platform's domain.

Meta competitors include TikTok, Nvidia, Microsoft, Unity Software, Roblex, and Snap. Snapchat's parent company, Snap, just added AR functions to its latest version of smart-glasses called Spectacles. Other competitors include LinkedIn, Google, Apple, Twitter, and Pinterest. A recent study compared Meta to LinkedIn, Google, Apple, Twitter, and Pinterest on nine management and marketing variables. The findings are provided in Exhibit 7. Note that Meta ranks lowest on variables 2, 3, 4 and 6, implying that Meta has some problems. Overall, as indicated in column 10, Meta's score of 38 is not good; only Twitter and Pinterest were ranked worse on the nine variables.

EXHIBIT 7 Comparing Meta vs Rival Firms (Ranking 1 = Best; 6 = Worst)

	Variables									
	1	2	3	4	5	6	7	8	9	10
Meta	3	6	6	6	6	3	3	2	3	38
LinkedIn	1	4	4	4	4	1	1	3	1	23
Google	2	2	3	1	2	2	2	1	2	17
Apple	4	1	1	2	1	4	5	4	5	27
Twitter	5	5	5	5	5	5	4	5	4	43
Pinterest	6	3	2	3	3	6	6	6	6	41

(*Continued*)

EXHIBIT 7 (*Continued*)

Variables

1. Effectiveness of CEO
2. Product Quality
3. Do Customers Recommend Company Products to Friends?
4. Pricing
5. Customer Service
6. Overall Culture
7. Do Employees Recommend Company Products to Friends?
8. How Happy Are the Women Employees at the Firm?
9. How Happy Are Minority Employees at the Firm?
10. Summed Score (lower sum the better)

Source: Based on https://www.comparably.com/companies/meta/competitors

Exhibit 8 reveals that as of October 2021, Facebook had more active users than YouTube, WhatsApp, and Instagram.

EXHIBIT 8 **A Comparison of Social Networks: Number of Active Users in October 2021 (in Millions)**

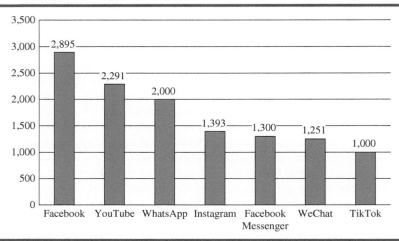

Source: Based on Study_id9711_facebook-statista-dossier.pdf, p. 8.

Apple Inc.

Apple announced in 2021 that it will block the ability of Facebook to target a significant segment of its users. Apple's plans for late 2022 are to enter the metaverse, virtual reality, and AR industries with a head-mounted device or smart-glasses that some analysts say has the potential to be the next biggest thing since the iPhone. With its own microchips and operating system, Apple plans to quickly build a moat around its AR business just as it did with the iPhone. The Apple product is expected to be superior to the Microsoft AR device called the HoloLens 2 headset or even Meta's Oculus brand. AR headsets and potential smart-glasses are part of a new phenomenon known as "spatial computing." Apple believes plans to capitalize on its own ecosystem where watches, phones, tablets, and computers "talk to each other" will be linked with its new AR glasses and related products. Samsung, Sony, and other firms do not have an ecosystem anything comparable to Apple.

To achieve the light, sleekness needed in smart-glasses, Apple likely will use its smartphone, tablets, watches, and iPads to do most of the computing being used by the smart-glasses. If companies such as Meta Platforms are successful at building a software-based metaverse, then Apple headsets, watches, smart-glasses, and other products may become the primary way that users access Facebook, WhatsApp, and Instagram.

External Issues

Thousands of companies ranging from Chipotle Mexican Grill to Verizon Communications to Nike are positioning themselves to capitalize on the upcoming metaverse world. No one is quite certain what the future entails for metaverse, but as you see in the case, even huge companies such as Microsoft are going "all in" on the promise of a profitable metaverse environment. Meta Platforms thus faces rivals on all fronts, from traditional companies like LinkedIn and Twitter to newcomers like Microsoft and Apple.

Millions of people now spend a good part of their days on social media. Millions of people check their social media feeds as soon as they wake up in the morning. Given the pervasiveness of social media, marketers and businesses today flock to social platforms in the hope of connecting with their target customers. However, it is challenging for any firm to stand out unless that company has a clear social media marketing strategy. Staying updated on the latest social media trends can help fuel your strategy and make you stand out in the crowd.

TikTok recently launched several useful tools, like ads and business profiles, aimed specifically at businesses. TikTok is set to become one of the main platforms that brands can use to reach millennials and Gen Z. Some analysts report that ads on the Pinterest platform can generate twice the return on ad spend for retail brands compared with other social media channels. Analysts also report that the potential advertising audience on Snapchat has increased notably. Social networks such as Instagram Storefronts are continuously evolving to become retail platforms.

HubSpot recently reported that the main social media goals of most marketers in 2022 is to reach new audiences, grow relationships with customers, and boost customer service. Previously, these goals focused more on boosting sales and advertising products. So, there is a clear shift going whereby brands are using social media as a channel for fostering deeper customer relations, rather than just for advertising.

Some reports are that about 80 percent of all online content already is anchored in video; using video content has become critical to staying relevant in the social media domain. However, long videos are out of favor, whereas short videos are mandatory. The success of Stories, Reels, and TikTok confirm that engaging, short videos are now the preferred choice of consumers.

Although the adoption of virtual reality in social media may still be at an early stage, AR filters are now being used on several major platforms like Snapchat and Instagram. Companies will increasingly use AR because it enhances reality by adding digital elements and changing the way things actually look. Consumers can use AR to try out products beforehand. AR can boost click-through rates by as much as 33 percent.

Social media networks are becoming major platforms for delivering customer service. According to Gartner, 60 percent of all customer service requests will be sorted out by means of digital channels by 2023. According to HubSpot, Twitter and Instagram will become especially important to B2B businesses. In 2022, about 70 percent of businesses plan to increase their investment on Twitter, whereas 63 percent of B2B businesses planned to increase their spending on Instagram compared with 49 percent of B2B brands planned to increase their investment on Facebook (https://influencermarketinghub.com/social-media-trends/).

Conclusion

CEO Mark Zuckerberg at Meta Platforms needs a clear strategic plan because his company faces scores of competitors of all sizes, facing the company from all directions. The lingering pandemic is a major concern for the movie industry. External threats from companies like Microsoft, TikTok, Apple, and Twitter are gaining momentum in the social media metaverse industry.

Zuckerberg knows the basic underlying external opportunities and threats facing Meta, as well as the basic internal strengths and weaknesses, but he needs to know the relative importance of those factors. He also needs to know the relative attractiveness of alternative strategies to be derived from those underlying external and internal factors. In other words, Zuckerberg needs strategy analyses performed, including IFE Matrix, EFE Matrix, SWOT, IE Matrix, perceptual mapping, EPS-EBIT analysis, and projected financial statement analysis.

Let's say that Zuckerberg hires you to develop a comprehensive strategic plan for Meta Platforms. Begin with developing an effective vision and mission statement, which as you see early in the case the company needs assistance on in this area, and include a new, improved organizational chart, which the case also reveals the company needs assistance on improving. Perform the analysis that is requested, develop some recommendations with associated costs, and present your findings and research to your professor and fellow students.

How can Meta Platforms adapt to an ever-changing world? Should Meta diversify by acquiring firms such as Electronic Arts in the video gaming industry? How can Meta more effectively gain customers in developing nations without what some reports contend to date has been somewhat unethical tactics. What does Meta need to do in the next 3 years to effectively adapt to becoming a profitable company over the next 3 decades?

References

1. Patrick Seitz, "Welcome to the Metaverse," *Investor's Business Daily*, November 1, 2021, pp. A1, A9.
2. https://about.facebook.com/meta/
3. https://www.wsj.com/articles/facebook-free-india-data-charges-11643035284
4. https://www.wsj.com/market-data/quotes/FB/company-people
5. https://www.comparably.com/companies/meta/competitors
6. https://influencermarketinghub.com/social-media-trends/
7. Meta Platforms' 2021 *Form 10K*.

Electronic Arts, Inc., 2022

www.ea.com, (NASDAQ: EA)

Headquartered in Redwood City, California, Electronic Arts (EA) is the second-largest (behind Activision Blizzard) video game company in the Americas and Europe. Just behind EA is Take-Two Interactive and Ubisoft. EA owns major gaming studios in Canada (EA Tiburon and EA Vancouver in Burnaby and BioWare in Edmonton), and EA Romania in Bucharest, and studios in the United States such as Stockholm and Respawn Entertainment in Los Angeles. EA is a global leader in digital interactive entertainment having more than 450 million registered players globally.

EA's best-selling video game is *FIFA* but other popular EA video games are *Rocket Arena* developed by Finai Strike Games and *It Takes Two* developed by Hazelight Studios. EA titles produced and marketed in 2021 include *Knockout City* by developer Velan Studios and *Lost in Random* by developer Zoink. These games play well on Microsoft Windows, Nintendo Switch, PlayStation 4 and 5, and Zbox One and Ebox Series X/S.

Other popular EA games include *Battlefield 2042, Mass Effect, Squadrons, Plants vs Zombies*, and *Command & Conquer*. Coming new in 2022 from EA is the game *RustHeart* by developer Glowmade. EA's games and content play well on numerous internet-connected consoles, mobile devices, and personal computers.

EA and the video gaming industry in general are performing well. For EA's fiscal 2022 that ended March 31, 2022, the firm had revenue of almost $7 billion. For the first 6 months of fiscal 2022, EA had about 100 million players engaged with the firm's EA SPORTS global football platform. The company's *Apex Legends* Season 9 and Season 10 reported the highest customer rates ever, and *The Battlefield 2042* game had 7.7 million players. EA's *Star Wars: Galaxy of Heroes* has more than 100 million active players to date.

In 2022, EA acquired from Warner Bros. the mobile game developer Playdemic Studios in Manchester, England. Although performing great right now, there are dozens of major rival firms working hard daily to capture some of EA's market share globally, so EA needs an excellent strategic plan to excel going forward. EA's international business is headquartered in Switzerland.

Copyright by Fred David Books LLC; written by Fred R. David.

History

EA was founded in 1982 by former Apple employee, Trip Hawkins. Up until 1987 when EA published *Skate or Die!,* the firm had published games developed by external individuals or companies. Mainly through acquisitions, EA shifted to internally developed games, including popular ones such as *Battlefield, Need for Speed, The Sims, Medal of Honor, Dragon Age, Army of Two*, and *Star Wars*. EA also produces sports titles such as *Madden 22, NBA Live*, NHL 21*FIFA 22*NHL 22, and *EA Sports UFC*. In 1991, Trip Hawkins stepped down as EA's CEO and was succeeded by Larry Probst.

In 2001, EA moved toward direct distribution of digital games and services with the acquisition of the popular online gaming site Pogo.com. In 2009, EA acquired the London-based social gaming startup Playfish company. In February 2007, Probst stepped down from being EA's CEO while remaining on the board of directors. John Riccitiello, who had worked at EA for several years previously, replaced Probst as CEO.

In the summer of 2021, EA suffered a data breach, with game and engine source codes taken from their servers, including the source for the *Frostbite Engine* and *FIFA 21*. The hackers began to extort EA for money in July, releasing small portions of the data to public forums and threatening to release more if their demands were not met. Since September 2013 and today, EA's CEO is Andrew Wilson. EA is performing great in a booming video-gaming industry, but dozens of small and large rival firms seek competitive advantage daily in this business.

EA's net bookings for fiscal 2022 that ended 3-31-22 were $7.515 billion, up 21 percent year-over-year. Other notable metrics from EA's fiscal 2022 were as follows:

1. Live services and other net bookings were up 17% year-over-year and represent 71% of total net bookings.
2. The EA player network grew 16% year-over-year to more than 580 million unique active accounts.
3. EA SPORTSTM FIFA had more than 150 million accounts.
4. FIFA Mobile just had the biggest Q4 ever with new unique players surging nearly 80% year-over-year.
5. *Apex LegendsTM* Season 12 set records for the highest engagement since launch.
6. *It Takes Two* won over 90 awards during FY22.

Vision/Mission

EA appears to not have a written vision or mission statement, at least not posted on the corporate website or in the most recent *Annual Report*. The company does talk about its purpose and beliefs as being composed of creativity, pioneering, passion, determination, learning, and teamwork, as you see at https://www.ea.com/about.

A possible vision statement for EA could read something like this:

"*We are a global, digital interactive entertainment company that develops, markets, produces, and delivers amazing video games and live services that can be played and watched on game consoles, PCs, mobile phones, tablets, and other devices.*"

Internal Issues

Organizational Structure

The company's current CFO and COO Blake Jorgensen will be stepping down by mid-2022, and to be replaced by studio head Laura Miele, while a search for a CFO will be launched. EA's top executives are listed and arrayed in Exhibit 1. Note there are three females among the eight persons. It appears from the executive titles that EA uses a functional (centralized) organized structure because there are no division or segment top persons by region or product, except for Natalie Altshuler.

EXHIBIT 1 EA's Top Executives and Probable Array

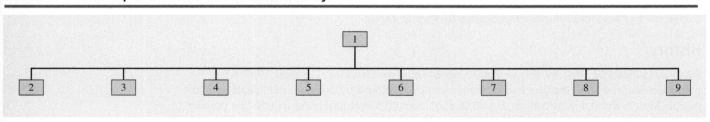

1. Andrew Wilson, CEO and Chairman of the Board
2. Blake Jorgensen, EVP and CFO
3. Laura Miele, EVP and COO
4. Ken Moss, Chief Technology Officer
5. Mala Singh, Chief People Officer
6. Jacob Schatz, Chief Legal Officer
7. Chris Bruzzo, Chief Experience Officer (basically Chief Marketing Officer)
8. Eric Kelly, VP and Chief Accounting Officer
9. Natalie Altshuler, VP, Head of EA SPORTS

Source: Based on information at https://www.ea.com/executives

R&D and Marketing

EA's R&D expenses for fiscal 2021 were $1,778 million, up $219 million or 14 percent from the prior fiscal year. The company's marketing and sales expenses for fiscal 2021 were $689 million, up $58 million or 9 percent from the prior fiscal year. For fiscal 2021, EA's advertising expense was $222 million, compared with $195 million and $271 million the prior 2 years.

EA's R&D expenses for fiscal 2022 were $2,186 million, up from $1,778 the prior fiscal year. The company's marketing and sales expenses for fiscal 2022 were $961 million, up from $689 million the prior fiscal year.

Strategy

EA's strategy is to continuously develop and provide amazing videos and live services offerings to more and more players across more and more platforms in more and more countries. EA is selling more and more games digitally and offering more and more live services. EA's portfolio includes company-owned brands, such as *Battlefield, The Sims, Apex Legends, Need for Speed,* and *Plants vs. Zombies*, and licensed brands, such as *FIFA, Madden NFL* and *Star Wars*.

EA's strategy is to grow primarily through acquisition, having acquired Glu Mobile, Inc. (Glu) for $2.3 billion in April 2021 and Codemasters Group Holdings plc for $1.2 billion in February 2021. Glu is speeding up EA's mobile growth with ongoing live services across multiple games and genres. Glu added substantial expertise in casual sports and lifestyle genres to new EA titles based on our intellectual property. Codemasters is speeding up EA's presence in racing, creating a global leader in racing entertainment.

EA markets and distributes across the spectrum. For example, EA console games and live services can be purchased through third-party storefronts such as the Apple App Store and Google Play. In fiscal 2021, EA's direct sales to Sony and Microsoft represented about 34 percent and 18 percent of total net revenue, respectively. EA's PC games and services can be downloaded directly through Origin, EA's digital storefront, as well as through third-party online download stores, such as Steam. EA has a partnership with Tencent Holdings Limited for *FIFA* Online in China and Nexon Co. Ltd. for FIFA Online in Korea.

In June 2022, EA released new features in its Madden NFL 23 game. That game now delivers the ultimate, authentic 11 versus 11 football simulation experience utilizing EA's new *Field*SENSE Gameplay System - only available on PlayStation®5 and Xbox Series X|S versions. EA players now have more control in their hands at all positions in every part of *Madden NFL 23*.

EA has historically obtained a significant portion of their revenue from sales related to one product, their largest and most popular game, FIFA, one of the best-selling games in the marketplace. Heavy dependence on one or a few products is such that if any events or circumstances such as cancellations or delayed launches impact those products, EA could incur financial troubles.

Diversity, Equity, and Inclusion (DEI)

In November 2021, EA released its *Impact Report* revealing the company's commitments and progress across DEI and sustainability issues. EA has several pages at its corporate website devoted to DEI as you see at https://www.ea.com/commitments/inclusion-and-diversity. EA is making continual progress hiring minorities and females. In fiscal 2021, EA published its first gender and racial/ethnic representation data report that allows all EA customers, employees, shareholders, and communities to measure EA's DEI progress. EA seemingly does everything it can to create an inclusive culture that welcomes different viewpoints and equip all employees with training and education that increases DEI understanding. EA is careful to assure pay equity across gender and racial and ethnic lines all the way from the entry level and to the executive level of the company. To assure continual progress on DEI, EA annually partners with an independent outside firm to review employees' pay and ensure that EA compensation policies, procedures, and practices are fair and free from unconscious bias, resulting in equitable pay.

By-Segment Information

EA reports its financial results in two categories: Full game and Live services and other. For example, for the 12 months that ended September 30, 2021, EA reported Full game revenues of $1.911 billion, up from $1.686 billion the previous 12 months and Live Services revenue of $4.485 billion, up from $3.904 billion the prior period. These results are an improvement over EA's fiscal 2021 results of those 12 months.

Full Game

For fiscal 2021, EA's revenues derived from digital full game downloads was $918 million, up from $811 million and $681 million the prior fiscal years, respectively. However, the company's net revenue attributable to packaged goods sales in fiscal 2021 was $695 million, down from $1,112 million and $1,076 million the prior fiscal years, respectively.

Based on information received from Microsoft and Sony, EA estimates that 62 percent of the company's total units sold during fiscal year 2021 were sold digitally, compared to 49 percent in both 2020 and 2019. For EA, costs associated with selling a game digitally is generally less than selling the same game through traditional retail and distribution channels. EA's total revenues for Full Game in fiscal 2021 was $1,613 million, mainly driven by *FIFA 21, Madden NFL 21, FIFA 20, Star Wars Jedi: Fallen Order*, and *Need for Speed Heat*.

Live Services

Live services entail EA offering players extra content, subscriptions, and other revenue generated outside of the sale of games themselves. EA's digital live services and other net revenue comprise 71 percent of the firm's total net revenue in fiscal 2021. The most popular EA live service is the extra content purchased within the Ultimate Team product, whereby players can collect current and former professional sports franchise players and build a personalized team. EA's net revenue from *Ultimate Team* comprised 29 percent of our total net revenue in fiscal 2021, with most of that coming from *FIFA Ultimate Team*.

In fiscal 2021, EA's live services included four more seasons of content for *Apex Legends*, expanding that product to the Nintendo Switch platform, and five additional content packs for *The Sims 4*. EA strives to connect players to their friends as the company promotes positive play in games and services, aiming to offer safe, fun, and inclusive environments in which to play.

For fiscal 2021, EA's revenue derived from live services and other was $4,016 million, up from $3,650 million and $3,157 million in the prior the fiscal years. EA's revenue from extra content sales for *Ultimate Team* was $1,623 million in fiscal 2021, up from $1,491 million and $1,369 million the prior fiscal years, with a substantial portion being derived from *FIFA Ultimate Team* but also *Apex Legends, The Sims 4*, and *Madden Ultimate Team*.

Exhibit 2 provides a synopsis of EA's fiscal 2021 and 2022 revenues by segment. Note the 35 percent decline in packaged goods in 2021, but increases in everything in fiscal 2022.

EXHIBIT 2 EA's Revenues by Segment (in Millions $)

	2020	2021	2022	Percentage Change 2020–2021
Revenue				
Full Game Downloads	$811	$918	$1,282	13
Packaged Goods	1,076	695	711	(35)
Full Game	1,887	1,613	1,993	(15)
Live Services and Other	3,650	4,016	4,998	10
Total	$5,537	$5,629	$6,991	02

Source: Based on the EA Fiscal 2021 *Form 10K*, p. 33; also https://s22.q4cdn.com/894350492/files/doc_financials/2022/q4/Q4-FY22-Earnings-Release-Final.pdf

By-Region Information

EA does report income by "domestic vs foreign" to pay taxes appropriately across countries. Exhibit 3 reveals that EA makes considerably more money from sources outside the United States than inside, which is interesting given Microsoft, Google, and Apple are based in the United States. Note the negative percentage changes being fairly dramatic.

EXHIBIT 3 EA's Net Income from Domestic Versus Foreign Sources (in Millions $)

	2020	2021	Percentage Change
Domestic	$380	$299	(21.3)
Foreign	1,128	718	(36.4)
Total	$1,508	$1,017	(32.6)

Source: Based on the EA Fiscal 2021 *Form 10K*, p. 64.

EA also reports revenue by North America versus International, as indicated in Exhibit 4. Note the increases in revenue as compared in Exhibit 4 to the decreases in net income.

EXHIBIT 4 EA's Revenues from North America Versus International (in Millions $)

	2020	2021	Percentage Change
North America	$2,270	$2,474	8.9
International	3,267	3,155	(3.4)
Total	$5,537	$5,629	1.7

Source: Based on the EA Fiscal 2021 *Form 10K*, p. 80.

By-Platform Information

EA provides a breakdown of its revenues by "type of platform" to monitor income in that manner. Exhibit 5 provides a breakdown of EA's revenues by platform. Note dramatic increases in revenues in all segments in fiscal 2022 following declines in 2021.

EXHIBIT 5 EA's Revenues by Platform (in Millions $)

	2020	2021	2022	Percentage Change 2020–2021
Console	$3,774	$3,716	$4,400	(1.5)
PC and Other	1,036	1,195	1,532	13.3
Mobile	727	718	1,059	(1.2)
Total	$5,537	$5,629	$6,991	1.7

Source: Based on the EA Fiscal 2021 *Form 10K*, p. 80; also https://s22.q4cdn.com/894350492/files/doc_financials/2022/q4/Q4-FY22-Earnings-Release-Final.pdf

EXHIBIT 6 A Histogram EA's Revenues by Platform (in Millions $)

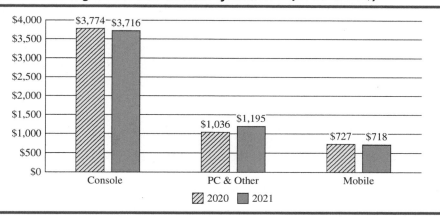

Source: Based on the EA Fiscal 2021 *Form 10K*, p. 80.

Finances

EA's fiscal 2021 ended on March 31, 2021. On November 2, 2022, EA released its Q2 2022 financial results for the period that ended September 30, 2021. Q2 2022 revenues were $1.826 billion compared to the prior year Q2 revenues of $1.151 billion. Net income for Q2 2022 was $294 million versus the prior year Q2 net income of $185 million. EA bought back 2.3 million shares of its stock in Q2 2022. However, EA's net income for the 12 months that ended September 3, 2021 declined to $785 million from $1,314 million the previous 12-month period.

In November 2020, EA declared a quarterly cash dividend of $0.17 per share of common stock and paid aggregate cash dividends of $98 million during the fiscal year ended March 31, 2021. EA is actively repurchasing its outstanding shares of stock, including purchasing 4.9 million shares or $651 million in fiscal 2021. Financial results for EA's fiscal year that ended March 31, 2021, included the following, as compared to the prior fiscal year:

- Total net revenue was $5,629 million, up 2 percent.
- Live services and other net revenue was $4,016 million, up 10 percent.
- Operating expenses were $3,089 million, up 13 percent.
- Operating income was $1,046 million, down 28 percent.
- Net income was $837 million, down 72 percent.

EA's recent income statements and balance sheets are provided for both fiscal 2021 and fiscal 2022 in Exhibit 7 and Exhibit 8, respectively. Note on the income statements the 2 percent increase in revenues but the 72 percent decline in net income. Note on the

EXHIBIT 7 EA's Recent Income Statements (in Millions $)

Income Statement	3/31/20	3/31/21	3/31/22	Percentage Change 2020–2021
Revenue (Sales)	$5,537	$5,629	$6,991	2%
Cost of Goods Sold	1,369	1,494	1,859	9%
Gross Profit	4,168	4,135	5,132	−1%
Operating Expenses	2,723	3,089	4,003	13%
EBIT (Operating Income)	1,445	1,046	1,129	−28%
Interest Expense	(63)	(29)	(48)	−146%
EBT	1,508	1,017	(1,081)	−33%
Tax	(1,531)	180	292	−112%
Nonrecurring Events	0	0	NA	NA
Net Income	$3,039	$837	$789	−72%

Source: Based on the EA Fiscal 2021 *Form 10K*, pp. 85–88; also, https://s22.q4cdn.com/894350492/files/doc_financials/2022/q4/Q4-FY22-Earnings-Release-Final.pdf

EXHIBIT 8 EA's Recent Balance Sheets (in Millions $)

Balance Sheet	3/31/20	3/31/21	3/31/22	Percentage Change
Assets				
Cash and Short-Term Investments	$3,768	$5,260	$2,732	40%
Accounts Receivable	461	521	650	13
Inventory	0	0	NA	NA
Other Current Assets	2,288	1,432	769	−37%
Total Current Assets	6,517	7,213	4,151	11%
Property Plant & Equipment	449	491	550	9%
Goodwill	1,885	2,868	5,387	52%
Intangibles	53	309	962	483%
Other Long-Term Assets	2,208	2,405	2,750	9%
Total Assets	**11,112**	**13,288**	**13,800**	**20%**
Liabilities				
Accounts Payable	68	96	101	41%
Other Current Liabilities	2,596	2,868	3,412	10%
Total Current Liabilities	2,664	2,964	3,513	11%
Long-Term Debt	397	1,876	1,878	373%
Other Long-Term Liabilities	590	608	784	3%
Total Liabilities	**3,651**	**5,448**	**6,175**	**49%**
Equity				
Common Stock	3	3	3	0%
Retained Earnings	7,508	7,887	7,607	5%
Treasury Stock	0	0	NA	NA
Paid in Capital & Other	(50)	(50)	15	0%
Total Equity	**7,461**	**7,840**	**7,625**	**5%**
Total Liabilities and Equity	**$11,112**	**$13,288**	**$13,800**	**20%**

Source: Based on the EA Fiscal 2021 *Form 10K*, pp. 85–88; also https://s22.q4cdn.com/894350492/files/doc_financials/2022/q4/Q4-FY22-Earnings-Release-Final.pdf

balance sheets that EA's long-term-debt increased 373 percent in fiscal 2021. Note in fiscal 2022 the increase in revenues but the decrease in net income. In the balance sheets, note the $2.5 billion increase in 2022 due to EA paying more than book (market) value for acquisition in fiscal 2022.

Competitors

The video-gaming entertainment industry is highly competitive and changes rapidly as new products, business models, and distribution channels are introduced. To be successful, EA has to anticipate consumer behavior years in advance to determine how their games and live services will be positioned in the market.

Major competitors in video-gaming industry include Activision Blizzard, Take-Two Interactive, Ubisoft, Epic Games, Naughty Dog, Valve, Tencent, Zynga, Netmarble, Warner Brothers, Sony, Microsoft, and Nintendo. All these firms develop games and services that operate on consoles, PCs, and/or mobile devices. Other companies such as Alphabet, Amazon, Apple, Facebook, and Microsoft also are developing and strengthening their interactive entertainment capabilities. With the growing metaverse and augmented reality (AR) phenomena, new entrants continue to emerge daily. New products are emerging such as smart-glasses and smart-headsets.

The website www.comparably.com recently compared EA to several of its key competitors on nine management and marketing variables. The results are provided in Exhibit 8. Note that EA ranks good only on "How Happy Are Minority Employees at the Firm." EA ranks last on five key categories as indicated by the number fives along the first row in Exhibit 9. Rival Activision Blizzard also ranks low on most categories. Overall, as indicated by the low summed scores in column 10, Naughty Dog and Value were ranked best overall, even though Naughty Dog was not ranked on variable 9.

EXHIBIT 9 Comparing EA Versus Rival Firms (Ranking 1 = Best; 6 = Worst)

	Variables									
	1	2	3	4	5	6	7	8	9	10
Electronic Arts	4	5	5	5	5	3	5	—	2	34
Activision Blizzard	3	4	4	4	4	5	4	—	3	31
Ubisoft	5	3	3	3	3	4	3	—	4	28
Value	2	1	3	3	2	2	2	—	1	16
Naughty Dog	1	2	1	1	1	1	1	—	—	08

Variables

1. Effectiveness of CEO
2. Product Quality
3. Do Customers Recommend Company Products to Friends?
4. Pricing
5. Customer Service
6. Overall Culture
7. Do Employees Recommend Company Products to Friends?
8. How Happy Are the Women Employees at the Firm?
9. How Happy Are Minority Employees at the Firm?
10. Summed Score (lower sum the better)

Source: Based on https://www.comparably.com/companies/activision-blizzard/competitors

EA has significant partnerships with some of the same competitor firms mentioned. For example, with Sony & Microsoft, EA is authorized to develop and distribute disc-based and digitally delivered software products and services compatible with PlayStation and Xbox consoles, respectively. With these firms, EA has the nonexclusive right to use, for a fixed term and in a designated territory, technology that is owned or licensed by Sony or Microsoft to publish EA games on their respective consoles. Various console manufacturers pay EA either a wholesale price or a royalty percentage on the revenue they derive from their sales of EA digital products and services.

The license agreements also require us to indemnify the console manufacturers for any loss, liability, and expense resulting from any claim against the console manufacturer regarding their games and services, including any claims for patent, copyright, or trademark infringement brought against the console manufacturer. Each license may be terminated by the console manufacturer if a breach or default by EA is not cured after they receive written notice from the console manufacturer, or if they become insolvent. The console manufacturers are not obligated to enter into license agreements with EA for any future consoles, products, or services.

EA has partnership agreements with Apple and Google to distribute EA products that are downloaded for mobile devices from third-party application storefronts. EA also has publishing partners in Asia such as with Tencent Holdings Limited and Nexon Co., Ltd to publish EA mobile and PC free-to-play games in certain countries, including China and Korea.

Activision Blizzard, Inc. (NASDAQ: ATVI)

Headquartered in Santa Monica, California, Activision Blizzard is a member of the *Fortune* 500 and S&P 500 and is one of the world's most successful video-gaming, interactive entertainment companies. Led by CEO Bobby Kotick, Activision Blizzard was founded in July 2008 through the merger of Activision, Inc. and Vivendi Games. Some popular video games produced by Activision Blizzard include *Call of Duty, Warzone, Diablo II: Resurrected, Diablo Immortal, World of Warcraft, Hearthstone, Mercenaries, Candy Crush,* and *Farm Heroes.* The company has recently been involved in numerous litigation suits involving allegations of infringed patents, unpaid royalties, sexual harassment, and employee discrimination. In July 2021, Activision Blizzard was sued by the California Department of Fair Employment and Housing, and soon after was investigated by the US Securities and Exchange Commission.

External Issues

The gaming, technology/internet, and entertainment industries are rapidly converging primarily due to booming growth in the industry that has attracted larger-than-EA, well-funded technology companies to pursue and strengthen their interactive entertainment capabilities. Hundreds of smaller-than-EA companies and entrepreneurs also are entering the business throughout the world. It is therefore increasingly difficult for EA to develop, market, and distribute products or services that are sufficiently amazing and engaging at effective price points. Consumers across all age groups are more and more demanding of the video games they spend time playing. Good is not good enough, and outstanding today may just be mediocre tomorrow, so EA and rival firms day (and night) work to survive and prosper in this industry.

EA's profitability depends on the success and availability of consoles, systems, and devices developed by third parties, coupled with EA's ability to develop commercially successful products and services for those devices. It is a challenge for EA to monitor and stay abreast of advancements in devices such as smart-glasses, advanced metaverse software, and new generation consoles to assure that EA products and live services will function properly on new products being introduced all the time.

There are many other external factors that represent opportunities and threats for EA, including the following:

1. The work-from-home expectation of employees globally curtails the creativity and innovativeness needed to develop video games collaboratively.
2. EA has a relatively small number of retail and distribution partners. Any trouble with these entities could spell trouble for EA.
3. It is increasingly difficult for EA to acquire the rights to publish and distribute games developed by third parties. EA has no control over their third-party storefronts, including digital storefronts, such as Microsoft's Xbox Store, Sony's PlayStation Store, Apple App Store, and Google Play Store.
4. Virtual and augmented reality (AR) and the metaverse are happening so quickly that EA is challenged to effectively anticipate evolving technology and future product development needs.
5. EA is dependent on consoles, systems, and devices that it does not produce, and these items are changing rapidly, often without EA being involved.
6. Negative perceptions about EA or any of its partners as related to DEI, sustainability, or anything could damage EA.
7. Security breaches, cyber threats, fraudulent activity, and data privacy concerns are increasingly a severe threat in the video-gaming industry.

Value Chain

The video game industry has a complex value chain that consists of six basic layers. As gaming has become more digital, companies function increasingly in two or more of the six layers:

1. Game development: includes programmers, designers, and artists that create games
2. Publishing: includes the marketing and advertising for a game
3. Distribution: includes both retail and digital channels and the packaging of games
4. Retailer: includes storefronts where games are sold
5. Customers/consumers: includes people of all ages who play video games
6. Hardware/platform manufacturers: includes producers of consoles, PCs, tablets, etc.

Consumer Behavior

The United States is the largest video gaming market with more than 150 million Americans playing games. China is number two and Japan is number three; then there is a significant drop off in the number of gamers per country, although there are millions of gamers across many countries worldwide. The average age of gamers is about 35, and the gender breakdown is about 59 percent male versus 41 percent female. US gamers tend to be conservative and are more likely to vote than nongamers.

Gamers like to go to conventions to see developers and publishers demonstrate their games directly to players and consumers and obtain feedback. New games are frequently introduced at conventions, such as the annual Gamescom in Cologne, Germany, and numerous PAX events. Some companies hold their own conventions, such as BlizzCon, QuakeCon, Nvision, and the X Shows.

Conclusion

EA needs an excellent strategic plan to guide its decision-making in the months and years to come. The video-gaming industry is booming but changing daily in terms of consumer behavior, technology, and huge rival firms moving to dominate the industry. Some of these firms are currently partners with EA and those partnerships could abruptly end for varied reasons.

EA continually assesses how its games are positioned as compared to rivals Activision Blizzard, Take-Two Interactive, Ubisoft, Epic Games, Tencent, Zynga, Netmarble, Warner Brothers, Sony, Microsoft, and Nintendo. All these firms develop games and services that operate on consoles, PCs, or mobile devices. Alphabet, Amazon, Apple, Facebook, and Microsoft are also becoming much more aggressive in the video-gaming industry as they develop and strengthen their interactive entertainment capabilities. With the growing metaverse and AR phenomena, new products are emerging such as smart-glasses and smart-headsets. Will EA's products play on the new hardware? Should EA make acquisitions to enter the hardware side of this industry?

It is important to consider when developing a strategic plan how the firm should allocate both its monetary and human capital resources. Factors to consider should include expansion and also divesture of certain segments to free up resources for more profitable segments. A careful analysis of the competitors and available opportunities across regions is needed along with EA's strengths and weaknesses to plot a strategy for the company moving forward. How aggressively should EA expand to other countries? Recall the company derives more revenue from outside the United States than from inside.

Remember, your job as the student is not to describe what EA is currently doing or what EA plans to do based on reading press releases or the company *Annual Report*, but rather your job is to consider that you have been hired by EA to develop and provide a 3-year strategic plan. EA's upper management, and in this case your classmates and professor, are looking for you (or paying you a high fee if hired by EA) to recommend what you feel is the best direction for the firm moving forward based on your strategic management research, knowledge, and expertise. Be reminded that shareholders of nearly all companies expect a minimum of 5 percent annual growth on both revenues and net income.

Consumers are increasingly price sensitive while at the same time demanding high quality in their games. Free is a good price and EA must contend with more and more free games that function based on advertising receipts. Should EA acquire one or more of its rival firms?

Prepare a clear 3-year strategic plan for EA indicating the direction you think will be most advantageous for management moving forward. Deciding how to allocate resources across regions is a difficult yet major challenge and job of a strategist. Prepare projected financial statements if possible to reveal your expectations regarding the financial impact of your proposed strategies.

References

1. Electronic Arts' Fiscal 2021 *Form 10K*.
2. https://www.ea.com/executives
3. https://www.comparably.com/companies/activision-blizzard/competitors
4. https://www.ea.com/commitments/inclusion-and-diversity
5. https://s22.q4cdn.com/894350492/files/doc_financials/2022/q4/Q4-FY22-Earnings-Release-Final.pdf

The TJX Companies, Inc., 2022

www.tjx.com, (NYSE: TJX)

Headquartered in Framingham, Massachusetts, and ranked 97th on the current *Fortune* 500 list of the largest US firms, TJX is the largest off-price chain of department stores in the US. TJX brands include T.J. Maxx, Marshalls, HomeGoods, Sierra, Winners in Canada, and HomeSense. TJX operates tjmaxx.com, marshalls.com, homegoods.com, and sierra.com, in the US; Winners, HomeSense, and Marshalls (combined, TJX Canada) in Canada; and T.K. Maxx in the UK, Ireland, Germany, Poland, Austria, the Netherlands, and Australia. TJX also operates HomeSense in the UK and Ireland, and tkmaxx.com in the UK (combined, TJX International).

Late in 2021, TJX operated 4,684 stores in nine countries, including 1,285 T.J. Maxx, 1,148 Marshalls, 850 HomeGoods, 55 Sierra, and 39 HomeSense stores. The company's Q3 2022 financials were excellent, but the company's fiscal 2021 financials were weak. Note, the TJX fiscal year ends each January 31.

As of 4-30-22 when TJX's Q1 2023 ended, the company operated 4,715 stores in nine countries, the United States, Canada, the United Kingdom, Ireland, Germany, Poland, Austria, the Netherlands, and Australia, and five e-commerce sites. These include 1,285 T.J. Maxx, 1,155 Marshalls, 859 HomeGoods, 60 Sierra, and 39 Homesense stores, as well as tjmaxx.com, marshalls.com, homegoods.com, and sierra.com, in the United States; 293 Winners, 148 HomeSense, and 106 Marshalls stores in Canada; 623 T.K. Maxx and 77 Homesense stores, as well as tkmaxx.com, in Europe; and 70 T.K. Maxx stores in Australia.

Copyright by Fred David Books LLC; written by Forest R. David.

History

In 1976, Ben Cammarata was general merchandising manager of Marshalls, but he was recruited by CEO Stanley Feldberg at discount retailer, Zayre Corporation, to launch a new off-price chain selling family apparel and home fashions. Under Cammarata and Feldberg's leadership, T.J. Maxx was born. Feldberg passed away in 2004.

TJX was initially part of Zayre, but the first T.J. Maxx store opened in Auburn, Massachusetts, as part of Zayre. In June 1989, Zayre was renamed The TJX Companies and began trading on the New York Stock Exchange. TJX reached 141st position in the 2004 *Fortune* 500 rankings, with almost $15 billion in revenue. In April 2008, TJX opened its first HomeSense store in the UK.

As of March 30, 2021, TJX had about 580 stores, mostly in Europe, that were temporarily closed due to COVID-19 government mandates. A few TJX milestones over the years are as follows:

1992 – HomeGoods was launched
1995 – TJX acquired Marshalls 496 stores
2001 – TJX launches HomeSense in Canada
2008 – TJX brings HomeSense to the UK
2015 – Marshalls opens its 1,000th store in the US while HomeGoods opens its 500th store
2016 – TJX opens its 500th store in Europe
2019 – TJX opens its 500th store in Canada

It is now 2022 and TJX is performing really well. TJX's fiscal year 2022 ended January 31, 2022. For Q3 2022 that ended October 30, 2021, TJX sales were $12.5 billion, an increase of 24 percent versus Q3 of fiscal 2021. TJX's net income for Q3 2022 was $1.0 billion. For the first nine months of fiscal 2022, TJX's sales were $34.7 billion, up 64 percent versus the first nine months of fiscal 2021.

Vision/Mission and Core Values

There is no written, published vision statement at TJX's corporate website or in the company's *Form 10K*, but the corporate website says: *"Our mission is to deliver great value to our customers every day."* The website www.comparably.com, however, provides a vision statement, mission statement, and set of core values for TJX, as follows (paraphrased):

Vision: *Our vision is to continually to grow TJX as a worldwide, off-price, excellent retailer.*

Mission: *Our mission is to provide excellent value to shoppers every day. We offer an ever-changing assortment of quality, fashionable, brand name, and designer merchandise. Our prices are generally 20 to 60 percent below prices charged at retail department stores, specialty stores, and online retailers on comparable merchandise. By providing value and a "treasure hunt," we reach and cater to customers across many income levels and demographic groups.*

Core Values: *We believe in honesty, integrity, and treating everybody with dignity and respect.*

Internal Issues

Strategy

TJX is one of the few large US brick-and-mortar retailers of apparel and home fashions to have expanded successfully internationally. With nearly 4,700 stores as the year 2020 begins, TJX states on their corporate website that they plan to expand their store base to 6,275 stores long term. TJX says all four major divisions or brands of the company have significant opportunity to further grow their store base over the long term. More specifically on their corporate website, TJX says it plans to increase the number of stores of Marmaxx (US) from 2,402 to 3,000, HomeGoods (includes HomeSense US) from 855 to 1,500, TJX Canada from 525 to 650, TJX International (Europe and Australia) from 742 to 1,125, with the total being 6,275.

Key components of TJX's strategy are opportunistic buying, inventory management, logistics, and flexible store layouts. TJX buyers that purchase merchandise from suppliers have the authority to make rapid decisions on price and quantity of merchandise to assure the company continuously gets great deals, so it in turn can give customers great deals. The selling floor space in every TJX store is flexible without walls or dividers to allow quick accommodation of whatever the empowered buyers buy. There are more than 1,100 TJX buyers globally operating from offices across four continents in 12 countries allowing merchandise to be "bought on the spot" in more than 100 countries in a variety of ways. TJX suppliers include roughly 21,000 manufacturers, retailers, and other vendors that provide TJX with substantial and diversified access to merchandise. TJX buyers pay promptly, often on the spot, and generally do not ask for typical retail concessions.

During Q1 of fiscal 2023 that ended 4-30-22, in the U.S., TJX added 1 TJ Maxx store, 7 Marshalls stores, 9 HomeGoods stores, 1 Sierra store, and kept the same 39 Homesense stores. In Q1 2023 in Canada, TJX added one HomeSense store but kept the same 293 Winners and the 106 Marshalls stores. During Q1 2023 in Europe, TJX added 5 new T.K. Maxx stores but kept the same 77 Homesense stores. During Q1 2023 in Australia, TJX added 2 new T.K. Maxx stores. So for the whole corporate system globally in Q3 2023, TJX added 26 net new stores, with 18 of those being in the U.S.

Inventory

TJX strives to create a "treasure hunt experience" in all their stores and to spur frequent customer visits. The company does this by offering customers a rapidly changing selection of merchandise. TJX has a rapid inventory turnover rate in their stores, regularly offering fresh selections of apparel and home fashions at excellent values. The company achieves this by using special inventory planning, purchasing, monitoring, markdown, distribution center storage, processing, handling, and shipping systems. TJX makes pricing, markdown, and inventory decisions centrally but continuously factors in local preferences and demographics. TJX precisely and effectively allocates the right merchandise at the right price to each store in its vast global network.

Organizational Structure

TJX operates using a strategic business unit (SBU) organizational structure because three of their top seven executives have the title group president. No specification is given on the corporate website or *Form 10K* regarding what each group entails, but the three groups likely correspond to three of the four reportable segments of the company as will be described. TJX's top executives are listed and arrayed as given in Exhibit 1. Notice there is a female chairperson and then all male executives.

EXHIBIT 1 TJX's Top Executives Listed and Arrayed

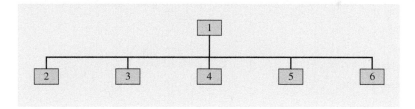

1. Carol Meyrowitz, Executive Chairman of the Board
2. Ernie Herrman, CEO and President
3. Ken Canestrari, Senior EVP and Group President of HomeGoods
4. Douglas Mizzi, Senior EVP and Group President of TJX Canada
5. Richard Sherr, Senior EVP and Group President perhaps of TJX International
6. Scott Goldenberg, Senior EVP and CFO

Source: Based on information at https://www.tjx.com/investors/governance/executive-officers

Segments

TJX has four reportable segments:

1. **Marmaxx** – this is Marshalls, T.J. Maxx, and Sierra in the US. There were 48 Sierra stores in the US at the end of fiscal 2021. The company differentiates Marshalls from T.J. Maxx in that T.J. Maxx has a high-end designer section called The Runway, whereas Marshalls offers a broader men's and junior's departments called the Cube.
2. **HomeGoods (US)** – with nearly 900 stores is an off-price retailer of home products; this segment includes HomeSense that offers larger furniture, ceiling lighting, and rugs.
3. **TJX Canada** – includes Winners, HomeSense, and Marshalls in Canada; Winners' product offerings are similar to T.J. Maxx in the US.
4. **TJX International** – includes the T.J. Maxx and HomeSense stores in Europe and Australia.

   Exhibit 2 reveals TJX's number of stores across the four segments mentioned.

EXHIBIT 2 TJX Number of Stores Across Its Four Segments

	Fiscal 2020	Fiscal 2021
Marmaxx		
T.J. Maxx	1,273	1,271
Marshalls	1,130	1,131
Total	2,403	2,402
HomeGoods	809	821
HomeSense	32	34
Total	841	855
Winners	279	280
HomeSense	137	143
Marshalls	97	102
Total	**513**	**525**

(Continued)

EXHIBIT 2 (*Continued*)

	Fiscal 2020	Fiscal 2021
TJX International		
T.K. Maxx Europe	594	602
UK	—	349
Ireland	—	26
Germany	—	154
Poland	—	46
Austria	—	14
Netherlands	—	13
HomeSense Europe	78	78
UK	—	76
Ireland	—	02
T.K. Maxx Australia	54	62
Total	**726**	**742**
Grand Total		**4,572**

Source: Based on the company's 2021 *Form 10K*, p. 7.

Exhibit 3 reveals TJX's revenues and profits across its four segments. Notice the weakest performing segment in the company in 2021 was TJX International.

EXHIBIT 3 TJX's Revenues and Profits Across Its Four Segments (in Millions)

		Fiscal 2020	Fiscal 2021
Marmaxx			
	Sales	$25,665	$19,363
	Profit	$3,470	$891
	Profit Margin	13.5	4.6
HomeGoods			
	Sales	$6,356	$6,096
	Profit	$681	$510
	Profit Margin	10.7	8.4
TJX Canada			
	Sales	$4,031	$2,836
	Profit	$516	$124
	Profit Margin	12.8	4.4
TJX International			
	Sales	$5,665	$3,842
	Profit	$307	$(504)
	Profit Margin	5.4	(13.1)

Source: Based on the company's 2021 *Form 10K*, p. 32–36.

Exhibit 4 reveals TJX's revenues by geographic region in percentage fiscal 2021. Note that 27 percent of TJX revenues are derived from the southern United States, a region that historically has lagged the Northeast and West on personal income and economic development. Nearly 80 percent of revenues are derived from the US, and nearly 90 percent are derived from the US and Canada, leaving significant room for international expansion.

EXHIBIT 4 TJX's Revenues by Region (Percentages)

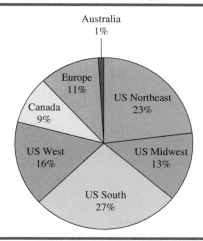

Source: Based on the company's 2021 *Form 10K*, p. 29.

Finances

Fiscal 2021 was a tough year for TJX. TJX's sales decreased 23 percent in fiscal 2021 to $32.1 billion, versus fiscal 2020 sales of $41.7 billion. TJX paid no dividends during the first nine months of fiscal 2021, and share repurchases were suspended in Q1 of fiscal 2021. TJX's net income was $0.1 billion in fiscal 2021 compared to $3.3 billion in fiscal 2020.

TJX's recent income statements and balance sheets are given in Exhibit 5 and Exhibit 6, respectively. Note the significant decline in both revenues and net income, coupled with a 138 percent increase in long-term-debt in fiscal 2021.

EXHIBIT 5 TJX's Recent Income Statements (in Thousands)

Income Statement	2/1/20	1/30/21		Percentage Change
Revenue (Sales)	$41,716,977	$32,136,962	⬇	−23
Cost of Goods Sold	29,845,780	24,533,815	⬇	−18%
Gross Profit	11,871,197	7,603,147	⬇	−36%
Operating Expenses	7,454,988	7,333,150	⬇	−2%
EBIT (Operating Income)	4,416,209	269,997	⬇	−94%
Interest Expense	10,026	180,734	⬆	1703%
EBT	4,406,183	89,263	⬇	−98%
Tax	1,133,990	(1,207)	—	—
Nonrecurring Events	0	0	—	—
Net Income	$3,272,193	$90,470	⬇	−97%

Source: Based on the TJX fiscal 2021 *Form 10K*, p. 4.

Diversity, Equity, Inclusion (DEI) and Sustainability

TJX list on their website a diversity wheel adapted from Johns Hopkins that includes seven diversity issues on the inner layer (i.e., age, gender identity, gender, race, sexual orientation, and more) and an outer layer to the wheel that includes issues such as income, religion, political beliefs, work experience, appearance, and more. In total, the outer layer includes eight issues related to diversity. TJX in 2021 accelerated its DEI efforts, especially as related to racial justice, and deployed a global strategy to drive these efforts. The main areas of this strategy include associate education, new training tools, honest conversations, special attention to recruitment of diverse individuals, and being inclusive.

With respect to associate education, starting in 2018, TJX instituted training programs with 190,000 associates, and a year later, the program was expanded to include training for the executive

EXHIBIT 6 TJX's Recent Balance Sheets (in Thousands)

Balance Sheet	2/1/20	1/31/21		Percentage Change
Assets				
Cash and Short-Term Investments	$3,216,752	$10,469,570	⬆	225%
Accounts Receivable	386,261	461,139	⬆	19%
Inventory	4,872,592	4,337,389	⬇	−11%
Other Current Assets	415,017	471,239	⬆	14%
Total Current Assets	8,890,622	15,739,337	⬆	77%
Property Plant & Equipment	5,325,048	5,036,096	⬇	−5%
Goodwill	95,546	98,998	⬆	4%
Intangibles	0	0	—	—
Other Long-Term Assets	9,833,787	9,939,124	⬆	1%
Total Assets	**24,145,003**	**30,813,555**	⬆	**28%**
Liabilities				
Accounts Payable	2,672,557	4,823,397	⬆	80%
Other Current Liabilities	4,477,690	5,980,271	⬆	34%
Total Current Liabilities	7,150,247	10,803,668	⬆	51%
Long-Term Debt	2,236,625	5,332,921	⬆	138%
Other Long-Term Liabilities	8,809,919	8,844,282	⬆	0%
Total Liabilities	**18,196,791**	**24,980,871**	⬆	**37%**
Equity				
Common Stock	1,199,100	1,204,698	⬆	0%
Retained Earnings	5,422,283	4,973,542	⬇	−8%
Treasury Stock	0	0	—	—
Paid in Capital & Other	(673,171)	(345,556)	⬇	−49%
Total Equity	**5,948,212**	**5,832,684**	⬇	**−2%**
Total Liabilities and Equity	**$24,145,003**	**$30,813,555**	⬆	**28%**

Source: Based on the TJX fiscal 2021 *Form 10K*, p. 6.

team and board of directors. TJX is also committed to expanding training programs where feedback is provided with better awareness and greater sensitivity. The review processes at TJX are increasingly designed to educate employees on unconscious bias and to be committed on inclusion. In 2021, 320,000 associates globally were invited to take part in a diversity survey to help gain data for TJX's commitment to its diversity programs.

Some interesting statistics associated with DEI as of 2021 at TJX: 78 percent of the global workforce is female with 67 percent of managerial position being held by females and 47 percent of employees ranked vice president and higher are female. More than 57 percent of the US workforce is people of color; however, this number drops to 34 percent and 13 percent for people of color holding managerial positions and 13 percent holding the rank of vice president or higher. However, 33 percent of the board members identify as racially or ethnically diverse. According to the Equal Employment Opportunity Commission, anyone nonwhite is considered to be of color and currently the number of nonwhite people in the workforce in the US is 57 percent.

During Q1 of fiscal 2023 that ended 4-30-22, TJX added four new environmental sustainability goals as follows: 1) Achieve net zero greenhouse gas (GHG) emissions in its operations by 2040, 2) Source 100% renewable energy in its operations by 2030, 3) Divert 85% of its operational waste from landfill by 2027, and 4) Shift 100% of the packaging for products developed in-house by its product design team to be reusable, recyclable, or contain sustainable materials by 2030.

Competitors

TJX competes with thousands of local, regional, national, and international department stores, as well as specialty, off-price, discount, warehouse, and outlet stores. Many of these competitors have physical stores, website ecommerce, and catalog offerings. Some of the largest and most direct competitors to TJX are L Brands, Ross Stores, The Gap, Burlington Stores, and Target.

With respect to the family clothing stores in the US market, this business alone is worth $92 billion with 27,000 businesses indicating just how fragmented the industry is and how many mom-and-pop stores are included. Ross Stores, TJX, and The Gap are the three largest family clothing stores in the US with market shares of 20, 19 and 8 percent, respectively. The remaining 53 percent of market share is derived from the other 27,000 businesses. However, as of early 2022, the market capitalization of TJX, Ross, and The Gap were $90, $40, and $7 billion, respectively, revealing the dominate position TJX has over its rivals with respect to stock price.

In August 2021, L Brands sold its Victoria's Secret stores and operations to L Brands' shareholders, creating a new public company named Victoria's Secret & Co. that has a NYSE ticker symbol of VSCO. Later in 2021, L Brands changed its name to match its primary business, Bath & Body Works, Inc. (NYSE: BBW).

The website www.comparably.com recently ranked TJX against some of its rival companies along nine management and marketing variables, as indicated in Exhibit 7. Note that TJX ranks number one (best) on "Effectiveness of CEO" but ranks worst on two variables: "How Happy Are the Women Employees at the Firm," and "How Happy are Minority Employees." Note that TJX overall ranks below (worse) than both L Brands and Target. Note that based on this analysis, Ross Stores has problems, being ranked the worst in six categories.

EXHIBIT 7 Comparing TJX with Rival Firms (Ranking 1 = Best; 6 = Worst)

	Variables									
	1	2	3	4	5	6	7	8	9	10
TJX	1	2	2	2	2	3	3	4	4	23
L Brands	2	3	3	3	3	1	1	1	1	18
Target	3	1	1	1	1	2	5	2	2	18
Ross Stores	4	3	4	4	4	4	4	3	3	33

Variables

1. Effectiveness of CEO
2. Product Quality
3. Do Customers Recommend Company Products to Friends?
4. Pricing
5. Customer Service
6. Overall Culture
7. Do Employees Recommend Company Products to Friends?
8. How Happy Are the Women Employees at the Firm?
9. How Happy Are Minority Employees at the Firm?
10. Summed Score (lower sum the better)

Source: Based on https://www.comparably.com/companies/tjx-companies/competitors

Ross Store, Inc. (NASDAQ: ROST)

Headquartered in Dublin, California, Ross Stores uses the brand name Ross Dress for Less. Ross operates 1,650 stores and 295 dd's Discount stores in 40 states in the US and Guam. Just like TJX but a bit larger and not outside the US, Ross sells brand-name clothing, shoes, accessories, and housewares at discount prices 20 to 60 percent off retail. Ross's fiscal 2020 revenues were $12.5 billion. The company is performing really well. For Q3 2021 that ended October 31, 2021, Ross reported net income of $385 million and sales of $4.6 billion, up 19 percent, with comparable store sales up 14 percent. Ross' CEO Barbara Rentler commented, "Ross' Q3 2021 sales and profitability significantly exceeded our expectations as consumers continued to purchase our broad assortment of great bargains (paraphrased)." In September and October 2021, the company opened 18 new Ross Dress for Less and 10 dd's DISCOUNTS stores across 15 different states, completing the corporate goal of opening 65 new stores in 2021.

The Gap, Inc. (NYSE: GPS)

Headquartered in San Francisco, California, Gap is the largest US specialty apparel company offering clothing, accessories, and personal care products for men, women, and children. Gap owns the brands Banana Republic, Old Navy, Athleta, and Gap. In 2021, Gap opened about 30 to 40 Old Navy and 20 to 30 Athleta stores but closed about 75 Gap and Banana Republic stores in North America.

Gap's smallest but best performing segment is Athleta that in Q3 2021 alone launched its Canadian online business and opened its first company-operated Canadian store in Vancouver and a second store in Toronto. New Athleta stores are coming soon in Costa Rica and Europe. Late in 2021, Athleta released its first item with Simone Biles, a limited edition Girl's hoodie, but more Biles releases were planned for spring 2022.

For the 39 weeks that ended October 31, 2021, Gap's revenues were $12.15 billion and net income was $272 million. These financial results were derived from 3,459 stores globally, including 1,257 Old Navy North America, 538 Gap North America, 335 Gap Asia, 11 Gap Europe, 461 Banana Republic North America, 51 Banana Republic Asia, and 220 Athleta North America, totaling 2,873 company-owned, plus 586 franchised stores.

Burlington Stores, Inc. (NYSE: BURL)

Headquartered in Burlington, New Jersey, and formerly Burlington Coat Factory, Burlington, is a US national discount department store retailer, and a division of Burlington Coat Factory Warehouse Corporation. The company operates about 800 stores in 45 states and Puerto Rico, and they all offer women's ready-to-wear apparel, menswear, youth apparel, baby, beauty, footwear, accessories, home, toys, gifts, and coats. Burlington today is performing well. For Q3 of 2021, Burlington's sales were $2.3 billion, up 30 percent compared with Q3 of fiscal 2019, while comparable store sales increased 16 percent. Net income was $14 million, down from $96 million in Q3 2019.

Target Corporation (NYSE: TGT)

Founded in 1946 and based in Minneapolis, Target operates more than 1,900 stores and through ecommerce. Target's Q3 2021 comparable sales grew 12.7 percent, on top of 20.7 percent growth the prior year. In 2021, Target's same-day services (Order Pickup, Drive Up, and Shipt) increased nearly 60 percent this year, on top of 200 percent last year. More than 95 percent of Target's Q3 2021 sales were fulfilled by its stores, and there are 1,926 Target locations in the US as of December 20, 2021.

External Issues

Exhibit 8 reveals the breakdown of the top revenue-generating products of this industry.

EXHIBIT 8 US Family Clothing Store Revenue Breakdown

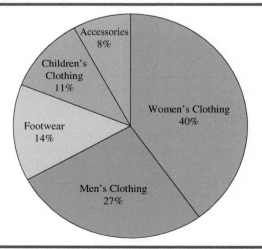

Source: Based on data from IBISWorld.

According to IBISWorld, women tend to purchase a wider variety of clothing articles to meet different occasions, partly explaining why women's clothing consists of 40 percent of the market. In both the women's and men's segments, casual clothing consisting of jeans, woven shirts, shorts, and even t-shirts are much more accepted now than they have been historically. These products are cheaper for the consumer, more comfortable to wear, and more practical than sports jackets, tailored slacks, dress shirts, neck ties, skirts, blouses, and more, especially during the warmer months.

Children clothes only account for 11 percent of industry revenue mostly because kids' clothing is cheaper on average than adult clothing. An attractive strategy for the industry with respect to children's clothing is to focus on high volume over higher price as kids tend to outgrow their clothes quickly. Growing children create an enormous opportunity for clothing stores because children's clothing is less discretionary; as they grow, children need new clothes that fit. Footwear and accessories sum to 22 percent of industry revenue with the accessories segment considered discretionary and more subject to the economy than footwear. Consumer spending online is steadily increasing, spurred on further by the COVID-19 pandemic, but the TJX business model is primarily reliant on brick-and-mortar stores.

Family Clothing Store Growth

Growth in the industry has been both volatile and sluggish from 2016 to 2021. Much of the volatility stems from a shift from traditional stores such as Sears, Belk, JCPenney, and traditional malls struggling and losing market share to luxury malls, specialty clothing stores and stores like TJX. Online retailers and supply chain concerns are also two major threats facing the industry moving forward. Growth from 2022 to 2026 is expected to be less than 2 percent for the industry as a whole, but niche providers will do exceptionally better than average. This is an excellent example of why having a detailed strategic plan and conducting business in the proper markets is more important than ever.

E-commerce

The global COVID pandemic accelerated retail apparel sales growing from 16 to 29 percent from the start of the pandemic to late 2021. McKinsey's *The State of Fashion* 2021 survey predicted growth on apparel e-commerce over 20 percent, with China leading the way, followed by Europe and the US. One drawback for firms shifting more to e-commerce is the lack of impulse buys; research reveals people tend to impulse buy more in person than online. With online sales of apparel, people are also unable to try on the merchandise before purchase. Nevertheless, e-commerce does allow new and existing firms to rapidly expand their footprints in a cost-effective manner.

Thrill of the Hunt

TJX has always prided itself on "The Thrill of the Hunt." Many times when visiting a TJX branded store, while the items are organized fairly well, they are disorganized enough to make exploring fun. New items can always be found in TJX because the store often purchases items that are not selling from other retailers, so people never know what the flavor of the day or week may be as they shop for items 50 percent off the retail price. For example, in the COVID height year of 2020 with zero online sales, Ross reported only a 4 percent decline in sales.

Conclusion

TJX reported a sales drop of more than 23 percent and net income drop of 97 percent during the COVID year that corresponded to the firm's fiscal 2021. Although revenues were not that much lower (23 percent) costs-of-good sold remained about the same. TJX prides itself on the thrill of the hunt, attracting people into stores to mingle and take their time browsing, so COVID was especially destructive. Trends favoring TJX moving forward are the reopening shopping centers in states and countries with less regulations, vaccines, and overall fatigue of COVID. TJX also has an excellent reputation for DEI, which if played properly, could encourage further support of the brand.

Moving forward, TJX needs to determine if the firm should begin to focus more online or continue with their present mix of online and brick-and-mortar stores options. In addition, while the firm has a presence outside of the US, there are tons of growth opportunities globally, so what balance of new stores in the US versus outside the US would be the most attractive for TJX? Help CEO Ernie Herrman design a 3-year strategic plan moving forward.

References

1. TJX's fiscal 2021 *Form 10K*.
2. IBISWorld documents.
3. https://www.comparably.com/companies/tjx-companies/competitors
4. www.comparably.com
5. https://www.tjx.com/investors/governance/executive-officers

Citigroup, Inc., 2022

www.citigroup.com, (NYSE: C)

Headquartered in New York City, Citigroup is one of the largest global investment banks and financial services corporations in the world. Citigroup's customers include individuals, corporations, governments, and institutions in North America, Latin America, Asia, Europe, the Middle East, and Africa. Citigroup today operates about 2,300 branches primarily in the US, Mexico, and Asia. Citigroup is ranked 33rd on the *Fortune* 500, has more than 200 million customer accounts, does business in more than 160 countries, and has about 200,000 employees.

In February 2021, Citigroup's CEO Michael Corbat was replaced by Jane Fisher, who became the first woman CEO of a Big Four bank in the US, that includes JPMorgan Chase, Wells Fargo, and Bank of America. In 2022, Citigroup divested its consumer banking, small-business, and middle-market banking operations in Mexico, following the company's similar closures around the world.

The banking industry is quickly becoming more digital, more diverse, and more competitive, as evidenced by the following nine trends expected for 2023–2025:

1. Increased and enhanced credit card offers and increased cross-selling
2. Increased and enhanced buy-now-pay-later offerings
3. Increased delinquencies and regulatory changes will drive collection digitization
4. The shift to 100% digital onboarding rather than branch banking; almost 50 percent of US retail bank customers are now digital-only.
5. Increased financial crime forcing banks to strengthen their defenses
6. Customer agent experience will matter even more in banking
7. Increased and enhanced auto lending
8. Increased and enhanced focus on cloud platforms
9. Increased competition from fintechs such as Square (Block) and Stripe and big tech firms such as Google and Apple, which are steadily staking claim to the payments and parts of the financial space.

Copyright by Fred David Books LLC; written by Fred R. David.

History

In the old days (1812), City Bank of New York was founded in New York City with Sam Osgood being elected as the first president of the company that today we call Citigroup. The original company name was changed to The National City Bank of New York in 1865 after it joined the new US national banking system. The company became the largest US bank by 1895 and the first contributor to the Federal Reserve Bank of New York in 1913. In 1914, the company opened the first overseas branch of a US bank in Buenos Aires, Argentina.

The company became the first US bank to surpass $1 billion in assets, the largest commercial bank in the world in 1929, the first major US bank to offer compound interest and savings (1921), unsecured personal loans (1928), customer checking accounts (1936), and the first to offer negotiable certificates of deposit (1961). The company we know today, Citigroup was formed in 1998 with the $140 billion merger of Citicorp and Travelers Group to create the world's largest financial services organization.

For the year 2021, Citigroup reported net income of $22 billion on revenues of $71.9 billion, compared to net income of $11 billion on revenues of $75.5 billion for the prior year. So revenues were down a lot but net income was up a lot in 2021. On 4-12-22, Citigroup reported net income for Q1 2022 of $4.3 billion and revenues of $19.2 billion, decreases from the company's Q1 2021's net income of $7.9 billion on revenues of $19.7 billion.

Vision/Mission

Citigroup appears not to have a published vision statement, but at the corporate website https://www.citigroup.com/citi/about/mission-and-value-proposition.html, Citigroup's mission (paraphrased) is as follows:

> *We strive to be a trusted partner for customers by responsibly providing financial services, safeguarding assets, lending money, making payments, and accessing capital markets on behalf of our clients. Here at Citigroup, we connect millions of people across hundreds of countries and cities. We protect individual and corporate savings, we help customers make the purchases, and we advise people on how to invest for future needs. We provide financing and support to local, state, national, and international governments. We serve all customers, near and far, responsibly and ethically, prudently managing risk, in order to earn and maintain the public's trust.*

Segments

Citigroup is organized into two segments: Global Consumer Banking (GCB) and Institutional Clients Group (ICG).

GCB Segment

The GCB segment deals primarily with serving individuals. This segment is also called Personal Banking and Wealth Management (PBWM) and includes all the banks' checking and savings accounts (called *retail banking*), Citi-branded credit cards, lending, and investment services through a network of local branches, offices, and electronic delivery systems. Citigroup is the world's largest credit card issuer. Within GCB, in Asia, more than 60 percent of personal loans at Citigroup are made digitally through Citi Quick Cash, Citi PayLite, Citi Flexibill, and the Grab app. In Mexico, Citibanamex is a leader in credit cards, with more than 40,000 exclusive agreements with retailers and businesses.

Within GCB or PBWM, Citi Retail Services provides private label and cobrand credit cards for retailers. The business of Citigroup serves about 80 million customers with iconic brands, including Best Buy, Exxon, Mobil, L.L. Bean, Macy's, Sears, Shell, The Home Depot, and Tractor Supply Company—and recently Meijer and Wayfair. Meijer is a privately owned and family-operated Midwestern retailer with more than 250 supercenters and grocery stores throughout the Midwest. Wayfair is a large online provider of home furnishings, décor, home improvement, housewares, and more.

Citigroup is the consumer credit card provider to half of the top 10 US ecommerce companies. Citi Retail Services generates purchase sales of more than $80 billion annually and manages a loan portfolio of over $50 billion.

Citigroup's PBWM revenues for Q1 2022 were $5.9 billion, down 1% versus the prior year. Within PBWM, US Personal Banking revenues of $4.0 billion decreased 1%. Branded Cards revenues of $2.1 billion decreased 1%. Retail Services revenues of $1.3 billion were largely unchanged. Retail Banking revenues of $595 million decreased 6%. Also within PBWM for Q1, Global Wealth Management revenues of $1.9 billion decreased 1%, primarily due to lower client activity in investments, particularly in Asia. Overall for Q1, PBWM net income of $1.9 billion decreased 23 percent.

ICG Segment

Citigroup's ICG segment deals primarily with serving companies, governments, and institutions. This segment comprises the company's fixed income and equity sales and trading, foreign exchange, prime brokerage, derivative, equity and fixed income research, corporate lending, investment banking and advisory, private banking, cash management, trade finance, and securities services to corporate, institutional, public sector, and high-net-worth clients. ICG at Citigroup includes six main business lines: Banking; Capital Markets and Advisory; Commercial Banking; Markets and Securities Services; Private Banking (part of Citi Wealth Management); and Treasury and Trade Solutions (TTS).

Citigroup's ICG segment has a physical presence in 96 countries, local trading desks in 77 markets and a custody network in 63 markets. Citigroup is involved in about $4 trillion in financial flows daily, supporting 90 percent of global *Fortune* 500 companies in their daily operations.

EXHIBIT 1 Citigroup's Revenues and Net Income by Segment (in Millions)

		2020	2021	Percentage Change
Institutional Clients Group				
Revenues by Product				
	Banking	$21,715	$23,253	07
	Securities	23,424	20,778	(11)
	Other	(51)	(144)	NM
	Total Revenues	45,088	43,887	(3)
	Net Income	$11,503	$15,880	36
Revenues by Region				
	North America	$17,476	$16,748	(4)
	EMEA	13,041	13,094	NM
	Latin America	4,981	4,946	(1)
	Asia	9,590	9,099	(5)
	Total Revenues	$45,088	$43,887	(3)
Global Consumer Banking or PBWM				
Revenues by Product				
	Retail Banking	$11,996	$10,776	(10)
	Cards	18,346	16,554	(10)
	Total Revenues	$30,342	$27,330	(10)
Revenues by region				
	North America	$19,284	$17,481	(9)
	Latin America	4,466	4,250	(5)
	Asia	6,592	5,599	(15)
	Total Revenues	30,342	27,330	(10)
	Net Income	$667	$6,057	808

Source: Based on https://www.citigroup.com/citi/news/2022/fourth-quarter-2021-earnings.htm

Segment Performance

Exhibit 1 reveals Citigroup's recent financial information reported by segment. Note mostly negative numbers in the far-right column, except for huge net income increases.

Citigroup's ICG revenues for Q1 2022 were $11.2 billion, down 2%, while ICG net income was $2.6 billion, down 51% from the prior year. More specifically within ICG for Q1 2022, Services revenues of $3.4 billion increased 15% versus the prior year. Treasury and Trade Solutions revenues of $2.6 billion increased 18%, Securities Services revenues of $858 million increased 6%, as net interest income grew 17%, driven by higher interest rates across currencies, and fee revenues grew 2% due to higher assets under custody. In addition, Markets revenues of $5.8 billion were down 2% while Fixed Income Markets revenues of $4.3 billion decreased 1%. ICG's Equity Markets revenues of $1.5 billion were down 4% compared to a very strong quarter in the prior year period. Also within ICG, Investment Banking revenues decreased 43%, Corporate Lending revenues of $689 million decreased 6%.

Organizational Structure

Citigroup's top executives are listed and arrayed in Exhibit 2. It appears from the job titles that Citigroup operates using a strategic business unit (SBU) organizational structure, with two units: Global Consumer Banking (GCB) and Institutional Clients Group (ICG). The title of CEO personal banking and wealth management likely should be changed to CEO Global Consumer Banking. Then, under those two by-customer-unit top persons should be arrayed by-region top persons to oversee vast regions.

EXHIBIT 2 Citigroup's Top Executives Listed and Arrayed

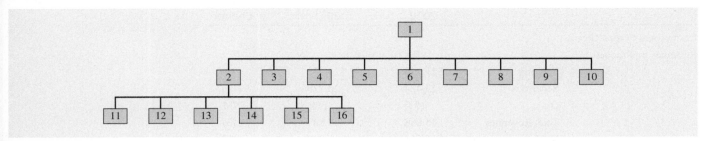

1. Jane Fraser, CEO of Citigroup
2. Karen Peetz, Chief Administrative Officer (CAO)
3. Margo Pilic, Chief of Staff in the Office of the CEO
4. Sara Wechter, Head of Human Resources
5. Mark Mason, CFO
6. Brent McIntosh, General Counsel and Corporate Secretary
7. Mary McNiff, Chief Compliance Officer
8. Jessica Roos, Chief Auditor

9. Edward Skyler, EVP Global Public Affairs
10. Mike Whitaker, Head of Enterprise Operations and Technology
11. Peter Babej, CEO Asia Pacific
12. Sunil Garg, CEO Citibank, North America
13. David Livingstone, CEO Europe, Middle East & Africa
14. Ernesto Torres Cantu, CEO Latin America
15. Anand Selva, CEO Personal Banking and Wealth Management
16. Paco Ybarra, CEO Institutional Clients Group

Source: Based on https://www.citigroup.com/citi/about/our_leaders.html. Numbers 11, 12, 13, 14, 15, and 16 report to number 2.

Strategy

In recent years (2021–2022), Citigroup is downsizing, having recently exited its consumer banking operations in 13 markets, including Australia, Bahrain, China, India, Indonesia, South Korea, Malaysia, the Philippines, Poland, Russia, Taiwan, Thailand, and Vietnam. Citigroup today operates its consumer banking business in only four markets outside the US: Hong Kong, Singapore, London, and the UAE.

Citigroup is strengthening its business in Mexico in their Institutional and Private Bank segments. The company is realigning its reporting structure to match its strategy, including the creation of the Personal Banking and Wealth Management and Legacy Franchises segments. This change will make it easier for the company's stakeholders to understand the performance of the company's core businesses.

Finance

Citigroup's recent income statements and balance sheets are provided in Exhibit 3 and Exhibit 4, respectively. Note for 2021 the company generated $71.9 billion in revenues and reported $22 billion in net income. The company's 2021 EPS was $10.14 and the company out $11.8 billion in dividends to shareholders.

EXHIBIT 3 Citigroup's Recent Income Statements (in Thousands)

Income Statement	12/31/20	12/31/21		Percentage Change
Revenues	**$75,501**	**$71,884**	⬇	**–5%**
Cost of Goods Sold	0	0	—	—
Gross Profit	75,501	71,884	⬇	–5%
Operating Expenses	61,869	44,415	⬇	–28%
EBIT	13,632	27,469	⬆	102%
Interest Expense	0	0	—	—
EBT	13,632	27,469	⬆	102%
Tax	2,525	5,451	⬆	116%
Nonrecurring Events	(60)	(66)	⬇	–10%
Net Income	**$11,047**	**$21,952**	⬆	**99%**

Source: Based on Citigroup's 2021 *Form 10K*.

EXHIBIT 4 Citigroup's Recent Balance Sheets (in Thousands)

Balance Sheet	12/31/20	12/31/21		Percentage Change
Assets				
Cash and Short-Term Investments	$26,349	$27,515	⇧	4%
Accounts Receivable	44,806	54,340	⇧	21%
Inventory	0	0	—	—
Other Current Assets	376,204	430,967	⇧	15%
Total Current Assets	447,359	512,822	⇧	15%
Property Plant & Equipment	0	0	—	—
Goodwill	22,162	21,299	⇩	–4%
Intangibles	4,747	4,495	⇩	–5%
Other Long-Term Assets	1,785,822	1,752,797	⇩	–2%
Total Assets	**$2,260,090**	**$2,291,413**	⇧	**1%**
Liabilities				
Accounts Payable	50,484	61,430	⇧	22%
Other Current Liabilities	1,737,720	1,772,937	⇧	2%
Total Current Liabilities	1,788,204	1,834,367	⇧	3%
Long-Term Debt	271,686	254,374	⇩	–6%
Other Long-Term Liabilities	0	0	—	—
Total Liabilities	**$2,059,890**	**$2,088,741**	⇧	**1%**
Equity				
Common Stock	31	31	⇩	0%
Retained Earnings	168,272	184,948	⇧	10%
Treasury Stock	(64,129)	(71,240)	⇩	–11%
Paid in Capital & Other	96,026	88,933	⇩	–7%
Total Equity	**$200,200**	**$202,672**	⇧	**1%**
Total Liabilities and Equity	**$2,260,090**	**$2,291,413**	⇧	**1%**

Source: Based on Citigroup's 2021 *Form 10K*.

Competitors

Citigroup's competitors include all the financial institutions in the US and even globally, so there are thousands. However, the largest rivals include Bank of America, JPMorgan Chase,

EXHIBIT 5 Rival Firms Compared Financially

	Citigroup (C)	JPMorgan Chase (JPM)	Bank of America (BAC)	Wells Fargo (WFC)
Market Capitalization	$128 billion	$462 billion	$370 billion	$216 billion
EPS	$10	$15	$3.6	$4.95
Revenue	$75 billion	$130 billion	$94 billion	$82 billion
Net Income	$21 billion	$46 billion	$31 billion	$20 billion
Total Debt	$473 billion	$609 billion	$533 billion	$204 billion
# Full-time Employees	223,000	271,000	208,000	249,000
Stock Price	$65	$146	$46	$56

Source: Based on https://finance.yahoo.com/quote/C?p=C&.tsrc=fin-srch

Goldman Sachs, CIT Group, and Wells Fargo. Exhibit 5 compares Citigroup with three rivals. Note that both JPMorgan Chase, Bank of America, and Wells Fargo are larger than Citigroup on market cap, revenue, and net income.

A recent study compared Citigroup on nine management and marketing variables to five rival companies and reported the findings provided in Exhibit 6. Note that Citigroup ranks overall good, but weak on variables number one (CEO effectiveness) and number five (Customer Service).

EXHIBIT 6 Comparing Citigroup with Rival Firms (Ranking 1 = Best; 6 = Worst)

	Variables									
	1	2	3	4	5	6	7	8	9	10
Citigroup	5	2	2	2	2	4	5	2	2	26
JPMorgan Chase	1	1	1	1	1	5	3	6	6	25
Bank of America	3	4	6	6	6	3	4	1	4	37
Wells Fargo	4	6	5	4	3	1	1	4	3	31
Goldman Sachs	2	3	3	3	4	2	2	3	5	27
CIT Group	6	5	4	5	5	6	6	5	1	43

Variables

1. Effectiveness of CEO
2. Product Quality
3. Do Customers Recommend Company Products to Friends?
4. Pricing
5. Customer Service
6. Overall Culture
7. Do Employees Recommend Company Products to Friends?
8. How Happy Are the Women Employees at the Firm?
9. How Happy Are Minority Employees at the Firm?
10. Summed Score (lower sum the better)

Source: Based on https://www.comparably.com/companies/citi/competitors

Exhibit 7 provides the percentage of market share of large US banks in 2021. Note that Citibank is the fourth largest.

Bank of America Corporation (BAC)

Headquartered in Charlotte, North Carolina, BAC provides banking, investment, savings, credit cards, and financial products and services for individuals, businesses, large corporations, and governments worldwide. BAC serves about 68 million consumer and small business clients with about 4,300 retail financial centers; about 17,000 ATMs; and digital banking platforms with about 40 million active users. BAC basically offers all the products and services that Citigroup offers,

EXHIBIT 7 Market Share Percentage of Large US Banks in June 2021 (by Total Assets)

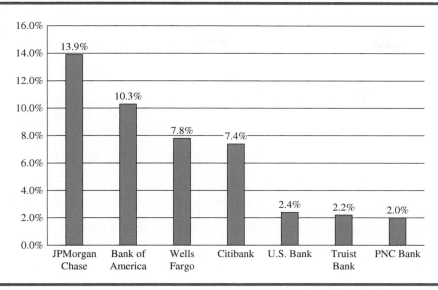

Source: Based on study_id51039_commercial-banks-in-the-united-states.pdf, p. 9.

with minor differences in fees, rates, basic organizational structure, and geographical dispersion of its offices. For example, BAC is much more dominant in the southern US, whereas Citigroup has a greater presence in the northern US.

JPMorgan Chase and Company (JPM)

Founded in 1799 and headquartered near Citigroup in New York City, JPM operates in four segments: Consumer and Community Banking (CCB), Corporate and Investment Bank (CIB), Commercial Banking (CB), and Asset and Wealth Management (AWM). These four segments collectively provide basically all the banking products and services that Citigroup provides, with minor differences in fees, rates, basic organizational structure, and geographical dispersion of its offices.

External Issues

The 2020–2021 pandemic ushered in a whole new era of strategic thinking for banks. The pandemic largely forced banks to abandon their historical reactive posture and become proactive, inventing and developing innovative products services. The pandemic forced banks to shift focus on the digital world and fintech, in particular.

Fintech (Financial Technology)

Fintech refers to digital financial activities, products, and services done without the assistance of a person, such as money transfers, depositing a check with your smartphone, bypassing a bank branch to apply for credit, raising money for a business start-up, managing investments, getting a loan, depositing checks, and more.

Start-up fintech companies such as Affirm seek to cut credit card companies such as Citigroup out of the online shopping process by offering consumers a secure immediate, short-term loan for purchases. Although rates can be higher than with credit cards, Affirm and other fintech companies offer a way for consumers with poor or no credit to make small and large purchases. Another company for example, Better Mortgage, offers a streamlined home mortgage process that bypasses traditional mortgage brokers such as Citigroup with a digital-only offering that can reward users with a verified preapproval letter within 24 hours of applying.

There are many other fintech companies, such as GreenSky, that links home improvement borrowers with banks. A company named Tala offers consumers in the developing world microloans and gives poor credit consumers better options than local banks.

The loan originator company Upstart makes the mortgage loan process simple by using different variables to determine creditworthiness, such as employment history and education. In many ways, fintech companies are disrupting lethargic, slow, expensive, traditional banking.

EXHIBIT 8 Top 10 Banking Trends in 2022

1. Apps are increasingly dominating peoples' lives. Banks are facing big strategic decisions on whether to compete or collaborate with these apps.
2. Banks are being expected to lead the way for the planet to become greener, so lead the way in a myriad of ways for companies to become more sustainable.
3. Fintechs are taking market share away from banks, so banks are scrambling to offer new and improved fintech products and services.
4. Banks are rethinking and revising and becoming more transparent with their fee structures due to "free" digital-only rival firms offering analogous bank products and services for free.
5. Banks are reinventing how they interact with customers to be more genuine, especially in digital spaces.
6. Crypto and digital currencies are here to stay, so banks are striving to embrace them, but how?
7. Banks are accelerating their usage of artificial intelligence and machine learning to gain zero waste and enhanced efficiency.
8. Banks are adapting to the consumer demand for payments to be anywhere, anytime, and anyhow.
9. Banks are generally embracing international markets more and seeking to make global acquisitions to achieve necessary levels of growth.
10. Competition among banks for exceptional talent has intensified to new levels.

Source: Based on https://www.accenture.com/us-en/insights/banking/top-10-trends-banking

Banking Trends in 2022–2024

The management consulting firm Accenture provides a summary of the top 10 trends in banking in 2022. These are summarized and paraphrased in Exhibit 8.

Exhibit 9 reveals the percentage value of loans by type made by commercial banks in the US in 2021. Note the largest is residential mortgages.

EXHIBIT 9 Percentage Value of Loans by Type Made by Commercial Banks in the US in 2021 (in Billions of US Dollars)

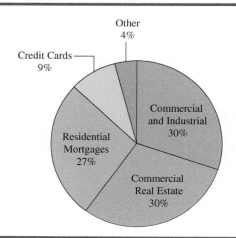

Source: Based on study_id51039_commercial-banks-in-the-united-states.pdf, p. 25.

Conclusion

CEO Jane Fraser at Citigroup needs a clear strategic plan because her company faces thousands of competitors of all sizes. Fraser knows the basic underlying external opportunities and threats facing Citigroup, as well as the basic internal strengths and weaknesses, but she needs to know the relative importance of those factors. She also needs to know the relative attractiveness of alternative strategies to be derived from those underlying external and internal factors. In other words, Fraser needs strategy analyses performed, including IFEM, EFEM, SWOT, IE Matrix, perceptual mapping, EPS-EBIT analysis, and projected financial statement analysis.

Let's say that Fraser hires you to develop a comprehensive strategic plan for Citigroup. Begin with developing an effective vision and mission statement, which as you see early in the case the company needs assistance on in this area, and include a new, improved organizational chart, which the case also reveals the company needs assistance on improving. Perform the analysis that is requested, develop some recommendations with associated costs, and present your findings and research to your professor and fellow students. How can Citigroup adapt to an ever-changing world? Should Citigroup continue divesting its international operations? What does Citigroup need to do in the next 3 years to effectively differentiate itself from rival banks and ultimately adapt to be a profitable company over the next three decades?

References

1. https://www.citigroup.com/citi/about/mission-and-value-proposition.html
2. https://www.citigroup.com/citi/about/our_leaders.html
3. https://finance.yahoo.com/quote/C?p=C&.tsrc=fin-srch
4. Citigroup's 2021 *Form 10K*.
5. https://www.accenture.com/us-en/insights/banking/top-10-trends-banking
6. Study_id51039_commercial-banks-in-the-united-states.pdf, p. 25.
7. https://www.citigroup.com/citi/news/2022/fourth-quarter-2021-earnings.htm
8. https://www.genpact.com/insight/article/nine-pivotal-trends-that-will-shape-banking-strategies-in-2022?gclid=CjwKCAjwtIaVBhBkEiwAsr7-cx9LlveX0bckN4tpJLpDlBwFo-TosDNYzOs9Grl5iSMWL6rMLLWfRBoCYioQAvD_BwE
9. https://www.comparably.com/companies/citi/competitors

JetBlue Airways Corporation, 2022

www.jetblue.com - (JBLU)

Incorporated in 1998 and headquartered in Long Island, New York, JetBlue is a low-cost airline that has grown to become the seventh-largest airline in North America. JetBlue operates about 65 Airbus A321 aircraft, 5 Airbus A220 aircraft, 15 Airbus A321 aircraft, 140 Airbus A320 aircraft, and 65 Embraer E190 aircraft, serving about 100 destinations in about 35 states in the US, the District of Columbia, Puerto Rico, the US Virgin Islands, and about 25 countries in the Caribbean and Latin America.

JetBlue in 2021 formed a partnership with American Airlines to facilitate connectivity for travelers in the Northeast US. JetBlue is New York's "Hometown Airline" and a leading carrier in Boston, Fort Lauderdale-Hollywood, Los Angeles, Orlando, and San Juan. JetBlue carries customers across the US, Caribbean and Latin America, and between New York and London. JetBlue's revenues increased from $2.9 billion in 2020 to $6.1 billion in 2021, while net income went from negative $1.35 billion to negative $182 million.

For Q1 of 2022 that ended 3-31-22, JetBlue reported a loss per share of ($0.79) or ($398 million) compared to a pre-tax income of $58 million in the first quarter of 2019. For Q1, JetBlue's capacity declined by 0.3% year over three and the company's revenue declined 7.2 percent year over three. For Q1, JetBlue's operating expenses per available seat mile increased 17.5 percent year over three. During Q1, JetBlue launched service to three new cities: Puerto Vallarta, Kansas City, and Milwaukee, and in Q2 began service to Asheville, NC, and Vancouver, Canada. JetBlue remains on track to operate almost 300 daily departures from New York City airports.

Copyright by Fred David Books LLC; written by Forest R. David.

History

JetBlue was founded in 1998 by David Neeleman under the name "NewAir." JetBlue's strategy from the beginning was to be a low-cost airline like Southwest but to offer more amenities. In May 2019, JetBlue and Southwest ranked "Highest in Customer Satisfaction Among Low-Cost Carriers" in a tie by J.D. Power in the North America Airline Satisfaction Study. JetBlue began flights from the US into Canada (Vancouver) in April 2021.

JetBlue's first major advertising campaign used phrases like "Unbelievable" and "We like you, too." Full-page newspaper ads touted low fares, new aircraft, leather seats, spacious legroom, and a customer-service-oriented staff committed to "bringing humanity back to air travel." JetBlue became the first airline to offer all passengers personalized in-flight entertainment. In April 2000, JetBlue installed flat screen monitors in every seatback, providing customers live access to more than 20 DirectTV channels at no additional cost.

In June 2022, JetBlue launched service from New York's John F. Kennedy International Airport to Vancouver International Airport, the company's first flight ever to Canada. JetBlue is now the only airline to serve Vancouver with nonstop service from New York-JFK. JetBlue continues to grow beyond the U.S. with over 30 international destinations now served in more than two dozen countries. On August 1, 2022, JetBlue officially won their battle with Frontier Airlines to acquire Spirit Airlines for $3.8 billion.

Internal Issues

Vision/Mission

JetBlue does not provide a vision or mission statement on its corporate website, but Exhibit 1 provides statements found on the internet for JetBlue.

Strategy

JetBlue and American Airlines established the Northeast Alliance (NEA) in February 2021 and since then have collectively grown quickly across New York and Boston. The two airlines now

EXHIBIT 1 JetBlue's Vision and Mission Statements

JetBlue's vision: *We continuously emphasize providing competitive rates for customers for all of our destinations.*

JetBlue's mission: *We aim to inspire humanity, in the air and on the ground, to join us in giving back to all communities we serve.*

Source: Based on https://www.comparably.com/companies/jetblue-airways/mission

have reciprocal loyalty benefits and are codesharing on 185 routes. In summer 2022, JetBlue began fully operating out of LaGuardia's (LGA) Terminal B, providing easy connections for customers traveling on the NEA.

In mid-2022, JetBlue began service to two new cities, Asheville, North Carolina, (AVL) and Vancouver (YVR). In 2022, JetBlue and American began offering up to 300 daily departures at JFK Airport, 195 of those operated by JetBlue—more flights than ever before. At LGA, JetBlue plans to operate about 50 of nearly 200 daily departures with American, more than tripling the company's flight count in 2019.

JetBlue in August 2022 successfully ended its battle with Frontier Airlines to acquire Spirit Airlines. In June 2022, JetBlue submitted a new proposal to the Board of Directors of Spirit (NYSE: SAVE) to acquire all of the outstanding common stock of Spirit, and additionally the proposal included the following incentives:

1. A $350 million ($3.20 per Spirit share) reverse break-up fee, payable to Spirit in the unlikely event the acquisition transaction is denied for antitrust reasons. This payment is an increase of $150 million, or $1.37 per Spirit share, to what JetBlue has previously offered to pay, and is $100 million greater than the amount being offer by Frontier.
2. A cash dividend of $164 million to Spirit stockholders to be paid promptly following the Spirit stockholder vote approving the combination between Spirit and JetBlue.
3. $31.50 per share in cash total to be paid, comprised of $30 per share in cash at the closing of the transaction and the prepayment of $1.50 per share of the reverse break-up fee.

Operational data for JetBlue is provided in Exhibit 2. Note mostly excellent positive numbers for 2021 as compared with 2020.

Organizational Structure
JetBlue's top executives are listed and arrayed in Exhibit 3. Note that Joanna Geraphty is COO, implying that the company uses a divisional-type organizational structure. However, it is unclear whether the divisions are by hub, region, or product. Note there are eight females among the top 15 persons.

Finance
JetBlue's recent income statements and balance sheets are provided in Exhibit 4 and Exhibit 5, respectively. Note the excellent revenue increases but the weak profitability numbers.

Segments
JetBlue basically does not have segments, but the company does provide a revenue breakdown as provided in Exhibit 6. Most airline companies have a separate category for freight, but JetBlue apparently does not carry freight.

EXHIBIT 2 JetBlue's Recent Operational Statistics

	2020	2021	Percentage Change
Number of passengers (thousands)	14,274	30,094	110.8
Available seat miles (ASMs) (millions)	32,689	54,113	65.5
Load factor	56.9%	76.0%	
Average fare	$191.42	$186.39	(2.6)
Departures	168,636	264,385	56.8
Average fuel cost per gallon	$1.53	$2.06	34.6
Fuel gallons consumed (millions)	412	696.	68.9
Average # full-time crewmembers	15,450	16,693	

Source: Based on http://blueir.investproductions.com/investor-relations/press-releases/2022/01-27-2022-120059203

EXHIBIT 3 JetBlue's Top Executives Listed and Arrayed

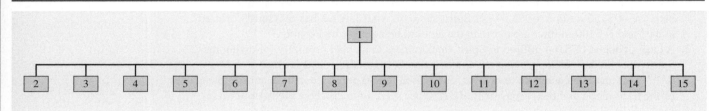

1. Robin Hayes, CEO
2. Joanna Geraghty, President and COO
3. Ursula Hurley, CFO
4. Tracy Lawlor, Chief Strategy and Business Development Officer
5. Doug McGraw, Chief Communications Officer
6. Brandon Nelson, General Counsel and Corporate Secretary
7. Jayne O'Brien, Head of Marketing and Loyalty
8. Lisa Reifer, Head of Finance and Treasury

9. Laurie Villa, Chief People Officer
10. Carol Clements, Chief Digital and Technology Officer
11. Dave Clark, Head of Revenue and Planning
12. Robert Land, Head of Government Affairs, Associate General Counsel
13. Edward Kayton, Head of Talent and Crewmember Experience
14. Warren Christie, Head of Safety, Security, and Fleet Operations
15. Amy Burr, President, JetBlue Technology Ventures

Source: Based on http://blueir.investproductions.com/investor-relations/corporate-governance/leadership

EXHIBIT 4 JetBlue's Recent Income Statements (in millions)

Income Statement	12/31/20	12/31/21		Percentage Change
Revenues	$2,957	$6,037	⬆	104%
Cost of Goods Sold	1,515	2,789	⬆	84%
Gross Profit	1,442	3,248	⬆	125%
Operating Expenses	3,156	3,328	⬆	5%
EBIT	(1,714)	(80)	—	—
Interest Expense	179	183	⬆	2%
EBT	(1,893)	(263)	—	—
Tax	(539)	(81)	—	—
Nonrecurring Events	0	0	—	—
Net Income	($1,354)	($182)	—	—

Source: Based on JetBlue's 2021 *Form 10K*, p. 67.

EXHIBIT 5 JetBlue's Recent Balance Sheets (in millions)

Balance Sheet	12/31/20	12/31/21		Percentage Change
Assets				
Cash and Short-Term Investments	$1,918	$2,018	⇧	5%
Accounts Receivable	98	207	⇧	111%
Inventory	71	74	⇧	4%
Other Current Assets	1,258	948	⇩	−25%
Total Current Assets	3,345	3,247	⇩	−3%
Property Plant & Equipment	8,399	8,814	⇧	5%
Goodwill	0	0	—	—
Intangibles	261	284	⇧	9%
Other Long-Term Assets	1,401	1,297	⇩	−7%
Total Assets	**$13,406**	**$13,642**	⇧	**2%**
Liabilities				
Accounts Payable	499	365	⇩	−27%
Other Current Liabilities	2,175	3,052	⇧	40%
Total Current Liabilities	2,674	3,417	⇧	28%
Long-Term Debt	5,165	4,341	⇩	−16%
Other Long-Term Liabilities	1,616	2,035	⇧	26%
Total Liabilities	**$9,455**	**$9,793**	⇧	**4%**
Equity				
Common Stock	5	5	⇩	0%
Retained Earnings	2,968	2,786	⇩	−6%
Treasury Stock	(1,981)	(1,989)	⇧	0%
Paid in Capital & Other	2,959	3,047	⇧	3%
Total Equity	**$3,951**	**$3,849**	⇩	**−3%**
Total Liabilities and Equity	**$13,406**	**$13,642**	⇧	**2%**

Source: Based on JetBlue's 2021 *Form 10K*, p. 65–66.

EXHIBIT 6 JetBlue's Revenue Breakdown (in millions)

	2020	2021	Percentage Change
Passenger	$2,733	$5,609	105.3
Other	$224	$428	91.4
Total	$2,957	$6,037	104.4

Source: Based on http://blueir.investproductions.com/investor-relations/press-releases/2022/01-27-2022-120059203

Competitors

Based in Miarmar, Florida, Spirit Airlines and Denver, Colorado-based Frontier Airlines tried to merge their operations in 2022, but JetBlue won the bidding war with Frontier. So, the new JetBlue + Spirit company—whose name has yet to be announced—pending final approval, will be the fifth-largest carrier in the US, behind the "Big Four": American, Delta, United, and Southwest.

JetBlue's competitors include Southwest Airlines, American Airlines, Delta, United Airlines, and Frontier Airlines. Based on domestic revenue passenger miles in late 2021, American Airlines is the largest US airline with a market share of 18.8 percent, followed by Southwest Airlines with 17.7 percent, Delta Airlines with 15.8 percent, and United Airlines with 12.3 percent; JetBlue had 5.2 percent market share, just below Spirit's 5.5 percent and just above Frontier's 3.5 percent.

A recent study compared JetBlue with four of its competitors on nine management and marketing variables and reported the findings provided in Exhibit 7. Note that JetBlue ranked last on six variables, revealing problems, as indicated by the number fives on Row 1 in Exhibit 7. Note on Row 2 that Southwest was ranked number one (best) on seven variables. On Row 3, note that Delta shows considerable strength. The analysis reveals that JetBlue faces formidable rival firms.

Exhibit 8 provides a comparison of JetBlue with several of its rival companies. Note that JetBlue is much smaller than its major rival firms.

EXHIBIT 7 Comparing JetBlue Versus Rival Firms (Ranking 1 = Best; 6 = Worst)

	Variables									
	1	2	3	4	5	6	7	8	9	10
JetBlue Airways	5	5	4	4	5	5	5	3	5	41
Southwest Airlines	1	2	1	1	1	1	1	1	2	11
Delta Airlines	2	1	2	2	2	2	2	2	1	16
American Airlines	3	3	3	3	4	4	5	3	3	31
United Airlines	3	4	5	5	4	3	3	4	4	35

Variables

1. Effectiveness of CEO
2. Product Quality
3. Do Customers Recommend Company Products to Friends?
4. Pricing
5. Customer Service
6. Overall Culture
7. Do Employees Recommend Company Products to Friends?
8. How Happy Are the Women Employees at the Firm?
9. How Happy Are Minority Employees at the Firm?
10. Summed Score (lower sum the better)

Source: Based on https://www.comparably.com/companies/jetblue-airways/competitors

EXHIBIT 8 JetBlue's Rival Firms Compared Financially

	JetBlue (JBLU)	Southwest (LUV)	United (UAL)	American (AAL)
Market Capitalization	$5.1 billion	$28 billion	$16 billion	$11.6 billion
EPS	−$0.57	$1.61	−$6.1	−$3.1
Revenue	$6.1 billion	$27 billion	$24 billion	$30 billion
Net Income	−$182 billion	$977 million.	−$2 billion	−$2 billion
Total Debt	$5 billion	$12 billion	$41 billion	$46 billion
Total Debt/Equity	126	117	816	51
Current Ratio	—	1.97	1.19	0.91
Stock Price	$16	$47	$46	$18
# Employees	16,690	55,100	84,100	123,000

Source: Based on https://finance.yahoo.com/quote/JBLU/key-statistics?p=JBLU

Exhibit 9 reveals the leading airlines in the US in 2020. Note that JetBlue had 6 percent market share.

EXHIBIT 9 Leading Airlines in the US by Domestic Market Share in 2020

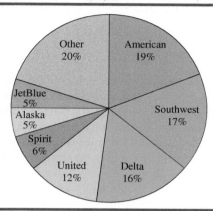

Source: Based on study_id33930_jetblue-airways-corporation-statista-dossier.pdf, p. 10.

Exhibit 10 reveals that back in 2020, JetBlue ranked just below Southwest in customer satisfaction on short-haul flights in North America.

EXHIBIT 10 Airline Satisfaction on Short-Haul Flights in North America in 2020

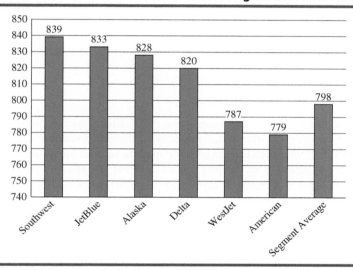

Source: Based on study_id33930_jetblue-airways-corporation-statista-dossier.pdf, p. 30.

Southwest Airlines

Incorporated in 1967 and headquartered in Dallas, Texas, Southwest operates a fleet of 728 Boeing 737 aircrafts, serving 121 destinations in 42 states, the District of Columbia, Puerto Rico, and 10 near-international countries, including Mexico, Jamaica, the Bahamas, Aruba, the Dominican Republic, Costa Rica, Belize, Cuba, the Cayman Islands, and Turks and Caicos. Southwest offers inflight entertainment and connectivity services on Wi-Fi–enabled aircrafts and a Rapid Rewards loyalty program in which program members earn points for dollars spent on Southwest base fares.

United Airlines Holdings

Headquartered in Chicago, Illinois, United Airlines provides air transportation services in North America, Asia, Europe, Africa, the Pacific, the Middle East, and Latin America. The company also sells fuel and offers catering, ground handling, and maintenance services for third parties. As indicated in Exhibit 8, United is more than three times larger than JetBlue.

American Airlines Group

Headquartered in Fort Worth, Texas, American Airlines provides air transportation services for passengers and cargo through its hubs in Charlotte, Chicago, Dallas/Fort Worth, Los Angeles, Miami, New York, Philadelphia, Phoenix, and Washington, DC. American also has hubs in London, Madrid, Seattle/Tacoma, Sydney, and Tokyo. The company operates about 900 aircraft.

External Issues

The number of US domestic leisure passengers on airlines is fast recovering toward prepandemic levels as vaccines are rolled out and consumers spend federal stimulus money. However, the number of business and international travelers are not growing, so major US airlines are redirecting much of their former business and international-oriented capacity to the domestic leisure market. Thus, air fares are staying relatively low since added business and international capacity is now competing for domestic leisure passengers. Analysts expect a recovery in business and international travel to occur late in 2022.

Airlines' biggest expense is jet fuel and its price closely tracks the movement of major oil benchmarks. In the first 11 months of 2021, the US West Texas Intermediate (WTI) averaged $67.6 per barrel, up 45.0 percent from the prior-year period. Analysts expect WTI crude prices are expected to average $67.87 per barrel in 2021 and $66.42 per barrel in 2022, according to the US Energy Information Administration in December 2021.

Global commercial airline passenger traffic, represented by revenue passenger kilometers (RPK), is expected to increase by 18 percent in 2021 and 51 percent in 2022. According to the International Air Transport Association (IATA), North America is expected to turn to profitability, while other regions are expected to operate under losses in 2022. IATA projects passenger capacity, represented by available seat kilometers (ASK) to increase 14.2 percent in 2021 and 25.2 percent in 2022. Considering both passengers and cargo, the overall weight load factor is expected to rise to 64.1 percent in 2022, just below what analysts say is the 65.9 breakeven point for any airline to be profitable in 2022.

Conclusion

CEO Robin Hayes needs a clear 3-year strategic plan for JetBlue. The new JetBlue-Spirit merger is aimed directly at Frontier's market areas. Intensity of competition and rivalry among airline firms is accelerating as companies and countries transition to zero emissions. The vision/mission and organizational structure sections of this case reveal that there is substantial room for improvement for JetBlue in both areas.

Hayes knows the basic underlying external opportunities and threats and internal strengths facing JetBlue, but he is unsure about the relative importance of those factors. He thus needs an external and internal assessment performed, anchored by development of an EFE Matrix and IFE Matrix as described in Chapter 3 and Chapter 4 of the David textbook. Hayes also needs to know the relative attractiveness of alternative strategies facing the company, so he needs a SWOT, BCG, and QSPM analyses performed as well.

Let's say Hayes asks you to develop the comprehensive strategic plan that he needs. In addition to the analyses mentioned, include in your report a perceptual map, a set of proposed recommendations with associated costs, and an EPS-EBIT analysis to reveal whether debt or stock or some combination of debt and stock is best to obtain the needed funds. Also include projected financial statements to show the expected impact on JetBlue if Hayes adopts your proposed strategic plan. What can JetBlue do to help assure top line (revenues) and bottom line (net income) 5+ percent annually in the years to come? Identify candidate airlines for JetBlue to acquire. If JetBlue should expand further organically (internally) into other regions, countries, and continents, include direction for Hayes in this regard.

All of JetBlue's top executives, board of directors, shareholders, and employees will benefit from and be thankful for your work developing and proposing a clear roadmap for their future. Good luck on this endeavor. We authors are confident you can do a wonderful job performing this task, following the guidelines presented in the David strategic management textbook and using the strategic planning template provided at www.strategyclub.com. Use the template to help CEO

Hayes best integrate Spirit's routes and culture with JetBlue's routes and culture. Additionally, how should JetBlue's new organizational structure be designed given the need to integrate Spirit executives into the array?

References

1. JetBlue's 2021 *Form 10K*.
2. study_id33930_jetblue-airways-corporation-statista-dossier.pdf, pp. 10, 30.
3. https://finance.yahoo.com/quote/JBLU/key-statistics?p=JBLU
4. https://www.comparably.com/companies/jetblue-airways/competitors
5. https://www.comparably.com/companies/jetblue-airways/mission
6. http://blueir.investproductions.com/investor-relations/press-releases/2022/01-27-2022-120059203
7. http://blueir.investproductions.com/investor-relations/corporate-governance/leadership

FedEx Corporation, 2022

www.fedex.com, (NYSE: FDX)

Headquartered in Memphis, Tennessee, FedEx is a global transportation, e-commerce, and business services company. FedEx's air delivery service today is named FedEx Express, and the company operates FedEx Ground and FedEx Office (originally known as Kinko's), FedEx Supply Chain, and FedEx Freight. FedEx is a major contractor of the US government, assisting the US Postal Service though is FedEx SmartPost operations.

Founded in Little Rock, Arkansas, in 1971, FedEx has operations in more than 220 countries and territories, linking more than 99 percent of the world's economies through the work of more than 600,000 team members around the world. FedEx has four segments: FedEx Express, FedEx Ground, FedEx Freight, and FedEx Other and Eliminations that in fiscal 2021 generated the following billions of dollars in revenue, $42.1, $30.5, $7.8, and $3.5, respectively, totaling $84 billion. The FedEx Other segment includes FedEx Logistics, FedEx Office, and ShopRunner.

In 2021, FedEx ranked 16th in *Fortune* magazine's "World's Most Admired Companies" list—the 21st consecutive year that FedEx has ranked among the top 20 in that list. FedEx is led by a famous exemplary strategist, Fred Smith. In mid-2021, FedEx agreed to purchase an additional 20 B767F aircraft, 10 of which will be delivered in 2024 and 10 of which will be delivered in 2025.

For FedEx's Q3 2022 that ended 2-28-22, the company reported revenues of $23.6 billion, up from $21.5 billion the prior year; and Q2 operating income of $1.33 billion, up 32 percent from the prior year. Also for its Q3, FedEx's revenue per shipment increased 19 percent and average daily shipments grew 2 percent from the prior year. So, FedEx is performing really well to date.

Copyright by Fred David Books LLC; written by Fred R. David.

History

In the 1960s, Frederick Smith was a student at Yale University when he developed a term paper where he proposed a transportation system specifically designed for urgent deliveries. Smith's professor did not like the idea, but Smith persisted, and after graduating and joining the US Marine Corp., Smith started his new business in 1973 in Memphis. He chose Memphis because of its location in the center of the country and its good weather.

Born in 1944 in Marks, Mississippi, Fred Smith graduated from Yale College in 1966 and joined the military to serve his country, even knowing that he one day planned to start FedEx. Smith served 4 years in the US Marines and completed two tours of duty in Vietnam—all before launching the original air-ground Federal Express network. Nearing age 80, Smith continues to serve as the chairman and CEO of FedEx today.

FedEx officially began operations on April 17, 1973, with 389 employees. That night, 14 small aircraft took off from Memphis and delivered 186 packages to 25 US cities from Rochester, New York, to Miami, Florida. FedEx did not show a profit until 1975 but soon became the gold standard, go-to carrier of high-priority packages and the standard for express shipping of almost anything anywhere.

FedEx's strategy for growth has historically been to acquire transportation companies in other countries; a few recent large acquisitions are detailed in Exhibit 1.

Internal Issues

Vision/Mission

FedEx appears to not have a written statement, but the company strives to abide by what it calls the Purple Promise: *"I will make every FedEx experience outstanding."* FedEx's mission statement is clearly provided on the corporate website and reads (paraphrased from https://www.fedex.com/content/dam/fedex/us-united-states/sustainability/gcrs/FedEx_2021_ESG_Report.pdf)

"FedEx strives to produce superior financial returns for its shareholders by providing rapid, global logistics and transportation services for both individuals and organizations. FedEx maintains the highest ethical and professional standards in performing all its operations and activities in towns, cities, and rural areas on nearly all continents."

EXHIBIT 1 Some Key FedEx Acquisitions in Recent Years

Year	Country	Company Acquired
2006	UK	ANC Holdings Ltd.
2007	China	DTW International Priority Express
2007	Hungary	Flying-Cargo Hungary Kft.
2011	India	Prakash Air Freight Pvt. Ltd. (PAFEX) and AFL Pvt. Ltd./Unifreight India Pvt. Ltd.
2011	Mexico	Servicios Nacionales Mupa, S.A. de C.V.
2012	Poland	Courier Opek Sp.z o.o. (Opek)
2012	France	TATEX
2012	Brazil	Rapidão Cometa
2014	South Africa, Zambia, etc.	Supaswift
2014	North America	Bongo International
2015	North America	GENCO
2016	Europe, Middle East, Africa	TNT Express

Source: Based on information at https://www.fedex.com/en-us/about/history.html

Strategy

FedEx plans to spend about $7.2 billion in 2022 on capital expenditures to increase capacity associated with higher volume levels, to modernize aircraft, and to invest further in productivity and safety. The company is also making investments over multiple years of about $1.5 billion to significantly expand the FedEx Express Indianapolis Hub and about $1.5 billion to modernize the FedEx Express Memphis World Hub. About half of FedEx's capital expenditures in 2022 are aimed to enhance its growth initiatives, including capital expenditures in 2022 of $1.7 billion for delivery of aircraft and related equipment and progress payments toward future aircraft deliveries at FedEx Express.

Organizational Structure

FedEx operates from a decentralized, divisional-by-process type organizational design. Exhibit 2 lists and arrays the FedEx top management team. Note the three divisional presidents and the legendary founder, now aged 80, Frederick Smith. Note also that FedEx has a COO, even though less than 40 percent of *Fortune* 500 companies today have a COO. Donald Colleran, President and CEO of FedEx Express, will retire in December 2022 after a nearly 40-year career at FedEx. Richard W. Smith, regional President of the Americas and EVP of Global Support, will succeed Colleran as President and CEO of FedEx Express.

EXHIBIT 2 FedEx's Top Executives Listed and Arrayed

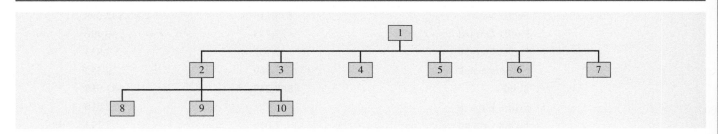

1. Frederick Smith, Chairman and CEO
2. Raj Subramaniam, President and COO
3. Mike Lenz, EVP and CFO
4. Mark Allen, EVP, General Counsel, and Secretary
5. Robert Carter, EVP, FedEx Information Services and CIO
6. Jill Brannon, EVP and Chief Sales Officer
7. Brie Carere, EVP, Chief Marketing and Communications Officer
8. Donald Colleran, President and CEO of FedEx Express
9. John Smith, President and CEO of FedEx Ground
10. Lance Moll, President and CEO of FedEx Freight

Source: Based on https://www.fedex.com/en-us/about/leadership/brie-carere.html

Segments

FedEx reports revenues and net income within four segments, described as follows:

1. *FedEx Express:* provides quick delivery to more than 220 countries and territories, connecting markets that comprise more than 99 percent of the world's gross domestic product (GDP). FedEx Express employs about 300,000 and has about 80,000 drop-off locations (including FedEx Office stores and FedEx OnSite locations, such as nearly 20,000 Walgreens, Dollar General, and Albertsons stores), 690 aircraft, and about 90,000 vehicles in its global network. This segment includes FedEx Custom Critical and FedEx Cross Border. FedEx Express offers domestic pickup-and-delivery services in France, UK, Australia, Brazil, Italy, Canada, Mexico, Poland, India, China, and South Africa.

2. *FedEx Ground:* provides small-package ground delivery services to any business address in the US and Canada, whereas FedEx Home Delivery service provides residential delivery to 100 percent of US residences and to almost 100 percent of residents in Canada. FedEx Ground Economy delivers high volumes of low-weight, less time-sensitive business-to-consumer packages.

3. *FedEx Freight:* provides less-than-truckload freight services across all lengths of haul to businesses and residences in the US, Puerto Rico, and US Virgin Islands. This segment includes FedEx Freight Priority, FedEx Freight Economy, and FedEx Freight Direct. FedEx Freight operates about 30,000 vehicles from a network of about 425 service centers and has nearly 50,000 employees.

4. Corporate, Other, and Eliminations

   a. *FedEx Office:* provides document and business services and retail access to the company's primary segments. FedEx Office operates nearly 2,500 customer-facing stores, providing convenient access to printing and shipping expertise with reliable service. About 350 FedEx Office locations are inside Walmart stores. This segment's activities are included in "Corporate, other and eliminations" in the company's segment reporting.

   b. *FedEx Logistics:* provides customs brokerage and global ocean and air freight forwarding through FedEx Trade Networks Transport and Brokerage, as well as integrated supply chain management solutions through FedEx Supply Chain. These activities are included in "Corporate, other and eliminations" in the company's segment reporting.

   c. *FedEx Services:* provides sales, marketing, information technology, communications, customer service, technical support, billing and collection services, and certain back-office functions to the company's primary segments.

Exhibit 3 provides FedEx financial data organized by segment. Note the dramatic increases. Exhibit 4 provides some recent critical financial ratios that FedEx monitors continuously. Note that the company's domestic operations are performing better than their international operations on some key variables. Note: FedEx's fiscal year ends each May 31.

EXHIBIT 3 FedEx's Revenues and Operating Income by Segment (in Millions)

	2020	2021
FedEx Express	$35,513	$42,078
FedEx Ground	22,733	30,496
FedEx Freight	7,102	7,833
Corporate and Other	3,869	9,552
Total	**$69,217**	**$83,959**
FedEx Express	996	2,810
FedEx Ground	2,014	3,193
FedEx Freight	580	1,005
Corporate and Other	(1,173)	(1,151)
Total	**$2,417**	**$5,857**

Source: Based on the FedEx 2021 *Form 10K*, p. 43, 55–65.

EXHIBIT 4 FedEx's Key Operating Variables (in Thousands)

	2020	2021
FedEx Express		
US Domestic Average Daily Package Volume	2,808	3,283
US Domestic Average Daily Package Volume	2,337	2,360
Average Daily Freight Pounds	19,880	19,869
US Domestic Revenue per Package	$18.30	$17.79
International Revenue per Package	$48.83	$49.03
FedEx Ground		
US Domestic Average Daily Package Volume	9,997	12,272
Revenue per Package	$8.93	9.70
FedEx Express and FedEx Ground		
US Domestic Average Daily Package Volume	15,983	18,953
Revenue per Pound	$1.38	$1.41
FedEx Freight		
Average Daily Shipments	72.5	76.2
Revenue per Shipment	$301.55	$313.67
Across All Segments		
Average Fuel Cost per Gallon	$2.69	$2.47

Source: Based on the FedEx 2021 *Form 10K*, pp. 46–47, 50.

Finances

FedEx's fiscal year ends each May 31. For Q2 2022 that ended November 30, 2021, FedEx reported revenues of $23.5 billion, up nicely from $20.6 billion the prior year period. Q3 2022 net income was $1.04 billion, down slightly from $1.30 billion the prior year period. During Q2 2022, FedEx announced it would repurchase another $5 billion of its common stock.

FedEx's recent income statements and balance sheets are provided in Exhibit 5 and Exhibit 6, respectively. Note the outstanding top line (Revenue) and bottom line (Net Income) increases.

EXHIBIT 5 FedEx's Recent Income Statements (in Millions)

Income Statement	5/31/20	5/31/21		Percentage Change
Revenue (Sales)	**$69,217**	**$83,959**	⇧	**21%**
Cost of Goods Sold	0	0	—	—
Gross Profit	69,217	83,959	⇧	21%
Operating Expenses	66,800	78,102	⇧	17%
EBIT (Operating Income)	2,417	5,857	⇧	142%
Interest Expense or (Credit)	748	(817)	—	—
EBT	1,669	6,674	⇧	300%
Tax	383	1,443	⇧	277%
Nonrecurring Events	0	0	—	—
Net Income	**$1,286**	**$5,231**	⇧	**307%**

Source: Based on the FedEx 2021 *Form 10K*, p. 80.

Diversity, Equity, and Inclusion (DEI) and Sustainability

In 2021, FedEx was ranked as one of "America's Most Responsible Companies" by *Newsweek*, ranking higher than any other "Travel, Transport and Logistics" company included on the list. In March 2021, FedEx announced plans to make its operations carbon-neutral by 2040 by investing $2 billion in sustainable energy initiatives, including $100 million for a new Yale Center for

EXHIBIT 6 FedEx's Recent Balance Sheets (in Millions)

Balance Sheet	5/31/20	5/31/21		Percentage Change
Assets				
Cash and Short-Term Investments	$4,881	$7,087	⬆	45%
Accounts Receivable	10,102	12,069	⬆	19%
Inventory	572	587	⬆	3%
Other Current Assets	828	837	⬆	1%
Total Current Assets	16,383	20,580	⬆	26%
Property Plant & Equipment	33,608	35,752	⬆	6%
Goodwill	6,372	6,992	⬆	10%
Intangibles	0	0	—	—
Other Long-Term Assets	17,174	19,453	⬆	13%
Total Assets	**$73,537**	**$82,777**	⬆	**13%**
Liabilities				
Accounts Payable	3,269	3,841	⬆	17%
Other Current Liabilities	7,075	9,819	⬆	39%
Total Current Liabilities	10,344	13,660	⬆	32%
Long-Term Debt	21,952	20,733	⬇	−6%
Other Long-Term Liabilities	22,946	24,216	⬆	6%
Total Liabilities	**$55,242**	**$58,609**	⬆	**6%**
Equity				
Common Stock	32	32	⬇	0%
Retained Earnings	25,216	29,817	⬆	18%
Treasury Stock	(9,162)	(8,430)	—	—
Paid in Capital & Other	2,209	2,749	⬆	24%
Total Equity	**$18,295**	**$24,168**	⬆	**32%**
Total Liabilities and Equity	**$73,537**	**$82,777**	⬆	**13%**

Source: Based on the FedEx 2021 *Form 10K*, pp. 78–79.

Natural Carbon Capture. Additionally, FedEx is upgrading its aircraft and ground transportation fleets to be totally electric by 2040, beginning by using General Motors's (GM) electric EV600 delivery vans. Milestones that FedEx is set to accomplish on the way to the 2040 objectives include that 50 percent of their vans will be electric by 2025 and 100 percent by 2030. In fact, on December 17, 2021, FedEx took delivery of its first five of an order of 500 electric Light Commercial Vehicles (eLCVs) from BrightDrop, a subsidiary of GM.

FedEx posts stories and accomplishments on its corporate website to show its commitment and progress on DEI issues. For example, more than 49 percent of the company's US workforce and 35.5 percent of their management team are minorities. Also, the company spent $13.3 billion in fiscal 2020 on diverse suppliers (81% small, 12% minority-owned, and 7% women-owned). FedEx was selected in 2019 by the National Gay and Lesbian Chamber of Commerce as Best-of-the-Best Corporation for Inclusion. Plus, FedEx was named one of *Forbes*' 2019 Best Employers for Diversity. The company recently established a DEI Depot, an online platform to create more awareness of DEI-related resources, events, and team member stories across operating companies.

FedEx publishes an annual *Environmental, Sustainability, and Governance (ESG)* Report to reveal its ESG strategies, goals, accomplishments and progress on ESG variables.

Competitors

FedEx competitors include DHL, C.H. Robinson, UPS, the US Postal Service, American Airlines Group, Delta Air Lines, and TNT. Exhibit 7 provides information regarding how FedEx ranks on nine quality variables, compared with some of its rival firms. Note that FedEx ranks number one on three variables: Customer Service, Happy Employees, and Minority Employees. FedEx ranks weakest on "Do Employees Recommend Company Products to Friends." Overall, note that FedEx is second-best behind DHL as indicated by the total score of 16 versus 15 (lower sum is better as you see in Column 10).

EXHIBIT 7 Comparing FedEx Versus Rival Firms (Ranking 1 = Best; 6 = Worst)

	Variables									
	1	2	3	4	5	6	7	8	9	10
FedEx	3	1	2	2	1	2	3	1	1	16
UPS	5	3	3	3	3	4	4	3	3	31
DHL	1	2	1	1	2	1	1	4	2	15
TNT	4	5	5	5	5	5	5	-	-	34+
CH Robinson	2	4	4	4	4	3	2	2	4	29

Variables

1. Effectiveness of CEO
2. Product Quality
3. Do Customers Recommend Company Products to Friends?
4. Pricing
5. Customer Service
6. Overall Culture
7. Do Employees Recommend Company Products to Friends?
8. How Happy Are the Women Employees at the Firm?
9. How Happy Are Minority Employees at the Firm?
10. Summed Score (lower sum the better)

Source: Based on https://www.comparably.com/companies/fedex/competitors

United Parcel Post (UPS)

Founded in 1907 in Seattle, Washington, UPS has 540,000 employees globally that work in more than 220 countries and territories working on the ground and managing 2,285 UPS delivery flights daily. As evidenced daily with thousands of clean, brown UPS trucks delivering packages to residences and businesses, UPS is a transportation and logistics leader. UPS owns or leases 576 aircraft to help deliver packages fast, globally, including seventy-five 757's, fifty-two A300's, seventy-eight 767's, forty-two MD-11's, and thirty-five 747's, all designed specifically for carrying packages and freight.

Located in Louisville, Kentucky, UPS's Worldport is the largest fully automated package handling facility in the world. Worldport measures 5.2 million square feet and serves more than 300 inbound and outbound flights daily and processes about 2 million packages per day. UPS owns and operates more than 250 large distribution centers globally. As showcased on the corporate website, UPS is moving rapidly to achieve carbon neutrality by 2050, including by 2025 to use 40 percent alternative fuel in its ground operations and 25 percent renewable electricity in its facilities.

UPS's Q3 2021 revenues were $23.2 billion, up 9.2 percent from the prior year and operating profits were $2.9 billion, up 22.6 percent. More specifically for Q3 2021, UPS's domestic revenues were $14.2 billion up 7.4 percent, and the company's international revenues were $4.72 billion, up 15.5 percent. The company also has a Supply Chain Solutions segment and Q3 2021 revenues were $4.26 billion, up 8.4 percent compared to the prior year.

DHL

Headquartered in Bonn, Germany, and owned by German logistics firm Deutsche Post, DHL is an international courier, package delivery, and express mail service that delivers more than

2 billion parcels per year. On January 1, 2022, DHL raised its rates for customers in the US by an average of 5.9 percent. DHL recently relocated its hub operations from Bergamo to Milan Malpensa Airport where the company has opened new logistics facilities.

DHL is well known for its yellow with red writing mail-delivery trucks and vans that go everywhere in Germany and almost everywhere in Europe. DHL's parent company, Deutsche Post AG is one of the world's largest courier companies. Deutsche Post generates more than $70 billion euros of revenue annually and is Europe's largest postal service transportation company.

External Issues

According to IBISWorld (https://my-ibisworld-com.fmarion.idm.oclc.org/us/en/industry/48-49/industry-at-a-glance), revenue in the mail and package transportation industry is expected to increase 4.2 percent annually to nearly $1.6 trillion over the next 5 years to 2026. Spurring this advance is increased consumer spending, manufacturing output, and trade. The US Postal Service (USPS) has a monopoly on the postal service industry (*IBISWorld Report 49111*), whereas United Parcel Service (UPS) and FedEx dominate the Courier and Local Delivery Services industry (*IBISWorld Report 49222*).

In the mail and package transportation industry, wages account for an estimated 28.5 percent of sector revenue in 2021, up from 26.8 percent in 2016. This industry is labor-intensive, and minimum wage rates are increasing nationally. Employees are needed to drive trucks, vans, and airplanes and to provide customer service, maintain equipment, and inspect and handle packages and cargo. The wages' share of overall expenses has slowly risen due to an increase in the number of employees. Companies such as FedEx are investing more in labor-saving technologies to manage this expense. They and UPS also increasingly hire independent contractors to control labor costs and carry out services when they themselves lack capacity.

Purchases of fuel and services account for almost 16 percent of revenue in the mail and package transportation industry. Fuel is crucial to the sector because it is needed to run cars, trucks, aircraft, trains, and ships. When oil prices rise, the price of fuel follows and industry purchases increase. Trucks deliver packages almost anywhere, and planes have the advantage of being the fastest mode of transport, despite being most expensive. Although historically volatile, the world price of crude oil is anticipated to rise over the next 5 years, which will likely boost fuel prices and sector fuel surcharge revenue. This is a reason, coupled with concern for global warming and carbon dioxide emissions, that FedEx and UPS are rapidly moving to utilization of all-electric delivery vehicles.

The increasing use of email and online services has hurt the mail and package transportation industry. FedEx, UPS, DHL, and TNT compete on price, speed, coverage, scope, and the reputation of achieving all these factors consistently. Up and down the value chain in this industry, there is competition between the various modes of transportation and various levels of competition within subsectors. However, price is the most important factor of competition. Companies that offer the lowest price often win because many customers only care that they receive the good or that it arrives at a location at a particular time.

Conclusion

Frederick Smith, Chairman and CEO of FedEx, has asked you to prepare a comprehensive 3-year strategic plan for his company. Smith is aware of the basic external and internal factors that impact his company, but he is unsure of the relative importance of various factors and the subsequent relative attractiveness of various alternative strategies. FedEx is performing admirably, but no firm has sufficient money or people to implement all strategies that could benefit the firm.

Based on your analysis of FedEx's external and internal situation, develop excellent alternative strategies for the company to pursue, and use QSPM analysis to help narrow down those options to "must do" recommendations for the future. You see in this case that FedEx has historically used acquisitions as its primary strategy to achieve 10+ annual percent growth in its Revenues and Net Income. What firm's globally do you believe FedEx should consider acquiring to expand its footprint further around the world?

Note on the FedEx balance sheets the company has more than $20 billion in long-term-debt but only $2.7 billion in paid-in-capital. How do you believe the company should finance its operations and acquisitions moving forward? Perform an EPS-EBIT analysis to determine the best mix of stock versus debt moving forward for the company to use. Also develop projected financial statements to reveal the expected impact of your proposed strategic plan for Smith.

References

1. https://www.fedex.com/en-us/about/history.html
2. FedEx 2021 *Form 10K*.
3. https://www.comparably.com/companies/fedex/competitors
4. https://my-ibisworld-com.fmarion.idm.oclc.org/us/en/industry/48-49/industry-at-a-glance
5. https://www.fedex.com/content/dam/fedex/us-united-states/sustainability/gcrs/ FedEx_2021_ESG_Report.pdf
6. https://www.fedex.com/en-us/about/leadership/brie-carere.html

Caterpillar, Inc., 2022

www.caterpillar.com, (NYSE: CAT)

Headquartered in Deerfield, Illinois, Caterpillar Inc. is the world's largest manufacturer of construction and mining equipment, diesel and natural gas engines, industrial gas turbines, and diesel-electric locomotives. In 2021, Caterpillar's revenue reached $51 billion, up 22 percent from $41.7 billion in 2020. The company's operating profit margin in 2021 was 13.5 percent, up from 10.9 percent the prior year.

Caterpillar machinery is distributed through a worldwide network of about 160 dealers (46 are in the US), which provide sales, rental, service, and aftermarket support to customers in more than 190 countries. About 60 percent of Caterpillar's revenue is generated outside of the US, mainly in Europe, Africa, and the Middle East (EAME) (25%) and in Asia/Pacific (25%). Caterpillar's number of full-time employees at year-end 2021 were 44,300 inside the US and 66,400 outside the US, compared to the prior year total of 40,300 and 57,000. The area with the largest percentage growth in number of employees in 2021 was Latin America going from 15,900 to 19,500, whereas EAME reported a slight decline in total number of employees in 2021.

Caterpillar Inc. has a strong customer base, a well-diversified brand portfolio, and a well-built production and distribution network. Caterpillar's core competencies include safety, quality, lean manufacturing and product development and having a competitive and flexible cost structure. In 2021 the company experienced strong end-user demand, and this is expected to continue into 2022. The company also expects profits margins to improve throughout 2022 as prices are increased to offset increases in manufacturing costs.

In January 2022, Caterpillar announced that Union Pacific Railroad (UPR) is purchasing 10 battery-electric locomotives from Progress Rail, a division of Caterpillar. The purchase is part of the largest investment in battery-electric technology by a large US railroad. Caterpillar builds EMD Joule electric locomotives that do not use fuel and emit zero exhaust emissions. UPR tested in rail yards in California and Nebraska, helping identify the locomotives' capabilities and challenges for broader deployment. UPR has a goal to reach net zero emissions by 2050. The new Cat locomotives are being manufactured in Muncie, Indiana, with the first units arriving to UPR in late 2023 and complete delivery anticipated in early 2024.

Copyright by Fred David Books LLC; written by Meredith E. David.

History

Founded in 1925 as Caterpillar Tractor Company, Caterpillar was reorganized in 1986 as Caterpillar Inc. For nearly a century, Caterpillar has offered products aimed at helping make the world a better place to live, including providing machines that built the Panama Canal and have protected more 11,000 miles of the world's greatest rivers. In 2020, Caterpillar launched a new mine management technology called MineStar Edge, which assesses, analyzes, and enhances an entire mining operation. In 2021, the company introduced a modified rotatory mixer called the RM400 Rotary Mixer, which provides 19 percent more power than its predecessor.

Caterpillar has made many company acquisitions over the years, including its most recent acquisition of the Oil and Gas Divisions of the Weir Group PLC in 2021 for about $375 million. This acquisition helped Caterpillar expand its offerings in the well service industry. One source of competitive advantage for Caterpillar is its services, and this is a key area of planned growth for the company. Caterpillar's services provide a source of company revenue throughout the lifecycle of Caterpillar products. The company is currently pursuing a goal to increase its Machinery, Energy, and Transportation services sales to $28 billion by 2026, which is double its 2016 baseline level.

Over the past several years, Caterpillar has begun making strategic efforts to increase its diversity, equity, and inclusion efforts (DEI) and to give back to communities in need. In 2021,

Caterpillar released its first *Diversity and Inclusion Report*. This report indicated that as of 2021, about 55 percent of independent directors of the board are women or racially diverse and about 63 percent of the CEO's direct reports are women or people of color.

Internal Issues

Vision/Mission/Core Values

Caterpillar does not provide a published vision or mission statement, but the company's purpose is stated (paraphrased): "Helping customers build a better world." The company strives to "make the planet a safer, more sustainable and better place to live." A possible vision or mission statement for Caterpillar could include the following excerpt (paraphrased) from the company website:

> *We are the global leading producer of construction and mining equipment, diesel and natural gas engines, industrial gas turbines and diesel-electric locomotives. We service all our equipment and use cutting-edge technology and decades of product expertise to help our customers succeed.*

Caterpillar's five key values are Integrity, Excellence (in Product and Service Quality), Teamwork, Commitment, and Sustainability. Caterpillar's code of conduct emphasizes how the company's values play out in everyday operations.

Segments

Caterpillar has five operating segments but operates principally through three main segments: Energy and Transportation, which comprises about 40 percent of sales; Construction Industries, which comprise more than 35 percent of sales; and Resource Industries, which comprise more than 15 percent of sales.

The Construction Industries segment manufacturers machinery such as asphalt pavers, backhoe loaders, excavators, earthmoving, building construction products, and pipelayers used by customers in infrastructure, forestry, and building construction. This segment includes the company's China Operations, Global Construction & Infrastructure, and Construction Industries Services divisions, as well as the Global Rental and Used Equipment Services group.

The company's Resource Industries segment manufactures and sells machinery for customers in mining, quarry, waste, and material handling. It also develops and sells technology products and services for customers' fleet management systems, equipment management analytics, and autonomous machine capabilities. Example products manufactured in this segment include hydraulic shovels, rotary drills, mining trucks, wheel dozers, landfill, and soil compactors. This segment includes the company's Integrated Components and Solutions Division, RI Operations and Products Division, Strategic Procurement and Planning Division and the RI Sales, and Services and Technology Division.

The Energy and Transportation segment of Caterpillar manufactures and sells products for customers in power generation, industrial, oil and gas, marine, rail, and industrial applications. Products include reciprocating engines, powered generator sets, turbines, diesel-electric locomotives and components, marine propulsion systems, and other transportation-related products, component parts, and services. This segment includes the Rail Division, Solar Turbines, Large Power Systems Division, Industrial Power Systems Division, Caterpillar Remanufacturing Division, Electric Power Division, and Caterpillar Oil and Gas and Marine Division.

The company's Services, Distribution and Digital segment includes these divisions: Americas Distribution, Service and Marketing; Asia Pacific Distribution; Europe Africa Middle East Eurasia; and Cat Digital and Product Support and Logistics. Exhibit 1 provides a breakdown of Caterpillar's recent revenues by segment. Note the 31 percent increase in Construction revenues in 2021, and the overall excellent Caterpillar performance.

Caterpillar reports revenues and operating income by region, as revealed in Exhibit 2. Note that most of the company business is done in North America and note the highest growth area was Latin America.

Organizational Structure

Caterpillar's top executives are listed and pictured nicely on the corporate website; these executives are arrayed in Exhibit 3. Note that the company operates using a strategic business unit (SBU) design as indicated by the group presidents. There are by-product divisional top persons

EXHIBIT 1 Caterpillar's Recent Revenues by Segment (in millions of dollars)

	2020	2021	Percentage Change
Construction Industries	$16,918	$22,106	31
Resource Industries	7,906	9,963	28
Energy & Transportation	17,470	20,287	16
Other	467	531	09
Corporate	(3,739)	(4,679)	-
Machinery, Energy & Transportation	39,022	48,188	23
Financial Products Segment	3,044	3,073	01
Corporate	(318)	(290)	-
Financial Services Revenues	2,726	2,783	02
Total	$41,748	$50,971	22

Source: Caterpillar's 2021 *Form 10K*, p. 30.

EXHIBIT 2 Caterpillar's Revenues and Operating Profit by Region (in Millions)

	2020	2021	Percent Change
	Revenues		
North America	$18,214	$22,023	21
Europe, Africa & Middle East	9,858	12,137	23
Asia/Pacific	10,244	11,725	14
Latin America	3,432	5,086	48
Total	$41,748	$50,971	22

Source: Based on Caterpillar's 2021 *Form 10K*, p. 30.

reporting to these group presidents. There is currently no COO position but likely there needs to be for the group presidents to report to in the array given in Exhibit 3.

EXHIBIT 3 Caterpillar's Top Executives Listed and Arrayed

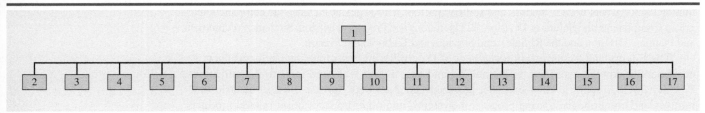

1. James Umpleby III, Chairman and CEO
2. Andrew Bonfield, CFO
3. Michael Marvel, Chief Accounting Officer
4. Karl Weiss, CTO and VP of Integrated Components and Solutions Division
5. Jamie Engstrom, CIO and VP of Global Information Services Division
6. Jennifer Driscoll, Director of Investor Relations
7. Eric Braun, Chief Compliance Officer
8. Cheryl Johnson, Chief Human Resources Officer
9. Suzette Long, Chief Legal Officer and General Counsel
10. Mathew Jones, Chief Audit Officer
11. Julie Lagacy, SVP of Enterprise Strategy Division and Chief Sustainability and Strategy Officer
12. Penny Naas, President of International Public Affairs and Sustainability
13. Ognjen Redzic, Chief Digital Officer and VP of Cat Digital Division
14. Joseph Creed, Group President of Energy and Transportation Segment
15. Bob De Lange, Group President of Services, Distribution and Digital
16. Anthony Fassino, Group President of Construction Industries Group
17. Denise Johnson, Group President of Resource Industries

Source: Based on https://www.caterpillar.com/en/company/governance/officers.html

Finance

Caterpillar's 2021 revenues were $51 billion, up 22 percent compared with $41.7 billion in 2020. There was higher end-user demand for equipment and services, and despite dealers having decreased their inventories $2.9 billion in 2020, these numbers remained flat in 2021. The company's 2021 operating profit margin was 13.5 percent, up from 10.9 percent in 2020. The company's recent income statements and balance sheets are provided in Exhibit 4 and Exhibit 5, respectively.

EXHIBIT 4 Caterpillar's Recent Income Statements (in Millions)

Income Statement	12/31/20	12/31/21		Percentage Change
Revenues	$41,748	$50,971	⇧	22%
Cost of Goods Sold	29,082	35,513	⇧	22%
Gross Profit	12,666	15,458	⇧	22%
Operating Expenses	8,113	8,580	⇧	6%
EBIT	4,553	6,878	⇧	51%
Interest Expense	558	(1,326)	⇩	−338%
EBT	3,995	8,204	⇧	105%
Tax	1,006	1,742	⇧	73%
Nonrecurring Events	14	31	⇧	121%
Net Income	$3,003	$6,493	⇧	116%

Source: Caterpillar's 4Q 2021 Earnings Release, p. 16.

EXHIBIT 5 Caterpillar's Recent Balance Sheets (in Millions)

Balance Sheet	12/31/20	12/31/21		Percentage Change
Assets				
Cash and Short-Term Investments	$9,352	$9,254	⇩	−1%
Accounts Receivable	16,780	17,375	⇧	4%
Inventory	11,402	14,038	⇧	23%
Other Current Assets	1,930	2,788	⇧	44%
Total Current Assets	39,464	43,455	⇧	10%
Property Plant & Equipment	12,401	12,090	⇩	−3%
Goodwill	6,394	6,324	⇩	−1%
Intangibles	1,308	1,042	⇩	−20%
Other Long-Term Assets	18,757	19,882	⇧	6%
Total Assets	**78,324**	**82,793**	⇧	**6%**
Liabilities				
Accounts Payable	6,128	8,154	⇧	33%
Other Current Liabilities	19,589	21,693	⇧	11%
Total Current Liabilities	25,717	29,847	⇧	16%
Long-Term Debt	25,999	26,033	⇧	0%
Other Long-Term Liabilities	11,230	10,397	⇩	−7%
Total Liabilities	**62,946**	**66,277**	⇧	**5%**
Equity				
Common Stock	6,230	6,398	⇧	3%
Retained Earnings	35,167	39,282	⇧	12%
Treasury Stock	(25,178)	(27,643)	⇧	10%
Paid in Capital & Other	(841)	(1,521)	⇧	81%
Total Equity	**15,378**	**16,516**	⇧	**7%**
Total Liabilities and Equity	**$78,324**	**$82,793**	⇧	**6%**

Source: Caterpillar's 4Q 2021 Earnings Release, p. 17.

Competitors

Caterpillar's competitors include Komatsu, Alamo Group, Deere & Company, Columbus McKinnon, Dresser-Rand, and Astec Industries (ASTE). Dresser-Rand is a private company. A recent study compared Caterpillar with four of its competitors and reported the findings provided in Exhibit 6. Note that Caterpillar ranks the best on three variables as indicated by the number-one rankings along the row, but the company is weak on CEO Effectiveness and Employees Recommending the Company. Caterpillar ranks next to last overall, as indicated by the summed score of 33. Caterpillar was ranked especially weak on Effectiveness of CEO and Overall Culture. The analysis reveals that Caterpillar's number-one competitor is John Deere, which overall scored better in Exhibit 6 as indicated in Column 10 by the lowest summed score.

EXHIBIT 6 Comparing Caterpillar Versus Rival Firms (Ranking 1 = Best; 6 = Worst)

	Variables									
	1	2	3	4	5	6	7	8	9	10
Caterpillar (CAT)	4	1	1	2	1	3	4	2	2	20
John Deere (DE)	3	2	2	1	2	2	2	1	1	16
Dresser-Rand	2	5	4	5	4	5	1	-	-	26+
Alamo Group (ALG)	3	3	3	3	3	1	3	-	-	19+
Columbus McKinnon (CMCO)	5	4	-	4	5	4	5	1	-	28+

Variables

1. Effectiveness of CEO
2. Product Quality
3. Do Customers Recommend Company Products to Friends?
4. Pricing
5. Customer Service
6. Overall Culture
7. Do Employees Recommend Company Products to Friends?
8. How Happy Are the Women Employees at the Firm?
9. How Happy Are Minority Employees at the Firm?
10. Summed Score (lower sum the better)

Source: Based on https://www.comparably.com/companies/caterpillar/competitors

Exhibit 7 provides a comparison of Caterpillar with several of its rival companies. Note that Caterpillar and Deere & Company are about the same size and perform in a similar manner.

As governments escalate their initiatives to decarbonize environments and economies, many companies are making fuel technology breakthroughs in new machinery and are switching their focus from diesel to alternative fuels in efforts to reach net-zero emissions.

EXHIBIT 7 Caterpillar's Rival Firms Compared Financially

	Caterpillar (CAT)	Deere & Co. (DE)	Alamo Group (ALG)	Columbus McK (CMCO)
Market Capitalization	$108 billion	$115 billion	$1.6 billion	$1.3 billion
EPS	$12	$19	$2.67	$1.00
Revenue	$51 billion	$44 billion	$1.3 billion	$840 million
Net Income	$6.5 billion	$6 billion	$69 million	$27 million
Total Debt	$38 billion	$49 billion	$311 million	$566 million
Total Debt/Equity	229	265	45	76
Current Ratio	1.46	2.19	3.25	1.91
# Full-time Employees	97,000	76,000	4,000	2,650
Stock Price	$200	$371	$136	$45

Source: Based on https://finance.yahoo.com/quote/CAT?p=CAT&.tsrc=fin-srch

Deere & Company (DE)

Headquartered in Moline, Illinois, and founded in 1837, Deere manufactures and distributes heavy and small equipment globally. The company's well-known brand name is John Deere. Deere is organized into four divisions: Production and Precision Agriculture, Small Agriculture and Turf, Construction and Forestry, and Financial Services. The Production and Precision Agriculture segment produces tractors, combines, cotton pickers and strippers, sugarcane harvesters, harvesting front-end equipment, sugarcane loaders, pull-behind scrapers, tillage and seeding equipment, sprayers, and grain growers. The Small Agriculture and Turf segment produces tractors, turf and utility equipment, riding lawn equipment, commercial mowing equipment, golf course equipment, and vehicles for mowing, tilling, snow and debris handling, aerating, residential, commercial, golf, sports turf care applications, and hay and forage equipment.

Deere's Construction and Forestry segment manufacturers and markets backhoe loaders, crawler dozers and loaders, four-wheel-drive loaders, excavators, motor graders, articulated dump trucks, landscape and skid-steer loaders, milling machines, pavers, compactors, rollers, crushers, screens, asphalt plants, log skidders, log feller bunchers, log loaders and forwarders, log harvesters, and attachments; and roadbuilding equipment. Deere's Financial Services segment finances sales and leases agriculture and dealer inventory for almost all its products.

In January 2022, Deere was sued by Forest River Farms in Forest River, North Dakota, regarding the right for farmers to repair Deere equipment.

External Issues

Caterpillar competes in the global construction equipment industry. Exhibit 8 reveals the global construction equipment market size from 2020 to 2025. Note the steady increase, which bodes well for Caterpillar. Note in Exhibit 9 that Caterpillar dominates the global market share chart.

EXHIBIT 8 The Global Construction Equipment Market Size, 2020 to 2025 (in Billion US Dollars)

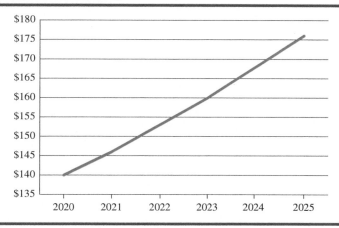

Source: Based on the 360researchreports.com, March 2021.

Conclusion

CEO James Umpleby at Caterpillar needs a clear strategic plan because his company faces fierce competitors, especially Deere & Company. Umpleby knows the basic underlying external opportunities and threats facing Caterpillar, as well as the basic internal strengths and weaknesses, but he needs to know the relative importance of those factors. He also needs to know the relative attractiveness of alternative strategies to be derived from those underlying external and internal factors. In other words, Umpleby needs strategy analyses performed, including IFEM, EFEM, SWOT, IE Matrix, perceptual mapping, EPS-EBIT analysis, and projected financial statement analysis.

Let's say that Umpleby hires you to develop a comprehensive strategic plan for Caterpillar. Begin with developing an effective vision and mission statement, which as you see in the case,

EXHIBIT 9 Construction Equipment Manufacturers' Global Market Share in 2020

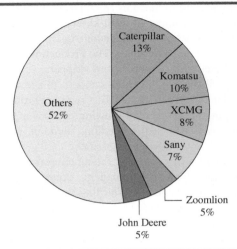

Source: Based on *International Construction*, May 2021, p. 28.

the company needs assistance on in this area. Also include a new, improved organizational chart, which the case also reveals the company needs assistance on improving. Perform the analysis that is requested, develop some recommendations with associated costs, and present your findings and research to your professor and fellow students.

How can Caterpillar adapt to an ever-changing world? Should Caterpillar expand more aggressively internationally? Which of the company's segments should be substantially invested in going forward, and which segment(s) should perhaps be divested? What does Caterpillar need to do in the next 3 years to effectively differentiate itself from rivals and ultimately adapt to be a profitable company over the next three decades?

References

1. www.caterpillar.com
2. Caterpillar's 2021 *Form 10K*.
3. https://www.caterpillar.com/en/company/governance/officers.html
4. https://finance.yahoo.com/quote/CAT?p=CAT&.tsrc=fin-srch
5. 360researchreports.com, March 2021.
6. *International Construction*, May 2021, p. 28.

Chevron Corporation, 2022

www.chevron.com, (NYSE: CVX)

Headquartered in San Ramon, California, Chevron is the number 2 integrated oil company in the US, behind Exxon Mobil; about 45 percent of the company's revenues are generated within the US. Chevron has 13,000 gas stations across the globe, with about 60 percent of them located in the US. Chevron is a vertically integrated oil and gas company that engages in global energy and chemical operations throughout the value chain, including exploring for and producing oil, transporting crude oil and natural gas, and refining and marketing oil and oil equivalents for sale to airlines, heavy industry firms, utility companies, and automobile-driving consumers through fuel stations and industrial channels under the Chevron, Texaco, and Caltex brands.

Active in more than 180 countries, Chevron is organized into two main segments: 1) Downstream and 2) Upstream operations. Downstream operations account for more than 75 percent of the company's revenue and include crude oil refining, transporting, and marketing of oil and refined products and making fuel and lubricant additives and commodity petrochemicals, as well as plastics for industrial needs. Upstream operations account for about 25 percent of revenue and include exploring for, producing, liquefying, and transporting crude oil and natural gas; about 75 percent of the revenue from the upstream operations comes from sources outside of the US.

To give you an idea of the extent of Chevron's operations, the percentage of involvement of the company in a few major projects are:

1. 50 percent equity ownership interest in Tengizchevroil (TCO), which operates the Tengiz and Korolev crude oil fields in Kazakhstan.
2. 30 percent interest in Petropiar, a joint stock company, which operates the heavy oil Huyapari Field and upgrading project in Venezuela's Orinoco Belt.
3. 39.2 percent interest in Petroboscan, a joint stock company, which operates the Boscan Field in Venezuela.
4. 15 percent interest in the Caspian Pipeline Consortium, which provides the critical export route for crude oil from both TCO and Karachaganak.
5. 36.4 percent interest in Angola LNG Limited, which processes and liquefies natural gas produced in Angola for delivery to international markets.
6. Noble Midstream, a fully consolidated subsidiary of Chevron, has equity investments in entities, which operate midstream assets in the US, including Advantage Pipeline LLC (50 percent), Delaware Crossing LLC (50 percent), EPIC Crude Holdings (30 percent), EPIC Y-Grade (15 percent), EPIC Propane (15 percent), and Saddlehorn Pipeline Co., LLC (20 percent).
7. 50 percent of Chevron Phillips Chemical Co. LLC. The other half is owned by Phillips 66.
8. 50 percent of GS Caltex Corp., a joint venture with GS Energy in South Korea that imports, refines, and markets petroleum products, petrochemicals, and lubricants.

Copyright by Fred David Books LLC; written by Meredith E. David.

History

A predecessor of Chevron, a business named Star Oil, discovered oil near Los Angeles in 1876. The 25 barrels of oil per day well marked the discovery of the Newhall Field. Star Oil's founders helped establish the oil industry in California. Chevron traces its beginning way back to 1879 when the company was originally founded under the name Pacific Coast Oil Company.

The company that eventually became Chevron originally was part of Standard Oil, but in 1911, the federal government broke Standard Oil into several pieces under the Sherman Antitrust Act. One of those pieces, Standard Oil Co. California eventually became Chevron. The Chevron name came into use for various retail products in the 1930s. Today, Chevron owns the Standard Oil trademark in 16 states in the western and southeastern United States.

In 2020 during the pandemic, Chevron considered a merger with rival ExxonMobil; that deal never happened but would have been one of the biggest corporate mergers in history. A combined Chevron and ExxonMobil would have been the second-largest oil company in the world. In 2021, Chevron began requiring some employees, namely expatriate employees, those working overseas, and workers on US-flagged ships, to receive COVID-19 vaccinations after having some outbreaks on offshore platforms in the Gulf of Mexico and Permian Basin.

In January 2022, Chevron decreased production in Kazakhstan's Tengiz Field due to protests that were motivated by heavy oil price increases. Also that month, Chevron ended all operations in Myanmar due to severe human rights abuses and deteriorating rule of law.

For Q1 2022 that ended 3-31-22, Chevron reported earnings of $6.3 billion, compared with $1.4 billion in Q1 2021. The company's revenues in Q1 2022 were $52 billion, compared to $31 billion in the year-ago period; their debt ratio and net debt ratio declined to 16.7 and 10.8 percent, respectively. The company's capital expenditures during Q1 2022 increased to $2.8 billion, 10 percent higher than the prior year. The total of full-year capital spending and announced acquisitions is expected to be more than 50 percent higher than 2021. All these results are quite positive for Chevron. Chevron's capital and exploratory expenditures during Q1 2022 were $2.8 billion, compared with $2.5 billion in 2021. Expenditures for upstream represented 88 percent of the company-wide total in 2022. Chevron is performing really well at the moment but many rival companies compete aggressively in the industry and the world is trying to transition away from oil and gas, so weaknesses and threats abound that should be considered in a comprehensive strategic plan.

Internal Issues

VIsion/Mission

Chevron's vision and mission statements are provided on the corporate website as indicated in Exhibit 1. Note that neither statement adheres well to the guidelines given in Chapter 1.

EXHIBIT 1 Chevron's Vision and Mission Statements

Vision: "*to be the global energy company most admired for its people, partnership and performance.*"

Mission: "*to develop the affordable, reliable, ever-cleaner energy that enables human progress.*"

Source: Based on https://www.chevron.com/about/the-chevron-way

Organizational Structure

Chevron's top executives are listed and arrayed in Exhibit 2. Note there is no COO, so basically all the top executives report to the CEO. There are as you see four group segment top persons, shown as numbers 15, 16, 17, and 18. These are likely group top persons with probably regional top persons reporting to them. Chevron should probably add a COO for these four group top persons to report to.

EXHIBIT 2 Chevron's Top Executives Listed and Arrayed

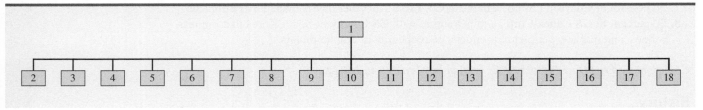

1. Michael K. Wirth, Chairman of the Board and CEO
2. Eimear P. Bonner, VP, Chief Technology Officer
3. Pierre R. Breber, VP and CFO
4. Mary A. Francis, Corporate Secretary and Chief Governance Officer
5. Rhonda J. Morris, VP and Chief Human Resources Officer
6. Marissa Badenhorst, VP, Health, Safety and Environment
7. Jeff B. Gustavson, VP, Lower Carbon Energies
8. David A. Inchausti, VP and Controller
9. Paul R. Antebi, VP and General Tax Counsel
10. Navin K. Mahajan, VP and Treasurer
11. Bruce L. Niemeyer, VP, Strategy and Sustainability
12. R. Hewitt Pate, VP and General Counsel
13. Jay R. Pryor, VP, Business Development
14. Albert (Al) Williams, VP, Corporate Affairs
15. Joseph C. Geagea, EVP of Technology, Projects and Services (TPS)
16. James W. Johnson, EVP, Upstream
17. Mark A. Nelson, EVP, Downstream and Chemicals
18. Colin Parfitt, VP, Midstream

Source: Based on https://www.chevron.com/about/leadership

Structure Update

In October 2022, Chevron changed it organizational structure significantly as described at https://www.chevron.com/investors/press-releases. Specifically, the company consolidated its Upstream, Midstream and Downstream business segments under a new EVP, Oil, Products & Gas, who now oversees the full value chain. A part of this change included Chevron consolidating into two Upstream regions – Americas Exploration & Production and International Exploration & Production. Also with the change, Chevron reorganized its Strategy & Sustainability, Corporate Affairs and Business Development functions under a new EVP, Strategy, Policy & Development. The structural changes were accompanied by the following new personnel appointments:

- Mark Nelson was named EVP, Strategy, Policy & Development
- Nigel Hearne was named EVP, Oil, Products & Gas
- Clay Neff was named President, International Exploration & Production
- Bruce Niemeyer was named President, Americas Exploration & Production
- Balaji Krishnamurthy was named VP, Chevron Strategy & Sustainability

Segments

The upstream part of the oil and gas industry is focused largely on getting hydrocarbons, crude oil and natural gas, mostly, out of the ground. Downstream is the end of the value chain and involves the selling of gasoline for cars, diesel fuel for trucks and boats and ships, and jet fuel for airliners.

Upstream

In Chevron's Upstream business, the 2020 acquisition of Noble Energy added assets in Texas's Permian Basin, Colorado's DJ Basin, and the Eastern Mediterranean. In 2020 alone, the company added about 5.67 million net exploration acres and 832 million barrels of net oil-equivalent proved reserves.

In Q1 2022, Chevron's worldwide net oil-equivalent production was 3.06 million barrels per day; the company's international production decreased 8 percent, but its US production increased 10 percent compared to the same period a year ago. Specifically, Chevron's US upstream operations earned $3.24 billion in Q1 2022, compared with $941 million a year earlier. The company's average sales price per barrel of crude oil and natural gas liquids was $77 in Q1 2022, up from $48 a year earlier, while the average sales price of natural gas was $4.10 per thousand cubic feet, up from $2.15 in Q1 the prior year. The company's net oil-equivalent production of 1.18 million barrels per day in Q1 2022 was up 109,000 barrels per day from the prior year, while the company's net natural gas production increased 11 percent to 1.83 billion cubic feet per day, compared to the prior year's first quarter.

In Q1 2022, Chevron's international upstream operations earned $3.70 billion, compared with $1.41 billion a year ago; the average sales price for crude oil and natural gas liquids in Q1 2022 was $93 per barrel, up from $56 the prior year; the average sales price of natural gas was $8.87 per thousand cubic feet in Q1, up from $4.72 in Q1 the prior year. However, Chevron's international upstream net oil-equivalent production of 1.88 million barrels per day in Q1 2022 was down 170,000 barrels per day from first quarter 2021, primarily due to expiration of the Rokan concession in Indonesia. The company's net liquids component of oil-equivalent production decreased 16 percent to 856,000 barrels per day in first quarter 2022, while net natural gas production of 6.12 billion cubic feet per day was largely unchanged compared to Q1 2021.

Downstream

Chevron's US downstream operations in Q1 2022 reported earnings of $486 million, compared with a loss of $130 million a year earlier. The increase was mainly due to higher earnings from the 50 percent-owned Chevron Phillips Chemical Company. The company's refinery crude oil input in Q1 2022 increased 4 percent to 915,000 barrels per day from the year-ago period, while refined product sales of 1.22 million barrels per day were up 16 percent from the year-ago period, mainly due to higher gasoline and jet fuel demand.

Chevron's International downstream operations reported a loss of $155 million in Q1 2022, compared with earnings of $135 million a year earlier. However, refinery crude oil input of 619,000 barrels per day internationally in Q1 2022 increased 15 percent from the year-ago period due to higher demand. Refined product sales of 1.33 million barrels per day in Q1 2022 increased 5 percent from the year-ago period.

In Chevron's Downstream business, their 2020 acquisition of Puma Energy (Australia) Holdings Pty Ltd., added a network of more than 360 company- and retailer-owned service stations, a commercial and industrial fuels business, and owned and leased seaboard import terminals and fuel distribution depots. Also in 2020, the company made excellent progress on GS Caltex's olefins mixed-feed cracker project at the Yeosu Refinery in South Korea.

Exhibit 3 provides Chevron's revenue breakdown by segment, followed by Exhibit 4 that provides similar data for the company's reported earnings. Note the dramatic increases in 2021 compared to Covid-19 2020.

EXHIBIT 3 **Chevron's Segment Revenues (in Millions $)**

Upstream		2020	2021
	US	14,577	29,219
	International	26,804	40,921
	Other	(15,070)	(26,148)
	Total	26,311	43,992
Downstream			
	US	32,589	57,209
	International	38,936	58,098
	Other	(3,442)	(3,817)
	Total	68,083	111,490
Other		77	124
Total Sales		94,471	155,606

Source: Based on Chevron's 2021 *Form 10K*, p. 76.

EXHIBIT 4 **Chevron's Segment Earnings (in Millions $)**

Upstream		2020	2021
	US	(1,608)	7,319
	International	(825)	8,499
	Total	(2,433)	15,818
Downstream			
	US	(571)	2,389
	International	618	525
	Total	47	2,914
Total of All		(2,386)	18,732
Other		(3,157)	(3,107)
Net Income (Loss)		(5,543)	15,625

Source: Based on Chevron's 2021 *Form 10K*, p. 32.

Exhibit 5 gives Chevron's sales by product in 2021.

EXHIBIT 5 **Chevron's Sales Volume of Refined Products Across Regions (Thousands of Barrels per Day) in 2021**

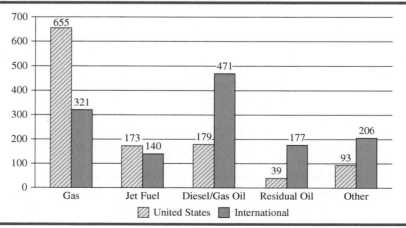

Source: Based on Chevron's 2021 *Form 10K*, p. 17.

Finances

Chevron's recent income statements and balance sheets are provided in Exhibit 6 and Exhibit 7, respectively. Note the huge increases in both revenues and net income.

EXHIBIT 6 Chevron's Recent Income Statements (in Millions $)

Income Statement	12/31/20	12/31/21		Percentage Change
Revenue (sales)	$94,692	$162,465	⬆	72%
Cost of Goods Sold	50,488	89,372	⬆	77%
Gross Profit	44,204	73,093	⬆	65%
Operating Expenses	50,960	50,742	⬇	0%
EBIT (operating Income)	(6,756)	22,351	—	—
Interest Expense	697	712	⬆	2%
EBT	(7,453)	21,639	—	—
Tax	(1,892)	5,950	—	—
Nonrecurring Events	18	(64)	⬇	–456%
Net Income	($5,543)	$15,625	—	—

Source: Based on Chevron's 2021 *Form 10K*, p. 58.

EXHIBIT 7 Chevron's Recent Balance Sheets (in Millions $)

Balance Sheet	12/31/20	12/31/21		Percentage Change
Assets				
Cash and Short-Term Investments	$5,596	$5,640	⬆	1%
Accounts Receivable	11,471	18,419	⬆	61%
Inventory	5,676	6,305	⬆	11%
Other Current Assets	3,335	3,374	⬆	1%
Total Current Assets	26,078	33,738	⬆	29%
Property Plant & Equipment	156,618	146,961	⬇	–6%
Goodwill	4,402	4,385	⬇	0%
Intangibles	0	0	—	—
Other Long-Term Assets	52,692	54,451	⬆	3%
Total Assets	239,790	239,535	⬇	0%
Liabilities				
Accounts Payable	10,950	16,454	⬆	50%
Other Current Liabilities	11,233	10,337	⬇	–8%
Total Current Liabilities	22,183	26,791	⬆	21%
Long-Term Debt	42,767	31,113	⬇	–27%
Other Long-Term Liabilities	42,114	41,691	⬇	–1%
Total Liabilities	107,064	99,595	⬇	–7%
Equity				
Common Stock	1,832	1,832	⬇	0%
Retained Earnings	160,377	165,546	⬆	3%
Treasury Stock	(41,498)	(41,464)	—	—
Paid in Capital & Other	12,015	14,026	⬆	17%
Total Equity	132,726	139,940	⬆	5%
Total Liabilities and Equity	$239,790	$239,535	⬇	0%

Source: Based on Chevron's 2021 *Form 10K*, p. 60.

EXHIBIT 8 Chevron's Earnings in Billions$

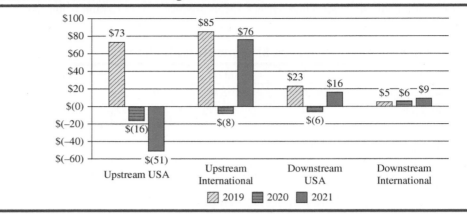

Source: Based on Chevron's 2021 *Form 10K*, p. 32.

Exhibit 8 illustrates Chevron's earnings for the last few years.

Competitors

Chevron's competitors include Phillips 66, ConocoPhillips, British Petroleum (BP), EOG Resources, Exxon-Mobil, Shell plc, and Koch Industries. A recent study compared Chevron with four of its competitors on nine management and marketing variables and reported the findings provided in Exhibit 9. Note that Chevron ranked badly on Pricing and Customer Service. The analysis reveals that Chevron's #1 competitor is Koch Industries that was ranked #1 in six of the nine categories.

EXHIBIT 9 Comparing Chevron Versus Rival Firms (Ranking 1 = Best; 6 = Worst)

	Variables									
	1	2	3	4	5	6	7	8	9	10
Chevron Corp.	2	4	3	5	5	2	1	2	2	26
ConocoPhillips	3	5	4	3	2	5	2	5	1	30
British Petroleum	5	3	5	4	3	4	4	4	3	35
Phillips66	4	2	1	2	4	3	5	3	5	29
Koch Industries	1	1	2	1	1	1	3	1	4	15

Variables

1. Effectiveness of CEO
2. Product Quality
3. Do Customers Recommend Company Products to Friends?
4. Pricing
5. Customer Service
6. Overall Culture
7. Do Employees Recommend Company Products to Friends?
8. How Happy are the Women Employees at the Firm?
9. How Happy are Minority Employees at the Firm?
10. Summed Score (lower sum the better)

Source: Based on https://www.comparably.com/companies/chevron-corporation/competitors

Exhibit 10 provides a comparison of Chevron with several of its rival companies. Note that only Exxon-Mobil is larger than Chevron. As governments and companies accelerate their initiatives to decarbonize and eventually reach net zero-emissions, many oil and gas companies are considering varied "renewable" options for the future.

EXHIBIT 10 Chevron's Rival Firms Compared Financially

	Chevron CVX	Exxon-Mobil XOM	ConocoPhillips COP	Shell plc SHEL
Market Capitalization	$263 billion	$335 billion	$121 billion	$206 billion
EPS	$8.14	$5.4	$6.1	$5.14
Revenue	$155 billion	$285 billion	$47 billion	$261 billion
Net Income	$16 billion	$23 billion	$8 billion	$20 billion
Total Debt	$37 billion	$57 billion	$20 billion	$90 billion
Total Debt/Equity	27	34	44	51
Current Ratio	NA	NA	1.34	1.35
Stock Price	$135	$79	$93	$55

Source: Based on https://finance.yahoo.com/quote/CVX?p=CVX&.tsrc=fin-srch

External Issues

In the US energy industry, there are four major industries: upstream, midstream, downstream, and energy services. The upstream segment has the largest share of revenue at 48.5 percent, followed by downstream at 25.6 percent, midstream at 20 percent, and energy services at 5.9 percent. However, in terms of earnings before interest and tax (EBIT) margins, the midstream segment reports the highest margins at 11.7 percent.

The US Energy Information Administration (EIA) projects $70+ crude oil prices in both 2022, according to its outlook published in December 2021. Considering this, in January 2022, the OPEC-Plus consortium agreed to raise their collective production by another 400,000 barrels a day. The European Commission, the executive arm of the EU, has published its aggressive goal to be carbon-neutral by 2050, insisting that fossil fuels be replaced with green energy.

Natural Gas

The EIA has published its forecast that liquid natural gas (LNG) prices to stay relatively flat at $3.94 per btu in 2022, after a dramatic upsurge in 2021, amid rising US LNG production and slowing growth in LNG exports. The International Energy Agency (IEA) reports that demand for LNG dropped 0.4 percent in 2021 and is expected to decline another 0.2 percent in 2022, as more electricity-generation capacity is replaced by renewable energy.

S&P Global Platts reports that the number of LNG pipeline projects will decline in 2022. As per January 2022 data, about 10.7 MMbtu of new natural gas pipeline capacity currently under construction will come online by the end of 2022, followed by an additional 8.9 MMbtu of additional capacity in 2023, and another 11.4 MMbtu in 2024.

Normal in the oil and gas industry, high prices normally lead to more supply and ultimately unravel those high prices. The year 2021, however, was abnormal as high prices were accompanied by continued supply cautiousness. This unusual circumstance is related to the transition to renewables, but fossil fuel demand suggests the transition may take longer to put into effect. For 2022, however, US crude oil supply (which came within a hair of 13 million barrels per day as recently as November 2019, and which stood at 11.5 million barrels per day in October 2021), may struggle to average better than 12 million barrels per day.

Analysts expect revenue growth in among oil and gas companies to slow to about 10 percent in 2022 after an excellent rebound in 2021. High oil prices should persist given expected supply cuts by the OPEC-Plus. As of January 2022, the US EIA global crude oil prices to average $71 per barrel in 2022, while the demand is also expected to exceed 100 million barrels per day by late 2022.

In December 2021, Federal Reserve Chair Jerome Powell indicated that the Fed would accelerate an end of its pandemic-era support, ending its pandemic-era bond purchases in March 2022, and pave the way for three-quarter-percentage-point interest rate hike that occurred in mid-2022. The US economy is expected to near full employment while the pace of inflation gets uncomfortably high.

Conclusion

CEO Michael Wirth needs a clear 3-year strategic plan for Chevron. Intensity of competition and rivalry among firms is accelerating as companies and countries transition to zero emissions. The vision/mission and organizational structure sections of this case reveal that there is substantial room for improvement for Chevron in both areas. Wirth knows the basic underlying external opportunities and threats and internal strengths facing Chevron, but he is unsure about the relative importance of those factors. He thus needs and external and internal assessment performed, anchored by development of an EFE Matrix and IFE Matrix as described in Chapter 3 and Chapter 4 of the David textbook. Wirth also needs to know the relative attractiveness of alternative strategies facing the company, so he needs a SWOT, BCG, and QSPM analyses performed.

During Q1 2022, Chevron announced its intent to acquire Renewable Energy Group, Inc. and Bunge North America, Inc., and announced its intent with Iwatani Corporation of America to build 30 hydrogen fueling stations in California, an investment in Carbon Clean, a global leader in cost-effective industrial carbon capture, and an agreement with Restore the Earth Foundation, Inc. on a carbon offsets reforestation project of up to 8,800 acres in Louisiana.

Let's say Wirth asks you to develop the comprehensive strategic plan that he needs. In addition to the analyses mentioned, include in your report a perceptual map, a set of proposed recommendations with associated costs, and an EPS-EBIT analysis to reveal whether debt or stock or some combination of debt and stock is best to obtain the needed funds. Also include projected financial statements to show the expected impact on Chevron if Wirth adopts your proposed strategic plan. What can Chevron do to help assure top line (revenues) and bottom line (net income) 5+ percent annually in the years to come? Identify candidate firms for Chevron to acquire. If Chevron should expand further organically (internally) into other regions, countries, and continents, include direction for Wirth in this regard.

All of Chevron's top executives, board of directors, shareholders, and employees will benefit from and be thankful for your work developing and proposing a clear roadmap for their future. Good luck on this endeavor. We authors are confident you can do a wonderful job performing this task, following the guidelines presented in the David strategic management textbook and using the strategic planning template provided at www.strategyclub.com.

References

1. https://www.chevron.com/about/the-chevron-way
2. www.chevron.com
3. https://www.chevron.com/about/leadership
4. https://www.comparably.com/companies/chevron-corporation/competitors
5. CFRAEquityResearch_UpstreamandDownstreamEnergy_Jan_27_2022.pdf
6. https://finance.yahoo.com/quote/CVX?p=CVX&.tsrc=fin-srch
7. Chevron's 2021 *Form 10K*.

Tyson Foods, Inc., 2022

www.ir.tyson.com, (NYSE: TSN)

Headquartered in Springdale, Arkansas, Tyson Foods (Tyson) is the world's second-largest processor and marketer of chicken, beef, and pork (behind JBS S.A.). Tyson exports more beef out of the US than any other company. With 137,000 employees and operations in 10 countries serving consumers and customers on five continents, Tyson produces many brand food products, such as Tyson, Jimmy Dean, Hillshire Farm, Ball Park, Wright, Aidellis, Pierre, Bryan, Reuben, Landshire, Russer, SteakEze, Original Philly, and State Fair.

Tyson is the leading protein provider to many national restaurant chains from quick-service to fine dining. Tyson grows, produces, packages, and sells meat products to schools, military bases, hospitals, nursing homes, locally, nationally, and globally. In fact, Tyson is the only company that sells chicken, beef, pork, and prepared foods products through all major retail distribution channels, including club stores, grocery stores, and discount stores.

Tyson's 2021 revenues were $47,049 million, up from $43,185 million the prior year. The company's net income for 2021 was $3,060 million versus $2,071 million the prior year. During fiscal 2021, the company reduced its total debt by about $2 billion.

Copyright by Fred David Books LLC; written by Fred R. David.

History

Tyson Foods was established by John W. Tyson in 1935. Tyson today employs about 145,000 including about 125,000 in the US. Tyson's locations expand across the globe but are concentrated in the Midwest, with 16 locations in Arkansas, 11 in Texas, 9 in Iowa, and the remainder mostly in the eastern US.

In mid-2017, Tyson Foods acquired AdvancePierre Foods to increase the company's portfolio of prepared foods and protein-packed brands. Late in 2018, Tyson acquired Keystone Foods, a leading supplier of meat products to the growing global foodservice industry. Early in 2019, Tyson acquired the Thai and European Operations of BRF S.A., including processing facilities in Thailand, the Netherlands, and the UK.

On June 2, 2021, Tyson's President and CEO Dean Banks stepped down and was replaced by Donnie King, the former COO who graduated from the University of Arkansas at Little Rock and has worked at Tyson for nearly 40 years.

Internal Issues

Vision/Mission

Tyson does not have a written vision or mission statement on the company website, but a purpose statement is given (paraphrased): *We strive to elevate the world's expectations for how much good food can do.*

The website https://www.comparably.com/companies/tyson-foods/mission gives the following vision and mission statements (paraphrased) for Tyson:

Vision: *To be the first choice globally for protein foods while maximizing shareholder value.*

Mission: *We are engaged in growing, processing, packaging, and marketing meat products as we pursue truth and integrity. We strive to create value for our shareholders, customers, employees, and communities.*

Recent Litigation

In recent years, Tyson has been implicated in several litigation cases. In mid-2020, *ProPublica* reported that Tyson had not implemented sufficient safety measures to protect its employees, such as physical distancing, plexiglass barriers, and wearing of face masks. Also about that time, China suspended imports of chicken from the Tyson Berry Street plant in Springdale. In August 2020, nearly 11,000 Tyson workers were confirmed to have COVID-19 (out of a workforce of more than 120,000), and company protocols were litigated.

In March 2019, Tyson issued a recall for 69,000 pounds of chicken strips potentially contaminated with pieces of metal, following six complaints and three alleged oral injuries. A recall for nearly 12 million pounds of chicken strips was issued in May 2019. In June 2019, Tyson recalled more than 190,000 pounds of chicken fritters which potentially contained hard plastic following reports from three consumers. In July 2021, Tyson recalled almost 9 million pounds of ready-to-eat (RTE), frozen, fully cooked chicken products that may be adulterated with *Listeria monocytogenes.*

In June 2020, Tyson was cooperating with the US Department of Justice on charges of price fixing and bid rigging in the poultry industry. Four poultry industry executives were indicted for conspiracy to engage in price fixing. In March 2021, Tyson paid $221.5 million to poultry buyers to settle the price-fixing claims.

Human Resources and Diversity

Among Tyson's 137,000 employees, about 120,000 work in the US, of whom about 114,000 are employed at production facilities and about 17,000 work in other countries, primarily in Thailand and China. About 33,000 employees in the US are members of various labor unions, compared with about 5,000 in other countries.

Tyson aims to cultivate a culture and vision that supports diversity, equity, and inclusion (DEI) as the company recruits, develops, and retains talent at every level. In fiscal 2021, Tyson hired their first chief DEI officer and established a company-wide DEI council. Also in fiscal 2021, Tyson added three new Business Resource Groups: African Ancestry Alliance, Asians and Allies, and LatinX.

Strategy

Tyson expects global protein consumption of beef, pork, and chicken to rise to about 95 billion pounds over the next 10 years. In response, Tyson plans to open 12 new plants between 2022 and 2024, increasing capacity by about 1.3 billion pounds. The construction of the 12 new plants includes nine chicken plants, two case ready beef and pork plants, and one new bacon plant. Tyson currently sells products in about 140 countries, especially in the US, Australia, Canada, Central America, Chile, China, the EU, the UK, Japan, Mexico, Malaysia, the Middle East, South Korea, Taiwan, and Thailand. The company expects to expand the 140 to 170 and beyond. Tyson's sales to customers in foreign countries for fiscal 2021 totaled $7 billion, including $4.9 billion related to export sales from the US. As the year 2022 begins, Tyson has about $1.4 billion in assets located outside the US, primarily Brazil, China, the EU, New Zealand, and Thailand.

Tyson plans to have 50 percent of its volume be value-added by the end of fiscal 2024. Between 2022 and 2025, Tyson is investing more than $1.3 billion in capital in new automation capabilities to increase yields and reduce labor costs and associated risks. Tyson also plans to save more than $250 million by using new digital solutions like artificial intelligence and predictive analytics to drive efficiency in operations, supply chain planning, logistics, and warehousing. Tyson's expectation and objective going forward is to achieve a 12 percent return on invested capital.

Walmart Inc. accounted for 18.3 percent of Tyson's 2021 sales and were important in all Tyson categories and segments. The company does try to manage seasonal demand being highest for beef, chicken, and certain prepared foods products, such as hot dogs and smoked sausage, generally in the spring and summer months and less during the winter months. In contrast, the demand for pork and certain other prepared foods products, such as prepared meals, meat dishes, appetizers and breakfast sausage, normally increase during the winter months, primarily due to the holiday season, whereas demand decreases during the spring and summer months. The bottom line, however, is that demand for all Tyson products is increasing and the company is "beefing up" to accommodate this demand.

Organizational Structure

Tyson's top executives are listed and arrayed in Exhibit 1. Note there is no COO, so apparently all top executives report to the CEO. Note also the Tyson array appears to be a strategic business unit (SBU) structure given the group president positions. Some analysts contend, however, that a divisional-by-product design or even as SBU design based on beef, chicken, pork, and packaged foods perhaps would be better and would match the financial reporting data in the company's *Form 10K.*

EXHIBIT 1 Tyson's Top Executives Listed and Arrayed

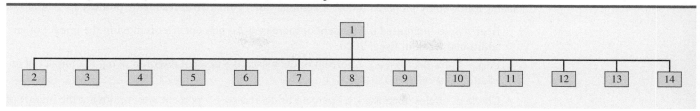

1. John Tyson, Chairperson of the Board
2. Donnie King, CEO and President
3. Stewart Glendinning, EVP and CFO
4. Jason Nichol, Chief Customer Officer
5. Ildefonso Silva, EVP, Business Services
6. John R. Tyson, EVP, Strategy and Chief Sustainability Officer
7. Johanna Soderstrom, EVP, Chief People Officer

8. Amy Tu, EVP, Chief Legal Officer and Secretary, Global Governance and Corporate Affairs
9. Scott Spradley, EVP, Chief Technology and Automation Officer
10. David Bray, Group President, Poultry
11. Shane Miller, Group President, Fresh Meats
12. Noelle O'Mara, Group President, Prepared Foods
13. Chris Langholz, President, International Business
14. Sandy Luckcuck, Global McDonald's Business Unit President

Source: Based on https://www.tysonfoods.com/who-we-are/our-people/leadership

Production/Operations

A summary of Tyson's manufacturing facilities are provided in Exhibit 2. Note the relatively low-capacity utilization rates.

EXHIBIT 2 Tyson's Manufacturing Facilities

Category	Number of Manufacturing Plants	Capacity Utilization Rate
Beef	14	78
Pork	07	88
Chicken	178	79
Prepared Foods	34	79

Source: Based on Tyson's 2021 *Form 10K*, p. 19.

Segments

Tyson's revenues and operating income by segment are provided in Exhibit 3. Note the declines in 2021 in operating income for pork and chicken, so the company made its money on beef and prepared foods. International/Other primarily includes the company's operations in Australia, China, Malaysia, Mexico, the Netherlands, South Korea, and Thailand.

EXHIBIT 3 Tyson's Revenues and Operating Income by Segment (in Millions $)

	Revenues		Operating Income	
	Fiscal 2020	Fiscal 2021	Fiscal 2020	Fiscal 2021
Product Category				
Beef	$15,742	$17,999	$1,580	$3,240
Pork	5,128	6,277	565	328
Chicken	13,234	13,733	122	(625)
Prepared Foods	8,532	8,853	743	1,456
International/Other	1,856	1,990	(2)	(3)
Intersegment	(1,307)	(1,803)	—	—
Total	$43,185	$47,049	$3,008	$4,396

Source: Based on https://ir.tyson.com/news/news-details/2021/Tyson-Foods-Reports-Strong-Fourth-Quarter-and-Fiscal-2021-Results/default.aspx

Tyson's percentage of food sold by category is illustrated in Exhibit 4. Note that chicken dominates followed by prepared foods. A summary of Tyson's 2021 results by product are as follows:

Beef – Sales increased 0.3 percent or increased 2.4 percent after removing the impact of an additional week in fiscal 2020.

Pork – Sales decreased 2.7 percent or decreased 0.8 percent after removing the impact of an additional week in 2020.

Chicken – Sales decreased 3.3 percent or decreased 1.5 percent after removing the impact of an additional week in 2020.

Prepared Foods – Sales decreased 5.4 percent or decreased 3.7 percent after removing the impact of an additional week in 2020.

EXHIBIT 4 Tyson's Percentage of Food by Sales 2021

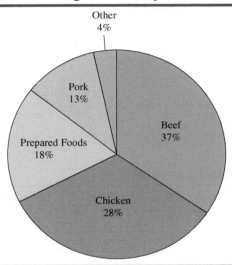

Other 4%
Pork 13%
Prepared Foods 18%
Beef 37%
Chicken 28%

Source: Based on https://ir.tyson.com/news/news-details/2021/Tyson-Foods-Reports-Strong-Fourth-Quarter-and-Fiscal-2021-Results/default.aspx

Tyson's revenues in by distribution channel are provided in Exhibit 5.

EXHIBIT 5 Tyson's Revenues by Distribution Channel (Percentages)

Fiscal	2020
Retail	48
Foodservice	28
International	14
Industrial/Other	10

Source: Based on Tyson's 2020 *Form 10K*.

Finances

Tyson's fiscal year always ends on the Saturday closest to September 30, so some years' data will include 52 weeks and some years 53 weeks. Tyson's recent income statements and balance sheets are provided in Exhibit 6 and Exhibit 7, respectively.

Competitors

Tyson faces more than a hundred rival firms, but the company's primary competitors include Hormel Foods, Bunge, Conagra Brands, Pilgrim's Pride, and Golden State Foods. A recent study compared Tyson with some of its competitors and reported the findings provided in Exhibit 8. Note that Tyson ranks good only on "Pricing," and Tyson ranks next to last overall, as indicated by the summed score of 33. Tyson was ranked especially weak on Effectiveness of CEO and Overall Culture. Hormel was ranked best overall even though that company was not ranked on variable 9.

EXHIBIT 6 Tyson's Recent Income Statements (in Millions)

Income Statement	10/2/20	10/2/21		Percentage Change
Revenue (Sales)	$43,185	$47,049	⬆	9%
Cost of Goods Sold	37,801	40,523	⬆	7%
Gross Profit	5,384	6,526	⬆	21%
Operating Expenses	2,376	2,130	⬇	−10%
EBIT (Operating Income)	3,008	4,396	⬆	46%
Interest Expense	344	355	⬆	3%
EBT	2,664	4,041	⬆	52%
Tax	593	981	⬆	65%
Nonrecurring Events	(10)	(13)	⬆	30%
Net Income	$2,061	$3,047	⬆	48%

Source: Based on Tyson's 2021 *Form 10K*, p. 44.

EXHIBIT 7 Tyson's Recent Balance Sheets (in Millions)

Balance Sheet	10/2/20	10/2/21		Percentage Change
Assets				
Cash and Short-Term Investments	$1,420	$2,507	⬆	77%
Accounts Receivable	1,952	2,400	⬆	23%
Inventory	3,859	4,382	⬆	14%
Other Current Assets	367	533	⬆	45%
Total Current Assets	7,598	9,822	⬆	29%
Property Plant & Equipment	7,596	7,837	⬆	3%
Goodwill	10,899	10,549	⬇	−3%
Intangibles	6,774	6,519	⬇	−4%
Other Long-Term Assets	1,589	1,582	⬇	0%
Total Assets	**34,456**	**36,309**	⬆	**5%**
Liabilities				
Accounts Payable	1,876	2,225	⬆	19%
Other Current Liabilities	2,358	4,100	⬆	74%
Total Current Liabilities	4,234	6,325	⬆	49%
Long-Term Debt	10,791	8,281	⬇	−23%
Other Long-Term Liabilities	4,045	3,849	⬇	−5%
Total Liabilities	**19,070**	**18,455**	⬇	**−3%**
Equity				
Common Stock	45	45	⬇	0%
Retained Earnings	17,502	15,100	⬇	−14%
Treasury Stock	(4,138)	(4,145)	⬆	0%
Paid in Capital & Other	1,977	6,854	⬆	247%
Total Equity	15,386	17,854	⬆	16%
Total Liabilities and Equity	**$34,456**	**$36,309**	⬆	**5%**

Source: Based on Tyson's 2021 *Form 10K*, p. 45.

Hormel Foods Corporation (NYSE: HRL)

A US food-processing company founded in 1891 in Austin, Minnesota, by George A. Hormel, Hormel ranked number one in five categories in Exhibit 8, and ranked best overall, as indicated by a summed score of 12. A competitor to Tyson, Hormel generates annual revenues across more than 80 countries and produces brands such as Skippy, SPAM, Hormel Natural Choice, Columbus, Applegate, Justin's, Wholly, Hormel Black Label, Planters, and more than 30 other popular products. Hormel in fiscal 2021 reported record net sales of $11.4 billion, up 19 percent. The company's organic net sales increased 14 percent. The company's operating income of $1.1 billion was up 2 percent from the prior year.

Hormel was on the "Global 2000 World's Best Employers" list by *Forbes* magazine for 3 years, is one of *Fortune* magazine's most admired companies and has appeared on *Corporate Responsibility* Magazine's "The 100 Best Corporate Citizens" list for 12 years. *Forbes* in December 2021 rated Hormel Foods as one of the world's top female-friendly companies. Hormel has long promoted and supported a female-friendly culture, including employee resource groups such as Hormel Foods Women in Leadership and Women's Insight Network. At Hormel, Jacinth Smiley was recently named chief financial officer and Wendy Watkins was appointed chief communications officer. Hormel's leadership and officer group includes 11 women, 5 at the senior leadership level, including Deanna Brady, group vice president of Refrigerated Foods, the company's largest business segment.

JBS S.A.

Headquartered in São Paulo, Brazil, JBS S.A. is the largest meat-processing company in the world, producing processed beef, chicken, and pork and also selling numerous by products from the processing of these meats. Having substantial operations in 15 countries and employing about 250,000, JBS owns Pilgrim's Pride that was ranked lowest in overall quality in Exhibit 8.

JBS is similar to Tyson in that JBS produces a vast array of fresh and frozen meats and prepared meals, under such brand names as Friboi, Swift, Seara, Pilgrim's Pride, Plumrose, Primo, among others. To promote sustainability of its entire business value chain, JBS owns numerous related businesses, such as leather, biodiesel, collagen, natural casings for cold cuts, hygiene and cleaning, metal packaging, transportation, and solid waste management operations. For example, JBS is the world's largest producer of leather.

EXHIBIT 8 Comparing Tyson Foods Versus Rival Firms (Ranking 1 = Best; 6 = Worst)

	Variables									
	1	2	3	4	5	6	7	8	9	10
Tyson Foods	5	4	3	2	3	5	4	4	3	33
Hormel Foods	1	2	2	3	1	1	1	1	-	12
Bunge	2	1	1	4	2	2	5	-	1	17
Conagra Brands	3	3	4	1	4	4	3	2	2	26
Pilgrim's Pride	4	4	5	5	5	3	2	3	3	34

Variables

1. Effectiveness of CEO
2. Product Quality
3. Do Customers Recommend Company Products to Friends?
4. Pricing
5. Customer Service
6. Overall Culture
7. Do Employees Recommend Company Products to Friends?
8. How Happy Are the Women Employees at the Firm?
9. How Happy Are Minority Employees at the Firm?
10. Summed Score (lower sum the better)

Source: Based on https://www.comparably.com/companies/tyson-foods/competitors

In late 2021, JBS made two substantial acquisitions:

1. Acquired King's Group and premium Italian charcuterie brands, strengthening the company's presence in the both the US and Europe. With this acquisition comes four production facilities in Italy and the iconic meat brands, Kings and Principe.
2. Acquired Bio Tech Foods, thus entering the cultivated protein market, and acquired the associated construction of a plant in Europe. JBS is building a research and development center in biotechnology and cultivated protein in Brazil.

External Issues

The world's population is projected to reach 10 billion people by 2050, and global demand for protein is expected to double in the next three decades. These projections bode well for Tyson and underlies the company's plans to grow both organically and through acquisitions, but there are numerous rival firms, internal problems must be corrected, and external threats must be managed. The US Department of Agriculture (USDA) forecasts that domestic protein production (beef, pork, chicken, and turkey) will increase slightly in 2022 versus 2021 levels. Specifically, the USDA projects the following:

Beef – Domestic production will decrease about 2 percent in 2022.

Pork – Domestic production will decrease about 2 percent in 2022.

Chicken – Domestic production will increase about 2 percent in 2022.

The plant-based meat industry is growing so rapidly that many larger food companies are entering this business, such as Hormel Foods new product line named Happy Little Plants, and Kroger introduced Simple Truth Plant Based, and Tyson Foods just launched a brand called Raised & Rooted, which comprises blended plant and beef patties, as well as 100% plant-based nuggets. Surveys suggest that 98 percent of the consumers who buy plant-based meat also buy animal meat, good news for Tyson. But there is a global trend toward consumers trying to eat healthier, and this includes eating less meat, which means less cholesterol being consumed.

Various sources report that meat and dairy are the major factors contributing to global warming. Estimates are that raising livestock globally accounts for between 14.5 and 18 percent of human-induced greenhouse gas emissions. Agriculture is one of the leading contributors to both methane and nitrous oxide emissions. Livestock reportedly uses 83 percent of farmland and produces 60 percent of agriculture's greenhouse gas emissions; yet, it provides just 18 percent of the food calories and 37 percent of protein required by humans. Besides the environmental impact of raising animals for food, the associated pain and suffering animals in the livestock industry endure is well documented. For example, historian, philosopher, and bestselling author Yuval Noah Harari has suggested that industrial farming is one of the worst crimes in history. (https://www.atlasandboots.com/travel-blog/countries-that-eat-the-most-meat/)

India consumes less meat per capita than any other country. Exhibit 9 reveals the 10 countries that consume the most meat per capita.

EXHIBIT 9 Countries that Consume the Most Meat per Capita

Country	Grams per Person per Day
1. Hong Kong SAR, China	419.6
2. Australia	318.5
3. US	315.5
4. Argentina	293.8
5. Bahamas	285.5
6. Samoa	280.0
7. New Zealand	277.8
8. French Polynesia	270.7
9. St. Lucia	272.6
10. Luxembourg	270.0

Source: Based on https://www.atlasandboots.com/travel-blog/countries-that-eat-the-most-meat/

EXHIBIT 10 Tyson's Revenues and Operating Income in Q2 2022 vs Q2 2021 (in Millions $)

	Revenues		Operating Income	
	2021	2022	2021	2022
Beef	$4,046	$5,034	$445	$638
Pork	1,477	1,565	67	59
Chicken	3,553	4,086	06	198
Prepared Foods	2,164	2,393	217	263
International/Other	487	565	(15)	(02)
Intersegment	(427)	(526)	NA	NA
Total	$11,300	$13,117	$720	$1,156

Source: Based on https://www.tysonfoods.com/news/news-releases/2022/5/tyson-foods-reports-second-quarter-2022-results

Conclusion

For Tyson's Q2 2022, the company reported dramatically increased revenues and net income across all meat products, as indicated in Exhibit 10. Note the dramatic increases, except for the profitability of pork.

Donnie King, CEO and President of Tyson, needs a clear strategic plan for the 2022–2026 period of time. The company has 12 new factories being completed in the 2022–2024 time period, but new countries and new customers are needed to sell this product. King is aware of the basic underlying external opportunities and threats and internal strengths and weaknesses facing Tyson but seeks input regarding the relative importance of each factor and the relative attractiveness of resultant alternative strategies. Let's say King asks you to prepare a comprehensive strategic plan for Tyson and present that to him and the company's top management team.

As part of your strategic analysis, include SWOT, IFEM, EFEM, IE Matrix, and QSPM analyses among your strategy formulation tools, and include perceptual mapping, EPS-EBIT analysis, corporate valuation analysis, and projected financial statements in the strategy implementation part of your overall analysis and presentation. What can Tyson do to improve its ranking among rival firms across the nine management and marketing variables included in Exhibit 8 of the case? To what extent should King be concerned about the shift toward consumption of more plant-based proteins in the diet of millions of persons? How concerned should Tyson be about reports that raising livestock globally contributes dramatically to increased carbon dioxide emissions globally?

Tyson is presently a financially strong firm, but internal weaknesses and external threats jeopardize long-term performance. Prepare a strategic plan that you are confident can lead Tyson to continued success as one of the world's most important providers of protein products.

References

1. Tyson's 2020 *Form 10K*.
2. Tyson's 2021 *Form 10K*.
3. https://www.comparably.com/companies/tyson-foods/competitors
4. https://ir.tyson.com/news/news-details/2021/Tyson-Foods-Reports-Strong-Fourth-Quarter-and-Fiscal-2021-Results/default.aspx

Constellation Brands, Inc., 2022

www.cbrands.com, (NYSE: STZ)

Headquartered in Victor, New York, Constellation Brands, Inc. is a *Fortune* 500 company that produces and markets beer, wine, and spirits internationally with operations in the US, Canada, Mexico, New Zealand, and Italy. The company owns some of the most iconic, high-end beer, wine, and spirits brands, including Corona, Modelo, Kim Crawford, Robert Mondavi, and SVEDKA Vodka, and although its products are sold in many countries, more than 95 percent of its sales are generated in the US. Constellation is the third-largest beer company and the fastest-growing large consumer-packaged goods company in the US. SVEDKA Vodka is the largest imported vodka brand in the US. Some of the company's high-end spirit brands include High West craft whiskeys and Casa Noble tequila.

Constellation is also the world's largest premium wine producer, owning more than 100 wine brands including some of the most well-known brands, such as Meiomi, Robert Mondavi, and Kim Crawford, which are produced using grapes sourced from independent growers in the world's premier wine-growing regions. Constellation's Wine and Spirits segment constitutes about 35 percent of the company's revenue. Constellation is the market leader of the high-growth, higher-end beer segment, owning many brands that are the market leaders, making them a preferred supplier to many of its customers, which include wholesale distributors, retailers, and on-premise locations.

Constellation's beer business has experienced growth for 11 consecutive years and represents more than 65 percent of the company's revenue. The Modelo brand had a successful 2021 with sales up 12 percent in fiscal year 2021; Corona was up 3 percent; and Pacifico sales increased 12 percent. The largest portion of the company's revenue is generated in the US, in part due to the company holding exclusive rights to produce, import, and sell Modelo and Corona, which are currently the number-three and number-six top-selling beer brands in the US, respectively.

In 2020, Constellation purchased Empathy Wines, a high-performing, digitally native wine brand and direct-to-consumer (DTC) platform. Empathy Wines produces high-quality, sustainably made wines, sold DTC through its eCommerce platform, powered by consumer insights and content-driven digital marketing. Constellation owns about 15 of the top 100 wine brands in the US. The company's advertising expenses for the years ended 2019 and 2020 were $700.8 million and $769.5 million, respectively.

Copyright by Fred David Books LLC; written by Meredith E. David.

History

Founded in 1945 by Marvin Sands under the name Canandaigua Industries Company, Constellation has grown rapidly through acquisitions and internal expansion. The company has product offerings across all segments of the alcohol beverage industry. The firm is today controlled by brothers Richard and Robert Sands, sons of Marvin.

Marvin Sands, the son of winemaker Mordecai (Mack) Sands, exited the Navy in 1945 and entered distilling by purchasing an old sauerkraut factory in Canandaigua, New York. His business struggled while making fruit wines in bulk for local bottlers in the eastern US. Marvin opened the Richard's Wine Cellar in Petersburg, Virginia, in 1951. In 1954 Marvin developed his own brand of "fortified" wine (190-proof brandy), and named it Richard's Wild Irish Rose, after his son Richard. Marvin Sands died in 1999, but his son, Richard, has been CEO of Constellation since 1993 and succeeded his father as chairman of the board of the company.

In 2004, Constellation acquired the Robert Mondavi Corporation for $988 million in cash. In 2013, Constellation acquired Grupo Modelo's US beer business from Anheuser-Busch InBev for about $5.2 billion. This purchase gave Constellation an exclusive license to import, market, and sell the Corona and Modelo brands in the US.

In 2015 and 2016 Constellation acquired the Meiomi and the Prisoner Wine Company businesses, the latter of which included a portfolio of five very-high-end wine brands. In 2015, Constellation sold its Canadian wine business, and in 2021, the company sold many of its lower-margin, low-growth wine and spirits brands. Divesting lower-end wine brands has helped Constellation pursue a strategy of focusing on premium wines and establish dominance as a market leader producer of premium, high-end beer, wine, and spirits. Constellation recently entered the cannabis industry by investing in a leading cannabis company, Canopy.

In March 2022, Constellation Brands introduced Next Round Cocktails, its first-ever ready-to-drink (RTD) and multi-serve boxed wine cocktails. Two flavors are offered: Salted Lime Margarita and Strawberry Lime Sangria, which guests can simply pour from the box over ice in a glass and enjoy. Constellation is trying to capitalize on the $696.5 million pre-mixed cocktails category and the $903.2 million premium boxed wine category. The Salted Lime Margarita contains 12.3 percent juice from concentrate while Next Round Cocktails Rosé Sangria contains 13.7 percent juice.

Internal Issues

Vision/Mission/Core Values

As provided in Exhibit 1, Constellation provides on its corporate website statements of vision, mission, and core values. There is substantial room for improvement in the statements based on Chapter 2 of the David strategic management textbook.

EXHIBIT 1 Constellation's Vision, Mission, and Core Values Statements (paraphrased)

Our Vision: *Worth Reaching For*

We go beyond the call of duty to provide more for consumers, shareholders, employees, and the communities where we live and work.

Our Mission: *Build Brands That People Love*

We strive to make people happy, to bring people together, and to elevate people's lives.

Our Values: *The Foundation of it All*

Our exemplary values have gotten us this far and will propel us to new heights moving forward.

Source: Based on https://www.cbrands.com/story

Operations

Constellation has one company-owned glass production plant in Mexico that services its beer brands. The company also operates 11 wineries in the US, 2 wineries in New Zealand, and 6 wineries in Italy, as well as four distilleries in the US for the production of spirits, two facilities for the production of its High West whiskey brand, and one facility each for Copper & Kings American brandies and for Nelson's Green Brier bourbon and whiskey products. Constellation owns or leases about 7,000 acres of vineyards in New Zealand, more than 10,00 acres in California, and about 1,300 acres in Italy.

Organizational Structure

Constellation's top executives are listed and arrayed in Exhibit 2. Note the company has two segments: Beer and Wine + Spirits. Note there is no COO, but there probably needs to be to reduce the CEO's span of control.

Finance

Constellation's fiscal year ends each February 28. The company's recent income statements and balance sheets are provided in Exhibit 3 and Exhibit 4, respectively. Note the company's substantially improved net income.

EXHIBIT 2 Constellation's Top Executives Listed and Arrayed

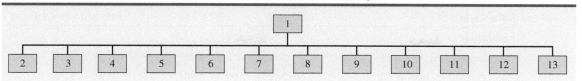

1. Bill Newlands, President, CEO, and Director
2. Tiffanie De Liberty, SVP, Chief Compliance Officer and General Counsel, Wine and Spirits
3. Kristen Klanow, VP, Associate General Counsel and Chief of Staff
4. Michael McGrew, EVP, Chief Communications Officer, CSR and Diversity Officer
5. Jim Bourdeau, Chief Legal Officer
6. Garth Hankinson, CFO & EVP
7. Tom Kane, EVP and Chief Human Resources Officer
8. Mallika Monteiro, EVP, Chief Growth, Strategy, and Digital Officer
9. Jim Sabia, EVP and Managing Director, Beer Division
10. Patty Yahn-Urlaub, SVP Investor Relations
11. Robert Hanson, President, Wine + Spirits Division
12. Paul Hetterich, EVP and President, Beer Division
13. Daniel Baima, President of Constellation Brands, Mexico

Source: Based on https://www.cbrands.com/story/leadership

EXHIBIT 3 Constellation's Recent Income Statements (in Millions)

Income Statement	2/28/20	2/28/21		Percentage Change
Revenue (Sales)	$8,344	$8,615	⬆	3%
Cost of Goods Sold	4,192	4,149	⬇	−1%
Gross Profit	4,152	4,466	⬆	8%
Operating Expenses	1,997	1,675	⬇	−16%
EBIT (Operating Income)	2,155	2,791	⬆	30%
Interest Expense	3,100	248	⬇	−92%
EBT	(945)	2,543	⬇	−369%
Tax	(966)	511	—	—
Nonrecurring Events	(33)	(34)	—	—
Net Income	($12)	$1,998	—	—

Source: Based on Constellation's 2021 *Form 10K*, p. 61.

EXHIBIT 4 Constellation's Recent Balance Sheets (in Millions)

Balance Sheet	2/28/20	2/28/21		Percentage Change
Assets				
Cash and Short-Term Investments	$81	$461	⬆	469%
Accounts Receivable	465	785	⬆	69%
Inventory	1,374	1,291	⬇	−6%
Other Current Assets	1,564	508	⬇	−68%
Total Current Assets	3,484	3,045	⬇	−13%
Property Plant & Equipment	5,333	5,822	⬆	9%
Goodwill	7,757	7,794	⬆	0%
Intangibles	2,719	2,732	⬆	0%
Other Long-Term Assets	8,030	7,712	⬇	−4%
Total Assets	**$27,323**	**$27,105**	⬇	**−1%**

(Continued)

EXHIBIT 4 *(Continued)*

Balance Sheet	2/28/20	2/28/21		Percentage Change
Liabilities				
Accounts Payable	558	460	⬇	–18%
Other Current Liabilities	1,754	809	⬇	–54%
Total Current Liabilities	2,312	1,269	⬇	–45%
Long-Term Debt	11,211	10,413	⬇	–7%
Other Long-Term Liabilities	1,326	1,494	⬆	13%
Total Liabilities	**14,849**	**13,176**	⬇	**–11%**
Equity				
Common Stock	2	2	⬇	0%
Retained Earnings	13,695	15,118	⬆	10%
Treasury Stock	(2,814)	(2,790)	—	—
Paid in Capital & Other	1,591	1,599	⬆	1%
Total Equity	**12,474**	**13,929**	⬆	**12%**
Total Liabilities and Equity	**$27,323**	**$27,105**	⬇	**–1%**

Source: Based on Constellation's 2021 *Form 10K*, p. 60.

Segments

Beer

Constellation is the number-one brewer and seller of imported beer in the US market. Constellation has the exclusive right to import, market, and sell the following Mexican brands in all 50 states of the US:

> Corona Brand Family, Modelo Brand Family, Other Import Brands
> Corona Extra, Corona Light, Modelo Especial Pacifico
> Corona Premier, Corona Refresca, Modelo Negra Victoria
> Corona Familiar, Corona Hard Seltzer, Modelo Chelada

Modelo Especial is the best-selling imported beer, third best-selling beer overall, and the fastest-growing major imported beer brand in the US. Corona Extra is the second-largest imported beer and sixth best-selling beer overall in the US. After introducing Corona Refresca in fiscal 2020, the company launched Corona Hard Seltzer in early fiscal 2021, and this brand soon became the number-four best-selling seltzer in the US. In fiscal 2022, the company added new flavors and introduced a second Corona Hard Seltzer variety pack, and then launched Corona Hard Seltzer Limonada in June of fiscal 2022.

Wine

As consumer disposable income increases globally as it is doing, the consumption of wine increases, benefiting Constellation. Constellation says the global wine market is expected to reach US$411,668.7 billion by 2022, or 27,057.6 million liters. Hypermarkets and supermarkets are the leading distribution channels for wine, accounting for a 41.1 percent share, followed by online trade (26 percent), food and drinks specialists (25 percent), others (6 percent), and convenience stores (3 percent).

Regionally, Europe accounts for 48 percent of the global wine market value, followed by Asia-Pacific (30 percent), the US (13 percent), rest of the world (8 percent), and the Middle East (1 percent). By type, still wine is the largest segment of the global wine market, accounting for 81 percent of the market value, followed by sparkling wine and fortified wine accounting for 16 percent and 3.1 percent, respectively.

In 2021, Constellation acquired a minority stake in Kerr Cellars, a portfolio of Napa Valley and Sonoma County wines. Constellation sold its Paul Masson Grande Amber Brandy brand to Sazerac Company Inc., in 2021 for US$267.4 million, and the same year sold a portion of its wine and spirits business to E. & J. Gallo Winery and received net cash proceeds of US$538.4 million and sold the New Zealand-based Nobilo Wine brand.

Spirits

The market for spirits such as brandy, gin and genever, rum, vodka, whisky, and cognac is growing, benefiting from a rapidly growing middle class and increasing income. Constellation expects the global spirits market to reach US$ 960,674 million by 2023 or 36,861.2 million liters. There is higher demand for spirits from regions like Asia-Pacific, which accounts for about 53 percent of the global value of the spirit market, followed by Europe (24 percent), the US (15 percent), the Middle East (1 percent), and rest of the world (7 percent). Vodka is the largest segment of the global spirits market, accounting for 68 percent of the market's total value, followed by Whisky (13 percent), Brandy (7 percent), Liqueurs (5 percent), Rum (3 percent), Tequila and Mezcal (2 percent), and Other (2 percent). In 2020, the Constellation acquired Copper & Kings American Brandy Company, a producer of American Brandy, absinthe, gin, and Destillare liqueurs.

Constellation's revenues by segment are provided in Exhibit 5. Note the rows where there are decreases.

EXHIBIT 5 Constellation's Revenues by Segment (in Millions)

	February 2020	February 2021
Beer	$5,615.9	$6,074.6
Wine and Spirits		
Wine	2,367.5	2,208.4
Spirits	360.1	331.9
Total Wine and Spirits	2,727.6	2,540.3
Canopy	(290.2)	378.6
Other	290.2	(378.6)
Total	$8,343.5	$8,614.9

Source: Based on Constellation's 2021 *Form 10K*, p. 6.

Constellation's sales and profits across segments are illustrated in Exhibit 6 and Exhibit 7, respectively.

EXHIBIT 6 Constellation's Sales Across Products (in Millions)

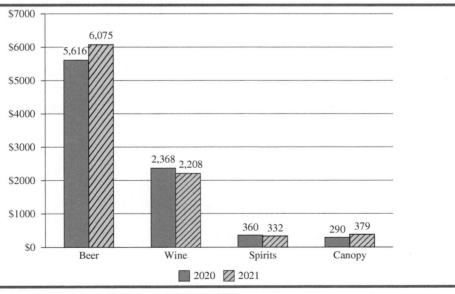

Source: Based on Constellation's 2021 *Annual Report*, p. 37.

Competitors

Constellation faces hundreds of competitors, but some of the largest are The Wine Group, E. & J. Gallo Winery, Trinchero Family Estates, Ste. Michelle Wine Estates, Treasury Wine Estates, Deutsch

EXHIBIT 7 Constellation's Gross Profit Across Products (in Millions)

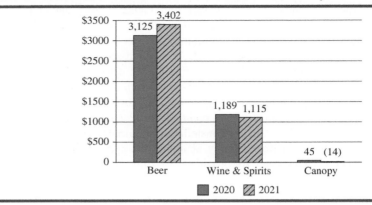

Source: Based on Constellation's 2021 *Annual Report*, p. 38.

Family Wine & Spirits, Anheuser-Busch InBev, Heineken, Molson Coors, Boston Beer Company, Mark Anthony, Beam Suntory, Diageo, Brown-Forman, Pernod Ricard, and Sazerac Company.

Founded in 1366 and headquartered in Leuven, Belgium, Anheuser-Busch InBev SA/NV is a subsidiary of AB InBev NV/SA. Anheuser produces, distributes, and sells beer, alcoholic beverages, and soft drinks worldwide. It offers about 500 beer brands, including Budweiser, Corona, and Stella Artois; Beck's, Hoegaarden, Leffe, and Michelob Ultra; and Aguila, Antarctica, Bud Light, Brahma, Cass, Castle, Castle Lite, Cristal, Harbin, Jupiler, Modelo Especial, Quilmes, Victoria, Sedrin, and Skol brands.

Exhibit 8 provides information regarding how Constellation ranks on nine quality variables, compared with two rival Wine and Spirits firms. Note that Constellation ranks number one only on variable 9. The company ranks worst number three of four variables: product quality, customer recommendation, pricing, and customer service. Overall, based on Column 10, note that Constellation ranks last as indicated by the total score of 21 (lower sum is better as you see in Column 10).

EXHIBIT 8 Comparing Constellation Versus Rival Wine and Spirits Firms (Ranking 1 = Best; 6 = Worst)

	Variables									
	1	2	3	4	5	6	7	8	9	10
Constellation	2	3	3	3	3	2	2	2	1	21
Diageo	1	2	2	2	2	1	1	1	2	14
Brown-Forman	3	1	1	1	1	3	3	3	3	19

Variables

1. Effectiveness of CEO
2. Product Quality
3. Do Customers Recommend Company Products to Friends?
4. Pricing
5. Customer Service
6. Overall Culture
7. Do Employees Recommend Company Products to Friends?
8. How Happy Are the Women Employees at the Firm?
9. How Happy Are Minority Employees at the Firm?
10. Summed Score (lower sum the better)

Source: Based on https://www.comparably.com/companies/constellation-brands/competitors

Exhibit 9 provides information regarding how Constellation ranks on nine quality variables, compared with three rival Beer firms. Note that Constellation ranks number one on no variables. The company ranks worst number four on overall culture. Overall, based on Column 10, note that Constellation ranks pretty low (lower sum is better as you see in Column 10). MillerCoors is private.

EXHIBIT 9 **Comparing Constellation Versus Rival Beer Firms (Ranking 1 = Best; 6 = Worst)**

	Variables									
	1	2	3	4	5	6	7	8	9	10
Constellation (STZ)	2	2	-	3	3	4	3	2	-	19+
Anheuser-Busch (BUD)	1	4	-	2	2	1	1	1	-	12+
MillerCoors	3	3	-	4	4	2	4	-	-	20+
Boston Beer Co.	4	1	-	1	1	3	2	-	-	12+

Variables

1. Effectiveness of CEO
2. Product Quality
3. Do Customers Recommend Company Products to Friends?
4. Pricing
5. Customer Service
6. Overall Culture
7. Do Employees Recommend Company Products to Friends?
8. How Happy Are the Women Employees at the Firm?
9. How Happy Are Minority Employees at the Firm?
10. Summed Score (lower sum the better)

Source: Based on https://www.comparably.com/companies/anheuser-busch/competitors

Exhibit 10 compares Constellation to rival companies on nine mostly financial variables.

EXHIBIT 10 **Constellation's Rival Firms Compared Financially**

	Constellation (STZ)	Anheuser (BUD)	Boston Beer (SAM)	Brown-Forman (BF-B)
Market Capitalization	$45 billion	$111 billion	$5.3 billion	$31 billion
EPS	−$0.3	$2.5	$8.0	$1.6
Revenue	$8.7 billion	$53 billion	$2.2 billion	$3.6 billion
Net Income	−53 million	$5 billion	$99 million	$2.4 billion
Total Debt	$10.4 billion	$90 billion	$63 million	$566 million
Total Debt/Equity	90	113	6.2	80
Current Ratio	1.5	—	1.51	5.15
# Full-time Employees	9,300	164,000	2,500	4,700
Stock Price	$235	$63	$432	$45

Source: Based on https://finance.yahoo.com/quote/STZ/profile?p=STZ

Brown-Forman Corporation (BF-B)

Founded in 1870 and headquartered in Louisville, Kentucky, Brown-Forman distills, bottles, imports, exports, markets, and sells various alcoholic beverages including spirits, wines, whisky spirits, whisky-based flavored liqueurs, ready-to-drink and ready-to-pour products, ready-to-drink cocktails, vodkas, tequilas, champagnes, brandy, bourbons, and liqueurs. The company's brand names include Jack Daniel's, Woodford Reserve, Old Forester, GlenDronach, Benriach, Glenglassaugh, Slane Irish Whiskey, Coopers' Craft, el Jimador, Herradura, New Mix, Pepe Lopez, Antiguo, Korbel Champagne, Sonoma-Cutrer, and Finlandia. The company has operations in the US, the UK, Germany, Australia, Mexico, and internationally.

External Issues

Sales of alcoholic drinks amount to $284,101 million in 2022 and are expected to grow annually by 7.45 percent. Volume is expected to amount to 34,940.5 million liters by 2025. The alcoholic drinks market is expected to show a volume growth of 2.9 percent in 2023. The global alcoholic beverages market size is expected to reach $2,797.05 billion by 2028.

The global alcohol beverage industry is growing and characterized by increasing number of breweries and wineries outlets, changing preference of consumers toward the drinks, especially for premium and super-premium drinks, rising trend of socializing and organizing parties among youngsters, rapid urbanization, inclinations toward flavored alcohol and mixed drinks, global rise in disposable income, and increased consumer demand for premium/super-premium products. Analysts indicate that the average American consumes 2.3 gallons of alcohol yearly.

Conclusion

In fiscal 2021, the US accounted for 97.5 percent of Constellation's revenue. High dependence on this one geographic region exposes the company to various risks such as economic downturn and political instability and additionally forgoes opportunities other regions of high growth potential. The case noted the high demand for spirits in the Asia-Pacific region. Should Constellation expand globally instead of relying 95+ percent on revenues from the US? If yes, how should the company do this most effectively? Are there large rival firms headquartered outside the US that Constellation should consider acquiring? What do you recommend?

References

1. https://www.cbrands.com/story
2. https://www.cbrands.com/story/leadership
3. Constellation's 2021 *Form 10K*.
4. https://www.comparably.com/companies/constellation-brands/competitors
5. https://finance.yahoo.com/quote/STZ/profile?p=STZ
6. https://www.comparably.com/companies/anheuser-busch/competitors
7. https://www.businesswire.com/news/home/20211124006101/en/Global-Alcoholic-Beverages-Market-Share-Size-Trends-Industry-Analysis-Forecast-Report-2021—2028—ResearchAndMarkets.com

Johnson Outdoors Inc., 2022

www.johnsonoutdoors.com, (NASDAQ: JOUT)

Headquartered in Racine, Wisconsin, Johnson Outdoors produces recreational watercraft, fishing equipment, diving equipment, camping gear, and outdoor clothing. Some well-known Johnson Outdoors brands include Old Town canoes and kayaks; Ocean Kayak; Carlisle paddles; Minn Kota fishing motors, batteries and anchors; Cannon downriggers; Humminbird marine electronics and charts; SCUBAPRO dive equipment; Jetboil outdoor cooking systems; and Eureka! camping and hiking equipment. Johnson Outdoors has about 1,400 employees, including 1,000 in the US; about 55 employees or 4 percent are members of a union, all of whom are located in Batam, Indonesia.

For fiscal year ending October 1, 2021, Johnson Outdoors reported a 26 percent increase in sales, operating profit grew 56.6 percent, and net income rose 51 percent over the prior fiscal year. The operating profits and net income were a record high, the firm's balance sheet shows zero debt, and dividends paid to shareholders increased.

Copyright by Fred David Books LLC; written by Fred R. David.

History

Johnson Outdoors was founded in 1970 by Samuel Curtis Johnson, Jr. who had four children, one of whom was Helen Johnson-Leipold, current chairman and CEO of Johnson Outdoors since 1999. This is a family run, but publicly held, company. The Johnson family owns about 75 percent of both classes of the company's common stock and additionally have a voting trust agreement covering about 96 percent of the outstanding class B common shares.

A segment of Johnson Outdoors, SCUBAPRO was founded in the US in 1963 by Gustav Dalla Valle and Dick Bonin to manufacture scuba gear. SCUBAPRO in 1997 became part of Johnson Outdoors. SCUBAPRO manufacturers all kinds of scuba equipment, from masks and fins to regulators and buoyancy compensators (BCs).

Jetboil is a lightweight gas fueled portable stove commonly used on camping trips. The company, Jetboil, was founded in 2001 by Dwight Aspinwall and Perry Dowst in New Hampshire when their product debuted at the 2003 Outdoor Retailers trade show. Since November 2012, Johnson Outdoors has owned Jetboil.

Johnson Outdoors acquired Eureka Tent Company in 1973, and in 2004, Johnson Outdoors acquired Old Town Canoe.

Internal Issues

Vision/Mission
Johnson Outdoors does not provide a written vision or mission statement on the corporate website, but a purpose statement is given, as follows: "*Find Your Awesome.*"

Organizational Structure
Johnson Outdoors gives no indication anywhere of the type of organizational structure the firm uses, and minimal information is even about the company's top management team. Only two persons clearly are designated as executives:

1. Helen Johnson-Leipold, Chairman and CEO
2. David Johnson, VP and CFO

Secrecy regarding the leadership positions and structure at Johnson Outdoors is somewhat unusual because this is a large firm. Presumably there would be a top manager for each segment (Fishing, Camping, Watercraft Recreation, and Diving), but this is unsure based on public information. Reviews of the effectiveness of the company's top managers is not too good, as indicated at the website https://www.comparably.com/companies/johnson-outdoors/leadership. The overall organizational culture at Johnson Outdoors is rated as not good, as indicated at the website https://www.comparably.com/companies/johnson-outdoors/leadership.

Manufacturing Operations

Exhibit 1 provides a location summary of Johnson Outdoors' manufacturing plants and office/distribution facilities. Note quite extensive reliance on outside-US manufacturing (the * indicates a production facility).

EXHIBIT 1 Johnson Outdoors' Manufacturing (Identified with an Asterisk) and Other Facilities

FISHING	DIVING	CAMPING
Alpharetta, Georgia	Barcelona, Spain	Binghamton, New York*
Eufaula, Alabama*	Antibes, France	Manchester, New Hampshire
Little Falls, Minnesota	Brussels, Belgium	Burlington, Ontario, Canada
Mankato, Minnesota*	Batam, Indonesia*	
Mexicali, Mexico*	Casarza Ligure, Italy*	
Toronto, Ontario, Canada	Chai Wan, Hong Kong	WATERCRAFT RECREATION
	Chatswood, Australia, El Cajon, California	Old Town, Maine*
	Nuremberg, Germany	Burlington, Ontario, Canada
	Zurich, Switzerland	

Source: Based on Johnson Outdoors' 2021 *Form 10K*, p. 15.

Segments

Johnson Outdoors has four reportable segments: Fishing, Camping, Watercraft Recreation, and Diving. Exhibit 2 reveals the company's revenues and operating income across segments. Note that Fishing comprises nearly 75 percent of the company's revenue. Also note the company is performing well.

EXHIBIT 2 Johnson Outdoors' Revenues and Operating Income by Segment (in Thousands)

	Revenues		Operating Income	
	2020	2021	2020	2021
Fishing	$449,878	$553,000	$95,884	$122,490
Camping	41,592	62,921	4,406	14,025
Watercraft Recreation	41,857	66,603	(329)	9,173
Diving	60,873	69,447	(2,576)	1,530
Other	9	(320)	(26,315)	(35,935)
Total	$594,209	$751,651	$71,070	$111,070

Source: Based on Johnson Outdoors' 2021 *Form 10K*, p. 19.

Exhibit 3 and Exhibit 4 reveal Johnson Outdoors' revenues across regions. Note heavy reliance on domestic markets, even though people globally enjoy fishing, camping, and water sports.

EXHIBIT 3 Johnson Outdoors' Revenues by Region (in Thousands)

	2020	2021
US	$525,204	$659,330
Europe	28,880	30,509
Canada	29,512	48,867
Other Regions	10,613	12,945
Total	$594,209	$751,651

Source: Based on Johnson Outdoors' 2021 *Form 10K*, p. F33.

EXHIBIT 4 A Histogram of Johnson Outdoors' Revenues by Region (in Thousands)

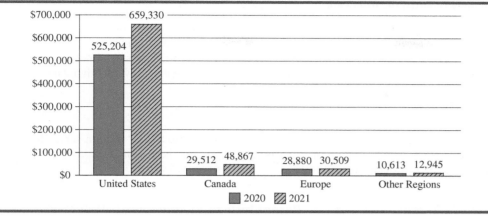

Source: Based on Johnson Outdoors' 2021 *Form 10K*, p. F33.

Fishing Segment

Johnson Outdoors has three fishing brands:

1. Minn Kota: electric motors, marine battery chargers, and shallow water anchors
2. Humminbird: sonar and GPS equipment for fish finding, plus navigation and marine cartography
3. Cannon: downriggers for controlled-depth fishing

Fishing brands are sold globally, with most sales coming from North America through large outdoor specialty retailers, such as Bass Pro Shops and Cabela's. However, thousands of retailers sell the company's fishing products. Fishing revenue increased 23 percent due to continued demand across all product lines.

Camping Segment

Johnson Outdoors has two camping brands:

1. Eureka!: tents of all sizes with accessories, camping furniture, camping stoves
2. Jetboil: portable outdoor cooking systems.

The company's fiscal 2021 Camping revenues grew 51 percent.

Watercraft Recreation Segment

Johnson Outdoors has three Watercraft Recreation brands:

1. Ocean Kayaks: kayaks and canoes of all size and type
2. Old Town: recreation, touring, angling and tripping products manufactured at the company facility in Old Town, Maine; includes personal flotation devices manufactured by third-party sources located in Asia and sold under the Old Town brand.
3. Carlisle Paddles: paddle produced mainly by third party sources located in North America and Asia.

The company's fiscal 2021 Watercraft Recreation sales rose 59 percent.

Diving Segment

Johnson Outdoors produces and markets scuba diving regulators, buoyancy compensators, dive computers and gauges, wetsuits, masks, fins, snorkels, and accessories for recreational divers—and sells and distributes them under the SCUBAPRO brand name. The company's fiscal 2021 Diving sales were up 14 percent.

Johnson Outdoors Q2 2022 that ended April 1, 2022 however was not exemplary primarily due to supply chain issues in the Fishing segment. Overall company sales were down 8 percent to $189.6 million for Q2, compared to the prior year Q2, led down by Fishing. The company's overall operating profit was down significantly too, to $15.4 million, from $36 million the prior year Q2, also led down by Fishing. And the company's Q2 2022 net income was $9.9 million, down from $27.8 million from the prior year Q2. Specifically for Q2 2022 by segment, the company reported the following:

- Fishing sales declined by 19 percent driven primarily by supply chain disruptions
- Camping revenue increased 35 percent, led by consumer tents and stoves
- Watercraft Recreation revenue grew 29 percent, led by the Sportsman line of products
- Diving sales increased 28 percent as more consumers resume travel to diving destinations.

Financial Summary

In fiscal 2021, Johnson Outdoors' revenue grew 26 percent to $751.7 million versus fiscal 2020 revenue of $594.2 million. Exhibit 5 and Exhibit 6 provide the recent company's income statements and balance sheets, respectively.

EXHIBIT 5 Johnson Outdoors' Recent Income Statements (in Thousands)

Income Statement	10/2/20	10/1/21		Percentage Change
Revenue (Sales)	$594,209	$751,651	⬆	26%
Cost of Goods Sold	329,216	417,526	⬆	27%
Gross Profit	264,993	334,125	⬆	26%
Operating Expenses	193,923	222,842	⬆	15%
EBIT (Operating Income)	71,070	111,283	⬆	57%
Interest Expense	(2,632)	(1,639)	—	—
EBT	73,702	112,922	⬆	53%
Tax	18,469	29,541	⬆	60%
Nonrecurring Events	0	0	—	—
Net Income	$55,233	$83,381	⬆	51%

Source: Based on Johnson Outdoors' 2021 *Form 10K*, p. F5.

EXHIBIT 6 Johnson Outdoors' Recent Balance Sheets (in Thousands)

Balance Sheet	10/2/20	10/1/21		Percentage Change
Assets				
Cash and Short-Term Investments	$212,437	$240,448	⬆	13%
Accounts Receivable	67,292	71,321	⬆	6%
Inventory	97,437	166,615	⬆	71%
Other Current Assets	11,372	12,880	⬆	13%
Total Current Assets	388,538	491,264	⬆	26%
Property Plant & Equipment	63,037	71,510	⬆	13%
Goodwill	11,184	11,221	⬆	0%
Intangibles	9,052	8,633	⬇	–5%
Other Long-Term Assets	74,215	91,659	⬆	24%
Total Assets	546,026	674,287	⬆	23%
Liabilities				
Accounts Payable	37,327	56,744	⬆	52%
Other Current Liabilities	68,280	80,826	⬆	18%
Total Current Liabilities	105,607	137,570	⬆	30%
Long-Term Debt	34,931	44,056	⬆	26%
Other Long-Term Liabilities	27,388	34,156	⬆	25%
Total Liabilities	167,926	215,782	⬆	28%

Balance Sheet	10/2/20	10/1/21		Percentage Change
Equity				
Common Stock	504	509	⇧	1%
Retained Earnings	296,431	370,501	⇧	25%
Treasury Stock	(2,220)	(2,790)	⇧	26%
Paid in Capital & Other	83,385	90,285	⇧	8%
Total Equity	378,100	458,505	⇧	21%
Total Liabilities and Equity	$546,026	$674,287	⇧	23%

Source: Based on Johnson Outdoors' 2021 *Form 10K*, p. F7.

Competition

Johnson Outdoors competes with many companies, but because fishing comprises 75 percent of the company's revenues, the firm's number-one competitor is Garmin. Exhibit 7, however, provides a list of Johnson Outdoors' key rival firms and products across the company's diverse array of fishing, camping, watercraft, and diving products.

EXHIBIT 7 Johnson Outdoors' Major Competitors and Their Brands

	Competing Brands	Manufacturer
Fishing		
Minn Kota	Motor Guide and Lowrance	Brunswick Corporation (NYSE: BC)
	Garmin	Garmin Ltd. (NYSE: GRMN)
Humminbird	Garmin and Navionics	Garmin Ltd.
	Lowrance, C-Map, Simrad	Navico, Inc.
	Raymarine	Teledyne FLIR
Cannon	Big Jon Sports	Amanda Pampu
	Walker and Scotty	Scotty Walker
Camping		
Eureka! Consumer	Anchor Industries, Aztec Tents, Coleman, Kelty	
Eureka! Commercial	North Face, Marmot, Big Agnes	
Eureka! Military	HDT, Alaska Structures, Camel, Outdoor Venture, Diamond Brand	
Jetboil	MSR, Vista Outdoor	
Watercraft Recreation		
Ocean Kayaks	Confluence Outdoor, Hobie Cat, Wenonah Canoe, Jackson Kayak	
Old Town	Legacy Paddlesports	
Carlisle Paddles		
Diving		
SCUBAPRO	Aqua Lung, Suunto, Atomic Aquatics, Oceanic, Cressi, Mares	

Source: Based on Johnson Outdoors' 2021 *Form 10K*, pp. 5, 6, and a variety of other sources.

Garmin Ltd.

Garmin International Inc. is a subsidiary of Garmin Ltd. (Nasdaq: GRMN). Incorporated in Schaffhausen, Switzerland, but with principal subsidiaries in the US, Taiwan, and the UK, Garmin Ltd. was founded in 1989 by Gary Burrell and Min Kao in Lenexa, Kansas, with headquarters in Olathe, Kansas. With more than 18,000 employees in 34 countries, Garmin produces GPS navigation and wearable technology for the automotive, aviation, marine, outdoor and fitness markets.

In January 2022, Garmin acquired Vesper Marine, a leading manufacturer of marine electronics equipment. In December 2021, the aircraft manufacturer Embraer named Garmin Supplier of the Year for the seventh straight year. Also in 2021, Garmin was named Manufacturer of the Year by the National Marine Electronics Association for the seventh consecutive year, and Garmin was ranked number one in avionics support for the 18th consecutive year by *Aviation International News*.

Garmin's vision, mission, and core values are clearly stated on the company's website (https://www.garmin.com/en-US/company/about-garmin/) paraphrased as follows:

Vision: *To be the global leader in a vast array of electronic products that offer compelling design, superior quality, and best value.*
Mission: *To create superior products for automotive, aviation, marine, outdoor, and sports that are integral in our customers' lives.*
Core Values: *Our organizational culture is based on complete honesty, integrity, and respect for associates, customers, and business partners. All our employees are dedicated to doing what is right and doing what we say we will do.*

Aqua Lung International

Headquartered in Paris, France, Aqua Lung is the world's largest manufacturer of scuba diving equipment and apparel. As described at https://us.aqualung.com/en/ourstory.html, the company was founded by Jacques Cousteau and Emille Gagnan 75 years ago and has a storied history. The company today manufacturers regulators, fins, snorkels, knives, masks, wetsuits, computers, gauges, buoyancy control devices (BCDs), footwear, dry suits, gloves, hoods, boots, flashlights, and even more products that scuba divers commonly need and use.

External Issues

Fishing

The global fishing equipment market is expected to increase at an annual 4 percent from 2021 to 2026, from $14 billion to $17 billion according to https://www.marketdataforecast.com/market-reports/fishing-equipment-market. This positive forecast is partly because due to the launch of new fishing equipment with superior technology by companies such as Johnson Outdoors. People are increasingly interested in leisure outdoor recreational activities such as fishing, which in many places globally is becoming a common social activity.

The Food and Agriculture Organization of the United Nations estimates that the global number of recreational fishers or anglers vary between 220 million and 700 million, to go along with about 350 million commercial anglers. Estimates are that only about 17 percent of the young people 18 years and younger have been involved in fishing, and this demographic accounts for less than 5 percent of all anglers (https://www.factmr.com/report/236/sports-fishing-equipment-market). Fishing is reported to be the 10th-most popular sport among women, who account for 26.8 percent of all anglers and 8 percent of the sports fishing population. Boding well for companies such as Johnson Outdoors is the resurgence of outdoor recreational activities with the gradual relaxation of lockdown regulations.

The National Sporting Goods Association reports that fishing currently ranks fourth in the most popular participation sports in the US, beating bicycling, bowling, basketball, golf, jogging, baseball, softball, soccer, football, and skiing. Only walking, swimming, and camping are generally rated to be more popular than fishing. Interestingly, fishing is more popular than golf and tennis combined. Johnson Outdoors is into both swimming and camping, so the external outlook is positive for the company.

The US Fish and Wildlife Service estimates that one out of every six Americans who are 16 and older enjoy fishing. The National Sporting Goods Association reports that the average angler in the US spends more than a US$ 1,000 annually for fishing-related expenses. North America is the leading market for sports-fishing equipment, led by the US, where consumers spend more than $800 million annually on fishing-related items.

Scuba Diving

The website https://www.scubadiving.com/dive-industry-news-announcements provides continuous updates and news in the scuba diving industry. For example, the Divers Alert Network (DAN) on January 21, 2022, at 7 p.m. on the DAN YouTube channel (https://www.youtube.com/channel/UCubVAUy6ROwzk2B5TQ_XttQ) begins a monthly 30- to 45-minute webinar series on dive research, risk mitigation, and medical services (i.e., on the third Thursday of every month). All certified divers are familiar with DAN.

According to https://medium.com/scubanomics/scuba-diving-participation-rate-statistics-36b9eecd8540, the scuba diving industry has been in slow decline for a decade. For example, there was a 5.5 percent decline in scuba diving participation in 2019 and a 6.6 percent decline in 2020. This decade-long downward trend reversed in 2021–2022 when countries opened borders and divers began to travel again. The decline pre-2021 and prepandemic was evidenced even by Johnson Outdoors' scuba diving division (SCUBAPRO) reporting a sharp drop in sales in 2020, while their three other divisions, fishing, camping, and watercraft, were booming. The dive industry and Johnson Outdoors' diving segment rebounded in 2021. Analysts report, however, that the dive industry in general is not attracting and retaining enough customers to grow—not good news for Johnson Outdoors Diving segment.

Camping

In contrast to diving, the popularity of camping was steadily growing prior to the pandemic but experienced aggressive growth across the US in 2021–2022. The *2021 North American Camping Report*, which surveyed US and Canadian campers' sentiments and behaviors on the outdoor recreation, reported that more than 86 million US households consider themselves campers and 48 million of those households took at least one camping trip in 2020, up more than 6 million over 2019 (https://www.prnewswire.com/news-releases/fresh-data-indicates-camping-interest-to-remain-high-in-2021-301273611.html).

Research reveals that campers are becoming more diverse than ever as the incidence of camping among nonwhite campers exceeds national representation. Specifically, 6 in 10 first-time campers in 2020 were diverse ethnic groups, and 61 percent of same-sex households camp with children, an increase of 12 percent over 2019. Additionally, more than 80 percent of campers today are working and schooling from the campground, turning RVs into working, liveable offices. People have turned to camping and the outdoors to make it through the pandemic and beyond. This is all good news for Johnson Outdoors' Camping segment.

Conclusion

CEO Helen Johnson-Leipold and CFO David Johnson need an excellent strategic plan. Let's say the two Johnson family executives ask you to prepare a roadmap for the future of Johnson Outdoors. Beginning with development of a vision and mission statement for the company, perform EFEM, IFEM, SWOT, IE Matrix, and QSPM analyses to determine the most important underlying external opportunities and threats facing the company and the most critical internal strengths and weaknesses. Determine the relative attractiveness of various alternative strategies that could benefit the company most. To give expected results of your proposed strategies (recommendations), develop and provide projected financial statements for Johnson Outdoors.

Given the headwinds the company faces in their Diving segment, do you believe divestiture is appropriate for that segment? If yes, how much money would you expect to receive for that segment? How would you redeploy those funds? Are there particular fishing-related companies that Johnson Outdoors should consider acquiring to reduce intensity of competition in that industry? The company's Camping segment has heavy tailwinds catapulting that segment along. How can Johnson-Leipold and Johnson best capitalize on that external opportunity? What can Johnson Outdoors do about its main segment, Fishing, that is being plagued by supply chain disruptions and dragging down company revenues and profits. Be sure to include with your strategic plan the expected net costs and the extent that you suggest the company use debt versus equity to raise needed capital.

References

1. Johnson Outdoors' 2021 *Form 10K*.
2. https://www.comparably.com/companies/johnson-outdoors/leadership
3. https://www.factmr.com/report/236/sports-fishing-equipment-market
4. https://www.marketdataforecast.com/market-reports/fishing-equipment-market
5. https://medium.com/scubanomics/scuba-diving-participation-rate-statistics-36b9eecd8540
6. https://www.youtube.com/channel/UCubVAUy6ROwzk2B5TQ_XttQ)
7. https://www.prnewswire.com/news-releases/fresh-data-indicates-camping-interest-to-remain-high-in-2021-301273611.html
8. www.johnsonoutdoors.com

Thor Industries, Inc., 2022

www.thorindustries.com, (NYSE: THO)

Headquartered in Elkhart, Indiana, Thor Industries (THOR) in North America manufactures recreational vehicles (RVs) including towables and motorized RVs under such brand names as Airstream, Heartland, Jayco, Crossroads, Redwood, Starcraft, Thor Motor Coach, Vanleigh, Venture, Entegra, CruiserRV, Highland Ridge RV, KZ RVs, Keystone RV, Dutchmen, and Livin Lite RV. In Europe, Thor has 25 more RV subsidiaries and brands such as Buccaneer, Burstner, Carado, Dethleffs, Eriba, Elddis, LMC, Hymer, Sunlight, Xplore, and Compass.

THOR is the largest RV manufacturer in the world, one of the largest RV manufacturers in Europe, and the largest RV manufacturer in North America. Demand exceeds supply for THOR products benefitting THOR. THOR's revenues for fiscal 2021 were $12.3 billion, up from $8.2 billion the prior year, and net income was $659 million, up from $222 million the prior year. **THOR's fiscal year ends July 31 every year**.

Copyright by Fred David Books LLC; written by Fred R. David.

History

THOR was founded in 1980 when Wade Thompson and Peter Orthwein acquired Airstream. THOR has a history of acquiring other companies almost annually. In 1986, THOR was listed on the New York Stock Exchange. That same year, *Forbes Magazine* ranked THOR sixth out of the 200 best small companies in America.

A few major acquisitions that THOR made over the years are as follows:

1982 – General Coach, a manufacturer of travel trailers and fifth wheels

1991 – National Coach, a manufacturer of RVs

1992 – Four Winds International, a producer of Class A and Class C RVs

1995 – Komfort Corporation, a builder of travel trailers and fifth wheels

2001 – Keystone RV, a manufacturer of RVs

2001 – Damon, a manufacturer of Class A motorhomes

2001 – Breckenridge, a builder of park trailers

2004 – Crossroads RV, a leader in towable RVs

2010 – Heartland RV Company, a large producer of towable RVs

2010 – SJC Industries, the second largest ambulance manufacturer in the US

2010 – Livin' Lite, a manufacturer of RVs

2010 – KZ Inc., a leading producer and marketer of towable RVs

2015 – Cruiser RV (CRV), a towable RV maker

2015 – DRV Luxury Suites, a luxury fifth-wheel maker

2016 – Jayco, that owns Starcraft RV, Highland Ridge, Entegra Coach, & Jay Flight

2016 – Erwin Hymer Group (EHG), one of Europes' largest makers of RVs

2020 – Tiffin Motor Homes, a manufacturer of luxury RVs

2021 – Aircel, a leading supplier of OEM and aftermarket RV parts and accessories

2021 – Elkhart Composites, produces Elkhart composite boards that go in RVs

Internal Issues

Vision/Mission

THOR does not have a written vision or mission statement provided on its corporate website or in the firm's *Form 10K*. However, a mission statement for THOR is provided at the website https://www.comparably.com/companies/thor-industries/mission as follows (paraphrased):

> *"To enhance the culture, visibility, desirability and enjoyment of the RV Experience."*

Strategy

Through acquisitions past, present, and in the future, THOR is an integrated company, owning suppliers, rival producers, and distributors of RVs. THOR exited the business of producing and selling buses, so the company is focused on RVs and vastly more on the manufacturing of RVs than the selling of RVs.

THOR is becoming more global, especially with regard to securing component parts for RVs. For example, in December 2021, THOR signed a binding Memorandum of Understanding with ZF Friedrichshafen AG ("ZF"), which specifies that the two parties will jointly develop a high voltage electric drive system for towable recreational vehicles ("eTrailer System"). This new system aims to extend the nominal range of an electric vehicle (EV) when towing a trailer. This product can be important in the RV industry because EVs experience a significant reduction in range when towing any load, including a trailer. A trailer equipped with the eTrailer System is designed to use its own power to move a towable at the same speed of the tow vehicle, allowing an electric tow vehicle to pull the trailer with minimal loss of range. THOR to date has not really embraced the rapid transition globally to EVs, but likely this will be the target of future acquisitions.

Diversity, Equity, and Inclusion (DEI)

Relative to most large corporations, there is not much DEI information provided on the THOR corporate website or in the company *Form 10K*.

Sustainability

Being in the camping business, THOR works hard to protect and preserve the health of our planet and conserve resources throughout their operations and through the development of programs like Pick-Up-America. THOR's manufacturing processes are more energy- and resource-efficient than ever before, with an emphasis on recycling and reducing the amount of waste that goes to landfills.

THOR has five environmental monitoring and reporting categories as follows: Greenhouse Gas (GHG), Restricted Substances and Chemicals (RSC), Solid Waste and Recycling (SWR), Volatile Organic Compounds (VOC), and Water. Using their fiscal year 2019 as their baseline, THOR regularly monitors and shows progress on each category. THOR has committed to achieve net-neutral GHG emissions in or before 2050, reaching the interim target of a 50 percent reduction in GHG emissions in or before 2030. By reducing waste and emissions, minimizing environmental impact, and promoting conservation everywhere, THOR has signed the UN Global Compact Business Ambition for 1.5°C Commitment.

Organizational Structure

THOR's top executives are listed and arrayed in Exhibit 1. Note there is a COO, which implies this is a divisional (decentralized) company, but it is unclear whether those divisions are by region

EXHIBIT 1 THOR's Top Executives Listed and Arrayed

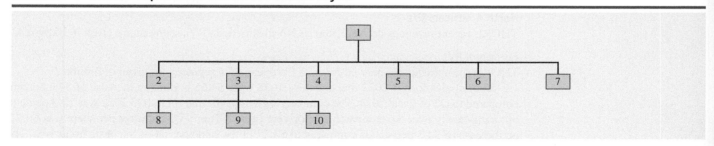

1. Robert Martin, President and CEO
2. Colleen Zuhl, SVP and CFO
3. Todd Woelfer, SVP and COO
4. Kennrth Julian, SVP of Administration and Human Resources
5. Josef Hjelmaker, Chief Innovation Officer
6. Trevor Gasper, VP and General Counsel
7. Mark Trinske, VP of Investor Relations
8. ABC, President North America
9. DEF, President South America
10. GHI, President Europe/Asia

Source: Based on https://ir.thorindustries.com/corporate-governance/management-team/default.aspx (Note that numbers 8, 9, and 10 report to number 3).

or product or subsidiary. Let's presume here that there are three regional presidents for North America, South America, and Europe/Asia, and that all three are female, to join Colleen Zuhl.

Segments

An RV is a vehicle that combines transportation and temporary living quarters for travel, recreation, and camping. RVs are generally categorized as motorhomes (motorized) and towables (towed behind family cars, vans, or pickups). The towable category includes travel trailers, fifth-wheel trailers, folding camp trailers, and truck campers, whereas the motorhome segment includes Type A, Type B, and Type C motorhomes.

Exhibit 2 and Exhibit 3 provide THOR's recent revenue information by segment. Note that North American Towables comprises slightly more than 50 percent of the total.

EXHIBIT 2 THOR's Revenues by Segment (in Thousands)

	2020	2021
RVs		
North American Towables	$4,140,482	$6,221,928
North American Motorized	1,390,098	2,669,391
European	2,485,391	3,200,079
Total	8,015,971	3,200,079
Other	234,481	373,174
Intercompany eliminations	(82,519)	(147,192)
Total	$8,167,933	$12,317,380

Source: Based on THOR's 2021 *Form 10K*, pp. 4 and 40.

EXHIBIT 3 A Histogram of THOR's Revenues by Segment (in Thousands)

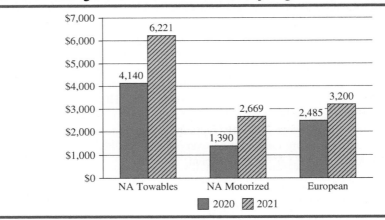

Source: Based on THOR's 2021 *Form 10K*, pp. 4 and 40.

North American RVs
THOR's recent revenues derived from its North American RVs segment are given in Exhibit 4.

European RVs
THOR's recent revenues derived from its European RVs segment are given in Exhibit 5.

Thor's sales for Q3 2022 that ended 4-30-22 were $4.66 billion, an increase of 34.6 percent compared to Q3 of fiscal 2021. The company's gross profit margin for Q3 2022 was 17.3 percent, up dramatically over the comparable prior-year period. Thor's Q3 earnings per share was $6.32, an increase of 92.1 percent as compared to $3.29 in the same period of the prior fiscal year. The company's consolidated RV backlog as of April 30, 2022 was $13.88 billion. Thor's addition of Airxcel back in September 2021 accounted for $154.0 million of the increase in net sales for Q3 2022. Specifically by segment for Q3 2022, Thor reported the following outstanding results in North America but decreases in the company's European business, as shown in Exhibit 6.

EXHIBIT 4 THOR's North American RVs Segment Revenues

	2020	2021
North American Towables		
Travel Trailers	$2,449,239	$3,791,235
Fifth Wheels	1,691,243	2,430,693
Total	4,140,482	6,221,928
North American Motorized		
Class A	495,520	1,052,982
Class B	776,191	1,266,624
Class C	118,387	349,785
Total	$1,390,098	$2,669,391

Source: Based on THOR's 2021 *Form 10K*, pp. 40, 42.
Note: Class A does not have access to the driver area, Classes B and C do have access.

EXHIBIT 5 THOR's European RVs Segment Revenues

	2020	2021
Motorcaravan	$1,505,353	$1,779,906
Campervan	433,398	779,755
Caravan	273,475	292,708
Other	273,165	347,710
Total	$2,485,391	$3,200,079

Source: Based on THOR's 2021 *Form 10K*, p. 44.

Note: Caravan is a nonmotorized, liveable, towable trailer; motorcaravans are caravans with their own motor/engine; campervans are like Class B vehicles from North America.

EXHIBIT 6 THOR's Q3 2022 Segment Results (in Thousands $)

Segment Results
North American Towable RVs

	Three Months Ended April 30,		% Change	2021	% Change
	2022	2021			
Net Sales	$ 2,640,137	$ 1,726,102	53.0	$ 4,491,327	52.9
Gross Profit	$ 453,907	$ 264,476	71.6	$ 711,980	74.0
Gross Profit Margin %	17.2	15.3		15.9	
Income Before Income Taxes	$ 326,697	$ 167,693	94.8	$ 456,752	90.2

North American Motorized RVs

	Three Months Ended April 30,		% Change	2020	% Change
	2022	2021			
Net Sales	$ 1,053,045	$ 775,393	35.8	$ 1,846,243	60.0
Gross Profit	$ 173,904	$ 96,288	80.6	$ 239,508	96.2
Gross Profit Margin %	16.5	12.4		13.0	
Income Before Income Taxes	$ 116,293	$ 54,780	112.3	$ 139,768	121.2

(Continued)

EXHIBIT 6 THOR's Q3 2022 Segment Results (in Thousands $) (*Continued*)

European RVs

	Three Months Ended April 30,		% Change			% Change
	2022	2021			2021	
Net Sales	$ 724,002	$ 894,240	(19.0)		$ 2,230,191	(6.7)
Gross Profit	$ 99,845	$ 120,159	(16.9)		$ 287,177	(10.4)
Gross Profit Margin %	13.8	13.4			12.9	
Income Before Income Taxes	$ 20,559	$ 43,993	(53.3)		$ 48,703	(74.9)

Source: Based on https://ir.thorindustries.com/investor-resources/press-releases/press-release-details/2022/
THOR-Industries-Delivers-Record-Third-Quarter-Net-Sales-And-Profitability/

Marketing and Distribution

THOR sells its RVs mainly through nonfranchised, independent dealers in the US, Canada, and Europe. There are about 2,400 of these dealers in the US and Canada and about 1,100 in Europe. Each THOR subsidiary has an independent wholesale salesforce that works closely with dealers. One dealer, FreedomRoads, accounts for about 13 percent of THOR's sales.

The largest RV retailer in the US, FreedomRoads, sells and rents new and used RVs through more than 100 locations in 30-plus states. FreedomRoads locations include Camping World stores and RV dealers that provide maintenance and repair services as well as financing for RVs. THOR almost never finances any dealer purchases.

As of 4-3-22, *Statistical Surveys, Inc.* reported THOR to be the #1 RV manufacturer within the North American Class B motorhome category. When combined with the company's European sales of campervans, which are European Class B equivalents, Thor is the global leader in this segment, which also is the fastest growing segment currently within the RV industry. Motor home industry retail registrations in the first calendar quarter of 2022 were below the record levels of 2021 but exceeded both 2020 and 2019 registrations in both North America and Germany. Analysts expect calendar year 2022 North American RV industry retail sales of between 460,000 and 480,000 units, which would represent one of the best years of North American RV retail sales on record.

Financial Issues

THOR's recent income statements and balance sheets are provided in Exhibit 7 and Exhibit 8, respectively.

Competitors

THOR's competitors include any companies in North America or Europe that design, manufacture, and market travel trailers, fifth-wheel trailers, Class A motorhomes, Class C motorhomes, and Class B motorhomes or components used in the manufacture of such vehicles. Three major rival firms

EXHIBIT 7 THOR's Recent Income Statements (in Thousands)

Income Statement	7/31/20	7/31/21		Percentage Change
Revenue (Sales)	$8,167,933	$12,317,380	⇧	51%
Cost of Goods Sold	7,049,726	10,422,407	⇧	48%
Gross Profit	1,118,207	1,894,973	⇧	69%
Operating Expenses	741,410	987,099	⇧	33%
EBIT (Operating Income)	376,797	907,874	⇧	141%
Interest Expense	103,901	63,293	⇩	–39%
EBT	272,896	844,581	⇧	209%
Tax	51,512	183,711	⇧	257%
Nonrecurring Events	1,590	(998)	—	—
Net Income	$222,974	$659,872	⇧	196%

Source: Based on THOR's 2021 *Form 10K*, p. F4.

EXHIBIT 8 THOR's Recent Balance Sheets (in Thousands)

Balance Sheet	7/31/20	7/31/21		Percentage Change
Assets				
Cash and Short-Term Investments	$538,519	$445,852	⇩	−17%
Accounts Receivable	814,227	949,932	⇧	17%
Inventory	716,305	1,369,384	⇧	91%
Other Current Assets	33,226	38,355	⇧	15%
Total Current Assets	2,102,277	2,803,523	⇧	33%
Property Plant & Equipment	1,107,649	1,185,131	⇧	7%
Goodwill	1,476,541	1,563,255	⇧	6%
Intangibles	914,724	937,171	⇧	2%
Other Long-Term Assets	170,269	165,008	⇩	−3%
Total Assets	5,771,460	6,654,088	⇧	15%
Liabilities				
Accounts Payable	636,506	915,045	⇧	44%
Other Current Liabilities	878,775	879,740	⇧	0%
Total Current Liabilities	1,515,281	1,794,785	⇧	18%
Long-Term Debt	1,652,831	1,594,821	⇩	−4%
Other Long-Term Liabilities	257,779	316,376	⇧	23%
Total Liabilities	3,425,891	3,705,982	⇧	8%
Equity				
Common Stock	6,540	6,565	⇧	0%
Retained Earnings	2,201,330	2,770,401	⇧	26%
Treasury Stock	(351,909)	(360,226)	—	—
Paid in Capital & Other	489,608	531,366	⇧	9%
Total Equity	2,345,569	2,948,106	⇧	26%
Total Liabilities and Equity	$5,771,460	$6,654,088	⇧	15%

Source: Based on THOR's 2021 *Form 10K*, p. F3.

are Winnebago Industries (WGO), LCI Industries (LCII), and The Shyft Group (SHYF). Statistical Surveys, Inc. reported that for the 6 months that ended June 30, 2021, THOR's combined US and Canadian market share was about 41.9 percent based on the revenue of travel trailers and fifth wheels combined and about 47.5 percent for motorhomes.

In Europe, THOR's major competitors are Trigano, Hobby/Fendt, Knaus Tabbert, and EHG. EHG's market share in Europe is about 24.5 percent for motorcaravans and campervans and about 17.5 percent for caravans. The word "caravan" in Europe refers to a nonmotorized travel trailer designed to be towed by a vehicle. Caravans and RVs in general in Europe are significantly smaller and lighter on average than in the US. Also in Europe, an "alcove" is more common, which as a sleeping area above the cab in a motorcaravan. About 40 percent of independent RV dealers in Europe sell the EHG brand exclusively.

According to https://www.comparably.com/companies/thor-industries/competitors, THOR's competitors include Harley-Davidson, Forest River, Jayco, Hero MotoCorp., and Winnebago Industries. A recent study compared THOR with some of its competitors and reported the findings provided in Exhibit 9. Note that THOR ranks excellent (number one) on four variables but ranks poorly on two variables (CEO Effectiveness and Overall Culture). Note also that the company's primary competitor, Winnebago, ranks last on the three variables it is compared on versus rivals.

EXHIBIT 9 Comparing THOR Versus Rival Firms (Ranking 1 = Best; 6 = Worst)

	Variables								
	1	2	3	4	5	6	7	8	9
THOR	4	2	1	1	1	4	1	3	17
Forest River	1	3	3	3	3	2	5	2	22
Hero MotoCorp	2	-	-	-	-	5	4	-	NA
Harley-Davidson	3	1	2	2	2	1	2	1	14
Jayco	5	4	4	4	4	3	3	-	NA
Winnebago Industries	6	-	-	-	-	6	6	-	NA

Variables

1. Effectiveness of CEO
2. Product Quality
3. Do Customers Recommend Company Products to Friends?
4. Pricing
5. Customer Service
6. Overall Culture
7. Do Employees Recommend Company Products to Friends?
8. How Happy Are the Women Employees at the Firm?
9. Summed Score (lower sum the better if all columns rated

Source: Based on https://www.comparably.com/companies/thor-industries/competitors

Winnebago Industries, Inc. (NYSE: WGO)

Headquartered in Forest City, Iowa, Winnebago Industries, Inc. is a leading North American manufacturer of motorized and towable RVs, motorhomes, travel trailers, fifth-wheel products, pontoons, inboard/outboard and sterndrive powerboats, and commercial community outreach vehicles under the Winnebago, Grand Design, Chris-Craft, Newmar, and Barletta brands. The company has multiple facilities in Iowa, Indiana, Minnesotas, and Florida.

Winnebago reported record fiscal 2021 record revenues of $3.6 billion, up a whopping 54.1 percent from $2.4 billion the prior year. The company's operating income was $407.4 million for fiscal 2021, compared to $113.8 million the prior year. Net income was $281.9 million, an increase of 358.8 percent compared to $61.4 million the prior year. Winnebago's fiscal 2021 revenues in their Towable segment were $2.0 billion, up 63.7 percent over the prior year. The company's fiscal 2021 revenues for the Motorhome segment were $1.5 billion, up 45.6 percent from the prior year.

Winnebago is working with the Science Based Target initiative and external validators to develop and enact a plan to achieve net-zero emissions by 2050. Winnebago's environmental sustainability goals include:

- Zero waste to landfill, with 90 percent diversion of waste by 2030.
- Net-zero greenhouse gas emissions by 2050.
- Reduce freshwater usage by 30 percent by 2050.
- Eco-friendly upgrade options to be available on all new products by 2025 and product lifecycle assessments by 2030.

Forest River, Inc.

Owned by Berkshire Hathaway and headquartered in Elkhart, Indiana, Forest River, Inc. has four manufacturing segments: RVs, Cargo Trailers, Pontoon Boats, Buses and Commercial Trucks. Within the RV segment, Forest River brand names include Coachmen, Park Models, Shasta, Dynamax, Palomino, East West, Forest River, and Prime Time. This is a private company, so financials and any substantive management, financial, or marketing information is not available, although the company website is excellent in regard to showcasing its different brands and models of products.

External Issues

Some RV campgrounds and repair facilities are reporting upward of a 50 percent increase in customers in 2021 versus the prior year as the pandemic slows down air travel but spurred RV travel. There are more first-time buyers of RVs in 2021 than in several decades. The RV Industry Association recently reported that suppliers are seeing as much as 170 percent increase in first-time RV buyers, with 46 million Americans planning on taking an RV trip within the next 12 months. It appears that people are taking the money they would normally spend on expensive vacations to instead buy an RV. Many guests at RV parks now are RVing while working remotely due to the coronavirus because many companies now allow employees to work from anywhere; people figure, why not work while traveling across the country? The pandemic definitely accelerated the popularity of RVing trends.

As a result of growing RVing popularity, the RV Industry Association is now forecasting total shipments for calendar 2021 to rising 34 percent to a new record high of 577,200 units, with an additional increase in shipments to more than 600,200 units in calendar 2022. With RV demand exceeding RV production in 2021, independent dealer inventory levels are at historically low levels. Dealer inventory may not return to more normalized levels until calendar 2023.

According to https://www.mordorintelligence.com/industry-reports/north-america-recreational-vehicle-market, the North American RV market was valued at $26.7 billion in 2020 but is anticipated to reach $35.7 billion by 2026, implying a 5 percent annual increase in revenues during the forecast period 2021–2026. Several factors spurring the increased popularity of RVing include the following:

1. Perceived safety of RV travel versus airplane travel and cruise ship vacationing
2. Desire to socially distance from others given the pandemic
3. Desire to get back to nature and spend more time with family and friends
4. More flexibility from companies regarding remote work
5. Rising levels of disposable income
6. Historically low interest rates

Conclusion

The RV Industry Association (https://www.rvia.org/reports-trends) reports that monthly RV shipments in November 2021 were 49,135, up 15.6 percent over November 2020, and 18.5 million Americans plan to travel in their RVs on their next vacation. Reports are that 43,881 towables were shipped from factories in November 2021, up 14 percent from the prior November, while 5,254 motorhomes were shipped out to dealers, up 30.4 percent. More than 600,000 RVs were manufactured in 2021, the most ever in a single year, according to RV Roadsigns.

Despite substantial tailwinds pushing the RV industry forward, THOR's CEO Robert Martin needs a clear strategic plan. Competitors such as Forest River and Winnebago are anxious to take market share away from THOR, by building what they say are better, more fuel-efficient, electric RVs at better prices across all sizes of motorhomes and towables. This industry is characterized by intense competition. Notice in the case that THOR has not mentioned a desire or plan to evolve into an electric-RV company, although this product is likely soon forthcoming.

As indicated in the History section of this case, THOR has used acquisition over the years as its primary growth strategy. Economies of scale are important in this industry. What additional acquisitions do you recommend THOR consider pursuing in the future? Or should THOR use more organic (internal) means to grow, by building additional factories to meet growing demand? Should THOR consider forward integration, perhaps selling vehicles online or developing exclusive franchise relationships or even launching a company-owned dealer network? These are all important questions that need to be answered from performing a comprehensive strategic planning analysis.

Develop for Martin a comprehensive strategic plan that can serve as a roadmap for THOR to follow over the next 3 to 5 years. Yes, there are nice tailwinds as consumers embrace camping and RVing more than ever, but fierce competitors stand everywhere along the roadway desiring to provide similar products with more value-added features to entice consumers. A clear vision, mission, and strategy for the future are needed to guide THOR to continued success in future years.

References

1. https://www.comparably.com/companies/thor-industries/competitors
2. THOR's 2021 *Form 10K*, p. 44.
3. https://www.mordorintelligence.com/industry-reports/north-america-recreational-vehicle-market
4. https://www.rvia.org/reports-trends
5. www.thorindustries.com

Apple Inc., 2022

www.apple.com, (NASDAQ: AAPL)

Apple is the world's largest corporation as of January 2022, based on market capitalization with a net worth of $3 trillion, which is $600 billion more than Microsoft and $1.3 trillion more than Amazon, the world's second- and third-largest firms, respectively. To reveal just how large Apple is and just how fast its growth has been, back in 2014 when a prior version of this case was included in the 16th edition, Apple was worth slightly more than $600 billion as the world's largest firm, with Exxon the world's second-largest firm valued at $400 billion. Today, Exxon is valued with a market capitalization of $282 billion.

Apple designs, manufacturers and markets the world's single-most popular smartphone, the iPhone, and the world's most popular tablet, the iPad. Apple also produces iCloud, Mac computers, watches, and other accessory devices. New for Apple in 2021 was the release of the iPhone 13 with the iPhone 14 released in 2022. Apple has developed a new "pro" branding for its higher-end iPhones and iPads. In addition, Apple has introduced its new M1 chip family included in the MacBook air and MacBook Pro laptops. This chip replaces the former Intel-based chips that caused the fans to run because Macs ran warm and were generally much slower than they are with the new chips. MacBook Pros released in 2021 with the new M1 pro chips were twice as fast as the Intel-based Macs only 1 year previously. Apple has made great strides in its wearable line now producing Series 7 on the watches. One significant strategic advantage of Apple is their ecosystem. Once a customer purchases an iPhone, there is high probability they will also purchase other Apple products.

In June 2022, Apple's updated 13-inch MacBook Pro with M2 became available for order on apple.com, the Apple Store app, and through Apple Authorized Resellers. The new machine is supercharged by the new M2 chip and features up to 24GB of memory, ProRes acceleration, and up to 20 hours of battery life, all in a compact design. The 13-inch MacBook Pro starts at $1,299 or $1,199 for education.

Copyright by Fred David Books LLC; written by Forest R. David.

History

Founded in 1976 by Steven Jobs and Steve Wozniak, Apple began as a personal computer company providing desktop computers for businesses and the home. The first computer, the Apple 1, was hand built by Wozniak and did not come with a keyboard or an outer case to protect the computer. The products were considered a kit, and users had to supply extra parts themselves. The Apple 1 sold for the interesting price of $666.66 or around $2,800 adjusted for inflation. Apple was incorporated in 1977 after Wozniak exited the business. The Apple II was first sold in 1977 and had the first major piece of business software, VisiCalc, a spreadsheet product.

Apple went public in 1980 for $22 a share and generated more money on its initial public offering (IPO) than any firm since Ford Motor Company 25 years earlier. Following a dispute with the board, Steven Jobs resigned from Apple in 1985 and started a new firm. With Jobs unaffiliated with Apple for the next 15 years, Apple experimented with various other products including CD players, digital cameras, and speakers among others. Throughout the 1990s, Apple experimented with several different product lines of personal computers with limited success. Apple's products were generally significantly more expensive than competitors, not compatible with much of the leading software or with the more popular Windows machines, and also were not able to multitask as well as Windows-based machines.

By 1996, Apple was struggling immensely, and the firm purchased Steve Jobs firm NeXT. After the board fired the existing CEO in 1997, Jobs was back acting as interim CEO of Apple. In the same year, Jobs identified Jonathan Ive and the two started working to rebuild Apple's products and brand name. After working for 25 years at Apple, Ive resigned his post. After several Mac upgrades and new software products like iMovie in 2001 Apple introduced the iPod and the firm sold 100 million units in 6 years. The year 2003 brought about the iTunes store, which enabled $0.99 downloads to iPods and remains an industry leader.

Apple launched the iPhone in 2008 and the iPad in 2010. In 2011, Steve Jobs passed away and current CEO Tim Cook now leads Apple. The major development for Apple recently is the advent of moving away from Intel processors to its own M family of chips in the MacBook laptop line. Rumors persist that Apple has new virtual reality technology that will possibly hit the market soon.

Internal Issues

Vision/Mission

Neither at its corporate website nor in its *Form 10K* does Apple have a vision or mission statement labeled as such. There are statements such as the following, however, that perhaps serve as Apple's vision and or mission (paraphrased):

Vision – *We strive to provide users of Apple products the best experience possible though innovative product designs and software.*

Mission – *We design the best personal computers in the world, along with OS X, iLife, iWork, and professional software. We lead the digital music revolution with iPods and iTunes online store. We developed and market the revolutionary iPhone. We are transforming the future of mobile media and computing devices with iPad.*

Organizational Structure

Apple's top executives are listed and arrayed in Exhibit 1. Note there is a COO, implying the company operates from a divisional (decentralized) design by product, region, or process. However, there are no divisional presidents, so it is unclear really what type structure Apple is using. A critical decision facing the company would be how best to organize, around regions, products, or processes. There should be divisional presidents reporting to #12, COO Jeff Williams. Regarding governance, note the CEO is not also Chair of the Board.

EXHIBIT 1 Apple's Top Executives Listed and Arrayed

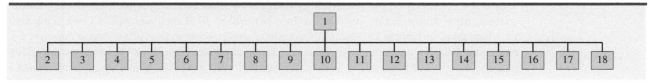

1. Tim Cook, CEO
2. Katherine Adams, SVP and General Counsel
3. Eddy Cue, SVP, Services
4. Craig Federighi, SVP, Software Engineering
5. John Giannandrea, SVP, Machine Learning and II Strategy
6. Greg "Joz" Joswiak, SVP, Worldwide Marketing
7. Sabih Khan, SVP Operations
8. Luca Maestri, SVP, CFO
9. Dierdre O'Brien, SVP, Retail + People
10. Johny Srouji, SVP, Hardware Technologies
11. John Ternus, SVP, Hardware Engineering
12. Jeff Williams, COO
13. Lisa Jackson, VP, Environment, Policy, and Social Initiatives
14. Stella Low, VP Communications
15. Isabel Ge Mahe, VP, Managing Director of Greater China
16. Tor Myhren, VP Marketing Communications
17. Adrian Perica, VP Corporate Development
18. Phil Schiller, Apple Fellow

Source: Based on https://www.apple.com/leadership/

Finance

Apple is performing exceptionally well financially. More than 10 years ago, financial analysts on TV were saying Apple was no longer a growth company, meaning it was so large that investors should not expect large gains in its stock price. However amazingly, Apple keeps growing as evidenced in Exhibit 2 with Revenues up 33 percent and Net Income up 65 percent. Since the start of 2014 when Apple was last used as a case in this textbook to early 2022, Apple stock is up 800 percent compared with 350 percent for the Nasdaq.

EXHIBIT 2 Apple's Recent Income Statements (in Millions)

Income Statement	9/26/20	9/25/21		Percentage Change
Revenue (Sales)	$274,515	$365,817	⇧	33%
Cost of Goods Sold	169,559	212,981	⇧	26%
Gross Profit	104,956	152,836	⇧	46%
Operating Expenses	38,668	43,887	⇧	13%
EBIT (Operating Income)	66,288	108,949	⇧	64%
Interest Expense	0	0	NA	NA
EBT	66,288	108,949	⇧	64%
Tax	9,680	14,527	⇧	50%
Nonrecurring Events	803	258	⇩	−68%
Net Income	$57,411	$94,680	⇧	65%

Source: Based on Apple's 2021 *Form 10K*, p. 30.

Apple paid about $14 billion in dividends 2019, 2020, and 2021, and repurchased $67, $72, and $85 billion, respectively, worth of common stock over the same time periods. Apple does not report these stock buyback transactions under treasury stock but deducts them from the retained earnings line on both the balance sheet and statement of cash flows as shown in Exhibit 3. This can be misleading for casual readers of Apple's financial statements noticing that treasury stock is zero and assuming the firm has not repurchased stock.

Strategy

Apple products are more expensive and tend to be more user-friendly than Windows, Android, and other operating systems but at the sacrifice of the user being able to customize or tailor the device for their specific needs. Apple's overriding strategy always has been to produce elegant, easy-to-use products, often at a premium price point. In a November 2014 interview, CEO Cook reiterated this when asked if having 15 percent of the global smartphone market share was a concern, by responding: "not all market share is equal, and Apple has never been about the most, we are about being the best." As of fiscal 2021, Apple still controls 15 percent of the global smartphone market.

Apple also has a culture of not collecting every detail about their users. For example, Apple does not read or store iMessages or FaceTime. Even if a government were to ask for this data, Apple could not provide it, they simply do not keep it on file. The latest version of iOS is more encrypted than ever. Out of respect for privacy, Apple forgoes potentially selling such information, as compared with other high-tech companies that collect massive amounts of information and sell it to potential advertisers. Apple historically has been an effective first mover but sometimes also a fast follower in the industry.

Keeping in line with its user-friendly products strategy, Apple must approve all third-party digital content through the App Store. Competitors like Android-based phones, tend to have less control over apps offered to their customers than does Apple. Apple prides itself on well-trained and knowledgeable salespersons who deliver excellent customer service. Apple invests heavily in R&D, more than $6 billion in 2014, which was up nearly 100 percent from 2012. However, by 2021 R&D had increased to $22 billion, which represents 6 percent of sales. For the last several years, Apple has allocated 6 to 7 percent of sales to R&D. Apple allocates nearly to the penny also 6 to 7 percent of sales to selling, general and administrative expenses, bringing annual operating expenses to 12 to 14 percent of sales, split evenly between the two categories.

A large push in Apple's strategy starting in 2021 was the introduction of the M family of chips for its Mac computers, moving away from Intel-based chips. Apple watches, iPhones, and iPads have long had Apple silicon powering them, and now Apple silicon moves into Mac machines much to the delight of Apple users everywhere. The transition away from rival firms who still are using Intel or other chip maker produced chips should bode well for Apple moving

EXHIBIT 3 Apple's Recent Balance Sheets (in Millions)

Balance Sheet	9/26/20	9/25/21		Percentage Change
Assets				
Cash and Short-Term Investments	$38,016	$34,940	⬇	−8%
Accounts Receivable	16,120	26,278	⬆	63%
Inventory	4,061	6,580	⬆	62%
Other Current Assets	85,516	67,038	⬇	−22%
Total Current Assets	143,713	134,836	⬇	−6%
Property Plant & Equipment	36,766	39,440	⬆	7%
Goodwill	0	0	—	—
Intangibles	0	0	—	—
Other Long-Term Assets	143,409	176,726	⬆	23%
Total Assets	**323,888**	**351,002**	⬆	**8%**
Liabilities				
Accounts Payable	42,296	54,763	⬆	29%
Other Current Liabilities	63,096	70,718	⬆	12%
Total Current Liabilities	105,392	125,481	⬆	19%
Long-Term Debt	98,667	109,106	⬆	11%
Other Long-Term Liabilities	54,490	53,325	⬇	−2%
Total Liabilities	**258,549**	**287,912**	⬆	**11%**
Equity				
Common Stock	50,779	57,365	⬆	13%
Retained Earnings	14,966	5,562	⬇	−63%
Treasury Stock	0	0	NA	NA
Paid in Capital & Other	(406)	163	NA	NA
Total Equity	**65,339**	**63,090**	⬇	**−3%**
Total Liabilities and Equity	**$323,888**	**$351,002**	⬆	**8%**

Source: Based on Apple's *Annual Report* 2021, p. 31.

forward. Backward-integrating to produce these chips should yield enormous strategic advantages and provide much needed control over chip suppliers.

Apple has historically been known for keeping its products simple with limited options for each item, and this remains true. There are currently two basic options for a Mac, the MacAir and the MacBook Pro; it is the same for the iPad and a similar story for watches and phones. This strategy is in stark contrast to many rivals who produce products all over the price spectrum. Apple also historically has done extensive outshoring and reshoring as the company does extensive business in dozens of foreign countries.

Diversity, Equity, Inclusion (DEI)

Apple's VP of inclusion and diversity, Barbara Whye stated in Apple's fiscal 2021 *Annual Report* that the company promotes a foundation of inclusion and diversity and is committed to rectifying any unintentional past injustices in hiring practices at Apple. Whye says Apple will continue to be a global pioneer in DEI issues and operate globally with humility and compassion. Among employees at Apple, people from underrepresented communities (URCs) increased 64 percent from 2014 to 2020, and today represents 50 percent of Apple's US workforce. Apple defines URCs as individuals that have had historically low representation in technology, including, in Apple's words, "Female, Black, Hispanic/Latinx, Multiracial, and Indigenous peoples." Between 2014 and 2020, Apple's percentage of females employed globally increased from 30 to 34 percent.

Exhibit 4 reveals the percentage of workers by race at Apple in the US, compared to US averages in 2020 based on race as follows: White, Hispanic/Latinx, Black, Asian, Two or more races, Indigenous, and Undeclared being 58, 19, 12, 6, 4, 1, and less than 1 percent, respectively.

To help aid in the firm's DEI efforts, Apple does the following: (1) provides excellent growth and development opportunities for URC (and all) employees, (2) provides an extended program for AppleCare team members whereby all employees can contribute lessons they have learned on the ground floor with engineering, marketing, upper management and beyond, and (3) provides classes at Apple University that promote DEI. For example, a new Race and Justice class is offered in the America speaker series that is available for all employees worldwide to take.

Additionally, Apple is focused on equal pay for all, a historically major problem for decades with people from URCs. Workers globally earn the same pay when performing the same job and have similar experience and performance. In the United States, the same practice is in place for all races and ethnicities, and Apple's policy is to never ask for salary history during the recruiting process. In 2020 the Arjuna Capital Gender Pay Scorecard awarded Apple the top ranking for pay equality.

EXHIBIT 4 Percentage of Workers by Self-Identified Race at Apple Over a 6-Year Span

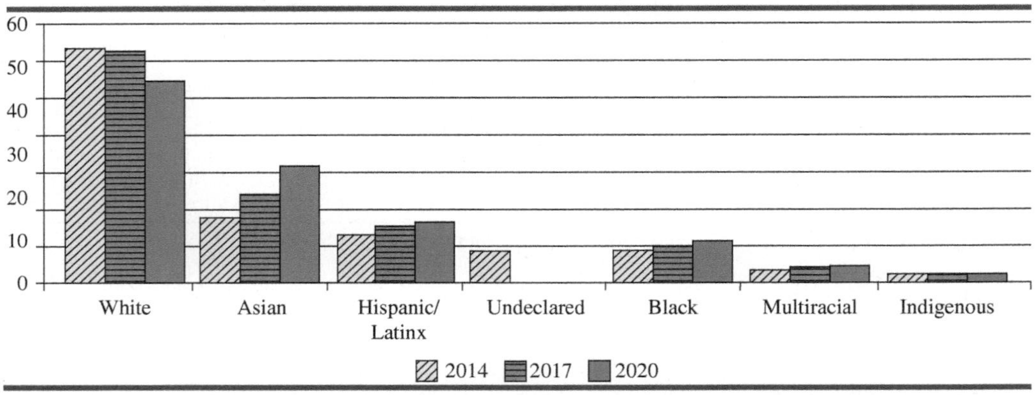

Source: Based on information Apple's DEI materials and information dispersed at www.apple.com

Segments

Apple reports revenues in five business segments presented in Exhibit 5. The firm also presents gross margin data in the *Annual Report* by two categories, Products and Services. In 2021 Apple reported a Products gross margin of $105 billion and a Services gross margin of $48 billion. Gross margin percentages were 35 and 70 percent, respectively. Without a major cost-of-goods-sold number associated with the Services, the gross margin is naturally higher than the corresponding number for Products.

Apple garnered 15 percent of the global phone sales in fiscal 2021, about the same percent the firm held in 2014, which is excellent considering new competitors have entered taking away market share from existing players. Apple's iPad sales account for 35 percent of the global market share of tablets in 2021.

Exhibit 5 reveals Apple's net sales by product or service. Apple has done a wonderful job with respect to services because it is the second-largest in net sales. Keep in mind, as previously mentioned, the profit margin is significantly higher with services. Surprising to some, wearables are the second-largest net sales category among Apple's products, higher than both Macs and iPads. Watches and other accessories such as keyboards, track pads, and ear buds cost significantly less than Macs and iPads per unit, but in total are larger revenue generators than the former two product classes.

Exhibit 6 reveals that the Americas, which includes from the tip of Canada to the southern tip of Argentina, account for 42 percent of fiscal 2021 net revenues. Apple does not provide detailed breakdowns on where in the Americas the revenues are generated. A key strategic decision for Apple is how aggressively the firm should target China, which is the world's second-largest economy that currently accounts for 19 percent of net sales for Apple.

EXHIBIT 5 Apple's Net Sales by Product/Service (in Millions)

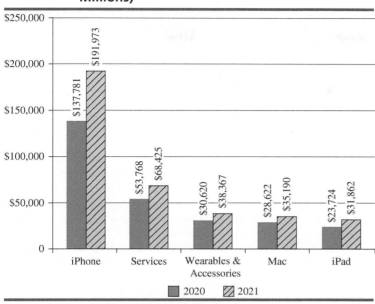

Source: Based on Apple's 2021 *Annual Report*, p. 21.

Competitors

Apple competes in a highly competitive and rapidly changing industry that is often associated with strong customer loyalty. Apple and rival firms typically roll out new smartphones, computers, and tablets annually. Many of Apple's rivals have prices 50 to 70 percent lower on comparable products. However, top rival Samsung's prices in the tablet and phone market of many of their top products are comparable with Apple prices. Competition for Apple should only increase in the future as rival firms are better able to duplicate Apple's products or even better able to persuade customers their products are just as good but significantly cheaper in price. Top competitors for Apple are revealed in detail in the respected product segments in the following sections.

Apple charges a premium for most of its product lines, but competitors often attempt to copy products, forcing Apple to file class action lawsuits for rivals that infringe on intellectual property. Most competitors in the industry compete on price. A customer can get an awful lot for their money by accepting products from different manufactures that will suit the needs of most

EXHIBIT 6 Apple's Net Sales Percentage Based on Geographic Region

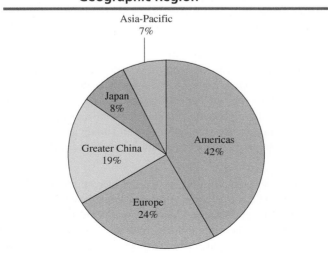

Source: Based on Apple's *Annual Report* 2021, p. 22.

customers. Such intense price competition may have actually helped Apple over the years by reducing competition because many of the top players from 10 years ago are no longer a significant factor because the main attraction of their products were price, and eventually they could no longer produce their products for a margin that made sense, as their most attractive differentiating strategy was continuingly lowering price. Of course, this strategy proved to be disaster for many former top rivals. This is one area where Apple has been exceptional, talking customers into buying products that have features and computing power they simply will never ever use at a price premium. However, despite many cheap alternatives, providing innovative products in a timely manner is a key success factor Apple has identified as evidenced by the firm's 50 percent of operating expenses or 7 percent of total revenues allocated to R&D.

Smartphones

The global smartphone industry as of 2022 is dominated by Samsung, Apple, Xiaomi, Oppo, and Vivo, representing a 70 percent market share. Samsung garners about 20 percent followed by Apple and Xiaomi with 15 percent each, and Vivo and Oppo with 10 percent as represented in Exhibit 7. Historically, and as recently as 2019, Huawei was commonly enjoying market shares close to Samsung, but recent effects from US trade bans and stiff competition have been devastating for Huawei.

EXHIBIT 7 Global SmartPhone Market Share, 2021

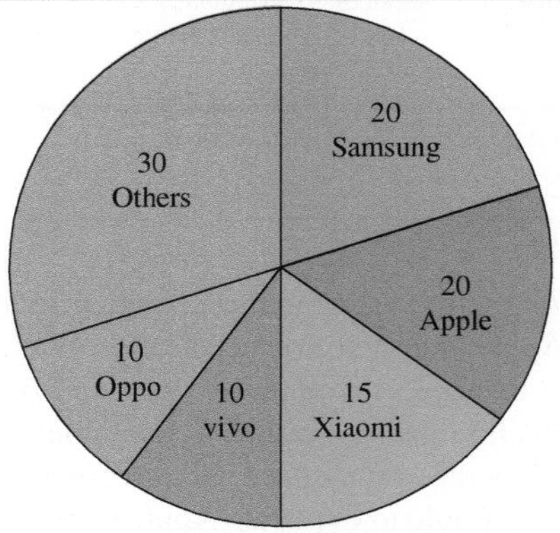

Source: Based on data from www.statistica.com

Samsung ships about 50 percent more phones than Apple, but Apple enjoys a profit from smartphones 2.5 times that of Samsung. Apple only has 35 percent more revenue than Samsung on smartphones. The differences are likely attributed to Apple not offering as many low-end smartphones as Samsung offers; Apple enjoys a significantly higher profit margin at the expense of extra volume. Other notable players in the smartphone industry in random order include: Sony, LG, Nokia, and Lenovo. Some of these firms just mentioned, although not major players, are large firms with the resources to enter the market on a moment's notice. Possibly, more concerning is that these firms could be positioning themselves for "the next big thing" in technology.

In the smartphone industry, Apple's iOS controls around 27 percent of the operating system market share with Android controlling about 73 percent. Yes, that adds to 100 percent, and there are other players offering operating systems, but they control less than 1 percent of this market. Apple has maintained their 27 percent for nearly a decade but more than 10 years ago in 2012, other key players in the mobile operating system market were Samsung, Nokia, BlackBerry, and Windows Phone, among others, all with operating systems of their own, and during this time, Android controlled a market share percentage about the same as Apple's. Apple, unwilling to allow rivals to use iOS, was a major opportunity for Android who capitalized by forcing every other operating system into extinction and upping their market share from 27 percent to 73 percent.

Tablets

The global tablet industry is dominated by some familiar faces that also dominate the smartphone market. However, Amazon and Lenovo are significantly larger players with respect to tablets than they are with smartphones. As mentioned previously, Apple is the market leader in tablets enjoying around a 35 percent market share. Samsung is the second-largest player with about a 20 percent market share. Amazon and Lenovo each control about 10 percent of the market share as of early 2022. Huawei controls 6 percent, which is down from the 10 percent share the firm enjoyed just 2 years prior, but the company is still competitive with tablets, so attributing the significant lost market share on smartphones to US trade bans is possibly over weighting that factor. With Huawei currently struggling, rival firms are certainly looking to take tablet market share away from Huawei. The remaining players in the tablet market control about 20 percent of the market. Notable names that round out the tablet market share include in no order: Microsoft, Asus, HP, LG, Acer, and several others.

Personal Computers

For the last 8 years into 2022, the PC market leaders based on shipments have been fairly stable. Lenovo and HP held about 18 percent each of the market in 2014, with Dell controlling 14 percent, Acer 8 percent, Asus 6 percent, and Apple 5 percent. Moving forward to 2022, the big loser has been Asus, dropping off the map, much to the benefit of Lenovo and HP, whose market shares increased to 24 percent for Lenovo and 22 percent for HP. Dell enjoyed 16 percent market share and Apple and Acer shared about 7 percent market share each. The other players in 2022 controlled about 22 percent jointly and represent a group of names most people are not familiar with; these brands are mostly local brands with the exception of Asus.

Although Apple shipped 7 percent of the PCs, the profit margins for high-end Apple products are much higher. Also, consider that the PC market data presented here is for all PCs, and within the PC market, there are many categories ranging from inexpensive basic PCs great for checking email, watching YouTube, browsing the internet, working on MS Office to high-end PCs like Apple products that offer great video creating to high-end Windows machines great for gaming. When analyzing a case such as Apple, it would be advantageous to focus on machines designed for the target Apple is marketing to and not the entire PC market in general. Also, one strategic issue for Apple moving forward is whether the company should produce a Mac designed for gaming. Many Apple customers are forced to purchase Windows-based machines for gaming applications.

Smartwatches and Wearables

In 2014, Samsung enjoyed a monopoly on smartwatches, controlling more than 70 percent of the market with the other firms enjoying the balance of 30 percent according to statistica.com. Smartwatches were in their infancy at this stage. The Apple smartwatch launched in 2015 and virtually instantly garnered a staggering 75 percent market share, dropping Samsung's share to miniscule 5 percent! Moving into 2022 as the smartwatch market matured, competitors did move in and erode Apple's monopolistic advantage, but as of 2022, Apple still controls a staggering 53 percent market share in smartwatches with top rival Samsung only moving up to a relatively paltry 11 percent market share.

A new name emerging with smartwatches not viewed with phones, tables, or PC is Garmin, who controls about 9 percent of the market. Other players make up the remaining 27 percent share. A possible rival is Fitbit who makes watches mainly for exercise applications. The synergies associated all four major products (i.e., phones, tablets, PCs, and wearables) are staggering and Apple has a stranglehold on the ecosystem. It could be argued the other major players viewed wearables as a fringe category and did not take this market seriously. With Apple controlling more than 50 percent, many watch customers may switch phones and PCs to Apple products moving forward. Ignoring the wearables segment could possibly be disastrous for the major names mentioned in phones, tablets, and PCs. What would you recommend Apple to do to capitalize further on this situation?

Cloud Storage

Cloud storage is becoming increasingly popular worldwide. Traditionally, many people were negligent on backing up their documents and files because it required a separate disk and time to save an item in another location. However, with the cloud, saving back up files are as simple as having the files in a dedicated folder on your existing device whether that device be a PC, phone, tablet, or watch. With Apple for example, any file on your desktop is also stored in Apple's iCloud by default. The files are both on your device and safe in the cloud. In addition to having the backup, cloud-saved material can be used from any device anywhere in the world with an internet connection and your login details. In fact, as many students know globally, professors commonly share class documents on a shared cloud folder for students.

The largest cloud providers worldwide by individual use are Google Drive, Apple iCloud, Microsoft OneDrive, Dropbox, and Amazon Drive Cloud, accounting for 40, 33, 20, 18, and 9 percent of the global use as of 2021, respectively. The reason these numbers add up to more than 100 percent are because many people use the services of more than one cloud provider. Cloud storage can be expensive if 1 TB is needed (in 2022 around $10 a month in the US), but many companies offer 5G of space for free, which is more than enough storage for documents.

External Issues

Global spending on PCs, tablets, mobile phones, and printers has been steady for nearly a decade. In 2012, $676 billion was spent on these devices, growing slightly more than $700 but falling back to $697 in 2020 before rocketing up to $802 billion in 2021, according to data provide by Statistica. Sales in 2021 were projected to finish the year around $821 billion with about 50 percent of spending being on smartphones, down from 73 percent allocation spent on smartphones in 2018.

Supply Chain

There has been a global shortage of parts especially semiconductor parts since the onset of the COVID pandemic in early 2020. Most of Apple's supplies, according to Apple, are available from multiple sources providing security for Apple and no overreliance on a single firm for critical component parts. However, several parts are only available from a single or few suppliers, placing increased stress and pressure on Apple in acquiring these parts in a timely manner. Many rival firms in the industry also want the same parts, which can cause price fluctuations that are not in Apple's favor. One aspect to consider about having many suppliers for similar products is that it likely produces excessive waste and increases disorganization; there are simply more moving parts that may be unnecessary.

It may be far better for Apple or any firm in the industry to have a supplier they can depend on, and form an excellent relationship with that single supplier. This is something to keep in mind when developing your 3-year plan for Apple. Could you imagine the cohesion case company McDonald's having multiple suppliers for soft drinks? As you can see, while having multiple suppliers for the same product may sound good on the surface, the benefits of McDonald's relationship with Coke may make you reconsider the attractiveness of multiple suppliers for one product.

Apple is increasingly using proprietary components not used by rivals in their products. The new A family of chips in iPhones and iPads are one such example, and the new M family of chips in the Macs are another, replacing the antiquated Intel family of chips. Apple even acknowledges that many of these custom components are derived from a single source. Most of Apple's outsourcing partners are located in Asia, but the United States and Ireland serve as home for manufacturing some Mac computers.

Conclusion

Apple competes in the highly competitive industry that produces phones, tablets, computers, watches, cloud storage, and related accessories. The competitors are wide ranging with the top competitors in one product such as phones differing significantly from another product such as watches. When analyzing the case, it is important to determine how Apple should allocate its resources across these product lines while remembering part of Apple's success is likely from the ecosystem, so the product categories are not independent of one another.

Another key area for Apple is with respect to R&D. Apple spends significant resources on R&D annually, and rumors are Apple will reveal new Apple glasses soon that will offer users a virtual reality experience. Virtual reality wearable devices on the head have been available for at least 10 years from various manufacturers but, to this point, have not become mainstream. Although a first mover on iPhones and iWatches and even PCs back in the early 1980s, Apple appears to be waiting to introduce their glasses.

To what extent should Apple backward-integrate by acquiring various key suppliers? Should the firm continue adding Apple Stores? Or should Apple get out of the retail store business and allow other stores and their online presence to generate sales? What do you recommend CEO Tim Cook do with respect to most of the manufacturing facilities being located in Asia? The firm is in desperate need for a 3-year strategic plan moving forward. Help Cook determine what new products or services Apple should develop and focus on in the future.

References

1. www.Statistica.com
2. Apple's fiscal 2021 *Annual Report* and *Form 10K*.
3. www.apple.com
4. https://www.apple.com/leadership/

International Business Machines (IBM) Corporation, 2022

www.ibm.com, (NYSE: IBM)

Headquartered in Armonk, New York, the International Business Machines (IBM) Corporation provides integrated solutions and products that use data, information technology (IT), and expertise in industries and business processes. With clients in nearly 175 countries, the company is divided into five segments: (1) Cloud and Cognitive Software (35 percent revenue), (2) Global Business Services (30 percent of revenue), (3) Global Technology Services (20 percent of revenue), (4) Systems (10 percent of revenue), and (5) Global Financing (less than 5 percent of revenue). About 45 percent of IBM's revenue comes from sales in the Americas, whereas 30 percent comes from sales in Europe, the Middle East, and Africa, and more than 20 percent of sales come from the Asia Pacific region.

IBM's Cloud and Cognitive Software segment offers software for customer information control systems and storage and analytics and integration software solutions for clients in banking, airline, and retail industries. This segment also offers middleware and data platform software, including Red Hat that enables the operation of clients' hybrid multicloud environments; and Cloud Paks, WebSphere distributed, and analytics platform software, such as DB2 distributed, information integration, and enterprise content management, as well as Internet of Things, Blockchain, and artificial intelligence (AI)/Watson platforms.

IBM's Global Business Services segment offers business consulting services; system integration, application management, maintenance, and support services for packaged software; and finance, procurement, talent and engagement, and industry-specific business process outsourcing services.

IBM's Global Technology Services segment provides IT infrastructure and platform services; and project, managed, outsourcing, and cloud-delivered services for enterprise IT infrastructure environments; and IT infrastructure support services.

IBM's Systems segment offers servers for businesses, cloud service providers, and scientific computing organizations; data storage products and solutions; and z/OS, an enterprise operating system, as well as Linux.

IBM's Global Financing segment provides lease, installment payment, loan financing, short-term working capital financing, and remanufacturing and remarketing services. The company collaborates with GK Software SE to enhance retail innovation and customer omnichannel experience with hybrid cloud technology; and with Apptio, Inc.

Copyright by Fred David Books LLC; written by Meredith E. David.

History

Incorporated in 1911 as the Computing-Tabulating-Recording Company, and in 1924 named IBM, the company became the largest office machine producer in the United States by 1940. In 1952, IBM introduced its first computer and then maintained nearly 80 percent market share through the 1960s and 1970s. Floppy disks were created by IBM in the early 1970s, and the first laser printer for computers was introduced by the company in 1975. In 1993, IBM hired a new, outsider CEO, Louis Gerstner.

In the 2000s, IBM acquired many companies, including 12 acquisitions in 2007 with an aggregate cost of $1,144,000,000, 13 acquisitions in 2008 with a total cost $889,000,000, and five additional acquisitions in 2009 with a total purchase price of $295,000,000, and 10 more acquisitions in 2010. Even today, in 2021, IBM acquired 15 companies, aimed primarily at strengthening the IBM's hybrid cloud and AI capabilities as part of a strategy to redefine the company as a hybrid cloud platform and AI company. Some of these acquisitions encompass outsourcing and reshoring operations as deemed necessary given the company's strategic planning process.

Several notable milestones in IBM's history are listed as follows (verbatim from IBM's website):

1953: The first heart and lung machine was produced by IBM and enabled the world's first successful open-heart surgery on a human.

1969: IBM builds the computers and software for the Apollo missions, landing Neil Armstrong and Buzz Aldrin on the moon and guiding them back to Earth.

1971: The world's first floppy disc was produced by IBM and eventually over 5 billion units were sold.

1973: The UPC bar code—IBM scientist Norman Woodland invents UPC bar codes, transforming the retail industry, with UPC codes tracking everything from clothing to flowers.

1980: IBM patents LASIK surgery and now millions of people enjoy improved vision.

1981: Computing goes mainstream with introduction of the IBM personal computer, revolutionizing society.

1997: IBM Deep Blue supercomputer defeats the best chess player in the world, leading to artificial intelligence (AI) that we know and use today.

Internal Issues

Vision/Mission

IBM does not have a formal vision statement, but a possible vision for IBM could include the wording from the company's website (paraphrased):

We are a hybrid cloud and AI company making investments to extend our innovation leadership into the future.

IBM does not have a formal mission statement, but the company makes the following statements on its website, which could serve as a possible mission for IBM (paraphrased):

We provide integrated solutions and products that leverage data and information technology with our hybrid cloud platform and AI technology. We enhance and support clients' digital transformations and help them engage with their customers and employees in new ways. We offer industry-leading consulting and IT implementation services, as well as cloud, digital and cognitive offerings, and enterprise systems and software, for customers globally.

Organizational Structure

IBM's top executives are listed and arrayed in Exhibit 1. Note the design appears to be divisional-by-product because there are no strategic business unit (SBU) group executives. Regarding governance, note that CEO Krishna is also Chairman of IBM's Board of Directors.

EXHIBIT 1 IBM's Top

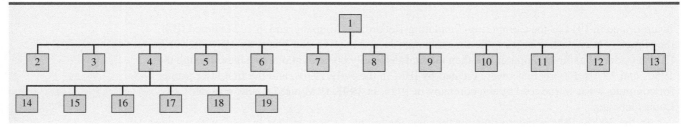

1. Arvind Krishna, Chairman & CEO
2. Jonathan H. Adashek, Chief Communications Officer & SVP, Marketing
3. Michelle H. Browdy, SVP, Legal and Regulatory Affairs, and General Counsel
4. Kelly Chambliss, SVP & COO, IBM Consulting
5. Gary Cohn, Vice Chairman of IBM
6. Mark Foster, Chairman, IBM Consulting
7. Dr. Darío Gil, SVP & Director of IBM Research
8. Kathryn Guarini, CIO
9. James J. Kavanaugh, SVP & CFO
10. Nickle LaMoreaux, SVP & Chief HRM Officer

11. Obed Louissaint, SVP, Transformation & Culture
12. Christina Montgomery, VP & Chief Privacy Officer
13. Roger Premo, General Manager, Strategy & Corporate Development
14. Ric Lewis, SVP, IBM Systems
15. Howard Boville, SVP, IBM Hybrid Cloud
16. Bob Lord, IBM SVP, The Weather Company & Alliances
17. Tom Rosamilia, SVP, IBM Software Chairman, North America
18. Rob Thomas, SVP, IBM Global Markets
19. John Granger, SVP, IBM Consulting

Note: Numbers 14 to 19 report to number 4.
Source: Based on https://www.ibm.com/investor/governance/senior-leadership

Segments

IBM has four segments: Software, Consulting, Infrastructure, and Financing. IBM's segment results for Q2 2021 are summarized in Exhibit 2. Note that the largest segment by far is Software and the smallest by far is Financing. Exhibit 3 shows the revenue information in a table. Exhibit 4 shows the revenue information in a bar graph.

EXHIBIT 2 IBM's Q4 2021 Segment Results

1. *Software (includes Hybrid Platform and Solutions, Transaction Processing)*

Total Revenues of $7.3 billion, up 8.2 percent
Hybrid Platform & Solutions up 7 percent
Red Hat up 19 percent
Automation up 13 percent
Data & AI up 1 percent
Security down 2 percent
Transaction Processing up 11 percent
Software segment hybrid cloud revenue up 22 percent

2. *Consulting (includes Business Transformation, Technology Consulting and Application Operations)*

Total Revenues of $4.7 billion, up 13.1 percent
Business Transformation up 18 percent
Technology Consulting up 14 percent
Application Operations up 6 percent
Consulting segment hybrid cloud revenue up 31 percent

3. *Infrastructure (includes Hybrid Infrastructure and Infrastructure Support)*

Total Revenues of $4.4 billion, down 0.2 percent
Hybrid Infrastructure flat
IBM Z down 6 percent
Distributed Infrastructure up 5 percent
Infrastructure Support down 1 percent
Infrastructure segment hybrid cloud revenue down 12 percent

4. *Financing (includes Client and Commercial Financing)*

Total Revenues of $0.2 billion, down 29.4 percent

Source: Based on https://www.ibm.com/investor/att/pdf/IBM-4Q21-Earnings-Press-Release.pdf

EXHIBIT 3 IBM's Full Year Segment Revenues (in Millions $)

	Revenues		Gross Profit Margin	
	2020	2021	2020	2021
Software	$22,927	$24,141	78.3	78.8
Consulting	16,257	17,844	29.3	28.0
Infrastructure	14,533	14,188	57.5	55.3
Financing	975	774	41.6	31.7
Other	488	404		
Total	$55,179	$57,350		

Source: Based on https://www.ibm.com/investor/att/pdf/IBM-4Q21-Earnings-Press-Release.pdf, p. 5.

Finance

IBM's recent income statements and balance sheets are provided in Exhibit 5 and Exhibit 6, respectively. Note the modest increases in revenue and net income in 2021, but a weakening balance sheet as indicated by all the down red arrows.

EXHIBIT 4 IBM's Revenues by Segment, 2020 Versus 2021 (in Millions $)

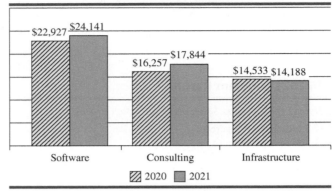

Source: Based on https://www.ibm.com/investor/att/pdf/IBM-4Q21-Earnings-Press-Release.pdf, p. 5.

EXHIBIT 5 IBM's Recent Income Statements (in Millions $)

Income Statement	12/31/20	12/31/21		Percentage Change
Revenues	$55,179	$57,350	⇧	4%
Cost of Goods Sold	24,314	25,864	⇧	6%
Gross Profit	30,865	31,486	⇧	2%
Operating Expenses	27,005	25,494	⇩	−6%
EBIT	3,860	5,992	⇧	55%
Interest Expense	1,288	1,155	⇩	−10%
EBT	2,572	4,837	⇧	88%
Tax	(1,360)	124	—	—
Nonrecurring Events	1,658	1,030	⇩	−38%
Net Income	$5,590	$5,743	⇧	3%

Source: Based on https://www.ibm.com/investor/att/pdf/IBM-4Q21-Earnings-Press-Release.pdf, p. 6.

EXHIBIT 6 IBM's Recent Balance Sheets (in Millions $)

Balance Sheet	12/31/20	12/31/21		Percentage Change
Assets				
Cash and Short-Term Investments	$13,188	$6,650	⇩	−50%
Accounts Receivable	17,377	15,770	⇩	−9%
Inventory	1,812	1,649	⇩	−9%
Other Current Assets	6,788	5,470	⇩	−19%
Total Current Assets	39,165	29,539	⇩	−25%
Property Plant & Equipment	6,205	5,694	⇩	−8%
Goodwill	53,765	55,643	⇧	3%
Intangibles	13,739	12,511	⇩	−9%
Other Long-Term Assets	43,097	28,614	⇩	−34%
Total Assets	**155,971**	**132,001**	⇩	**−15%**

Balance Sheet	12/31/20	12/31/21		Percentage Change
Liabilities				
Accounts Payable	4,033	3,955	⇩	−2%
Other Current Liabilities	35,836	29,664	⇩	−17%
Total Current Liabilities	39,869	33,619	⇩	−16%
Long-Term Debt	54,217	44,917	⇩	−17%
Other Long-Term Liabilities	41,158	34,469	⇩	−16%
Total Liabilities	**135,244**	**113,005**	⇩	**−16%**
Equity				
Common Stock	56,556	57,319	⇧	1%
Retained Earnings	162,717	154,209	⇩	−5%
Treasury Stock	(169,339)	(169,392)	⇧	0%
Paid in Capital & Other	(29,207)	(23,140)	⇩	−21%
Total Equity	**20,727**	**18,996**	⇩	**−8%**
Total Liabilities and Equity	**$155,971**	**$132,001**	⇩	**−15%**

Source: Based on https://www.ibm.com/investor/att/pdf/IBM-4Q21-Earnings-Press-Release.pdf, p. 6.

Competitors

IBM competitors include Google, Meta, Microsoft, Amazon, and Apple. Analysts recently compared IBM with several of its key competitors on nine management and marketing variables. The results are provided in Exhibit 7. Note that IBM ranks an impressive number one on five variables, including CEO Effectiveness. IBM ranks poorly however on three key categories as indicated by the number fives along the first row in Exhibit 7. Rival Meta Platforms ranks really low on four categories as indicated by the sixes on Row 3. Overall, as indicated by the low summed scores in Column 10, Google was ranked best overall, closely followed by IBM.

EXHIBIT 7 Comparing IBM Versus Rival Firms (Ranking 1 = Best; 6 = Worst)

	Variables									
	1	2	3	4	5	6	7	8	9	10
IBM	1	5	5	5	4	1	1	1	1	24
Meta Platforms	4	6	6	6	6	3	3	3	3	40
Microsoft	2	4	4	4	5	4	4	4	4	35
Amazon	6	2	2	3	1	5	6	5	5	35
Apple	5	1	1	3	2	6	5	6	6	33
Google	3	3	3	2	3	2	2	2	2	22

Variables

1. Effectiveness of CEO
2. Product Quality
3. Do Customers Recommend Company Products to Friends?
4. Pricing
5. Customer Service
6. Overall Culture
7. Do Employees Recommend Company Products to Friends?
8. How Happy Are the Women Employees at the Firm?
9. How Happy Are Minority Employees at the Firm?
10. Summed Score (lower sum the better)

Source: Based on https://www.comparably.com/companies/ibm/competitors

Exhibit 8 compares IBM to three rival companies. Note IBM is far less than half the size of all three rivals but still is a large company.

EXHIBIT 8 Rival Firms Compared Financially

	IBM (IBM)	Microsoft (MSFT)	Alphabet (GOOG)	Apple (AAPL)0
Market Capitalization	$121 billion	$2.3 trillion	$1.8 trillion	$2.83 trillion
EPS	$6.35	$9.4	$112	$6.01
Revenue	$57.3 billion	$185 billion	$257 billion	$378 billion
Net Income	$4.7 billion	$71 billion	$76 billion	$100 billion
Total Debt	$55 billion	$80 billion	$28 billion	$122 billion
Total Debt/Equity	290	50	11	170
Current Ratio	1.78	2.25	2.93	1.04
# Full-time Employees	270,000	181,000	156,500	100,000
Stock Price	$135	$304	$2,786	$174

Source: Based on https://finance.yahoo.com/quote/IBM?p=IBM&.tsrc=fin-srch

Microsoft

Based in Redmond, Washington, Microsoft provides software, services, devices, and solutions worldwide, including MS Office, Exchange, SharePoint, MS Teams, Office 365 Security and Compliance, Skype for Business, Client Access Licenses (CAL), Skype, Outlook.com, One-Drive, LinkedIn, and Dynamics 365, a set of cloud-based and on-premises business solutions for organizations and enterprise divisions. Microsoft licenses SQL, Windows Servers, Visual Studio, System Center, and related CALs; GitHub that provides a collaboration platform and code hosting service for developers; and Azure, a cloud platform. The company additionally provides consulting services related to Microsoft server and desktop solutions, as well as training and certification on Microsoft products.

Microsoft provides Windows original equipment manufacturer (OEM) licensing and licensing of the Windows operating system, Windows cloud services, Windows Internet of Things, MSN advertising, MS Surface, PC accessories, PCs, tablets, gaming and entertainment consoles, gaming, including Xbox, and MS Search, including Bing. Microsoft sells its products through OEMs, distributors, resellers, online stores, and retail stores. The company collaborates with Dynatrace, Inc., Morgan Stanley, Micro Focus, WPP plc, ACI Worldwide, Inc., and iCIMS, Inc., Avaya Holdings, and wejo Limited. Microsoft just acquired the video-game company Activision Blizzard for $68 billion.

Google

Headquartered in Mountain View, California, the parent company of Google, Alphabet Inc., is a gigantic search engine company that provides online advertising services globally. Alphabet operates in three segments: Google Services, Google Cloud, and Other Bets segments. Google Services provides Android, Chrome, Google Maps, Google Play, Search, and YouTube; subscription-based products; and Fitbit wearable devices, Google Nest home products, Pixel phones, and other devices, as well as in-app purchases and digital content. Google Cloud offers Google Workspace that includes cloud-based collaboration tools for enterprises, such as Gmail, Docs, Drive, Calendar and Meet; and other services for enterprise customers. The company's Other Bets segment sells health technology and internet services, as well as licensing and research and development services.

External Issues

IBM competes in what is called the high-performance computing (HPC) market globally. Exhibit 9 provides the expected revenue for various segments of HPC in 2024.

EXHIBIT 9 Expected Revenue of HPC Segments in 2024

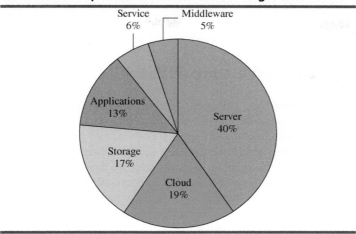

Source: Based on www.hyperionresearch.com, December 2020.

Conclusion

CEO Arvind Krishna needs a clear 3-year strategic plan for IMB. Gigantic rival firms facing IBM create high intensity of competition; rivalry among firms is accelerating as technology changes daily in this industry. The vision/mission and organizational structure sections of this case reveal that there is substantial room for improvement for IBM in both areas. Krishna knows the basic underlying external opportunities and threats and internal strengths facing IBM, but he is unsure about the relative importance of those factors. He thus needs an external and internal assessment performed, anchored by development of an EFE Matrix and IFE Matrix as described in Chapter 3 and Chapter 4 of the David textbook. Krishna also needs to know the relative attractiveness of alternative strategies facing the company, so he needs a SWOT, BCG, and QSPM analyses performed.

Let's say Krishna asks you to develop the comprehensive strategic plan that he needs. In addition to the analyses mentioned, include in your report a perceptual map, a set of proposed recommendations with associated costs, and an EPS-EBIT analysis to reveal whether debt or stock or some combination of debt and stock is best to obtain the needed funds. Also include projected financial statements to show the expected impact on IBM if Krishna adopts your proposed strategic plan. What additional acquisitions should IBM make to help assure top line (revenues) and bottom line (net income) 5+ percent annually in the years to come? Identify candidate firms for IBM to acquire. If IBM should expand further organically (internally) into other regions, countries, and continents, include direction for Krishna in this regard.

All of IBM's top executives, board of directors, shareholders, and employees will benefit from and be thankful for your work developing and proposing a clear roadmap for their future. Good luck on this endeavor. We authors are confident you can do a wonderful job performing this task, following the guidelines presented in the David strategic management textbook and using the strategic planning template provided at www.strategyclub.com.

References

1. https://www.ibm.com/investor/governance/senior-leadership
2. https://www.ibm.com/investor/att/pdf/IBM-4Q21-Earnings-Press-Release.pdf
3. https://www.comparably.com/companies/ibm/competitors
4. https://finance.yahoo.com/quote/IBM?p=IBM&.tsrc=fin-srch
5. IBM's 2021 *Form 10K*.
6. www.hyperionresearch.com, December 2020.

Colgate-Palmolive, 2022

www.colgatepalmolive.com; (NYSE: CL)

Headquartered in New York City, Colgate-Palmolive is a large global consumer products company specializing in the production and distribution of household, health care, personal care, and veterinary products. Colgate manufactures and sells consumer products worldwide through two segments: (1) Oral, Personal, and Home Care and (2) Pet Nutrition.

Colgate's Oral, Personal, and Home Care segment produces and markets to retailers, wholesalers, and distributors of toothpaste, toothbrushes, mouthwash, bar and liquid hand soaps, shower gels, shampoos, conditioners, deodorants and antiperspirants, skin health products, dishwashing detergents, fabric conditioners, household cleaners, and other similar items. Colgate sells its products in more than 200 countries and territories.

Colgate's Pet Nutrition segment produces and offers to pet supply retailers, veterinarians, and eCommerce retailers pet nutrition products for everyday nutritional needs; and a range of therapeutic products to manage disease conditions in dogs and cats. Trademarks in this segment include Colgate, Palmolive, elmex, hello, meridol, Sorriso, Tom's of Maine, EltaMD, Filorga, Irish Spring, Lady Speed Stick, PCA Skin, Protex, Sanex, Softsoap, Speed Stick, Ajax, Axion, Fabuloso, Murphy, Soupline, and Suavitel, as well as Hill's Science Diet and Hill's Prescription Diet. Colgate has a partnership with Verily Life Sciences LLC to advance oral health research.

Colgate-Palmolive has long been in intense competition with Procter & Gamble (P&G), the world's largest soap and detergent maker. P&G's Tide laundry detergent debuted in 1946 and millions of consumers turned from Colgate's soaps to the new product. Colgate also lost its number-one position in the toothpaste market when P&G added fluoride to its toothpaste (Colgate has since reclaimed the number-one sales position). In the mid-1950s as television debuted, Colgate-Palmolive competed with P&G as a sponsor of many soap operas, such as *The Doctors*. Excellent, updated Colgate financial charts illustrating the company's sales and net income across regions and products is provided at the website: https://investor.colgatepalmolive.com/financial-information/financial-highlights.

Copyright by Fred David Books LLC; written by Meredith E. David.

History

William Colgate, a devout Baptist English immigrant soap and candlemaker established in 1806 a starch, soap, and candle factory in New York City under the name William Colgate & Company. In the 1840s, the company began selling individual cakes of soap in uniform weights. In 1857, Colgate passed away, and the company was reorganized as Colgate & Company under the management of his devout Baptist son Samuel Colgate, who did not want to continue the business but thought it would be the right thing to do. In 1872, the company debuted Cashmere Bouquet, a perfumed soap.

In 1873, the company introduced its first Colgate toothpaste, an aromatic toothpaste sold in jars. In 1896, the company sold the first toothpaste in a tube, named Colgate Ribbon Dental Cream (invented by dentist Washington Sheffield). By 1908, the company initiated mass sales of toothpaste in tubes. William Colgate's other son, James Boorman Colgate, became a primary trustee of Colgate University.

While the Colgate company was growing, in Milwaukee, Wisconsin, the B. J. Johnson Company was making a soap by combining palm oil and olive oil, hence PalmOlive. The soap became so popular the Johnson Company was renamed Palmolive in 1917. In the early 1900s, Palmolive was the world's best-selling soap. George Henry Lesch, President, CEO, and Chairman of the Board of Colgate-Palmolive in the 1960s and 1970s transformed the firm into a fast-growing, modern company.

In 2005, Colgate sold some of its underperforming brands, including Fab, Dynamo, Arctic Power, ABC, Cold Power, and Fresh Start, and the license for the Ajax brand for laundry detergents in the US, Canada, and Puerto Rico as part of an overall plan to focus on higher margin oral, personal, and pet care products. In 2020, Colgate-Palmolive acquired Hello Products LLC, a fastest-growing, premium oral care brand in the US.

Today, Colgate has numerous subsidiary organizations in 200 countries, but the company's stock is publicly listed in just three countries: US, India, and Pakistan. Colgate-Palmolive's chief manufacturing plant is located in Burlington, New Jersey, and provides fragrance and flavor oils for the company's facilities around the world.

Internal Issues

Vision/Mission

Colgate does not have a published vision or mission statement available on its corporate website, but statements can be found on the internet as indicated in Exhibit 1.

EXHIBIT 1 Colgate's Vision and Mission Statement (Paraphrased)

Vision – *Our core values of Caring, Global Teamwork and Continuous Improvement are the foundation for our future initiatives.*

Mission – *We are committed to serving others with compassion, integrity, and honesty in all situations. We listen with respect to others, value diversity, and are committed to protect the global environment. We strive to enhance the communities where our employees live and work and to be compliant globally with government laws and regulations.*

Source: https://www.comparably.com/companies/colgate-palmolive/mission

Organizational Structure

Colgate's top executives are listed and arrayed in Exhibit 2. The design is divisional-by-region, but there probably needs to be a COO, unless perhaps the Chief of Staff serves as COO. Note there are seven females among the top 22 persons which from an organizational culture perspective that is excellent in comparison to rival companies.

EXHIBIT 2 Colgate's Top Executives Listed and Arrayed

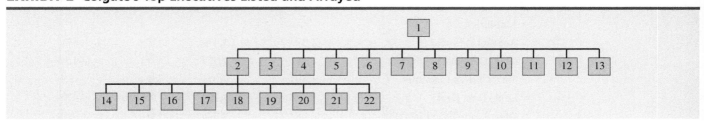

1. Noel Wallace, Chairman, President, and CEO
2. John Kooyman, Chief of Staff
3. Al Lee, Chief Internal Governance Officer
4. Sally Massey, Chief Human Resources Officer
5. Jennifer Daniels, Chief Legal Officer and Secretary
6. Stanley Sutula III, Chief Financial Officer
7. Michael Corbo, Chief Supply Chain Officer
8. Patricia Verduin, Chief Technology Officer
9. Mike Crowe, Chief Information Officer
10. Iain Kielty, VP, Global Budget & Financial Planning
11. John Faucher, Chief Investor Relations Officer, and SVP, M&A
12. Paula Davis, VP & Chief Communications Officer
13. Brigitte King, Chief Digital Officer
14. Prabha Parameswaran, Group President, Growth and Strategy
15. Panagiotis Tsourapas, Group President, Europe and Developing Markets
16. Peter Brons-Poulsen, President, Europe
17. Juan Pablo Zamorano, President, Latin America
18. Maria Paula Capuzzo, President, Colgate-Africa/Eurasia
19. Mukul Deoras, President, Asia-Pacific
20. Jesper Nordengaard, President, Colgate-North America
21. Jean-Luc Fischer, President, Colgate-Europe
22. John Hazlin, President, Hill's Pet Nutrition

Note: Numbers 14 to 22 perhaps report to number 2, if number 2 serves as a COO.

Source: Based on https://www.colgatepalmolive.com/en-us/who-we-are/our-leadership-team

Finance

Colgate's recent income statements and balance sheets are provided in Exhibit 3 and Exhibit 4, respectively.

EXHIBIT 3 Colgate's Recent Income Statements (in Millions)

Income Statement	12/31/20	12/31/21		Percentage Change
Revenue (Sales)	$16,471	$17,421	⇧	6%
Cost of Goods Sold	6,454	7,046	⇧	9%
Gross Profit	10,017	10,375	⇧	4%
Operating Expenses	6,132	7,043	⇧	15%
EBIT (Operating Income)	3,885	3,332	⇩	−14%
Interest Expense	238	245	⇧	3%
EBT	3,647	3,087	⇩	−15%
Tax	787	749	⇩	−5%
Nonrecurring Events	(237)	(213)	—	—
Net Income	$2,623	$2,125	⇩	−19%

Source: Based on https://investor.colgatepalmolive.com/node/39741/html Also, Colgate's 2021 *Annual Report,* p. 72.

EXHIBIT 4 Colgate's Recent Balance Sheets (in Millions)

Balance Sheet	12/31/20	12/31/21		Percentage Change
Assets				
Cash and Short-Term Investments	$888	$832	⇩	−6%
Accounts Receivable	1,264	1,297	⇧	3%
Inventory	1,673	1,692	⇧	1%
Other Current Assets	513	586	⇧	14%
Total Current Assets	4,338	4,407	⇧	2%
Property Plant & Equipment	3,716	3,730	⇧	0%
Goodwill	3,824	3,284	⇩	−14%
Intangibles	2,894	2,462	⇩	−15%
Other Long-Term Assets	1,148	1,157	⇧	1%
Total Assets	**15,920**	**15,040**	⇩	**−6%**
Liabilities				
Accounts Payable	1,393	1,479	⇧	6%
Other Current Liabilities	3,011	2,572	⇩	−15%
Total Current Liabilities	4,404	4,051	⇩	−8%
Long-Term Debt	7,334	7,194	⇩	−2%
Other Long-Term Liabilities	3,081	2,824	⇩	−8%
Total Liabilities	**14,819**	**14,069**	⇩	**−5%**
Equity				
Common Stock	1,466	1,466	⇩	0%
Retained Earnings	23,699	24,350	⇧	3%
Treasury Stock	(23,045)	(24,089)	⇧	5%
Paid in Capital & Other	(1,019)	(756)	NA	NA
Total Equity	**1,101**	**971**	⇩	**−12%**
Total Liabilities and Equity	**$15,920**	**$15,040**	⇩	**−6%**

Source: Based on https://investor.colgatepalmolive.com/node/39741/html. Also, Colgate's 2021 *Annual Report,* p. 73.

Segments

Colgate is transparent in providing financial information by segment, both by region and by product. Colgate's two primary segments are 1) Oral, Personal, and Home Care and 2) Pet Nutrition.

Exhibit 5 provides a breakdown of Colgate's segment financial results for 2021 versus 2020. Note slight declines in the North America segment, suggesting that the best growth opportunities for the company may lie outside North America.

EXHIBIT 5 Colgate's Financials by Segment (in Millions)

		2020	2021
Revenues			
Oral, Personal and Home Care			
	North America	3,741	3,694
	Latin America	3,418	3,663
	Europe	2,747	2,841
	Asia-Pacific	2,701	2,867
	Africa/Eurasia	981	1,045
Total Oral, Personal and Home Care		13,588	14,110
Pet Nutrition		2,883	3,311
Total Revenues		16,471	17,421
Operating Profit			
Oral, Personal and Home Care			
	North America	988	754
	Latin America	975	1,012
	Europe	652	682
	Asia-Pacific	773	844
	Africa/Eurasia	206	203
Total Oral, Personal and Home Care		3,594	3,495
Pet Nutrition		793	901
Corporate		(502)	(1,064)
Total Operating Profit		$3,885	$3,332

Source: Based on https://investor.colgatepalmolive.com/news-releases/news-release-details/colgate-announces-4th-quarter-and-full-year-2021-results

Exhibit 6 illustrates Colgate's percent sales by product segment. Note the decline in Home Care compared with the increase in Pet Nutrition.

EXHIBIT 6 Colgate's Percentage of Sales by Segment

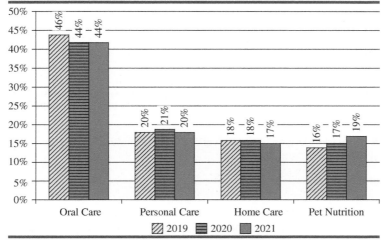

Source: Based on Colgate's 2021 *Annual Report*, p. 75.

Marketing

For household products companies like Colgate, advertising remained relatively consistent as a percentage of total SG&A at close to 33 percent, but in 2021 increased to 35 percent as companies increased advertising efforts in anticipation of the recovering economy and increased consumption. Companies also advertise to fend off competitors and tap into new markets.

People in developed countries in particular are spending less time with traditional television and moving to digital media. The firm eMarketer reports that individuals aged 18 and older spend more than 52 percent of their daily media time on digital media (about 6.5 hours per day) and only about 28 percent of their daily total media time watching television (3.5 hours per day).

The vast amount of data generated by social media and other companies regarding consumer behavior benefits firms like Colgate that obtain tremendous insight into how to allocate advertising expenditures to generate the greatest return. US companies especially are pushing personalized advertising within digital media to target younger demographics. In contrast, in many emerging markets, companies such as Colgate are still using television to communicate with consumers.

Competitors

Colgate's competitors include Johnson & Johnson, Unilever, Clorox, Kimberly-Clark, and Procter & Gamble. Analysts recently compared Colgate with several of its key competitors on nine management and marketing variables. The results are provided in Exhibit 7. Note that Colgate ranks an impressive number one on five variables versus its competitors. Overall, as indicated by the low summed scores in Column 10, Colgate was ranked best overall, closely followed by Johnson & Johnson. Colgate could promote this excellence going forward in their marketing efforts.

EXHIBIT 7 Comparing Colgate Versus Rival Firms (Ranking 1 = Best; 6 = Worst)

	Variables									
	1	2	3	4	5	6	7	8	9	10
Colgate-Palmolive	3	1	1	2	1	1	3	4	1	17
Johnson & Johnson	1	5	3	3	3	2	1	2	2	22
Unilever	2	4	2	5	4	3	2	6	4	32
Kimberly-Clark	4	3	5	6	6	4	4	3	3	38
Procter & Gamble	5	6	6	4	5	6	5	5	5	47
Clorox	6	2	4	1	2	5	6	1	6	33

Variables

1. Effectiveness of CEO
2. Product Quality
3. Do Customers Recommend Company Products to Friends?
4. Pricing
5. Customer Service
6. Overall Culture
7. Do Employees Recommend Company Products to Friends?
8. How Happy Are the Women Employees at the Firm?
9. How Happy Are Minority Employees at the Firm?
10. Summed Score (lower sum the better)

Source: Based on https://www.comparably.com/companies/colgate-palmolive/competitors

Exhibit 8 compares Colgate to three rival companies. Note that Colgate is much smaller than its major rival firms.

Procter & Gamble (P&G)

Founded in 1837 and headquartered in Cincinnati, Ohio, P&G is one of the largest branded consumer-packaged-goods company in the world, providing famous brand name products, such as Tide detergent and Olay, to consumers in North and Latin America, Europe, the Asia-Pacific, Greater

EXHIBIT 8 Colgate's Rival Firms Compared Financially

	Colgate (CL)	P&G (PG)	J&J (JNJ)	Unilever Plc (UL)
Market Capitalization	$66 billion	$380 billion	$435 billion	$132 billion
EPS	$2.55	$5.7	$7.81	$2.63
Revenue	$14.4 billion	$78 billion	$94 billion	$52 billion
Net Income	$2.2 billion	$14 billion	$21 billion	$6 billion
Total Debt	$7.3 billion	$36 billion	$34 billion	$30 billion
Total Debt/Equity	746	80	48	152
Current Ratio	1.1	0.67	2.93	0.70
Stock Price	$78	$158	$165	$51

Source: Based on https://finance.yahoo.com/quote/CL?p=CL&.tsrc=fin-srch

China, India, the Middle East, and Africa. P&G operates in five segments: (1) Beauty, (2) Grooming, (3) Healthcare, (4) Fabric & Home Care, and (5) Baby, Feminine & Family Care. P&G's Beauty segment produces, markets, and distributes conditioners, shampoos, styling aids, antiperspirants and deodorants, soaps, and skin care products under brand names that include Head & Shoulders, Herbal Essences, Pantene, Rejoice, Olay, Old Spice, Safeguard, Secret, and SK-II brands. The other segments are also massive and profitable. As indicated in Exhibit 8, P&G is five times larger than Colgate and five times more profitable, and, thus, a fierce global competitor.

Unilever PLC

Incorporated in 1894 and based in London, UK, Unilever is a large global consumer goods company supplying households and businesses in Asia, Africa, the Middle East, Turkey, Russia, Ukraine, Belarus, the Americas, and Europe. Unilever's Beauty & Personal Care and Home Care segments compete with Colgate. The Beauty & Personal Care segment provides skin care and hair care products, deodorants, and skin cleansing products under such brand names as Axe, Clear, Dove, Lifebuoy, Lux, Pond's, Rexona, Signal, Suave, Sunsilk, TRESemmé, and Vaseline. The Home Care segment provides a wide array of fabric solutions, and home care and hygiene products under the Cif, Omo, Persil, Domestos, Seventh Generation, and Sunlight brands.

Pet Industry Competitors

Colgate offers its Hill's Science Diet brand of products in the pet food market, but other household products manufacturers also compete in the pet industry, including Church & Dwight with its Arm & Hammer cat litter products, and Clorox with its Fresh Step and Scoop Away brands of cat litter. Most other pet industry participants are food companies, including General Mills (Blue Buffalo), Mars (Pedigree, Royal Canin), Nestlé (Purina), and J.M. Smucker (Rachael Ray Nutrish, Nature's Recipe, Milk-Bone).

External Issues

The COVID-19 pandemic resulted in a huge increase in demand for household products, particularly disinfectants, hand sanitizers, toilet tissue, paper towels, facial tissue, laundry detergent, and cleaning tools. Interestingly, sales for these products remain elevated versus prepandemic levels for the following two reasons: consumers have formed habits amid the pandemic and working from home is the new normal for many professionals, which supports demand for household products.

For household products companies like Colgate, international markets present a growth opportunity due to a growing middle class and relatively low household penetration. In developing countries, urbanization and improvements in living conditions bode well for the consumer staples industry because they can increase the per-capita consumption of basic household products. Analysts report that Latin America and Asia-Pacific offer the best prospects for long-term growth, but Eastern Europe is also important for some companies because GDP, disposable income, and population growth are outpacing those of the United States and Western Europe. Compared with the other industries in the consumer staples sector, household products companies do more business in international markets, comprising about 50 percent or more of sales from the three largest participants (Procter

& Gamble, Colgate-Palmolive, and Kimberly-Clark) in the industry. The bottom line is that household products companies are focusing on opportunities outside their home markets in 2021–2025.

In the US, there were 142,000 fewer babies born in 2020 versus 2019, representative of a cultural shift toward focusing on one's career over an intimate relationship, as well as more women entering the workforce as the gender pay gap narrows (especially in leadership positions that require more time at work). Millennials completing major milestones later in life than previous generations could also be a contributing factor.

The Pet Industry

Analysts forecast that the total US pet expenditure will increase at a 6.6 percent annual rate due to favorable demographic trends described previously, the surge of new pet parents during the pandemic, and the shift to higher-end pet foods and treats. The largest provider of preventive veterinary medicine in the US, Banfield Pet Hospital confirms the huge boom in US pet ownership, reporting that 9.2 percent more juvenile dogs and 12.4 percent more juvenile cats were brought in to Banfield for veterinary visits in 2020 compared to 2019. Barfield says this is the first increase in the percentage of juvenile pets seen at the practice in 10 years.

Conclusion

CEO Noel Wallace needs a clear 3-year strategic plan for Colgate. P&G and J&J and Unilever are pursuing strategies to take away Colgate's market share. Intensity of competition and rivalry among consumer staples firms are accelerating as companies roll product lines out globally and develop new and improved products. The vision/mission and organizational structure sections of this case reveal that there is substantial room for improvement for Colgate in both areas.

Wallace knows the basic underlying external opportunities and threats and internal strengths facing Colgate, but he is unsure about the relative importance of those factors. He thus needs an external and internal assessment performed, anchored by development of an EFE Matrix and IFE Matrix as described in Chapter 3 and Chapter 4 of the David textbook. Wallace also needs to know the relative attractiveness of alternative strategies facing the company, so he needs a SWOT, BCG, and QSPM analyses performed.

Let's say Wallace asks you to develop the comprehensive strategic plan that he needs. In addition to the analyses mentioned, include in your report a perceptual map, a set of proposed recommendations with associated costs, and an EPS-EBIT analysis to reveal whether debt or stock or some combination of debt and stock is best to obtain the needed funds. Also include projected financial statements to show the expected impact on Colgate if Wallace adopts your proposed strategic plan. What can Colgate do to help assure top line (revenues) and bottom line (net income) 5 + percent annually in the years to come? Identify candidate airlines for Colgate to acquire. If Colgate should expand further organically (internally) into other regions, countries, and continents, include direction for Wallace in this regard.

All of Colgate's top executives, board of directors, shareholders, and employees will benefit from and be thankful for your work developing and proposing a clear roadmap for their future. Good luck on this endeavor. We authors are confident you can do a wonderful job performing this task, following the guidelines presented in the David strategic management textbook and using the strategic planning template provided at www.strategyclub.com.

References

1. Colgate's 2021 *Form 10K*.
2. https://www.comparably.com/companies/colgate-palmolive/competitors
3. https://www.colgatepalmolive.com/en-us/who-we-are/our-leadership-team
4. https://www.comparably.com/companies/colgate-palmolive/mission
5. https://investor.colgatepalmolive.com/news-releases/news-release-details/colgate-announces-4th-quarter-and-full-year-2021-results
6. CFRAEquityResearch_HouseholdProducts_Jan_11_2022.pdf
7. https://investor.colgatepalmolive.com/node/39741/html. Also, Colgate's 2021 *Annual Report*, pp. 72 & 73.
8. https://investor.colgatepalmolive.com/financial-information/financial-highlights
9. https://finance.yahoo.com/quote/CL?p=CL&.tsrc=fin-srch

Helen of Troy Limited, 2022

www.helenoftroy.com, (NASDAQ: HELE)

Headquartered Hamilton, Bermuda, but with US operations based in El Paso, Texas, Helen of Troy Limited is a worldwide diversified, consumer-products company that designs, develops, and markets (but does not manufacture) health and beauty products and housewares under such brands as Revlon (licensed), Honeywell, Brut, and Vicks. The company was named for the Greek mythology woman Helen (pronounced Helene) of Troy, sometimes called Beautiful Helen or Helen of Sparta, who was considered the most beautiful woman in the world. "Helene" was supposedly the daughter of Zeus and Leda. About 70 percent of all Helen of Troy products are manufactured by and obtained from suppliers in China.

With 1,750 employees, Helen of Troy designs, develops, imports, markets, and distributes brand-name products in three reportable business segments: (1) Home and Outdoor, 2) Health & Wellness, and (3) Beauty. The company's Home & Outdoor segment offers food and beverage preparation tools such as storage containers, household cleaning products, shower and bathroom accessories, feeding and drinking products, child seating, cleaning tools, nursery accessories, insulated water bottles, jugs, drinkware, travel mugs, and food containers under brand names such as OXO, Good Grips, Hydro Flask, and Soft Works. For fiscal 2022, this segment reported revenues of $865.8 million, up 19 percent from the prior year. Corporations of late are finding it difficult to manage diversified activities, and many are divesting (spinning off) various segments to become more homogeneous, which is a strategy that Helen of Troy may want to consider in the future.

The company's Health and Wellness segment offers thermometers, blood pressure monitors, humidifiers, faucet mount and pitcher-based water filtration systems, air purifiers, heaters, fans, humidifiers and dehumidifiers under brand names that include PUR, Honeywell, Braun, and Vicks. For fiscal 2022, this segment reported revenues of $890.2 million, comprising 42.4 percent of the company's total sales. Helen of Troy is a diversified company.

The company's Beauty segment offers hair, facial and skin care appliances (both retail and professional), grooming brushes, tools and decorative hair accessories, liquid hair styling, treatment and conditioning products, shampoos, skin care products, fragrances, deodorants and antiperspirants under brand names that include Hot Tools, Brut, Pert, Sure, Infusium 23, Revlon, and Bed Head. For fiscal 2022, this segment reported revenues of $580.4 million, up 20.6 percent from the prior year.

Copyright by Fred David Books LLC; written by Fred R. David.

History

Helen of Troy was founded by Jerry Rubin in 1968 as a wig store in downtown El Paso. By 1975 the company was in the hair appliance business, supplying salons with hair dryers, curling irons, and other items. The company began trading on the NASDAQ in 1972 and reorganized in Bermuda in 1994. For fiscal 2022, the company reported $2.23 billion in sales and had more than 1,700 full-time employees around the world. During its 50+ years, the company has grown organically (internally) as well as through acquisition.

Helen of Troy's fiscal year ends on February 28. For fiscal 2022, company-wide sales increased 22.9 percent, to $2,223 million, compared to $2,098 million for the prior year. For fiscal 2022, the company's operating income decreased 3.2 percent to $272.5 million, compared to $281.4 million the prior year. During fiscal 2022, the company divested (sold) its Personal Care business, so for the 9 months (Q1, Q2, Q3) that ended November 30, 2021, company sales were $1.641 billion, up 3.3 percent from the prior year period; net income was $183 million, down from $231 million the prior year 9-month period.

Internal Issues

Vision/Mission/Core Values

Helen of Troy states on its corporate website that its purpose is *"to elevate lives and soar together."* That is all that is provided regarding a vision or mission statement. However, at the website https://www.comparably.com/companies/helen-of-troy/mission, a vision and mission statement and a set of core values (to help establish a desired organizational culture), are provided as follows (all paraphrased):

> Vision – *We are led by our exceptional employees who feel and act like dedicated owners; we cultivate careers and celebrate shared success as we create long-term sustainable value together.*

> Mission – *We acquire and build world-class brands and products that elevate people's lives everywhere, every day; we function as a close-knit family of leading consumer products and brands marketed in over 75 countries.*

> Core Values – *We believe in Mutual Respect, Ingenuity, Shared Success, and Exceptional People*

Diversity, Equity, and Inclusion (DEI) and Sustainability

The corporate webpage https://www.helenoftroy.com/esg/ details Helen of Troy's extensive efforts on both DEI and sustainability, anchored by an annual *Environmental, Social, and Governance (ESG) Report* that details initiatives and progress on varied DEI and sustainability fronts. For example regarding sustainability, the company has recycled more than 180,000 metric tons of metal, paper fiber, electronics and other miscellaneous waste in their distribution centers. Regarding DEI, the company has created a new DEI top management leadership position.

No Helen of Troy US employees are members of a union, but a few of their employees in Europe are covered by collective arrangements. The company has never experienced a work stoppage and contends they have satisfactory working relations with all employees.

Organizational Structure and Governance

Helen of Troy's top executives are listed and arrayed in Exhibit 1. Note there are divisional-by-product presidents, which likely is an excellent structure for the company. There is no COO, so apparently the divisional presidents report directly to the CEO, along with all functional-level executives, which perhaps is too large a span of control for the CEO.

In May 2022 Helen of Troy appointed Tabata Gomez and Elena Otero to their Board of Directors. Ms. Gomez is President of Hand Tools, Accessories & Storage Group for Stanley Black & Decker Inc. while Ms. Otero recently retired from her position as Chief Marketing Officer, eCommerce Officer and Strategy Officer for the international business at Clorox Company. With the additions of Ms. Gomez and Ms. Otero, Helen of Troy's Board of Directors is comprised of ten directors, nine of whom are independent, but will return to nine directors when Director Gary Abromovitz soon retires.

Marketing and R&D

For millions of consumers, a brand is more than a name—it's a lifestyle whereby an individual develops loyalty to a product or service. From a household products company, brand is one

EXHIBIT 1 Helen of Troy's Leadership Personnel Listed and Arrayed

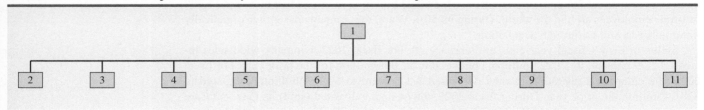

1. Julien Mininberg, CEO
2. Matthew Osberg, CFO
3. Jay Caron, Chief Supply Chain Officer
4. Harish Ramani, CIO
5. Ronald Anderskow, President, Beauty
6. Christophe Coudray, President, Health & Home

7. Nicolar Lanus, President, International
8. Larry Witt, President, Housewares
9. Jack Jancin, SVP, Corporate Business Development
10. Tessa Juge, SVP, General Counsel
11. Lisa Kidd, SVP, Chief People Officer

Source: Based on https://investor.helenoftroy.com/governance/leadership-team/default.aspx

of best ways for a firm to build subscription-type revenue for a product. A strong brand name spurs consumer loyalty, which in turn creates opportunity for increased pricing flexibility and product line extensions. Helen of Troy has an excellent brand name, especially with rights to use the Revlon name, but the company must capitalize on this better, especially with outside-the-US efforts.

Helen of Troy sells products in more than 90 countries, but company sales within the United States comprise about 79 percent of total sales. The company sells products through mass merchandisers such as Amazon, drugstore chains such as CVS, warehouse clubs such as Costco, home improvement stores such as Lowes, grocery stores such as Kroger, specialty stores, beauty supply retailers, e-commerce retailers, wholesalers, and various types of distributors, as well as directly to consumers. "Helene" has outside and sales representatives and internal marketing, category management, engineering, creative services, and customer and consumer service staff.

The company's largest customer, Amazon, accounted for 20, 18, and 16 percent of the firm's total revenue in fiscal 2021, 2020, and 2019, respectively. Sales to the company's second-largest customer, Walmart, accounted for 13, 14, and 16 percent of total sales in fiscal 2021, 2020, and 2019, respectively. Helen of Troy's third-largest customer is Target, and they accounted for about 11, 9, and 10 percent of total sales in fiscal 2021, 2020, and 2019, respectively. Sales to the company's top five customers accounted for about 52, 50, and 51 percent of total revenue in fiscal 2021, 2020, and 2019, respectively.

Be reminded that Helen of Troy does not own Revlon but licenses Revlon's trademark for hair care appliances and tools (the "Revlon License"). The company in 2021 made investments of $98.7 million to extend the Revlon License and use the trademark royalty-free for the next 100 years, paying a one-time, up-front license fee of $72.5 million. Other trademarks used or owned by Helen include Braun, Vicks, Bed Head, OXO, Osprey, PUR, Drybar, and Hot Tools.

Helen of Troy's advertising costs were $96.4 million, $110.7 million, $71.4 million, and $62.4 million during fiscal 2022, 2021, 2020, and 2019, respectively. The company's R&D expenses were $37.2 million, $30.6 million, $17.8 million, and $13.0 million during fiscal 2022, 2021, 2020, and 2019, respectively.

Segments

Analogous to the organizational structure illustrated in Exhibit 1, Helen of Troy operates in three reportable business segments, as will be described. Exhibit 2 and Exhibit 3 provide a revenue and operating income breakdown by segment. Exhibit 4 and Exhibit 5 provide a revenue and percentage breakdown of revenues by region, respectively. Note that fiscal 2022 was an excellent year for the company except for the Health and Wellness segment. Recall that Helen's fiscal year ends the last day of February.

EXHIBIT 2 Helen of Troy's Revenues by Segment (in Thousands)

	Fiscal 2019	Fiscal 2020	Fiscal 2021	Fiscal 2022
Home & Outdoor	$523,807	$640,965	$727,354	$865,844
Health & Wellness	695,217	685,397	890,191	777,080
Beauty	345,127	381,070	481,254	580,431
Total	$1,564,151	$1,707,432	$2,098,799	$2,223,355

Source: Based on Helen of Troy's fiscal 2022 *Form 10K*, p. 42.

EXHIBIT 3 Helen of Troy's Operating Income by Segment (in Millions)

	Fiscal 2020	Fiscal 2021	Fiscal 2022
Home & Outdoor	$123.1	$122.5	$134,9
Health & Wellness	68.2	94.1	39.2
Beauty	(13.1)	64.9	98.4
Total	$178.2	$281.5	$272.5

Source: Based on Helen of Troy's fiscal 2022 *Form 10K*, p. 50.

Home and Outdoor: Provides a broad range of consumer products for the home and for food preparation, including cooking and cleaning. There are five categories of products in this segment: (1) Food Preparation and Storage, (2) Coffee and Tea, (3) Cleaning and Bath, (4) Infant and Toddler, and (5) Hot and Cold Beverage and Food Containers.

Health and Wellness: Provides healthcare and home products including healthcare devices, water-filtration systems, and small home appliances. There are three categories of products in this segment: (1) Health Care, (2) Water Filtration, and (3) Home Environment.

Beauty: Provides personal care products such as hair styling appliances, grooming tools, decorative haircare accessories, and personal care and grooming products. There are two categories of products in this segment: (1) Appliances and Accessories and (2) Personal and Hair Care.

The overreliance on the United States for revenue is potentially disastrous for Helen of Troy as rival firms gain economies of scale that could enable them to lower prices and defend territories effectively. The overreliance seen in Exhibit 4 and Exhibit 5 is especially troublesome because household and beauty products sell well globally, can be introduced relatively easily globally, and as developing nations become more prosperous, their citizens are seeking new household products. Helen of Troy should be there with the offerings.

Financial Information

Instead of ever paying out cash dividends to shareholders, Helen of Troy retains earnings to provide funds for the operation and growth of the business. This is considered to be wise by many analysts because dividends are double-taxed considering the company pays taxes on the income

EXHIBIT 4 Helen of Troy's Revenues by Region (in Thousands)

	2020	2021	2022
United States	$1,357,345	$1,666,324	$1,738,099
Canada	74,417	92,150	101,617
EMEA	138,858	183,398	214,583
Asia Pacific	99,378	118,000	109,750
Latin America	40,434	38,927	59,306
Total	$1,707,432	$2,098,799	$1,223,355

Source: Based on Helen of Troy's fiscal 2022 *Form 10K*, p. 107.

Note: EMEA is Europe, Middle East, and Africa.

EXHIBIT 5 Helen of Troy's Revenues by Region (in Percentages)

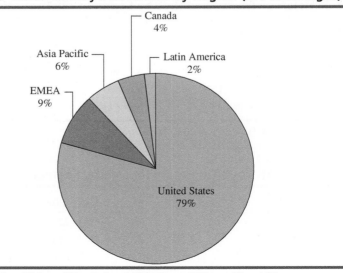

Source: Based on Helen of Troy's fiscal 2021 *Form 10K*, pp. 67 and 98.

Note: EMEA is Europe, Middle East, and Africa.

and then the recipient pays taxes on the proceeds. Perhaps the company could more aggressively in the future use these funds to penetrate global markets deeper.

As indicated in Exhibit 6, the company's sales revenue increased $391.4 million, or 5.9 percent in fiscal 2022, to $2,223 million, compared with $2,098 million the previous year. As indicated in Exhibit 7, the company's long-term debt versus paid-in-capital is reasonable.

EXHIBIT 6 Helen of Troy's Recent Income Statements (in Thousands)

Income Statement	2/28/20	2/28/21		2/28/22
Revenue (Sales)	$1,707,432	$2,098,799	⇧	$2,223,355
Cost of Goods Sold	972,966	1,171,497	⇧	1,270,168
Gross Profit	734,466	927,302	⇧	953,187
Operating Expenses	556,215	645,814	⇧	680,637
EBIT (Operating Income)	178,251	281,488	⇧	262,550
Interest Expense	12,311	12,058	⇩	12,844
EBT	165,940	269,430	⇧	259,966
Tax	13,607	15,484	⇧	36,202
Nonrecurring Events	0	0	—	—
Net Income	$152,333	$253,946	⇧	$223,764

Source: Based on Helen of Troy's fiscal 2022 *Form 10K*, pp. 72 & 68.

EXHIBIT 7 Helen of Troy's Recent Balance Sheets (in Thousands)

Balance Sheet	2/28/20	2/28/21		2/28/22
Assets				
Cash and Short-Term Investments	$24,467	$45,120	⇧	33,381
Accounts Receivable	348,032	382,449	⇧	457,623
Inventory	256,311	481,611	⇧	557,992
Other Current Assets	54,026	62,757	⇧	33,084
Total Current Assets	682,836	971,937	⇧	1,082,080
Property Plant & Equipment	132,107	136,535	⇧	205,378
Goodwill	739,901	739,901	⇩	948,873
Intangibles	300,952	357,264	⇧	537,846
Other Long-Term Assets	48,087	57,851	⇧	1,131,354
Total Assets	**1,903,883**	**2,263,488**	⇧	**2,823,451**
Liabilities				
Accounts Payable	152,674	334,807	⇧	308,178
Other Current Liabilities	186,222	280,085	⇧	294,512
,222Total Current Liabilities	338,896	614,892	⇧	602,690
Long-Term Debt	337,421	341,746	⇧	811,332
Other Long-Term Liabilities	65,843	67,503	⇧	684,780
Total Liabilities	**742,160**	**1,024,141**	⇧	**1,496,112**
Equity				
Common Stock	2,519	2,441	⇩	2,380
Retained Earnings	898,166	965,166	⇧	1,021,017
Treasury Stock	0	0	—	0—
Paid in Capital & Other	261,038	271,740	⇧	303,942
Total Equity	**1,161,723**	**1,239,347**	⇧	**1,327,339**
Total Liabilities and Equity	**$1,903,883**	**$2,263,488**	⇧	**$2,823,451**

Source: Based on Helen of Troy's fiscal 2022 *Form 10K*, p. 71.

Competitors

Helen of Troy is a diversified company, so it has more than 100 primary competitors, as revealed in Exhibit 8 organized by segment. Other serious competitors include Mary Kay, USANA Health Sciences, Rodan + Fields (R + F), Avon, L'Oreal, and Beautycounter.

EXHIBIT 8 Helen of Troy's Competitors by Segment According to the Company

Segment	Competitors
Housewares	Lifetime Brands (KitchenAid), Newell Brands, Simple Human, Yeti Holdings, Bradshaw Home
Health & Home	Exergen Corp., Omron Healthcare, Crane Engineering, Newell Brands, Lasko Products, Clorox Co. (Brita), Zero Tech., Vornado Air
Beauty	Conair, Spectrum Brands Holdings (Remington), Newell Brands, Procter & Gamble, Unilever, Colgate-Palmolive, Coty, Dyson Ltd.

Source: Based on the Helen of Troy fiscal 2021 *Form 10K*, p. 7.

Exhibit 9 provides a market share percentage breakdown of leading hair appliances brands in the United States in 2018. Note that Conair is the largest competitor on this chart. Note in Exhibit 10 that Nu Skin Enterprises and Church & Dwight are the largest competitors.

EXHIBIT 9 Market Share of the Leading Hair Appliance Brands in the United States

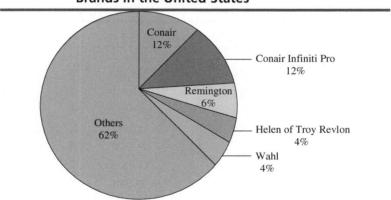

Source: Based on *Drug Store News*, August 26, 2018 Edition, p. 38.

EXHIBIT 10 Top Competitors of Helen of Troy

Company	# Employees	$ Revenue (in millions)
Helen of Troy	1,750	$2,000
Conair	3,471	2,000
USANA Health Sciences	1,911	1,000
Nu Skin Enterprises	24,900	2,000
GWA Group	665	120
Voyant Beauty	3,500	698
McBride	4,300	910
Sunbeam	1,128	223
Church & Dwight Co.	4,800	$4,000

Source: Based on https://www.zoominfo.com/c/helen-of-troy-limited/44108449

External Issues

All Helen of Troy products are manufactured by third-party, unaffiliated companies, and 80 percent of these producers are located in the Far East, primarily China. This concentration and reliance on one geographic area of the world for most of your inventory exposes the company to risks, including:

1. Global public health crises such as the pandemic could hamper securement of product,
2. Supply bottlenecks anywhere globally could hamper securement of product,
3. Political unrest across countries,
4. Changes in labor availability and cost across countries,
5. Changes in laws, taxes, regulations, treaties, tariffs, customs, and trade barriers across countries,
6. Changes in shipping costs via ocean cargo carriers and airline cargo, and
7. Currency exchange fluctuations such as the Chinese Renminbi versus the US dollar.

Analysts expect demand for household products to remain high versus prepandemic levels due to (1) increased work-from-home activities that lead to more surfaces being cleaned, more dishes being washed, and more bathroom products being used, (2) shifting consumer preferences and loyalty to brands because research suggests it takes only 66 days to form a new habit; and (3) as economies improve, consumers are trading up and favoring premium over value brands. COVID-19 resulted in a historic increase in demand for household products, particularly disinfectants, hand sanitizers, toilet tissue, paper towels, facial tissue, laundry detergent, and cleaning tools. Because consumers are now more aware of the need for cleanliness, demand for these products is expected to remain permanently elevated compared with prepandemic levels.

A negative trend for the household and personal care products industry and especially the baby-care segment is that 142,000 fewer babies were born in the United States in 2020 versus 2019, according to census data. There were 3.6 million births in 2020, a 4 percent drop from 2019 and in line with the number of births back in 1980.

Labor pressures and higher raw material and transportation costs are plaguing the homewares and personal care product industries. For example, pulp, which is the main raw material used in most paper-based products and packaging, is surging. On average, producers paid 11 percent more for pulp, paper, and allied products in June 2021 compared to the same period last year, according to the US Bureau of Labor Statistics. Transportation costs are also rising rapidly, driven by (1) a robust economic recovery, (2) a shortage of truck drivers, and (3) higher fuel expenses. According to the Cass Truckload Linehaul Index, which tracks per-mile truckload linehaul rates (independent of fuel), freight rates were up 14.5 percent in June 2021 compared to the same period the previous year.

In developing countries, urbanization and improvements in living conditions are increasing the per-capita consumption of basic household products. Latin America and Asia-Pacific offer the outstanding prospects for long-term growth, and Helen of Troy is deficient in these areas. There are many areas of the world where GDP, disposable income, and population growth are outpacing those of the United States and Western Europe, and Helen of Troy should capitalize on these opportunities.

Conclusion

CEO Julien Mininberg at Helen of Troy needs a clear strategic plan for the future because his company faces scores of competitors of all sizes, located everywhere, globally. And his company relies exclusively on outside manufacturers for everything his company sells, and 80 percent of those producers are located in China or the Far East. Supply disruptions due to the pandemic and labor shortages and political uneasiness across countries are plaguing his company and industry. Additionally, many Helen of Troy shareholders are beginning to question whether the company should divest (spinoff) products or segments to become more homogeneous, as is a common trend today among diversified firms in many industries. It has simply become increasingly difficult for a company to be an expert on many different products, ranging in the case of Helen of Troy from coffee to appliances. What products/segments do you believe the company should divest, if any, and for how much, and how should the company redeploy those incoming funds?

For most companies in the household products industry, international markets comprise 50 percent or more of sales from the firm's basic products since they have universal appeal but not for Helen of Troy. To expand their markets worldwide, Helen of Troy could establish partnerships and joint ventures with local companies and retailers to more effectively enter foreign markets to learn diverse customs, tastes, and regulatory issues of a market from partners. This is exactly what Procter & Gamble, Colgate Palmolive, and Kimberly Clark do globally in the household and personal care products industry.

Mininberg knows the basic underlying external opportunities and threats facing his company, as well as the basic internal strengths and weaknesses, but he needs to know the relative importance of those factors. He also needs to know the relative attractiveness of alternative strategies to be derived from those underlying external and internal factors. In other words, Mininberg needs strategy analyses performed, including IFEM, EFEM, SWOT, IE Matrix, perceptual mapping, EPS-EBIT analysis, and projected financial statement analysis. Let's say that Mininberg hires you to develop a comprehensive strategic plan for his company. Beginning with improved vision and mission statements, perform the analysis that is requested, develop some recommendations with associated costs, and present your findings and research to your professor and fellow students.

References

1. *Drug Store News*, August 26, 2018 Edition, p. 38.
2. https://www.zoominfo.com/c/helen-of-troy-limited/44108449
3. Helen of Troy's fiscal 2021 and fiscal 2022 *Form 10K*.
4. S&P Industry Surveys, CFRAEquityResearch_HouseholdProductsProviders_Aug_19_2021.pdf
5. https://investor.helenoftroy.com/governance/leadership-team/default.aspx
6. www.helenoftroy.com

The American Red Cross, 2022

https://www.redcross.org/

Headquartered in Washington, DC, the American Red Cross (ARC) is one of the nation's premier humanitarian organizations. In 2021, the Red Cross served more than 2.1 million meals, provided over 200,000 overnight shelter and hotel stays, and assisted more than 20,000 people each day. As a nonprofit organization, the ARC is dependent on donations. Its top donors each donate more than $3 million annually and include companies such as Amazon, Lowe's Corporation, Walmart, and Wells Fargo. The ARC states on its website that the organization is proud to report that an average of 90 percent of all donations are directly invested in delivering care and comfort to those in need.

ARC is the premier emergency response organization in the United States, bringing shelter, food, and comfort to people affected by disasters, large and small. ARC collects lifesaving donated blood and supplies it to patients everywhere and provides support to personnel at military bases globally and to their families. ARC trains individuals and groups in CPR, first aid, and other skills, and provides assistance worldwide with critical disaster response, preparedness and disease prevention efforts. ARC annually mobilizes thousands of volunteers and appreciates the generosity of donors. For example, along the US-Mexico border, ARC helps refugees, migrants and asylum seekers, as described at the website: https://www.redcross.org/about-us/news-and-events/news/how-does-the-american-red-cross-help-migrants.html.

Copyrighted by Fred David Books LLC; written by Meredith E. David.

History

Founded by Clara Barton on May 21, 1881, ARC has been serving people in need for more than 140 years. During the First World War and until the end of the Second World War, the ARC focused its efforts on providing services to veterans, staffing hospitals and ambulance companies, and providing related services such as recruiting the nearly 20,000 registered nurses needed to serve the military during the war and recruiting nurses for assistance during the worldwide influenza epidemic of 1918. In the 1940s, the ARC developed the first nationwide civilian blood program in the United States. Since then, the ARC has provided lifesaving services, including supplying more than 40 percent of blood and blood-related products in the United States.

ARC states on its website the following (paraphrased):

American Red Cross employees, supporters, and volunteers provide compassionate care in five key areas:
- People affected by disasters in America
- Support for members of the military and their families
- Blood collection, processing and distribution
- Health and safety education and training, and
- International relief and development.

Internal Issues

Vision Statement
ARC states on its website that the vision of the organization is (paraphrased): *"Our vision to use our strong network of volunteers, donors and partners, to always be there in times of need. We aspire to turn compassion into action so that people around the world receive care, shelter and hope before, during and after disasters, and so that every person in the U.S. has access to safe blood when needed, and so that U.S. armed services members and their families have support in times of need."*

Mission Statement

ARC states on its website that its mission is (paraphrased): "*We are on a mission to prevent and alleviate human suffering in emergency situations by mobilizing the power of volunteers and the generosity of donors.*"

Core Values

ARC's values center on being compassionate, collaborative, creative, credible, and committed.

Organizational Structure

ARC is led mainly by two key individuals: (1) the Chair of the Board and (2) the President and CEO. The ARC's Board of Governors provides strategic oversight and direction to the organization. The Chair of the Board leads in the governance and oversight of the organization, and the President and CEO leads the business operations and executes strategies.

ARC's top executives are listed and arrayed in Exhibit 1. Note 7 of the 14 persons are female. Note there are no divisional-by-region presidents or head persons, so the organization seems to operate using a decentralized, divisional-by-product design, with three segments: Training, Biomedical, and Humanitarian.

EXHIBIT 1 ARC's Top Executives Listed and Arrayed

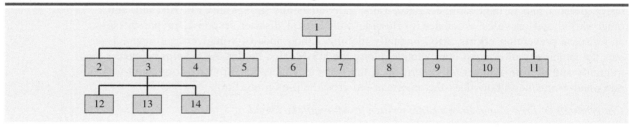

1. Bonnie McElveen-Hunter, Chair of the Board
2. Gail J. McGovern, President and CEO
3. Cliff Holtz, COO
4. Brian J. Rhoa, CFO
5. Jennifer L. Hawkins, Corporate Secretary and Chief of Staff
6. Phyllis Harris, General Counsel
7. Adrienne Alberts, Chief Diversity Officer
8. Shaun P. Gilmore, Chief Transformation Officer
9. Melissa B. Hurst, Chief Human Resources Officer
10. Sajit Joseph, Chief Innovation Officer
11. Rosemary McGillan, Chief Marketing and Communications Officer
12. Jack McMaster, President, Training Services
13. James "Chris" Hrouda, President, Biomedical Services
14. Harvey Johnson, President, Humanitarian Services

Source: Based on https://www.redcross.org/about-us/who-we-are/leadership.html

Note: Numbers 12, 13, and 14 report to number 3.

Commitment to Diversity, Equity, and Inclusion (DEI)

ARC updated its Equal Employment Opportunity and Commitment (EEO/C) to Diversity statement in March 2021. The organization appears to have a strong commitment to DEI-related matters for example, by establishing the National Diversity Advisory Council, which consists of a team of external DEI thought leaders from across the country who work together to provide guidance to the organization. The organization even has a mission and vision statement specifically for its DEI commitment.

The ARC's DEI vision (paraphrased) is to "*have a diverse, high-performing range of employees and volunteers who work in a collaborative, inclusive and respectful environment that facilitates and fosters culturally competent service delivery.*"

The ARC's DEI mission is (paraphrased): "*to deliver our products and services in a consistent, timely, and culturally competent manner.*"

Factors Related to COVID-19

The ARC reports that since the beginning of the COVID-19 pandemic, the organization has suffered from a 10 percent decline in the number of donors. The pandemic has also created an increased demand for blood. The ARC supplies nearly 40 percent of the US blood supply. Thus, it is reasonable to assume that a decline in the number of people willing to donate would most likely have a harmful impact on the organization.

In January 2022, the ARC declared the first-ever "National Blood Crisis," and has since increased its marketing expenditures and attempts to increase donations. In early 2022, the ARC partnered with the NFL to encourage people to donate blood. Donors were entered to win a free trip to the 2022 Super Bowl.

Segments

ARC's revenues come from four main sources: (1) Revenues from products and services, (2) Contributions, (3) Investment income, and (4) Other revenue.

As indicated in Exhibit 2, total ARC operating revenue and gains for fiscal year 2020 were $2,907.4 million, while total operating expenses were $2,751.6 million. Net assets were $1,812.2 million.

Finance

ARC's recent income statements and balance sheets are provided in Exhibit 3 and Exhibit 4, respectively.

EXHIBIT 2 ARC's Revenues and Expenses by Segment (in Thousands $)

		2020
Revenues		
Products & Services		1,840.0
Contributions		
	Corporate, Foundation & Individual Giving	549.9
	Contracts, Including Federal Government	128.1
	Legacies & Bequests	125.7
	Donated Materials & Services	84.1
	United Way & Combined Federated Campaign	33.5
	Total	936.3
Investment Income & Other		131.1
Total Revenues		2,907.4
Expenses		
Biomedical Services		1,766.6
Domestic Disaster Services		427.6
Fundraising		172.7
Training Services		122.9
Management & General		89.5
International Relief & Development Services		82.1
Service to the Armed Services		65.3
Community Services		24.9
	Total	2,751.6
Net Income		$155.8

EXHIBIT 3 ARC's Recent Income Statements (in Millions $)

Income Statement	6/30/20	6/30/21		Percentage Change
Revenue (Sales)	$2,907,386	$3,130,644	⇧	8%
Cost of Goods Sold	0	0	—	—
Gross Profit	2,907,386	3,130,644	⇧	8%
Operating Expenses	2,751,585	2,836,486	⇧	3%
EBIT (Operating Income)	155,801	294,158	⇧	89%
Interest Expense	0	0	—	—
EBT	155,801	294,158	⇧	89%
Tax	0	0	—	—
Nonrecurring Events	0	0	—	—
Net Income	$155,801	$294,158	⇧	89%

Source: Based on https://www.redcross.org/content/dam/redcross/about-us/publications/2020-publications/fy20-annual-report.pdf. Also, ARC 2021 *Annual Report*, p. 4.

EXHIBIT 4 ARC's Recent Balance Sheets (in Thousands $)

Balance Sheet	6/30/20	6/30/21		Percentage Change
Assets				
Cash and Short-Term Investments	$235,415	$205,148	⇩	−13%
Accounts Receivable	286,464	226,657	⇩	−21%
Inventory	46,998	47,394	⇧	1%
Other Current Assets	433,800	638,770	⇧	47%
Total Current Assets	1,002,677	1,117,969	⇧	11%
Property Plant & Equipment	755,519	728,858	⇩	−4%
Goodwill	0	0	—	—
Intangibles	0	0	—	—
Other Long-Term Assets	1,508,703	1,821,673	⇧	21%
Total Assets	**3,266,899**	**3,668,500**	⇧	**12%**
Liabilities				
Accounts Payable	253,123	299,798	⇧	18%
Other Current Liabilities	213,703	194,553	⇩	−9%
Total Current Liabilities	466,826	494,351	⇧	6%
Long-Term Debt	596,132	383,420	⇩	−36%
Other Long-Term Liabilities	391,726	422,342	⇧	8%
Total Liabilities	**1,454,684**	**1,300,113**	⇩	**−11%**
Equity				
Common Stock	0	0	—	—
Retained Earnings	0	0	—	—
Treasury Stock	0	0	—	—
Paid in Capital & Other	1,812,215	2,368,387	⇧	31%
Total Equity	**1,812,215**	**2,368,387**	⇧	**31%**
Total Liabilities and Equity	$3,266,899	$3,668,500	⇧	12%

Source: Based on ARC 2021 *Annual Report*, p. 3.

ARC's revenues from contributions are illustrated in Exhibit 5, and the organization's revenues from all sources are illustrated in Exhibit 6.

Competitors

In the sense that people decide what charities to support and not support with their donations, ARC has hundreds of competitors. Several of ARC's rival charities, although no charity has the same vision and mission as ARC, include Feeding America, The Salvation Army, Direct Relief, America Cares, and United Way.

Feeding America
Founded in 1979 and headquartered in Chicago, Illinois, the charity organization named Feeding America is the largest hunger-relief organization in the United States, and the largest or second-largest charity in the United States by revenues. The organization has more than 200 food banks, 21 statewide food bank associations, and more than 60,000 partner agencies, food pantries, and meal programs. The organization annually helps provide 6.6 billion meals to millions of people. Feeding America also supports programs that prevent food waste, improve food security, and advocates for legislation that protects people from going hungry.

EXHIBIT 5 ARC's Revenues from Contributions Only (in Thousands)

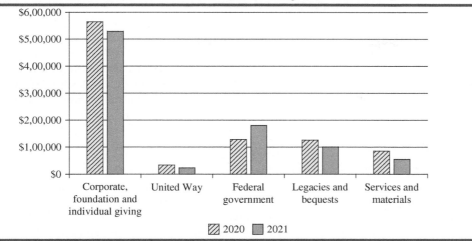

Source: Based on ARC's 2021 *Annual Report*, p. 4.

EXHIBIT 6 ARC's Revenues from Products, Services, Other, and Contributions

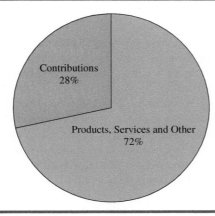

Source: Based on ARC's 2021 *Annual Report*, p. 4.

Direct Relief

Headquartered in Santa Barbara, California, and founded in 1945, Direct Relief is a nonprofit charity that provides emergency medical assistance and disaster relief in the United States and internationally. In May 2020, Direct Relief began partnering with FedEx Cares to ship personal protective equipment (PPE) to underserved communities around the United States and Mexico. Whenever there is a hurricane, typhoon, earthquake, volcano, wildfires, and any natural disaster, Direct Relief goes into action to assist. Direct Relief receives donations and has total revenue of more than $1 billion annually.

Americares

Headquartered in Stamford, Connecticut, and founded in 1975, Americares is a global nonprofit humanitarian organization that responds to individuals affected by poverty, disaster, or crisis. The organization addresses poverty, disasters, or crises with medicine, medical supplies, and health programs. The organization has offices in the Philippines, Tanzania, Puerto Rico, Colombia, El Salvador, Haiti, India, Liberia, Nepal, and other countries. Americares serves nearly 170 countries and goes into action whenever there is catastrophic suffering anywhere.

United Way

Headquartered in Alexandria, Virginia, and founded in 1887, United Way is a global humanitarian fundraising organization. The way the organization functions is that each local United Way is run independently and incorporated separately as a 501c(3) organization. Each affiliate office is led by local staff and volunteers and has its own board of directors, independent of United Way Worldwide or a parent organization.

United Way raises funds primarily through company-sanctioned workplace campaigns, where the employer solicits contributions from their employees that can be paid through automatic payroll deductions. In fact, nearly 60 percent of United Way's donations come through payroll deductions, while about 20 percent are obtained from corporate donations. United Way annually donates millions of dollars to many charities and organizations, such as American Cancer Society, Big Brothers/Big Sisters, Catholic Charities, The Salvation Army, Girl Scouts, and Boy Scouts, and probably even the ARC.

External Issues

In January 2022, ARC announced that the organization and the United States are facing a national blood crisis, its worst blood shortage in over a decade according to ARC, posing a concerning risk to patient care. Hundreds of doctors nationwide have been forced to make difficult decisions about who receives blood transfusions and who will need to wait. Blood and platelet donations are critically needed to help prevent further delays in vital medical treatments.

ARC asks all Americans to roll up their sleeve to help ensure people receive the care they need. Anyone can make an appointment to give blood or platelets by using the ARC Blood Donor App or by visiting RedCrossBlood.org or by calling 1-800-RED CROSS (1-800-733-2767).

Conclusion

CEO Gail McGovern needs a clear 3-year strategic plan for ARC. Hundreds of charities and even churches compete for donations for individuals, companies, and organizations. The vision/mission and organizational structure sections of this case reveal there is substantial room for improvement for ARC in both areas.

McGovern knows the basic underlying external opportunities and threats and internal strengths facing ARC, but she is unsure about the relative importance of those factors. She thus needs an external and internal assessment performed, anchored by development of an EFE Matrix and IFE Matrix as described in Chapter 3 and Chapter 4 of the David textbook. McGovern also needs to know the relative attractiveness of alternative strategies facing the company, so she needs a SWOT, BCG, and QSPM analyses performed.

Let's say CEO McGovern asks you to develop the comprehensive strategic plan that she needs. In addition to the analyses mentioned, include in your report a perceptual map, a set of proposed recommendations with associated costs, and an EPS-EBIT analysis to reveal whether debt or stock or some combination of debt and stock is best to obtain the needed funds. Also include projected financial statements to show the expected impact on ARC if McGovern adopts your proposed strategic plan.

All of ARC's top executives, board of directors, shareholders, and employees will benefit from and be thankful for your work developing and proposing a clear roadmap for their future. Good luck on this endeavor. We authors are confident you can do a wonderful job performing this task, following the guidelines presented in the David strategic management textbook and using the strategic planning template provided at www.strategyclub.com.

References

1. https://www.redcross.org/content/dam/redcross/National/history-full-history.pdf
2. https://www.redcross.org/about-us/news-and-events/press-release/2022/blood-donors-needed-now-as-omicron-intensifies.html
3. https://www.redcross.org/content/dam/redcross/about-us/publications/2020-publications/fy20-annual-report.pdf
4. American Red Cross 2021 *Annual Report*.

US Postal Service (USPS), 2022

https://about.usps.com/who/

Headquartered in Washington, DC, USPS is an independent federal nonprofit organization that provides global mail delivery products and services for all Americans. USPS is one of the few government agencies explicitly authorized by the US Constitution; various US presidents started most other federal agencies. USPS is highly unionized and has almost 560,000 career employees and about 140,000 noncareer employees. As of January 2022, a first-class stamp cost 58 cents.

USPS has exclusive "letter" delivery responsibilities within the United States and operates under a universal service obligation (USO). Although not explicitly defined, USO is broadly outlined in statute and includes multiple dimensions: geographic scope, range of products, access to services and facilities, delivery frequency, affordable and uniform pricing, service quality, and security of the mail. Rival organizations may claim to voluntarily provide delivery on a broad basis, but USPS is the only carrier legally required to provide universal mail delivery services to all Americans.

USPS competes against FedEx, United Parcel Service (UPS), Amazon, and DHL, as well as email platforms such as Google, AOL, Yahoo, and Hotmail. With more than 34,000 retail locations and one of the most frequently visited websites in the federal government, usps.com, USPS has annual operating revenue of more than $71 billion and delivers 48 percent of the world's mail. USPS is one of the nation's largest employers and operates one of the world's largest computer networks.

On July 6, 2022, USPS made available its newest stamp, a Forever stamp, to commemorate the former First Lady, Nancy Reagan, as shown in the photo.

USPS needs help. Despite striving to be financially self-sufficient, in FY 2021, USPS reported a $4.9 billion loss, on the heels of FY 2020's loss of $9.2 billion, adding to 15 years of losses totaling $92 billion. As you read this case and plan to prepare a comprehensive strategic plan for USPS, consider the following idea:

> *An analyst recently proposed that the USPS should consider phasing out city and rural deliveries over time and let all Americans eventually simply have a free local post office box, and they go get mail from their P.O. box, rather than the USPS delivering mail for millions of Americans to both individuals' physical address and to their P.O. box. Exhibit 1 provides some relevant recent information on this issue. Note the number of P.O. boxes versus the number of physical delivery spots. The analyst contends that if USPS could migrate to an all P.O. box business model within a decade, thus avoiding the need for thousands of vehicles and millions of gallons of fuel used, and needing far fewer employees, then the price of a first-class stamp could drop dramatically, perhaps to 17 cents instead of 58 cents. With this proposal, USPS would need to build more central post offices, but perhaps could compete better with email and rival firms, and cease incurring billion-dollar losses annually.*

Read this case, conduct your own research, and determine whether the analyst's proposal is feasible or even possible.

Copyright by Fred David Books LLC; written by Fred R. David.

History

USPS was founded in 1775 during the Second Continental Congress when Benjamin Franklin was appointed the first postmaster general, after serving in a similar position for the American colonies when they were controlled by Great Britain. The Post Office Department was created in 1792 with the passage of the Postal Service Act. USPS was transformed in 1970 into the US Postal Service as an independent federal government agency.

EXHIBIT 1 USPS's Residential Delivery Points in 2021 Versus 2020 (in Actual Units)

	2020	2021
City	84,233,373	84,775,116
Rural	45,320,604	46,475,650
P.O. Box	16,015,289	16,020,228
Highway Contact	3,050,749	3,106,794
Total	148,620,015	150,377,788

Source: Based on USPS FY2021 *Annual Report*, p. 27.

For the last two decades, Republicans have been discussing the idea of privatizing the US Postal Service because the organization loses billions of dollars every year. For example, President Trump's administration proposed turning USPS into "a private postal operator" as part of a June 2018 governmental reorganization plan, but this idea never gained sufficient support. On December 17, 2017, President Trump criticized the postal service's relationship with Amazon, saying: "Why is the United States Post Office, which is losing many billions of dollars a year, while charging Amazon and others so little to deliver their packages, making Amazon richer and the Post Office dumber and poorer? Should be charging MUCH MORE!"

USPS's postage prices seem high, but as indicated in Exhibit 2, they are relatively low compared to analogous prices in other countries. In FY 2021, the retail price for a first-class mail one-ounce stamp was raised $0.03 to $0.58 and continued to be one of the lowest letter-mail postage rates among industrialized countries. Historical comparative data is given in Exhibit 2. Maybe all countries should consider the analyst's proposal mentioned previously, but maybe not, pending your strategic analysis.

EXHIBIT 2 Prices of a First-Class Stamp in Various Countries on October 14, 2020

United States	$ 0.55
Australia	0.79
Japan	0.80
Canada	0.81
Germany	0.94
UK	0.99
France	1,67
Italy	3.29
Average	1.23

Source: Based on https://about.usps.com/what/strategic-plans/delivering-for-america/assets/USPS_Delivering-For-America.pdf, p.17.

Internal Issues

Vision/Mission

The USPS vision (paraphrased) is *"to deliver customer value that binds the nation together in a digital age."*

The USPS mission (paraphrased) is *"to serve the American people with prompt, affordable, reliable, secure universal postal services as described in the organization's USO, making full use of evolving technologies."*

Diversity, Equity, and Inclusion (DEI)

According to the USPS FY 2021 *Annual Report*, minorities comprise 52 percent and women comprise 47 percent of the total USPS workforce. Additionally, minorities comprise 38 percent and women comprise 37 percent of senior USPS management positions. About 29 percent of USPS workers are Black, 13 percent are Hispanic, and 8 percent are Asian. In comparison, according to 2018 Census Bureau data of the national workforce, Black Americans make up 13 percent, Hispanic Americans 17 percent, and Asian Americans 6 percent. Also, USPS is a leading employer of veterans that comprise slightly more than 10 percent of its workforce, nearly double the national rate of 5.7 percent according to the Bureau of Labor Statistics.

In 2021, USPS was ranked the top federal agency in *Black EOE Journal, Hispanic Network* magazine, and *Professional Woman's* magazine Additionally, the Postal Service received the Readers' Choice Award as a top 20 government employer in *Equal Employment Opportunity* magazine, *Woman Engineer* magazine, *Minority Engineer* magazine, and *Careers & the disABLED* magazine.

Objectives and Performance

In its 5-year strategic plan posted on the USPS website, four objectives or goals (paraphrased) are given, as follows:

Deliver a World-Class Customer Experience

Mobilize and Empower Employees

Continuously Innovate

Invest in Future Technology

Exhibit 3 provides a summary of USPS's performance and operations in 2021 versus the prior year. Note the decline in total mail and package volume in 2021 but the increase in total delivery points.

EXHIBIT 3 USPS's Performance Highlights (in Millions)

	2020	2021	Percentage Change
Total mail and package volume	$129,171	$128,861	(0.2)
Total revenue	73,225	77,069	5.2
Total expenses	82,401	81,999	(0.5)
Net loss	(9,176)	(4,930)	(46.3)
PP&E purchases	1,810	1,872	3.4
Debt	14,000	11,000	(21.4)
Capital contributions from US government	3,132	13,132	319.3
Deficit since 1971 reorganization	(83,840)	(88,812)	5.9
Total net deficiency	(80,708)	(75,680)	(6.2)
(in actual units)			
# of career employees	495,941	516,636	4.2
# of precareer employees	148,092	136,531	(7.8)
Total delivery points	161,374,152	163,139,167	1.1
Change in delivery points	$1,472,840	$1,765,015	19.8

Source: Based on the USPS FY 2021 *Annual Report,* p. 1.

Organizational Structure and Segments

For decades up through 2020, USPS operated under a structure in which core and supporting functions were managed in a decentralized fashion within each of seven regions, called areas. Each area's oversight included retail, processing, logistics, and delivery operations, as well as business functions, such as human resources, marketing, finance, and communications. Each area was managed independently by an area vice president (AVP). The AVPs reported to the COO. Each area had districts reporting to them for a total of 67 districts across the nation.

This structure all changed in 2021 when USPS created three core operating units: (1) Retail and Delivery Operations, (2) Logistics and Processing Operations, and (3) Commerce and Business Solutions, described as follows:

Retail and Delivery: Accept and deliver mail and packages efficiently with high level of customer satisfaction. Two headquarters organizations—Delivery Operations and Retail & Post Office Operations—will oversee four operational areas (Atlantic, Southern, Central and Pacific). Within the four Retail & Delivery Areas, 67 Postal Districts have been consolidated to 50 Districts. New

District territories closely align to state boundaries. Districts align with the communities the Postal Service serves and provide familiar boundaries for employees, customers, and stakeholders.

Logistics and Processing: Process and move mail and packages efficiently to all delivery points. The operations are divided into two processing regions with 13 divisions and four logistics divisions, each geographically aligned with Retail & Delivery areas, with a total of 13 divisions shared across the regions. No divisions or regions span across more than one area.

Commerce and Business: now aligned around four key functions. Business Solutions fully utilizes our digital, physical, and logistics infrastructure to develop innovative solutions for customers' evolving shipping needs. Business Development cultivates strong operational relationships with shipping customers to drive long-term growth. Transportation Strategy drives an efficient and reliable transportation network, with a focus on improving contract systems, processes, and performance to drive an operationally precise network. The Facilities group maintains and leverages our real estate infrastructure to maximize opportunities.

USPS's top executives are listed and arrayed in Exhibit 4.

EXHIBIT 4 USPS's Top Executives Listed and Arrayed

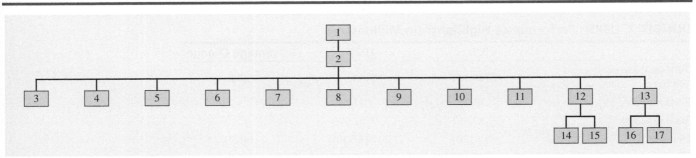

1. Ron Bloom, Chair, Board of Governors
2. Louis DeJoy, Postmaster General and CEO
3. Joshua Colin, Chief Retail & Delivery Officer and EVP
4. Isaac Cronkhite, Chief Logistics & Processing Operations Officer and EVP
5. Jacqueline Krage Strako, Chief Commerce & Business Solutions Officer and EVP
6. Schott Bombaugh, Chief Technology Officer and EVP
7. Pritha Mehra, Chief Information Officer and EVP
8. Steven Monteith, Chief Customer & Marketing Officer and EVP
9. Joseph Corbett, CFO and EVP
10. Douglas Tulino, Deputy Postmaster General and Chief HRO
11. Thomas Marshall, General Counsel and EVP
12. Larry Munoz, VP Regional Processing Operations Western
13. Dane Coleman, VP Regional Processing Operations Eastern
14. Eric Henry, VP Area Retail & Delivery Operations Central
15. Eduardo Ruiz, VP Area Retail & Delivery Regional Operations WestPac
16. Tim Costello, VP Area Retail & Delivery Operations Southern
17. Salvatore Vacca, VP Area Retail & Delivery Operations Atlantic

Note: Numbers 14 and 15 report to number 12; numbers 16 and 17 report to number 13.
Source: Based on https://about.usps.com/who/leadership/pmg-exec-leadership-team.htm

As indicated in Exhibit 5, USPS reports the organization's revenues in six categories: (1) First-Class Mail, (2) Marketing Mail, (3) Shipping and Packages, (4) International, (5) Periodicals, and (6) Other. Note where there are increases and decreases. The analyst's plan mentioned at the beginning of this case would likely say that the decreases are partly or largely due to the price being too high for basic postage, which they say could be reduced dramatically with evolution to an all P.O. box type business model. Exhibit 6 provides an illustration of USPS's revenues across segments.

EXHIBIT 5 USPS's Revenues and Number of Pieces by Segment (in Millions)

	Revenue ($)		Number of Pieces	
	2020	2021	2020	2021
First-Class Mail	$23,781	$23,281	52,628	50,695
Marketing Mail	13,909	14,590	64,004	66,200
Shipping & Packages	28,529	32,013	7,325	7,578
International	2,408	2,223	742	409
Periodicals	1,024	942	4,006	3,679
Other	3,472	3,960	466	300
Total	$73,123	$77,009	129,171	128,171

Source: Based on https://about.usps.com/newsroom/national-releases/2021/1110-usps-reports-fiscal-year-2021-results.htm

EXHIBIT 6 USPS's Revenues Across Segments

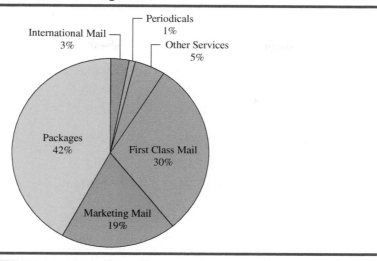

Source: Based on the USPS FY2021 *Annual Report*, p. 25.

Finance

USPS has a stated goal to reach annual breakeven operations by 2024. Specifically, USPS shows a graph at https://about.usps.com/what/strategic-plans/delivering-for-america/assets/USPS_Delivering-For-America.pdf (p. 7) whereby it plans to have a $1.7 billion surplus in 2024, followed by 8 years of similar surpluses. However, as indicated in Exhibit 7, USPS is losing money.

EXHIBIT 7 USPS's Annual Losses in Billions of Dollars in Last Decade

Year	Loss
2012	$15.9
2013	5.0
2014	5.5
2015	5.1
2016	5.6
2017	2.7
2018	3.9
2019	8.8
2020	9.2
2021	$4.9

Source: Based on https://about.usps.com/what/strategic-plans/delivering-for-america/assets/USPS_Delivering-For-America.pdf, p.20.

USPS' recent income statements and balance sheets are provided in Exhibit 8 and Exhibit 9, respectively. Note the annual substantial losses.

Strategy and Sustainability

USPS published the "Delivering for America" plan on March 23, 2021, establishing a 10-year vision for transforming the organization into a high-performing, profitable entity. Within this plan, USPS intends to invest $40 billion to fund a new vehicle fleet, processing equipment and automation, facility improvements, retail and delivery operation upgrades, and better information technology—all designed to put USPS employees in the best possible position to succeed.

EXHIBIT 8 USPS's Recent Income Statements (in Millions)

Income Statement	12/31/20	12/31/21		Percentage Change
Revenue (Sales)	$73,133	$77,041	⇧	5%
Cost of Goods Sold	8,814	9,652	⇧	10%
Gross Profit	64,319	67,389	⇧	5%
Operating Expenses	73,373	72,192	⇩	–2%
EBIT (Operating Income)	(9,054)	(4,803)	—	—
Interest Expense	122	127	⇧	4%
EBT	(9,176)	(4,930)	—	—
Tax	0	0	—	—
Nonrecurring Events	0	0	—	—
Net Income	($9,176)	($4,930)	—	—

Source: Based on the USPS FY2021 *Annual Report*, p. 24.

EXHIBIT 9 USPS's Recent Balance Sheets (in Millions)

Balance Sheet	12/31/20	12/31/21		Percentage Change
Assets				
Cash and Short-Term Investments	$14,358	$23,858	⇧	66%
Accounts Receivable	0	0	—	—
Inventory	0	0	—	—
Other Current Assets	0	0	—	—
Total Current Assets	14,358	23,858	⇧	66%
Property Plant & Equipment	14,567	14,778	⇧	1%
Goodwill	0	0	—	—
Intangibles	0	0	—	—
Other Long-Term Assets	6,979	7,769	⇧	11%
Total Assets	**35,904**	**46,405**	⇧	**29%**
Liabilities				
Accounts Payable	51,865	56,975	⇧	10%
Other Current Liabilities	31,657	33,089	⇧	5%
Total Current Liabilities	83,522	90,064	⇧	8%
Long-Term Debt	14,000	11,000	⇩	–21%
Other Long-Term Liabilities	19,090	21,021	⇧	10%
Total Liabilities	**116,612**	**122,085**	⇧	**5%**
Equity				
Common Stock	0	0	—	—
Retained Earnings	0	0	—	—

Balance Sheet	12/31/20	12/31/21		Percentage Change
Treasury Stock	0	0	—	—
Paid in Capital & Other	(80,708)	(75,680)	—	—
Total Equity	**(80,708)**	**(75,680)**	—	—
Total Liabilities and Equity	**$35,904**	**$46,405**	⇧	**29%**

Source: Based on the USPS FY2021 *Annual Report*, p. 24.

As opposed to just letters, the mailed package market has experienced unprecedented growth, and this growth is projected to continue for years to come. USPS estimates the US parcel market to grow 6 to 11 percent annually from 2020 to 2025. Online sales have also surged while shipping durations have been reduced. Customers select 1- or 2-day service for 72 percent of their parcel shipments on average, but this percentage could be as high as 90 percent by 2025.

USPS plans to change its existing service standards for First-Class Mail Letters and Flats from a current 1- to 3-day service standard within the continental United States to a 1- to 5-day service standard. This change would enable 43 percent of that portion First-Class Mail, which is currently transported through the air, to shift to surface transportation. USPS owns no planes.

USPS is investing heavily in 50,000 to 165,000 next-generation delivery vehicles (NGDV) over the next 10 years. In addition to being all electric, these vehicles will include advanced safety and comfort features and will increase delivery efficiency by providing additional loading and cargo space, and provide a safer, more reliable environment for postal carriers. USPS will continue to make use of commercial-off-the- shelf (COTS) vehicle acquisitions. USPS expects its delivery fleet of vehicles to be fully electric by 2035. USPS says it needs from Congress an additional investment of about $8 billion to electrify their delivery vehicle fleet to the maximum extent that is operationally feasible.

Competitors

USPS's primary competitors are United Parcel Service (UPS) and FedEx. Exhibit 10 provides a financial comparison between these two rival companies. Note that UPS is three times larger than FedEx.

EXHIBIT 10 USPS's Rival Firms Compared Financially

	FedEx Corp. (FDX)	United Parcel Service (UPS)	US Postal Service (USPS)
Market Capitalization	$59 billion	$182 billion	—
EPS	$18	$ 14.7	
Revenue	$90 billion	$97 billion	$77 billion
Net Income	$4.9 billion	$12.9 billion	–$4.9 billion
Total Debt	$37 billion	$25 billion	
Total Debt/Equity	148	179	
Current Ratio	1.5	1.4	
# of Full-time Employees	384,000	534,000	516,000
Stock Price	$222	$209	—

Source: Based on https://finance.yahoo.com/quote/FDX/key-statistics?p=FDX

Federal Express
Based in Memphis, Tennessee, and founded in 1971, FedEx has four segments. The first segment, FedEx Express, offers express transportation, small-package ground delivery, and freight and time-critical transportation services; and cross-border e-commerce transportation services. The company's FedEx Ground segment provides day-certain delivery services to businesses and

residences. The company's FedEx Freight segment offers less-than-truckload freight transportation services. As of June 2021, this third segment had about 29,000 vehicles and 400 service centers. Lastly, the company's FedEx Services segment provides sales, marketing, information technology, communications, customer service, technical support, billing and collection, and back-office function services.

United Parcel Service (UPS)

Founded in 1907 and headquartered in Atlanta, Georgia, UPS provides letter and package delivery, transportation, logistics, and financial services. UPS operates through three segments: (1) US Domestic Package, (2) International Package, and (3) Supply Chain & Freight. The US Domestic Package segment offers time-definite delivery of letters, documents, small packages, and palletized freight through air and ground services in the United States. The International Package segment provides guaranteed day and time-definite international shipping services in Europe, Asia/ Pacific, Canada, Latin America, the Indian subcontinent, the Middle East, and Africa.

UPS's Supply Chain and Freight segment provides international air and ocean freight forwarding, customs brokerage, distribution, mail, and consulting services in about 200 countries and territories; and less-than-truckload and truckload services to customers in North America. This segment also offers truckload brokerage services; supply chain solutions to the health-care and life sciences industry; shipping, visibility, and billing technologies; and financial and insurance services. UPS operates about 127,000 package cars, vans, tractors, and motorcycles; and owns 58,000 containers used to transport cargo in its aircraft.

External Issues

Exhibit 11 provides six key external trends facing USPS.

EXHIBIT 11 Six External Trends Facing USPS

1. USPS's domestic mail revenue declined from $60.6 billion in FY 2007 to $38.7 in FY 2020, a decline of more than $21.9 billion (36 percent) or an average annual decline of 2.8 percent, including a decline of more than 8 percent during the COVID-19 pandemic in FY 2020.
2. USPS's first-class mail volume provides the greatest contribution toward covering the costs of maintaining our universal service network but declined by 45 percent from FY 2007 to FY 2021.
3. USPS's number of delivery points are growing on average by more than 1 million each year. The result has been that pieces per delivery point per day dropped from 5.6 pieces of mail and packages in FY 2006 to 3.0 pieces in FY 2020, reinforcing that USPS is delivering less mail to more delivery points each year.
4. USPS expects its total volume to decline by 36 percent and total pieces per delivery to decline to 1.7 by FY 2030.
5. Being solely reliant on external carriers, USPS's air transportation comes with a high price and significant risk, despite 43 percent of Priority Mail, 42 percent of first-class packages, and more than 21 percent of first-class mail are transported via air.
6. USPS employees pay taxes into Medicare, with $35 billion in combined payments since 1983, being the second-largest contributor into Medicare. Yet unlike virtually any other entity that offers and funds RHB, we are not permitted to make Medicare enrollment mandatory for our retirees who receive RHB.

Source: Based on https://about.usps.com/what/strategic-plans/delivering-for-america/assets/USPS_ Delivering-For-America.pdf, p. 9.

Conclusion

Postmaster General and CEO Louis DeJoy needs a clear 3-year strategic plan for USPS. The case reveals that USPS is most profitable delivering packages, but its rivals are strengthening their efforts in this area. Intensity of competition and rivalry among firms and USPS is accelerating as companies and countries transition to zero emissions and email rather than snail-mail.

DeJoy knows the basic underlying external opportunities and threats and internal strengths facing USPS, but he is unsure about the relative importance of those factors. He thus needs and external and internal assessment performed, anchored by development of an EFE Matrix and IFE Matrix as described in Chapter 3 and Chapter 4 of the David textbook. DeJoy also needs to know the relative attractiveness of alternative strategies facing the company, so he needs a SWOT, BCG, and QSPM analyses performed. DeJoy is particularly interested to know whether a comprehensive strategic planning analysis will support the analyst's contention described at the beginning of this case regarding USPS transitioning to a business model using all P.O. boxes within a decade. Exhibit 12 provides additional information regarding this decision.

EXHIBIT 12 USPS'S Residential and Business Delivery Points in 2021

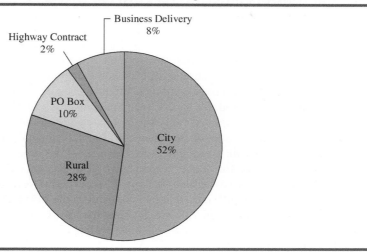

Source: Based on the USPS FY2021 *Annual Report,* p. 27.

Let's say DeJoy asks you to develop the comprehensive strategic plan that he needs. In addition to the analyses mentioned, also include projected financial statements to show the expected impact on USPS if DeJoy adopts your proposed strategic plan. All of USPS's top executives, board of directors, and employees will benefit from and be thankful for your work developing and proposing a clear roadmap for their future. Good luck on this endeavor. We authors are confident you can do a wonderful job performing this task, following the guidelines presented in the David strategic management textbook and using the strategic planning template provided at www.strategyclub.com.

References

1. https://about.usps.com/strategic-planning/five-year-strategic-plan-2017-2021.pdf
2. https://about.usps.com/what/strategic-plans/delivering-for-america/assets/USPS_Delivering-For-America.pdf
3. https://about.usps.com/what/financials/annual-reports/fy2021.pdf
4. USPS FY 2021 *Annual Report.*
5. https://about.usps.com/newsroom/national-releases/2021/1110-usps-reports-fiscal-year-2021-results.htm
6. https://finance.yahoo.com/quote/FDX/key-statistics?p=FDX
7. https://about.usps.com/who/leadership/pmg-exec-leadership-team.htm

Singapore Airlines Group, 2022

www.singaporeair.com, (OTCMTS: SINGY)

Headquartered in Singapore, Singapore Airlines Group (SIA) is practically tied for the 4th largest airline in the world based on market capitalization as of January 2022. In fact, Singapore Airlines is worth $1.5 billion as of January 2022, more than American Airlines despite American serving 350 destinations. The high valuation is reflective of Singapore Air's outstanding quality provided. Privately-held (and rival) Emirates Airline is often considered a peer of Singapore Air, based on the quality of service offered. Mr. Goh Choon Phong is the CEO of Singapore Air.

Providing what many consider to be the best passenger airline flying experience on the planet, Singapore Air has received numerous awards. In 2020 alone, the company was voted top airline in Asia by *Trip Advisor, Travel + Leisure Magazine* (USA based) voted the airline the world's best international airline for the 25th consecutive year, *Business Traveler* (Asia-Pacific based) voted Singapore Airlines best airline for the 29th consecutive year. In 2021, *Fortune Magazine* ranked Singapore Air the 34th most admired company in the world, and 2nd most admired airline. Malaysia Airlines and Singapore Air, two rival (but friendly) airlines, in November 2021 launched a Vaccinated Travel Lane (VTL) arrangement, providing customers with seamless travel for long-distance business or leisure travel.

Also in November 2021, Malaysia Airlines and Singapore Air reactivated and expanded their codeshare arrangement between Singapore and Kuala Lumpur, Malaysia, expanding it to include 15 domestic points in Malaysia, seven destinations in Europe, and two cities in South Africa. Singapore Air customers now can connect on Malaysia Air services out of Kuala Lumpur to 15 new destinations in Malaysia: Alor Setar, Bintulu, Johor Bahru, Kota Kinabalu, Kuala Terengganu, Kuantan, Kuching, Labuan, Langkawi, Miri, Penang, Sandakan, Sibu, and Tawau. And Malaysia Air customers can now connect on Singapore Air's flights from Singapore to seven cities in Europe: Barcelona, Copenhagen, Frankfurt, Moscow, Munich, Rome, and Zurich – as well as Cape Town and Johannesburg in South Africa.

Copyright by Fred David Books LLC; written by Forest R. David.

History

Singapore Air traces its history to 1947 when the airline was known as Malaysian Airways Limited (MAL) servicing three flights from Singapore to Kala Lumpur, Ipoh, and Penang in Malaysia. It was not until 1971 that the firm flew their first transcontinental flight from Singapore to London, and in 1972 the airline split into two companies: 1) Malaysian Airline System and 2) Singapore Airlines.

Singapore Air grew rapidly in the 1970s and 1980s purchasing both Boeing 747s and Airbus A300s; the company moved its operations to the new Singapore Changi Airport in 1981. From 1997 to 2003, the company did not purchase any new aircraft before adding the Airbus A340 ultra long-range plane in 2003. In 2007, Singapore Air took delivery of the world's first Airbus A380. The company invested $150 million in 2013 and another $80 million in 2015 to improve its premium seating offerings.

In December 2021, Singapore Air agreed to purchase from Airbus seven new A350F freighter aircraft, with options to order another five aircraft, with deliveries to begin in Q4 of 2025. Singapore Air will be the first airline to operate this new generation widebody freighter aircraft. With the agreement, Singapore Air swaps out the new aircraft with 15 A320neo and two A350-900 passenger aircraft that are in the company's current fleet. The new A350F can carry a similar volume of cargo as the Boeing 747-400F that Singapore Air is phasing out of its fleet. The A350-900 burns up to 40 percent less fuel on similar flights. The new aircraft enable Singapore Air to 1) maintain an exceptionally young fleet of aircraft, 2) strengthen its freight-hauling capabilities, and 3) meet is carbon emission targets upcoming in this decade.

Internal Issues

Vision/Mission

Singapore Air does not have a published vision statement, but an analyst recently offered the following vision statement for the company:

Vision statement – *We strive to be the best airline anywhere for customers, and to offer the best workplace anywhere for employees, and to be an outstanding corporate citizen of the world.*

Singapore Air provides a mission statement in their 2021 *Annual Report*, paraphrased as follows:

Mission statement: *"We are committed to offering exceptional air travel services globally, while providing employees great pay and benefits, and providing excellent returns to our shareholders."*

Corporate Wellness

Singapore Air recently partnered with a health and wellness firm, California-based Golden Door, to provided health-focused meals, exercise, stretching, relaxation, sleeping and well-being options to Singapore Air customers on board its flights between Singapore and the USA. Some of these non-stop flights can extend to nearly 19 hours. Singapore Air now use Golden Door on its flights to the United States to assure that passengers experience enhanced corporate wellness to the extent possible, including nutrition, rest, exercise, sleep, and mental and physical relaxation.

Singapore Air's SVP for Customer Experience, Mr. Yeoh Phee Teik says: "Our long-standing commitment to corporate wellness has led us to work with Golden Door's experts to maximize wellness services to our passengers." Singapore Air's non-stop flights to and from Los Angeles, New York, and San Francisco and other cities in America have also now been designated as Vaccinated Travel Lane flights, allowing eligible customers quarantine-free entry into Singapore.

Organizational Structure

Based on the titles of top executives at Singapore Air, the company likely operates from a divisional-by-product organizational design, with the four segments being: 1) Commercial, 2) Cargo, 3) Engineering, and 4) Scoot. The company's top managers are listed and arrayed in Exhibit 1. Note there are three females among seventeen executives.

EXHIBIT 1 Singapore's Top Executives Listed and Arrayed

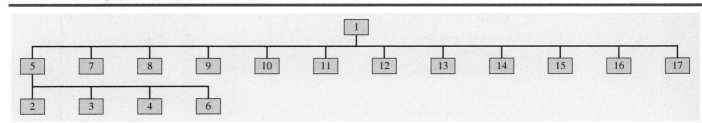

1. Goh Choon Phong, CEO
2. Lee Lik Hsin, EVP Commercial
3. Ng Chin Hwee, CEO of SIA Engineering
4. Campbell Wilson, CEO Scoot
5. Mak Swee Wah, EVP Operations
6. Chin Yau Seng, SVP Cargo
7. Tan Kai Ping, EVP Finance and Strategy
8. Lau Hwa Peng, SVP Engineering
9. Lee Wen Fen, SVP Corporate Planning (female)

10. Vanessa Ng Wee Leng, SVP Human Resources (female)
11. Jo-Ann Tan, SVP Marketing Planning (female)
12. Marvin Tan, SVP Customer Services and Operations
13. Tan Pee Tech, SVP Cabin Crew
14. Leslie Thng, SVP Sales and Marketing
15. Captain Quay Chew Eng, SVP Flight Operations
16. George Wang, SVP Information Technology
17. Yeoh Phee Teik, SVP Customer Experience

Source: Based on https://www.singaporeair.com/en_UK/sg/about-us/information-for-investors/management-team/

Finance

Two of the highest expense items for firms in the airline industry are fuel and labor, with many firms having labor costs nearly equal to fuel costs. Using fiscal 2020 data instead of 2021 since the firm was able to operate most of fiscal 2020, fuel costs accounted for 35 percent of Singapore Air's expenses and labor costs comprised 14 percent.

Singapore Air's fiscal years ends every March 31. Exhibit 2 reveals that Singapore Air, like many airlines, was severely hurt during the Covid pandemic. Note that sales for Singapore Air declined 76 percent in fiscal 2021. The firm reported a net loss of $169 million in fiscal 2020 followed by a net loss of $4.283 billion in fiscal 2021. Note the huge improvement in fiscal 2022 but still the net income loss of $962 million.

EXHIBIT 2 Singapore Air's Recent Income Statements (in Millions)

Income Statement	3/31/20	3/31/21		3/31/22
Revenue (Sales)	$15,976	$3,816	⇩	$7,615
Cost of Goods Sold	0	0	NA	0
Gross Profit	15,976	3,816	⇩	7,615
Operating Expenses	15,917	6,329	⇩	8,225
EBIT (Operating Income)	59	(2,513)	⇩	(610)
Interest Expense	279	(232)	⇩	
EBT	(220)	(2,280)	⇩	
Tax	(51)	(674)	⇧	
Non-Recurring Events	0	(2,677)	NA	
Net Income	($169)	($4,283)	⇩	(962)

Source: Based on Singapore Airline's 2021 *Form 10K*, p 58 - 59. Also, https://www.singaporeair.com/saar5/pdf/Investor-Relations/Financial-Results/News-Release/nr-q4fy2122.pdf

Exhibit 3 provides recent balance sheets for Singapore Air over the same time frame. Note the company was able to raise cash and reduce current liabilities, but retained earnings dropped 30 percent mostly from the significant loss in net income.

EXHIBIT 3 Singapore Air's Recent Balance Sheets (in Millions)

Balance Sheet	3/31/20	3/31/21		Percent Change
Assets				
Cash and Short Term Investments	$2,685	$7,783	⇧	190%
Accounts Receivable	1,151	1,057	⇩	−8%
Inventory	239	194	⇩	−19%
Other Current Assets	768	638	⇩	−17%
Total Current Assets	4,843	9,672	⇧	100%
Property Plant & Equipment	25,486	23,483	⇩	−8%
Goodwill	0	0	NA	NA
Intangibles	487	301	⇩	−38%
Other Long-Term Assets	2,897	4,125	⇧	42%
Total Assets	**33,713**	**37,581**	⇧	**11%**
Liabilities				
Accounts Payable	69	95	⇧	38%
Other Current Liabilities	10,933	5,618	⇩	−49%
Total Current Liabilities	11,002	5,713	⇩	−48%

Balance Sheet	3/31/20	3/31/21		Percent Change
Long-Term Debt	11,102	13,445	⇧	21%
Other Long-Term Liabilities	1,876	2,145	⇧	14%
Total Liabilities	**23,980**	**21,303**	⇩	**−11%**
Equity				
Common Stock	1,856	7,180	⇧	287%
Retained Earnings	7,614	5,363	⇩	−30%
Treasury Stock	(156)	(133)	⇩	−15%
Paid in Capital & Other	419	3,868	⇧	823%
Total Equity	**9,733**	**16,278**	⇧	**67%**
Total Liabilities and Equity	**$33,713**	**$37,581**	⇧	**11%**

Source: Based on Singapore Airline's 2021 *Form 10K*, p. 113.

Strategy

Moving into 2023 and beyond, Singapore Airlines will be operating with two airline brands, Singapore Airlines and Scoot. The legacy carrier Singapore Airlines is positioned for long haul flights across the globe and offers full service while Scoot is a low cost airline provider focusing on more regional flights. SIA has an investment in Vistara, an Indian airline that allows for a multi hub strategy. Vistara expects to increase its aircraft fleet from 47 in 2021 to 70 by 2023. SIA is also expanding its omnichannel platform through its KrisShop, and KrisFlyer which serves as SIA's loyalty program. KrisPay serves as the group's digital wallet.

Sustainability

The airline industry has a large negative impact on the environment. Singapore Air has committed itself to net zero carbon emissions by 2050. The firm continually invests in new aircraft, adopts low carbon technologies, and searches for carbon offsets of the highest quality. Singapore Air's customers can calculate and make contributions to their portion of the emissions of the flight. The firm continues to install solar panels on its rooftops that can deliver 18 percent of the firm's energy needs. The company has extensive water management policies and saves water through collection devices and harvesting of rainwater. The company's work on water has earned it the PUB Water Efficiency Building certificates on four of its buildings. Meals on flights are now using reusable materials rather than throw away containers and leftover food is saved and produced into pellets that are used as fuel in other industries. The company provides an elaborate annual *Sustainability Report* on its corporate website.

Segments

Singapore Air operates in four main divisions: Singapore Air, SilkAir, Scoot, and Sia Engineering. The legacy business is Singapore Air that serves 47 destinations, with SilkAir serving 5 and Scoot serving 18 destinations. Singapore Air serves the entire world, including three destinations in the United States and twelve destinations in Europe. SilkAir is focused and only serves 5 cities in Southeast Asia but no airports in China; and Scoot serves Southeast Asia, China, Australia, and Japan. SilkAir only has 1 current aircraft in service because their fleet of 6 Boeing 737 Max are not currently in service. Singapore Air operates 113 aircraft and Scoot operates 47.

The company's Engineering segment/division serves as maintenance for Singapore Air and many other airlines around the region. Exhibit 4 provides the breakdown of how the company obtains its revenue. Note over 80 percent is derived from the main airline and only 3 percent is derived from SIA Engineering. Exhibit 5 provides revenues based on product category; passenger revenue normally dominates all revenues for the firm. Exhibit 6 reveals the geographic markets served by the airline with the most revenue being generated from East Asia. Note the Americas produce substantial revenues but profit margins may not be as high for this region as flights are extremely long distances.

EXHIBIT 4 Singapore Air's Percent Revenue by Division

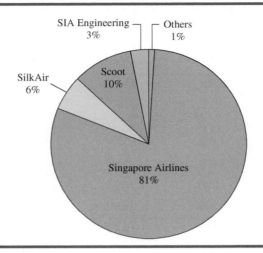

Source: Based on Singapore Air's 2021 *Annual Report*, p. 54.

EXHIBIT 5 Singapore Air's Revenue by Product Category (in Millions)

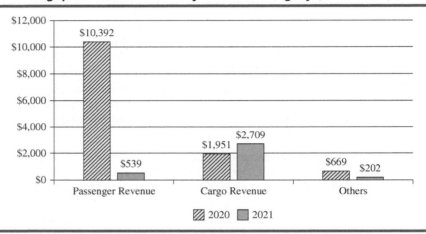

Source: Based on Singapore Air's 2021 *Annual Report*, p. 60.

EXHIBIT 6 Singapore Air's Revenue by Region (in Millions)

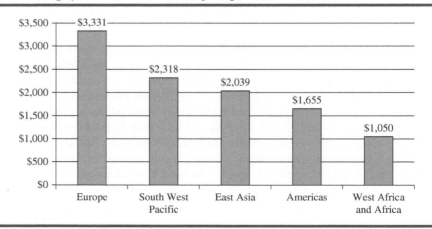

Source: Based on Singapore Air's 2021 *Annual Report*, p. 61.

SilkAir

In 2021, SilkAir, the regional airline of Singapore Air, was under the process of being merged into Singapore Air as the firm attempted to better integrate it's airlines. Full integration of this airline was completed in 2021. Look for future data on financial statements to reflect this change, but be sure to account for the integration in any analysis regarding the case moving forward.

Scoot

Scoot is the low-cost subsidiary of Singapore Air serving far less airports and focusing on economy/value-minded travelers. During the pandemic, Scoot was able to shift its resources more from offing passenger service to providing cargo service. Also during 2021, Scoot received service to six Indonesian cities from SilkAir, bringing the total destinations served in Indonesia to 18 for Scoot. During the height of the pandemic in 2020, Scoot was flying cargo-only flights with cargo in the belly of the aircraft, and also was strapping cargo onto passenger seats. Eventually Scoot removed all passenger seats on its A320 aircraft which doubled its cargo capacity. Scoot offered repatriation flights for many during 2020.

Singapore Airlines (SIA) Engineering Company (SIAEC)

SIAEC provides maintenance services to 30 airports across seven countries in the Asia Pacific region. The segment provides services to 80 international airlines with six hangers in Singapore and three hangers in the Philippines. SIAEC itself consists of 23 subsidiaries and joint ventures with partners from around the region. While this segment was severely impacted during Covid because grounded planes did not need regularly scheduled maintenance, the segment did purchase Cebu Pacific's stake in Singapore Air Philippines providing SIAEC 100 percent ownership in this subsidiary. The division is currently investing heavily in new digitalization and automation.

Competitors

Singapore Air competes with many airlines around the world, but the airline competes most directly with Emirates Airlines, due to the markets it prominently serves and by the quality of upscale service. Many of the top airlines provided in Exhibit 7 are not direct competitors with Singapore Air. Exhibit 7 reveals the top airlines by market capitalization. Emirates is not listed as the company is private. Note, the market capitalization value may not correlate exactly with the size of the airline with respect to planes owned or markets served.

EXHIBIT 7 Corporate Value of the Top Airlines in the World (in Billions)

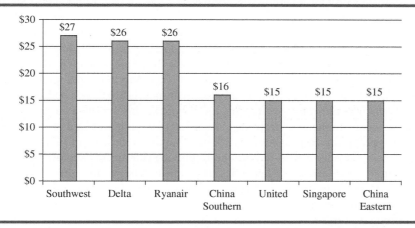

Source: Based on information collected from the individual respected ticker information on Yahoo Finance, January 2022.

Emirates Group

The name "Emirates Group" includes two entities: 1) the well-known Emirates Airline and 2) the aviation services company Dubai National Air Transport Association (dnata). Headquartered in Garhoud, Dubai, UAE near the Dubai International Airport, Emirates Airline (or simply Emirates) is the state-owned global airline of Dubai. The largest airline in the Middle East, Emirates provides passenger and freight services to about 100 countries, while dnata provides ground handling, cargo, catering, and travel services in 35 countries. (Note: Emirates Airlines and dnata do not form a group according to International Financial Reporting Standards (IFRS), so much of Emirates Group's *Annual Report* presents separate data for the two entities, but the name "Emirates Group" refers to the two entities combined). Emirates is known for its high-quality service that is similar to the service Singapore Air provides. Both airlines also serve many of the same markets.

More than twenty brands of the Emirates Group are described at the corporate website at https://www.theemiratesgroup.com, including everything from catering to food services to travel agencies to ground handling and cargo services – so this is a diversified, backward and forward integrated, well-managed, fast-growing group. Today, Emirates serves 155 airports in 81 countries from its hub in Dubai.

China Southern Airlines Company Limited

Headquartered in Guangzhou, China, China Southern has been the largest airline in China for 43 years running as of 2022 transporting more than 150 million passengers annually and is ranked 2nd globally in number of passengers transported annually. The company is in the top 10 globally with respect to cargo and mail carried. China Southern maintains this volume of traffic through its 860 aircraft that include such jets as the Boeing 787 Dreamliner, Airbus 380 and Airbus 320 and many smaller aircraft for medium haul flights. The firm serves 3,000 daily flights to 224 destinations. Close partners with China Southern include American Airlines and Qatar Airways. Guangzhou has become the top airport for travel to Australia and Southeast Asia, also two of the top markets for Singapore Air. China Southern in 2020 was the first airline in Asia and third in the world to be certified by IATA for its efforts on green flights and catering service reducing waste. The firm reported revenues of $25 billion in 2019 and $14 billion in 2020.

External Issues

How Do Airlines Make Money?

Airlines receive the bulk of their revenue from tickets, but also generate income from fees, food, credit cards, frequent-flyer programs, moving cargo, and at times government bailouts. Singapore Air uses all these means to generate revenue. Business travelers on average account for about 12 percent of global airline-ticketed passengers, but can account for 60 to 75 percent of revenues, as business class tickets can cost upwards of 10 times the price of coach. Corporations are often willing to pay for business class flights as they view having rested and less-stressed employees arriving at a location to be worth the additional cost of business class travel. Although the advent of Zoom and other means of video conferencing is curtailing business travel significantly, video conferencing is nothing new; there has been significant demand for business travel for the last 20 years.

Affluent travelers are a significant source of income for airlines as they often purchase business class seating; you cannot Zoom as a replacement for a fancy vacation. To take advantage of business and high-end vacation travelers, airlines are catering more and more to business class customers. Even firms that were traditionally low cost such as Southwest Airlines based in Texas, USA and RyanAir in Europe are competing more aggressively for these customers.

Airlines benefit immensely from their frequent flier programs and also from credit cards linked to these programs. High-income customers tend to purchase more flights with these cards. Also, using these cards for day-to-day purchases provide significant data for marketing and strategy. Surprisingly, these frequent flier miles programs can be worth more than the airlines that own them. They are so profitable in fact that airlines are able to offer more attractive pricing on tickets and more and better routes. Many of the rewards earned by customers are not redeemed further profiting the airlines.

Personalized Websites

Customers today demand increased flexibility and options in the products and services they buy; people are demanding increased flexibility regarding how they purchase airline tickets. This shift in buying behavior has challenged airlines to produce increasingly modern websites that are even more user friendly and personalized. Surprisingly, low-cost carriers are performing significantly better than full-service carriers with respect to having home pages that are dynamic and effective in nature. Offering customers customizable features, nudging tactics, personalized widgets, and much more creates a meaningful experience and helps increase brand loyalty.

Video Conferencing

While you cannot have a fun vacation video conferencing, you certainly can hold a meeting or attend a conference via video conferencing. Airlines have long thrived on the high-priced business class seats as business professionals jetted across the skies for business meetings. MS Teams, Zoom, and many other video-conference platforms replaced business travel during Covid and it is still unclear whether business travel will return to its pre-pandemic percentage numbers.

Conclusion

As the pandemic expectedly moderates, consumer demand for both business and leisure air travel is returning and growing upwards of five percent annually even as video conferencing and online meetings become the new normal. Exhibit 8 provides recent operating statistics for the company,

EXHIBIT 8 Recent Operating Statistics For Singapore Air

Singapore Airlines (and SilkAir)		
	2021–2022	2020–2021
Passengers carried (thousand)	$3,388	$514
Revenue passenger-km (million)	19,177.7	2,669.0
Available seat-km (million)	58,748.1	19,493.0
Passenger load factor (%)	32.6	13.7
Scoot		
Passengers carried (thousand)	502	82
Revenue passenger-km (million)	1,486.8	221.6
Available seat-km (million)	9,822.2	2,228.2
Passenger load factor (%)	15.1	9.9
Group Airlines (passenger)		
Passengers carried (thousand)		
Revenue passenger-km (million)		
Available seat-km (million)		
Passenger load factor (%)		
Passenger yield (cents/pkm)		
Revenue per available seat-km (cents/ask)		
Group Airlines (Cargo)		
Cargo and mail carried (million kg)	1,046.0	734.0
Cargo load (million tonne-km)	5,941.0	4,111.9
Gross capacity (million tonne-km)	7,195.3	4,795.1
Employee Productivity (Average)		
Singapore Airlines (and SilkAir)		
Average number of employees	14,534	16,772
Capacity per employee (tonne-km)	914,731	406,688
Revenue per employee ($)	$486,315	$207,369

Source: Based on https://www.singaporeair.com/saar5/pdf/Investor-Relations/Financial-Results/News-Release/nr-q4fy2122.pdf

Singapore Air is competing on upscale flights and low-cost carrier flights with the firm's Scoot brand. Should Singapore Air attempt to compete on both business models, or should the firm attempt to expand its legacy carrier offerings of Singapore Air? Recall from the case, the company offers service to less than five US cities. Also, take note of the firm's engineering arm which provides air service maintenance to many rival firms and only generates 3 percent of revenue for the company as a whole. Would it be more advantageous to stop offering this service to rival airlines and shift excess resources to expanding the Singapore fleet?

CEO Goh Choon Phong needs a clear 3-year strategic plan for Singapore Air. Intensity of competition and rivalry among firms such as Emirates Airlines and Malaysia Air are accelerating. The vision/mission and organizational structure sections of this case reveal that there is substantial room for improvement for Singapore Air in both areas. CEO Phong knows the basic underlying external opportunities and threats and internal strengths facing Singapore Air, but he is unsure about the relative importance of those factors. He thus needs an external and internal assessment performed, anchored by development of an EFE Matrix and IFE Matrix as described in Chapter 3 and Chapter 4 of the David textbook. CEO Phong also needs to know the relative attractiveness of alternative strategies facing the company, so he needs SWOT, BCG, and QSPM analyses performed.

Lets say CEO Phong asks you to develop the comprehensive strategic plan that he needs. In addition to the analyses mentioned above, include in your report a perceptual map, a set of proposed recommendations with associated costs, and an EPS-EBIT analysis to reveal whether debt or stock or some combination of debt and stock is best to obtain the needed funds. Also include projected financial statements to show the expected impact on Singapore Air if CEO Phong adopts your proposed strategic plan. If further acquisitions are needed by Singapore Air to grow its top line (revenues) and bottom line (net income) 5+ percent annually in the years to come, identify the best candidate firms for Singapore Air to acquire. If Singapore should expand further organically (internally) into other regions, countries, and continents, include direction for CEO Phong in this regard.

All of Singapore Air's top executives, board of directions, drivers, shareholders, and employees will benefit from and be thankful for your work developing and proposing a clear roadmap for their future. Good luck on this endeavor. We authors are confident you can do a wonderful job performing this task, following the guidelines presented in the David strategic management textbook, and using the strategic planning template provided at www.strategyclub.com.

References

1. www.statista.com
2. Singapore Airline's fiscal 2021 *Annual Report* and *Form 10K*.
3. www.finance.yahoo.com
4. https://www.theemiratesgroup.com
5. https://www.singaporeair.com/en_UK/sg/about-us/information-for-investors/management-team/
6. www.singaporeair.com
7. https://www.singaporeair.com/saar5/pdf/Investor-Relations/Financial-Results/News-Release/nr-q4fy2122.pdf

Danone S.A., 2022

www.danone.com, (OTCQX: DANOY)

Headquartered in Paris, France, Danone, sometimes spelled Dannon in English, is a large food-producing company specializing in dairy products and is the second-most valuable dairy firm in the world trailing only the Chinese firm, Yili Group, headquartered in Hohhot, Inner Mongolia. Based on sales among dairy producers, Danone is closer to fourth globally. Danone derives revenues globally, but the top three nations where revenues are derived from are the United States, China, and France. Fully 53 percent of Danone's 2020 revenues were from Europe, United States, and Canada, with the remaining 43 percent coming from the rest of the world.

Danone reported 24.6 billion euros in 2020 revenues, down from 25.3 billion euros in 2019. Danone has three main business categories: (1) Essential Dairy and Plant-Based, (2) Specialized Nutrition, and (3) Waters. Top global brands in the first segment include Danone Yogurt, Activia, Oikos, Delight, Danonino, Silk and others. In the second segment, top water brands owned by Danone include Aqua, Bonafont, evian, Volvic, and Hayat among others. Danone's third segment nutrition business focuses mostly on baby foods.

In 2020, Danone sold Vega, a Canadian and US-based plant-based food brand to a private-equity firm in the United States. This was an interesting move because Danone's rival Nestle is focusing heavily on plant-based products. Possibly Danone is exiting certain areas and plans to focus on its more traditional product lines. A few quick facts about Danone are:

1. The company's products are available in 120+ countries.
2. The percentage breakdown of revenues by segment for Danone are 54%, 31%, and 15% for (1) Essential Diary and Plant-Based, (2) Specialized Nutrition, and (3) Waters, respectively.
3. The company has 100,000+ employees in more than 55 countries.
4. The company's top three brands are Aptaml, Activia, and Danone.
5. The company has 23.6 billion in annual sales in euros.

Copyright by Fred David Books LLC; written by Forest R. David.

History

Danone traces its history to a pharmacy in Barcelona, Spain, in 1919 with the creating of the first yogurt. For many decades yogurt was all Danone was known for. The new product was derived from many people in Spain at the time suffering from intestinal problems that were associated with poor nutrition. The lactic ferments of yogurt helped many people overcome these problems and explains why the product we associate today with food was originally offered only at the drug store.

Danone began operations in France in 1929 and in the United States in 1942, a destructive year for much of the world. In 1970, Danone became France's largest baby food and beverage producer after the acquisition of evian known for its bottled water, Kronenbourg known for its beer, and two other firms. In the 1990s, Danone acquired several companies in Eastern Europe, Latin America, and Asia Amoy, including a Hong Kong-based soy sauce and frozen foods company.

The current form of Danone started taking shape in 2007 with the sale of its biscuits business to Kraft Foods and the acquisition of Royal Numico, at the time a global leader in medical and baby nutrition. Shifting resources around is one of the top jobs of a strategist. In 2014, Danone was ahead of its time with the recommendation of then CEO and chair of the board Franck Riboud, to separate the functions of the chair and the CEO. Riboud remained as chair but relinquished his CEO duties to Emmanuel Faber. The company has recently, however, once again allowed the chair and CEO to be the same person. Danone's operations in the United States and Canada received a B Corp Certification in 2018, 2 years ahead of schedule, which measures a firm's social and environmental impact.

Internal Issues

Vision/Mission

Danone reports a mission statement on its website that is one sentence in length and can be paraphrased as "*We provide healthy food to as many people as possible.*" The firm also provides a vision paraphrased as (Danone: Helping Our Planet With Healthy Foods), but that statement does not address the question "what do we wish to become." Danone's vision instead strikes a balance between the interconnectivity of the planet and people's health and encourages people to seek sustainable eating and drinking habits while protecting the earth. The company claims that 90 percent of the volume of its products are healthy.

Finance

Danone is a profitable company with net income of €2,028 million in 2019 and almost identical net income of €2,030 million in 2020 however a 2 percent drop in net income in 2021 was reported despite a 3 percent increase in revenues. Exhibit 1 reveals the Income Statements for Danone for fiscal years 2020 and 2021. Exhibit 2 reveals Danone's revenues over a 10-year period.

EXHIBIT 1 Danone's Recent Income Statements (in Millions, €)

Income Statement	12/31/20	12/31/21		Percent Change
Revenue (Sales)	€ 23,620	€ 24,281	⇧	3%
Cost of Goods Sold	12,267	12,760	⇧	4%
Gross Profit	11,353	11,521	⇧	1%
Operating Expenses	8,555	9,264	⇧	8%
EBIT (Operating Income)	2,798	2,257	⇩	−19%
Interest Expense	310	262	⇩	−15%
EBT	2,488	1,995	⇩	−20%
Tax	762	589	⇩	−23%
Non-Recurring Events	304	586	⇧	93%
Net Income	€ 2,030	€ 1,992	⇩	−2%

Source: Based on the 2021 Danone *Annual Report*, p. 4.

EXHIBIT 2 Danone's Revenues Over Time (in Millions, €)

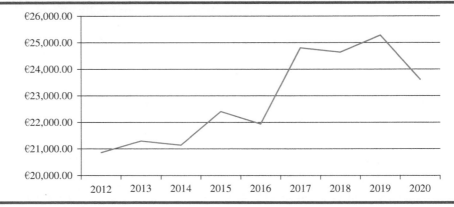

Source: Based on information at a variety of sources.

Danone's recent Balance Sheets are provided in Exhibit 3. The firm reports that more than half of its assets are in the form of goodwill and intangibles; the company has over €12 billion in long-term debt.

EXHIBIT 3 Danone's Recent Balance Sheets (in Millions, €)

Balance Sheet	12/31/20	12/31/21		Percent Change
Assets				
Cash and Short Term Investments	€ 593	€ 659	⬆	11%
Accounts Receivable	2,608	2,862	⬆	10%
Inventory	1,840	1,982	⬆	8%
Other Current Assets	5,597	6,553	⬆	17%
Total Current Assets	10,638	12,056	⬆	13%
Property Plant & Equipment	6,572	6,843	⬆	4%
Goodwill	17,106	17,871	⬆	4%
Intangibles	6,020	6,182	⬆	3%
Other Long-Term Assets	2,440	2,468	⬆	1%
Total Assets	**42,776**	**45,420**	⬆	**6%**
Liabilities				
Accounts Payable	3,467	7,080	⬆	104%
Other Current Liabilities	6,871	3,998	⬇	−42%
Total Current Liabilities	10,338	11,078	⬆	7%
Long-Term Debt	12,343	12,537	⬆	2%
Other Long-Term Liabilities	3,798	4,430	⬆	17%
Total Liabilities	**26,479**	**28,045**	⬆	**6%**
Equity				
Common Stock	172	172	⬇	0%
Retained Earnings	17,374	18,038	⬆	4%
Treasury Stock	(1,595)	(2,380)	⬆	49%
Paid in Capital & Other	346	1,545	⬆	347%
Total Equity	**16,297**	**17,375**	⬆	**7%**
Total Liabilities and Equity	**€ 42,776**	**€ 45,420**	⬆	**6%**

Source: Based on the 2021 Danone *Annual Report*, p. 5.
https://www.danone.com/content/dam/danone-corp/danone-com/investors/en-consolidated-accounts/2021/Danone_2021_full_year_consolidated_financial_statements.pdf

Strategy

Danone is committed to providing excellent nourishment to the world while protecting the environment at the same time. Danone 2030 is the name of the firm's strategy moving forward to execute the mission of the company. Within this strategy, nine long-term goals of the company correlate nicely with the 2030 Sustainable Development Goals of the United Nations. The first long-term goal is to "provide excellent food experiences through innovation." In 2020, 36 percent of Danone's revenue was derived from products launched less than 2 years prior. The firm's plant-based business yielded sales of €2.2 billion in 2020 with expectations to grow to €5 billion by 2025. The €2.2 billion sounds large but only represents around 10 percent of Danone's revenues.

Danone's second stated goal is to "maintain profitability growth while being environmentally sustainable." In 2020, carbon dioxide cost per share at the company dropped 4 percent. Danone is "committed to obtaining many certifications" as its third goal and enjoyed 13 additional certifications in 2020 with goals to be 100 percent certified by 2025. Product categories that received certifications in 2020 include dairy and plant-based with two such certifications, specialized nutrition, waters, and other products as well.

Danone's fourth goal is to "meet the health needs of people." Top accomplishment in 2020 was a number-one ranking in marketing for breastmilk substitutes. The firm has five additional goals that all are related to the four outlined here dealing with healthy eating and becoming more environmentally sustainable.

Segments

Danone operates in three different segments: (1) Early Life Nutrition, Dairy and Plant-Based Products (EDP), (2) Specialized Nutrition, and (3) Waters. The firm is committed to being a healthy food provider to the world. Under the dairy and plant-based products notable brands of Danone include Danone, Oikos, Activia, International Delight, Silk, Danonino, alpro, Actimel and more. The firm is increasingly moving into plant-based foods and drinks. One such example is the Silk line of milk products derived from soy, almonds, and other plant-based products.

Danone's water line includes the world-famous brand evian, but there are many others including AQUA, Mizone, Bonafont, Volvic, Hayat, Font Vella, and more. The top three brands according to Danone are AQUA, Mizone, and evian. Danone is ranked second in the world in packaged waters by volume. Danone claims to be number one in Europe in medical nutrition and number 2 worldwide in early life nutrition with the top three countries by sales of this division being: China, the UK, and France.

Exhibit 4 reveals Danone's sales by product and service. The company's EDP segment generates more sales than the other two divisions combined. However, with respect to operating profits, the Specialized Nutrition segment reported profits of €1.8 billion in 2020 compared to €1.3 billion for EDP. The company's Waters segment only generated €251 million in operating profit in 2020 for a margin of 7 percent. The Specialized Nutrition profit margin is 25 percent and EDP is 10 percent based on 2020 numbers.

EXHIBIT 4 Danone's Net Sales by Product/Service (in Millions, €)

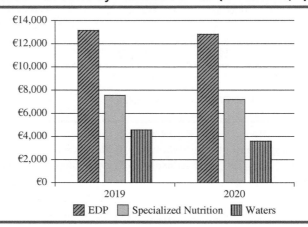

Source: Based on the 2021 Danone *Annual Report*, p. 3.

Exhibit 5 reveals Danone's sales by region. Sales for Europe, United States, and Canada (Noram = North America) represent about 58 percent of companywide sales depending on the year. Profit margins are around 14 percent for both regions. Note from Exhibit 6 the company's booming water sales increase in 2021.

EXHIBIT 5 Danone's Sales by Region (in Millions, €)

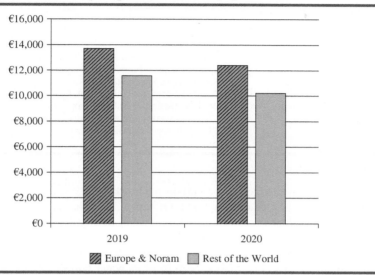

Source: Based on the 2020 Danone *Annual Report*, p. 5.

EXHIBIT 6 Danone's Sales by Product and by Region (in Millions, €)

	2020	2021	Percentage Change
EDP	€12,823	€13,090	2.1
Specialized Nutrition	7,192	7,230	0.5
Water	3,605	3,961	9.9
Total	23,620	24,281	2.8
Europe and North America	13,408	13,762	2.6
Rest of the World	€10,212	€10,520	3.0

Source: Based on https://www.danone.com/content/dam/danone-corp/danone-com/medias/medias-en/2022/corporatepressreleases/pr-danone-fy-2021.pdf

Organizational Structure

Danone's top executives are listed and arrayed in Exhibit 7. Note the company appears to operate from a divisional-by-region organizational structure. This would make sense for the company. The regional top executives report to COO Henri Bruxelles.

Competitors

Danone faces hundreds of rival companies from small local firms to large global manufacturers such as Nestle. Other large competitors include Kraft Heinz, PepsiCo, Unilever, and Mondelez International.

Nestle S.A. (OTCMKTS: NSRGY)

Headquartered in Vevey, Vaud, Switzerland, and founded by Henri Nestle, the global company named Nestle S.A. is a huge, rival firm to Danone, competing on waters, baby food, milk products, and many other products. Both companies also talk the talk on plant-based options. Consumers debate on whether Danone or Nestle's sparking water is better, S. Pellegrino or Perrier. Actually, both brands are Nestle products, along with many other local brands of sparkling

EXHIBIT 7 Danone's Top Executives Listed and Arrayed

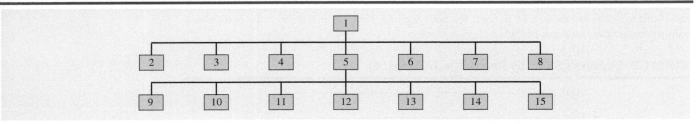

1. Gilles Antoine de Saint-Affrique, CEO
2. Bertrand Austruy, Chief Human Resources Officer
3. Cecile Cabanis, EVP, CFO
4. Shane Grant, CEO, North America
5. Henri Bruxelles, COO
6. Juergen Esser, CFO, Tech and Data
7. Nicolas Gausseres, Chief Executive of the Danone Ecosystem Fund
8. Nigyar Makhmudova, Chief Growth Officer

9. Veronique Penchienati-Bosetta, CEO, International
10. Charlie Cappetti, President, CIS and Turkey
11. Silvia Davila, President, Latin America
12. Jean-Marc Magnaudet, President, Specialized Nutrition
13. Floris Wesseling, President, Europe
14. Corine Tap, President, Asia, Africa and Middle-East
15. Bruno Chevot, President, Greater China and Oceania

Source: Based on https://craft.co/danone/executives

waters. This segment has pledged to be carbon neutral by 2025 with S. Pellegrino and Aqua Panna pledging to be carbon neutral by 2022. Of course, this carbon neutrality likely does not include shipping the product to stores as providing water through a pipeline still remains much more economically friendly both on transporting and on packaging.

Nestle is committed to a waste-free future through offering recyclable or reusable packaging and currently Nestle uses recycled plastic in most of its water bottles. Maintaining the theme of plant-based, the new product Buxton is being tested in the UK. Buxton is a plant-infused water that blends spring water, plant polyphenols, and minerals with fruit flavors. This segment reported $6.4 billion in sales in 2020 and accounted for 7.6 percent of companywide sales.

Nestle's milk-product segment reported $11 billion in sales accounting for 13 percent of corporate sales in 2020. Nestle recently divested its US ice cream business. The firm is aggressively marketing less dairy, less meat, and increased plant-based products in their other segments, while still operating a billion-dollar business within this milk product segment. Nestle promotes its plant-based alternatives with notable brands such as Nesfit, Nido, Coffee mate, nesQuno, Carnation, Moca, and La Lechera.

With a growing number of people worldwide being lactose intolerant and a more health-minded public, brands owned by Nestle include Ninho, Nesfit Sabor Natural, and Carnation all launched plant-based products in 2020. Carnation, a thick fatty and sweet condensed milk product, is now offering a plant-based option that importantly tastes good.

One of Nestle's largest brands is Gerber, but NAN, illume, and Cerelac are also blockbuster brands owned by Nestle. Nestle's NAN supplements are designed to be a replacement or as a supplement for a mother's breast milk. Baby formula Belsol was produced with coordination with Alibaba's innovation center and the product (according to Nestle's *Annual Report*) is claimed to be tailored for Chinese babies. BrainXpert is a drink product that, according to Nestle is "clinically proven" to increase brain functioning in people with cognitive difficulties which research reveals affects about 20 percent of people globally older than age 65. Other Nestle products focus on food allergies and supporting healthy mitochondria.

Yili Group

Based in China, Yili is the most valuable dairy brand in the world according to data presented in Exhibit 8. The firm competes globally. In Europe for example, Yili has a partnership with Sterilgarda Alimenti, the largest dairy firm in Italy. Yili has an R&D center in the Netherlands. Yili works jointly with some of the leading universities in the United States. Yili sells liquid milk, powdered milk, yogurt, ice cream, cheese, and bottled water. Yili has been consecutively ranked number one in the Asian dairy industry in the past several years and is the largest dairy company in China, offering the most comprehensive range of products.

External Issues

There is a growing awareness worldwide to unhealthy eating, especially when it comes to sugars, processed foods, and animal fats. Many different governments (local, regional, and national) have

EXHIBIT 8 Brand Value of Dairy Processors in 2020 (in Millions, $)

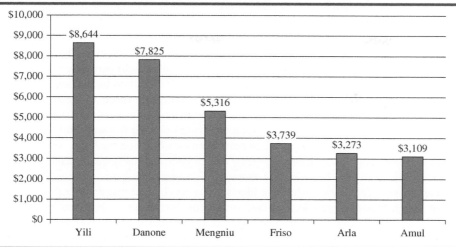

Source: Based on information at *Statistica*. Also, the *Danone Report Study ID 27158*, p. 4.

(or plan to) increased taxes or flat out banned unhealthy items. Taxes are viewed by governments much like tobacco taxes as a way not only to curb citizens' consumption but also as an additional means of revenues. New York City in 2014 banned most sugary drinks 16 ounces (500 mL) and larger from being served. Former NBA star Yao Ming is campaigning in his home country of China to promote healthier eating and exercise habits. Mexico recently passed legislation to significantly tax both sugary drinks and high-calorie items such as candy. Increasing obesity is a major problem among the world's population. Processed sugar negatively impacts the body by increasing your chances of tooth decay, obesity, and diabetes and additionally can significantly increase one's chances of getting heart disease and even cancer. In fact a study in the *Journal of the American Medical Association* reported people who intake 17 to 21 percent of their calories from added sugar had more than four times the chance of dying from cardiovascular disease than someone limiting their added sugar intake to 8 percent of total calorie intake. Scientific tests reveal that sugar is basically a food for cancer cells and people that drink two soft drinks a week are 87 percent more likely to develop pancreatic cancer. For comparison, a Nestle Butterfinger and Baby Ruth contains 29 and 33 grams of sugar, respectively, and a can of cola contains about 39 grams of sugar. Sugar is also believed to be damaging to a person's skin, looks, and overall mood.

Plant Protein Growth in the United States

Plant proteins are growing rapidly in popularity around the world, and by some estimates, plant-based protein will consist of one third of the protein market by 2054. Most of the data is currently from the United States, but the plant-based trend is expected to grow globally as well. Growth in traditional foods hovers around 2 percent, but if the prediction holds of 33 percent of all protein being derived from plants by 2054, it would represent monumental growth for players in the plant-based protein industry. But consumers are after the protein, not simply plants, as 25 percent of Americans feel increased protein is beneficial and up to 50 percent of Americans check the ingredient list for the source of proteins.

In 2019, plant-based meat sales rose more than 20 percent, and according the S&P's *Industry Surveys*, plant-based meat sales outpaced animal meat sales in 2020 partly due to several meat plants closing down in 2020 from the pandemic. While the research presented is for Americans, there is strong evidence that plant-based proteins are extremely popular in other regions around the world. In fact, more than 45 percent of Americans believe plant-based proteins are healthier than animal-based, and 30 percent of Americans enjoy meat-free days in their diet. However, only 6 percent of Americans are categorized as true vegetarians.

Flavor Enhancers

There is a growing awareness of sugar's harmful effects on people, in particular high-fructose corn syrup and salt. Hershey for example is replacing high-fructose corn syrup in some of its products with sugar, making the firm a high-profile example of the move away from high-fructose corn syrup that may fuel weight gain and diabetes.

In the food and beverage industry, soda accounts for a majority of the market for high-fructose corn syrup. Hunt's ketchup is an example product that switched to more sugar, but then switched back to corn syrup, seeing no change in the sales of Hunt's. The US Food and Drug Administration (FDA) has denied requests by some companies to have their sweetening agent renamed "corn sugar" on nutrition labels. In addition, the FDA proposed forcing food companies to add the percentage daily allotment of sugar on all nutrition labels in July 2015, similar to the percentage of the daily allowance of salt, fat, and other ingredients that are listed. As of 2021, labels in the United States still only refer to the amount of sugars in grams not percentages of daily allowance. However, many customers can associate the meaning of a percent much more readily than a simple weight of measurement such as grams or ounces presenting a threat for food companies moving forward if this law is enacted. In addition to corn syrup, any added sugar can have dramatic effects on the body. All added sugars are linked to diabetes, tooth decay, heart problems, weight gain, and many other health problems.

In response to sugar being harmful, there is growing global demand for artificial sweeteners as a means to reduce calories, not raise blood sugar levels, and just an overall healthier choice than raw sugar. However, research to date is not conclusive, and some studies reveal artificial sweeteners are similar to raw sugar once ingested. Europe has banned several artificial sweetener products such as Stevia and aspartame from lack on conclusive research, but other nations such as Japan and the United States have been using the same sweeteners for decades. Nevertheless, there is a growing public awareness toward both raw and artificial sugars.

Another common flavor enhancer found in food is salt. Table salt has been linked to water retention, high blood pressure, stomach cancer, osteoporosis, and killing of beneficial bacterial in the body. Many medical researchers recommend limiting salt consumption to 6 grams per day; however, the World Health Organization suggests the average person consumes between 9 and 12 grams of salt daily. Many food companies are attempting to reduce the amount of sodium in their products as global awareness increases on the harmful effects of a high salt diet. Nestle, for example is experimenting with reducing both salt and sugar from its foods and replacing them with natural flavorings.

Conclusion

The dairy business in many nations is struggling because people simply do not drink as much milk as they once did. Dairy is often viewed as unhealthy, high in fat and sugars. Possibly the most famous yogurt firm in the world, Danone is subject to these external trends in dairy. The firm also produces many nondairy options that serve as dairy substitutes such as their Silk brand of milk. Although Danone competes heavily in the water business, the firm does not seem to have a significant market share on mineral waters or flavored waters. Waters, the smallest revenue segment for Danone, is also the smallest profit margin at 7 percent. Baby foods and other medical based products are additional revenue streams for Danone and come with a much higher profit margin of around 25 percent.

How should Danone proceed moving forward? Note that more than half the revenues are derived from Europe and North America. Should the firm integrate current products more into the Asian markets? Or should the firm expand its plant-based businesses anticipating further reductions in dairy consumption? Danone could also develop new dairy-based products targeted for the most profitable markets of Europe and North America. Deciding how to shift resources around is an important consideration for CEO Antoine de Saint-Affrique. What would you recommend CEO Grupo Bimbo do going forward? Help the CEO by developing a 3-year strategic plan for Danone that includes a new vision statement and mission statement as well.

References

1. www.statistica.com
2. Danone's corporate website. https://www.danone.com/about-danone/at-a-glance/danone-data.html
3. Danone's 2020 and 2021 *Annual Report*.
4. https://craft.co/danone/executives
5. S&P's *Industry Surveys* for food manufacturers.
6. The *Danone Report Study ID 27158*, p. 4.
7. https://www.danone.com/content/dam/danone-corp/danone-com/medias/medias-en/2022/corporatepressreleases/pr-danone-fy-2021.pdf

Grupo Bimbo S.A.B. de C.V., 2022

www.grupobimbo.com; (BIMBO on the Mexico Exchange; BMBOY on the US exchange)

Headquartered in Mexico City, Mexico, Grupo Bimbo (Bimbo) is the self-proclaimed largest baking company in the world and is also an important player in the global snack market. Serving 33 nations with 203 bakeries and plants through 1,700 sales centers, people around the world enjoy the over 13,000 Bimbo products and more than 100 Bimbo Brands. The firm offers bagels, muffins, bread, cakes, cookies, salty snacks, confectionery products, and much more. The firm has 133,000 employees.

Bimbo is committed to creating a better world by increasing universal values that help communities grow. The company has 3 million points of sale globally, so customers enjoy Bimbo products on every continent except Australia and Antarctica. Some of the most popular Bimbo brands in Mexico and Central America are Coronado, Tia Rosa, Thomas, Entenmann's, Sanissimo, La Corona Chocolates, Sara Lee, Takis, Wonder, and more. The brand Wonder is owned by Flowers in the United States, which is discussed in the competitor section of the case.

In North America, Bimbo acquired Canada Bread in 2014 and Vachon, the leading pastry company in Canada a year later. Top brands in the North American market are also some of the top brands in the Mexican market, but unique brands to the North American market are Sara Lee, Hostess, Sun-Maid, Cinnabon, and more. Many of these firms readers will recognize as traditional and famous products from their childhood that have exchanged hands between various companies and are now controlled by Bimbo. Who would have thought that Sara Lee and Hostess would be owned by a Mexican based company, but they are today.

Bimbo is well established in South America with a presence in six nations with 30 brands, many of which are enjoyed in Central America and Mexico, too. Bimbo has largely entered the South American market through acquisitions. Bimbo has operations in eight European nations and in Morocco and South Africa. Bimbo's expansion into Europe has been more recent mostly dating to 2017 through mergers. Bimbo entered China in 2006 and has a presence in six Asian nations.

For Bimbo's Q1 2022 than ended 3-31-22, the company reported record sales of 93,321 million pesos, an increase of 17.7 percent, due to strong volume and price/mix performance across every region. For Q1 2022 compared to the prior year Q1, the company's net income increased 10.4 percent and its return on equity reached a record 15.8 percent. Also during Q1 2022, Bimbo divested (sold) its confectionery business, "Ricolino," in order to focus more on its baking and snacks industries.

For the sixth consecutive year, Ethisphere Institute in 2022 named Grupo Bimbo as one of the World's Most Ethical Companies.

Copyright by Fred David Books LLC; written by Forest R. David.

History

Bimbo traces its roots to 1943 when the company was founded serving white and rye breads along with toast. In 1948, the firm added sweets, buns, and pound cakes to the lineup. In the 1950s, the firm started offering sweets in three flavors, strawberry, orange, and chocolate, and in the 1960s, the Gansito product was introduced that was a chocolate covered cake stuffed with strawberry jelly, cream, and topped with chocolate. After growing and adding new products in the 1970s and 1980s, Bimbo expanded south of Mexico in the 1990s by acquiring many firms. Bimbo has used an acquisition strategy through much of its history and continues to do so even today. The firm acquired a Spanish firm in 2006 that also gained access to the Chinese market.

The Year 2021

Bimbo's overall sales in 2021 reached a record level at Ps. 348,887 million, an increase of 5.4 percent. The company's operating income grew 34.3 percent. During 2021, Bimbo successfully completed six strategic acquisitions: two in the United States, two in India, one in Spain, and one in Brazil. For 2021, Bimbo's Return on Equity reached its highest level for more than 10 years, at 15.2 percent. For the eighth consecutive year, Bimbo in 2021 was ranked number one in Merco's 2021 ranking as the Most Responsible Company in environmental, sustainability, and governance in Mexico.

Internal Issues

Vision/Mission

Bimbo does not have a published vision statement. Bimbo has a written mission on their *Annual Report* that can best be paraphrased as "*providing nutritious and tasty snacks and bakery items for everyone.*"

Organizational Structure

Bimbo provides only limited information about its top executives. Bimbo's top executives are listed and arrayed in Exhibit 1.

EXHIBIT 1   Bimbo's Top Executives Listed and Arrayed

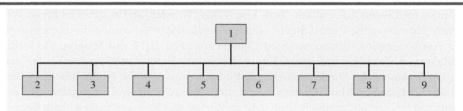

1. Daniel Servitje Montull, Chair and CEO
2. Diego Cuevas, CFO
3. RaA Servitje, CIO
4. Juan Barrena, Chief People Officer
5. Gabino Carbajal, EVP

6. Javier Franco, EVP
7. Pablo Huerta, EVP
8. Rafael Romero, EVP
9. José Goyenaga, Chief Auditing Officer

Source: Based on https://finance.yahoo.com/quote/BIMBOA.MX/profile?p=BIMBOA.MX

Finance

Bimbo's recent income statements and balance sheets are provided in Exhibit 2 and Exhibit 3, respectively.

EXHIBIT 2   Grupo Bimbo's Recent Income Statements (in Millions, Pesos)

Income Statement	12/31/20	12/31/21		Percentage Change
Revenue (Sales)	₱331,051	₱348,887	⇧	5%
Cost of Goods Sold	152,608	163,575	⇧	7%
Gross Profit	178,443	185,312	⇧	4%
Operating Expenses	153,035	151,187	⇩	−1%
EBIT (Operating Income)	25,408	34,125	⇧	34%
Interest Expense	8,665	7,773	⇩	−10%
EBT	16,743	26,352	⇧	57%
Tax	6,192	8,969	⇧	45%
Nonrecurring Events	0	0	—	—
Net Income	₱10,551	₱17,383	⇧	65%

Source: Based on Grupo Bimbo's 2021 *Annual Report* and their *Q4 Report*, p. 9.

EXHIBIT 3   **Grupo Bimbo's Recent Balance Sheets (in Millions, Pesos)**

Balance Sheet	12/31/20	12/31/21		Percentage Change
Assets				
Cash and Short-Term Investments	₱9,268	₱8,747	⇩	−6%
Accounts Receivable	27,487	27,170	⇩	−1%
Inventory	10,893	13,710	⇧	26%
Other Current Assets	2,955	3,784	⇧	28%
Total Current Assets	50,603	53,411	⇧	6%
Property Plant & Equipment	91,248	103,891	⇧	14%
Goodwill	0	0	—	—
Intangibles	127,419	139,483	⇧	9%
Other Long-Term Assets	38,380	40,854	⇧	6%
Total Assets	**307,650**	**337,639**	⇧	**10%**
Liabilities				
Accounts Payable	26,679	37,278	⇧	40%
Other Current Liabilities	34,586	43,482	⇧	26%
Total Current Liabilities	61,265	80,760	⇧	32%
Long-Term Debt	84,629	82,230	⇩	−3%
Other Long-Term Liabilities	73,746	73,043	⇩	−1%
Total Liabilities	**219,640**	**236,033**	⇧	**7%**
Equity				
Common Stock	4,061	4,506	⇧	11%
Retained Earnings	64,265	81,648	⇧	27%
Treasury Stock	0	0	—	—
Paid in Capital & Other	19,684	15,452	⇩	−21%
Total Equity	**88,010**	**101,606**	⇧	**15%**
Total Liabilities and Equity	**₱307,650**	**₱337,639**	⇧	**10%**

Source: Based on Grupo Bimbo's 2021 *Annual Report*, and their Q4 Report, p. 9.

Strategy Shift to Organic and Healthiness

Bimbo lists 11 product categories on their website: Sliced bread, Buns and Rolls, Pastries, Snack Cakes, Cookies, Toasted Bread, English Muffins, Bagels, Tortillas and Flatbreads, Salty Snacks, and Confectionery. Refer to the external section of the case to see how these product categories stack up based on global demand in Exhibit 9. Across the board, Bimbo is committed to making the products healthier. As reported on the 2021 *Annual Report*, Bimbo claims 93 percent global compliance toward meeting the recommended limits in regard to added sugars, fats, trans fats, and sodium in their products with 100 percent compliance expected by 2023. The global recommendations are by product category, so a snack cake would be allowed to have significant added sugar based on the product, which still presents a problem moving forward in a growing health conscious minded public globally.

To address the healthy food issue, Bimbo responded with 77 initiatives launched in 2020. Examples of these products include Oroweat Organics for Kids. The Oroweat is the flagship brand for healthy eating and owns a 10 percent market share in the US market and is branded as Arnold on the US East Coast. The products are claimed to be whole wheat and have important sources of A, D, and E vitamins.

Segments

Bimbo's sales by region for 2021 versus 2020 are given in Exhibit 4. Note the overall 5.4 percent increase.

EXHIBIT 4 Bimbo's Recent Sales by Region (in Millions, Pesos)

	2020	2021	Percentage Change
North America	176,395	176,275	(0.1)
Mexico	104,593	118,661	13.5
Europe/Asia	30,029	34,195	13.9
Latin America	29,081	31,376	7.9
Total	331,051	348,887	5.4

Source: Based on https://grupobimbo-com-assets.s3.amazonaws.com/s3fs-public/reportes-2022/Grupo%20 Bimbo%20Reports%204Q21%20Results.pdf?VersionId=f1RXH2VlO3TwRnoSw7dEn4IXjgW8oQVp

Competitors

General Mills (NYSE: GIS)

Headquartered in Minneapolis, Minnesota, General Mills (GIS) competes with Bimbo by producing and marketing food products worldwide through five segments: (1) North America Retail, (2) Convenience Stores, (3) Europe and Australia, (4) Asia and Latin America, and (5) Pet. GIS's revenues increased from $17.6 billion to $18.6 billion from 2019 to 2021. Some of the firms most popular brands include cereals including Cheerios, ice cream including Haagen-Dazs, yogurt including Yoplait, and many more. In fact, GIS is expanding its cereal business, which may come as a surprise to some as cereals are high carbs and high sugar and global trends are moving away from such items. Top GIS brands include Cheerios, Cinnamon Toast Crunch, Lucky Charms, Chex, Total, and Wheaties. Top products considered meals include Helper, Old El Paso, Wanchai Ferry, V. Peral, Green Giant, and Yoki. The firm competes in the highly competitive frozen pizza business with brands Annie's and Totinos. GIS competes with Bimbo on many similar product lines.

Flowers Foods (NYSE: FLO)

Headquartered in Thomasville, Georgia, Flowers Foods is one of the largest bakeries in the United States with 46 bakeries that produce a wide range of bakery foods for both retail customers and food service providers. Top brands include Nature's Own, Dave's Killer Bread, Canyon Bakehouse, Sunbeam, Wonder, Merita, European Bakers, Bunny, Mi Casa, and more. Mi Casa produces both corn and flour tortillas intruding on some of Bimbo's most sought-after products. Dave's Killer Bread according to the company is the number-one organic bread brand in the United States and prides itself on USDA organic and non-GMO products with no artificial ingredients or preservatives.

Flowers has operations across the United States but is heavily proportioned in the southeastern United States, with 42 percent of sales being derived from supermarkets and 33 percent are from mass merchandisers. Branded retail products as the ones named account for 66 percent of sales. Flowers reported a sales decrease of 1.3 percent in fiscal 2021 to $4.3 billion, but net income increased 35 percent to $206 million, although adjusted net income decreased 5.3 percent to $263 million.

Analysts recently compared Bimbo to Flowers Foods on nine management and marketing variables. The results are provided in Exhibit 5. Note that Bimbo's CEO Servitje ranks an impressive number one. Overall, Bimbo was ranked number one impressively on five variables.

EXHIBIT 5 Comparing Bimbo to Flowers Foods (Ranking 1 = Best; 6 = Worst)

	Variables									
	1	2	3	4	5	6	7	8	9	10
Grupo Bimbo	1	2	2	2	1	1	1	2	1	13
Flowers Foods	2	1	1	1	2	2	2	1	-	11+

Variables

1. Effectiveness of CEO
2. Product Quality
3. Do Customers Recommend Company Products to Friends?
4. Pricing
5. Customer Service
6. Overall Culture
7. Do Employees Recommend Company Products to Friends?
8. How Happy Are the Women Employees at the Firm?
9. How Happy Are Minority Employees at the Firm?
10. Summed Score (lower sum the better)

Source: Based on https://www.comparably.com/companies/bimbo-bakeries/competitors

Exhibit 6 compares Bimbo to both General Mills and Flowers Foods. Note that Bimbo is gigantic in terms of revenues versus these two rival firms.

EXHIBIT 6 Grupo Bimbo and Rival Firms Compared Financially

	General Mills (GIS)	Flowers Foods (FLO)	Grupo Bimbo (BMBOY)
Market Capitalization	$41 billion	$6 billion	$15 billion
EPS	$2.55	$0.97	$0.63
Revenue	$18.6 billion	$4.3 billion	$336 billion
Net Income	$2.2 billion	$209 million	$14 billion
Total Debt	$17.7 billion	$1.2 billion	$120 billion
Total Debt/Equity	122	84	125
Current Ratio	0.85	1.43	0.72
Full Time Employees	35,000	10,000	134,000
Stock Price	$68	$28	$14

Source: Based on https://finance.yahoo.com/quote/GIS/profile?p=GIS

External Issues

Exhibit 7 reveals the global market growth of bread and bakery products through 2025. Despite possible trends toward more healthy eating and less consumption of carbs, the overall trend for breads and bakery items globally is sound. The expected annual rate of increase through 2025 is about 4.5 percent. These numbers are average so a firm with the reputation and quality of Bimbo should exceed these growth numbers with a quality strategy and good management. This chart does not detail what locations in the world growth will be the highest or what products among bread, cakes, cookies and the like will have the higher growth rates and more importantly the higher profit margins. As a strategist this is your job to position Bimbo well to take advantage of this wonderful opportunity.

Exhibit 8 reveals the top 15 markets for bread and cereal products globally based on sales. Note China leads the world with 32 percent share out of the 15 nations listed and has double the revenue share as second place India. The top four nations are also the top four most populous nations in the world but not in proportion to bakery revenue consumption. For example, China

EXHIBIT 7 **Global Market Estimates of Bread and Bakery Product Consumption (in Millions of Tons)**

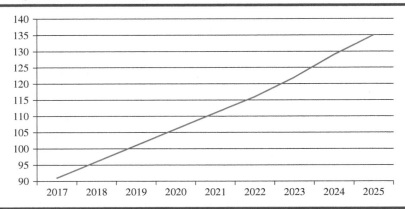

Source: Based on study_id36527_bread-and-bakery-products-us-statista-dossier.pdf, page 2.

EXHIBIT 8 **Revenue Percentage of Bread and Cereal Products Consumed Across Countries**

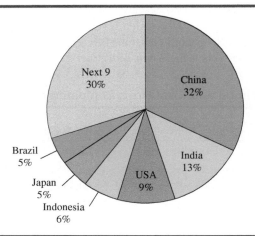

Source: Based on study_id36527_bread-and-bakery-products-us-statista-dossier.pdf, p. 3.

and India are close on population each representing around 18 percent of the global population, yet China is a far more lucrative market than India. The United States represents 4.2 percent of the global population to Indonesia's 3.5 percent, but the United States generates 63 percent more revenue from bakery goods than Indonesia. Grupo is strategically positioned well to market to the US market.

Exhibit 9 reports sales of select bakery products in the United States. Note that bagels and English muffins, two products Bimbo produces, are not nearly as good sellers as others listed in the exhibit. This does not indicate they are poor business choices because there may not be much competition on these product lines. Fresh bread leads all categories with annual sales around $14 billion. Cookies enter as second and are an interesting business option for firms because the shelf life is much longer than breads and variety is almost limitless.

Whole Grains

According to the Mayo Clinic, whole grains are healthy options if a person is looking to incorporate complex carbohydrates into their diet or simply to enjoy carbs without feeling overly guilty. Grains are known to be high in fiber, which aids in not feeling hungry and which in return helps on not overeating and gaining weight. In addition, whole grains can reduce heart disease, some cancers, and even diabetes. It is recommended that 50 percent of all grains consumed be whole grains. What defines whole grains from other grains is that with whole grains all parts of the seed is ground into the flour. An easy example would be brown rice with the germ and bran (husk)

EXHIBIT 9 2020 United States Bakery Sales by Selected Bakery Category (in millions USD)

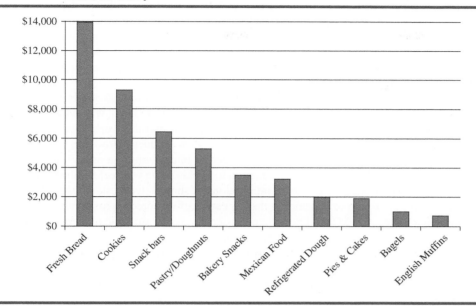

Source: Based on study_id36527_bread-and-bakery-products-us-statista-dossier.pdf page 9.

attached is considered a whole grain, while the same product with the husk removed would not be considered a whole grain. Refined grains have the germ and bran removed. This process removes many of the nutrients including much of the fiber but does increase shelf life and many people consider refined grains to taste better. White rice is an example of a refined grain. A marketing technique is to add some nutrients back after the refined stage and calling the product enriched grains.

Dangers of Sugar

Enjoying whole foods that are high in sugar such as whole grains or fresh fruits and vegetables are likely okay to eat for most people. The high fiber, minerals, antioxidants, calcium, protein, and other nutrients are vital. The body digests these foods slowly and have been shown to even reduce some chronic diseases. But what about added sugar that food makers add to products to extend shelf life and to increase flavor. How much added sugar is too much? The American Heart Association recommends that women limit their intake to 100 calories of added sugar or 24 grams a day, and men are recommended to limit their intake to 36 grams of added sugar. Growing public sugar awareness, either added or through refined grains, is a major threat moving forward for firm's competing in this market. Many governments have instituted legislation to tax or reduce sugar intake on top of simply general public awareness.

Potential Taxes and Health-Minded Public

There is a growing awareness worldwide of unhealthy eating, especially when it comes to sugars, processed foods, and animal fats. Many different governments (local, regional and national) have (or plan to) increased taxes or flat out banned unhealthy items. Taxes are viewed by governments much like tobacco taxes as a way not only to curb citizens' consumption but also as an additional means of revenues. Increasing obesity is a major problem. Processed sugar negatively impacts the body by increasing your chances of tooth decay, obesity, and diabetes and additionally can significantly increase one's chances of getting heart disease and even cancer. In fact, a recent study in the *Journal of the American Medical Association* reported people who intake 17 to 21 percent of their calories from added sugar had more than four times the chance of dying from cardiovascular disease than someone limiting their added sugar intake to 8 percent of total calorie intake. Scientific tests reveal that sugar is basically a food for cancer cells and people that drink two soft drinks a week are 87 percent more likely to develop pancreatic cancer. For comparison, a Nestle Butterfinger and Baby Ruth contains 29 and 33 grams of sugar respectively, and a can of cola contains about 39 grams of sugar. Sugar is also believed to be damaging to skin, looks, and overall mood.

Conclusion

Bimbo, the self-proclaimed largest baking firm in the world, needs a detailed strategic plan. From reading the case, you learned Bimbo has used an aggressive acquisition strategy to enter new markets across the globe especially into Europe. What are your thoughts on Bimbo so eagerly leaving the Mexican, Central American, US, and Canadian markets it knows so well and shifting resources to Europe and Asian markets? Would Bimbo be better off expanding further in the United States or adding new product lines in the United States?

Bimbo produces products in 11 categories, but most all the products are based on grains, and many are not based on whole grains and many product lines are laden with added sugars. Of course, this is the business Bimbo is in, and many people around the world love sweet sugary cakes, and there is likely always a place and market for such products. However, what strategies would you put in place if we saw a 10 percent reduction in consumption of such items? Could Bimbo survive currently if this 10 percent reduction took place? Do you feel Bimbo should invest more in development or marketing whole grain options or should sweets stay "sweet?"

There is a lot for Bimbo to consider in the allocation of resources across both product lines and geographic regions. CEO Daniel Servitje needs a clear 3-year strategic plan for Bimbo. General Mills and Flowers Foods are pursuing strategies to take away Bimbo's market share. Intensity of competition and rivalry among baking firms are accelerating as companies roll product lines out globally and develop new and improved products. The vision/mission and organizational structure sections of this case reveal that there is substantial room for improvement for Bimbo in both areas.

Servitje knows the basic underlying external opportunities and threats and internal strengths facing Bimbo, but he is unsure about the relative importance of those factors. He thus needs an external and internal assessment performed, anchored by development of an EFE Matrix and IFE Matrix as described in Chapter 3 and Chapter 4 of the David textbook. Servitje also needs to know the relative attractiveness of alternative strategies facing the company, so he needs a SWOT, BCG, and QSPM analyses performed.

Let's say Servitje asks you to develop the comprehensive strategic plan that he needs. In addition to the analyses mentioned, include in your report a perceptual map, a set of proposed recommendations with associated costs, and an EPS-EBIT analysis to reveal whether debt or stock or some combination of debt and stock is best to obtain the needed funds. Also include projected financial statements to show the expected impact on Bimbo if Servitje adopts your proposed strategic plan. What can Bimbo do to help assure top line (revenues) and bottom line (net income) 5+ percent annually in the years to come? Identify particular companies for Bimbo to acquire. If Bimbo should expand further organically (internally) into other regions, countries, and continents, include direction for Servitje in this regard.

References

1. Statistica.com
2. Grupo Bimbo's Website www.grupobimbo.com.
3. Group Bimbo's 2021 *Annual Report* and their Q4 Report.
4. Flowers Foods' Website.
5. https://www.comparably.com/companies/bimbo-bakeries/competitors
6. https://finance.yahoo.com/quote/GIS/profile?p=GIS
7. https://www.health.harvard.edu/heart-health/the-sweet-danger-of-sugar
8. https://www.mayoclinic.org/healthy-lifestyle/nutrition-and-healthy-eating/in-depth/whole-grains/art-20047826
9. study_id36527_bread-and-bakery-products-us-statista-dossier.pdf, p. 2.
10. study_id36527_bread-and-bakery-products-us-statista-dossier.pdf, p 9.
11. study_id36527_bread-and-bakery-products-us-statista-dossier.pdf, p. 3.
12. https://grupobimbo-com-assets.s3.amazonaws.com/s3fs-public/reportes-2022/Grupo%20Bimbo%20Reports%204Q21%20Results.pdf?VersionId=flRXH2VlO3TwRnoSw7dEn4IXjgW8oQVp, p. 3.
13. https://finance.yahoo.com/quote/BIMBOA.MX/profile?p=BIMBOA.MX

GlaxoSmithKline plc, 2022

www.gsk.com; (NYSE: GSK)

Headquartered in London, England, GlaxoSmithKline (Glaxo) is the sixth-largest pharmaceutical company in the world, behind Pfizer, Novartis, Roche, Sanofi, and Merck. Glaxo creates, discovers, develops, manufactures, and markets pharmaceutical products, vaccines, over-the-counter medicines, and health-related consumer products globally. Glaxo operates through four segments: (1) Pharmaceuticals, (2) Pharmaceuticals R&D, (3) Vaccines, and (4) Consumer Healthcare.

Glaxo's pharmaceutical products are aimed at areas that include respiratory, HIV, immuno-inflammation, oncology, antiviral, central nervous system, cardiovascular and urogenital, metabolic, antibacterial, and dermatology. The company offers consumer health-care products in wellness, oral health, nutrition, and skin health categories, including nasal sprays, tablets, syrups, lozenges, gum and transdermal patches, caplets, infant syrup drops, liquid filled suspension, wipes, gels, effervescents, toothpastes, toothbrushes, mouthwashes, denture adhesives and cleansers, topical creams and nonmedicated patches, lip balm, gummies, and soft chews.

Copyright by Fred David Books LLC; written by Forest R. David.

History

Glaxo traces its beginning back to Joseph Nathan and Co. in 1873 being a general trading company in Wellington, New Zealand. In 1904, the company began producing a dried-milk baby food from excess milk produced on dairy farms near Bunnythorpe. The product was first known as Defiance, then as Glaxo (from *lacto*), and sold with the slogan "Glaxo builds bonnie babies." The company's first pharmaceutical product, released in 1924, was vitamin D.

Glaxo and Burroughs Wellcome merged in 1995, to form Glaxo Wellcome plc, and the company acquired the California-based Affymax. By 1999, Glaxo Wellcome had become the world's third-largest pharmaceutical company by revenues (behind Novartis and Merck), with a global market share of around 4 percent. Notable products included Imigran (for the treatment of migraine), Ventolin (for the treatment of asthma), Zovirax (for the treatment of cold sores), Retrovir and Epivir (for the treatment of AIDS), and Amoxicillin (for the treatment of infections).

Glaxo Wellcome and SmithKline Beecham merged in 2000 forming GlaxoSmithKline with global headquarters at GSK House, Brentford, London. In 2009, Glaxo acquired Stiefel Laboratories, which was then the world's largest independent dermatology drug company, enabling us to become a leader in skincare. Glaxo developed the first malaria vaccine, RTS.S, which it said in 2014 would be sold for 5 percent above cost.

During 2021, Glaxo had three major product approvals: Apretude HIV long-acting medicine for prevention, Xevudy for COVID-19, and Jemperli for endometrial cancer. As 2021 ended, Glaxo had a strong pipeline of 21 vaccines and 43 medicines, many offering great treatment for patients, and of which 22 were in pivotal trials.

In mid-2022, GSK acquired Affinivax, Inc., a clinical-stage biopharmaceutical company based in Cambridge, Massachusetts, for $3.3 billion. Affinivax is developing a novel class of vaccines for pneumococcal diseases such as pneumonia, meningitis, bloodstream infections, and milder diseases such as sinusitis and otitis media. Affinivax also has developed the Multiple Antigen Presenting System (MAPS) technology that enables broader coverage against prevalent pneumococcal serotypes and potentially creating higher immunogenicity than current vaccines. Affinivax's most advanced vaccine candidate (AFX3772) includes 24 pneumococcal polysaccharides plus two conserved pneumococcal proteins (compared to up to 20 serotypes in currently approved vaccines). Affinivax has a 30-plus valent pneumococcal candidate vaccine in development.

Internal Issues

Vision/Mission

Glaxo does not have a published vision or mission statement, but the following statement (paraphrased) is given at the corporate website:

> *We are an international healthcare company that strives to improve the quality of human life by helping people do more, feel better, live longer.*

Organizational Structure

Glaxo's top executives are listed and arrayed in Exhibit 1. Note there likely needs to be a COO for positions 10, 11, 12, and 13 to report to, rather than all top executives reporting to the CEO.

EXHIBIT 1 Glaxo's Top Executives Listed and Arrayed

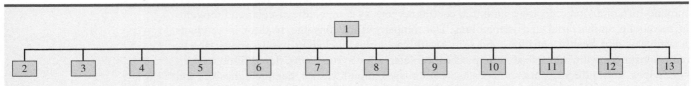

1. Dame Emma Walmsley, CEO
2. Iain Mackay, CFO
3. Dr. Hal Barron, Chief Scientific Officer and President, R&D
4. Diana Conrad, Chief People Officer
5. James Ford, SVP and General Counsel
6. Tony Wood, Chief Scientific Officer Designate
7. Phil Thomson, President, Global Affairs

8. Sally Jackson, SVP, Global Communications and CEO Office
9. Shobie Ramakrishnan, Chief Digital and Technology Officer
10. Regis Simard, President, Pharmaceuticals Supply Chain
11. Roger Connor, President, Vaccines and Global Health
12. Brian McNamara, CEO, GSK Consumer Healthcare
13. Deborah Waterhouse, CEO, ViiV Healthcare

Source: Based on https://www.gsk.com/en-gb/about-us/gsk-leadership-team/

Segments

Glaxo operates through three segments: (1) Pharmaceuticals, (2) Vaccines, and (3) Consumer Healthcare. For 2021, Pharmaceuticals operating profit was £4,681 million, up 12 percent; Vaccines operating profit was £2,256 million, down 17 percent; and Consumer Healthcare operating profit was £2,239 million, up 1 percent.

Exhibit 2, Exhibit 3, and Exhibit 4 give segment sales for 2021 versus 2020.

Exhibit 5 and Exhibit 6 illustrate Glaxo's 2021 sales by percentages and in British pounds, respectively.

EXHIBIT 2 Glaxo's Sales in its Pharmaceutical Segment (in Millions)

	2021	Percentage Growth from Prior Year
Pharmaceutical		
Respiratory	£2,863	21
HIV	4,777	(2)
Immuno-inflammation	885	22
Oncology	489	31
Pandemic	958	-
New and Specialty	9,972	20
Established Pharmaceuticals	7,757	(11)
Total	17,729	4
United States	8,442	13
Europe	3,934	(4)
International	5,353	(3)
Total	£17,729	4

Source: Based on https://www.gsk.com/media/7377/fy-2021-results-announcement.pdf

EXHIBIT 3 Glaxo's Sales in its Vaccines Segment (in Millions)

	2021	Percentage Growth from Prior Year
Meningitis	£961	(7)
Influenza	679	(7)
Shingles	1,721	(13)
Established Vaccines	2,970	(8)
Subtotal	6,331	(9)
Pandemic Vaccines	447	-
Total Vaccines	6,778	(3)
United States	3,472	(6)
Europe	1,436	-
International	1,870	1
Total	£6,778	(3)

Source: Based on https://www.gsk.com/media/7377/fy-2021-results-announcement.pdf

EXHIBIT 4 Glaxo's Sales in its Consumer Healthcare Segment (in Millions)

	2021	Percentage Growth from Prior Year
Oral health	£2,732	(1)
Pain relief	2,276	3
Vitamins, minerals, and supplements	1,512	-
Respiratory health	1,133	(6)
Digestive health and other	1,803	(1)
Total	9,456	(1)
Brands divested/under view	151	(71)
Total	9,607	(4)
United States	3,179	(7)
Europe	2,468	(6)
International	3,960	(1)
Total	£9,607	(4)

Source: Based on https://www.gsk.com/media/7377/fy-2021-results-announcement.pdf. Also, the GSK 2021 *Annual Report*, p. 55. Also, https://www.gsk.com/media/7377/fy-2021-results-announcement.pdf

EXHIBIT 5 Glaxo's 2021 Sales by Product in Percentages

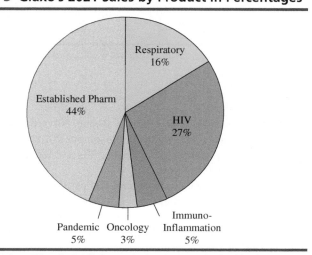

Source: Based on Glaxo's Q4 Release; https://www.gsk.com/media/7377/fy-2021-results-announcement.pdf, p. 47.

EXHIBIT 6 Glaxo's 2021 Sales by Millions of British Pounds

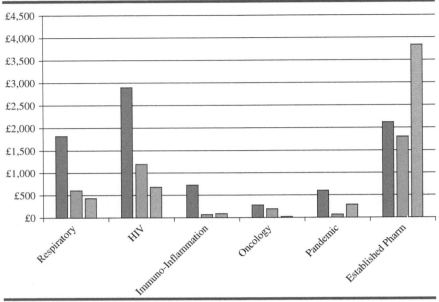

Source: Based on Glaxo's Q4 Release; https://www.gsk.com/media/7377/fy-2021-results-announcement.pdf, p. 47.

Finance

Glaxo's recent income statements and balance sheets are provided in Exhibit 7 and Exhibit 8 respectively.

EXHIBIT 7 Glaxo's Recent Income Statements (in Millions, £)

Income Statement	12/31/20	12/31/21		Percentage Change
Revenue (Sales)	£34,099	£34,114	⇧	0%
Cost of Goods Sold	11,704	11,603	⇩	−1%
Gross Profit	22,395	22,511	⇧	1%
Operating Expenses	14,612	16,310	⇧	12%
EBIT (Operating Income)	7,783	6,201	⇩	−20%
Interest Expense	815	759	⇩	−7%
EBT	6,968	5,442	⇩	−22%
Tax	580	346	⇩	−40%
Nonrecurring Events	0	0	—	—
Net Income	6,388	5,096	⇩	−20%

Source: Based on Glaxo's Q4 Release, p. 45. https://www.gsk.com/media/7377/fy-2021-results-announcement.pdf

Competitors

Glaxo's competitors include Johnson & Johnson, Roche, Novartis, Sanofi, Merck, AstraZeneca, and Pfizer. In terms of market capitalization in November 2021, the five largest pharmaceutical firms were J&J at $429 billion, followed by Roche, Pfizer, Merck, and Novartis at $184 billion. Glaxo's market cap is about $109 billion.

Analysts recently compared Glaxo to several competitors on nine management and marketing variables. The results are provided in Exhibit 9. Note that Glaxo ranks an impressive number one on six variables versus its competitors. Overall, as indicated by the low summed scores in Column 10, Glaxo was ranked best overall, closely followed by Merck. Glaxo could promote this excellence going forward in their marketing efforts.

EXHIBIT 8 Glaxo's Recent Balance Sheets (in Millions, £)

Balance Sheet	12/31/20	12/31/21		Percentage Change
Assets				
Cash and Short-Term Investments	£6,292	£4,274	⇩	−32%
Accounts Receivable	6,952	7,860	⇧	13%
Inventory	5,996	5,783	⇩	−4%
Other Current Assets	1,007	757	⇩	−25%
Total Current Assets	20,247	18,674	⇩	−8%
Property Plant & Equipment	10,176	9,932	⇩	−2%
Goodwill	10,597	10,552	⇩	0%
Intangibles	29,824	30,079	⇧	1%
Other Long-Term Assets	9,587	9,866	⇧	3%
Total Assets	**80,431**	**79,103**	⇩	**−2%**
Liabilities				
Accounts Payable	15,840	17,554	⇧	11%
Other Current Liabilities	6,308	6,116	⇩	−3%
Total Current Liabilities	22,148	23,670	⇧	7%
Long-Term Debt	23,425	20,572	⇩	−12%
Other Long-Term Liabilities	14,050	13,519	⇩	−4%
Total Liabilities	**59,623**	**57,761**	⇩	**−3%**
Equity				
Common Stock	1,346	1,347	⇧	0%
Retained Earnings	6,755	7,944	⇧	18%
Treasury Stock	0	0	—	—
Paid in Capital & Other	12,707	12,051	⇩	−5%
Total Equity	**20,808**	**21,342**	⇧	**3%**
Total Liabilities and Equity	**£80,431**	**£79,103**	⇩	**−2%**

Source: Based on Glaxo's Q4 Release, p. 51. https://www.gsk.com/media/7377/fy-2021-results-announcement.pdf

EXHIBIT 9 Comparing Glaxo Versus Rival Firms (Ranking 1 = Best; 6 = Worst)

	Variables									
	1	2	3	4	5	6	7	8	9	10
GlaxoSmithK	1	1	2	1	3	1	1	1	3	14
Sanofi	2	3	4	4	4	2	4	4	2	29
Merck	3	4	1	3	1	3	3	2	1	21
Pfizer	4	2	3	2	2	4	2	3	4	26

Variables

1. Effectiveness of CEO
2. Product Quality
3. Do Customers Recommend Company Products to Friends?
4. Pricing
5. Customer Service
6. Overall Culture
7. Do Employees Recommend Company Products to Friends?
8. How Happy Are the Women Employees at the Firm?
9. How Happy Are Minority Employees at the Firm?
10. Summed Score (lower sum the better)

Source: Based on https://www.comparably.com/companies/gsk/competitors

EXHIBIT 10 Glaxo's Rival Firms Compared Financially

	Glaxo (GSK)	Pfizer (PFE)	Merck (MRK)	Sanofi (SNY)
Market Capitalization	$109 billion	$272 billion	$192 billion	$132 billion
EPS	$2.35	$3.85	$5.14	$2.81
Revenue	$34 billion	$81 billion	$49 billion	$39 billion
Net Income	$4.4 billion	$22.4 billion	$12 billion	$6.2 billion
Total Debt	$24.2 billion	$40 billion	$26 billion	—
Total Debt/Equity	113	52	49	—
Current Ratio	0.79	—	—	—
Stock Price	$43	$49	$76	$52

Source: Based on https://finance.yahoo.com/quote/GSK?p=GSK&.tsrc=fin-srch

Exhibit 10 compares Glaxo to three rival companies. Note that Glaxo is smaller than its major rival firms.

Pfizer Inc.

Founded in 1849 and headquartered in New York City, Pfizer discovers, develops, manufactures, markets, distributes, and sells biopharmaceutical products globally. The company offers medicines and vaccines in various therapeutic areas, including cardiovascular metabolic and pain under the Eliquis, Chantix/Champix, and Premarin family brands; biologics, small molecules, immunotherapies, and biosimilars under the Ibrance, Xtandi, Sutent, Inlyta, Retacrit, Lorbrena, and Braftovi brands; and sterile injectable and anti-infective medicines under the Sulperazon, Medrol, Zithromax, Vfend, and Panzyga brands. Pfizer also provides medicines and vaccines in areas such as pneumococcal disease, meningococcal disease, tick-borne encephalitis, and COVID-19 under the Prevnar 13/Prevenar 13 (pediatric/adult), Nimenrix, FSME/IMMUN-TicoVac, Trumenba, and the Pfizer-BioNTech COVID-19 vaccine brands; biosimilars for chronic immune and inflammatory diseases under the Xeljanz, Enbrel, Inflectra, and Eucrisa/Staquis brands; and amyloidosis, hemophilia, and endocrine diseases under the Vyndaqel/Vyndamax, BeneFIX, and Genotropin brands.

Merck & Company

Founded in 1891 and headquartered in Kenilworth, New Jersey, Merck has two segments: Pharmaceutical and Animal Health. The Pharmaceutical segment offers products in oncology, hospital acute care, immunology, neuroscience, virology, cardiovascular, diabetes, and women's health, as well as vaccine products. Merck's Animal Health segment discovers, develops, manufactures, and markets veterinary pharmaceuticals, vaccines, and health management solutions and services, as well as digitally connected identification, traceability, and monitoring products. Merck has collaborations with AstraZeneca PLC; Bayer AG; Eisai Co., Ltd.; Synthekine Inc., Ridgeback Biotherapeutics, Hummingbird Bioscience Pte. Ltd, and Gilead Sciences.

External Issues

Prescription drug sales globally are forecast to grow at 6.4 percent annually from 2021 to 2026, hitting $1.4 trillion in 2026. EvaluatePharma expects AbbVie to overtake Roche to be the leading prescription drug company in 2026, with sales of $59 billion. Various trends spurring this growth include the aging population, lengthening of life expectancy, increasing economic development globally, and rising consumer expectations will drive long-term demand for better quality drugs in the years ahead.

Oncology

A key strategy decision for pharmaceutical companies is deciding where to compete across a diverse range of therapeutic areas. Oncology is the largest therapy area globally in terms of prescription drug sales with a 16.7 percent share among all types of illnesses. Four key oncology drugs make up about 20 percent of sales: Merck's Keytruda, Johnson & Johnson's Darzalex, Bristol-Myers Squibb's Opdivo, and AstraZeneca's Tagrisso. EvaluatePharma forecasts oncology to account for 22 percent of prescription drug sales in 2026.

Generic Drugs

Drugs continually come off patent protection, opening the door for generic drugs; the market is turning more and more toward generic substitution. Generic medicines globally account for the majority of total medication dispensed, while contributing only a fraction of the cost. In 2020, global spending on unbranded generic medicines reached $113.8 billion, according to IQVIA.

Key companies in the generic drugs market include Viatris, Teva Pharmaceuticals, and Sun Pharmaceutical, plus some of the large pharmaceutical companies also have their own generic arm. For example, Sandoz is Novartis generic arm segment. India is the largest provider of generic drugs globally, exporting to major markets, including the United States (accounts for roughly 40 percent of US generic drugs imported) and the EU.

India-based generic companies will continue to take market share from developed nations' firms due to lower production costs. Chinese pharmaceutical companies are shifting some of their resources away from generics into more lucrative innovative drugs.

A total of 444 generic drugs were approved as of August 2021 in the United States (754 in 2020), while the number of Europe's total generic drug approvals stood at 11 as of October 2021, compared with 22 approved in 2020. Worldwide sales of generic drugs are expected to grow by 3.8 percent annually through 2026 period to $99 billion and make up about 8 percent of total prescription drug sales.

COVID Treatments

Pharmaceutical companies are continually in search of COVID-19 treatments. For example, Sotrovimab, an antibody drug developed by GSK and Vir Biotechnology, recently showed a 79 percent reduction in risk of hospitalization or death in its Phase III trial, and received the US Food and Drug Administration authorization of its use for mild- to-moderate COVID-19 in May 2021. In October 2021, Merck sought emergency use authorization for its COVID-19 treatment pill, called Molnupiravir, following positive interim results, which showed the orally administered drug was able to lower the risk of death and hospitalization by half.

Conclusion

CEO Dame Emma Walmsley needs a clear 3-year strategic plan for Glaxo. Intensity of competition and rivalry among firms is accelerating as companies and countries transition to zero emissions. The vision/mission and organizational structure sections of this case reveal that there is substantial room for improvement for Glaxo in both areas. Walmsley knows the basic underlying external opportunities and threats and internal strengths facing Glaxo, but she is unsure about the relative importance of those factors. She thus needs an external and internal assessment performed, anchored by development of an EFE Matrix and IFE Matrix as described in Chapter 3 and Chapter 4 of the David textbook. Walmsley also needs to know the relative attractiveness of alternative strategies facing the company, so she needs a SWOT, BCG, and QSPM analyses performed.

Let's say Walmsley asks you to develop the comprehensive strategic plan that she needs. In addition to the analyses mentioned, include in your report a perceptual map, a set of proposed recommendations with associated costs, and an EPS-EBIT analysis to reveal whether debt or stock or some combination of debt and stock is best to obtain the needed funds. Also include projected financial statements to show the expected impact on Glaxo if Walmsley adopts your proposed strategic plan. What can Glaxo do to help assure top line (revenues) and bottom line (net income) 5+ percent annually in the years to come? Identify candidate firms for Glaxo to acquire. If Glaxo should expand further organically (internally) into other regions, countries, and continents, include direction for Walmsley in this regard.

All of Glaxo's top executives, board of directors, shareholders, and employees will benefit from and be thankful for your work developing and proposing a clear roadmap for their future. Good luck on this endeavor. We authors are confident you can do a wonderful job performing this task, following the guidelines presented in the David strategic management textbook and using the strategic planning template provided at www.strategyclub.com.

References

1. https://finance.yahoo.com/quote/GSK?p=GSK&.tsrc=fin-srch
2. https://www.comparably.com/companies/gsk/competitors
3. Glaxo's 2021 *Annual Report.*
4. https://www.gsk.com/media/7377/fy-2021-results-announcement.pdf
5. https://www.gsk.com/en-gb/about-us/gsk-leadership-team/
6. https://www.gsk.com/media/7377/fy-2021-results-announcement.pdf

Glossary

Acquisition When a large organization purchases (acquires) a smaller firm; a merger.

Actionable responses Meaningful in terms of having strategic implications; suggestive of potential strategies to capitalize on or compensate for.

Activity ratios Inventory turnover and average collection period measure how effectively a firm is using its resources.

Aggressive Quadrant In a SPACE matrix analysis, when the firm's directional vector points in the upper-right quadrant, the firm should pursue aggressive strategies.

Annual objectives Short-term milestones that organizations must achieve to reach long-term objectives.

Attractiveness Scores (AS) In a QSPM, the numerical value (rating) that indicates the relative attractiveness of each strategy given a single internal or external factor.

Auditing The accounting process that firms undertake to have their financial statements reviewed for accuracy to assure compliance with the law and IRS code.

Avatars Digital objects that can become "you" or "anyone" or "anything" and interact with you as if you and the entity are together.

Backward integration A strategy seeking ownership or increased control of a firm's suppliers, such as a manufacturer acquiring its raw material source firms.

Balanced scorecard A framework of desired objectives; derives its name from the need of firms to "balance" quantitative (such as financial ratios and percentages) with qualitative (such as for employee morale and business ethics) objectives that are often used in strategy evaluation.

Bankruptcy A legal document that allows a firm to avoid major debt obligations and void union contracts to survive and regroup as a firm. There are five major types: Chapter 7, Chapter 9, Chapter 11, Chapter 12, and Chapter 13.

Benchmarking A management technique associated with value chain analysis, whereby a firm compares itself on a wide variety of performance-related criteria against the best firms in the industry, thus establishing standards of excellence.

Black Swan events Highly unpredictable yet profound events, such as the COVID-19 pandemic.

Blue ocean strategy Actions that aim to target a new market where competition is not yet present, thus creating a "blue ocean" as opposed to a red ocean where many firms are competing often on price and the gains of one firm are often at the expense of another. Blue ocean strategy is similar to being a first mover seeking market space not yet used by rivals.

Board of directors A group of individuals above the CEO who have oversight and guidance over management and who care for shareholders' interests; sometimes called governance.

Book value Number of shares outstanding multiplied by stock price.

Boston Consulting Group (BCG) Matrix A four-quadrant, strategic planning analytical tool that places an organization's various divisions as circles in a display (similar to the IE Matrix) based on two key dimensions: relative market share position and industry growth rate. The diagram's four quadrants (Stars, Question Marks, Cash Cows, Question Marks) each have different strategy implications.

Bribe A gift bestowed to influence a recipient's conduct.

Bribery Offering, giving, receiving, or soliciting of any item of value to influence the actions of an official or other person in discharge of a public or legal duty.

Business analytics An MIS technique designed to analyze huge volumes of data to help executives make decisions; sometimes called *predictive analytics* or *data mining*.

Business ethics Principles of behavior and conduct a firm may institute to minimize wrongdoing among employees and managers.

Business portfolio Autonomous divisions (or profit centers or segments) of an organization as represented by circles in BCG and IE matrices.

Capacity utilization The extent to which a manufacturing plant's output reaches its potential output; the higher the capacity utilization the better because otherwise equipment may sit idle.

Capital budgeting A basic function of finance; the allocation and reallocation of capital and resources to projects, products, assets, and divisions of an organization.

Capital structure The proportion of debt-to-equity on a balance sheet; performing an EPS/EBIT analysis is a common way to determine the appropriate capital structure needed.

Cash cows A quadrant in the BCG Matrix for divisions that have a high relative market share position but compete in a low-growth industry; they generate cash in excess of their needs are are often milked; this is the lower-left quadrant.

Champions Individuals most strongly identified with a firm's new idea, product, or service and whose futures are linked to its success.

Chief Information Officer (CIO) More an external manager compared with a CTO; focuses on the firm's technical, information gathering, and social media relationship with diverse external stakeholders.

Chief Technology Officer (CTO) More an internal manager compared with a CIO; focuses on technical issues such as data acquisition, data processing, decision-support systems, and software and hardware acquisition.

Code of business ethics A written document specifying expected employee and manager behavior and conduct in an organization.

Collaborative machines   Robots used in manufacturing operations; these robots are flexible, capable of doing a variety of tasks.

Combination strategy   The pursuit of a combination of two or more strategies simultaneously.

Competitive advantage   Anything a firm does especially well, compared to rival firms. For example, when a firm can do something that rival firms cannot do, or owns something that rival firms desire, that can represent a competitive advantage.

Competitive Intelligence (CI)   A systematic and ethical process for gathering and analyzing information about the competition's activities and general business trends to further a business's own goals (SCIP website).

Competitive Position (CP)   One of four dimensions or axes of the SPACE Matrix; determines an organization's competitiveness, using such factors as market share, product quality, product life cycle, customer loyalty, capacity utilization, technological know-how, and control over suppliers and distributors.

Competitive Profile Matrix (CPM)   A widely used strategic planning analytical tool designed to identify a firm's major competitors and its particular strengths and weaknesses in relation to a sample firm's strategic position.

Competitive Quadrant   In a SPACE Matrix analysis, when the firm's directional vector points in the lower-right quadrant it suggests that the firm should pursue competitive strategies such as horizontal integration.

Concern for employees   A component of the mission statement; are employees a valuable asset to the firm?

Concern for public image   A component of the mission statement; is the firm responsive to social, community, and environmental concerns?

Concern for survival, growth, and profitability   A component of the mission statement; does the firm strive to survive, grow, and (if for-profit) be profitable?

Conflict   A disagreement between two or more parties on one or more issues.

Conservative Quadrant   In a SPACE Matrix analysis, when the firm's directional vector points in the upper-left quadrant it suggests that the firm should pursue conservative strategies such as market penetration.

Contingency plans   Alternative plans that can be put into effect if certain key events do not occur as expected.

Controlling   A basic function of management; includes all of those activities undertaken to ensure that actual operations conform to planned operations.

Core competence   A value chain activity that a firm performs especially well.

Core values statement   A document that specifies a firm's commitment to integrity, fairness, discipline, equal employment opportunity, teamwork, accountability, continuous improvement, or other such exemplary attributes.

Cost leadership   One of Michael Porter's strategy dimensions that involves a firm producing standardized products at a very low per-unit cost for consumers who are price sensitive.

Creed statement   Another name for mission statement; a declaration of an organization's "reason for being." It answers the pivotal question, "What is our business?"

Culture   The set of shared values, beliefs, attitudes, customs, norms, personalities, heroes, and heroines that describe a firm. Strategists should strive to preserve, emphasize, and build on these aspects.

Customers   A component of the mission statement; individuals who purchase a firm's products or services.

Data mining   A business technique that uses software to mine huge volumes of data, such as a firm's interaction with its customers, suppliers, distributors, employees, rival firms, and more to help executives make decisions; sometimes called *business analytics*.

Decision stage   Stage 3 of the strategy formulation analytical framework that involves development of the Quantitative Strategic Planning Matrix (QSPM). A QSPM uses input information from Stage 1 to objectively evaluate feasible alternative strategies identified in Stage 2. A QSPM reveals the relative attractiveness of alternative strategies and thus provides objective basis for selecting specific strategies.

Defensive Quadrant   In a SPACE Matrix analysis, when the firm's directional vector goes into the lower-left quadrant it suggests that the firm should pursue defensive strategies such as retrenchment.

De-integration   Reducing the pursuit of backward integration; instead of owning suppliers, companies negotiate with several outside suppliers.

Differentiation   One of Michael Porter's strategy dimensions that involves a firm producing products and services considered unique industrywide and directed at consumers who are relatively price insensitive.

Directional vector   In a SPACE Matrix analysis, this line begins at the origin and goes into one of four quadrants, revealing the type of strategies recommended for the organization: aggressive, competitive, defensive, or conservative.

Discount   If an acquiring firm pays less for another firm than the firm's stock price multiplied by its number of shares of stock outstanding (book value or market value), then that amount minus the actual purchase price is called a discount.

Distinctive competence   A firm's strengths that cannot be easily matched or imitated by competitors. One of the nine basic components needed for inclusion in a mission statement.

Diversification strategies   When a firm enters a new business or industry, either related and unrelated to its existing business or industry. Related diversification is when the old versus new business value chains possess competitively valuable cross-business strategic fits; unrelated diversification is when the old versus new business value chains are so dissimilar that no competitively valuable cross-business relationships exist.

Divestiture Selling a division or part of an organization.

Dividend decisions A basic function of finance; concerns issues such as the percentage of earnings paid to stockholders, the stability of dividends paid over time, and the repurchase or issuance of stock.

Divisional (decentralized) structure This type of organizational design is based on having various profit centers or segments by geographic area, by product or service, by customer, or by process. With a divisional structure, functional activities are performed both centrally and in each separate division.

Dogs A quadrant in the BCG Matrix for divisions that have a low relative market share position and compete in a low-growth industry; this is the lower-right quadrant.

Empirical indicators Refers to three characteristics of resources (rare, hard to imitate, not easily substitutable) that enable a firm to gain and sustain competitive advantage.

Employability Refers to having developed the skills used by businesses, including the actual tools, techniques, and concepts learned by students using this text.

Employee stock ownership plans (ESOP) A tax-qualified, defined-contribution, employee-benefit plan whereby employees purchase stock of the company through borrowed money or cash contributions.

Empowerment The act of strengthening employees' sense of shared ownership by encouraging them to participate in decision-making and rewarding them for doing so.

Environment The surroundings in which an organization operates, including air, water, land, natural resources, flora, fauna, humans, and their interrelation.

Environmental management system (EMS) When a firm or municipality operates using "green" policies, practices, and procedures as outlined by ISO 14001.

Environmental scanning Process of conducting research and gathering and assimilating external information; also referred to as *external audit*.

EPS/EBIT analysis A financial technique to determine whether debt, stock, or a combination of debt and stock is the best alternative for raising capital to implement strategies.

External audit Process of identifying and evaluating trends and events beyond the control of a single firm, in areas such as social, cultural, demographic technology, economic, political, and competition; reveals key opportunities and threats confronting an organization, so managers can better formulate strategies.

External Factor Evaluation (EFE) Matrix A widely used strategic planning analytical tool designed to summarize and evaluate economic, social, cultural, demographic, environmental, political, governmental, legal, technological, and competitive information.

External forces (1) Economic forces; (2) social, cultural, demographic, and natural environment forces; (3) political, governmental, and legal forces; (4) technological forces; and (5) competitive forces.

External opportunities Economic, social, cultural, demographic, environmental, political, legal, governmental, technological, and competitive trends, events, or facts that could significantly benefit an organization in the future.

External threats Economic, social, cultural, demographic, environmental, political, legal, governmental, technological, and competitive trends, events, or facts that could significantly harm an organization in the future.

Feng shui In China, this term refers to the practice of harnessing natural forces, which can impact how you arrange office furniture.

Financial objectives Include desired results growth in revenues, growth in earnings, higher dividends, larger profit margins, greater return on investment, higher earnings per share, a rising stock price, improved cash flow, and so on.

Financial Position (FP) One of four dimensions or axes of the SPACE Matrix that determines an organization's financial strength, considering such factors as return on investment, leverage, liquidity, working capital, and cash flow.

Financial ratio analysis Quantitative calculations that reveal the financial condition of a firm and exemplify the complexity of relationships among the functional areas of business. For example, a declining return on investment or profit margin ratio could be the result of ineffective marketing, poor management policies, research and development errors, or a weak management information system. Ratios are usually compared to industry averages, to prior time periods, or to rival firms.

Financing decision A basic function of finance; determines the best capital structure for the firm and includes examining various methods by which the firm can raise capital (e.g., by issuing stock, increasing debt, selling assets, or using a combination of these approaches).

First-mover advantages The benefits a firm may achieve by entering a new market or developing a new product or service before rival firms.

Forward integration A strategy that involves gaining ownership or increased control over distributors or retailers, such as a manufacturer opening its own chain of stores.

Franchising An effective means of implementing forward integration whereby a franchisee purchases the right to own one or more stores or restaurants of a chain firm.

Friendly merger If the merger or acquisition is desired by both firms.

Functional structure A type of organizational design that groups tasks and activities by business function, such as production/operations, marketing, finance/accounting, research and development, and management information systems.

Future shock High anxiety that results when the nature, types, and speed of changes overpower an individual's or organization's ability and capacity to adapt.

Generally accepted accounting principles (GAAP) A set of procedures or rules used by accountants, particularly in the United States, to develop financial statements.

Generally accepted auditing standards (GAAS) A set of accounting standards used by independent auditors to evaluate an organization's financial statements.

Generic strategies Michael Porter's strategy breakdown; consists of three strategies: cost leadership, differentiation, and focus.

Glass ceiling A term used to refer to the artificial barrier that women and minorities face in moving into upper levels of management.

Global strategy Designing, producing, and marketing products with global needs in mind, instead of solely considering individual countries.

Globalization A process of doing business worldwide, so strategic decisions are made based on global profitability of the firm rather than just domestic considerations.

Goodwill If a firm acquires another firm and pays more than the book value (market value), then the additional amount paid is called a *premium* and becomes goodwill, which is a line item on the assets portion of a balance sheet.

Governance The act of oversight and direction, especially in association with the duties of a board of directors.

Grand Strategy Matrix A four-quadrant, two-axis tool for formulating alternative strategies. All organizations can be positioned in one of this matrix's four strategy quadrants, based on their position on two evaluative dimensions: competitive position and market (industry) growth. Strategy suggestions ensue depending on which quadrant the firm is located.

Growth ratios Measures such as the percentage increase or decrease in revenue or profit from one period to the next are important comparisons.

Guanxi In China, business behavior is based on "personal relations."

Horizontal consistency of objectives Objectives need to be compatible across functions; for example, if marketing wants to sell 10 percent more, then production must produce 10 percent more.

Horizontal integration Acquiring a rival firm.

Hostile takeover If the merger or acquisition is not desired by both firms.

Human resource management (HRM) Also called *personnel management*; a basic function of management; includes activities such as recruiting, interviewing, testing, selecting, orienting, training, developing, caring for, evaluating, rewarding, disciplining, promoting, transferring, demoting, and dismissing employees, as well as managing union relations.

Industry analysis Another term for external audit; conducting research to gather and assimilate external information.

Industry growth rate The vertical axis in a BCG Matrix; the average percentage increase or decrease in sales or revenues this year (versus last year) for a given industry.

Industry position (IP) One of four dimensions or axes of the SPACE Matrix that determines how strong or weak a firm's industry is, considering such factors as growth potential, profit potential, financial stability, extent leveraged, resource utilization, ease of entry into market, productivity, and capacity utilization.

Information technology (IT) The development, maintenance, and use of computer systems, software, and networks for the processing and distribution of data.

Inhwa A South Korean term for activities that involve concern for harmony based on respect of hierarchical relationships, including obedience to authority.

Initial public offering (IPO) When a private firm goes public by selling its shares of stock to the public to raise capital.

Input stage Stage 1 of the strategy formulation analytical framework that summarizes the basic input information needed to formulate strategies; consists of an EFEM, CPM, and IFEM.

Integration strategies Includes forward integration, backward integration, and horizontal integration (sometimes collectively referred to as *vertical integration strategies*).

Intensive strategies Includes market development, market penetration, and product development.

Internal audit The process of gathering and assimilating information about the firm's management, marketing, finance/accounting, production/operations, R&D, and MIS operations. The purpose is to identify, evaluate, and prioritize a firm's strengths and weaknesses.

Internal-External (IE) Matrix A nine-quadrant, strategic planning analytical tool that places an organization's various divisions as circles in a display (similar to the BCG Matrix) based on two key dimensions: the segment's IFE total weighted scores on the x-axis and the segment's EFE total weighted scores on the y-axis. The diagram is divided into three major regions that have different strategy implications: grow and build, hold and maintain, or harvest or divest.

Internal Factor Evaluation (IFE) Matrix A strategy formulation tool that summarizes and evaluates a firm's major strengths and weaknesses in the functional areas of a business and provides a basis for identifying and evaluating relationships among those areas.

Internal strengths An organization's controllable activities that are performed especially well, such as in areas that include finance, marketing, management, accounting, and MIS, across a firm's products, regions, stores, and facilities.

Internal weaknesses An organization's controllable activities that are performed especially poorly, such as in areas that include finance, marketing, management, accounting, and MIS, across a firm's products, regions, stores, or facilities.

International financial reporting standards (IFRS) A set of procedures or rules used by accountants, particularly outside the United States, to develop financial statements.

International firms Firms that conduct business outside their own country.

Intuition Using one's cognition without evident rational thought or analysis; based on past experience, judgment, and feelings; essential to making good strategic decisions but must not be relied on heavily in lieu of objective analysis.

Investment decision Also called *capital budgeting*; a basic function of finance; the allocation and reallocation of capital and resources to projects, products, assets, and divisions of an organization.

ISO 14000 A series of voluntary standards in the environmental field whereby a firm minimizes harmful effects on the environment caused by its activities and continually monitors and improves its own environmental performance.

ISO 14001 A set of standards adopted by thousands of firms worldwide to certify to their constituencies that they are conducting business in an environmentally friendly manner. These standards offer a universal technical standard for environmental compliance that more and more firms are requiring not only of themselves but also of their suppliers and distributors.

Joint venture A strategy that occurs when two or more companies form a temporary partnership, consortium, or business for the purpose of capitalizing on some opportunity.

Leverage ratios The debt-to-equity ratio and debt-to-total assets ratio measure the extent to which a firm has been financed by debt.

Leveraged buyout (LBO) When the outstanding shares of a corporation are bought by the company's management and other private investors using borrowed funds.

Liquidation Selling all of a company's assets, in parts, for their tangible worth.

Liquidity ratios The current ratio and quick ratio measure a firm's ability to meet short-term cash obligations.

Long-range planning Deciding on future actions, objectives, and policies with the aim to optimize for tomorrow the trends of today; less effective and comprehensive than strategic planning.

Long-term objectives Specific results that an organization seeks to achieve (in more than 1 year) in pursuing its basic vision, mission, or strategy.

Management The active engagement in four managerial activities including planning, organizing, motivating, and controlling.

Management information system (MIS) A system that gathers, assimilates, evaluates, and converts external and internal data (facts, figures, and trends) into useful information for decision-making.

Market capitalization Number of shares outstanding multiplied by stock price.

Market development Introducing present products or services into new geographic areas.

Market penetration Increasing market share for present products or services in present markets through greater marketing efforts.

Market segmentation Using demographic, geographic, psychographic, or behavioral characteristics of consumers to divide a market into distinct subsets of customers that differ from one another in product needs and buying habits.

Market value Number of shares outstanding multiplied by stock price.

Marketing The process of defining, anticipating, and fulfilling consumers' needs and wants.

Marketing mix variables Product, place, promotion, and price.

Marketing research The systematic gathering, recording, and analyzing of data about problems, practices, and issues related to the marketing of goods and services.

Markets A component of the mission statement; geographic locations where a firm competes.

Matching When an organization matches its internal strengths and weaknesses with its external opportunities and threats using, for example, the SWOT, SPACE, BCG, IE, or GRAND Matrices.

Matching stage Stage 2 of the strategy formulation framework that focuses on generating feasible alternative strategies by aligning internal with external factors by using five matrices: BCG, IE, SWOT, GRAND, and SPACE.

Matrix structure This type of organizational design places functional activities along the top row and divisional projects or units along the left side to create a rubric where managers have two bosses—both a functional boss and a project boss—thus creating the need for extensive vertical and horizontal flows of authority and communication.

Measuring organizational performance Activity 2 in the strategy evaluation process; includes comparing expected results to actual results, investigating deviations from plans, evaluating individual performance, and examining progress being made toward meeting stated objectives.

Merger When two organizations of about equal size unite to form one enterprise; an acquisition.

Metaverse An online 3D, virtual or augmented reality (AR) world where individuals, companies, and organizations can interact and share quality time with others and spend money as avatars on products and services.

Mission statement An enduring statement of purpose that distinguish one business from other similar firms; a statement that identifies the scope of a firm's operations in product and market terms and addresses the question "What is our business?" A declaration of an organization's "reason for being."

Mission statement components (1) Customers; (2) products and services; (3) markets; (4) technology; (5) concern for survival, growth, and profitability; (6) philosophy; (7) distinctive competence; (8) concern for public image; and (9) concern for employees.

Motivating A basic function of management; the process of influencing and leading people to accomplish specific objectives.

Multinational firms Firms that conduct business outside their own country.

Nemaswashio U.S. managers in Japan have to be careful about this phenomenon, whereby Japanese workers expect supervisors to alert them privately of changes rather than informing them in a meeting.

Organic growth A term denoting strategies that aim for a firm to build or grow from within rather than through acquisition.

Organizational culture A pattern of behavior developed by an organization over time as it learns to cope with its problem of external adaptation and internal integration and that has worked well enough to be considered valid and to be taught to new members as the correct way to perceive, think, and feel in the firm.

Organizing A basic function of management; the process of arranging duties and responsibilities in a coherent manner to determine who does what and who reports to whom.

Outsourcing Refers to the practice of firms using or paying other firms to perform certain activities, such as managing payroll, call centers, or even R&D.

Outstanding shares method A method for determining the cash worth of a firm by multiplying the number of shares outstanding by the market price per share; also called *book value, market value*, or *market capitalization*.

Perceptual map Also called *product-positioning map*; a two-dimensional, four-quadrant marketing tool designed to position a firm versus its rival firms in a schematic diagram to better determine effective marketing strategies.

PESTEL The acronym for the six external forces that impact organizations: Political, Economic, Sociocultural, Technological, Environmental, and Legal.

Philosophy A component of the mission statement; the basic beliefs, values, aspirations, and ethical priorities of the firm.

Phubbing (short for phone snubbing), which occurs when a manager uses or is distracted by his/her cell phone during time spent with an employee, albeit during a meeting, at lunch, or in other workplace settings, has shown that boss phubbing negatively impacts employee job performance

Planning A basic function of management; the process of deciding ahead of time the strategies to be pursued and actions to be taken in the future.

Policies The means by which annual objectives will be achieved. Policies include guidelines, rules, and procedures established to support efforts to achieve stated objectives. Policies are guides to decision-making and address repetitive or recurring situations.

Porter's Five-Forces Model A theoretical model devised by Michael Porter, who suggests that the nature of competitiveness in a given industry can be viewed as a composite of five forces: rivalry among competing firms, potential entry of new competitors, potential development of substitute products, bargaining power of suppliers, and bargaining power of consumers.

Portfolio analysis A tool that compares divisions of a firm to determine how best to allocate resources among those divisions.

Positioning Designing a marketing mix (product, price, place, promotion) that offers unique value to target customers.

Premium If an acquiring firm pays more for another firm than that firm's stock price multiplied by its number of shares of stock outstanding (book value or market value), then the overage is called a premium.

Price-earnings ratio method This method involves dividing the market price of the firm's common stock by the annual earnings per share and multiplying this number by the firm's average net income for the past 5 years.

Private-equity firm An investment management company that purchases outright or provides venture capital to another firm, generally taking that other firm from public to private, and commonly then managing that other firm with the intent to increase that firm's performance and value.

Product development Increased sales by improving or modifying present products or services.

Production/operations The portion of a business consisting of the activities that transform inputs (raw materials, labor, capital, machines, and facilities) into finished goods and services.

Products or services A component of the mission statement; commodities or benefits provided by a firm.

Profitability ratios The profit margin ratio and return on investment ratio measure the profitability of a firm's operations.

Projected financial statement analysis A financial technique that enables a firm to forecast the expected financial results of various strategies and approaches; involves developing income statements and balance sheets for future periods of time.

Promotion Includes many marketing activities, such as advertising, sales promotion, public relations, personal selling, and direct marketing, designed to attract customers in a firm's target market(s).

Protectionism When countries impose tariffs, taxes, and regulations on firms outside the country to favor their own companies and people.

Quantitative Strategic Planning Matrix (QSPM) An analytical technique designed to determine the relative attractiveness of feasible alternative actions. This technique comprises Stage 3 of the strategy formulation analytical framework; it objectively indicates which alternative strategies are best.

Question marks A quadrant in the BCG Matrix for divisions that have a low relative market share position but compete in a high-growth industry; this is the upper-right quadrant; firms generally must decide whether to strengthen such divisions or sell them (hence, a question is at hand).

Recommendation Any alternative strategy that is selected for implementation.

Recommendations Page The page in a strategic planning case project where recommendations are listed along with an estimated dollar (respective currency) amount for the expected cost (or savings) of each recommendation over the next three years.

Reconciliatory   With regard to mission statements, the need for the statement to be sufficiently broad to "reconcile" differences effectively among diverse stakeholders; to appeal to a firm's customers, employees, shareholders, and creditors rather than alienate any group.

Reengineering   Reconfiguring or redesigning work, jobs, and processes in a firm, for the purpose of improving cost, quality, service, and speed.

Related diversification   When a firm acquires a new business whose value chain possesses competitively valuable cross-business strategic fits.

Relative market share position   The horizontal axis in a BCG Matrix, which is the firm's particular segment's market share (or revenues or number of stores) divided by the industry leader's analogous number.

Reshoring   Refers to U.S. companies working offshore but planning to move some of their manufacturing back to the United States.

Resistance to change   A natural human tendency to be wary of new policies or strategies due to potential negative consequences; if not managed then this could result in sabotaging production machines, absenteeism, filing unfounded grievances, and an unwillingness to cooperate.

Resource allocation   A central strategy implementation activity that entails distributing financial, physical, human, and technological assets to allow for strategy execution.

Resource-based view (RBV)   An approach that suggests internal resources to be more important for a firm than external factors in achieving and sustaining competitive advantage.

Restructuring   Modifying the firm's chain of command and reporting channels to improve efficiency and effectiveness.

Retreats   Formal meetings commonly held off premises to discuss and update a firm's strategic plan; done away from the work site to encourage more creativity and candor from participants.

Retrenchment   When an organization regroups through cost and asset reduction to reverse declining sales and profits.

Reviewing the underlying bases of an organization's strategy   Activity 1 in the strategy evaluation process; entails a firm developing a revised EFE Matrix and IFE Matrix to determine if corrective actions are needed.

Revised EFE Matrix   Part of activity 1 in the strategy evaluation process whereby a firm reassesses its previously determined external opportunities and threats.

Revised IFE Matrix   Part of activity 1 in the strategy evaluation process whereby a firm reassesses its previously determined internal strengths and weaknesses.

Sexual harassment   Unwelcome sexual advances, requests for sexual favors, and other verbal or physical conduct of a sexual nature; this activity is illegal, unethical, and detrimental to any organization and can result in expensive lawsuits, lower morale, and reduced productivity.

SO strategies   Strategies that result from matching a firm's internal strengths with its external opportunities.

Social responsibility   Actions an organization takes beyond what is legally required to protect or enhance the well-being of living things.

Special purpose acquisition company (SPAC)   A public company listed on a stock exchange that acquires (merges with) a private company, enabling the private company to raise equity capital and to become a public firm with its own stock symbol, without that private firm going through the traditional initial public offering (IPO) process.

ST strategies   Strategies that result from matching a firm's internal strengths with its external threats.

Stability Position (SP)   One of four dimensions or axes of the SPACE Matrix that determines how stable or unstable a firm's industry is, considering such factors as technological changes, rate of inflation, demand of variability, price range of competing products, barriers to entry into market, competitive pressure, ease of exit from market, price elasticity of demand, and risk involved in business.

Stakeholders   The individuals and groups of individuals who have a special stake or claim on the company, such as a firm's customers, employees, shareholders, and creditors.

Stars   A quadrant in the BCG Matrix for divisions that have a high relative market share position and compete in a high-growth industry; this is the upper-left quadrant.

Strategic business unit (SBU) structure   This type of organizational design groups similar divisions together into units; widely used when a firm has many divisions or segments to reduce span of control reporting to a COO.

Strategic management   The art and science of formulating, implementing, and evaluating cross-functional decisions that enable an organization to achieve its objectives.

Strategic management model   A framework or illustration of the strategic management process; a clear and practical approach for formulating, implementing, and evaluating strategies.

Strategic management process   The process of formulating, implementing, and evaluating strategies as revealed in the comprehensive model, that begins with vision or mission development and ends with strategy evaluation and feedback.

Strategic objectives   Desired results such as a larger market share, quicker on-time delivery than rivals, shorter design-to-market times than rivals, lower costs than rivals, higher product quality than rivals, wider geographic coverage than rivals, achieving technological leadership, and consistently getting new or improved products to market ahead of rivals.

Strategic planning   The process of formulating an organization's game plan; in a corporate setting, this term may refer to the whole strategic management process.

Strategic Position and Action Evaluation (SPACE) Matrix   Indicates whether aggressive, conservative, defensive, or competitive strategies are most appropriate for a given organization.

The axes of this matrix represent two internal dimensions (financial position [FP] and competitive position [CP]) and two external dimensions (stability position [SP] and industry position [IP]). These four factors are perhaps the most important determinants of an organization's overall strategic position.

Strategies The means by which long-term objectives will be achieved. Business strategies may include geographic expansion, diversification, acquisition, product development, market penetration, retrenchment, divestiture, liquidation, and joint ventures.

Strategists The person(s) responsible for formulating and implementing a firm's strategic plan, including the CEO, president, owner of a business, head coach, governor, chancellor, or the top management team in a firm.

Strategy evaluation Stage 3 in the strategic management process. The three fundamental strategy evaluation activities are review external and internal factors that are the bases for current strategies, measure performance, and take corrective actions; strategies need to be evaluated regularly because external and internal factors constantly change.

Strategy formulation Stage 1 in the strategic management process; includes developing a vision or mission, identifying an organization's external opportunities and threats, determining internal strengths and weaknesses, establishing long-term objectives, generating alternative strategies, and choosing particular strategies to pursue.

Strategy formulation analytical framework A three-stage, nine-matrix array of tools widely used for strategic planning as a guide: (stage 1: input stage; stage 2: matching stage; stage 3: decision stage).

Strategy implementation Stage 2 of the strategic management process. Activities include establishing annual objectives, devising policies, motivating employees, allocating resources, developing a culture supported by strategy, creating an effective organizational structure, redirecting marketing efforts, preparing budgets, developing and using information systems, and linking employee compensation to organizational performance.

Strengths-Weaknesses-Opportunities-Threats (SWOT) Matrix The most widely used of all strategic planning matrices; matches a firm's internal strengths and weaknesses with its external opportunities and threats to generate four types of strategies: SO (strengths-opportunities) Strategies, WO (weaknesses-opportunities) Strategies, ST (strengths-threats) Strategies, and WT (weaknesses-threats) Strategies.

Sum Total Attractiveness Scores (STAS) In a QSPM, this is the sum of the Total Attractiveness Scores in each strategy column; value reveals which strategy is most attractive in each set of alternatives.

Sustainability The extent that an organization's operations and actions protect, mend, and preserve, rather than harm or destroy, the natural environment.

Sustainability report A form of annual report produced by organizations to reveal their progress and activities aimed at helping, rather than harming, the natural environment.

Sustained competitive advantage Maintaining what a firm does especially well, compared to rival firms—by continually adapting to changes in external trends and events and internal capabilities, competencies, and resources and effectively formulating, implementing, and evaluating strategies that capitalize on those factors.

Synergy The $2 + 2 = 5$ effect; when everyone pulls together as a team, the results can exceed individuals working separately.

Tactics The actions that bring to life or execute the formulated strategies.

Taking corrective actions Activity 3 in the strategy evaluation process; involves a firm making changes to competitively reposition a firm for the future.

Target market analysis Engaging in marketing research to examine and evaluate the needs and wants of selected groups of customers.

Technology A component of the mission statement; is the firm technologically current?

Test marketing An activity to determine ahead of time whether a certain product or service or selling approach will be cost effective; also used to forecast future sales of new products.

Total Attractiveness Scores (TAS) In a QSPM, the product of multiplying the weights by the Attractiveness Scores in each row. The values indicate the relative attractiveness of each alternative strategy, considering only the impact of the adjacent external or internal critical success factor.

Treasury stock An item in the equity portion of a balance sheet that reveals the dollar amount of the firm's common stock owned by the company itself.

Triple-bottom-line Organizational performance in terms of "people," "planet," and "profits," in which success depends on (1) the financial bottom line, (2) the social bottom line, and (3) the natural environment bottom line.

Turnaround strategy A retrenchment strategy designed to fortify an organization's basic distinctive competencies by regrouping through cost and asset reduction to reverse declining sales and profits.

Unrelated diversification When a firm acquires a new business whose value chains are so dissimilar that no competitively valuable cross-business relationships exist.

Value chain The business of a firm, where total revenues minus total costs of all activities undertaken to develop, produce, and market a product or service yields value.

Value chain analysis (VCA) The process whereby a firm determines the costs associated with organizational activities from purchasing raw materials to manufacturing product(s) to marketing those products and compares these costs to rival firms using benchmarking.

Vertical consistency of objectives Compatibility of objectives from the CEO (corporate level) down to the presidents (divisional level) on down to the managers (functional level).

Vertical integration A combination of three strategies: backward, forward, and horizontal integration, allowing a firm to gain control over distributors, suppliers, or competitors, respectively.

Vision statement A one-sentence statement that answers the question, "What do we want to become?"

Wa In Japan, this term stresses group harmony and social cohesion.

Whistleblowing The act of telling authorities about some unethical or illegal activities occurring within an organization of which a person is aware.

WO strategies Strategies that result from matching a firm's internal weaknesses with its external opportunities.

Workplace romance An intimate relationship between two truly consenting employees, as opposed to sexual harassment, which the EEOC defines broadly as unwelcome sexual advances, requests for sexual favors, and other verbal or physical conduct of a sexual nature.

WT strategies Strategies that result from matching a firm's internal weaknesses with its external threats.

Name Index

Subject Index